GALE
ENCYCLOPEDIA OF
MULTICULTURAL
AMERICA

GALE
ENCYCLOPEDIA OF
MULTICULTURAL
AMERICA

volume 2
Irish Americans – Yupiat Index

Contributing Editor
RUDOLPH J. VECOLI

Edited by
JUDY GALENS
ANNA SHEETS
ROBYN V. YOUNG

Endorsed by *EMIE Bulletin* of the Ethnic Materials
Information Exchange Round Table,
American Library Association.

Gale Research Inc.

An International Thomson Publishing Company

Changing the Way the World Learns

NEW YORK • LONDON • BONN • BOSTON • DETROIT • MADRID
MELBOURNE • MEXICO CITY • PARIS • SINGAPORE • TOKYO
TORONTO • WASHINGTON • ALBANY NY • BELMONT CA • CINCINNATI OH

STAFF

Judy Galens, Anna Sheets, Robyn V. Young, *Editors*

Neil Schlager, *Managing Editor, Multicultural Team*
Sharon Malinowski, *Editor*
Dawn R. Barry, Melissa Walsh Doig, Jeffrey Lehman, *Associate Editors*

Victoria B. Cariappa, *Research Manager*
Barbara McNeil, *Research Specialist*
Maria Bryson, *Research Associate*

Mary Beth Trimper, *Production Director*
Evi Seoud, *Assistant Production Manager*
Shanna Heilveil, *Production Assistant*

Marlene H. Lasky, *Permissions Manager*
Diane Cooper, *Permissions Associate*

Cynthia Baldwin, *Product Design Manager*
Tracey Rowens, *Art Director*

⊗™ This book is printed on acid-free paper that meets the minimum requirements
of American National Standard for Information Sciences-
Permanence Paper for Printed Library Materials, ANSI Z39.48-1984.

♻ This book is printed on recycled paper that meets Environmental Protection Agency Standards.

ISBN 0-8103-9163-5
Vol 2 ISBN 0-8103-9165-1

Library of Congress Cataloging-in-Publication Data

Gale encyclopedia of multicultural America / Judy Galens, Anna J.
Sheets, Robyn V. Young, editors.
    p. cm.
    Includes bibliographical references and index.
    ISBN 0-8103-9164-3. -- ISBN 0-8103-9165-1 (pbk.)
    1. Ethnology--United States--Encyclopedias. 2. Pluralism (Social
sciences)--United States--Encyclopedias. I. Galens, Judy, 1968-
. II. Sheets, Anna J. (Anna Jean), 1970- . III. Young, Robyn V.,
1958- .
E184.A1G14 1995   95-23341
305.8'00973--dc20   CIP

I(T)P™ Gale Research Inc., an International Thomson Publishing Company.
         ITP logo is a trademark under license.

CONTENTS

Volume 1

Volume 2

Based upon a need for comprehensive reference sources in the area of multiculturalism in public, high school, and academic libraries, Gale presents the *Gale Encyclopedia of Multicultural America*. This source contains over one hundred signed original essays, each addressing a distinct ethnic, ethnoreligious, or Native American group in the United States. The articles, which range from 5,000 words to 20,000 words in length, are arranged alphabetically.

SCOPE

The groups included in the *Gale Encyclopedia of Multicultural America* were selected according to two principal criteria: the magnitude of each ethnic group based on the 1990 U.S. Census, and the recommendations of an advisory board regarding widely studied groups in high schools and universities. To meet the needs of students and researchers, the editors and advisory board therefore chose to include some groups that have relatively small populations. The majority of the articles were written by scholars and writers with a special interest in and knowledge of the ethnic groups about which they were writing. Once the essays were completed, additional scholars were asked to review the essays for comprehensiveness, factual accuracy, and objectivity.

The editors have attempted to make the *Gale Encyclopedia of Multicultural America* as inclusive as possible. Its scope encompasses peoples from Africa, Asia, the Caribbean, Central America, Europe, the Middle East, North America, the Pacific Islands, and South America; thus the *Gale Encyclopedia of Multicultural America* recognizes the history, culture, and contributions of established ethnic groups, such as English Americans and French Americans, as well as newer Americans who have been previously overlooked in studies of American ethnic groups, like Hmong Americans and Guatemalan Americans. Moreover, certain ethnoreligious groups, such as the Amish, are included as well.

Because America's cultural diversity is not limited to immigrant groups, the *Gale Encyclopedia of Multicultural America* also contains essays on Native American groups, representing regions

The *Gale Encyclopedia of Multicultural America* has been endorsed by *EMIE Bulletin* of the Ethnic Materials Information Exchange Round Table, American Library Association.

from throughout the United States. The richness of their heritage and the importance of their historical role in the United States require their inclusion in any discussion of multiculturalism. As a full-scale treatment of Native Americans was not possible in this publication, twelve groups were chosen for inclusion based on their cultural diversity, geographical representation, and the recommendations of the advisory board.

There are two chapters devoted to peoples from Subsaharan Africa. Because the vast majority of people in the United States from this region identified themselves as African American in the 1990 U.S. Census, there is a lengthy essay entitled "African Americans" that represents persons of multiple ancestry. An essay on Nigerian Americans, who are a relatively recent immigration group and therefore have a history in the United States that is quite different from other African immigrants, is included as well. According to the 1990 U.S. Census, there were 91,688 people of Nigerian descent in the United States that year, making Nigerians the single largest American immigrant group from a specific country in Subsaharan Africa.

FORMAT

While each essay contained in the *Gale Encyclopedia of Multicultural America* includes information on the country of origin and circumstances surrounding major immigration waves (if applicable), the primary focus of these essays is on that group's experiences in the United States, specifically in the areas of acculturation and assimilation, family and community dynamics, language, religion, employment and economic traditions, politics and government, and significant contributions. Wherever possible, each entry also features directory listings of periodicals, radio and television stations, organizations and associations, and museums and research centers to aid the user in conducting additional research. Each entry also contains sources for further study that are both useful and accessible. Every essay is designed for ease of use by students, teachers, librarians, and the general public, with the articles divided into clearly marked headings and subheadings. This method of organization makes it easy to find specific types of information within an essay, and it also facilitates comparisons between groups.

ADDITIONAL FEATURES

In addition to a general subject index, which provides reference to significant terms, people, places, movements, events, and organizations, the *Gale Encyclopedia of Multicultural America* contains a general bibliography of over 100 books and periodicals, compiled by Vladimir Wertsman of the Ethnic Materials Information Exchange Round Table, American Library Association. These sources do not replicate those listed in each entry; rather, they are concerned with more general works in the field of multicultural studies. The text is highlighted by 171 photographs.

ACKNOWLEDGEMENTS

The editors gratefully acknowledge contributing editor and author of the introduction Rudolph J. Vecoli, as well as the members of the advisory board, especially Vladimir Wertsman for his relentless enthusiasm and support; Neil Schlager and the Multicultural Team, particularly Sharon Malinowski for her guidance, skill, and generous spirit; Jeffrey Muhr and Roger Valade for their technical expertise; Wiley M. Woodard for his extensive research; and the many scholars who reviewed the essays, including Arnold Alanen, Wanni Anderson, Kay A. Averette, Carlota Cárdenas de Dwyer, Araxie Churukian, Oralia Garza de Cortés, Lou Gretch-Cumbo, Kyung-Sun Lim, Joel Monture, Kirin Narayan, Chia Ning, Sorya Poc, Claire Quintal, Martha Ratliff, Akiko Tani, Robert Thacker, Nadeen M. Thomas, Rudolph J. Vecoli, and Vladimir Wertsman. Although we are indebted to these individuals for their efforts, we also recognize that the ultimate responsibility for this publication is ours as the editors.

SUGGESTIONS ARE WELCOME

The editors welcome your suggestions on any aspect of this work. Please send comments to: The Editor, *Gale Encyclopedia of Multicultural America*, Gale Research Inc., 835 Penobscot Bldg., 645 Griswold St., Detroit, MI 48226-4094; or call 1-800-347-GALE; or fax to (313) 961-6741.

The editors wish to thank the permissions managers of the companies that assisted us in securing reprint rights. The following list acknowledges the copyright holders who have granted us permission to reprint material in this edition of the *Gale Encyclopedia of Multicultural America*. Every effort has been made to trace the copyright holders, but if omissions have been made, please contact the editors.

COPYRIGHTED PHOTOGRAPHY

The photographs and illustrations appearing in the *Gale Encyclopedia of Multicultural America* were received from the following sources:

Cover Photographs: **UPI/Bettmann:** The Joy of Citizenship; Against the Sky: **The Bettmann Archive:** Leaving Ellis Island.

Courtesy of Village Historique Acadien: page 3; **Courtesy of David Richmond:** page 7; **AP/Wide World Photos, Inc.:** pages 27, 47, 58, 67, 85, 90, 102, 106, 132, 153, 229, 232, 267, 286, 333, 505, 571, 599, 644, 727, 737, 830, 860, 924, 1050, 1132, 1151, 1168, 1175, 1218, 1278, 1303, 1316, 1369, 1413, 1425; **Courtesy of Skip Mason/Digging It Up Photo Archives:** page 32; **The Bettmann Archive:** pages 44, 660, 769, 1119, 1231, 1337; **UPI/Bettmann:** pages 73, 272, 305, 317, 386, 391, 398, 432, 436, 487, 568, 636, 652, 694, 732, 753, 801, 871, 873, 881, 890, 943, 955, 1011, 1019, 1026, 1092, 1138, 1146, 1163, 1245, 1276, 1285, 1301, 1366, 1381, 1384; © **Ann Trulove/Unicorn Stock Photos:** page 76; A Project Save Photograph Courtesy of Kay Danielian Megerdichian: page 112; © **Michael Newman/PhotoEdit:** page 118; **Courtesy of Rudi VonBriel:** page 127; © **Frances M. Roberts/Levine & Roberts:** pages 166, 330, 722, 1045, 1182; **Courtesy of The Gousse Family Photographs:** page 189; © **Suzanne L. Murphy:** pages 200, 1190, 1235, 1328; © **Richard B. Levine/Levine & Roberts:** pages 205, 902, 978, 1062, 1078; **Courtesy of Culver Pictures:** page 212; © **Robert Ginn/PhotoEdit:** page 275; © **Oscar C. Williams:** pages 290, 792, 1356; © **Gary Conner/PhotoEdit:** pages 303, 520, 605, 803, 842, 1332; © **Elaine S. Queery:** pages 321, 1121; © **1975 The Saul Zaentz Company:** page 355; © **Aneal Vohra/Unicorn Stock Photos:** pages 376, 401, 415, 713, 716, 788, 1074, 1224; **Courtesy of Dr. John M. Nielsen, Professor at Dana College:** page 413; © **Charlotte Kahler:** pages 428; © **Dennis MacDonald/PhotoEdit:** 440; © **Audrey Gottlieb:** pages 452, 457, 494, 580, 587, 1059; © **Gale Zucker:** pages 478, 1110; © **Rick Baker/Unicorn Stock Photos:** page 481; **Courtesy of Tyler Photo Illustrators:** pages 509, 1193; **Courtesy of The Tuomi Family Photographs/Balch Institute for Ethnic Studies:**

ADVISORY BOARD

CONTRIBUTORS

Nabeel Abraham
Professor of Anthropology
Henry Ford Community College
Dearborn, Michigan

June Granatir Alexander
Adjunct Assistant Professor
Russian and East European Studies
University of Cincinnati
Cincinnati, Ohio

Donald Altschiller
Freelance Writer
Cambridge, Massachusetts

Diane Andreassi
Freelance Writer
Livonia, Michigan

Carl L. Bankston III
Professor, Department of Sociology
Louisiana State University
Baton Rouge, Louisiana

Diane Benson
Tlingit Actress and Writer
Eagle River, Alaska

Barbara Bigelow
Freelance Writer
White Lake, Michigan

D.L. Birchfield
Editor and Writer
Oklahoma City, Oklahoma

Herbert Brinks
Professor, Department of History
Calvin College
Grand Rapids, Michigan

Sean Buffington
Professor, Department of Ethnic Studies
University of Michigan
Ann Arbor, Michigan

Phyllis Burson
Independent Consultant
Silver Spring, Maryland

Helen Caver
Associate Professor and Librarian
Jacksonville State University
Jacksonville, Alabama

Cida S. Chase
Professor of Spanish
Oklahoma State University
Stillwater, Oklahoma

Clark Colahan
Professor of Spanish
Whitman College
Walla Walla, Washington

Robert J. Conley
Freelance Writer
Tahlequah, Oklahoma

Jane Cook
Freelance Writer
Green Bay, Wisconsin

Paul Cox
Dean, General Education and Honors
Brigham Young University
Provo, Utah

Ken Cuthbertson
Queen's Alumni Review
Queen's University
Kingston, Ontario, Canada

Rosetta Sharp Dean
Counselor and Writer
Anniston, Alabama

Stanley E. Easton
Professor of Japanese
Jacksonville State University
Jacksonville, Alabama

Lucien Ellington
Professor of Japanese
University of Tennessee-Chattanooga
Chattanooga, Tennessee

Jessie L. Embry
Oral History Program Director
Charles Redd Center for Western Studies
Brigham Young University
Provo, Utah

Allen Englekirk
Professor of Spanish
Gonzaga University
Spokane, Washington

Marianne Fedunkiw
Freelance Writer
Toronto, Ontario, Canada

Mary Gillis
Freelance Writer
Huntington Woods, Michigan

Edward Gobetz
Executive Director
Slovenian Research Center of America, Inc.
Willoughby Hills, Ohio

Mark A. Granquist
Assistant Professor of Religion
Saint Olaf College
Northfield, Minnesota

Derek Green
Freelance Writer
Ann Arbor, Michigan

Paula Hajar
Freelance Writer
New York, New York

Loretta Hall
Freelance Writer
Albuquerque, New Mexico

Sheldon Hanft
Professor, Department of History
Appalachian State University
Boone, North Carolina

Evan Heimlich
Assistant Coordinator
Multicultural Resource Center
The University of Kansas
Lawrence, Kansas

Mary A. Hess
Teaching Assistant
Integrated Arts and Humanities
Michigan State University
Lansing, Michigan

Laurie Hillstrom
Freelance Writer
Pleasant Ridge, Michigan

Maria Hong
Freelance Writer
Austin, Texas

Ed Ifkovic
Writer and Lecturer
Hartford, Connecticut

Alphine Jefferson
Professor, Department of History
The College of Wooster
Wooster, Ohio

Syd Jones
Freelance Writer and Novelist
Aptos, California

Jane Jurgens
Assistant Professor
Learning Resources Center
St. Cloud State University
St. Cloud, Minnesota

Jim Kamp
Freelance Writer and Editor
Royal Oak, Michigan

Oscar Kawagley
Assistant Professor of Education
College of Liberal Arts, UAF
Fairbanks, Alaska

Vituat Kipel
Librarian, Slavic and Baltic Division
The New York Public Library
New York, New York

Donald B. Kraybill
Professor, Department of Sociology
Elizabethtown College
Elizabethtown, Pennsylvania

Ken Kurson
Freelance Writer
New York, New York

Odd S. Lovoll
Professor of Scandinavian American Studies
Saint Olaf College
Northfield, Minnesota

Jacqueline A. McLeod
Freelance Writer
Michigan State University
East Lansing, Michigan

Paul Robert Magosci
Director and Chief Executive Officer
Multicultural History Society of Ontario
Toronto, Ontario, Canada

William Maxwell
Contributing Editor
A Gathering of the Tribes Magazine
New York, New York

H. Brett Melendy
University Archivist
San Jose State University
San Jose, California

Mona Mikhail
Professor, Department of Near Eastern Languages
and Literatures
New York University
New York, New York

Christine Molinari
Manuscript Editor
The University of Chicago Press
Chicago, Illinois

Lloyd Mulraine
Professor of English
Jacksonville State University
Jacksonville, Alabama

Jeremy Mumford
Assistant News Editor
Courtroom Television Network
New York, New York

N. Samuel Murrell
Professor of Religion and Black Studies
The College of Wooster
Wooster, Ohio

Amy Nash
Freelance Writer
Minneapolis, Minnesota

John Mark Nielson
Professor of English
Dana College
Blair, Nebraska

Ernest E. Norden
Professor, Division of Spanish and Portuguese
Baylor University
Waco, Texas

John F. Packel, II
Freelance Writer
Brooklyn, New York

Tinaz Pavri
Freelance Writer
Columbus, Ohio

Richard Perrin
Librarian, Reference and Instructional Services
Timme Library
Ferris State University
Big Rapids, Michigan

Peter L. Peterson
Professor of History
West Texas A&M
Canyon, Texas

George E. Pozzetta
Professor, Department of History
University of Florida
Gainesville, Florida

Brendan Rapple
Reference Librarian/Education Bibliographer
O'Neill Library
Boston College
Boston, Massachusetts

Megan Ratner
Freelance Writer
New York, New York

La Vern J. Rippley
Professor of German
Saint Olaf College
Northfield, Minnesota

Julio César Rodríguez
Freelance Writer
Walla Walla, Washington

Lorene Roy
Associate Professor and Minority Liaison Officer
The University of Texas at Austin
Austin, Texas

Kwasi Sarkodie-Mensah
Chief Reference Librarian
O'Neill Library
Boston College
Boston, Massachusetts

Leo Schelbert
Professor, Department of History
University of Illinois at Chicago
Chicago, Illinois

Mary C. Sengstock
Professor, Department of Sociology
Wayne State University
Detroit, Michigan

Stefan Smagula
Freelance Writer
Austin, Texas

Bosiljka Stevanovic
Principal Librarian
Donnell Library Center
World Languages Collection
The New York Public Library
New York, New York

Andris Straumanis
Freelance Writer
New Brighton, Minnesota

Pamela Sturner
Freelance Writer
New Haven, Connecticut

Mark Swartz
Manuscript Editor
The University of Chicago Press
Chicago, Illinois

Harold T. Takooshian
Professor, Division of Social Sciences
Fordham University
New York, New York

Felix Unaeze
Head Librarian
Reference and Instructional
    Services Department
Timme Library
Ferris State University
Big Rapids, Michigan

Steven Béla Várdy
Professor and Director,
    Department of History
Duquesne University
Pittsburgh, Pennsylvania

Ling-chi Wang
Professor, Asian American Studies
Department of Ethnic Studies
University of California, Berkeley
Berkeley, California

K. Marianne Wargelin
Freelance Writer
Minneapolis, Minnesota

Vladimir Wertsman
Chair of Publishing in Multicultural Materials
Ethnic Materials Information Exchange
American Library Association
New York, New York

Mary T. Williams
Associate Professor
Jacksonville State University
Jacksonville, Alabama

Elaine Winters
Freelance Writer
Berkeley, California

Eveline Yang
Manager, Information Delivery Program
Auraria Library
Denver, Colorado

Eleanor Yu
Deputy News Editor
Courtroom Television Network
New York, New York

INTRODUCTION

RUDOLPH J. VECOLI

The term multiculturalism has recently come into usage to describe a society characterized by a diversity of cultures. Religion, language, customs, traditions, and values are some of the components of culture, but more importantly culture is the lens through which one perceives and interprets the world. When a shared culture forms the basis for a "sense of peoplehood," based on consciousness of a common past, we can speak of a group possessing an ethnicity. As employed here, ethnicity is not transmitted genetically from generation to generation; nor is it unchanging over time. Rather, ethnicity is invented or constructed in response to particular historical circumstances and changes as circumstances change. "Race," a sub-category of ethnicity, is not a biological reality but a cultural construction. While in its most intimate form an ethnic group may be based on face-to-face relationships, a politicized ethnicity mobilizes its followers far beyond the circle of personal acquaintances. Joined with aspirations for political self-determination, ethnicity can become full-blown nationalism. In this essay, ethnicity will be used to identify groups or communities that are differentiated by religious, racial, or cultural characteristics and that possess a sense of peoplehood.

The "Multicultural America" to which this encyclopedia is dedicated is the product of the mingling of many different peoples over the course of several hundred years in what is now the

United States. Cultural diversity was characteristic of this continent prior to the coming of European colonists and African slaves. The indigenous inhabitants of North America who numbered an estimated 4.5 million in 1500 were divided into hundreds of tribes with distinctive cultures, languages, and religions. Although the numbers of "Indians," as they were named by Europeans, declined precipitously through the nineteenth century, their population has rebounded in the twentieth century. Both as members of their particular tribes (a form of ethnicity), Navajo, Ojibwa, Choctaw, etc., and as American Indians (a form of panethnicity), they are very much a part of today's cultural and ethnic pluralism.

Most Americans, however, are descendants of immigrants. Since the sixteenth century, from the earliest Spanish settlement at St. Augustine, Florida, the process of repeopling this continent has gone on apace. Some 600,000 Europeans and Africans were recruited or enslaved and transported across the Atlantic Ocean in the colonial period to what was to become the United States. The first census of 1790 revealed the high degree of diversity that already marked the American population. Almost 19 percent were of African ancestry, another 12 percent Scottish and Scotch-Irish, ten percent German, with smaller numbers of French, Irish, Welsh, and Sephardic Jews. The census did not include American Indians. The English, sometimes described as the "founding people," only comprised 48 percent of the total. At the time of its birth in 1776, the United States was already a "complex ethnic mosaic," with a wide variety of communities differentiated by culture, language, race, and religion.

The present United States includes not only the original thirteen colonies, but lands that were subsequently purchased or conquered. Through this territorial expansion, other peoples were brought within the boundaries of the republic; these included, in addition to many Native American tribes, French, Hawaiian, Inuit, Mexican, and Puerto Rican, among others. Since 1790, population growth, other than by natural increase, has come primarily through three massive waves of immigration. During the first wave (1841-1890), almost 15 million immigrants arrived: over four million Germans, three million each of Irish and British (English, Scottish, and Welsh), and one million Scandinavians. A second wave (1891-1920) brought an additional 18 million immigrants: almost four million from Italy, 3.6 million from Austria-Hungary, and three

million from Russia. In addition, over two million Canadians, Anglo and French, immigrated prior to 1920. The intervening decades, from 1920 to 1945, marked a hiatus in immigration due to restrictive policies, economic depression, and war. A modest post-World War II influx of refugees was followed by a new surge subsequent to changes in immigration policy in 1965. Totalling approximately 16 million—and still in progress, this third wave encompassed some four million from Mexico, another four million from Central and South America and the Caribbean, and roughly six million from Asia. While almost 90 percent of the first two waves originated in Europe, only 12 percent of the third did.

Immigration has introduced an enormous diversity of cultures into American society. The 1990 U.S. Census report on ancestry provides a fascinating portrait of the complex ethnic origins of the American people. Responses to the question, "What is your ancestry or ethnic origin?," were tabulated for 215 ancestry groups. The largest ancestry groups reported were, in order of magnitude, German, Irish, English, and African American, all over 20 million.

Other groups reporting over six million were Italian, Mexican, French, Polish, Native American, Dutch, and Scotch-Irish, while another 28 groups reported over one million each. Scanning the roster of ancestries one is struck by the plethora of smaller groups: Hmong, Maltese, Honduran, Carpatho-Rusyns, and Nigerian, among scores of others. Interestingly enough, only five percent identified themselves simply as "American"—and less than one percent as "white."

Immigration also contributed to the transformation of the religious character of the United States. Its original Protestantism (itself divided among many denominations and sects) was both reinforced by the arrival of millions of Lutherans, Methodists, Presbyterians, etc., and diluted by the heavy influx of Roman Catholics—first the Irish and Germans, then Eastern Europeans and Italians, and more recently Hispanics. These immigrants have made Roman Catholicism the largest single denomination in the country. Meanwhile, Slavic Christian and Jewish immigrants from Central and Eastern Europe established Judaism and Orthodoxy as major American religious bodies. As a consequence of Near Eastern immigration—and the conversion of many African Americans to Islam—there are currently some three million Muslims in the United States. Smaller numbers of Buddhists, Hindus, and followers of other religions have also arrived. In many American cities, houses of worship now include mosques and temples as well as churches and synagogues. Such religious pluralism is an important source of American multiculturalism.

The immigration and naturalization policies pursued by a country are a key to understanding its self-conception as a nation. By determining who to admit to residence and citizenship, the dominant element defines the future ethnic and racial composition of the population and the body politic. Each of the three great waves of immigration inspired much soul-searching and intense debate over the consequences for the republic. If the capacity of American society to absorb some 55 million immigrants over the course of a century and a half is impressive, it is also true that American history has been punctuated by ugly episodes of nativism and xenophobia. With the possible exception of the British, it is difficult to find an immigrant group that has not been subject to some degree of prejudice and discrimination. From their early encounters with Native Americans and Africans, Anglo-Americans established "whiteness" as an essential marker of difference and superiority. The Naturalization Act of 1790, for example, specified that citizenship was to be available to "any alien, being a free white person." By this provision not only were blacks ineligible for naturalization, but also future immigrants who were deemed not to be "white." The greater the likeness of immigrants to the Anglo-American type (e.g., British Protestants), the more readily they were welcomed.

Not all Anglo-Americans were racists or xenophobes. Citing Christian and democratic ideals of universal brotherhood, many advocated the abolition of slavery and the rights of freedmen—freedom of religion and cultural tolerance. Debates over immigration policy brought these contrasting views of the republic into collision. The ideal of America as an asylum for the oppressed of the world has exerted a powerful influence for a liberal reception of newcomers. Emma Lazarus's sonnet, which began "Give me your tired, your poor, your huddled masses yearning to breathe free, the wretched refuse of your teeming shore," struck a responsive chord among many Anglo-Americans. Moreover, American capitalism depended upon the rural workers of Europe, French Canada, Mexico, and Asia to man its factories and mines. Nonetheless, many Americans have regarded immigration as posing a threat to social stability, the jobs of native white workers, honest politics, and American cultural—even biological—integrity. The strength of anti-immigrant movements has waxed and waned with the volume of immigration, but even more with fluctuations in the state of the economy and society. Although the targets of nativist attacks have changed over time, a constant theme has been the danger posed by foreigners to American values and institutions.

Irish Catholics, for example, were viewed as minions of the Pope and enemies of the Protestant character of the country. A Protestant Crusade culminated with the formation of the American (or "Know-Nothing") Party in 1854, whose battle cry was "America for the Americans!" While the Know-Nothing movement was swallowed up by sectional conflict culminating in the Civil War, anti-Catholicism continued to be a powerful strain of nativism well into the twentieth century.

Despite such episodes of xenophobia, during its first century of existence, the United States welcomed all newcomers with minimal regulation. In 1882, however, two laws initiated a progressive tightening of restrictions upon immigration. The first established qualitative health and moral standards by excluding criminals, prostitutes, lunatics, idiots, and paupers. The second, the Chinese Exclusion Act, the culmination of an anti-Chinese movement centered on the West Coast, denied admission to Chinese laborers and barred Chinese immigrants from acquiring citizenship. Following the enactment of this law, agitation for exclusion of Asians continued as the Japanese and others arrived, culminating in the provision of the Immigration Law of 1924, which denied entry to aliens ineligible for citizenship (those who were not deemed "white"). It was not until 1952 that a combination of international politics and democratic idealism finally resulted in the elimination of all racial restrictions from American immigration and naturalization policies.

In the late nineteenth century, "scientific" racialism, which asserted the superiority of Anglo-Saxons, was embraced by many Americans as justification for imperialism and immigration restriction. At that time a second immigrant wave was beginning to bring peoples from eastern Europe, the Balkans, and the Mediterranean into the country. Nativists campaigned for a literacy test and other measures to restrict the entry of these that "inferior races." Proponents of a liberal immigration policy defeated such efforts until World War I created a xenophobic climate which not only insured the passage of the literacy test, but prepared the way for the Immigration Acts of 1921 and 1924. Inspired by racialist ideas, these laws established national quota systems designed to drastically reduce the number of southern and eastern Europeans entering the United States and to bar Asians entirely. In essence, the statutes sought to freeze the biological and ethnic identity of the American people by protecting them from contamination from abroad.

Until 1965 the United States pursued this restrictive and racist immigration policy. The Immigration Act of 1965 did away with the national origins quota system and opened the country to immigration from throughout the world, establishing preferences for family members of American citizens and resident aliens, skilled workers, and refugees. The unforeseen consequence of the law of 1965 was the third wave of immigration. Not only did the annual volume of immigration increase steadily to the current level of one million or more arrivals each year, but the majority of the immigrants now came from Asia and Latin America. During the 1980s, they accounted for 85 percent of the total number of immigrants, with Mexicans, Chinese, Filipinos, and Koreans being the largest contingents.

The cumulative impact of an immigration of 16 plus millions since 1965 has aroused intense concerns regarding the demographic, cultural, and racial future of the American people. The skin color, languages, and lifestyles of the newcomers triggered a latent xenophobia in the American psyche. While eschewing the overt racism of earlier years, advocates of tighter restriction have warned that if current rates of immigration continue, the "minorities" (persons of African, Asian, and "Hispanic" ancestry) will make up about half of the American population by the year 2050.

A particular cause of anxiety is the number of undocumented immigrants (estimated at 200,000-300,000 per year). Contrary to popular belief, the majority of these individuals do not cross the border from Mexico, but enter the country with either student or tourist visas and simply stay—many are Europeans and Asians. The Immigration Reform and Control Act (IRCA) of 1986 sought to solve the problem by extending amnesty for undocumented immigrants under certain conditions and imposing penalties on employers who hired undocumented immigrants, while making special provisions for temporary agricultural migrant workers. Although over three million persons qualified for consideration for amnesty, employer sanctions failed for lack of effective enforcement, and the number of undocumented immigrants has not decreased. Congress subsequently enacted the Immigration Act of 1990, which established a cap of 700,000 immigrants per year, maintained preferences based on family reunification, and expanded the number of skilled workers to be admitted. Immigration, however, has continued to be a hotly debated issue. Responding to the nativist mood of the country, politicians have advocated measures to limit access of legal as well as undocumented immigrants to Medicare and other welfare benefits. A constitutional amendment was even proposed that would deny citizenship to American-born children of undocumented residents.

Forebodings about an "unprecedented immigrant invasion," however, appear exaggerated. In the early 1900s, the rate of immigration (the number of immigrants measured against the total population) was ten per every thousand; in the 1980s the rate was only 3.5 per every thousand. While the number of foreign-born individuals in the United States reached an all-time high of almost 20 million in 1990, they accounted for only eight percent of the population as compared with 14.7 per cent in 1910. In other words, the statistical impact of contemporary immigration has been of a much smaller magnitude than that of the past. A persuasive argument has also been made that immigrants, legal and undocumented, contribute more than they take from the American economy and that they pay more in taxes than they receive in social services. As in the past, immigrants are being made scapegoats for the country's problems.

Among the most difficult questions facing students of American history are: how have these tens of millions of immigrants with such differing cultures incorporated into American society?; and what changes have they wrought in the character of that society? The concepts of acculturation and assimilation are helpful in understanding the processes whereby immigrants have adapted to the new society. Applying Milton Gordon's theory, acculturation is the process whereby newcomers assume American cultural attributes, such as the English language, manners, and values, while assimilation is the process of their incorporation into the social networks (work, residence, leisure, families) of the host society. These changes have not come quickly or easily. Many immigrants have experienced only limited acculturation and practically no assimilation during their lifetimes. Among the factors that have affected these processes are race, ethnicity, class, gender, and character of settlement.

The most important factor, however, has been the willingness of the dominant ethnic group (Anglo-Americans) to accept the foreigners. Since they have wielded political and social power, Anglo-Americans have been able to decide who to include and who to exclude. Race (essentially skin color) has been the major barrier to acceptance; thus Asians and Mexicans, as well as African Americans and Native Americans, have in the past been excluded from full integration into the mainstream. At various times, religion, language, and nationality have constituted impediments to incorporation. Social class has also strongly affected interactions among various ethnic groups. Historically, American society has been highly stratified with a close congruence between class and ethnicity, i.e., Anglo-Americans tend to belong to the upper class, northern and western Europeans to the middle class, and southern and eastern Europeans and African Americans to the working class. The metaphor of a "vertical mosaic" has utility in conceptualizing American society. A high degree of segregation (residential, occupational, leisure) within the vertical mosaic has severely limited acculturation and assimilation across class and ethnic lines. However, within a particular social class, various immigrant groups have often interacted at work, in neighborhoods, at churches and saloons, and in the process have engaged in what one historian has described as "Americanization from the bottom up."

Gender has also been a factor since the status of women within the general American society, as well as within their particular ethnic groups, has affected their assimilative and acculturative experiences. Wide variations exist among groups as to the degree to which women are restricted to traditional roles or have freedom to pursue opportunities in the larger society. The density and location of immigrant settlements have also influenced the rate and character of incorporation into the mainstream culture. Concentrated urban settlements and isolated rural settlements, by limiting contacts between the immigrants and others, tend to inhibit the processes of acculturation and assimilation.

An independent variable in these processes, however, is the determination of immigrants themselves whether or not to shed their cultures and become simply Americans. By and large, they are not willing or able to do so. Rather, they cling, often tenaciously, to their old world traditions,

languages, and beliefs. Through chain migrations, relatives and friends have regrouped in cities, towns, and the countryside for mutual assistance and to maintain their customary ways. Establishing churches, societies, newspapers, and other institutions, they have built communities and have developed an enlarged sense of peoplehood. Thus, ethnicity (although related to nationalist movements in countries of origin) in large part has emerged from the immigrants' attempt to cope with life in this pluralist society. While they cannot transplant their Old Country ways intact to the Dakota prairie or the Chicago slums, theirs is a selective adaptation, in which they have taken from American culture that which they needed and have kept from their traditional culture that which they valued. Rather than becoming Anglo-Americans, they became ethnic Americans of various kinds.

Assimilation and acculturation have progressed over the course of several generations. The children and grandchildren of the immigrants have retained less of their ancestral cultures (languages are first to go, customs and traditions often follow) and have assumed more mainstream attributes. Yet many have retained, to a greater or lesser degree, a sense of identity and affiliation with a particular ethnic group. Conceived of not as a finite culture brought over in immigrant trunks, but as a mode of accommodation to the dominant culture, ethnicity persists even when the cultural content changes.

We might also ask to *what* have the descendants been assimilating and acculturating. Some have argued that there is an American core culture, essentially British in origin, in which immigrants and their offspring are absorbed. However, if one compares the "mainstream culture" of Americans today (music, food, literature, mass media) with that of one or two centuries ago, it is obvious that it is not Anglo-American (even the American English language has undergone enormous changes from British English). Rather, mainstream culture embodies and reflects the spectrum of immigrant and indigenous ethnic cultures that make up American society. It is the product of syncretism, the melding of different, sometimes contradictory and discordant elements. Multiculturalism is not a museum of immigrant cultures, but rather this complex of the living, vibrant ethnicities of contemporary America.

If Americans share an ideological heritage deriving from the ideals of the American Revolution, such ideals have not been merely abstract principles handed down unchanged from the eighteenth century to the present. Immigrant and indigenous ethnic groups, taking these ideals at face value, have employed them as weapons to combat ethnic and racial prejudice and economic exploitation. If America was the Promised Land, for many the promise was realized only after prolonged and collective struggles. Through labor and civil rights movements, they have contributed to keeping alive and enlarging the ideals of justice, freedom, and equality. If America transformed the immigrants and indigenous ethnic groups, they have also transformed America.

How have Americans conceived of this polyglot, kaleidoscopic society? Over the centuries, several models of a social order, comprised of a variety of ethnic and racial groups, have competed for dominance. An early form was a society based on caste—a society divided into those who were free and those who were not free. Such a social order existed in the South for two hundred years. While the Civil War destroyed slavery, the Jim Crow system of racial segregation maintained a caste system for another hundred years. But the caste model was not limited to black-white relations in the southern states. Industrial capitalism also created a caste-like structure in the North. For a century prior to the New Deal, power, wealth, and status were concentrated in the hands of an Anglo-American elite, while the workers, comprised largely of immigrants and their children, were the helots of the farms and the factories. The caste model collapsed in both the North and the South in the twentieth century before the onslaught of economic expansion, technological change, and geographic and social mobility.

Anglo-conformity has been a favored model through much of our history. Convinced of their cultural and even biological superiority, Anglo-Americans have demanded that Native Americans, African Americans, and immigrants abandon their distinctive linguistic, cultural, and religious traits and conform (in so far as they are capable) to the Anglo model. But at the same time that they demanded conformity to their values and lifestyles, Anglo-Americans erected barriers that severely limited social intercourse with those they regarded as inferior. The ideology of Anglo-conformity has particularly influenced educational policies. A prime objective of the American public school system has been the assimilation of "alien" children to Anglo-American middle class values and behaviors. In recent years, Anglo-conformity has taken the form of

opposition to bilingual education. A vigorous campaign has been waged for a constitutional amendment that would make English the official language of the United States.

A competing model, the Melting Pot, symbolized the process whereby the foreign elements were to be transmuted into a new American race. There have been many variants of this ideology of assimilation, including one in which the Anglo-American is the cook stirring and determining the ingredients, but the prevailing concept has been that a distinctive amalgam of all the varied cultures and peoples would emerge from the crucible. Expressing confidence in the capacity of America to assimilate all newcomers, the Melting Pot ideology provided the rationale for a liberal immigration policy. Although the Melting Pot ideology came under sharp attack in the 1960s as a coercive policy of assimilation, the increased immigration of recent years and the related anxiety over national unity has brought it back into favor in certain academic and political circles.

In response to pressures for 100 percent Americanization during World War I, the model of Cultural Pluralism has been offered as an alternative to the Melting Pot. In this model, while sharing a common American citizenship and loyalty, ethnic groups would maintain and foster their particular languages and cultures. The metaphors employed for the cultural pluralism model have included a symphony orchestra, a flower garden, a mosaic, and a stew or salad. All suggest a reconciliation of diversity with an encompassing harmony and coherence. The fortunes of the pluralist model have fluctuated with the national mood. During the 1930s, when cultural democracy was in vogue, pluralist ideas were popular. Again during the period of the "new ethnicity" of the 1960s and the 1970s, cultural pluralism attracted a considerable following. In recent years, heightened fears that American society was fragmenting caused many to reject pluralism for a return to the Melting Pot.

As the United States approaches the twenty-first century its future as an ethnically plural society is hotly contested. Is the United States more diverse today than in the past? Is the unity of society threatened by its diversity? Are the centrifugal forces in American society more powerful than the centripetal? The old models of Anglo-conformity, the Melting Pot, and Cultural Pluralism have lost their explanatory and symbolic value. We need a new model, a new definition of our identity as a people, which will encompass our expanding multiculturalism and which will define us as a multiethnic people in the context of a multiethnic world. We need a compelling paradigm that will command the faith of all Americans because it embraces them in their many-splendored diversity within a just society.

SUGGESTED READINGS

On acculturation and assimilation, Milton Gordon's *Assimilation in American Life: The Role of Race, Religion, and National Origins* (1964) provides a useful theoretical framework. For a discussion of the concept of ethnicity, see Kathleen Neils Conzen, et al. "The Invention of Ethnicity: A Perspective from the USA," *Journal of American Ethnic History*, 12 (Fall 1992). *Harvard Encyclopedia of American Ethnic Groups*, ed. Stephan Thernstrom (Cambridge, MA, 1980) is a standard reference work with articles on themes as well as specific groups; see especially the essay by Philip Gleason. "American Identity and Americanization." Roger Daniels' *Coming to America: A History of Immigration and Ethnicity in American Life* (New York, 1991) is the most comprehensive and up-to-date history. For a comparative history of ethnic groups see Ronald Takaki's *A Different Mirror: A History of Multicultural America* (1993). On post-1965 immigration, David Reimers' *Still the Golden Door: The Third World Comes to America* (1985), is an excellent overview. A classic work on nativism is John Higham's, *Strangers in the Land: Patterns of American Nativism: 1860-1925* (1963), but see also David H. Bennett's *The Party of Fear: From Nativist Movements to the New Right in American History* (1988). On the Anglo-American elite see E. Digby Baltzell's *The Protestant Establishment: Aristocracy and Caste in America* (1964).

IRISH AMERICANS

by
**Brendan A.
Rapple**

The Irish have been present in the United States for hundreds of years and, accordingly, have had more opportunity than many other ethnic groups to assimilate to the wider society. Each successive generation has become more integrated with the dominant culture.

OVERVIEW

The island of Ireland lies west of Great Britain across the Irish Sea and St. George's Channel. It is divided into two separate political entities: the independent Republic of Ireland, and Northern Ireland, a constituent of the United Kingdom. Dublin is the capital of the former, Belfast of the latter. The country is divided into four provinces: Leinster, Munster, Connaught, and Ulster. All of the first three and part of the fourth are situated within the Republic of Ireland. Ulster is made up of nine counties; the northeastern six constitute Northern Ireland. The area of the Republic of Ireland is 27,137 square miles, that of Northern Ireland is 5,458 square miles. The entire island, with a total area of 32,595 square miles, is a little larger than the state of Maine. The population of the Republic of Ireland in 1991 was approximately 3,523,401, that of Northern Ireland 1,569,971. About 95 percent of the Republic's population is Roman Catholic; most of the rest are Protestant. Over 25 percent of Northern Ireland's population is Roman Catholic; about 23 percent is Presbyterian; about 18 percent belongs to the Church of Ireland; the rest are members of other churches or of no stated denomination.

This 1929 photograph shows an Irish family after their arrival in New York City.

HISTORY

Ireland was occupied by Celtic peoples, who came to be known as Gaels, sometime between 600 and 400 B.C. The Romans never invaded Ireland so the Gaels remained isolated and were able to develop a distinct culture. In the fifth century A.D. St. Patrick came to Ireland and introduced the Gaels to Christianity. Thus began a great religious and cultural period for the country. While the rest of Europe was swiftly declining into the Dark Ages, Irish monasteries—preserving the Greek and Latin of the ancient world—not only became great centers of learning, but also sent many famous missionaries to the Continent. Toward the end of the eighth century Vikings invaded Ireland and for over two centuries battled with the Irish. Finally in 1014 the Irish under King Brian Boru soundly defeated the Viking forces at the Battle of Clontarf. An important legacy of the Viking invasion was the establishment of such cities as Dublin, Cork, Waterford, Limerick, and Wexford. In the second half of the twelfth century King Henry II began the English Lordship of Ireland and the challenge of the Anglo-Norman Conquest commenced. By the close of the medieval period many of the Anglo-Norman invaders had been absorbed into the Gaelic population.

English kings traveled to Ireland on several occasions to effect order and increase allegiance to the Crown. The English were generally too occupied with the Hundred Years War (1337-1453) and with the War of the Roses (1455-1485) to deal adequately with the Irish, however. By the sixteenth century English control over Ireland was limited to a small area of land surrounding Dublin. Consequently, Henry VIII and his successors endeavored to force the Irish to submit through military incursions and by "planting" large areas of Ireland with settlers loyal to England. A forceful resistance to the English reconquest of Ireland was led by the Northern chieftain Hugh O'Neill at the end of the sixteenth century. Following O'Neill's defeat in 1603 and his subsequent flight to the Continent, the Crown commenced the large-scale plantation of Ulster with English settlers; Scottish Presbyterians soon followed. During the seventeenth century Ireland, continuing its steady decline, came increasingly under England's rule. In 1641 the Irish allied themselves to the Stuart cause; however, after the defeat and execution of King Charles I in 1649 Cromwell and his Puritans devastated much of Ireland, massacred thousands, and parceled out vast tracts of land to their soldiers and followers. Hoping to regain some of their property, the Catholic Irish sided with the Catholic James II of England but their fortunes further declined when James was defeated by William of Orange at the Battle of the Boyne in 1690. To keep the Irish subservient and powerless the English enacted a series of brutal penal laws, which succeeded so well that eighteenth century Catholic Ireland was economically and socially wasted.

In 1800, two years after the defeat of the rebellion of Protestant and Catholic United Irishmen led by Wolfe Tone, the Act of Union was passed combining Great Britain and Ireland into one United Kingdom. The Catholic Emancipation Act followed in 1829 chiefly due to the activities of the Irish politician Daniel O'Connell. During the 1830s and 1840s a new nationalist movement, Young Ireland, arose. A rebellion that it launched in 1848, however, was easily defeated. The second half of the 1840s was one of the grimmest periods in Irish history. Due to the great famine caused by the crop failure of Ireland's staple food—the potato—millions died or emigrated. The second half of the nineteenth century saw increased nationalistic demands for self-government and land reform, most notably in the activities of the Home Rule Movement under the leadership of Charles Stewart Parnell. Though home rule was finally passed in 1914, it was deferred because of the onset of World War I. On Easter Monday in 1916 a small force of Irish nationalists rebelled in Dublin against British rule. The rising was a military failure and had little support among the public. However, the harsh response of the British government and particularly its execution of the rising's leaders won many over to the cause. After the Anglo-Irish Treaty was signed in 1921, the Irish Free State, whose constitutional status was tied to the British Commonwealth and required allegiance to the Crown, was established. The Free State was composed of 26 of Ireland's 32 counties, the other six remained part of Britain. In 1949 the 26 counties became the Republic of Ireland, an independent nation. Although the Republic has consistently maintained its claim over the six counties of the U.K.'s Northern Ireland and declared its wish to reunite the whole island into a sovereign nation, in recent decades it has placed more emphasis on economic and social rather than nationalistic issues. Nevertheless, the status of the six counties of Northern Ireland remains a highly critical concern for politicians in Dublin, Belfast, and London.

IRISH EMIGRATION

The Irish like to boast that St. Brendan sailed to America almost a millennium before Christopher Columbus; but even if St. Brendan did not make it to the New World, Galway-born William Ayers was one of Columbus's crew in 1492. During the seventeenth century the majority of the Irish immigrants to America were Catholics. Most were poor, many coming as indentured servants, others under agreements to reimburse their fare sometime after arrival, a minority somehow managing to pay their own way. A small number were more prosperous and came seeking adventure. Still others were among the thousands who were exiled to the West Indies by Cromwell during the 1640s and later made their way to America. There was an increase in Irish immigration during the eighteenth century, though the numbers were still relatively small. Most of the century's arrivals were Presbyterians from the northern province of Ulster who had originally been sent there from Scotland as colonists by the British crown. Many of these, dissenters from the established Protestant church, came to America fleeing religious discrimination. In later years, especially in the second half of the nineteenth century, it was common to assign the term Scotch-Irish to these Ulster Protestant immigrants, although they thought of themselves as strictly Irish. There were also numerous Irish Quaker immigrants, as well as some Protestants from the south. A significant minority of eighteenth century immigrants were southern Catholics. Most of the these were escaping the appalling social and economic conditions as well as the draconian penal laws enacted by the British to annihilate the Celtic heritage and the religion of the Catholic majority. Some of these Catholic arrivals in America in time converted to Protestantism after encountering severe anti-papist discrimination as well as an absence of Catholic churches and priests. The preferred destinations of most of the eighteenth century Irish immigrants were New England, Maryland, Pennsylvania, the Carolinas, and Virginia.

IMMIGRATION UNTIL THE FAMINE YEARS

In the early years of the nineteenth century Protestants, many of whom were skilled tradesmen, continued to account for the majority of Irish immigrants. There were also numerous political refugees especially after the abortive United Irishmen uprising of 1798. However, by the 1820s and 1830s the overwhelming majority of those fleeing the country were unskilled Catholic peasant laborers. By this time Ireland was becoming Europe's most densely populated country, the population having increased from about three million in 1725 to over eight million by 1841. The land could not support such a number. One of the main problems was the absence of the practice of primogeniture among the Irish. Family farms or plots were divided again and again until individual allotments were often so small—perhaps only one or two acres in size—that they were of little use in raising a family. Conditions worsened when, in the wake of a post-Napoleonic Wars agricultural depression, many Irish were evicted from the land they had leased as tenants because the landlords wanted it used for grazing. The concurrent great rise in population left thousands of discontented landless Irish eager to seek new horizons. Moreover, the increase in industrialization had all but ended the modest amount of domestic weaving and spinning that had helped to supplement the income of some families. In addition, famine was never distant—a number of severe potato failures occurred during the 1820s and 1830s before the major famine of the 1840s.

As the passage from Britain to the Canadian Maritimes was substantially cheaper than that to the United States, many Irish immigrants came first to Canada, landing at Quebec, Montreal, or Halifax and then sailed or even walked down into America. After about 1840, however, most immigrants sailed from Ireland to an American port. Whereas most of the Irish Catholic immigrants during the eighteenth century became engaged in some sort of farming occupation, those in the subsequent century tended to remain in such urban centers as Boston, New York, and Philadelphia or in the textile towns where their unskilled labor could be readily utilized. The immigrants were impoverished but usually not as destitute as those who came during the famine. Many readily found jobs building roads or canals such as the Erie. Still, times were tough for most of them, especially the Catholics who frequently found themselves a minority and targets of discrimination in an overwhelmingly Protestant nation.

FROM FAMINE YEARS TO THE PRESENT

It was the cataclysmic Potato Famine of 1845-1851, one of the most severe disasters in Irish history, that initiated the greatest departure of Irish immigrants to the United States. The potato constituted the main dietary staple for most Irish and when the blight struck a number of successive harvests social and economic disintegration ensued. As many as 1.5 million individuals perished of starvation and the diverse epidemics that accompanied the famine. A great number of the survivors emigrated, many of them to the United States From the beginning of the famine in the mid-1840s until 1860 about 1.7 million Irish immigrated to the United States mainly from the provinces of Connaught and Munster. In the latter part of the century, though the numbers fell from the highs of the famine years, the influx from Ireland continued to be large. While families predominated during the Famine exodus, single people now accounted for a far higher proportion of the immigrants. By 1880 more single women than single men were immigrants. It has been estimated that from 1820 to 1900 about four million Irish immigrated to the United States.

Though the majority of Irish immigrants continued to inhabit urban centers, principally in the northeast but also in such cities as Chicago, New Orleans, and San Francisco, a significant minority went further afield. Only a small number went west to engage in farming, however. Most Irish immigrants were indeed peasants, but few had the money to purchase land or had sufficient skill and experience to make a success of large-scale agriculture. Still, despite the great exploitation, oppression, and hardships suffered by many nineteenth-century Irish immigrants, the majority endured and their occupational mobility began to improve slowly. Their prowess and patriotic fervor in the Civil War helped to diminish anti-Irish bigotry and discrimination. As the years went by, the occupational caliber of Irish immigrants gradually improved in line with the slow amelioration of conditions in Ireland. By the end of the century a high proportion were skilled or semi-skilled laborers or had trades. Moreover, these immigrants were greatly aided by the Irish American infrastructure that awaited them. While life was still harsh for most immigrants, the parochial schools, charitable societies, workers' organizations, and social clubs aided their entry into a society that still frequently discriminated against Irish Catholics. Furthermore, the influx of even poorer southern and eastern European immigrants helped the Irish attain increased status.

In the twentieth century immigration from Ireland has ebbed and flowed. After World War I Irish immigration to the United States was high. After Congress passed legislation limiting immigration during the 1920s, however, the numbers declined. Numbers for the 1930s were particularly low. After World War II numbers again increased; but the 1960s saw emigration from Ireland falling dramatically as a result of new quota laws restricting northern Europeans. Accordingly, the number of Irish-born legal residents now in the United States is far lower than it was in the mid-twentieth century. From the 1980s onward, however, there has been an unprecedented influx of undocumented Irish immigrants, especially to such traditionally Irish centers as New York, Boston, Chicago, and San Francisco. These have been mainly young, well-educated individuals who have left an economically troubled country with one of the highest rates of unemployment in the European Community (EC). They prefer to work illegally in the United States, frequently in Irish-owned businesses, as bartenders, construction workers, nannies, and food servers, exposed to the dangers of exploitation and apprehension by the law, rather than remain on the dole at home. Their number is unknown, though the figure is estimated to be between 100,000 and 150,000.

ACCULTURATION AND ASSIMILATION

The Irish have been present in the United States for hundreds of years and, accordingly, have had more opportunity than many other ethnic groups to assimilate into the wider society. Each successive generation has become more integrated with the dominant culture. In the eighteenth century the Protestant Irish relatively easily became acculturated and socially accepted. However, it was far more difficult for the vast numbers of Catholic Irish who flooded into the United States in the post-famine decades to coalesce with the mainstream. Negative stereotypes imported from England characterizing the Irish as pugnacious, drunken, semi-savages were common and endured for at least the rest of the nineteenth century. Multitudes of cartoons depicting the Irish as small, ugly, simian creatures armed with liquor and a shillelagh pervaded the press, and such terms as "paddywagons," "shenanigans," "shanty Irish" gained popularity. Despite the effects of these offensive images, compounded by poverty and ignorance,

the Catholic Irish immigrants possessed important advantages. They arrived in great numbers; most were able to speak English; and their Western European culture was similar to American culture. These factors clearly allowed the Irish Catholics to blend in far more easily than some other ethnic groups. Even their Catholicism, once disdained by so many, came to be accepted in time. Though some prejudices still linger, Catholicism is now an important part of American culture.

Today it is no longer easy to define precisely what is meant by an Irish American ethnic identity. This is especially so for later generations. Intermarriage has played a major role in this blurring of ethnic lines. The process of assimilating has also been facilitated by the great migration in recent decades of the Irish from their ethnic enclaves in the cities to the suburbs and rural regions. Greater participation in the multicultural public school system with a corresponding decline in parochial school attendance has played a significant role as well; another major factor has been the great decrease of immigrants from Ireland due to immigration laws disfavoring Europeans. Today, with 38,760,000 Americans claiming Irish ancestry (according to the 1990 census), American society as a whole associates few connotations—positive or negative—with this group. Among these immigrants and their ancestors, however, there is still great pride and a certain prestige in being Irish.

"The first time I saw the Statue of Liberty all the people were rushing to the side of the boat. 'Look at her, look at her,' and in all kinds of tongues. 'There she is, there she is,' like it was somebody who was greeting them."

Elizabeth Phillips in 1920, cited in *Ellis Island: An Illustrated History of the Immigrant Experience,* edited by Ivan Chermayeff et al. (New York: Macmillan, 1991).

Still, there exists in some circles the belief that the Irish are less cultured, less advanced intellectually, and more politically reactionary and even bigoted than some other ethnic groups. The results of numerous polls show, however, that Catholic Irish Americans are among the best educated and most liberal in the United States. Moreover, they are well represented in law, medicine, academia, and other prestigious professions, and they continue to be upwardly socially mobile. Traditionally prominent in the Democratic ranks of city and local politics, many, especially since the Kennedy presidency, have now attained high positions in the federal government. Countless more have become top civil servants. Irish acceptability has also grown in line with the greater respect afforded by many Americans to the advances made by the Republic of Ireland in the twentieth century.

TRADITIONAL MUSIC, SONG, AND DANCE

Ireland's cultural heritage, with its diverse customs, traditions, folklore, mythology, music, and dance, is one of the richest and most distinctive in Europe. Rapid modernization and the extensive homogenization of western societies, however, has rendered much of this heritage obsolete or, at best, only vaguely perceived in contemporary Ireland. With their extensive assimilation into American culture there has been a decline in continuity and appreciation of the domestic cultural heritage among Irish Americans as well. Nevertheless, there exist many elements in the Irish American culture that are truly unique and lend this group a distinct cultural character.

Irish music and song brought to America by generations of immigrants have played a seminal role in the development of America's folk and country music. Elements of traditional Irish ballads introduced during the seventeenth and eighteenth centuries are easily discernible in many American folk songs. Irish fiddle music of this period is an important root of American country music. This earlier music became part of a rural tradition. Much of what was carried to America by the great waves of Irish immigration during the nineteenth century, on the other hand, became an important facet of America's urban folk scene. With the folk music revival of the 1960s came a heightened appreciation of Irish music in both its American and indigenous forms. Today Irish music is extremely popular not only among Irish Americans but among many Americans in general. Many learn to play such Irish instruments as the pipes, tin whistle, flute, fiddle, concertina, harp, and the bodhrán. Many also attend Irish céilithe and dance to traditional reels, jigs, hornpipes.

ST. PATRICK'S DAY

March 17 is the feast of St. Patrick, the most important holiday of the year for Irish Americans. St. Patrick, about whose life and chronology little definite is known, is the patron saint of Ireland. A Romano-Briton missionary, perhaps from Wales, St. Patrick is honored for spreading Christianity throughout Ireland in the fifth century. Though Irish Americans of all creeds are particularly prominent on St. Patrick's Day, the holiday is now so ubiquitous that individuals of many other ethnic groups participate in the festivities. Many cities and towns hold St. Patrick's Day celebrations, parties, and, above all, parades. One of the oldest observances in the United States took place in Boston in 1737 under the auspices of the Charitable Irish Society. It was organized by Protestant Irish. Boston, especially in the districts of South Boston, still holds great celebrations each year, though the holiday is now more closely identified with Catholic Irish. The largest and most famous parade is held in New York City, with the first parade in that city dating back to 1762. In the early years this parade was organized by the Friendly Sons of St. Patrick; in 1838 the Ancient Order of Hibernians became sponsor, and that group still holds the sponsorship today. New York's main cathedral is dedicated to St. Patrick. Most people celebrating St. Patrick's Day strive to wear something green, Ireland's national color. Green dye is often put in food and drink. The mayor of Chicago regularly has the Chicago River dyed green for the day. If people cannot find a shamrock to wear they carry representations of that plant. According to legend the shamrock, with its three leaves on the single stalk, was used by St. Patrick to explain the mystery of the Christian Trinity to the pagan Irish. In Ireland St. Patrick's Day, though still celebrated with enthusiasm, tends to be somewhat more subdued than in the United States due to a greater appreciation of the religious significance of the feast.

TRADITIONAL CLOTHING

Hardly any true folk costume is still worn in Ireland. The brat, a black hooded woolen cloak, is sometimes seen on old women in County Cork. During the nineteenth century the shawl was found by many women to be a cheaper substitute for the cloak and even today older rural women might be shawled. The heavy white báinín pullovers, traditionally worn in the west and northwest of Ireland by fishermen whose sweaters each bore a unique and identifiable cable pattern, is now frequently seen throughout the nation. Traditional homespun tweed trousers are still sometimes worn by Aran Islander men. In America the Irish rarely wear any traditional costume. The main exception is the kilt which is some-

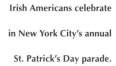

Irish Americans celebrate in New York City's annual St. Patrick's Day parade.

times worn by members of *céilí* bands and traditional Irish dancers. This plaid skirt is actually Scottish, however, and was adopted in the early twentieth century during the Gaelic Revival.

FOOD

For the most part Irish Americans eat generic American food as well as the cuisine of other ethnic groups. Many Irish Americans do cook some of the dishes that make up the distinctive Irish cuisine, which is frequently served in Irish restaurants and pubs throughout America. There is a good market for the many shops in America that sell such Irish favorites as rashers (bacon), bangers (sausages), black and white pudding, and soda bread. Potatoes have traditionally constituted the staple of the Irish diet. The Irish also consume such dairy products as butter, milk, and cheese in large quantities. Many eat oatmeal stirabout or porridge for breakfast. Irish stew is a favorite dish. Smoked Irish salmon, imported from Ireland, is a popular delicacy. Other traditional foods include: soda bread, made with flour, soda, buttermilk, and salt (sometimes with raisins); coddle, a dish originating in Dublin that is prepared with bacon, sausages, onions, and potatoes; and *drisheens*, made from sheep's blood, milk, bread crumbs, and chopped mutton suet. Corned beef and cabbage, sometimes served with juniper berries, was a traditional meal in many parts of Ireland on Easter Sunday and is still con-

sumed by many Irish Americans on this and other days. Boxty bread, a potato bread marked with a cross, is still eaten by some on Halloween or the eve of All Saint's Day. Also on the table at Halloween are colcannon, a mixture of cabbage or kale and mashed potatoes with a lucky coin placed inside, and barmbrack, an unleavened cake made with raisins, sultanas, and currants. A ring is always placed inside the barmbrack and it is said that whoever receives the slice containing the ring will be married within the year. Tea, served at all times of the day or night, is probably the most popular Irish beverage. Irish coffee, made from whiskey and coffee, is truly an Irish American invention and is not drunk much in Ireland. Though Scotch and whiskey are synonymous to many in other countries, the Irish believe that their whiskey, *uisce beatha* (the water of life), is a finer drink. Irish stout, particularly the Guinness variety, is well-known throughout the world.

PROVERBS

Sceitheann fíon fírinne (Wine reveals the truth); *Níl aon tinteán mar do thinteán féin* (There's no fireside like your own fireside); *Más maith leat tú a cháineadh, pós* (Marry, if you wish to be criticized); *Mol an óige agus tiocfaidh sí* (Give praise to the young and they will flourish); *An té a bhíos fial roinneann Dia leis* (God shares with the generous); *Is maith an scáthán súil charad* (The eye of a friend is a good mirror); *Is fada an bóthar nach mbíonn casadh ann* (It's a long road that has no turn); *Giorraíonn beirt bóthar* (Two people shorten the road).

HEALTH AND MENTAL HEALTH ISSUES

The health of Irish Americans is influenced by the same factors affecting other ethnic groups in the western world: old age, pollution, stress, excessive use of tobacco and alcohol, overly rich diet, employment and other economic problems, discord in marriage and personal relationships, and so on. The chief cause of death is heart-related diseases, exacerbated by the Irish fondness for a rich diet traditionally high in fat and caloric content. Alcohol plays a strong role in Irish American social life, and alcohol-related illnesses are common—the rate of alcoholism is high. Irish Americans also have an above-average rate of mental health diseases, with organic psychosis and schizophrenia being particularly prevalent.

In the earlier days of emigration the Irish, like numerous other groups, brought their folk medical remedies to America. Most of these, especially those associated with herbs, are unknown to the majority of contemporary Irish Americans; however, a number of traditional medical beliefs survive. In order to maintain good health and prevent illness many Irish recommend wearing holy medals and scapulars, blessing the throat, never going to bed with wet hair, never sitting in a draft, taking laxatives regularly, wearing camphor about the neck in influenza season, taking tonics and extra vitamins, enjoying bountiful exercise and fresh air, and avoiding physicians except when quite ill. Some traditional treatments are still used, such as painting a sore throat with iodine or soothing it with lemon and honey, putting a poultice of sugar and bread or soap on a boil, drinking hot whiskeys with cloves and honey for coughs or colds, and rubbing Vicks on the chest or breathing in hot Balsam vapors, also for coughs and colds.

Just as other groups in America, the Irish worry about the ever rising cost of medical care. Many would like improved medical insurance plans, whether national or private. The thousands of undocumented Irish throughout the United States who are not medically insured are particularly apprehensive of the frequently high expense of medical treatment.

LANGUAGE

Irish is a Celtic language of Indo-European origin, related to the ancient language of the Gauls. Lin-

guistic scholars usually consider at least four distinct stages in the development of Irish: Old Irish (c. 600-900); Middle Irish (c. 900-1400); Early Modern Irish (c.1400-1600); and Modern Irish (c.1600-present). There are three fairly distinct dialects, those of Ulster, Munster, and Connaught. Beginning in the nineteenth century, Irish—until then widely spoken throughout Ireland—began a rapid decline mainly due to the Anglicization policies of the British government. Since the founding of the Irish Free State in 1921, however, the authorities have made great efforts to promote the widespread usage of Irish. Under the Constitution of the Republic of Ireland, Irish is decreed as the official language, though special recognition is given to English. Irish is still extensively taught in most schools. The result is that competence in Irish as well as general interest in the language is higher today than at any time in the Republic's history. Nevertheless, despite all efforts to render Irish a living national language, it is clear that it remains the daily language of communication for only about four percent of the population, most of whom live in small *Gaeltacht* (southwest, west, and northwest) areas. Only a tiny number of Northern Ireland's population speak Irish.

The decline in the usage of Irish and the triumph of English as the first language for most Irish throughout the nineteenth century, though undoubtedly a great loss for nationalistic and cultural reasons, proved to be a boon to Irish immigrants to the United States. Almost alone among new immigrants, apart from those from the British Isles, most spoke the language of their adopted country. Today, there is a resurgence of interest in Irish among many Irish Americans. In cities such as New York, Chicago, Boston, and San Francisco, classes in learning Irish are extremely popular. A growing number of American colleges and universities now offer courses in Irish language.

GREETINGS AND OTHER REPRESENTATIVE EXPRESSIONS

Dia dhuit ("dee-ah guit")—Hello; *Conas atá tú?* ("kunus ah-thaw thoo")—How are you; *Fáilte romhat!* ("fawilteh rowth")—Welcome; *Cad as duit?* ("kawd oss dit")—Where are you from; *Gabh mo leithscéal* ("gauw muh leshgale")—Excuse me; *Le do thoil* ("leh duh hull")—Please; *Tá dhá thaobh ar an scéa* ("thaw gaw hayv air un shgale")—There's something to be said on both sides; *Más toil le Dia* ("maws tule leh dee-ah")—God willing; *Tá sé ceart to leor* ("thaw shay k-yarth guh lore") It's all right; *Beidh lá eile ag an bPaorach!* ("beg law eleh egg un fairoch")—Better luck next time; *Buíochas le Dia* ("bu-ee-kus leh dee-ah")—Thank God; *Is fusa a rá ná a dhéanamh* ("iss fusa ah raw naw ah yea-anav")—Easier said than done; *Go raibh míle maith agat* ("guh row meela moh ugut")—Thank you very much; *Slán agat go fóill* ("slawn ugut guh fowil")—Good-bye for the present.

FAMILY AND COMMUNITY DYNAMICS

It is difficult to discuss the Irish American family in isolation from the broader society. Irish assimilation into the American culture has been occurring for a long time and has been quite comprehensive.

MARRIAGE

Traditionally the average age of marriage for the Irish was older than for numerous other groups. Many delayed getting married, wishing first to attain a sufficient economic level. Large numbers did not marry at all, deciding to remain celibate, some for religious reasons, others, it has been suggested, due to a certain embarrassment about sex. Today delayed marriages are less common and there is probably less sexual dysfunction both within and outside marriage. Furthermore, those Irish whose families have long been established in America tend to have a more accepting attitude towards divorce than do the more recently arrived Irish. Many young Irish Americans are more inclined than their elders to look favorably on divorce. The negative attitude of the Catholic church toward divorce still affects perceptions, however. Many Irish Americans, even those who obtain a civil divorce, seek to procure a church annulment of their marriages so that they may remarry within Catholicism. Though Irish Americans frequently intermarry with other groups there remains a strong leaning toward marrying within one's own religion.

WAKES

In remote times in Ireland the Irish generally treated death in a boisterous and playful manner. It is possible that the storytelling, music playing, singing, dancing, feasting, and playing of wake diversions during the two or three days the dead person was laid out prior to burial owed something to pre-Christian funeral games. Such activity may also have stemmed in part from a welcoming of death by an exploited and destitute people. Today, however, wakes among Irish Americans are much more sedate and respectable and generally last only one night. The main purpose of a wake is for relatives, neighbors, and friends to visit in order to pay their respects to the dead person and to offer condolences to the family. Though food and drink are still invariably offered to visitors, the traditional over-indulgence of eating and drinking rarely occurs. In years past the dead body was laid out on a bed in the person's own house. Today the wake often takes place in a funeral home with the body lying in a casket. Catholic dead often have rosary beads entwined in their crossed hands, and some are dressed in the brown habit or shroud of the Franciscan Third Order. Flowers and candles are usually placed about the casket. The laid-out corpse always has somebody standing beside it. This is mainly out of respect for the dead person. Many years ago, however, there was a practical reason for watching the body, namely to guard it from the predations of body-snatchers who would sell it to medical schools. The *caoine* or keening of women over the corpse is no longer heard in America. This custom has also, except for rare occasions, died out in Ireland. It is common for visitors to a wake to say a short silent prayer for the soul of the dead person.

WOMEN

The traditional Irish American mother remained at home to take care of the household. Female dominance of domestic life was common and the mother generally played a disproportionate role in raising the children. Not all Irish women were tied to the house, however. Many were also active in community oriented projects, such as charity activities, parochial work, and caring for the old and sick. In addition, many others displayed great independence and resolve last century when, fleeing the famine and terrible conditions in Ireland, they emigrated alone to the United States, a bold act for women of the period. This will and determination remains one of the most dominant character traits of contemporary Irish American females. Modern Irish American women are as likely, if not more so, to be as successful as their peers from other groups. Few today are content to devote their lives to traditional housework, with the great majority working in either part-time or full-time jobs. Great numbers have thrived in such professional spheres as academia, law, business, politics, and a variety of other occupations.

CHILDREN

Irish American families have traditionally been large. Today many families still tend to produce an above-average number of children. This may be due in part to the continued adherence of many Irish to the teachings of the Catholic church on contraception. How Irish Americans rear their children depends to a great extent on the socio-economic background of the family. Generally, however, children are treated firmly but kindly. They are taught to be polite, obey their parents, and defer to authority. The mother often plays the dominant role in raising children and imparting values; the father is frequently a distant figure. In many families negative reinforcement, such as shaming, belittling, ridiculing, and embarrassing children, is as common as positive reinforcement. There has always been a tendency to imbue children with a strong sense of public respectability. It even has been argued that this desire to be thought respectable has deterred many Irish from taking chances and has impeded their success. Overt affection displayed by parents toward their children is not as prevalent as in some other ethnic groups.

EDUCATION

In earlier generations more attention was often paid to the education of sons than to that of daughters. It was generally thought that girls would become homemakers and that even if some did have a job such work would be considered secondary to their household duties. Today, however, though some Irish parents, particularly mothers, still "spoil" or indulge their sons, the education of daughters is a major concern.

Irish American families encourage achievement in school. In this they follow the traditional respect of the Irish for education. This dates back to when Irish monks helped preserve Latin and Greek learning in Europe, as well as the English language itself, by copying manuscripts during the fifth through eighth centuries when Ireland attained the name of "Island of Saints and Scholars." In addition, Irish Americans well understand that academic success facilitates achievement in wider social and economic spheres. The result is that Irish Catholics are among the top groups in the United States for educational attainment. They are more likely than any other white gentile ethnic group to go to college and are also more likely than most other ethnic groups to pursue graduate academic and professional degrees. While many Irish attend public schools, colleges, and universities, numerous others go to Catholic educational institutions. During the nineteenth century, however, many Irish parochial schools placed a greater emphasis on preventing Irish children from seduction by what many felt to be the Protestant ethos of the public schools. There is strong evidence that attendance at today's Catholic educational institutions, many of which have high standards, facilitates high levels of educational achievement and upward social mobility. Contrary to some beliefs, they are not deterrents to either academic or economic success. Among the most renowned Catholic universities attended by Irish Americans are Boston College and the University of Notre Dame.

RELIGION

Some early Catholic Irish immigrants converted to the pervasive Protestantism in America. However, the vast majority of subsequent Catholic immigrants, many holding their religion to be an intrinsic part of their Irish heritage as well as a safeguard against America's Anglo establishment, held steadfastly to their faith and, in so doing, helped Roman Catholicism grow into one of America's most powerful institutions. Since the late eighteenth century many aspects of American Catholicism have possessed a distinctly Irish character. A disproportionate number of Irish names may be found among America's past and present Catholic clergy. Scores of Irish laymen have been at the forefront of American Catholic affairs. The Irish have been particularly energetic supporters of the more concrete manifestations of their church and have established throughout America great numbers of Catholic schools, colleges, universities, hospitals, community centers, and orphanages, as well as churches, cathedrals, convents, and seminaries.

Until the mid-twentieth century, the life of Catholic Irish Americans revolved around their parish. Many children went to parochial schools, and the clergy organized such activities as sports, dances, and community services. There was little local politics without the participation of the priests. The clergy knew all the families in the community and there was great pressure to conform to the norms of the tightly knit parish. The parish priest, generally the best-educated individual of the congregation, was usually the dominant community leader. At a time when there were far fewer social workers, guidance counselors, and psychologists, parishioners flocked to their priest in times of trouble. Today the typical parish is less closed mainly due to the falling off in religious practice over the last decades of the twentieth century and the increased mainstreaming of parishioners. Nevertheless, there still remains a strong identification of many Catholic Irish with their parish.

The American Catholic church has undergone great changes since the 1960s, due largely to the innovations introduced by the Second Vatican Council. Some Catholic Irish Americans, wishing to preserve their inherited church practices, have been dismayed by the transformation. Some, alienated by the modernization of the liturgy, have been offended by what they consider a diminution of the mystery and venerability of church ritual with respect to the introduction of the vernacular, new hymns, and guitar playing at services. Some have attempted to preserve the traditional liturgy by joining conservative breakaway sects, and others have adopted different branches of Christianity.

Most Irish Americans have embraced the recent developments, however. The traditional Irish obedience to ecclesiastical authority is no longer certain as Rome asserts an uncompromising stance on many issues. Many Irish Catholics are now far more inclined to question doctrines and take issue with teachings on such subjects as abortion, contraception, divorce, priestly celibacy, and female priests. Certain members of the clergy have shown discontent; priests, nuns, and brothers have been leaving their orders in large numbers and there has been a concurrent decline in Irish vocations to the religious life. The numbers of Irish receiving the sacraments and attending mass and other church services have substantially declined; and many have abandoned puritan attitudes toward lifestyle issues, especially sex. Nevertheless, most Irish American Catholics are still faithful to many teachings of their church, and continue to identify as Catholics despite some disagreements with Vatican teachings.

EMPLOYMENT AND ECONOMIC TRADITIONS

The great majority of Catholic Irish immigrants in the eighteenth and the first half of the nineteenth century languished at the bottom of America's economic ladder as unskilled laborers. Though some were farm workers, many more worked in such areas as mining, quarrying, bridge and canal building, and railway construction. So many Irish were killed working on the railroad that it was commonly speculated that "there was an Irishman buried under every tie." Others were dockworkers, ironworkers, factory-hands, bartenders, carters, street cleaners, hod-carriers, and waiters. Irish women generally worked in menial occupations. Multitudes were employed as domestic servants in Anglo-Protestant households, while others worked as unskilled laborers in New England textile mills. Some Irish became quite successful but their numbers were few. The handful who attained white-collar status were frequently shopkeepers and small businessmen. There was an exceedingly meager number of Irish professionals. Those Irish who made the long trip to the western states tended to have somewhat more prestigious jobs than their compatriots in the East and North. This is due in part to the large numbers of Chinese in the West who did much of the manual laboring work. Many Irish participated in the California Gold Rush.

In the years after the Civil War the occupational lot of the Irish began to improve as more entered skilled trades. Many moved into managerial positions in the railroad, iron, construction, and other industries. Some went into business for themselves, especially in the building and contracting sectors. Numerous others became police officers, firefighters, streetcar conductors, clerks, and post-office workers. The Irish held many leadership positions in the trade union movement. Entertainment and athletics were other fields in which they began to attain greater recognition. It was more difficult for Irish women to move into higher prestige jobs, as there were far fewer opportunities for women in general at this time. Still, many attained upward occupational mobility by becoming teachers, nurses, and secretaries. Many Irish American nuns held positions of responsibility in hospitals, schools, and other Catholic social institutions.

By the beginning of the twentieth century Catholic Irish Americans were clearly ascending the occupational ladder. Though most remained members of the working class, large numbers moved into the ranks of the lower middle classes. Throughout the century this improvement in socioeconomic status has continued. Today the Irish are well represented in academia, medicine, law, government service, politics, finance, banking, insurance, journalism, the entertainment industry, the Catholic clergy, and most other professions.

POLITICS AND GOVERNMENT

The vast majority of Irish Catholic immigrants to the United States during the eighteenth and nineteenth centuries arrived as Democrats, a political stance imbued by years of oppression at the hands of the British. Not surprisingly, most favored the democratic policies of Thomas Jefferson and their vote greatly assisted his election to the presidency in 1801. Their political inclinations were again manifest in 1829 in their support for the populist politics of Democrat Andrew Jackson, America's seventh president and the nation's first of Irish (Protestant) background. Understanding that they were clearly unable to match the Anglo-Protestant establishment in the world of business and economics, Irish Catholics, many of whom entered the United States with fundamental political experience gained through mass agitation movements at home, realized that politics would provide them with a potent vehicle for attaining influence and power. In the years after the Civil War the Irish metier for political activity became increasingly evident. To many today the Irish control of New York's Tammany Hall, the center of the city's Democratic Party, is a resolute symbol of their powerful and sometimes dubious involvement in American urban politics. Though graft, cronyism, and corruption were once an integral part of many of their political "machines" in New York and other cities, Irish politicians were frequently more successful than their Anglo-Protestant counterparts in reaching the people, feeding the poor, helping the more unfortunate obtain jobs, and organizing other practical social welfare activities. The Irish political "machine" generally had a strong democratic, reformist, and pragmatic agenda, which frequently extended to Jews, Italians, Germans, Poles, and other nationalities.

The phenomenon of Irish domination of the political life of numerous cities continued well into the twentieth century. Two extremely influential and powerful figures of the old "machine" style were James Michael Curley (1874-1958), mayor of Boston for four terms, and Richard J. Daley, mayor of Chicago from 1954 to 1976. Irish involvement in both state and national politics also gained prominence in the twentieth century. Alfred Emanuel Smith (1873-1944), the grandson of Irish immigrants, was the first Irish Catholic to receive the nomination of a major party (Democratic) in a presidential election; he was defeated by Herbert Hoover. An Irish Catholic reached the White House in 1960 with the election of the Democrat John Fitzgerald Kennedy, who was assassinated in 1963. His brother, Senator Robert F. Kennedy, another prominent Democratic politician who served as attorney general in the Kennedy administration, was assassinated in 1968. A third brother, Edward, has been one of the most liberal and effective champions of social reform in the history of the Senate. Two other twentieth century Presidents, Richard M. Nixon and Ronald Reagan (both Republicans) were of Irish Protestant background. Numerous other Irish American politicians have gained state and national attention in recent decades. Both Mike Mansfield and George J. Mitchell were Senate majority leaders. Thomas O'Neill and Thomas S. Foley both served as Speaker of the House of Representatives. Another influential politician and 1976 presidential candidate was Eugene J. McCarthy of Minnesota.

Despite the notable presence this century of such influential reactionaries as the demagogue Father Charles Coughlin and the Communist-baiter Senator Joseph McCarthy, Catholic Irish Americans are among the most likely to advocate the right of free speech. They also tend to be more supportive of liberal issues than many other white ethnic groups. For example, they have traditionally promoted such causes as racial equality, welfare programs, environmental issues, and gun control. Irish Americans have been and still are among the most stalwart supporters of the Democratic Party. Beginning in the late twentieth century, however, there has been a movement by some toward the Republican Party.

ARMED FORCES

The Irish, either as regulars or as volunteers, have served in all of America's wars. They fought with distinction in the Revolutionary War, most siding with Washington. It is estimated that as many as 38 percent of Washington's army was composed of

Irish Americans, even though they made up only 10 percent of the population. Of the generals, 26 were Irish, 15 of whom were born in Ireland. In the Civil War most Irish sided with the Union and great numbers fought in the Yankee armies. "The Fighting 69th" was probably the most famous Irish regimental unit, though 38 other Union regiments had "Irish" in their names. The contribution of the Irish to the Confederate cause was also significant. As many as 40,000 Confederate soldiers were born in Ireland and numerous others were of Irish ancestry. Irish Americans continued to fight in America's armies in subsequent wars and were particularly prominent, with many gaining decorations, in the two World Wars, the Korean War, and the Vietnam War. Their ready and distinguished participation in America's military conflicts has helped the Irish to gain respectability in the eyes of generations of other Americans and to assimilate into mainstream American life.

LABOR MOVEMENT

The Irish have contributed greatly to the labor movement in America. Their struggle for American workers' rights began as an outgrowth of their fight against oppression in Ireland. American capitalist injustice in industry was not too different in principle from persecution by English landlords at home. Even in the antebellum years the Irish were active in workers' organizations, many of which were clandestine, but it was during the second half of the nineteenth century that their involvement in labor activities became especially prominent. Particularly well known are the activities of the Molly Maguires, anthracite coal miners of Pennsylvania who in the 1860s and 1870s violently resisted the mostly English, Scottish, and Welsh mine bosses. Found guilty of nine murders, ten Mollies were hanged in 1876. This did not deter Irish involvement in American labor activities, however. Terrence V. Powderly (1849-1924), the son of an Irish immigrant, was for years leader of the Knights of Labor, the first national labor organization, which was founded in 1869. He later became commissioner general of immigration. Peter James McGuire (1852-1906), a carpenter, was another leading union activist. A founder of the American Federation of Labor, he was its secretary and first vice-president. He is perhaps best known today as the "Father of Labor Day." Irish women have also been prominent in America's labor movement. The Cork-born Mary Harris ("Mother") Jones (1830-1930), after losing all her possessions in the Chicago fire of 1871, began a 50-year involvement in organizing labor unions and in striving to improve workers' conditions and wages throughout the United States. Today, a nationally circulated magazine devoted to liberal issues bears her name. Another famous Irish female in the labor movement was Elizabeth Gurley Flynn (1890-1964) who co-founded the American Civil Liberties Union in 1920 and later became head of the U.S. Communist party. Kerry-born Michael Joseph Quill (1905-1966) founded the Transport Workers Union of America in 1934 and was its first president. In 1937 Joe Curran became the National Maritime Union's first president. George Meany (1894-1979), grandson of an Irish immigrant, was president of the combined American Federation of Labor and Congress of Industrial Organizations (AFL-CIO) from 1955 to 1979. Irish American participation in America's unions and labor movement has been and continues to be of vital importance and benefit to the well-being of American society.

IRISH AMERICAN INTEREST IN NORTHERN IRELAND

The attention of many Irish Americans of different generations has been sharply focused on the political affairs of Ireland ever since the Catholic civil rights movement began in Northern Ireland in the late 1960s. This movement was a response to decades of institutionalized and private discrimination against Catholics in this region since the creation of Northern Ireland as part of the United Kingdom in 1921. This discrimination by the Protestant majority was pervasive in such spheres as voting, housing, and employment. For the past three decades Northern Ireland has been convulsed by political upheaval, the frequently controversial tactics of an occupying force of British soldiers, Protestant and Catholic paramilitary activity, riots, killings, bombings, hunger strikes, internment without trial, and patent violations of human rights. The reactions of numerous Irish Americans have been forceful. In 1970 the Northern Ireland Aid Committee (NORAID) was formed to provide material help to Catholics in Northern Ireland. The Irish National Caucus, a Washington-based lobbying group, has been vociferous in its call for a British withdrawal from Northern Ireland and for a reunification of the whole nation. Many Irish American politicians have campaigned intensely to find a settlement to Northern Ireland's problems. Among the most prominent have been Senator Edward Kennedy of

Massachusetts, Senator Daniel P. Moynihan of New York, former Speaker of the House of Representatives Tip O'Neill, and former Governor of New York Hugh Carey. These and other Irish American politicians and lobbying groups have consistently exerted pressure on successive administrations to use their influence with London, Belfast, and Dublin to help amend human rights abuses in Northern Ireland and to aid in the provision of social and economic justice in that region. After the Anglo-Irish Agreement was reached in England in November 1985 Congress, responding in part to pressure from Irish Americans, passed a multi-billion-dollar aid bill for Northern Ireland. The future of this region is by no means clear, despite the recent cease-fire by the Irish Republican Army (IRA), but it is expected that Irish Americans will continue influence the policy of the major players in this conflict.

INDIVIDUAL AND GROUP CONTRIBUTIONS

It would constitute a thoroughly invidious task to provide a comprehensive record of the vast number of Irish Americans who have attained prominence over the past few centuries. The following list is necessarily selective, and countless other individuals might also have been named.

ARTS

There have been numerous Irish Americans who have achieved prominence in the arts. In the fine arts, for example, the following three achieved particular fame: Mathew Brady (1823-1896), Civil War photographer; James E. Kelly (1855-1933), sculptor; Georgia O'Keeffe (1887-1986), painter. Others include: Mathew Carey (1760-1839), author, book publisher, and political economist; Edgar Allan Poe (1809-1849), one of the greatest figures in American literature; Ring Lardner (1885-1933), short story writer and sports journalist; Mary O'Hara Alsop (1885-1980), popular novelist who focused on animal life; Eugene O'Neill (1888-1953), one of America's most eminent playwrights; F. Scott Fitzgerald (1896-1940), popular novelist and short story writer; James T. Farrell (1904-1979), author whose work, notably his Studs Lonigan trilogy, centered on working-class Irish American families on Chicago's South Side; John O'Hara (1905-1970), novelist and short story writer; Mary McCarthy (1912-1989), novelist and critic; Mary Flannery O'Connor (1925-1964), novelist and short story writer of the American South; and William F. Buckley (1925-), editor, critic, commentator, and novelist.

BUSINESS AND FINANCE

Numerous Irish Americans have made their mark in the world of business and finance: William Russell (1812-1872), founder of the Pony Express; William Russell Grace (1832-1904), entrepreneur and first Roman Catholic mayor of New York; John Philip Holland (1840-1914), Clare-born father of the modern submarine; Anthony Nicholas Brady (1843-1913), wealthy industrialist whose interests extended from railroads to electric companies; Andrew Mellon (1855-1937), banker, art collector, and philanthropist; Samuel S. McClure (1857-1949), leading journalist and newspaper publisher; Henry Ford (1863-1947), auto manufacturer; James A. Farrell (1863-1943), head of United States Steel Corporation; and Howard Hughes (1905-1976), wealthy and eccentric industrialist, aerospace manufacturer, and movie maker.

EDUCATION

John R. Gregg (1867-1948), inventor of the Gregg system of shorthand; and William Heard Kilpatrick (1871-1965), philosopher and leader in the Progressive Education movement, are among prominent Irish American Educators.

ENTERTAINMENT

A great number of Irish Americans have attained distinction in the entertainment industry: Victor Herbert (1859-1924), Dublin-born conductor and popular composer of operettas; Will Rogers (1879-1935), humorist and actor; John McCormack (1884-1945), popular Westmeath-born tenor; Buster Keaton (1895-1966), famous silent film comedian; Emmett Kelly (1898-1979), well-known circus clown; James Cagney (1899-1986), a movie actor; John Ford (1895-1973), who was born Sean Aloysius O'Feeny, was a film director; Spencer Tracy (1900-67), movie actor; Ed Sullivan (1901-1974), newspaper columnist and television personality; Bing Crosby (1901-1977), singer and movie and radio actor; Pat O'Brien (1900-1983), movie, radio, and television actor; John Huston (1906-1987), film director; John Wayne (1907-1979), movie actor; Errol Flynn (1909-1959), swashbuckling movie actor; Maureen O'Sullivan (1911-), movie actor; Gene Kelly (1912-), dancer, actor, singer; Tyrone Power (1913-1958), movie actor; Mickey Rooney (1920-), movie actor; Maureen O'Hara (1920-), movie actor; Carroll O'Connor (1924-), television actor; Grace Kelly (1929-1982), movie actor and later Princess of Monaco; Jack Nicholson (1937-), movie actor; and Mia Farrow (1945-), movie actor.

LABOR

Activists in the labor movement not mentioned already include: Leonora Barry (1849-1923), feminist and activist for women's suffrage; Mary Kenney O'Sullivan (1864-1943), active labor organizer; and Daniel Tobin (1875-1955), president of the Teamsters Union and a leader of the American Federation of Labor.

MILITARY

Several Irish Americans who have won renown in the military field have been mentioned. Others include: Lydia Barrington Darragh (1729-1789), Dublin-born heroine of the Revolutionary War and spy for George Washington; John Barry (1745-1803), Wexford-born "Father of the American Navy"; Margaret Corbin (1751-1800), heroine of the Revolutionary War; General Douglas MacArthur (1880-1964), leader of the Allied forces in the Pacific during World War II; William J. Donovan (1883-1959), World War I hero and later founder of the Office of Strategic Services; and Audie Murphy (1924-1971), the United States's most decorated soldier of World War II and later movie actor.

POLITICS AND LAW

The fields of politics and law have had more than their share of eminent Irish Americans; the following few may be added to those named earlier: Sir Thomas Dongan (1634-1715), Irish-born governor of New York in 1682; Sir William Johnson (1715-1774), army officer and superintendent of Indian Affairs; Pierce Butler (1744-1822), Carlow-born American political leader who signed the U.S. Constitution; Nellie Tayloe Ross (1876-1977), first female governor (of Wyoming 1925-1927) and first female director of the Mint (1933-1953); Sandra Day O'Connor (1930-), the first

female Supreme Court Justice; and William G. Brennan (1906-), Supreme Court Justice.

RELIGION

Famous Irish American religious leaders include: Archbishop John Joseph Hughes (1797-1864), first Roman Catholic archbishop of New York; John McCloskey (1810-1885), first American cardinal of the Roman Catholic church; James Gibbons (1834-1921), Francis Joseph Spellman (1889-1967), Richard J. Cushing (1895-1970), and Terence Cooke (1921-1983), all Roman Catholic cardinals; Archbishop Fulton John Sheen (1895-1979), charismatic Roman Catholic church leader; Father Andrew Greeley (1928-), priest, sociologist, and novelist. Two famous humanitarians are Father Edward Joseph Flanagan (1886-1948), Roman Catholic priest who worked with homeless boys and who founded Boys Town in Nebraska; and Thomas A. Dooley (1927-1961), medical doctor who performed great humanitarian work in southeast Asia.

SPORTS

Irish Americans have been eminent in sports as well, including: John L. Sullivan (1858-1918), James John "Gentleman Jim" Corbett (1866-1933), Jack Dempsey (1895-1983), and Gene Tunney (1898-1978), all heavyweight boxing champions; Babe Ruth (1895-1948), baseball player; Ben Hogan (1912-), golfer; Maureen "Little Mo" Connolly (1934-1969), tennis star who won the U.S. women's singles championship three times; and Jimmy Connors (1952-), another famous tennis player.

MEDIA

PRINT

Irish America Magazine.

Established in 1984, the magazine publishes information about Ireland and Irish Americans, including book, play, and film reviews.

Address: Irish America, Inc., 432 Park Avenue South, No. 1000, New York, New York 10016-8013.

Irish Echo.

Established in 1928, this publication contains articles of interest to the Irish community.

Contact: Jane M. Duffin, Editor.
Address: 803 East Willow Grove Avenue, Wyndmoor, Pennsylvania 19038.
Telephone: (215) 836-4900.
Fax: (215) 836-1929.

Irish Herald.

Established in 1962, this newspaper covers Irish American interests.

Contact: John Whooley, Editor.
Address: Irish Enterprises, 2123 Market Street, San Francisco, California 94114.

Stars and Harp.

Carries profiles of Irish Americans and their contributions to the formation of the United States.

Contact: Joseph F. O'Connor, Editor.
Address: American Irish Bicentennial Committee, 3917 Moss Drive, Annandale, Virginia 22003.
Telephone: (703) 354-4721.

RADIO

WFUV-FM (90.7).

"Míle Fáilte" presented by Séamus Blake, Saturdays 8:00 a.m. to 9:00 a.m.; "A Thousand Welcomes" presented by Kathleen Biggins, Saturdays 9:00 a.m. to 12:00 p.m.; "Ceol na nGael" presented by Eileen Fitzsimons and Marianna McGillicuddy, Sundays 12:00 p.m. to 4:00 p.m.

Contact: Chuck Singleton, Program Director.
Address: Fordham University, Bronx, New York 10458.
Telephone: (718) 817-4550.
Fax: (718) 365-9815.

WGBH-FM (89.7).

Celtic program presented by Brian O'Donovan, Sundays 12:00 to 2:00 p.m.

Contact: Martin Miller, Programming Director.
Address: 125 Western Avenue, Boston, Massachusetts 02134.
Telephone: (617) 492-2777.
Fax: (617) 787-0714.

WNTN-AM (1550).

"The Sound of Erin," Saturdays 10:30 a.m. to 7:00 p.m.

Contact: John Curran or Bernie McCarthy.
Address: P.O. Box 12, Belmont, Massachusetts 02178.
Telephone: (617) 484-2275 (John Curran); (617) 326-4159 (Bernie McCarthy).

WPNA-AM (1490).

Irish programming each Saturday 8:00 a.m. to 1:00 p.m., 6:30 p.m. to 9:00 p.m.

Contact: Bud Sullivan, the Hagerty Family, Mike O'Connor, Mike Shevlin, or Joe Brett.
Address: Alliance Communications, Inc., Radio Station WPNA, 408 South Oak Park Avenue, Oak Park, Illinois 60302.
Telephone: (708) 974-0108 (Bud Sullivan); (708) 834-8110 (the Hagerty Family); (708) 771-2228 (Mike O'Connor); (708) 282-7035 (Mike Shevlin); (312) 746-4561 (Joe Brett).

ORGANIZATIONS AND ASSOCIATIONS

American Irish Historical Society (AIHS).

The goal of the AIHS is to promote awareness among Americans of Irish descent of their history, culture, and heritage. To attain that end the AIHS presents lectures, readings, musical events, and art exhibitions. Each year the Society awards its gold medal to an individual who best reflects the Society's ideals. The Society's journal, *The Recorder,* is published semi-annually in the winter and summer, and contains articles on a wide range of Irish American and Irish topics with a primary focus on the contribution of the Irish in American history.

Contact: Thomas Michael Horan, Executive Director.
Address: 991 Fifth Avenue, New York, New York 10028.
Telephone: (212) 288-2263.

Ancient Order of Hibernians in America (AOH).

Founded in Ireland in the early sixteenth century the AOH established its first American branch in New York City in 1836. Today the AOH, its membership almost 200,000, is the largest Irish American organization with divisions throughout the country. Originally founded to protect the Catholic faith of its members, the AOH still has this as one of its chief aims. It also seeks to promote an awareness throughout America of all aspects of Irish life and culture. The AOH publishes a bimonthly newspaper, *The National Hibernian Digest*.

Contact: Thomas D. McNabb, Secretary.

Address: 31 Logan Street, Auburn, New York 13021.

Telephone: (315) 252-3895.

Irish American Cultural Association (IACA).

Promotes the study and appreciation of Irish culture.

Contact: Thomas R. McCarthy, President.

Address: 10415 South Western, Chicago, Illinois 60643.

Telephone: (312) 238-7150.

Irish American Cultural Institute (IACI).

Founded in 1962 this non-profit foundation, whose purposes are non-political and non-religious, fosters the exploration of the Irish experience in Ireland and America. Among its programs are: Irish Perceptions, which facilitates tours and presentations in America of leading Irish actors, lecturers, musicians, and artists; Irish Way, which takes American high school students on a summer educational tour of Ireland; Art and Literary Awards, which provides grants aimed at stimulating the arts in Ireland; and the Irish Research Fund, which supports scholarly work by citizens of any country that illuminates the Irish American experience. IACI also awards a visiting fellowship in Irish Studies at University College, Galway, and scholarships for American undergraduate students to the University of Limerick. IACI publishes *Éire-Ireland*, a quarterly scholarly journal of Irish studies, and *Dúcas*, a bimonthly newsletter. The Institute has 15 chapters throughout the U.S.

Contact: James S. Rogers, Director of Operations.

Address: University of St. Thomas, 2115 Summit Avenue, Mail No. 5026, St. Paul, Minnesota 55105-1096.

Telephone: (612) 962-6040.

Fax: (612) 962-6043.

Irish Genealogical Society (IGS).

Promotes and encourages the study of Irish genealogy and other types of Irish studies.

Contact: Joseph M. Glynn, Jr., Director.

Address: 21 Hanson Avenue, Somerville, Massachusetts 02143.

Telephone: (617) 666-0877.

Irish Heritage Foundation (IHF).

Promotes Irish heritage and cultural awareness in the United States.

Contact: John Whooley, President.

Address: 2123 Market Street, San Francisco, California 94114.

Telephone: (415) 621-2200.

Irish National Caucus.

Founded in 1974, the Irish National Caucus, with a membership of about 200,000 Irish Americans, is a powerful lobbying group that seeks to publicize the violations of human rights in Ireland among Americans. Though it does not support any specific solution to the Irish problem, its ultimate objective is to achieve, by political, legal, and non-violent means, a peaceful Ireland free of British rule.

Contact: Fr. Sean McManus, President.

Address: 413 East Capitol Street, S.E., Washington, D.C. 20003.

Telephone: (202) 544-0568.

Fax: (202) 543-2491.

MUSEUMS AND RESEARCH CENTERS

American Irish Historical Society.

The library of the AIHS coontains more than 30,000 volumes together with major manuscript and archival collections. It is probably the premier repository of library materials on the Irish in America. The library is open to the public by appointment.

Contact: Alec Ormsby.

Address: 991 Fifth Avenue, New York, New York 10028.

Telephone: (212) 288-2263.

An Claidheamh Soluis—The Irish Arts Center.

Aims to develop an understanding of Irish culture and arts among the Irish, Americans, and others. It offers a variety of courses in such subjects as Irish language, history, literature, dance, and traditional music. It has an excellent resident theater company. It also sponsors Irish dances, poetry-readings, lectures, and concerts. In addition, the Center publishes the monthly newsletter *Irish Arts—Ealaíona Éireannacha*.

Contact: Nye Heron, Executive Director.

Address: 553 West 51st Street, New York, New York 10019.
Telephone: (212) 757-3318.
Fax: (212) 247-0930.

Boston Public Library.

With more than 6,000,000 volumes, this library is one of the nation's major research libraries. It has particularly strong holdings, including numerous important manuscript and archival collections, relating to many aspects of the national and local history of the Irish in America. Irish American literature and music are also well represented.

Contact: Gunars Rutkovskis, Assistant Director, Resources and Research Library Services.
Address: Boylston Street, Boston, Massachusetts 02117-0286.
Telephone: (617) 536-5400.

Georgetown University, Joseph Mark Lauinger Library, Special Collections.

Contact: George M. Barringer, Head of Special Collections Division; or Nicholas B. Scheetz, Manuscript Librarian.
Address: 3700 O Street N.W., D.C. 20057-1006.
Telephone: (202) 687-7444.
Fax: (202) 687-7501.

Irish American Heritage Museum.

The exhibits, artifacts, and archives of this museum's collection cover many aspects of the Irish American experience from the earliest immigrants up to the present. There are plans to move the museum's research library of Irish American material from its present location at The College of St. Rose in Albany, New York, to the museum itself.

Contact: Monique Desormeau.
Address: Route 145, East Durham, New York 12423.
Telephone: (518) 634-7494.

John J. Burns Library, Boston College, Special Collections and Archives.

The Irish collection at Boston College's Burns Library is widely regarded as one of the most comprehensive collections of its kind outside of Ireland. Burns is also recognized for its extensive and important holdings in materials relating to Irish America. Included in the collection are papers of former Speaker of the House Tip O'Neill, the archives of the Charitable Irish Society (1889-present), and the Eire Society of Boston (founded 1937), George D. Cahill (some 600 letters and ephemera, 1857-1900) and Patrick A. Collins (some 100 letters, 1880-1882) collections. Numerous other books and periodicals and several more manuscript collections relate to the history of the Irish, particularly in Boston.

Contact: Robert K. O'Neill, Burns Librarian.
Address: Chestnut Hill, Massachusetts 02167.
Telephone: (617) 552-3282.
Fax: (617) 552-2465.

St. John's University, Special Collections.

Contact: Szilvia E. Szmuk, Special Collections Librarian.
Address: Grand Central and Utopia Pkwys, Jamaica, New York 11439.
Telephone: (718) 990-6737.
Fax: (718) 380-0353.

SOURCES FOR ADDITIONAL STUDY

Blessing, Patrick J. *The Irish in America: A Guide to the Literature and the Manuscript Collections.* Washington, D.C.: Catholic University of America, 1992.

Bradley, Ann Kathleen. *History of the Irish in America.* Secaucus, New Jersey: Chartwell, 1986.

Eleuterio-Comer, Susan K. *Irish American Material Culture: A Directory of Collections, Sites, and Festivals in the United States and Canada.* Westport, Connecticut: Greenwood, 1988.

Feagin, Joe R., and Clairece Booher Feagin. "Irish Americans," in their *Racial and Ethnic Relations,* fourth edition. Englewood Cliffs, New Jersey: Prentice Hall, 1993; pp. 85-114.

Greeley, Andrew M. *That Most Distressful Nation: The Taming of the American Irish.* Chicago: Quadrangle, 1972.

Griffin, William D. *The Book of Irish Americans.* New York: Times Books, 1990.

Horgan, Ellen Somers. "The American Catholic Irish Family," in *Ethnic Families in America: Patterns and Variations*, third edition, edited by Charles H. Mindel, Robert W. Habenstein, and Roosevelt Wright, Jr. New York: Elsevier, 1988; pp. 45-75.

The Irish in America: Emigration, Assimilation and Impact, Volume 4 of *Irish Studies*, edited by P. J. Drudy. Cambridge: Cambridge University Press, 1985.

McCaffrey, Lawrence J. *Textures of Irish America.* Syracuse, New York: Syracuse University Press, 1992.

Shannon, William V. *The American Irish.* New York: Macmillan, 1963.

The Iroquois have
been willing to adapt
to a changing world,
but they have
resisted efforts to
substitute a
European culture for
their own heritage.

IROQUOIS
by
Loretta Hall
CONFEDERACY

OVERVIEW

The Iroquois Confederacy, an association of six linguistically related tribes in the northeastern woodlands, was a sophisticated society of some 5,500 people when the first white explorers encountered it at the beginning of the seventeenth century. The 1990 Census counted 49,038 Iroquois living in the United States, making them the country's eighth most populous Native American group. Although Iroquoian tribes own seven reservations in New York state and one in Wisconsin, the majority of the people live off the reservations. An additional 5,000 Iroquois reside in Canada, where there are two Iroquoian reservations. The people are not averse to adopting new technology when it is beneficial, but they want to maintain their own traditional identity.

HISTORY

The "Five Tribes" that first joined to form the Iroquois Confederacy, or League, were the Mohawk, Oneida, Onondaga, Cayuga, and Seneca (listed in order from east to west according to where they lived in an area that roughly corresponds to central New York state). They called themselves Haudenosaunee (pronounced "hoo-dee-noh-SHAW-nee"), or people of the longhouse, referring to the construction of their homes, in which extended families of up to 50 people lived together in bark-covered, wooden-framed houses that were 50 to 150 feet long. They also envisioned their extended community as occupying a symbolic longhouse some 300 miles long, with the Mohawks guarding the eastern door and the Seneca the western.

The origin of the name Iroquois is uncertain, although it seems to have involved French adaptations of Indian words. Among the possibilities that have been suggested are a blending of *hiro* (an Iroquois word used to conclude a speech) and *koué* (an exclamation); *ierokwa* ("they who smoke"); *iakwai* ("bear"); or the Algonquian words *irin* ("real") and *ako* ("snake") with the French *ois* termination.

The Mohawk called themselves Ganiengehaka, or "people of the flint country." Their warriors, armed with flint arrows, were known to be overpowering; their enemies called them *Mowak*, meaning "man eaters." The name Oneida means "people of the standing stone," referring to a large rock that, according to legend, appeared wherever the people moved, to give them directions. The Onondaga ("people of the hills"), the Cayuga ("where they land the boats"), and the Seneca ("the people of the big hill") named themselves by describing their homelands.

Because the Algonquian people living on both sides of the Iroquois corridor are of a different culture and linguistic stock, it appears likely that the Iroquois migrated into this area at some time. No evidence has been found to indicate where they came from, however. The Cherokee Indians, whose historic homeland was in the southeastern United States, belong to the same linguistic group and share some other links with the Iroquois. Where and when they may have lived near each other is unknown.

Despite their common culture and language, relations among the Five Tribes deteriorated to a state of near-constant warfare in ancient times. The infighting, in turn, made them vulnerable to attacks from the surrounding Algonquian tribes. This period, known in the Iroquois oral tradition as the "darktimes," reached a nadir during the reign of a psychotic Onondaga chief named Todadaho. Legend has it that he was a cannibal who ate from bowls made from the skulls of his victims, that he knew and saw everything, that his hair contained a tangle of snakes, and that he could kill with only a Medusa-like look.

Into this terrible era, however, entered two heroic figures. Deganawidah came from his Huron homeland in the north, travelling unchallenged among the hostile Iroquois. Finally, he encountered a violent, cannibalistic Onondagan. According to legend, Deganawidah watched through a hole in the roof while the man prepared to cook his latest victim. Seeing the stranger's face reflected in the cooking pot, the barbarian assumed it to be his own image. He was struck by the thought that the beauty of the face was incompatible with the horrendous practice of cannibalism and immediately forsook the practice. He went outside to dispose of the corpse, and when he returned to his lodge he met Deganawidah. The foreigner's words of peace and righteousness were so powerful that the man became a loyal disciple and helped spread the message.

Deganawidah named his disciple Hiawatha, meaning "he who combs," and sent him to confront Todadaho and remove the snakes from the chief's hair. After enduring terrible hardships at his adversary's hands, and after convincing the other Iroquoian chiefs to accept the Good Message, Hiawatha finally convinced Todadaho as well. On the banks of Onondaga Lake, sometime between 1350 and 1600, Deganawidah established the Iroquois Confederacy, a league of nations that shared a positive code of values and lived in mutual harmony. Out of respect, the Iroquois refer to him as the Peacemaker.

When the first white explorers arrived in the early seventeenth century, they found the settled, agricultural society of the Iroquois a contrast to the nomadic culture of the neighboring Algonquians.

RELATIONSHIP BETWEEN THE IROQUOIS AND NON-INDIANS

The French had established a presence in Canada for over 50 years before they met the Iroquois. During that period, the Iroquois began to acquire European trade goods through raids on other Indian tribes. They found the metal axes, knives, hoes, and kettles far superior to their implements of stone, bone, shell, and wood. Woven cloth began to replace the animal skins usually used for clothing materials.

The recurring raids prompted the French to help their Indian allies attack the Iroquois in 1609, opening a new technological era for the people of the Confederacy. French body armor was made of metal, whereas that of the Iroquois was made of slatted wood. Furthermore, the French fought with firearms, while traditional Iroquois weapons were bows and arrows, stone tomahawks, and wooden warclubs.

In response to European influence, the Iroquois gradually changed their military tactics to incorporate stealth, surprise, and ambush. Their motives for fighting also changed. In the past, they had fought for prestige or revenge, or to obtain goods or captives; now they fought for economic advantage, seeking control over bountiful beaver hunting grounds or perhaps a stash of beaver skins to trade for European goods.

Although it provided the Indians with better tools, European incursion into the territory was disastrous for the indigenous people. In the 1690s alone, the Iroquois lost between 1,600 and 2,000 people in fighting with other Indian tribes. In addition, European diseases such as smallpox, measles, influenza, lung infections, and even the common cold took a heavy toll on them since they had developed no immunity and knew no cures.

These seventeenth century population devastations prompted the Iroquois people to turn increasingly to their traditional practice of adopting outsiders into their tribes to replace members who had died from violence or illness. While some captives were unmercifully tortured to death, others were adopted into Iroquois families (the leading clanswomen decided prisoners' fates, sometimes basing their decision on the manner in which a relative of theirs had been killed). The adopted person, who was sometimes the opposite gender or of a significantly different age than the deceased Indian he replaced, was treated with the same affection, given the same rights, and expected to fulfill the same duties as his predecessor.

Most, if not all, of the Indians who were educated by the English returned to their native cultures at the first opportunity. Many colonists, on the other hand, chose to become Indians, either by joining Indian society voluntarily, by not trying to escape from captivity, or by staying with their Indian captors in the wake of peace treaties that gave them the freedom to return home.

Early in the eighteenth century the Tuscarora, another Iroquoian-speaking tribe living in North Carolina, moved into the territory occupied by the Confederacy. They had rebelled against the encroachment of colonial settlers, against continual fraudulent treatment by traders, and against repeated raids that took their people for the slave trade. They suffered a terrible defeat, with hundreds of their people killed and hundreds more enslaved. Those who escaped such fates made their way north and became the sixth nation of the Iroquois League.

The first half of the eighteenth century was a period of rebuilding. The Iroquois made peace with the French and established themselves in a neutral position between the French and the English. This strategy lasted until the French and Indian War erupted in 1754; though the Confederacy was officially neutral, the Mohawk sided with the English, and the Seneca with the French.

Before long, another conflict arose among the European colonists, and the Iroquois were faced with the American Revolutionary War. Again, the various tribes failed to agree on which side to support. Without unanimous agreement on a common position, each nation in the Confederacy was free to pursue its own course. The Oneida fought on the side of the colonists, eventually earning official commendation from George Washington for their assistance. A major faction of the Mohawk sided with the British and recruited other Iroquois warriors to their cause. The League as a political entity was severely damaged by the conflict, and the war itself brought death and devastation to the member tribes. After the war, American retaliatory raids destroyed Iroquois towns and crops, and drove the people from their homelands.

The Six Nations remained fragmented in political, social, and religious ways throughout the nineteenth century. The development of the New Religion, beginning in 1799, helped revitalize the traditional culture and facilitated the transition to reservation life. Finally, beginning in the 1950s, the Mohawk, Seneca, and Tuscarora became involved in major land disputes over power-production and flood-control projects proposed by the New York State Power Authority and the United States Army Corps of Engineers. Paired with the social climate favoring ethnic assertion in the mid-twentieth century, these land disputes helped foster a resurgence in Iroquois solidarity.

KEY ISSUES

The Iroquois see themselves as a sovereign nation, not as merely another ethnic group within the United States population, and gaining further recognition of that status is a major objective. They have asserted their position in interesting ways. For example, when the United States declared war on Germany in 1917, the Iroquois Confederacy issued its own independent declaration and claimed status as an allied nation in the war effort. In 1949 a Haudenosaunee delegation attended groundbreaking ceremonies for the United Nations building in New York City. Iroquois statesmen and athletes use Haudenosaunee passports as they travel around the world.

Protecting the land is another priority. After New York state attempted to condemn a portion of the Seneca's land for use in building a highway, a federal court ruled in the 1970s that the state would have to negotiate with the Iroquois as equal sovereigns. In another land issue, the St. Regis (Akwesasne) Mohawk reservation has been affected by off-reservation pollution sources, including a neighboring toxic-waste dump and nearby air-fouling industrial plants.

Resolving the question of gambling on the reservations is also an important issue. In 1990 the controversy erupted into a gun battle that left two Mohawk dead. The Onondaga Council of Chiefs issued a "Memorandum on Tribal Sovereignty" that said: "These businesses have corrupted our people and we are appalled at the Longhouse people who have become part of these activities. They have thrown aside the values of our ancient confederacy for personal gain" (*The Onondaga Council of Chiefs Memorandum on Tribal Sovereignty*). On the other hand, the Oneida tribe saw a dramatic decrease in unemployment after building a bingo hall in 1985; first year profits of over $5 million were used by the tribe to acquire additional land adjacent to the reservation.

ACCULTURATION AND ASSIMILATION

TRADITIONAL CULTURE

Even before the Europeans came to America, the Iroquois were an agricultural society. The men set out on hunting expeditions in dugout or bark canoes to provide meat and hides, while the women tended to the farming. They were a relaxed society with a minimum of rules. The people laughed easily, favoring a sense of the paradoxical.

The longhouses in which they lived were constructed with a vestibule at each end that was available for use by all residents. Within the body

In this 1948 photograph, Benjamin Cohen, assistant secretary general of the United Nations, smokes a peace pipe as Iroquois representatives pledge their support for the U.N.

of the house, a central corridor eight feet wide separated two banks of compartments. Each compartment, measuring about 13 feet by six feet, was occupied by a nuclear family. A wooden platform about a foot above the ground served as a bed by night and chair by day; some compartments included small bunks for children. An overhead shelf held personal belongings. Every 20 feet along the central corridor, a fire pit served the two families living on its opposite sides. Bark or hide doors at the ends of the buildings were attached at the top; these openings and the smoke holes in the roof 15 to 20 feet above each hearth provided the only ventilation.

Villages of 300 to 600 people were protected by a triple-walled stockade of wooden stakes 15 to 20 feet tall. About every 15 years the nearby supplies of wild game and firewood would become depleted, and the farmed soil would become exhausted. During a period of two years or so, the men would find and clear an alternate site for the village, which would then be completely rebuilt.

The primary crops, revered as gifts from the Creator, were called the "Three Sisters": Corn provided stalks for climbing bean vines, while squash plants controlled weeds by covering the soil. The complimentary nutrient needs and soil-replenishing characteristics of the three crops extended the useful life of each set of fields. In addition to providing food, the corn plants were used to make a variety of other goods. From the stalks were made medicine-storing tubes, corn syrup, toy warclubs and spears, and straws for teaching children to count. Corn husks were fashioned into lamps, kindling, mattresses, clotheslines, baskets, shoes, and dolls. Animal skins were smoked over corn cob fires.

Although bows and arrows tipped with flint or bone were the primary hunting weapons, blow guns were used for smaller prey. Made from the hollowed stem of swamp alder, blow guns were about six feet long and one inch thick, with a half-inch bore; the arrows were two and a half feet long.

Elm bark was put to many useful purposes, including constructing houses, building canoes, and fashioning containers. Baskets were woven of various materials, including black ash splints. Pottery vessels were decorated with angular combinations of parallel lines.

Wampum (cylindrical beads about one-fourth inch long and one-eighth inch in diameter) was very important in the Iroquois culture. The beads were made of quahog, or large, hard-shell clam shells and could only be obtained through trading or as tribute payments from coastal tribes. White and purple beads were made from the different sections of the shells. Although the beads were used as ornamentation on clothing, wampum had several more important uses. Strings of the beads were used in mourning rituals or to identify a messenger as an official representative of his nation. Wampum belts served as symbols of authority or of contract. Patterns or figures woven into wampum belts recorded the terms of treaties; duplicate belts were given to each of the contracting parties. Because of its important uses, wampum became a valuable commodity and was sometimes used as a form of currency in trading.

Traditional Iroquois games ranged from lively field contests like lacrosse to more sedentary activities involving the bouncing of dried fruit-pit "dice" from a wooden bowl. The games were played both as entertainment and as elements of periodic ceremonies. A favorite winter game called "snow-snake" involved throwing a long wooden rod and seeing how far it would slide down an icy track smoothed out on a snowy field.

The Iroquois had no stringed musical instruments. The only wind instrument, the wooden "courting flute," had six finger stops and was blown from the end. Single-tone rhythm instruments provided the only musical accompaniment for ceremonial dancing and singing. Rattles were made by placing dried corn kernels inside various materials including turtle shells, gourds, bison horns, or folded, dried bark. The traditional drum was about six inches in diameter, made like a wooden pail, and covered with stretched animal skin; just the right amount of water was sealed inside to produce the desired tone when the drum was tapped with a stick.

ACCULTURATION AND TRANSFORMATION OF CULTURE

The Iroquois have been willing to adapt to a changing world, but they have resisted efforts to substitute a European culture for their own heritage. For example, in 1745 the Reverend David Brainerd proposed to live among them for two years to help them build a Christian church and become accustomed to the weekly worship cycle. They were direct in declining his offer: "We are Indians and don't wish to be transformed into white men. The English are our Brethren, but we never promised to become what they are" (James Axtell, *The European and the Indian: Essays in the Ethnohistory of Colonial North America.* [New York: Oxford University Press, 1981] p. 78).

Yet changes were inevitable. In 1798 a Quaker delegation worked among the Seneca, teaching them to read and write. They also instructed them in modern farming methods and encouraged men to work on the farms, which represented a major cultural shift. A respected Seneca warrior named Gaiantwaka, known as The Cornplanter, helped bring about this change, as did his half brother, Ganiodayo (Handsome Lake).

More Iroquois began to accept the concept of private ownership of land; historically, tribal lands were held in common, although individuals might have the right to farm certain parcels during their lifetime. During the nineteenth century, the Iroquois sold large amounts of land in exchange for useful trade goods. Leading chiefs were sometimes induced to support such sales by the offer of lifetime pensions. Shrinking land holdings made hunting increasingly difficult and left the men with little to do, which contributed to the Quakers' success in turning them to agricultural work. Families were encouraged to leave the longhouses and live separately on small farms so the men could work in their fields without being embarrassed by being seen doing women's work. Today, longhouses are used only for religious and ceremonial purposes.

In the mid-1800s a rather abrupt change occurred in the style of artwork used to decorate clothing with beads, quills, and embroidery. Rather than the traditional patterns of curving lines and scrolls, designs became representational images of plants and flowers, influenced by the floral style prominent among the seventeenth- and eighteenth-century French.

Eventually, the Onondaga discovered that non-Indians would be willing to pay to see their ceremonial dances, and they experimented with public performances. In 1893 the annual Green Corn Festival was delayed several weeks for the convenience of the audience, and the council house was filled three times with spectators who paid 15 cents admission. The contemporary historian William M. Beauchamp wrote, "Of course, this deprived the feast of all religious force, and made it a mere show; nor did it quite satisfy those who saw it" ("Notes on Onondaga Dances," *An Iroquois Source Book, Volume 2*, edited by Elisabeth Tooker. [New York: Garland Publishing, 1985] p. 183).

As was the case with other Native Americans, much of the friction between the Iroquois and non-Indians has involved different attitudes toward land. During the 1950s and 1960s the long-standing disparity was brought into sharp focus during the planning and construction of the Kinzua Dam, which flooded over 9,000 acres of Seneca Land. The Indians fought the dam, claiming it violated the treaty between the Six Nations and the United States. The government reimbursed the tribe financially, but the reservation was disrupted. The grave of the revered Cornplanter had to be moved to accommodate the dam; his descendant Harriett Pierce commented, "The White man views land for its money value. We Indians have a spiritual tie with the earth, a reverence for it that Whites don't share and can hardly understand" (Alvin M. Josephy, Jr., *Now That the Buffalo's Gone: A Study of Today's American Indians* [New York: Alfred A. Knoph, 1982] p. 129).

Traditional values are sustained on the various Iroquois reservations. The ancient languages are spoken and taught, traditional ceremonies are observed, and baskets are woven. Material wealth is not characteristic of reservation Indians, but Tonawanda Seneca Chief Corbett Sundown, keeper of the Iroquois "spiritual fire," disputes the assessment that the people are poor. He told a *National Geographic* writer: "We're rich people without any money, that's all. You say we ought to set up industries and factories. Well, we just don't want them. How're you going to grow potatoes and sweet corn on concrete? You call that progress? To me "progress" is a dirty word" (Arden Harvey, "The Fire that Never Dies," *National Geographic* [September 1987] p. 398).

MISCONCEPTIONS AND STEREOTYPES

"Hiawatha" is one of the most widely recognized Indian names among non-Indian Americans, thanks to Henry Wadsworth Longfellow. Unfortunately, his character is a classic case of mistaken identity. The real subject of the poem, an Ojibwe hero named Nanabozho, was confused with the Iroquoian Hiawatha in a mid-nineteenth century work by Henry Rowe Schoolcraft that inspired Longfellow.

The Longfellow poem, at least, presented a sympathetic image of an Iroquois-named character. In his eloquent history of the Tuscarora Indians, Chief Elias Johnson wrote in 1881: "Almost any portrait that we see of an Indian, he is represented with tomahawk and scalping knife in hand, as if they possess no other but a barbarous nature. Christian nations might with equal justice be always represented with cannon and balls, swords and pistols, as the emblems of their employment and their prevailing tastes" (Elias Johnson, *Legends, Traditions and Laws of the Iroquois, or Six Nations, and History of the Tuscarora Indians* [New York: AMS Press, 1978 (reprint of 1881 edition)] p. 13).

CUISINE

Corn is the traditional staple of the Haudenosaunee diet. It was baked or boiled and eaten on or off the cob; the kernels were mashed and either fried, baked in a kettle, or spread on corn leaves that were folded and boiled as tamales. Some varieties of corn were processed into hominy by boiling the kernels in a weak lye solution of hardwood ashes and water. Bread, pudding, dumplings, and cooked cereal were made from cornmeal. Parched corn coffee was brewed by mixing roasted corn with boiling water.

Besides corn, and the beans and squash they raised with it, the Iroquois people ate a wide variety of other plant foods. Wild fruits, nuts, and roots were gathered to supplement the cultivated crops. Berries were dried for year-round use. Maple sap was used for sweetening, but salt was not commonly used.

The traditional diet featured over 30 types of meat, including deer, bear, beaver, rabbit, and squirrel. Fresh meat was enjoyed during the hunting season, and some was smoked or dried and used to embellish corn dishes during the rest of the year. The Iroquois used the region's waterways extensively for transportation, but fish was relatively unimportant as food.

TRADITIONAL CLOTHING

The fundamental item of men's clothing was a breechcloth made of a strip of deerskin or fabric. Passing between the legs, it was secured by a waist belt, and decorated flaps of the breechcloth hung in the front and back. The belt, or sash, was a favorite article; sometimes worn only around the waist, and sometimes also over the left shoulder, it was woven on a loom or on the fingers, and might be decorated with beadwork.

The basic item of women's clothing was a short petticoat. Other items that were worn by both sexes included a fringed, sleeveless tunic, separate sleeves (connected to each other by thongs, but not connected to the tunic), leggings, moccasins, and a robe or blanket. Clothing was adorned with moosehair embroidery featuring curved line figures with coiled ends. Decorated pouches for carrying personal items completed the costumes. Women used burden straps, worn across the forehead, to support litters carried on their backs.

By the end of the eighteenth century, trade cloth replaced deerskin as the basic clothing material. Imported glass beads replaced porcupine quills as decorative elements.

FESTIVALS

The annual cycle consists of six regular festivals, which are still observed among the Iroquois. In addition, ceremonies are held as needed for wakes, memorial feasts, burials, adoptions, or sealing of friendships.

The new year began with the Mid-Winter Festival, which was held in late January or early February when the men returned from the fall hunt. It lasted five days, followed by another two or three days of game playing. This was a time of spiritual cleansing and renewal, and included a ritual cleaning of homes. Public confessions were made, and penitents touched a wampum belt as a pledge of reform. Playing a traditional dice game

commemorated the struggle between the Creator and his evil twin brother for control over the earth. Thanks were offered to the Creator for protection during the past year. Dreams were always considered to be supernatural messages, and everyone was obliged to help the dreamer by fulfilling the needs or desires expressed in the dream; particular attention was devoted to dream guessing during the Mid-Winter Festival. On a pre-festival day, names were conferred on babies, young adults, and adoptees so they could participate in the upcoming ceremonies.

In the spring, when the sap rose, it was time for the Thanks-to-the-Maple Festival. This one-day celebration included social dances and the ceremonial burning of tobacco at the base of a maple tree.

In May or June, corn seeds saved from the previous year were blessed at the Corn Planting Ceremony. This was a half-day observance in which the Creator was thanked and spirit forces were implored for sufficient rain and moderate sun.

Ripening strawberries in June signaled time for the Strawberry Festival. Dancers mimicked the motions of berry pickers. This one-day celebration was a time for giving thanks.

In August or early September, the corn was ready to eat. This event was marked by the Green Corn Festival, which involved ceremonies on four successive mornings. The first day included general thanksgiving, a Feather Dance honoring those who worked to put on the festival, and the naming of children. The second day saw more dances and the bestowing of names on young adults and adoptees. The third day was dedicated to personal commitment and sacrifice, and included a communal burning of tobacco. Speeches and dancing were followed by a feast. On the fourth day the ceremonial dice game was played as it was at the Mid-Winter Festival. Finally, the women who worked the fields sang thanksgiving for the crops.

When all the crops had been harvested and stored away, and before the men left for the fall hunt, the Harvest Festival was held. This one-day celebration took place in October.

The use of masks, or "false faces," is a major component of Iroquois rituals. They symbolized spirit forces that were represented by the person wearing the mask at festivals or healing ceremonies. One group of spirits was depicted by masks carved from living trees, while another group was represented by masks made from braided corn husks. Miniature corn husk masks, three inches across or less, were kept as personal charms; in ancient times the miniatures were also made of clay or stone.

DEATH AND BURIAL CUSTOMS

When a person died, everyone who had similar names gave them up until a period of mourning was completed. Later, if another person was adopted into the clan, he was often given the name of the deceased person whose place he took.

A wake was held the night following a death. After a midnight meal, the best orators of the village spoke about the deceased, and about life and death in general. The body was placed on a scaffold for several days on the chance that the person only appeared dead and might revive, which happened occasionally. After decomposition began the remains might be buried, or the cleaned bones might be housed in or near the family lodge. When the village relocated, all of the unburied skeletons were interred in a common grave. By the end of the nineteenth century, burials were conducted according to European customs.

Upon death both the soul and the ghost left the body. Using food and tools offered by the survivors, the soul journeyed to the land of the dead. The ghost, on the other hand, became a spiritual inhabitant of the village. At a yearly Feast of the Dead, tobacco and songs were offered to the resident ghosts.

HEALTH AND MENTAL HEALTH ISSUES

Traditional Iroquois rituals addressed both physical and mental health issues. Medicine men (or women) used herbs and natural ointments to treat maladies including fevers, coughs, and snake bites. Wounds were cleaned, broken bones were set, and medicinal emetics were administered.

Another type of healer, known as a conjurer, sang incantations to combat maladies caused through witchcraft. They might remove an affliction from the patient's body by blowing or sucking. Twice a year groups of False Faces visited each house in the village, waving pine boughs and dispelling illness. Shamans were empowered to combat disorders caused by evil spirits.

In the realm of mental health, modern psychologists see the value in the Iroquois practice of dream guessing. Everyone in the community had a responsibility to resolve conflicts and unmet needs made evident through any person's dreams.

LANGUAGE

The six Iroquoian dialects are similar enough to allow easy conversation. The Mohawk and Oneida are quite similar, as are the Cayuga and Seneca; the Onondaga and Tuscarora are each different from the five others. One common characteristic is the lack of labial sounds formed by bringing the lips together.

The language is rich in words for tangible things, but lacking in abstract expressions. A 1901 treatise noted, "for the varieties, sexes, and ages of a single animal they would have a multitude of terms, but no general word for animal. Or they would have words for good man, good woman, good dog, but no word for goodness" (Lewis H. Morgan, *League of the Ho-de-no-sau-nee or Iroquois* [New Haven: Human Relations Area Files, 1954] p. 243).

Historically, the Iroquois language was oral. In the mid-1800s a Congregational missionary named Asher Wright devised a written version using the English alphabet and edited a Seneca newspaper. During the latter half of the 1900s, written dictionaries and grammar texts have been developed for teaching the languages on the reservations. However, Barbara Graymont noted at the 1965 Conference on Iroquois Research that no written material existed in Tuscarora, other than an "unreadable" nineteenth century hymnal (Barbara Graymont, "Problems of Tuscarora Language Survival," *Iroquois Culture, History, and Prehistory* [Albany: The University of the State of New York, 1967] pp. 27-8).

Graymont reported a revival of interest in keeping the language alive. A young person had told her that parents had not taught his generation the language but had used it among themselves when they didn't want the children to know what they were saying. On the other hand, she noted that during the land disputes with the State Power Authority of New York about 1958, Indians involved in a passive resistance campaign relied on their native language to avoid being understood by State police officers and to foil telephone wiretaps.

GREETINGS AND OTHER POPULAR EXPRESSIONS

Some of the basic Mohawk expressions are: *shé:kon* ("SHAY kohn") or *kwé kwé* ("KWAY KWAY")—hello; *hén* ("hun")—yes; *iáh* ("yah")—no; *niá:wen* ("nee AH wun")—thank you.

FAMILY AND COMMUNITY DYNAMICS

CLAN AND FAMILY STRUCTURE

The Iroquois tribes were organized into eight clans, which were grouped in two moieties: Wolf, Bear, Beaver, and Turtle; and Deer, Snipe, Heron, and Hawk. In ancient times, intermarriage was not allowed within each four-clan group, but eventually intermarriage was only forbidden within each clan. Tribal affiliation did not affect clan membership; for example, all Wolf clan members were considered to be blood relatives, regardless of whether they were members of the Mohawk, Seneca, or other Iroquois tribes. At birth, each person became a member of the clan of his or her mother.

Within a tribe, each clan was led by the clan mother, who was usually the oldest woman in the group. In consultation with the other women, the clan mother chose one or more men to serve as clan chiefs. Each chief was appointed for life but the clan mother and her advisors could remove him from office for poor behavior or dereliction of duty.

MARRIAGE

Traditionally, a man and woman wishing to marry would tell their parents, who would arrange a joint meeting of relatives to discuss the suitability of the two people for marriage to each other. If no objections arose during the discussion, a day was chosen for the marriage feast. On the appointed day the woman's relatives would bring her to the groom's home for the festivities. Following the meal, elders from the groom's family spoke to the bride about wifely duties, and elders from the bride's family told the groom about husbandly responsibilities. Then the two began their new life together.

In ancient times adultery was rare. When it was discovered, the woman was punished by whipping, but the man was not punished. If a couple decided to separate, both of their families would be called to a council. The parties would state their reasons for wanting a divorce, and the elders would try to work out a reconciliation. If those efforts failed, the marriage ended. In ancient times, fathers kept their sons and mothers kept their daughters when a divorce occurred; by the early eighteenth century, however, mothers typically kept all of the children.

CHILDREARING

Children were valued among the Iroquois; because of the matrilineal society, daughters were somewhat more prized than sons. The birth of a couple's first child was welcomed with a feast at the mother's family home. The couple stayed there a few days, and then returned to their own home to prepare another feast.

Birthing took place in a hut located outside the village. As her time drew near, the mother and a few other women withdrew to the hut and remained there until a few days after the birth. Until he was able to walk, an Iroquois baby spent his days secured to a cradleboard, which his mother would hang from a tree branch while she worked in the fields.

Babies were named at birth; when the child reached puberty, an adult name was given. Names referred to natural phenomena (such as the moon or thunder), landscape features, occupations, and social or ceremonial roles; animal names were very rare. Some examples of the meanings of names are: In the Center of the Sky, Hanging Flower, He Carries News, and Mighty Speaker. A person was never addressed by his name during conversation; when speaking about a person, especially to a relative, the name was only used if he could not otherwise be clearly identified by terms of relation or the context of the discussion.

Mothers had primary responsibility for raising their children and teaching them good behavior. In keeping with the easy-going nature of Haudenosaunee society, children learned informally from their family and clan elders. Children were not spanked, but they might be punished by splashing water in their faces. Difficult children might be frightened into better behavior by a visit from someone wearing the mask of Longnose, the cannibal clown.

Puberty marked the time of acceptance into adult membership in the society. On the occasion of her first menses, a girl would retire to an isolated hut for the duration of her period. She was required to perform difficult tasks, such as chopping hardwood with a dull axe, and was prohibited from eating certain foods. The period of initiation for a young man was more lengthy; when his voice began to change, he went to live in a secluded cabin in the forest for up to a year. An old man or woman took responsibility for overseeing his well-being. He ate sparsely, and his time was spent in physically demanding activities such as running, swimming, bathing in icy water, and scraping his shins with a stone. His quest was completed when he was visited by his spirit, which would remain with him during his adult life.

EDUCATION

A speaker at the 1963 American Anthropological Association convention described the Iroquois as "virtually 100% literate today" (Cara E. Richards, "Women Use the Law, Men Suffer From It: Differential Acculturation Among the Onondaga Indians in the 1950's & 60's," *Iroquois Women: An Anthology* [Ohsweken, Ontario: Iroqrafts Ltd, 1990] p. 167). The 1980 Census found that 60 percent of the Iroquois over the age of 25 were high school graduates, and nine percent were college graduates.

Iroquois children attending reservation schools learn not only the subjects typically taught at non-Indian schools, but also study their tribal culture and history. The stated goals of the Akwesasne Freedom School, for example, are "to facilitate learning so that the students will have a good self-concept as Indians, promote self-reliance, promote respect for the skills of living in harmony with others and the environment and master the academic and/or vocational skills necessary in a dualistic society" (*The Native North American Almanac*, edited by David Champagne [Detroit: Gale Research, 1994] p. 886).

RELIGION

From ancient times the Haudenosaunee believed that a powerful spirit called Orenda permeated the universe. He created everything that is good and useful. The Evil Spirit made things that are poisonous, but the Great Spirit gained control of the world.

During the seventeenth century, French Jesuit missionaries converted many of the Iroquois to Catholicism. Kateri Tekakwitha, who was baptized in 1635, became the first Native American nun. She was extraordinarily devout; since her death many visions and miraculous cures have been attributed to her intervention. She was beatified by the Catholic Church in 1980 and is a candidate for canonization to sainthood.

In 1710 three Mohawk chiefs, along with another from the Mahicans, visited Queen Anne in England to ask for military assistance against the French and for Anglican missionaries to teach

their people. As the years passed, Quakers, Baptists, Methodists, and an interdenominational Protestant group called the New York Missionary Society joined the effort of proselytizing the Iroquois. An intense rivalry developed between the pagan and Christian factions. In fact, in 1823 a group of Oneidas led by Eleazar Williams, a Mohawk from Canada who had become an Episcopalian minister, left their New York homeland and moved to Wisconsin, where they established a reservation.

In 1799, amidst the Christian missionary efforts, a revival of the ancient Longhouse religion developed. A Seneca known as Handsome Lake had spent much of his life in dissolute living and fell gravely ill when he was about 65 years old. He expected to die, but instead, he experienced a profound vision and recovered. Inspired, he began to spread the Good Word among his fellow Iroquois. The New Religion was essentially a revitalization of the ancient pagan beliefs, although some Quaker influence can be detected.

Major tenets of the New Religion included shunning of alcoholic beverages, abandonment of beliefs in witchcraft and love potions, and denunciation of abortion. The fact that Handsome Lake's message had come in a dream gave it a profound impact among the Haudenosaunee. The religion was instrumental in showing many Iroquois how to retain their own culture while adapting to a world dominated by non-Indians.

The Longhouse religion continues to be a major spiritual focus among the Iroquois people. Some adhere solely to its practice, while others maintain a parallel membership in a Christian church.

EMPLOYMENT AND ECONOMIC TRADITIONS

Although the Haudenosaunee's bond to the land remains, most no longer live as farmers. Census data from 1980 show that two-thirds of the Iroquois people lived in urban areas. About half of those living outside urban settings actually lived on reservations. Ties to the homeland and the tribal culture are strong, however, and those who live off the reservation return from time to time to visit relatives and to spiritually renew themselves.

In a modern rendition of their ancient sojourns away from the village to hunt, Iroquois

men today may support their families by living and working in a city but returning home periodically. In particular, there is a cohesive group of Indians, including many Mohawk, living in Brooklyn during the week but returning to their families on weekends.

Iroquois men, especially Mohawk, are famous as ironworkers in construction. They walk steel girders high in the air unhampered by any fear of heights. Consequently, they are in demand around the country for skyscraper and bridge building projects, which have included such landmarks as the World Trade Center and the Golden Gate Bridge. Fathers pass their ironworking tools on to their sons (or sometimes daughters) in an atmosphere reminiscent of ancient rituals.

The 1980 census indicated that about nine percent of the employed Iroquois were engaged in construction, although over half of the men of the St. Regis Mohawk Reservation are members of the ironworker union. Factory work was actually the largest occupation, accounting for one-fourth of the jobs held by Iroquois people. Nineteen percent of the employed Iroquois worked in "professional and related services," including health and education. Another 13 percent were engaged in retail trade.

Cara E. Richards of Cornell University conducted an acculturation study focusing on the Onondaga tribe during the 1950s and early 1960s (Richards, pp. 164-67). At that time 70 percent of the tribal women who held jobs worked as domestics in off-reservation homes. This put them in the position of interacting with upper- and middle-class families in home environments that exposed them to radio and television programs, non-Indian lifestyles, modern home appliances, and even different types of foods. Onondaga men, on the other hand, worked primarily in factories or on construction sites. Although they interacted with non-Indian men, there was little exchange of cultural information. Differential patterns of acculturation resulted, in which the women were more comfortable and successful in relating to non-Indian agencies, including law enforcement.

Economic activity varies markedly among the various Iroquois reservations. For example, the Onondaga reservation does not offer services for tourists, but the Mohawk welcome tourists to their museum and marinas.

POLITICS AND GOVERNMENT

The Great Peace forged by Deganawidah and Hiawatha produced an unwritten but clearly defined framework for the Iroquois Confederacy (a written constitution was developed about 1850). Three principles, each with dual meanings, formed the foundation of the League government. The Good Word signified righteousness in action as well as in thought and speech; it also required justice through the balancing of rights and obligations. The principle of Health referred to maintaining a sound mind in a sound body; it also involved peace among individuals and between groups. Thirdly, Power meant physical, military, or civil authority; it also denoted spiritual power. The founders envisioned the resulting peace spreading beyond the original League members, so that eventually all people would live in cooperation. Law and order remained the internal concern of each tribe, but the League legally prohibited cannibalism.

Under the structure of the Confederacy, the 50 clan chiefs (called sachems) from all the tribes came together to confer about questions of common concern. The successor of the Onondaga chief Todadaho served as a chairman who oversaw the discussion, which continued until a unanimous decision was reached. If no consensus could be achieved, each tribe was free to follow an independent course on that matter.

The League functioned well for generations, fostering peace among the Six Nations. Even when the tribes failed to agree regarding an external dispute, such as one between the French and the Dutch, they would find a way to fight their respective enemies without confronting another League tribe. However, they were unable to do this during the American Revolution. The Confederacy nearly collapsed in the wake of that war, and traditionalists are still trying to rebuild it. During the latter half of the twentieth century, it has strengthened significantly.

In 1802 the Mohawks living within the United States officially discarded their traditional clan-based structure and established an elective tribal government. In 1848 a faction of Senecas instituted a similar change, establishing the Seneca Nation. Voting rights were denied to Seneca women, who had historically chosen the tribal leaders; women's suffrage was not reinstated until 1964. Other tribes eventually followed suit, either abandoning their ancestral governments or modifying them to incorporate elections. Traditionalists clung to the ancient structure, however, and today two competing sets of governments exist on several reservations. Violence occasionally erupts between the opposing factions.

The United States government has tried in various ways to relocate, assimilate, or disband Indian tribes. A core group of the Iroquois people has steadfastly resisted these efforts. In 1831 some Seneca and Cayuga moved to Indian Territory (now Oklahoma) as part of the federal removal effort; other Iroquois factions held their ground until the policy was overturned in 1842 and ownership of some of the Seneca land was restored. In 1924 Congress passed legislation conferring U.S. citizenship to all American Indians; the Haudenosaunee rejected such status.

The Iroquois have actively worked to reclaim sacred artifacts and ancestral remains from museums. In 1972 a moratorium was enacted prohibiting archaeologists from excavating native burial sites in New York state; tribal members would be notified to arrange proper reburials for remains unearthed accidentally. Wampum belts held by the New York State Museum in Albany were removed from public display in deference to the Indians' belief that they should not be treated as curiosities, and were finally returned to the Onondagas (as Keeper of the Central Fire for the Iroquois League) in 1989. Years of effort were rewarded in the early 1990s when the Smithsonian Institution and its National Museum of the American Indian committed to returning human remains, burial artifacts, sacred objects, and other articles of cultural patrimony to Indian tribes.

INDIVIDUAL AND GROUP CONTRIBUTIONS

Although disputed by some, there is significant evidence that the Iroquois Confederacy served as a model or inspiration for the U.S. Constitution. Benjamin Franklin and Thomas Paine were well acquainted with the League. John Rutledge, chairman of the committee that wrote the first draft of the Constitution, began the process by quoting some passages from the Haudenosaunee Great Law. The Iroquois form of government was based on democracy and personal freedom, and included elements equivalent to the modern political tools of initiative, referendum, and recall. In 1987 Senator Daniel Inouye sponsored a resolution that would commemorate the Iroquois' contributions to the formation of the federal government.

Many Iroquois people have made notable contributions to society and culture that transcend political boundaries. A dramatic example is Oren Lyons (1930-), an Onondaga chief who has led political delegations to numerous countries in support of the rights of indigenous people. Twice named an All-American lacrosse goal-keeper, he led his 1957 team at Syracuse University to an undefeated season and was eventually enrolled in the sport's Hall of Fame. He was a successful amateur boxer in both the U.S. Army and in the Golden Gloves competition. He worked as a commercial artist for several years before returning to the reservation to assume his position as faithkeeper. An author and illustrator, he has served as Chairman of American Studies at the State University of New York (SUNY) at Buffalo and as publisher of *Daybreak*, a national quarterly newspaper of Native American views. In 1992 he became the first indigenous leader to have addressed the United Nations General Assembly.

ACADEMIA AND SCHOLARSHIP

Arthur C. Parker (Seneca, 1881-1955) was a leading authority on Iroquois culture as well as museum administration. He joined the New York State Museum at Albany as an archeologist in 1906 and became director of the Rochester Museum of Arts and Sciences in 1925. He wrote 14 major books and hundreds of articles.

Dr. John Mohawk (Seneca) teaches Native American law and history at SUNY in Buffalo. He has written extensively on the Iroquois philosophy and approach to government. He founded *Akwesasne Notes*, a quarterly activist magazine, and the Indigenous Press Network, a computerized news service focusing on Indian affairs.

The poetry of Roberta Hill Whiteman (Oneida) has been published in anthologies and magazines including *American Poetry Review*. She has been involved with Poets-in-the-Schools programs in at least seven states and has taught at the University of Wisconsin-Eau Claire.

GOVERNMENT AND PUBLIC INVOLVEMENT

Robert L. Bennett (Oneida) and Louis R. Bruce Jr. (Mohawk) served in the 1960s and early 1970s as commissioner of the United States Bureau of Indian Affairs. Ely Parker (Seneca, 1828-1895), the first Native American to hold that post, had been appointed by Ulysses S. Grant in 1869.

Katsi Cook (Mohawk), a midwife and lecturer on women's health, is active is the Akwesasne Environment Project. Her health-related writings have appeared in national magazines as well as in medical books.

Amber Coverdale Sumrall (Mohawk), a writer and poet, has been active in the Sanctuary Movement. She also lectures and teaches workshops on the topic of disabilities.

Tahnahga (Mohawk) has a degree in Rehabilitation Counseling; she incorporates traditional Native American healing methods into her work with chemical dependency. She also uses her talent as a poet and storyteller to show Indian youth how to use visions and dreaming to enhance their lives.

VISUAL ARTS AND LITERATURE

Richard Hill (1950-) followed his father's footsteps and became an ironworker in construction before enrolling in the Art Institute of Chicago. His watercolor paintings include a series on Iroquois culture, and he has also documented the culture through photography. Since the early 1970s he has curated numerous art shows, prepared museum exhibits for such clients as the Smithsonian Institution, and written many articles about history and art. A past Director of the North American Indian Museums Association, he has also taught at the State University of New York at Buffalo.

Maurice Kenny (Mohawk), a poet nominated for the Pulitzer prize, received the American Book Award in 1984 for *The Mama Poems*. His work has been widely anthologized, and he has been Writer-in-Residence at North County Community College in Saranac Lake, New York. He is described as having "a distinctive voice, one shaped by the rhythms of Mohawk life and speech, yet one which defines and moves beyond cultural boundaries" (Joseph Bruchac, *New Voices from the Longhouse: An Anthology of Contemporary Iroquois Writing* [Greenfield Center, NY: Greenfield Review Press, 1989] p. 161). He has also received the National Public Radio Award for Broadcasting.

Daniel Thompson (Mohawk, 1953-) has been a photographer, graphic artist, and editor of several publications including the *Northeast Indian Quarterly* published by Cornell University. He writes poetry in both English and Mohawk and is working to devise an improved written form for the Mohawk language. He has also served as news director for the Mohawk radio station.

Using the knowledge she acquired when earning bachelor's and master's degrees in zoology, Carol Snow (Seneca) has written and illustrated a dozen reports on endangered and rare species for the Bureau of Land Management. As an artist, in 1980 she created a technique incorporating ink and acrylic paint, which she employed in her renderings of Native American and wildlife themes.

Tuscarora sculptor Duffy Wilson works in both wood and stone. Tom Huff, another stone sculptor, is also a writer and poet; he served as editor of the Institute of American Indian Arts' literary journal in 1979. Alex Jacobs (Mohawk), whose sculptures, paintings, and prints can be found in New York galleries, has had his written works included in several Native American poetry and literature anthologies.

MEDIA

PRINT

Akwesasne Notes.
This quarterly magazine is published by the Mohawk tribe.

Contact: Mark Narsisian, Editor.
Address: P.O. Box 196, Rooseveltown, NY 13683-0196.
Telephone: (518) 358-9535.

Indian Time.
Weekly newspaper that covers local news of the Akwesasne Mohawk Nation.

Contact: Jann Day, Editor.
Address: P.O. Box 196, Rooseveltown, NY 13683-0196.
Telephone: (518) 358-9535.

Kalihwisaks ("She Looks for News").
Published by the Oneida Nation in Wisconsin, this bi-weekly newspaper covers tribal news at the local, state, and national levels.

Contact: Keith Skenandore, Managing Editor.
Address: P.O. Box 365, Oneida, WI 54155-0365.
Telephone: (414) 869-4395.

Ka Ri Wen Ha Wi.
This monthly newsletter contains reservation news and items about the Akwesasne Library/Cultural Center.

Contact: Sarah Hamill, Editor.
Address: R.R. 1, Box 14 C, Hogansburg, NY 13655.
Telephone: (518) 358-2240.

The Seneca Nation of Indians Official Newsletter.
Quarterly publication that prints news and special interest pieces about the Seneca Nation.

Contact: Debbie Hoag, Editor.
Address: P.O. Box 231, Salamanca, NY 14779-0231.
Telephone: (716) 945-1790.

RADIO

CKON.
This FM radio station is owned and operated by the Mohawk tribe on the St. Regis Reservation in New York. It broadcasts music 24 hours a day, including country, adult contemporary, rock, and blues segments. In addition, it airs hourly local news summaries, community announcements (sometimes in Mohawk or French) three times a day, and live coverage of local lacrosse games.

Contact: Stuart Wood, Station Manager.
Address: P.O. Box 140, Rooseveltown, NY 13683-0140.
Telephone: (518) 358-3426.

ORGANIZATIONS AND ASSOCIATIONS

The Onondaga Nation.
Contact: Chief Leon Shenandoah.
Address: P. O. Box 152, Onondaga Reservation, Nedrow, NY 13120.
Telephone: (315) 469-8507.

St. Regis Mohawk Tribe.
Contact: Joseph Gray, Public Information Director.
Address: Community Building, Hogansburg, NY 13655.
Telephone: (518) 358-2272.

The Seneca Nation, Allegany Reservation.
Contact: Dennis Bowen Sr., President.
Address: P.O. Box 321, Salamanca, NY 14779.
Telephone: (716) 945-1790.

The Seneca Nation of Indians, Cattaraugus Reservation.
Contact: Adrian Stevens, Treasurer.
Address: P.O. Box 268, Irving, NY 14081.
Telephone: (716) 532-3341.

Tonawanda Band of Senecas.
Contact: Darwin Hill.

Address: 7027 Meadville Road, Basom, NY 14013.
Telephone: (716) 542-4600.

MUSEUMS AND RESEARCH CENTERS

The Akwesasne Museum.
Displays traditional Mohawk artifacts and basketry, contemporary Iroquois artifacts, and ethnological exhibitions.

Contact: Carol White, Director.
Address: R.R. 1, Box 14 C, Hogansburg, NY 13655.
Telephone: (518) 358-2461.

The Iroquois Indian Museum.
Features the history of the Iroquois and displays contemporary arts and crafts. A library is available for research.

Contact: James Schafer, Director.
Address: P.O. Box 7, Howes Cave, NY 12092.
Telephone: (518) 296-8949.

The National Shrine of the Blessed Kateri Tekakwitha and Native American Exhibit.
Displays artifacts and maintains the only completely excavated and staked-out Iroquois village in the United States.

Contact: Fr. Jim Plavcan.
Address: P.O. Box 627, Fonda, NY 12068.
Telephone: (518) 853-3646.

The Oneida Nation Museum.
Preserves the culture of the Wisconsin tribe and serves as a point of contact for the Oneida Reservation.

Contact: Denise Vigue, Director.
Address: P.O. Box 365, Oneida, WI 54155-0365.
Telephone: (414) 869-2768.

The Rochester Museum and Science Center.
Offers changing exhibits as well as a permanent display, "At the Western Door," that focuses on relations between the Seneca Indians and European colonists. Also on display are a furnished 1790s Seneca cabin, six life-size figure tableaus, and over 2,000 artifacts.

Contact: Richard C. Shultz, Director.
Address: 657 East Avenue, P.O. Box 1480, Rochester, NY 14603-1480.
Telephone: (716) 271-1880.

The Seneca-Iroquois National Museum.
Located on the Allegany Reservation, this museum houses 300,000 articles portraying the life and culture of the Seneca and other Iroquois Indians, including wampum belts, costumes, games, and modern art.

Contact: Museum Director.
Address: P.O. Box 442, Salamanca, NY 14779.
Telephone: (716) 945-1738.

SOURCES FOR ADDITIONAL STUDY

Arden, Harvey. "The Fire That Never Dies," *National Geographic*, September 1987.

Axtell, James. *The European and the Indian: Essays in the Ethnohistory of Colonial North America.* New York: Oxford University Press, 1981.

A Basic Call to Consciousness. Rooseveltown, NY: Akwesasne Notes, 1978.

Bruchac, Joseph. *New Voices from the Longhouse: An Anthology of Contemporary Iroquois Writing.* Greenfield Center, N.Y.: Greenfield Review Press, 1989.

The Native North American Almanac, edited by David Champagne. Detroit: Gale Research Inc., 1994.

"Indian Roots of American Democracy," *Northeast Indian Quarterly,* edited by Jose Barreiro. Winter/Spring, 1987/1988.

An Iroquois Source Book, Volumes 1 and 2, edited by Elisabeth Tooker. New York: Garland Publishing, Inc., 1985.

Iroquois Women: An Anthology, edited by W. G. Spittal. Ohsweken, Ontario: Iroqrafts Ltd, 1990.

Johnson, Elias. *Legends, Traditions and Laws of the Iroquois, or Six Nations, and History of the Tuscarora Indians.* New York: AMS Press, 1978 (reprint of 1881 edition).

Josephy, Alvin M., Jr. *Now That the Buffalo's Gone: A Study of Today's American Indians.* New York: Alfred A. Knopf, 1982.

ITALIAN

by
George Pozzetta

AMERICANS

The family (*la famiglia*) rested at the heart of Italian society. Family solidarity was the major bulwark from which the rural population confronted a harsh society, and the family unit (including blood relatives and relatives by marriage) became the center of allegiances.

OVERVIEW

Moored by Alpine mountains in the north, the boot-shaped Italian peninsula juts into the central Mediterranean Sea. Along its European frontier, Italy shares borders with France, Switzerland, Austria, and Slovenia. The nation's land mass, which includes the two major islands of Sicily and Sardinia and numerous smaller ones, measures 116,324 square miles (301,200 square kilometers)—almost exactly double the size of the state of Florida. Italy's population in 1991 stood at 57.6 million. With the exception of the broad north Italian Plain at the foot of the Alps, the peninsula is crosscut through much of its length by the Apennine mountain chain. The obstacles created by the highlands, valleys, and gorges found in the mountain regions fostered strong cultural and linguistic differences.

HISTORY

Italy's modern state traces its mythological roots to the founding of the city of Rome in 753 B.C. More historically verified is the fact that the Romans engaged in territorial expansion and conquest of neighboring lands, devising effective colonization policies that ultimately sustained a widespread realm. By 172 B.C., Rome controlled all of the Italian peninsula and began moving outward into the Mediterranean basin. At its peak, the Roman empire extended from the British Isles to the Euphrates River. The *Pax Romana* began to crumble, however, by the end of the first century A.D. The sack of Rome by the Visigoths in 410 A.D. presaged the more complete disintegration of the empire in the later fifth and sixth centuries. With its political integration shattered, the country remained fragmented until the late nineteenth century. Italy was, in the view of many Europeans, a "mere geographic expression."

Italy is a relatively young nation state, achieving full unification only during the *Risorgimento* of 1860-1870. Prior to this, the peninsula consisted of often mutually antagonistic kingdoms, duchies, city-states, and principalities. Some of these regions had a history of autonomous rule, while others came under the periodic control of foreign powers as a result of recurrent wars and shifting political alliances. Over the centuries, therefore, powerful regional loyalties emerged, and persisted well after unification. Although local cultural variations remained notable, the most significant internal distinctions have been those stemming from the contrast between a relatively prosperous, cosmopolitan, urban North and a socially backward, economically depressed, agricultural South.

Southern Italy (*Mezzogiorno*), the source of more than 75 percent of immigration to the United States, was an impoverished region possessing a highly stratified, virtually feudal society. The bulk of the population consisted of artisans (*artigiani*), petty landowners or sharecroppers (*contadini*), and farm laborers (*giornalieri*), all of whom eked out meager existences. For reasons of security and health, residents typically clustered in hill towns situated away from farm land. Each day required long walks to family plots, adding to the toil that framed daily lives. Families typically worked as collective units to ensure survival. Angelo Pellegrini, who became a successful immigrant, remembered his sharecropping family: "The central, dominating fact of our existence was continuous, inadequately rewarded labor.... Education beyond the third grade was out of the question.... At eight or nine years of age, if not sooner, the peasant child is old enough to bend his neck to the yoke and fix his eyes upon the soil in which he must grub for bread. I did not know it then, but I know it now, that is a cruel, man-made destiny from which there is yet no immediate hope of escape." (Angelo Pellegrini, *Immigrant's Return*. New York: Macmillan, 1952; pp. 11, 21.)

The impact of unification on the South was disastrous. The new constitution heavily favored the North, especially in its tax policies, industrial subsidies, and land programs. The hard-pressed peasantry shouldered an increased share of national expenses, while attempting to compete in markets dominated more and more by outside capitalist intrusions. These burdens only exacerbated existing problems of poor soil, absentee landlords, inadequate investment, disease, and high rates of illiteracy. With cruel irony, as livelihoods became increasingly precarious, population totals soared. Italy jumped from 25 million residents in 1861 to 33 million in 1901 to more than 35 million in 1911, despite the massive migration already underway.

EARLY IMMIGRATION

An exodus of southerners from the peninsula began in the 1880s. Commencing in the regions of Calabria, Campania, Apulia, and Basilicata, and spreading after 1900 to Sicily, Italian emigration became a torrent of humanity. From 1876-1924, more than 4.5 million Italians arrived in the United States, and over two million came in the years 1901-1910 alone. Despite these massive numbers, it should be noted that roughly two-thirds of Italian migration went elsewhere, especially to Europe and South America. Immigration to the United States before and after this period accounted for approximately one million additional arrivals—a considerable movement in its own right—but the era of mass migration remains central to the Italian immigrant experience.

Yet, there were important precursors. Italian explorers and sailors venturing outward in the employ of other nations touched America in its earliest beginnings. The most famous was, of course, Christopher Columbus, a Genoese mariner sailing for Spain. Other seafarers such as John Cabot (Giovanni Caboto), Giovanni da Verrazzano, and Amerigo Vespucci, and important missionaries such as Eusebio Chino and Fra Marco da Nizza, also played roles in early exploration and settlement.

After the American Revolution, a small flow of largely northern-Italian skilled artisans, painters, sculptors, musicians, and dancers came to the new nation, filling economic niches. With the failure of the early nineteenth-century liberal revolutions, these immigrants were joined by a trickle of political refugees, the most famous of whom was Giuseppe Garibaldi. By the second half of the century, American cities also typically included Italian street entertainers, tradesmen, statuette makers, and stone workers, who often established the first beachheads of settlement for the migrations to come. Many of these pioneers were merely extending generations-old migratory patterns that had earlier brought them through Europe. An old Italian proverb instructed: *Chi esce riesce* (He who leaves succeeds).

This initial Italian movement dispersed widely throughout America, but its numbers were too small to constitute a significant presence. By 1850, the heaviest concentration was in Louisiana (only 915 people), the result of Sicilian migration to New Orleans and its environs. Within a decade, California contained the highest total of any state—a mere 2,805—and New York, soon to become home to millions of Italian immigrants, counted 1,862.

Everything changed with mass migration, the first phase of which consisted primarily of temporary migrants—"sojourners"—who desired immediate employment, maximum savings, and quick repatriation. The movement was predominately composed of young, single men of prime working age (15-35) who clustered in America's urban centers. Multiple trips were commonplace and ties to American society, such as learning English, securing citizenship, and acquiring property, were minimal. With eyes focused on the old-world *paese* (village), a total of at least half of the sojourners returned to Italy, although in some years rates were much higher. Such mobility earned Italians the sobriquet "birds of passage," a label that persisted until women and families began to migrate and settlement became increasingly permanent in the years following 1910.

Migrants brought with them their family-centered peasant cultures and their fiercely local identifications, or *campanilismo*. They typically viewed themselves as residents of particular villages or regions, not as "Italians." The organizational and residential life of early communities reflected these facts, as people limited their associations largely to kin and *paesani* fellow villagers. The proliferation of narrowly based mutual aid societies and *festas* (*feste*, or feast days) honoring local patron saints were manifestations of these tendencies. Gradually, as immigrants acclimated to the American milieu, in which others regarded them simply as Italians, and as they increasingly interacted with fellow immigrants, *campanilismo* gave way to a more national identity. Group-wide

organization and identity, nonetheless, have always been difficult to achieve.

THE EMERGENCE OF "LITTLE ITALIES"

In terms of settlement, immigrants were (and are) highly concentrated. Using kin and village-based chain migration networks to form "Little Italies," they clustered heavily in cities in the Northeast region (the Mid-Atlantic and New England states) and the Midwest, with outposts in California and Louisiana. More than 90 percent settled in only 11 states—New York, New Jersey, Pennsylvania, Massachusetts, California, Connecticut, Illinois, Ohio, Michigan, Missouri, and Louisiana—and approximately 90 percent congregated in urban areas. These patterns largely hold true today, although immigrants have branched out to locations such as Arizona and Florida. In every settlement area, there has been, over time, a slow but steady shift from central cities to suburbs.

Immigrants often sought out Little Italies as a result of the hostility they encountered in American society. As a despised minority rooted in the working class and seemingly resistant to assimilation, Italians suffered widespread discrimination in housing and employment. American responses to the immigrants occasionally took uglier forms as Italians became the victims of intimidation and violence, the most notorious incident being the 1890 lynching of 11 Italians in New Orleans. Italian mass migration coincided with the growth of a nativism that identified southern and eastern Europeans as undesirable elements. Inspired by the pseudo-scientific findings of eugenics and social Darwinism, turn-of-the-century nativists often branded southern Italians as especially inferior. Powerful stereotypes centering on poverty, clannishness, illiteracy, high disease rates, and an alleged proclivity toward criminal activities underscored the view that southern Italians were a degenerate "race" that should be denied entry to America. Criticism of Italians became integral to the successful legislative drives to enact the nativist Literacy Test in 1917 and National Origins Acts in 1921 and 1924.

Within Little Italies, immigrants created New World societies. A network of Italian language institutions—newspapers, theaters, churches, mutual aid societies, recreational clubs, and debating societies—helped fuel an emerging Italian-American ethnic culture. Aspects of the folk, popular, and high culture intermixed in this milieu yielding an array of entertainment options.

Saloons or club buildings in larger urban centers often featured traditional puppet and marionette shows while immigrant men sipped wines and played card games of *mora*, *briscola*, and *tresette*. By the early 1900s, a lively Italian language theater brought entertainment to thousands and sustained the careers of professional acting troupes and noted performers such as the comedic genius Eduardo Migliacco, known as "Farfariello." On a more informal level, Italian coffee houses often presented light comedies, heroic tragedies, and dialect plays sponsored by drama clubs. Italian opera was a staple in most American urban centers, and working-class Italian music halls attracted customers by offering renditions of Neapolitan or Sicilian songs and dances. Band performances and choral recitals were regularly staged on the streets of Italian settlements. Although illiteracy rates among immigrants often ran well above 50 percent, newcomers in larger cities had access to Italian language bookstores stocked with poetry, short stories, novels, and nonfiction. In 1906 one New York bookseller published a catalogue of 176 pages to advertise his merchandise.

"My first impression when I got there, I tell you the God's truth, you're in a dream. It's like in heaven. You don't know what it is. You're so happy there in America."

Felice Taldone in 1924, cited in *Ellis Island: An Illustrated History of the Immigrant Experience*, edited by Ivan Chermayeff et al. (New York: Macmillan, 1991).

The cultural patterns of Little Italies were constantly evolving, providing for a dynamic interplay between older forms brought from Italy and new inventions forged in the United States. Many immigrants attempted to recreate old-world celebrations and rituals upon arrival in the United States, but those that directly competed with American forms soon fell away. The celebration of Epiphany (January 6), for example, was the principal Christmas time festivity in Italy, featuring the visit of *La Befana*, a kindly old witch who brought presents for children. In the United States the more popular Christmas Eve and Santa Claus displaced this tradition.

Even those cultural forms more sheltered from American society were contested. Immigrant settlements were not homogenous entities. Various members of the community fought for the right to define the group, and the ongoing struggle for dominance invariably employed cultural symbols and events. The commercial and political elites (*prominenti*)—usually aided by the Italian Catholic clergy—sought to promote Italian nationalism as a means of self-advancement. These forces invested great energy in celebrations of Italian national holidays (such as *venti di settembre*, which commemorated Italian unification), and in the erection of statutes to such Italian heroes as Columbus, the poet Dante, and military leader Giuseppe Garibaldi.

These activities were challenged by a variety of leftist radicals (*sovversivi*), who sought very different cultural and political goals. Anarchists, socialists, and syndicalists such as Carlo Tresca and Arturo Giovannitti considered Italian Americans as part of the world proletariat and celebrated holidays (*Primo Maggio*—May Day) and heroes (Gaetano Bresci, the assassin of Italian King Umberto) reflecting this image. These symbols also played roles in mass strikes and worker demonstrations led by the radicals. Meanwhile, the majority of Italian Americans continued to draw much of their identity from the peasant cultures of the old-world *paese*. Columbus Day, the preeminent Italian American ethnic celebration, typically blended elements of all these components, with multiple parades and competing banquets, balls, and public presentations.

World War I proved an ambiguous interlude for Italian immigrants. Italy's alliance with the United States and the service of many immigrants in the U.S. military precipitated some level of American acceptance. The war also produced, however, countervailing pressures that generated more intense nationalism among Italians and powerful drives toward assimilation—"100 percent Americanism"—in the wider society. Immigration restrictions after 1924 halted Italian immigration, although the foreign-born presence remained strong (the 1930 census recorded 1,623,000 Italian-born residents—the group's historic high). As new arrivals slowed and the second generation matured during the 1920s and 1930s, the group changed.

Several critical developments shaped the character of Italian America during the interwar years. National prohibition provided lucrative illegal markets, which some Italian Americans successfully exploited through bootlegging operations. During the 1920s, the "gangster" image of Italians (exemplified by Al Capone) was perpetuated through films and popular literature. The celebrated case of Nicola Sacco and Bartolomeo Vanzetti further molded the group's national image, underwriting the conception of Italians as dangerous radicals.

The Great Depression overshadowed earlier economic gains, often forcing Italian Americans back into their family-centered ethnic communities. Here, the emerging second generation found itself in frequent conflict with the first. Heavily influenced by the traditional *contadino* culture passed on from their parents, the second generation uneasily straddled two worlds. Traditional notions of proper behavior, stressing collective responsibilities toward the family, strict chastity and domestic roles for females, rigid chaperonage and courting codes, and male dominance, clashed with the more individualist, consumer-driven American values children learned in schools, stores, and on the streets. Problems of marginality, lack of self-esteem, rebellion, and delinquency were the outcomes.

Partly because of these dynamics, the community structures of Little Italies began to change. The more Americanized second generation began to turn away from older, Italian-language institutions founded by immigrants, many of which collapsed during the depression. Italian theaters and music halls, for example, largely gave way to vaudeville, nickelodeons, organized sports, and radio programming. During the 1920s and 1930s, these transformations were also influenced by Benito Mussolini's fascist regime, which sponsored propaganda campaigns designed to attract the support of Italian Americans. The *prominenti* generally supported these initiatives, often inserting fascist symbols (the black shirt), songs ("Giovinezza"—the fascist anthem), and holidays (the anniversary of the March on Rome) into the ichnography and pageantry of America's Little Italies. A small, but vocal, anti-fascist element existed in opposition, and it substituted counter values and emblems. Memorials to Giacomo Matteotti, a socialist deputy murdered by fascists, and renditions of *Bandiera Rossa* and *Inno di Garibaldi* became fixtures of anti-fascist festivities. Thus, the cultural world of Italian America remained divided.

Any questions concerning loyalties to the United States were firmly answered when Italy declared war on the United States in 1941, and Italian Americans rushed to aid the American struggle against the Axis Powers. More than 500,000 Italian Americans joined the U.S. military, serving in all theaters, including the Italian campaign. The war effort and ensuing anti-communist crusade stressed conformity, loyalty, and

An Italian immigrant family arrives at Ellis Island, New York.

patriotism, and in the 1940s and 1950s it appeared that Italian Americans had comfortably settled into the melting pot. The second generation especially benefitted from its war service and the postwar economic expansion as it yielded new levels of acceptance and integration. In the 1950s, they experienced substantial social mobility and embraced mass consumerism and middle-class values.

Since the end of World War II, more than 600,000 Italian immigrants have arrived in the United States. A large percentage came shortly after passage of the Immigration Act of 1965, at which time yearly totals of Italian immigrants averaged about 23,000. Beginning in 1974, the numbers steadily declined as a result of improved economic conditions in Italy and changing policies in other immigrant-receiving nations. In 1990 only 3,300 Italian immigrants were admitted to the United States, but 831,922 Italian-born residents remained in the country, guaranteeing that Italian language and culture are still part of the American cultural mosaic.

ACCULTURATION AND ASSIMILATION

Assimilation takes place at many different levels, but for the individual, it is likely that few captured the essence of the experience better than

Rosa Cavalleri. Cavalleri came from the Italian town of Cuggiono in 1884 as a frightened young woman, joining her husband in a mining camp in remote Missouri. After undergoing numerous tribulations, Cavalleri settled in Chicago, where she cleaned floors and bathrooms, while remarrying and successfully raising a family. As Cavalleri neared death in 1943, she mused: "Only one wish more I have: I'd love to go in *Italia* again before I die. Now I speak English good like an American I could go anywhere—where millionaires go and high people. I would look the high people in the face and ask them questions I'd like to know. I wouldn't be afraid now—not of anybody. I'd be proud I come from America and speak English. I would go to Bugiarno [Cuggiono] and see the people and talk to the bosses in the silk factory.... I could talk to the *Superiora* now. I'd tell her, `Why you were so mean—you threw me out that poor girl whose heart was so kind toward you? You think you'll go to heaven like that?' I'd scold them like that now. I wouldn't be afraid. They wouldn't hurt me now I come from America. Me, that's why I love America. That's what I learned in America: not to be afraid." (Marie Hall Ets, *Rosa: The Life of an Italian Immigrant*. Minneapolis: University of Minnesota Press, 1970; p. 254.)

The integration of Italians like Cavalleri into American life was a result of changes in both the group and the larger society. Italians were beginning to make a commitment to permanent settlement. This process was substantially underway by 1910, cresting in the 1920s when new immigration fell off. After this, perpetuation of the old-world public culture became increasingly difficult, although the family-based value structure was more resilient. During the 1920s and 1930s, the second generation continued to display many of its hallmarks: children of immigrants still held largely blue-collar occupations and were underrepresented in schools, tied to Little Italy residences, and attracted to in-group marriages—choices that demonstrated the continuing power of parental mores.

Changing contexts, however, diminished the "social distance" separating Italians from other Americans. In the 1930s, second-generation Italian Americans joined forces with others in labor unions and lobbied for benefits. They also began to make political gains as part of the Democratic Party's New Deal coalition. Also for the first time, the national popular culture began to include Italian Americans among its heroes. In music, sports, politics, and cinema the careers of Frank Sinatra, Joe DiMaggio, Fiorello LaGuardia, Frank Capra, and Don Ameche suggested that national attitudes toward Italians were in transition.

World War II was a critical benchmark in the acceptance of Italian Americans. Their whole-hearted support of America's cause and their disproportionately high ratio of service in the military legitimized them in American eyes. The war also transformed many Little Italies, as men and women left for military service or to work in war industries. Upon their return, many newly affluent Italian Americans left for suburban locations and fresh opportunities, further eroding the institutions and *contadino* culture that once thrived in ethnic settlements.

The Cold War pushed the group further into the mainstream as Italian Americans joined in the anti-communist fervor gripping the nation. Simultaneously, structural changes in the economy vastly expanded the availability of white collar, managerial positions, and Italian Americans jumped to take advantage. Beginning in the 1950s, they pursued higher education in greater numbers than ever before, many receiving aid as a result of the G.I. Bill. Such developments put them into more immediate and positive contact with other Americans, who exhibited greater acceptance in the postwar years.

Ironically, a resurgent Italian American ethnicity emerged at the same time, as the group experienced increasing integration into the larger society. Italian Americans were active participants in the ethnic revival of the 1960s and 1970s. As American core values came under assault in the midst of Vietnam, Watergate, and the rising counterculture, and the nation's urban centers became torn by riots and civil protest, Italian Americans felt especially vulnerable and besieged. Unlike other ethnic groups, they had remained in urban enclaves, manifesting high rates of home ownership, where they now found themselves in contact and conflict with African Americans. Many interpreted the ensuing clashes in cultural terms, seeing themselves as an embattled minority defending traditional values in the face of new compensatory government programs. In response, ethnic traditions surrounding family, neighborhood, and homes gained heightened visibility and strength. New Italian American organizations and publications fostering ethnic identity came into being, and many old rituals experienced a resurgence, most notably the celebration of the *feste*.

Intermarriage rates increased after the 1950s, especially among the third and fourth generations who were now coming of age. By 1991, the group's overall in-marriage rate was just under 33 percent, above the average of 26 percent for other ethnic groups. But among those born after 1940—by now a majority—the rate was only 20 percent, and these marriages crossed both ethnic and religious lines. Once a marginalized, despised minority, Italian Americans are now among the most highly accepted groups according to national surveys measuring "social distance" indicators (Italians ranked fourteenth in 1926, but fifth in 1977). All of the statistical data point to a high level of structural assimilation in American society, although Italian American ethnicity has not disappeared.

That Italian American identity has lost much of its former negative weight is suggested further by recent census figures for ancestry group claiming. The 1980 census recorded 12.1 million individuals who claimed Italian ancestry (5.4 percent of national population). By 1990 this figure had risen to 14.7 million (5.9 percent), indicating that ethnicity remains an important and acceptable component of self-identification for substantial numbers of Italian Americans.

Despite strong evidence of integration, Italian Americans retain distinguishing characteristics. They are still geographically concentrated in the old settlement areas, and they display a pronounced attachment to the values of domesticity and family loyalty. Italian Americans still rely heavily on personal and kin networks in residential choices, visiting patterns, and general social interaction. Perhaps most distinctive, the group continues to suffer from stereotypes associating it with criminal behavior, especially in the form of organized crime and the mafia. These images have persisted despite research documenting that Italian Americans possess crime rates no higher than other segments of American society, and that organized crime is a multi-ethnic enterprise in which Italian Americans play a very small role. Television and film images of Italian Americans continue to emphasize criminals, "lovable or laughable dimwits" who engage in dead-end jobs, and heavy-accented, obese "Mamas" with their pasta pots.

These representations have influenced the movement of Italian Americans into the highest levels of corporate and political life. The innuendos of criminal ties advanced during Geraldine Ferraro's candidacy for vice-president in 1984 and during Mario Cuomo's aborted presidential bids illustrate the political repercussions of these stereotypes, and many Italian Americans believe that bias has kept them underrepresented in the top echelons of the business world. Since the 1970s, such organizations as the Americans of Italian Descent, the Sons of Italy in America, and the National Italian American Foundation have mounted broad-based anti-defamation campaigns protesting such negative imagery.

HOLIDAYS

The major national holidays of Italy—*Festa della Republica* [June 5], *Festa dell'Unità Nazionale* (November 6), and *Festa del Lavoro* (May 1)—are no longer occasions of public celebration among Italian Americans. Some religious holidays, such as *Epifania di Gesù* (January 6), receive only passing notice. Most Italian Americans celebrate Christmas Day, New Year's Day, and Easter Day, but usually without any particular ethnic character. The principal occasions of public celebration typically revolve around Columbus Day, the quintessential Italian American national holiday, and the *feste* honoring patron saints. In both cases, these events have, in general, become multi-day celebrations virtually devoid of any religious or Italian national connotation, involving numerous non-Italians.

Italian immigrants utilized traditional costumes, folk songs, folklore, and dances for special events, but like many aspects of Italian life, they were so regionally specific that they defy easy characterization. Perhaps the most commonly recognized folk dance, the *tarantella*, for example, is Neapolitan, with little diffusion elsewhere in the peninsula.

CUISINE

The difficult conditions of daily life in Italy dictated frugal eating habits. Most peasants consumed simple meals based on whatever vegetables or grains (lentils, peas, fava beans, corn, tomatoes, onions, and wild greens) were prevalent in each region. A staple for most common folk was coarse black bread. Pasta was a luxury, and peasants typically ate meat only two or three times a year on special holidays. Italian cuisine was—and still is—regionally distinctive, and even festive meals varied widely. The traditional Christmas dish in Piedmont was *agnolotti* (ravioli), while *anguille* (eels) were served in Campania, *sopa friu-*

lana (celery soup) in Friuli, and *bovoloni* (fat snails) in Vicenza.

In the United States, many immigrants planted small backyard garden plots to supplement the table and continued to raise cows, chickens, and goats whenever possible. Outdoor brick ovens were commonplace, serving as clear ethnic markers of Italian residences. With improved economic conditions, pastas, meats, sugar, and coffee were consumed more frequently. One New York City immigrant remembered asking, "Who could afford to eat spaghetti more than once a week [in Italy]? In America no one starved, though a family earned no more than five or six dollars a week.... Don't you remember how our *paesani* here in America ate to their hearts delight till they were belching like pigs, and how they dumped mountains of uneaten food out the window? We were not poor in America; we just had a little less than others." (Leonard Covello, *The Social Background of the Italo-American School Child*. Totowa, New Jersey: Rowman and Littlefield, 1972; p. 295.)

"Italian cooking" in the United States has come to mean southern-Italian, especially Neapolitan, cuisine, which is rich in tomato sauces, heavily spiced, and pasta-based. Spaghetti and meatballs (not generally known in Italy) and pizza are perhaps the quintessential Italian dishes in the United States. More recently, northern Italian cooking—characterized by rice (*risotto*) and corn (*polenta*) dishes and butter-based recipes—has become increasingly common in homes and restaurants. Garlic (*aglio*), olive oil (*olio d'oliva*), mushrooms (*funghi*), and nuts (*nochi*) of various types are common ingredients found in Italian cooking. Wine (*vino*), consumed in moderate amounts, is a staple. Overall, Italian dishes have become so popular that they have been accepted into the nation's dietary repertoire, but not in strictly old-world forms. Americanized dishes are generally milder in their spicing and more standardized than old-world fare.

HEALTH AND MENTAL HEALTH ISSUES

A number of Italian American organizations have supported the Cooley's Anemia Foundation to fund research into Thalassemia, once thought to be a sickle cell anemia confined to persons of Mediterranean ancestry. Recent research has demonstrated the fallacy of this belief, however, and contributions have largely ceased.

LANGUAGE

Italian is a Romance language derived directly from Latin; it utilizes the Latin alphabet, but the letters "j," "k," "w," "x," and "y" are found only in words of foreign origin. "Standard" Italian—based on the Tuscan dialect—is a relatively recent invention, and was not used universally until well into the twentieth century. Numerous dialects were the dominant linguistic feature during the years of mass immigration.

Italian dialects did not simply possess different tonalities or inflections. Some were languages in their own right, with separate vocabularies and, for a few, fully developed literatures (e.g., Venetian, Piedmontese, and Sicilian). Italy's mountainous terrain produced conditions in which proximate areas often possessed mutually unintelligible languages. For example, the word for "today" in standard Italian is *oggi*, but *ancheuj* in Piedmontese, *uncuó* in Venetian, *ste iorne* in Sicilian, and *oji* in Calabrian. Similarly, "children" in Italian is *bambini*, but it becomes *cit* in Piedomontese, *fruz* in Friulian, *guagliuni* in Neapolitan, *zitedi* in Calabrian, and *picciriddi* in Sicilian. Thus, language facilitated *campanilismo*, further fragmenting the emerging Italian American world.

Very soon after the Italians' arrival, all dialects became infused with Americanisms, quickly creating a new form of communication often intelligible only to immigrants. The new patois was neither Italian nor English, and it included such words as *giobba* for job, *grossiera* for grocery, *bosso* for boss, *marachetta* for market, *baccausa* for outhouse, *ticchetto* for ticket, *bisiniss* for business, *trocco* for truck, *sciabola* for shovel, *loffare* for the verb to loaf, and *carpetto* for carpet. Angelo Massari, who immigrated to Tampa, Florida, in 1902, described preparations in his Sicilian village prior to leaving it: "I used to interview people who had returned from America. I asked them thousands of questions, how America was, what they did in Tampa, what kind of work was to be had.... One of them told me the language was English, and I asked him how to say one word or another in that language. I got these wonderful samples of a Sicilian-American English from him: *tu sei un boia, gud morni, olraiti, giachese, misti, sciusi, bred, iessi, bud* [you are a boy, good morning, alright, jacket, mister, excuse me, bread, yes, but]. He told me also that in order to ask for work, one had to say, `Se misti gari giobbi fo mi?' [Say, mister got a job for me?]." (Angelo Massari, *The Wonderful Life* of *Angelo Massari*, translated by Arthur Massolo. New York: Exposition Press, 1965; pp. 46-47.)

Italian proverbs tend to reflect the conditions of peasant and immigrant lives: Work hard, work always, and you will never know hunger; He who leaves the old way for the new knows what he loses but knows not what he will find; Buy oxen and marry women from your village only; The wolf changes his skin but not his vice; The village is all the world; Do not miss the Saint's day, he helps you and provides at all times; Tell me who your friends are and I will tell you what you are; He who respects others will be respected.

FAMILY AND COMMUNITY DYNAMICS

The family (*la famiglia*) rested at the heart of Italian society. Family solidarity was the major bulwark from which the rural population confronted a harsh society, and the family unit (including blood relatives and relatives by marriage) became the center of allegiances. Economically and socially, the family functioned as a collective enterprise, an "all-inclusive social world" in which the individual was subordinated to the larger entity. Parents expected children to assist them at an early age by providing gainful labor, and family values stressed respect for the elderly, obedience to parents, hard work, and deference to authority.

The traditional Italian family was "father-headed, but mother-centered." In public, the father was the uncontested authority figure and wives were expected to defer to their husbands. At home, however, females exercised considerable authority as wives and mothers, and played central roles in sustaining familial networks. Still, male children occupied a favored position of superiority over females, and strong family mores governed female behavior. Women's activities were largely confined to the home, and strict rules limited their public behavior, including access to education and outside employment. Formal rituals of courting, chaperonage, and arranged marriages strictly governed relations between the sexes. Above all, protection of female chastity was critical to maintaining family honor.

Family and kin networks also guided migration patterns, directing precise village flows to specific destinations. During sojourner migrations, the work of women in home villages sustained the family well-being in Italy and allowed male workers to actively compete in the world labor market. In America, the extended family became an important network for relatives to seek and receive assistance. Thus, migration and settlement operated within a context of family considerations.

Attempts to transfer traditional family customs to America engendered considerable tension between generations. More educated and Americanized children ventured to bridge two worlds in which the individualist notions of American society often clashed with their parents' family-centered ethos. Still, strong patterns of in-marriage characterized the second generation, and many of their parents' cultural values were successfully inculcated. These carryovers resulted in a strong attachment to neighborhoods and families, consistent deference to authority, and blue-collar work choices. The second generation, however, began to adopt American practices in terms of family life (seen, for example, in smaller family size and English language usage), and the collective nature of the unit began to break down as the generations advanced.

EDUCATION

The peasant culture placed little value on formal instruction, seeking instead to have children contribute as soon as possible to family earnings. From the peasant perspective, education consisted primarily of passing along moral and social values through parental instruction (the term *buon educato* means "well-raised or behaved"). In southern Italy, formal education was seldom a means of upward mobility since public schools were not institutions of the people. They were poorly organized and supported, administered by a distrusted northern bureaucracy, and perceived as alien to the goals of family solidarity. Proverbs such as "Do not let your children become better than you" spoke to these perceptions, and high rates of illiteracy testified to their power.

These attitudes remained strong among immigrants in America, many of whom planned a quick repatriation and saw little reason to lose children's wages. Parents also worried about the individualist values taught in American public schools. The saying "America took from us our children" was a common lament. Thus, truancy rates among Italians were high, especially among girls, for whom education had always been regarded as unnecessary since tradition dictated a path of marriage, motherhood, and homemaking.

Italian Americans honor

St. Amato in this Queens,

New York, parade.

Antagonism toward schools was derived not only from culture, but also from economic need and realistic judgments about mobility possibilities. Given the constricted employment options open to immigrants (largely confined to manual, unskilled labor), and the need for family members to contribute economically, extended schooling offered few rewards. From the parental viewpoint, anything threatening the family's collective strength was dangerous. Generations frequently clashed over demands to terminate formal education and find work, turn over earnings, and otherwise assist the family financially in other ways. Prior to World War I, less than one percent of Italian children were enrolled in high school.

As the second generation came of age in the 1920s and 1930s, and America moved toward a service economy, however, education received greater acceptance. Although the children of immigrants generally remained entrenched in the working class (though frequently as skilled workers), they extended their education, often attending vocational schools, and could be found among the nation's clerks, bookkeepers, managers, and sales personnel. The economic downturn occasioned by the depression resulted in increased educational opportunities for some immigrants since job prospects were limited.

Italian Americans were well situated in post-World War II America to take advantage of the national expansion of secondary and higher edu-

cation. They hastened to enroll in G.I. Bill programs and in the 1950s and 1960s began to send sons and daughters to colleges. By the 1970s, Italian Americans averaged about 12 years of formal education; in 1991 the group slightly surpassed the national mean of 12.7 years.

RELIGION

Although Italian immigrants were overwhelmingly Roman Catholic, their faith was a personal, folk religion of feast days and peasant traditions that often had little to do with formal dogma or rituals. As such, its practices differed greatly from those encountered in America's Irish-dominated Catholic Church. Unlike Irish Americans, most Italians possessed no great reverence for priests (who had sometimes been among the oppressors in Italy) or the institutions of the official Church, and they disliked what they regarded as the impersonal, puritanical, and overly doctrinal Irish approach to religion. As in Italy, men continued to manifest anticlerical traditions and to attend church only on selected occasions, such as weddings and funerals.

For their part, the Irish clergy generally regarded Italians as indifferent Catholics—even pagans—and often relegated them to basement services. The Irish American hierarchy agonized over the "Italian Problem," and suspicion and mistrust initially characterized relations between the groups, leading to defections among the immigrant generation and demands for separate parishes. A disproportionately low presence of Italian Americans in the church leadership today is at least partially a legacy of this strained relationship. Protestant missionaries were not unaware of these developments. Many attempted to win converts, but met with very little success. With the establishment of "national parishes," however, the Catholic Church hit firmer ground, and Italian parishes proliferated after 1900. In many settlements, parish churches became focal points providing a sense of ethnic identity, a range of social services, and a source of community adhesion.

Italian immigrant Catholicism centered on the local patron saints and the beliefs, superstitions, and practices associated with the *feste*. The *feste* not only assisted in perpetuating local identities, but they also served as a means for public expression of immigrant faith. In the early years, feast days replicated those of the homeland. Festivals were occasions for great celebration, complete with music, parades, dancing, eating, and fireworks displays. At the high point, statues of local saints such as San Rocco, San Giuseppe, or San Gennaro, were carried through the streets of Little Italies in a procession. New Yorker Richard Gambino recalled the feast days of his youth: "Not long ago there were many such street *feste*. Their aromas of food, the sight of burly men swaying from side to side and lurching forward under the weight of enormous statues of exotic Madonnas and saints laden with money and gifts, the music of Italian bands in uniforms with dark-peaked caps, white shirts, and black ties and the bright arches of colored lights spanning the city streets.... True to the spirit of *campanilismo*, each group of *paesani* in New York had its *festa*.... Three *feste* were larger than the others. Sicilians, especially from the region of Agrigento, went all out for the huge September festival of San Gandolfo. In July, thousands turned out to honor the Madonna del Carmine. And in the fall, Neapolitans paid their respect to the patron of their mother city, San Gennaro." (Richard Gambino, *Blood of My Blood: The Dilemma of the Italian Americans*. Garden City, New York: Anchor Press, 1975; pp. 242-243.)

Worshippers lined the streets as processions moved toward the parish church, and they vied to pin money on the statue, place gifts on platforms, or make various penances (walking barefoot, crawling, licking the church floor [*lingua strascinuni*], reciting certain prayers). Irish prelates frequently attempted to ban such events, viewing them as pagan rituals and public spectacles. A cluster of beliefs focusing on the folk world of magic, witches, ghosts, and demons further estranged Italians from the church hierarchy. Many immigrants were convinced, for example, of the existence of the evil eye (*malocchio* or *jettatura*), and believed that wearing certain symbols, the most potent of which were associated with horns (*corni*) or garlic amulets, provided protection from its power.

As the second and subsequent generations grew to maturity, most strictly old-world forms of religious observance and belief were discarded, leading to what some have called the "hibernization" of Italian American Catholicism. Many feast day celebrations remain, although, in some cases, they have been transformed into mass cultural events which draw thousands of non-Italians. The San Gennaro *feste* in Manhattan's Little Italy is a case in point: once celebrated only by Neapolitans, it now attracts heterogeneous crowds from hundreds of miles away.

EMPLOYMENT AND ECONOMIC TRADITIONS

Throughout the years of mass migration, Italians clustered heavily in the ranks of unskilled, manual labor. In part, this seems to have resulted from cultural preference—men favored outdoor jobs dovetailing old-world skills—and immigrant strategies that sought readily available employment in order to return quickly to Italy with nest eggs. But American employers also imposed the choice of positions since many regarded Italians as unsuited for indoor work or heavy industry. Immigrants thus frequently engaged in seasonal work on construction sites and railroads and in mines and public works projects. Male employment often operated under the "boss system" in which countrymen (*padroni*) served as middlemen between gangs of immigrant workers and American employers. Married women generally worked at home, either concentrating on family tasks or other home-based jobs such as keeping boarders, attending to industrial homework, or assisting in family-run stores. In larger urban centers, unmarried women worked outside the home in garment, artificial flower, and costume jewelry factories, and in sweatshops and canneries, often laboring together in all-Italian groups.

Some Little Italies were large enough to support a full economic structure of their own. In these locations, small import stores, shops, restaurants, fish merchants, and flower traders proliferated, offering opportunities for upward mobility within the ethnic enclave. In many cities, Italians dominated certain urban trades such as fruit and vegetable peddling, confectioniering, rag picking, shoe-shining, ice-cream vending, and stevedoring. A portion of the immigrants were skilled artisans who typically replicated their old-world crafts of shoemaking and repairing, tailoring, carpentry, and barbering.

The dense concentration of Italian Americans in blue-collar occupations persisted into the second generation, deriving from deliberate career choices, attitudes toward formal education, and the economic dynamics of the nation. Italians had begun to make advances out of the unskilled ranks during the prosperous 1920s, but many gains were overshadowed during the Great Depression. Partially in response to these conditions, Italians—both men and women—moved heavily into organized labor during the 1930s, finding the CIO industrial unions especially attractive. Union memberships among Italian Americans rose significantly; by 1937, the AFL International Ladies Garment Workers Union (with vice president Luigi Antonini) counted nearly 100,000 Italian members in the New York City area alone. At the same time, women were becoming a presence in service and clerical positions.

The occupational choices of Italian Americans shifted radically after World War II, when structural changes in the American economy facilitated openings in more white collar occupations. Italian Americans were strategically situated to take advantage of these economic shifts, being clustered in the urban areas where economic expansion took place and ready to move into higher education. Since the 1960s, Italian Americans have become solidly grounded in the middle-class, managerial, and professional ranks. As a group, by 1991 they had equalled or surpassed national averages in income and occupational prestige.

POLITICS AND GOVERNMENT

Italians were slow to take part in the American political process. Due to the temporary nature of early migration, few took the time to achieve naturalization in order to vote. Anti-government attitudes, exemplified in the *ladro governo* ("the government as thief") outlook, also limited participation. Hence, Italian voters did not initially translate into political clout. Early political activity took place at the urban machine level, where immigrants typically encountered Irish Democratic bosses offering favors in return for support, but often blocking out aspiring Italian politicians. In such cities, those Italians seeking office frequently drifted to the Republican Party.

Naturalization rates increased during the 1920s, but the next decade was marked by a political watershed. During the 1930s, Italian Americans joined the Democratic New Deal coalition, many becoming politically active for the first time in doing so. The careers of independent/some-time-Republican Fiorello LaGuardia and leftist Vito Marcantonio benefitted from this expansion. As a concentrated urban group with strong union

ties, Italians constituted an important component of President Franklin Roosevelt's national support. The Democratic hold on Italians was somewhat shaken by Roosevelt's "dagger in the back" speech condemning Italy's attack on France in 1940, but, overall, the group maintained its strong commitment to the Party. In the early 1970s, only 17 percent of Italian Americans were registered Republicans (45 percent were registered Democrats), although many began to vote Republican in recent presidential elections. Both President Ronald Reagan and President George Bush were supported by strong Italian-American majorities. Overall, the group has moved from the left toward the political center. By 1991, Italian American voter registrations were 35 percent Republican and 32 percent Democratic.

The political ascent of Italian Americans came after World War II with the maturation of the second and third generations, the acquisition of increased education and greater wealth, and a higher level of acceptance by the wider society. Italian Americans were well-represented in city and state offices and had begun to penetrate the middle ranks of the federal government, especially the judicial system. By the 1970s and 1980s, there were Italian American cabinet members, governors, federal judges, and state legislators. Only four Italian Americans sat in Congress during the 1930s, but more than 30 served in the 1980s; in 1987 there were three U.S. Senators. The candidacy of Geraldine Ferraro for the Democratic vice presidency in 1984, the high profile of New York governor Mario Cuomo in American political discourse, and the appointment of Antonin Scalia to the Supreme Court are indicative of the group's political importance.

Since World War II, most Italian Americans have remained largely uninvolved in—even ignorant of—the political affairs of Italy, no doubt a legacy of World War II and the earlier brush with fascism. They have been very responsive, however, to appeals for relief assistance during periodic natural disasters such as floods and earthquakes.

INDIVIDUAL AND GROUP CONTRIBUTIONS

Italians constitute such a large and diverse group that notable individuals have appeared in virtually every aspect of American life.

ACADEMIA

Lorenzo Da Ponte (1747-1838), taught courses on Italian literature at Columbia University and sponsored the first Italian opera house in Manhattan in the 1830s. Prior to becoming president of Yale University in 1977, A. Bartlett Giamatti (1938-1989) was a distinguished scholar of English and comparative literature. He resigned his presidency to become the commissioner of the National Baseball League. Peter Sammartino (1904-1992) taught at the City College of New York and Columbia University before founding Fairleigh Dickinson University. He published 14 books on various aspects of education.

BUSINESS

Amadeo P. Giannini (1870-1949) began a storefront bank in the Italian North Beach section of San Francisco in 1904. Immediately after the 1906 earthquake he began granting loans to residents to rebuild. Later, Giannini pioneered in branch banking and in financing the early film industry. Giannini's Bank of America eventually became the largest bank in the United States. Lido Anthony "Lee" Iacocca (1924-) became president of Ford Motor Company in 1970. Iacocca left Ford after eight years to take over the ailing Chrysler Corporation, which was near bankruptcy. He rescued the company, in part through his personal television ads which made his face instantly recognizable. Iacocca also spent four years as chairman of the Statue of Liberty/Ellis Island Foundation, which supported the refurbishment of these national monuments.

FILM, TELEVISION, AND THEATER

Frank Capra (1897-1991) directed more than 20 feature films and won three Academy Awards for Best Director. His films, stamped with an upbeat optimism, became known as "Capra-corn." Capra won his Oscars for *It Happened One Night* (1934), *Mr. Deeds Goes to Town* (1936), and *You Can't Take it With You* (1938), but he is also well known for *Lost Horizon* (1937), *Mr. Smith Goes to Washington* (1939), and *It's a Wonderful Life* (1947). In addition to directing, Capra served four terms as president of the Academy of Motion Picture Arts and Sciences and three terms as president of the Screen Directors Guild. Francis Ford Coppola (1939-) earned international fame as director of *The Godfather* (1972), an adaptation of Mario Puzo's best selling novel. The film won several Academy Awards, including Best Picture. Among numerous other films, Coppola has made two sequels to *The Godfather*; the second film of this trilogy, released in 1974, also won multiple awards, including an Academy Award for Best Picture.

Martin Scorcese (1942-), film director and screenwriter, directed *Mean Streets* (1973), *Taxi Driver* (1976), *Raging Bull* (1980), and *Good Fellas* (1990), among others, all of which draw from the urban, ethnic milieu of his youth. Sylvester Stallone (1946-), actor, screenwriter, and director, has gained fame in each of these categories. He is perhaps best known as the title character in both *Rocky* (1976), which won an Academy Award for Best Picture (and spawned four sequels), and the *Rambo* series. Don Ameche (1908-1993), whose career spanned several decades, performed in vaudeville, appeared on radio serials ("The Chase and Sanborn Hour"), and starred in feature films. Ameche first achieved national acclaim in *The Story of Alexander Graham Bell* (1941) and appeared in many films, earning an Academy Award for Best Supporting Actor for his performance in *Cocoon* (1986). Ernest Borgnine (born Ermes Effron Borgnino, 1915-) spent his early acting career portraying villains, such as the brutal prison guard in *From Here to Eternity*, but captured the hearts of Americans with his sensitive portrayal of a Bronx butcher in *Marty* (1956), for which he won an Academy Award. Borgnine also appeared on network television as Lieutenant Commander Quintin McHale on "McHale's Navy," a comedy series that ran on ABC from 1962 to 1965. Liza Minnelli (1946-), stage, television, and motion picture actress and vocalist, won an Academy Award for *Cabaret* (1972), an Emmy for *Liza with a Z* (1972), and a Tony Award for *The Act* (1977).

LITERATURE

Pietro DiDonato (1911-1992) published the classic Italian immigrant novel, *Christ in Concrete*, in 1939 to critical acclaim. He captured to the immigrant experience in later works, including *Three Circles of Light* (1960) and *Life of Mother Cabrini* (1960). Novelist Jerre Mangione (1909-) wrote *Mount Allegro* (1943), an autobiographical work describing his upbringing among Sicilian Americans in Rochester, New York. Mangione is also noted for his *Reunion in Sicily* (1950), *An Ethnic at Large* (1978), and *La Storia: Five Centuries of the Italian American Experience* (1992), with Ben Morreale. Gay Talese (1932-), began his career as a reporter for the *New York Times*, but later earned fame for his national bestsellers, including *The Kingdom and the Power* (1969), *Honor Thy Father* (1971), and *Thy Neighbor's Wife* (1980). Talese's *Unto the Sons* (1992) dealt with his own family's immigrant experience. The poetry of Lawrence Ferlinghetti (1919-) captured the essence of the Beat Generation during the 1950s and 1960s. His San Francisco bookstore, City Lights Books, became a gathering place for literary activists. John Ciardi (1916-1986), poet, translator, and literary critic, published over 40 books of poetry and criticism and profoundly impacted the literary world as the long-time poetry editor of the *Saturday Review*. Ciardi's translation of Dante's *Divine Comedy* is regarded as definitive. Novelist Mario Puzo (1920-) published two critical successes, *Dark Arena* (1955) and *The Fortunate Pilgrim* (1965), prior to *The Godfather* in 1969, which sold over ten million copies and reached vast audiences in its film adaptations. Helen Barolini (1925-), poet, essayist, and novelist, explored the experiences of Italian-American women in her *Umbertina* (1979) and *The Dream Book* (1985).

MUSIC AND ENTERTAINMENT

Francis Albert "Frank" Sinatra (1915-), began singing with the Harry James Band in the late 1930s, moved to the Tommy Dorsey Band, and then became America's first teenage idol in the early 1940s, rising to stardom as a "crooner." Moving into film, Sinatra established a new career in acting that was launched in 1946. He won an Academy Award for his performance in *From Here to Eternity* in 1953. Since 1954, Sinatra has made 31 films, released at least 800 records, and participated in numerous charity affairs.

Mario Lanza (1921-1959) was a famous tenor who appeared on radio, in concert, on recordings, and in motion pictures. Vocalist and television star Perry Como (born Pierino Roland Como, 1913-) hosted one of America's most popular television shows in the 1950s. Frank Zappa (1940-1993), musician, vocalist, and composer, founded the influential rock group Mothers of Invention in the 1960s. Noted for his social satire and musical inventiveness, Zappa was named Pop Musician of the Year for three years in a row in 1970-1972.

POLITICS

Fiorello LaGuardia (1882-1947) gained national fame as an energetic mayor of New York City, in which capacity he served for three terms (1934-

1945). Earlier, LaGuardia sat for six terms as a Republican representative in the U.S. Congress. Known as "The Little Flower," LaGuardia earned a reputation as an incorruptible, hard working, and humane administrator. John O. Pastore (1912-) was the first Italian American to be elected a state governor (Rhode Island, 1945). In 1950, he represented that state in the U.S. Senate. Geraldine Ferraro (1935-) was the first American woman nominated for vice president by a major political party in 1984 when she ran with Democratic presidential candidate Walter Mondale. Her earlier career included service as assistant district attorney in New York and two terms in the U.S. Congress. Mario Cuomo (1932-) was elected governor of New York in 1982 and has been reelected twice since then. Prior to his election as governor, Cuomo served as lieutenant governor and New York's secretary of state.

John J. Sirica (1904-1992), chief federal judge, U.S. District Court for the District of Columbia, presided over the Watergate trials. He was named *Time* magazine's Man of the Year in 1973. Antonin Scalia (1936-) became the first Italian American to sit on the U.S. Supreme Court when he was appointed Associate Justice in 1986. Rudolph W. Giuliani (1944-), served for many years as U.S. Attorney for the southern district of New York and waged war against organized crime and public corruption. In 1993, he was elected mayor of New York City.

RELIGION

Father Eusebio Chino (Kino) (1645-1711) was a Jesuit priest who worked among the native people of Mexico and Arizona for three decades, establishing more than 20 mission churches, exploring wide areas, and introducing new methods of agriculture and animal-raising. Francesca Xavier Cabrini (1850-1917), the first American to be sainted by the Roman Catholic Church, worked with poor Italian immigrants throughout North and South America, opening schools, orphanages, hospitals, clinics, and novitiates for her Missionary Sisters of the Sacred Heart.

SCIENCE AND TECHNOLOGY

Enrico Fermi (1901-1954), a refugee from Benito Mussolini's fascist regime, is regarded as the "father of atomic energy." Fermi was awarded the 1938 Nobel Prize in physics for his identification of new radioactive elements produced by neutron bombardment. He worked with the Manhattan Project during World War II to produce the first atomic bomb, achieving the world's first self-sustaining chain reaction on December 2, 1942. Salvador Luria (1912-1991) was a pioneer of molecular biology and genetic engineering. In 1969, while he was a faculty member at the Massachusetts Institute of Technology, Luria was awarded the Nobel Prize for his work on viruses. Rita Levi-Montalcini (1909-) was awarded a Nobel Prize in 1986 for her work in cell biology and cancer research. Emilio Segre (1905-1989), a student of Fermi, received the 1959 Nobel Prize in physics for his discovery of the antiproton.

SPORTS

Joseph "Joe" DiMaggio (1914-), the "Yankee Clipper," was voted the Greatest Living Player in baseball. DiMaggio set his 56 consecutive game hitting streak in 1941. (The record still stands.) In a career spanning 1936 to 1951, DiMaggio led the New York Yankees to ten world championships and retired with a .325 lifetime batting average. At the time of his death, Vincent Lombardi (1913-1970) was the winningest coach in professional football, and the personification of tenacity and commitment in American sports. As head coach of the Green Bay Packers, Lombardi led the team to numerous conference, league, and world titles during the 1960s, including two Super Bowls in 1967 and 1968. Rocky Marciano (born Rocco Francis Marchegiano, 1924-1969) was the only undefeated heavyweight boxing champion, winning all his fights. Known as the "Brockton Bomber," Marciano won the heavyweight championship over Jersey Joe Walcott in 1952 and held it until his voluntary retirement in 1956. Rocky Graziano (born Rocco Barbella, 1922-), middleweight boxing champion, is best known for his classic bouts with Tony Zale. Lawrence "Yogi" Berra (1925-), a Baseball Hall of Fame member who played for the New York Yankees as catcher for 17 years, enjoyed a career that lasted from 1946 to 1963. He also coached and managed several professional baseball teams, including the New York Mets and the Houston Astros. Joseph Garagiola (1926-) played with the St. Louis Cardinals (1946-1951) and several other Major League clubs.

VISUAL ARTS

Frank Stella (1936-) pioneered the development of "minimal art," involving three-dimensional, "shaped" paintings and sculpture. His work has been exhibited in museums around the world. Constantino Brumidi (1805-1880), a political exile from the liberal revolutions of the 1840s, became known as "the Michelangelo of the United States Capitol." Brumidi painted the interior of the dome of the Capitol in Washington, D.C., from 1865 to 1866, as well as numerous other areas of the building. Ralph Fasanella (1914-) a self-taught primitive painter whose work has been compared to that of Grandma Moses, is grounded in his immigrant backgrounds.

MEDIA

PRINT

Since the mid-1800s, more than 2,000 Italian American newspapers have been established, representing a full range of ideological, religious, professional, and commercial interests. As of 1980, about 50 newspapers were still in print.

America Oggi (America Today).

Currently the only Italian-language daily newspaper in the United States.

Contact: Andrea Mantineo, Editor.

Address: 41 Bergentine Avenue, Westwood, New Jersey 07675.

Telephone: (201) 695-5608.

Fra Noi (Among Us).

A monthly publication in a bilingual format by the Catholic Scalabrini order; features articles on issues primarily of interest to Chicago's Italian community.

Contact: Paul Basile, Editor.

Address: 263 North York Road, Elmhurst, Illinois 60126.

Telephone: (708) 782-4440.

Italian Americana: Cultural and Historical Review.

An international journal published semi-annually by the University of Rhode Island's College of Continuing Education.

Contact: Carol Bonomo Albright, Editor.

Address: 199 Promenade Street, Providence, Rhode Island 02908.

Italian Tribune News.

Publishes a heavily illustrated journal that features articles weekly in English on Italian culture and Italian American contributions.

Contact: Joan Alagna, Editor.

Address: 427 Bloomfield Avenue, Newark, New Jersey 07107.

Telephone: (201) 485-6000.

Fax: (201) 485-8967.

The Italian Voice (La Voce Italiana).

Provides regional, national, and local news coverage; published weekly in English.

Contact: Cesarina A. Earl, Editor.

Address: P.O. Box 9, Totowa, New Jersey 07511.

Telephone: (201) 942-5028.

OSIA News: National Publication of the Supreme Lodge, Order Sons of Italy in America.

Concentrates on broad issues of concern to the Order Sons of Italy in America and is published monthly in English and Italian.

Contact: Albert A. Maino, Editor.

Address: 41 Austin Street, Worcester, Massachusetts 01609.

Sons of Italy Times.

Publishes news bi-weekly concerning the activities of Sons of Italy lodges and the civic, professional, and charitable interests of the membership.

Contact: John B. Acchione III, Editor.

Address: 414 Walnut Street, Philadelphia, Pennsylvania 19106.

Telephone: (215) 592-1713.

VIA: Voices in Italian Americana.

A literary journal published by Purdue University.

Contact: Anthony J. Tamburri, Editor.

Address: West Lafayette, Indiana 47987.

RADIO

WHLD-AM.

Broadcasts eight hours of Italian-language programming a week.

Contact: Paul Butler.

Address: 2692 Staley Road, Grand Island, New York 14072.

Telephone: (716) 773-1270.

WLUV-AM.

Broadcasts seven hours of Italian-language shows per week.

Contact: Walter Solarz.

Address: 2625 Country Road 95, Palm Harbor, Florida 34684.

Telephone: (813) 786-1723.

WSBC-AM.

Presents seven hours of Italian-language programming each week.

Contact: Roy Bellavia.

Address: 4949 West Belmont Avenue, Chicago, Illinois 60641.

Telephone: (312) 282-9722.

WSRF-AM.

Features 12 hours of Italian-language programming weekly.

Contact: John Tenaglia.

Address: 3000 S.W. 60th Avenue, Ft. Lauderdale, Florida 33314.

Telephone: (305) 581-1580.

WUNR-AM.

Features 12 hours of programs of ethnic interest.

Contact: Herbert S. Hoffman.

Address: 160 North Washington Street, Boston, Massachusetts 02114.

Telephone: (617) 367-9003.

ORGANIZATIONS AND ASSOCIATIONS

America-Italy Society (AIS).

Fosters friendship between Italy and the United States based upon mutual appreciation of their respective contributions to science, art, music, literature, law, and government.

Contact: Gianfranco Monacelli, President.

Address: 3 East 48th Street, New York, New York 10017.

Telephone: (212) 838-1560.

American Committee on Italian Migration.

A non-profit social service organization advocating equitable immigration legislation and aiding newly arrived Italian immigrants. It sponsors conferences, publishes a newsletter, and disseminates information beneficial to new Italian Americans.

Contact: Rev. Joseph Cogo.

Address: 373 Fifth Avenue, New York, New York 10016.

Telephone: (212) 679-4650.

American Italian Historical Association.

Founded in 1966 by a group of academics as a professional organization interested in promoting basic research into the Italian American experience; encourages the collection and preservation of primary source materials, and supports the teaching of Italian American history.

Contact: Dr. Jerome Krase, President.

Address: 209 Flagg Place, Staten Island, New York 10304.

Italian Cultural Exchange in the United States (ICE).

Promotes knowledge and appreciation of Italian culture among Americans.

Contact: Professor Salvatore R. Tocci, Executive Director.

Address: 27 Barrow Street, New York, New York 10014.

Telephone: (212) 255-0528.

Italian Historical Society of America.

Perpetuates Italian heritage in America and gathers historical data on Americans of Italian descent.

Contact: Dr. John J. LaCorte, Director.

Address: 111 Columbia Heights, Brooklyn, New York 11201.

Telephone: (718) 852-2929.

Joint Civic Committee of Italian Americans.

A nonprofit organization that plans and coordinates civic, educational, and social welfare activities serving the interests of Italian Americans in the Chicago area.

Contact: Anthony Sorrentino.

Address: 127 North Dearborn Street, Chicago, Illinois 60602.

Telephone: (312) 372-6788.

The National Italian American Foundation.

A nonprofit organization designed to promote the history, heritage, and accomplishments of Italian Americans and to foster programs advancing the interests of the Italian American community.

Contact: Dr. Fred Rotandaro, Executive Director.

Address: 666 Eleventh Street, N.W., Suite 800, Washington, D.C. 20001-4596.

Telephone: (202) 638-0220.

Order Sons of Italy in America (OSIA).

Established in 1905, the organization is composed of lodges located throughout the United States. It seeks to preserve and disseminate information on Italian culture and encourages the involvement of its members in all civic, charitable, patriotic, and youth activities. OSIA is committed to supporting Italian-American cultural events and fighting discrimination.

Address: 219 E Street, N.E., Washington, D.C., 20002.

Telephone: (202) 547-2900.

MUSEUMS AND RESEARCH CENTERS

American Italian Renaissance Foundation.

Focuses on the contributions of Italian Americans in Louisiana. Its research library also includes the wide-ranging Giovanni Schiavo collection.

Contact: Joseph Maselli, Director.

Address: 537 South Peters Street, New Orleans, Louisiana 70130.

Telephone: (504) 891-1904.

The Balch Institute for Ethnic Studies.

Contains many documents addressing the Italian American experience in Pennsylvania and elsewhere, most notably the Leonard Covello collection. A published guide to the holdings is available.

Contact: Pamela Nelson, Associate Curator/Registrar.

Address: 18 South Seventh Street, Philadelphia, Pennsylvania 19106.

Telephone: (215) 925-8090.

The Center for Migration Studies.

Houses a vast collection of materials depicting Italian American activities. It features extensive records of Italian American Catholic parishes staffed by the Scalabrini order. The center also provides published guides to its collections.

Contact: Dr. Lydio Tomasi, Director.

Address: 209 Flagg Place, Staten Island, New York, 10304.

Telephone: (718) 351-8800.

Immigration History Research Center (IHRC), University of Minnesota.

IHRC is the nation's most important repository for research materials dealing with the Italian American experience. The center holds major documentary collections representing a wide cross-section of Italian American life, numerous newspapers, and many published works. A published guide is available.

Contact: Dr. Rudolph J. Vecoli, Director.

Address: 826 Berry Street, St. Paul, Minnesota 55114.

Telephone: (612) 627-4208.

The New York Public Library, Manuscripts Division.

Holds many collections relevant to the Italian American experience, most notably the papers of Fiorello LaGuardia, Vito Marcantonio, Gino C. Speranza, and Carlo Tresca.

Address: 42nd Street and Fifth Avenue, New York, New York 10036.

Telephone: (212) 930-1018.

SOURCES FOR ADDITIONAL STUDY

Alba, Richard. *Italian Americans: Into the Twilight of Ethnicity*. Englewood Cliffs, New Jersey: Prentice-Hall, 1985.

Battistella, Graziano. *Italian Americans in the '80s: A Sociodemographic Profile*. New York: Center for Migration Studies, 1989.

DeConde, Alexander. *Half Bitter, Half Sweet: An Excursion into Italian American History*. New York: Charles Scribner's Sons, 1971.

Gabaccia, Donna. "Italian American Women: A Review Essay," *Italian Americana*, Volume 12, No. 1 (Fall/Winter 1993); pp. 38-61.

Gambino, Richard. *Blood of My Blood*. New York: Anchor, 1975.

Mangione, Jerre, and Ben Morriale. *La Storia: Five Centuries of the Italian American Experience*. New York: HarperCollins, 1992.

Orsi, Robert A. *The Madonna of 115th Street: Faith and Community in Italian Harlem, 1880-1950*. New Haven: Yale University Press, 1988.

Pozzetta, George E., "From Immigrants to Ethnics: The Italian American Experience," *Journal of American Ethnic History*, Volume 9, No. 1 (Fall 1989); pp. 67-95.

Vecoli, Rudolph J. "The Search for Italian American Identity: Continuity and Change," in *Italian Americans: New Perspectives in Italian Immigration and Ethnicity*, edited by Lydio Tomasi. Staten Island: Center for Migration Studies, 1985; pp. 88-112.

JAMAICAN AMERICANS

by
Samuel Murrell

First generation
Jamaican Americans
cherish traditional
family values, such
as practicing
religion, respecting
elders and marital
vows, being with
one's family in times
of need, supporting
one's family, and
correcting and
punishing one's
disobedient children.

OVERVIEW

One of the four large islands of the Caribbean archipelago, Jamaica measures 4,441 square miles, slightly smaller than the size of Connecticut. Its mountainous terrain, which exceeds 7,400 feet at its Blue Mountain peak, makes traveling from one end of the island to another more interesting than one would expect. Jamaica's northern shores are lined by many miles of lovely white sand beaches that attract thousands of American, Canadian, and a growing number of European tourists annually. Kingston, the capital and largest English-speaking city south of Miami, is Jamaica's chief commercial and administrative center. The island is well known for its rich-tasting Blue Mountain coffee and its bauxite mining and aluminum processing industries.

Jamaica's motto, "Out of Many One People," is a national ideal for its diverse population of 2,506,000 in 1990. As many as 90 percent of all Jamaicans can lay claim to African ancestry. About 26 percent of the population is mixed and approximately nine percent is composed of people of Chinese, European, and East Indian descent. Intermarriage among races over centuries accounts for the diverse physical features of Jamaicans. In addition to English, many Jamaicans speak *Patois* (pronounced patwa)—or what Jamaican intellectuals call Jamaican Talk—a mixture of English and

African dialects. Jamaica was once called a "Christian country" because approximately 80 percent of its citizens have some form of association with Christianity. Protestants have traditionally outnumbered Catholics by a wide margin and Rastafarianism, a twentieth-century religious movement, claims a following of approximately eight percent of the population. A number of small Afro-Caribbean, Asian, and Middle-eastern religious groups also exist in Jamaica.

HISTORY

As early as 600 A.D., Jamaica was settled by Arawaks who called the island Xaymaca. In 1494 Columbus claimed the island for Spain and in 1509, Juan de Esquivel began transporting Jamaican Arawaks to Hispaniola as slaves. Within a few decades, the original population, which was made extinct by European disease, kidnapping, enslavement, and genocidal methods of war, was later replaced by Africans. From 1509 until the early 1660s Jamaica served as a sparsely populated Spanish-held way station for galleons en route to Cuba and the Spanish Main. It became the headquarters for pirate ships. Whoever controlled the island controlled much of the Southern Atlantic Ocean and the Caribbean Sea. After a failed expedition to the larger Spanish Caribbean, British Admiral Penn and General Vernables captured the island in 1655 and driving off the Spaniards. Later Spain officially ceded Jamaica to Britain at the Treaty of Madrid, and the British then left the island to the pirates until 1670. During this time, some of the Spaniards' black slaves fled to the hills. Known as *Maroons*, they were an organized band of fierce-fighting fugitive slaves who hampered British rule until a peace treaty was executed with them in 1738.

Britain turned the island into a vast sugar plantation based on slave labor. Since the British one-crop sugar economy in Barbados was in sharp decline by 1650, many planters in Barbados relocated to Jamaica with their slaves. They were followed by hundreds of British colonizers and hundreds of thousands of enslaved Africans. By 1730 Jamaica's 75,000 slaves produced 15,500 tons of sugar and the island replaced Barbados as Britain's most prized colony. In 1808 the slave population exceeded 324,000 and produced 78,000 tons of sugar. Oliver Cromwell's government attempted to balance the white to black population ratio by shipping criminals, prisoners of war, prostitutes, and other undesirable persons to Jamaica as a

form of punishment and as indentured servants. However, when the slave trade was abolished in 1807, blacks outnumbered whites by as many as ten to one.

Prior to 1834, when slavery was abolished, blacks in Jamaica fought a bitter and often futile battle to free themselves from the savage institution of slavery. The *Maroons* were well known as Jamaica's only successful black resistance movement. For centuries, they menaced British troops, looted plantations, and carried off slave recruits to the precipitous mountains in retaliation against abuses. Their successful guerrilla warfare abated in 1739 and 1795 when *Maroon* chiefs signed peace treaties with the British government.

As the anti-slavery campaign in Britain heated up in 1830 the slave population gathered in large numbers in Afro-Christian Baptist circles—the most vocal anti-slavery organization in Jamaica—in anticipation of freedom. A different kind of revolt called the Baptist War occurred in Jamaica in 1831. Sam Sharpe, a black Baptist lay preacher, perceived that "free paper" had come but the government was concealing it from the slaves. He led a large revolt in western Jamaica, which resulted in massive destruction of property and a bloody and brutal repression by the government. It is believed that this violent slave resistance, the unprofitability of slavery, and mounting pressure from abolitionists, forced Britain to abolish the institution in 1834.

MODERN ERA

Blacks in post-emancipation Jamaica lived in freedom but had no rights or access to property. They were exploited by the white ruling class and treated with contempt by British governors, whose fiscal policies were designed only to benefit whites. In 1865, the unheeded plea of the peasant masses for farm land erupted into a second major revolt, the Morant Bay Rebellion. This was led by Paul Bogle and supported by George William Gordon, Baptist leaders who became two of Jamaica's national heroes. The suppression of the rebellion by the ruling class was ruthless. A blood thirsty Governor Eyre court-marshaled and executed almost 400 suspects, including dozens of innocent Baptist peasants. In the aftermath, the British government appointed a Royal Commission of Inquiry, which found Eyre's penalty "excessive, barbarous, reckless, and criminal." On December 1, 1865, the secretaries of state for the colonies tore up the Jamaican Constitution and recommended a Crown Colony government for the island. The new political system limited the powers of the governor and the Assembly and allowed Britain to retain direct control over the legislative and executive decisions of the colony. Adversely, however, the Crown Colony government inhibited national leadership and allowed the colonials to dominate and exploit the black masses.

As late as the 1930s the political system continued to be closed to most Jamaicans. In the post World War I period, blacks voiced their discontent by supporting trade unions and other organizations led by young political activists such as Dr. Love (a Jamaican physician and anti-colonialist), Marcus Moziah Garvey, Brian Alves, A.G.S. Coombs, and Alexander Bustamante. The lingering unameliorated political inequity and economic hardship led to the 1938 rebellion in which the working class staged a national strike when the West Indian Sugar Company (WISCO) failed to keep its promises of new jobs, higher wages, and better working conditions in its new massive, centralized factory in Westmoreland. Garvey, Bustamante, William Grant, and Norman Manley played key roles in this organized political agitation, which resulted in better workers' compensation. The strike also put new political leaders in the spotlight and renewed interest in political change. The Peoples' National Party (PNP) and the Jamaica Labour Party (JLP) were born in the throes of these upheavals under the Westminster form of government. It was not until 1944 that the country was granted limited self-government and adult suffrage. The Westminster system created the two-party parliamentary democracy that led Jamaica into independence in 1962; it is in effect today under a prime minister, elected by the people, and a governor general (a Jamaican) who represents the Queen.

THE FIRST JAMAICAN AMERICANS

The documented history of black emigration from Jamaica and other Caribbean islands into the United States dates back to 1619 when 20 voluntary indentured workers arrived in Jamestown, Virginia, on a Dutch frigate. They lived and worked as "free persons" even when a Portuguese vessel arrived with the first shipload of blacks enslaved in 1629. Since Jamaica was a major way station and clearing house for slaves en route to North America, the history of Jamaican immigration in the United States is inseparably tied to slavery and post-emancipation migration.

After 1838, European and American colonies in the Caribbean with expanding sugar industries imported large numbers of immigrants to meet their acute labor shortage. Large numbers of Jamaicans were recruited to work in Panama and Costa Rica in the 1850s. After slavery was abolished in the United States in 1865, American planters imported temporary workers, called "swallow migrants," to harvest crops on an annual basis. These workers, many of them Jamaicans, returned to their countries after harvest. Between 1881 and the beginning of World War I, the United States recruited over 250,000 workers from the Caribbean, 90,000 of whom were Jamaicans, to work on the Panama Canal. During both world wars, the United States again recruited Jamaican men for service on various American bases in the region.

SIGNIFICANT IMMIGRATION WAVES

Since the turn of the twentieth century, three distinct waves of Caribbean immigration into the United States have occurred—most of these immigrants came from Jamaica. The first wave took place between 1900 and the 1920s, bringing a modest number of Caribbean immigrants. Official black immigration increased from 412 in 1899 to 12,245 in 1924, although the actual number of black aliens entering the United States yearly was twice as high. By 1930, 178,000 documented first-generation blacks and their children lived in the United States. About 100,000 were from the British Caribbean, including Jamaica. The second and weakest immigration wave occurred between the 1930s and the new immigration policy of the mid-1960s. The McCarran-Walter Act reaffirmed and upheld the quota bill, which discriminated against black immigrants and allowed only 100 Jamaicans into the U.S. annually. During this period, larger numbers of Jamaicans migrated to Britain rather than to the United States due to the immigration restrictions.

The final and largest wave of immigration began in 1965 and continues to the present. This wave began after Britain restricted immigration in its former black Commonwealth colonies. The 1965 Hart-Celler Immigration Reform Act changed the U.S. immigration policy and, inadvertently, opened the way for a surge in immigration from the Caribbean. In 1976, Jamaicans again relocated to the United States in large numbers after Congress increased immigration from the Western Hemisphere to a maximum of 20,000 persons per country. Although about 10,000 Jamaicans migrated to the United States legally from 1960 to 1965, the number skyrocketed in succeeding years—62,700 (1966-1970), 61,500 (1971-1975), 80,600 (1976-1980) and 81,700 (1981-1984)—to an aggregate of about 300,000 documented immigrants in just under a quarter of a century.

At present, Jamaicans are the largest group of American immigrants from the English-speaking Caribbean. However, it is difficult to verify the exact number of Jamaican Americans in this country. The 1990 census placed the total number of documented Jamaican Americans at 435,025, but the high Jamaican illegal alien phenomenon and the Jamaican attitude toward census response may increase that number to 800,000 to 1,000,000 Jamaicans living in the United States. Government statistics report that 186,430 Jamaicans live in New York, but the number is closer to 600,000.

Currently, Jamaican migration is so large that it has caused a national crisis in Jamaica. The exodus has resulted in a serious brain drain and an acute shortage of professionals, such as skilled workers, technicians, doctors, lawyers, and managers, in essential services in Jamaica. For example, the mail often takes one to three months to reach its final destination because of a shortage of postal service supervisors. During the 1970s and early 1980s about 15 percent of the population left the country. In the early 1990s the government began offering incentives to persons with technical, business, and managerial skills to return to Jamaica for short periods of time to aid in management and technical skills training.

REASONS FOR MIGRATING

Jamaicans migrate to the United States for many socio-economic reasons. Migration is encouraged by economic hardship caused by a failing economy based upon plantation agriculture, lack of economic diversity, and scarcity of professional and skilled jobs. Since the nineteenth century Jamaica has had a very poor land distribution track record. The uneven allotment of arable crown lands and old plantations left farmers without a sufficient plot for subsistence or cash crop farming, which contributed to high unemployment statistics and economic hardship. During the 1970s the standard of living declined due to economic inflation and

low salaries. When companies and corporations lost confidence in Michael Manley's Democratic Socialist government and his anti-American rhetoric and close business ties to Cuba, the flight of capital from Jamaica and the shift in U.S. capital investments worsened the situation. Jamaica's huge foreign debt and the International Monetary Fund's (IMF) restructuring of the economy further exacerbated the island's economic woes in the 1980s and 1990s. An increase in crime, fueled by unemployment and aggravated by the exporting of criminals from the United States back to Jamaica, forced thousands of Jamaicans to flee the island for safety. Today, unemployment and under-employment continue to rise above 50 percent, wages continue to fall, the dollar weakens, and the cost of goods and services continues to increase.

The Jamaican mentality that one must "go ah foreign" and "return to him country" to "show off" evidence of success has become a rite of passage for thousands of Jamaicans. This began when the United States imported Jamaicans to work on various projects in the 1800s and early twentieth century. Before long, Jamaicans saw migration as an attractive solution to the harsh social and economic conditions on the island. Since 1930 an important part of Rastafarian theology is the idea of repatriation to Africa in order to escape oppression in "Babylon." However, many Rastas conveniently "followed the star" of the Yankee dollar instead of the "Star of David" (Emperor Haile Selassie of Ethiopia). After 1966, Ethiopia as a haven for Rastafari faded in the bright lights of U.S. metropolitan centers. In addition, many Jamaican students and trainees study at American institutions. Not all return to Jamaica upon completion of their studies. Many stay because of the lack of job opportunities at home and an entrenched British-colonial bias among Jamaica's elite against American education.

SETTLEMENT

Of the Jamaicans documented in the 1990 census 410,933 reported at least one specific ancestry. Of this number 94.5 percent are persons of first ancestry, and the remaining 5.5 percent are of second ancestry. The regional composition is as follows: 59 percent live in the Northeast; 4.8 percent in the Midwest; 30.6 percent in the South; and 5.6 percent in the West. The Northeast and the South have the largest number of immigrants and are home to most illegal Jamaicans in the United States. Jamaicans refer to Miami and

Brooklyn colloquially as "Kingston 22" and "Little Jamaica" respectively. Accessibility, family connections, the help of friends or church, jobs, group psychology (including gangs), access to college and university education, and weather conditions explain the heavy concentration of Jamaican immigrants along the eastern coast.

Jamaicans have a saying, "Anywhere you go in the world you meet a Jamaican." According to the 1990 census, there are Jamaicans in every state in the Union. The census shows that regionally, there are 30,327 in New England, 223,310 in the middle Atlantic, 18,163 in east north central, 2,698 in the west north central, 121,260 in the south Atlantic, 2,882 in the east south central, 9,117 in the west south central, 2,696 in the mountain region, and 21,571 in the Pacific region.

ACCULTURATION AND ASSIMILATION

Jamaican immigrants generally have four options once they arrive in the United States. The first option is to remain a "bird of passage" by viewing oneself as a temporary alien accumulating some Yankee dollars to return home. The second option is to immerse one self within the culture and work for the improvement of the African American community. The third option is to settle in white suburbs, secure a good-paying job at a white institution or company, and live a life of being the conspicuous black family in town who enhances the diversity of the community. The fourth option is to engage in academic and professional training while intending to return to Jamaica upon completion. Most early Jamaican immigrants chose the first option because they did not intend to become part of the American mainstream. However, since the 1970s more Jamaicans have sought permanent residence in the United States because of social and economic problems back home.

In addition to adjusting to severe weather variations, especially in northern states, Jamaican immigrants must make many other adjustments to American society. First, they must adjust to their new citizenship or residency. Those who are naturalized American citizens often wrestle with the issue of a split national allegiance to Jamaica and to the United States. Immigrants who are resident aliens enjoy the same privileges as all legal residents and are generally more settled than illegal aliens, who exist in a state of vulnerability—a voice-with-no-vote status in the United States. Thousands of Jamaican American professionals, academics, and skilled workers fall in this category.

A second adjustment must be made to the cultural traditions and social roles of racial or ethnic groups with which the immigrants must identify. Today, Jamaicans enter a more prosperous society than that left behind. However, the first and second waves of immigrants suffered much of the racial prejudices of Jim Crow laws and the economy of pre-civil rights United States. Recent immigrants may not encounter the older blatant forms of segregation, but they suffer from the effects of subtle discrimination and stereotypical perceptions based upon color and ethnicity. Although Jamaica is not immune to color distinctions, immigrants to the United States become much more conscious of their blackness (often as a disadvantage) than they did back home in Jamaica, where blacks are the majority and many are highly respected leaders. In the United States, they must adjust to living in communities where blacks are treated as a numerical, political, social, and economic minority.

Third, Jamaicans also must learn to adjust to life in some of America's toughest neighborhoods. They become street-wise very early and learn where to walk and work, and which apartment buildings and neighborhoods to live in. Occasionally, they become victims of inner-city crimes, but many Jamaican youths have penetrated the gangs and drug culture in New York City, Miami, Los Angeles, Washington, D.C., and Boston. Some are named in organized-crime raids by the FBI and other law-enforcement bodies. Finally, because of their large numbers in many U.S. neighborhoods, uninformed Americans often classify any foreign black with a different accent as Jamaican. When Africans, Haitians, Barbadians, and other groups commit felonies, Jamaicans are often de facto implicated in the act by the media.

CULTURE

Jamaica's ethnic distinctions are not as large as those of Trinidad, Guyana, or the United States, but Jamaicans are rich in cultural traditions and ethnic diversity. Although the population is predominantly black, small enclaves of East Indians, Chinese, Lebanese, Europeans, Jews, and other ethnic groups enhance the rich cultural heritage of the country. The motto "Out of Many One People" brings Jamaicans together to celebrate a

This Jamaican American woman is participating in an ethnic festival.

occurs on October 17, during which local communities come alive with music, folk dance, and colorful dress. Politicians or other prominent citizens give speeches and pay tribute to fallen heroes at National Heroes' Park. The Independence Day celebration is Jamaica's grandest holiday. Between March and August, the Jamaica Cultural Development Commission offers an interesting array of colorful events that exhibit local talents, featuring visual arts, performing arts, and entertainment. On the first Monday in August, a profusion of color and excitement fills the air as community cultural groups showcase their abilities, and preachers and politicians thunder patriotic sermons and speeches. This culminates with the spectacular Grand Gala in Kingston. Jamaican Americans usually observe these holidays by staging their own local activities, such as traveling to Jamaica for the Big Splash. On Labor Day, Jamaican Americans join other Caribbean people during the Carnival celebration in New York.

wide range of local, national, and international cultural events throughout the year.

FESTIVALS

The Accompong Maroon festival is kicked off in Accompong, St. Elizabeth, in January. The annual Jamaica Carnival takes place in April and May in Kingston and Negril, respectively; and the Labor Day celebration is observed on May 23. In June, there is a Jamaica Festival National Heroes Tribute at National Heroes' Park, in anticipation of National Heroes Day, celebrated on October 17. The Jamaica Festival Performing Arts Final also takes place in June, and the Jamaica Festival Amateur Culinary Arts, as well as the Jamaica Festival Popular Song Contest, are staged at the National Arena in July. Independence Day observed in August is the most celebrated cultural event in Jamaica. The Portland Jamboree follows Independence Day, providing ten days of colorful street parades, parties, street dancing, cultural and sporting events, fashion and cabaret shows.

HOLIDAYS

Jamaicans celebrate religious holidays like Christmas, Good Friday, New Year's Day, Ash Wednesday, and Easter Monday. Additional holidays include Bob Marley's Birthday (in February) and Boxing Day. The National Heroes Day celebration

MUSIC

Many Jamaican festivals celebrate Jamaica's rich musical tradition. In the 1960s, Count Ossie merged native Jamaican, Afro-Caribbean, and Afro-American musical rhythms with rock and other influences to create a distinctively black music called "reggae." This music, which the Rastafarians and Bob Marley popularized, is a plea for liberation and a journey into black consciousness and African pride. Like calypso, reggae began as a working-class medium of expression and social commentary. Reggae is the first distinctly Caribbean music to become global in scope. Each August, Jamaica stages its internationally acclaimed music festival at the Jamworld Center in Kingston. Over the five-day period, the premier music festival of the Caribbean attracts over 200,000 visitors. Each year it features top reggae stars like Ziggy Marley, Jimmy Cliff, Third World, and Stevie Wonder. This is followed immediately by the Reggae Sunfest at the Bob Marley Performing Center in Montego Bay. In the post Lenten period, the streets of Kingston come alive to the pulsating sounds of calypso and soca music. For nine emotionally charged days, local and international artists treat revelers to the best of reggae, soca and calypso "under the tents." During this time, thousands of glittering costumed celebrants revel and dance through the streets in a festive mood. The National Mento Yard is kicked off in Manchester in October with a potpourri of traditional and cultural folk forms which have contributed to Jamaica's rich cultural heritage. Many of these cultural events are observed by Jamaican Americans in local public celebrations or in the privacy of their homes.

DANCE AND SONGS

Jamaica is known worldwide for its African folk dances, Jan Canoe and Accompong. Jamaica's carnival Jump-up is now very popular in Kingston and Ocho Rios. The National Dance Theater (NDTC), established temporarily in 1962, is a world-renowned troupe that celebrates the unique traditional dance and rich musical heritage of Jamaica and the other Caribbean islands. Under the distinguished leadership of Professor Rex Nettleford, NDTC has made many tours to the United States, Britain, Canada and other countries.

Jamaica also has many other musical forms. Calypso and soca music sway the body of festive dancers to a mixture of Afro-Caribbean rhythms with witty lyrics and heavy metal or finely tuned steel drums. There is also "dub poetry" or chanted verses, "dance hall" music (with rap rhythms, reggae beat, and rude or suggestive lyrics), and Ska, with its emotionally charged, celebrative beat. Jamaican Americans listen to a great variety of music: jazz, reggae, calypso, soca, ska, rap, classical music, gospel and "high-church" choirs.

CUISINE

The national dish in Jamaica is *ackee and saltfish* (codfish), but curried goat and rice, and fried fish and *bammy* (a flat, baked cassava bread) are just as popular and delicious. A large variety of dishes are known for their spicy nature. Patties, which are hot and spicy, turtle soup, and pepper pot may contain meats such as pork and beef, as well as greens such as okra and kale. Spices such as pimento or allspice, ginger, and peppers are used commonly in a number of dishes. Other Jamaican American foods are: plantain, rice and peas, cowfoot, goat head, jerk chicken, pork, oxtail soup, stew peas and rice, run-down, liver and green bananas, *calaloo* and dumplings, *mannish water* from goat's intestine, and hard dough bread and pastries.

Dessert is usually fruit or a dish containing fruit. An example is *matrimony*, which is a mixture of orange sections, star apples, or guavas in coconut cream with guava cheese melted over it. Other desserts are cornmeal pudding, sweet potato pud-ding, totoes, plantain tarts, and many other "sweet-tooth" favorites. Coffee and tea are popular nonalcoholic beverages, as are carrot juice, roots, and Irish or sea moss, while rum, Red Stripe Beer, Dragon and Guinness stouts are the national alcoholic beverages. In Miami and New York City, especially Flatbush, Nostrand, Utica, and Church Avenues, one sees groceries filled with a variety of other Caribbean foods, including sugar cane, jelly coconut, and yarns, and black American foods that Jamaicans use for supplementary dishes.

TRADITIONAL COSTUMES

Jamaica's traditional folk costume for women is a bandana skirt worn with a white blouse with a ruffled neck and sleeves, adorned with embroidery depicting various Jamaican images. A head tie made of the same bandana material is also worn. Men wear a shirt that is also made of the same fabric. The colors of the national flag are black, green, and gold. However, because of the popularity of the clothes and colors of Rastafari, many people mistake Rastas' colors (red, green, and gold) as Jamaica's national colors. Jamaicans wear their costumes on Independence Day, National Heroes Day, and other national celebrations. In New York, Jamaican Americans participate in the Caribbean Carnival Jamboree and dress in lavish and colorful costumes during the festive celebration.

SPORTS

Jamaica's primary sports are cricket and soccer. Cricket is more than a sport in Jamaica; it is like a religion, a rallying point for the spirit of patriotism, Caribbean unity and pride, and an occasion for national and individual heroism. Other national sports include horse racing, tennis, basketball, netball, track and field, and triathlon. Some local sports specifically designed for tourists are golf, boating, diving, fishing, and polo.

HEALTH AND MENTAL HEALTH ISSUES

There are no documented medical problems that are unique to Jamaicans. In the 1950s and 1960s, polio appeared in some communities but was later contained by medical treatment. Since the 1980s, drug abuse, alcoholism, and AIDS have also plagued Jamaicans. Crime and economic hardship have taken a heavy toll on the health and life expectancy in Jamaica during the last two decades.

In 1994, the government of Jamaica admitted that most violent crimes committed in the country are drug related. Many of the Caribbean drug kingpins in New York City and Jamaica were trained in the slums of Kingston. The distribution and use of marijuana and crack cocaine accompany Jamaican gang members to New York, New Jersey, Pennsylvania, Florida, Massachusetts, California, and West Virginia, thus perpetuating drug abuse problems.

LANGUAGE

English, Jamaica's official language, is spoken with many variations ranging from British English to Jamaican *Patois*, which is now a language of its own. Jamaicans adapt their speech to the social context of the moment. They speak English in formal discourse or political discussions and shift to Patois in informal conversation and gossip. A large number of people from rural Jamaica, however, experience great difficulty in switching to standard English in formal conversation. In addition, thousands of Jamaicans who live in Brooklyn, speak mainly *Patois*. In recent years, the Rastafarians have developed their own non-Western vocabulary and Afro-Jamaican way of speaking.

JAMAICAN PROVERBS AND SAYINGS

Before the 1960s, working-class Jamaicans used numerous *Patois* sayings and verbal expressions, which were usually scorned by the upper-class people, and not easily understood by foreigners. In more recent years, the language and its proverbial expressions have been used by most Jamaicans. The use of animal characters is quite frequent in Jamaican proverbs: "When Jon Crow wan go a lowered, im sey a cool breeze tek im;" "When tiger wan' nyam, him seh him favor puss;" "Cow seh siddung nuh mean ress;" "Every dawg have im day;" "Yu see yu neighbor beard on fire, yu tek water an wet yu own;" "When man can't dance, him say music no good;" "One time nuh fool, but two times fool, him a damn fool;" "Mi t'row mi corn but mi nuh call nuh fowl;" "One one cocoa full basket."

There are many Anglicized African proverbs that are popular in Jamaica: When the mouse laughs at the cat there is a hole nearby; No matter how long the night, the day is sure to come; No one tests the depth of a river with both feet; He who is bitten by a snake fears a lizard; If you are greedy in conversation you lose the wisdom of your friend; When a fowl is eating your neighbor's corn, drive it away or someday it will eat yours. Often, the purpose of these sayings is to give caution, play with social and political conventions, make uncomplimentary remarks, crack smutty jokes, or give a new twist to a conversation. They are also used to teach morality, values, and modes of conduct.

GREETINGS AND OTHER EXPRESSIONS

Some casual colloquial Jamaican greetings are: "Cool man;" "Wah the man ah seh?" "How di dahta doin'?" "Me soon come man" (See you soon); "Likle more" (See you later); "How you doin' man?" "Wah 'appen man?" "Mawning Sah!" "How yu deh do?" Some Rastafari greetings are: "Hail the man," "I an I," "Selassi I," "Jah, Ras Tafari," and "Hey me bredren" (hello brother).

FAMILY AND COMMUNITY DYNAMICS

First generation Jamaican Americans cherish traditional family values, such as practicing religion, respecting elders and marital vows, being with one's family in times of need, supporting one's family, and correcting and punishing one's disobedient children. The emotional bond between parents and children is very strong, often stronger than between spouses. Parents with legal status often are active in civic and political affairs and take an interest in their children's education by joining the PTA, attending open school board meetings, and participating in programs designed to address racism, crime, and poor SATs. Jamaica was once proud of its high literacy rate but the constant migration of teachers and other professionals has taken a heavy toll on the school system and educational achievement since the 1970s.

Unfortunately, the modern Jamaican immigrant family is plagued by many problems. Immigration restrictions and financial limitations make it difficult for an entire family to migrate to the United States simultaneously and to keep their family values intact. One parent often precedes the other family members by many years. Jamaican women are more likely than men to migrate to the United States first. The filing of papers for family members becomes a top priority five to ten years after one becomes a permanent citizen. In some cases, during such long periods of separation, parents, especially men, sever ties with their Jamaican family and begin new ones in the United States. Before they migrate, mothers are forced to leave their children with relatives, grandparents, or friends. These children are often left unsupervised in Jamaica and are introduced to drugs and crime at a young age. They rarely remain in school and others who do become very disruptive because they believe they are in the process of migrating and see no need to complete their studies. When they join their parents in inner-city communities in the United States, Jamaican American children are often left on their own for many hours a day while their single parent, who lacks the family support that they had back home, works more than one job to make ends meet. The net result is that a significant number of Jamaican American families suffer a fair amount of dysfunction as part of the migration phenomenon. The situation is rather acute among blue-collar immigrants who migrate to the United States. Quite often, their children find it difficult to adjust to the new social setting and the resentment which they encounter from students and teachers in the American school environment.

WEDDINGS

Most Jamaican American weddings follow Christian tradition. an engagement period lasts a few months or years. Traditionally, in Jamaica the bride's parents were responsible for supplying the bridal gown and the reception; the groom and his parents provided the ring and the new home. In the United States, substantial variation in this practice exists due to changes in family structure and values. In many cases, the parties are already cohabiting and the wedding ceremony, often performed by a judge or Justice of the Peace, only legalizes the relationship. However, lovers who are practicing Christians do not live together before marriage and the wedding ceremony is performed in a chapel or church. Traditionally, the bride wears white as a sign of chastity, and large numbers of people are invited to observe the ceremony. In rural Jamaica, weddings are community events—the community feels that they are a part of the couple's life and they view a public invitation to observe the ceremony also as an invitation to attend the reception, which includes lots of food and a large supply of rum and other beverages. In the United States, however, the ceremony and reception are kept within a small circle of close friends and relatives.

The wedding menu usually includes traditional Jamaican cuisine. It starts off with *mannish water*—a soup made from goat tripe (intestine). Guests are often given a choice of curry goat and white rice, rice and peas or kidney beans with fried chicken, or stewed chicken or beef for the main course. A light salad is served with the meal along with sorrel or rum punch. After the meal, the wedding cake is cut and served to the guests. It is usually a black cake with dried fruits presoaked in rum or wine and decorated with icing. Among the poorer people, port wine is used for toasting the couple. Some weddings include dancing by the bride and groom as well as guests and revelry, which can go into the wee hours of the morning.

BAPTISMS

Jamaicans practice two types of baptisms: infant baptism and adult baptism. Among Catholics, Anglicans, Lutherans, Presbyterians, Disciples of Christ, and Methodists, an infant is baptized into the body of believers and of Christ by sprinkling water on its head. When the child reaches the age of accountability, a confirmation ceremony is performed. In other Protestant-Christian and Afro-Caribbean Christian traditions, the infant is blessed at "dedication" but baptized only after faith is confessed voluntarily in Christ. In this baptism by immersion, the "initiate" is submerged bodily under the water by a minister of religion or elder of the faith, in a river, the sea, or a baptismal font located near the sanctuary.

FUNERALS

Jamaican funeral rituals and beliefs are influenced by African, Caribbean, and European-Christian traditions. The basic West African-Jamaican and Christian beliefs concerning death are as follows: the individual has three components—body, soul, and spirit; death marks the end of mortal life and the passage into immortality; at death, the spirit returns to the Supreme God where it joins other spirits; and the deceased's shadow or *duppy* wanders for several days, after which it is laid to rest through special rites. Consequently, Jamaican Christians and Afro-centric religions (Myalism, Pocomania, Shango) bury their dead after performing special rites or a formal church service. A Catholic priest gives the last rites to the dying and may offer a mass for a soul that departed to purgatory before making peace with God. In Jamaica, the high-church Protestants have stately funerals for their communicants who are prominent citi-

This Jamaican American displays a flowered headdress.

zens. Around election time, these funerals are usually attended by high-ranking government officials and distinguished persons in the community. On the night before the funeral, there is a wake for the dead in which friends and family come to offer condolences, sing dirges, and "drink up."

A highlight of the funeral in Afro-centric religions is the "Nine Night" service, conducted to ensure that the shadow of the deceased does not return on the ninth evening after death to visit with family members. In most funerals, it is a custom for men to carry the corpse in a coffin on their shoulders. During the funeral, a phase of ritual mourning and howling in a sorrowful manner occurs. An offering of libation and sacrifices accompanies communication with the deceased at the gravesite. A phase of ritual joy mixed with mourning precedes and follows the interment, which is concluded with a second ceremony at the gravesite. Funeral rites involve dancing, singing, music, and grand incantations. There are often elaborate superstitious grave decorations to fend off evil spirits or bad omens from the deceased who lived a wicked life.

INTERACTION WITH OTHER GROUPS

Working-class Jamaican Americans have certain characteristics that set them apart from other groups. They dress differently (especially the Rastas), speak with a different accent, favor certain types of foods, often love loud music and in some

parts of New York City and Miami live as a self-contained group with distinct social and economic habits. They use special verbal expressions and linguistic codes to communicate (mostly in *Patois*). They are a hard-working and confident people, proud of their Jamaican heritage and the international reputation Jamaica receives from reggae and sports. Although often described as very assertive and not easily dominated, Jamaican immigrants generally establish good relations with other groups in their community. Jamaicans own or operate most of the successful Caribbean businesses in communities where they live. They are able to maintain strong friendly social, religious, economic, and political ties with both black and white American institutions and communities simultaneously. Many of the Caribbean nurses and nurses aides are Jamaican; and Jamaican American scholars and professionals establish collegial relations at American universities, colleges, and other institutions of learning.

On the other hand, Jamaican immigrants and native-born African Americans often misunderstand each other as a result of stereotypes and misconceptions, which often leads to intraracial conflict. For example, some Jamaicans believe that their attitudes of hard work, community building, and family values are superior to that of African Americans. Jamaicans see themselves as more ambitious and greater achievers than African Americans. Caribbean people also believe that they have healthier relations with whites than that of their counterparts because they do not carry anti-white rhetoric into all social, political, and economic discussions. Some American blacks see Jamaicans as selfish intruders, idle unsanitary Rasta drug dealers, and criminals who are making it more difficult for African Americans to find jobs and live peacefully in their neighborhoods. The fact that Jamaican Americans have dual national allegiance and, as a result, often pursue a different social and political agenda from other African Americans, adds to the misunderstanding.

Evidence shows that with time, many of the differences between African Americans and Jamaican Americans will become less distinct. Marriage patterns, for example, demonstrate that first-generation Jamaicans marry and have relations with other Jamaicans, while second and third generations tend to marry African Americans as well. This is due to their contact in school, interaction in their living environments, and that the second and third generation Jamaican Americans have lived in the United States all their lives and share very similar life experiences with African Americans. The combined efforts of Jamaicans and African Americans to deal with racial incidences and injustice in their neighborhoods also helps to improve relations.

RELIGION

The majority of Jamaica's population is Christian with small Hindu, Muslim, Jewish, and Bahai communities. The older, established Christian denominations are Baptist, Methodist, Anglican, Roman Catholic, Moravian, and the United Church (Presbyterian and Congregationalist). Jamaica's most vibrant religious experience comes from the less formal or liturgical Protestant religious confessions: the Pentecostals, Church of God, Associated Gospel Assembly, Open Bible Standard Churches, Seventh Day Adventist, Jehovah Witnesses, the Missionary church, and a number of independent churches all of which are called "Evangelical."

A number of African Caribbean revivalist religious groups also exist in Jamaica, which survived under slavery. Among these are Myalism, Bedwardism (founded by Alexander Bedward in 1920), Pocomania Kurnina, Nativism or the Native Baptist church, and Rastafarianism. Myalism is a religion with African origins. It is one of the oldest religions from Africa and involves the practice of magic and spirit possession. It is community-centered and refuses to accept negatives in life such as sickness, failure, and oppression. Kumina, which is related to Mayalism, began around 1730. Membership into Kumina "bands" is inherited at birth rather than by conversion or voluntary membership. The Native Baptist church began as an indigenous church among black American slaves who were taken to Jamaica by their owners when they migrated to the island as Baptist loyalists. One of the distinguishing characteristics of the Native Baptist church is immersion baptism.

Rastafari is Jamaica's most famous Afro-Caribbean religion. It was founded in 1930 by wandering Jamaican preachers who were inspired by the teachings of Marcus Garvey, a political activist. Rastas established their beliefs on messianic interpretations of Christian scripture and the idea that Haile Selassie, the former Emperor of Ethiopia, is divine. Distinguishing features of Rastafari are the wearing of dread locks and loose-fitting clothes. The movement has made its presence felt on every continent. There are about 800,000 Rastas and Rasta supporters in the United States, about 80,000 of whom live in Brooklyn.

EMPLOYMENT AND ECONOMIC TRADITIONS

Jamaican American employment is quite diverse. A large number of older Jamaican women work for low wages taking care of predominantly white senior citizens in American metropolitan cities. However, many Jamaican Americans bring technical and professional skills with them to the United States, which often allow them to secure better paying jobs than other blacks. Before 1970, white institutions and corporations tended to hire skilled and highly educated Jamaicans in preference to black Americans. This gave American blacks the distinct impression that Jamaicans were specially favored in the job market. There is no documented evidence, however, that Jamaicans are better educated or more productive workers than black Americans.

Both Caribbean and American blacks suffer job discrimination in the United States. Jamaican immigrants who are illegal aliens or who are in a transitional stage of residency are particularly vulnerable to injustice and exploitation. Often, unskilled immigrants work for long hours in two or three part-time low-paying jobs in order to survive. However, a significant number of Jamaican Americans are successful in entrepreneurial enterprises. In New York City, many have benefitted from affirmative action policies in housing and jobs in Flatbush, Crown Heights, Bedford Stuyvesant, and elsewhere. Some Jamaicans have used the open enrollment at the City University of New York to improve their skills in order to obtain higher paying jobs and upward mobility.

After the late 1970s, Jamaican businesses in New York City proliferated, including grocery stores, parlors, and shops, restaurants, travel agencies, realtor brokerages, bakeries, bars, beauty salons, music and record shops, and disco and dance clubs. A number of Jamaicans are subcontractors in building construction, masonry, carpentry, woodwork and cabinet making, electrical wiring, plumbing, heating and central air installations, printing, typing and stenographic services. Jamaican professional businesses include computer consulting and training in word processing, law firms, private medical practices, immigration agents or counselors. Con artists, beggars, hustlers, and drug traffickers also engage in parallel market economic activities.

Crime has become such a way of life in Jamaica that in the post independence period, both of the ruling parties, the JLP and the PNP, recruited gangsters to "eliminate" opponents in electoral districts, stuff ballot boxes to control election results, hand pick the tenants for scarce housing, launder money, and funnel government jobs to supporters. Since the late 1970s, the gangs have had almost unlimited power in Jamaica and are now bodyguards for government officials. They prey on the defenseless and vulnerable and compete with rivals for turf, both in Jamaica and the United States. In recent years, the U.S. government has adopted a policy of deporting violent Jamaican criminals who are now a serious menace to national security.

POLITICS AND GOVERNMENT

Jamaicans have been involved in issues of political significance in the United States since the early 1800s. In 1827, Jamaican-born John B. Russwurm co-founded and co-edited the first black press in America, *Freedom's Journal*. Russwurm's vocal political views and anti-slavery criticism forced him to leave the paper under pressure from contributors and his own colleagues. After slavery was abolished in the British West Indies in 1834, a number of Jamaicans supported the Back to Africa movement and worked for the abolition of American slavery in collaboration with their black counterparts in the United States.

This political activity led to the founding of the Pan-African Movement, which Marcus Garvey and W.E.B. Dubois championed. Garvey attracted the largest single political gathering in American history prior to the Civil Rights March on Washington. He spurred blacks in Harlem into political action with self-confidence and black pride. He established the Universal Negro Improvement Association (UNIA), which helped to cement the bonds of racial consciousness between American and Caribbean blacks. The majority of Garvey's UNIA in the United States comprised West Indians, especially from Jamaica. Garvey's movement intimidated the National Association for the Advancement of Colored People (NAACP), which envied the power and

support that Garvey enjoyed before he was arrested on charges of alleged embezzlement and later incarcerated in Atlanta, Georgia. After Garvey was deported in the late 1920s, he established the Peoples' Political Party (PPP), which called for many reforms, including minimum wages, guaranteed employment, social security benefits, workers' compensation, the expropriation of private lands for public use, land reform, and the creation of a Jamaican university. While working in the American political context, W. A. Domingo, a Jamaican-born Harlem Renaissance figure and writer, supported black rights and advocated Jamaican independence in the Caribbean. Domingo did not want to emphasize the differences between African Americans and West Indian Americans, because both are black and experience some of the same effects of racial oppression and discrimination.

The influences of Jamaican politics and culture on places like New York City, East Orange, Miami, and elsewhere extend beyond the mere establishment of cultural enclaves. Jamaicans were very vocal and assertive during the early twentieth century black struggle, often paving the way for new black professional opportunities not previously open to blacks. Jamaican Americans who experience racial discrimination in the workplace, in their neighborhoods, and in their communities, combine political efforts to address the concerns of the entire black population. In the 1930s, Jamaican-U.S. political activity reached a new level as Jamaican, Trinidadians, Guyanese, and other Caribbean immigrants began playing an important role in the Democratic Party in New York City. In more recent times, Una Clarke, a Jamaican-born educator who won one of New York's predominantly Caribbean districts, rose to be one of the prominent Jamaican American politicians in New York.

POLITICAL RELATIONS WITH JAMAICA

Jamaica and the United States have never engaged in a major military confrontation. U.S. involvement in Jamaica includes little intervention. There has never been a need for a "Bay of Pigs" invasion, as in Cuba, a "vertical insertion," as in Grenada, or a military occupation as in Haiti and the Dominican Republic. The United States did not contemplate annexing Jamaica as it did with Puerto Rico and Cuba in the Spanish Cuban American War of 1898. The United States also did not have military bases in Jamaica as it did in Trinidad. The relationship between Kingston and

Washington has been very cordial, except for a period under Michael Manley's administration. Today, American tourists frequently visit the island in large numbers, adding substantially to the economy. A busy flow of air traffic exists between Jamaica and United States as Jamaicans make frequent business trips to the United States. Immigrants make regular remittances to family and relatives in Jamaica and visit their "land of origin" regularly. Many of them maintain dual residence and vote in local elections.

In recent decades, the U.S. government has used economic and diplomatic clout to influence political and fiscal direction in Jamaica. In the late 1970s and 1980s, the U.S. government used clandestine activities to destabilize Manley's democratic socialist government. Consequently, Washington came under heavy criticism from Jamaican political analysts and politicians for supporting political violence in Jamaica during elections.

MILITARY

Jamaican membership in the U.S. Armed Forces began during World War I and continued during World War II. Jamaicans both in America and on the island were recruited for service in Europe and some of them were stationed at U.S. bases in the region. Since then, Jamaican Americans have worked in many different wings of the Armed Forces. During the Gulf War, the Head of the Joint Chiefs of Staff, General Colin Powell (born in New York City in 1937) was recognized as the America's most eminent second-generation Jamaican American. He served his country in the Armed Forces with academic and political distinction. He became a household name under the Bush administration and earned the admiration and respect of the nation; Random House has paid the retired four-star general $6.5 million to publish his memoirs.

INDIVIDUAL AND GROUP CONTRIBUTIONS

Jamaican immigrants contribute substantially to American political, cultural, religious, and educational life. Jamaican-born writers, athletes, teachers, musicians, poets, journalists, artists, professors, sports writers, actors, and other professionals who have lived in the United States have greatly enriched the American culture in many ways.

ACADEMIA

Jamaican-born John B. Russwurm was one of the first blacks to enter an American academy; he graduated with a B.A. from Baldwin College in 1826; Russwurm distinguished himself as the co-founder of *Freedom's Journal*, black America's first newspaper. Jamaican-born Leonard Barrett lived most of his adult life in the United States and taught at Temple University and other institutions for more than 30 years. Jamaican-born Orlando Patterson, professor of sociology at Harvard University, and economist George Beckford are recognized as leading social scientists in America.

FILM, TELEVISION, THEATER, AND OTHER VISUAL ARTS

Jamaicans have made contributions to the film and television industry in the United States. Louise Bennett-Coverly, better known as "Miss Lou," Jamaica's premier and world-renowned folklorist, has lived and performed in the United States for many years. She was born in Kingston, Jamaica, in 1919 and became a performer of stories, songs, and rhymes. At the age of 14, she began to write and dramatize poems using *patois* rather than standard English. In 1966, she will mark her sixtieth anniversary as a performer of poetry, story, and song. For her 50 years of contribution to Caribbean culture, she was named Jamaica's national poet and poet laureate in 1986. Her dramatic style, physical presence, and debonair theatrical equity have made her a legend in Jamaican and Jamaican American theater and has brought distinction to Jamaican *patois* on stage.

Other Jamaican American folklorists like Ranny Williams and Leonie Forbes have made a substantial contribution to the performing arts. Choreographer, scholar, literature laureate, and performer, Rex Nettleford, now vice chancellor of the University of the West Indies, has taken the Caribbean's premier National Dance Theater Company (NDTC) around the world and performed with distinction. The NDTC has won several awards and made several tours of the United States. The Sister Theater Group has also made several U.S. tours. The comedian Oliver Samuels has starred in *Oliver At Large* and *Doctors in Paradise*.

JOURNALISM

Modern Jamaican American journalists who have lived and studied in the United States are John

Maxwell, John Heame, Barbara Gloudon (former editor of the *Jamaica Gleaner* and the *Star*), Ronnie Thwaites, Adrian Robinson, Dennis Hall, and Morris Cargill (columnist). Carl Williams, editor and founder of *Black Culture* (1989), lives and works in the United States. Winston Smith, who lives in Brooklyn, works with *The Paper*.

LITERATURE

A number of contemporary Jamaican American scholars are well known in the field of literature. Claude McKay migrated from Jamaica to the United States in 1912 and became an important voice in the Harlem Renaissance; he wrote many novels, among them *Banana Bottom* and *This Island*. Many Jamaican poets have distinguished themselves in the field of literature: Adriza Mandiela wrote *Life of the Caribbean Immigrant, Living in America*. Louise Bennett-Coverly, poet laureate, has written dozens of poems and books on Caribbean life. Two literature laureates and scholars, Rex Nettleford and Sir Arthur Lewis, are well known in the United States. Afoa Cooper, Lillian Allen, Oliver Senior, Mutabaruka, Linton Kwasii Johnson, Gene Binta, Breeze, Opaimer Adisa, D'Janette Sears, Michael Smith, and a-dziao Simba, who wrote *25.40 P.M. Past Morning*, are only a few of the dozens of outstanding Jamaican American poets of modern times. Sheila Winter taught literature at Princeton University and Sir John Mordecai was a visiting professor at the same institution.

MUSIC

Well-known Rasta artists are: The Wailers, Big Youth, We the People, Ras Michael and the Sons of Negus, Peter Tosh, The I Threes, Light of Saba, and United Africa. Reggae rhythms are so popular and powerful that jazz musicians in Jamaica and the United States—Herbie Mann, Sonny Rollins, Roberta Flack, Johnny Nash, Eric Clapton, and Lennie Hibbert—are exploiting the potential of Rasta music with huge financial success. Other well-known Jamaican music stars are: Marjorie Wiley, a Jamaican folklorist, musician, and dancer; Marcia Griffiths, Tiger, Shine Head, and Freddie McGregor.

SPORTS

A number of Jamaicans and Jamaican Americans have excelled in international competition and carried home many trophies. Sir Herbert McDonald was an Olympian; Donald Quarrie won the 200, and the 4 x 100 meters Olympics Gold Medal; and Marlene Ottey won the 200 and the 4 x 100 meters. Some of the world's most outstanding cricketers were Jamaicans; they include: O. J. Collier Smith, Alfred Valentine, Roy Gilcrist, Michael Holding, Easton McMorris, Franze Alexander, and George Headley, who was born in Panama in 1909, transported to Cuba, grew up in Jamaica and lived in the United States.

MEDIA

PRINT

Caribbean Newsletter.

This quarterly acts as the voice of Friends for Jamaica, which supports Jamaican workers. Contains articles on political, economic, social, and agricultural issues.

Address: Friends for Jamaica, Box 20392, Cathedral Finance Station, New York, New York 10025.

The Correspondent.

A quarterly publication of the Congress of Racial Equality. Preserves and promotes the philosophical tenets initiated by Marcus Garvey; provides news and information concerning the right of blacks to govern themselves in areas that are demographically and geographically defined as theirs.

Contact: George W. Holmes, Editor.
Address: 30 Cooper Square, New York, New York 10003.
Telephone: (212) 598-4000.

There are many other newspapers and tabloids in the United States that cater to the Jamaican population in America. The journal *Cimmarron*, published by the City University of New York, discusses a variety of Caribbean issues, as does the Afro-centric magazine, *Black Culture*. *Everybody's Magazine* has a very wide readership, as does *New York Carib News*, founded in 1981 by Karl Rodney, the former president of the Jamaican Progressive Party. Additional publications include *Viewpoint* and *The Paper*. These publications provide news about different aspects of Jamaican life such as politics, current events, sports, and other issues of importance to the Caribbean. Newspapers also cover issues and concerns facing Caribbean Americans in the United States. The

Jamaica Gleaner and *The Star* are favorite daily papers in Miami and New York City.

RADIO AND TELEVISION

Jamaicans in the United States and Jamaica also receive up-to-the-minute news on CNN, C-Span, and other television stations in the international network. At the same time, the Jamaica Broadcasting Corporation (JBC) and Jamaican radio stations (like RJR) supply Jamaican Americans with current news of the island.

ORGANIZATIONS AND ASSOCIATIONS

Various organizations and funds exist to help Jamaican Americans. These include the St. Vincent Benefit and Education Fund, Jamaican Nurses Association and the Jamaican Policemen's School Alumni Association of New York. The Worker's Liberation League (WLL), founded in 1974, was once viewed as a communist party but it worked for the social and economic justice of blacks in New York City. The Brooklyn Council on the Arts, Caribbean Festival, The Jamaican Association of Greater Cleveland, The Cleveland Cricket Club, The New York Cricket Club (of Brooklyn), and The Third World Foundation located in Chicago are additional Jamaican organizations. Several Jamaican American clubs and organizations comprise alumni of several high schools in Jamaica. Alumni organizations include, MICA Old Student Association (MOSA), Cornwall College Association (CCA), St. Hughes High School Alumni Association (SHHAA), and the Montego Bay Boys Alumni Association (MBBAA).

SOURCES FOR ADDITIONAL STUDY

Alleyne, Mervyn C. *Roots of Jamaican Culture.* London: Pluto Press, 1988.

Blake, Judith. *Family Structure in Jamaica: The Social Context of Reproduction.* New York: The Free Press of Gencoe Inc., 1961.

Blustein, Howard L., Kathryn T. Johnson, et al. *Area Handbook for Jamaica.* Washington, D.C.: Federal Research Division, Library of Congress, 1976.

Campbell, Marvis C. *The Maroons of Jamaica 1655-1796: A History of Resistance, Collaboration and Betrayal.* Massachusetts: Bergin & Publishers Inc., 1988.

Carty, Hilary S. *Folk Dances of Jamaica: An Insight.* London: Dance Books, 1988.

Henriques, Fernado. *Jamaica: Land of Wood and Water.* London: Mac Gibbon & Kee, 1957.

Kessner, Thomas, and Betty Boyd Caroli. *Today's Immigrants: Their Stories; A New Look at the Newest Americans.* New York: Oxford University Press, 1982.

Luntta, Karl. *Jamaica Handbook.* California: Moon Publications, 1991.

Nicholas, Tracy. *Rastafari: A Way of Life.* New York; Arbor Books, 1979.

The economic position and socioeconomic mobility of Japanese Americans is much higher now than at any time in American history.

JAPANESE AMERICANS

by
Stanley E. Easton
and Lucien
Ellington

OVERVIEW

A country slightly larger than the United Kingdom (about the size of California), Japan lies off the eastern coast of the Asian continent. An archipelago, Japan consists of four main islands—Honshū, Hokkaidō, Kyūshū, and Shikoku—as well as 3,900 smaller islands. Japan has a total land area of 145,825 square miles (377,688 square kilometers). Much of Japan is extremely mountainous and almost the entire population lives on only one-sixth of the total land area. Of all the world's major nations, the Japanese have the highest population density per square mile of habitable land. Japan has virtually no natural resources except those found in the sea. To Japan's north, the nearest foreign soil is the Russian-controlled island of Sakhalin while the People's Republic of China and South Korea lie to the west of Japan.

The word, "Japan," is actually a Portuguese misunderstanding of the Chinese pronunciation of the Chinese term for the country. The actual name for the country is Nippon or Nihon ("source of the sun"). Japan has a population of approximately 124 million people. By the standards of other nations, the Japanese are one of the most homogeneous people on earth. Under two million foreigners (less than one percent of the total Japanese population) live in Japan. Koreans constitute well over one-half of resident minorities. There are also two indigenous minority groups in Japan, the Ainu and the Burakumin. The Ainu, a Caucasian people, number around 24,381 and live mainly in special reservations in central Hokkaidō. Ethnically, the approximately two million Burakumin are no different than other Japanese, but have traditionally engaged in low status occupations; and although they have the same legal status as their fellow citizens, they are often discriminated against. Shinto, an indigenous religion, is the most popular spiritual practice in Japan, followed by Buddhism, a Korean and Chinese import. Followers of other religions constitute less than one percent of the Japanese population. Culturally, the Japanese are children of China but have their own rich native culture and have also borrowed extensively from Western countries. Tokyo is Japan's capital and largest city. The national flag of Japan is a crimson disc, symbolizing the rising sun, in the center of a white field.

HISTORY

The oldest identified human remains found in Japan date from upper Paleolithic times of the last glacial period, about 30,000 B.C. While there is some dispute, most historians believe that political unity in Japan occurred at the end of the third century or the beginning of the fourth century A.D. The Yamato chiefs who unified the country developed an imperial line, which is the oldest in the world. However, early in Japanese history, emperors lost political authority. Compared to China, ancient and medieval Japan was undeveloped culturally. From early in Japanese history many Chinese imports including architecture, agricultural methods, Confucianism, and Buddhism profoundly influenced the Japanese. The Japanese established a pattern that still exists of selectively importing foreign customs and adapting them to the archipelago.

Medieval and early modern Japan was marked by long periods of incessant warfare as rival families struggled for power. While power struggles were still occurring, the Japanese had their first contact with Europe when Portuguese traders landed off southern Kyūshū in 1543. In 1603, through military conquest, Tokugawa Ieyasu established himself as ruler of the entire country. Early in the Tokugawa era, foreigners were expelled from Japan and the country was largely isolated from the rest of the world until Commodore Matthew C. Perry of the U.S. Navy forced Japan to open its doors in 1853.

THE MODERN ERA

Japan's modern history began in 1868 when a number of citizens led by Satsuma and Chosū domains overthrew the Tokugawas. In the decades that followed Japan feverishly modernized in an attempt to end Western efforts at dominance. By the early twentieth century, Japan possessed a rapidly industrializing economy and a strong military. At first the rest of Asia was excited by Japan's rise. However, the militarization of Japan in the 1930s, and Japan's attempt to dominate the rest of Asia, resulted in the Pacific War that pitted much of Asia and a number of Western countries (including the United States) against Japan. In August 1945, a devastated Japan accepted the surrender terms of the Allied powers. The subsequent American occupation resulted in major political and economic change as Japan became a democracy, renounced militarism, and resumed its impressive economic growth. Today, Japan is a stable democracy among the world's economic superpowers.

MIGRATION TO HAWAII AND AMERICA

In 1835, American settlers established the sugar plantation system in Hawaii, which was then an independent monarchy. The sugar plantations required large numbers of workers to cultivate and harvest the cane fields and to operate the sugar refineries. Beginning in 1852, the plantation owners imported Chinese laborers. In many ways, this "coolie" trade resembled the African slave trade.

By 1865, many of the Chinese were leaving the plantations for other jobs. Hawaii's foreign minister, a sugar planter, wrote to an American businessman in Japan seeking Japanese agricultural workers. On May 17, 1868, the *Scioto* sailed from Yokohama for Honolulu with 148 Japanese—141 men, six women, and two children—aboard. These laborers included samurai, cooks, *sake* brewers, potters, printers, tailors, wood workers, and one hairdresser. Plantation labor was harsh; the monthly wage was $4, of which the planters withheld 50 percent. The ten-hour work days were hard on the soft hands of potters, printers, and tailors. Forty of these first Japanese farm laborers returned to Japan before completion of their three-year contracts. Once back home, 39 of them signed a public statement charging the planters with cruelty and breach of contract.

On May 27, 1869, the Pacific Mail Company's *China* brought a party of samurai, farmers, tradesmen, and four women to San Francisco.

These Japanese had been displaced from their homes by the ending of the Tokugawa shogunate and the restoration of the Meiji emperor. Followers of lord Matsudaira Katamori established the 600-acre Wakamatsu Tea and Silk Farm Colony on the Sacramento River at Placerville. The colony failed in less than two years because the mulberry trees and tea seedlings perished in the dry California soil. A few of the settlers returned to Japan while the rest drifted away from the colony seeking new beginnings. Such were the origins of the first-generation Japanese (*Issei*) on Hawaiian and American shores.

EFFORTS TO BAN JAPANESE IMMIGRATION

The U. S. Congress passed the Chinese Exclusion Act in 1882, prohibiting further Chinese immigration. In 1886, Hawaii and Japan signed a labor convention that led to large numbers of Japanese contract workers in Hawaii and student laborers in California. The increase of Japanese in California gave rise to an anti-Japanese movement and a 1906 San Francisco school board order segregating Japanese American students. Ninety-three students of Japanese ancestry and a number of Korean students were ordered to attend the school for Chinese. The Japanese government was insulted. President Theodore Roosevelt, wishing to maintain harmonious relations with Japan, condemned anti-Japanese agitation and the school segregation order. He advocated naturalization of the Issei, but never sponsored introduction of a bill to accomplish it. Political reaction against Roosevelt in California was fierce. Several anti-Japanese bills were introduced in the California legislature in 1907. President Roosevelt called San Francisco school officials and California legislative leaders to Washington. After a week of negotiations, the Californians agreed to allow most Japanese children (excluding overage students and those with limited English) to attend regular public schools. Roosevelt promised to limit Japanese labor immigration. In late 1907 and early 1908 Japan and the United States corresponded on the matter. Japan agreed to stop issuing passports to laborers in the United States. The United States allowed Japanese who had already been to America to return and agreed to accept immediate family members of Japanese workers already in the country. This was the so-called "Gentlemen's Agreement."

Under the Gentlemen's Agreement some Japanese migration to the United States continued. Between 1908 and 1924, many of the immigrants were women brought by husbands who had returned to Japan to marry. Between 1909 and 1920, the number of married Japanese women doubled in Hawaii and quadrupled on the mainland. Most of the Japanese women who migrated to Hawaii and the United States during that period were "picture brides." Marriages were arranged by parents. Go-betweens brokered agreements between families. Couples were married while the bride was in Japan and the groom was in the United States. Husband and wife met for the first time upon their arrival at the pier in Honolulu, San Francisco, or Seattle, using photographs to identify one another. This wave of immigration changed the nature of the Japanese American community from a male migrant laborer community to a family-oriented people seeking permanent settlement.

By 1924, many Americans favored restricting immigration through a quota system aimed primarily at restricting European immigration without discriminating against any country. Such a bill passed the U. S. House of Representatives in April 1924. U.S. Senator Hiram Johnson of California, however, wanted a ban on all immigration from Japan. Hoping to avoid offending the Japanese government further, Secretary of State Charles Evans Hughes asked the Japanese ambassador to write a letter summarizing the Gentlemen's Agreement of 1907-1908 since its provisions were not widely known. Ambassador Masanao Hanihara wrote the letter and included an appeal to the senators to reject any bill halting Japanese immigration. He referred to "the grave consequences" that exclusion would have upon relations between his country and the United States. Senator Henry Cabot Lodge of Massachusetts, who chaired the Foreign Relations Committee, called Hanihara's letter a "veiled threat" and led the Senate to incorporate Japanese exclusion into the immigration bill. President Coolidge signed the Immigration Act of 1924, including the ban on further Japanese immigration, into law on May 24. Japanese immigration was curtailed until 1952, except for post World War II Japanese brides of U.S. servicemen.

POST WORLD WAR II IMMIGRATION

In 1952 the McCarran-Walter Act allowed immigration from South and East Asia. The new law ended Japanese exclusion, but was still racially discriminatory. Asian countries were allowed 100 immigrants each, while immigration from European countries was determined by the national

Japanese immigrants
arrive in San Francisco,
California, in 1920.

origins quotas of the Immigration Act of 1924. The McCarran-Walter Act also repealed the racial clauses in the naturalization law of 1790 that forbade non-white immigrants from obtaining American citizenship. Over 46,000 Japanese immigrants, including many elderly Issei, became naturalized citizens by 1965.

The Immigration Act of 1965 abolished the national origin quotas and annually permitted the admission of 170,000 immigrants from the Eastern Hemisphere and 120,000 from the Western Hemisphere. Twenty thousand immigrants per year per Asian country were allowed to enter the United States. This law opened the way for the second wave of Asian immigration and resulted in a new composition of the Asian American population. In 1960, 52 percent of the Asian American population were Japanese American. In 1985 only 15 percent of Asian Americans were Japanese. Between 1965 and 1985, there were nearly four times as many Asian immigrants as there had been between 1849 and 1965.

JAPANESE AMERICANS TODAY

According to the 1990 census figures, there were 847,562 Japanese Americans in the United States. About 723,000 of the Japanese Americans lived in the West, 312,989 of those in California. Today there are Japanese Americans located in each of the 50 states.

Recent decades have brought not only legal and institutional changes but positive attitudinal change on the part of many white Americans toward Japanese Americans. The combination of legal and attitudinal change, along with the higher levels of education that Japanese Americans tend to attain, compared to whites, have resulted in a reversal of the dismal situation of overeducated and underemployed Japanese Americans that existed in the 1930s. Today, substantial numbers of Japanese Americans are employed by corporations and are members of professions that require college educations. Still, however, Japanese Americans experience problems that are a direct result of racially based misperceptions that some members of the majority population hold.

Many white Americans, particularly well-educated white Americans, think of Japanese Americans as a "model minority" because of their reputation for hard work and their high educational attainment. Despite this reputation, many Japanese as well as other Asian Americans complain that they are stereotyped as good technicians but not aggressive enough to occupy top managerial and leadership positions. Anti-Asian graffiti can sometimes be found at top universities where at least some white students voice jealousy and resentment toward perceived Asian American academic success.

Recent economic competition between the United States and Japan has resulted in a rise in anti-Japanese sentiment on the part of many Americans. The 1982 murder of Vincent Chin, a young Chinese man in Detroit, by two auto workers who mistook him to be a Japanese is one grisly example of these sentiments. Third- and fourth-generation Japanese Americans often cite incidents of fellow Americans making anti-Japanese statements in their presence or mistaking them for Japanese nationals.

The issue of cultural revitalization is not related to racial attitudes but is still serious to many Japanese Americans. Because of the amazing success of Japan's economy since World War II, the number of Japanese immigrating annually has been far below the 20,000 quota allotted to Japan. In recent years, Japanese immigrants have constituted less than two percent of all Asian immigrants. As a result, the Japanese towns of large American cities are not being culturally renewed and many second- and third-generation Japanese have moved to the suburbs. Many third- and fourth-generation Japanese Americans are not literate in the Japanese language. Unlike the lingering prejudices toward Japanese Americans, the over-assimilation problem may very well have no ultimate solution.

ACCULTURATION AND ASSIMILATION

In the United States, Japanese Americans built Buddhist temples and Christian churches. They built halls to serve as language schools and as places for dramas, films, judo lessons, poetry readings, potlucks, and parties. They constructed sumō rings, baseball fields, and bath houses. They also established hotels, restaurants, bars, and billiard parlors. Japanese Americans opened shops to provide Japanese food and herbal medicines.

The Issei faced many restrictions. They were excluded from some occupations, could not own land, and could not become U.S. citizens. They faced discrimination and prejudice. The Issei's pleasure was in seeing the success of their children. Despite their poverty, the Issei developed large, close-knit families. They encouraged their children (Nisei) to become educated and obtain white collar jobs rather than stay in farming communities. This drove the Nisei into close associations and friendships with Caucasians. The Nisei were educated in American schools and learned white middle-class American values. Hierarchical thinking, characteristic of Japanese culture, led to pressure to achieve academically and to compete successfully in the larger Caucasian-dominated society.

Between 1915 and 1967 the proportion of Japanese Americans living in predominantly Japanese American neighborhoods fell from 30 percent to four percent. With the end of World War II, prejudice and discrimination against Japanese Americans declined. The majority of Nisei now live in largely Caucasian neighborhoods. Their children (Sansei) have been schooled there and have mostly Caucasian associations. A majority of Sansei are unfamiliar with the Japanese American world characterized by intimate primary, communal association, and close social control. They rarely see members of their clan. Their world has been that of Little League and fraternities and sororities. Whereas only ten percent of Nisei married outside their ethnic group, about 50 percent of the Sansei did.

Many Sansei long to know more about their cultural roots, although the ways of their grandparents are alien to them. They are concerned over the demise of Japanese values. They seek to preserve their Japanese culture through service to the Japanese community at centers for the elderly, participation in community festivals, involvement with Asian political and legal organizations, and patronizing Japanese arts.

In *Japanese Americans*, sociologist Harry Kitano observed that Japanese Americans developed a congruent Japanese culture within the framework of American society. This was due to necessity rather than choice, since there was little opportunity for the first Japanese immigrants to enter into the social structure of the larger com-

munity. Now most Japanese Americans can enter into that social structure. Nisei and Sansei continue to identify themselves as Japanese Americans, but that identity is of little importance to them as members and partakers of a larger society that is not hostile toward them as it was to the Issei. The degree to which Japanese Americans have been assimilated into the predominant culture is unusual for a nonwhite group. Coexistence between Japanese and American cultures has been successful due to the willingness of both cultures to accommodate to one another.

Japanese American history brings us to some critical questions. What the future holds for fourth-generation Japanese Americans (the Yonsei) is unclear. The Japanese American ethnic community may disappear in that generation, or complete assimilation may bring about the demise of the values that pushed Japanese Americans to socioeconomic success. It is uncertain whether the Yonsei will retain their Japanese characteristics and inculcate them in the next generation.

TRANSPLANTED TRADITIONS

In Japanese American communities many Japanese still celebrate New Year's Day very much in the manner the Issei did, following the customs of Meiji-era Japan. New Year is a time for debts to be paid and quarrels to be settled. It is an occasion when houses are cleaned, baths are taken, and new clothes are worn. On New Year's Eve, many Japanese Americans go to temples and shrines. Shinto shrines are especially popular. Just inside the red tori gate, worshippers wash their hands and rinse their mouths with water from the special basin. Then a priest cleanses them by sprinkling water from a leafy branch on them and blesses them by waving a wand of white prayer papers. The people sip sake, receive amulets (charms), and give money.

In Japanese American homes where the traditions are observed, New Year's offerings are set in various places of honor around the house. The offering consists of two *mochi* (rice cakes), a strip of *konbu* (seaweed), and a citrus arranged on a "happiness paper" depicting one or all of the seven gods of good luck. The offerings symbolize harmony and happiness from generation to generation.

At breakfast on New Year's Day many Japanese Americans eat *ozoni*, a toasted *mochi*, in a broth with other ingredients such as vegetables and fish. *Mochi* is eaten for strength and family cohesiveness. Sometimes children compete with each other to see if they can eat *mochi* equal to the number of their years.

Friends, neighbors, and family members visit one another on New Year's Day. Special foods served include *kuromame* (black beans), *kazunoko* (herring eggs), *konbumaki* (seaweed roll), *kinton* (mashed sweet potato and chestnut), and *kamaboko* (fish cakes). Also, *sushi* (rice rolled in seaweed), *nishime* (vegetables cooked in stock), *sashimi* (raw fish), and cooked red snapper are commonly provided for New Year's guests. At many celebrations the Japanese cheer of "*Banzai! Banzai! Banzai!*" rings out. That salute, which originated around 200 B.C.E., means 10,000 years.

HEALTH AND MENTAL HEALTH ISSUES

As a rule, Japanese Americans are healthier than other Americans. Japanese Americans have the lowest infant death rate of any ethnic group in the United States In 1986, 86 percent of babies born to Japanese American mothers were born to women who had received early prenatal care, compared to 79 percent for Caucasians and 76 percent for all races. Relatively few Japanese American infants have low birth weight and only eight percent of Japanese American births were preterm, compared to ten percent for all races in 1987. Asian Americans have fewer birth defects than Native Americans, Caucasians, or African Americans, but more than Hispanic Americans. Asian and Pacific Islanders were two percent of the U.S. population in 1981-1988, but accounted for only one percent of all U.S. AIDS cases during that period. In October of 1987 less than one percent of drug abuse clients in the United States were Asian Americans.

A study comparing the health status of Japanese and Caucasians over the age of 60 in Hawaii revealed that better health could be predicted from younger age, higher family income, maintenance of work role, and Japanese ethnicity (Marvelu R. Peterson and others, "A Cross-Cultural Health Study of Japanese and Caucasian Elders in Hawaii," *International Journal of Aging and Human Development*, Volume 21, 1985, pp. 267-279). The better health of Japanese Americans in Hawaii may be due to cultural values such as the priority of family interests over those of the individual, reverence for elders, and obligation to care for elders.

Many Japanese Americans consider the use of mental health services as shameful. They tend to use them only as a last resort in severe disorders, such as schizophrenia. Japanese Americans underuse mental health services in comparison to other ethnic groups. They believe the causes of mental illness to be associated with organic factors, a lack of will power, and morbid thinking. They tend to seek help from family members or close friends, rather than from mental health professionals. Further, since Japanese Americans tend to somaticize psychological problems, they may seek help from traditional medical practitioners instead of mental health professionals. There are, however, a number of Japanese American psychiatrists in practice today, indicating greater acceptance of the need for professional mental health care.

LANGUAGE

The Japanese language is unique and has no close relationship to any other language, such as English does to German, or French does to Spanish. It is a popular misconception that Japanese and Chinese are similar. Although many kanji, or ideograms, were borrowed from classical Chinese, the two spoken languages do not have a single basic feature in common. The origins of Japanese are obscure, and only Korean can be considered to belong to the same linguistic family. Spoken Japanese was in existence long before kanji reached Japan. While there is some variation in dialect throughout Japan, variance in pronunciation and vocabulary is, in general, quite small.

Japanese is easy to pronounce and bears some similarity to the Romance languages. The five short vowels in Japanese order are "a," "e," "i," "o," and "u." They are pronounced clearly and crisply. The same vowels in the long form are pronounced by doubling the single vowel and making a continuous sound equal to two identical short vowels. Japanese consonants approximately resemble English.

Some useful daily expressions include: *Ohayōgozaimasu*—good morning; *Konnichiwa*—hello; *Kombanwa*—good evening; *Sayōnara*—good-bye; *Oyasumi nasai*—good night; *Okaeri nasai*—welcome home; *O-genki desu ka*—how are you; *Dōmo arigatō gozaimasu*—thank you very much; *Chotto matte kudasai*—wait just a moment please.

Many linguists believe that Japanese is the world's most difficult written language. Written Japanese consists of three types of characters: kanji, hiragana, and katakana. Kanji, which means "Chinese characters," are ideograms, or pictorial representations of ideas. Kanji were imported into Japan sometime during the fifth century A.D. from China via Korea. Although there are said to be some 48,000 kanji in existence, roughly 4,000 characters are commonly used. The Ministry of Education identified 1,850 kanji (called tōyō kanji) in 1946 as essential for official and general public use. In 1981 this list was superseded by a similar but larger one (called jōyō kanji) containing 1,945 characters. These are taught to all students in elementary and secondary school. Kanji are used in writing the main parts of a sentence such as verbs and nouns, as well as names. Kanji are the most difficult written Japanese characters, requiring as many as 23 separate strokes.

Since spoken Japanese existed before kanji reached Japan, the Japanese adopted the Chinese ideograms to represent spoken Japanese words of the same or related meanings. Since the sounds of Japanese words signifying the ideas were not the same as the sounds of the Chinese words, it became important to develop a writing system to represent the Japanese sound. Therefore, the Japanese developed two sets of characters, hiragana and katakana, from original Chinese characters. Each kana, as these two systems are called, is a separate phonetic syllabary and each hiragana character has a corresponding katakana character. Hiragana and katakana characters are similar to English letters in that each character represents a separate phonetic sound. Hiragana are used in writing verb endings, adverbs, conjunctions, and various sentence particles and are written in a cursive, smooth style. Katakana, which are used mainly in writing foreign words, are written in a more angular, stiff style. Both hiragana and katakana are easy to write compared with kanji. In modern written Japanese, kanji, hiragana, and katakana are combined. Traditionally, Japanese is written vertically and read from top to bottom and right to left. Now, most business writing is done horizontally because it is easier to include numerals and English words. Even though the written language is illogical, in many ways, it has aesthetic appeal and contributes to a feeling on the part of many Japanese that they are unique among the world's peoples. For a variety of reasons, including negative pressures by the majority population and a lack of new Japanese immigrants in the United States, many third- and fourth-generation Japanese Americans do not know the language of their ancestors.

FAMILY AND COMMUNITY DYNAMICS

Communalism did not develop in overseas Japanese communities as it did among the overseas Chinese. In the fifteenth and sixteenth centuries Japan's land-based lineage community gave way to downsized extended families. Only the eldest son and his family remained in the parental household. Other sons established separate "branch" households when they married. In Japan, a national consciousness arose while in China, the primary allegiance remained to the clan-based village or community. Thus, Japanese immigrants were prepared to form families and rear children in a manner similar to that of white Americans. The "picture bride" system brought several thousand Japanese women to the United States to establish nuclear branch families.

The "picture bride" system was fraught with misrepresentation. Often old photographs were used to hide the age of a prospective bride and the men sometimes were photographed in borrowed suits. The system led to a degree of disillusionment and incompatibility in marriages. The women were trapped, unable to return to Japan. Nevertheless, these women persevered for themselves and their families and transmitted Japanese culture through child rearing. The Issei women were also workers. They worked for wages or shared labor on family farms. Two-income families found it easier to rent or purchase land.

By 1930, second-generation Japanese Americans constituted 52 percent of the continental U.S. population of their ethnic group. In the years preceding World War II, most Nisei were children and young people, attempting to adapt to their adopted country in spite of the troubled lives of their parents. For many young people the adaptation problem was made even more ambiguous because their parents, concerned that their children would not have a future in the United States, registered their offspring as citizens of Japan. By 1940, over half of the Nisei held Japanese as well as American citizenship. Most of the Nisei did not want to remain on family farms or in the roadside vegetable business and with the strong encouragement of their parents obtained high school, and in many cases, university educations. Discrimination against Japanese Americans, coupled with the shortage of jobs during the Great Depression, thwarted many Nisei dreams.

The dual-career family seems to be the norm for Sansei households. Recently, spousal abuse has surfaced as an issue. If it was a problem in previous generations, it was not public knowledge. In San Francisco an Asian women's shelter has been established, largely by third-generation Asian women.

In Japanese tradition, a crane represents 1,000 years. On special birthdays 1,000 hand-folded red *origami* cranes are displayed to convey wishes for a long life. Certain birthdays are of greater importance because they are thought to be auspicious or calamitous years in a person's life. For men, the forty-second birthday is considered the most calamitous. For women it is the thirty-third year. Especially festive celebrations are held on these birthdays to ward off misfortune. The sixty-first birthday is the beginning of the auspicious years and the beginning of a person's second childhood. Traditionally, a person in his or her second childhood wears a crimson cap. The seventy-seventh birthday is marked by the wearing of a loose red coat (*chanchan ko*) over one's clothes. The most auspicious birthday is the eighty-eighth, when the honoree wears both the crimson cap and the *chanchan ko*.

At a wedding dinner, a whole red snapper is displayed at the head table. The fish represents happiness and must be served whole because cutting it would mean eliminating some happiness. Silver and golden wedding anniversaries are also occasions for festive celebrations.

RELIGION

While virtually all Issei came to the United States as Buddhists, Christian missionaries worked at converting the immigrants from the very beginning. The Methodists were particularly successful in this effort and records of the Pacific Japanese Provisional Conference of the Methodist Church indicate that three immigrants from Japan were converted in 1877, 11 years before Japan legally allowed citizens to emigrate. In the beginning the Japanese, even though they understood no Chinese, were segregated into Chinese churches. By the latter part of the nineteenth century and the early years of the twentieth century, separate Japanese Christian churches and missions were established in various California cities as well as in Tacoma, Washington, and Denver, Colorado. These early Japanese Christian organizations usually offered night English classes and social activities as well. While Methodism remained, other denominations such as Presbyterians, Baptists, Congregationalists, Episcopalians, and Catholics also claimed converts.

Organized Buddhism was somewhat slow in attempting to minister to the spiritual needs of Japanese Americans. The first record of Japanese Buddhist priests in the United States was in 1893 when four of them attended the World Parliament of Religions in Chicago. The priests had limited contact, however, with Japanese Americans. The success of one San Francisco Methodist minister, Yasuzo Shimizu, in winning converts stimulated a Japanese American to return to his native land and pressure priests of the Nishi Honganji sect of the Jodo Shinshu denomination to begin establishing Buddhist churches in the United States. The arrival in San Francisco of two Nishi Honganji priests, Shuyei Sonoda and Kukuryo Nishijima, on September 2, 1899, is regarded as the founding date for the Buddhist Churches of America. By the early years of the twentieth century, a number of Buddhist churches were founded on the West Coast. Today, Jodo Shinshu, organized as the Buddhist Churches of America with headquarters in San Francisco, is the dominant Buddhist denomination in the United States. However, Zen, Nichiren, and Shingon sects of Buddhism are represented in various cities throughout the United States. While only a minuscule number of Japanese Americans practice Zen Buddhism, this particular sect has exercised a profound influence on many artists, musicians, philosophers, and writers who are members of the majority American population.

Because of cultural assimilation it is difficult to obtain statistics on the religious practices of Japanese Americans. However, followers of Christianity are probably more numerous than Buddhists.

EMPLOYMENT AND ECONOMIC TRADITIONS

The Issei, who came to the United States in the late 1800s and early twentieth century, worked on the West Coast as contract seasonal agricultural workers, on the railroad, and in canneries. For the most part, working conditions were abysmal; and because of racism and pressure by organized labor, Issei were barred from factory and office work. As a result many Japanese Americans created small businesses such as hotels and restaurants to serve their own ethnic group or became small vegetable farmers. The term "ethnic economy" is often used to describe the activities of pre-World War II Japanese Americans. While Japanese produce interests sold to the majority population from the beginning, the grower, wholesaler, and retailer networks were Issei. Issei were remarkably successful in both of these endeavors for several different reasons. Small businessmen, farmers, their families, and work associates toiled an incredible number of hours and saved much of what was earned. Also, the Issei community was well organized, and small businesses and farms could rely upon their tightly knit ethnic group for capital, labor, and business opportunities. Ethnic solidarity paid off economically for Japanese Americans. By the eve of World War II, 75 percent of Seattle's Japanese residents were involved in small business, and Japanese farmers were responsible for the production of the majority of vegetables in Los Angeles County.

Japanese economic success caused a substantial white backlash spearheaded by elements of the majority population who felt their livelihoods threatened. Unions were consistently anti-Japanese for a variety of reasons and California agricultural groups assumed leadership roles in the land limitation laws. The laws resulted, between 1920 and 1925, in the number of acres owned by Issei declining from 74,769 to 41,898 and the acreage leased plummeting from 192,150 to 76,797.

POST WORLD WAR II ECONOMIC CHANGES

No event in history has resulted in more economic change for Japanese Americans than World War II. Before the war Japanese Americans constituted mostly a self-contained ethnic economy. The internment of Japanese Americans and societal changes in attitudes toward Japanese destroyed much of the pre-war economic status quo. Since the war a minority of Japanese Americans have been employed in Japanese American-owned businesses. Many Japanese American farmers, because of the internment, either sold their land or never were able to lease their pre-war holdings again. As a result of the internment, Japanese Americans also sold or closed many family businesses. A comparison of pre-war and post-war economic statistics in Los Angeles and Seattle illustrates these major changes. Before World War II, Japanese Americans in Seattle operated 206 hotels, 140 grocery stores, 94 cleaning establishments, 64 market stands and 57 wholesale produce houses. After World War II, only a handful of these businesses remained. In Los Angeles, 72 percent of Japanese Americans were employed in family enterprises before World War II. By the late 1940s, only 17.5 percent of Japanese Americans earned their livelihood through family businesses.

While these economic changes were largely forced upon Japanese Americans because of the events surrounding the internment, other societal factors also contributed to the end of the Japanese American ethnic economy. The pre-war racial prejudice against Japanese Americans declined substantially in the late 1940s and 1950s. Japan no longer constituted a geo-political threat; many Americans were becoming more sympathetic about the issue of minority rights; and Japanese American West Coast agricultural interests no longer were seen as threatening by other Americans. As a result of these events, the large majority of Japanese Americans in the post-war years have experienced assimilation into the larger economy.

THE CONTEMPORARY ECONOMIC POSITION OF JAPANESE AMERICANS

Today, because of the changes in the post-war years, Japanese Americans are well-represented in both the professions and corporate economy. The pre-war discrimination against university-educated Japanese Americans is largely ended. Japanese Americans today have higher levels of education on average than the majority population and comparable to slightly higher incomes. Studies documenting the absence of Asian Americans from top corporate management and public sector administrative positions provide some evidence that there is some sort of "glass-ceiling" for Japanese Americans still present in the larger economy. Still, the economic position and socioeconomic mobility of Japanese Americans is much higher now than at any time in American history.

POLITICS AND GOVERNMENT

JAPANESE AMERICAN LABOR MOVEMENTS

In February 1903, 500 Japanese and 200 Mexican farm workers in Oxnard, California, formed the Japanese Mexican Labor Association, the first farm workers union in California history. Led by Kozaburo Baba, the union called a strike for better wages and working conditions. By March 1903, membership had grown to 1,200 members, about 90 percent of the work force. On March 23 a Mexican striker was shot and killed and two Mexicans and two Japanese were wounded in a confrontation with the Western Agricultural Contracting Company, the major labor contractor. Negotiations led to a settlement by the end of March. Despite such effective organization and leadership, however, the American Federation of Labor denied the Japanese Mexican Labor Association a charter, due to its opposition to Asians.

In Hawaii there were 20 strikes by Japanese plantation workers in 1900 alone. In 1908 the Higher Wage Association asked for an increase from $18 to $22.50 per month. In May 1909, 7,000 Japanese workers struck all major plantations on Oahu. The strike lasted four months. The planters branded the strike as the work of agitators and evicted the strikers from plantation-owned homes. By June, over 5,000 displaced Japanese were living in makeshift shelters in downtown Honolulu. The leaders of the Higher Wage Association were arrested, jailed, and tried on conspiracy charges. The Association called off the strike about two weeks before their leadership was convicted.

In 1920 the Japanese Federation of Labor struck the Hawaiian plantations for higher wages, better working conditions, and an end to discriminatory wages based on race and ethnic background. The strike lasted six months and cost the plantation owners an estimated $11.5 million. The union saw their cause as part of the American way. Hawaii's ruling class—the plantation owners and their allies—called the strike anti-American and painted it as a movement to take control of the sugar industry. The planters evicted over 12,000 workers from their homes. Many deaths resulted from unsanitary conditions in the tent cities that arose.

WARTIME INTERNMENT OF JAPANESE AMERICANS

The great plantation strike of 1920 generated fears within the U.S. government that the labor movement in Hawaii was part of a Japanese plot to take over the territory. Japanese Americans accounted for about 40 percent of the Hawaiian population in the 1920s and 1930s. Beginning in the 1920s, the U.S. Army viewed the presence of Japanese in the Hawaiian Islands as a military threat. The army formulated plans for the declaration of martial law, registration of enemy aliens, internment of Japanese who were considered security risks, and controls over labor. On the afternoon of December 7, 1941, the United States declared martial law, suspension of *habeas corpus*,

and restrictions on civil liberties, following the attack by the Japanese navy on U.S. naval and army bases at Pearl Harbor.

Immediately after the bombing of Pearl Harbor American officials in Hawaii began rounding up Japanese Americans. A concentration camp was established on Sand Island, a flat, barren, coral island at the mouth of Pearl Harbor. Terror and punishment were applied to the internees. Terror techniques included strip searches, frequent roll calls, threats to shoot, and excessive display of firepower by the guards who were armed with machine guns and pistols. The prisoners were often forced to eat in the rain, use dirty utensils, and sleep in tents. Ultimately, the army held 1,466 Japanese Americans in Hawaii and sent 1,875 to mainland camps such as Fort Lincoln (North Dakota), Fort Missoula (Montana), Santa Fe (New Mexico), and Crystal City (Texas).

General Delos Emmons, military governor of Hawaii, recognized that Japanese American labor was essential to the territory's economic survival. Therefore, he resisted pressure from Washington to intern more Japanese Americans. Those Japanese Americans in Hawaii who were not interned were required to carry alien registration cards at all times. They were to observe a curfew that applied only to them and were forbidden to write or publish attacks or threats against the U.S. government.

On the U. S. mainland, Japanese Americans were not considered essential to the economy or the war effort. On February 19, 1942, President Franklin D. Roosevelt signed Executive Order 9066 authorizing the army to designate military areas from which "any or all persons may be excluded" and to provide transportation, food, and shelter for persons so excluded. Lt. General John L. DeWitt, commander of the Western Defense Command, issued proclamations dividing Washington, Oregon, California, and Arizona into military areas from which enemy aliens and all Japanese Americans would be excluded. These proclamations also laid down a curfew between 8:00 p.m. and 6:00 a.m. for enemy aliens and all Japanese, aliens and citizens alike.

RESPONSES TO THE INTERNMENT

While some in the majority population objected to the oppressive treatment of loyal American residents and citizens, most Americans either approved or were neutral about the actions of our government. Wartime American propaganda about the Japanese reflected long-held racist attitudes of many Americans. While cartoonists depicted Germans as buffoons, Japanese were typically caricatured as apes or monkeys.

On December 7, 1941, there were about 1,500 Nisei recruits in U.S. Army units in Hawaii. On December 10 the army disarmed them and confined them to quarters under armed guard. Two days later they were re-armed and placed on beach patrol. On June 5, 1942, after rounding them up and disarming them again, the army organized 1,432 Japanese American soldiers into the Hawaiian Provisional Battalion and shipped them to Camp McCoy, Wisconsin. There, they trained for seven months, initially with wooden guns. The Nisei from Hawaii were joined by other Japanese American soldiers, mostly volunteers and draftees from mainland concentration camps, to form the segregated 100th Infantry Battalion and the 442nd Regimental Combat Team. Many Nisei argued that serving the United States in war against Japan and her Axis allies would prove their loyalty and worth as citizens and overcome the discrimination from which they suffered. In all, about 33,000 Japanese Americans served the United States' cause in World War II.

Other patriotic Japanese Americans saw the situation differently. In 1943, about 200 Nisei at the Heart Mountain concentration camp in Wyoming formed the Fair Play Committee (FPC) to resist conscription into the armed services. The FPC published a manifesto that read in part, "We, the Nisei, have been complacent and too inarticulate to the unconstitutional acts that we were subjected to. If ever there was a time or cause for decisive action, IT IS NOW!" The Fair Play Committee protested denial of their rights as citizens without due process, without any charges being filed against them, and without any evidence of wrongdoing on their part. In June 1944, at the end of the largest draft resistance trial in U.S. history, 63 Nisei resisters were sentenced to three years in prison. On Christmas Eve 1947, President Harry S Truman pardoned them.

From the beginning, Japanese Americans sought to right the wrong of interning up to 120,000 innocent civilians. Mitsuye Endo agreed to serve as the test case against the internment program in 1942. On December 18, 1944, the U.S. Supreme Court unanimously declared the detention of Japanese Americans unconstitutional and ordered Endo's immediate release. One day before the ruling, and in anticipation of it, the Western Defense Command of the U.S. Army announced the termination of its exclusion of loyal Japanese Americans from the West Coast, effective January 2, 1945.

After the war, many Japanese Americans returned home from the camps or the armed services and went to work to secure their rights and redress the wrongs committed against them. In Hawaii, Daniel K. Inouye, a decorated veteran, entered politics. He served in the U.S. House of Representatives from 1959 to 1962. He was elected to the U.S. Senate in 1962. Along with three other Japanese American legislators (Senator Spark M. Matsunaga of Hawaii and Representatives Norman Y. Mineta and Robert T. Matsui of California), Inouye sponsored a bill to apologize for the wartime internment and offer cash payments of $20,000 (tax-free) to each of the 60,000 victims still living. Congress enacted the bill in 1988, but because Congress failed to appropriate the necessary funds, a second bill had to be passed in 1989 to assure the payments.

INDIVIDUAL AND GROUP CONTRIBUTIONS

ACADEMIA

Harry H. L. Kitano (1926-), a native of San Francisco, is a professor of sociology at UCLA, where he holds an endowed chair in Japanese American studies.

ARCHITECTURE

Minoru Yamasaki (1912-1986) designed the World Trade Center in New York City. Its twin towers, erected in 1970-1977, rise 110 stories high.

ART

Perhaps the most famous Japanese American sculptor was Isamu Noguchi. His work extended beyond sculpture to include important architectural projects and stage designs, including designs for the Martha Graham Dance Company.

Ruth Asawa (1926-) is a Nisei artist known for her wire mesh sculptures and bronzed "baker's clay" sculptures. She is co-founder of the School of the Arts Foundation in San Francisco.

Isami Doi (1903-1965) exhibited his art works widely. Born and reared in Hawaii, he studied art at the University of Hawaii, Columbia University, and in Paris.

Toyo Miyatake (1895-1979) was a noted photographic artist and a leader in the Los Angeles Little Tokyo Community. During World War II, he and his family were interned at Manzanar, California, where he was allowed to take photographs documenting life in the camp. After the war he reopened his studio.

FILM, MUSIC, AND ENTERTAINMENT

Philip Kan Gotanda (1949-), a playwright, musician, and director, is best known for musicals and plays about the Japanese American experience and family life. His plays include *The Avocado Kid*, *The Wash*, *A Song for a Nisei Fisherman*, *Bullet Headed Birds*, *The Dream of Kitamura*, *Yohen*, *Yankee Dawg You Die*, and *American Tatoo*.

Sessue Hayakawa (1890-1973) was a leading figure in silent films. After an absence of many years, he returned to Hollywood filmmaking in the 1950s and won an Academy Award for his portrayal of Colonel Saito in *The Bridge on the River Kwai*.

Hiroshima is a Sansei pop music group which blends traditional Japanese instruments into jazz.

Makoto (Mako) Iwamatsu (1933-) was the founding artistic director of the East West Players, an Asian American theater company in Los Angeles. He was nominated for an Academy Award for his supporting role as a Chinese coolie in *The Sand Pebbles*.

Nobu McCarthy (1938-) was a Hollywood star in the 1950s and is currently artistic director of the East West Players in Los Angeles. Her early film roles were mostly stereotypical (geisha girls and "lotus blossoms"). In the 1970s and 1980s, she appeared in more rounded roles in *Farewell to Manzanar*, *The Karate Kid, Part II*, and *The Wash*.

Midori (1971-) is a celebrated violinist who has performed with many of the world's great orchestras.

Noriyuki "Pat" Morita (1932-) became a major television and film actor in the 1980s. In 1984 he starred as Miyagi, a kind-hearted karate instructor, in *The Karate Kid*, and was nominated for an Academy Award for best supporting actor.

Sono Osato (1919-) is an important dancer who worked with Diaghilev, the Ballet Russe, Balanchine, Tutor, Fokine, Massine, the American Ballet Theatre, and performed in the original production of the Jerome Robbins/Leonard Bernstein *On The Town*.

Seiji Ozawa (1935-), conductor, became music director of the San Francisco Symphony Orchestra in 1970 and the Boston Symphony Orchestra in 1973.

Pat Suzuki (c. 1930-), singer and actress, was the first Nisei to star in a Broadway musical, Rodgers and Hammerstein's *Flower Drum Song*, in 1958.

Miyoshi Umeki (1929-) received an Academy Award as best supporting actress in 1957 for her role in *Sayonara*.

GOVERNMENT

John Fujio Aiso (1909-1987) was director of the Military Intelligence Service Language School which trained about 6,000 persons in Japanese for intelligence work during World War II. In 1953 he became the first Japanese American judge.

George Ryoichi Ariyoshi (1926-) served as governor of Hawaii from 1973 to 1986. He was the first Japanese American lieutenant governor and governor in U.S. history.

S. I. Hayakawa (1906-1992), a professor of English, gained national attention for his strong stand against dissident students during his tenure as president of San Francisco State College (1968-1973). He served as a Republican U.S. Senator from California from 1977 to 1983.

Daniel K. Inouye (1924-) of Hawaii was the first Nisei elected to the U.S. Congress. A Democrat, he served in the House of Representatives from 1959 to 1962. He was elected to the U.S. Senate in 1962. He was a decorated veteran of the 442nd Regimental Combat Team during World War II.

Clarence Takeya Arai (1901-1964), a Seattle lawyer, was a key figure in the founding of the Japanese American Citizens League. He was active in Republican politics in the state of Washington in the 1930s. He and his family were sent to the relocation camp at Minidoka, Idaho, during World War II.

JOURNALISM

James Hattori is a television correspondent for CBS News.

Harvey Saburo Hayashi (1866-1943) was both a physician and newspaper editor for the rural Japanese American community of Holualoa in Kona, Hawaii. He founded the *Kona Hankyo* in 1897. The newspaper was published for the next 40 years and reached a circulation of 500 at its peak.

William K. "Bill" Hosokawa (1915-) has served as a writer and editor for the *Denver Post.* He is the principal historian for the Japanese American Citizens League. During his wartime internment at Heart Mountain, Wyoming, he edited the *Heart Mountain Sentinel.*

Ken Kashiwahara (1940-) is a television correspondent for ABC News and one of the first Asian American journalists to work in network television.

James Yoshinori Sakamoto (1903-1955) began the first Nisei newspaper, the *American Courier,* in 1928. He was a strong supporter of the Japanese American Citizens League from its beginning and served as its national president from 1936 to 1938.

LAW

Lance A. Ito (1950-), Los Angeles County superior court judge, is a highly respected jurist who gained national prominence as the judge in the O. J. Simpson murder trial.

LITERATURE

Velina Hasu Houston (1957-) is known for her plays and poetry reflecting on the experiences of Japanese American women and her own experience as a multiracial Asian woman. Her plays include *Asa Ga Kimashita, American Dreams, Tea,* and *Thirst.*

Jun Atushi Iwamatsu (1908-) is best known as author and illustrator of children's books. He has been runner-up for the Caldecott Medal for *Crow Boy* (1956), *Umbrella* (1959), and *Seashore Story* (1968). He has held several one-man exhibitions of his paintings.

Tooru J. Kanagawa (1906-), a journalist and decorated veteran of the 442nd Regimental Combat Team, published his first novel at the age of 83. His novel, *Sushi and Sourdough,* is based on his youth in Juneau, Alaska.

Toshio Mori (1910-1980) chronicled the lives of Japanese Americans in numerous short stories and six novels. Most of his writings, however, remain unpublished.

SCIENCE

Leo Esaki (1925-) is a Nobel Prize-winning physicist who invented the tunnel diode while working for the Sony Corporation in Japan. In 1960, Esaki immigrated to the United States to work at IBM's Watson Research Center in Yorktown Heights, New York.

Makio Murayama (1912-), a biochemist, received the 1969 Association for Sickle Cell Anemia award and the 1972 Martin Luther King, Jr. medical achievement award for his research in sickle cell anemia.

Hideyo Noguchi (1876-1928), a microbiologist, devoted his life to fighting diseases such as bubonic plague, syphilis, Rocky Mountain spotted fever, and yellow fever.

Jokichi Takamine (1854-1922) was a chemist who developed a starch-digesting enzyme (*Takadiastase*), which was useful in medicines. In 1901 he isolated adrenaline from the supradrenal gland and was the first scientist to discover gland hormones in pure form.

SPORTS

Kristi Yamaguchi (1971-), a figure skater, won the women's gold medal in figure skating at the 1993 Winter Olympics in Albertville, France.

MEDIA

PRINT

Chicago Shimpo.
A bi-lingual publication from Takeo F. Sugano.

Contact: Art Morimitsu and Kayoko Kawaguchi, Editors.
Address: 4670 North Manor Avenue, Chicago, Illinois 60625.
Telephone: (312) 478-6170.
Fax: (312) 478-9360.

The Hawaii Hochi.
A bilingual publication from Paul S. Yempuku.

Contact: Mitsunori Shoji, Editor.
Address: P. O. Box 17430, Honolulu, Hawaii 96817.
Telephone: (808) 845-2255.

Hokubei Mainichi.
An English-language publication from J. Akira Matsuo.

Contact: Atsuyo Hiramato, Editor.
Address: 1746 Post Street, San Francisco, California 94115.
Telephone: (415) 567-7324.
Fax: (415) 567-3926.

Japan-America Society Bulletin.
Published by the Japan-America Society of Washington, Inc., informs members of coming cultural and educational events; carries articles on U.S.-Japan relations.

Contact: Patricia Keams, Editor.
Address: 606 18th Street, N.W., Washington, D.C. 20006.
Telephone: (202) 289-8290.

Japanese American Yellow Pages.
Annual directory of Japanese businesses, residents, visitors, and U.S. companies of interest to the Japanese community. Includes information on companies, officials, and tourism, restaurants, shopping, transportation, medical services, entertainment, sports, recreation, cultural and business organizations and services.

Contact: Raymond Otani, Publisher.
Address: 151-23 34th Avenue, Flushing, New York 11363.
Telephone: (718) 463-2100.
Fax: (718) 358-3298.

Japanese Beach Press.
A Japanese-language publication.

Contact: Atsuko Chambers, Editor and Publisher.
Address: 777 Ala Moana Boulevard, Honolulu, Hawaii 96805.
Telephone: (808) 848-1414.

Japanese Lifestyle.
Offers lifestyle information for Japanese living in America.

Contact: Susan Meadow, Editor and Publisher.
Address: 126 Library Lane, Mamaroneck, New York 10543.
Telephone: (914) 381-4740.

Kashu Mainichi.
A bilingual publication from Hiro E. Hishiki.

Contact: Jitsuo Kikunaga, Editor.
Address: 706 East First Street, Los Angeles, California 90012.
Telephone: (213) 628-4686.

New York Nichibei.
Bilingual weekly newspaper founded in 1945.

Contact: Isaku Kida or Edward Moran, Editors.
Address: Japanese American News Corp., 396 Broadway, Suite 301-B, New York, New York 10013.
Telephone: (212) 226-9555.

Nichibei Times.
A bilingual publication from Nichi Bei Times Company.

Contact: I. Namekawa and Michi Oriuma, Editors.
Address: 2211 Bush Street, San Francisco, California 94119.

North American Post.
A bilingual tri-weekly founded in 1946.

Contact: Akiku Kusunose, Editor.
Address: North American Post Publishing, Inc., P.O. Box 3173, Seattle, Washington 98114.
Telephone: (206) 623-0100.
Fax: (206) 625-1424.

Northwest Nikkei.
An English-language monthly newspaper serving the Japanese American community in the Pacific.

Contact: S. Taniguchi, Editor.
Address: North American Post Publishing, Inc., P. O. Box 3173, Seattle, Washington 98114.
Telephone: (206) 623-0100.
Fax: (206) 625-1424.

Pacific Citizen.
A bilingual weekly publication of the Japanese American Citizens League.

Contact: Richard Suenaga, Editor.
Address: 941 East Third Street, No. 200, Los Angeles, California 90013.
Telephone: (213) 626-6936.
Fax: (213) 626-8213.

Rafu Shimpo.
A bilingual publication from Michael Komai.

Contact: Naomi Hirahara, Editor.
Address: 259 South Los Angeles Street, Los Angeles, California 90012.
Telephone: (213) 629-2231.

RADIO

The following radio stations offer programming in Japanese language: KOHO-AM, Honolulu, Hawaii; KZOO-AM, Honolulu, Hawaii; KTYM-AM, Inglewood, California; KEST-AM, San Francisco, California; KUAM-AM, Agana, Guam; KIPA-AM, Hilo, Hawaii; KPUA-AM, Hilo, Hawaii; KMVI-AM, Wailuku, Hawaii; WAMH-FM, Amherst, Massachusetts; WZLY-FM, Wellesley, Massachusetts; WCAR-AM, Livonia, Michigan; WBXL-FM, Baldwinsville, New York; and KKMO-AM, Tacoma, Washington.

TELEVISION

The following television stations offer programming in Japanese language: KDOC-TV, Anaheim, California; KTSF, Brisbane, California; KHNL, Hilo, Hawaii; and WNYC-TV, New York City, New York.

ORGANIZATIONS AND ASSOCIATIONS

Japan-America Society of Chicago (JASC).

Promotes inter-cultural contact and encourages trade between U.S. and Japanese citizenry; preserves the cultural and ethnic heritage of Japanese Americans.

Contact: Dr. Richard P. Soter, Executive Director.
Address: 225 West Wacker Drive, Suite 2250, Chicago, Illinois 60606.
Telephone: (312) 263-3049.

Japanese American Citizens League.

Educational, civil, and human rights organization founded in 1929 with 115 chapters and 25,000 members.

Address: 1765 Sutter Street, San Francisco, California 94115.
Telephone: (415) 921-5225.
Fax: (415) 931-4671.

Japan Hour Broadcasting.

Founded in 1974, it produces radio and television programs in Japanese for Japanese residents in the United States, and English language programs on Japan to promote American understanding of Japan and U.S.-Japanese relations.

Contact: Raymond Otami, Executive Director.
Address: 151-23 34th Avenue, Flushing, New York 11354.

Japan Society (JS).

Organization for individuals, institutions, and corporations representing the business, professional, and academic worlds in Japan and the United States; promotes exchange of ideas to enhance mutual understanding.

Contact: William H. Gleysteen, Jr., President.
Address: 333 East 47th Street, New York, New York 10017.
Telephone: (212) 832-1155.
Fax: (212) 755-6752.

Nippon Club.

Organization for persons who take special interest in Japanese affairs.

Contact: Tsutomu Karino, Vice President and Secretary.
Address: 145 West 57th Street, New York, New York 10019.
Telephone: (212) 581-2223.

MUSEUMS AND RESEARCH CENTERS

Japanese American Cultural and Community Center.

A performing and visual arts center founded in 1980.

Address: 244 South San Pedro, Room 505, Los Angeles, California 90012.

Japanese American Curriculum Project.

Address: 414 East Third Avenue, San Mateo, California 94401.

Japanese American National Museum.

The first national museum dedicated to preserving and sharing the history of Japanese Americans.

Address: 369 East First Street, Los Angeles, California 90012.

Japanese American Society for Legal Studies.

Contact: Professor Daniel H. Foote.
Address: University of Washington Law School, JB-20, Seattle, Washington 98105.

U.S.-Japan Culture Center (USJCC).

Seeks to promote mutual understanding between the United States and Japan; to help the public, scholars, government officials, and businesspersons of both countries increase their knowledge of U.S.-Japan relations.

Contact: Mikio Kanda, Executive Director.

Address: 2600 Virginia Avenue, N.W., Suite 711, Washington, D.C. 20037.

Telephone: (202) 342-5800.

SOURCES FOR ADDITIONAL STUDY

Ellington, Lucien. *Japan: Tradition and Change.* White Plains, New York: Longman, 1990.

Hosokawa, Bill. *Nisei: The Quiet Americans.* New York: William Morrow, Inc., 1969.

Japan: An Illustrated Encyclopedia. Tokyo, Japan: Kodansha, 1993.

Japanese American History: An A to Z Reference from 1868 to the Present. New York: Facts on File, 1993.

Kitano, Henry E. *Japanese Americans: The Evolution of a Subculture.* Englewood Cliffs, New Jersey: Prentice-Hall, 1969.

Lyman, Stanford M. *Chinatown and Little Tokyo: Power, Conflict, and Community Among Chinese and Japanese Immigrants in America.* Millwood, New York: Associated Faculty Press, 1986.

Montero, Darrel. *Japanese Americans: Changing Patterns of Ethnic Affiliation Over Three Generations.* Boulder, Colorado: Westview Press, 1980.

Nakano, Mei T. *Japanese American Women: Three Generations 1890-1990.* Berkeley, California: Mina Press, 1990.

Takaki, Ronald. *Strangers from a Different Shore: A History of Asian Americans.* Boston: Little, Brown and Company, 1989.

JEWISH AMERICANS

by
Jim Kamp

Jews have enjoyed greater acceptance in America than in any other country and have figured prominently in American culture and politics.

OVERVIEW

Jews represent a group of people rather than a distinct race or ethnicity. Although Jews originally came from the Middle East, many races and peoples have mixed together in Jewish communities over the centuries, especially after the Jews were forced out of Palestine in the second century C.E. What binds the group together is a common Jewish heritage as passed down from generation to generation. For many Jews, the binding force is Judaism, a term usually referring to the Jewish religion but sometimes used to refer to all Jews. There are, however, Jewish atheists and agnostics, and one does not have to be religious to be Jewish. In general, one is Jewish if born of a Jewish mother or if he or she converts to Judaism.

Most Jews consider the State of Israel the Jewish homeland. Located in the Middle East with a land mass of 7,992 square miles, Israel is only slighter larger than New Jersey. It is bounded by Lebanon in the north, by Syria and Jordan in the east, by Egypt in the southwest, and by the Mediterranean Sea in the west. With a population of approximately 4.2 million Jews, Israel is home to about one third of the world Jewry, estimated at 12.9 million at the end of 1992. However, not all Jews consider Israel home. Some feel the United States, with 5.8 million Jews, is the de facto home of Jews, evidenced in part by the fact that Israel is sometimes called "Little America" because of its similarities to the United States. Accounting for more than three-fourths of the world Jewry, Israel and the United States represent the two major Jewish population regions.

Although Jews comprise less than three percent of the American population, Jews have generally had a disproportionately larger representation in American government, business, academia, and entertainment. American Jews have suffered their share of setbacks and have had to combat anti-Semitism during the early twentieth century. On the whole, however, Jews have enjoyed greater acceptance in America than in any other country and have figured prominently in American culture and politics.

HISTORY

Jewish history dates back 4,000 years to the time of Abraham, the biblical figure credited for introducing the belief in a single God. Abraham's monotheism not only marked the beginning of Judaism, but of Christianity and Islam as well. Following God's instructions, Abraham led his family out of Mesopotamia to Canaan, later renamed Palestine, then Israel. Abraham and his descendants were called Hebrews. ("Hebrew" is derived from "Eber," which means "from the other side." This is a reference to the fact that Abraham came from the "other side" of the Euphrates River.) According to the Bible, God made a covenant with Abraham promising that if the Hebrews followed God's commandments, they would become a great nation in the land of Canaan. Subsequently, Hebrews referred to themselves as "God's chosen people."

After Abraham, the Hebrews were led by Abraham's son Isaac, then by Isaac's son Jacob. Jacob, also known as "Israel" ("Champion of God"), was the father of 12 sons, who became leaders of the 12 tribes of Israel. For hundreds of years these tribes lived in Canaan and comprised all of Hebrew civilization. By about 1700 B.C.E., food shortages compelled the Hebrews to leave Canaan for Egypt, where they were social outcasts and were eventually forced into slavery by pharaoh Ramses II around 1280 B.C.E. From these bleak conditions emerged perhaps the greatest leader of the Jews, Moses. In about 1225 B.C.E., Moses led the Hebrews out of Egypt (the Exodus) into the Sinai Desert, where Moses is said to have received the Ten Commandments from God on Mount Sinai. For 40 years the Israelites lived in the desert, obeying God's commandments.

After Moses, Joshua led the Israelites back into Canaan, now called Palestine, representing the "Promised Land." There the people were ruled by benevolent Judges and later by Kings until social tensions after the death of King Solomon caused the Israelites to break apart. Ten tribes organized into the northern kingdom of Israel, while the other two tribes formed the southern kingdom of Judah. The people of Israel, however, lost much of their Hebrew identity after the Assyrians invaded the northern kingdom in 721 B.C.E. By contrast, when the people of Judah, or Jews, were captured by Babylonians in 586 B.C.E., these Jews remained faithful to their traditions and to the Ten Commandments. Fifty years later Jews returned to Palestine after the Persians defeated the Babylonians.

For centuries Jewish culture thrived in Palestine until the Roman occupation beginning in 63 B.C.E. For more than 100 years Jews endured life with the oppressive, violent Romans. By 70 C.E., when the Romans destroyed the Jewish Temple in Jerusalem, Jews had begun migrating to the outer regions of the Roman Empire, including the Near East, North Africa, and southwestern, central, and eastern Europe. In 135 C.E. the Romans officially banned Judaism, which marked the beginning of the diaspora, or the dispersal of Jews. Forced out of Palestine, Jews in exile concentrated less on establishing a unified homeland and more on maintaining Judaism through biblical scholarship and community life.

EUROPEAN LIFE

European Jews are divided mainly between the Jews of Spain and Portugal, the Sephardim, and the Jews from German-speaking countries in central and eastern Europe, the Ashkenazim. The distinction between the Sephardim and Ashkenazim—Hebrew terms for Spanish and German Jews—continues to be the major classification of Jews, with 75 percent of today's world Jewry being Ashkenazic. In medieval Europe, Sephardic Jews enjoyed the most freedom and cultural acceptance. Between the ninth and fifteenth centuries Sephardic Jews made significant cultural and literary contributions to Spain while it was under Islamic rule. By contrast, Ashkenazic Jews in the north lived uneasily among Christians, who saw Jews as "Christ killers" and who resented Jews for thinking of themselves as a chosen people. Christians subjected Jews to violence and destroyed Jewish communities beginning with the First Crusade in 1096. Jewish populations were driven from

England and France in the thirteenth and fourteenth centuries. By the beginning of the Spanish Inquisition in 1492, Jews from Spain faced similar oppression, violence, and expulsion from Spanish Christians. As a result, Sephardic Jews spread out to Mediterranean countries, while the majority of Ashkenazic Jews moved east to Poland, which became the center of European Jewry.

In Poland, Jews were permitted to create a series of councils and courts that together represented a minority self-government within the country. In individual Jewish communities, the *kehillah* was the governing structure comprised of elected leaders who oversaw volunteer organizations involved in all aspects of social and religious life in the community. The disintegration of the Polish state in the eighteenth century, however, disrupted community life and caused many to emigrate. By the nineteenth century, Jews in eastern Europe were primarily split between Prussia, Austria, and Russia. The governments in these countries, however, oppressed Jews through military conscription, taxation, and expulsion. Though relatively impoverished, the four million Jews in the Pale of Settlement (a region encompassing eastern Poland and western Russia) maintained their Jewish traditions through close community life.

By contrast, Jews in Western Europe fared much better economically and socially as they gained acceptance in England, France, and Austria-Hungary after the Protestant Reformation. Northern European cities with large Protestant populations such as London, Hamburg, and Amsterdam increasingly opened their doors to Jews. In order to fully assimilate and become citizens, these Jews sometimes had to renounce Jewish laws, self-government, and the quest for nationhood. Still, many Jews were eager to comply, some even becoming Christians. As a result, many western European Jews attained significant wealth and status, generally through banking and trade. In addition to material prosperity, German Jews also enjoyed a period of heightened cultural activity during the Jewish Enlightenment of the eighteenth and early nineteenth centuries, a period marked by free inquiry and increased political activism. Political turmoil by the mid-nineteenth century, however, brought upheaval to Jewish communities, prompting many to emigrate.

IMMIGRATION WAVES

The first Jewish immigrants to settle in the United States were 23 Sephardic Jews who arrived in New Amsterdam (later known as New York) in 1654. Although this group of men, women, and children from Dutch Brazil initially faced resistance from Governor Peter Stuyvesant, they were allowed to settle after Jews in Amsterdam applied pressure on the Dutch West India Company, Stuyvesant's employer. In addition to Spain, Sephardic Jews came from various Mediterranean countries as well as from England, Holland, and the Balkans. The number of Jews in Colonial America grew slowly but steadily so that by 1776 there were approximately 2,500 Jews in America.

The wave of German Jewish immigrants during the mid-nineteenth century represented the first major Jewish population explosion in America. While there were just 6,000 Jews in the United States in 1826, the number of American Jews climbed above 50,000 by 1850 and rose to 150,000 only a decade later. The German Jews actually came from Germany and various other central European countries, including Bavaria, Bohemia, Moravia, and western Poland. Challenges to the monarchies of central Europe in the 1840s caused considerable social unrest, particularly in rural villages. While wealthy Jews could afford to escape the turbulence by moving to cities such as Vienna or Berlin, poorer Jews could not. Consequently, many chose to immigrate to America.

The largest wave of Jewish immigrants were eastern European Jews who came to America between 1881 and 1924. During these years one third of the Jewish population in eastern Europe emigrated because of changing political and economic conditions. The assassination of Russian Tsar Alexander II in 1881 ushered in a new era of violence and anti-Jewish sentiment. Pogroms, or massacres, by the Slavs against the Jews had occurred since the mid-seventeenth century, but the pogroms of 1881 and 1882 were particularly numerous and intense, wiping out entire villages and killing hundreds of Jews. Also, industrialization made it difficult for Jewish peddlers, merchants, and artisans to sustain themselves economically. As a result, a mass exodus of Jews from eastern Europe occurred, with approximately 90 percent bound for America. During the late nineteenth and early twentieth centuries, tens and sometimes hundreds of thousands of Jews arrived in America annually. The immigration of some 2.4 million eastern European Jews boosted the American Jewish population from roughly a quarter million in 1881 to 4.5 million by 1924.

The Immigration Restriction Act of 1924 decreased the annual Jewish immigration from more than 100,000 to about 10,000. Subsequently, U.S. immigration policy remained strict, even during World War II when the need to emigrate was a matter of life and death for German Jews. The 150,000 Jews who managed to immigrate to America between 1935 and 1941 were primarily middle-class, middle-aged professionals and businessmen. These refugees from Nazi Germany represented a different type of immigrant from the young, working-class Jews who emigrated from eastern Europe at the turn of the century. After a period of increased immigration during and immediately following World War II (within the quotas set by Congress), Jewish immigration leveled off for several decades. The most recent immigration wave occurred during the 1980s, when political and economic changes in the Soviet Union prompted hundreds of thousands of Soviet Jews to come to Israel and America. The American quotas by this time had risen to 40,000 Jews per year. This immigration wave of Soviet Jews has been the largest since the immigration of Russian Jews at the turn of the century.

Jewish population in relation to the general U.S. population peaked in 1937 at 3.7 percent. Limits on immigration and a Jewish birthrate of less than two children per family—lower than the national average—have lowered the Jewish proportion of the American population to under three percent. This proportion has remained relatively stable, even as the American Jewish population approached six million in the 1990s.

SETTLEMENT PATTERNS

The Sephardic Jews who settled in the American colonies established themselves in cities along the eastern seaboard. From the mid-seventeenth to the mid-eighteenth centuries, the largest Jewish population centers were in New York, Newport, Savannah, Philadelphia, and Charleston, the only cities with synagogues during the period. Jewish businessmen from these cities were supported by influential businessmen from Sephardic communities in London and Amsterdam.

The influx of German Jews in the nineteenth century contributed to the westward expansion of the Jewish population in the United States. By the mid-nineteenth century, there were approximately 160 Jewish communities from New York to California, with Jewish population centers in the major hubs along the trade routes from east to west. Cities such as Cleveland, Chicago, Cincinnati, and St. Louis all became centers of Jewish business, cultural, and religious life. Jewish peddlers and retailers also followed the economic growth of the cotton industry in the South and the discovery of gold in the West. Most of the Jewish immigrants from this period were young, single Germans hoping to escape unfavorable economic conditions and repressive legislation that restricted marriage. Individuals from the same community would typically immigrate together and continue their congregation in the New World.

The wave of eastern European Jews at the turn of the century gravitated toward big cities in the East and Midwest. The result was that by 1920 Jews had their greatest population centers in New York, Newark, Cleveland, Philadelphia, Boston, Baltimore, Pittsburgh, Chicago, St. Louis, and Detroit. Within these cities, eastern European Jews established their own communities and maintained their cultural heritage and identity much more so than nineteenth-century German Jews, who were eager to assimilate into American culture.

Jewish settlement trends in the twentieth century have shown population decreases in the midwest and increases in cities such as Los Angeles and Miami. During the 1930s and 1940s, refugees from Nazi Germany predominantly settled in Manhattan's West Side and Washington Heights as well as in Chicago and San Francisco. After World War II the population of American Jews decreased in midwestern cities such as Chicago, Detroit, and Cleveland and increased in Los Angeles, Miami, and Washington, D.C. For each major city with a significant Jewish population, there has been a steady postwar trend of outward movement toward the suburbs. The young and middle-aged professionals have led this movement, while working-class, Orthodox, and older Jews continue to inhabit the old neighborhoods closer to the city.

By the end of 1992, the largest Jewish population centers were in New York City (1.45 million), Los Angeles (490,000), Chicago (261,000), Philadelphia (250,000), Boston (228,000), San Francisco Bay Area (210,000), Miami (189,000), and Washington, D.C. (165,000).

ACCULTURATION AND ASSIMILATION

Until the late nineteenth century, Jewish settlers desired and found it relatively easy to assimilate into American society. Jews had left Europe because of poor social and economic conditions and were eager to establish themselves in an open, expanding society. Occasionally, Jews would have to combat anti-Semitism and negative stereotypes of "dirty Jews," but for the most part Americans appreciated the goods and services provided by Jewish merchants. The religious freedom guaranteed by the U.S. Constitution coupled with the increasing prosperity of nineteenth-century German Jews enabled Jews to enjoy considerable acceptance in American society.

The basic division between Jews during the nineteenth century was between Polish and German congregations. However, in large population centers such as New York, subgroups emerged to accommodate the local traditions of various Dutch, Bavarian, English, or Bohemian Jews. The desire to assimilate to American culture was felt in the larger synagogues, where decorations were added and sermons were changed from German to English or abandoned altogether.

Beginning in 1881, the immigration of eastern European Jews marked the first significant resistance to acculturation. These immigrants tended to be poor, and they settled in tight-knit communities where they retained the traditions and customs from the old world. They consciously avoided assimilation into American culture and continued to speak Yiddish, a mixture of Hebrew and medieval German that further separated them from other Americans. Some American institutions applied pressure to assimilate into mainstream culture by banning the use of Yiddish in public programs. But the ban was removed by the turn of the century as efforts to limit Americanization became more popular. Increasingly, rapid assimilation into American culture was viewed as unnecessary and harmful to Jewish identity. Still, a conflict remained between younger and older generation Jews over how much Americanization was desirable.

STEREOTYPES, ANTI-SEMITISM, AND DISCRIMINATION

The arrival of eastern European immigrants prompted the first significant tide of anti-Semitism in America. During the 1880s, clubs and resorts that once welcomed Jews began to exclude them. European anti-Semitism influenced a growing number of Americans to adopt various negative stereotypes of Jews as clannish, greedy, parasitic, vulgar, and physically inferior. To mitigate these sentiments, Americanized Jews developed aid societies to provide jobs and relief funds to help eastern European Jews fit into American society. In addition, American-born German Jews fought against restrictive legislation and formed philanthropic societies that funded schools, hospitals, and libraries for eastern European Jews. The hope was that if the hundreds of thousands of newly arriving Russian Jews had access to homes, jobs, and health care, the decreased burden on American public institutions would ease ethnic tensions.

Despite efforts by Americanized Jews to reduce ethnic hatred and stereotyping, discrimination against Jews continued into the twentieth century. Housing restrictions and covenants against Jews became more common just prior to World War I. During the 1920s and 1930s, Jews faced significant difficulty obtaining employment in large corporations or in fields such as journalism. Jews were also increasingly subjected to restrictive quotas in higher education. In particular, Jewish enrollment dropped by as much as 50 percent at Ivy League schools such as Harvard and Yale during the 1920s. By the 1930s most private institutions had Jewish quota policies in place. In politics, one of the motivating forces behind the Immigration Restriction Act of 1924 was the negative image that some held of immigrant Russian Jews, who were thought to live a lowly, animal-like existence. This "dirty Jew" stereotype was based on a perception of ghetto Jews, who were forced to endure squalid living conditions out of economic necessity. Another stereotype was of the Jew as Communist sympathizer and revolutionary, a characterization stemming from the belief that Jews were responsible for the Russian Revolution. All of these negative stereotypes were reinforced in American literature of the 1920s and 1930s. Authors such as Thomas Wolf, F. Scott Fitzgerald, and Ernest Hemingway all depicted Jewish caricatures in their novels, while poets such as T.S. Eliot and Ezra Pound freely expressed their anti-Semitism.

Fueled by a Worldwide Depression and the rise of German Nazism, Jewish discrimination and anti-Semitism reached a peak during the 1930s. One of the more influential American voices of anti-Semitism was Roman Catholic priest Charles E. Coughlin, who argued that the Nazi attack on Jews was justified because of the communist tendencies of Jews. Coughlin blamed New York Jews for the hard economic times, a message intended to appeal to Coughlin's Detroit audience of industrial workers hurt by the Depression.

At the end of World War II, when the atrocities of the Nazi Holocaust became widely known, anti-Semitism in America diminished considerably. Though some Jews in academia lost appointments as a result of Communist fears instigated by Senator Joseph McCarthy, Jews generally enjoyed improved social conditions after 1945. Returning war veterans on the G.I. Bill created a demand for college professors that Jews helped fulfill, and entrance quotas restricting admission of Jewish students at universities were gradually abandoned. As discrimination waned, Jews enjoyed substantial representation in academia, business, entertainment, and such professions as finance, law, and medicine. In short, Jews during the postwar years resumed their positions as contributing and often leading members of American society.

TRADITIONS, CUSTOMS, AND BELIEFS

Immigrant Jews passed on Jewish traditions in the home, but subsequent generations have relied on religious schools to teach the traditions. These schools have helped Jewish parents accommodate their goal of having their children become familiar with Jewish tradition without interfering with their children's integration into American culture. Today, many Jewish children attend congregation school a few days a week for three to five years. During this time, they learn Hebrew and discover the essential traditions and customs of Jewish culture.

Jewish traditions and customs primarily derive from the practice of Judaism. The most important Jewish traditions stem from the *mitzvot,* which are the 613 holy obligations found in the Torah and Talmud. Consisting of 248 positive commandments (Thou shall's) and 365 negative commandments (Thou shall not's), these commandments fall into three categories: *Edot,* or "testimonies," are rules that help Jews bear witness to their faith (e.g., rules on what garments to wear); *Mishpatim* (judgments) are rules of behavior found in most religions (e.g., the rule against stealing); and *Hukim* (statutes) are divine rules that humans cannot fully understand (e.g., dietary rules). No one person can possibly fulfill all 613 *mitzvot* since they include laws for different people in different situations. Even the most Orthodox Jew in modern times is expected to observe less than half of the obligations.

The basic beliefs common to all Jews, except atheists and agnostics, were articulated by Moses Maimonides (1135-1204). Known as the Thir-

teen Principles of the Faith, they are: (1) God alone is the creator; (2) God is One; (3) God is without physical form; (4) God is eternal; (5) humans pray only to God; (6) the words of the prophets are true; (7) the greatest prophet was Moses; (8) today's Torah is the one God gave to Moses; (9) the Torah will not be replaced; (10) God knows people's thoughts; (11) the good are rewarded and the evil are punished; (12) the Messiah will come; and, (13) the dead will be revived. Although most of the Jewish faithful share these broad beliefs, there is no specific requirement to commit all 13 to memory.

CUISINE

There is no specific Jewish cuisine, only lists of permissible and impermissible foods for Orthodox Jews and others who observe *kashrut.* Delineated in the Book of Leviticus and dating back to 1200 B.C.E., *kashrut* is a system of food laws for eating *kosher* foods and avoiding *trefa* foods. *Kosher* foods are simply ones that are, by law, fit for Jews; they include fruits, vegetables, grains, meat from cud-chewing mammals with split hooves (e.g., sheep, cows, goats), fish with scales and fins (e.g., salmon, herring, perch), domesticated birds (e.g., chicken, turkey, duck), and milk and eggs from kosher mammals and birds. *Trefa* foods are forbidden by Jewish law, simply because of biblical decree, not because such foods are unfit for human consumption; they include meat from unkosher mammals (e.g., pork, rabbit, horse), birds of prey (e.g., owls, eagles), and water animals that do not have both scales and fins (e.g., lobster, crab, squid). *Kashrut* also prescribes that the slaughter of animals shall be painless. Thus, a Jewish butcher (*shohet*) studies the anatomy of animals to learn the precise spot where killing may occur instantaneously. After the animal is killed, the blood must be completely drained and any diseased portions removed. Finally, kashrut involves keeping meat and milk separate. Because of the biblical commandment not to "stew a kid in its mother's milk," Jewish law has interpreted this to mean that meat and dairy products cannot be prepared or consumed together.

HOLIDAYS

Because there is a separate Jewish calendar based on the lunar cycle, Jewish holidays occur on different secular days every year. The first holiday of the Jewish year is the celebration of the new year,

Rosh Hashanah, which occurs sometime in September or October. It is a ten-day period in which Jews reflect on their lives during the previous year. Three basic themes are associated with this holiday: the anniversary of the creation of the world; the day of judgment; and the renewal of the covenant between God and Israel. On the night before the beginning of *Rosh Hashanah*, one popular custom is to eat honey-dipped apples so that the new year will be a sweet one. *Yom Kippur*, the "Day of Atonement," occurs at the end of *Rosh Hashanah*. For 25 hours observant Jews fast while seeking forgiveness from God and from those against whom they have sinned. There are five services at the synagogue throughout the day, most centering on the themes of forgiveness and renewal.

In the winter, usually in December, Jews celebrate the festival of *Hanukkah*. This is a joyous eight-day period that marks the time when in 164 B.C.E. the Jews, led by Judah the Maccabee, successfully reclaimed the Temple in Jerusalem from the Syrians. When the Maccabbees prepared to light the perpetual flame in the Temple, they only found one jar of oil, enough for only one day. Miraculously, the oil lasted eight days until a new supply of oil arrived. Thus, the celebration of Hanukkah, also known as the Festival of Lights, involves lighting a candle for each night of the festival, one on the first night, two on the second, and so forth. Over time, Hanukkah has become a time of family celebration with games and presents for children.

Other holidays and festivals round out the Jewish year. In late winter Jews celebrate *Purim*, a period of great drinking and eating to commemorate the biblical time when God helped Esther save the Jews from the evil, tyrannical Haman, who wanted to destroy the Jews. In late March or early April, Jews participate in the week-long festival of Passover, which marks the Jewish Exodus from Egypt. The Passover Supper, or *Seder*, is the central feature of this celebration and is a gathering of family and friends (with room for the "unexpected guest") who eat a traditional meal of unleavened bread, parsley, apples, nuts, cinnamon, raisins, and wine. Seven weeks after Passover, *Shavout* is celebrated, marking the giving of the Torah by God and the season of wheat harvest. In autumn Jews celebrate *Sukkot*, an eight-day festival honoring the time when the Israelites spent 40 years in the desert after the Exodus and before returning to Palestine. Because the Israelites spent 40 years living in the wilderness, this holiday season is celebrated by living for eight days in a temporary home called a *sukkah*. Though a *sukkah* is small and typically does not protect well against the increasingly harsh fall weather, Jews are expected to be joyous and grateful for all that God has provided.

HEALTH AND MENTAL HEALTH ISSUES

Before coming to America, Jews living in small communities in Europe occasionally suffered from amaurotic idiocy, an inherited pathology attributed to inbreeding. During the early twentieth century, when the largest waves of Jewish immigrants arrived in America, Russian Jewish immigrants were afflicted with nervous disorders, suicides, and tuberculosis more often than other immigrants. Despite these afflictions, Jews had a lower death rate than other immigrants at the time. Recently, the National Foundation for Jewish Genetic Diseases published a list of the seven most common genetic diseases suffered by Jews:

Bloom Syndrome: a disease causing shortness in height (usually less than five feet), redness of skin, and susceptibility to respiratory tract and ear infections. Affected men often experience infertility and both sexes have an increased risk of cancer. Just over 100 cases have been reported since the disease was discovered in 1954, but one in 120 Jews are carriers and children from two carriers have a 25 percent chance of contracting the disease.

Familial Dysautonomia: a congenital disease of the nervous system resulting in stunted growth, increased tolerance of pain, and lack of tears. One in 50 Ashkenazi Jews in America carries the gene, and the risk of recurrence in affected families is 25 percent.

Gaucher Disease: a disease that in its mildest form—the form common to Jews—is characterized by easy bruising, orthopedic problems, anemia, and a variety of other symptoms. The more advanced forms of the disease are fatal but rare and not concentrated in any one ethnic group. One out of 25 Ashkenazi Jews carries the recessive gene, and one in 2,500 Jewish babies is afflicted.

Mucolipidosis IV: a recently discovered disease (1974) involving the deterioration of the central nervous system in babies who later develop mild or more severe retardation. Thus far only handful of cases have been reported, all by Ashkenazi Jews. The disease only occurs when both parents are carriers, with 25 percent of babies from such parents being affected.

Niemann-Pick Disease: a usually fatal disease characterized by a buildup of fatty materials causing enlargement of the spleen, emaciation, and degradation of the central nervous system. Afflicted babies typically die before the age of three, but survival into young adulthood is possible in milder cases. The disease affects about 25 Ashkenazi Jews each year in the United States.

Tay-Sachs Disease: a biochemical disorder causing retardation in babies as early as the fourth month and leading to a deterioration of the central nervous system that ends in death, usually between the ages of five and eight. Approximately one in 25 Jews is a carrier, with the risk that 25 percent of babies from two carriers will have Tay-Sachs. Screening techniques have enabled carriers to bring only normal babies to term.

Torsion Dystonia: a disease involving an increasing loss of motor control coupled with normal to superior intelligence affecting children between the ages of four and 16. One in 70 Ashkenazi Jews in America is a carrier, with one out of every 20,000 Jewish babies developing the disease.

LANGUAGE

One of the strongest unifying links between Jews throughout the world is the Hebrew language. From the time of Abraham in 2000 B.C.E. until the Babylonians captured Judah in 586 B.C.E., Hebrew was the everyday language of Jews. Since then, Jews have generally adopted the vernacular of the societies in which they have resided, including Arabic, German, Russian, and English. Hebrew continued to be spoken and read, but primarily in sacred contexts. Most of the Torah is written in Hebrew, and religious services are mostly in Hebrew, though Progressive synagogues will make greater use of the language of the community. The use of Hebrew in religious worship enables Jews from all parts of the world to enjoy a common bond. In the twentieth century, Hebrew regained its status as an everyday language in Israel, where it is the official language.

During the diaspora, as Jews left Palestine to settle in various parts of Europe, two distinctly Jewish languages emerged. The Sephardic Jews of Spain and Portugal developed Ladino, a mixture of Spanish and Hebrew, while Ashkenazic Jews in central and eastern Europe spoke Yiddish, a combination of medieval German and Hebrew. These two languages were spoken by immigrants when they came to America, but were not typically passed on to the next generation. The exception to this occurred during the turn of the century when Russian Jews helped Yiddish gain a strong foothold in America through Yiddish newspapers and theater. At its high point in 1920, Yiddish was spoken by half of the Jewish population in America. By 1940, however, the proportion of American Jews who spoke Yiddish had dropped to one-third, and its presence as a world language was severely threatened by the Holocaust, which killed most of the Yiddish-speaking Jews. Today, a small but growing minority of Jews are attempting to revitalize Yiddish as a language uniquely capable of transmitting Jewish cultural heritage.

GREETINGS AND OTHER POPULAR EXPRESSIONS

Commonly heard expressions are: *Shalom*—Peace (a general greeting); *Shalom lekha*—Hello/Goodbye (an everyday greeting); *Barukh ha-ha*—Blessed be the one who comes (a general welcome to guests often used at weddings or circumcisions); *Mazel tov*—Good luck (a wish for luck commonly used at births, *bar mitzvahs*, and weddings); *Lehayyim*—To life/Cheers (a traditional toast wishing someone good health); *Ad me'ah ve-esrim shana*—May you live until 120 (an expression meaning good wishes for a long life); *Tizkeh le-shanim*—Long life to you (an expression wishing someone happy birthday or happy anniversary); *Hag same'ah*—A happy holiday (a general holiday greeting used for all Jewish festivals); *L'shana tova*—Good year (a shortened version of "may you be inscribed in the Book of Life for a good year," which is wished during Rosh Hashanah).

FAMILY AND COMMUNITY DYNAMICS

As Jews have spread to Europe and America after being forced out of Palestine, their cultural heritage has depended on strong family and community relations. One of the chief ways in which Jews, particularly Orthodox Jews, have maintained family and community values has been through the keeping of *Shabat*, the Sabbath. Observing *Shabat*, or "the day of delight," is one of the Ten Commandments and is essentially a matter of taking a break from work to devote one day of the week to rest, contemplation, and family and community togetherness. Just prior to Sabbath, which lasts from sunset on Friday to late Saturday night, the family must complete all the preparations for the day because no work should be done once the Sabbath begins. Traditionally, the mother starts the Sabbath by lighting candles and saying a special prayer. Afterward, the family attends a short service in the synagogue, then returns home for a meal and lighthearted conversation, perhaps even singing. The following morning the community gathers in the synagogue for the most important religious service of the week. On Saturday afternoon observant Jews will continue to refrain from work and either make social visits or spend time in quiet reflection. A ceremony called *havdalah* (distinction) takes place Saturday night, marking the end of Sabbath and the beginning of the new week.

The relative importance of *Shabat* and the synagogue for American Jews has declined over the years. In fact, the history of Jews in America reflects an ongoing secularization of Jewish values. Beginning in the nineteenth century, the Jewish community center developed as an important nonsectarian counterpart to the synagogue. Modeled after the Young Men's Hebrew Association, Jewish community centers became dominated by the 1920s by professionals who wanted to establish a central place for younger Jews to acquire such American values as humanism and self-development. While such community centers continue to play a role in Jewish population areas, many of today's American Jews no longer associate with a synagogue or community center, but may live in a Jewish neighborhood as the only outward sign of their Jewish identity.

COURTSHIP AND MARRIAGE

According to Judaism, marriage is the fulfillment of one of God's purposes for human beings. Consequently, all Jews are intended to experience both the joy and hardship of matrimony, including rabbis. To facilitate the finding of a mate, the matchmaker plays a role in Jewish society of bringing together suitable but perhaps reluctant individuals. The matchmaker only helps the process along; the final choice must be made freely by both partners according to Jewish law.

Traditionally, intermarriage between Jews and Gentiles has been forbidden. A Jew who married a Christian faced ostracism from family and community. Jews who immigrated to America during the Colonial period and after, however, intermarried with non-Jews with relative impunity. This tolerance of religious freedom lasted until the 1880s when the arrival of Russian Jews ushered in a conservative era with a more traditional view of marriage. For the first half of the twentieth century, intermarriage among Jews remained low, with only about five percent choosing to marry non-Jews. By the 1960s and 1970s, however, intermarriage became more common, with as many as 20 to 30 percent of Jews choosing non-Jewish mates.

BIRTHS, WEDDINGS, AND FUNERALS

Jewish babies usually receive two names, an everyday name and a Hebrew name used in the synagogue and on religious documents. The naming of the baby occurs after birth at a baby-naming service or, for many male babies, when they are circumcised. Since the emergence of Judaism some 4,000 years ago, Jews have observed the tradition of *brit milah* (covenant of circumcision). Although the practice of cutting the foreskin of male babies probably served a hygienic purpose originally, circumcision has come to represent the beginning of life in the Jewish community. To be sure, many non-Jews are circumcised, and being born of a Jewish mother is sufficient to make a baby Jewish. Nonetheless, circumcision is traditionally associated with the keeping of the covenant between Abraham and God as well as with physical and ethical purity. The *brit milah* must occur eight days after birth, unless the baby is sick. The ceremony takes place in the home and is usually performed by a *mohel*, an observant Jew who may be a rabbi, doctor, or simply one skilled in the technique. After the circumcision, which occurs very quickly and without much pain, a celebration of food, prayers, and blessings follows.

Bar mitzvah, which varies according to local traditions (Ashkenazic, Sephardic, or Oriental) is the ceremony that initiates the young Jewish male into the religious community. By reading in the synagogue, he becomes an adult. According to Talmudic tradition, this ususally occurs at the age of 13. Following the reading in the synagogue, there is a celebration (*seudat mitzavah*). In the twentieth century, the *bas* or *bat mitzvah* has been introduced for young girls; however, this occurs more frequently in the Reform and Conservative groups than the Orthodox ones.

This boy reads from the Torah during his Bar Mitzvah.

Jewish weddings are marked by several distinct traditions. The ceremony occurs under a *huppah*, a canopy open on all four sides, symbolizing the openness of the bride and groom's new home. The huppah can be placed in a home or outdoors but is most often used in a synagogue. Under the *huppah*, the bride circles the groom a set number of times, the couple is blessed, and they both drink from the same cup of wine, a sharing which demonstrates that from this point forward they will share a life together. The heart of the ceremony, the only part required to make the marriage legally binding, occurs next. The groom places a ring on the right-hand index finger of the bride, proclaiming, "Behold you are consecrated to me by this ring according to the law of Moses and Israel." If at least two witnesses observe her accept the ring, the marriage is complete. The ceremony is rounded out by the signing of the marriage contract (the *ketubah*), the singing of seven blessings (the *Sheva brahot*), and the traditional smashing of the glass by the husband. Breaking a glass symbolizes the destruction of the Temple in Jerusalem and the fact that the couple will have to face hard times together. When the glass is broken, guests exclaim, "*Mazel tov*" (good luck), and a wedding feast ensues.

Jewish funerals and mourning are characterized by a sense of frankness toward the reality of death. Funerals occur soon after a person dies, usually within a day or two unless family travel plans or the observance of Sabbath delays the service for an extra day. Arrangements for the deceased are handled by the *hevra kadisha* (holy society), which is a volunteer organization within the synagogue responsible for preparing the body. Such preparation does not involve make-up or embalming but instead consists of dressing the person in white, perhaps wrapping the deceased with his or her prayer cloth, or *tallit*. In modern times, the *hevra kadisha* are sometimes assisted by professionals, but not for profit. The ceremony is usually short and is followed by burial at the cemetery, where family members will recite the *Kaddish,* a traditional prayer celebrating God and life.

For Orthodox survivors, four stages of mourning have evolved over the years which encourage expression of grief so that the healing process may occur without delay. From the time a person dies until the funeral, mourners cease working, gather together, and do not generally receive visitors, primarily because any comfort at this point is premature and only causes unnecessary strain. The second stage occurs during the first week after the funeral, when the family observes *shiva*. At this time, mourners do not generally work but open their homes to visitors who offer their sympathy. The next stage is *shaloshim*, which lasts for three weeks after shiva and is marked by a resumption of work and other obligations, but entertainment is avoided. Finally, there is a last phase of light mourning for spouses or immediate family members that ends 11 months after the funeral. By the anniversary of a person's death, mourning is complete.

WOMEN'S ROLES

Jewish culture over the years has been male-dominated. Women's roles were limited to household activity, including raising children and performing minor religious functions, such as lighting the Sabbath candles. Although women are subject to the same negative biblical commandments as men, they are not expected to observe the same positive commandments. For example, men are expected to pray three times a day at fixed times, while women only pray once at a time of their choosing. This difference has been variously attributed to the demanding nature of women's household duties and to men's higher proclivity to sin. For centuries, women could not study the Torah and could not receive a formal education. While Orthodox Jews have eased their stance against education for women, they have nevertheless maintained that women should serve a secondary role to their husbands. Other Jews have taken a more liberal view, holding that women are equals who can fully participate in religious ceremonies. In Reform and Conservative Judaism, women are permitted to become rabbis. Many Jewish women rabbis played a role in the American feminist movement of the 1960s and 1970s. The movement liberated women from having to serve traditional roles, and Jewish women such as Congresswoman Bella Abzug and authors Gloria Steinem and Betty Friedan paved the way for women to enter a variety of fields once dominated by men.

EDUCATION

For years Jews have placed strong emphasis on the importance of education. In the nineteenth century, the ability to read gave German Jewish immigrants a competitive edge over other German immigrants. Later, American-born Jews pursued education as a means of entering such professions as law and medicine. Although Jews currently represent less than three percent of the American population, the proportion of Jews in academia has been significantly higher since World War II, with Jews comprising ten percent of the teaching faculty at American universities. By 1973, nearly 60 percent of all Jewish graduate students were enrolled in the nation's top ten institutions of higher learning. Approximately 20 to 30 percent of the leading scholars who taught at such universities were Jewish.

Religious education was once taught in a *heder*, an eastern European elementary school for boys. While girls generally did not have access to formal education, boys would attend the *heder* all day long, studying the Hebrew prayerbook and the Torah. In America, the *heder* played a secondary role to public schools. As priorities changed with acculturation, the *heder* diminished in significance. However, the Talmud Torah school, a charitable school first established in Europe, began to usurp the role of the *heder* as a place for Judaic instruction. Today, a number of Jewish children attend some type of religious school a few hours each week for three to five years in order to learn Jewish history, traditions, and customs as well as the Hebrew language.

PHILANTHROPIC TRADITIONS

The Jewish philanthropic tradition reaches back to biblical times when Israeli Jews practiced

tzedakah, or charity, as one of their primary duties in life. One common form of *tzedakah* was to allocate a portion of the harvest for the poor, who were free to take crops from certain parts of a farm. During the Middle Ages, Jewish self-governing communities called *kehillahs* would ensure that the community's poor would have the basic necessities of life. The spirit of the *kehillah* survived into the twentieth century in the form of *landsmanshaft*, separate societies existing within congregations in cities such as New York. The *landsmanshaft* were comprised of townspeople from congregations who pooled resources to provide such benefits as insurance, cemetery rights, free loans, and sick pay.

While the tradition of lending assistance began in the synagogue, over the years philanthropic organizations became increasingly independent. Organizations such as the Order of B'nai B'rith and the Young Men's Hebrew Association became major sponsors of charitable projects. These and other benevolent societies were responsible for the establishment of Jewish orphanages, hospitals, and retirement homes in major cities across the United States throughout the nineteenth century.

"Everybody had something to give me for help. It wasn't a question of money, it was a question of being a human being to a human being. And in those days people were apparently that way. There were so many nice people that were trying to help us when we came to this country."

Clara Larsen in 1908, cited in *Ellis Island: An Illustrated History of the Immigrant Experience,* edited by Ivan Chermayeff et al. (New York: Macmillan, 1991).

Jewish philanthropy increased tremendously during the twentieth century. Scientific philanthropy—a method of providing aid through modern methods and without assistance from religious institutions—gained favor at the turn of the century in response to the problem of helping settle the large waves of Russian immigrant Jews. One outgrowth of this movement was the establishment of the National Conference of Jewish Charities, which formed national agencies to deal with immigrant issues. During World War I, Jewish philanthropic efforts were consolidated through the establishment of the American Jewish Joint Distribution Committee, an organization formed to provide relief to eastern European Jews suffering from famine and pogroms. By raising more than $66 million by 1922, the Committee was able to expand its relief efforts to include health care and economic reconstruction programs that reached some 700,000 Jews in need of assistance. Several organizations supplied economic relief to European Jews during and after World War II. One such organization, the United Jewish Appeal, was initially established to help Holocaust survivors and to promote Israel as a homeland for Jews. During the postwar decades, however, it has blossomed into the largest private charity in America, providing financial aid to Israel and Jews worldwide. In recent decades, the Jewish philanthropic tradition has extended beyond the Jewish community. Mazon, for example, was founded in the 1980s as a national hunger relief organization that is funded by Jews who voluntarily donate three percent of the costs of such celebrations as weddings and *bar mitzvahs*.

RELIGION

The basic message of Judaism is that there is one all-powerful God. Originally established as a response to polytheism and idol worship, Judaism has been quite successful in perpetuating its belief in monotheism in that it is the parent religion of both Christianity and Islam. The basic difference between these three religions centers on the Messiah, or savior of the world. While Christians believe the Messiah was Jesus Christ and Muslims believe in several divinely inspired prophets, the greatest being Mohammed, Jews believe the Messiah has not yet appeared.

The centerpiece of Judaism is the Torah. Strictly speaking, the Torah refers to the first five books of the Bible (Five Books of Moses), but it can also mean the entire Bible or all of Jewish law, including the Talmud and the Midrash. The Talmud is oral law handed down through the generations that interprets the written law, or Torah. The Talmud consists of the Mishnah, which is the text version of the oral law as compiled by Rabbi Judah the Patriarch in 200 C.E., and the Gemara, which is the collected commentary on the Mishnah. The Midrash refers to the collection of stories or sermons, or *midrashim*, which interpret biblical passages. Taken as a whole, Jewish law is known as *halahah*, which guides all aspects of Jewish life.

Two other vital components of Judaism are the rabbi and the synagogue. Since the Middle Ages, rabbis served as spiritual leaders of communities. Though equal with the rest of humanity in the eyes of God, the rabbi was chosen by the community as an authority on Jewish law. Rabbis were paid to teach, preach, and judge religious and civic matters. While the role of the rabbi was well established in Europe, American synagogues were reluctant to preserve the social and economic position of rabbis. Congregation members no longer felt the need for such an authoritative figure. Consequently, some congregations hired ministers rather than rabbis in order to restrict the influence of their religious leaders. Today, many congregations continue to be led by rabbis who perform traditional duties as well as a variety of other functions, including visiting the sick and attending to wedding and funeral services. The synagogue is the place for Jewish worship, study, and social meetings. Although synagogues have generally played a secondary role to Jewish secular organizations in America, the postwar years saw a revival in the importance of the synagogue in Jewish life. The synagogue expanded to become the center of community life and the organization through which Jewish children developed a Jewish identity. Membership in synagogues rose dramatically, though attendance at services did not increase proportionately.

Though not known as such, Jews were all basically Orthodox until the French Revolution. Orthodoxy as a separate branch of Judaism developed in eastern and central Europe during the eighteenth and nineteenth centuries when the Jewish Enlightenment and Emancipation ushered in a new era of freedom of thought and living. Rejecting such changes, Orthodox Jews sought to maintain Jewish traditions through strict observance of Jewish law as expressed in the Torah. While most Jewish immigrants were Orthodox when they arrived in the United States, economic pressure and differences in social climate between Europe and America caused many to abandon Orthodoxy. As a result, Orthodox Judaism has only been practiced by a small minority of American Jews. (Roughly ten percent of American Jews are Orthodox, 30 percent are Reform, and 40 percent are Conservative.) The survival of Orthodox Judaism is due in part to its tolerance of American ways and modern educational practices, which have appealed to middle-class Jews. Other factors include the founding of Yeshiva College in 1928 and the development of an Orthodox parochial school system, which grew from just 17 schools in the 1930s to more than 400 schools by the 1970s.

For many years, the dominant branch of American Judaism has been Reform. Though some Jews maintain that Judaism has always been Reform, Reform Judaism as a distinct segment of Judaism can be traced to eighteenth-century German Jewish Enlightenment. Some Reform synagogues began to appear in Germany in the early nineteenth century, but Reform Judaism gained its largest following among German Jews who immigrated to America during the mid-nineteenth century. Unlike Orthodox Jews, members of Reform Judaism view Jewish laws as adaptable to the changing needs of cultures over time. As a result, Reform Jews look to the Bible for basic moral principles. They do not believe in a literal reading of the Bible and have felt free to ignore outdated passages, such as those that make reference to animal sacrifice. In general, Reform Judaism represents the most liberal strain of Judaism: Reform was the first to let women become rabbis (1972); it is accepting of intermarriage and converts; and it does not stress such traditional teachings as the coming of the Messiah or the need for separate nationhood (Israel). These liberal views reflect Reform's emphasis on reason over tradition, a shift that represents a transformation of the traditional Jewish identity into a Jewish American identity.

With a theological perspective that falls somewhere between Orthodoxy and Reform, Conservative Judaism has become the largest branch of American Judaism. Conservative Judaism first developed in nineteenth-century Germany and later gained an American following by the early 1900s. The American roots of this branch of Judaism can be traced to the 1887 founding in New York City of the Jewish Theological Seminary, which has since become the center of Conservative Judaism and home to the world's largest repository of books on Judaism and Jewish life. With its blend of tradition and openness to change within the confines of Jewish law, Conservative Judaism steadily attracted new members until World War II, when membership sharply increased and ultimately attained its current status as the largest branch of Judaism in America. Theologically, Conservatives look to the Talmud and its interpretations of the Torah as an example of their own views on the evolving nature of Jewish law. As long as change does not violate the basic tenets outlined in the Torah, change is welcomed by Conservatives. Thus, religious ceremonies do not have to be in Hebrew, and women can serve as rabbis. Because Conservatives have not formally articulated their ideology, individual congregations are able to style themselves around the needs of the community.

Another segment of American Judaism is Reconstructionist Judaism, which is sometimes lumped together with Reform and Conservative Judaism as Progressive Judaism. Developed in the 1920s and 1930s by Mordecai M. Kaplan and influenced by the thinking of American pragmatist philosopher John Dewey, Reconstructionism emphasizes Democratic culture and humanistic values. Reconstructionists value Jewish traditions not merely for their religious significance, but because such traditions reflect Jewish culture. Thus, Judaism is more a way of life than a religion. Reconstructionists may learn Hebrew, observe Jewish holidays, and eat kosher foods, but not out of a sense of obligation but as a way of preserving Jewish culture. Of the four major branches of Judaism, Reconstructionism has the smallest following.

Although most American-born Jews do not practice traditional Judaism or attend religious services, nearly three-fourths of American Jews align themselves with either Reform or Conservative Judaism.

EMPLOYMENT AND ECONOMIC TRADITIONS

Over the years, Jews have attained a high level of economic prosperity through keen business sense and dedication to hard work. Such prosperity has been achieved over the course of several generations, dating back to medieval Europe when Jews first became associated with the world of finance and trade. Because they were not allowed to hire Gentiles and were excluded from craft guilds, Jews took on the jobs that Christians found repugnant, such as money-lending and tax-collecting. In time Jews became involved in trade and the clothing business as well. By the time the Sephardic Jews began settling in America in the seventeenth and eighteenth centuries, most earned their livings as independent retailers; they were bakers, tailors, merchants, and small business owners.

Jews in the mid-nineteenth century were predominantly tailors or peddlers. Many of those who worked in the city were tailors or were otherwise affiliated with the garment business. Those who sought their fortune outside of the city were usually peddlers, who played a key role in bringing merchandise from the city to the country. The successful peddler could eventually earn enough to set up his own retail store on the outskirts of town or in rural areas. Credit was at the heart of the emerging network of these retail businesses. German Jews were the chief creditors at the time, and they would minimize their credit risks by dealing with relatives whenever possible. The close connection between creditor and businessman led to the emergence of a Jewish business elite between 1860 and 1880 that had established profitable ventures in such fields as investment banking, the garment industry, shoe manufacturing, and meat processing. By the end of the century, American Jews were no longer primarily tailors or peddlers (those trades represented just three percent and one percent, respectively, of American Jews in the 1890 census). Instead, Jews had attained a substantial measure of wealth by becoming retailers, bankers, brokers, wholesalers, accountants, bookkeepers, and clerks; together, these occupations represented 67 percent of all American Jews in the 1890 census.

The immigration of Russian Jews in the early twentieth century brought vast numbers of workers into the clothing industry in large cities. Newly arriving immigrants would work in the factories for long hours, often 70 or more hours a week, honing their skills and developing their own specialties. As with the German Jews before them, the Russian Jews worked their way into more affluent positions over the years, becoming business owners and professionals. While German Jews comprised the majority of the 1,000 clothing manufacturers in the late nineteenth century, by the eve of the World War I Russian Jews owned more than 16,000 garment factories and employed more than 200,000 Russian Jews. The slowing of immigration during and immediately after World War I coupled with increasing wages in the garment industry enabled Russian Jews to raise their standard of living and attain the same socio-economic status as German Jews by the 1920s.

The educated professional has long been a highly valued member of Jewish culture. The entrepreneurial success of first-generation Jews enabled subsequent generations to move into the professional ranks of society. In large eastern and midwestern cities such as New York and Cleveland, the disproportionate share of Jewish doctors, lawyers, and dentists represented two to three times the proportion of the Jewish population in those cities. For example, Jews in the 1930s comprised 25 percent of the population of New York City, yet accounted for 65 percent of all lawyers and judges in the city.

As with the general population, Jews enjoyed considerable economic prosperity during the Postwar years. After World War II, the institutional discrimination against Jews that had developed during the first part of the twentieth century disappeared. With unprecedented access to education and advancement in American society, younger Jews entered colleges and embarked upon successful professional careers at about twice the rate of the preceding generation. Rather than gravitating toward the clothing industry, as many of their parents and grandparents had done, postwar Jews turned to a range of fields, including management, communications, real estate, entertainment, and academia.

POLITICS AND GOVERNMENT

Since the first Jews arrived in Colonial America, Jews have enjoyed a high degree of political freedom and have taken an active role in politics and government. Although early Jewish settlers in America faced some political and social discrimination, laws restricting Jewish religious and business activities were generally not enforced. By 1740, Parliament granted Jewish aliens the right to citizenship without having to take a Christian oath. After America gained its independence, the Mikveh Israel Congregation urged the Constitutional Convention to make a provision guaranteeing the freedom of religious expression, which became a reality with the passage of the First Amendment in 1789. Since then, Jews have been involved in all levels of American civic and political life, with the presidency being the only office a Jew has not held. By 1992, Jews held 33 seats in the U.S. House of Representatives and a full ten percent of the Senate. The Republican congressional victories in 1994 reduced the number of Jews in the House to 24, while the retirement of Democrat Howard Metzenbaum brought the number of Jewish senators to nine.

Over the years Jews have developed a rich political tradition of fighting for social justice as liberals and radicals primarily affiliated with the Democratic party. Jews have been staunch supporters of Democratic political leaders. When in 1944 President Roosevelt's New Deal policies caused the president to lose popularity, 90 percent of Jews continued to support him. The tendency to side with an unpopular liberal candidate continued through 1972, when Democratic presidential candidate George McGovern won only 38 percent of the popular vote, but garnered more than 60 percent of the Jewish vote. The majority of Jews have continued their allegiance to the Democratic party, even during the 1980s when Republicans Ronald Reagan and George Bush won the presidency in landslide victories. Beginning in the 1970s, however, a growing number of Jews abandoned liberal politics in favor of pragmatism and conservatism. Leading this movement were Nathan Glazer, Irving Kristol, Sidney Hook, and Milton Friedman.

UNIONS AND SOCIALISM

The more radical Jewish political activists have been involved in unions and socialism. During the first part of the twentieth century, Jewish union leaders had strong ties to the Socialist party and the Jewish Socialist Federation. This support reflected a socialist leaning on the part of several Russian Jews who had participated in the failed Russian Revolution of 1905. The Socialist party enjoyed its greatest success in New York City between 1914 and 1917 when Socialist Meyer London was elected to represent the Lower East Side in the U.S. Congress and more than a dozen Socialists won seats in city government.

Influenced by eastern European socialist thought and American free enterprise, Jews found themselves on both sides of the labor disputes of the early twentieth century. The clothing industry provided the battleground. For a time Russian Jewish manufacturers refused to recognize unions, many of which contained a significant proportion of Jewish members. Tensions came to a head during two major strikes: The "uprising of twenty thousand," which involved Jewish and Italian young women striking against shirtwaist manufacturers in 1909, and "the great revolt," a massive strike in 1911 involving thousands of cloak makers. Both strikes pitted thugs and police against union workers. The workers received community support from various Jewish benefactors, ranging from wealthy women who posted bail for the arrested workers to lawyers and community leaders who helped mediate settlements. As a result of the strikes, the work week was lowered to 50 hours and permanent mediation procedures were established. Two key unions at the time were the International Ladies Garment Workers Union and the Amalgamated Clothing Workers Union, both of which included a significant proportion of Jewish members. Another union with significant Jewish membership was Arbeter Ring, or Workmen's Circle. With approximately 80,000 Jewish families on board by the mid-1920s, this union provided health care and cemetery services and involved itself in Yiddish culture by sponsoring Yiddish newspapers, schools, and theaters.

MILITARY PARTICIPATION

Throughout American history, Jews have served with distinction in the U.S. military. Of the approximately 2,500 Jews in America during the Revolutionary War, hundreds fought against the British while others supported the struggle for independence by refusing to recognize British authority. Just as the Civil War divided North against South, so too did it divide the American Jews. While most Jewish soldiers served in the Union army, many Jews in the South remained loyal to the Confederate cause. Several prominent Jews supported the South, notably Judah P. Benjamin, the Confederate Secretary of War and Secretary of State. Jews also figured prominently in the two world wars, with 250,000 Jews participating in World War I and 550,000 in World War II.

The participation of Jews in America's major wars demonstrates that while they are generally known as a peaceful people, Jews are prepared to fight for just causes. For some Jewish Americans, this principle extends beyond national concerns. The Jewish Defense League (JDL), for example, is a militant organization established in New York in 1968 by radical Rabbi Meir Kahane. The JDL's guiding principle is "Never Again," a reference to the Nazi Holocaust. The group's method of combatting worldwide anti-Semitism with violence has made the JDL controversial among Jews and non-Jews alike.

ISRAEL

For centuries Jews have sustained a commitment to establishing a homeland for Jews at some point. The longing to return to Zion, the hill on which Jerusalem was built, remained a vague dream until 1896, when Theodor Herzl wrote *The Jewish State*, which called for modern Palestine to be the home for Hebrew culture. The following year the first Zionist Congress convened in Basle, which along with Herzl's book marked the beginning of Zionism as an official movement. By 1914, some 12,000 American Jews had become Zionists. The movement was bolstered by the 1934 publication of Conservative Mordecai M. Kaplan's influential *Judaism as a Civilization*, which argued that Judaism as a religion reflected the totality of the

U.S. Senator Alfonse D'Amato (left center), comedian Jackie Mason (center), and others celebrate the annual Salute to Israel Parade in New York City.

Jewish people's consciousness. As such, Kaplan asserted that Jewish culture deserved its own central location, Palestine. After World War II, the effort to establish a Jewish state was helped considerably when the British gave the United Nations control of Palestine. In November of 1947 the United Nations approved a resolution to partition Palestine into Arab and Jewish regions. When Israel declared itself a nation on May 14, 1948, President Harry Truman decided to officially recognize Israel, despite a longstanding warning from the U.S. State Department that such recognition could anger oil-producing Arab countries.

Since the late 1930s American Jews have contributed billions of dollars in aid to help Israel deal with its immigration burdens and tenuous relations with Arab neighbors. While the periods of military strife in 1948, 1967, and 1973 brought forth the greatest contributions from the American Jewish community, financial support for various philanthropic projects has been steady over the years.

INDIVIDUAL AND GROUP CONTRIBUTIONS

Countless Jews have made significant contributions to American culture over the years. Only a partial listing of notable names is possible.

ACADEMIA

Jews have been particularly influential in academia, with ten percent of faculty at American universities comprised of Jews, the number rising to 30 percent at America's top ten universities. Notable Jewish scholars include historians Daniel J. Boorstin (1914-), Henry L. Feingold (1931-), Oscar Handlin (1915-), Jacob Rader Marcus (b. 1896), Abram Sachar (b. 1899), and Barbara Tuchman (1912-), linguist Noam Chomsky (1928-), Russian literature and Slavic language experts Maurice Friedman (1929-) and Roman Jakobson (b. 1896), Zionist scholar and activist Ben Halpern (1912-), and philosophers Ernest Nagel (1901-1985), a logical positivist influential in the philosophy of science, and Norman Lamm (1927-), Yeshiva University president and founder of the orthodox periodical *Tradition*.

FILM, TELEVISION, AND THEATER

Jews have had an enormous influence in Hollywood. By the 1930s Jews dominated the film industry as almost all of the major production companies were owned and operated by eastern European Jews. These companies include Columbia (Jack and Harry Cohn), Goldwyn (Samuel Goldwyn), Metro-Goldwyn-Mayer (Louis B. Mayer and Marcus Loew), Paramount (Jesse Lasky, Adolph Zukor, and Barney Balaban), Twentieth Century-Fox (Sol Brill and William Fox), United

Artists (Al Lichtman), Universal (Carl Laemmle), and Warner Brothers (Sam, Jack, Albert, and Harry Warner).

Actors/performers: The Marx Brothers—Chico (Leonard; 1887-1961), Harpo (Adolph; 1888-1964), Groucho (Julius; 1890-1977), Gummo (Milton; 1894-1977), and Zeppo (Herbert; 1901-1979); Jack Benny (Benjamin Kubelsky; 1894-1974); George Burns (Nathan Birnbaum; 1896-); Milton Berle (Milton Berlinger; 1908-); Danny Kaye (Daniel David Kominski; 1913-1987); Kirk Douglas (Issur Danielovitch; 1918-); Walter Matthau (1920-); Shelly Winters (Shirley Schrift; 1923-); Lauren Bacall (Betty Joan Perske; 1924-); Sammy Davis, Jr. (1925-1990); Gene Wilder (Jerome Silberman; 1935-); and Dustin Hoffman (1937-).

Directors: Carl Reiner (1922-); Mel Brooks (Melvyn Kaminsky; 1926-); Stanley Kubrick (1928-); Woody Allen (Allen Konigsberg; 1935-); and Steven Spielberg (1947-).

GOVERNMENT

Mordecai M. Noah (1785-1851) was the most widely known Jewish political figure of the first half of the nineteenth century. A controversial figure, Noah was U.S. consul in Tunis from 1813 to 1815, when he was recalled for apparently mismanaging funds. He went on to serve as an editor, sheriff, and judge. In 1825 he created a refuge for Jews when he purchased Grand Island in Niagara River. The refuge city, of which Noah proclaimed himself governor, was to be a step toward the establishment of a permanent state for Jews.

In 1916 the first Jew joined the U.S. Supreme Court, noted legal scholar Louis Brandeis (1856-1941), whose liberalism and Jewish heritage sparked a heated five-month Congressional battle over his nomination. After his confirmation, Brandeis used his power to help Zionism gain acceptance among Jews and non-Jews alike. Other prominent Jewish Supreme Court jurists include Benjamin Cardozo (1870-1938), a legal realist whose opinions foreshadowed the liberalism of the Warren court, and Felix Frankfurter (1882-1965), who prior to his Supreme Court appointment had been influential in promoting New Deal policies as a key advisor to President Franklin D. Roosevelt.

After the 1994 elections, nine Jews were members of the U.S. Senate: Barbara Boxer (California), Russell Feingold (Wisconsin), Diane Feinstein (California), Herbert Kohl (Wisconsin), Frank Lautenberg (New Jersey), Carl Levin (Michigan), Joseph Lieberman (Connecticut), Arlen Specter (Pennsylvania), and Paul Wellstone (Minnesota). With the exception of Specter, all are Democrats.

JOURNALISM

During the late nineteenth century Joseph Pulitzer operated a chain of newspapers, many of which often featured stories of public corruption. After his death in 1911, he left funds for the Columbia University School of Journalism and for the coveted annual prizes in his name. Since then, many Jewish journalists have won the Pulitzer Prize, including ABC news commentator Carl Bernstein (1944-), *Washington Post* columnist David Broder (1929-), syndicated columnist and satirist Art Buchwald (1925-), syndicated columnist Ellen Goodman (1927-), former *New York Times* reporter and author David Halberstam (1934-), journalist Seymour Hersh (1937-), *New York Times* columnist Anthony Lewis (1927-), former *New York Times* reporter and Harvard journalism professor Anthony J. Lukas (1933-), *New York Times* executive editor and author A. M. Rosenthal (1922-), stylist, humorist, and former presidential speech writer William Safire (1929-), *New York Times* reporter Sydney Schanberg (1934-), and journalist and political historian Theodore H. White (1915-). Other notable Jewish journalists include sportscaster Howard Cosell (William Howard Cohen; 1920-1995), *Village Voice* columnist Nat Hentoff (1925-), NBC television journalist Marvin Kalb (1930-), financial columnist Sylvia Porter (Sylvia Feldman; 1913-), investigative journalist I. F. Stone (Isador Feinstein; 1907-), "60 Minutes" television journalist Mike Wallace (Myron Leon Wallace; 1918-), and television journalist Barbara Walters (1931-).

LITERATURE

Novelists: Saul Bellow (Solomon Bellows; 1915-) —*The Adventures of Augie March* and *Mr. Sammler's Planet*; E. L. Doctorow (1931-)—*Ragtime* and *Billy Bathgate*; Stanley Elkin (1930-); Joseph Heller (1923-)—*Catch 22*; Erica Jong (Erica Mann; 1942-)—*Fear of Flying*; Jerzy Kosinski (1933-1991)—*Being There*; Ira Levin (1929-)—*Rosemary's Baby* and *Boys from Brazil*; Norman Mailer (1923-)—*The Naked and the Dead* and *Tough Guys Don't Dance*; Bernard Malamud

(1914-1986)—*The Natural* and *The Fixer*; Cynthia Ozick (1928-)—*The Pagan Rabbi*; Philip Roth (1933-)—*Portnoy's Complaint*; Isaac Bashevis Singer (1904-1991)—*In My Father's House*; Leon Uris (1924-)—*Exodus*; Nathaniel West (Nathan Weinstein; 1903-1940)—*Miss Lonelyhearts* and *The Day of the Locust*; and Herman Wouk (1915-) —*The Caine Mutiny* and *War and Remembrance*.

Playwrights: Lillian Hellman (1907-1984)— *Children's Hour* and *The Little Foxes*; David Mamet (1947-)—*American Buffalo* and *Glengarry Glen Ross*; and Arthur Miller (1915-)—*Death of a Salesman* and *The Crucible*.

Poets: Allen Ginsberg (1926-)—"Howl" and "Kaddish;" Stanley Kunitz (1905-)—"Green Ways;" and Howard Nemerov (1920-1991).

Essayists/critics: Irving Howe (1920-)— *World of Our Fathers* and *How We Lived*; Alfred Kazin (1915-)—*New York Jew*; Susan Sontag (1933-)—*Against Interpretation*; and Elie Wiesel (1928-)—*Night*.

MUSIC

Broadway and popular composers: Irving Berlin (1888-1989)—"Blue Skies," "God Bless America," and "White Christmas;" George Gershwin (1898-1937)—*Of Thee I Sing* and *Porgy and Bess* (musicals) and "Rhapsody in Blue;" Richard Rodgers (1902-1979)—*Oklahoma!*, *Carousel*, *South Pacific*, *The King and I*, and *The Sound of Music* (musicals; with Oscar Hammerstein II); Benny Goodman (1909-1986)—"Let's Dance" and "Tiger Rag" (swing band music); pianist, composer, and conductor Leonard Bernstein (1918-1990)—*West Side Story* and *Candide* (musicals) and *On the Waterfront* (film score); Burt Bacharach (1929-); Herb Alpert (1935-); and Marvin Hamlisch (1944-).

Classical performers/composers: pianist Arthur Rubinstein (1887-1982); violinist Jascha Heifetz (1901-1987); pianist Vladimir Horowitz (1904-1989); violinist Nathan Milstein (1904-1992); violinist Itzhak Perlman (1945-); operatic soprano Beverly Sills (Belle Silverman; 1929-); and composer Aaron Copeland (1900-1990).

Popular songwriters/performers: Bob Dylan (Robert Zimmerman; 1941-)—"Like a Rolling Stone" and "Blowing in the Wind;" Neil Diamond (1941-)—"Solitary Man" and "I'm a Believer;" Carole King (Carole Klein; 1941-)— "You've Got a Friend" and "Been to Canaan;" Paul Simon (1941-); Art Garfunkel (1941-); and Barbra Streisand (1942-).

SCIENCE AND TECHNOLOGY

Perhaps the best known thinker of the twentieth century is Albert Einstein (1879-1955), the German Jewish physicist who had completed his most important scientific work before coming to America in 1934. Though best known for his theory of relativity, for which he won the Nobel Prize in 1922, Einstein played a critical role in American history as part of team of scientists who researched atomic power during World War II. At that time, Jewish emigres joined native-born Jews in the famous Los Alamos nuclear project that led to the explosion of the first atomic bomb in 1945. Robert Oppenheimer (1904-1967), Lewis Strauss, and I.I. Rabi (b. 1898), all American-born Jews, teamed up with such Jewish immigrant scientists as Einstein, Enrico Fermi (1901-1954), Leo Szilard, Theodor von Karman, and John von Neumann. Einstein was part of "brain drain" of Jews from Nazi Germany that also included psychoanalysts Erich Fromm (1900-1980), Bruno Bettelheim (1903-1990), and Erik Erikson (1902-), as well as social scientists Hannah Arendt (1906-1975) and Leo Strauss (1899-1973).

Other American Jews made notable contributions to science as well. Albert Michelson, who measured the speed of light, was the first American to win the Nobel Peace Prize. Jonas Salk (1914-1995) and Albert Sabin (1906-1993) discovered polio vaccines during the 1950s, and Robert Hofstadter (1916-1970) won the Nobel Prize for creating a device for measuring the size and shape of neutrons and protons. Medical science pioneer Joseph Goldberger (1874-1929) laid the foundation for modern nutritional science with his study of the dietary habits of poor whites and blacks in the South. Finally, chemist Isaac Asimov (1920-1992) popularized science with his 500 fiction and non-fiction books on science.

SPORTS

Children of Jewish immigrants at the turn of the century gravitated toward sports to break up the routine of daily life. Boxing was especially popular, with Jewish boxing champions Abe Attell (Albert Knoehr; 1884-1969), Barney Ross (Barnet Rasofsky; 1909-1967), and Benny Leonard (Benjamin Leiner; 1896-1947), all hailing from New York's Lower East Side. Other world champions from various weight classes for two years or more include Benny Bass (1904-1975), Robert Cohen (1930-), Jackie Fields (Jacob Finkelstein; 1908-), Alphonse Halimi (1932-), Louis "Kid" Kaplan (1902-1970),

Battling Levinsky (Barney Lebrowitz; 1891-1949), Ted Lewis (Gershon Mendeloff; 1894-1970), Al McCoy (Al Rudolph; b. 1894), Charley Phil Rosenberg (Charles Green; 1901-), "Slapsie" Maxie Rosenbloom (1904-1976), and Corporal Izzy Schwartz (1902-).

Beyond boxing, Jews have made their mark in many other sports as well. The Jewish Sports Hall of Fame in Israel incudes the following Americans: Red Auerbach (basketball), Isaac Berger (weightlifting), Hank Greenberg (baseball), George Gulak (gymnastics), Irving Jaffe (ice skating), Sandy Koufax (baseball), Sid Luckman (football), Walter Miller (horse racing), Dick Savitt (tennis), Mark Spitz (swimming), and Sylvia Wene Martin (bowling).

MEDIA

PRINT

Commentary.
An organ of the American Jewish Committee and published monthly, this influential Jewish magazine addresses religious, political, social, and cultural topics.

Contact: Norman Podhoretz, Editor.

Address: 165 East 56th Street, New York, New York 10022.

Telephone: (212) 751-4000.

Jewish Forward.
Published in English and Yiddish by the Forward Association. With a circulation of 25,000, the daily paper covers local, national, and international news, with special emphasis on Jewish life.

Contact: Mordecai Shtrigler, Editor.

Address: 45 East 33rd Street, New York, New York 10016.

Telephone: (212) 889-8200.

Jewish Press.
A national weekly newspaper covering issues and events related to Jewish life. Established in 1949, it has a circulation of 174,000.

Contact: Jerry Greenwald, Editor.

Address: 338 Third Avenue, Brooklyn, New York 11215.

Telephone: (718) 330-1100.

Nashreeye B'nei Torah.
A bimonthly journal published by the Iranian B'Nei Torah Movement that carries articles on Jewish history, tradition, and culture for Iranian Jews.

Contact: Rabbi Joseph Zargari.

Address: P.O. Box 351476, Los Angeles, California 90035.

Telephone: (310) 652-2115.

Reform Judaism.
An organ of Union of American Hebrew Congregations, this quarterly concentrates on religious, political, and cultural issues of concern to Reform Jews.

Contact: Aron Hirt-Manheimer, Editor.

Address: 838 Fifth Avenue, New York, New York 10021.

Telephone: (212) 249-0100.

The Sentinel.
An English-language weekly paper established in 1911 with a circulation of 46,000. It publishes local, national, and international news stories and commentary as well as listings of events of interest to the Jewish community.

Contact: Jack I. Fishbein, Editor and Publisher.

Address: 150 North Michigan Avenue, Suite 2025, Chicago, Illinois 60601.

Telephone: (312) 407-0060.

RADIO

More than a dozen Jewish radio programs are broadcast weekly in cities across the United States. Typically lasting one to two hours, the programs are found on such stations as the following:

KCSN-FM.
Address: 18111 Nordhoff Street, Northridge, California 91330.

Telephone: (818) 885-3089.

KERA-FM.
Address: 3000 Harry Hines, Dallas, Texas 75201.

Telephone: (214) 871-1390.

KUXL-AM.
Address: 5730 Duluth Street, Golden Valley, Minnesota 55422.

Telephone: (612) 544-3196.

WCLV-FM.
Address: 26501 Emery Industrial Parkway, Cleveland, Ohio 44128.

Telephone: (216) 464-0900.

WMUA-FM.

Address: 105 Campus Center, University of Massachusetts, Amherst, Massachusetts 01003.

Telephone: (413) 545-2876.

TELEVISION

There are several Jewish television broadcasting stations, including:

Israel Broadcasting Authority.

Address: 1101 30th Street, Washington, D.C. 20007.

Telephone: (202) 338-6091.

Israel Broadcasting Authority Radio and Television.

Address: 10 Rockefeller Plaza, New York, New York 10020.

Telephone: (212) 265-6330.

Jewish Television Network.

Address: 617 South Olive Street, Suite 515, Los Angeles, California 90014.

Telephone: (213) 614-0972.

Jewish Video Cleveland.

Address: Jewish Community Federation, 1750 Euclid Avenue, Cleveland, Ohio 44115.

Telephone: (216) 566-9200.

Tele-Israel.

Cable channels 23, 24, 25, and M in New York City.

Telephone: (212) 620-7041.

ORGANIZATIONS AND ASSOCIATIONS

American Jewish Committee (AJC).

Founded in 1906, the AJC is an influential organization dedicated to the protection of religious and civil rights. Representing more than 600 Jewish American communities, the AJC sponsors educational programs, maintains its own library, and publishes the noted journal, *Commentary*.

Contact: David Harris, Executive Vice President.

Address: c/o Institute of Human Relations, 165 East 56th Street, New York, New York 10022.

Telephone: (212) 751-4000.

American Jewish Joint Distribution Committee (JDC).

Founded 1914, the JDC is a charitable organization created by the American Jewish Relief Committee, the Central Committee for Relief of Jews of the Union of Orthodox Congregations, and the People's Relief Committee. In addition to providing economic assistance to needy Jews in 25 countries, the organization fosters community development through an assortment of educational, religious, cultural, and medical programs with an annual budget of $90 million.

Contact: Michael Schneider, Executive Vice President.

Address: 711 Third Avenue, New York, New York 10017.

Telephone: (212) 687-6200.

Anti-Defamation League of B'nai B'rith (ADL).

Founded in 1913, the ADL was created by B'nai B'rith, an international organization founded in 1843 to foster Jewish unity and protect human rights. The ADL was established to counter the rising tide of anti-Semitism during the early twentieth century, but it has since expanded its focus to protect against defamation of any group of people. Though the ADL has broadened its mission and sought to improve interfaith relations, one of the group's primary goals is to further American understanding of Israel. The ADL sponsors a number of bulletins, including its *Anti-Defamation League Bulletin*, as well as articles, monographs, and educational materials.

Contact: Abraham H. Foxman, Director.

Address: 823 United Nations Plaza, New York, New York 10017.

Telephone: (212) 490-2525.

92nd Street Young Men's and Young Women's Hebrew Association (YM-YWHA).

Founded in 1874, the YM-YWHA resulted from the merger between the Young Men's Hebrew Association, the Young Women's Hebrew Association, and the Clara de Hirsch Residence. It provides Jewish cultural, social, educational, and recreational programs for 300,000 Jews in New York City. The association serves a variety of functions by maintaining several facilities in New

York, including residence facilities for Jewish men and women between 18 and 27, men's and women's health clubs, swimming pools, gymnasiums, and a library containing more than 30,000 volumes on Jewish life and thought. Scholarships are also offered to Jewish undergraduate and graduate students.

Contact: Sol Adler, Executive Director.

Address: 1395 Lexington Avenue, New York, New York 10128.

Telephone: (212) 427-6000.

World Jewish Congress, American Section (WJC).

Founded 1936, the WJC is an international organization representing three million Jews in 68 countries. The American Section of the WJC represents 23 Jewish organizations. Guided by its mission to protect human rights worldwide, the WJC serves a consultative capacity with various international governing bodies, including the United Nations, UNESCO, UNICEF, International Labour Organization, and Council of Europe. The WJC is responsible for such periodicals as *World Jewry, Journal of Jewish Sociology* and *Patterns of Prejudice*.

Contact: Elan Steinberg, Executive Director.

Address: 501 Madison Avenue, 17th Floor, New York, New York 10022.

Telephone: (212) 755-5770.

MUSEUMS AND RESEARCH CENTERS

American Jewish Historical Society.

Founded in 1892 in an effort to gather, organize, and disseminate information and memorabilia related to the history of American Jews. The society has a library with more than ten million books, documents, manuscripts, pictures, and miniatures.

Contact: Justin L. Wyner, President.

Address: 2 Thornton Road, Waltham, Massachusetts 02154.

Telephone: (617) 891-8110.

Holocaust Memorial Museum.

Sponsored by the President's Commission on the Holocaust and the U.S. Holocaust Memorial Council, it presents a moving tribute to the millions of Jews who perished in Nazi concentration camps during World War II. Opened in 1994, the museum features photographs, documents, and video.

Contact: Sam Eskenazi, Public Information Director.

Address: 100 Raoul Wallenberg Place, S.W., Washington, D.C. 20024-2150.

Telephone: (212) 488-0400.

The Jewish Museum.

Boasts the largest collection in the Western Hemisphere of materials related to Jewish life. Covering 40 centuries, the collection features paintings, drawings, prints, sculpture, ceremonial objects, coins, broadcast material, and historical documents.

Contact: Anne Scher, Director of Public Relations.

Address: 1109 Fifth Avenue, New York, New York 10128.

Telephone: (212) 423-3200.

Leo Baeck Institute.

A research center dedicated to the preservation and study of materials related to the culture and socio-economic history of German-speaking Jews of the nineteenth and twentieth centuries. The institute maintains a library with more than 500 unpublished memoirs and 60,000 volumes on the German Jewish experience from the Jewish Enlightenment to the emergence of National Socialism. There is also an art collection featuring more than 3,000 works by German-Jewish artists.

Contact: Robert A. Jacobs, Executive Director.

Address: 129 East 73rd Street, New York, New York 10021.

Telephone: (212) 744-6400.

YIVO Institute for Jewish Research.

A secular research institute dedicated to scholarship on all aspects of the American Jewish experience, with particular emphasis on Yiddish language and literature. Established in 1925, the institute has gathered a massive collection of some 22 million documents, photographs, manuscripts, audiovisuals, and other items related to Jewish life.

Contact: Allan Nadler, Interim Director.

Address: 1048 Fifth Avenue, New York, New York 10028.

Telephone: (212) 535-6700.

SOURCES FOR ADDITIONAL STUDY

Dimont, Max I. *The Jews in America: The Roots, History, and Destiny of American Jews*. New York: Simon & Schuster, 1978.

Glazer, Nathan. *American Judaism*. Chicago: University of Chicago Press, 1972.

Golden, Harry. *The Greatest Jewish City in the World*. Garden City, New York: Doubleday, 1972.

Hertzberg, Arthur. *The Jews in America: Four Centuries of an Uneasy Encounter*. New York: Simon & Schuster, 1989.

Howe, Irving. *World of Our Fathers*. New York: Harcourt Brace Jovanovich, 1976.

Kushner, Harold. *To Life! A Celebration of Jewish Being and Thinking*. Boston: Little, Brown, 1993.

Sachar, Howard. *A History of Jews in America*. New York: Knopf, 1992.

Silberman, Charles E. *A Certain People: American Jews and Their Lives Today*. New York: Summit Books, 1985.

Sklare, Marshall. *America's Jews*. New York: Random House, 1971.

Waskow, Arthur I. *Seasons of Our Joy: A Handbook of Jewish Festivals*. New York: Summit Books, 1986.

KOREAN

by
Amy Nash

AMERICANS

Coming from a traditional society greatly influenced by the Confucian principle of placing elders, family, and community before the individual, Korean immigrants struggle to make sense of the American concept of individual freedom.

OVERVIEW

Known to its people as *Choson* (Land of Morning Calm), Korea occupies a mountainous peninsula in eastern Asia. Stretching southward from Manchuria and Siberia for close to 600 miles (966 kilometers), it extends down to the Korea Strait. China lies to Korea's west, separated from the peninsula by the Yellow Sea. Japan lies to its east on the other side of the Sea of Japan.

Western societies have traditionally viewed the Korean peninsula as a remote region of the world. They have often referred to it as "The Hermit Kingdom" because it remained isolated from the West until the nineteenth century. Yet it actually holds a central position on the globe, neighboring three major world powers—the former Soviet Union, China, and Japan.

At the end of World War II in 1945, the United States and the Soviet Union divided the peninsula along the 38th Parallel into two zones of occupation—a Soviet controlled region in the north and an American controlled one in the south. In 1948, North Korea (the Democratic People's Republic of Korea) and South Korea (the Republic of Korea) were officially established. North Korea is run by a Communist government, with Pyongyang as its capital city. South Korea's government is an emergent democracy, and Seoul—Korea's largest city—is its capital.

An estimated 67 million people live on the Korean peninsula, with a population of approximately 43.9 million in South Korea and another 23.1 million residing in North Korea. Together they are racially and linguistically homogeneous. They are the ethnic descendants of a Tungusic branch of the Ural-Altaic family. Their spoken language, Korean, is a Uralic language with similarities to Japanese, Mongolian, Hungarian, and Finnish.

EARLY HISTORY

In its 5,000-year history, Korea has suffered over 900 invasions from outside peoples. Accordingly, the Korean people have found it necessary to defend fiercely their identity as a separate culture. Tungusic tribes from the Altai mountain region in central Asia made the peninsula their home during the Neolithic period around 4000 B.C. These tribes brought with them primitive religious and cultural practices, such as the east Asian religion of shamanism. By the fourth century B.C. several wall-town states throughout the peninsula were large enough to be recognized by China. The most advanced of these, Old Choson, was located in the basin of the Liao and Taedong rivers, where Pyongyang is situated today. China invaded Choson in the third century B.C. and maintained a strong cultural influence over the peninsula for the next 400 years.

Historians commonly refer to the first period of recorded Korean history (53 B.C.-668 A.D.) as the Period of the Three Kingdoms. These kingdoms were Koguryo, Paekche, and Silla. Toward the end of the seventh century A.D. Silla conquered Koguryo and Paekche and united the peninsula under the Silla dynasty. This period saw many advancements in literature, art, and science. Buddhism, which had reached Korea by way of China, was practiced by virtually all of Silla society. By the mid-eighth century the Silla people began using woodblock printing to reproduce sutras and Confucian writings.

In 900, the three kingdoms divided again. Within 36 years the Koguryo kingdom took control, and its leader, General Wang Kon, established the Koryo dynasty. The word Korea comes from this dynastic name. During Koryo's 400-year reign, artistic, scientific, and literary achievements advanced further. Improving upon earlier Chinese printing methods, Korea became the first country in the world to use movable cast metal type in 1234. Medical knowledge also developed

during the thirteenth century. Evolving out of local Korean folk remedies and Chinese practices, Korean medical science was recorded in books such as *Emergency Remedies of Folk Medicine* and *Folk Remedies of Samhwaja*.

Mongolian forces invaded Koryo in 1231 and occupied the kingdom until 1368. The Chinese Ming dynasty forced the Mongols back to the far north. This struggle eventually led to the fall of Koryo in 1392, when General Yi Song-Gye revolted against the king and founded the Yi dynasty. In control until the early twentieth century, it proved to be Korea's longest reigning dynasty and one of the most enduring regimes in history. The increasingly militant Buddhist state of the former Koryo dynasty yielded to the thinking of the new Choson kingdom, which was ruled by civilians who devotedly followed Confucian principles. Confucianism is not a religion but a philosophy of life and ethics that stresses an individual's sense of duty to family members and society as a whole. The Yi regime emphasized hierarchical relationships, with highest respect given to family elders, the monarch, and China as the older, more established country.

The Yi dynasty remained peaceful until 1592, when Japan invaded the peninsula. Chinese soldiers helped Korea seize control over its land from the Japanese armies. Japan attacked again in 1597, but Korea was able to force its withdrawal by the end of the year. Still, the country was left in tatters from the war. Korea suffered more attacks in 1627 and 1636, this time at the hands of the Manchus, who later conquered China. Western scientific, technological, and religious influences began to make their way to Korea during this period, by way of China. France, Great Britain, and the United States had already begun to dominate areas within China and other Asian countries. Calling Korea "The Hermit Kingdom" because of its closed-door policy toward non-Chinese foreigners, Western countries became interested in the peninsula in the nineteenth century.

In 1832 an English merchant ship landed off the coast of Chungchong province, and in 1846 three French warships landed in the same area. Eight years later two armed Russian ships sailed along the Hamgyong coast and killed a few Korean civilians before leaving the region. In 1866 the U.S.S. *General Sherman* sailed up the Taedong River to Pyongyang. The crew's goal of drawing up a trade agreement was thwarted by an enraged mob of Koreans who set fire to the ship, killing everyone aboard. Five U.S. warships appeared near the

Korean island of Kanghwa the following year and also were fought off. Korean animosity toward Western countries stemmed largely from their awareness of China's troubles with these same nations, particularly Great Britain, which had devastated China during the First Opium War of 1839-1842. Despite Korean resistance, Japan forced the country to open to trade in 1876. In 1882 Korea reluctantly agreed to trade with the United States.

For two centuries China and Japan fought for control over Asia. China's defeat in the Sino-Japanese War (1894-1895) greatly weakened Chinese dominance. After this victory Japan invaded the Korean peninsula. Korean students from American-founded schools resented this invasion. These schools had become a place to learn about democracy and national liberation. The Japanese army despised the American missionaries who had established these schools but knew better than to confront citizens of the powerful U.S. government. Instead, they took advantage of Korean citizens and outlawed Korean customs. Korea turned to Russia for financial support and protection. What followed was a ten-year struggle between Russia and Japan for control over the Korean peninsula. The Russo-Japanese War of 1904-1905 ended in another Japanese victory. U.S. president Theodore Roosevelt mediated the treaty agreement and won a Nobel Peace Prize for his role in creating the Treaty of Portsmouth. Korea became a protectorate of Japan, and Japan officially annexed the country in 1910.

MODERN HISTORY

During its 35 years as a Japanese colony, Korea experienced major economic and social developments, such as soil improvement, updated methods of farming, and industrialization in the north. Japan modernized the country along Western lines, but Korea did not reap the benefits. Japan used half of the Korean rice crop for its own industry. Most Korean farmers were forced off their land. All Korean schools and temples were controlled by the Japanese. By the 1930s Koreans were forced to worship at Shinto shrines, speak Japanese in schools, and adopt Japanese names. Japan also prevented them from publishing Korean newspapers and organizing their own intellectual and political groups.

Thousands of Koreans participated in demonstrations against the Japanese government. These marches were mostly peaceful, but some led to violence. On March 1, 1919, a group of 33 prominent Koreans in Seoul issued a proclamation of independence. Close to 500,000 Koreans, including students, teachers, and members of religious groups, organized demonstrations in the streets, protesting against Japanese rule. This mass demonstration, which became known as the March First Movement, lasted two months until the Japanese government suppressed it and expanded the size of its police force in Korea by 10,000. According to conservative estimates from Japanese reports, the Japanese police killed 7,509 Koreans, wounded 15,961, and imprisoned another 46,948 in the process of quelling the movement.

Japan sided with Nazi Germany during World War II. The Japanese government put Koreans to work in munitions plants, airplane factories, and coal mines in Japan. Before the war, Korean nationalists living outside of the country (in Siberia, Manchuria, China, and the United States) organized independence efforts, often using guerrilla tactics against the Japanese. One of these nationalists residing in the United States, Syngman Rhee, went on to become the first president of South Korea. Another Korean who was making a name for himself as a rebel was Kim Song-Je. Born in 1912 near Pyongyang, Kim spent most of his childhood in Manchuria and took the pseudonym Kim Il Sung in 1930, and organized one of the first anti-Japanese guerrilla units in Antu, Manchuria, on April 25, 1932, and became North Korea's first president. North Koreans still celebrate April 25 as the founding date of the Korean People's Army.

When Japan attacked Pearl Harbor, Hawaii, on December 7, 1941, bringing the United States into World War II, the Korean provisional government created by such nationalists as Syngman Rhee finally had an opportunity to take a stand against Japan. On December 8, this provisional government declared war on Japan and formed the Restoration Army to fight alongside the Allies in the Pacific theater.

When Japan surrendered to the Allies on August 15, 1945, ending the Japanese occupation of Korea, Koreans took to the streets in celebration of the end of 36 years under oppressive rule. But the freedom they expected did not follow. The Soviet Union immediately occupied Pyongyang, Hamhung, and other major northern cities. The United States followed by stationing troops in southern Korea. This division, which was supposed to have been a temporary measure, remained a source of turbulence and tragedy for Koreans at the dawn of the twenty-first century..

In the months that followed the end of World War II, postwar international decisions were made without the consent of the Korean people. The Soviet Union set up a provisional Communist government in northern Korea, and the United States created a provisional republican government in the South. In 1948 the Republic of Korea was founded south of the 38th Parallel, followed by the establishment of the Democratic People's Republic of Korea in the North. Both governments claimed authority over the entire peninsula and tempted fate by crossing the border at various points along the 38th Parallel.

On June 25, 1950, North Korea launched a surprise attack on South Korea, beginning a costly, bloody, three-year struggle known as the Korean War. It was perhaps the most tragic period in modern history for the Korean people. In the end, neither side achieved victory. On July 27, 1953, in the town of Panmunjom, the two sides signed an armistice designating a cease-fire line along the 38th Parallel and establishing a surrounding 2.5-mile-wide (four-kilometer-wide) demilitarized zone, which remains the boundary between the two Koreas. The war left the peninsula a wasteland. An estimated four million soldiers were killed or wounded, and approximately 1 million civilians died.

Both Koreas moved swiftly to rebuild after the war and have emerged into modern, industrialized nations. North Korea, which was more industrialized than South Korea before the war, restored the production of goods to prewar levels within three years. North Korea's economy and industry suffered in the latter part of the twentieth century, however, as a result of the break-up of the Soviet Union, one of its major trading partners. South Korea has evolved from a rural to post-industrial society since the 1960s. It has become an important exporter of products such as Hyundai cars, GoldStar televisions, and Samsung VCRs. In the late 1980s the United States was the second largest exporter to South Korea, after Japan. In 1989, South Korea was the seventh largest exporter country to the United States.

Kim Il Sung ruled as a Communist dictator in North Korea for more than four decades, until his death in July 1994. South Korea, on the other hand, has undergone several political upheavals since the Korean War. South Koreans have become increasingly dissatisfied with the U.S.-South Korea alliance and with the presence of U.S. troops in the country. Corruption in the government and the lack of free elections have caused many student uprisings. President Kim Young-Sam, who took office in February 1993, has instituted economic reforms and an aggressive anti-corruption campaign. As of 1995, it was too soon to tell if his programs would bring the country closer to a true democracy.

All measures introduced to reunify the Korean peninsula have ended in a stalemate. U.S. concern over North Korea's nuclear weapons program during the 1990s has threatened to increase tensions between the two Koreas. North Korea's refusal to allow full international inspection of its nuclear facilities brought the United States close to proposing a resolution for a United Nations economic embargo against North Korea in June 1994. Before sanctions were implemented, former U.S. President Jimmy Carter met with the North Korean government and reported back that the country would be willing to freeze all activity that produces fuel for nuclear weapons if Washington would initiate high-level talks. In the past, planned meetings between the two Korean governments have broken down. Officials were cautiously hopeful that this time would be different, until Kim Il Sung's death once again put negotiations between the two countries on hold. Reunification remains the most pressing issue on the minds of virtually all Koreans.

THE FIRST KOREANS IN AMERICA

The first recorded emigration of Koreans from their homeland occurred in the eighth century, when thousands moved to Japan. Korean communities also existed in China as early as the ninth century. By the middle of the nineteenth century, the Yenpien section of Manchuria and the Maritime provinces of Russia became home to many Koreans escaping famine on the peninsula. Emigration was illegal in Korea, but by the end of the century, 23,000 Koreans were living in the Maritime provinces. Natural disasters, poverty, high taxes, and government oppression were given as their reasons for leaving. As Japanese control over the peninsula began to spread, so did Korean discontent. The United States became a refuge for a small number of Koreans at the end of the nineteenth century. Three Korean political refugees moved to America in 1885. Five more arrived in 1899 but were mistaken for Chinese. Between 1890-1905, 64 Koreans had traveled to Hawaii to attend Christian mission schools. Most of these students returned to Korea after completing their studies.

SIGNIFICANT IMMIGRATION WAVES

The first major wave of Korean immigrants to the United States began in 1903, when Hawaiian sugar plantation owners offered Koreans the opportunity to work on their plantations. By 1835 sugar had become the main crop produced on the Hawaiian Islands, largely due to the prolific yield of the Koloa Plantation on the island of Kauai. Initially the sugar planters hired native Hawaiians to work as contract laborers on the plantations. By 1850 the native population had declined, the laborers became increasingly dissatisfied with the hard work, and the demand for sugar continued to grow. The resulting labor shortage forced the planters to form the Royal Hawaiian Agricultural Society to recruit outside sources of labor. Hawaii was not yet a part of the United States, and contract labor was therefore still legal. In 1852, the first immigrant laborers arrived in Hawaii from China. By the time the United States annexed Hawaii in 1898, 50,000 Chinese immigrants lived in Hawaii. Low wages, long work days, and poor treatment caused many Chinese laborers to leave the plantations in order to find work in the cities. The sugar planters then began to recruit Japanese immigrants to supplement the work force on the plantations.

In 1900 Hawaii became an official U.S. territory, making it legal for the Chinese and Japanese workers to go on strike. Many of them did. America's Chinese Exclusion Act of 1882 prohibited immigration of Chinese people to the United States. When Hawaii became a U.S. territory, Chinese workers were not allowed to immigrate to Hawaii. To offset another labor shortage and weaken the unions, Hawaiian sugar planters turned to Korea. In 1902 growers sent a representative to San Francisco to meet with Horace Allen, the American ambassador to Korea. Allen began recruiting Koreans to work on the plantations with the help of David William Deshler, an American businessman living in Korea. Deshler owned a steamship service that operated between Korea and Japan. The Hawaiian Sugar Planters Association paid Deshler 55 dollars for each Korean recruited. The Deshler Bank, set up in the Korean seaside town of Inchon, provided loans of 100 dollars to each immigrant for transportation.

With conditions worsening in their homeland, the offer appealed to a great number of Koreans. They would be paid a monthly wage of 16 dollars; receive free housing, health care, and English lessons; and would enjoy a warmer climate. Newspaper advertisements and posters promoted Hawaii as paradise and America as a land of gold and dreams. Recruiters used the slogan *Kaeguk chinch wi* ("the country is open, go forward") to encourage potential recruits. American missionaries also helped persuade Koreans with stories of how life in the West would make them better Christians. Reverend George Heber Jones of the Methodist Episcopal Church in Inchon was one of the more well-known American preachers who encouraged Koreans to go to Hawaii.

In December 1902, 121 Koreans left their homeland aboard the U.S.S. *Gaelic,* and all but 19 of the recruits (who failed their medical examinations in Japan) arrived in Honolulu on January 13, 1903. This original group included 56 men, 21 women, and 25 children. Over 7,000 Korean immigrants joined them on the Hawaiian sugar plantations within two years. Most of these immigrants were bachelors or had left their families behind. They hoped to save their wages and return to Korea to share the wealth with their families. With the higher cost of living in Hawaii, only about 2,000 Koreans were able to return to Korea. By 1905 the Japanese government banned emigration from the peninsula because so many Koreans were leaving to avoid Japanese oppression.

The next wave of Korean immigration to the United States occurred when Japan issued the Gentlemen's Agreement of 1907. This pact forbade further immigration of Japanese and Korean workers but included a clause that allowed wives to rejoin their husbands already in the United States. This law initiated the "picture bride" system, enabling immigrant men to have wives and families in America. Of the 7,296 Korean immigrants in Hawaii, only 613 of them were women. To improve the male/female ratio, Korean village matchmakers and the groom's family selected the women to contact. The men exchanged photographs with the prospective brides, and when a match was agreed upon, the groom's family would write the bride's name into the family register to legalize the union. The bride would then travel to the United States by boat and meet her new husband. Marriage ceremonies were often performed on the boat, so that the women could touch American soil as legal wives of the immigrants. Between 1910 and 1924, over 1,000 Korean picture brides came to the United States, mostly to Hawaii. These women were motivated to become picture brides by the opportunities for education and wealth they heard existed in America. Traditional Korean society placed many restrictions on women. Education, travel, and careers were not open to them at home.

The picture brides, however, did not find America paved with gold. Many discovered that their husbands were much older than they looked in the pictures. In fact, an alarming number of these women became widows at a very young age. They faced hard work and long hours, leaving little free time to learn English. In her introduction to *Making Waves: An Anthology of Writings By and About Asian American Women* (Boston: Beacon Press, 1989; p. 9), Sucheta Mazumdar recounts Anna Choi's description of her life in Hawaii as a picture bride: "I arose at four o'clock in the morning, and we took a truck to the sugar cane fields, eating breakfast on the way. Work in the sugar plantations was back breaking. It involved cutting canes, watering, and pulling out weeds.... The sugar cane fields were endless and twice the height of myself. Now that I look back, I *thank goodness* for the height for if I had seen how far the fields stretched I probably would have fainted from knowing how much work was ahead."

In the years between 1907 and World War II, a few Korean political refugees and students also came to the United States. Some were members of a secret Korean patriotic society called *Sinminhoe* (New People's Society). To escape persecution by the Japanese government, they crossed the Yalu River and took trains to Shanghai. From there, they made their way to America. By 1924, 541 Koreans living in America claimed to be political refugees. Among the political activists residing in the United States at this time were

Ahn Chang Ho, Pak Yong-Man, and Syngman Rhee, the future first president of South Korea. Rhee immigrated to the United States as a student and earned a doctorate from Princeton University in 1910. He returned to Korea to organize a protest against the Japanese. He then came back to the United States to avoid arrest and remained there until the end of World War II. During his years in America, he founded one of the major Korean independence movements.

Korean emigration was discouraged by the South Korean government after World War II, and North Korea forbade any kind of emigration. Most of the Koreans who did immigrate to the United States after the war were women. The quota system created by the U.S. Office of Immigration in the 1940s allowed between 105 and 150 immigrants from each of the Asian nations into the country. This law favored immigrants with post-secondary education, technical training, and specialized skills. Most of the Koreans allowed to immigrate were women with nursing training. The War Brides Act of 1945 also helped women and children obtain papers to immigrate.

More women who had married American soldiers were allowed into the United States after the Korean War. By this time, Koreans and all Asians in America were able to acquire citizenship through naturalization as a result of the McCarran-Walter Act of 1952. Foreign adoption of Korean babies also began at the end of the

Korean War. The war had left thousands of children orphaned in Korea. Over 100,000 South Korean children have been adopted abroad since the war, and roughly two-thirds of these children have been adopted by American families. An estimated 10,000 Korean children have been adopted by Minnesota families alone. Criticized by other countries for running a "baby mill," the South Korean government began to phase out the practice in the 1990s. Although adopting children is traditionally frowned upon in Korean society, social workers are attempting to encourage domestic adoption.

RECENT IMMIGRATION

In 1965 the U.S. Congress passed the Immigration and Naturalization Act. The quota system was replaced with a preference system that gave priority to immigration applications from relatives of U.S. citizens and from professionals with skills needed by the United States. Thousands of South Korean doctors and nurses took advantage of the new law. They moved to America and took jobs in understaffed, inner-city hospitals. Koreans with science and technological backgrounds also were encouraged to immigrate. These new immigrants came from middle-class and upper-class families, unlike the earlier immigrants. The portion of the law informally known as the "Brothers and Sisters Act" has also been a factor in the dramatic increase in the Korean American population. In 1960, 10,000 Koreans were living in the United States. By 1985 the number had increased to 500,000. According to the U.S. Department of Commerce's 1990 Census of Population, 836,987 Korean Americans had settled in the United States. The *1991 Statistical Yearbook* of the Immigration and Naturalization Service states that 26,518 Koreans were admitted to the United States in 1991, making up 1.5 percent of the total immigrants arriving in America that year.

SETTLEMENT

Virtually all of the first Koreans who immigrated to the United States settled in Hawaii and the West Coast. As Korean immigrants working on the Hawaiian sugar plantations became increasingly frustrated by the harsh conditions, they moved to cities and opened restaurants, vegetable stands, and small stores, or worked as carpenters and tailors. Some returned to Korea if they could save the money for transportation. Approximate-ly 1,000 Korean plantation workers remigrated to the U.S. mainland by 1907. They settled in San Francisco or moved farther inland to Utah to work in the copper mines, to Colorado and Wyoming to work in the coal mines, and to Arizona to work on the railroads. Some Koreans moved as far north as Alaska and found jobs in the salmon fisheries. The majority of those who remigrated, however, settled in California.

Recent Korean immigrants have settled in concentrated areas around the country. In 1970 the highest percentage of Korean Americans lived in California, followed by Hawaii, New York, Illinois, Pennsylvania, and Washington. In 1990 the U.S. Census reported 260,822 Korean Americans in California, 93,145 Korean immigrants in New York, 42,167 in Illinois, 38,087 in New Jersey, 35,281 in Texas, 32,918 in Washington, and 32,362 in Virginia. Maryland, Hawaii, and Pennsylvania each have over 25,000 Korean American residents. Every state has at least a small population of Korean Americans. Most Koreans who settle in the United States reside in large cities where jobs are available and Korean communities have been established. Koreatowns have developed in areas such as the Olympic Boulevard neighborhood west of downtown Los Angeles, where over 150,000 Korean Americans live. The Flushing, Woodside, and Jackson Heights neighborhoods within the New York City borough of Queens also have substantial Korean American populations. Unlike the early immigrants, later immigrants generally traveled to America to take up permanent residence. Korean American professionals who can afford it have begun moving to the suburbs.

ACCULTURATION AND ASSIMILATION

Like all immigrants arriving in the United States, Koreans have had to make major adjustments to live in a country that is vastly different from their homeland. Coming from a traditional society greatly influenced by the Confucian principle of placing elders, family, and community before the individual, Korean immigrants struggle to make sense of the American concept of individual freedom. Since the first immigrants arrived in Hawaii, Korean Americans have preserved their identity by creating organizations, such as Korean Christian churches and Korean schools. The Korean word *han*, used to describe an anguished feeling of being far from what you want, accurately conveys the longing that accompanies most Koreans to America. Korean American organizations provide a sense of community for new immigrants and a way to alleviate this longing.

TRADITIONS, CUSTOMS, BELIEFS

Korean immigrants bring with them a culture that incorporates aspects of Chinese, Indian, Japanese, and Western cultures. These influences have filtered into Korean society throughout its long history. Yet Koreans have also maintained native elements of their literature, art, music, and way of life. The result is a wonderful collage of elements, both foreign and indigenous to the peninsula. Korean Americans tend to maintain aspects of their culture, while also adopting elements of mainstream America.

LITERATURE, ART, AND MUSIC

Korean literature draws from Chinese and Japanese roots but has its own distinctive features. Poems, romances, and short stories represent only a portion of the breadth of the Korean literary tradition. This tradition includes both folk and highly advanced literary writings and works written in Chinese, as well as Korean. Korean poems, called *hyangga*, dating back to the sixth century, were written in Chinese characters. Hyangga were sung by Buddhist monks for religious purposes. Korean myths and legends were first recorded in Chinese in the thirteenth century. The first literary work written in the Korean alphabet, *hangul*, was the *Songs of Flying Dragons*, a multivolume account written between 1445 and 1447 by King Sejong's father during the Yi dynasty. Novels began to appear in the seventeenth century. Among the best known are Ho Kyun's *Life of Hong Kiltong* and *Spring Fragrance*, written anonymously in the eighteenth century.

Chinese, Japanese, and Korean art forms have many similarities, but Korea has also preserved its own creative elements in this field. Korean art is characterized by simple forms, subdued colors, humor, and natural images. Korea is known for its ceramics, especially the celadon. This highly sophisticated form of pottery was first introduced during the Koryo dynasty.

Korean music incorporates Confucian rituals, court music, Buddhist chants, and folk music. Ancient instruments used for court music include zithers, flutes, reed instruments, and percussion. Folk music, which usually includes dancing, is played with a *chango* (a drum shaped like an hourglass) and a loud trumpet-like oboe. *P'ansori*, stories first sung by wandering bards in the late Choson dynasty, are an early form of Korean folk music. Modern Korean composers often draw from Western classical music. Korean American musicians, like Jin Hi Kim, use traditional Korean elements in their compositions. Kim is a *komungo* harpist who came to the United States in her twenties. She incorporates traditional Korean musical styles with other non-Western styles. Kim is one of the leaders in the No World Improvisations movement, which promotes the performance and composition of new improvisational music.

SPORTS

Several sports native to Korea have become popular around the world. For instance, *tae kwon do*, a method of self-defense that originated in Korea more than 2,000 years ago, has now become a commonly taught form of karate in the United States. It involves more sharp, quick kicking than the Japanese style of karate. It was a demonstration sport in the 1988 Summer Olympics in Seoul.

SPECIAL EVENTS

The importance placed on family in Korean society is apparent from the way special events in family members' lives are celebrated. Traditionally, parents—with the help of a marriage broker or go-between—chose their children's marriage partners. The parents also planned and prepared the wedding ceremony. Female relatives spent days preparing special dishes for the wedding feast and making the wedding clothes. The picture bride system used to increase the population of Korean American females in Hawaii is one example of how this traditional system was maintained in America. While still common in rural areas of Korea, these customs are no longer standard practice in cities. Similarly, Korean Americans, who generally come from urban areas, usually allow their children to choose their own spouses. As members of Christian churches, most modern Korean Americans have Western-style wedding ceremonies and wear Western-style bridal gowns and formal suits. Another event that Koreans traditionally celebrate with great flourish is a baby's first birthday. The child is dressed in a traditional costume and seated amidst rice cakes, cookies, and fruits. Friends and relatives offer the child objects,

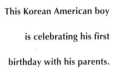

each one symbolizing a different career. A pen represents a writing career, and a coin signifies a career in finance. The first object the child picks up is said to indicate his or her future profession.

PRESERVING TRADITION

Korean culture is maintained within Korean American communities through church organizations, Korean schools, and Korean-culture camps. Since the beginning of this century, Korean Protestant churches have offered classes in Korean culture and language. In 1990 an estimated 490 Korean-language schools operated in the United States. Approximately 31,000 students attend these schools, which are run by 3,700 teachers. Classes are held during the week and sometimes on the weekends. The April/May 1994 issue of *The U.S.-Korea Review* lists 19 summer Korean-culture camps across the country. Located predominantly in California, Minnesota, New Jersey, and New York, these camps offer Korean American children, usually adoptees, an opportunity to learn about their heritage with other Korean American children.

CUISINE

Korean cooking is similar to other Asian cuisines. Like the Chinese and Japanese, Koreans eat with chopsticks. Common ingredients in Korean food, such as tofu, soy sauce, rice, and a wide variety of vegetables, are also staples in other far eastern cuisines. But Korean food is also distinct in many ways. It is often highly seasoned, including combinations of garlic, ginger, red or black pepper, scallions, soy sauce, sesame seeds, and sesame oil. Blander grain dishes such as rice, barley, or noodles offset the heat of the spices. Red meat is scarce in both North and South Korea and typically is reserved for special occasions. Koreans do not usually designate certain foods as breakfast, lunch, or dinner dishes. A standard meal consists of rice, soup, *kimchi* (a spicy Korean pickle), vegetables, and broiled or grilled meat or fish. Fresh fruit is usually served at the end of a meal. *Kimchi* is considered the national dish and is served at virtually every meal. Made from cabbage, turnips, radishes, or cucumber, *kimchi* can be prepared many ways, from mild to very spicy. Korean cuisine includes many different kinds of *namul* (salads). A common type of *namul* is *sukju namul*, or bean sprout salad. Made with bean sprouts, soy sauce, vinegar, sesame oil, black pepper, and other ingredients, it is easy to make and serve. A common soup served at breakfast is *kamja guk* (potato soup). It is often spiced with chopped onion and chunks of tofu. Koreans serve *mandu* (Korean dumplings) at winter celebrations. They are deep-fried wonton skins, usually filled with beef, cabbage, bean sprouts, onions, and other ingredients. Another common Korean dish is *chap ch'ae* (mixed vegetables with noodles). This popular stir-fry dish features cellophane noodles, which are made from mung beans and prepared with vegetables in a wok.

TRADITIONAL CLOTHING

Traditional Korean clothing is rarely worn in either the United States or in Korea on a daily basis. Modern Western-style clothes are standard attire in most of South Korea, with the exception of some rural areas. During holidays, however, Koreans in both the United States and Korea often wear traditional costumes. Women may wear a *chi-ma* (a long skirt, usually pleated and full) and *cho-gori* (a short jacket top worn over a skirt) during New Year's celebrations. Traditional attire for men includes long white overcoats and horsehair hats or colorful silk baggy trousers known as *paji*.

MAJOR HOLIDAYS

Koreans in both the United States and Korea celebrate several important days throughout the year. Following Buddhist and Confucian traditions, Koreans begin the new year with an elaborate three-day celebration called *Sol*. Family members dress in traditional clothing and pay homage to the oldest members of the family. The festivities include several feasts, kite-flying, board games, and various rituals intended to ward off evil spirits.

The first full moon is also an ancient day of worship. Torches are kept burning all night, and often people set off firecrackers to scare away evil spirits. *Yadu Nal* (Shampoo Day) is celebrated on June 15. Families bathe in streams or waterfalls to protect them from fevers. *Chusok* (Thanksgiving Harvest) is celebrated in autumn to give thanks for the harvest. *Kimchi* is also prepared for the winter at this time. Other traditional holidays observed in many Korean American households include Buddha's birthday on April 8, Korean Memorial Day on June 6, Father's Day on June 15, Constitution Day in South Korea on July 17, and Korean National Foundation Day on October 3. Korean American Christians also observe major religious holidays such as Easter and Christmas.

PREJUDICE AND STEREOTYPES

Anti-Asian prejudice first erupted in the United States when Chinese and Japanese immigrants began arriving in the nineteenth century. Early Korean immigrants suffered discrimination but were not specifically targeted until they became a significant percentage of the population. Americans generally knew nothing about Korea when Koreans first came to the United States. What little information they could find was written by non-Asians and claimed Western superiority over Asian cultures. William Griffis' *Corea: The Hermit Kingdom*, Alexis Krausse's *The Far East*, and Isabella Bird Bishop's *Korea and Her Neighbors* are examples of books that perpetuated the myth of Western superiority. American writer Jack London was also responsible for giving Americans an unfavorable view of Korea. As a war correspondent covering the Russo-Japanese conflict in 1904, London voiced his opinions in dispatches that appeared on the front pages of newspapers across the country. In an article entitled "The Yellow Peril" (*San Francisco Examiner*, September 25, 1904; p. 44), London wrote that "the Korean is the perfect type of inefficiency—of utter worthlessness."

Anti-Asian sentiments grew during the early twentieth century when San Francisco workers accused Koreans, along with Japanese and Chinese immigrants, of stealing jobs because the immigrants would work for lower wages. Restaurants refused to serve Asian customers, and Asians were often forced to sit in segregated corners of movie theaters. Violent white gangs harassed Korean Americans in California, and the government did nothing to help the victims. In fact, California laws in the first few decades of the twentieth century supported anti-Asian attitudes. Asian students were banned from attending public schools in white districts in 1906. The 1913 Webb-Heney Land Law prohibited Asians from owning property, and the Oriental Exclusion Act of 1924 banned all Asian immigration to the United States for close to 30 years.

Korean Americans continue to be discriminated against in the job market, often receiving lower pay and having fewer opportunities for promotion than non-Asian co-workers. The view of Korean Americans as "super immigrants" has also caused discord. Korean American success stories in business and education have led to resentment from outside groups. These stories are often exaggerated. Rumors that the U.S. government gives Korean immigrants money when they arrive are untrue. Only refugees receive aid from the U.S. government, and very few Korean immigrants qualify as refugees. Also, statistics that show the mean income of Korean American families to be higher than that of the general public are misleading because most Korean Americans live in large cities where the cost of living is much higher. These stereotypes have led to boycotts of Korean greengrocers in Brooklyn, Chicago, and elsewhere. In the April 1992 Los Angeles uprising that followed the verdict in the trial of African American assault victim Rodney King's attackers, black rioters targeted Korean grocers, destroying countless Korean American businesses. Korean immigrants refer to this tragic episode as the *Sa-i-kup'ok-dong* (April 28 riots). Korean Americans have come to represent wealth, greed, materialism, and arrogance because they have started businesses in inner-city neighborhoods that have been abandoned by corporations. The people still living in these neighborhoods often use the Korean small businessperson as a scapegoat for their anger against corporate America. Organizations such as the Korea Society in New York and the Korean Youth and Community Center in Los Angeles have begun to address these issues.

HEALTH AND MENTAL HEALTH ISSUES

Korean Americans hold a prominent position in the field of medical science. The proportionally large number of Korean American doctors and nurses attest to this fact. Data on the status of the health of Korean Americans is limited. Asian Americans in general have a longer life expectancy than Americans as a whole. Job-related stress and other factors have contributed to mental health problems within the Korean American community. Most Korean Americans receive health insurance through their employers. New immigrants and the elderly, however, often do not have access to medical care because of language barriers. Organizations such as the Korean Health Education Information and Referral in Los Angeles address this problem.

LANGUAGE

Virtually every citizen in North and South Korea is an ethnic Korean and speaks Korean. Spoken for over 5,000 years, the Korean language was first written in the mid-fifteenth century when King Sejong invented the phonetically-based alphabet known as *hangul* ("the great writing"). The King created the alphabet so that all Korean people, not just the aristocracy who knew Chinese char-

acters, could learn to read and write. As a result both North and South Korea have among the highest literacy rates in the world.

While most second- and third-generation Korean immigrants speak English exclusively, new immigrants often know little or no English. As time goes by, they begin to learn necessary English phrases. The earliest Korean immigrants in Hawaii learned a form of English known as pidgin English, which incorporated phrases in English, Chinese, Japanese, Korean, Filipino, and Portuguese—all languages spoken by the different ethnic groups working on the plantations. Learning English is crucial for new immigrants who hope to become successful members of the larger American community. Yet most Korean American parents also hope to preserve their heritage by sending their American-born children to Korean-language schools.

Several American universities offer undergraduate, graduate, and doctoral programs in Korean language and Korean studies. These universities include Brigham Young University, Columbia University, Cornell University, Harvard University, the University of Hawaii, Manoa, and the University of Washington, Seattle.

GREETINGS AND OTHER POPULAR EXPRESSIONS

The following greetings are translated phonetically from the *hangul* alphabet according to the McCune-Reischauer System of Romanization: *Annyonghasipnigga*—Hello (formal greeting); *Yoboseyo*—Hello (informal greeting); *Annyonghi kasipsio*—Good-bye (staying); *Annyonghi kyeshipsio*—Good-bye (leaving); *Put'akhamnida*—Please; *Komapsumnida*—Thank you; *Ch'onmaneyo*—You're welcome; *Sillyehamnida*—Excuse me; *Ye*—Yes; *Aniyo*—No; *Sehae e pok mani padu sipsiyo!*—Happy New Year!; *Man sei!*—Hurrah! Long live our country! Ten thousand years!; *Kuh reh!*—That is so! True!

FAMILY AND COMMUNITY DYNAMICS

Historically, the family-kinship system was an extremely integral part of Korean society. The male head of a household played a dominant role, as did the oldest members of the family. Parents practiced control over their children's lives, arranging their marriages and choosing their careers. The eldest son was responsible for taking care of parents in their old age. Inheritances also went to the son. These systems have changed in modern Korea, particularly in cities, but the family remains very important to Koreans in their homeland and in America. Parents still pressure their children to marry someone who has a good relationship with the family. Children—both male and female—usually are responsible for the care of elderly parents, although the government has begun to carry some of the financial burden. Tight family bonds continue to exist among Korean Americans. The current U.S. immigration laws encourage these bonds by favoring family reunions. Korean Americans who invite relatives to come to the States have a responsibility to help the new immigrants adjust to their new home. Korean American families often include extended family members. The average Korean American household consists of more members than the average American family. The 1980 U.S. Census Bureau reported an average of 4.3 members in the Korean American household, compared to an average of 2.7 persons in the American household at large. The family ties also extend to strong networks of support within Korean American communities.

PUBLIC ASSISTANCE

Because of the well-defined familial structure in Korean society, Koreans traditionally rely less on public assistance. Receiving welfare is often considered to be disgraceful. Family support, however, began to break down in the 1980s and 1990s. Larger numbers of recent Korean immigrants, particularly the elderly, are in need of assistance. Organizations within the Korean community have begun to address this problem. The Korean Youth and Community Center in Los Angeles offers numerous programs and activities for children and their families who have recently immigrated or are economically disadvantaged. Services include employment assistance and placement, family and youth counseling, and education and tutorial programs.

MODERN MARRIAGE AND DIVORCE

In Korean American communities, the marriage bond has in some ways become stronger than filial piety. While honoring one's parents remains important, physical distance and cultural barriers between Korean Americans and their parents have shifted priorities. Because Korean Americans are less likely to have arranged marriages than their ancestors, marrying outside of the Korean community has become increasingly common. Recent surveys show that Korean American women in college are expressing a preference for mates from other ethnic groups.

Traditionally Koreans have frowned upon divorce. Even with the marriages arranged through the picture bride system in Hawaii, few ended in divorce. Recent statistics suggest that the stigma against divorce no longer exists. The divorce rate among Korean Americans has reached and is possibly surpassing the national average. Exhaustion due to working extremely long hours in order to survive contributes to failed marriages. Women in particular suffer from stress. They often work long hours in garment factories or managing small businesses and are also responsible for running their households. Again, Korean American community organizations attempt to address these problems in order to make life in America more fulfilling.

EDUCATION

Koreans have always valued education, and Korean Americans place a strong emphasis on academic achievement. Employment in the civil service, which required passing extremely difficult qualifying examinations, was considered to be the most successful career path to take. Koreans take great pride in their educational achievements. Recent immigrants are strongly motivated to perform well in school and come to the United States better educated than the general population in Korea. Korean American parents pressure their children to perform well. In 1980, 78.1 percent of Korean Americans over the age of 25 had at least a high school education, compared with 66.5 percent of Americans overall. While 33.7 percent of Korean Americans had four or more years of college education, only 16.2 percent of the general U.S. population did.

Korean society gives priority to the education of males. Many of the Korean women who chose to come to the United States as picture brides hoped to find more educational opportunities than they were offered in their home country. In the United States, the bias in favor of educating males persists. Of all Korean American males over 25, 90 percent were high school graduates in 1980. Only 70.6 percent of Korean American women had high school educations. In 1980, 52.4 percent of Korean American males had attended four or more years of college, compared with 22 percent of Korean American females. It is a common stereotype that Korean Americans excel in math and science. Although this is often true, they tend to perform well in all subjects.

ROLE OF WOMEN

Korean husbands traditionally work outside the home, while their wives take full-time responsibility for the children and household. Living in a modern industrialized nation, South Korean women do have full-time jobs today, especially in urban areas. Still, the majority of full-time female employees in South Korea are unmarried. In the United States, economic needs often require both parents to work. Running the household, however, usually remains solely the responsibility of the woman. Second-, third-, and fourth-generation Korean American women face conflicts between traditional familial values and mainstream American culture. These women have more opportunities than their mothers and grandmothers. Some of them have careers as lawyers, doctors, teachers, and businesswomen, but most have behind-the-scenes positions or are clerks, typists, and cashiers. Korean American women, like American women in general, are still discriminated against in the job market. Modern Korean immigrant women often come to the United States with professional skills but are forced to work in garment factories or as store clerks because of the language barrier.

The view that Korean American women are passive also persists. Contrary to popular perceptions, Korean American women have a long history of political activism. Unfortunately their work has gone largely unrecorded. Korean female immigrants played a significant role in organizing protests against Japanese occupation both in Korea and America. They established organizations like the Korean Women's Patriotic League, wrote for Korean newspapers, and raised $200,000 for the cause by working on plantations, doing needlework, and selling candies. They also participated in labor strikes on the Hawaiian plantations. Korean American women of the 1990s joined other Asian American women in fighting unfair work practices in the hotel, garment, and food-packaging industries. Korean American women also participate fully in efforts to reunify Korea.

RELIGION

Throughout Korea's long history, religion has played a prominent role in the lives of the its citizens. A variety of faiths have been practiced on the peninsula, the most common being shamanism, Buddhism, and Christianity.

Shamanism, the country's oldest religion, involves the worship of nature; the sun, mountains, rocks, and trees each hold sacred positions. Based on a belief in good and evil spirits that can only be appeased by priests or medicine men called shamans, early shamanism incorporated pottery making and dances such as the *muchon*, which was performed as part of a ceremony to worship the heavens.

China brought Buddhism to Korea sometime between the fourth and seventh centuries A.D. This religion, based on the teachings of the ancient Indian philosopher Siddhartha Gautama (Buddha), has as its premise that suffering in life is inherent and that one can be freed from it by mental and moral self-purification.

Christianity first reached Korea in the seventeenth century, again by way of China where Portuguese missionaries came to promote Catholicism. American Protestant missionaries arrived in Korea in the nineteenth century. The Korean government persecuted these missionaries because the laws of Christianity went against Confucian social order. By the mid-1990s, the majority of South Koreans were still Buddhists, but an estimated 30 percent of the population practiced some type of Christianity.

KOREAN AMERICAN CHRISTIANITY

Of the original 7,000 Korean immigrants in the United States, only 400 were Christian. Those 400 immediately formed congregations in Hawaii, and by 1918 close to 40 percent of the Korean immigrants had converted to Christianity. Koreans immigrants relied heavily on their churches as community centers. After Sunday service, immigrants spoke Korean, socialized, discussed problems of immigrant life, and organized political rallies for Korean independence. The churches also served as educational centers, providing classes in writing and reading Korean. They remain an integral part of the Korean immigrant community. In 1990 there were an estimated 2,000 Korean Protestant churches in the United States. Most Korean Protestants are evangelical Christians, who study the Bible extensively and follow the word of the gospel closely. In large cities like Los Angeles, New York, and Chicago, Korean Protestants have their own buildings and hold several services a week. The Oriental Mission Church and

Youngnak Presbyterian Church in Los Angeles are two of the largest Korean Protestant churches in America with 5,000 members each. Most Koreans in the United States today practice Protestantism.

Over two million Catholics live in South Korea. The Korean American Catholic Community was established by Korean immigrants in the 1960s. The first Korean Catholic center opened in Orange County, California, in 1977. As of 1995, an estimated 35,000 Korean Americans practiced Catholicism. Most Korean American Catholic parishes are part of larger American Catholic parishes.

KOREAN BUDDHISM IN AMERICA

Although Buddhism has undergone many upheavals on the Korean peninsula, nearly 14 million South Koreans practice Buddhism today. A Buddhist monk named Soh Kyongbo founded Korean Buddhism in the United States in 1964. Most Korean American Buddhists belong to the Chogye sect. Prominent Buddhist organizations in the United States include the Zen Lotus Society in Ann Arbor, Michigan, the Korean Buddhist Temple Association, the Young Buddhist Union in Los Angeles, the Buddhists Concerned with Social Justice and World Peace, the Western Buddhist Monk's Association, the Southern California Buddhist Temples Association, and several Son and Dharma centers across the country. According to the Korean Buddhist Temple Association's reports, there were 60 temples in the United States and Canada in 1990. The Young Buddhist Union holds an annual arts festival where Buddhist monks dance, sing, read Son poetry, perform comedy sketches, plays, and piano recitals. Still, Buddhism has not become widespread in the United States and is often viewed as a cult.

EMPLOYMENT AND ECONOMIC TRADITIONS

Early Korean immigrants living on the West Coast were restricted from many types of employment. Discriminatory laws prohibited Asian immigrants from applying for citizenship, which meant that they were ineligible for positions in most professional fields. They took jobs with low pay and little advancement potential, working as busboys, waiters, gardeners, janitors, and domestic help in cities. Outside the cities, they worked on farms and in railroad "gangs." Many Korean immigrants opened restaurants, laundries, barbershops, grocery stores, tobacco shops, bakeries, and other retail shops. With the changes in immigration laws after World War II, Korean immigrants have been able to move into more professional fields such as medicine, dentistry, architecture, and science. Recent immigrants, those who have come to America since 1965, are mostly college-educated, with professional skills. The language barrier, however, often prevents new immigrants from finding jobs within their fields. Korean doctors often work as orderlies and nurses' assistants. In 1978, only 35 percent of Korean teachers, administrators, and other professionals were working in their respective fields in Los Angeles.

According to the U.S. Census Bureau's *Asian and Pacific Islander Population in the United States: 1980 Report*, the average Korean American household income was $22,500, which was higher than the average household income for Americans overall ($20,300). However, Korean Americans have, on the average, more persons living in each household and, as noted earlier, tend to live in urban areas where the cost of living is higher. The same report indicates that 13.1 percent of Korean American families had incomes below the poverty level, which is higher than the 9.6 percent reported for the total U.S. population. Asian American adults have lower unemployment rates than the U.S. adult population overall. In 1980 the U.S. Census Bureau also reported that 24 percent of Korean Americans age 16 or older held managerial or professional positions; 26 percent had technical, sales, or administrative jobs; 16 percent worked in service fields; nine percent held precision production, crafts, or repair jobs; 19 percent were laborers or operators; and six percent were unemployed.

SMALL BUSINESSES

Out of economic need, large numbers of recent Korean immigrants start their own businesses. Most of these immigrants did not run small businesses in Korea. In 1977, 33 percent of Korean American families owned small businesses, such as vegetable stands, grocery stores, service stations, and liquor stores. As a whole, they have a high success rate. In the 1980s an estimated 95 percent of all dry-cleaning stores in Chicago were owned by Korean immigrants. By 1990, 15,500 Korean-owned stores were in operation in New York City alone. Since then, a recession and internal competition has slowed the growth. New Korean immigrants are opening businesses in cities other than New York, Los Angeles, and Chicago, where the competition is less fierce.

ECONOMIC ORGANIZATIONS

Support within Korean communities has contributed to the success of small businesses. Recent immigrants still use the ancient Korean loan system, based on the *kye*, a sum of money shared by a group of business owners. A new grocer, for instance, will be allowed to use the money for one year and keep the profits. The *kye* is then passed to the next person who needs it. Organizations like the Korean Produce Association in New York and the Koryo Village Center in Oakland, California, are another source of support for new immigrants hoping to set up their own businesses.

POLITICS AND GOVERNMENT

Koreans have a general distrust of central governments. Historically, individual citizens have had little power in Korea and have suffered through scores of tragic episodes at the hands of other governments controlling the peninsula. As a result, most Korean immigrants come to America unaccustomed to participation in the democratic process. Discriminatory laws against Asian Americans on the West Coast have contributed to this distrust. Korean American communities have traditionally isolated themselves, relying on their family and neighborhood networks. Korean American participation in these grass-roots organizations and in U.S. government politics in general is growing and evolving slowly.

GRASS-ROOTS ORGANIZATIONS

From the church meetings on Hawaiian plantations in the early 1900s to the efforts of the Black-Korean Alliance in the 1990s, Korean immigrants have created settings to voice their opinions. Racial tensions within Korean American communities have led to the establishment of several grass-roots organizations. The Black-Korean Alliance in Los Angeles and the Korea Society in New York have set up programs to educate the two ethnic groups about each other's cultures. In 1993, the Korea Society launched its Kids to Korea program. Designed to improve the strained relationship between the Korean and African American communities, the program enabled 16 African American high school students from New York City and Los Angeles to travel to South Korea in order to learn about its people, culture, and history. This successful program has been expanded to include students from other cities. The Korea Society also sponsors a program called Project Bridge in Washington, D.C., which offers classes in both Korean and African American cultures.

UNION ACTIVITY

While research experts have studied extensively the economic development and work patterns of Korean American professionals and entrepreneurs, the general American public knows little about Korean immigrant laborers. Yet since the beginning of the twentieth century, American industries have employed Koreans. By the 1990s, Korean Americans had begun to join forces with other Asian Americans to educate themselves about labor unions and their rights. Founded in 1983, the Asian Immigrant Women Advocates (AIWA) organizes Chinese and Vietnamese garment workers and Korean hotel maids and electronics assemblers in the Oakland, California, area. They have staged demonstrations and rallies to draw attention to the unfair labor practices within the garment, hotel management, and electronics industries. The Korean Immigrant Worker Advocates (KIWA) in Los Angeles is another group that is bringing labor issues to the forefront. The KIWA is unique among Asian American organizations in Los Angeles because most of the members of its board of directors are workers themselves.

VOTING PATTERNS

Studies have shown that voter participation among Korean Americans is low. Historically, Korean immigrants have rarely been active in election campaigns and have seldom made financial contributions to individual candidates. Groups such as the Coalition for Korean American Voters (CKAV) in New York are working hard to address this problem. In just three years CKAV has registered 3,000 voters and sponsored programs that educate Korean immigrants about local and national government. The coalition's efforts include airing public service announcements on Korean American television channels, establishing a college internship program to foster community service and leadership skills in students, and joining forces with other Asian American organizations to increase Asian American involvement in government.

MILITARY PARTICIPATION

In his book *Strangers from a Different Shore: A History of Asian Americans*, Ronald Takaki describes the plight of a Korean immigrant named Easurk Emsen Charr. He was drafted and served in the U.S. Army during World War I. Afterward he argued in court that as a U.S. military veteran, he should be entitled to citizenship and the opportunity to own land in California. The court ruled that the military should not have drafted him because he was Asian and therefore ineligible for American citizenship. Despite such discriminatory treatment, Korean Americans were eager to volunteer for military service during World War II. Doing so gave them a chance to support the American effort to curtail Japanese imperialism. Some Korean Americans served as language teachers and translators, and 100 Korean immigrants joined the California Home Guard in Los Angeles. They also participated in Red Cross relief operations. The American government, however, was somewhat suspicious of Korean-immigrant support because Koreans were technically still part of the Japanese empire. In Hawaii, Korean immigrants were referred to as "enemy aliens" and banned from working on military bases. Today, many Korean American men and women hold positions in the military.

INVOLVEMENT IN POLITICS OF KOREAN PENINSULA

Since Koreans first began immigrating to the United States, they have remained active in the politics of their homeland. Studies have shown that Korean Americans are generally more actively involved in the politics of Korea than in that of their new home. The lives of early Korean immigrants revolved around the Korean independence movement. In the 1960s Korean Americans staged mass demonstrations and relief efforts in response to the massacre of civilians by the South Korean dictatorship in Kwangju, the capital of South Cholla province. Today virtually every Korean American organization supports reunification of the peninsula. Groups such as the Korea Church Coalition for Peace, Justice, and Reunification were formed specifically for this purpose.

Other American-based organizations, including the Council for Democracy in Korea, seek to educate the public about the political affairs of Korea.

INDIVIDUAL AND GROUP CONTRIBUTIONS

EDUCATION

Margaret K. Pai (1916-) taught English at Kailua, Roosevelt, and Farrington high schools on the Hawaiian island of Oahu for many years. Her father, Do In Kwon, immigrated to Hawaii to work on the sugar plantations in the early 1900s. Her mother, Hee Kyung Lee, was a picture bride and met and married her husband in Hawaii at age 18. Since retiring, Margaret Pai has been writing short Hawaiian legends, poems, and personal reminiscences, including *The Dreams of Two Yi-Men* (1989), a vivid account of her parents' experiences as early Korean immigrants in America.

Elaine H. Kim (1943-) is a professor of Asian American studies and faculty assistant for the status of women at the University of California-Berkeley. She is also president of the Association for Asian American Studies and founder of the Asian Immigrant Women Advocates and Asian Women United of California. Kim is the author of *Asian American Literature: An Introduction to the Writings and their Social Context.*

FILM, VIDEO, TELEVISION, THEATER, AND MUSIC

Peter Hyun (1906-) worked in the American theater for many years. He was a stage manager for Eva LeGallienne's Civic Repertory Theatre in New York, director of the Children's Theatre of the New York Federal Theater, and organizer and director of the Studio Players in Cambridge, Massachusetts. During World War II, he served as a language specialist in the U.S. Army. After settling in Oxnard, California, he taught English to immigrant students from Asia. He is the author of *Man Sei!: The Making of a Korean American* (1986), a personal account of growing up as the son of a leader in the Korean independence movement.

Nam June Paik (1932-) has built a worldwide reputation as a composer of electronic music and producer of avant-garde "action concerts." He grew up in Seoul and earned a degree in aesthetics at the University of Tokyo before meeting American composer John Cage in Germany. His interest in American electronic music brought him to the United States. His work has been exhibited at the Museum of Modern Art, the Whitney Museum, and the Kitchen Museum, all in New York City, the Metropolitan Museum in Tokyo, and the Museum of Contemporary Art in Chicago. Among his video credits are *TV Buddha* (1974) and *Video Fish* (1975). He also produced a program called *Good Morning, Mr. Orwell*, which was broadcast live simultaneously in San Francisco, New York, and Paris on New Year's Day 1984 as a tribute to George Orwell's novel *1984*.

Myung-Whun Chung (1953-) was born in Seoul into a family of talented musicians. He made his piano debut at age seven with the Seoul Philharmonic Orchestra and then moved with his family to the United States five years later. He studied piano at the Mannes School of Music and conducting at the Juilliard School of Music in New York City. He has served as assistant conductor of the Los Angeles Philharmonic Orchestra, music director and principal conductor for the Radio Symphony Orchestra in Saarbrucken, Germany, and principal guest conductor of the Teatro Comunale in Florence, Italy. He is now music director and conductor for the Opera de la Bastille, located in the legendary French prison.

Margaret Cho (1968-) is a second-generation comedian who has broken barriers and stereotypes with her numerous television and film appearances. In 1994 Cho became the first Asian American to star in her own television show, the ABC-sitcom *All-American Family*, which centered on a Korean American family.

GOVERNMENT AND COMMUNITY ACTIVISM

Herbert Y. C. Choy (1916-) became the first Asian American to be appointed to the federal bench in 1971. Educated at the University of Hawaii and Harvard University, he practiced law in Honolulu for 25 years. He served as attorney general of the Territory of Hawaii in 1957 and 1958 and continued his law practice until President Richard Nixon appointed him to the U.S. Court of Appeals.

Grace Lyu-Volckhausen comes from a family of female activists. Her mother and grandmother were members of organizations supporting women's needs in Korea. Moving to New York in the late 1950s to study international and human relations at New York University, Lyu-Volckhausen established an outreach center for women at a YWCA in Queens in the 1960s. The program now offers sewing classes, after-school recreation for children, counseling for battered women, and discussion groups. She has served on the New York City Commission on the Status of Women, on the Mayor's Ethnic Council, and on Governor Mario Cuomo's Garment Advisory Council. Still chairperson of her YWCA youth committee in the mid-1990s, she also worked with the New York mortgage agency to provide affordable housing for minorities.

INDUSTRY

Kim Hyung-Soon (1884-1968) immigrated to the United States in 1914 and started a small produce and nursery wholesale business in California with his friend Kim Ho. The Kim Brothers Company developed into a huge orchard, nursery, and fruit-packing shed business. Kim is credited with having developed new varieties of peaches known as "fuzzless peaches," or "Le Grand" and "Sun Grand." He also crossed the peach with the plum and developed the nectarine. Kim helped establish the Korean Community Center in Los Angeles and the Korean Foundation, a fund that offers scholarships to students of Korean ancestry.

LITERATURE

Younghill Kang (1903-1972) was one of the first Korean writers to offer Americans a first hand, English-language account of growing up in occupied Korea. He wrote his first novel, *The Grass Roof* (1931), after spending many years struggling to survive as an immigrant living in San Francisco and New York. He later taught comparative literature at New York University and devoted the rest of his life to fighting racism in the United States and political oppression in his homeland.

Kim Young Ik (1920-) is the author of several novels and stories for children and adults. His books have won numerous awards and have been translated into many languages. They include *The Happy Days* (1960), *The Divine Gourd* (1962), *Love in Winter* (1962), *Blue in the Seed* (1964), and *The Wedding Shoes* (1984).

Marie G. Lee (1964-) is at the forefront of the current boom in children's literature being written by and about Korean Americans. Raised in Hibbing, Minnesota, she graduated from Brown

University and lives in New York City. She is the author of the young adult novel *Finding My Voice* (1992), which won the 1993 Friends of American Writers Award. Her other young adult novels include *If It Hadn't Been for Yoon Jun* (1993) and *Saying Goodbye* (1994). Her work has appeared in many publications, including *The New York Times* and the *Asian/Pacific American Journal*, as well as several anthologies. She is president of the Board of Directors of the Asian American Writers' Workshop and a member of PEN and the Asian American Arts Alliance.

SPORTS AND MEDICINE

Dr. Sammy Lee (1920-) has made a name for himself in both sports and medicine. He won the gold medal for ten-meter platform diving in the 1948 Olympic Games in London and again in the 1952 Games in Helsinki, along with a bronze medal in three-meter springboard diving. He received his M.D. in 1947 and practiced medicine in Korea as part of the U.S. Army Medical Corps. Lee was named outstanding American athlete in 1953 by the Amateur Athletic Union and inducted into the International Swimming Hall of Fame in 1968. He served on the President's Council on Physical Fitness and Sports from 1971 to 1980 and coached the U.S. diving team for the 1960 and 1964 Olympics. He has also been named Outstanding American of Korean Ancestry twice—by the American Korean Society in 1967 and the League of Korean Americans in 1986. After retiring from sports, he ran a private practice in Orange, California, for many years.

MEDIA

PRINT

Korean Culture.
Published quarterly by the Korean Cultural Center of the Korean Consulate General in Los Angeles.

Contact: Robert E. Buswell, Jr., Editor in Chief.
Address: 5505 Wilshire Boulevard, Los Angeles, California 90036.
Telephone: (213) 936-7141.

The New Korea.
A bilingual magazine published weekly for the Korean American community.

Contact: Woon-Ha Kim, Editor and Publisher.
Address: 505 South Serrano Avenue, Los Angeles, California 90020.
Telephone: (213) 382-9345.
Fax: (213) 382-1678.

The U.S.-Korea Review.
The bimonthly newsletter of the Korea Society, it is designed to improve the depth and breadth of information, news, and analysis in U.S.-Korea relations. It features chronologies of current affairs and trends in trade and business. It also includes literary excerpts and reviews.

Contact: David L. Kim, Editor.
Address: 412 First Street, S.E., Washington, D.C. 20003.
Telephone: (202) 863-2963.
Fax: (202) 863-2965.

RADIO

FM Seoul.
Programs are broadcast in both Korean and English.

Address: 129 North Vermont Avenue, Los Angeles, California 90004.
Telephone: (213) 389-1000.

KBC-Radio.
Contact: Jung Hyun Chai.
Address: 42-22 27th Street, Long Island City, New York 11101.
Telephone: (718) 482-1111.
Fax: (718) 643-0479.

Radio Korea NY.
Contact: Byung Woo Kim.
Address: 44 East 32nd Street, New York, New York 10016.
Telephone: (212) 685-1480.
Fax: (212) 685-6947.

Radio Korea U.S.A.
Programs are broadcast in Korean.

Address: 2001 West Olympic Boulevard, Los Angeles, California 90006.
Telephone: (213) 487-1300.

TELEVISION

KBC-TV.
Contact: Jung Hyun Chai.

Address: 42-22 27th Street, Long Island City, New York 11101.

Telephone: (718) 482-1111.

Fax: (718) 643-0479.

KMBC-TV.

Address: 3434 West Sixth Street, Suite 300, Los Angeles, California 90020.

Telephone: (213) 368-7700.

Korean Cultural Television.

Contact: Seung Ho Ha.

Address: 111 West 30th Street, New York, New York 10001.

Telephone: (212) 971-0212.

Fax: (212) 629-0982.

K-TAN, Inc.

Address: 101 North Vermont Avenue, Los Angeles, California 90004.

Telephone: (213) 365-6500.

KTE-TV.

Address: 625 South Kingsley Drive, Los Angeles, California 90005.

Telephone: (213) 382-6700.

ORGANIZATIONS AND ASSOCIATIONS

Coalition for Korean American Voters, Inc.

Founded in 1991, this nonprofit, nonpartisan, volunteer organization promotes voter registration and education of Korean Americans in the New York City metropolitan area.

Contact: Johnny Im, Coordinator.

Address: 38 West 32nd Street, Suite 904, New York, New York 10002.

Telephone: (212) 967-8428.

Fax: (212) 967-8652.

The Korean American Coalition.

Founded in 1983, this organization seeks to bring together Korean communities within the United States through fundraising and educational programs. It also sponsors programs designed to educate non-Koreans about Korean culture. The coalition publishes a monthly newsletter called the *KAC Newsletter.*

Contact: Jerry C. Yu, President.

Address: 610 South Harvard Street, Suite 111, Los Angeles, California 90005.

Telephone: (213) 380-6175.

The Korean Culture Camp.

Founded in 1975 as the first such camp in the nation, the Minnesota Korean Culture Camp is also believed to be the largest Korean camp in the United States. The camp was started to build self-esteem in Korean children through a study of their heritage. During the five day or evening sessions, children from around the country are taught by Korean adults, eat traditional Korean food, and learn about Korean art, music, language, dance, and *tae kwon do.*

Contact: Carol Green.

Address: 2551 Hayes Street, N.E., Minneapolis, Minnesota 55418.

Telephone: (612) 789-6314.

Korean Scientists and Engineers Association in America.

Founded in 1971, this professional organization promotes mutuality among Korean and American scientists and engineers. It seeks to strengthen a scientific, technological, and industrial bond between the two countries through its programs, speakers bureau, and library facilities.

Contact: Moo Young-Han, President.

Address: 6261 Executive Boulevard, Rockville, Maryland 20852.

Telephone: (301) 984-7048.

The Korea Society (U.S.-Korea Society).

The Korea Society is the result of the 1993 merger of the work and programs of the New York-based Korea Society and the U.S.-Korea Foundation based in Washington, D.C. This nonprofit organization is dedicated to strengthening the bonds of awareness, understanding, and cooperation between the United States and Korea, and among Koreans, Korean Americans, and all other Americans. The society's efforts extend to education, public policy, business, the arts, and the media. Its Washington branch publishes *The U.S.-Korea Review.*

Contact: Frederick F. Carriere, Executive Director.

Address: 950 Third Avenue, Eighth Floor, New York, New York 10022.

Telephone: (212) 759-7525.

Fax: (212) 759-7530.

MUSEUMS AND RESEARCH CENTERS

Korean Cultural Center.

Founded in 1980, this cultural center offers programs that introduce Korean culture, society, history, and arts to the American public. It organizes exhibitions, lectures, symposiums, and multicultural festivals. The center houses a 10,000-volume library and an art museum and gallery. *Korean Culture Magazine* is published by the center.

Contact: Joon Ho Lee, Director.

Address: 5505 Wilshire Boulevard, Los Angeles, California 90036.

Telephone: (213) 936-7141.

Fax: (213) 936-5712.

The Korea Economic Institute of America.

Founded in 1982, this educational group includes politicians, academics, trade organizations, banks, and other Americans concerned with the Korean economy. The institute publishes a quarterly update on economic issues in Korea.

Contact: W. Robert Warne, President.

Address: 1101 Vermont Avenue, N.W., Suite 401, Washington, D.C. 20005.

Telephone: (202) 371-0690.

Korean Institute of Minnesota.

Founded in 1973, this nonprofit organization is dedicated to preserving Korean language and culture. It brings together Korean American and adoptive families with a variety of classes and social opportunities for all ages.

Contact: Yoonju Park, Director.

Address: P.O. Box 8094, St. Paul, Minnesota 55108.

Telephone: (612) 644-3251.

SOURCES FOR ADDITIONAL STUDY

The Korean American Community: Present and Future, edited by Tae-Hwan Kwak and Seong Hyong Lee. Seoul: Kyungnam University Press, 1991.

Lehrer, Brian. *The Korean Americans*. New York: Chelsea House Publishers, 1988.

Making Waves: An Anthology of Writings By and About Asian American Women, edited by Asian Women United of California. Boston: Beacon Press, 1989.

Mangiafico, Luciano. *Contemporary American Immigrants: Patterns of Filipino, Korean, and Chinese Settlement in the United States*. New York: Praeger Publishers, 1988.

New Immigrants in New York, edited by Nancy Foner. New York: Columbia University Press, 1987.

Pai, Margaret. *The Dreams of Two Yi-Min*. Honolulu: University of Hawaii Press, 1989.

Patterson, Wayne. *The Korean Frontier in America: Immigration to Hawaii, 1896-1910*. Honolulu: University of Hawaii Press, 1988.

Patterson, Wayne, and Hyung-Chan Kim. *Koreans in America*. Minneapolis: Lerner Publications, 1992.

The State of Asian America: Activism and Resistance in the 1990s, edited by Karin Aguilar-San Juan. Boston: South End Press, 1994.

Takaki, Ronald. *Strangers from a Different Shore: A History of Asian Americans*. Boston: Little, Brown, 1989.

LAOTIAN AMERICANS

by
Carl L. Bankston III

OVERVIEW

Located in Southeast Asia, Laos measures approximately 91,400 square miles (236,800 square kilometers), making it slightly larger than the state of Utah. The country shares its borders with Thailand in the southwest, Cambodia in the south, Burma in the west, China in the north, and Vietnam in the east. Laos has a tropical climate, with a rainy season that lasts from May to November and a dry season that lasts from December to April.

Laos has about 4,400,000 residents and an estimated population growth rate of 2.2 percent each year. Minority groups in this small, mountainous country include the Mon-Khmer, the Yao, and the Hmong. Approximately 85 to 90 percent of employed persons in Laos work in subsistence agriculture. Rice is the country's principal crop; other significant agricultural products include corn, tobacco, and tea. The majority of Laotians practice Theravada Buddhism, a form of Buddhism popular in Cambodia, Thailand, Burma, and Sri Lanka. In Laos, however, Buddhism is heavily influenced by the cult of *phi* (spirits) and Hinduism.

The Laotian flag has three horizonal bands, with red stripes at the top and bottom and a blue stripe in the middle. A large white disk is centered in the blue band. Many Laotian Americans identify more with the pre-1975 flag of the Kingdom of Laos than with the present-day flag of the country. This flag was red, with a three-headed white elephant situated on a five-step pedestal, under a white parasol. The elephant was symbolic of the ancient kingdom of Laos, known as "The Kingdom of a Million Elephants." The parasol represented the monarchy and the five steps of the pedestal symbolized the five main precepts of Buddhism.

HISTORY

Laotians trace their ancestry to the T'ai people, an ethnolinguistic group that migrated south from China beginning in the sixth century. Originally part of the Khmer (Cambodian) empire, Laos achieved independence in 1353 when Fa Ngum, a prince from the city of Luang Prabang, claimed a large territory from the declining empire and declared himself king, calling the newly established state Lan Xang, or "The Kingdom of a Million Elephants." Luang Prabang was the nation's capital for 200 years until, in 1563, a later king, Setthalhiralh, moved the capital to Vientiane, which serves as the capital of Laos today.

The Lao kingdom reached its height in the late 1600s, under King Souligna Vongsa. After his death in 1694, three claimants to the throne broke the kingdom into three distinct principalities, the kingdoms of Vientiane, Luang Prabang, and Champassak. Each kingdom struggled for power, causing the weakened Lao states to become vulnerable to the more powerful nations of Siam (Thailand) and Vietnam. While the Siamese took Vientiane, the Vietnamese took other parts of Laos. By the mid 1800s, almost all of northern Laos was controlled by Vietnam, and almost all the southern and central parts of the country were controlled by Thailand. Only the area around Luang Prabang remained independent.

MODERN ERA

Vietnam suffered from its own internal problems in the late 1700s and early 1800s, and in 1859 French Admiral Rigault de Genouilly attacked and seized Saigon. By 1862, the emperor of Vietnam was forced to recognize French possession of the southern provinces, and 21 years later, Vietnam became a French colony.

In 1893 the French entered Thailand's Chao Phya River and forced the king to relinquish Thailand's suzerainty over Laos. Four years later, King Oun-Kham of Luang Prabang was forced to seek the help of France against invaders from China and, consequently, Luang Prabang also fell to France's growing Indochinese empire. Laos then became a protectorate, or colony, of France. By 1899, Vientiane had become the administrative capital of French Laos with French commissioners holding administrative power in all the provinces.

Although there were some local rebellions against French rule—mainly by the tribes of the hills and mountains—widespread Laotian resistance to the French did not begin until after World War II, when Japan, which had assumed control over Indochina during the war years, was defeated. In 1945 the Laotian prime minister, Prince Phetsarath, declared Laos an independent kingdom and formed a group known as the Lao Issara, or "Free Lao." Some Laotians supported a return to French colonization, feeling that their country was not ready for immediate independence. The Lao Issara, however, were strongly opposed to French rule in Laos. The prime minister's half-brother, Prince Souphanuvong, called for armed resistance and sought support from the anti-French movement in neighboring Vietnam, the Viet Minh, led by Ho Chi Minh. This Laotian political group became known as the Pathet Lao ("Lao Nation").

The Viet Minh defeated French troops at Dien Bien Phu in 1954. Afterward, an international conference held in Geneva separated Vietnam at the 17th parallel to prevent Ho Chi Minh's communist government from assuming control over the entire nation. Many Laotians supported the Viet Minh and, when North Vietnam invaded South Vietnam in 1959, Laos was drawn into the war.

The United States also became involved in the war to deter the spread of Communism in Southeast Asia. In Laos, American forces provided tactical and economic support to the royal government but were unsuccessful in their efforts. U.S. troops withdrew from the area in 1973 and South Vietnam fell to its northern enemy in April 1975. Later that same year, Pathet Lao forces overthrew the Laotian government, renaming the country the Lao People's Democratic Republic. Thousands of Laotians fled to Thailand where they were placed in refugee camps.

SIGNIFICANT IMMIGRATION WAVES

While there was some migration from Laos to the United States prior to 1975, the immigrants were so few that there is no official record of them. Available records do suggest, however, that they were highly professional and technically proficient. After 1975, thousands of Laotian people fled their homeland for the United States; the passage of the Indochina Migration and Refugee Assistance Act of 1975 by Congress aided them in this effort. Early Laotian immigrants included former government administrators, soldiers from the royal army, and shopkeepers. More recent immigrants from Laos included farmers and villagers who were not as educated as their predecessors.

While large numbers of Vietnamese and Cambodians began to settle in the United States almost immediately after socialist governments came to power in the spring of 1975, Laotian refugees did not begin to arrive in America in great numbers until the following year. In contrast to the 126,000 Vietnamese and 4,600 Cambodians who arrived in 1975, only 800 refugees from Laos were admitted into the United States. This is partially due to the fact that the new Laotian government obtained power in a relatively peaceful manner, despite fighting between the Hmong and the Pathet Lao. Moreover, the U.S. government was reluctant to accept refugees who had fled Laos for bordering Thailand, many of whom U.S. officials viewed as economic migrants rather than refugees from political oppression.

In 1976, 10,200 refugees from Laos, who had fled across the border into Thailand, were admitted to the United States. The number of Laotian refugees dipped to only 400 in 1977 and then climbed to 8,000 in 1978. In the years between 1979 and 1981, the number of Laotians entering the United States increased dramatically, due to international attention given to the plight of Indochinese refugees in the late 1970s and to the family unification program, which allowed refugees already in the United States to sponsor their relatives. During these three years, about 105,000 people from Laos resettled in America: 30,200 in 1979, 55,500 in 1980, and 19,300 in 1981. Although migration from Laos to America never again achieved the stature of this period, the resettlement of Laotians in the United States continued throughout the late 1980s and early 1990s.

GEOGRAPHIC DISTRIBUTION OF LAOTIAN AMERICANS

According to the U.S. Census, in 1990 there were about 150,000 Laotian Americans living in the United States. (This figure does not include the Hmong and other minority groups from Laos.) The majority of Laotian Americans (58,058) lived in California, primarily in Fresno (7,750), San Diego (6,261), Sacramento (4,885), and Stockton (4,045). Texas held the second largest number of Laotian Americans (9,332), with the majority living in Amarillo (1,188) and Denton (1,512). Minnesota and Washington State had the third and fourth largest Laotian American populations, with 6,831 and 6,191 residents, respectively. Thirty-four percent (2,325) of Minnesota's Laotian American population lived in Minneapolis and 46 percent (2,819) of Washington's Laotian American community lived in Seattle.

ACCULTURATION AND ASSIMILATION

While few Laotian residents live in cities, Laotian Americans are an overwhelmingly urban people, with most living in large metropolitan centers. Of the 171,577 people in America born in Laos (this figure includes both ethnic Laotians and Hmong and excludes members of both groups born in America), 164,892 people (96 percent) lived in urban areas in 1990. The remaining four percent lived in rural communities. This is largely due to the fact that the vast majority of Laotians who immigrated to the United States were unaccustomed to an industrial society and spoke either very little or no English; they migrated to urban areas where they could find work that did not require many skills or language proficiency.

As a group, Laotian Americans are substantially younger than the national average. In 1990, the median age for Laotian Americans was 20.4 years while the median age for other Americans was 34.1 years. Moreover, Laotian Americans have larger families than other Americans. In 1990, the average number of people in each Laotian American family was 5.01 members, compared to an average of 3.06 members in white American families and 3.48 members in African American families. These figures demonstrate that Laotian Americans are a dynamic, rapidly growing community.

Because Laotian Americans are relatively new members of American society, it is difficult to predict to what extent they will assimilate. According to interviews given by Laotian Americans, however, it is apparent that many individuals have had to alter their viewpoints consider-

A Laotian American weaver (left) demonstrates how to use a loom to a student.

ably to better adapt to American society. For example, such common "American" acts as touching, kissing, slapping someone on the back, waving, pointing one's feet at another person, and looking directly into someone's eyes are considered rude in Laotian culture. As Saelle Sio Lai has explained in John Tenhula's *Voices from Southeast Asia*, "Some of the Laotian customs I can use in my own way and some I must forget."

The majority of Laotian Americans have maintained a low profile in the United States. Consequently, few Americans have much knowledge of Laotian culture and people and, as a result, there are few stereotypes—positive or negative—regarding Laotian Americans.

LAOTIAN AMERICAN VALUES

Many Laotian Americans have retained the values they brought with them from their homeland. Most significant among these values is the practice of Buddhism, which pervades every aspect of Laotian American life. While individual Laotian Americans may not follow all Buddhist teachings, its philosophy serves as a behavorial guide.

The family is also highly important to Laotian Americans. In Laos, where the majority of people work in agriculture, families often work together to produce the goods necessary for their livelihood. In the United States, this practice has been altered somewhat since the majority of Laot-

ian Americans work outside the home in urban communities. Nonetheless, Laotian Americans often live in close proximity to their extended family and such family values as respect for one's parents have remained constant. Laotian American children are expected to respect and care for their parents throughout their adult life.

Education has also become extremely important among Laotian Americans. Often, the family's future is dependent upon their children's success in school. "My husband and I always remind [our children] to study first, study hard, not play, not go out without permission from us," explained one Laotian American woman in *Voices from Southeast Asia*, "We tell them that we want to go to school, too, but we have to work to feed them. We sacrifice for them, and the only thing they can pay back is to study well."

LAOTIAN PROVERBS

Laotian proverbs often express an earthy and practical sort of folk wisdom that is rooted in the experiences of generations of hard-working farmers. The Lao have brought countless proverbs to America with them, including the following examples: if you're shy with your teacher, you'll have no knowledge; If you're shy with your lover, you'll have no bedmate; Don't teach a crocodile how to swim; Keep your ears to the fields and your eyes on the farm; If you have money, you can talk; if you have wood, you can build your house;

Water a stump and you get nothing; Speech is silver, silence is gold; Follow the old people to avoid the bite of a dog; It's easy to find friends who'll eat with you, but hard to find one who'll die with you; It's easy to bend a young twig, but hard to bend an old tree.

FESTIVALS

Most Laotian holidays and festivals have religious origins. The Lao word for "festival," *boon*, literally means "merit" or "good deed." Scheduled according to the lunar calendar, festivals usually take place at Buddhist temples, making it difficult for Laotian Americans to participate due to the limited availability of monks and temples in the United States. Two of the most important festivals are the *Pha Vet*, which commemorates the life of the Buddha in the fourth lunar month, and the *Boon Bang Fay*, or "rocket festival." Held in the sixth month to celebrate the Buddha, it is marked by fireworks displays.

CUISINE

Laotian cuisine is spicy. Most meals contain either rice (*khao*) or rice noodles (*khao poon*). The rice may be glutinous (*khao nyao*) or nonglutinous (*khao chao*), but glutinous, or "sticky," rice is the food most often associated with Laotian cuisine. The rice is accompanied by meat, fish, and vegetables. Meats are often chopped, pounded, and spiced to make a dish known as *lap*, and fish is usually eaten with a special sauce called *nam ba*. The sticky rice is usually taken in the thumb and first three fingers and used to scoop up other foods. A papaya salad spiced with hot peppers, which is known as *tam mak hoong* to Laotians and *som tam* to Thais, is a popular snack food.

Many Laotian Americans still eat Lao-style foods at home. These dishes are also available at most Thai restaurants, since the cooking of northeastern Thailand is almost identical to that of Laos. Sticky rice and other ingredients for Lao foods are likewise available at most stores that specialize in Asian foods. In areas that have large Laotian American communities, there are also a number of Lao markets where these ingredients may be purchased.

TRADITIONAL DRESS

On special occasions marked by the *sookhwan* ceremony, some Laotian American women wear traditional costumes. The staple of their attire is the *sinh*, a skirt made from a piece of silk brocade about two yards long that is wrapped around the waist. It is often held in place by a belt made of silver buckles or rings. Accompanying the *sinh* is a shawl, or a strip of material, which is draped over the left shoulder and under the right arm. Some Laotian American men wear ethnic costumes at weddings, especially during the *sookhwan* ritual, and on stage during a *maw lam* performance, when actors sometimes don the *sampot*, or baggy trousers worn in Laos before French occupation.

"My children will surely be influenced by their scholastic environment and be Americanized very fast. I can't and don't intend to stop this natural process. I just want them not to forget their own culture. The ideal is the combination of the positive traits of the two cultures."

A Laotian refugee, cited in John Tenhula, *Voices from Southeast Asia: Experience in the United States* (New York: Holmes & Meier, 1991).

HEALTH AND MENTAL HEALTH ISSUES

Traditional Laotian medicine involves massages and herbal cures. Practitioners of traditional medicine may be laypeople or monks. Since sickness is seen as a problem of spiritual essence, the *khwan*, chants, and healing rituals are often used to cure illnesses. Although some traditional Lao medicine may be found in the United States, particularly in places that have large Laotian American communities, the practice of mainstream western medicine in America appears to be much more common.

Laotian Americans are more likely to visit a community clinic than any other type of medical establishment. As new arrivals, their mental health generally follows a pattern common to refugees. The first year in the United States tends to be a period of euphoria at having reached their destination. The second year tends to be a time of psychological shock, producing feelings of helplessness as the strangeness of the new environment becomes apparent. New Laotian Americans usually begin to adjust during the third or fourth year in the States.

LANGUAGE

Lao is a tonal language; therefore, the meaning of a word is determined by the tone or pitch at which it is spoken. Although the tones vary somewhat from one part of the country to another, the dialect of the capital, Vientiane, is considered standard Lao. In Vientiane there are six tones: low, mid, high, rising, high falling, and low falling. Changing the tone of a word makes it a different word. The sound "kow," pronounced much like the English "cow," spoken with a high tone means "an occasion, a time." "Kow" spoken with a rising tone means "white." Spoken with a mid tone, this word means "news." These tones give the Lao language a musical quality, so that its speakers often sound like they are singing or reciting melodic poetry.

The Lao alphabet is phonetic, meaning that each Lao letter stands for a sound. Lao writing has 27 consonant symbols that are used for 21 consonant sounds. There are more symbols than sounds because different consonants are used to begin words of different tones. The Lao alphabet also has 38 vowel symbols, representing 24 vowel sounds. These 24 sounds are made up of nine simple vowels and three diphthongs (vowels made up of two vowel sounds), each of which has a short form and a long form. The sounds are written with more than 24 symbols because some of them are written differently at the end of a word and in the middle of a word. All Lao words end in a vowel or in a consonant sound similar to the English "k," "p," "t," "m," "n," or "ng." Some English diphthongs (including "th" and "oh") do not exist in the Lao phonetic system. This is why some Laotian Americans who learned English as a second language may occasionally pronounce "fish" as "fit" or "stiff" as "stip."

The graceful, curving letters of the Laotian alphabet are based on the Khmer (Cambodian) alphabet, which, in turn, was developed from an ancient writing system in India. Although the Lao writing system is not the same as the Thai writing system, the two are very similar, and anyone who can read one language can read the other with only a little instruction.

GREETINGS AND OTHER POPULAR EXPRESSIONS

Common Laotian American greetings and expressions include: *Sabai dee baw*—How are you? (literally, are you well?); *Koy sabai dee*—I'm well; *Jao day*—And how are you? (used when responding to *Sabai dee*); *Pai sai*—Where are you going? (used as a greeting); *Kawp jai*—Thank you; *Kaw toht*—Excuse me; *Baw pen nyang*—You're welcome, never mind (literally, it's nothing); *Ma gin khao*—Come eat! (literally, come eat rice); *Sab baw*—Is the food good?; *Sab eelee*—It's delicious.

LAOTIAN AMERICAN LITERATURE

Most Laotian literature consists of oral tales and religious texts. Laotian oral literature often takes the form of poetry and is sung or chanted to the accompaniment of a hand-held bamboo pipe organ called the *khene* (pronounced like the word "can" in American English). Such poetry is most often used in theater, or opera, known as *maw lam*. The *maw lam leuang*, or "story *maw lam*," is similar to European opera; a cast of actors in costume sing and act out a story, often drawn from historical or religious legend. *Maw lam khoo*, or "*maw lam* of couples," involves a young man and a young woman. The man flirts with the woman through inventive methods and she refuses him with witty verse responses. *Maw lam chote*, or "*maw lam* competition," is a competition in verse sung between two people of the same gender, in which each challenges the other by asking questions or beginning a story that the other must finish. In *maw lam dio*, or "*maw lam* alone," a single narrator sings about almost any topic.

Among the many legends and folktales told by Laotians and Laotian Americans, the stories about the character Xieng Mieng are among the most popular. Xieng Mieng is a trickster figure who plays pranks on people of various social classes. Other popular tales involve legends taken from Buddhist writings, especially the *Sip Sat*, stories about the last ten lives of the Buddha before he was reborn and achieved enlightenment. All Laotian religious literature is made up of the same Buddhist texts used by other Theravada Buddhists. These include the *Jataka*, the five *Vinaya*, the *Dighanikaya*, and the *Abhidamma*, all of which are scriptures written in Pali, an ancient language from India still used for religious purposes in countries practicing Theravada Buddhism. Verses in Pali known as the *parittam* are also important to Laotian Buddhists and are chanted by monks to protect people from a variety of dangers.

In the United States, Laotian monks have successfully retained Laotian religious literature. In addition, secular legends and stories, told through the medium of *maw lam*, may be heard at gatherings in cities with large Laotian American communities.

FAMILY AND COMMUNITY DYNAMICS

In Laos, men represent their family in village affairs, while women are responsible for running the household and controlling the financial affairs of the family. Among Laotian Americans, however, female employment is an important source of family income, and it is common for Laotian American women to work outside the home. Fifty percent of Laotian American women and 58 percent of Laotian American men participate in the American labor force. Because of the relative equality between men and women in Laotian American society, many Laotian American men share responsibility for completing household tasks. While Laotian American men almost always hold the official positions of leadership in community organizations, women are also quite active in their communities and are often important (though usually unacknowledged) decision makers.

The most common family arrangement in Laos is that of a nuclear family that lives in close proximity to their extended family. In the United States, extended families have, in many cases, become even more important to Laotian Americans for social and financial support. This interdependence may account for the low divorce rate among Laotian Americans. In 1990, only about four percent of Laotian Americans over the age of 15 who had been married were divorced, while nearly 12 percent of the American population over 15 years of age who had been married were divorced.

The practice of dating is also new to Laotian American immigrants, as it simply was not done in their homeland. In Laos couples usually come to know one another in the course of village life. In the United States, however, many young people date, although this custom is not always embraced by their parents.

EDUCATION

Since Laotian Americans are such a young group, their prospects for continuing adaptation are good, especially considering the scholastic successes of Laotian American children. In *The Boat People and Achievement in America*, an influential book on the academic achievement of young Indochinese Americans, Nathan Caplan, John K. Whitmore, and Marcella H. Choy asserted that refugee children, including Laotians, "spoke almost no English when they came, and they attend predominantly inner-city schools whose reputations for good education are poor. Yet by 1982, we find that the Indochinese had already begun to move ahead of other minorities on a national basis, and, two years later, their children are already doing very well on national tests."

Despite these accomplishments, few Laotian American young people attend college; this may be attributed to the economic disadvantages of their families. Only 26.3 percent of Laotian Americans (not counting the Hmong) between the ages of 18 and 24 attended college in 1990 (compared to 39.5 percent of white Americans and 28.1 percent of African Americans). Laotian American young people also had relatively high dropout rates; 12.2 percent of Laotian Americans between the ages of 16 and 19 were neither high school graduates nor enrolled in school in 1990 (compared to 9.8 percent of white Americans and 13.7 percent of African Americans).

IMPORTANT RITUALS

Many Laotian Americans retain the ritual practices of their culture. The most common of all Laotian rituals is the *baci* (pronounced "bah-see") or *sookhwan*, which is performed at important occasions. The word *sookhwan* may be interpreted as "the invitation of the *khwan*" or "the calling of the *khwan*." The *khwan* are 32 spirits that are believed to watch over the 32 organs of the human body. Together, the *khwan* are thought to constitute the spiritual essence of a person. The *baci* is a ritual binding of the spirits to their possessor. Even Laotians who do not believe in the existence of the *khwan* will usually participate in the *baci* as a means of expressing goodwill and good luck to others.

In the *baci* ceremony, a respected person, usually an older man who has been a monk, invokes the *khwan* in a loud, songlike voice. He calls on the spirits of all present to cease wandering and to return to the bodies of those present. He then asks the *khwan* to bring well-being and happiness with them and to share in the feast that will follow. After the invocation to the *khwan* is finished, the celebrants take pieces of cotton thread from silver platters covered with food, and tie them around each other's wrists to bind the *khwan* in place. While tying the thread, they will wish one another health and prosperity. Often an egg is placed in the palm of someone whose wrist is being bound, as a symbol of fertility. Some of the threads must be left on for three days, and when they are removed they must be broken or untied, not cut. Non-Laotians are not only welcomed to this ceremony, they are frequently treated as guests of honor.

WEDDINGS

The *khwan* is also significant to traditional Laotian wedding ceremonies. When a couple adheres to Laotian traditions strictly, the groom goes to the bride's house the day before the wedding feast, where monks await with bowls of water. The bride and groom's wrists are tied together with a long cotton thread, which is looped around the bowls of water and then tied to the wrists of the monks. The next morning, friends and relatives of the couple sprinkle them with the water and then hold a *baci* ceremony. Afterward, the couple is seated together in front of all the guests and the monks chant prayers to bless the marriage.

RELIGION

In Laos almost all lowland Laotians are Buddhists, and the temple, or *wat*, is the center of village life. Most Laotian Americans are Buddhists as well, although many have converted to Protestant Christianity, especially in areas where there are no large Laotian concentrations to sustain traditional religious practices. Laotian American Buddhist temples are frequently established in converted garages, private homes, and other makeshift religious centers.

Buddhism is divided into two schools of thought. The "Northern School," known as Mahayana Buddhism, is a school of Buddhism most often found in China, Japan, Tibet, Korea, and Vietnam. The "Southern School," or Theravada Buddhism, is predominant in Laos, Thailand, Cambodia, Burma, and Sri Lanka. Theravada Buddhists stress the importance of becoming a monk and achieving *Nirvana*, an ideal state in which an individual transcends suffering. Mahayana Buddhists rely more on *Bodhisattvas*, enlightened beings who delay achieving *Nirvana* in order to help others become enlightened.

Essential to the Buddhist faith is the belief that all worldly things are impermanent. Those who are not aware of this concept become attached to worldly things, and this leads to suffering. Their suffering continues as the soul goes through a cycle of rebirths, and they are continually drawn back to worldly desires. An individual may break this cycle by overcoming desire through meditation and a moral, disciplined life. The soul that successfully overcomes all worldly desires reaches *Nirvana*.

Also significant to Buddhism is *karma*, which is form of spiritual accounting: good deeds performed in this life enable the soul to be reborn in better circumstances; bad deeds cause the soul to be reborn in worse circumstances. Accordingly, performing good deeds, or "making merit," is important to all Laotians and Laotian Americans. One can make merit through acts of kindness; however, becoming a monk or supporting monks or a temple are considered the best methods for making merit. All Laotian men are expected to become monks, usually in early manhood, before marriage. It is also common for older men, especially widowers, to become monks. Laotian women may become nuns, although nuns are not as respected as monks. In Laos, some men are not able to fulfill their religious duty of entering the temple for a time. This is even more difficult for Laotian American men because of demands in the workplace and the scarcity of temples in the United States. Laotian American monks sometimes share temples with Thai American or Cambodian American monks, since the latter also adhere to Theravada Buddhism.

A belief in spirits, or *phi* (pronounced like the English word "pea"), dates back to the time before the Lao were introduced to Buddhism. Since then, the spirit cult has become a part of popular Buddhist practices in Laos. Some of these spirits are "ghosts," the spirits of human beings following death. Other *phi* are benevolent guardians of people and places or malevolent beings who cause harm and suffering.

EMPLOYMENT AND ECONOMIC TRADITIONS

Although Laotian Americans have earned a reputation as hardworking people, many find themselves among the most disadvantaged in their new country. In 1990, while one out of every ten Americans lived below the poverty line, about one out of every three Laotian Americans lived below the poverty line. The median household income of Laotian Americans in that year was only $23,019, compared to $30,056 for other Americans. Unemployment among Laotian Americans is high (9.3 percent in 1990), and those with jobs tend to be concentrated in manual labor. Fully 44 percent of employed Laotian Americans held jobs classified as "operators, fabricators, and laborers" in 1990.

Many of the economic hardships of people in this ethnic group stem from their newness in America and from difficulties in making the change from life in a predominantly agricultural country to a highly industrialized country. Nearly 34 percent of Laotian Americans over the age of 25 had not completed fifth grade in 1990, compared to 2.7 percent of other Americans. While 75.2 percent of all adult Americans had completed high school, only 40 percent of adult Laotian Americans had finished high school. With regard to higher education, over 20 percent of Americans over 25 had finished college, while only about five percent of adult Laotian Americans were college graduates.

Learning English has hindered the economic adjustment of Laotian Americans. Over two-thirds (68 percent) of Laotians over five years of age reported that they did not speak English very well in 1990. While adult education programs and classes in English as a second language in community colleges and other institutions have helped, the transition has not been easy.

Despite their economic difficulties, Laotian Americans generally have positive views of life in the United States, probably because they tend to contrast life in America with their experiences in war-ravaged Laos.

POLITICS AND GOVERNMENT

As a group, Laotian Americans are very concerned about occurrences in their homeland and many would like to return but are unable to because of Laos's communist government. Laotian Americans have not yet become very active in American politics. At present, their first priority appears to be achieving economic independence. In general, they tend to have a positive view of American society and government, as might be expected of recent political refugees.

INDIVIDUAL AND GROUP CONTRIBUTIONS

Although Laotian Americans are relatively new to the United States, many professional individuals have made significant contributions to the Laotian American community and American society in general, specifically in professions requiring strong communication skills. Many Laotian American professionals are multilingual and serve as interpreters, negotiators, counselors,

This Laotian American girl is selling garlic at a farmer's market in Minnesota.

organization executives, and educators. For example, Banlang Phommasouvanh (1946-), a respected Laotian American educator, is the founder and executive director of the Lao Parent and Teacher Association. As such, she assists in promoting Lao culture, language, and arts through classes and support services. In 1990, Phommasouvanh received the Minnesota Governor's Commendation, Assisting the Pacific Minnesotans, State Council of Asia. In 1988, Lee Pao Xiong (1966-) served as an intern in the U.S. Senate. That same year, he was one of 25 people chosen in a nationwide competition to attend the International Peace and Justice Seminar. From 1991 to 1993, Xiong was executive director of the Hmong Youth Association of Minnesota. Currently, he is executive director of the Hmong American Partnership in St. Paul, Minnesota. William Joua Xiong (1963-), who is proficient in Lao, Hmong, Thai, English, and French, served as an interpreter and translator at the U.S. Embassy in Bangkok in 1979. Presently a guidance counselor, he is also co-author of the *English-Hmong Dictionary* (1983).

MEDIA

PRINT

Because Laotian Americans are still establishing themselves in the United States, there are very few Laotian publications. Worthy of mention is the monthly, multilingual publication *New Life*, which has attained a wide readership among Laotian Americans. Published by the federal government, it provides international news and articles covering American culture and institutions. *New Life* circulates 35,000 copies in Vietnamese, 10,000 in Lao, and 5,000 in Cambodian.

Khosana.

Contains academic news of Thai, Laotian, and Cambodian studies.

Contact: Michael R. Rhum, Editor.
Address: Association for Asian Studies, Thailand-Laos-Cambodia Studies Group, Department of Anthropology, Northern Illinois University, Dekalb, Illinois 60115.
Telephone: (815) 753-8577.

ORGANIZATIONS AND ASSOCIATIONS

Most Laotian organizations in the United States were established to help Laotian Americans adapt to life in a new country. Therefore, these organizations concentrate heavily on providing English language tutoring, job counseling, psychological counseling, and other social services.

Lao Assistance Center of Minneapolis.

Provides social services to the Laotian American community in Minneapolis.

Contact: Manivah Foun, Executive Director.
Address: 1015 Olson Memorial Highway, Minneapolis, Minnesota 55405.
Telephone: (612) 374-4967.

Lao Coalition.

Located in Washington State, this organization coordinates the activities of ten Laotian organizations (including Hmong organizations and organizations of other minority groups from Laos). The Coalition also provides social services, including transitional counseling, transportation, and tutoring. This is probably the best source for information on the Laotian American community of Washington.

Contact: Udong Sayasana, President.
Address: 4713 Rainier Avenue, Seattle, Washington 98118.
Telephone: (206) 723-8440.

Lao Family Community, Inc.

Provides training in English as a second language, vocational education, a variety of youth programs, and a gang prevention program for people from Laos and other countries in Southeast Asia.

Contact: Pheng Lo.
Address: 807 North Joaquin, Stockton, California 95202.
Telephone: (209) 466-0721.

Lao Lane Xang.

A Lao cultural and social service organization with chapters in most areas that have large Laotian communities. It hosts annual meetings that gather Laotian American community leaders from various parts of the United States.

Contact: Khamsang Thaviseth, President.
Address: 5150 Cloverdale, Seattle, Washington 98118.
Telephone: (206) 723-8440.

Migration and Refugee Services.

Provides social services such as English language training and help in finding employment to the Laotian community in western Louisiana.

Contact: Khamla Luangsouphom, Diocese of Lafayette.
Address: 1408 Carmel Avenue, Lafayette, Louisiana 70501.
Telephone: (318) 261-5535.

National Association for the Education and Advancement of Cambodian, Laotian, and Vietnamese Americans (NAFEA).

Seeks to provide equal educational opportunities for and advance the rights of Indochinese Americans; acknowledge and publicize contributions of Indochinese in American schools, culture, and society; and encourage appreciation of Indochinese cultures, peoples, education, and language.

Contact: Ngoc Diep Nguyen, President.
Address: Illinois Research Center, 1855 Mt. Prospect Road, Des Plaines, Illinois 60018.
Telephone: (708) 803-3112.

MUSEUMS AND RESEARCH CENTERS

Laotian Cultural and Research Center (LCRC).

Individuals interested in preserving Laotian culture by collecting documents that illustrate the history of Laos. Maintains library of more than 500 items.

Contact: Seng Chidhalay, President.

Address: 1413 Meriday Lane, Santa Ana, California 92706.

Telephone: (714) 541-4533.

SOURCES FOR ADDITIONAL STUDY

Caplan, Nathan, John K. Whitmore, and Marcella H. Choy. *The Boat People and Achievement in America: A Study of Family Life and Cultural Values*. Ann Arbor: University of Michigan Press, 1989.

Proudfoot, Robert. *Even the Birds Don't Sound the Same Here: The Laotian Refugees' Search for Heart in American Culture*. New York: Peter Lang Publishing, 1990.

Stuart-Fox, Martin. *Laos: Politics, Economics, and Society*. Boulder, Colorado: Lynne Rienner Publishers, 1986.

Tenhula, John. *Voices from Southeast Asia: The Refugee Experience in the United States*. New York and London: Holmes & Meier, 1991.

The majority of Latvians who came to the United States after World War II had received at least some higher education in their homeland. Many were already academic or cultural leaders, and they placed high value on education for their children.

LATVIAN AMERICANS

by
Andris Straumanis

OVERVIEW

Latvia is situated in Eastern Europe on the Baltic Sea, bordered by Estonia to the north, Russia to the east, Belarus to the southeast, and Lithuania to the south. With a population in 1993 of about 2.6 million and a surface area of 24,903 square miles (64,600 square kilometers), Latvia—one of the three Baltic nations—is larger than Estonia but smaller than Lithuania. Nearly 69 percent of Latvia's population lives in cities, especially the capital, Rīga, which is home to about a third of the nation's people.

Although Latvia has always had a diverse population, the country's ethnic composition has become a growing issue among Latvians concerned with preservation of their culture. In 1993, according to Latvian government statistics, 53.5 percent of inhabitants were ethnic Latvians, while 33.5 percent were Russians. In some regions, particularly in southeastern Latvia as well as in the capital city of Rīga, ethnic Russians outnumber ethnic Latvians. Other ethnic groups often found in Latvia include Belarussians, Estonians, Germans, Gypsies, Jews, Lithuanians, Poles, and Ukrainians. The leading religions in Latvia include Lutheran, Russian Orthodox, and Roman Catholic. The official language of the country is Latvian, and the national flag consists of three horizontal stripes (maroon on top and bottom, white in the middle).

HISTORY

Latvia's experience as an independent nation has been limited. Inhabited as early as 9000 B.C., the region now called Latvia only began taking on a national identity in the mid-nineteenth century. The Latvians' ancestors—early tribes of Couronians, Latgallians, Livs, Selonians, and Semgallians—were established in the area by about 1500 B.C. Through the centuries, these pagan tribes gradually developed their society and culture, but beginning in the late twelfth and early thirteenth centuries they came under subjugation from German invasions. In particular, the Teutonic Knights of the Holy Roman Empire forcibly Christianized the tribes and built an economic and political system that continued in power until the twentieth century. The Germans were responsible for the growth of Rīga, established in 1201, as an important Baltic Sea port that continues today to serve as a transportation link between western Europe and Russia.

As the Russian Empire expanded in the 1600s, German military control of the Baltic region weakened. Beginning in the 1620s and into the 1700s, the northern part of Latvia was under Swedish rule, while the south and the east came under Polish-Lithuanian domination. Only the Duchy of Courland, in western Latvia by the Baltic Sea, maintained some independence. The Duchy of Courland even managed to briefly extend its influence beyond its home, establishing colonies in Gambia in Africa (1651) and on the Caribbean Sea island of Tobago (1654).

With the signing of the Treaty of Nystad in 1721, settling the Great Northern War between Russia and Sweden, the region that would later become Latvia came under the political and military rule of the Russian czar. Its economy, however, continued to be controlled by German barons who lived off the labor of Latvian peasants. Latvians began to gain some economic power after 1819, when serfs in the Baltic provinces were emancipated by the Russians.

Industrialization and the emergence of the so-called "National Awakening" in the late nineteenth century created discontent among Latvians over their social and political relationships with the Russians and the Germans. That discontent led to the 1905 Revolution in Latvia. Although the revolution failed, it served to bring together the Latvian working class and intelligentsia and to heighten hopes for independence. A year after the 1917 Russian Revolution, Latvia declared its independence and was a sovereign nation until its occupation by Soviet troops in 1940. In June of 1941, during the final three days of the Russian occupation of Rīga before its fall to the Germans, an estimated 30,000 Latvians were shepherded onto boxcars and deported to Siberia. Thousands died in what is now known among Latvians as the *Baigais gads* ("The Year of Terror"). "Liberated" by German troops in 1941, Latvia again fell under Soviet rule by the end of World War II. Forcefully incorporated into the Soviet Union, Latvia only regained independence in 1991 with the collapse of the Soviet Union.

THE FIRST LATVIANS IN AMERICA

Some historical evidence suggests that the first Latvians in North America may have settled with Swedish and Finnish migrants in the area of Delaware and Pennsylvania around 1640. In the late 1600s, a group from the island of Tobago migrated to Massachusetts. Latvians were also among the thousands of fortune seekers who headed to California during the 1849 Gold Rush. Two histories of Latvians in America claim that Mārtiņš Buciņš, believed to be a Latvian sailor, was among the first to die during the American Civil War.

SIGNIFICANT IMMIGRATION WAVES

Latvian American immigrants consist of two distinct groups: those immigrants—often called *veclatvieši*, or Old Latvians—who settled in the United States before World War II, and those who arrived after the war. Immigration before World War II is generally divided into three phases. The first phase began in 1888 with the arrival of several young men in Boston. (Among them was Jēkabs Zībergs [1863-1963], who became one of the most important Latvian American community leaders in the pre-World War II era.) Like other Latvian immigrants who followed in the early years of the twentieth century, these men journeyed to America in search of their fortunes—or to escape being drafted into the Russian czar's army. Politically, the early immigrants were further divided into two groups: one devoted to the creation of an independent Latvia; the other, influenced by socialism, concerned with freeing Latvian workers from the oppression of imperial Russia. This division was mirrored in Latvian American society.

The early immigrants were usually young, single men, although some single women and families also came to the States at the end of the nineteenth century. They settled primarily in East Coast and Midwest cities, such as Boston, New York, Philadelphia, Cleveland, and Chicago, as well as in some cities on the West Coast, including Seattle, Portland, and San Francisco. Scattered immigrants also settled in rural areas, although usually not in great enough numbers to form long-lasting communities. In most cities, in fact, Latvians were so few in number that they failed to create the sort of ethnic neighborhoods for which other groups, such as the Italians or Poles, are known. Only in the Roxbury district of Boston did an urban Latvian neighborhood develop. Latvians also attempted to create a rural colony in Lincoln County in north central Wisconsin, but political differences and hard economic conditions sapped the community of its members, which at one point is said to have numbered about 2,000. The first Lutheran church built by Latvians in America was erected in Lincoln County in 1906.

Among the early wave of immigrants were several hundred Latvian Baptists who also settled in various East Coast locations. Perhaps the best-known Latvian Baptist settlement was in Bucks County, Pennsylvania, not far from Philadelphia, where beginning in 1906 a community was formed that eventually grew to about 100 individuals.

The next wave of immigration of Old Latvians began around 1906, following the failed 1905 Revolution in the Latvian province of the Russian empire. Many Latvian political leaders, as well as rank-and-file revolutionaries, faced certain death if caught by Russian soldiers, so they chose instead to emigrate and to continue the revolutionary movement from abroad. Most of the revolutionaries who arrived in the United States had more radical political views than the earlier Latvian immigrants, and this resulted in splits not only between conservative and leftist Latvians but also among the leftists themselves.

With the beginning of World War I, Latvia became a battleground between German and Russian forces. Latvian migration came to a halt until the aftermath of the 1917 Russian Revolution, when many revolutionary Latvians returned to their homeland to work for the creation of a Bolshevik government (a forerunner to the Communist party) in Latvia as well as in Moscow. Among those returning was Fricis Roziņš (1870-1919), a radical Marxist philosopher who had immigrated to America in 1913. He returned in 1917 to head a short-lived Latvian Soviet government. A few nationalist Latvian Americans returned to Latvia after the country declared independence in 1918.

The next wave of immigration was more of a trickle. U.S. immigration quotas put in place in 1924 limited the number of Latvians who could settle in America, while the creation of a free Latvia and the promise of better economic times in the homeland—coupled with the Great Depression in the United States—generally discouraged immigration.

The number of Latvians who journeyed to America before World War II is difficult to determine. Figures compiled by Francis J. Brown and Joseph Slabey Roucek, published in 1937, show that 4,309 Latvians came to the States before 1900; 8,544 from 1901-1910; 2,776 from 1911-1914; 730 from 1915-1919; 3,399 from 1921-1930; and 519 from 1930-1936. Until the 1930 census, the U.S. government lumped Latvians in with Lithuanians and Russians. Ten years later, the census counted 34,656 people of Latvian origin, about 54 percent of them foreign-born.

World War II's ravages of Latvia turned many Latvians into refugees. Fearing the Soviet communists, they headed to western Europe. By the end of the war, an estimated 240,000 Latvians—more than a tenth of the country's population—were camped in Displaced Persons (DP) facilities in Germany, Austria, and other countries. About half were eventually repatriated to Latvia, but the rest resettled in Germany, England, Sweden, Australia, Canada, and the United States, as well as in other countries. As documented by Andris Skreija in his unpublished thesis on Latvian refugees, an estimated 40,000 Latvians immigrated to the United States from 1949 to 1951 with the help of the U.S. government and various social service and religious organizations. Many of these Latvians had been members of the professional class in their homeland, but in America they often had to take jobs as farmhands, custodians, or builders until they managed to find better paying positions.

Most Latvian DPs settled in larger cities, such as New York, Boston, Philadelphia, and Chicago. As with the Old Latvians, the DPs failed to create neighborhoods and had to rely on social events, the telephone, the mail, and the press to create a sense of community. In a few eastern cities, the newer immigrants found that some Old Latvian colonies remained active. (Some organizations and congregations begun by the Old Latvians, such as the Philadelphia Society of Free Letts, founded in 1892, continue to operate today.) In most cases, however, the Latvian DPs had to start from scratch and within a few years had managed to create a rather complete social and cultural world that included schools, credit unions, choirs, dance groups, theater troupes, publishers and book sellers, churches, veterans' groups, and political organizations.

Unlike the Old Latvians, many of whom considered themselves immigrants, the Latvian DPs saw themselves as living in *trimda*, or exile, and dreamed of the day they could return to a free Latvia. Since the reestablishment of an independent Latvia in 1991, however, few have returned, although about 9,000 have declared dual citizenship as a way to offer political support to the reemerging nation. Many frequently travel to their homeland and provide financial and material support for relatives and various organizations. A number of Latvian Americans have been elected to the *Saeima*, or Parliament, in Latvia. According to the 1990 report of the U.S. Bureau of the Census, a total of 75,747 persons claimed Latvian ancestry, 27,540 of whom were born abroad. From 1980 to 1990, the census reports, 1,006 Latvians arrived in the United States.

ACCULTURATION AND ASSIMILATION

The Latvians of the pre-World War II immigration are generally thought to have assimilated quickly into the American mainstream, while the exiles of the post-World War II period have maintained their ethnic distinctiveness but now are facing deepening concerns about their future.

In a 1919 article in *Literary Digest*, the attitude of Latvians (or Letts, as they were known then) toward acculturation was described thus: "Their first aim, except among the radical element, is to secure admission to American citizenship. Their children all are educated in our public schools, and the second generation of Letts are thorough Americans in the majority" ("Letts in the United States," *Literary Digest*, 21 June 1919; p. 37). While it may be true that many of the Old Latvians were eager to seek American citizenship,

In this 1949 photograph, a Latvian immigrant explains the meaning of the American flag to his daughter upon their arrival in the United States.

many also continued to keep up their interest in Latvia, especially between 1918 and 1920, when Latvia declared and fought for independence. At the same time, as the *Literary Digest* article noted, some Latvians who held leftist political views may have resisted becoming part of the American system. In 1919, for example, about 1,000 Latvians were among those immigrants who helped found the Communist Party of America.

Except for the political radicals among them, pre-World War II Latvian immigrants tended to assimilate easily. According to Brown and Roucek, 60.9 percent of the 20,673 foreign-born Latvians in the United States had been naturalized by 1930, while another 10.5 percent had declared their intention to be naturalized. Most Latvians, like other immigrants, started out in low-paying, unskilled jobs, but over the years gained experience and higher socioeconomic status. A report of the Committee on Racial Groups of the Massachusetts Bay Tercentenary Inc., written about 1930, had this to say about the Latvians in Massachusetts: "The Lettish people cannot be classified among the rich, but neither are they poor. Many of them own their own homes. Partly due to the fact that the Letts are scattered, there are no Lettish banks, corporations, or big businesses that are worth mentioning. The same is true of the professional workers. Mostly, they are skilled workers, such as carpenters, machinists, painters, wood finishers, tool makers, railroad workers, garage mechanics. Some of them, however, have taken up farming as their chosen profession and are successful farmers" (Committee on Racial Groups of the Massachusetts Bay Tercentenary Inc., *Historical Review*, 1930).

Latvians did not experience much of the stereotyping that plagued southern, central, and eastern European immigrants during the early twentieth century. This is most likely due to the fact that the Latvians were a little-known group. In one incident in Boston in 1908, however, Latvians as a group briefly made the front pages of local newspapers after three Latvians robbed a saloon at gunpoint. The newspaper coverage, the Boston-based magazine *Arena* complained, made the Latvians look like "a bloodthirsty, murderous people, lawless, criminal and altogether undesirable citizens" (Andris Straumanis, "'This Sudden Spasm of Newspaper Hostility': Stereotyping of Latvian Immigrants in Boston Newspapers, 1908," *Ethnic Forum*, Volume 13, No. 2, and Volume 14, No. 1, 1993-1994).

The arrival of the Latvian DPs after World War II sparked an era of heightened ethnic maintenance. Fiercely anticommunist, they saw the Soviet occupation of their homeland not only as an infringement on their right to autonomy but also as an effort to eradicate Latvians altogether. Migration of Russians and other non-Latvian groups into Latvia, part of a Soviet effort at "Russification," became a threat to Latvian culture. Latvian DPs in the United States reacted by launching a number of political and cultural movements to fight assimilation and help make Americans aware of Latvia's plight. Weekend Latvian schools were organized in several cities, while summer camps offered children and adults cultural immersion. *Runāsim latviski* ("Let's speak Latvian") was as much a political statement as an expression of cultural preservation. Marriage outside of the Latvian group often was discouraged, because it might mean that children of mixed couples would not learn the language.

As with the Old Latvians, few cultural misconceptions exist about post-World War II Latvians. Indeed the biggest difficulties Latvians have faced are their small numbers and the erasure, before 1991, of Latvia from many world maps. As a result, few Americans know anything about Latvians—and often confuse Europe's Balkan states with the Baltic countries, of which Latvia is a part.

TRADITIONS, CUSTOMS, AND BELIEFS

Like many other ethnic groups, the Latvians in the United States have adopted some American ways, but they also maintain a cultural heritage from the homeland. Until the late nineteenth century, when industrialization created demand for workers in several Latvian cities, Latvians remained rural. As a result, many of the traditions, customs, and beliefs still acknowledged by Latvian Americans are based on agricultural life. Others are drawn from more ancient Latvian culture. For example, in the Latvian tradition, a bride-to-be proved her worthiness by knitting many intricately designed wool mittens, as well as linen handkerchiefs and wool socks. The more she had in her dowry, the more worthy she might appear to her suitor. In the States, wool mittens and socks are sometimes used as adornments in wedding ceremonies.

Among the Latvian people's strongest traditions are their songs, called *dainas*, and their interest in folk culture. The *dainas*—simple verses that tell old stories and reveal the wisdom of centuries of Latvian culture—were handed down orally over generations. Beginning in the nineteenth century, as interest in Latvian nationalism grew, folklorists transcribed about 900,000 of these songs, culminating in a multi-volume collection compiled by Krisjānis Barons (1835-1923). Even at the end of the twentieth century, dozens of Latvian ensembles maintained the musical tradition in the United States, often performing at community events and in ethnic festivals. On a grander scale, Latvians in America and in Latvia have organized song festivals that feature performances of traditional folk songs and dances, choral music, and even musicals and plays. These song festivals serve as a ritual, reminding Latvians of their common ideals. The first such festival was held in Latvia in 1873; the tradition has since been carried on in the States, beginning in Chicago in 1953.

CUISINE

Traditional Latvian foods include *pīrāgi*, pastry stuffed with bacon or ham; *Jāṇu siers*, a cheese usually made for the Midsummer Eve's holiday; various soups; sauerkraut; potato salad; smoked fish and eel; and beer. At major celebrations, such as holidays and birthdays, a popular sweetbread— the *kliņģeris*, flavored with raisins and cardamom and shaped like a large pretzel—is served. Because of the work involved in preparing many of these dishes, as well as the difficulty in obtaining some

ingredients, many of these foods are now prepared only for special occasions. The foods tend to be rich, although Latvian Americans have been known to modify recipes by using lower-fat ingredients and less salt.

TRADITIONAL COSTUMES

Folk costumes are worn by Latvian Americans primarily when performing in song groups or dance troupes. Men's costumes are characterized by monotone (white, gray, or black) wool trousers and coats, white shirts, and black boots. Women's costumes usually include an embroidered white linen blouse and a colorful ankle-length wool skirt. Both men and women wear wide, bright belts and silver jewelry. Unmarried women wear a *vaiņags* (crown) on their heads, while married women wear a cap or kerchief. The designs of costumes are characteristic of specific locales in Latvia.

HOLIDAYS CELEBRATED BY LATVIAN AMERICANS

Latvian Christians observe Easter and Christmas in the Catholic tradition—they attend church services and get together with relatives and friends. At Easter, eggs are colored using onion skins rather than paint. The skins are wrapped around uncooked eggs, which are then boiled. One Easter dinner custom is to play a game to determine

whose egg is strongest: two people each hold an egg, the ends of the eggs are knocked together, and the person whose egg does not break goes on to challenge someone else. At Christmas, an evergreen tree is brought into the home and decorated. Before Christmas gifts are opened, a line of poetry or words from a song are recited. At New Year's, some Latvians still observe a custom of "pouring one's fortune." The person who wishes to know what his or her fortune will be in the New Year pours a ladle filled with molten lead into a bucket of cold water. The shape of the hardened lead is then examined to determine the future.

Perhaps the favorite Latvian holiday, however, comes in June, during the summer solstice—the longest day of the year. Called *Jāņi* (also known as St. John's Eve or Midsummer's Eve), in Latvia the day was a traditional celebration of nature's fertility. An elaborate feast was prepared—including the symbolic *Jāņu siers*, a rich cheese—and the home was decorated with oak leaves and flowers. The celebration, featuring bonfires and sing-alongs, lasted through the night and well into the following morning. In the United States, many of these customs survive; in modern Latvia, *Jāņi* is an official three-day holiday.

HEALTH AND MENTAL HEALTH ISSUES

Latvians in the United States have largely accepted modern medical treatments, although some folk cures are still used by some families. A number of Latvians have entered the medical profession. In addition to health insurance offered through their place of employment or through government programs, many Latvians also have joined the Latvian Relief Fund of America (*Amerikas latviešu palīdzības fonds*), founded in 1952. No illnesses specific to Latvian Americans are known.

LANGUAGE

Latvian, along with Lithuanian, is considered part of the small Baltic language group of the Indo-European family. It is one of the oldest languages still spoken in Europe. Latvian uses the Latin alphabet, although the letters "q," "w," "x," and "y" are not part of the alphabet. In addition, Latvian uses diacritical marks on some letters ("ā," "č," "ē," "ģ," "ī," "ķ," "ļ," "ņ," "ŗ," "š," "ū," and "ž") to differentiate long or soft sounds from short or hard sounds. Latvian words are stressed on the first syllable, and written Latvian is largely phonetic.

Due to Latvia's location and its history, the country's language has been influenced by German, Russian, and Swedish. During the 50-year occupation of Latvia by the former Soviet Union, the influence of Russian became particularly strong. A few dialects in addition to standard Latvian can still be heard in Latvia, most notably Latgallian, spoken in the heavily Catholic southeastern province of Latgale. In the United States, Latvian cultural leaders and schools have battled against the encroachment of English into their mother tongue; since Latvia regained independence in 1991 and declared Latvian rather than Russian the official language, more and more English words are creeping into Latvian.

Latvian continues to be used in the United States most widely among the first generation of post-World War II immigrants. According to the 1990 U.S. Census Bureau report, about 13 percent of those persons who claim Latvian ancestry—most of them aged 65 and older—said they do not speak English very well. Among second and third generation Latvian Americans, usage has dropped significantly, in some cases because of intermarriage. Latvian is still used in church services in many congregations, although some churches have begun to use English as a way to attract and serve non-Latvian speakers. In the United States, only one Latvian-language newspaper is published (the semi-weekly *Laiks* of Brooklyn, New York), but there are several small Latvian-language magazines and numerous church newsletters.

GREETINGS AND OTHER POPULAR EXPRESSIONS

Perhaps the most widespread salutation in Latvian is *Sveiks!* ("svayks")—Greetings! It is commonly used when greeting friends but is also seen on bumper stickers on cars driven by Latvian Americans. Other terms include: *Apsveicu* ("ap-svay-tsu")—Congratulations; *Atā* ("a-tah")—Goodbye; *Daudz laimes dzimšanas dienā* ("daudz laimes dzim-shan-as dien-ah")—Happy birthday; *Labdien* ("labdien")—Good day; *Labrīt* ("labreet")—Good morning; *Labvakar* ("labvakar")—Good evening; *Lūdzu* ("loodz-u")—Please; *Paldies* ("pal-dies")—Thank you; *Priecīgus svētkus* ("prie-tsee-gus sveht-kus")—Happy holidays, used at Christmastime; *Uz redzēšanos* ("uz redz-eh-shan-os")—Until we meet again.

FAMILY AND COMMUNITY DYNAMICS

Latvians in the United States tend to have small nuclear families, usually not exceeding two adults and two children. According to the 1990 census, a total of 37,574 households of Latvian ancestry were reported. Of those, 12,341 had only one family member (32.8 percent); 14,211 (37.8 percent) had two; 5,010 (13.3 percent) had three; and 3,985 (10.6 percent) had four. A total of 86.9 percent of children under the age of 18 were living with two parents. Most families are middle-class; the median household income in 1989 was $38,586. Four percent of Latvian families received public assistance in 1989.

Within the post-World War II Latvian emigre population, young men and women have been encouraged to seek each other out in the hope that new Latvian families would result. For some youth, however, the close-knit nature of Latvian community life made it difficult to transform longtime acquaintances into romantic involvement. Others, perhaps realizing that their involvement in the Latvian community would make a relationship outside the ethnic group difficult, seem to have deliberately sought out Latvian mates. But because the rate of marriage to non-Latvians has continued to increase over the years, older Latvians have become concerned that Latvian culture in the United States might be threatened. At one point in the early 1970s, it was even suggested that Latvian newspapers should not carry announcements of marriages involving non-Latvians. Among Latvian men, according to the 1990 census, 62.3 percent were married, one percent were separated, and 6.4 percent were divorced. Among women, 50.9 percent were married, one percent were separated, and 8.8 percent were divorced.

THE ROLE OF WOMEN

Latvia extended broad democracy to its inhabitants and guaranteed equal rights to women. In the States, women have often been placed in such traditional roles as homemaker and cook. Despite their accomplishments in the professions, women for many years were not seen at the helm of the most influential local and national Latvian institutions. In recent years, however, that has been changing. For example, the Latvian newspaper *Laiks*, published since 1949, is now edited by a woman, Baiba Bičole.

EDUCATION

The Old Latvians, while recognizing the value of education, did not appear to want or to be able to afford college degrees. By 1911—more than 20 years after the first Latvian immigrants had arrived in the United States—only two individuals had obtained American university degrees, the first one being a woman, Anna Enke, who studied at the University of Chicago.

The majority of Latvians who came to the United States after World War II had received at least some higher education in their homeland. Many were already academic or cultural leaders, and they placed high value on education for their children. The 1990 census indicates that about 34 percent of people claiming Latvian ancestry had earned bachelor's degrees or higher. Between 1940 and 1982, according to a 1984 study, 28 percent of Latvian men outside the Soviet Union who had earned bachelor's degrees studied in the engineering sciences, while another 15.6 percent studied in the humanities. Among women, 22.5 percent studied humanities and 16.9 percent studied medicine.

RELIGION

In 1935, 55.1 percent of religious Latvians followed the Lutheran faith, 24.4 percent were Roman Catholic, and 8.9 percent were Greek Orthodox (*Cross Road Country—Latvia*, edited by Edgars Dunsdorfs [Waverly, Iowa: Latvju Grāmata, 1953]; p. 360). Although it is difficult to obtain accurate figures, the majority of Latvians in the United States follow the Lutheran faith, but there also are adherents of the Catholic and Baptist faiths, as well as a small group of *dievturi*, followers of a folk religion.

The first Latvian Lutheran church service in the United States was organized by the Boston Latvian Society in 1891. The earliest known congregation, St. John's Latvian Evangelical Lutheran Church, was formed in 1893 in Philadelphia and continued to operate more than a century later. The Rev. Hans Rebane (1862-1911) became the first Latvian Lutheran minister ordained in America. Rebane, of Estonian and Latvian heritage, also served Estonian and German congregations. Together with Jēkabs Zībergs, he began *Amerikas Vēstnesis* (*America's Herald*, 1896-1920), a nationalist and religiously oriented newspaper based in Boston; Zībergs also published an almanac and other religious materials. In a few short years, additional Latvian congregations were established in New York, Philadelphia, Baltimore, Cleveland, Chicago, northern Wisconsin, San Francisco, and other locations. Radical Latvians in the United States criticized these early churchgoers; to them, the church in Latvia—largely controlled by German-appointed pastors—contributed to the oppression of Latvian peasants. By World War II, only a few congregations remained, but the arrival of Latvian DPs beginning in 1949 gave them new life.

Latvian Lutheran DPs saw theirs as a church in exile. Although a Lutheran church still existed back in Latvia, its activities were suppressed by the Soviet regime. The Latvian Lutheran church in the United States remains conservative but in many cities has become a focus of community activity. Many congregations have organized Saturday or Sunday schools offering language and cultural heritage lessons in addition to religious instruction. In cities where Latvians acquired their own church buildings, the facilities often double as cultural centers where concerts or other programs might be presented.

A key issue for Lutheran clergy has been whether they can continue to preach Christianity at the expense of Latvian ethnic maintenance. Attempts by some pastors to introduce English into religious instruction have in the past been met by resistance. Like other Latvian social and cultural institutions in the United States, the Lutheran church is concerned about decreasing membership, which erodes both the vitality of congregations as well as their financial base. According to Latvian statistics published in 1993, the number of church members totaled 26,265 in 1978, but dropped steadily to 18,557 over the next 15 years.

Latvian Baptists were also active in the States by the late 1880s. The first Latvian Baptist congregation was founded in Philadelphia in 1900; by 1908 congregations were also meeting in Boston, Chicago, and New York, as well as in Bucks County, Pennsylvania. Latvian Baptists published a number of magazines and newsletters before World War II, including the monthly *Amerikas Latvietis* (*America's Latvian*, 1902-1905) and *Jaunā Tēvija* (*The New Fatherland*, 1913-1917).

Latvian American Catholic groups also sprang up after World War II, but they were not large enough in any city to have their own church. Latvian Catholics are represented by the American Latvian Catholic Association (*Amerikas latviešu katoļu apvienība*), formed in 1954.

Also active in the United States are the *dievturi*, followers of a folk religion registered as the Latvian Church Dievturi Inc., which developed in the 1920s in Latvia. The *dievturi* look to ancient Latvian culture, particularly folk songs, for their beliefs and are credited for their efforts in maintaining old folkways.

EMPLOYMENT AND ECONOMIC TRADITIONS

Many of the Old Latvians who left their homeland were either farmers or factory workers. Upon arriving in the United States, they at first took jobs as unskilled laborers; later, however, some moved into management and professional positions. Unlike the Old Latvians, many of the DPs had held professional positions in Latvia before migrating to America. Most, however, were unable to immediately resume their professional careers—at least until they had mastered English and proven their qualifications.

According to the 1990 census, 38,132 persons of Latvian ancestry were counted in the nation's civilian labor force, of which 1,653 (4.2 percent) were unemployed. About 48 percent of Latvians in the labor force had positions in management and the professions; 30 percent had jobs in technical, sales, and administrative support occupations. Almost three-fourths of the Latvians in the labor force worked in the private sector, about 16 percent had jobs in government and education, and about 10 percent were self-employed.

Like other Americans, Latvians were among those affected by the economic recession of the late 1980s and early 1990s. When a family was forced to relocate to other parts of the mainland States in search of employment, the move sometimes had a dramatic effect on Latvian social and cultural life. In Minneapolis, for example, when two young but large families had to move in the mid-1980s, their departure resulted in enrollment in the small Latvian Saturday school being trimmed by about a third.

POLITICS AND GOVERNMENT

Latvian Americans have always been politically active. Before Latvia declared its independence, radical Old Latvians were particularly active in working for the creation of a socialist government in their homeland as well as in the United States. The first Latvian socialist organization, the Lettish Workingmen's Society, was started in Boston in 1893. By World War I, almost every city where Latvians could be found also had at least one socialist club. With the arrival of revolutionary Latvians after the failed 1905 Revolution, Latvian radicalism moved farther to the left. Latvians were among those immigrants who helped form the American communist movement in 1919. Radicals produced a number of newspapers and other publications, but the most important was the Boston-based weekly *Strādnieks* (*The Worker*, 1906-1919). The failure to establish a permanent socialist government in Latvia following the 1917 Russian Revolution—compounded by U.S. government repression of radical activities during the "Red Scare" of the 1920s—largely put an end to Latvian radical activity in America.

The radicals were opposed by nationalist Latvians who sought independence for their homeland. Under the leadership of Jēkabs Zībergs, Christopher Roos (1887-1963), and others, the nationalists organized in 1917 to support the American World War I military effort by selling Liberty Bonds. The American National Latvian

League (*Amerikas latviešu tautiskā savienība* [ALTS]) was formed the next year in Boston to represent Latvian interests in the United States. When their homeland declared independence later in 1918, ALTS representatives urged America to recognize the new nation of Latvia; *de jure* recognition came in 1922.

Soviet occupation of Latvia during World War II was criticized by nationalist Latvians in the States, who sought to inform the American public about atrocities committed by the Russians. The arrival of Latvian DPs after the war heightened political activity among Latvian Americans. A number of Latvian civic and political organizations were founded, including the American Latvian Association in 1951 and the American Latvian Republican National Federation in 1961. Latvians also joined with Estonians and Lithuanians to form groups such as the Baltic Appeal to the United Nations (BATUN), to press world governments to oppose Soviet power in their homelands.

Officially, the U.S. government never recognized the incorporation of the Baltic countries into the Soviet Union. Attempts by U.S. diplomats to ease tensions with the Soviets usually drew swift criticism from the Baltic groups. At election time, the Republican party tended to evoke more support from Latvians than the Democrats—particularly among the first generation of Latvian immigrants, who felt the Republicans had a stronger anticommunist foreign policy platform. Within the Latvian community, efforts during the 1970s and 1980s by some Latvian Americans to establish cultural exchanges with Soviet Latvia were viewed with suspicion and criticism.

Reestablishment of Latvian independence in 1991 opened the door to direct political involvement in the homeland. Latvian immigrants and their descendants were allowed to reclaim their pre-World War II citizenship and voting rights; by May of 1993 more than 8,700 Latvian Americans held dual U.S. and Latvian citizenship, according to American Latvian Association statistics. In June of 1993, during the first free democratic elections after the end of Soviet rule, a number of Latvian Americans were elected to Parliament. Among them were twin brothers Olģerts Pavlovskis (1934-) and Valdis Pavlovskis (1934-) both of whom returned to Latvia to take government posts.

INDIVIDUAL AND GROUP CONTRIBUTIONS

Latvians have made a number of contributions to America culture and society. The following sections list some of their achievements.

ART

Florida's famed Coral Castle, a sculpture garden carved from coral, was created over a 30-year period by Edward Leedskalnin (1887-1951), a Latvian immigrant. Leedskalnin, jilted by the girl he wanted to marry, journeyed to the United States and decided to build the sculpture garden as a testament to his love for her. The garden (located in Homestead, Florida) was completed in 1940 and was placed on the National Register of Historical Places in 1984.

EDUCATION

Edgars Andersons (1920-1989) was a prolific historian who taught at San Jose State University in California. A specialist in European and early American history, he received a Distinguished Academic Achievement Award in 1978. Oswald Tippo (b. 1911), a botanist by training, held several top academic posts during his career, including chancellor of the University of Massachusetts at Amherst.

FILM, TELEVISION, AND THEATER

Actress Rutanya Alda (1942-) has appeared in numerous film, stage, and television productions, including *The Long Goodbye* (1973), *Pat Garrett and Billy the Kid* (1973), *The Deer Hunter* (1978), and *Prancer* (1989). Actor Buddy Ebsen (b. 1908), best known for his television roles as Jed Clampett in *The Beverly Hillbillies* and as the title character in *Barnaby Jones*, is of Latvian and Danish parentage. Chicagoan Mārīte Ozere (1944-) was crowned Miss U.S.A. in 1965. Actress Laila Robins has appeared in several feature films, including *Planes, Trains & Automobiles* (1987), *A Walk on the Moon* (1987), *An Innocent Man* (1989), and *Welcome Home, Roxy Carmichael* (1990). Anita Stewart (1895-1961) appeared in the silent movies *Hollywood* (1923) and *Never the Twain Shall Meet* (1925).

INDUSTRY

Augusts Krastiņš (1859-1942) began building gasoline-powered automobiles in 1896, several years before Henry Ford. The Cleveland, Ohio-based Krastin Automobile Company operated until 1904. Leon "Jake" Swirbul was a cofounder of the Grumman Aircraft Company and helped lead the company's production of fighter planes for the U.S. Navy during World War II. In 1946 Swirbul became president of the company, which is now part of Northrop Grumman Corporation.

LITERATURE AND JOURNALISM

Anšlevs Eglītis (1906-1993), a novelist and movie critic, wrote many popular Latvian books and was a frequent contributor to the Latvian American newspaper *Laiks*. Jānis Freivalds (1944-) has worked as a journalist, consultant, and entrepreneur. In 1978 he published a novel, *The Famine Plot*. Peter Kihss (1912-1984) spent nearly 50 years working as a journalist, including 30 years for the *New York Times*.

MUSIC

Several Latvian Americans have made significant contributions to symphonic music and opera, such as concert pianist Artūrs Ozoliņš (1946-), who has recorded with the Toronto Symphony Orchestra, and composer Gundaris Pone (1932-1993), whose work received international recognition but whose radical politics did not endear him to Latvian Americans. Alternative pop singer-songwriter Ingrid Karklins (1957-) of Austin, Texas, has released two albums, *A Darker Passion* (1992) and *Anima Mundi* (1994), some of which draws inspiration from traditional Latvian instruments and songs. The Quags, a Latvian rock group in Philadelphia, have also embarked on a recording career.

SCIENCE

John Akerman (1897-1972), a professor of aeronautics, had a long career teaching and researching at the University of Minnesota. Akerman Hall on the Minneapolis campus is named in his honor. Lectures about the Star of Bethlehem by retired astronomy professor Kārlis Kaufmanis (1910-) have become a popular Christmas attraction in Minnesota. Mārtiņš Straumanis (1898-1973) was a professor of metallurgy at the University of Missouri at Rolla.

SPORTS

Latvians in America and in Latvia have become ardent fans of the San Jose Sharks team of the National Hockey League. Two Latvians, goalie Arturs Irbe (1967-) and defenseman Sandis Ozolinsh (1972-), were acquired by the team in 1991. Gundars Vetra (c. 1967-) was the first Latvian to play for a National Basketball Association team. He was recruited by the Minnesota Timberwolves after playing for the Russian-led Unified Team in the 1992 Olympics.

MEDIA

PRINT

Baltic Observer.

A popular newspaper among those who do not read Latvian fluently, the English-language weekly is published in Rīga and covers all three Baltic countries.

Laiks (Time).

A semi-weekly Latvian-language newspaper published in Brooklyn, New York.

Latvian Dimensions.

Published by the American Latvian Association, it offers a national perspective on issues of interest to Latvians.

Contact: Mārtiņš Zvaners, Editor.

Address: American Latvian Association, P.O. Box 4578, 400 Hurley Avenue, Rockville, Maryland 20849-4578.

Telephone: (301) 340-8732.

RADIO

WVVX-FM (103.1).

Chicago Association of Latvian Organizations (*Čikāgas latviešu organizāciju apvienība*) sponsors a program.

Contact: Juris Valainis.

Address: 5020 West Lake Shore Drive, Wonder Lake, Illinois 60097.

Telephone: (815) 728-0028.

ORGANIZATIONS AND ASSOCIATIONS

American Latvian Association (*Amerikas latviešu apvienība*, ALA).

Founded in 1951, the ALA is the largest Latvian association in the United States; it has about

9,000 members and represents approximately 160 organizations. In the past, it served as an umbrella organization that coordinated the political, cultural, and educational activities of Latvian communities and lobbied the U.S. government for legislation and policies supporting independence for Latvia. Since independence was achieved, the ALA has given increased attention to welfare and education efforts in Latvia.

Contact: Ints Rupners, President.

Address: P.O. Box 4578, 400 Hurley Avenue, Rockville, Maryland 20849-4578.

Telephone: (301) 340-1914.

Fax: (301) 762-5438.

American Latvian Catholic Association (*Amerikas latviešu katoļu apvienība*, ALKA).

Founded in 1954, the ALKA represents the interests of Latvians of the Roman Catholic faith, many of whom trace their heritage to the Latgale province in southeastern Latvia.

Contact: Zigfrīds Zadvinskis, Chairman.

Address: 2235 Ontonagon Street, S.E., Grand Rapids, Michigan 49506.

Telephone: (616) 949-3126.

American Latvian Youth Association (*Amerikas latviešu jaunatnes apvienība*, ALJA).

Founded in 1952 and incorporated in 1964, the ALJA is a national organization for Latvian youth, generally those under age 30. It has served as a voice for its members in the exile community. During the 1970s and 1980s, it was especially active on the political front, organizing demonstrations at the Soviet embassy in Washington, D.C., and in other locations. Some former officers of the association have gone on to other leadership posts in the Latvian American community as well as in newly independent Latvia.

Contact: Pēteris Zards, Chairman.

Address: 10 Lois Lane, Katonah, New York 10536.

Telephone: (914) 232-2192.

Latvian Evangelical Lutheran Church in America (*Latviešu evaņģeliski luteriskā baznīca Amerikā*, LELBA).

Founded in 1975, the LELBA carries on the work of a Latvian American church association formed in 1957. Before 1975, local Latvian Lutheran congregations belonged to one of the U.S. churches, such as the American Lutheran Church. Since then, many have dropped their ties to U.S. churches and now are only members of LELBA. As of 1994, LELBA included 53 congregations in the United States; not all congregations, however, have their own churches or ministers.

Contact: Rev. Uldis Cepure, Chairman of the Board.

Address: 2140 Orkla Drive, Golden Valley, Minnesota 55427.

Telephone: (612) 546-3712.

Latvian Welfare Association (*Daugavas Vanagi*).

Founded in 1945 in Belgium, this is a global organization of war veterans—primarily those who fought in the two Latvian divisions organized during the German occupation of Latvia in World War II. Aside from offering support for disabled Latvian veterans, *Daugavas Vanagi* also supports cultural and educational efforts and works to preserve the history of the Latvian military. The organization has national and local chapters in several countries.

Contact: Andrejs Spārniņš, Chairman.

Address: 3220 Rankin Road, Minneapolis, Minnesota 55418.

Telephone: (612) 781-7132.

Fax: (612) 789-2602.

MUSEUMS AND RESEARCH CENTERS

Balch Institute for Ethnic Studies.

Houses Latvian material in its archives, including some records of St. John's Latvian Evangelical Lutheran Church.

Contact: John Tenhula, President.

Address: 18 South Seventh Street, Philadelphia, Pennsylvania 10106.

Telephone: (215) 925-8090.

Hoover Institution.

Houses a Russian and East European collection that includes some material on Latvians in the United States.

Address: Stanford University, Stanford, California 94305.

Immigration History Research Center.

Devoted to collecting archival materials concerning eastern, central, and southern European immigrants, as well as immigrants from the Middle East, the *IHRC* continues to expand its Latvian collection of books, newspapers, serials, and manuscripts. In 1993 the center embarked on a two-year project to organize materials pertaining to Displaced Persons from Latvia and Ukraine.

Contact: Joel Wurl, Curator.

Address: University of Minnesota, 826 Berry Street, St. Paul, Minnesota 55114.

Telephone: (612) 627-4208.

Latvian Museum.

Housed in the Latvian Lutheran Church in Rockville, Maryland, the museum opened in 1980 and provides an overview of Latvian life in the homeland and in exile.

Address: 400 Hurley Avenue, Rockville, Maryland 20850.

Latvian Studies Center.

Serves as a focus for students of Latvian heritage. It includes a growing library and archives of Latvian materials that have been donated to the center by Latvians from throughout the country.

Contact: Maira Bundža.

Address: Western Michigan University, 1702 Fraternity Village Drive, Kalamazoo, Michigan 49006.

Telephone: (616) 343-1922.

Fax: (616) 343-0704.

SOURCES FOR ADDITIONAL STUDY

Akmentiņš, Osvalds. *Latvians in Bicentennial America.* Waverly, Iowa: Latvju Grāmata, 1976.

Andersons, Edgars, and M. G. Slavenas. "The Latvian and Lithuanian Press," *The Ethnic Press in the United States: A Historical Analysis and Handbook,* edited by Sally M. Miller. Westport, Connecticut: Greenwood Press, 1987; pp. 229-245.

The Baltic States: A Reference Book. Tallinn, Estonia: Tallinn Book Printers, 1991.

Brown, Francis J., and Joseph Slabey Roucek. *Our Racial and National Minorities: Their History, Contributions, and Present Problems.* New York: Prentice-Hall, 1937.

Cross Road Country—Latvia, edited by Edgars Andersons. Waverly, Iowa: Latvju Grāmata, 1953.

Kārklis, Maruta, Līga Streips, and Laimonis Streips. *The Latvians in America, 1640-1973: A Chronology and Fact Book.* Dobbs Ferry, New York: Oceana Publications, 1974.

Kaslas, Bronis J. *The Baltic Nations—The Quest for Regional Integration and Political Liberty.* Pittston, Pennsylvania: Euraamerica Press, 1976.

Lieven, Anatoly. *The Baltic Revolution: Estonia, Latvia, Lithuania and the Path to Independence.* New Haven, Connecticut: Yale University Press, 1993.

Misiunas, Romuald J., and Rein Taagepera. *The Baltic States: Years of Dependence, 1940-1980.* Berkeley: University of California Press, 1983.

Šīmanis, Vito Vitauts. *Latvia.* St. Charles, Illinois: Book Latvia, 1984.

Straumanis, Alfreds. "Latvian American Theatre," *Ethnic Theatre in the United States,* edited by Maxine Schwartz Seller. Westport, Connecticut: Greenwood Press, 1983; pp. 277-318.

LITHUANIAN AMERICANS

by
Mark A.
Granquist

Slowly, as the immigrants began to settle permanently in the United States, family, religious, and community institutions were formed. A growing sense of nationalism within the community allowed the Lithuanians to see themselves as a people separate from the Poles and the Russians.

OVERVIEW

Located in northeastern Europe on the east coast of the Baltic Sea, Lithuania is the most southern of the Baltic Republics—a trio of countries that was formed in 1918. Lithuania measures 25,174 square miles (64,445 square kilometers) and is bordered by Latvia to the north, Belarus to the east, and Russia and Poland to the south and southwest. Its capital is Vilnius, which has a population of 590,000, making it the largest city in the country.

The 1993 census estimated the population of Lithuania at just over 3.75 million people; approximately 80 percent of the citizens are ethnic Lithuanians, 9 percent are Russians, and the remaining 11 percent are largely of Polish, Latvian, and Ukrainian descent. Roman Catholics constitute the largest religious group in Lithuania (85 percent), with smaller numbers of Lutherans, Orthodox Christians, and Jews. The official language of the country is Lithuanian, and the country's flag consists of three equal horizontal bands—yellow on the top, green in the middle, and red on the bottom.

HISTORY

The Lithuanians are ethnically part of the Baltic group of Indo-European peoples, most closely related to the Prussians (a people with Polish and German roots who populated a former northern European state) and the Latvians. The Lithuanians settled along the Neman River perhaps as early as 1500 B.C., founding small agricultural settlements in the area's thick forests. The eastward expansion of medieval German Christianity—under the guise of the crusading religious-military Teutonic Order—brought a number of important changes to the Lithuanians. This outside pressure forced the Lithuanians to unite and sparked Lithuanian expansion south and eastward, into the Belarus and Kievan territories.

Lithuania soon became one of the largest kingdoms in medieval Europe and remained pagan despite attempts by the Catholics and the Orthodox church to Christianize it. The region forged a close alliance with Poland, and the two crowns united in 1386. Lithuania accepted Roman Catholicism at that time, and the combined forces began to push back German incursions, most notably at the battle of Tannenberg-Grünberg in 1410. By 1569 the union of Lithuania and Poland was complete, and the Polish language and culture began to dominate the Lithuanian upper classes, although the peasantry remained culturally and linguistically Lithuanian.

The rise of Russia, combined with the weakness of the Polish-Lithuanian state, led to increasing Russian domination of Lithuania in the eighteenth century. This movement was completed in 1795, when the Russians executed their third division of Poland, effectively ending Polish sovereignty. Some of the northern regions of the division's Lithuanian-speaking territory came under German control as a part of East Prussia. Russia attempted a program of so-called "Russification" of the Baltic states throughout the next century, including the prohibition of Lithuanian language and literature, the imposition of Russian legal codes, and the forcible integration of Uniate (or Byzantine Rite) Catholicism into the Orthodox church. Lithuanian consciousness was maintained in ethnic regional cultures and through a variety of linguistic groupings, but not with a particular sense of national feeling. Beginning in the 1880s, however, a rising nationalistic movement emerged, challenging both Polish cultural domination and Russian governmental controls. With the Revolution of 1905 and the organization of the *Lietuvių Socialistaų Partija Amerikoje* (Lithuanian Socialist Party of America), a Lithuanian assembly convened and demanded a greater degree of territorial and cultural autonomy.

Russian rule of Lithuania came to an end with the German invasion and occupation of the territory during World War I, and 1918 marked the proclamation of the Lithuanian Republic. Achieving actual independence proved more complicated, with opposing forces of Germany, Poland, and the Soviet Union involved, but within two years the region was exercising self-rule.

The dawn of World War II brought political upheaval to Lithuania. In 1940 the Soviet Union took over control of the country—only to lose it to the Germans from 1941 to 1944. Soviet forces then retook Lithuania, though many thousands of Lithuanian refugees fled westward along with the retreating German army. Soviet authorities ordered the deportation of many Lithuanian people from their homeland and from eastern Europe in general between 1945 and 1949, at which time they also collectivized Lithuanian agriculture. During the late 1980s, growing Lithuanian nationalism forced the communists to grant concessions, and, after two years of contention with Soviet authorities, Lithuania finally declared its independence in 1991.

SIGNIFICANT IMMIGRATION WAVES

A number of Lithuanians immigrated to the New World before the American Revolution. The first may have been a Lithuanian physician, Dr. Aleksandras Kursius, who is believed to have lived in New York as early as 1660. Most of the other Lithuanians who ventured to the Americas during this period were members of the noble class or practitioners of particular trades. The first really significant wave of Lithuanian immigration to the United States began in the late 1860s, after the Civil War. During the late nineteenth and early twentieth centuries, an estimated 300,000 Lithuanians journeyed to America—a flow that was later halted by the combined effects of World War I, the restriction of immigration into the United States, and the achievement in 1918 of Lithuanian independence. This number is hard to document fully because census records did not officially recognize Lithuanians as a separate nationality until the twentieth century, and the country's people may have been reported as Russian, Polish, or Jewish.

Several key factors brought about the first surge of Lithuanian immigration to the United States. These included the abolition of serfdom in 1861, which resulted in a rise in Lithuania's free population; the growth of transportation, espe-

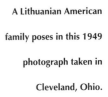
A Lithuanian American family poses in this 1949 photograph taken in Cleveland, Ohio.

cially railroads; and a famine that broke out in the country in the 1860s. Later, other conditions, such as a depressed farm economy and increased Russian repression, prompted even more Lithuanians to leave their home soil. In 1930 the U.S. Census Bureau listed 193,600 Lithuanians in the United States. This figure represents six percent of the total population of Lithuania at the time.

The initial wave of immigrants to the United States can also be viewed as part of a larger movement of the Lithuanian peasantry off the land, in search of a better life. Lithuanian peasants moved into Russia and western Europe as agricultural and industrial workers, often intending to return to their native country when they had earned enough money. Their pattern was cyclical, with the numbers of migrating workers shifting along with the seasons and economic cycles. This wave of intra-European immigration consisted mostly of young males, either single or having left their families behind; approximately 48 percent of them were illiterate.

The second wave of immigration had a greater impact on U.S. census figures. Following World War II, a flood of displaced refugees fled west to escape the Russian reoccupation of Lithuania. Eventually 30,000 *Dipukai* (war refugees or displaced persons) settled in the United States, primarily in cities in the East and the Midwest. These immigrants included many trained and educated leaders and professionals who hoped to return someday to Lithuania. The heightening of tensions between the United States and the Soviet Union—known as the Cold War—dampened these expectations, and many Lithuanians sought to create a semipermanent life in the United States. By 1990 the U.S. Bureau of the Census listed 811,865 Americans claiming "Lithuanian" as a first or second ancestry.

SETTLEMENT PATTERNS

The main areas of Lithuanian settlement in the United States included industrial towns of the Northeast, the larger cities of the Northeast and the Midwest, and the coal fields of Pennsylvania and southern Illinois. According to the 1930 census report, only about 13 percent of Lithuanians lived in rural areas, and even fewer—about two percent—were involved in agriculture.

Many of the first immigrants were very mobile, searching for work all over the United States and returning to Lithuania from time to time. Slowly, however, settlement patterns became apparent, and stable Lithuanian American communities were established in the smaller industrial towns in Massachusetts, Connecticut, New Jersey, and Pennsylvania. But by 1930 almost 50 percent of all Lithuanian Americans lived in just ten metropolitan areas. The large cities of Chicago, Cleveland, Detroit, Pittsburgh, New York, and Boston saw the greatest rise in

Lithuanian American population. Nearly 20 percent of all Lithuanian immigrants settled in Chicago alone.

When the World War II refugees started entering the United States after 1945, they set up their own communities in many of the same areas as the previous immigrants. The 1990 census lists the leading areas of Lithuanian American settlement as Illinois (109,400), Pennsylvania (103,200), New York (70,300), Massachusetts (68,400), California (63,800), and New Jersey (49,800).

"It was kind of bad for awhile till we got to know people and speak the language and quit being called greenhorns. People say, you ought to preserve your own heritage or something, but all we could think of was, we didn't want to be different, we wanted to be like the rest of the Americans."

Walter Wallace in 1923, cited in *Ellis Island: An Illustrated History of the Immigrant Experience,* edited by Ivan Chermayeff et al. (New York: Macmillan, 1991).

RELATIONS WITH SETTLED AMERICANS

Lithuanian immigrants were seen by settled Anglo-Americans as part of the "immigration problem" of the late nineteenth century: the poverty and illiteracy of many of the new arrivals, their Eastern European language and culture, and their devotion to Roman Catholicism put them at a distinct disadvantage in a country where scores of immigrant groups were competing for jobs, housing, and a better life—the so-called "American Dream." Because Lithuanians often took low-paying, unskilled laboring positions, they were not considered as "desirable" as other immigrants. In addition, their involvement in the U.S. labor movement at the turn of the twentieth century led to even more discrimination and resentment from a frightened and suspicious American public. (Lithuanians played an important role in the growth of the United Mine Workers Union and the United Garment Workers Union and were involved in labor unrest in the meat packing and steel industries.)

Throughout the twentieth century, however, Lithuanian Americans began to climb up the economic ladder and gain an important place in their local communities. This mobility allowed them to enter the American mainstream. Members of the

post-1945 immigration surge—with their fierce opposition to Russian communism and their middle-class professionalism—have adjusted smoothly and rapidly to the American way of life.

ACCULTURATION AND ASSIMILATION

In 1930 only about 47 percent of Lithuanian immigrants had become American citizens, despite the formation of Lithuanian citizens clubs to promote naturalization. But with their rise toward economic and social success in the twentieth century, Lithuanian Americans began to adapt more easily to life in the States. The American-born second generation, which by 1930 made up the majority of the immigrant community, assimilated much more quickly than their predecessors.

But along with assimilation came the development of an extensive network of immigrant institutions that sought to preserve and advance the immigrant community's native traditions. Foremost among these institutions were the Lithuanian parishes of the Roman Catholic church, which were joined together by various religious orders and lay and clerical organizations. Each immigrant community also boasted numerous immigrant social and fraternal organizations, newspapers, and workers' societies, all of which helped to buttress an immigrant identity.

Two important developments in Lithuania led to the growth of a strong Lithuanian American ethnic identity: the late nineteenth-century rise of Lithuanian national consciousness and the achievement of Lithuanian independence in 1920. Lithuanian Americans were staunch supporters of their newly independent homeland during the 1920s and 1930s, and some even returned to assist in the restructuring of the country's economy and government.

The post-World War II wave of Lithuanian immigrants—the *Dipukai*—also experienced a surge of Lithuanian consciousness. These later immigrants saw themselves as an exiled community and clung to their memory of two decades of freedom in Lithuania. They developed an extensive network of schools, churches, and cultural institutions for the maintenance of Lithuanian identity in the United States. But among the second and third generations of this community, assimilation and acculturation have taken deep hold; ethnic identity, while still important, is no longer central to the community's existence. Given the mass of those American citizens who claim at least partial Lithuanian heritage, most observers feel that this ethnic identity will not be completely forgotten, but many of the institutions that maintained the earlier generations of immigrants have declined in numbers and vitality.

CUISINE

Lithuanian cuisine is influenced by the foods of the land itself and by the various cuisines of its neighbors. More than the other Baltic nations, Lithuanian cooking looks to the east and the south, having much in common with the cooking of Russia, Belarus, and the Ukraine; this is not surprising, as these were the directions taken by the expansion of the medieval kingdom of Lithuania. Lithuanian recipes rely heavily on pork, potatoes, and dairy products such as eggs, milk, cream, and butter. (One specialty is a white cottage-type cheese called *suris*.) Dark, flavorful mushrooms, herring, eels, sausages, and dark rye breads are also central to the Lithuanian diet. Holiday foods included jellied pigs feet, goose stuffed with prunes, and roasted suckling pig.

TRADITIONAL DRESS

The colorful regional dress of Lithuania was used at times of festivals, market days, and special events in the old country. Some immigrants may have brought these costumes with them when they immigrated, but the wearing of such dress was not common in the United States, except for ethnic festivals. The daily working clothes of the immigrants never really differed from that of other Americans holding the same positions.

HOLIDAYS CELEBRATED BY LITHUANIAN AMERICANS

Along with the traditional Catholic and American holidays, there are several festival days of special significance to the Lithuanian American community. February 16 is Lithuanian Independence Day, marking the formal declaration of independence in 1918. September 8 is known as Lithuanian Kingdom Day. Roman Catholics celebrate the Feast of St. Casimir on March 4, with special celebrations led by the Knights of Lithuania fraternal organization.

HEALTH AND MENTAL HEALTH ISSUES

With the formation of a solid Lithuanian American community at the end of the nineteenth century, the need for health care among immigrants became a key issue. Immigrant fraternal and benefit societies sought to provide help for sick or injured Lithuanians, as did social and charitable organizations. Roman Catholics organized Holy Cross Hospital in Chicago, as well as homes for the aged and infirm. Many of these activities came under the control of Lithuanian Roman Catholic orders, especially the Sisters of St. Casimir. Few Lithuanian medical professionals set up practice in the United States until after 1945, when a postwar influx of Lithuanian doctors from the European refugee community took place.

LANGUAGE

The Lithuanian language—a part of the Baltic branch of the Indo-European language family—is closely related to Latvian and the now-extinct language known as Old Prussian. Wider relationships, whether to German or the Slavic languages, are difficult to establish. Spoken Lithuanian is a very ancient language; it maintains many early features of speech and grammar that other Indo-European languages have lost. Although written Lithuanian came into existence in the sixteenth century, strong Polish cultural influences and Russian Imperial domination effectively suppressed the development of Lithuanian as a written, literary language—at least until the rise of Lithuanian nationalism in the late nineteenth century.

Lithuanian is divided into Low and High dialects, with numerous subdialects. The language uses 11 vowels ("a," "ą," "e," "ę," "ė," "i," "į," "y," "o," "u," "ų," "ū") along with six diphthongs ("ai," "au," "ei," "ui," ie," and "uo"). In addition to most of the standard consonants of the English language, Lithuanian makes use of "č," "š, and "ž," however, the consonants "f" and "h" and the combination "ch" are used only in foreign words.

The preservation of the Lithuanian language was a key concern among the initial wave of immigrants to the United States. The cultural domination of the Poles led to considerable dissension among the members of the Lithuanian American community. Especially in the Roman Catholic church, Polish prevailed as the official language used in worship and religious education, a practice that came under bitter attack from

Lithuanian Americans. Religious organizations and their priests were divided along this issue; eventually, however, the Polophile party lost, and modern Lithuanian became the language of the community. The later immigrants who came after World War II have worked to keep the Lithuanian language alive within the community by developing a network of schools to encourage the preservation of the language. There are still quite a few Lithuanian American publications issued at least partially in Lithuanian, including some local Lithuanian daily newspapers. Several universities and colleges offer Lithuanian language courses, including Yale University, University of Illinois-Chicago, Indiana University-Bloomington, Tulane University, Cornell University, and Ohio State University. There are also dozens of public libraries with Lithuanian language collections, including the Los Angeles Public Library, Chicago Public Library, Donnell Library Center at the New York Public Library, Ennoch Pratt Free Library, and the Detroit Public Library.

GREETINGS AND OTHER POPULAR EXPRESSIONS

Common Lithuanian greetings and other expressions include: *labą rytą* ("lahba reehta")—good morning; *labą vakara* ("lahba vahkahra")—good evening; *labanaktis* ("lahba-nahktees")—good night; *sudievu* ("sood-yeeh-voo")—goodbye; *kaip tamsta gyvuoji* ("kaip tahmstah geeh-vu-oyee")—how are you; *labai gerai* ("lahbai gar-ai")—quite well; *dėkui* ("deh-kooy")—thanks; *atsiprašau* ("aht-see-prah-show")—excuse me; *sveikas* ("say-kahs")—welcome; *taip* ("taip")—yes; *ne* ("nah")—no; *turiu eiti* ("toor-i-oo ay-tee")—I must go.

FAMILY AND COMMUNITY DYNAMICS

During the first wave of Lithuanian immigration to the United States, a stable immigrant community developed rather slowly. Since many of the first immigrants were young males seeking temporary employment, an immigrant community identity was hard to establish. Long hours, grinding poverty, and isolation increased the pressures that fragmented the immigrants. Slowly, as the immigrants began to settle permanently in the United States, family, religious, and community institutions were formed. A growing sense of national-ism within the community allowed the Lithuanians to see themselves as a people separate from the Poles and the Russians.

The immigrant community of the early twentieth century was beginning to mature, with second and third generations rapidly becoming Americanized. The arrival of Lithuanian refugees after World War II brought a fresh wave of immigrants and an intensified sense of Lithuanian nationalism. The size and strength of the Lithuanian American community has allowed its people to maintain a certain sense of ethnic heritage, even as the immigrant population evolves and its succeeding generations become thoroughly Americanized.

INTERACTION WITH OTHER ETHNIC GROUPS

In the late eighteenth and early nineteenth centuries, the Lithuanian American community was closely tied to the Polish community. Since the borders of these nations were fluid—and since a long history of Polish religious and cultural dominance existed in Lithuania—Polish American and Lithuanian American immigrants tended to settle in many of the same areas of the United States. The early struggle for Lithuanians in America involved a move away from the Polish community and toward the definition of a pure Lithuanian national and ethnic identity. In later years a significant relationship developed between Lithuanian Americans and the other Baltic immigrants, Estonians and Latvians. These groups banded together in the interest of freeing the Baltic Republics from Soviet rule: their solidarity is especially evident in the creation of groups such as the Joint Baltic-American National Committee (1961) and other joint organizations.

EDUCATION

Like many other immigrant groups, Lithuanians have seen that the road to success in America lies with education. Many of the immigrants, especially before 1920, arrived in the States as illiterate peasants. Despite their limited resources, the community soon established a system of parochial schools among the Lithuanian Roman Catholic parishes in the United States, many of which were run by the Sisters of St. Casimir. A smaller network of Lithuanian American Roman Catholic high schools and academies appeared later, numbering approximately ten by 1940.

Responding to a plea from the immigrant community, the Marian Fathers opened a high school and college in Hinsdale, Illinois, in 1926. Later the college was relocated to Thompson, Connecticut, and renamed Marianapolis College. Another early center of Lithuanian education was Indiana's Valparaiso University. Though not an ethnic institution, this university attracted a number of Lithuanian students early in the twentieth century; between 1902 and 1915 the school graduated 29 Lithuanian doctors, 15 lawyers, and 14 engineers. Lithuanian refugees of World War II—many of whom were highly educated, skilled professionals—exhibited an intense interest in education. Their main educational contribution to the community was the formation of a series of Lithuanian schools to transmit Lithuanian language and culture to succeeding generations of Lithuanian Americans.

WOMEN'S ROLES

Coming from an extremely traditional agricultural society, the first wave of Lithuanian immigrants brought with them a very rigid set of beliefs about women's roles in the community. Male domination of the family was a given, and women's roles were strictly defined. This social system was very hard for the immigrants to maintain in the United States, especially in the urban areas where the majority of the immigrants settled. As the immigrants became assimilated into the mainstream of American life, women's roles began to change and grow, though not without stress and conflict. One new independent role for women came through the formation of Lithuanian American religious orders, which afforded Lithuanian women a leading role in the immigrant religious community, and beyond: they headed parochial schools and established institutions of mercy, such as hospitals, orphanages, and nursing homes. Later, lay women's organizations—such as the American Lithuanian Roman Catholic Women's Alliance (founded in 1914) and the Federation of Lithuanian Women's Clubs (founded in 1947)—began to spring up in Lithuanian American communities, further empowering the female population.

RELIGION

The large majority of Lithuanian immigrants to America were Roman Catholics; there were also small numbers of Lutherans, Jews, and Orthodox Christians. The dominance of Roman Catholicism in the Lithuanian American community is even more pronounced because of the influence of Catholicism in the formation of the institutions of Lithuanian identity. However, the Roman Catholic presence was neither monolithic nor universal, and significant tensions existed within the Catholic community.

Lithuania adopted Roman Catholicism along the lines of its western neighbor, Poland, and for many centuries Lithuanian Catholicism was Polish in language and orientation. Lithuanian was considered to be a barbarous language, unworthy of religious use, so Polish was used for all official religious business. This dominance in religious matters extended to the immigrant communities of America as well; early Lithuanian immigrants tended to merge into Polish-language Roman Catholic parishes, and Polish-leaning priests dominated many of the early institutions of the Lithuanian American community.

But the rising tide of Lithuanian nationalism and ethnic identity toward the end of the nineteenth century sparked profound changes in the Lithuanian American religious community. Under the leadership of Aleksandras Burba, a priest from Lithuania, some Lithuanian Americans began to pull away from Polish parishes and Polish-dominated institutions and establish their own Lithuanian parishes. More than 100 Lithuanian parishes were formed by 1920. This movement created considerable tension within the immigrant community but also helped heighten and define a sense of ethnic consciousness among Lithuanian Americans. Not all Lithuanians wanted to distance themselves from Polish Roman Catholicism though, and divisiveness soon clouded the ranks of many Lithuanian American institutions and organizations.

The development of Lithuanian Roman Catholicism took hold early in the twentieth century, cementing a Lithuanian ethnic consciousness in America. Many of these efforts were led by an immigrant priest, Father Antanas Staniukynas, who formed the Lithuanian American Roman Catholic Priest's League in 1909. Staniukynas also contributed to the establishment of religious orders in the immigrant community, including the Sisters of St. Casimir and an American branch of the Lithuanian Marian Fathers. Around the same time, many lay Roman Catholic organizations were also founded; fraternal and social organizations were formed for men, women, workers, students, and other lay groups. But probably the most lasting and impressive achievement was the formation of a large parochial school system in affiliation with the Lithuanian American Roman Catholic parishes, a system run largely by the immigrant religious orders.

Religious life in the United States was not without conflict for the Lithuanian Roman Catholics. The old style of autocratic priestly leadership soon gave way to the realities of a democratic and pluralistic America, and the laity demanded an increased role in parish government. After 1945 the influx of war refugees brought new members to Lithuanian American Roman Catholicism; new religious orders, such as the Sisters of the Immaculate Conception and the Lithuanian Franciscan and Jesuit priestly orders were also established.

In 1914 the Lithuanian National Catholic Church was formed in Scranton, Pennsylvania. This movement, which broke away from the Roman Catholic hierarchy in the United States, stressed the national dimension of Lithuanian Catholicism. Lithuanian National Catholic parishes flourished in areas of heavy Lithuanian settlement early in the twentieth century.

Lithuanian Lutherans hailed mainly from the northern and western areas of Lithuania, areas that had been influenced by German and Latvian Lutheranism. The Lutheran reformation—a sixteenth-century Protestant reform movement—took hold in Lithuania until it was largely eliminated by the counter-reformation, yet over the centuries a small Lutheran minority remained. When these immigrants came to America during the initial surge of Lithuanian immigration, they tended to develop separate Lutheran congregations apart from the mainstream Lithuanian American community. The German-speaking Lutheran Missouri Synod sponsored several pastors who sought to reach out to this community. After 1945 a second wave of Lithuanian Lutherans formed the Lithuanian Evangelical Lutheran Church in Exile, headquartered near Chicago. This church has 19 congregations and 10,000 members worldwide.

Although a sizable Jewish community was established in Lithuania prior to World War II, it was forced to coexist with the Christian ethic of the country's wider Roman Catholic world. Many members of the Lithuanian Jewish community immigrated to America during the latter part of the nineteenth century and formed their own communities in the United States, mainly in the cities of the Northeast and the Midwest. One estimate from about 1940 puts the number of Lithuanian American Jews at around 25,000. During the assimilation process, these communities became affiliated with the larger Jewish communities throughout the United States. At the same time back in Europe, the Nazi-engineered Holocaust of World War II had a devastating effect on the Lithuanian Jewish community, leaving it almost completely destroyed by war's end.

EMPLOYMENT AND ECONOMIC TRADITIONS

The first wave of Lithuanian immigration, which ended around 1920, included mostly unskilled and often illiterate immigrants who settled in the cities and coal fields of the East and the Midwest and provided the raw muscle power of urban American factories; they were especially drawn to the garment trade in the East, the steel mills and forges of the Midwest, and the packing houses of Chicago and Omaha. Other immigrants opened businesses within their communities, supplying the growing needs of Lithuanian Americans.

To assist their people in the economic transition to life in the United States, the immigrants established many institutions, including fraternal and benefit societies and building and loan associations. The fraternal societies assisted needy immigrants and provided inexpensive insurance and death benefit protection. The building and loan associations met the immigrants' banking needs and helped them to purchase their own homes. By 1920 there were at least 30 such associations within the Lithuanian immigrant community.

The war refugees who came to the United States after 1945 were a different class of immigrants, mainly educated and professional. Although they had been the leaders of an independent Lithuania from 1918 to 1940, many of these new immigrants had difficulty finding suitable employment in the United States. The language barrier and professional differences meant that many of them had to take positions that were beneath their level of training and education. These refugees were an enterprising group, however, and they began a tradition of economic success in the United States.

POLITICS AND GOVERNMENT

Much of the initial political activity of the Lithuanian Americans was confined to the immigrant community itself, as immigrants sought to define themselves, especially in terms of the rising tide of Lithuanian nationalism that dominated the latter part of the nineteenth century. But slowly the immigrant community began to look outside itself toward the wider American world. The first examples of immigrant political activity came in areas that directly affected the new immigrants—namely labor issues and the condition of American relations with the new Lithuanian state. Lithuanians were active in the formation of some of the American labor unions, especially in coal mining and the garment trade. For some, this activity grew into a wider push for socialism (a political and economic doctrine espousing collective rather than private ownership of property), especially with the formation of the Lithuanian Socialist Party of America in 1905. This prewar socialism collapsed, though, after 1918, as the so-called "Red Scare" put great pressure on all socialist groups. The first major political push among Lithuanian Americans came after 1918, when they tried to influence American foreign policy to recognize and support Lithuanian independence.

Since the Lithuanian immigrant community was mostly urban and working class, many Lithuanians aligned themselves with the Democratic party during the twentieth century. Although they were not a real force in national politics, Lithuanian Americans used their numbers to dominate local politics, electing local officials, state legislators, judges, and occasionally members of the U.S. House of Representatives. In turn they became loyal supporters of the local Democratic political machines in areas such as Chicago, Cleveland, and Detroit. In many communities Lithuanians formed their own Democratic clubs for the support of political and ethnic priorities. A smaller number of Lithuanians were attracted to the Republican party, especially after 1945. Along with some members of the other Baltic groups, these Lithuanians blamed the Democrats for the "betrayal" of Lithuanian independence in the Yalta agreement of 1945, which extended Soviet territories to the West. Post-World War II immigrants, because of their strongly anticommunist feelings, favored mostly the Republicans.

UNION ACTIVITY

Lithuanian immigrants were involved in a number of industries that saw a great deal of union activity at the end of the nineteenth century. The Lithuanian coal miners of Pennsylvania and Illinois became members of the United Mine Workers unions, and local unions of Lithuanian garment workers soon merged with either the Amalgamated Clothing Workers Union or the United Garment Workers Union. In other industries, such as steel or meat packing, union organization was slower, but Lithuanian workers were an omnipresent force in labor agitation. A number of nationalist, Roman Catholic, and socialist immigrant organizations were developed to provide support to laborers. Socialist and radical workers groups, such as the Industrial Workers of the World (IWW), succeeded in recruiting Lithuanian workers in the first part of the twentieth century, but these groups declined rapidly after 1920. The Lithuanian community was generally sympathetic to the union cause and supported their fellow immigrants during labor unrest.

MILITARY

Lithuanians have served in the American armed forces in every war since the Civil War; in that war 373 Lithuanians fought on the Union side, and 44 fought on the side of the Confederacy. Lithuanian Americans were especially interested in both World Wars, since they directly influenced the fate of Lithuanian independence. In 1918 a group of 200 Lithuanian Americans who had served in the American military went to Lithuania to help in the fight for freedom.

RELATIONS WITH LITHUANIA

Relations with Lithuania have always been important to the Lithuanian American community. Tensions ran especially high among Lithuanians in the United States during those periods when the Russian state had control over Lithuania. Immigrant communities in America were fertile ground for nationalistic sentiment, and during the last decades of the nineteenth century many radical Lithuanian nationalists sought refuge in the United States from political oppression in Russia. Most Lithuanian Americans supported the nationalist cause, although a small group of radical communists backed Soviet attempts to forcibly annex Lithuania to the Soviet Union.

Lithuanian Americans protest Soviet policies concerning the Baltic States in this 1990 photograph.

When Lithuania was declared a republic in 1918, the immigrant community supported independence with financial, military, and political help. A number of the leaders of independent Lithuania had even lived and studied for a time in the United States. Lithuanian Americans pressured the American government to recognize Lithuanian independence and support Lithuanian border claims in the dispute with Poland. This support of the homeland helped strengthen Lithuanian American group solidarity in the United States during the 1920s and 1930s.

With the Soviet invasion of Lithuania in 1940, the Lithuanian American community had new cause for common action. War refugees from Lithuania flooded the United States after 1945, and many new groups and organizations were formed to rally for an independent Lithuania— and to support this cause with money and publicity. Lithuanian Americans worked to keep the dream of an independent Lithuania alive with publicity, lobbying efforts, and various political and cultural activities. These actions moved Lithuanian Americans into the wider sphere of the Lithuanian exile community worldwide, uniting American organizations with others in Europe and elsewhere. Agitation efforts also brought Lithuanian Americans into closer contact with other Baltic Americans, with whom they shared the dream of independence for the Baltic states.

INDIVIDUAL AND GROUP CONTRIBUTIONS

BUSINESS AND INDUSTRY

Lane Bryant (1879-1951), born Lena Himmelstein, arrived in New York in 1895 and began working in the garment industry. With the help of her second husband, Lithuanian-born Albert Maislin (1879-1923), Bryant expanded her business, introducing the first maternity wear and later manufacturing larger-sized women's clothing. The family of Nicholas Pritzker, a Lithuanian immigrant born in 1871, started numerous businesses that now comprise the Hyatt Corporation.

FILM

Actor Laurence Harvey (1928-1973) was born Laurynas Skinkis in Lithuania. He had an active career in England and the United States, appearing in such films as *Room at the Top*, *Butterfield 8*, and *The Manchurian Candidate*. Charles Bronson (1920-), born Casimir Businskis, is a popular movie actor known for his action roles in such movies as *The Great Escape, Once Upon a Time in the West, Death Wish,* and *Hard Times.* Actress Ruta Lee, born Ruta Kilmonis, appeared in the 1950s and 1960s motion pictures *Witness for the Prosecution, Marjorie Morningstar,* and *Operation Eichmann.*

GOVERNMENT

Alexander Bruce Bialaski, an American of Lithuanian descent, was the first director of the Federal Bureau of Investigation (FBI), serving in that capacity from 1912 to 1919. Sydney Hillman (1887-1946), a Lithuanian Jewish immigrant, was the leader of the Amalgamated Clothing Workers Union for over 30 years. He moved into the national political arena in 1941, when he became director of the U.S. Office of Production Management.

PHOTOGRAPHY

Lithuanian photographer and journalist Vitas Valaitis (1931-1965) worked for several major publications, including *Newsweek, Saturday Evening Post,* and *U.S. News and World Report,* and won numerous prizes for his work.

SOCIAL ISSUES

Father Jonas Zilinskas (1870-1932) was instrumental in developing the Lithuanian Alliance of America and served as its president. Emma Goldman (1869-1940) was a radical anarchist and supporter of communism. She immigrated to America in 1886 and quickly became a leader in radical movements in the United States. Her bold lectures promoting atheism, revolution, birth control, and "free love" often led to trouble with the authorities. Goldman was imprisoned in 1917 and deported to Russia in 1919. An early supporter of Soviet ideals, she eventually grew disenchanted with the course of the revolution. When she died in 1940 her body was returned to the United States for burial.

SPORTS

Johnny Unitas (1933-) was one of the greatest quarterbacks in the National Football League (NFL). As a star player for the Baltimore Colts in the 1960s, he set a number of professional records and was repeatedly named to the all-star team. Dick Butkas (1942-), a key player for the Chicago Bears during the 1960s and 1970s, is widely regarded as the best middle-linebacker ever to play professional football. Johnny Podres (1932-) pitched for the Brooklyn Dodgers and other professional baseball teams. Jack Sharkey (born Juozas Žukauskas; 1902-) was a World Heavyweight champion boxer whose career peaked in the 1920s and 1930s. Billie Burke, born Vincas Burkauskas, made her mark as a professional golfer on the women's circuit. Vitas Gerulaitis (1954-1994) was a top-ranked tennis professional whose career flourished in the 1970s and 1980s.

THEATER

Elizabeth Swados (1951-) is an award-winning composer, writer, and director whose works include the Broadway musicals *Doonesbury* and *The Beautiful Lady*. She has also written music for many classical dramatic productions and television specials.

VISUAL ARTS

Victor D. Brenner (1871-1924; surname originally Baranauskas) designed the Lincoln penny in 1909. Many of the first Lincoln pennies, now collector's items, bear his initials, "VDB."

PRINT

Bridges.

A Lithuanian American news journal.

Contact: Rimantas Stirbys, Editor.

Address: 2715 East Allegheny Avenue, Philadelphia, Pennsylvania 19134.

Telephone: (215) 739-9353.

Fax: (215) 739-6587.

Dirva (The Field).

Lithuanian-language newspaper that contains items of interest to the Lithuanian community.

Contact: Vytautas Gedgaudas, Editor.

Address: Viltis, Inc., 19807 Cherokee Avenue, Cleveland, Ohio 44119-1090.

Telephone: (216) 531-8150.

Fax: (216) 531-8428.

Draugas (The Friend).

Newspaper published by the Lithuanian Catholic Press Society.

Contact: Rev. Francis Garsva, Editor.

Address: 4545 West 63rd Street, Chicago, Illinois 60629.

Telephone: (312) 585-9500.

Fax: (312) 585-8284.

Garsas (The Echo).

Published by the Lithuanian Alliance of America, this monthly bilingual publication contains general news for and about the Lithuanian American community.

Contact: Florence Eckert, Editor.

Address: 71-73 South Washington Street, Wilkes Barre, Pennsylvania 18701.

Telephone: (717) 823-8876.

I Laisve (Toward Freedom).

Lithuanian-language magazine of politics that contains articles of interest to the Lithuanian community.

Contact: Vacys Rociunas, Editor.

Address: Friends of the Lithuanian Front, 1634 49th Avenue, Cicero, Illinois 60650.

Journal of Baltic Studies.

Published by the Association for the Advancement of Baltic Studies, this quarterly provides a forum for scholarly discussion of topics regarding the Baltic Republics and their peoples.

Contact: William Urban and Roger Noel, Editors.

Address: Executive Offices of the ARABS, 111 Knob Hill Road, Hacketstown, NJ 07840.

Lietuviu Dienos (Lithuanian Days).

A general interest, bilingual monthly publication that covers Lithuania and the Lithuanian American community.

Contact: Ruta Skurius, Editor.

Address: 4364 Sunset Boulevard, Hollywood, California 90029.

Telephone: (213) 664-2919.

Lituanus: Lithuanian Quarterly Journal of Arts and Sciences.

Established in 1954, this quarterly publication features scholarly articles about Lithuania and Lithuanians around the world. Published by the Lituanus Foundation, Inc.

Address: P.O. Box 9318, Chicago, Illinois 60690.

Metmenys.

Lithuanian-language scholarly publication.

Contact: Vytautas Kavolis, Editor.

Address: A M & M Publications, 7338 South Sacramento, Chicago, Illinois 60629.

Telephone: (312) 436-5369.

Nepriklausoma Lietuva.

Weekly Lithuanian newspaper.

Contact: B. Nagys, Editor.

Address: Lithuanian Publishing Co., 7722 George Street, La Salle, Quebec, Canada H8P 1C4.

Telephone: (514) 366-6220.

Sandara (The League).

Monthly fraternal magazine published by the Lithuanian National League of America in English and Lithuanian; first published in 1914.

Contact: G. J. Lazauskas, Editor.

Address: P.O. Box 241, Addison, Illinois 60101.

Telephone: (708) 543-8198.

Fax: (312) 735-8793.

Tevyne.

Weekly Lithuanian interest newspaper published by the Lithuanian Alliance of America.

Address: 307 West 30th Street, New York, New York 10001.

Telephone: (212) 563-2210.

World Lithuanian.

Established in 1953 by the Lithuanian World Community, Inc., this is a monthly publication that seeks to unite Lithuanians around the world for ethnic solidarity.

Address: 6804 Maplewood Avenue, Chicago, Illinois 60629.

Telephone: (312) 776-4028.

RADIO

KGUS-FM.

One hour of Lithuanian programming weekly.

Address: Box 1089, 208$\frac{1}{2}$ Broadway, Hot Springs, Arkansas 71901.

Telephone: (501) 624-5425.

KTYM.

One-half hour of Lithuanian programming weekly.

Address: 6803 West Boulevard, Inglewood, California 90302.

Telephone: (213) 678-3731.

WCEV.

Seven hours of Lithuanian programming weekly.

Address: 5356 West Belmont Avenue, Cicero, Illinois 60641.

Telephone: (312) 282-6700.

WPIT.

One hour of Lithuanian programming weekly.

Address: 200 Gateway Towers, Pittsburgh, Pennsylvania 15222.

Telephone: (412) 281-1900.

WRYM.

One hour of Lithuanian programming weekly.

Address: 1056 Willard Street, Newington, Connecticut 06111.

Telephone: (203) 666-5646.

ORGANIZATIONS AND ASSOCIATIONS

Institute of Lithuanian Studies (ILS).

Seeks to sponsor and encourage research on Lithuanian language, literature, folklore, history, and other fields related to Lithuania and its culture.

Contact: Violeta Kelertas, President.
Address: University of Illinois at Chicago, Department of Slavic and Baltic Studies (m/c 306), 601 South Morgan, Chicago, Illinois 60607-7110.
Telephone: (312) 996-4412.

Lithuanian Alliance of America.

Founded in 1886, the LAA was one of the first social organizations established by Lithuanians in America. Though originally a fraternal benefit association, the alliance quickly became the center of organized Lithuanian life in the United States, especially in the early part of the twentieth century.

Contact: Algirdas Budreckis, Executive Secretary.
Address: 307 West 30th Street, New York, New York 10001.
Telephone: (212) 524-5529.

Lithuanian American Community (LAC).

Founded in 1952, this organization focuses on educational and cultural activities, sponsoring regional cultural festivals, providing grants and scholarships to support academic and cultural activities, and calling for freedom in Lithuania.

Contact: Joseph Gaila, President.
Address: 2713 West 71st Street, Chicago, Illinois 60629.
Telephone: (312) 436-0197.

Lithuanian American Council (LAC).

Founded in 1940, the LAC functions as an umbrella organization to coordinate the work of Lithuanian American groups, clubs, and religious and fraternal organizations. Its primary purpose is to unite the Lithuanian American community and to advance Lithuanian independence.

Contact: Grozvydas Lazauskas, President.
Address: 6500 South Pulaski, Chicago, Illinois 60629.
Telephone: (312) 735-6677.

Lithuanian National Foundation (LNF).

Collects, researches, analyzes, and disseminates information on Lithuania and the Lithuanian nation.

Contact: J. Giedraitis, President.
Address: 351 Highland Road, Brooklyn, New York 11207.
Telephone: (718) 277-0682.

Lithuanian Roman Catholic Alliance of America (LRCAA).

Founded in 1886, the LRCAA is one of the original immigrant organizations in the immigrant community; it functions to strengthen Roman Catholicism within the Lithuanian American community.

Contact: Thomas E. Mack, President.
Address: 71-73 South Washington Street, Wilkes-Barre, Pennsylvania 18703.
Telephone: (717) 823-8876.

Lithuanian World Community (LWC).

Founded in 1949, LWC is the largest ethnic organization for the Lithuanian community in exile. It was formed by immigrants who fled Lithuania following the Soviet takeover during World War II. It seeks to unite the Lithuanian exile community around the world and helps maintain an extensive Lithuanian educational presence in the United States.

Contact: V. J. Bieliauskas, President.
Address: 14911 127th Street, Lemont, Illinois 60439.
Telephone: (708) 257-8457.

Lituanus Foundation (LF).

Organizes, sponsors, and publishes research material on the language, history, politics, geography, economics, folklore, literature, and arts of Lithuania and the Baltic States.

Contact: J. K. Kucenas, Business Manager/Treasurer.
Address: 6621 South Troy Street, Chicago, Illinois 60629-2913.
Telephone: (312) 434-0706.

National Lithuanian Society of America (NSLA).

Fosters Lithuanian fine arts, handicraft, cultural, and educational activities. Publishes bimonthly newsletter.

Contact: Dr. Leon K. Leonas, President.
Address: 13400 Parker Road, Lemont, Illinois 60439.
Telephone: (708) 301-8183.

MUSEUMS AND RESEARCH CENTERS

Balzekas Museum of Lithuanian Culture.

A museum and research library dedicated to the study of Lithuania and Lithuanian Americans. Displays feature Lithuanian art, collectibles, and memorabilia.

Contact: Stanley Balzekas, Jr., Director.

Address: 6500 South Pulaski Road, Chicago, Illinois 60629.

Telephone: (312) 582-6500.

Immigration History Research Center.

Located at the University of Minnesota, it is a valuable library and archival resource on eastern and southern Europeans, including Lithuanians. In addition to serials and newspapers, the center has a large holding of books and monographs on the immigrant community, along with archival resources and manuscripts.

Contact: Dr. Rudolph Vecoli, Director.

Address: 826 Berry Street, St. Paul, Minnesota 55114.

Telephone: (612) 627-4208.

Lithuanian American Cultural Archives.

Run by the Lithuanian Marian Fathers, it focuses on Lithuanians in America. It has an extensive collection of early materials on the immigrant community, especially on Lithuanians in the Northeast and Middle Atlantic states.

Address: Thurber Road, Putnam, Connecticut 06260.

Telephone: (203) 928-9317.

Lithuanian Museum.

Founded to promote and further an understanding of the Lithuanian American immigrant experience, it sponsors both permanent and traveling exhibits and also houses a library. The Lithuanian Museum is affiliated with the World Lithuanian Archives, a major repository of materials by and about the Lithuanian American community, gathered by the Lithuanian Jesuit Fathers Provincial House in Chicago.

Contact: Nijole Mackevincius, Director.

Address: 5620 South Claremont Avenue, Chicago, Illinois 60636.

Telephone: (312) 434-4545.

Van Pelt Library, University of Pennsylvania.

The library houses one of the largest collections of materials about Lithuania and Lithuanian Americans in the United States.

Address: 3420 Walnut Street, Philadelphia, Pennsylvania 19104.

Telephone: (215) 898-7088.

SOURCES FOR ADDITIONAL STUDY

Alilunas, Leo J. *Lithuanians in the United States: Selected Studies*. San Francisco: R&E Research Associates, 1978.

Budreckis, Algirdas. *The Lithuanians in America, 1651-1975: A Chronology and Factbook*. Dobbs Ferry, New York: Oceana Publications, Inc., 1975.

Encyclopedia Lithuanica, six volumes, edited by Simas Suziedelius. Boston: Juozas Kapocius, 1970-78.

Fainhauz, David. *Lithuanians in the U.S.A.: Aspects of Ethnic Identity*. Chicago: Lithuanian Library Press, Inc., 1991.

Kantautas, Adam. *A Lithuanian Bibliography*. Edmonton, Alberta, Canada: University of Alberta Press, 1975.

Kučas, Antanas. *Lithuanians in America*. San Francisco: R&E Research Associates, 1975.

Lithuanian Cooking. New York: Darbininkas, 1976.

Roucek, Joseph. "Lithuanian Americans," in *One America: The History, Contributions, and Present Problems of Our Racial and National Minorities*, revised edition, edited by Joseph Slabey Roucek and Francis Brown. New York: Prentice Hall, 1945; p. 186.

Wolkovich-Valkavičius, William. "Toward a Historiography of Lithuanian Immigrants to the United States," *Immigration History Newsletter*, Volume 15, No. 2 (November 1983); pp. 7-10.

MALTESE AMERICANS

by
Diane Andreassi

The greatest number of Maltese people came to the United States during the first decades of the twentieth century. Their move coincided with the discharge of skilled workers from the Royal British Dockyard in 1919 following the end of the World War I.

OVERVIEW

A European country often called "the mouse that roars," Malta is also referred to as "the island of sunshine and history." Malta covers 122 square miles in the center of the Mediterranean Sea and is comprised of three inhabited islands: Malta, Gozo, and Comino. Malta, 17 miles long and about nine miles across, is the largest of the three islands. Gozo, the northern island, is 35 square miles and is known for its grottoes, copper beaches, and the third-largest church dome in the world. Comino, at one square mile, has a small population and is located between Malta and Gozo. The uninhabited islands in the archipelago are Filfla and St. Paul's. The topography of Malta lacks mountains and rivers, but the island is characterized by a series of low hills with terraced fields.

The weather, more than any other feature, has made Malta a key tourist resort in the center of the Mediterranean. It never snows in Malta, and the total average rainfall is 20 inches annually. The summers are warm and breezy and the winters are mild, with an average winter temperature of 54 degrees. About 606,000 tourists from all over the world, including the United States and Europe, arrive annually. Tourists boost the economy significantly by spending approximately $3.6 million each year on the island. The Maltese weather and lifestyle also call for afternoon breaks, when shop owners close and the island people rest. Everything resumes again later in the day, when the sun is not as tiring. The climate, sea, and terrain also provide perfect backdrops for movies; for instance, the movie "Popeye" was filmed on the island in the 1980s.

Malta is located 58 miles south of Sicily and 180 miles north of North Africa. The total population is 350,000, which places it among the most densely populated countries in the world. Ninety-six percent of the population is of Maltese descent, two percent are British, and the remaining people are of various other heritages. The chief languages are Maltese, English, and Italian. Ninety-seven percent of the population is Roman Catholic. A high priority is placed on education, bringing the literacy rate to 96 percent. Education is mandatory for Maltese children from age 5 to 16, and by age four there is already almost 100 percent enrollment. Instruction is available in state as well as private schools, with the private sector catering to about 27 percent of the total population.

HISTORY

The first Maltese were late Stone Age farmers who immigrated to Malta from Sicily before 4000 B.C. Structures believed to be temples were the biggest reward of these early people, and their remains can be seen in the megalithic buildings. At least one underground temple catacomb has been associated with the cult of a Mother Goddess. By the year 2000 B.C. these early arrivers were replaced by bronze-using warrior-farmers of the Alpine race who likely arrived from southern Italy.

Phoenicians were to follow during the Iron Age period around 800 B.C., and they were succeeded by Carthaginians. Due to the Punic Wars, Malta became part of the Roman Empire, and inhabitants were well treated by the conquerors. During this time, the Maltese enjoyed peace and prosperity based on a well-developed agricultural economy. Aghlabite Arabs, by way of Sicily, invaded Malta in 870. Then came Count Roger, a Norman who conquered the Arabs in Sicily and brought Malta back into the Christian and European orbit. For four-and-a-half centuries, beginning in 1090, Malta's history was nearly identical to that of Sicily.

In 1530 Malta was granted as a fief to the Order of St. John of Jerusalem, who as the Knights of Malta defended Christianity against Islam and fortified the island. The Knights of Malta were responsible for building grand churches and palaces, especially in the city of Valletta, Malta's capital. The decline of the order hastened when Napoleon landed with his Republican Army in 1798; however, the insurrection of the Maltese that same year brought the end of the French rule. Malta was granted to Britain in 1814. The British built a first-class dockyard and concentrated her fleet on Malta's magnificent harbors.

Malta's strategic position in the Mediterranean Sea made the islands an important ally during World War II. This key location also made Malta a target for overwhelming bombing by Germany and Italy during the war. Surviving the unrelenting attacks, the Maltese people were awarded the George Cross by English prime minister Winston Churchill for their fortitude and dogged determination. Evidence of the bombings, including buildings reduced to rubble and torn up streets, was still apparent decades after the war. The island became independent after a 164-year British occupancy. In 1974 Malta became a Republic.

MODERN ERA

Malta has limited natural resources, and the land is not suited to agriculture. The small size of the country and its isolation dissuades industrialization. Economic growth was spurred until the eighteenth century by a low rate of population growth, income gained from trade of cotton, and the European estates of the Knights of St. John. This began to unravel, however, following the era of the Napoleonic Wars, when an economic downswing was coupled with a surge in population. Early in the nineteenth century the government tried to obtain an ideal population—220,000 inhabitants by the twentieth century. As part of this plan, the government encouraged immigration to other British colonies in the Mediterranean and to the West Indies. The Maltese preferred northern Africa, and by 1885, 36,0000 Maltese immigrants moved to Algeria, Egypt, Tunis, and Tripoli. The rise in cheap native labor in northern Africa later pushed the Maltese people to find other locations in which to settle.

THE FIRST MALTESE IN AMERICA

The earliest Maltese settlers in the United States came in the mid-eighteenth century, mostly to

New Orleans. These settlers were sometimes regarded as Italians, and in fact tombstones often mistakenly noted the deceased as "natives of Malta, Italy." The burial grounds were inscribed with such common Maltese names as Ferruggia (Farrugia), Pace, and Grima. By 1855 there were 116 Maltese living in the United States. In the 1860s, it was estimated that between five and ten Maltese came to the United States every year. The majority of the migrants were agricultural workers, and in New Orleans the majority worked as market gardeners and vegetable dealers.

The greatest number of Maltese people came to the United States during the first decades of the twentieth century. Their move coincided with the discharge of skilled workers from the Royal British Dockyard in 1919 following the end of the World War I. More than 1,300 Maltese immigrated to the United States in the first quarter of 1920, and most found work in automobile manufacturing. The *Detroit Free Press* reported in October 1920 that Detroit had the largest Maltese population in the United States, at 5,000 residents. In 1922, the *Detroit Free Press* reported that the only Maltese colony in the United States was in Detroit. Over the next few years it is believed that more than 15,000 Maltese people settled in the United States and became citizens. They apparently intended to stay for a short time and return home. However, opportunities in America seemed more plentiful and stable than the uncertainties at home, and many Maltese people remained in the United States. By 1928 New York had an estimated 9,000 Maltese immigrants. San Francisco also had a large Maltese population.

After World War II, the Maltese government launched a program to pay passage costs to Maltese willing to emigrate and remain abroad for at least two years. As a result, a surge of Maltese left their homeland. In 1954, a reported 11,447 Maltese left the islands. This program enticed approximately 8,000 Maltese to come to the United States between 1947 and 1977. For more than a century Malta's government encouraged emigration because of the tiny size of the overpopulated island nation.

SETTLEMENT
Settlement in the United States was concentrated in Detroit, New York City, San Francisco, and Chicago. It has been estimated that more than 70,000 Maltese immigrants and their descendants were living in the United States by the mid-

1990s. The largest estimated communities are the more than 44,000 Maltese in the Detroit area and the 20,000 Maltese in New York City, most of them in Astoria, Queens.

ACCULTURATION AND ASSIMILATION

Possibly due to the small size of their nation and the large numbers of countries that once occupied the islands, the Maltese are often ignored or confused with other nationalities when studies are done. However, signs of Malta can be seen in fire stations in most cities, small and large, throughout the United States. Firefighters are identified by a badge that designates their company. The majority of badges worn by firefighters take the shape of the Maltese Cross, which is an eight-sided emblem of protection and badge of honor. The history of the cross goes back to the Knights of St. John, who courageously fought for possession of the Holy Land.

Malta's involvement with the United Nations is substantial. The island country became a full member in December 1964 after gaining independence from Great Britain. Issues Malta has been involved in, or spearheaded, include the Law of the Sea Convention in 1981; the United Nations Conference on the Aged; and an initiative to raise questions about the effects of climate change.

Although the people of the Maltese islands are not particularly well known, there are a number of Maltese influences in United States culture. For instance, many people are familiar with the Maltese, a tiny fluffy white dog. The movie *The Maltese Falcon*, a drama about a detective trying to find a priceless statue, is a classic part of American cinema, although another movie, *The Maltese Bippy*, is less known. Oftentimes people with the surname Maltese are Italian by heritage, not Maltese.

TRADITIONS, CUSTOMS, AND BELIEFS
Maltese have traditions and folklore dating back centuries. They are wide and varied—and mostly forgotten today. One popular belief was that if someone gave you "the evil eye," you would have bad luck. To rid their houses of those bad spirits, some Maltese would undergo an elaborate ritual involving old dried olive branches, which were

blessed on Palm Sunday in place of the palm branches commonly used in the United States on the Sunday before Easter. The Maltese would burn the olive branches in a pan and spread the incense through every room of their houses, saying a special prayer and hoping the evil spirit would be chased away.

In other folklore tradition, some Maltese believed women who were menstruating could taint new wine, so they were banned from the cellar while wine was made. The same thinking was applied to making bread.

Others thought bad luck would follow if you dropped a knife. Another sign of bad luck was the sighting of a black moth. Good luck was sure to come when a white moth was seen, however. Some believed, also, that you should never kill a moth.

The tradition of matchmaking involved an elaborate sequence of events. For instance, if a young woman were ready for marriage, her parents would place a flower pot on the front porch. A matchmaker would take note and alert the single men about her availability. Interested suitors would then tell the matchmaker they wanted to marry. The matchmaker would next approach the father of the prospective bride and obtain his blessing.

In the United States a matchmaker was not involved. However, during the first half of the twentieth century, men interested in marrying a Maltese girl still spoke to the girl's father, and in

some cases brothers and other members of her family, for permission to marry. This tradition has faded with time.

Most of these customs and beliefs were gradually forgotten as the Maltese people were assimilated into American society. However, some lingered even if they were only jokingly remembered.

CUISINE

Maltese cuisine involves a tasty mixture with many influences. Garlic is a mainstay. The most popular Maltese dish is *pastitsi*, made of a flaky dough similar to the filo dough used by Greeks. A meat or ricotta cheese mixture is wrapped inside the dough enclave, which is usually about the size of a hand. The ricotta mixture includes ricotta cheese, egg, grated cheese, salt, and pepper. The meat mixture has ground beef, onion, tomato paste, peas, salt, pepper, and curry powder. This cheese or meat mixture also can be cooked in a pie form and served as a meal. Baked macaroni, *imquarrun fil forn*, is another popular dish. The macaroni is cooked in salt water. The sauce includes ground beef, tomato paste, garlic powder, eggs, grated cheese, and a dash of curry powder. This dish can be served without baking, in which case it is called *mostoccoli*.

Rabbit cooked in various ways, including stew, is a Maltese mainstay on the island and in the United States. Pastas with ricotta and tomato sauce are common meals, too. Fish is extremely popular, likely because of the abundance available from Mediterranean Sea. Fried cod, octopus stew, and tuna are typically on the menu. Stuffed artichoke and eggplant are regular meals as well.

For dessert or treats, date slices, or *imqaret*, are found in most Maltese homes in Malta and the United States. This deliciously deep fried pastry has dates, orange and lemon extract, anisette, chopped nuts, orange rind, and lemon rind. Cream-filled or ricotta-filled cannoli shells are common, too. These Maltese sweets are often served at functions like showers, weddings, and baptisms.

TRADITIONAL COSTUMES

Up until the 1950s some of the women in Maltese villages wore a *ghonella*, or *faldetta*, a black dress with a black cape with a hard board black veil. In the modern era many of the fashions are dictated by Italian styles. In the United States, Maltese Americans wear typically the same fashions as others.

MALTESE DANCES AND SONGS

The traditional Maltese dance is an interpretive routine called *miltija*, which describes the victory of the Maltese over the Turks in 1565. Old-time singing was called *ghana*. This involves a bantering, oftentimes between two people who good-heartedly tease each other. They use rhyme and jokes in a relay of comments about each other. Maltese folk singer Namru Station was best known for this form of singing.

HOLIDAYS CELEBRATED BY MALTESE AMERICANS

The Maltese love festivals, and between May and October almost every town and village in Malta and Gozo celebrates the feast day of its patron saint. The *festa* is the most important day in each village, where the church is the focal point of the event. The churches are elaborately decorated with flowers. Gold, silver, and crystal chandeliers are placed on display as a backdrop for the statue of the patron saint. After three days of preparation, the statue is carried shoulder-high along the streets of the city or village in a parade-like procession, including bands and church bells. Since the Maltese specialize in making elaborate fire-

works, colorful displays are part of the party. Cities and villages compete with one another to put on the best show. Maltese in the United States privately commemorate and remember the patron saint of their town, but gone are the big festivals and fireworks.

Since the country is officially Roman Catholic, the Catholic traditions and celebrations dominate in the Maltese culture. Holy days include Christmas, Easter, and an annual observance of February 10, which is the day St. Paul, Malta's patron saint, shipwrecked on the island. Legend has it that when he was shipwrecked with his crew, the people made a bonfire to make them warm. Later, a viper snake came out of the wood and went toward St. Paul. The people were awed that this man had escaped the ravages of the seas, and they were curious to see what would happen with the snake. When he was not bitten, the people thought for sure this man was God. He told them, "I am not a God, but I came to talk to you about God."

Other public holidays in Malta include January 1, New Year's Day; March 19, St. Joseph's feast day; March 29, Good Friday; March 31, Freedom Day; May 1, May Day; June 7, Sette Giugno; June 29, St. Peter and St. Paul feast day; August 15, the Assumption of the Blessed Virgin Mary; September 8, Our Lady of Victories or Victory Day; September 21, Independence Day; December 8, the Immaculate Conception of the Blessed Virgin Mary; December 13, Republic Day; and December 25, Christmas Day.

On patriotic days, the Maltese flag is flown. It has two vertical stripes, white in the hoist and red in the fly. A sign of the George Cross awarded to Malta by His Majesty King George the Sixth on the April 15, 1942, is carried, edged with red in the canton of the white stripe. According to tradition the national colors were given to the Maltese by Count Roger in 1090. Roger the Norman had landed in Malta to oust the Arabs from the island. Out of regard for their hospitality, Roger gave the Maltese part of the pennant of the Hautevilles to serve as their colors.

PROVERBS

Unless the baby cries, he or she will not be put to the mother's breast; Build your reputation and go to sleep; Who I see you with is who I see you as; Little by little the jar will fill; Essence comes in small bottles; Cut the tail of a donkey and it's still a donkey; If you want it to be it never will be; I'll be there if I'm not dead; A friend in the market is better than your money in the hope chest; God does not pay every Saturday; He who waits will sooner or later be happy; Only God knows when death and rain will happen; Always hold onto the words of the elderly to show respect and to gain from their wisdom.

HEALTH AND MENTAL HEALTH ISSUES

Many Maltese people have been stricken with thalassemia. It is also called Mediterranean anemia, because it usually strikes people from that region. In the United States most cases occur in Americans of Maltese, Italian, Greek, Portuguese, or Levantine background. Thalassemia refers to a group of hereditary disorders of the control of globin synthesis, causing too much or too little synthesis of either the alpha or the beta globin chains. In some cases a wrong kind of chain is produced. In beta-thalassemia deficient amounts of beta chains are produced, and in hemoglobin-Lepore thalassemia the beta chain grows longer than the normal 146 amino acids. When the gene is taken from only one parent, a mild anemia usually results; however, when the gene is from both parents the results are devastating. This blood disease is usually discovered during infancy.

LANGUAGE

Like its people and history, the Maltese language is varied. It is Semitic, chiefly Arabic, written in the Roman alphabet, with words and phrases taken from the Italian, Spanish, English, Greek, and some French. The official languages in Malta are Maltese and English. Many people also speak Italian. When English is spoken it is often heard with a British accent, likely a leftover of the 164-year British occupancy of the country.

GREETINGS AND OTHER POPULAR EXPRESSIONS

Typical Maltese greetings and other expressions include: *bongu* ("bon-ju")—good morning; *bonswa* ("bon-swar")—good night; *grazzi* ("grats-ee")—thank you; *taf titkellem bl-Ingliz?* ("tarf tit-kell-lem bilin-gleez")—do you speak English?; *kemm?* ("kem")—how much? The word *sahha* ("sa-ha") can be used as a greeting, as good-bye, or as a toast—it is the Maltese equivalent of "good health."

FAMILY AND COMMUNITY DYNAMICS

There were many changes in the family structure when the first Maltese immigrants came to the United States. Typically, the patriarchs came to the United States without their families. Sometimes they would bring sons, but the wives and children were often left on the homeland. The plan was that they would bring their entire family after they established themselves in their new country and were more financially stable. Oftentimes years lapsed before the entire family was reunited. In other cases, single men came to the United States and lived with relatives, or close family friends who had come to the country earlier. They lived in communities that were heavily populated by other Maltese and often married Maltese women who came to America with their families. These Maltese couples then raised a generation of full-blooded Maltese children who had never lived in the mother country. In downtown Detroit and neighboring Highland Park, the largest Maltese community in the United States, there was a heavily populated Maltese area. However, by the 1970s many, but certainly not all, the Maltese in this area began moving to Detroit suburbs.

Maltese family members were usually very close, and aunts, uncles, and cousins were often regarded as immediate family. Before 1980 most Maltese families were large, with four or more children as the norm. In later years, however, the Maltese, like most other ethnic groups in the United States, were beginning to have smaller families, with two or three children commonly found in each household.

There were a number of gathering places, like clubs, where immigrants and first-generation Maltese could find camaraderie. New immigrants also turned to the Maltese clubs and organizations for information and direction on life in their new country. They were a good place to meet other Maltese, who spoke the language and could help in the assimilation process.

WEDDINGS

A Maltese bridal shower is usually very elaborate, with a multi-course meal and a sweet table. The party often is held in a hall or banquet room to accommodate the large number of family and friends who are invited. In Malta the typical wedding is based on the Roman Catholic mass. The bride would be accompanied by several bridesmaids and the groom had one male, the best man, at his side. In the United States, however, the Maltese wedding is usually dictated by typical traditions followed in the United States.

BAPTISMS

Again the Roman Catholic religion dictates much of what happens at baptisms. A *parrina,* or godmother, and a *parrinu,* or godfather, are chosen. Usually, these people are close family members, like brothers or sisters of the baby's parents. In Malta a party celebration with tables of cookies, ice creams, and drinks will follow the religious ceremony. However, as the customs changed in their new country, the Maltese Americans adopted new traditions, like having a full meal at the party after the baptism.

FUNERALS

The Maltese in the United States have adopted the wake tradition. In Malta when a person died they were usually buried within 24 hours, and very few people were embalmed. In the villages during the early part of the twentieth century, a local person would visit the home, clean the body, and dress the deceased. This person usually was on the lowest rung of the social ladder. Superstition prevailed, and some people were afraid of the undertaker to the point that when village people saw him walking down the street they would walk on the other side of the road. As time passed, however, these traditions faded in Malta and most certainly were not followed in the United States.

RELIGION

Malta's strong Roman Catholic history has been imprinted on those who came to the United States. The religion dates back to a cadre of important visitors to the island, including the Apostle Paul, who was shipwrecked on the island in 60 A.D. The hospitality shown to him by the locals was well documented in the Acts of the Apostles, Chapters 27 and 28, in the New Testament of the Bible. "The natives showed us extraordinary kindness by lighting a fire and gathering us all around it, for it had begun to rain and was growing cold," a passage reads.

Malta's historical and religious background was also greatly influenced by the Knights of the Order of St. John during the eleventh century. In the Holy Land the Order's original duties were to care for the sick and wounded Christians. The Knights became soldiers of Christ and maintained huge estates in the Holy Land. With the loss of their headquarters, Acre, to the Moslems in 1291, however, the Knights withdrew to Rhodes. They were shields against the Turks until 1522, when Suleiman the Magnificent ousted the Knights from Rhodes. In 1530 they moved to Malta. They quickly improved trade and commerce on the islands by building new hospitals and erecting strong fortifications. Although heavily outnumbered, the Knights fought off an attack by Suleiman during the Great Siege of 1565. They were assisted by Maltese and Sicilian reinforcements. The Turks retreated and the Knights of St. John protected southern Europe and Christendom. A blossoming era in culture, architecture, and the arts followed, when the fortress city, Valletta, was built. The fall of the Ottoman Empire marked the end of the military life of the Order. To this day, 97 percent of the Maltese are Roman Catholic.

In the United States the Maltese maintain their strong devotion to the Catholic church by attending mass weekly and becoming active in their local parishes. Since attendance among Maltese Americans is high, church is another common place where they meet one another. For instance, in San Francisco, St. Paul of the Shipwreck Church at 1122 Jamestown Avenue is heavily populated by Maltese. And in Detroit, the Maltese have attended St. Paul's Maltese Church since the 1920s.

EMPLOYMENT AND ECONOMIC TRADITIONS

Many of the Maltese who came to the Detroit area worked on the assembly line at one of the three automakers, Ford Motor Company, General Motors, and Chrysler Corporation. Other Maltese immigrants worked at various jobs on ships, in restaurants and hotels, selling real estate, and in religious orders as priests and nuns.

POLITICS AND GOVERNMENT

The Maltese government is a Republic with a president and prime minister. The major political

This Maltese American woman is participating in a parade in New York City.

stone in the wool trade between Barbary and the United States because it received wool from different ports in North Africa for shipment to America. Later, American tobacco was shipped to Barbary and Sicily through Malta. About 1,500 Maltese were employed in making cigars, which were exported to Italy, Barbary, Turkey, and the Greek Islands. Malta also imported petroleum, rum, pepper, flour, logwood, pitch, resin, turpentine, coffee, sugar, cloves, codfish, wheat, cheese, butter, and lard. Meanwhile, the island nation exported to America items like olive oil, lemons, sulphur, ivory, salt, rags, goat skins, stoneware, soap, squills, sponges, and donkeys of the largest and most valuable race in the Mediterranean.

INDIVIDUAL AND GROUP CONTRIBUTIONS

ACADEMIA

Professor Paul Vassallo, formerly of Marsa, Malta, headed a consortium of eight universities in the Washington, D.C. area. The Washington Research Library Consortium is a national model of the U.S. government that demonstrates how university libraries can keep up with the volume of new material. Vassallo, born in 1932, immigrated to the United States when he was 15 years old. His mother and siblings lived in the Detroit area.

FILM, TELEVISION, AND THEATER

Joseph Calleia, a Maltese native and actor, appeared in a number of Hollywood movies, including *Wild Is the Wind* in 1957.

MILITARY

Joseph Borg went to the United States at the time of the American Revolution. He was described as having been a sea captain who fought in many battles for American independence.

Brigadier General Patrick P. Caruana commanded the 50 B-52 bombers flying out of Saudi Arabia, England, Spain, and the Indian Ocean during the Persian Gulf War of 1991. The fleet pounded the Iraqis incessantly and helped break their morale. Caruana, a St. Louis resident, was also a KC-135 tanker pilot in Vietnam and commanded the 17th Air Division and its fleet of bombers refueling tankers and spy planes.

parties are the Malta Labor Party and the Nationalist Party. In Malta, the first American consul was nominated in 1796, which made Malta among the first countries to have a consular office of the United States.

MILITARY

Maltese involvement in supporting the United States during war dates back to at least the American Revolution. Maltese seamen enlisted in the French navy, which was supporting the colonists against Great Britain. About 1,800 Maltese sailors went to Toulon to join the French in this effort.

RELATIONS WITH MALTA

During the first decade of the nineteenth century American ships brought a variety of goods to Malta, including flour, rice, pepper, salted meat, rum, tobacco, and mahogany wood from Boston and Baltimore, as well as dried fruits, cotton, wax, pearls, goat hides, coffee, potatoes, drugs, and sponges from Smyrne and the Greek archipelago. During 1808, 33 American vessels entered Valletta, Malta's capital city. Trade would rise and fall cyclically. Malta's biggest boon of American shipping was during the Crimean War, between 1854 and 1856, when Great Britain and France were fighting Russia. Malta also emerged as a stepping

MUSIC

Oreste Kirkop, an opera singer, appeared in *Student Prince*. Legend had it that he was encouraged to change his name to increase his fame, but he refused to take the suggestion and instead returned to Malta.

SCIENCE AND TECHNOLOGY

John Schembri, a Pacific Bell employee, has two patents to his name and a third pending. He holds degrees in electronics, engineering, mathematics, and industrial relations and is a recognized expert in the design and application of optical fiber transmissions systems.

VISUAL ARTS

The Liberty Bell was made in England in 1751 for the Assembly of the Province of Pennsylvania, to be used in the State House of the City of Philadelphia. However, when it was being tested, the bell cracked. It was recast in Philadelphia by John Pass (a Maltese immigrant) and John Stow, who added a small amount of copper to make it less brittle. Pass appears in the painting "The Bell's First Note," which hangs in the United States National Museum of the Smithsonian Institution in Washington, D.C. Although Pass is not a Maltese surname, there is no doubt about his heritage: the speaker of the Pennsylvania Assembly referred to him as hailing from Malta. It is likely that his name in Malta was Pace, and he either changed it, or it was misspelled in documents.

MEDIA

PRINT

Malta Gazetta.

Address: 27-20 Hoyt Avenue South, Astoria, New York 11102.

The Maltese Herald.

Address: Maltese American Foundation, 570 Park Avenue, Marysville, Ohio 43040.

The Maltese News.

Address: 2600 Saulino Court, Dearborn, Michigan 48120.

ORGANIZATIONS AND ASSOCIATIONS

American Association, Sovereign Military Order of Malta.

Address: 1011 First Avenue, Room 1500, New York, New York 10022.

Committee for Maltese Unity, Inc.

Address: P.O. Box 456, Mount Vernon, New York 10551.

Friends of Malta Society, Inc.

Address: 3009 Schoenherr Road, Warren, Michigan 48093.

Institute of Maltese American Affairs.

Address: Malta Overseas Press News Service, Allied Newspapers Limited, Malta House, 36 Cooper Avenue, Dumont, New Jersey 07628.

Malta Club of Macomb.

Address: 31024 Jefferson Avenue, St. Clair Shores, Michigan 48082.

Maltese American Association of L.I., Inc.

Address: 1486 Lydia Avenue, Elmont, New York 11003.

Maltese American Benevolent Society.

Address: 1832 Michigan Avenue, Detroit, Michigan 48216.

Telephone: (313) 961-8393.

Maltese American Club.

Address: 5221 Oakman Boulevard, Dearborn, Michigan 48216.

Telephone: (313) 846-7077.

Maltese American Community Club.

Address: 17929 Eton Avenue, Dearborn Heights, Michigan 48215.

Maltese American Foundation.

Address: 2074 Ridgewood Road, Medina, Ohio 44256.

Maltese American Friendship Society, Inc.

Address: 32-57 45th Street, Astoria, New York 11103.

Maltese American League.

Address: 1977 Le Blanc Street, Lincoln Park, Michigan 48146.

Maltese-American Social Club of San Francisco, Inc.

Address: 1769 Oakdale Avenue, San Francisco, California 94134.

Maltese International.

Address: 10 Columbus, Berea, Ohio 44017.

Maltese Social Club.

Address: 27-20 Hoyt Avenue South, Astoria, New York 11102.

Maltese Union Club.

Address: 246 Eighth Avenue, New York, New York 10011.

San Pablo Rectory.

Address: 550 122nd Street, Ocean Maraton, Florida 33050.

Sons of Malta Social Club, Inc.

Address: 233 East 32nd Street, New York, New York 10016.

MUSEUMS AND RESEARCH CENTERS

Maltese American Benevolent Society.

Contains a library covering Maltese issues, concerns, and background.

Address: 1832 Michigan Avenue, Detroit, Michigan 48226.

SOURCES FOR ADDITIONAL STUDY

Dobie, Edith. *Malta's Road to Independence*. Norman: University of Oklahoma Press, 1967.

Early Relations Between Malta and U.S.A. Valletta, Malta: Midsea Books, Ltd., 1976.

The Epic of Malta. Odhams Press Limited, (n.d.).

Luke, Harry. *Malta: An Account and an Appreciation*, second edition. [London], 1968.

The Malta Yearbook. Sliema, Malta: De La Salle Brothers Publications, 1991.

Price, Charles A. *Malta and the Maltese: A Study in Nineteenth Century Migration*. Melbourne, Australia, 1954.

MEXICAN AMERICANS

by
**Allan Englekirk
and Marguerite
Marín**

By 1990 over one-
half million
Hispanic-owned
businesses existed in
the United States,
the majority of them
in California and
controlled by
Mexican Americans.

OVERVIEW

Mexico, or Estados Unidos Mexicanos, is bordered by the United States to the north, the Gulf of Mexico to the east, Guatemala, Belize, and the Caribbean Sea to the southeast, and the Pacific to the south and west. The northwest portion of Mexico, called Baja California, is separated from the rest of the nation by the Gulf of California. The Sierra Madre, an extension of the Rocky Mountain chain, divides into the Oriental range to the east and the Occidental range to the west. The central highlands, where the majority of Mexico's 75 million people live, lies in between these two mountain systems. Overall, Mexico occupies 759,530 square miles.

HISTORY

The earliest inhabitants of Mexico are believed to have been hunters who migrated from Asia approximately 18,000 years ago. Over time, these early peoples built highly organized civilizations, such as the Olmec, Teotihuacan, Mayan, Toltec, Zapotec, Mixtec, and Aztec societies, the majority of which were accomplished in art, architecture, mathematics, astronomy, and agriculture. In 1517 Spanish explorer Francisco Fernández de Córdoba discovered the Yucatán, a peninsula located in the southeast of Mexico. By 1521 the Spanish conquistador Hernando Cortéz had managed to conquer the Aztec empire, the most powerful Indian nation in Mexico at the time. For the next 300 years, Mexico, or New Spain, would remain under colonial rule.

Spain's generally repressive colonial regime stifled the growth of commerce and industry, monitored or censored the dissemination of new and possibly revolutionary ideas, and limited access to meaningful political power to anyone but native-born Spaniards. An unequal distribution of land and wealth developed and, as the nation grew in numbers, the disproportion between the rich and poor continued to increase, as did a sense of social unrest among the most neglected of its populace. Their discontent resulted in a successful revolt against Spain in 1821.

In the latter part of the nineteenth century, under the 30-year authoritarian rule of Porfirio Díaz, noticeable industrialization occurred in Mexico, financed in large part by foreigners. Mining was revitalized and foreign trade increased. Dynamic growth brought relative prosperity to many economic sectors of various regions of the country, complemented by increased levels of employment. As the century ended, however, a vast majority of the nation's inhabitants had realized little if any improvement in their standard of living. Those residing in rural areas struggled to produce enough to survive from their own small parcels of land, or, much more likely, worked under a debt-peonage system, farming lands owned by someone infinitely wealthier than they were. Most residents of urban areas, if they were lucky enough to have full employment, worked long hours under poor conditions for extremely low wages and lived in housing and neighborhoods that fostered diseases. The economic depression of 1907 soured the aspirations of the small but growing middle class and brought financial disaster to the newest members of the upper class (Ramón Ruiz, *Triumphs and Tragedy*, pp. 310-13).

Though he was able to manipulate his reelection in 1910, opposition to the Díaz regime was strong, and when small rebellions began to proliferate in the northern states of the nation, he resigned his post in 1911 and left the country. After Francisco Madero, the newly elected president, failed to define an agenda to satisfy the several disparate groups in Mexico, he likewise agreed to self-exile but was assassinated by supporters of General Victoriano de la Huerta, the man who next assumed national leadership. Violence escalated into a bloody and prolonged civil war known as the Revolution of 1910. The turmoil and bloodshed motivat-

ed some people from all levels of society to flee the country, most often northward to the United States.

By the early 1920s, though relative peace had been restored, the social and economic reforms that had become associated with the revolution were still unrealized, chief among them the redistribution of land to a greater percentage of the populace. From the perspective of the government-controlled political party, first designated as the PNR (Partido Nacional Revolucionario/National Revolutionary Party), and finally, in 1946, as the PRI (Partido Revolucionario Institucional/Institutional Revolutionary Party), a nonviolent revolution was to continue until the goals related to social and economic justice were attained (Ruiz, p. 423). National presidents focused on promoting growth in the industrial sector, but the opening of new jobs did not keep pace with the employment needs of a rapidly expanding population.

Since the 1950s, economic conditions in Mexico have improved at a gradual pace. Expanding industrialization has provided additional jobs for greater numbers of workers and increased oil production has brought in needed foreign currencies. The projected benefits from commercial accords such as the North American Free Trade Agreement have yet to materialize, but continued growth of international trade with other Latin American nations may invigorate areas of economic investment and production. Continued single-party rule by the PRI, high levels of unemployment, underemployment, low wages, and the many social problems related to a prolonged period of intense urbanization—coupled with the need for renewed efforts at land redistribution in certain areas of the country—remain as sources of concern for the government and causes of unrest for a significant segment of the population. In increasing proportions since the late 1970s, those people unable to find dependable sources of employment or subsistence wages have moved to the northern borderlands and crossed into the United States, where the economic prospects are more promising. To reverse this movement of manpower out of the country, future administrations in Mexico will have to continue to promote the expansion of economic growth to all regions in the country and the creation of new jobs in the public and private sectors.

THE MEXICAN-AMERICAN WAR AND MEXICAN IMMIGRATION TO THE UNITED STATES

The Mexican government initially promoted

American settlement in parts of the territory now known as Texas in the 1820s to bolster the regional economy. As the proportion of North American settlers in these lands multiplied, however, they began to request greater local autonomy, feared the possibility that Mexico might outlaw slavery, and resented the imposition of taxes from the government in Mexico City (Oscar Martínez, *The Handbook of Hispanic Cultures in the United States History*, p. 263). Sporadic insurrections occurred after a new president, General Antonio López de Santa Anna, imposed restrictive controls on commerce between the Anglos living on Mexican land and the United States, and these uprisings precipitated an armed response by the Mexican army. Santa Anna seized the Alamo in San Antonio but was later defeated in the Battle of San Jacinto. Santa Anna later signed the Velasco Agreement in Washington D.C., which formally recognized the independence of present-day Texas. After returning to Mexico, however, he was quick to join other military leaders who rejected the accord.

Relations between the United States and Mexico remained strained, at best, during the late 1830s and early 1840s. The Lone Star Republic was admitted to the Union as the State of Texas in 1845; shortly thereafter the frequency of border skirmishes between the two countries increased. U.S. forces responded to these clashes by moving into New Mexico and California in 1846, as well as southward into Mexico. The capture of Mexico City was the final significant armed conflict.

War between Mexico and the United States ended with the Treaty of Guadalupe Hidalgo in 1848 in which Mexico surrendered 890,000 square miles, close to one-half of its territory. Six years later, in order to finish construction of a transcontinental railway, the United States purchased an additional 30,000 square miles of Mexican land for $10 million. This acquisition was made final through the Gadsden Treaty of 1854 (Carlos Cortés, *Harvard Encyclopedia of American Ethnic Groups*, p. 701).

Approximately 80,000 Mexicans resided in the territory transferred to the United States at the conclusion of the Mexican-American War, the greatest numbers of whom were located in present-day New Mexico and California. Only a small proportion of the total, slightly over 2,000, decided to return to their country of origin after the signing of the treaty. Those who remained north of the border were guaranteed citizenship after two years, along with other privileges and responsibilities related to this status.

SIGNIFICANT IMMIGRATION WAVES

When compared to various periods of the twentieth century, Mexican immigration to the United States between 1850 and 1900 was relatively low. The discovery of gold in the Sierra Nevada of California in 1849 was an initial stimulus for this migration, as was the expansion of copper mining in Arizona beginning in the 1860s. During this same period and on into the twentieth century, ranching and agriculture lured many inhabitants of the northern and central states of Mexico to Texas. By 1900 approximately 500,000 people of Mexican ancestry lived in the United States, principally in the areas originally populated by Spaniards and Mexicans prior to 1848. Roughly 100,000 of these residents were born in Mexico; the remainder were second-generation inhabitants of these regions and their offspring.

A combination of factors contributed to sequential pronounced rises in Mexican migration to the United States during the first three decades of the twentieth century. The Reclamation Act of 1902, which expanded acreage for farming through new irrigation projects, spurred the need for more agricultural laborers. The Mexican Revolution of 1910 and the aftermath of political instability and social violence caused many to flee northward across the border for their safety, and the growth of the U.S. economy in the 1920s attracted additional numbers of immigrants. Though the wages received by most Mexican migrants in these decades were quite low, they were considerably higher than the salaries paid for comparable work in Mexico. Most importantly, the number of jobs for foreign laborers seemed unlimited, especially during World War I and on into the early 1920s.

Only 31,000 Mexicans migrated to the United States in the first decade of the twentieth century, but the next two ten-year periods manifested markedly higher numbers, especially from 1920 to 1929, when almost 500,000 people of Mexican ancestry entered the country. However, since the frontier was virtually open to anyone wishing to cross it until the creation of the Border Patrol in 1924, immigration figures for years prior to this date are of dubious legitimacy. The actual number may be appreciably higher (Cortés, p. 699). Rural areas of California, Arizona, New Mexico, Colorado, and Texas attracted a vast majority of these migrants, but during the years of World War I, mounting numbers of newcomers moved to the upper midwestern states, mainly to the region around Chicago. They were attracted by jobs in industry, railroads, steelmills, and meat-packing.

In these initial periods of heavy immigration, it was most common for Mexican males to cross the border for work and return to Mexico periodically with whatever profits they were able to accumulate over several months. Alternatively, they remained in the United States for a longer duration and sent money southward to family members; between 1917 and 1929, Mexican migrants to the United States sent over $10 million to relatives in their home country (Carey McWilliams, *North from Mexico*, [New York: Praeger, 1990], p. 171). During these same decades, men might also establish residency in the United States and return for their families, though still quite often with the ultimate objective of returning to Mexico permanently in a not-too-distant future. It is estimated that about one-half of those immigrants who entered the United States from 1900 to 1930 returned to Mexico (Matt S. Meier and Feliciano Rivera, *Mexican Americans/American Mexicans*, [New York: Hill and Wang, 1993], p. 129).

Mexican immigration to the United States decreased considerably in the 1930s due to the economic depression of this decade. Though approximately 30,000 Mexicans entered the United States during these years, over 500,000 left the country, most of them forced to do so because of the Repatriation Program, which sought to extradite those Mexicans without proper documentation. The Mexican government since the 1870s had attempted to encourage reverse migration to Mexico. In the 1930s jobs and/or land were promised to those who would return, but when this commitment was not fulfilled, many families or individuals moved back to the border towns of the north and often attempted again to return to the United States (Richard Griswold del Castillo, *La familia*, p. 59).

With the exception of the decade of Word War II, legal immigration from Mexico to the United States since 1940 has remained at or above the high levels of 1910 to 1930. Despite federal legislation to limit the numbers of immigrants from most countries to the United States in the 1960s and 1970s, Mexican migrants crossing the border totaled 453,937 and 640,294 for the two decades. It is estimated that approximately one million entered the United States legally between 1981 and 1990. The number of undocumented workers has increased consistently since the 1960s; approximately one million people of this category were deported annually to Mexico in the late 1980s and early 1990s, a proportion of this figure representing individuals deported more than once (Meier and Rivera, pp. 192-95). The availability of jobs in the United States, coupled with high rates of unemployment and periodic slowdowns in the Mexican economy, served to encourage this continued migration northward.

SETTLEMENT PATTERNS

Though in 1900 a vast majority of people of Mexican ancestry lived in rural areas, by 1920, 40 percent of the Mexican American population resided in cities or towns. In 1990 the estimated proportion had risen to 94 percent (Meier and Rivera, p. 250). Los Angeles had among the highest number of Hispanics of major cities of the world and by far the greatest proportion of its population was Mexican in origin.

According to the 1990 U.S. Census Bureau report, approximately 12 million people of Mexican ancestry lived in the United States, a figure which represented 4.7 percent of the total national population and 61.2 percent of the total Hispanic population in the country. Over 66 percent of the people of Mexican ancestry were born in the United States, while 7.5 percent of the total were naturalized citizens. The Pacific states, led by California, held 47.8 percent of the 12 million; 30 percent lived in the West Central states, led by Texas. The states with the highest populations of Mexican Americans are, in descending sequence: California, Texas, Illinois, Arizona, New Mexico, Colorado, Florida, and Washington.

MEXICAN AMERICANS AND ANGLO AMERICANS: THE GRADUAL MOVE TO MUTUAL ACCEPTANCE

Mexicans who held tracts of land of any appreciable size in Texas, California, and New Mexico prior to 1848 were angered and alienated when they began to lose their properties because of alterations made in the 1848 treaty after its signing or because of other unethical tactics used by Anglo Americans to obtain their land. Luis Falcón and Dan Gilbarg identify the procedures employed to acquire two-thirds of the lands once held by Spanish or Mexican families in New Mexico: "Traditional claims were rejected, and original owners were required to prove their ownership in court. The procedures of these courts were biased against the original owners: the burden of proof fell on them, the courts were conducted in English and in locations less accessible to Mexican landowners, and standards of legal proof were based on U.S. law rather than Mexican law under which the land had originally been acquired" (Luis Falcón and Dan Gilbarg, *The Handbook … Sociology*, p. 58). Small landholders were particularly vulnerable. Land companies often successfully appropriated the holdings of isolated Mexican villagers who neglected to register their land claims in the appropriate governmental offices or failed to pay sometimes burdensome new taxes demanded on their properties. In some instances, these taxes were increased to excessive levels for Mexicans, then lowered after they were forced to sell their holdings to Anglo American families or land agents (Cortés, p. 707).

The response of many Mexicans in the southwestern United States to the Anglo American presence was retaliatory violence. In New Mexico, Las Gorras Blancas, a vigilante group, destroyed rail lines and the properties of lumber and cattle interests in an attempt to convince these forces to move elsewhere (Griswold del Castillo, p. 13). In Texas, the decade-long Cortina War started in 1859. After shooting a deputy sheriff for arresting one of his former servants for no apparently just reason, Juan Nepomuceno Cortina and some followers conducted a prolonged series of raids on ranches and small towns around Brownsville, in part to avenge the deputy's act but also because he believed that since shortly after their arrival in the region Anglo Americans had scorned and insulted Mexican locals. In defense of Mexican property rights, Cortina declared: "Our personal enemies shall not possess our lands until they have fattened it with their gore" (McWilliams, pp. 104-05). Most Mexicans perceived Anglo Americans to be "arrogant, overbearing, aggressive, conniving, rude, unreliable and dishonest" because of the unscrupulous actions of some (McWilliams, p. 89).

Disfavor on the part of some Anglo Americans with Mexicans was evident before 1848, but it intensified thereafter. Besides a small minority of well-to-do Mexican families with extensive landholdings, the preponderant number of residents in the territories ceded to the United States in 1848 were of humble origin and negligible financial resources. As greater numbers came north in search of work, the wages of those Mexicans already working in the United States were held down due to the abundant supply of labor, and the standard of living of most of these indi-

viduals consequently remained at the same low level for decade upon decade. Though not all Anglo Americans living in the same areas inhabited by Mexicans were appreciably better off, a definite economic disparity existed and was one of the reasons for a division to develop between the two cultures.

Other differences made this division more pronounced, however. Whereas the immigrants from Mexico were predominantly Catholic, most of the people who settled in Texas, California, and the other territories were of Protestant sects. The religious wars on the European continent between these creeds were not too distant in the past to be forgotten. Perhaps most importantly for some, however, the new majority society was decidedly of North European origin and of light skin color. In contrast, most Mexicans living in or moving to these newly acquired lands of the United States were *mestizos* (people of mixed Spanish and Indian ancestry), and a significant percentage of those who immigrated from the northern states of Mexico were primarily of Indian ancestry. The sentiments of a sizable portion of western settlers in the United States in the mid-1800s about the indigenous civilizations whose lands they were slowly appropriating were quite negative. In the words of McWilliams, "Indians were a conquered race despised by Anglo Americans" and "Mexicans were constantly equated with Indians" by the most race-conscious of the early Anglo American westerners (McWilliams, p. 190).

The number of immigrants increased considerably in the first decades of the twentieth century. Though employers in mining, agriculture, and various industries were more than pleased to see ever larger numbers of migrant workers cross the border each year, Anglo American laborers in the same occupations as these immigrants blamed the newcomers for holding their wages down and viewed them as strike busters. Moreover, when urbanization became more pronounced in the 1920s and Mexicans in the Southwest began moving to the major cities, many people in these urban centers perceived these Hispanics as part of the cause of higher crime rates, increased vagrancy, and violence. City chambers of commerce, local welfare agencies, nativist organizations, and various labor unions all began to call for controls on Mexican migration. Bills to place a limit on their immigration were proposed in Congress in the 1920s, but never ratified (Cortés, p. 703). Massive unemployment in the 1930s prompted the initiation of the Repatriation Program. Many of the Mexicans who left the country had lived in the United States for over ten years and had started American-born families. Their mandated eviction was a tragic experience that led to a bitter realization: it was clear to those involved that they were only welcome in the United States when the economy needed their labors. This would not be the last time this fact would be dramatized to Mexicans and Mexican Americans in such humiliating fashion.

Approximately 350,000 children born in the United States of Mexican immigrants or Mexican American parents fought in World War II, and a proportionately high number won medals of honor, but relations between Mexican American and Anglo American citizens remained tense in the 1940s. In 1942 in Los Angeles, the purported beating of eleven sailors by a group of Mexican American youths sparked a prolonged retaliation by servicemen and civilians against Hispanics wearing "zoot suits," distinctive clothing interpreted by some Anglo Americans in the city to symbolize a rebellious attitude by the younger Mexican Americans. Many injuries occurred on both sides and the riots in Los Angeles spread to several other metropolitan centers nationwide (Meier and Rivera, p. 164).

After the war, despite the fact that thousands of Mexican Americans lost their lives in battle, many Hispanics remained segregated in neighborhoods out of sight to Anglo American society. They attended segregated schools, ate in segregated restaurants, sat in specially designated areas of theaters, and swam in pools on "colored" days only (Cortés, pp. 707-09). Though in the 1950s several southwestern states attempted to rebuild old sections of certain towns of Spanish heritage to romanticize the local Hispanic traditions, the apparent respect for the Hispanic past in this region of the country contrasted "harshly with the actual behavior of the community toward persons of Mexican descent" (McWilliams, p. 47). Increased tourism, rather than pride in the multicultural heritage of these areas, might have been the primary factor for most reconstruction programs.

Only in the 1960s, when the civil rights of most minorities in the United States were brought under scrutiny, did the negative attitudes of many citizens toward Mexican Americans begin to be called into question. In 1970 the U.S. Commission on Civil Rights proclaimed that Mexican Americans had been denied equal treatment by the legal and judicial systems in the United States

(Cortés, p. 714). The press coverage given to the efforts of César Chávez to improve the wages and working conditions of agricultural workers and the vital ideas emerging from the Chicano movement of the 1970s raised the consciousness of non-Hispanic U.S. citizens to the social and economic issues of importance to the Mexican American population of the country. The *Teatro Campesino* of Luis Valdez dramatized visually for audiences the barriers of prejudice faced by most Mexican Americans in the land once possessed by their ancestors.

A significant majority of U.S. citizens in the 1990s recognized that Mexican Americans represent a segment of the population whose contributions to the nation's society have been and will be valuable and praiseworthy. Upward mobility has brought a better life to a minority of Mexican Americans and increased acceptance by some who might previously have repudiated them. Inequalities and discrimination have not disappeared, however, and remain as legitimate and vexing sources of discontent for a significant segment of this Hispanic community. As reasons for misunderstanding or discord diminish, both cultures will realize greater rewards.

ACCULTURATION AND ASSIMILATION

Most immigrant groups in America to a lesser or greater extent have attempted to maintain their distinctive cultural ways. However, the general pattern has been that with each successive generation the use of the mother tongue and the immigrant culture diminishes. Mexican Americans do not fit this pattern for a number of reasons. First of all one must consider their historical experience— particularly their "charter member" status within the United States. Some Mexican Americans can trace their ancestry back ten generations. The ancestors of many Mexican Americans living in rural Colorado and northern New Mexico predate the Anglo American presence in that region. Many have not acculturated; some speak English with difficulty and appear to be more traditionally oriented than the newly arrived Mexican immigrant (Joan Moore and Henry Pachón, *Hispanics in the United States,* p. 92). Second, Mexican immigration has been a constant pattern throughout the twentieth century. As a result, each successive wave of Mexican immigration has served to reinforce certain aspects of Mexican culture and maintain and encourage the use of the Spanish language within the United States. In addition, intermarriage between immigrant males and Mexican American women has encouraged the maintenance of Spanish. Immigrants have also encouraged the continuous growth of Spanish language enterprises such as the Spanish-language media, print as well as electronic, and small businesses that cater to the Spanish-speaking community. In fact, McLemore has stated that Mexican Americans "have been the primary contributors to the maintenance of the Spanish language over a comparatively long period of time" (*Ethnic Relations in America*, p. 261).

The size and the distribution of the ethnic group also plays a dominant role in the persistence of traditional cultural patterns. The 1990 census indicates that there are approximately 21,000,000 Hispanic Americans residing in the United States, so about one out of every ten Americans is of Hispanic origin. Mexican Americans form the largest group of Hispanic Americans, at over 12,000,000. Not all speak Spanish, but most have some familiarity with the language, and many who speak English in the larger society will often speak Spanish at home. While most are concentrated in the southwestern United States, there has been a greater integration of Mexican Americans into the larger society, and the vast majority are likely to live in communities with high concentrations of inhabitants of their same ethnic identity. Thus, the potential for interaction with other Mexican Americans is extremely high. Many, on a daily basis, will work, go to school, go to church, and attend various community events with other Mexican Americans. This continuous interaction over the years has served to perpetuate certain elements of Mexican and Mexican American culture.

The Mexican Americans' close proximity to their homeland is yet another factor resulting in their slower rate of assimilation. Since the United States shares a 2,000 mile border with Mexico, Mexican Americans are in a truly unique position. Over the years, the children and grandchildren of Mexican immigrants have been able to maintain close ties with the "old country." Many have the opportunity to visit Mexico on a relatively frequent basis. On extended trips, they may travel to the interior of Mexico, or, if their time is limited, they can visit the border region. These return visits to the old country are not once-in-a-lifetime opportunities as has been the case for most European immigrants who settled in America. Many Mexican Americans are able to maintain strong cultural ties through their contacts with friends and extended family in Mexico (Richard Schaefer, *Racial and Ethnic Groups*, p. 277).

MEXICAN AMERICAN TERMS OF IDENTITY

In the 1990s, two terms were widely used to identify Spanish-speaking people: Hispanic and Latino. The latter term appears to be growing in acceptance, especially by younger people who reject the Hispanic identification. The popular use of "Hispanic" grew out of the federal government's efforts, beginning with the 1980 census, to identify and count all people of Spanish-speaking backgrounds with origins from the western hemisphere. Since the term was employed in most federal government reports, the media soon appropriated it and popularized its use. Some members of the Hispanic community have employed the term to create political alliances among all ethnic groups with ties to the Spanish language. However, according to the Latino National Political Survey, the majority of respondents indicated that they defined their identities in terms of place of origin. Among those of Mexican origin who were born in the United States, 62 percent identified themselves as Mexican; 28 percent as Hispanic or Latino; and ten percent as American (P. Kivisto, *Americans All*, pp. 386-87).

Terms of identity vary greatly from region to region and from generation to generation. Traditionally, residents of northern New Mexico have referred to themselves as Spanish Americans or *Hispanos*, terms which are essentially a reflection of their early ancestors from "New Spain" who settled the region. Persons from Texas, in the recent past, have referred to themselves as Latin Americans, although there is growing use of the term "Tejano" by Texas residents of Mexican ancestry. The identification of Mexican is more commonly used in the Los Angeles area. More recently, the identification of Mexican American has gained in popularity.

In general, varying group identities are a reflection of the changing self-definitions of an ethnic group. The term "Chicano" is perhaps the best example of this social process. Chicano appeared in the mid-1960s as a political term of choice primarily among the young. The term identified an individual actively promoting social change within the context of the social movements of the 1960s and 1970s. To the older generation and the more affluent, to be identified as a "Chicano" was an insult. In the past the term specifically referred to the unsophisticated immigrant. However, to the generation of political activists, their term of ethnic identity came to signify a sense of pride in one's community and heritage. Thus, as Kivisto states, group identities are social constructs that "human beings are continually renegotiating and articulating" (Kivisto, p. 18).

RESISTANCE TO ASSIMILATION

Following the Mexican-American War, increasing violence perpetrated by Anglo Americans made Mexicans and Mexican Americans intensely aware of their subordinate status within the American Southwest. They did not have equal protection under the law, despite the guarantees of the Treaty of Guadalupe Hidalgo and the U.S. Constitution, and several laws were passed to specifically control their way of life. According to Griswold del Castillo: "A Sunday Law imposed fines ranging from ten to 500 dollars for engaging in `barbarous or noisy amusements' which were listed as bullfights, horse races, cockfights, and other tradition Californio amusements. At the same time, a vagrancy law called `the Greaser Law' was passed.... This law imposed fines and jail sentences on unemployed Mexican-Americans who, at the discretion of local authorities, could be called vagrants" (*The Los Angeles Barrio: A Social History*, p. 115). When Mexican Americans defied Anglo Americans and their newly established laws, lynchings, murders, and kangaroo trials were quite common as Anglo Americans asserted their dominance.

In an attempt to cope with their second-class status, Mexican Americans created a variety of social and political organizations, many of which promoted ethnic solidarity. As sociologist Gordon Allport has noted, one of the results of ethnic persecution is the strengthening of ethnic ties. Within their group, ethnic minorities "can laugh and deride their persecutors, celebrate their own heros and holidays" (*The Nature of Prejudice*, p. 149).

Before the turn of the twentieth century at least 16 Spanish-language newspapers were established in Los Angeles. The Mexican American press took the lead in condemning discrimination against their community. For example, in 1858 the editor of *El Clamor Público* denounced the theft of California lands by Anglo Americans and urged nonconformity to Anglo American culture and domination. The Mexican American press also developed a sense of ethnic solidarity by reporting on such cultural events as Mexican Independence Day and Cinco de Mayo, which celebrates the defeat of the French forces in Mexico in 1862.

The concept of "La Raza" was also promoted by the newspapers of the time. Its use by the Spanish-language press was evidence of a new kind of ethnic identity. The term connoted racial, spiritual, and blood ties to all Latin American people, ties particularly to Mexico. In addition, a number of social and political associations began to reinforce ethnic identity. Griswold del Castillo notes that between 1850 and 1900 at least 15 associations were established in Los Angeles. Their purposes were social and political. However, they overwhelmingly promoted Mexican nationalist sentiments (p. 135).

During the 1960s the Chicano movement specifically challenged assimilationist orientations within the larger society as well as within the Mexican American community itself. The ideology of the Chicano movement, particularly for Mexican American college students, called into question the idea of conformity to "Anglo American" cultural ideals. The beliefs promoted by the movement articulated a sense of personal worth and pride in common history and culture by emphasizing Chicano contributions to American society. The activists also reevaluated former symbols of shame associated with their heritage, culture, and physical appearance. Activists took great care in pronouncing Spanish names and words with the proper accent. Monolingual English-speaking Chicanos took courses to learn Spanish. Cultural relics and artifacts were resurrected. Items such as *sarapes* (serapes, or shawls) and *huaraches* (sandals), as well as other clothing symbolic of Mexican American culture, were displayed and worn with pride. A new perception of self-worth and pride in one's heritage prevailed among the adherents of the Chicano movement. This perspective was not only indicative of a newfound image and self-concept; it was also an assertion of dignity within a society that regarded Chicanos and their cultural symbols as inferior (Marguerite Marín, *Social Protest in an Urban Barrio*, pp. 114-120).

The ethnic movements of the 1960s and 1970s brought to the fore the contemporary debate concerning cultural pluralism. The ethnic movements of this period argued that assimilating into American society entailed the loss of distinctive identities, cultures, and languages. Assimilation was defined as a virtual assault on the way of life of American ethnic minority groups. As a result, a concerted effort is under way to understand, albeit only within certain segments of American society, the internal and external dynamics of the many peoples that make up the American mosaic.

MISCONCEPTIONS AND STEREOTYPES

The first major wave of Mexican immigration during the twentieth century triggered physical as well as verbal attacks by white Americans. Immigrant labor camps were raided by whites espousing white supremacist beliefs. By 1911 certain politicians lobbied against further Mexican immigration. The Dillingham Commission argued that Mexicans were undesirable as future citizens. Nativist scholars and politicians feared "mongrelization" as a by-product of contact with Mexicans, and in 1925 a Princeton economics professor even spoke of the future elimination of Anglo Americans by interbreeding with Mexicans (Feagin and Feagin, p. 265). These themes reemerged in 1928 when a congressional committee attempted to set limits on immigration from the Western Hemisphere. Congressman John Box called for restrictions on Mexican immigration because the Mexican was a product of mixing by the Spaniard and "low-grade" Indians. This mixture, according to Boxer, was an obstacle to participation in American democracy.

The image of the Mexican American male possessing innate criminal tendencies emerged during the World War II era. For example, in 1943, following the Zoot Suit Riots, the Los Angeles Sheriff's Department issued a report alleging that the Mexican American's desire to spill blood was an inborn characteristic. Further, the report concluded that Mexican Americans were violent because of their Indian blood (Feagin and Feagin, p. 265). And as late as 1969, a California judge ruling in an incest case reiterated similar racist beliefs. He stated in court: "Mexican people ... think it is perfectly all right to act like an animal. We ought to send you out of this country.... You are lower than animals ... maybe Hitler was right. The animals in our society probably ought to be destroyed" (Feagin and Feagin, p. 266).

One of the most persistent stereotypes is the image of simplemindedness. In 1982 the U.S. Department of Defense issued a report explaining that lower test scores for Hispanics and African Americans as compared to white Americans were due to genetic differences as well as cultural differences. During the same year, the National Educational Testing Service, surprised by the excellent performance of 18 Mexican American students attending Garfield High School (a school situated in one of Los Angeles' poorest Mexican American communities), demanded that all retake the exam. Allegations of cheating by the students was the reasoning of the testing administrators. The students eventually did re-take the exam; once again they received excellent scores.

TRADITIONAL HEALTH CARE BELIEFS AND PRACTICES

A majority of Mexican immigrants and Mexican Americans relied most frequently on traditional medical beliefs and practices to resolve health problems up through the first decade of the twentieth century. In some situations, a physical ailment might easily be alleviated or eliminated by herbs or other natural medicines or remedies. These cures, prescribed most often by mothers or grandmothers, represented the accumulated knowledge gained from personal experience or observation of others passed down from generation to generation. On those occasions in which relief from a specific affliction was not achieved through home remedies, however, individuals or families might solicit the assistance of a *curandero* (folk curer) or other type of folk healer.

In general, all folk healers possessed a certain *don*, or God-given gift or ability, that provided them the power to restore the health of others. They might accomplish this through the use of herbs (*yerberos*, or herbalists), massages or oils, and/or the aid of the spirit of another more powerful healer serving as a medium between this more potent spirit and the afflicted person (Leo R. Chávez and Victor M. Torres, *The Handbook ... Anthropology*, p. 227). Alternatively, some used cards to divine an illness or to prescribe a remedy (Chávez and Torres, pp. 229-30).

Curanderos have also been used to cure ailments more readily recognizable to the medical establishment in the United States. It was not uncommon for some Mexican Americans to seek assistance from both a *curandero* and a physician. Several factors prompted the first generations of Mexican Americans in the late nineteenth and early twentieth centuries to rely more readily on folk healers than on practitioners of the U.S. medical community. The geographic isolation of the rural areas in which they settled or the segregated neighborhoods in which they lived in the cities combined with limited financial resources to restrict the options available to most people or families for several generations. Even those with ready access to medical assistance often were more confident in relying on a local curandero because of the faith their parents and grandparents had placed in these traditional curers or because of the more personal approach they employed. In many cases, the healers were likely to be acquainted with the family and involved relatives in the evaluation or treatment of an illness (Trotter, p. 44). The emotional bond established by the folk healer with the patient was a consistent and compelling element promoting greater trust in these traditional health providers.

"I went to the doctor. He made me get undressed and put on a little robe. He examined my hands and knees. Then he told me I had rheumatism. I already knew that! He said he couldn't do anything for me, just give me a shot. He charged me $15; now I go to him only when I feel real sick and need the drugs. Otherwise I go see [a healer]. I don't know why but I have more confidence and faith in him. He gives me herbs, and I feel fine."

Cited from Robert Trotter, *Curanderismo*, p. 51.

As more Mexican Americans emigrated to large cities and greater numbers moved into more integrated settings, a higher percentage of them came to depend on practitioners and services of the U.S. medical community, occasioned either by easier access to these facilities, by the availability of medical insurance through their employers, or because of decreasing contact with families maintaining ties to traditional health practices. By the 1950s, research revealed that the primary source of health care for a dominant percentage of Mexican Americans had become doctors and clinics of the modern medical establishment. Surveys in the 1970s and 1980s in various urban areas of California suggested that as low as five percent of those polled had consulted a folk healer to resolve a health problem. Other studies showed that though close to 50 percent in some mixed urban and rural areas expressed faith in

curanderos, over 90 percent of the same sample proclaimed confidence in medical doctors (*Family and Mental Health in the Mexican American Community*, edited by Susan E. Keefe and J. Manuel Casas, pp. 10-11).

Though their importance among Mexican Americans has diminished considerably over the last century, folk healers remain as a viable source for assistance with illness. J. Diego Vigil asserts that "some very acculturated Latinos accept the validity of diagnoses and traditional cures" of these healers (Chávez and Torres, p. 223). Second-generation families living in rural areas may have easier access to curanderos and therefore use them more frequently, and these curers may still consult with urban dwellers whose family medical doctors, despite the advances in contemporary medicine, are ineffective in treating a given ailment.

HEALTH PROBLEMS OF THE MEXICAN AMERICAN COMMUNITY

Though Mexican Americans manifest no congenital diseases that are group-specific, the rates at which they contract certain maladies are considerably above the national average. Some of these diseases are more evident among certain sectors of the Mexican American population, while others are common to the entire community.

The incidence of diabetes is greater among obese persons and studies have shown that one-third of all Mexican Americans fall in this category, the highest rate among Hispanics in the United States. Among those of the 45-74 age group, 23.9 percent had diabetes. Poor eating habits and/or inadequate diets contributed directly to its prevalence (Chávez and Torres, p. 235).

According to recent studies, 14 percent of all AIDS cases in the United States occurred among the Hispanic community and, as a group, they were 2.7 times more likely to contract this disease than Anglo Americans. Evidence of higher rates of AIDS within the migrant farmworking community (a considerable proportion of which is still Mexican or Mexican American) became more pronounced in the 1990s. The mobile nature of existence of this specific populace facilitates its dissemination, as does a lower frequency of condom use (Chávez and Torres, p. 236). Farmworkers are also at higher risk of exposure to tuberculosis. In comparison to the overall population of the United States, they are six times as likely to fall victim to this disease.

Alcoholism afflicts Hispanics at two to three times the national average. Mexican Americans and Puerto Ricans suffer the highest rates. Alcohol abuse is eight percent to 12 percent higher for all age groups among Mexican Americans as compared to "non-Hispanic whites" in these same categories (*The Statistical Record ...*, p. 434). The highest frequencies occur in those families of low economic stability, and many of those afflicted are unaware of, or ineligible for, treatment programs. Cirrhosis of the liver is the most common cause of death for these specific individuals. The frequency level for this disease is 40 percent higher among Mexican Americans than among Anglo Americans.

The underutilization of medical services represents one of the most pressing health issues among a significant proportion of the Mexican American population. For second-generation families whose contacts with Anglo American society have been limited and whose disposable income is low, such fundamental considerations as inadequate language skills, lack of transportation, or inability to pay for services reduce the possibilities for using or even seeking health care facilities. Public health facilities have decreased in number in some urban zones of heavy Hispanic population. In rural areas, medical assistance may be too distant, poorly staffed, or offer medical technologies of limited capacity to detect or cure more complex ailments. Preventative health measures are a privilege too expensive to consider for those whose income is at survival-level.

MENTAL HEALTH

Research in the 1960s in Texas and California revealed that the proportionate number of Mexicans and Mexican Americans receiving psychiatric assistance in public facilities was significantly lower than their overall population in these areas. The findings in Texas prompted sociologist E. G. Jaco to suggest that Mexican Americans might in fact suffer less from mental illnesses than the Anglo American population, a premise that seemed to contradict generally held assumptions regarding immigrant groups and their families raised in foreign countries—specifically, that individuals of such groups were more likely than people of the dominant culture in a given society to exhibit a higher prevalence of mental disorders due to the psychological stress and tension generated by the immigration experience, discrimination, and the acculturation process in general.

Jaco proposed that the existence of strong, supportive family ties among the Mexican and Mexican American population might explain the lower proportion of patients of this ethnic community at these facilities, but other theories have since been put forth. The most often-repeated assertions, some of which have been posited with little or insufficient supporting material to defend their contentions, have suggested that: Mexican and Mexican Americans are more tolerant of psychiatric disorders than Anglo Americans and seek assistance with lower frequency; they suffer from just as many disorders but manifest these conditions more often in criminal behavior, alcoholism and other addictions; they are too proud or sensitive to expose such psychological problems, especially in facilities staffed mainly by Anglo Americans; they utilize priests and family physicians instead of public health specialists or they return to Mexico to seek a cure.

LANGUAGE

Spanish has remained the principal, if not sole, language of almost all Mexicans in the southwestern United States for many decades after the signing of the Treaty of Guadalupe Hidalgo. Since the overwhelming majority of the first generations of Mexican immigrants moved to areas already populated predominantly by people of their heritage and worked side-by-side with these individuals in the same jobs, the need for them to learn more than rudimentary English was of minor importance. Proximity to Mexico and the continued entry of additional immigrants constantly revitalized the culture and native language of those who chose to become permanent residents of the United States.

In the twentieth century, as the proportion of second- and third-generation Mexican American families increased and some of their members moved into a wider range of professions in which more of their co-workers were non-Hispanic, proficiency in English became practical and necessary for many. In addition, heightening exposure of the younger generations of Mexican Americans to Anglo American education meant that English became a fundamental part of their curriculum. Moreover, the use of Spanish in and outside the classroom was strongly discouraged and sometimes even prohibited in many school systems until mid-century and beyond. Of equally substantial and enduring impact, English was introduced to ever greater numbers of Hispanic households by means of television. Though few lower income Mexican American families could afford this form of entertainment in the 1950s, it had entered most living rooms by the end of the next decade and brought the language (as well as other aspects) of Anglo American culture nightly to the ears of a growing Mexican American audience.

The persistence of high immigration levels did not allow Spanish to disappear from this community, regardless of the encroachments made by English in their public and private lives, and the Chicano movement of the late 1960s and 1970s renewed the pride of many Mexican Americans in their heritage and in the Spanish language. In the 1980s there were still over 100 Spanish-language newspapers in circulation within the United States, approximately 500 radio stations, and 130 television stations whose programming was partially or completely in Spanish.

MEXICAN SPANISH AND THE LANGUAGE OF MEXICAN AMERICANS

Some families in more remote parts of northern New Mexico still speak a Spanish quite similar to the language spoken in Spain at the time of the arrival of the first conquistadors in the Americas. On the other hand, later immigrants, like their immediate ancestors, speak Mexican Spanish. This language differs from Castilian Spanish in the pronunciation of certain consonants and consonant and vowel combinations but is more strikingly distinct in aspects of vocabulary, where the influence of pre-Columbian indigenous languages have added to the language spoken in Mexico. Such words most often apply to agriculture and the natural world. For example, the native word for "grass," *zacate*, replaced the Spanish word *hierba*, and *guajolote* and *tecolote*, of Indian derivation, replaced the Spanish words for "turkey" and "owl."

The Spanish spoken by Mexican Americans is "a spoken and informal dialect" (González-Berry, p. 304). It varies to some extent depending on the rural or urban identity of the speaker, his/her economic standing, length of time in the United States, and level of education. Though some scholars have maintained that Mexican American Spanish may be separated or differentiated by geographic zone in the United States, the intramigration among these areas has made a clear delineation between them difficult. In general terms, it is characterized by and distinguished

from Mexican Spanish in differences between the enunciation of certain sounds. For example, whereas the standard Spanish words for "soldier" and the pronoun "you" are respectively *soldado* and *usted*, the corresponding words in Mexican American Spanish for many speakers have altered to *soldau* and *usté* through the elimination of the consonant of the last syllable. Transformations of certain verb conjugations are evident also in Mexican American Spanish, such as the shift from *decía* ("I/she/he/you were saying") to *dijía* (González-Berry, p. 305). Markedly evident also is the incorporation of English words to Spanish, with the appropriate orthographic changes to make the specific terminology more similar in sound to Spanish, for example, *troca* for "truck," *parquear* for "park," or *lonche* for "lunch."

Still prevalent among various urban groups of young Mexican Americans is the use of *caló*, a variation of Mexican Spanish which employs slang from Mexican Spanish, African American English, and Anglo American English to create a new vocabulary. It was used much more extensively in urban settings in the Southwest during the 1940s and 1950s by members of the younger generation who wished to set themselves apart from their parents. As González-Berry illustrates, the combination of languages used in *caló* make it comprehensible only to those who use it, as may be seen by the phrase *gasofla pá la ranfla*—"gas for the car" (p. 306).

Those Mexican Americans who have been exposed extensively to English and Spanish and employ both languages actively in speaking or writing may move from one language to another within a given sentence, a linguistic phenomenon referred to as "code-switching." The alternation may be caused by a momentary memory lapse by the speaker, with use of proper nouns, or when a specific word has no exact equivalent in the other language. The result occasioned by one or more of these factors might be a sentence such as: "*Mucha gente no sabe* where Magnolia Street is" ("Many people don't know where Magnolia Street is") (Lipski, *The Hispanic American Almanac*, p. 224). This linguistic tendency was once perceived in a negative light, and in the case of some speakers is indicative of lexical deficiencies. An expanding percentage of Mexican Americans, however, are now "coordinate bilinguals," able to separate English from Spanish completely and use either language effectively and persuasively depending upon the situation or need (Olivia Arrieta, *The Handbook … Anthropology*, p. 166). Code-switching when employed by these bilinguals by no means signifies confusion or insufficient linguistic aptitude to distinguish between the two languages but rather an attempt to use the most appropriate phrase to convey a certain word or notion (Lipski, p. 224).

LANGUAGE ISSUES

Despite high levels of Mexican immigration and strong pride in their Hispanic heritage, the primary language of Mexican Americans is English, and with each new generation born in the United States the use of Spanish becomes less frequent in many families. U.S. Census Bureau statistics for 1976 revealed that 68 percent of the Mexican American population possessed good language proficiency in English. According to Meier, polls taken in the 1990s indicate that though 90 percent of those Mexican Americans questioned asserted an ability to speak and comprehend Spanish, only 5.3 percent confirmed that they spoke the language at home (p. 245). Census figures for 1990 calculate that though 65 percent of Mexican Americans "speak a language other than English," 97.8 percent of those persons five years of age and over professed to an "ability to speak English" (1990 Census of Population—Persons of Hispanic Origin in the United States, p. 86).

In addition to the factor of progressive acculturation, these figures also in part reflect the effect of bilingual education programs nationwide, programs that began in significant numbers in the late 1960s with passage of the Bilingual Education Act of 1968 but multiplied considerably in the 1970s due to a decision rendered by the U.S. Supreme Court in the case of Lau v. Nichols in 1974. This verdict affirmed that those schools not able or willing to provide language instruction to children of immigrants whose skills in English were deficient were acting in violation of the Civil Rights Act of 1964 and the Fourteenth Amendment to the Constitution. By the close of the 1970s there were still four states in which bilingual instruction was forbidden. Spending for these classes had increased to $107 million (Cortés, p. 715).

The movement to bilingual instruction in the public schools was not received positively by all sectors of society in the United States in this period, however. Towards the end of the 1970s and in the initial years of the 1980s, various individuals and organizations set out to reverse a perceived trend towards bilingualism and/or biculturalism/multiculturalism in the United States, which they saw as a threat to the dominant Anglo American culture. In 1978 Emmy Shafer established the organization English Only and in 1983 United States English was founded, a group whose annual budget is now $5 million with a membership of 400,000. One of the priorities of this second group has been to secure passage of the English Language Amendment, thereby declaring English as the official language in the United States. Though they had not achieved this goal at the national level as of 1995, 21 states had passed legislation to this effect. Opponents of these proposals assert that the United States has never been monolingual or monocultural and that attempts to establish national or local restrictive language policies are anti-immigrationist and racist.

Though virtually all Mexican Americans endorse the need to learn English and have supported programs in bilingual instruction as a prerequisite to academic and professional advance in the United States, many have found fault with the "language immersion" or "transitional" approaches employed in a large percentage of bilingual programs, which place little or no importance on the retention of the students' native language or culture as they learn English. A method far less commonly employed but defended more positively by many Mexican Americans is "maintenance bilingual instruction," a technique that utilizes the speaker's language of origin to teach English but never abandons the use of the native language nor denies the importance of the student's ethnicity. The goal of this popular alternative is to make the learner totally functional in the two languages in terms of reading, writing, and speaking (Arreta, p. 186). The English Plus proposal endorsed by the League of Latin American Citizens (LULAC), which asserts the necessity of acquiring fluency in English for Hispanics yet also reaffirms the importance of maintaining identity with Hispanic values, has received the support of many Hispanic groups in the United States.

FAMILY AND COMMUNITY DYNAMICS

The average size of the Mexican American family in 1989 was 4.1 persons, as compared to 3.1 for non-Hispanic and 3.8 for all Hispanic families residing in the United States. Though the birth rate among Mexican American women remains high in comparison to the national average and 43 percent of the Mexican American population was 14 years of age or under in 1989, the size of this family has declined slowly over the past generations. In 1991, among Mexican-origin families in the United States, 73.5 percent were headed by married couples, and 19.1 percent were female-headed, a figure approximately three percent higher than for non-Hispanic groupings. Among female-headed families, 49 percent were below the poverty line in terms of income. According to the 1990 census, 7.8 percent of Mexican American men over 15 years of age were divorced, as opposed to 6.4 percent of the women in this same category. In 1989 13.5 percent of Mexican American households received public assistance. The mean for this specific income per household was $4,359 (*1990 Census of Population …*).

Intermarriage between Mexicans/Mexican Americans and Anglo Americans was prevalent in the mid-nineteenth century and increased slowly in subsequent generations. After World War II, due in part to a slow movement towards residential integration and greater and more widespread social mobility, the incidence of intermarriage increased at more rapid rates, especially in urban settings. In the mid 1980s in the states of the Southwest of highest Hispanic population, intermarriage rates varied from nine to 27 percent in Texas, 27 to 29 percent in New Mexico, and 51 to 55 percent in California (Rosina Becerra, in Mindel, *Ethnic Families in America: Patterns and Variations*, p. 156). Male exogamy was slightly higher than female exogamy for the same period and occurred most frequently among third-generation Mexican Americans.

TRADITION AND CHANGE IN FAMILY STRUCTURE AND ROLES

In the mid-nineteenth century *la familia*, or the extended family, included aunts and uncles, as well as grandparents and even great grandparents. Beyond these direct familial ties between generations, *compadres* (co-parents) were most often an integral part of these groupings, as were adopted children and intimate friends, in many instances. As close, personal friends of the mother or father of a child, the *padrinos* (godfathers) or *madrinas* (godmothers) developed a special relationship with their *ahijados* (godchildren), a relationship that started in definitive terms at his/her baptism. From this point forward, in most instances, they provided emotional, financial , or any other form

of assistance or advice their *ahijados* might require past that afforded by their actual parents, especially in times of family crisis. They were also essential participants in all events of social or religious importance to the godchild and maintained strong bonds with their *compadres* or *comadres*— lasting friendships based upon mutual admiration and support. As much as any immediate family member, godparents contributed to strong family unity (Griswold del Castillo, p. 42).

A patriarchal hierarchy prescribed a system of male dominance in the traditional family. As the authority figure, the husband was the principal, if not the sole, breadwinner. He made the important social and economic decisions and was the protector of the family's integrity. Wives had general control over household matters but were expected to be obedient and submissive to their husbands (Maxine Baca Zinn, *The Handbook … Sociology*, p. 164). Though the wife might perform work outside the household, this was usually an acceptable alternative only in cases of extreme economic duress. In such cases, her efforts were limited to a restricted number of options, almost always of a part-time nature, and contributed nothing to improve her subservient status within the house. This division of authority established between man and wife was perpetuated by their offspring. Girls were taught distinct behavior patterns and were encouraged to adopt specifically defined aspirations quite different from their brothers, beginning at an early age. Motherhood was the ideal objective of all young girls and the primary virtue of all those who achieved it (Zinn, p. 167).

This system of mutual dependence and respect for elders created a close-knit family unit. Family honor and unity were of paramount significance. If problems arose for individual members, the immediate or extended family could be relied upon to resolve the issue. Important decisions were always made with first consideration given to the needs of the group rather than the individual. Traditional social and religious practices passed from one generation to the next virtually unchanged because they were perceived as intrinsic values to the family's cultural heritage.

While extended family households are less common today, the importance of the family as a unit and the ties between these units and their extended members remains strong. Newly arrived immigrants generally continue to seek out relatives in the United States, as did the initial generations after 1848, and may rely upon these individuals and their families for temporary residence as well as assistance in arranging employment, especially in rural regions. Though in a majority of instances each successive generation born in the United States tends to exhibit reduced dependence on extended kin, birthdays, baptisms, marriages, and other family celebrations bring relatives together with a pronounced regularity (Robert R. Alvarez, Jr., *The Hispanic American Almanac*, p. 171).

Modifications also have occurred in the pattern of male dominance and division of work by gender within these families. In the United States in the generations immediately subsequent to 1848, economic necessities provided the initial impulse toward a more egalitarian relationship between husband and wife. The specific forms of employment assumed by the Mexican American husband in the southwestern region during these years frequently made his absence necessary from the household for long periods of time; while drovers, miners, farmworkers, and other laborers often strayed considerable distances from their families in pursuit of work or in performing their labors, the wife was left as the authority figure. Though the male almost always assumed total control upon his return, accommodations or compromise might alter the structure of power within the family somewhat, and it was not uncommon for women to continue to exert a more pronounced role in decision making in those families where this pattern of male absence was prolonged and repetitive (Griswold del Castillo, p. 34).

As a growing proportion of Mexican American women moved into the full-time labor force in the early decades of the twentieth century and thereafter, alterations in role patterns and the division of responsibilities were manifested in greater frequencies. Though in some cases, especially in the early years of the century, the family was less male dominant, equal hours of work outside the house for the wife generally helped to initiate a progressively more egalitarian arrangement with the family structure.

The contemporary Mexican American family exhibits a wide range of decision making patterns, including that of male-authoritarianism. Most, but not all, studies in the 1980s and early 1990s have concluded that both parents generally share in the day-to-day management of the family and in determining responses to matters of critical importance to this unit. Among others, Ybarra contends that "egalitarianism is the predominant conjugal role arrangement in Chicano families" (*Journal of Marriage and Family* 1982, p. 177). The mother, as before, is generally seen as the individual most responsible for meeting the domestic needs of husband and children, but in those families in which she has become the disciplinarian, she has frequently found this role is in conflict with her traditional identity as nurturer (Chavira-Prado, p. 258). Alvarez contends that, as in many contemporary cultures, though women most often have taken on new and varied roles, men have altered little with respect to their low participatory level related to household chores (*The Handbook ...*, p. 165). Despite the fact that actual family dynamics reveal general egalitarianism, deference to the father as the ultimate authority remains the ideal behavior pattern (Alvarez, *The Hispanic American Almanac*, p. 172).

CHILDREARING AND DATING PRACTICES

Fairly rigid sex roles were maintained for Mexican American children well into the twentieth century. Beginning in colonial times in Mexico, young girls were taught the tasks and skills of their mother from an early age. The eldest daughter was initially always given the chore of caring for her younger siblings, but, after reaching puberty, the eldest brother replaced her in this responsibility (Becerra, pp. 149-50).

Whereas girls, up through adolescence, were restricted in their activities and spent much time together with their sisters at home, boys of the same age group were given more liberties and were allowed to venture outside the household with peers. There were rules of proper etiquette that prevailed in large cities and small towns for dating. Chaperoning was most common, if not required. Young unwed women were to be perceived by the community as the ideal figures in terms of social behavior. Adolescent boys, on the other hand, were not monitored as closely. The male was seen as "a fledgling (sic) macho who must be allowed to venture out of the home so he may test his wings and establish a masculine identity" (Alfredo Mirandé and Evangelina Enríquez, *La Chicana: The Mexican-American Woman*, 1979, p. 114).

Teen marriages were most prevalent in Mexican American families into the first decades of the twentieth century. The premarital procedures involved in joining a couple in matrimony varied depending on the social background of the families. Up until the 1920s and perhaps later in rural areas, a *portador* (go-between) would deliver a written proposal of marriage to the father of the would-be bride. Fathers decided on the acceptability of the suitor based on the apparent moral respectability of the young man and his family, and though the opinions of his spouse and daughter were important in the final decision as to marriage, the father might often overrule the wishes of either or both of these individuals (Williams, pp. 27-30).

Except among the most traditional Mexican American families, childrearing and dating practices have changed substantially over the past few generations. Among other studies finding similar conclusions, Jesse T. Zapata and Pat T. Jaramillo have found that parents rarely ascribe pronounced roles determined by sex to their children (*Hispanic Journal of Behavioral Sciences* 3, No. 3, p. 286). Family commitments or responsibilities may still curtail the social activities of young girls more than boys, but equal privileges within the family arrangement are the norm rather than the exception. Girls may be monitored more closely in their dating patterns, but few of the restrictions that once prevailed now determine their behavior. Premarital chastity is still expected of young Chicanas, but as Mirandé and Enríquez affirmed, though "premarital virginity prevails ... its enforcement may prove more difficult today than in the past" (p. 114). Parents have far-reduced and sometimes incidental influence with regard to the selection of marriage partners for their offspring, except in the most traditional families, but their sentiments on the issue are most always considered of significance.

EDUCATION

The desire of low-income migrant families from Mexico to provide their children with opportunities for education in the late 1800s and early 1900s was counterbalanced by more fundamental needs: the wages paid these immigrants for their labors in the fields, mines, factories, or railways were most often so low that families needed the additional income provided by their children to meet the basic necessities required for survival. Attendance at the primary level of instruction was relatively high, provided that schools were available in the predominantly rural areas where the first generations of Mexican immigrants resided. But progress past this level and on into secondary schools was less common because of economic factors. The mobile nature of farm and railworker families made it difficult for children to maintain a continuity in their schooling. Finally, the schools and

teachers in these rural areas were of inferior quality. It was hard for parents to maintain a positive attitude about the long-range significance of attending classes since it quickly became apparent to most that, as with other families before them, it would only be a matter of time before economic factors would force them to pull their children out of classes or at least reduce the number of hours or days that they could attend school.

Low-income immigrant families, as well as those with greater financial stability whose children consequently had a better chance of staying in school, were dissuaded from adopting a more positive attitude toward the U.S. educational system because of the tendency of teachers and administrators to deny the existence or importance of Catholic or Hispanic traditions in favor of those held by the majority population. The assimilationist philosophy endorsed by the public school system was designed "to shape desirable behaviors for functioning in America" and encourage uniformity of perspective regardless of differences in the ethnic heritage among the student population (Guadalupe San Miguel, Jr., *The Handbook ... Anthropology*, p. 293). Texts as well as curricula in the public schools well into the twentieth century disregarded or acknowledged only minimally the role and/or contributions of minority peoples to the socioeconomic historic development of the United States.

Religious orders staffed most Catholic schools in the latter decades of the nineteenth century, many of which were located in areas of high Mexican and Mexican American population. Though not founded specifically to educate Hispanics, these schools attracted significant numbers of Mexican Americans because of their religious orientation. However, as public education facilities began to proliferate at the end of the century, an ever-smaller percentage of Chicanos attended parochial schools, either because of easier access to public institutions or because of the cost factor involved with Catholic education (San Miguel, p. 293). By the 1960s, though the Mexican American population of the United States was close to 90 percent Catholic, only 15 percent of Spanish-surname students in Los Angeles attended grades one through six in Catholic institutions, whereas in San Antonio 21 percent attended grades one through eight (Grebler, p. 475). The proportion of Mexican Americans in parochial schools in the 1990s remains at similar or lower levels.

Beginning in the first decades of the twentieth century and continuing thereafter, as greater numbers of Mexican Americans moved to an urban setting, the opportunities for public school education increased measurably. Alternative sources of employment were more plentiful in the cities, and, though a majority of Mexican Americans continued to experience wage discrimination during these decades, the possible advantages of higher levels of education related to salary and employment options made academic preparation more attractive. Segregated educational facilities were the rule, however, until mid-century and beyond. The suits brought by *Menendez v. Westminster School District* in Southern California and *Delgado v. Bastrop Independent School District* represented important steps in the 1940s toward the outlawing of segregation, but some school systems practiced "integration" by joining Mexican American and Afro American students rather than combining these minorities with predominantly Anglo American students (Cortés, p. 718). The separate educational facilities provided to minority students were most often poorly maintained, staffed by undertrained instructors, and provided with inadequate supplies.

As segregated facilities have slowly diminished over time, Mexican Americans who have entered integrated schools have often been classified as "learning disabled" because of linguistic deficiencies or inadequate academic preparation afforded by their previous learning institutions. This factor has caused many of these students to be channeled into "developmentally appropriate" classes or curricular tracks (San Miguel, p. 303). It was only in the late 1960s that the judicial system took steps to mandate the establishment of bilingual programs in education, but continued strong funding for these programs has been challenged by many groups at national and local levels. The pedagogical approach adopted by the vast majority of bilingual programs has stressed rapid conversion to the use of English without regard for the maintenance of skills in the native languages of first- and second-generation immigrants.

Leaders of the Chicano movement focused much of their energies on educational issues. They emphasized the need to lower the high school dropout rate, expand the number of bilingual/bicultural programs, increase the availability of fellowships for Mexican Americans at the college level, support the recruitment of higher percentages of Hispanic instructors and administrators at all levels of the educational system, and diversify class offerings by establishing new courses and programs in Chicano studies (Cortés, p. 718). Several student organizations have evolved to provide forums for the discussion and wider propagation of issues fundamental to improving educational opportunities for Mexican American students. In 1969 a conference at the University of California, Santa Barbara, attempted to unite many of these organizations under MECHA (*Movimiento Estudiantil Chicano de Aztlán*—Chicano Student Movement of Aztlán). A *Plan de Santa Barbara* (Santa Barbara Plan) was formulated related to the procedures necessary for the development of degree programs in Chicano studies (Meier, in McWilliams, p. 287). Strategies emerging from this reunion and other meetings of an academic focus among Mexican Americans have resulted in the creation of a growing number of Chicano studies programs nationwide. These programs feature courses and curricula of more definitive relevance to students at advanced education levels. In 1972 the National Association of Chicano Studies (NACS) was founded, an organization for college students and professors that sponsors annual conferences oriented to social, economic, literary, and other themes pertinent to Mexican Americans. A special session of the annual meeting in 1982 brought under discussion the need to champion recognition and participation by Mexican American women in this organization, a goal that has been accomplished in large part since that time (Teresa Córdova, *The Handbook … Sociology*, p. 185).

According to U.S. Census Bureau estimates for 1991, 50.5 percent of the "Mexican-origin" population 35 years of age and over had completed four years of high school or more, and 7.4 percent of this same age category had attended four years of college or more. As of 1985, 27.8 percent of women in the United States designated under the identical classification had studied four years or more in high school, whereas 4.6 percent had continued on to four or more years of college. Significant differences existed between first- and second-generation families and their levels of educational attainment in 1988: 34 percent of the first generation received a high school degree while 65 percent of the next generation reached this level (Steven F. Arvizu, *The Handbook … Anthropology*, p. 288). Though the number of Hispanics with advanced degrees remains low, this number has risen in a consistent, albeit slow, pattern since the 1970s.

THE ROLE OF WOMEN

Beginning in the late 1960s and in increasing proportions thereafter, Mexican American women began to write about themes directly oriented to the socioeconomic and political challenges that had confronted them over many generations: gender/race-based discriminatory practices in almost all areas of the labor market; inequities in educational opportunities and lack of sufficient local or federal support to alter this situation; the specific needs of Chicana women in poor Mexican American neighborhoods (health care, physical abuse, and unemployment, among others); Chicana prisoner abuse and rights; welfare rights and child care issues; lack of equitable political enfranchisement; and the virtual nonexistence of gender-specific political representation at local, state, or national levels (Córdova, pp. 177-80).

In the 1970s and early 1980s a significant number of Mexican American women were intrigued, but most often not attracted, by the ideas emerging from the women's movement in the United States. Though, as Maria Gonzalez affirms, it "provided the example and the language with which Hispanic women could challenge traditional attitudes towards women's roles," several basic perspectives identified with the movement were seen in a negative light by most Mexican American women. While they were aware of the need to react to oppression from within and without the Mexican American community, they judged the declarations of Anglo American feminists as somewhat excessive in their demands for independence and self-autonomy and contended that such stances, if adopted by Chicanas, might function to disrupt the unity of the Mexican American family. They also were disenchanted by a perceived racism that was made evident to them from occurrences at various national women's association conferences. As synthesized by María González: "What has emerged from Hispanic women's experience with feminism is an acknowledgment by Hispanic feminists of pride in their traditional heritage but with a realistic attitude toward its limitations, as well as an acknowledgment of the limitations of feminism" (*The Hispanic-American Almanac*, p. 356).

Since the 1960s many notable advances for women and women's issues within the Mexican American community have been made. Melba J. T. Vásquez cites two studies (Gándara and Avery) of the 1980s on "high-achieving" Chicanas that suggest a dilemma of a different dimension for these women when set in the context of Mexican American social history in the United States. In both studies, it was revealed that, as opposed to Anglo American professional women, Mexican American women in industry, academia, and politics married at significantly lower rates and, of those who married, only 56 percent of them had children. Avery concluded that for these specific females, "the conflicts involved in maintaining roles within and outside the home may be perceived as too overwhelming and the availability of male partners of comparable educational backgrounds may be limited" (quoted in Vásquez in *Chicano Psychology*, second edition, edited by Joe L. Martínez and Richard H. Mendoza, p. 42).

For the pronounced majority of Chicanas, however, the move to a position of equality in North American society has yet to begin or is hardly commencing. Insufficient opportunity for an adequate education to allow them to compete in an increasingly challenging job market condemns too many of them to unemployment, underemployment, or work in professions with little promise for upward mobility and jobs with decent salaries. Many Chicanas remain in oppressed situations within their own community, held back by gender-based traditions that deny them a chance to alter their role and define a new identity. The positive advances of the minority of Mexican American women must be viewed by the majority, however, as a promise for a better future.

CUISINE

The basic diet of the inhabitants of Mexico has changed little from the beginning years of recorded human history in the area to the present period. Corn, beans, squash, and tomatoes were staples until the arrival of the Spaniards in the early 1500s. The culinary preferences of these Europeans, plus the addition of some items from trade centered in Manila brought pork, beef, rice, and various spices, among other foods, to the diet of this region.

Pork and beef, in steaks or stews, along with chicken, were the meats eaten in those areas from which migration to the United States was highest in 1848 and subsequent decades. This same cuisine forms the day-to-day food of most contemporary Mexican Americans: prepared with tomato-based sauces flavored by a variety of chiles and/or spices or herbs such as cumin and cilantro, one of these meats is generally served with rice, beans, and corn tortillas.

On festive occasions such as religious holidays or family reunions, one or more of the following traditional meals consumed in Mexico are prepared by most Mexican American families: *tamales* (shredded and spiced pork or beef caked within cornmeal and wrapped in a corn husk before steaming); *enchiladas* (corn tortillas lightly fried in oil then wrapped around sliced chicken, shredded beef, cheese, or ground beef and various spices and coated with a tomato and chile sauce before baking); *mole* (most often chicken, but sometimes pork, combined with a sauce of chiles, chocolate, ground sesame or pumpkin seeds, garlic, and various other spices, slow-cooked under a low flame on the stove); *chilaquiles* (dried tortilla chips complemented by cheeses, chile, and perhaps *chorizo*—spiced sausage—and/or chicken and a tomato-based sauce of green or red chile stirred into a hash-like dish on the stove); *chiles rellenos* (green chiles stuffed with a white cheese and fried in an egg batter that adheres to the chiles); and *posole* (a soup-like stew which contains hominy as its essential ingredient, as well as stew meat and various spices).

Though some ingredients of the meals described above are at times somewhat difficult to find in major supermarkets in the United States, the proximity of Mexico makes it possible for small markets that specialize in Mexican food to obtain and sell these items at a reasonable price.

TRADITIONAL CLOTHING

The clothing identified as most traditional by Mexicans and Mexican Americans and, according to Olga Nájera-Ramírez, recognized as "official national symbols of Mexico," is now worn most frequently at festivals of historic importance to these people. Men dress as *charros*, or Mexican cowboys, and wear wide-brimmed *sombreros* along with tailored jackets and pants lined with silver or shining metal buttons. Women dress in *China Poblana* outfits, which include a white peasant blouse and a flaring red skirt adorned with sequins of different colors. This apparel is linked most closely in socio-historical terms to people of more humble origin in Mexico.

HOLIDAYS CELEBRATED BY MEXICAN AMERICANS

Two secular holidays of national importance in Mexico are celebrated by a significant number of Mexican Americans. Mexican Independence Day is celebrated on the 16th of September. Commemorating the date that the priest Miguel Hidalgo y Costilla initiated the war for liberation from Spain with the *grito*, or call to battle, "Viva Mexico y mueran los gachupines" ("Long live Mexico and death to all *gachupines*"—a derogatory term for Spaniards used during the colonial period and afterwards), part of the festivities may include the pronouncement of the grito and/or a mass with *mariachis* (Mexican street bands), followed possibly by a speech or parade. In that the central idea related to this date is ethnic solidarity, many of the participants wear the *charro* and *China Poblana* outfits. Along with traditional plates such as *mole*, other condiments and food served on this date traditionally stress the colors of the Mexican flag: white, red, and green. These items may include rice, limes, avocados, chopped tomatoes, peppers, and onions (Eunice Romero Gwynn and Douglas Gwynn *The Handbook ... Anthropology*, p. 366).

Perhaps the most widely recognized Mexican holiday celebrated by Mexicans and Mexican Americans residing in the United States, as well as by other Hispanics nationwide, commemorates the victory of Mexican troops in the Battle of Puebla over the invading French army on May 5, 1862. The Cinco de Mayo celebration may include parades or other festivities and, as with Independence Day, reinforces for many Mexican Americans a sense of ethnic brotherhood. Many Anglo Americans join in commemorating this date, though its historic importance is known by only a negligible number of revellers.

RELIGION

Approximately 75 percent of the Mexican American population are of the Catholic faith, and in the southwestern United States over two-thirds of the Catholics are Mexican or Mexican American (Julián Samora, *A History of the Mexican-American People*, p. 232). Despite their numerical importance within this church, however, the first Mexican American bishop was not ordained until 1970 and, as of 1992, only 19 of 360 bishops in the country were of Hispanic origin. In recent decades, attempts have been made by church hierarchy to establish a stronger bond between Mexican Americans and the Catholic church in the United States, but various factors and events over time since 1848 created a rift that remains clearly defined between this specific laity and the

Rene Poblano, a member of the Xipe Totec Aztec dance group, blows through a conch shell to celebrate Cinco de Mayo in this 1993 photograph.

institutional church with which they are nominally affiliated (Silvia Novo Pena, *The Hispanic-American Almanac*, p. 367).

MEXICAN AMERICANS AND THE CATHOLIC CHURCH IN THE UNITED STATES

The presence of the Catholic church on Mexico's northern frontier was weak throughout the first half of the nineteenth century, due in part to the attempts of liberals to reduce its economic and political power nationwide, but also because of the death, departure. or expulsion of Spanish clerics from the region and the failure of the church to replace them (Cortés, p. 710). By 1846 there were only 16 Catholic priests in the lands that were to become the states of California, Arizona, and New Mexico (Alberto L. Pulido, in *Perspectives in Mexican American Studies* IV, p. 106).

Beginning in the colonial period, and increasingly so in the nineteenth century, Mexicans living in the rural areas of this region evolved a "self-reliant," popular religiosity. Though based upon fundamental Catholic tenets, this form of religion manifested practices that deviated in notable ways from those endorsed by the institutional church, especially so after 1848 (Moisés Sandoval, *On the Move: A History of the Hispanic Church in the United States*, p. 21). Home altars and devotional tables became the center of prayer for this isolated laity, and parents or grandparents often instructed the younger members of the family in religious matters. Feasts, festivities, and processions to honor saints or events of historical religious significance became the principal means for local believers to share religion on a community level. Pilgrimages to shrines took on added importance for those hoping for divine intervention in times of despair (Anthony Stevens-Arroyo and Ana María Díaz-Stevens, *The Handbook ... Sociology*, p. 270). A more pronounced devotion to certain saints or the Virgin Mary in one of her various identities frequently dominated a believer's prayers. Religious brotherhoods, such as *Los Hermanos Penitentes* (the Confraternity of Our Father, Jesus of Nazarene) in northern New Mexico and southern Colorado—operating in the absence of priests—directed holy ceremonies for those in the surrounding communities, taught doctrine to the young, and conducted penitential rituals (Sandoval, p. 22).

By the mid-1850s the lands taken over by the United States were included in newly created dioceses placed under the control of bishops and vicars whose origin or heritage, much like the newly ordained clergy of the period, most frequently was European. These leaders were prompt to voice protests over the religious practices of the Mexican laity and priests in their regions and soon proposed several basic reforms. Though they had been prohibited since 1833, the collection of tithes was called for in most dioceses and set fees were established for church marriages, burials, and baptisms. Processions and other public demonstrations of faith not under the direct control of the church were discouraged. Festive religious celebrations often were condemned as immoral and those who selected not to worship or to do so in services not tied officially to the institutional church were chastised. In New Mexico the French apostolic vicar of the Santa Fe diocese, Jean Baptiste Lamy, actively sought to curtail the activities and power of the penitents and replaced or excommunicated several priests who failed to follow his dictates, among them Father Antonio José Martínez of Taos, who, despite being excommunicated, continued to perform services in a small chapel in his parish (Mirandé, p. 136).

Thus, although they had been guaranteed the right to maintain their religious preferences and practices in 1848, as the nineteenth century ended it was progressively more evident to most Mexican and Mexican American Catholics that they had no institutional voice at any level in the American Catholic church and that the religious traditions they had come to deem important and essential to their convictions were considered inappropriate, if not unacceptable, in the estimation of the Euroamerican Catholic laity and clergy in the United States.

It was not until the mid-1940s that the institutional Catholic church in the United States began to devise strategies and programs to meet the pastoral and social needs of Mexican Americans and other Hispanics. In 1944 meetings and seminars were organized for delegates of western and southwestern dioceses at the request of Robert E. Lucey and Urban J. Vehr, the archbishops of San Antonio and Denver, respectively, to analyze the scope and effectiveness of the church's efforts in these areas (Sandoval, p. 47). In 1945 the Bishop's Committee for the Spanish-speaking was formed, the objectives of which were to construct clinics, improve housing and educational and employment opportunities, and eliminate discrimination.

Hispanic priests increased in numbers slowly during the 1950s and 1960s, and beginning in 1969, some of these pastors organized the PADRES (Priests Associated for Religious, Educational, and Social Rights) to help strengthen the voice of their ethnic community within the national Catholic church (Novo Pena, p. 367). Fifty nuns in 1971 united to form *Las Hermanas* and proclaimed a similar agenda. In response to pressure from these and other associations, a Secretariat of Hispanic Affairs was created within the church to coordinate activities of Hispanic clergy across the country. Three national meetings (*Encuentros*) between Spanish-speaking leaders and higher clerics in the church were held in 1972, 1977, and 1985. Though not all participants involved in these meetings viewed them in positive terms, Sandoval concludes that they provided a means for Hispanics to "come face to face with the top levels of authority in the church to express their frustrations and demands for equality and opportunity in the community of believers. The encuentros have legitimized protest and demonstrated the Church's willingness to listen to the oppressed" (*Fronteras: A History of the Latin American Church in the United States*, p. 431).

One of the most dynamic forces to bring about change between Mexican Americans and the Catholic church and its clergy in the United States was the Chicano movement of the 1960s and early 1970s. In seeking to define their unique identity within North American society by affirming a strong sense of pride in their Spanish and indigenous American heritage, leaders of this movement also condemned U.S. institutions that they believed had fostered or condoned the oppression of Mexican Americans in the past and present. In the early 1970s, the activist group *Católicos por la Raza* dramatized their discontent over lingering evidence of segregation in the church and its failure to bring about reforms to correct inequities in society by organizing a Christmas Eve demonstration. Many of the participants were arrested, but their sentiments were publicized (Meier, p. 227).

By the 1990s, an expanding proportion of Mexican Americans were mainstream Catholics and no longer sensed the same isolation or separation that their parents or grandparents likely experienced. According to Sandoval, however, the basic reality is the same as before: "Hispanics ... remain a people apart. They continue to cling to their culture and maintain at least some of their religious traditions. There is `social distance' between them and the institutional Church. For some it is a vague discomfort of not feeling at home. For others, it is the perception that the clergy are not interested in them. Moreover, Hispanics in the main have no role in ministry: episcopal, clerical, religious or lay. They are the objects of ministry rather than its agents" (p. 131).

RELIGIOUS FESTIVALS AND RITUALS

Various rituals and festivals of Spanish or Mexican Catholic origin continue to represent an important spiritual element in the lives of many contemporary Mexican Americans. In some instances, these public manifestations of faith have remained virtually unchanged since 1848 or before, but the number of those believers who practice them is decreasing with each new generation. The degree to which any single family participates in these activities depends on the nature of their religious convictions and the level of contact they maintain with more tradition-oriented members of churches of the Mexican American Catholic community.

One of the most symbolic celebrations for many Mexican Americans is the Feast of Our Lady of Guadalupe on December 12th. The festivity commemorates the apparitions of the Virgin Mary to a converted Christian Indian, Juan Diego, in Mexico on the hill of Tepeyac (located within the boundaries of present-day Mexico City) on this same date in 1521. Though she had identified herself as the Virgin Mary to Diego, in appearing before him she spoke his language, Nahuatl, related herself to indigenous deities and, most importantly, was of a skin color similar to his. In the years immediately after her apparition countless thousands of Indians who had previously sought to maintain their native religions converted to the Catholic faith, seeing the coming of the Virgin in a new identity as a symbolic act of supreme consequence.

To commemorate the day of the Virgin's final apparition to Juan Diego on December 12th, some Mexican Americans may rise early and unite at some high point in the area (symbolic of the hill at Tepeyac) and sing "Las Mañanitas," a traditional song which, according to Elizondo, in this festivity represents the Mexican Americans' "proclamation of new life" (*Galilean Journey: The Mexican-American Promise*, p. 44). A special mass is said and roses are an important part of the celebration; most families take these flowers to the service and place them at the altar of the Virgin. Some Mexican Americans, on a given year, may make a pilgrimage to the Basilica of Our Lady of Guadalupe in Mexico City. The importance of the Virgin Mary to Mexican Americans and Hispanics in general cannot be overstated, as affirmed by Silvia Novo Pena: "For the males she is the understanding mother who forgives and intercedes for her errant sons; for the women she sympathizes with the early travails of a mother, sister, or daughter" (p. 381).

Ceremonies and rituals in recognition of events related to the birth and death of Jesus Christ are an essential part of the religious calendar of many Mexican Americans. During the nine days prior to Christmas Day, masses are said at dawn and the festivities of "Las Posadas" honor the arrival of Mary and Joseph to Bethlehem and their search for lodging at an inn (*posada*). Dressing in clothing similar to that likely worn by these personages, a couple visits designated houses of friends or other family members on consecutive nights. It is common for the participants to read dialogues that recreate the probable conversation between the Holy Family and the innkeepers. Though the contemporary Mary and Joseph, like those whom they represent, are denied entry each night, after the dialogues and other ritual acts are completed they may return to the house and unite with friends and family for fellowship. On the ninth night, which is Christmas Eve, Mary and Joseph visit a house that accepts their request for a night's lodging. All those who participated in the events of prior evenings generally attend the *Misa de Gallo* (Midnight Mass), which usually starts with a procession down the main aisle during which two godparents carry a statue of the Christ Child to a manger near the front altar (Samora, p. 227). Festivities include the sharing of food and drink to celebrate the arrival of Mary and Joseph at the inn where the Christ child will be born. During the evening, in most instances, those children present break a *piñata* (a paper maché figure often in the shape of a farm animal filled with candy and hung from a high spot in the house). In all, these joyous events serve to prepare the human spirit for the arrival of the Christ Savior. Christmas Day is spent at home with members of the extended family, and traditional Mexican dishes are principal elements of the menu (Nájera-Ramírez, p. 337).

The final significant event of the Christmas season is *El Día de los Reyes Magos* (Three Kings' Day) on January 6th, when children receive gifts to mark the arrival of the Magi and their offerings for the Christ Child. The night before this special date children leave a note in one of their shoes explaining their behavior during the past year, followed by a list of requests for specific gifts. The shoes often are filled with straw and left under the bed or on a windowsill, along with water, symbolically to provide sustenance to the camels of the kings. In doing so, "they are taught to be mindful of animals and to experience the joy of gratitude" (Samora, p. 227). On the evening of January 6th, families and close friends of this group unite to cut and share a special bread of circular shape with the figure of the infant, Jesus Christ, in the center.

Activities throughout the Hispanic world also occur to recall the last days of Christ's life on earth. *El Miércoles de Ceniza* (Ash Wednesday), according to Samora, is of particular importance to Mexican Americans "as they reflect on their ties to the earth as a mestizo people" (p. 227). By receiving the imprint of a cross on their foreheads during mass on this day, like Catholics of all countries, they acknowledge the pain and suffering of Christ on the cross and "profess publicly the Christian faith with an awareness of their human sinfulness and limitations." On Good Friday in many parishes, *La Procesión de las Tres Caídas* (The Procession of the Three Falls), in conjunction with religious services brings to the memory of those in attendance the agony associated with Christ's journey to Calvary. Families may visit a statue or altar of Our Lady of Sorrows, a Virgin Mary with tears of anguish for her Son in His last moments on earth. The Mexican American mother, in visiting the statue, demonstrates her pity for the Virgin on this anniversary day. On Easter Sunday, another procession commemorates the reunion of the resurrected Christ and His mother. The burning of an effigy of Judas may also form part of the religious activities (Samora, p. 228).

FUNERALS

Rituals practiced in Spain and colonial Mexico associated with the death of family members are still preserved by some Mexican American families. After passing, the body of the deceased may be dressed in special clothing (*la mortaja*) and remain in the family home overnight, making it possible for relatives and friends to pay respects to the departing soul. Food is generally served at this *velorio* (wake). For years to follow on this same date, those people who attended the *velorio* may reunite to affirm once again their bonds to the deceased person. On the day of burial, the family accompanies the body to the grave, frequently singing songs of a religious theme. Flowers are thrown into the grave and the entire family generally stays at the site until the casket is completely covered. Mexican American families whose deceased members were born in Mexico may sometimes arrange for the body to be transported back to his/her town of origin. It was once customary for the spouse and certain family members to wear black clothing for varying periods and make *promesas* (vows) to honor the dead. This is still the practice with a reduced number of families, but the length of time of mourning differs considerably from group to group. Most significant is the perspective on death held by many Mexican and Mexican American Catholics that, rather than an end, death is seen as "a new beginning" (Stevens-Arroyo and Díaz Stevens, p. 379).

PROTESTANTISM AND OTHER FAITHS

The Anglo American settlers who immigrated in the early nineteenth century to the area of present-day Texas were predominantly of Protestant faith, as were those who in later decades travelled to California and most other regions north of the Rio Grande. Over time, they converted a small number of Mexican Americans to Protestantism. By the 1960s three percent of the Mexican American population were members of Protestant denominations (Cortés, p. 711). Increased efforts in social outreach projects, pronounced support of farmworker protest campaigns, and expanded evangelism, coupled with the continued dissatisfaction of many Mexican Americans with the relative lack of recognition accorded them locally or institutionally, have contributed to a considerable expansion in the proportion of Mexican Americans who have converted to Protestant sects. Pentecostal groups have also attracted growing numbers of Mexican Americans.

EMPLOYMENT AND ECONOMIC TRADITIONS

Mining, agriculture, transportation, and ranching attracted the highest numbers of Mexican immigrants and Mexican Americans in search of work in the United States from shortly after the mid-nineteenth century through the first decades of the twentieth century. As these sectors of the economy grew in importance, their demand for low-wage laborers multiplied, and the completion of local and transcontinental rail lines expanded the markets for ranchers and farmers in this region, prompting further increases in demands for additional workers (Mirandé, p. 29). Laws limiting or excluding Chinese and Japanese immigration made jobs even more abundant for others in certain regions of the western United States. For the Mexican immigrant, repeated downturns in the Mexican economy and the socio-political turbulence related to the Revolution of 1910 made "the North" an attractive location for at least temporary residence.

A reduced percentage of Mexican landowners and merchants crossed into the United States in this early period during the years of the Mexican Revolution. Many were successful in establishing businesses in Mexican American neighborhoods in the Southwest. With more years of formal education in their background than the majority of immigrants in this same period, this minority frequently provided jobs and political leadership within their newly adopted communities (Meier, p. 109).

Though mining, ranching, and transportation employed many new immigrants, the highest percentage of foreign workers were drawn to agriculture, mostly in Texas and California, but also in parts of New Mexico, Arizona, and Colorado. By 1930, 41 percent of the agricultural laborers in the Southwest were Mexicans or Mexican Americans (Cortés, p. 708). Eight-, ten-, or twelve-hour workdays, with few if any days of rest, combined with generally high temperatures to make this work in the fields or orchards extremely demanding and wearing in physical terms. Housing made available to laborers by their employers was of inferior quality. Unsanitary and confining living quarters facilitated the spread of disease. Clean drinking water was not easily accessible and indoor plumbing was uncommon. In areas of colder climate, inadequate heating was the norm. The transitory nature of this work was most difficult on immigrant families, whose children very seldom had the opportunity to attend anything but makeshift schools on a temporary basis and were most often forced, for economic reasons, to begin work in the fields at a young age.

The decade of the 1930s brought severe cutbacks in hiring in agriculture and other industries due to worldwide economic depression. High levels of unemployment nationwide made immigrant labor expendable. Those workers not of U.S. origin were deported in large numbers; over 500,000 were forced to return to Mexico during this ten-year period. Frequently, families were separated: parents of foreign citizenship were returned to their home countries, whereas their children, if born in the United States, and thus, American citizens, sometimes remained in their country of birth with relatives or family friends, hoping for the prompt return of their parents.

Less than ten years after the first of these deportations, however, labor shortages caused by World War II—principally in agriculture—stimulated a renewed need for immigrant labor. To resolve this matter, the governments of the United States and Mexico signed an agreement in 1942 that initiated the *bracero* (someone who works with their arms or *brazos*) program, which allocated temporary work visas to Mexican immigrants seeking farm work in the Southwest. From 1942 to 1948, over 200,000 laborers entered the United States to work in California agribusiness and, in reduced numbers, in the rail industry and other sectors. Though cancelled in 1948, the program was renewed shortly thereafter and continued in force until 1964 when, in part because of socio-political pressures related to the civil rights movement, the U.S. Congress decided against any further extensions of the agreement. Accusations of farmworkers against their employers related to substandard housing and work conditions had been confirmed by studies conducted by the Labor Department in the 1950s; agencies such as the National Council of Churches of Christ in America, the National Catholic Welfare Council, and the National Consumers League had spoken out against these infringements and made many U.S. citizens more fully aware of the abuses repeatedly suffered by these workers.

A major portion of the braceros working in the United States from 1942 to 1964 returned to Mexico, but it is estimated that eight percent of these workers, roughly 750,000, remained in the Southwest to raise families and establish permanent residency or citizenship (Meier, p. 184). To those who participated in this program and to other immigrant Mexican laborers who had come northward for work in this period, it became evident once again, as in the 1930s, that when low-wage workers were needed, they were welcome in the United States. When the demand for laborers diminished, however, their presence was not wanted by significant numbers of the majority community.

Wages for Mexican and Mexican American farmworkers continued at inequitable, low levels and living and work conditions failed to improve to any marked degree in the decades subsequent to the 1960s. Strikes and boycotts organized by César Chávez further publicized the injustices perpetrated by many employers in this rural industry. The formation of the United Farm Workers union gave somewhat greater strength to migrant labor demands, but unfair practices by employers still remain a source of grievance in the fields (Meier, p. 210).

DIVERSIFICATION OF EMPLOYMENT OPPORTUNITIES

Noticeable beginning in the 1920s and increasing measurably in the years after World War II was a shift in the Hispanic labor force in the United States, especially by second- and third-generation Mexican Americans, away from their initial sources of employment into a wider range of occupations. Many of these workers were attracted to other regions of the country. The midwestern states, particularly Illinois, offered jobs in meatpacking and manufacturing to mounting numbers of Mexican Americans seeking alternatives to the transient life of field work. By 1990 only 2.9 percent of the Mexican American working population were employed in agriculture and forestry, with less than one percent in the mining industry. Professional and health and education services employed 20.3 percent of this specific labor force, while 16.4 percent had service occupations and 15.9 percent were in manufacturing. Over 16 percent held managerial and professional specialty positions (*The Statistical Record of Hispanic Americans*, p. 534).

The small Mexican American entrepreneurial sector—evident beginning in the second decade of the 1900s—expanded considerably after World War II. By 1990 over one-half million Hispanic-owned businesses existed in the United States, the majority of them in California and controlled by Mexican Americans. Earnings for these commercial concerns approached $100 billion annually and contributed to the growth of the Mexican American middle class (Meier, p. 253).

Mexican American women entered the labor market as farmworkers, laundresses, and domestics in representative numbers starting in the first decades of the twentieth century. By 1930, 15 percent had employment, and 45 percent of this total worked in domestic and personal service, with smaller percentages in textile and food processing industries, agriculture, or sales (Cortés, pp. 708, 713). The proportion of Mexican American women in the labor force increased substantially in the decades that followed, reaching 21 percent by 1950 and over 50 percent by 1990 (Falcón and Gilbarg, p. 64). In 1991 the sectors of the national economy with highest levels of employment for Mexican American women were technical, sales, and administrative support, including clerical positions at 39 percent, followed by jobs in service occupations at 27 percent. Fourteen percent were in managerial and professional specialty classifications (*The Statistical Record ...*, p. 508). Though Mexican American women are employed at approximately the same percentage as non-Hispanic women, their earnings are 82 percent of the income of this other group (Meier, p. 262). In general, as asserted by many contemporary sociologists, Mexican American women have had to overcome the triple oppression of class, race, and gender in seeking employment.

Despite the diversification in employment into other sectors of the national economy detailed above, wages have remained low for most members of the Mexican American community. Though well over 50 percent of the families had two wage earners and 15 percent had three workers, as of 1990, the median family income was $23,240, considerably lower than the national average. The median incomes for Mexican American males and females were below those of most other Hispanic groups: while Puerto Rican males and females earned $18,193 and $11,702 respectively, the corresponding wages for Mexican American men and women were $12,894 and $9,286. Unemployment rates for the two genders were 11.7 percent and 9.2 percent (Falcón and Gilbarg, p. 64).

In the early 1990s jobs in manufacturing in the national economy declined, whereas service and information technology hirings increased. Service sector jobs respond more immediately to cyclical trends, and because a large percentage of Mexican Americans are in this line of employment, they are among the first exposed to periodic declines in the contemporary job market. High dropout rates at the high school level and low numbers of Mexican American youth that graduate from two- or four-year colleges allow but a small percentage of Mexican Americans to qualify for positions in the information technology sector. Low educational attainment in general continues to place them consistently at entry-level positions and makes progress to higher rank or pay more difficult. The plant closings of many manufacturing industries in the Southwest, and specifically in southern California in the early 1990s, have forced many thousands of Mexican Americans to look for jobs in other lines of work, but again, low levels of education or technical training limit the alternatives open to these individuals.

POLITICS AND GOVERNMENT

Political participation by Mexican Americans historically has been limited by discrimination. In the early Southwest before 1910, small numbers of Mexican Americans held offices in territorial and state legislatures in California, Colorado, and New Mexico. However, they were usually handpicked by the dominant Anglo Americans of these regions. In other cases, Anglo American businessmen who controlled the railroads, mines, and large ranches dominated the state and local politics of the Southwest. The existing political structure was manipulated to benefit these interests. During the first decades of the twentieth century—to insure Anglo American political control—participation in the voting process for Mexican Americans was maintained at a minimum with the use of various discriminatory devices. Restrictive policies included the poll tax, literacy tests, all-white primaries, and coercion. In this atmosphere it is not surprising that few Mexican Americans voted (Feagin and Feagin, p. 274).

While political participation was limited, Miguel Tirado points out that during the early part of the twentieth century Mexican Americans formed protective organizations—*mutualistas* (mutual aid societies)—which were quite similar to those that developed among European immigrant groups. Members of these organizations found that by pooling their resources they could provide each other with funeral and insurance benefits as well as other forms of assistance. For example, the Lázaro Cardenas Society was formed in Los Angeles soon after World War I to improve municipal facilities available to Mexican Americans (*Aztlán*, 1970, p. 55). By the 1920s it became evident to Mexican Americans that if their interests were to be protected political power was essential.

However, even as Mexican Americans began to adapt to the political and social traditions of the United States they were still viewed as "foreigners" by the larger society. Thus, they set out to demonstrate that they were true Americans. This orientation was reflected in the goals of the emerging organizations of the early twentieth century. The *Orden Hijos de América* (Order of the Sons of America), established in 1921 in San Antonio, Texas, by members of a small emerging middle class, restricted its goals to that of "training members for citizenship." Membership was consequently limited to "citizens of the United States of Mexican or Spanish extraction" (Moore and Cuellar, 1970, p. 41). According to Moore and Cuellar, this orientation strongly suggested that Mexican Americans "were more trustworthy to Anglos than Mexican nationals, and also more deserving of the benefits of American life." Thus, as an organization consisting of upwardly mobile individuals, OSA attempted to demonstrate to the larger community that they were people to be respected. To understand the group's motives, the OSA must be placed within the social climate of the era. Their orientation was a reflection of the social and economic vulnerability of Mexican Americans during the 1920s.

The OSA functioned for approximately ten years. Disagreements about the goals and direction of the group soon lead to schisms. However, the splintering of OSA led to the development of a new organization—the League of Latin American Citizens (LULAC). The theme of unity and the need to provide a united front to the Anglo American community guided the group's decision to call itself LULAC. It also limited its membership to U.S. citizens. LULAC gained power among the Mexican American middle class and it ultimately became their strongest advocate (Moore and Cuellar, p. 41).

THE POLITICIZATION OF MEXICAN AMERICANS

The events of World War II would prove to be a turning point in the Mexican American's bid for expanded political participation. This confrontation profoundly affected Mexican Americans, first by exposing those who served in the armed services to social climates where they were regarded as equals. Secondly, the needs of the industrial wartime economy drew many Mexican Americans into the nation's urban centers seeking employment, thus fostering a greater participation

in larger society. In essence, their participation in the war effort at home and abroad served as a solidifying force, setting the stage for political activism (Moore and Pachón, p. 178).

Many political groups organized by returning Mexican American veterans emerged to challenge segregation and other forms of discriminatory practices in American life. The Community Service Organization (CSO) is one example. It was founded in 1947 to promote social change within the Mexican American communities of Los Angeles. The founding members set out to improve social conditions by promoting participation in the political process. CSO was determined to elect individuals responsive to the needs of the Mexican American community. It met with some success. Through the efforts of CSO, the East Los Angeles community elected the first Mexican American to the city council since 1881 (Tirado, pp. 62-66).

The political activism of this period is also exemplified by the actions of the G.I. Forum, the

Mexican American Political Association (MAPA), and the Political Association of Spanish-Speaking Organizations (PASSO). Established in 1948, the G.I. Forum emerged to protest the refusal of cemeteries and mortuaries in Three Rivers, Texas, to bury the body of a Mexican American World War II veteran. This incident focused national attention on the discriminatory conditions of Mexican Americans in Texas. The Forum later turned its attention to mainstream politics by organizing voter registration drives and get-out-the-vote campaigns (C. F. García and R. O. de la Garza, *The Chicano Political Experience: Three Perspectives*, p. 29).

Created in 1960, MAPA marks yet another stage of political activism. It was one of the first organizations to clearly articulate ethnic political goals. According to the MAPA Fourth Annual Convention Program, "An organization was needed that would be proudly Mexican American, openly political, and necessarily bipartisan" (Moore and Pachón, p. 179). MAPA met with success. It helped elect several Mexican Americans to office (Garcia and de la Garza, p. 31). PASSO, created a few years earlier in Texas, and MAPA were political groups organized essentially to lobby at the party level for Mexican American interests. Both organizations carried out voter education and registration drives; however, they were primarily oriented toward winning concessions for Mexican Americans at the party level (Moore and Cuellar, p. 45).

In the 1970s, unhappy with both the Democratic and Republican parties, some Mexican Americans opted for an entirely different political strategy. They set out to create an alternative political party—La Raza Unida (LRU). Established in Texas in 1970, the LRU had remarkable successes. Most notable were the party's achievements in Crystal City, Texas, a community of approximately 10,000 where many LRU candidates won control of the city council and the school board. These newly elected officials in turn hired more Mexican American teachers, staff, and administrators. They also instituted bilingual programs and added Mexican American history to the school curriculum. The newly elected officials also made changes throughout the city government, including the police department, to rectify years of neglect by city officials (John Shockley, *Chicano Revolt in a Texas Town*).

The LRU then sent organizers throughout the Southwest in efforts to duplicate their success in South Texas. LRU candidates were placed on many local and statewide ballots, but they were unable to generate the type of support that led to their success in Crystal City. After the mid-1970s, the LRU rapidly declined. Its decline was the result of several factors. Internal ideological splintering and personality conflicts played a part, but harassment and repression of the party was the most significant force (Carlos Muñoz, *Youth, Identity, Power: The Chicano Movement*, 1989).

The LRU is but one of many groups that contributed to the growth of the Chicano Movement during the 1960s and 1970s. Mexican Americans became much more vocal and militant in their demands for social change. Many groups emerged to address such issues as the rights of farmworkers, inferior education, employment opportunities, health care, women's rights, reform within the welfare system and the Catholic church, police brutality, and community self-determination.

National attention during this period focused on the actions of La Alianza Federal de Mercedes (Federal Alliance of Land Grants) and the United Farmworkers of America (UFW). Reies López Tijerina and the members of La Alianza demanded the return of stolen lands to the indigenous peoples of northern New Mexico. In 1966 La Alianza occupied a part of the Kit Carson National Forest in New Mexico. Arrested for trespassing, Tijerina spent the next few years awaiting trial. In 1975 the land dispute was partially resolved when about 1,000 acres of the forest were transferred to 75 Mexican American families (Shaefer, p. 283).

The notable organizing efforts of César Chávez, Dolores Huerta, and the UFW brought the plight of the farmworker to national attention and served as a mobilizing force for many Americans of all walks of life. The UFW's first success was the grape boycott beginning in 1965, which carried the struggle of the farmworkers into the households of many Americans. With the overwhelming refusal to buy table grapes by many American households, the UFW was able to negotiate its first union contract with California growers (the first union contract in the history of California farm labor). During the late 1980s, the UFW altered its labor unionizing strategies by addressing the issue of pestiticide use in agricultural production.

From the Mexican American communities of Denver, Colorado, emerged the Crusade for Justice led by Corky Gonzales. This organization was primarily concerned with civil rights issues of urban Mexican Americans; however, it was also one of the first groups to advocate and promote issues of cultural diversity. During 1969 and 1970, the Crusade for Justice was instrumental in organizing a series of Chicano youth liberation conferences, bringing together hundreds of young Chicanos from throughout the nation and generating a series of discussions concerning the question of ethnic identity (Rodolfo Acuña, *Occupied America*, pp. 241-43).

By the late 1960s high school and college students were calling for social change within the educational system. The high school "blowouts" of East Los Angeles in 1968 galvanized student discontent. Chicano high school students walked out of their classes in mass, demanding quality education and local community control of their schools. In several other communities students staged similar events. High school students abandoned their classes in Riverside, California; Denver, Colorado; Crystal City and San Antonio, Texas; and several other cities with high concentrations of Mexican Americans. College students also mobilized. In the Los Angeles area, college students came together to support the high school walkouts and the students' demands for a quality education. Throughout the Southwest, college students were instrumental in establishing the first Chicano studies programs and educational opportunities programs on many college campuses (Acuña, p. 243).

In 1968 the Mexican-American Legal Defense and Education Fund (MALDEF) was established by several Mexican American lawyers to protect the constitutional rights of Mexican Americans. Although it does not endorse political candidates, it has made itself felt in the political sphere much like the NAACP has for African Americans. In addition to providing legal advocacy, MALDEF has been involved in litigation involving illegal employment practices, immigrant's rights, biased testing in school settings, educational segregation, inequalities in school financing, and voting rights issues. As of the 1990s, MALDEF has emerged as the primary civil rights group advocating on behalf of Mexican Americans.

MEXICAN AMERICAN VOTING PATTERNS AND ELECTED OFFICIALS

Mexican American voting behavior has traditionally been Democratic, especially at the presidential level. According to the Latino National Political Survey (1992), 59.6 percent of all Mexican Americans identify themselves as Democrats, 16 percent as Republican, and 24.4 as belonging to independent parties. As members of the Democratic Party, they have played a significant role in several elections. In 1960 John F. Kennedy won an estimated 85 percent of the Mexican American vote, which allowed him to win the states of New Mexico and Texas. To insure Kennedy's victory, "Viva Kennedy" clubs were formed throughout the Southwest, promoting voter education and registration drives. In 1964 Lyndon B. Johnson won an estimated 90 percent, and in 1968 Herbert Humphrey won 87 percent of the Mexican American vote (Feagin and Feagin, p. 275).

While Mexican Americans played a significant role in the above elections, there are several factors that have worked against the growth of Mexican American participation in the political process. First, they are a young population, which means that many are below the voting age. Second, a relatively large segment of the population is ineligible to vote because they are not citizens.

Even among those who are eligible to vote, the turnout of 46 percent (for all Hispanics) in the November 1988 elections was 15 percent lower than for non-Hispanics. Third, lower socioeconomic status serves as an obstacle for many Mexican Americans. The educational attainment of Mexican Americans is still far below the general population and the poverty rates are much higher for Mexican Americans than the general population. Thus, many Mexican Americans have not had the opportunity to develop the skills necessary to participate in the voting process. Consequently, Mexican Americans are presented with formidable obstacles that prevent the development of political strength and greatly hinder the election of Mexican American officials (Maurilio Vigil, *The Handbook ... Sociology*, pp. 81-82).

While the percentage of Mexican American elected officials is not representative of their total U.S. population, significant changes have taken place since the mid-1960s. The number of state legislators in 1950 with Spanish surnames totaled 20. By the late 1980s the number had increased to 90. In 1991 the National Roster of Hispanic Elected Officials reported 3,754 elected officials in the five southwestern states, mostly of Mexican American ancestry, and 4,202 Latino elected officials nationwide. The increase in Mexican American officials is due in part to the Twenty-fourth Amendment, which banned the poll tax and eliminated the English-only literacy requirements for voting in some states. Redistricting following the 1980 census, as well as a substantial growth in the Mexican American population, have also contributed to the rise in the number of Mexican American elected officials (Feagin and Feagin, p. 274).

FEDERAL LEGISLATION AND NATIONAL POLICY

With the slow yet steadily increasing number of Mexican American elected officials, significant pieces of federal legislation have been introduced and enacted into law. During the recent past, Mexican American lawmakers have supported the creation of the federal Fair Employment Practices Commission, the Civil Rights Act of 1964, the Voting Rights Act of 1965, and the subsequent series of civil rights and affirmative action legislation. In 1968 the Bilingual Education Act was passed into federal law; in 1974 subsequent amendments were sponsored by New Mexico Congressman Joseph Montoya. That same year,

Congress, with the urging of many Hispanic and non-Hispanic elected officials alike, encouraged the adoption of bilingual or multilingual ballots where census data documented a substantial number of non-English-speaking people.

In 1976 the Congressional Hispanic Caucus was created with the election of several Hispanics to the House of Representatives. Since then, the caucus has acted as a viable force within Congress, consistently supporting legislation on behalf of Mexican Americans and other disadvantaged groups (Vigil, pp. 91-92). Two of the most prominent public policies affecting Mexican Americans and Hispanics in general are immigration reform and the "English as Official Language" policy. Although the members of the caucus did not agree with each other on the specific initiatives of the policies, both of these issues were and continue to be a high priority for the caucus.

MILITARY STATUS

According to the 1990 census, there are 59,631 Mexican American men over the age of 16 serving in the armed forces, 7,924 of whom are naturalized citizens, while the remainder are native-born. The number of Mexican American women in the armed services is significantly lower; 5,025 native-born Chicanas are active members of the military.

INDIVIDUAL AND GROUP CONTRIBUTIONS

Mexican Americans have made significant and lasting contributions to virtually every element of American culture and society. The following individuals represent merely a sample of this growing community's achievements.

BUSINESS

Born to undocumented Mexican parents in Miami, Arizona, Romana Acosta Bañuelos (1925-) was deported at the age six during the Repatriation Program of the 1930s. After returning to the United States at age 19, she converted a small tortilla factory into Romana's Mexican Food Products, a multimillion-dollar firm. In 1971 she became the first Mexican American to serve as treasurer of the United States.

EDUCATION

Born in Albuquerque, New Mexico, George I. Sánchez (1906-1972) directed his energies to improving the quality of education available to Mexican Americans as well as defending their civil rights. *Forgotten People: A Study of New Mexico* (1940), one of his many publications, revealed the inadequacies of the educational system for Mexican Americans in his home state. Sánchez served as president of LULAC and, in 1956, founded the American Council of Spanish-Speaking People, a civil rights organization.

FILM, TELEVISION, AND THEATER

Mexican American dancer and choreographer José Arcadia Limón (1908-1972) was a pioneer of modern dance and choreography. Edward James Olmos (1947-), received critical acclaim for his portrayal of the *pachuco* in the stage and film version of Luis Valdez's *Zoot Suit* and for his role as Jaime Escalante in the film *Stand and Deliver*. In addition to his appearances in other movies of merit, Olmos starred in "Miami Vice," a popular television series of the 1980s. Paul Rodríguez, who has worked in a number of television series and movies, is perhaps the most popular and widely recognized comedian of Mexican descent in the United States. The head of his own company, Paul Rodríguez Productions, in 1986 he released his first comedy album entitled "You're in America Now, Speak Spanish." The son of Mexican migrant farmworkers, Luis Valdez (1940-) is the founding director of the Teatro Campesino, an acting troupe that was originally organized to dramatize the oppressive existence of the migrant worker. In addition to directing the stage and film version of *Zoot Suit,* he wrote and directed the film *La Bamba,* about the Mexican American rock star Ritchie Valens.

FOLKLORE

Born in Brownsville, Texas, Americo Paredes (1915-) achieved national and international recognition for his research and scholarship in the area of folklore and Mexican American popular culture and served as president of the American Folklore Society. Among his many noteworthy publications are *Folktales in Mexico* (1970) and *A Texas Mexican Cancionero* (1976).

LABOR

César Chávez (1927-1993) was born in Yuma, Arizona, to a farmworking family. Chávez attended over 30 schools as a youth because of the mobile pattern of existence of migrant agriculture. In 1962, after working as a community organizer in the CSO, he moved to Delano, California, and soon became the head of the United Farm Workers, AFL-CIO. From the mid-1960s to his death, Chavez dedicated his life to improving the living conditions, wages, and bargaining power of Mexican and Mexican American farmworkers by means of organized work stoppages, demonstrations, hunger strikes, and boycotts.

LITERATURE

Lucha Corpi (1945-) is a notable poet and novelist whose works often address the struggles of women in contemporary society. Primarily known as a poet, she is perhaps best known for her series "The Mariana Poems," which appear in her *Palabras de mediodia/Noon Words* (1980). Rolando Hinojosa (1929-) was one of the first Chicano writers to achieve national as well as international fame. His *Estampas del valle y otras obras: Sketches of the Valley and Other Works,* a series of "sketches" that portrayed Mexican American life in a fictional town in Texas, won the Premio Quinto Sol for Chicano literature. Another of his works on the same theme, *Klail City y sus alrededores,* won the prestigious international award, Premio Casa de las Americas, in 1976. Born in Linares, Mexico, in 1907, literary critic Luis Leal is one of the most productive, most respected, and most honored scholars of Latin American and Chicano literature. In addition to teaching at numerous universities, he has written some 16 books and edited dozens of others.

MUSIC

Eduardo Mata (1942-) is among the most respected conductors in the world. The former director and conductor emeritus of the Dallas Symphony Orchestra, he was awarded the White House Hispanic Heritage Award in 1991. Singer and musician Lydia Mendoza (1916-) was the first interpreter of rural popular Tejano and border music to acquire star status through her many recordings. Grammy Award-winning Tejano singer and entertainer Selena Quintanilla Perez (1971-1995), best known as Selena, had achieved international fame at the time of her brutal murder in April 1995.

POLITICS

After her election as a state assemblywoman in California in 1982, Gloria Molina (1948-) was voted into the Los Angeles City Council in 1987. In 1991 she was elected to the Los Angeles County Board of Supervisors, thus becoming the first Hispanic in California to be selected by voters to serve at these three levels of government.

RELIGION

The first Mexican American to be named as a bishop of the Catholic church in the United States, Patrick F. Flores (1929-) worked in the diocese of Galveston-Houston and became the director of the Bishop's Committee for the Spanish-Speaking. He has been a strong defender of the civil rights of Hispanics in the United States for over four decades and has won many honors for these efforts, including the Ellis Island Medal of Honor in 1986.

SCIENCE

A renowned physicist and educator, Mexican American Alberto Vinicio Baez (1912-) and his coresearcher, Paul Kirkpatrick, developed the Kirkpatrick-Baez Lamar x-ray telescope, which was later approved for flight on the Freedom Space Station. A pioneer in x-ray radiation, optics, and microscopy, Baez has also made noteworthy achievements in the field of environmental education; he has served as chairman of the Committee on Teaching Sciences of the International Council of Science Unions and as chairman emeritus of Community Education, International Union for the Conservation of Nature and Natural Resources, Glantz, Switzerland. Chemist Mario Molina (1943-) earned national prominence by theorizing, with fellow chemist F. Sherwood Rowland, that chlorofluorocarbons deplete the Earth's ozone layer.

MEDIA

PRINT

El Chicano.

Contact: Linette Jueneman, Editor.

Address: P.O. Box 6247, San Bernadino, California 92412.

Telephone: (909) 381-9898.

Mexican American Sun.

Contact: Delores Sanches, Editor.
Address: 2500 South Atlantic Boulevard, Building B, Los Angeles, California 90040.
Telephone: (213) 263-5743.

El Mundo.

Contact: Anna Parker, Editor.
Address: 630 20th Street, Oakland, California 94612.
Telephone: (510) 763-1120.

Saludos Hispanos.

Contact: Maureen Herring, Editor.
Address: 41-550 Eclectic Avenue, Suite 260, Palm Desert, California 92260.
Telephone: (619) 776-1206.

El Sol.

Contact: Christine Flores, Editor.
Address: 750 Northwest Grand Avenue, Phoenix, Arizona 85007.
Telephone: (602) 257-1746.

RADIO

KLAX-FM.

Founded in 1993, dominates Spanish-speaking market.

Contact: Susan Page, Director of Operations; Alfredo Rodríguez, General Manager.
Address: 5700 West Sunset Boulevard, Los Angeles, California 90028.
Telephone: (213) 466-3001.

KQTL-AM.

Covers Southern Arizona and Northern Mexico.

Contact: Bertha Gallego, Director of Operations; Raul B. Gamez, General Manager.
Address: P.O. Box 1511, Tucson, Arizona 85702.
Telephone: (602) 628-1200.

KXKS-AM.

Founded in 1969, but went to all-Spanish format in 1982. 10,000 watts, covers 150 miles out from center of Albuquerque.

Contact: Bertha Gallego, Director of Operations; Kelly Cunningham, General Manager.
Address: 6320 Zuni S.E., Albuquerque, New Mexico 87108.
Telephone: (505) 265-8331.

WIND-AM.

Contact: Blanca Cerda, Director of Operations.
Address: 625 North Michigan, Third Floor, Chicago, Ilinois 60611.
Telephone: (312) 751-5560.

TELEVISION

KDB-59 (Telemundo Affiliate).

Contact: Darlene Nevarez, Director of Operations/Traffic Manager.
Address: 6320 Zuni S.E., Albuquerque, New Mexico 87108.
Telephone: (505) 265-8331.

KHRR-40 (Telemundo Affiliate).

Contact: Lupe López, Director of Operations/Traffic Manager.
Address: 2919 East Broadway, Tucson, Arizona 85716.
Telephone: (520) 322-6888.

KINT-26 (Univision Affiliate).

Contact: Silvia Martínez, Director of Operations.
Address: 5426 North Mesa, El Paso, Texas 79912.
Telephone: (915) 581-1126.

KLUZ-41 (Univision Affiliate).

Contact: Marcela Medina, Director of Operations.
Address: 2725 Broadbelt Parkway N.E., Albuquerque, New Mexico 87107.
Telephone: (505) 344-5589.

KMEX-34 (Univision Affiliate).

Contact: Jorge Belón, Director of Operations.
Address: 6701 Center Drive West, 15th Floor, Los Angeles, California 90045.
Telephone: (310) 216-3434.

KSTS-48 (Telemundo Affiliate).

Contact: Enrique Pérez, Director of Operations.
Address: 2349 Bering Drive, San Jose, California 95131.
Telephone: (415) 285-4848.

KTMD-48 (Telemundo Affiliate).

Contact: Darlene Stephens, Director of Operations.
Address: 3903 Stoneybrooke, Houston, Texas 70063.
Telephone: (713) 974-4848.

KWEX-41 (Univision Affiliate).

Contact: Lillian Almendarez, Director of Operations.

Address: 411 East Durango, San Antonio, Texas 78204.

Telephone: (210) 227-4141.

WGBO-66 (Univision Affiliate).

Contact: Paul Yewowsski, Director of Operations.

Address: 541 North Fairbanks, 11th Floor, Chicago, Illinois 60611.

Telephone: (312) 751-6666.

WSNS-44 (Telemundo Affiliate).

Contact: David Cordoba, Director of Operations.

Address: 431 Grant Place, Chicago, Illinois 60614.

Telephone: (312) 929-1200.

ORGANIZATIONS AND ASSOCIATIONS

Comisión Femenil Mexicana Nacional, Inc. (National Mexican Women's Commission)

Founded in 1970. Current membership: 5,000, in 23 chapters. Supports increased rights and opportunities for Hispanic women in education, politics and labor. Publication: *La Mujer* (*The Woman*); semiannual.

Contact: Nina Aguyo-Sorkin, Director.

Address: 379 South Loma Drive, Los Angeles, California 90017.

Telephone: (213) 484-1515.

Mexican American Legal Defense and Education Fund.

Founded in San Antonio in 1968 in response to a historical pattern of discrimination against Mexican Americans. Protects and promotes the rights of over 25 million Latinos in the United States in employment, education, immigration, political access, and language through litigation and community education.

Contact: Antonia Hernández, President.

Address: 634 South Spring Street, 11th Floor, Los Angeles, California 90014.

Telephone: (213) 629-2512.

National Association for Chicano and Chicana Studies, NACCS National Office.

Founded in 1971. Membership of over 300 consists of college professors, graduate and undergraduate students, and diverse others whose professional or personal interests center on sociological, historical, political or literary themes or concerns pertaining to Mexican Americans. Sponsors annual conference and publishes selected proceedings.

Contact: Dr. Carlos Maldonado, Director.

Address: Chicano Education Program, Eastern Washington University, MS 170, Cheney, Washington 99004.

Telephone: (509) 359-2404.

National Council of La Raza.

The nation's largest constituency-based Hispanic organization. Exists to reduce poverty and discrimination and improve life opportunities for all Hispanics nationally. Nearly 200 formal affiliates serve 37 states, Puerto Rico and the District of Columbia. Programmatic efforts focus on civil rights, education, health, housing and community development, employment and training, immigration and poverty.

Contact: Lisa Navarrete, Director.

Address: 1111 19th Street N.W., Suite 1000, Washington, D.C. 20036.

Telephone: (202) 785-1670.

Southwest Voter Registration Education Project.

Founded in 1975. Conducts nonpartisan voter registration drives, compiles research on Hispanic and native American voting patterns and works to eliminate gerrymandered voting districts. Publication: *National Hispanic Voter Registration Campaign*. Regional planning committees publish newsletters.

Contact: Lydia Camarillo, Director.

Address: 403 East Commerce Street, Suite 220, San Antonio, Texas 78205.

Telephone: (210) 222-0224.

MUSEUMS AND RESEARCH CENTERS

Arizona State University Hispanic Research Center.

Established: 1985. Staff: 15. Budget: $350,000. Main goals: to conduct basic and applied research on a broad range of topics related to Hispanic populations, particularly Mexican Americans; to disseminate research findings to the academic community and the public; and to provide public service in areas of importance to Hispanics. Publication: *The Bilingual Press*.

Contact: Felipe Castro.

Address: Box 2702, Tempe, Arizona 85287.

Telephone: (602) 965-3990.

Guadalupe Cultural Arts Center.

Latino arts and cultural institution. Sponsors instructional programming and presentations.

Contact: Pedro A. Rodríguez, Executive Director.

Address: 1300 Guadalupe Street, San Antonio, Texas 78207.

Telephone: (210) 271-3151.

Mexic-Arte Multicultural Works.

Exhibits include work of Mexican artists, pre-Cortez implements, and photographs of the Mexican Revolution.

Contact: Herlinda Zamora, Director.

Address: 419 Congress Avenue, Austin, Texas 78701.

Telephone: (512) 480-9373.

Mexican Fine Arts Center Museum.

Collections of Mexican art as well as presentations of current and past Mexican literary works.

Contact: Carlos Tortellero, Director.

Address: 1852 West 19th Street, Chicago, Illinois 60608.

Telephone: (312) 738-1503.

Mexican Museum.

Pre-Hispanic, colonial, folk, Mexican, and Mexican American fine arts. Permanent collection as well as temporary exhibits.

Contact: Marie Acosta-Colón, Executive Director.

Address: Fort Mason Building D., Laguna and Marina Boulevard, San Francisco, California 94123.

Telephone: (415) 441-0404.

Plaza de La Raza.

Offers instruction in theater, dance, music, visual and communication arts. Exhibits include Mexican American folk art of surrounding region.

Contact: Rose Cano, Executive Director.

Address: 3540 North Mission Road, Los Angeles, California 90031.

Telephone: (213) 223-2475.

University of California, Los Angeles Chicano Studies Research Center.

Promotes the study and dissemination of knowledge on the experience of people of Mexican descent and other Latinos in the United States. Publication: *Aztlán: A Journal of Chicano Studies*.

Contact: Dr. Guillermo Hernández, Director.

Address: 180 Haines, Los Angeles, California 90024.

Telephone: (310) 825-2363.

University of California, Santa Barbara Center for Chicano Studies.

Supports and conducts research on historical and contemporary issues related to Mexican-origin population of the United States. Encourages and facilitates academic investigations and training of minority students. Sponsors events that increase public awareness and appreciation of Mexican and Mexican American culture.

Contact: Dr. Denise Segura, Director.

Address: Centro Building 406, Santa Barbara, California 93106.

Telephone: (805) 893-2226.

University of New Mexico Southwest Hispanic Research Institute/Chicano Studies.

Established in 1980. Coordinates and conducts investigations of interdisciplinary scope. Visiting Scholars Program funded by Rockefeller Foundation provides economic support to scholarly research of regional focus. Sponsors colloquium series that allows faculty to present findings of research to academic and local community. Publications: *Working Paper Series*.

Contact: Dr. Eligio R. Padilla, Director.

Address: 1829 Sigma Chi, Albuquerque, New Mexico 87131.

Telephone: (505) 277-2965.

University of Texas at Austin Center for Mexican American Studies.

Provides financial and technical support for research by faculty and graduate students. Offers courses as part of Ethnic Studies curriculum of College of Liberal Arts. Publication: *Monograph Series*.

Contact: Dr. Gil Cardenas, Director.

Address: West Mall Building, Fifth Floor, Austin, Texas 78712.

Telephone: (512) 471-4557.

SOURCES FOR ADDITIONAL STUDY

Acuña, Rodolfo. *Occupied America: A History of Chicanos,* third edition. New York: Harper & Row, 1988.

Durán, Livie Isauro, and H. Russell Bernard. *Introduction to Chicano Studies,* second edition. New York: Macmillan Publishing Co., 1982.

Grebler, Leo, Joan W. Moore, and Ralph Guzman. *The Mexican-American People: The Nation's Second Largest Minority.* New York: Free Press, 1970.

The Handbook of Hispanic Cultures in the United States, four volumes, edited by Nicolás Kanellos and Claudio Esteva-Fabregat. Houston: Arte Público Press, 1993.

Kanellos, Nicolás. *The Hispanic-American Almanac.* Detroit: Gale Research, Inc., 1993.

McWilliams, Carey. *North from Mexico: The Spanish-Speaking People of the United States,* updated by Matt S. Meier. New York: Praeger, 1990.

Meier, Matt S., and Feliciano Rivera. *Mexican Americans/American Mexicans.* New York: Hill & Wang, 1993.

Mirandé, Alfredo. *The Chicano Experience: An Alternative Perspective.* South Bend, Indiana: University of Notre Dame Press, 1985.

Samora, Julián, and Patricia Vandel Simon. *A History of the Mexican-American People.* South Bend: University of Notre Dame Press, 1993.

Mormons believe that through marriages performed in the temple, families are sealed for eternity. While most American Mormon families live with just the nuclear family, they value the extended family, living and dead.

Mormons

by

Jessie L. Embry

Overview

Scholars disagree on whether Mormons, members of the Church of Jesus Christ of Latter-day Saints (LDS), can rightly be considered an ethnic group. Using survey results, sociologist Armand Mauss shows that Mormons are typical Americans. Canadian anthropologist Keith Parry, however, contends that Mormons have a distinctive lifestyle and language that set them apart from mainstream America. Much of the Mormon identity comes from its history. Members accept the Book of Mormon as a religious history of a people who saw the United States as a land of promise where Christ's church could be restored before His second coming. As historian Dean May explains, "The Mormons have been influenced subsequently by ritual tales of privation, wandering, and delivery under God's hand, precisely as the Jews have been influenced by their stories of the Exodus. A significant consequence of this tradition has been the development of an enduring sense of territoriality that has given a distinctive cast to Mormon group consciousness. It differentiates the Mormons from members of other sects and lends support to the judgment of [Catholic] sociologist Thomas F. O'Dea that the Mormons `represent the clearest example to be found in our national history of the evolution of a native and indigenously developed ethnic minority'" (*The Harvard Encyclopedia of American Ethnic Groups*, 1980).

The Mormon church has grown to be more than an American religious denomination. Its 8,000,000-person membership in 1991 nearly covered the world and only half (4,336,000) lived in the United States. Of the one million converts in 1988 and 1989, 60 percent of them were from Mexico and Central and South America. Still, Utah is 77 percent Mormon, but only about one-eighth of the church members (1,363,000) live there.

HISTORY

The founder of the Mormon church in the United States, Joseph Smith, Jr., was the third son of a New England farming family. When he was a teenager, he attended a religious revival where his family lived in upstate New York. Confused by the different religions, Smith prayed for direction in 1820 and over the next few years recorded several personal revelations. He organized his first church on April 6, 1830. Members accepted him as a prophet who could speak the will of the Lord. As the church grew and developed, he received additional revelations that the Mormons view as scripture; these teachings are recorded in the Doctrine and Covenants known as the *Book of Mormon*.

From his New York base, Smith sent his followers out to seek converts; the majority of growth during this period occurred in Ohio. One of the first groups went to share the *Book of Mormon* with the Native Americans. When there were more Mormons in Ohio than in New York, Smith received a revelation that the church should move west. The first group arrived in Kirtland, Ohio, a few miles east of Cleveland, early in 1831. For the next seven years, Kirtland served as the church headquarters, and the Latter-day Saints built their first temple there.

But Smith made it clear that Kirtland was only a temporary home. In time, he predicted, God would ask Mormons to establish "Zion," a "New Jerusalem" to prepare for the millennium—the return of the Savior who would usher in a 1,000-year reign of peace. During the summer of 1831 Smith declared that this Zion would be established in Jackson County, Missouri. So Mormons started to gather there. However, tension arose between the Mormons, who opposed slavery, and slaveholding immigrants from Tennessee and Kentucky. The Mormons' claims that the territory was their promised land, their voting together as a bloc, and their communal living posed a threat to the Missourians' lifestyle, and the Mormons were eventually forced from the state.

The Mormons moved to Illinois and settled on undeveloped land along the Mississippi River known as Commerce. They renamed the area Nauvoo and started building a city. The Mormons received a liberal charter from the state that allowed them to have their own militia and courts. From here Smith continued to send out missionaries. Those sent to England were very successful, and soon immigrants from there as well as Canada and other areas of the United States arrived and helped establish what became the second largest city in Illinois. The Saints again started to build a temple. Smith continued to receive revelations.

One of Smith's revelations, plural marriage, caused special problems for the Mormons. Historians do not know when Smith received this revelation; there is some evidence that he married his first plural wife, Fanny Alger, in 1831. He did not write down the revelation until 1843, when he attempted to convince his first wife, Emma Hales Smith, of the principle. Although Smith and some of his closest followers practiced polygamy in Nauvoo, the church did not publicly announce the doctrine until 1852, after the Mormons moved to Utah. Some Mormons who knew of the doctrine opposed the practice and in June 1844 published a newspaper expressing their views of Smith as a fallen prophet. Using the powers granted by Nauvoo's charter, Smith destroyed not only the newspaper but also the press. The city courts released him, but the state arrested him for treason. As Smith, his brother Hyrum, and other church leaders were held in jail awaiting trial, a mob broke into the jail and killed Joseph and Hyrum Smith on June 27, 1844.

Following the death of their leader, Brigham Young (1801-1877), the president of the Council of Twelve Apostles, gained the trust of most of Smith's followers. Some Mormons reported that when Young spoke to them he sounded like Smith. These people saw this as a heavenly manifestation that Young was to be the next leader. Eventually, he became church president. Young led the work to complete the temple in Nauvoo and continued to give the members the ordinances he learned from Smith.

Problems between the Mormons and the local residents continued, and by February 1846, the Mormons began to leave Illinois, heading first for Nebraska and then to Salt Lake Valley. Isolated from the rest of the nation, Brigham Young and the Mormons set out to establish "Zion in the tops of the mountains," following Smith's visions. He planned Salt Lake City and other communities using Smith's Plat of Zion, a grid system. He encouraged the Mormons to be self-sufficient and created an independent commonwealth. He sent settlers to southern Utah, where they attempted to raise cotton and manufacture iron so they would not have to depend on outsiders for these goods. He asked communities to live the "United Order," wherein people shared resources. Communities had varying success for several years, but eventually most communal attempts failed because most Mormons supported the American ideal of free enterprise. Eventually the church adopted free-enterprise policies. The Mormons completed the first temple in the area in St. George, Utah, in 1877. The Salt Lake Temple, which has become a symbol of Mormonism, took 40 years—from ground breaking to dedication—to complete. It was dedicated on April 6, 1893.

Young also announced for the first time publicly that the church endorsed plural marriage. In 1852 Apostle Orson Pratt delivered a discourse on the virtues of plural marriage. While church members now knew the church sanctioned polygamy, most of the Latter-day Saints did not practice it. The practice of polygamy varied by community, apparently based on how strongly local leaders encouraged it. Current research suggests that around 20 percent of the Mormons belonged to plural families.

Because of the Mormons' practice of polygamy and their political and economical isolation, many Americans questioned their loyalty to the nation. In 1857 the U.S. government sent an army to Utah with a federal appointee, Alfred Cumming of Georgia, to replace Brigham Young as governor of the territory. Although the groups resolved the problem peacefully and Cumming took office, the Mormons still contended with the U.S. government. In 1862 Congress passed the Morrill Act, the first legislation against polygamy, and continued to strengthen those laws for the next 25 years. The Edmunds Act (1882) was a series of amendments that strengthened the Morrill Act. It made cohabitation illegal; federal officials only had to prove that husband and wives were living together and not that multiple marriages had been performed for the law to have been broken. Polygamists were disenfranchised and could not hold political office. When the Edmunds Act did not control polygamy, Congress passed the Edmund-Tucker Act (1887), which

abolished women's suffrage, required plural wives to testify against their husbands, and allowed the federal government to acquire all church property. The government began plans to confiscate the property, including the temples, in 1890. Church President Wilford Woodruff then issued a "Manifesto" stating that the church would no longer practice polygamy. In 1904 church President Joseph F. Smith presented a second manifesto that disciplined those who continued to practice polygamy or perform plural marriages.

SETTLEMENT

As Mormons arrived in Utah's Great Basin, Brigham Young sent them throughout the West. Although some colonies were short lived, Mormon communities extended from southern Idaho to San Bernardino, California. During the years when the federal government arrested polygamists, Mormons also moved into northern Mexico and southern Alberta, Canada. Young and the presidents who followed him also sent missionaries throughout the United States and northern Europe. The church encouraged the new converts to "gather to Zion." Church-sponsored ships carried emigrants across the Atlantic. Once in the United States, converts traveled by rail as far as possible and then continued by wagon. Some groups who could not afford wagons pulled two-wheeled handcarts. The church established an endowment, the Perpetual Emigrating Fund, to help the new arrivals.

The church encouraged the newcomers to assimilate as quickly as possible. They learned English and the Mormon way of life. Brigham Young proposed an alphabet that spelled English phonetically. Although it was never adopted, the alphabet demonstrated the church's attempt to assimilate newcomers. European immigrants were allowed at first to attend congregations speaking their native languages but were encouraged also to attend the congregation in which they lived, which usually spoke English. In 1903, when a disagreement developed over the celebration of a Swedish holiday, the First Presidency emphasized, "The counsel of the church to all Saints of foreign birth who come here is that they should learn to speak English when possible, adopt the manners and customs of the American people, fit themselves to become good and loyal citizens of this country, and by their good works show that they are true and faithful Latter-day Saints."

Additional factors worked for assimilation in Mormon society; those already in Utah understood the desire of the newcomers to be in Zion

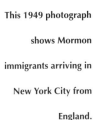

This 1949 photograph shows Mormon immigrants arriving in New York City from England.

and felt a religious obligation to accept and love their brothers and sisters in the gospel. With all groups working together, European immigrants often married out of their cultural groups. So while Salt Lake City's foreign-born population during the 1880s ran as high as 80 percent, there were very few conflicts. Mormon immigrants assimilated into the mainstream of Mormonism's unique culture in one generation.

Throughout the late nineteenth and early twentieth centuries, Mormons remained concentrated in the intermountain west. The agricultural and mining depression of the 1920s and the nationwide depression of the 1930s forced some Mormons to leave the area looking for employment. During World War II, Utah's population increased as the government developed military bases and supported wartime industries. In the 1990s, while Mormons can be found throughout the United States, there is still a high concentration in the intermountain west.

MORMON RELATIONS WITH OTHER AMERICANS

During the nineteenth century, most Americans saw the Mormon church as an eccentric religion that practiced polygamy, voted as a bloc, and lived together. Following the issuing of the Manifesto, though, Mormons not only abandoned polygamy but also gave up many of their unique economic and political practices. In order for Utah to become a state, the federal government required the church to dissolve its political arm, the People's Party. Most Mormons became Republicans and Democrats like the rest of the nation. The church gave up its communal and cooperative efforts and embraced the capitalist economy.

As time passed Mormonism became, as historian Jan Shipps described, "the Reader's Digest church" because members seemed to fit the American ideal. While there are still some misgivings about the church's claims to be the only true church, most Americans now see Mormons as law abiding, peaceful people who embrace all aspects of American life. This image improved in 1978 when the church abandoned its policy that blacks could not hold its lay priesthood.

FUTURE OF THE MORMON CHURCH

One major problem facing the Mormon church is its growing international membership, both worldwide and in American ethnic communities. Church leaders face the dilemma of separating gospel values from the American secular traditions that they have interwoven into Mormon culture. Before the priesthood revelation, there was an informal rule in many missions that they should not recruit blacks. As a result, only a limited number of African Americans joined. After 1978, missionaries actively ministered among blacks, and increasing numbers of African Americans are joining the religion. Hispanic Americans and Asian Americans are also becoming members. Polynesian Americans who joined the church in the islands are immigrating to the United States and bringing extended family members. Not all of them are Mormons, but some join after they have arrived. The church has also continued its efforts, although on a lesser scale, to convert Native Americans.

While the northern European immigrants assimilated in one generation, these new members maintain their language and much of their cultural identity. The Mormon church has tried various approaches to help these members, including establishing separate congregations, integrating them into existing congregations without translation support, and facilitating partial integration— allowing them to "fuse" their culture with the Mormon lifestyle. In the 1960s, for example, church President Spencer W. Kimball (1895-1985) actively organized Indian congregations (generally called Lamanite branches), and congregations of other ethnic groups, including a Chinese branch and a German-speaking ward in Salt Lake City, were formed. In the early 1970s, church leaders again questioned the utility of sponsoring separate branches and urged the integration of ethnic members into the church. However, before the end of the decade, a Basic Unit plan encouraged ethnic branches again. In practice the church's policy has vacillated because neither ethnic branches nor integrated wards have met the needs of all church members. Language and cultural barriers often weaken the ties of religion. Questions about how to resolve these issues still face the Mormon leadership.

In addition, church leaders uphold family values and gender roles that some Americans question. Many see the Mormon church as a conservative voice similar to the South's Bible Belt, and even some Mormons question these conservative stands. In 1993 and 1994 the church excommunicated intellectuals who questioned some basic tenets such as not ordaining women to the priesthood, the historicity of the *Book of Mormon*, and the role of church leaders.

FAMILY AND COMMUNITY DYNAMICS

Mormons believe that through marriages performed in the temple, families are sealed for eter-

nity. While most American Mormon families live with just the nuclear family, they value the extended family, living and dead. They feel that the temple "saving ordinances" such as baptism, a special "endowment" session, and marriages are also essential for family members who have died. Since these ordinances can only be performed on earth, living Mormons perform them as proxies for deceased relatives. To facilitate this, church leaders encourage Mormons to research their genealogies and collect the names of their deceased relatives.

The LDS church has emphasized family worship, including family scripture reading and weekly family meetings (now called family home evenings) for decades. The practice of family gatherings started in the Granite Stake in the Salt Lake Valley in 1909. Church leaders instructed families to set aside time to learn the gospel, participate in activities, sing songs, read the scriptures together, play games, and enjoy refreshments. Six years later in 1915, the First Presidency of the church announced its official endorsement of the church program. They asked "presidents of stakes and bishops throughout the church [to] set aside one evening each month for a "Home Evening" where "fathers and mothers may gather their boys and girls about them in the home and teach them the word of the Lord." The church formalized the program in 1965 as the "family home evening" program. General church leaders encouraged local leaders to set aside Monday for the weekly meeting, prohibited ward or stake meetings that night, and provided lesson and activity manuals to assist families in their time together.

Mormons also encourage daily family prayer. In a survey of Utah adults by sociologist Stan Albrecht, 42 percent of lifetime Mormons reported having "daily" family prayer, with another 27 percent specifying "often." The comparable figures for converts were 45 percent and 23 percent respectively. While the number of those answering "never" or "only on special occasions" were higher (31 percent for lifetime members and 32 percent for converts), Utah Mormons prayed as families more often than Utah Catholics and Protestants, who collectively reported that 16 percent had daily family prayer, 13 percent less frequently, and 71 percent "never" or "only for special occasions."

Church leaders encourage Mormons to be self-sufficient. Since 1930, the church has operated its own welfare system to help members in need. Leaders ask members to fast once a month and donate the money they would have spent on those meals to help the needy. However, leaders also encourage members to use their own resources and seek their extended families' assistance before coming to the church for aid. To help in times of emergency, leaders ask members to maintain a year's supply of food and other necessities. During the 1930s, the church claimed that it could support its own members, but studies showed that members depended on the federal programs to a greater extent than other Americans. Church members continue to use federal and church programs, but the goal of self-reliance endures.

Church policy discourages teenagers from dating until they are 16 years old. Leaders also encourage no serious dating until after young men serve a two-year full-time mission when they are 19. Leaders stress that young people should marry other Mormons within their own racial group. The 1978 issue of the *Church News* that announced the change in policy toward blacks holding the priesthood included an article restating that the church still discouraged interracial marriages. It pointed out that marriage is always difficult and even more so when the partners come from different backgrounds. While the topic is not discussed as much in the general church, single Mormons from ethnic groups are frequently confused by the church's counsel to marry within the church and to marry someone from their ethnic groups when they do not find potential marriage partners who are Mormons and who belong to their cultural backgrounds.

The church teaches that sexual intercourse outside marriage is a sin. As a result, Mormon women marry at slightly younger ages than other Americans, while men marry at about the same age as the national average. Most Mormons marry rather than cohabit. As divorce has become more acceptable in the United States, more Mormons are separating. Utah has a higher divorce rate than the national average. Some studies show Mormons are more likely to separate in the first five years and less likely to divorce after five years of marriage.

Mormons believe all people existed as spirits before they were born and that to progress they needed to come to this earth to receive a body and to be tested. Many believe that the spirits on the other side need to be provided bodies. For that reason, the church discourages birth control and suggests that Mormons have large families;

Latter-day Saints have families larger than the U.S. average. Mormon church leaders also speak against abortion. They view ending a pregnancy as "one of the most ... sinful practices of this day." The only allowable exceptions are where "incest or rape was involved, or where competent medical authorities certify that the life of the mother is in jeopardy, or that a severely defective fetus cannot survive birth."

Mormons value children and provide training for them in the home and in the church. Traditional Mormon gender roles have changed along with overall American values as society has evolved in the twentieth century. But there are still differences in the training of boys and girls. Boys receive the priesthood when they are 12 years old and progress through priesthood offices. Church leaders ask all young men to serve a two-year mission when they are 19 years old. They receive the temple endowment before leaving on their missions. Girls, however, do not have the same advancement. They are allowed but not encouraged to go on missions, and they do not go until they are 21. Young women who serve missions receive the temple ordinances before they leave. Most women attend the temple for the first time just before their marriages. In marriage, a woman is sealed to her husband, and the church teaches that the man, the priesthood holder, is the head of the home; leaders discourage women from working outside the home. While many women work, studies show that women in Utah are more likely to work part time and many Mormon Utah women stay at home.

Despite rather conservative family status for women, however, Utah was the second state (after Wyoming) to give women the right to vote. Although Congress took suffrage away with the Edmunds-Tucker Act, some women continued to campaign for suffrage and were active in the national suffrage movements. The Utah State Constitution gave women back the vote in 1896. Some women, especially those involved in suffrage, became active in political parties. Historically Mormon women have been involved in community health, social welfare, and adoption programs; the best known of these is the Relief Society.

EDUCATION

Mormons place a high value on education. Joseph Smith established a School of the Prophets and stressed the importance of learning, and Mormon scripture encourages members to "seek learning even by study and also by faith." Once the Mormons arrived in Utah, they established and sponsored the first schools on all levels in the state. Formal statehood brought public education, and gradually the church closed or transferred to the state most of its high schools (or academies). Weber State University in Ogden, Utah; Snow College in Ephraim, Utah; and Dixie College in St. George, Utah, are examples of state-sponsored institutions that were first established as Mormon academies. The church did not abandon all of its educational facilities, however. It still sponsors Brigham Young University, a four-year college with a large campus in Provo, Utah, as well as a smaller campus in Laie, Hawaii. It also operates a two-year junior college in Rexburg, Idaho, LDS Business College in Salt Lake City, and high schools and smaller colleges throughout the world in areas with limited public education.

With the closing of its academies, the church feared the loss of religious instruction. To provide the spiritual training other than that provided at Sunday activities, the church established seminaries at high schools and institutes at universities. The first seminary was established at Granite High School in Salt Lake City in 1912; the first institute was created at the University of Idaho in Moscow in 1926.

The Mormons' emphasis on education has led to an educated Mormon populace in the United States. In 1984 sociologists Stan L. Albrecht and Tim B. Heaton found that over half Mormon men (53.5 percent) had some post high school education as compared to 36.7 percent of American men; 44.3 percent of Mormon women had similar training, contrasting with only 27.7 percent of American women overall.

HOLIDAYS

For the most part, American Mormons observe only the national holidays that other Americans celebrate. The exception is July 24, Pioneer Day, in honor of the day that Brigham Young entered the Salt Lake Valley in 1847. This date is a state holiday in Utah, and residents celebrate with parades and fireworks. With the emphasis Mormons place on their history, members throughout the United States celebrate Pioneer Day on a smaller scale.

HEALTH AND MENTAL HEALTH ISSUES

Mormons consider the Word of Wisdom, a revelation received by Joseph Smith, to be a command-ment from God. According to Mormon tradition, in 1833 Emma Smith questioned male church leaders using chewing tobacco and spitting in her home. As a result, Joseph Smith asked the Lord for guidance and received Section 89 of the Doctrine and Covenants. It cautioned against "wine and strong drinks," tobacco, and "hot drinks." It also said meat should be "used sparingly" and urged the use of grains, especially "wheat for man," and herbs. When the revelation was first received, the church considered it only advice; violation did not restrict church membership. During the 1890s, though, church leaders started emphasizing the Word of Wisdom more. They led the prohibition fight in Utah and discouraged the use of alcoholic drinks. In 1921 church president Heber J. Grant made obeying the Word of Wisdom a requirement to enter the temple. The church interpreted the revelation to forbid coffee, tea, tobacco, and alcohol, but it does not stress other elements of the teaching, including guidelines about the use of meat and grains.

Strict adherence to the Word of Wisdom has led to greater health among Mormons. Studies have found that Mormons in Utah have fewer cases of diseases, especially cancers, and suggest this may be because they do not use tobacco or alcohol. One study declared that Mormons showed that one-third of the cancers in the United States could be prevented by avoiding these substances. Mormons also helped in cancer research through their high birth rate and the keeping of genealogical records. University of Utah professors have encoded this information and identified high-risk cancer patients. In addition, information provided by the Mormons helped lead to the identification of a gene that frequently occurs in colon cancer patients.

Nineteenth-century Mormon health practices and problems were similar to those of other Americans at the time. Mormons suffered a high rate of infant morality and death from infectious diseases. Their initial mistrust of the medical profession was also common. Some early Mormons believed in herbal treatments. Many practiced faith healing. Leaders encouraged members to depend more on the power of God than on doctors. In the church's early days, men and women gave blessings as a way of healing. Usually women blessed other women at the time of childbirth. Now the church only authorizes men holding the priesthood to give blessings.

Mormon health practices have changed over the years. Some modifications developed in response to changes in American views. After the Mormons moved to Utah, Brigham Young encouraged members to go to doctors for medical treatment. His suggestion slightly preceded the general American shift to greater support of the medical profession. Young asked second-generation Mormons to return to the East to study medicine, and men and women responded. While leaders still stressed faith healing, they also encouraged members to seek the assistance of secular medicine.

Around the turn of the century, Mormons participated in public health programs that were popular throughout the United States. Church leaders encouraged voluntary vaccination programs and supported quarantines. The women's organization, the Relief Society, sponsored maternal and child health programs. It also held milk clinics and organized "Swat the Fly" campaigns. The women worked closely with the state government to implement the services Congress provided through the 1920s Sheppherd-Towner Act. Under this law, the stake Relief Society in Cottonwood opened a maternity hospital and other church groups provided layettes and promoted pregnancy and well-baby care.

The Mormon church also sponsored hospitals in Utah to provide assistance to the sick. The Relief Society started the Deseret Hospital in 1882. When that hospital closed 10 years later, members worked to raise money for the W. H. Grover Latter-day Saint Hospital that opened in 1905. The Mormon church owned and operated hospitals in Utah and Idaho until the 1980s, when the leaders turned these hospitals over to a newly created private institution, the Intermountain Health Corporation.

By the end of the twentieth century, Mormons depended as much on doctors as on other members. While blessings at the time of illness continue, leaders recommend that members seek medical advice. Physician and historian Lester Bush concludes, "With regard to most aspects of medical practice, Mormons are indeed no longer a `peculiar people'" (*Health and Medicine Among the Mormons: Science, Sense, and Scripture*, 1993). There are some minor differences though. Early in the century the Utah state legislature voted against compulsory vaccinations. Later that decision was reversed, but for years Utah had higher cases of smallpox than the rest of the nation because vaccinations were not required. Utah has also resisted water fluoridation. In 1972 the First Presidency asked members to study the issue and make their own decision, but they did not express support. As a result, much of Utah's water is not fluoridated, and children have more cavities.

RELIGION

Though Mormons are found throughout the world, the church is thoroughly American. That is true especially of its leadership. While the church has appointed local leaders that represent its worldwide membership, the most influential, the First Presidency and the Council of Twelve, are all white American males. When a president dies, the senior member of the Council of Twelve replaces him, so future church leaders will come from this group. The two Quorums of Seventies are also General Authorities in the church. The First Quorum is appointed for life and in 1993 included 35 men. Only eight of its members are not from the United States. The Second Quorum is appointed for a five-year term. Of 43 men in 1993, only 14 are not Americans. Since nearly all the General Authorities are Americans, the body tends to represent that perspective.

Mormons attend geographically structured congregations known as wards. In Utah a ward might include only a few blocks; in other areas, wards might encompass an entire middle-sized or metropolitan city. In Utah boundaries frequently split neighborhoods, and there is very little contact outside assigned wards. Wards support religious and social life by sponsoring athletic events, parties, and other activities for all age groups. Five to six wards form a unit known as a stake, which is similar to a diocese.

The importance of "going to church" has changed for Mormons over time. Historian Jan Shipps described the changes in Mormon religious practice: "Hypothetical Saints [travelling to the nineteenth century] ... in a time machine would have been astonished to find so few Saints at sacrament meeting because the twentieth century sacrament meeting is a visible worship sign, whereas in the pioneer era more expressive worship signs were irrigation canals or neatly built or nicely decorated houses or good crops of sugar beets. More significant, living in the nineteenth century was the sign of citizenship in God's elect nation" (*Mormonism: The Story of a New Religious Tradition*, 1985). As the Mormons gave up such distinctive practices as polygamy and the United Orders, the responsibility of "boundary maintenance" shifted from the church to the individual. According to Shipps,

"The LDS dietary, behavior, and dress codes" are now important boundary markers, while correspondingly, "worship activity ... seems almost mandatory."

The importance of attending worship services is reflected in contemporary Mormon church statistics. For example, a 1980-1981 study shows that 68 percent of lifetime Mormons in Utah attend church on a weekly basis. Converts are even more devout: 74 percent attend weekly. Sociologist Armand Mauss's study of general U.S. surveys found that 58 percent of Mormons go to church weekly compared to only 29 percent of other Americans. On Sundays Mormons attend a three-hour block of meetings that includes a general worship service—known as sacrament meeting—for everyone. Adults and teenagers attend Sunday School classes. Men and women then split; women attend Relief Society and men attend priesthood meeting. Teenage girls attend Young Women, and teenage boys attend priesthood classes. Children between the ages of three and twelve go to Primary. A nursery serves those between eighteen months and three years of age. Before 1981, Mormons scattered meetings throughout the week. Partly because of the gasoline shortage of the late 1970s, these meetings were consolidated into today's Sunday block. The church leaders hoped this would not only cut down travel time but allow families more time to be together.

Mormons also develop a sense of community by working together in the wards. The only paid full-time clergy in the church are the General Authorities. Ward and stake leaders accept positions to serve as bishop (similar to a pastor or priest), stake president (similar to a bishop in the Catholic church), and staff for other church organizations. Catholic sociologist Thomas F. O'Dea in his extensive study of the Mormons observed that the church's lay ministry means "the church has provided a job for everyone to do and, perhaps more important, has provided a formal context in which it is to be done. The result is a wide distribution of activity, responsibility, and prestige" (The Mormons, 1957). O'Dea explained lay structure has historical roots. Mormonism came into being "when lay responsibility in church government was widespread and developed in circumstances that demanded lay participation for the survival of the group and the carrying-out of the program.... If western conditions caused older and established churches to make use of laymen, a new and struggling religious movement had all

the more reason to do so, and no inhibiting traditions." Mormonism's already expansive definition of priesthood continued to broaden, becoming universal for men after 1978.

TEMPLES

Early Mormon meeting houses and temples were works of art. The architecture was often similar to Gothic chapels and represented the feeling that the Saints were giving the best to the Lord. The Salt Lake Temple, often seen as the symbol of Mormonism, is a classic example; but the church has had a mixed record of preserving these historic treasures. In the late 1960s local residents along with state citizens fought to prevent the church from tearing down the Heber City, Utah, tabernacle that had served as a meeting place for the Wasatch Stake. Just a few years later similar groups were unable to preserve the Coalville, Utah, tabernacle. In the late 1970s the church preserved the outside of the Logan Temple but gutted the interior. It maintained the original murals in the Salt Lake and Manti temples. In 1994 the church announced plans to convert the tabernacle in Vernal, Utah, into a temple.

Mormon temples provide a special worship atmosphere for members; meeting houses are more practical. They include a chapel for worship, a cultural hall for sports and theater, classrooms, a kitchen, and a library. In the early days the buildings were still decorative; now there is more emphasis on utilitarianism. The church provides standard architectural plans that can be adapted for individual needs. New temples are built to serve functional needs. A good contrast that shows the changes is to compare the Salt Lake Temple with its granite towers and symbolism with the simple concrete design of the Provo, Utah, and Ogden, Utah, temples.

EMPLOYMENT AND ECONOMIC TRADITIONS

Mormons have a variety of occupations. Sociologist Wade Dewey Roof and theologian William McKinney examined religious "streams" in the "circulation of the saints." The "upward movement" from one social and economic class to another is one of these streams. They concluded that the Mormon church moved from the bottom of the lowest scale in the 1940s, based on education, family income, occupational prestige, and perceived social class, to the highest in the middle category by the 1980s.

POLITICS AND GOVERNMENT

Since the breakup of the People's Party, the Mormon church leaders claim to speak out only on political issues that they consider to be of moral concern. In 1968 the church opposed the sale of liquor by the drink, supported Sunday closing laws, and favored right-to-work laws. The Mormon church also took a stand opposing the Equal Rights Amendment (ERA) in the 1970s. While LDS women were split, the church's Relief Society came out against the amendment and in October 1976 a First Presidency statement opposed the ERA. The church's stand influenced the vote in Utah, Florida, Virginia, and Illinois and affected states such as Idaho that attempted to reverse their ratification of the amendment.

Besides opposing the ERA, Mormons attended state activities for the International Women's Year. Mormons tended to vote as a bloc against what they saw as liberal proposals. The Mormon church also made national news when an outspoken supporter of the ERA, Sonia Johnson, was excommunicated from the Mormon church. The Mormon Women's Forum, a group of Mormon feminists seeking to reform the church, looks at what its members see as the suppressive influence of the church on Mormon women and examines such issues as the ordination of women to the priesthood.

The First Presidency also spoke out against the location of the MX missile system in Utah and Nevada in 1981. The church issued a statement declaring, "Our fathers came to this western area to establish a base from which to carry the gospel of peace to the peoples of the earth." It continued, "It is ironic, and a denial of the very essentials of that gospel, that in this same general area there should be a mammoth weapons system potentially capable of destroying much of civilization." The federal government then suggested moving the project to Wyoming and later abandoned the project altogether.

The Mormon church also spoke out on other issues. Leaders came out strongly against abortion. Utah passed one of the most pro-life legislation packages in the United States in 1991. In 1992

Sandra and Jerald Tanner pose outside their Salt Lake City, Utah, home and bookstore, where they sell Mormon literature.

the LDS church opposed a pari-mutuel betting proposal in the state of Utah; several General Authorities mentioned this subject in the October General Conference just before the election. The measure was defeated.

Other than speaking out on issues and encouraging members to vote and be involved in the political process, Mormon leaders do not officially support any political party. Almost half of the American Mormon population are Republicans. The rest are independents, Democrats, and small political party members. Mormons tend to be conservative no matter which political party they belong to.

MILITARY

One of Joseph Smith's Articles of Faith, a 13-statement creed of belief, says that Mormons believe in being "subject" to governments and "honoring" the laws of the land. Church leaders asked members to participate in the armed forces of their countries, even when that meant that Mormons fought against each other. During World War II and the Korean and Vietnamese conflicts, Mormon leaders restricted the missionary efforts and discouraged draft dodgers and conscientious objectors. Mormons have changed the way that they view wars. In the early church, Latter-day Saints looked for the Second Coming of Jesus Christ. They viewed the Civil War as the beginning of the "wars and rumors of wars" that were prophesied would proceed the millennium. Mormons saw the Spanish American War that came immediately after Utah received statehood as a chance to prove their loyalty to America. Like other Americans, Mormons saw World War I as a "just war" to end all wars. World War II was seen as a necessary battle to save democracy and remove dictators.

INDIVIDUAL AND GROUP CONTRIBUTIONS

ACADEMIA

Laurel Thatcher Ulrich won the Pulitzer Prize for nonfiction for her book A Midwife's Tale: The Life of Martha Ballard, Based on Her diary, 1785-1812. Ulrich is a professor of history at the University of New Hampshire. Mormons also publish scholarly journals that deal with various aspects of LDS life. The first journal addressed to the intellectual community was Brigham Young University Studies (1959). In 1966 scholars formed Dialogue: A Journal of Mormon Thought, an independent voice, despite disapproval from many in the church's hierarchy. Other autonomous periodicals followed including the Journal of Mormon History (1974), Exponent II (1974), and Sunstone (1975). The Mormon History Association publishes the Journal of Mormon History. The rest are published by small groups devoted to the need for an independent organ for Mormon scholars.

ART AND MUSIC

President Spencer W. Kimball (1895-1985) encouraged Mormons to develop an art form of their own. Mormons have attempted to do this throughout the church's history. They formed musical groups, especially bands, during the nineteenth century. They also participated in choral singing on a local and churchwide basis. Several Mormon regional choirs are very successful. The best-known choir is the Mormon Tabernacle Choir that presents a weekly program on CBS Radio and Television. Mormons have also encouraged plays and theatrical productions. In 1861 the church built the Salt Lake Theater that was the center of drama in the Rocky Mountain West for years. Dramas have continued on a local and churchwide basis over the years. The church also sponsors pageants depicting the Mormon past at

historic sites throughout the United States. The most noted is the Hill Cumorah Pageant near Palmyra, New York, which enacts the history of the Book of Mormon and Joseph Smith's early life.

Mormons have used motion pictures as missionary and teaching tools. One of the first was Man's Search for Happiness, produced for the 1967 World's Fair in New York City. Since then, the church has produced television specials and other motion pictures. In 1993, for example, the church started showing Legacy, a dramatic presentation of early Mormon history, in the restored Hotel Utah, now known as the Joseph Smith Memorial Building.

Mormon artists have used their talents to express church messages. During the 1880s and 1890s, Mormon painters went as missionaries to Paris to learn the impressionist art. They returned to paint murals for the Salt Lake Temple. Other Mormon painters contributed stained glass windows and other paintings to chapels. As the church has grown worldwide, artists from many countries have adapted their native art forms to portray Mormon themes. The church-owned Museum of Church History and Art sponsors art competitions to help collect and display the art produced from around the world. Brigham Young University has a large collection of painting and sculpture in its Museum of Art.

CHURCH ADMINISTRATION

Amy Brown Lyman (1872-1959) served on the Relief Society general board and as president of that organization from 1940 to 1944. Lyman was active in church and state welfare programs. James O. Mason (1930-) worked in the LDS church welfare services and then in the Utah Department of Health. In 1989 he was appointed head of the U.S. Public Health Service. He retired from the federal government in 1992 and was called to be a member of the Second Quorum of Seventy in the LDS church. Eliza R. Snow (1804-1887) served as secretary of the Relief Society in Nauvoo, Illinois, and president in Utah. Snow wrote poems; some are LDS hymns. She was a plural wife of Joseph Smith, and after Smith's death, she became a plural wife of Brigham Young. Emmaline Blanche Wells (1828-1921) was editor of the Women's Exponent for nearly four decades and general president of the Relief Society for over a decade. Active in women's suffrage, she was a friend of Elizabeth Cady Stanton and Susan B. Anthony.

JOURNALISM

Since the early church, Mormons have published newspapers and magazines. Some important U.S. publications include the *Evening and Morning Star* (Independence, Missouri, 1832-1833; Kirtland, Ohio, 1833-1834), the *Times and Seasons* (Nauvoo, Illinois, 1839-1946); and the *Frontier Guardian* (Kanesville, Iowa, 1849-1852). Once in Utah the Mormons started a newspaper, the *Deseret News* (1850-) that is ongoing. Women established a quasi-Mormon women's paper, the *Woman's Exponent* (1872-1914). It was replaced by an official magazine, the *Relief Society Magazine* (1914-1970). The church also sponsored a Sunday School magazine, the *Juvenile Instructor*, a young women's magazine, and the *Children's Friend*. The general church magazine was the *Improvement Era* (1897-1970). In 1970 the church started three new magazines, the *Ensign* for adults, the *New Era* for teenagers, and the *Friend* for children.

LITERATURE

Mormons have also written novels, stories, and poems about the LDS experience. Vardis Fisher (1895-1968) wrote from a Mormon background. Others with Latter-day Saint backgrounds who wrote about Mormon themes include Samuel Taylor (1906-), Virginia Sorsensen (1912-1992), and Maurine Whipple (1904-1993). Another contemporary Mormon author is Levi Peterson (1933-), who writes novels (*Backslider*) and short stories (*Canyons of Grace*). Mormon authors formed the Association of Mormon Letters to promote literary study.

SCIENCE AND TECHNOLOGY

Mormons have also been involved in technological inventions, although most of these innovations have had little to do with their Mormon past. One exception is the development of irrigation. The community-minded Mormons worked out a system to share water in the arid west. They developed irrigation companies and ways to share the limited water resources. Later other Mormons improved these methods and shared them throughout the United States and the world. John A. Widstoe (1872-1952) was among the first Mormons who went east in the 1890s to study science at secular universities. Widstoe directed the Utah Agricultural Experiment Station and was a professor of chemistry at the Utah State Agricultural College. He developed dry farming and irrigation methods. Henry Eyring (1901-1981), a chemist, developed the absolute rate theory of chemical reactions and received the National Medal of Science. He served as president of several leading scientific organizations. Harvey Fletcher (1884-1981), a physicist, worked for Bell Labs and helped develop stereophonic reproduction. James Chipman Fletcher (1919-1992) was the director of NASA from 1971 to 1977. He was asked to return to that position after the Challenger disaster and remained from 1986 to 1989.

POLITICS AND GOVERNMENT

Terrell H. Bell (1921-) was the secretary of education in the early 1980s under President Ronald Reagan. Ezra Taft Benson (1899-1994) served as president of the LDS church. Benson also served as secretary of agriculture under President Dwight D. Eisenhower and was active in farm organizations. David M. Kennedy (1925-), a banker, was the secretary of the treasury under president Richard Nixon from 1969-1971, an ambassador-at-large from 1971-1973, and the ambassador to NATO from 1972-1973. He later became an ambassador-at-large for the LDS church. Rex Lee (1935-) was U.S. solicitor general. In 1989 he became president of Brigham Young University. George Romney (1912-) was president and general manager of American Motors (1954-1962), governor of the state of Michigan (1963-1967), and a candidate for the Republican presidential nomination in 1968. Stewart L. Udall (1920-) served as secretary of the interior in the 1960s under President John F. Kennedy.

SPORTS

Many Mormons have achieved fame in athletics. These include professional baseball players such as Dale Murphy, basketball players such as Danny Ainge, football players such as Steve Young, and golfers such as Johnny Miller. Mormons have also excelled in amateur sports, including athletes Henry Marsh, Doug Padilla, Ed Eyestone, and Jay Silvester in track and field. So many Latter-day Saints have excelled in sports it would be impossible to list them.

MEDIA

PRINT

Affinity.
Monthly publication of the Affirmation/Gay and Lesbian Mormons.

Contact: Marty Beaudet, Editor.

Address: P.O. Box 46022, Los Angeles, California 90046.

Telephone: (213) 255-7251.

Church News.

A weekly publication that includes the activities of Mormons worldwide. It is published as an insert in the Mormon-owned *Deseret News*.

Contact: Dell Van Orden, Editor.

Address: 34 East 100 South, Salt Lake City, Utah 84110.

Dialog: A Journal of Mormon Thought.

Quarterly scholarly journal examining the relevance of religion to secular life and expressing Mormon culture.

Contact: Martha Bradley, Editor.

Address: P.O. Box 658, Salt Lake City, Utah 84110-0658.

Telephone: (801) 363-9988.

Ensign.

A monthly magazine published by the Mormon church for its adult English-speaking members. It includes a message from the First Presidency and articles concerning LDS life and members. A section includes "News of the Church."

Contact: Jay M. Todd, Editor.

Address: 50 East North Temple, 23rd Floor, Salt Lake City, Utah 84150.

Exponent II.

Quarterly newspaper for Mormon women.

Contact: Susan L. Paxman, Editor.

Address: P.O. Box 37, Arlington, Massachusetts 02174.

Telephone: (617) 862-1928.

Fax: (617) 868-3464.

Friend.

An LDS church magazine for children. Its stories and articles provide information for youth ages three to 12.

Contact: Vivian Paulsen, Editor.

Address: 50 East North Temple, 23rd Floor, Salt Lake City, Utah 84150.

New Era.

A Mormon publication for teenagers and young adults. Its articles focus on the concerns of young people.

Contact: Richard M. Romney, Editor.

Address: 50 East North Temple, 23rd Floor, Salt Lake City, Utah 84150.

Sunstone: Mormon Experience, Scholarship, Issues, and Art.

Magazine published by Sunstone Foundation, which also sponsors symposiums in the United States. (In 1992 the Mormon church's First Presidency and Council of Twelve issued a statement cautioning against Mormons participating in symposiums, and many felt this referred to Sunstone.)

Contact: Elbert Peck, Editor.

Address: 331 South Rio Grande, Suite 30, Salt Lake City, Utah 84101.

Telephone: (801) 355-5926.

Fax: (801) 355-4043.

This People: Exploring LDS Issues and Personalities.

Quarterly magazine for members of the LDS church.

Contact: William B. Smart, Editor.

Address: Utah Alliance Publishing, P.O. Box 2250, Salt Lake City, Utah 84110.

Telephone: (801) 581-0881.

Fax: (801) 581-0881.

RADIO

Bonneville LDS Radio Network.

The media corporation owned by the LDS church; provides a 24-hour radio service that is sent by satellite to church members who own satellite receivers. It is also repeated by a few stations across the nation as an FM sideband service.

Contact: Richard Linford.

Address: P.O. Box 1160, Salt Lake City, Utah 84110-1160.

Telephone: (801) 575-7505.

Bonneville International also operates radio stations throughout the United States: KIRO-AM (710) and KIRO-FM (100.7) in Seattle, Washington; KOIT-FM (96.5) and KOIT-AM (1260) in San Francisco, California; KBIG-FM (104.3) in Los Angeles, California; KSL-AM (1160) in Salt Lake City, Utah; KPSN-FM (96.9) and KIDR-AM (740) in Phoenix, Arizona; KMBZ-AM (980) and KLTH-FM (99.7) in Shawnee Mission, Kansas; KZPS-FM (92.5) and KAAM-AM (1310) in Dallas, Texas; WTMX-FM (101.9) in Skokie, Illinois; and WMXV-FM (105.1) in New York City. These are commercial stations. At least one station in each operating area carries the CBS broadcast

"Music and the Spoken Word," and some carry one or more sessions of the LDS General Conference.

LDS Public Communications.

Produces a weekly "News of the Church of Jesus Christ of Latter-day Saints" and other public affairs programs that are packaged and sent to radio stations.

Contact: Gerry Pond, Producer.

Address: LDS Church Headquarters, 50 East North Temple, Salt Lake City, Utah 84150.

TELEVISION, BROADCAST, AND CABLE SERVICES

Bonneville International Corporation.

Operates two television stations, KIRO-TV, Channel 7 in Seattle, Washington, and KSL-TV in Salt Lake City, Utah. These operate as commercial stations and do not regularly carry unique Mormon programming. The LDS church Public Communications airs shows on the cable system religious station VISIONS.

Address: LDS Church Headquarters, 50 East North Temple, Salt Lake City, Utah 84150.

ORGANIZATIONS AND ASSOCIATIONS

Affirmation/Gay and Lesbian Mormons.

Members of the Mormon church; friends, relatives, and interested individuals whose purpose is to promote understanding, tolerance, and acceptance of gay men and lesbians as full, equal, and worthy members of the church and society. Studies ways of reconciling sexual orientation with traditional Mormon beliefs.

Contact: Irwin Phelps, Executive Director.

Address: P.O. Box 46022, Los Angeles, California 90046.

Telephone: (213) 255-7251.

Mormon History Association.

Promotes the study of the Mormon past. It publishes the *Journal of Mormon History*, a biannual scholarly publication.

Contact: Craig and Suzanne Foster, Executive Secretaries.

Address: 2470 North 1000 West, Layton, Utah.

The Society for the Scientific Study of Mormon Life.

Encourages the study of Mormon life.

Contact: Lynn Payne, Secretary-Treasurer.

Address: Sociology Department, A 800 SWKT, Brigham Young University, Provo, Utah 84602.

SOURCES FOR ADDITIONAL STUDY

Alexander, Thomas G. *Mormonism in Transition: A History of the Latter-day Saints, 1890-1930.* Urbana: University of Illinois Press, 1986.

Allen, James B., and Glen M. Leonard. *The Story of the Latter-day Saints,* second edition. Salt Lake City: Deseret Books, 1992.

Arrington, Leonard J., and Davis Bitton. *The Mormon Experience.* New York: Alfred A. Knopf, 1979.

Bush, Lester E. *Health and Medicine Among the Mormons: Science, Sense, and Scripture.* New York: Crossroads, 1993.

Cornwall, Marie, Tim B. Heaton, and Lawrence A. Young. *Contemporary Mormonism: Social Science Perspectives.* Urbana: University of Illinois Press, 1994.

Hansen, Klaus J. *Mormonism and the American Experience.* Chicago: University of Chicago Press, 1981.

Hill, Marvin S. *Quest for Refuge: The Mormon Flight from American Pluralism.* Salt Lake City: Signature Books, 1989.

Ludlow, Daniel H. *Encyclopedia of Mormonism.* New York: Macmillan, 1992.

Mauss, Armand L. *The Angel and the Beehive: The Mormon Struggle with Assimilation.* Urbana: University of Illinois Press, 1994.

Shipps, Jan. *Mormonism: The Story of a New Religious Tradition.* Urbana: University of Illinois Press, 1985.

NAVAJOS

by
D. L. Birchfield

> Because they have remained relatively isolated from the centers of population, because they have been able to hold onto a large part of their ancestral homeland, and because of the great distances and poor roads within the region, Navajos have been more successful than most Native Americans in retaining their culture, language, and customs.

OVERVIEW

The Navajo Nation covers a territory larger than the combined states of Massachusetts, New Hampshire, and Vermont. It is the largest reservation-based Indian nation within the United States, both in land area and population. More than 200,000 Navajos live on the 24,000 square miles of the Navajo Nation. The Navajo's name for themselves is *Dine*, meaning "the people." "Navajo" is the name they were called by the Zunis, and later by the Spanish, the Mexicans, and non-Native Americans. In 1969 the Navajo Tribal Council officially designated the nation the "Navajo Nation."

HISTORY

In the early nineteenth century, Navajos lived in what is now New Mexico in an area that was under Spanish colonial rule. Navajos lived too far from the colonists, who were concentrated in the upper Rio Grande Valley, to be subjected to the disruption of their lives that the Pueblos suffered at the hands of the Spanish. At times the Navajo were allied with the Spanish against other Indians, principally the Utes; other times the Spanish joined forces with the Utes and fought the Navajo. For the Navajo, the most important by-product of Spanish colonization in New Mexico

was the introduction of horses and sheep; the smooth, long-staple, non-oily wool of the Spanish churro sheep would prove ideal for weaving. When the United States claimed that it had acquired an interest in Navajo land by virtue of having won a war with Mexico in 1848, the Navajo were not particularly impressed. But when the U.S. Army arrived in force at the conclusion of the American Civil War, matters took a grim turn for the Navajo. In a scorched-earth campaign, led by Colonel Kit Carson, the Navajo homeland was devastated. Half of the Navajo, demoralized and starving, surrendered to the army and were marched 370 miles to the Bosque Redondo concentration camp on the Pecos River, where many of them died—2,000 of them in one year alone from smallpox. After four years of imprisonment they were allowed to return to their homeland in 1868, now reduced to one-tenth its original size by treaty that same year. They began rebuilding their lives and their herds, virtually unnoticed in an area that most Americans considered worthless desert wasteland.

MODERN ERA

Modern Navajos remain in their ancestral homelands in Arizona, New Mexico, and Utah. In both the 1980 and 1990 census, Arizona and New Mexico ranked third and fourth, respectively, for the largest number of Native American residents within each state. The contemporary government of the Navajo is the Navajo Nation in Window Rock, Arizona. The Navajo Nation comprises approximately 16 million acres, mostly in northeastern Arizona, but including portions of northwestern New Mexico and southeastern Utah. It is a land of vast spaces and only a few all-weather roads. Eighty-eight percent of the reservation is without telephone service and many areas do not have electricity.

The local unit of Navajo government is called the Chapter. There are more than one hundred Chapter Houses throughout the nation, which serve as local administrative centers for geographical regions. Before the 1990 tribal elections, the tribal council system of government was reorganized into executive, legislative, and judicial branches. In 1990 Navajos elected a tribal president for the first time, rather than a tribal chairman. The tribal budget exceeds $100 million annually, with much of the revenue coming from mineral leases.

The Navajo reservation, as created by treaty in 1868, encompassed only about ten percent of the ancestral Navajo homeland. The land base soon tripled in size, largely by the addition of large blocks of land by executive orders of presidents of the United States during the late nineteenth century, when Americans still considered most of the desert Southwest to be undesirable land. Dozens of small increments were also added by various methods until the middle of the twentieth century.

Navajos of the mid-1990s were still adjusting the boundaries of their nation, especially by trading land in an attempt to create contiguous blocks in an area called the Checkerboard, which lies along the eastern boundary of the Navajo Nation. More than 30,000 Navajos live in this 7,000-square-mile area of northwestern New Mexico. They are interspersed with Anglo and Mexican stock raisers and involved in a nightmare of legal tangles regarding title to the land, where there are 14 different kinds of land ownership. The problems originated in the nineteenth century, when railroad companies were granted rights of way consisting of alternating sections of land. They were complicated by partial allotments of 160-acre parcels of land to some individual Navajos, the reacquisition of some parcels by the federal government as public domain land, and other factors. Crownpoint is the home of the Eastern Navajo Agency, the Navajo administrative headquarters for the Checkerboard. As recently as 1991 the Navajo were still attempting to consolidate the Checkerboard, exchanging 20,000 acres in order to achieve 80,000 acres of consolidation.

There are three isolated portions of the nation in New Mexico—satellite reservations known as the Ramah Navajo, the Canoncito Navajo, and the Alamo Navajo. Canoncito was first settled around 1818. Ramah and Alamo had their origins in the late 1860s when some Navajos settled in these areas on their way back toward the Navajo homeland from imprisonment at the U.S. Army concentration camp at Bosque Redondo; approximately half the Navajo had been incarcerated there. Ramah is rural and is a bastion of traditional Navajo life. More than 1,500 Navajos live at Ramah, which is between the pueblos of Zuni and Acoma, near the El Malpais National Monument. More than 1,700 Navajos live at Canoncito, which is to the east of Mt. Taylor near the pueblos of Laguna and Isleta, and more than 2,000 live at Alamo, which is south of the pueblos of Acoma and Laguna.

FIRST NAVAJOS IN AMERICA

Navajos and Apaches, as members of the Athapaskan language family, are generally believed to have been among the last peoples to have crossed the land bridge from Siberia to Alaska thousands of years ago during the last Ice Age. The Athapaskan language family is one of the most widely dispersed language families in North America, and most of its members still reside in the far north in Alaska and Canada.

SETTLEMENT

It is not known, and will probably never be known, exactly when the Navajo and Apache (Southwestern Athapaskans) began migrating from the far north to the Southwest or what route they took. Linguists who study changes in language and then estimate how long related languages have been separated have offered the year 1000 A.D. as an approximate date for the beginning of the migration. It is clear, however, that the Southwestern Athapaskan did not arrive in the Southwest until at least the end of the fourteenth century. Until that time what is now known as the Navajo homeland was inhabited by one of the most remarkable civilizations of ancient people in North America, the Anasazi. Anasazi ruins are among the most spectacular ruins in North America—especially their elaborate cliff dwellings, such as the ones at Mesa Verde National Park, and such communities as Chaco Canyon, where multistory stone masonry apartment buildings and large underground kivas can still be seen today.

Scholars originally thought that the arrival of the Southern Athapaskan in the Southwest was a factor in the collapse of the Anasazi civilization. It is now known that the Anasazi expanded to a point where they had stretched the delicate balance of existence in their fragile, arid environment to where it could not withstand the severe, prolonged droughts that occurred at the end of the fourteenth century. In all likelihood, the Anasazi had moved close to the more dependable sources of water along the watershed of the upper Rio Grande River and had reestablished themselves as the Pueblo peoples by the time the Navajo entered the Southwest. The Navajo then claimed this empty land as their own. They first settled in what they call *Dinetah* (among the Navajo), in the far northwestern corner of what is now New Mexico. After they acquired sheep and horses from the Spanish—which revolutionized their lives—and acquired cultural and material attributes from the Pueblos—which further enhanced their ability to adjust to the environment of the Southwest—the Navajo then spread out into all of *Dine Bikeyah*, "the Navajo country."

ACCULTURATION AND ASSIMILATION

Because they have remained relatively isolated from the centers of population, because they have been able to hold onto a large part of their ancestral homeland, and because of the great distances and poor roads within the region, Navajos have been more successful than most Native Americans in retaining their culture, language, and customs. Until early in the twentieth century Navajos were also able to carry out their traditional way of life and support themselves with their livestock, remaining relatively unnoticed by the dominant culture. Boarding schools, the proliferation of automobiles and roads, and federal land management policies—especially regarding traditional Navajo grazing practices—have all made the reservation a different place than what it was in the late nineteenth century. As late as 1950 paved roads ended at the fringes of the reservation at Shiprock, Cameron, and Window Rock. Even wagons were not widely used until the early 1930s. By 1974, however, almost two-thirds of all Navajo households owned an automobile. Navajos are finding ways to use some changes to support traditional culture, such as the adult education program at Navajo Community College, which assists in teaching the skills that new Navajo medicine men must acquire in order to serve their communities. Bilingual education programs, and broadcast and publishing programs, in the Navajo language are also using the tools of change to preserve and strengthen traditional cultural values and language.

TRADITIONS, CUSTOMS, AND BELIEFS

Navajo traditional life has remained strong. In 1941 an anthropologist interviewed an entire community of several hundred Navajos and could not find even one adult over the age of 35 who had not received traditional medical care from a "singer," a Navajo medicine man called a *Hataali*. Today, when a new health care facility is built on the reservation it includes a room for the traditional practice of medicine by members of the Navajo Medicine Man's Association. Virtually all of the 3,600 Navajo who served in World War II underwent the cleansing of the Enemyway ceremony upon their return from the war. There are 24 chantway ceremonies performed by singers. Some last up to nine days and require the assistance of dozens of helpers, especially dancers. Twelve hundred different sandpainting designs are available to the medicine men for the chantways.

Large numbers of Navajos also tend to identify themselves as Christians, with most of them mixing elements of both traditional belief and Christianity. In a 1976 survey, between 25 and 50 percent called themselves Christians, the percentage varying widely by region and gender. Twenty-five thousand Navajos belong to the Native American Church, and thousands more attend its peyote ceremonies but do not belong to the church. In the late 1960s the tribal council approved the religious use of peyote, ending 27 years of persecution. The Native American Church had originally gained a stronghold on the Ute Mountain Reservation, which adjoins the Navajo Nation on the northeast. In 1936 the church began to spread to the south into the Navajo Nation, and it grew strong among the Navajo in the 1940s.

HOLIDAYS CELEBRATED BY NAVAJOS

The premier annual events open to visitors are the Navajo Fairs. One of the largest is the Northern Navajo Fair, ordinarily held on the first weekend in October, at Shiprock, New Mexico. The dance competition powwow draws dancers from throughout the continent. Another large Navajo Fair is held annually at Window Rock, usually during the first week in July. Other Navajo fairs are also held at other times during the year. All-Indian Rodeos are also popular, as are competition powwows.

NAVAJO DANCES AND SONGS

Except for powwow competition dances and singing, most Navajo traditional dances and songs are a part of healing ceremonies, at which visitors are allowed only with the permission of the family. Photography and video or tape recording of the ceremonies are not permitted without the express authorization of the healers. Charlotte Heth of the Department of Ethnomusicology, University of California, Los Angeles, noted in a chapter of *Native America: Portrait of the Peoples*, that "Apache and Navajo song style are similar: tense, nasal voices; rhythmic pulsation; clear articulation of words in alternating sections with vocables. Both Apache Crown Dancers and Navajo Yeibichei (Night Chant) dancers wear masks and sing partially in falsetto or in voices imitating the supernaturals."

HEALTH AND MENTAL HEALTH ISSUES

Four full-service Indian hospitals are located in northwestern New Mexico. The one at Gallup is the largest in the region. The others are at

Crownpoint, Shiprock, and Zuni. In northern Arizona, full-service Indian hospitals are located at Fort Defiance, Winslow, Tuba City, and Keams Canyon. Indian Health Centers (facilities staffed by health professionals, open at least 40 hours per week, and catering to the general public) are located at Ft. Wingate and Tohatchi in northwestern New Mexico and at Greasewood, Toyei, Dilkon, Shonto, Kayenta, Many Farms, Teec Nos Pos, and Chinle in Arizona. Indian Health Stations (facilities staffed by health professionals and catering to the general public, but open only limited hours, often only one day per week) are located at Toadlena, Naschitti, Navajo, Pinedale, Pueblo Pintado, Ojo Encino, Torreon, Rincon, and Bacca in northwestern New Mexico and at Gray Mountain, Pinon, Dinnebito Dam, Red Lake, Page, Coppermine, Kaibito, Dinnehotso, Rock Point, Rough Rock, and Lukachukai in Arizona. Indian School Health Centers (facilities meeting the same criteria as Indian Health Centers, but catering primarily to school populations) are located at Crownpoint, Sanostee, and Shiprock in northwestern New Mexico and at Leupp, Tuba City, Holbrook, and Chinle in Arizona. Additionally, non-Indian hospitals are located in Flagstaff, Winslow, and Holbrook in Arizona, in Gallup, Rehoboth, Grants, and Farmington in New Mexico, in Durango and Cortez in Colorado, and in Goulding, Utah. In keeping with the recent trend throughout the United States, Navajos are now administering many of their own health care facilities, taking over their operation from the Public Health Service. The Navajo Tribal Health Authority also plans to develop an American Indian medical school at Shiprock, New Mexico.

Traditional Navajo healers are called *Hataali*, or "singers." Traditional Navajo medical practice treats the whole person, not just the illness, and is not conducted in isolation but in a ceremony that includes the patient's relatives. The ceremony can last from three to nine days depending upon the illness being treated and the ceremony to be performed. Illness to the Navajo means that there is disharmony in the universe. Proper order is restored with sand paintings in a cleansing and healing ceremony. There are approximately 1,200 designs that can be used; most can be created within the size of the average hogan floor, about six feet by six feet, though some are as large as 12 feet in diameter and some as small as one foot in diameter. The *Hataali* may have several helpers in the creation of the intricate patterns. Dancers also assist the *Hataali*. In some ceremonies, such

as the nine-day Yei-Bei-Chei, 15 or 16 teams of 11 members each dance throughout the night while the singer and his helpers chant prayers. When the painting is ready the patient sits in the middle of it. The singer then transforms the orderliness of the painting, symbolic of its cleanliness, goodness, and harmony, into the patient and puts the illness from the patient into the painting. The sand painting is then discarded. Many years of apprenticeship are required to learn the designs of the sand paintings and the songs that accompany them, skills that have been passed down through many generations. Most *Hataali* are able to perform only a few of the many ceremonies practiced by the Navajo, because each ceremony takes so long to learn. Sand painting is now also done for commercial purposes at public displays, but the paintings are not the same ones used in the healing rituals.

LANGUAGE

The Athapaskan language family has four branches: Northern Athapaskan; Southwestern Athapaskan; Pacific Coast Athapaskan; and Eyak, a southeast Alaska isolate. The Athapaskan language family is one of three families within the *Na-Dene* language phylum. (The other two, the Tlingit family and the Haida family, are language isolates in the far north, Tlingit in southeast Alaska, and Haida in British Columbia.) *Na-Dene* is one of the most widely distributed language phyla in North America. The Southwestern Athapaskan language, sometimes called Apachean, has seven dialects: Navajo, Western Apache, Chiricahua, Mescalero, Jicarilla, Lipan, and Kiowa-Apache. In 1987 approximately 125,000 Navajos on the reservation still spoke Navajo fluently.

FAMILY AND COMMUNITY DYNAMICS

No tribe in North America has been more vigorously studied by anthropologists than the Navajo. When a man marries, he moves into the household of the wife's extended family. The Navajo say that a Navajo family consists of a grandmother, her married daughters and their spouses and children, and an anthropologist. A Navajo is "born to" the mother's clan and "born for" the father's clan. The importance of clans, the membership of which is dispersed throughout the nation for each clan, has gradually diminished in favor of the increasingly important role of the Chapter House, the significance of which is based on the geographical proximity of its members. Traditional prohibitions against marrying within one's own clan are beginning to break down. The girl's puberty ceremony, her *kinaalda*, is a major event in Navajo family life. Navajos maintain strong ties with relatives, even when they leave the reservation. It is not uncommon for Navajos working in urban centers to send money home to relatives. On the reservation, an extended family may have only one wage-earning worker. Other family members busy themselves with traditional endeavors, from stock tending to weaving.

From the late 1860s until the 1960s, the local trading post was the preeminent financial and commercial institution for most Navajos, serving as a local bank (where silver and turquoise could be pawned), a post office, and a store. One of the most famous, Hubbell's Trading Post, is now a national monument. Traders served the community as interpreters, business managers, funeral directors, grave diggers, and gossip columnists. The automobile and big discount stores in the urban centers at the fringes of the nation have greatly diminished the role of the trading posts.

TRADITIONAL CRAFTS

Navajo jewelry, especially work done in silver and turquoise, is internationally famous. Navajo silversmithing dates from 1853, when a Mexican silversmith arrived at Fort Defiance in what is now Arizona. The Navajo 'Atsidi Sani learned the craft from him and taught it to others. By 1867 several Navajos were working with silver, and by 1880 they had begun to combine turquoise with their designs. At the turn of the century the Fred Harvey Company asked Navajo silversmiths to make lighter pieces for the tourist trade and guaranteed them a sales outlet. Today silversmithing is a widespread craft practiced by many Navajos.

Weaving is also an important economic activity throughout the nation. Navajo weaving has undergone many changes in designs. Navajos are continually creating new ones, and various locations within the nation have become famous for particular types of rugs and patterns. Weaving underwent a revival in the 1920s, when Chinle weavers introduced the multicolored Wide Ruins, Crystal, and Pine Springs patterns. The rug weavers auction at Crownpoint is known world-wide. The Navajo Nation owns the Navajo Nation Arts and Crafts Enterprise at Window Rock, where customers can be assured of purchasing authentic Indian crafts made by Indian people.

EDUCATION

An 1868 treaty provided for schools for Navajo children. The number of schools increased greatly after compulsory school attendance was mandated in 1887. In 1907 a Navajo headman in Utah was imprisoned without trial for a year and a half for speaking out against forced removal of local children to the Shiprock Boarding School. Others were strongly in favor of schools, especially after 19 influential Navajo headmen were exposed to the outside world at the 1893 World's Columbian Exposition in Chicago.

Until 1896 Navajo schools were operated by missionaries, who were frequently more interested in attempting to eradicate the Navajo religion, culture, and language than in educating their charges. Due to great distances and few roads, boarding schools had to be established, which subjected children to the trauma of being removed from their families and their cultures for extended periods of time. Instruction was conducted only in English. With the secularization of the federally maintained Navajo public school system in 1896 civil servants replaced the missionaries, but lack of understanding and appreciation of Navajo culture—and instruction only in English—continued to be the norm. Some religious-affiliated schools continue to the present day, but they display a greater appreciation for Navajo culture and traditions than their nineteenth-century predecessors. By 1958, 93 percent of Navajo children were in school.

In the 1960s Navajos began to exercise much stronger management of their children's education with the establishment of community-controlled contract schools. The Rough Rock Demonstration School was the first of these schools. It introduced bilingual education for young children, the adult training of Navajo medicine men, and other innovative programs based on the perceived needs of the local community.

In 1969 the Navajo established Navajo Community College, the first college operated by Indians. At first located at Many Farms High School, it moved to Tsaile, Arizona, with the opening of its new campus in 1974; there is a branch campus in Shiprock, New Mexico. In 1972 the College of Ganado, a junior college in Ganado, Arizona, was incorporated as a successor to the Ganado Mission School. Following the lead of the Navajo, there are now a total of 29 Indian institutions of higher education in the United States, all members of an American Indian higher education consortium. Navajo Community College Press is a leading native-owned academic press. A number of state supported baccalaureate institutions are located near the Navajo Nation. These include branch campuses of the University of New Mexico at Gallup and Farmington, Northern Arizona University at Flagstaff, and Ft. Lewis College in Durango, Colorado. In 1987 more than 4,000 Navajos were attending college.

EMPLOYMENT AND ECONOMIC TRADITIONS

Nearly every Navajo extended family has members who engage in silversmithing and weaving as a matter of occasional economic enterprise. Farming and stock raising are still important in the economic life of the nation. But the largest employers of Navajo people are the federal and tribal governments. The Navajo have their own parks and recreation department, fish and wildlife department, police department, educational programs, and health service, as well as many other jobs in tribal government and administration. Many federal agencies have offices either on or near the reservation. Other Navajos are employed at the tribally operated electronics plant at Fort Defiance, Arizona, and at the Navajo Forest Products Industry, an $11 million sawmill also run by the tribe. It is located at Navajo, New Mexico, the only industrial town on the reservation, which was created and planned to serve the needs of its industry.

Until the early twentieth century Navajos were able to continue deriving their livelihood from their traditional practices of stockraising. Since the 1920s fewer and fewer Navajos have been able to maintain themselves in this manner. Chronic high rates of unemployment and dependency on governmental assistance have gradually replaced the traditional way of life. In 1941 Navajos had earned only $150,000 from industry, but World War II was a boon time for the economy, giving the Navajo a taste for money and what it could buy. More than half the Navajo 19 and older had wartime jobs; in 1943 they earned $5 million. After the war in the late 1940s the annual family income averaged $400.

By 1973 a study released by the Navajo Office of Program Development found that only 20,000 people were employed on the reservation, of which 71 percent were Navajos. Nine communities were found to account for 84 percent of the jobs held by Navajo people: Shiprock, 3,616; Chinle, 2,284; Window Rock, 2,100; Ft. Defiance, 1,925; Tuba City, 1,762; Crownpoint, 1,149; Navajo, 697; Kayenta, 571; and Ganado, 311. Public service jobs—health, education, and government—were found to account for nearly three-fourths of all employment on the reservation. In 1975 the Navajo unemployment rate was 67 percent. Median Navajo annual household income declined during the 1970s, standing at $2,520 in 1979. In 1991 the unemployment rate was 36 percent.

Since the late 1960s, developing projects have been diversifying employment within the Navajo Nation. The Navajo Indian Irrigation Project (NIIP) is projected to irrigate 110,000 acres of cropland from water impounded in the upper San Juan River basin, using open canals, pipelines, lift stations, and overhead sprinkler systems. The Navajo Agricultural Products Industry (NAPI), a tribal enterprise, manages the program. It includes agribusiness plant sites, grazing lands and a feedlot for cattle production, and an experimental research station. Instituted by act of Congress in 1962, the first 10,000 acres were brought into irrigation in 1976, producing crops of barley and cabbage. By 1981 the total irrigated acreage had increased to 40,000 acres, and crop diversification had added alfalfa, pinto beans, corn, and milo. In 1982 a cattle feedlot operation began to make use of grain and forage crop production. NAPI showed its first profit in 1986. By 1991 more than half of the projected acreage had been brought under irrigation. A coal-gasification plant near Burnham and Navajo-Exxon uranium leases, along with the irrigation project, are making northwestern New Mexico and the eastern portion of the Navajo reservation the focus of new economic activity. Uranium mining, however, has produced health risks, including alarmingly high rates of cancer. In 1979 a broken tailings dam belonging to United Nuclear Corporation at Church Rock, New Mexico, discharged 100 million gallons of radioactive water into the Puerco River—the largest release of radioactivity in United States history.

The Navajo people's biggest economic ventures have been coal leases. By 1970 the Navajo Nation had the largest coal mine in the world.

The 1964 and 1966 Black Mesa coal leases to Peabody Coal Company have become a source of controversy within the nation, as more and more Navajos decry the scouring of their land, the displacement of families for the sake of mining activity, and the threat to sacred places posed by mining operations.

Tourism accounts for a significant amount of economic activity and helps provide a number of Navajos with employment. The Navajo Nation maintains four campgrounds: Monument Valley, Four Corners, Tsaile South Shore south of Lukachukai, and Little Colorado River. Other economic ventures under way include shopping centers and motels. Hunting and fishing provide economic activity and jobs in the portion of the reservation lying in northwestern New Mexico, where 16 lakes offer fishing for trout, channel catfish, bass, northern pike, and bluegill. Hunting permits may be obtained for deer, turkey, bear, and small game.

POLITICS AND GOVERNMENT

The basic unit of local government in the Navajo Nation is the Chapter, each with its own Chapter House. The Chapter system was created in 1922 as a means of addressing agricultural problems at a local level. Before the 1920s, the nation had no centrally organized tribal government. Like many other Indian nations, the tribe was forced to create a central authority by the United States. For the Navajo, the seminal event was the discovery of oil on the reservation in 1921, after which the United States desired some centralized governmental authority for the Navajo for the purpose of executing oil leases, largely for the benefit of non-Navajos. At first the Bureau of Indian Affairs appointed three Navajos to execute mineral leases. In 1923 this arrangement gave way to a plan for each of several Navajo agencies to provide representatives for the Navajo government. After World War II the Navajo Tribal Council became recognized as the Navajo government.

MILITARY

Navajos have served with distinction in the armed forces of the United States in every war in the twentieth century, including World War I, even though they—and other reservation Indians—did not become citizens of the United States until citizenship was extended to them by an act of Congress in 1924. Their most heralded service, however, came during World War II in the U.S. Marine Corps, when they employed the Navajo language for military communication in the field as the Marines stormed Japanese-held islands in the Pacific. They have become known to posterity as the Navajo Code Talkers.

Philip Johnson, born to missionaries and raised on the Navajo reservation, is credited with a leading role in the formation of the Navajo Code Talkers. As a child he learned fluent Navajo, as well as Navajo culture and traditions. At the age of nine he served as interpreter for a Navajo delegation that traveled to Washington, D.C., to present Navajo grievances to President Theodore Roosevelt. After serving in World War I, Johnson was a civil engineer in California. When war broke out with Japan in 1941, Johnson learned that the military hoped to develop a code using American Indians as signalmen. He met with Marine Corps and Army Signal Corps officers and arranged a demonstration of Navajo as a code language. The demonstration took place on February 28, 1942, at Camp Elliott with the cooperation of four Navajos from Los Angeles and one who was in the Navy in San Diego.

"On the wind-beaten plains once lived my ancestors. / In the days of peaceful moods, / they wandered and hunted.... / Now, from the wind-beaten plains, only their dust rises."

From the poem "Ancestors" by Grey Cohoe, on the rising consciousness of the American Indian.

Within a year the Marine Corps authorized the program, which at first was classified as top secret. Johnson, though over age, was allowed to enlist in the Corps and was assigned to help supervise the establishment of the program at Camp Pendleton in Oceanside, California. In May 1942 the Marine Corps, with the approval of the Navajo Tribal Council, began recruiting Navajo men at Window Rock, Arizona, for the program. The first group to receive training consisted of 29 Navajos who underwent basic boot camp training at the San Diego Marine Corps Recruit Depot. They were then sent for four weeks to the Field Signal Battalion Training Center at Camp Pendleton, where they received 176 hours of instruction in basic communications procedures and equipment. They were later deployed to Guadalcanal, where their use of the Navajo language for radio communication in the field proved so effective that recruitment for the program was expanded. Eventually, approximately 400 Navajo Code Talkers saw duty in the Pacific in the Marine Corps. By the end of the war they had been assigned to all six Marine divisions in the Pacific and had taken part in every assault—from Guadalcanal in 1943 to Okinawa in 1945. Today the surviving Navajo Code Talkers maintain an active veterans' organization. In 1969, at the Fourth Marine Division Association reunion in Chicago, they were presented with a medallion specially minted in commemoration of their services.

RELATIONS WITH THE UNITED STATES

Much friction has resulted between the Navajo and the United States over the management of Navajo livestock grazing. The original Navajo Reservation in 1868 encompassed only a small portion of the ancestral Navajo rangelands. The size of the reservation tripled between 1868 and the mid-1930s by 14 additions of blocks of land from 1878 to 1934. This would give the appearance of a rapidly expanding amount of rangeland available to the Navajo. In fact, just the opposite was true.

When the Navajo returned to their homeland from the Bosque Redondo in 1869, the government issued them 1,000 goats and 14,000 sheep to begin replacing the herds that American frontiersman Kit Carson had either slaughtered or confiscated. In 1870 the Navajo were issued an additional 10,000 sheep. With practically no Anglo encroachment on their ancestral rangeland, reservation boundaries had little meaning. The Navajo spread out over their old estate and their herds began increasing. The Bureau of Indian Affairs forbade the selling of breeding stock, eager to see the Navajo regain self-sufficiency. The Navajo population increased steadily, from an estimated 10,000 to 12,000 in 1868 to nearly 40,000 by 1930, and their herds increased accordingly, though there were large fluctuations in the numbers year by year due to occasional drought and disease. At the same time the appropriation of the ancestral rangelands outside the reservation boundaries by Anglo cattle operations and other interests had accelerated, forcing the Navajo onto an ever smaller amount of range. By the 1920s a serious soil erosion problem on the reservation was being blamed on overgrazing. The Navajo tried to alleviate the problem by seeking more land and renewed access to the ancestral rangelands from which they had gradually been forced. The United States believed that a solution to the problem was to force Navajo livestock reductions by killing the animals it deemed to be unnecessary. Thus began a 20-year conflict between the Navajo and the United States, in which the U.S. government, in attempting to implement its policies, found itself disrupting traditional Navajo economic, social, and political life to a far greater extent than at any time in the past.

The tool of the government in this matter was the creation of land management districts, first established in 1936 and adjusted to their preset boundaries in 1955. In attempting to change Navajo livestock practices, the U.S. government subverted and altered Navajo culture in the process. Today the federal land management districts on the reservation are still important factors in Navajo livestock practices. The grazing committees of the Navaho Chapter Houses must work closely with the districts to set the herd size for each range. The extreme turmoil that the stock reduction crisis caused in traditional Navajo life—and the tactics used by the U.S. government to subvert traditional Navajo culture and government during the height of the crisis in the 1930s and 1940s—are the subject of an extensive, detailed study by Richard White, *The Roots of Dependency: Subsistence, Environmental, and Social Change Among the Choctaws, Pawnees, and Navajos.*

Indians in Arizona and New Mexico were not allowed to vote in state and national elections until 1948. In 1957 Utah finally allowed Indians living on reservations to vote—the last remaining state to do so. It required a 1976 U.S. Supreme Court ruling to force Apache County, Arizona, where the population was 70 percent Navajo, to allow Navajos to serve on its board of supervisors. As of 1984 no Native American had ever been elected to public office in Utah. In that year the U.S. Department of Justice ordered San Juan County, Utah, where the population was 50 percent Navajo, to redistrict. The next year a Navajo was elected county commissioner.

The most divisive issue among the Navajo in recent years, and the cause of the greatest strain in relations with the United States, has been the so-called "Navajo-Hopi Land Dispute," in which thousands of Navajos have been forced to relocate from lands that were jointly held by the two tribes since 1882. Many prominent Navajos and some prominent Hopis believe that the relocation of the Navajo and the division of the 1882 Joint Use Area has been undertaken by the U.S. government for the benefit of the American extraction industry, so that valuable mineral deposits within the area can be strip-mined.

INDIVIDUAL AND GROUP CONTRIBUTIONS

ACADEMIA

Among the first Navajos to earn a Ph.D., Ned Hatathli (1923-1972) was the first president of the Navajo Community College—the first college owned and operated by the Navajo people. Annie Dodge Wauneka (1910-) is a public health educator responsible for largely eliminating tuberculosis among the Navajo Indians. Wauneka was later elected to the Navajo Tribal Council and was the first Native American to receive the Presidential Medal of Freedom. Peterson Zah (1937-) is an educator and leader who has devoted his life to serving the Navajo people and retaining Navajo culture, especially among young people. In 1990 Zah was elected the first president of the Navajo people; he was later awarded the Humanitarian Award from the City of Albuquerque and an honorary doctorate from Santa Fe College.

ART

Harrison Begay (1917-) is one of the most famous of all Navajo painters. Noted for their sinuous delicacy of line, meticulous detail, restrained palette, and elegance of composition, his watercolors and silkscreen prints have won 13 major awards. Carl Nelson Gorman (1907-) is a prominent Navajo artist whose oil paintings and silk screening have won acclaim for their divergence from traditional Indian art forms. His contributions to Navajo and Native American art and culture inspired the dedication of the Carl Gorman Museum at Tecumseh Center at the University of California at Davis. Rudolpf Carl Gorman (1931-) is one of the most prominent contemporary Native American artists of the twentieth century. His art combines the traditional with the nontraditional in style and form.

LITERATURE

Navajo author Vee Browne has achieved national recognition with her retellings of Navajo creation stories. Her books have included *Monster Slayer* and *Monster Birds*, a children's biography of Osage international ballet star Maria Tallchief, and a volume in a new series of Native American animal stories from Scholastic books. Her honors include the prestigious Western Heritage Award from the Cowboy Hall of Fame and Western Heritage Center in 1990. A guidance counselor by training, Browne is active in helping emerging Native American writers hone their skills and find outlets for their work, serving as a mentor in the Wordcraft Circle of Native American Mentor and Apprentice Writers. She has also served on the 1994-1996 National Advisory Caucus for Wordcraft Circle.

Elizabeth Woody (1959-), born on the Navajo Nation but raised mostly in the Pacific Northwest, has been influenced by the Pacific Northwest tribes as well as her Navajo heritage. She returned to the Southwest to study poetry and art at the Institute of American Indian Arts in Santa Fe, New Mexico. Her first volume of poetry, *Hand Into Stone*, published in 1988, won the American Book Award. Her other books include *Luminaries of the Humble* and *Seven Hands, Seven Hearts*. Woody's poetry has been anthologized in *Returning the Gift* and *Durable Breath*; her short fiction, "Home Cooking," has been anthologized in *Talking Leaves*; her nonfiction, "Warm Springs," has been anthologized in *Native America*. Woody now teaches at the Institute of American Indian Arts. Her illustrations can be found in Sherman Alexie's *Old Shirts & New Skins*, and her art has been the subject of a five-week exhibit at the Tula Foundation Gallery in Atlanta, Georgia.

Actress/writer Geraldine Keams has appeared in several films, including *The Outlaw Josey Wales*, and has been published in *Sun Tracks* and *The Remembered Earth*. Jean Natoni has published her work in *The Remembered Earth*, as have Aaron Yava, a Navajo/Hopi, and Genevieve Yazzie. Yava's drawing have appeared in *Border Towns of the Navajo Nation*, *Man to Send Rain Clouds*, and *A Good Journey*. Yazzie's work is also featured in *New America*, and she worked on the Navajo-English dictionary project.

Rex Jim, a highly regarded medicine man, is the first author to have published a volume of poetry in Navajo, with no translation, with a major university press (*Ahi'Ni'Nikisheegiizh*, Princeton University Press). Jim's fiction and non-fiction have also been published by Rock Point Community School in the Navajo Nation and include such works as "Naakaiiahgoo Tazhdiya" and "Living from Livestock."

Laura Tohe's volume of poetry, *Making Friends with Water*, was published by Nosila Press, and her poetry and nonfiction have appeared in such publications as *Nebraska Humanities*, *Blue Mesa Review*, and *Platte Valley Review*. Tohe received her Ph.D. in English literature from the University of Nebraska and teaches at the University of Arizona. Tohe's latest project is a children's play for the Omaha Emmy Gifford Children's theater. Like Vee Browne, Tohe is a mentor in the Wordcraft Circle program and is also a member of its 1994-1996 National Advisory Caucus.

Lucy Tapahonso (1953-) is the author of four books of poetry, including *Saanii Dahataa*. She is an assistant professor at the University of Kansas at Lawrence. Della Frank lives and works on the Navajo Nation. Her poetry has appeared in such publications as *Blue Mesa Review* and *Studies in American Indian Literature* and has been anthologized in *Neon Powwow* and *Returning the Gift*. She is co-author of *Duststorms: Poems From Two Navajo Women*. Rachael Arviso (Navajo and Zuni) lives and works on the Navajo Reservation; her short fiction has been anthologized in *Neon Powwow*. Esther G. Belini's poetry also appeared in *Neon Powwow*; she received her B.A. degree from the University of California at Berkeley.

Other Navajos whose work has been anthologized in *Neon Powwow* include Dan L. Crank, Nancy Maryboy, Irvin Morris, Patroclus Eugene Savino, Brent Toadlena, Gertrude Walters, and Floyd D. Yazzie. Aaron Carr (Navajo and Laguna Pueblo) has published poetry and short stories in *The Remembered Earth* anthology, in *Sun Tracks*, and in *Planet Quarterly*. Bernadette Chato's work has appeared in *New America* and *The Remembered Earth*. Grey Cohoe's work has appeared in several anthologies, including *Whispering Wind*, *The Remembered Earth*, and *The American Indian Speaks*. Larry Emerson's column "Red Dawn" appeared in a number of Indian newspapers, and his work has been anthologized in *New America* and *The Remembered Earth*. Nia Francisco, who has taught at the Navajo Community College, has been published in *Southwest: A Contemporary Anthology*, *College English*, *The Remembered Earth*, *Cafe Solo*, *New America*, and *Southwest Women's Poetry Exchange*.

SCIENCE

Nuclear physicist and educator Fred Begay (1932-) has served as a member of the technical staff at the Los Alamos National Laboratory since 1971. His research is directed primarily toward the use of laser, electron, and ion beams to demonstrate the application of thermonuclear fusion; this technique will provide future economical and environmentally safe and clean power sources.

Media

Aborigine.
Address: P.O. Box 892, Gallup, New Mexico 87301.

Americans Before Columbus.
Address: 318 Elm Street, Albuquerque, New Mexico 87012.

Bear Track.
Address: 1202 West Thomas Road, Phoenix, Arizona 85013.

Broncos Monthly News.
Address: Sanostee Rural Station, Shiprock, New Mexico 87420.

Center for Indian Education News.
Address: 302 Farmer Education Building, Room 302, Tempe, Arizona 85287.

Dine' Baa-Hani'.
Address: Box 527, Ft. Defiance, Arizona 86504.

Dinehligai News.
Address: P.O. Box 1835, Tuba City, Arizona 86045.

DNA in Action.
Address: DNA Legal Services, Window Rock, Arizona 86515.

Farmington Daily Times.
Address: P.O. Box 450, Farmington, New Mexico 87499-0450.

Four Directions.
Address: 1812 Las Lomas N.E., Albuquerque, New Mexico 87131.

Graduate Indian Center Newsletter.
Address: 4520 Montgomery N.E., Suite 1B, Albuquerque, New Mexico 97109.

ICAP Newsletter.
Address: Arizona State University, Tempe, Arizona 85281.

Indian Arizona.
Address: 4560 North 19th Avenue, Suite 200, Phoenix, Arizona 85015-4113.

Indian Education Update.
Address: 2121 South Mill Avenue, Suite 218, Tempe, Arizona 85282.

Indian Extension News.
Address: New Mexico State University, Las Cruces, New Mexico 88001.

Indian Life.
Address: 1664 East Campo Bello Drive, Phoenix, Arizona 85022.

Indian Quest.
Address: 708 South Lindon Lane, Tempe, Arizona 85281.

Indian Resources Development Newsletter.
Address: P.O. Box 30003, Las Cruces, New Mexico 88003-0003.

Indian Voice.
Address: 9169 Coors Road, N.W., Box 10146, Albuquerque, New Mexico 87184.

Institute of American Indian Arts Newsletter.
Address: P.O. Box 20007, Santa Fe, New Mexico 87504.

Journal of American Indian Education.
Address: Arizona State University, Tempe, Arizona 82581.

Kachina Messenger.
Address: P.O. Box 1210, Gallup, New Mexico 87301.

Native American Smoke Signals.
Address: 13282 Central Avenue, P.O. Box 515, Mayer, Arizona 86333.

Native Images.
Address: P.O. Box 1624, Tempe, Arizona 85280.

Native Peoples Magazine.
Address: 1833 North Third Street, Phoenix, Arizona 85004.

Navajo.

Covers history, art, culture, events, and people relevant to the Navajo Indians.

Contact: Michael Benson, Editor.

Address: Box 1245, Window Rock, Arizona 86515.

Telephone: (602) 729-2233.

Navajo Assistance.

Address: P.O. Box 96, Gallup, New Mexico 87301.

Navajo Nation Enquiry.

Address: P.O. Box 490, Window Rock, Arizona 86515.

Navajo Times.

Weekly newspaper that contains articles of interest to the American Indian community and the Navajo people.

Contact: Tom Arviso, Jr., Editor.

Address: Box 310, Window Rock, Arizona 86515.

Telephone: (602) 871-6641.

Fax: (602) 871-6177.

Rough Rock News.

Address: Demonstration School, Chinle, Arizona 86503.

Sandpainter.

Address: P.O. Box 791, Chinle, Arizona 86503.

Southwest Native News.

Address: P.O. Box 1990, Tuba City, Arizona 86045.

Southwind Native News.

Address: P.O. Box 40176, Albuquerque, New Mexico 87196.

Thunderbird.

Address: Albuquerque Indian School, 1000 Indian School Road N.W., Albuquerque, New Mexico 87103.

Tsa'aszi'.

Address: P.O. Box 12, Pine Hill, New Mexico 87321.

Uts'ittisctaan'i.

Address: Northern Arizona University, Campus Box 5630, Flagstaff, Arizona 86011.

RADIO

KCIE-FM (90.5).

Address: P.O. Box 603, Dulce, New Mexico 87528.

KENN.

Address: P.O. Box 1558, Farmington, New Mexico 87499-1558.

KGAK.

Address: 401 East Coal Road, Gallup, New Mexico 87301-6099.

KGHR-FM (91.5).

Address: P.O. Box 160, Tuba City, Arizona 86045.

KHAC-AM (1110).

Address: Drawer F, Window Rock, Arizona 86515.

KNNB-FM (88.1).

Address: P.O. Box 310, Whitewater, Arizona 85941.

KPGE.

Address: P.O. Box 00, Page, Arizona 80640-1969.

KPLZ.

Address: 816 Sixth Street, Parker, Arizona 85344-4599.

KSHI-FM (90.9).

Address: P.O. Box 339, Zuni, New Mexico 87327.

KTDB-FM (89.7).

National Public Radio (NPR) affiliate with Indian cultural affairs format.

Contact: Bernard J. Bustos, Station Manager/Chief Engineer.

Address: P.O. Box 40, Drawer B, Pine Hill, New Mexico 87357.

Telephone: (505) 775-3215.

KTNN-AM (660).

Format is contemporary country with traditional and contemporary Native American music.

Contact: Roy Hubbell, General Manager.

Address: P.O. Box 2569, Window Rock, Arizona 86515.

Telephone: (602) 871-2582.

Fax: (602) 871-3479.

ORGANIZATIONS AND ASSOCIATIONS

Arizona Commission for Indian Affairs.
Address: 1623 West Adams, Phoenix, Arizona 85007.

Indian Community Center.
Address: 200 West Maxwell, Gallup, New Mexico 87017.

Indian Education Center.
Address: Arizona State University, Tempe, Arizona 85281.

Navajo Code Talkers Association.
Contact: Albert Smith, President.
Address: P.O. Box 1395, 103 West Highway 66, Gallup, New Mexico 87301.
Telephone: (505) 722-5267.

Navajo Nation.
Address: P.O. Box 308, Window Rock, Arizona 86515.
Telephone: (602) 871-6352.
Fax: (602) 871-4025.

Navajo Tourism Office.
Address: P.O. Box 663, Window Rock, Arizona 86515.
Telephone: (602) 871-6436.
Fax: (602) 871-7381.

New Mexico Commission on Indian Affairs.
Address: 330 East Palace Avenue, Santa Fe, New Mexico 87501.

New Mexico Indian Advisory Commission.
Address: Box 1667, Albuquerque, New Mexico 87107.

MUSEUMS AND RESEARCH CENTERS

Albuquerque Museum and Maxwell Museum in Albuquerque, New Mexico; American Research Museum, Ethnology Museum, Fine Arts Museum, Hall of the Modern Indian, Institute of American Indian Arts, and Navajo Ceremonial Arts Museum in Santa Fe, New Mexico; Art Center in Roswell, New Mexico; Black Water Draw Museum in Portales, New Mexico; Coronado Monument in Bernalillo, New Mexico; Hubbell Trading Post National Historic Site in Ganado, Arizona; Heard Museum of Anthropology in Phoenix, Arizona; Milicent Rogers Museum in Taos, New Mexico; Navajo National Monument in Tonalea, Arizona; Navajo Tribal Museum in Window Rock, Arizona; Northern Arizona Museum in Flagstaff; and the State Museum of Arizona in Tempe.

SOURCES FOR ADDITIONAL STUDY

Bailey, Garrick, and Roberta Glenn Bailey. *A History of the Navajos: The Reservation Years*. Santa Fe, New Mexico: School of American Research Press, 1986.

Benedek, Emily. *The Wind Won't Know Me: A History of the Navajo-Hopi Land Dispute*. New York: Alfred A. Knopf, 1992.

Correll, J. Lee. *Through White Men's Eyes: A Contribution to Navajo History (A Chronological Record of the Navajo People from Earliest Times to the Treaty of June 1, 1968)*; six volumes. Window Rock, Arizona: Navajo Heritage Center, 1979.

Forbes, Jack D. *Apache, Navaho, and Spaniard*. Norman: University of Oklahoma Press, 1969; with new introduction, 1994.

Goodman, James M. *The Navajo Atlas: Environments, Resources, People, and History of the Dine Bikeyah*, drawings and cartographic assistance by Mary E. Goodman. Norman: University of Oklahoma Press, 1982.

Iverson, Peter. *The Navajos: A Critical Bibliography*. Bloomington: Indiana University Press, 1976.

Navajo History, Vol. 1, edited by Ethelou Yazzie. Many Farms, Arizona: Navajo Community College Press for the Navajo Curriculum Center, Rough Rock Demonstration School, 1971.

Thompson, Gerald. *The Army and the Navajo*. Tucson: University of Arizona Press, 1976.

Trimble, Stephen. *The People: Indians of the American Southwest*. Santa Fe, New Mexico: Sar Press, 1993.

Underhill, Ruth. *The Navajos*. Norman: University of Oklahoma Press, 1967.

Warriors: Navajo Code Talkers, photographs by Kenji Kawano, foreword by Carl Gorman, introduction by Benis M. Frank. Flagstaff, Arizona: Northland Publishing, 1990.

White, Richard. *The Roots of Dependency: Subsistence, Environment, and Social Change Among the Choctaws, Pawnees, and Navajos*. Lincoln: University of Nebraska Press, 1983.

NICARAGUAN AMERICANS

by
Stefan Smagula

For Nicaraguan Americans, the central plazas of Nicaraguan towns may have been replaced by shopping centers and malls, but traditions do not change as easily as one's locale. Having only recently arrived in the United States, most Nicaraguan Americans have maintained their traditions and beliefs.

OVERVIEW

Bordered on the north by Honduras, on the south by Costa Rica, on the east by the Caribbean Sea, and on the west by the Pacific Ocean, Nicaragua is Central America's largest nation. Within its triangular borders there are 57,089 square miles (147,900 square kilometers), making Nicaragua the size of Iowa. Dividing the Caribbean lowlands from the Pacific coast is a range of volcanic mountains whose highest peak, Pico Mogoton, 6,913 feet above sea level, is near the Honduran border. The 3,000-square-mile Lake Nicaragua is the largest lake in Central America, and because it was once part of the Pacific Ocean, it is the only place in the world where freshwater sharks, swordfish, and sea horses live. The Caribbean lowlands, which extend inland from the Mosquito Coast, make up half the national territory, but most of Nicaragua's population has always been concentrated near the fertile Pacific coast.

In 1970 about two million people were living in Nicaragua. In 1995 the population could reach 4.5 million, and by 2025 the population could be over nine million, according to the United Nations Department of International Economic and Social Affairs. The population grows 3.4 percent each year, according to the Inter-American Development Bank. *Mestizos*—people of mixed Spanish-indigenous ancestry—make up about 77 percent of Nicaragua's population. Another ten percent are of European descent, nine percent are of African descent, and four percent are indigenous. However, these numbers oversimplify the complex racial, cultural, and ethnic makeup of a country where, before the Spanish conquest, there lived at least nine distinct indigenous peoples.

In the mid-1990s, the main cultural-racial groups were *mestizos, indígenas,* English- and Garífuna-speaking Afro-Karib people, and a small Caucasian elite class. Among the groups living on the Atlantic coast that are commonly defined as indigenous are the Miskito, Sumu, and Rama. The Miskito are not exactly an indigenous group, but a mixture of indigenous peoples and all the travellers who have passed through the Mosquito Coast over the last two centuries. The Sumu and Rama are indigenous people who probably originated in South America. The Garífuna, known historically as the "Black Karibs," are the descendants of escaped African slaves and Karib Indians who intermarried on the island of St. Vincent, where they lived until the British transported them forcibly to the Caribbean coast of Central America in 1796. The Caucasian elite is formed by a small, but typically wealthy, group of people whose ancestors came from Europe—usually Spain, Germany, France, and England. There are minorities of Chinese, Arabs, Cubans, Russians, and others in Nicaragua today.

Indígena, or indigenous, is a cultural and linguistic designation, not merely a racial term. The term "indigenous" refers to people who not only have ancestors who came from Central or South America but who self-consciously identify themselves with a specific indigenous group or tribe, speak the language, and practice the customs of that group. It is possible to be entirely indigenous in the racial sense and to be *mestizo. Mestizos* are culturally, linguistically, and often racially mixed people. The word *mestizo* means "mixed race" in Spanish and refers to the race of people that has resulted from hundreds of years of assimilation and intermarriage between Spanish and indigenous people.

About 88 percent of the entire country is nominally Roman Catholic. Many Nicaraguans, especially in rural areas, practice a syncretist form of religion that combines indigenous religious beliefs with Catholicism. A small but growing percentage of the country belongs to evangelical, Pentecostal, and fundamentalist Protestant churches.

HISTORY

Archaeologists working in El Bosque, Estelí, Nicaragua unearthed a pile of Mastodon and Megatherium bones that suggest that prehistoric people used El Bosque as a slaughter site as many as 20,000 to 30,000 years ago. The bones at El Bosque are among the oldest known evidence of a prehistoric human presence in Central America. Archaeologists and others have theorized that the ancestors of the people who lived long ago at El Bosque—and of all indigenous people in the Americas—originally came from Asia across an ice- or land-bridge between Siberia and Alaska. Aside from archeological and geological evidence, there are also some genetic similarities between Asians and indigenous Americans that support the idea of the Asian origin of indigenous American peoples.

INDIGENOUS SOCIETIES

Many thousands of years after the first people arrived in North America between 5000 and 2000 B.C., the Mayan empire first began to develop along the Caribbean coast, and eventually its influence spread through a network of city-states that stretched from present-day southern Mexico into Honduras, just north of Nicaragua. The ancient Maya produced many intellectual and artistic accomplishments. They invented the first system of writing in the New World, developed a sophisticated knowledge of astronomy and mathematics, worshipped at brightly painted temples of stone, lived in large city-like centers, and sustained a rigid and highly structured society. The many Mayan temples and stone-paved roads that remain are testimony to the beauty, ingenuity, and durability of ancient Mayan architecture and engineering. But the Mayan culture that flowered so brilliantly was the same culture that waged the brutal civil wars that may have contributed to the sudden and mysterious downfall of the Mayan empire around 900 A.D. The descendants of the ancient Maya live today in Guatemala and the Yucatán Peninsula in southern Mexico. The influence of the ancient Maya is ubiquitous throughout Central America, and many Mayan-language words are present in the everyday Spanish spoken in modern Nicaragua.

After the fall of the Maya, the Aztecs, a Nahuat-speaking group who originated in northern Mexico, came into full power. They eventually established a series of allegiances that spread from Mexico to El Salvador. The Nicarao and some of the other indigenous groups of Nicaragua may have originally fled south to Nicaragua in order to avoid subjugation by the aggressive Aztecs. These migrating groups of people brought with them the Aztec language and culture, both of which persist in various forms today in Nicaragua.

COLONIAL PERIOD

Before the Spanish conquest in the early 1520s, Nicaragua was inhabited by numerous competing indigenous groups that probably originally came from both the North and the South. Among them were the Niquiranos, the Nicarao (also known as the Nahual or Nagual), the Chorotega, the Chontales (or Mames), the Miskito, the Sumu (or Sumo), the Voto, the Suerre, and the Guetar. The invading Spaniards and the epidemics that followed the conquest all but eradicated the Nicarao, Chorotega, Chontales, Voto, Suerre, Guetar, and numerous other indigenous Nicaraguan peoples. Having been decimated by war and disease, their societies in shambles, the surviving indigenous people were often forced to learn Spanish, to convert to Catholicism, and to work under slavelike conditions for the benefit of the Spanish colonizers and missionary priests. Over the years, many of these indigenous people assimilated and intermarried into Spanish colonial society, forming the racial-cultural group called *mestizo*.

Although a few Nicarao persisted in Nicaragua until the mid-twentieth century, their descendants are now only vaguely aware of their ethnic identity. Unlike the Nicarao, whose culture has been subsumed by mestizo culture, some indigenous groups in Nicaragua have maintained their language, culture, and ethnic identity. Through a combination of fierce resistance to Hispanic control and isolation in the Caribbean lowlands, the Miskito, the Sumu, and the Rama have managed to survive and maintain their ethnic identity into the present.

INDEPENDENCE

From the time of the conquest until 1821, Spain controlled most of Nicaragua. British colonizers controlled some areas along the Caribbean coast. Nicaragua gained independence from Spain first in 1821 as part of the Mexican empire and later as part of the Central American Federation. By 1838 the Federation had collapsed, and rival conservative and liberal factions had begun violent struggles for power in Nicaragua. The rivalry was as much based on political differences as it was on *localismo*—the provincial hatred between Grenada and Leon, the two oldest colonial cities in Nicaragua. In the mid-1800s the United States and Britain aggravated the liberal-conservative feud when the two nations competed for control over a potential transoceanic canal route that would have crossed Nicaragua via the San Juan River and Lake Nicaragua.

In 1855 liberal leader General Francisco de Castellón invited a well-known Tennessee-born adventurer named William Walker to come to Nicaragua as a peaceful "colonist" with the understanding that Walker was to be the defender of the liberals. However, when Walker arrived with a gang of 58 mercenaries named the "American Phalanx of Immortals," he promptly ended the civil war and declared himself president of Nicaragua. The same day he took office, he issued four decrees: the first was an agreement to borrow money from abroad with the Nicaraguan territory as collateral; the second confiscated the property of the conservatives, for sale to U.S. citizens; the third made English the official language of the country; and the fourth reinstated slavery.

Walker next attempted to conquer the other four Central American republics, but a combined effort by the Central American armies eventually forced his retreat in May of 1857. Fortunately for Walker, there was a U.S. ship waiting to take him back to New Orleans, where he was given a hero's welcome. Completely discredited by the Walker incident, the liberals lost control to the conservatives, who established the Nicaraguan capital in Managua. The conservative government was stable but not democratic. In November of 1857, Walker led another failed invasion of Nicaragua and once again was shipped safely back to the United States. Three years later Walker made his third attempt to achieve "manifest destiny," but this time a British ship overcame him and turned him over to the Honduran government; a Honduran firing squad ended Walker's life. It was just the beginning of a long era of U.S. intervention in Nicaraguan politics.

MODERN NICARAGUA

In recent years the people of Nicaragua have suffered many disasters, both natural and man-made. Hurricanes, severe earthquakes, dictatorships, revolution, counterrevolution, famines, epidemics, civil war, volcanic eruptions, and foreign machination have all besieged Nicaragua. In 1909 the U.S. government supported a revolution that ousted liberal General Jose Santos Zelaya and instated conservative rule. In 1912 popular revolt against the conservatives led to U.S. Marine intervention, and the Marines essentially did not leave Nicaragua until 1933, after fighting a guerrilla war against General Augusto Cesar Sandino and his followers. At the request of their commander, General Anastasio Somoza, the U.S.-trained Nicaraguan National Guard killed General Sandino.

Somoza seized control of Nicaragua in 1936 and was the country's dictatorial ruler until his assassination by young poet Rigoberto Lopez in 1956. Somoza's sons, Luis Somoza Debayle and Anastasio Somoza Debayle, who both spoke English and were educated in the United States, assumed control of the country. When Luis, better known as Tachito, died a natural death in 1967, Anastasio became leader.

After a severe earthquake leveled Managua in 1972, Anastasio Somoza's detractors claimed that Somoza had embezzled many millions of dollars of earthquake-relief money. Popular dissatisfaction with the perceived widespread corruption and brutality of the Somoza regime, coupled with anger over what many believed was the Somoza-directed murder of opposition leader Pedro Joaquin Chamorro in 1978, prompted nationwide uprisings that led to civil war. The Marxist guerrillas of the Sandinista National Liberation Front (FSLN) led the anti-Somoza fighting. The Sandinistas, who take their name from General Sandino, took power on July 9, 1979 and set up a broad-based coalition government. On July 17, 1979 Somoza, along with many of the top-ranking government officials, fled with their families to Miami, Florida. The coalition government soon broke up when the leadership of the Roman Catholic church, industrialists, and moderate politicians all opposed the FSLN's Marxist elements. Somoza later moved from Miami to Paraguay, where he was assassinated.

POST-REVOLUTION U.S. INVOLVEMENT IN NICARAGUA

President Ronald Reagan imposed an economic embargo against Nicaragua, citing what he saw as the threat of Marxism and Communism in the "backyard" of the United States. Despite a thorough campaign of misinformation by the U.S. Department of State, which denied American support for anti-Sandinistas, the U.S. government secretly aided anti-Sandinista guerrillas, or "Contras." Exiled Nicaraguan Contra leaders who lived in Miami worked together with high-ranking officials in the Marines, the Central Intelligence Agency (CIA), and the National Security Council (NSC) to supply weapons and money to the Contras at a time when Congress had passed a law banning U.S. government support for the Contras. This affair was partially brought to light in 1986 when then-Attorney General Edwin Meese discovered that much of the money for the Contras came from a secret arms-for-hostages deal between the United States and Iran. Marine Lt. Col. Oliver North and other high-ranking officials in the CIA and NSC were later convicted of crimes ranging from perjury to conspiracy to defraud the U.S. government. Presidents Reagan and Bush denied prior knowledge of the Iran-Contra affair, as the scandal came to be called. In 1992 President Bush pardoned all of the high-ranking officials who were involved with the scandal.

FLEDGLING DEMOCRACY

FSLN leader Daniel Ortega Saavedra was elected president of Nicaragua in 1984, but much of the opposition boycotted the election. As fighting against the U.S.-funded Contras continued to grow more and more severe, economic and civil rights conditions began to deteriorate in Nicaragua, prompting many former Sandinista supporters to flee to the United States and Costa Rica.

Violeta Barrios de Chamorro, wife of slain anti-Somoza leader Pedro Joaquin Chamorro, was elected president in February 1990. She is a conservative who is moderately opposed to the Sandinistas. After Chamorro's election the U.S. trade embargo was lifted, and in November 1993, in response to Chamorro's pledge to place the army under non-Sandinista control, President Bill Clinton approved $40 million in aid for Nicaragua. Chamorro attempted to achieve peace by giving amnesty to both sides for crimes committed during the civil war, but later clashes between the Sandinista-controlled army and "recontras" have revived old anxieties among Nicaraguans.

Sixteen years after the Sandinista revolution, Nicaragua was still in a desperate situation. There were an estimated 1,500 recontras, former right-wing rebels, fighting for land rights. The annual per capita income in 1994 was $540, less than it was in 1960, according to the University of Central America. Some 60 percent of Nicaraguans were unemployed, and 70 percent lived in extreme poverty, according to United Nations estimates. The infant mortality rate was the highest in Central America: 81 deaths per 1,000 live births. Nicaragua had an external debt of about $14 billion and suffered from inflation. In a mid-1990s poll in Nicaragua, 50 percent of the respondents said that Nicaragua was better off under the brutal Somoza regime, and only seven percent said that the country was better off under Chamorro, according to Canadian magazine *Maclean's*.

FIRST NICARAGUANS IN THE UNITED STATES

Little is known about the first Nicaraguans to immigrate to the United States. One early visitor was Padre Augustín Vigil, a priest from Granada, Nicaragua, who served as William Walker's ambassador to the United States. Padre Vigil lived in Washington, D.C., sometime between 1856 and 1857. The U.S. Census Bureau did not keep separate statistics for individual Central American countries until 1960. Pre-1960 census reports simply lumped Nicaraguans together with all Spanish-surnamed people. Estimates of the number of undocumented early immigrants are not available. Available statistics show a great deal of variation from decade to decade. Documented migration to the United States from Central America rose from 500 individuals entering between 1890 and 1900 to 8,000 individuals between 1900 and 1910. U.S. demand for labor increased during World War I, and 17,000 Central Americans entered the United States legally between 1910 and 1920. Due to 1920s legislation that restricted the flow of immigrants from the Western Hemisphere, the number of Central American immigrants dropped to 6,000 during the 1930s (Nora Hamilton and Norma Stoltz Chinchilla, "Central American Migration: A Framework Analysis," *Latin American Research Review*, Volume 26, No. 1; p. 81). In general, early migration from Nicaragua to the United States was facilitated by Nicaragua's political and economic dependency upon the United States.

Nicaragua's dependence upon the United States has fostered in the Nicaraguans a "perverse esteem" for the United States, according to Judith Thurman in an article written for the *New Yorker*. Esteem for the United States, whether perverse or not, is certainly one of the main factors that has attracted Nicaraguans to move north. Across Central America the United States is thought of as a *país de maravillas* or "country of marvels," where everyone is wealthy, or at least upwardly mobile.

Nearly 7,500 Nicaraguans immigrated legally into the United States between 1967 and 1976. In 1970, 28,620 Nicaraguans were living in the United States, according to the U.S. Census Bureau. Over 90 percent of Nicaraguan immigrants self-reported as "white" on the 1970 census. Most Nicaraguan immigrants during the late 1960s were women: there were only 60 male Nicaraguan immigrants for every 100 female immigrants during this period (Ann Orlov and Reed Veda, "Central and South Americans," *Harvard Encyclopedia of American Ethnic Groups* [Cambridge: Harvard University Press, 1980]; pp. 210-217). This male-to-female ratio may be explained by the large number of Central American women who came to the United States to work as domestic servants so that they could send money home to Nicaragua. Most immigrants during this period settled in urban areas, and many went to live in Los Angeles and San Francisco, California.

DOCUMENTED IMMIGRATION DURING AND AFTER THE SANDINISTA REVOLUTION

The 1979 revolution triggered the largest waves of Nicaraguan immigrants. Documented immigration increased two to three times after the revolution, and undocumented immigration rose dramatically. Migration to the United States occurred in three waves. The first wave took place during the time of the revolution, when the wealthy families closely associated with the Somoza regime fled to Miami. Perhaps as many as 20,000 Nicaraguans immigrated to Miami during this period. After the revolution there was a period of repatriation, when people who had left Nicaragua to avoid the conflicts returned home. The second wave occurred during the early 1980s, when the Nicaraguan government was reorganized. Many non-Sandinista members of the coalition as well as industrialists whose companies had been seized by the state left the country—some ending up in the United States. In the mid-1980s, fighting between the Sandinistas and the U.S.-supported Contras became more severe, which caused the country's economic and civil rights conditions to worsen significantly. The real wage paid to workers, for example, declined by over 90 percent from 1981 to 1987, according Sandinista figures, and the opposition newspaper was heavily censored. This economic chaos and social repression prompted the third and largest wave of immigrants to date. Over 62 percent of the total documented immigration from 1979 to 1988 occurred after 1984 (Edward Funkhouser, "Migration from Nicaragua: Some Recent Evidence," *World Development*, Volume 20, No. 8, 1992; p. 1210). The immigrants in the third wave tended to be young men of all classes fleeing the involuntary military draft and poorer families seeking to escape harsh economic conditions and violence.

The three waves together brought the documented population of all Nicaraguans in the United States to 202,658, with a large percentage of that number, 168,659, having been born in Nicaragua, according to the 1990 U.S. Census. However, some sources say that in the late 1980s there were probably about 175,000 documented and undocumented Nicaraguans in Miami alone.

Between 1982 and 1992, approximately ten percent to 12 percent of the population of Nicaragua left their native country. The largest numbers of people went to Costa Rica, but hundreds of thousands went to the United States, Honduras, and Guatemala. Between 1979 and 1988, 45,964 Nicaraguans emigrated to Costa Rica legally, and another 24,000 people were classified as refugees, as reported by the Nicaraguan Instituto Nacional de Estadísticas y Censos. During almost the same period, 21,417 Nicaraguans entered the United States legally, according to the Immigration and Naturalization Service's *Statistical Yearbook*. In 1988 over 44,000 people, or 1.5 percent of the population of 3.6 million, left Nicaragua, according to the Nicaraguan Instituto Nacional de Estadísticas y Censos.

When the Sandinistas tried to relocate the Miskitos away from the war zones, thousands of Miskitos fled to Honduras and Costa Rica to avoid what they felt was mistreatment by the Hispanic Sandinistas. Large numbers of Miskitos also joined the Contras in Honduras. It is not known whether Miskitos traveled in large numbers to the United States, and the same is true of the Garífuna. There is reportedly a Garífuna community living in Houston, Texas, and some of them may be Nicaraguan.

UNDOCUMENTED IMMIGRATION

The majority of Nicaraguans have entered the United States without the knowledge of immigration authorities. Because most Nicaraguan immigrants are undocumented, and therefore deportable, collecting information about them is difficult. When the Immigration Reform and Control Act of 1986 offered amnesty to all undocumented immigrants who could prove that they had entered the United States before 1982, 15,900 Nicaraguans applied for amnesty. This is more than double the number of Nicaraguans who entered the country legally between 1979 and 1982. According to several studies, the number of amnesty applicants suggests that there were about 200,000 Nicaraguans living in the United States during the mid-1980s (Funkhouser, p. 1210). The true number of Nicaraguan immigrants can only be estimated, but in 1995 it was probably over 250,000.

ENTERING THE UNITED STATES ILLEGALLY

Aimed at reducing the numbers of illegal immigrants to the United States, the 1986 Immigration Reform and Control Act had little effect on the numbers of immigrants who entered the United States—it just drove the flow of undocumented immigrants deeper underground and made it more difficult for them to find work once in the United States. Even before the law was passed, large numbers of Nicaraguans were forced to cross the Mexican-United States border illegally with the help of *coyotes*, a Spanish colloquial term for the people who illegally transport immigrants into the United States. After the law was passed, and border control was stepped up, the *coyotes* began to charge more money.

Undocumented Nicaraguans who enter the United States typically cross Honduras, Guatemala, and Mexico before they reach the United States. *Coyotes*, so called because they often prey upon the people they are transporting, rob, rape, enslave, and sometimes even kill the immigrants they carry. The illegal immigrants are known colloquially as *mojados* or wetbacks, illegals, and *pollos*—Spanish for "chickens," the prey of *coyotes*. Sometimes the *coyotes* recruit the *pollos* inside of Nicaragua, even offering to take the immigrant across the border on family credit; otherwise the immigrant gets to the Mexican-United States border on her or his own and then contacts and pays the *coyote*. Whatever the case, the journey is always dangerous and expensive. *Coyotes* charge from between $400 to $1,500 per person—depending upon the distance involved and the current demand—to take the *pollo* into the United States. The entire journey from Nicaragua to

Los Angeles, for example, easily could cost $2,000 to $2,500, after paying the *mordidas*, or bribes to Mexican officials at control posts on Mexican highways, the *coyote*'s fee, food, and transportation costs. This is an enormous sum of money for most people in Nicaragua, where the average person makes about $540 dollars a year.

The border towns of Tijuana and El Paso are the crossing points favored by undocumenteds. These towns are notorious for drug cartels and prostitution rings in which many Central American immigrants, Nicaraguans among them, are forced to work. One chapter in *Miami: Secretos de un exilio*, a book written by a Nicaraguan who traveled in the United States, tells the tale of one woman and her four children who narrowly escaped tragedy when they tried to cross at El Paso. The family flew into Mexico City and then traveled to a border town where she claimed the Mexican police robbed her of all the money she had, $970, and even took the clothes of her small children. Penniless, friendless, and homeless, the woman had almost given up hope when a family member living in Miami was able to help her and her children to reach Miami, where she filed a claim for political asylum. The INS allowed her to remain in the United States until her claim could be heard by the court—a process that could take years.

Not every woman who attempts to cross the border illegally has family in the United States and not every woman makes it across the border. Some must struggle to survive waiting on tables at bars or working as prostitutes in the rough bordertowns like Ciudad Juarez, Matamoros, and Nuevo Laredo, hoping to someday save enough to cross into *el norte*, or "the north," as the United States is known. The number of Central American women who are raped in transit to the United States is unknown because most women are too ashamed to tell even family or friends about the crime, but many estimate that rape, along with robbery, is common. On the U.S. side of the border, undocumented immigrants cannot report assault, rape, or exploitation in the cantinas, manual-labor jobs, or the sweatshops that employ them for fear of being deported by the *migra*, as the INS is known in California, Texas, and Florida.

SETTLEMENT PATTERNS

Miami, the capital of the exile, is the center of Nicaraguan American life. The ousted dictator Anastasio Somoza was the first of about 175,000 Nicaraguans who overwhelmed Miami in the 1980s. A small city called Sweetwater, about 16 miles from Miami, has been dubbed "Little Managua" by the locals because of the large number of Nicaraguans who settled there. Nicaraguans have also created communities in other large urban centers where Hispanics live, such as Los Angeles and San Francisco. Smaller numbers of Nicaraguans live in large cities in Texas. All these cities have significant Spanish-speaking populations, and it is possible to work and live in areas where Spanish is spoken. This facilitates networking and the sense of community among the recent immigrants, many of whom speak little English. In 1990, soon after Chamorro was elected, a caravan of cars and buses left Miami headed for Nicaragua, according to several newspaper reports. But only a small portion of the total number of Nicaraguan Americans were repatriated.

REACTION TO NICARAGUAN IMMIGRANTS

Many Americans wished that more Nicaraguans would return to Nicaragua. In 1994, tensions between the haves and have-nots, and between the "legals," and the "illegals," led to the passage of Proposition 187 in California, which would prohibit undocumented immigrants from benefitting from publicly funded services like nonemergency health care and education. Similar legislation banning undocumented immigrant children from public schools was passed in Texas but was eventually overthrown by the U.S. Supreme Court. It is not known whether Proposition 187 will actually survive the constitutional challenge recently posed to it by the federal government.

The recent animosity toward immigrants in California is in contrast to the welcome that Nicaraguan immigrants received in the early days of the first wave after the revolution. President Reagan painted the Nicaraguan revolution in stark cold-war tones: the Sandinistas were Marxists and Communists who were going destabilize the Central American isthmus through their close alignment with Communist Cuba and the Soviet Union. According to this cold-war scenario, Nicaraguan immigrants were refugees and exiles who had escaped the Communist regime and therefore deserved political asylum and assistance. Even though the political affiliation of the parent country is not supposed to enter into questions of asylum, Nicaraguan applicants were granted political asylum about 50 percent of the time in 1987.

Salvadorans fleeing similar conditions received asylum only three percent of the time in 1987.

During the mid- to late 1980s, in an attempt to make up for what they saw as wrong-headed American immigration laws and foreign policy in Central America, some Americans banded together to support Central Americans and Central American refugees. Over 80 municipal governments created U.S.-Nicaraguan sister city agreements. The U.S. cities sent medical supplies, food, and farming materials to their counterpart cities in Nicaragua. Some churches created what were called "sanctuaries" for undocumented immigrants. The churches offered support and shelter to Central American immigrants. During this period Central American refugee centers appeared in nearly every large urban center in America.

Key issues facing Nicaraguans staying permanently in the United States are questions of identity. They wonder, for example, whether they are considered refugees or immigrants, or whether they are merely living in exile. CARACEN, one of the leading Central American assistance groups, reflected this shift in identity when it recently changed its name from Central American Refugee Center to Central American Resource Center. Another key issue is the return of millions of dollars' worth of property seized by the Sandinistas under a law that gave the government the right to seize property if the owner was absent from Nicaragua for more than 60 days. Many of the former owners of the seized property are now citizens of the United States and are attempting to regain title through U.S. law.

MYTHS AND STEREOTYPES

The most common myth pertaining to Nicaraguan Americans is that they are all former *Somocistas*, as the followers of Somoza are called. This is untrue. Despite significant cultural differences among Hispanics Nicaraguans are often perceived to be no different from other Hispanics and are thus subject to the same prejudices and stereotypes as other Hispanics. Some common stereotypes are that Hispanics are docile, ignorant, and easily led. On the West Coast and in the Southwest, Mexican Americans and Central Americans have been called "greasers," "beans," "beaners," and "spics" by people of other ethnic groups. According to one stereotype, Hispanics stay within their own group and always protect their own people. A phrase common in the schools and streets of Cali-

fornia expresses this stereotype: "If you crush one bean, the whole burrito comes after you."

Undocumented Hispanic immigrants are also portrayed as ignorant workers who enjoy being exploited. In an article about the Southwest's dependence on undocumented workers published by the *Wall Street Journal* in 1985, the author wrote: "But Mexican nationals ... happily dangle in branches and power lines for the minimum wage" (*Wall Street Journal*, May 7, 1985; p. 10). Common among leftist American writers in the 1980s was the stereotype of the happy, friendly Nicaraguan: "But most of all I like the people— their friendliness, their openness, their courage" (Rita Golden Gelman, *Inside Nicaragua: Young People's Dreams and Fears* [New York: Franklin Watts, 1988], p. 128).

ACCULTURATION AND ASSIMILATION

For Nicaraguan Americans, the central plazas of Nicaraguan towns may have been replaced by shopping centers and malls, but traditions do not change as easily as one's locale. Having only recently arrived in the United States, most Nicaraguan Americans have maintained their traditions and beliefs. Because the Nicaraguan American community in San Francisco, for instance, is relatively diffuse, Nicaraguan Americans there are assimilating into a pan-Latino culture more rapidly than they are assimilating into non-Latino culture.

BELIEFS, CUSTOMS, AND MYTHS

Some of the Nicaraguan people's beliefs and traditions date back to pre-Columbian times, and others appeared during colonial times. Most are a mixture of both pre- and post-Colombian culture. *La Llorona* is the name of a legendary woman-spirit who walks along streets and paths on dark nights sighing and sobbing over the children she lost during the time of the Spanish conquest. One version of the legend has it that her children were killed by an earthquake; another says that the children's Spanish father stole them away from her. This may be related to the Mexican legend of La Malinche, the lover and assistant of conquistador Cortés.

There are many folk beliefs in Nicaraguan culture. One belief says that if a person who has walked in the sun for many hours looks at a child with sun-irritated eyes, that child will be "infected with the sun" and will suffer from fever and diarrhea. The treatment is difficult unless the person who has infected the child is known. If the person is known, the treatment is simple: wrap the child in a sweaty shirt that has been worn by the person who originally infected him or her, and hours later the child will be healthy.

LA PURÍSIMA

Until recently, *La Purísima* was a holiday celebrated only in Nicaragua. Now it is also celebrated in Los Angeles, Miami, and other Nicaraguan American communities. The holiday takes place from the last days in November until the night of the seventh of December, which is called the *Noche de Gritería*, or "Night of the Shouting." All through the week women make all sorts of intricate traditional sweets and drinks that are exchanged during the last night. The centerpiece of the holiday is a small statue of the Virgin Mary covered with decorations of flowers, fruits, lights, and candles. Each night the family prays together in front of the statue. Then on the last night, neighbors, friends, and families go traveling from house to house in a secular-religious celebration that takes its name from the shouts raised in honor of the Virgin Mary: "Long live the Conception of Mary!" and "Who causes so much joy? The Conception of Maria!" are heard in the streets. Groups of people also sing traditional religious songs in front of the statue of the Virgin. Typically, the *gritería* culminates at midnight with the explosions of bombs and the reports of thousands of pistols shot into the air.

SEMANA SANTA

In Nicaragua, *Semana Santa*, or Holy Week, a major summer holiday, is a time for relaxing at the beach or vacationing. This holiday may still be celebrated by Nicaraguan Americans. On Easter Sunday villagers all over Nicaragua gather beneath bowers made of palm leaves decorated with fruits, vegetables, and flowers. Accompanied by a brass band, the villagers walk slowly around the town. At the head of the parade are people dressed as symbolic characters: Hebrew elders and Apostles. The Apostles carry a life-size statue of Christ. The procession usually ends up in a public square in front of the town's church, where there is food for sale and carnival-like concessions.

VELORIOS

The observation of a *velorio*, or funeral party, after a person's death is an old tradition with Hispanic origins. During the *velorio* the family and friends of the deceased gather to share their grief. The relatives and close friends sit in the same room as the deceased and maintain a silent prayer vigil throughout the night until morning. Others at the *velorio* talk in small groups to distract themselves from fatigue, tell picaresque stories, drink liquor, eat large amounts of food, and even gamble. Sometimes, after hours of drinking, the *velorio* ends in a raucous, drunken fight. Following the *velorio*, the body is taken to the cemetery in a funeral procession with a brass band. The mourners follow the casket on foot to the cemetery.

The *velorios de los santos*, or *velorios* of the saints are similar affairs in which small candles are lit on altars, festive decorations are hung, and prayers are made, accompanied by music and sometimes drunkenness. The most famous funeral procession of a saint is the procession of Managua's Saint Domingo. In this noisy and colorful parade, a tiny statue of the saint is carried to "sanctuary" in the hills of Managua. Marimbas, dancers, fireworks, and a carnival atmosphere mark the event.

SPORTS

The national sport of Nicaragua is baseball. The first organized baseball game in Nicaragua took place in 1892. For more than two decades in the early part of the twentieth century, U.S. Marines were stationed in Nicaragua. One result of the U.S. Marine occupation is Nicaragua's widespread fascination with baseball. In Nicaragua, the word for baseball is *béisbol* ("bays-bole"). Men and boys in small towns play baseball with whatever equipment they can muster—sometimes they use tough Nicaraguan grapefruits (for which the Nicaraguan word is *grapefruit*), or even an old sock rolled up around a rock, instead of a ball. There is also a professional league. At least five Nicaraguans who may have started by playing with rolled up socks later played for the major leagues in the United States. Cockfighting, a sport in which two trained cocks fight each other, is also popular among Nicaraguans. Men gather around the fighting birds to cheer their favorites and to make bets on the animals, who fight sometimes to their death.

PROVERBS

Seemingly innocuous, the following Nicaraguan proverbs and sayings reveal quite a bit about Nicaragua and Nicaraguans: *Con eme-omo-de-odo, se consigue todo*—With manners, everything can

be obtained; *Cada uno tiene su modo de matar pulgas*—Everyone has her or his manner of killing fleas; *De todos modos, moros son todos*—At any rate, *moros* are everyone (A "*moro*" is the color white with dark brown grease stains and may refer in a negative way to *mestizos*.); *El último mono se ahoga*—The last monkey drowns (Figuratively, the last in line will not receive her or his portion of food.); *No creer en santos que orinan*—Don't believe in saints that urinate; *Voltearse la tortilla*—The tortilla is flipped (Refers to the way that tortillas are cooked. This is said when one party has fallen and another is ruling.); *Tamal con queso, comida de preso*—Tamale with cheese, food of the prisoner (Tamales are made of meat and cornmeal wrapped in cornhusks or banana leaves).

CUISINE

The importance of corn to traditional Nicaraguan cuisine, religion, and folklore cannot be overstated. To a large extent, the traditional cuisine of Nicaragua consists of varied and imaginative ways of preparing corn, or *maíz*. Nearly every part of the plant is used—from the fungus that grows on the corn to the husk that covers the cob—and nearly every type of dish and beverage is made of corn. Breakfast cereals, breads, drinks that taste a bit like coffee, puddings, desserts, porridges, and even beer are made from corn. Beans are also important. Unlike most of Central America, which prefers black beans, Nicaraguans tend to eat red beans. While everyday cuisine is based upon abundant corn and beans, the *criollo* ("cree-o-yo"), or Creole, cuisine is based more on meats and sauces that are Nicaraguan adaptations of Spanish and European dishes. The scarcity and high cost of meats in Nicaragua has put meats normally out of reach of everyone but the upper classes. In the United States, where meat is more abundant, Nicaraguans probably eat more meat dishes.

The small, round, unleavened *tortilla* ("tortiya"), made of ground and processed corn, is the daily staple of Nicaraguans. The *tortilla* is bread, spoon, and plate for Central Americans. Traditionally made at home by hand, *tortillas* are made by machines in the United States and sold in supermarkets all over California, the Southwest, and in southern Florida.

The *tamal* ("tahmahl") is a bit of corn dough with seasoned meat, sweet chocolate or vegetables, wrapped inside of a corn husk or a banana leaf before it is steamed or boiled. The national *tamal* is called *nacatamal* ("naca-tahmahl") and consists of pork, chicken, or turkey, various vegetables, mint, and hot peppers, all combined with a corn dough made with sour orange juice. A small amount of this mixture is put inside of an individual corn husk or banana leaf and then folded or rolled and sealed before cooking. Restaurants in Miami have signs in their windows that say: "Nacatamales and other Nicaraguan Foods." According to Angélica Vivas, author of

Cocina Nica, "The silent nacatamal says more about the history of Nicaragua than all the pages of don José Dolores Gámez" (Angélica Vivas, *Cocina Nica* [Managua: Ministerio de Cultura], p. 17). Gámez was a chronicler of Nicaraguan colonial history.

Red bean soup is the most typical soup of Nicaragua. It is made from red beans boiled with garlic, onion, pork, and sweet red pepper. The soup is poured into a bowl, and then an egg is cracked into the hot soup. The heat of the soup partially cooks the egg.

Desserts called *almibares* ("almeebarays") consist of honey- and syrup-coated fruits such as mango, mamey, jocote, papaya, and marañon. *Almibares* are eaten all over the country during *Semana Santa*. Many corn-based desserts also exist. For example, *motlatl atol* ("moetlahtel ahtol") is a yellow pudding-like dessert made from corn, milk, sugar and a fruit, which is also eaten during *Semana Santa*. Chocolate, which is native to Central America, is used not only in sweet drinks and desserts but as a flavoring for meat dishes.

HEALTH AND MENTAL HEALTH ISSUES

Because so many are undocumented immigrants, and so many work in clandestine jobs for low wages, many poorer Nicaraguan Americans have no health insurance. Those who have health insurance are either professionals who are covered through their employers or are successfully self-employed.

Nicaraguan-educated doctors came to the United States only to find out that without a U.S. medical degree, all those years of study and training were worth almost nothing. Those who had studied in the United States were more fortunate and could more easily transfer their experience to a job in the states. Frustrated by their situation, some Nicaraguan-educated doctors in Miami founded clandestine clinics to serve the uninsured Nicaraguan American population. These clinics do not appear in telephone books and do not advertise. During the time of the Contra war, some of the medical supplies that were headed for the fighting in Honduras ended up in some of these clandestine clinics, according to a Nicaraguan journalist. Other Nicaraguan-educated doctors found illegal work in clinics that agreed to let them work at wages far below normal.

Nicaraguans, like all people native to the Americas and the Pacific Basin, are genetically prone to develop a small birthmark called a Mongoloid spot. The spot is a small, oval bluish mark found at the base of the spine on babies. Eventually this spot disappears, leaving no trace. In some cases a similar pigmentation, called Nevus of Ota, can appear on the cheeks or on the sclera of the eyes. Nevus of Ota is disfiguring, but usually not debilitating.

According to a study conducted in Los Angeles and published in 1992, post-traumatic stress disorder (PTSD) is common among Nicaraguan immigrant children who have witnessed or experienced violence. Fifteen of the 31 Central American children studied had witnessed violence. Of the children who both witnessed violence and lost contact with a caregiver, 100 percent suffered from some form of PTSD. The combined stress of living in guerrilla war conditions, forced emigration and impoverished living conditions in the United States cause many Nicaraguan refugee children to suffer from the symptoms of PTSD, including nightmares, nervousness, insomnia, loss of appetite, and tearfulness.

"The Nicaraguan's worst fear is not the fear of losing a job, but the fear of getting sick."

A Nicaraguan American pediatrician in Miami (from Guillermo Corés Domínguez, *Miami: secretos de un exilio*. Managua: El Amanecer, 1986).

The indigenous medicine of Nicaragua is one part magical and one part rational. For every illness there is a specific therapy, usually of vegetal origin. Many potent botanical medicines are part of the traditional medicine—some of them, like the leaves of the coca plant, which are the source of cocaine, have been recognized as potent pharmaceuticals by Western science and medicine. The various leaves, roots, berries, etc. are usually made into a tea that the ill person drinks or a poultice that is applied to the body. Certain foods, like *atol* made from corn, are also believed to have specific curative properties.

La Hechicería, or the belief that some people have supernatural powers, is common among Nicaraguans and stems from indigenous beliefs. Those who practice *hechicería* are known as *brujos* ("brew-hose") or *brujas* ("brew-has"). *Brujos* are believed to have the power to transform themselves into animals, like tigers and dogs, and they are also believed to have the power to heal others.

LANGUAGE

Spanish is the language spoken by most Nicaraguans, but several indigenous groups speak their own languages, sometimes in addition to Spanish or English. The Miskito, Sumu, and Rama on the Atlantic coast all speak related, but distinct, languages. Many Garífuna also speak an Afro-Karib language of their own, sometimes in addition to Spanish and English. It is not known how many Garífuna or indigenous people have immigrated to the United States.

Nicaraguan Spanish has several distinguishing characteristics. The Nicaraguan accent dates back to the sixteenth century in Andalusia, and the relative isolation of Nicaragua meant that the accent did not change in the same ways that the Andalusian accent has. For example Nicaraguans have a tendency to replace the "s" sound with an "h" sound when speaking. Nicaraguans also tend to use grammatical constructions that are now rare in most other Spanish-speaking countries. For example: ¡Y quien sos vos!—And who are you! uses "vos," an antiquated form of "you." Some linguists have noted that onomatopoeic words are common in Nicaragua.

Nicaraguan Spanish also has many indigenous influences. Until the nineteenth century a hybrid form of Nahuat-Spanish was the common language of Nicaragua. Today Nahuat, Mangue, and Maya words and syntax can be found in everyday speech. As the words for two tropical fruits, mamey and papaya, testify, Nicaraguan Spanish has some Caribbean influences. Béisbol and daime ("dime") attest to Nicaragua's long association with the United States. However, the greatest number of Nicaraguanisms come from Aztec and Nahuat languages. An example of a Spanish-Aztec hybrid word is chibola, the Nicaraguan word for bottled soda. It is formed from two words: Chi, meaning small in Aztec, and bola, meaning ball in Spanish. Nicaraguan Americans and other Spanish-speaking newcomers in cities like Miami soon learn to speak "Spanglish"—a combination of Spanish and English. For example: "Have a nice day, Señor." This type of language usage is so common that it can be heard on Spanish-language radio shows and television.

The most novel contribution Nicaragua has made to the Spanish language is the word jodido ("ho-dee-doe") and its many variants. Jodido stems from the most vulgar and indecent of all verbs in Latin American use that describe the act of sexual intercourse. Strangely enough, jodido has been used so commonly in Nicaragua by all classes of people that the word has lost much of its original obscenity and now means something like "bothered" or "screwed."

GREETINGS

Buenos Días (Spanish), Pain lalahurám (Miskito), and Buiti binafi (Garífuna) mean "Good day." ¿Qué tal, amiga? (Spanish), Naksá? (Miskito), and Numá ¿Ida biñá gia (Garífuna) are translated as "How's it going, friend?" Bendiga, mami (Spanish) and Busó da (Miskito) mean "Bless you, mother." ¿Como te llamas? (Spanish) and ¿Ka gia biri? (Garífuna) mean "What's your name?" Adios (Spanish), Asabé (Miskito), and Ayó (Garífuna) all mean "Good-bye."

FAMILY AND COMMUNITY DYNAMICS

Partly because of tradition, and partly because of the Catholic prohibition against birth control and abortion, Nicaraguan American families tend to be larger than is typical in the United States. The tradition of larger families may have its origin in Nicaragua's agricultural economy, where more children meant more help to plant and harvest. In the 1960s and early 1970s, few families immigrated together—two-thirds of all Nicaraguan Americans were women. As the reasons for immigration changed over the years, single women gave way to more families and widowed women with children. Sometimes families spanning three generations immigrated together. When immigrants are fleeing from violence and economic problems, as Nicaraguans were in the 1980s, they want to take as many loved ones with them as they can. When the goal is to make money to send home, as it was in the late 1960s, immigrants tend to migrate alone. No records of the number of Nicaraguan American families who receive public assistance exist, but the number is probably fairly small, because many Nicaraguans are undocumented and are not eligible for any public assistance.

INTERMARRIAGE

In a 1989 San Francisco study of birth records, out of 192 Nicaraguan-born mothers living in San Francisco, 12.5 percent had children with men born in the United States; 56 percent had children with men born in Nicaragua. Nicaraguan-born women were much more likely (28.1 percent) to have children with Mexican- or other Latin American-born men than they were with U.S.-born men. The same study showed that the degree of intermixing between Nicaraguan Americans and other groups is higher than the degree of intermixing between Mexican Americans and other groups. This implies that Nicaraguan Americans, in San Francisco at least, are less likely than Mexican Americans to retain a distinct nationality-based identity (Steven P. Wallace, "The New Urban Latinos, Central Americans in a Mexican Immigrant Environment," *Urban Affairs Quarterly*, Volume 25, No. 2, December 1989; pp. 252-255).

Divisions are deep among Nicaraguan American families and communities. The Sandinista revolution split sister from brother, mother from daughter, and friend from friend. Attitudes for or against the Sandinistas undermined efforts to create cohesive communities in cities like Los Angeles, where Casa Nicaragua, a Nicaraguan American social and political organization, was burned down in 1982, supposedly by Somocistas. However, as Nicaraguan Americans have become more assimilated, the political differences that have divided the community are dissipating. Relatives of the deposed dictator Somoza own a chain of Nicaraguan restaurants in Miami, and these restaurants have become gathering places for a diverse group of Nicaraguans. Speaking of the restaurant, one Nicaraguan American man said: "The Somozas own it and nobody cares. Everybody goes there—Somocistas, Sandinistas, Cubans, Americans. Because in Miami, the war is over. Our children are not even Nicaraguans" (Marc Fisher, "Home, Sweetwater, Home," *Mother Jones,* Volume 13, No. 10, December 1988; p. 40).

EDUCATION

Many Nicaraguan families venture to the United States in order to improve their own or their children's education. It has been common for the wealthier families in Nicaragua to send their children to boarding schools and universities in the United States and Europe. There is no information on typical courses of study among Nicaraguan Americans.

INTERGROUP RELATIONS

Tension exists in Miami between Nicaraguan Americans and African Americans. African American resentment over what they saw as preferential treatment being given to the newly arrived Nicaraguans led, in part, to African American riots in Miami in 1989. African Americans perceived that the Cuban Americans, who have most of the political control in Miami, were looking after Nicaraguan American interests at the cost of African American interests.

RELIGION

Nicaraguan Americans are overwhelmingly Roman Catholic, and Nicaragua's Catholicism is very much centered around the Virgin Mary. There are small numbers of evangelical, Pentecostal, and fundamentalist Protestants. Most, if not all, of Nicaragua's 60 or 70 Jewish families left the country during and after the Sandinista revolution. They cited anti-Semitic harassment by FSLN soldiers as the main reason for leaving. One Managuan synagogue was firebombed, reportedly by people who identified themselves as members of the FSLN. Some of these Nicaraguan Jewish families came to live in the United States. Changes in worshipping practices since Nicaraguans have begun arriving in the United States are not documented.

EMPLOYMENT AND ECONOMIC TRADITIONS

As undocumented immigrants, most Nicaraguan Americans work in clandestine jobs with neither social security nor unemployment benefits. Over the years diverse groups of Nicaraguans have immigrated to the United States—some were doctors or bankers with university educations, and some were 15-year-old boys fleeing the draft. As a group, though, they all have one thing in common: the majority of them are undocumented. Regardless of degrees, experience, and prior social standing, the undocumented Nicaraguan American must take whatever job is available, and usually these jobs are unskilled manual or service-related jobs that, because they are clandestine, sometimes pay below the federally mandated minimum wage.

The Nicaraguans who left Nicaragua between 1979 and 1988 tended to be of working age and were more likely to have been employed in a white-collar occupation before leaving Nicaragua, according to a statistical study published in 1992. They also tended to be from wealthier, larger, better educated families compared to nonmigrating Nicaraguans: 64.2 percent of the immigrants had a secondary education, compared to 43.3 percent of all families surveyed in Managua. About 14 percent of the migrants had a university education, according to the same study (Funkhouser, p. 1211).

Nicaraguan Americans typically find work by word of mouth through family or friends who have established themselves in the community, and they tend to work in specific niches that are related to these unofficial word-of-mouth networks. In San Francisco between 1984 and 1985, for example, it was common for Nicaraguan American men to work as janitors. Nearly nineteen percent of Nicaraguan men worked as building cleaners, according to one San Francisco study that tallied the occupations of Nicaraguan-born men who listed their occupations on their children's birth certificates. Another 21.6 percent of Nicaraguan-born men worked in operations and fabrications, 10.8 percent worked at production and repair, and 1.1 percent worked as farmers, bringing the total percentage of Nicaraguan Americans who worked at blue-collar jobs to 33.5 percent. Nicaraguan Americans were also much less likely to work as food-service laborers than were other Central Americans. Only 6.5 percent of the Nicaraguan Americans worked in food service, compared to 34.5 percent of Guatemalan Americans. Nicaraguan Americans were much more likely to work in white-collar jobs: 36.3 percent held administrative or other white-collar positions, compared to 6.9 percent of the Guatemalan Americans. This discrepancy may be the result of differences in education between Nicaraguans and Guatemalans. Similar information about Nicaraguan American women in the workplace is not available, though many sources say that Central American women commonly work in textiles and housecleaning.

Each year, Nicaraguan Americans send millions of dollars home to their families in Nicaragua. Thirty-six percent of Managuan households with relatives abroad received an average of $79 each month, according to a Sandinista government source. In 1988, Nicaraguan Americans sent somewhere between $50 million and $80 million to Nicaragua, making this nearly the second largest source of foreign exchange in Nicaragua. Coffee exports bring in the most money: $84 million in 1988. The amount of money sent home to Nicaragua has probably increased since 1988.

POLITICS AND GOVERNMENT

Shortly after the revolution, Nicaraguan exiles living in America who were politically opposed to the Sandinistas organized an anti-Sandinista guerrilla army that had its base in Miami and Honduras. Many of the guerrillas and guerrilla leaders were former National Guardsmen or closely associated with the Somoza regime. The Somoza regime's long affiliation with the U.S. government meant that some Nicaraguan exiles already had well-placed U.S. government contacts and friends before they arrived in the United States. U.S.-government support of the Contras grew out of some of these relationships. Secret CIA involvement in the Contras' affairs dates back to at least 1981, according to Edgar Chamorro, former leader of the Contras, in his 1987 book *Packaging the Contras*. In a Senate subcommittee hearing in 1988, Octaviano Cesar, a Contra leader, admitted that the Contras had smuggled drugs into the United States for a profit, but he blamed it on the U.S. Congress, which cut off aid to the Contras in 1984. Notes taken by Marine Lt. Col. Oliver North suggest that North knew about the drug running and that the profits may have been as high as $14 million.

In 1987, about 2,000 Nicaraguan Americans protested publicly against the Immigration Reform and Control Act of 1986, which they said prevented the majority of Nicaraguans from remaining in the United States. About two months later, Attorney General Edwin Meese signed an order that permitted Nicaraguans to stay in the United States "for the present." Two years later, in 1989, the INS changed its regulations in order to streamline its operations. The result was that fewer Nicaraguan refugees received working permits. Nicaraguans who applied for political asylum in the 1980s received preferential treatment. Up to 80 percent of the Nicaraguan asylum applicants were granted asylum in certain years. Only a few nationalities, like the Poles and Armenians, received asylum at such a high rate.

INDIVIDUAL AND GROUP CONTRIBUTIONS

What follows is an eclectic listing of individuals who have contributed in various ways to American culture and society.

ACADEMIA

Author of "El mito de paraiso perdido en la literatura nicaragüense en los Estados Unidos" ("The Myth of Paradise Lost in Nicaraguan Literature in the United States") published in *El Pez y la Serpiente* in 1989, Nicasio Urbina is a writer and an assistant professor in the department of Spanish and Portuguese at Tulane University in Louisiana. Born in 1958 in Buenos Aires, Argentina, to parents of Nicaraguan ancestry, Urbina was educated at Florida International University and at Georgetown University. He has been a member of the Modern Language Association since 1984 and has received numerous scholarships and fellowships throughout his academic career.

Eddy O. Rios Olivares was born in Nicaragua in 1942 and educated in Minnesota and Puerto Rico. He has conducted microbiological research in Nicaragua and at the Universidad Central Del Caribe in Puerto Rico, where he is professor and chairman of the department of microbiology. He has received various grants and research awards for his antitumor research.

ARTS

Guillermo Ortega Chamorro (Gil Ortegacham), an actor and musician who lives in Brooklyn, New York, was born in 1909 in San Jorge, Rivas, Nicaragua. Chamorro performed in *The Blood Wedding* on off-off-Broadway in 1987 and 1988. Educated in Nicaragua and at New York University, Chamorro has made many contributions to New York City radio and drama.

HEALTH CARE

Born in Managua in 1940, Norma F. Wilson is an obstetrical/gynecological nurse practitioner who lives in Kansas City. Wilson belongs to many professional associations and organizations relating to public health, family planning, and minority health. The Seward County Republican Women named her one of the women of the year in 1988.

Born in Managua in 1937, Rolando Emilio Lacayo is a physician and surgeon who specializes in gynecology, infertility, and obstetrics. Lacayo was educated in Nicaragua, the United States, and Mexico. From 1970 to 1971 he was an instructor in gynecology and obstetrics at Baylor College in Houston, Texas. He is a member of the American Medical Association, a junior fellow of the American College of Obstetrics and Gynecology, and currently practices medicine in Miami, Florida.

LITERATURE

Pancho Aguila was born Roberto Ignacio Zelaya in 1945 in Managua. Aguila immigrated to the United States in 1947 and wrote and read in coffeehouses in San Francisco during the late 1960s until he was arrested and sentenced to life in prison in 1969. He escaped from prison in 1972 and was reapprehended five months later. While in prison, he has written five books of poetry and has contributed to several periodicals.

Horacio Aguirre is the publisher and editor of *Diario las Américas*, the leading conservative Spanish-language newspaper in Miami. In 1970 he was named man of the year by *Revista Conservadora del Pensamiento Centroamericano*. Horacio's brother, Francisco Aguirre, has been called the godfather of the Contras. Francisco is a former National Guard colonel and has lived in exile in Washington, D.C., since 1947. He is well known in CIA and U.S. Department of State circles.

POLITICS AND BUSINESS

President of the Nicaraguan American Banker's and Businessman's Association, educated at Notre Dame, and a commercial banker in Miami, Roberto Arguello is one of the most visible Nicaraguan Americans. In 1990 Arguello took time off from banking to lobby in Washington on behalf the Nicaraguan government. In the late 1980s, he was a vocal opponent of the U.S. refugee policy for Nicaraguans.

Nadia Pallais is a resident of Miami and in 1988 was the Dade County government's spokeswoman for the Hispanic media. Pallais immigrated to the United States from Nicaragua in 1979. She is the mother of four daughters.

SOCIAL WORK

Born in 1943 in Mexico to a Nicaraguan father and a Mexican mother, Carmela Gloria Lacayo has worked for many years to improve the lives of the poor and elderly. Lacayo established the National Association for Hispanic Elderly and founded Hispanas Organized for Political Equality. She has been appointed to a number of political positions, including vice-chair of the Democratic National Committee, member of the Census Bureau on Minority Populations, and an advisor on Social Security reform.

SPORTS

Nicaraguan American pitcher Dennis Martinez is a native of Grenada, Nicaragua. In 1976 Martinez became the first Nicaraguan ever to play in major league baseball. In 1990 he signed a three-year contract with the Montreal Expos that paid him more than $3 million per season. In an interview with *Sports Illustrated*, Martinez said that when he broke into the big leagues and told people that he was from Nicaragua, they didn't know where it was. In 1991 he pitched a perfect game against the Los Angeles Dodgers. He has narrowly missed winning the Cy Young award several times. During his off-seasons in Miami, Martinez has put his celebrity among baseball-loving Nicaraguan Americans to good use by participating in drug-prevention programs for young Nicaraguan Americans in Miami.

MEDIA

PRINT

Diario las Américas.
Leading conservative Spanish-language paper in Miami; printed in Spanish.

Contact: Horacio Aguirre, Editor.
Address: 2900 Northwest 39th Street, Miami, Florida 33142.
Telephone: (305) 633-3341.

La Estrella de Nicaragua.
Newspaper published in Spanish by and for Nicaraguan Americans in Miami, Florida.

Telephone: (305) 386-6491.

Nicaraguan Perspectives.
Quarterly political science journal of Nicaragua Information Center.

Address: Box 1004, Berkeley, California 94701-1004.

Voz Summary.
Summary of Nicaraguan news from shortwave radio.

Address: Box 8151, Kansas City, Missouri 64112.
Telephone: (816) 561-0125.

RADIO

WZOR-AM (1490).
Broadcasts programs for the Hispanic community in Immokalee, Florida. Programming is specifically for Nicaraguan Americans.

Contact: Jose Quiatanilla, Station Manager.
Address: 2105 West Immokalee Drive, Immokalee, Florida 33934.

ORGANIZATIONS AND ASSOCIATIONS

American Nicaraguan Foundation.
Address: 444 Brickell Avenue, Miami, Florida.
Telephone: (305) 375-9248.

Nicaragua Center for Community Action (NICCA).
Publishes quarterly journal with news and analysis about Nicaragua and the Nicaraguan solidarity movement.

Address: 2140 Shattuck Avenue, Box 2063, Berkeley, California 94704.
Telephone: (501) 428-2146.

Nicaraguan American Women Civic Association.
Contact: Mauritza Herrera.
Address: 961 Northwest Second Street, Miami, Florida 33128.
Telephone: (305) 326-7700.

Nicaraguan Interfaith Committee for Action (NICA).
NICA is concerned with the problems of Nicaragua and with taking action to alleviate them;

the organization also sponsors Nicaraguans in the United States.

Contact: Janine Chayoga, Director.

Address: 942 Market Street, San Francisco, California 94102.

Telephone: (415) 433-0657.

MUSEUMS AND RESEARCH CENTERS

Dallas Museum of Art.

The museum displays an extensive collection of pre-Columbian and eighteenth- to twentieth-century textiles, censers, and other art objects from the Nicaraguan area.

Contact: Karen Zelanka, Associate Registrar, Permanent Collection.

Address: 1717 Harwood, Dallas, Texas 75201.

Telephone: (214) 922-1200.

Fax: (214) 954-0174.

Documentation Exchange.

Formerly known as the Central America Resource Center, the Documentation Exchange maintains a library of information on human rights and social conditions in many countries, including Nicaragua. Also produces biweekly compilations of current news articles on Central America called NewsPaks.

Contact: Charlotte McCann, Editor.

Address: P.O. Box 2327, Austin, Texas 78768.

Telephone: (512) 476-9841.

Fax: (512) 476-0130.

The Nattie Lee Benson Latin American Collection.

Located at the University of Texas at Austin, this renowned collection consists of Nicaraguan books, books about Nicaragua, and resources relating to Nicaraguan Americans. Excellent electronic information resources.

Contact: Laura Gutiérrez-Witt, Head Librarian.

Address: Sid Richardson Hall 1.109, General Libraries, University of Texas, Austin, Texas 78713-7330.

Telephone: (512) 471-3818.

Nicaraguan Information Center.

Maintains a library of 100 volumes, videotapes, slides, magazines, newspapers and microfilms on Nicaragua.

Contact: Amanda Velazquez, President.

Address: P.O. Box 607, St. Charles, Missouri 63301.

Telephone: (314) 946-8721.

The UT-LANIC Server.

Managed by the Institute of Latin American Studies at the University of Texas at Austin. The UT-LANIC Server is accessible on the Internet. It provides access to academic databases and information services worldwide, as well as information from and about Latin America. To reach UT-LANIC Server via World Wide Web browser: http://lanic.utexas.edu; via Gopher client: lanic. utexas.edu.

Contact: Laura Gutiérrez-Witt, Head Librarian.

Address: Sid Richardson Hall 1.109, General Libraries, University of Texas, Austin, Texas 78713-7330.

Telephone: (512) 495-4520.

SOURCES FOR ADDITIONAL STUDY

Boyer, Edward J. "Nicaraguans in L.A.: A Lively Political Debating Society," *Los Angeles Times*, February 20, 1984; pp. 1, 3.

Chamorro, Edgar. *Packaging the Contras: A Case of CIA Disinformation*. New York: Institute for Media Analysis, 1987.

Chavez, Leo Ralph. "Outside the Imagined Community: Undocumented Settlers and Experiences of Incorporation," *American Ethnologist*, May 1991; pp. 257-278.

Cortés Domínguez, Guillermo. *Miami: secretos de un exilio*. Managua: El Amanecer, 1986.

Crawley, Eduardo. *Nicaragua in Perspective*. New York: St. Martin's Press, 1979.

Fins, Antonio. "For Exiled Nicaraguans, Just Where Is Home?" *Business Week*, March 26, 1990; pp. 28D-28K.

Fisher, Marc. "Home, Sweetwater, Home," *Mother Jones*, 13, No. 10, December 1988; pp. 35-40.

Funkhouser, Edward. "Migration from Nicaragua: Some Recent Evidence," *World Development*, 20, No. 8, 1992; pp. 1209-18.

Gelman, Rita Golden. *Inside Nicaragua, Young People's Dreams and Fears*. New York: Franklin Watts, 1988.

Hamill, Pete. "Any Happy Returns?" *Esquire*, July 1990; pp. 33-34.

Marks, Copeland. *False Tongues and Sunday Bread: A Guatemalan and Mayan Cookbook*. New York: M. Evans and Company, Inc., 1985.

Misconceptions about U.S. Policy Toward Nicaragua (Department of State Publication 9417, Inter-American Series 117). Washington, D.C.: Department of State, 1985.

Petzinger, Thomas, Jr., Mark Zieman, Bryan Burrough, and Dianna Solis. "Vital Resources: Illegal Immigrants Are Backbone of Economy in States of Southwest," *Wall Street Journal*, May 7, 1985; pp. 1, 10.

Scanlan, David. "Just Like Old Times: The Civil War May Be Only a Memory, But Nicaraguans Are Still Suffering," *Maclean's*, January 17, 1994; p. 32.

Thurman, Judith. "Dry Season," *New Yorker*, March 14, 1988; pp. 44-78.

NIGERIAN AMERICANS

by
Kwasi Sarkodie-
Mensah

While in their native country large families are common, Nigerian Americans have fewer children so that they will be able to give them the best education possible. The early immigrants were educated people and they instilled in their children the importance of education as a component of a successful life.

OVERVIEW

With an area of 356,669 square miles (923,768 square kilometers), Nigeria's size approximately equals the combined areas of New Mexico, Arizona and California. A coastal state on the shores of the Gulf of Guinea in West Africa, Nigeria is bounded by Niger to the north, Benin to the west, Cameroon to the east and southeast, and Chad to the northeast.

The November 1991 population census put Nigeria's population at 88,514,501. Nigeria's population is extremely diverse—more than 250 ethnic groups are identified. Ten ethnic groups account for 80 percent of Nigeria's population. English is the official language; however, Yoruba, Ibo, and Hausa represent the principal languages, joined by Kanuri, Fulani, Nupe, Tiv, Edo, Ijaw and Ibibio. Like many other African countries, the distribution of religion can be broken down into three major areas: Christians, Muslims, and animists. In Nigeria, 47 percent of the population practice Islam, while about 36 percent practice Christianity, and 17 percent practice animism or traditional African religion. Nigeria's national flag, believed to have been designed by Taiwo Akinkunmi—a Nigerian student in London, consists of a field of green, white, and green, divided into three equal parts. Green represents the agricultural richness of the nation, while the white stands for unity and peace.

HISTORY

The name Nigeria was coined by Lord Lugard's wife in 1897 in honor of the 2,600-mile-long Niger River. The first Europeans to reach Nigeria were the Portuguese in the fifteenth century. In 1553, the first English ships landed at the Bight of Benin, then known as the "Slave Coast." The present day Nigeria came into existence in 1914, when the Colony of Lagos, the Protectorate of Southern Nigeria, and the protectorate of Northern Nigeria were amalgamated. Even before the arrival of Europeans, the many nationalities or ethnic groups were highly organized and had law and order. There were village groups, clans, emirates, states, kingdoms, and some empires. The Kanem-Bornu empire goes as far back as the tenth century. The Oyo Empire, founded in the late fourteenth century by Oranmiyan, a Prince of Ile-Ife, had a powerful army and maintained diplomatic contact with other kingdoms in the area. The Fulani Empire was established in 1803 by the *jihad*, or holy war against the rulers of the Hausa states by Usman Dan Fodio; it went on to become one of the most powerful kingdoms. Within two decades, parts of the Oyo Empire, Bornu, and Nupe were added by conquest to the Fulani Empire. Though there was no centralized governments, trade and commercial activities existed. Intermarriages flourished among the various groups.

One of the most prosperous trades even before the arrival of the Europeans was the slave trade. It was common practice in many African civilizations to sell war captives, delinquent children, and the handicapped; and Nigeria was no exception. With the arrival of the Europeans, slavery became more lucrative. Intertribal wars were encouraged by the Europeans so that more captured slaves could be sent to the New World. The British Parliament abolished slavery in 1807.

MODERN ERA

When the mouth of the Niger River was discovered in 1830, the British heightened their economic expansion into the interior of the country. Formal administration of any part of Nigeria goes back to 1861 when Lagos, a vital component of the lucrative palm oil trade, was ceded to the British Crown. At the Berlin Conference of 1884-1885, geographical units and artificial borders were created in Africa by European powers without any consideration of cultural or ethnic homogeneity. Britain acquired what is now Nigeria as a result of this scramble for Africa. In 1914 the various protectorates were consolidated into one colony, the Protectorate of Nigeria.

After World War II, nationalism rose in Nigeria. Under the leadership of Nnamdi Azikiwe, Obafemi Awolowo, and Alhaji Sir Abubakar Tafawa Balewa, Nigerians began to ask for self-determination and increased participation in the governmental process on a regional level. On October 1, 1960, Nigeria became an independent country, but this independence brought about a series of political crises. Nigeria enjoyed civilian rule for six years until January 15, 1966 when, in one of the bloodiest coups in Africa, the military took over the government of Tafawa Balewa, assassinated him and replaced him with General J. Aguiyi-Ironsi. Later that month Ironsi was killed in a counter-coup, and replaced by General Yakubu Gowon. In early 1967 the distribution of petroleum revenues between the government and the Eastern Region, where the majority of Ibos come from, sparked a conflict. Gowon proposed to abolish the regions of Nigeria and replace them with 12 states. Colonel Ojukwu, a soldier from the Ibo tribe, announced the secession of the Eastern Region, and declared a Republic of Biafra. Events following this declaration resulted in the Biafra War, one of the most deadly civil wars in Africa, claiming the lives of over two million Nigerians.

Gowon was overthrown in a bloodless military coup on July 29, 1975, when he was attending a summit meeting of the Organization of African Unity. Brigadier General Murtala Ramat Muhammed became the leader of the government. He started a popular purging of the members of the previous government and announced a return of the country to civilian rule. On February 13, 1976 Muhammed was assassinated during a coup attempt. Lieutenant General Olusegun Obasanjo, chief-of-staff of the armed forces in Muhammed's government became the new head of state. In 1978 Nigeria produced a new constitution similar to that of the United States.

The country returned to civilian rule in 1979 when Alhaji Shehu Shagari was sworn in as president on October 1. Shagari's government ended on New Year's Eve 1983 when he was ousted by a group of soldiers, led by Major-General Muhammadu Buhari. Buhari introduced stringent measures to curb corruption. He imprisoned many former government officials found guilty of corruption. Under Buhari's government, the death penalty was reintroduced in Nigeria and freedom of the press was rigorously restricted. Many newspapers were banned and many journalists were imprisoned or tortured.

On August 27, 1985, Major General Ibrahim Babaginda led a bloodless coup d'etat, deposing Buhari as the head of state. Babaginda promised to restore human rights, establish a democratically elected government, and eradicate corruption, which has always been a part of Nigerian politics. Babaginda not only violated his promises, but imprisoned journalists who stood up for the truth. After repeatedly postponing, altering, or scrapping timetables for a return to a democratically elected government, Babaginda annulled the results of the elections held in June 1993, which were won by his opponent Chief Moshood Abiola. Under pressure, Babaginda resigned and left power in the hands of a handpicked and widely opposed interim government headed by Ernest Shonekan, who was prominent in business and supported Babaginda.

THE FIRST NIGERIANS IN AMERICA

Compared with other ethnic groups in America, the presence of Nigerian Americans in the United States does not date back very far. However if the slave trade is considered, then Nigerians have been part of the American society as far back as the eighteenth century. Even though Nigerian Americans of the modern era do not want to be associated with slavery and put in the same category as African Americans, history bears witness to the fact that the coastal regions of modern day Nigeria were referred to as the Slave Coast. Nigeria provided a vast percentage of the Africans who were bitterly separated from their families and forced into slavery by European entrepreneurs.

World War I expanded the horizons of many Africans. Though European colonial masters wanted Africans in their territories to receive an African-based education with emphasis on rural development, Africans wanted to go abroad to study. In the early parts of the twentieth century, it was traditional for Nigerians to travel to European countries such as the United Kingdom and Germany to receive an education and to return to their countries. Two dynamic programs emerged after the war: Marcus Garvey's military platform of Africa for Africans, and W. E. B. Dubois' Pan African movement. The colonial powers in Africa feared that the strong ideas of identity and freedom preached by both Garvey and Dubois would turn the Africans against their colonial masters.

The United States became a center of attraction for Nigerian nationalists who later became the revolutionary leaders. The Nigerians who came to the United States to study saw the white person in the same light as a black individual; white people were subjected to the same grandeur and malaise of human nature and were in no way superior to black people. The most prominent Nigerian symbolizing the spirit of freedom and human respect was the late Chief Dr. Nnamdi Azikiwe, first President of Nigeria and first indigenous governor-general of Nigeria. Arriving in the United States by boat in 1925, Zik, as he was affectionately referred to, entered Storer College and later transferred to Lincoln University and Howard University. While in the United States, Zik experienced racial prejudice and worked as a dishwasher, a coal miner, and a boxer to survive the difficult times in America. However, he later became a professor at several prestigious American institutions. Two other Nigerians from the Eastern Region used their American education in the 1930s to bring change to their people. Professor Eyo Ita and Mbonu Ojike became influential leaders in Nigerian national politics.

SIGNIFICANT IMMIGRATION WAVES

In its 1935 annual report, the New York-based Institute of International Education indicated that in 1926 there were three documented Nigerian students in United States universities. In its subsequent reports, the number of students increased to 22 in 1944. A steady increase in Nigerians continued when the oil boom in the 1970s made Nigeria one of the wealthiest nations in Africa and many came to the United States to study. Most students were sponsored by their parents and relatives both in Nigeria and in the United States, while others obtained financial assistance from universities and colleges in the United States. In the late 1970s and 1980s Nigeria was among the top six countries in the number of students sent to study in the United States. While many returned home, in the 1980s when Nigeria's economy began to decline at a tragic rate, many Nigerians remained in the United States and obtained citizenship. After becoming citizens many Nigerian Americans brought their relatives into the United States. According to

1990 census figures, there were approximately 91,688 people of Nigerian ancestry living in the United States.

SETTLEMENT

Nigerian Americans, like many Africans migrating into the United States, are willing to settle almost anywhere. Family relations, colleges or universities previously attended by relatives and friends, and the weather are three major considerations for settlement by Nigerian Americans. Early Nigerians coming to the United States went to schools in the southern United States. Large metropolitan areas attract modern day Nigerian Americans, many of whom hold prestigious professional jobs. Poor economic conditions have forced many highly educated Nigerian Americans to take up odd jobs. In many metropolitan areas, Nigerian Americans with one or several graduate degrees are taxi drivers or security officers. The heaviest concentrations of Nigerian Americans are found in Texas, California, New York, Maryland, Illinois, New Jersey, and Georgia.

ACCULTURATION AND ASSIMILATION

Mention the name Nigeria, and the average American conjures up the image of the jungle and children living in squalor. This perception is largely due to the erroneous depiction of Africa by Hollywood and the tendency of the American media to publicize only catastrophic events in Nigeria. Nigeria as a country defies easy generalization because the people are as varied as the cultural differences that characterize them as a nation. Nigerian Americans come from a wide variety of rich backgrounds not only in financial terms but in societal values. Despite the negative stereotypes Nigerian Americans have maintained their pride and cultural identity, and contribute immensely to the American society at large.

TRADITIONS, CUSTOMS, AND BELIEFS

Nigerians have a variety of traditions and lore dating back to antiquity. For example, peeking at the eggs on which a hen is sitting was believed to make you blind. Singing while bathing could result in a parent's death. A pregnant woman who ate pork could have a baby with a mouth like that of a pig. Among the Yoruba it was believed that there were spirits hidden in rivers and hills in various cities. Since these spirits were there to protect the people, they were not to be disturbed on certain days of the week. In almost all Nigerian societies, there is a strong belief that most disease and death are caused supernaturally, by witchcraft, curses, or charms. Witches are usually elderly women. For a long time the Ibos believed that twins were an abomination and killed them at birth. Among some of the Hausa people, it was believed that marrying a Yoruba woman could result in mystical dangers such as serious sickness or even death. As the immigrants became acculturated into the American society, these beliefs and superstitions were forgotten.

In many Nigerian cultures elders are supposed to be served first during a meal but leave food in the bowl for the children to eat as leftovers. The proverb, "the elder who consumes all his food will wash his own dishes," attests to this belief. However, in many Nigerian American homes children are served before adults, an indication of the Western influence whereby the needs of the child come first.

PROVERBS

The following are some common Nigerian proverbs: The voyager must necessarily return home; Death does not recognize a king; A foreign land knows no celebrity; An elephant is a hare in another town; The race of life is never tiresome; The nocturnal toad does not run during the day in vain; A child who does not know the mother does not run out to welcome her; If birds do not seek a cause for quarrel, the sky is wide enough for them to fly without interference; It is not a problem to offer a drink of wine to a monkey, but the problem is to take away the cup from him; Many words do not fill a basket; Truth is better than money; If the elephant does not have enough to eat in the forest, it puts the forest to shame.

There is a mine of proverbs in Pidgin English: "Man wey fool na him loss" (It is the fool that loses); "Lion de sick no be say goat fit go salute am for house" (Just because the lion is sick does not mean the goat can go to the lion's house to greet him); "Monkey no fine but im mamma like am so" (The monkey may not look handsome, but his mother likes him as he is); "Cow wey no get tail na God dey drive him fly" (God drives away the flies from the cow without a tail).

CUISINE

Ask anyone who has tasted Nigerian cuisine, and one answer is almost guaranteed—hot. There is no typical Nigerian American dish. Among the Yoruba, a meal may consist of two dishes: a starch form of dough derived from corn or guinea corn, or mashed vegetables that may be served with stew. The stew is prepared in typical Yoruba way using palm oil, meat, chicken, or other game cooked with many spices and vegetables, flavored with onions or bitterleaf leaves. A common Yoruba food is *Garri*, made from the roots of *cassava* (manioc).

Among the Ibo people, *cassava*, *cocoyam* (taro), potato, corn, okra, beans, peanuts, and pumpkins are common foods. In the northern part of Nigeria, grains constitute a good component of the diet. *Tuo* ("tu-wo") is a common dish in the north, and is eaten with different types of soup and sauce made from onions, peppers, tomatoes, okra, meat, or fish.

Akara ("ah-ka-ra"), Nigerian bean cakes, are fried patties made with uncooked, pulverized black-eye peas ground into a batter with onion, tomatoes, eggs, and chili peppers. *Egusi* ("e-goo-she") soup is a hot fiery soup made from *Egusi* seeds—pumpkin seeds can be substituted. Other ingredients required for a typical Egusi soup include okra, hot peppers, onions, any type of meat, poultry, or fish, palm oil, leafy greens, tomato paste, and salt. *Chinchin* ("chin-chin"), are fried pastries made from flour mixed with baking powder, salt, nutmeg, butter, sugar, and eggs. *Kulikuli* ("cooley-cooley"), or peanut balls, are made from roasted peanuts (called ground nuts in Nigeria), peanut oil, onions, salt, and cayenne pepper. *Moi-moi* ("moy-moy") is a savory pate made from black-eyed beans, onions, vegetable oil, tomato paste, parsley or fresh vegetables, salt, and pepper. Okra soup is based on meat, smoked fish, seafood and vegetables, and okra. This dish is similar to New Orleans gumbo. Pounded *Yam Fufu* is made from boiled yams pounded in a mortar with a pestle, and served with meat or fish stew and vegetable or okra soup.

TRADITIONAL COSTUMES

Men from various Nigerian groups wear *Sokoto* ("show-kowtow"), a pair of loose-fitting trousers, a *buba* ("boo-bah") or loose-fitting overshirt, and a cap. Yoruba men wear *agbada* ("ah-bah-dah"), which is flowing robe worn to the ankle. It covers an undervest with no sleeves, and a pair of baggy pants. The women wear a wide piece of cloth that goes from below the neck to the ankles. A blouse hanging to the waist is worn over it. A head tie and a thin veil are also worn. Nigerian Americans wear their traditional costumes on special occasions such as National Day, October 1.

NIGERIAN DANCES AND SONGS

Nigerian Americans boast of a wealth of traditional and modern music and dances because dancing and music form a focal point in life. At birth and death, on happy and sad occasions, and in worship, dancing and music are present. Traditionally in many Nigerian societies, men and women did not dance together. Western education and influence have changed this tradition, though Nigerian Americans who want to recreate their culture retain this separation.

Drums form an integral part in Nigerian dances and music. Juju music, a very popular form of music from Yorubaland is a slow, spaced, and very relaxed guitar-based music. Highlife music is popular in all parts of West Africa, including Nigeria. Highlife music usually consists of brass, vocals, percussion, drums, double bass, and electric guitar. Nigerians from the North practicing Islam enjoy music that has origins in North Africa. Such music is varied, but the instruments commonly used include trumpets, flutes, long brass horns, percussion frame drums, cymbals, and kettle drums.

Nigerian Americans returning from visits to Nigeria bring back with them both contemporary and old music in various formats. Nigerian Americans enjoy music from all over the world. In addition to American and British music, reggae, calypso, and Zairian music are popular.

HOLIDAYS CELEBRATED BY NIGERIAN AMERICANS

The major public holidays in Nigeria are: New Year's Day; *Id al Fitr*—end of Ramadan; Easter; *Id al-Kabir*—Feast of the Sacrifice; *Mouloud*—birth of the Prophet Mohammed; National or Independence Day—October 1; and Christmas. Nigerian Americans also celebrate the major public holidays in the United States.

National Day is one of the most important holidays for Nigerian Americans celebrating the independence of Nigeria from colonial rule. A whole week of cultural, educational, and political events are scheduled. Activities include lectures on Nigeria, traditional Nigerian dances and music, fashion shows, story telling, myths and legends from various Nigerian communities. Many Nigerian Americans volunteer to talk to neighborhood school children about Nigeria and the African continent at large. When the holiday proper falls on a weekday, parties and other festive celebrations are held on the weekend. The parties and festivities culminating in the celebration of Nigerian's independence are open invitations to Nigerians, people of other African descents, and others associated in one way or the other with Nigerian living in the United States. In New York, for example, the staff of the Nigerian Consulate attend these festivities.

For Moslem Nigerian Americans, *Id al-Fitr* or the end of the Moslem fasting season is the second most important holiday in the Islamic calendar. For the approximately 30 days of Ramadan, Moslems are expected to fast from dawn to sunset. They also abstain from sex, drink, tobacco, and other activities that result in physical pleasure. To celebrate *Id al-Fitr*, Moslems say the special feast prayer in a community format and give special alms to the poor. Nigerian American Moslems also share food and gifts with relatives and friends, and children receive gifts of all kinds.

There are many other holidays and festivities observed by Nigerian Americans to preserve their cultural heritage. Ibos in large metropolitan areas make it a point to celebrate the New Yam Festival every year. Traditionally, the yam has been the symbol of the prowess of the Ibo man. Just before midnight, the *ezejis* or elders offer prayers of thanksgiving and break kola nuts. Drums are played while blessings are offered. Other participants perform libation using Scotch or other similar liquor by pouring from a ram's horn. During the ceremony, prayers are addressed to an almighty being, and to the ancestral gods who control the soil, through whose constant kindness and guidance yams and other foods of the land bear fruit. The ceremony also includes dancing, eating, and exchange of greetings.

HEALTH AND MENTAL HEALTH ISSUES

There are no documented health problems or medical conditions specific to Nigeria Americans. However, like all black people, Nigerian Americans are susceptible to sickle cell anemia, an abnormal hereditary variation in the structure of hemoglobin, a protein found in the red blood cell.

A 1994 deportation victory by a Nigerian immigrant brought the health issue of female circumcision to light. Lydia Oluroro won a deportation case in Portland, Oregon. If she had been sent home, her two children could have had their clitoris and part of their labia minora cut. Nigerian Americans reacted differently to this decision; some praised it, and others expressed concern that Americans might consider female circumcision a common practice in all of Nigeria. This issue is definitely going to be a future health concern among Nigerian Americans.

LANGUAGE

English is the official language in Nigeria, but it is estimated that there are between 250 and 400 distinct languages. There are three major ethnic languages in Nigeria: Yoruba, Ibo, and Hausa. Yoruba is spoken by over 15 million people, primarily in Southwestern Nigeria. Belonging to the Kwa group of languages, Yoruba is a tonal tongue. Depending on the tone used, the same combination of sounds may convey different meanings. Ibo is also spoken by over 15 million people in Nigeria. Formerly considered as a Kwa language, recent research has placed Ibo in the Benue-Congo family of languages. Hausa is spoken in the Northern part of Nigeria, and is considered to be the most widely spoken language in Africa. It is a member of the Chad group of languages frequently assigned to the Hamitic subfamily of the Hamito-Semitic family of languages.

Pidgin English has become the unofficial language in many African countries and Nigeria is no exception. It can be loosely defined as a hybrid of exogenous and indigenous languages. It has become the most popular medium of intergroup communication in various heterogenous communities in Nigeria. Nigerian Americans from different tribal entities who may not communicate in English can communicate with each other in Pidgin English.

First generation of Nigerian Americans speak their native languages at home and when interacting with people from the same tribal groups. English words have found their way into most of the traditional languages spoken by Nigerian Americans. Children born into Nigerian American homes speak English and may learn the native languages if their parents teach them or speak the languages at home. Since English is the official language in Nigeria, and is used for instruction in schools, many Nigerian Americans prefer to have their children learn English as well possible so that upon returning home, the children will be able to communicate with others or do better in schools. The American accent acquired by younger Nigerian Americans is of spectacular interest to people in their home country.

It has been proposed several times that Nigeria needs an African language as its official language. This laudable desire may never become a reality because there are too many languages and dialects to consider. The existence of the diverse tribal and cultural groups makes it hard to single out one native language as the national language.

GREETINGS AND OTHER POPULAR EXPRESSIONS

Common Yoruba expressions include: *Bawo ni?* ("baa wo knee")—Hi, how are things?; *Daadaa ni* ("daadaa knee")—Fine. Common Hausa expressions include: *Sannu* ("sa nu")—Hi; *Lafiya?* ("la fee ya")—Are you well?. Common Ibo expressions include: *Ezigbo ututu*—Good morning; *Kedu ka imere?*—How do you do?; *Gini bu aha gi?*— What is your name? Popular expressions in Pidgin English are varied: "How now?"—How are you? or How is the going?; "Which thing you want?"— What do you want? "How body?"—How are you health-wise?

FAMILY AND COMMUNITY DYNAMICS

The first Nigerians came to the United States for educational purposes. Since transportation costs were high, it was common for them to leave their family behind. Painful as this separation was, it also afforded them the opportunity to concentrate on their studies. They saved money and later sent for their wives or children. In some cases, though, Nigerians sponsored by governmental agencies were accompanied by their families. In the modern era, Nigerians who migrated to America were sponsored by their families. Nigerian Americans have always had the reputation of living comfortable lives and maintaining high standards of living. Their industrious nature has made it possible for a great majority of them to purchase cars and houses, or rent nice apartments.

There is no typical Nigeria American household decoration. Depending on which region in Nigeria they come from, Nigerian Americans decorate their houses with various art forms. Many of them bring such artifacts when they travel home to visit. Other Nigerian Americans become so westernized that their households do not have any indication of their heritage.

Africans in general have strong family commitments. It is traditional in Nigeria to have extended families. Unannounced visits are always welcome, and meals are shared even if no prior knowledge of the visit was given. Nigerian Americans continue this tradition. However, as a result of hectic work schedules and economic realities, it is common for Nigerian Americans to make a phone call before paying visits to relatives or friends.

"**D**on't misunderstand me. I love America. The freedom, tolerance, and respect of differences that are a part of everyday public life are some of the first things a visitor to America notices. But I also saw a public school system disconnected from society's most important institution—the family. In Nigeria, with all its political and social problems, the family remains strong, and by doing so helps to define the social and economic expectations of the nation."

Jide Nzelibe, a graduate of St. John's College in Annapolis and Woodrow Wilson School of Public and International Affairs at Princeton University (from "A Nigerian Immigrant Is Shocked by His U.S. High School," *Policy Review*, fall 1993, p. 43).

Traditionally, in many Nigerian communities, a man marries as many wives as possible. However, Nigerian Americans marry only one wife. While in their native country large families are common, Nigerian Americans have fewer children so that they will be able to give them the best education possible. The early immigrants were educated people and they instilled in their children the importance of education as a component of a successful life. Over half of Nigerian Americans between the age 18 and 24 go to four-year universities and obtain bachelor degrees. About 33 percent of Nigerian Americans 25 years and over who entered the United States between 1980 and 1990 received masters degree. Close to ten percent received doctoral degrees. About 50 percent of women aged 25 or older received their bachelor degrees. Masters and doctoral degrees for women in the same age group were 32 percent and 52 percent.

Years ago in Nigeria it was traditional for women to stay home and take care of children; however in modern times, both in the United States and at home, educational opportunities are opened equally to men and women. The areas of specialization are not delineated between the sexes.

Children are required by tradition to be obedient to their parents and other adults. For example, a child can never contradict his or her parents; and the left hand cannot be used to accept money from parents, or as a gesture of respectful communication. Nigerian Americans try to maintain these traditional values, but as a result of peer pressure in American society, young Nigerian Americans resist this type of strict discipline from their parents. Even though children are treated equally in Nigerian American families, girls are usually the center of attention for several reasons. With teenage pregnancies on the rise in the United States, many parents seem to keep a closer eye on their female children. As part of sex education, many Nigerian American parents alert their male children to the problem of teenage pregnancy and its ensuing responsibilities.

WEDDINGS

Different groups in Nigeria have different types of weddings. Usually, marriages are a combination of the traditional and the modern. Even though the traditional marriage ceremonies seem to be fading, many Nigerian Americans continue to perform it at home and then perform a Western-type wedding in a church or a court of law.

Among the Yoruba for example, on the day of the traditional marriage, there is feasting, dancing, and merriment. At nightfall, the senior wives in the family of the groom go to the house of the bride's family to ask for the bride. At the door, the senior wives in the house of the bride ask for a door opening fee before they are allowed in the house. In addition to this initial fee, there are several others to be paid—the children's fee, the wives' fee, and the load-carrying fee. The family of the bride must be completely satisfied with the amount of monies given before the bride can be taken away. The senior members of the bride's family pray for and bless her, and then release her to the head of the delegation. A senior wife from the groom's family carries the bride on her back to the new husband's home. The feet of the new wife have to cleaned before she can enter the house. This symbolizes that the new wife is clean and is on the threshold of a new life altogether.

When there are no close relatives of the bride and the groom in the United States, friends take on the roles of the various participants in the traditional wedding. After the traditional wedding, if the couple practices Christianity, the ceremony is performed according to the tradition of the church. Friends, relatives, an well-wishers from the home country and across the United States are invited to the ceremony. Though many guests may stay in hotels, according to the African tradition of hospitality, friends and relatives of the couple living in the immediate surroundings will house and feed the visitors free of charge. The accompanying wedding reception is a stupendous feast of African cuisine, traditional and modern music and dancing, and an ostentatious display of both African and American costumes.

CHILD NAMING CEREMONIES

In many Nigerian American homes the child naming ceremony is even more important than the baptism. Among the Ibos, when a child is born, the parents set a time for this ceremony to take place and friends, relatives, and well wishers are invited to this event. Grandmothers traditionally prepare the dish that will be served, but in modern times all the women in the household take part in the preparation of the food. At the ceremony benches are arranged in a rectangular form with a lamp placed at the center, and guests are ushered in by the new mother. Kola nuts (the greatest symbol of Ibo hospitality) are served followed by palm wine. When the guests have had enough to drink, the new mother asks her mother to serve the food, which is usually a combination of rice, *garri,* yams, or *fufu,* and soup and stew made with stock-fish, ordinary fish, meat, and other types of game meat. After the meal, more palm wine is served. The host, usually the most senior man in the household, then repeats one or more proverbs, orders the baby to be brought, and places the baby in the lap. The grandmother gives a name, followed by the child's father, and then the baby's mother. Guests can also suggest names. After more drinking and celebration the guests depart and the household gathers to review the suggested names and to select one, which becomes the name of the child. Possible Ibo names include: *Adachi* (the daughter of God); *Akachukwu* (God's hand); *Nwanyioma* (beautiful lady); and *Ndidikanma* (patience is the best).

The Yoruba naming ceremony takes place on the ninth day after birth for boys, and on the seventh day for girls. Twins are named on the eighth day. By tradition the mother and the child leave the house for the first time on the day the naming ceremony takes place. Relatives, friends and well wishers join together to eat, drink, and make merry. Gifts are lavished on the newborn and the parents. An elder performs the naming ceremony using Kola nuts, a bowl of water, pepper, oil, salt, honey, and liquor. Each of these items stands for a special life symbol: Kola nuts are for good fortune; water symbolizes purity; oil symbolizes power and health; salt symbolizes intelligence and wisdom; honey symbolizes happiness, and liquor stands for wealth and prosperity. The baby tastes each of the above, as do all the people present. The name of the child is chosen before the ceremony. After dipping his hand in a bowl of water, the person officiating at the ceremony touches the forehead of the baby and whispers the name into the baby's ears, and then shouts it aloud for all around to hear. Some Yoruba names are: *Jumoke* (loved by all); *Amonke* (to know her is to pet her); *Modupe* (thanks); *Foluke* (in the hands of God); and *Ajayi* (born face downwards). Nigerian Americans preserve the traditional ceremonies, modifying as needed. For example, an older relative or friend plays the role of the grandmother when the real grandmother of the child is unable to be present.

After the traditional naming ceremony, if the family is Christian, another day is set aside for the child to be baptized in church. Hausa children born to Islamic parents are given personal names of Moslem origin. The Moslem name is often followed by the father's given name. Surnames have been adopted by a few Hausa people, especially those educated abroad. Some given Hausa names are: *Tanko* (a boy born after successive girls); *Labaran* (a boy born in the month of the Ramadan); *Gagare* (unconquerable); and *Afere* (a girl born tiny).

FUNERALS

The African concept of death is considered a transition, not an end. The Ibos, Yoruba, and the Hausa, including those practicing the Christian and Islamic religions, believe in reincarnation. Even though Western education and religion may have changed many traditional African beliefs, many Nigerian Americans hold on to those beliefs. Thus, if a person dies, he is born into another life completely different from the one he had. In addition to our visible world, there is believed to be another world where ancestors dwell and exert influence on the daily activities of the living. In many Nigerian societies, when a person dies, the entire community becomes aware of the death almost immediately. Wailing and crying from family members and unrelated people fill the town or village where the death occurs.

Funeral traditions vary in Nigeria according to group. For example, at the funeral of the Kalabari people of Eastern Nigeria, unless a person dies from what are considered abominable causes such as witchcraft, drowning, or at childbirth, every adult receives an *Ede* funeral, which consists of laying the body in state and dressing the chief mourners. Traditionally the dead were buried the day after death. In the case of an older person, a whole week of ceremonial mourning was set aside. In modern times, the dead are kept in the mortuary up to eight weeks or more so that elaborate preparations can take place and relatives both local and abroad could come to the funeral. The initial wake is usually held on a Friday, and the burial takes places on a Saturday. After elaborate traditional burial ceremonies, those who practice Christianity are taken to the church for the established funeral rites before the corpses are taken to the cemetery. A week after that the final wake is held on a Friday, and the funeral dance and ceremonies on a Saturday. The day of the final funeral is filled with elaborate activities; relatives of the dead person dress up in expensive garments.

Many Nigerian Americans prefer to be buried in Nigeria when they die. For this reason they buy enough life insurance to cover the transportation of their bodies home. Bodies in the United States are usually kept in the funeral homes till the wake is done. When the body is flown home, in addition to the traditional burial ceremonies, Nigerian Americans who practice Christianity will be buried according to established rites. Nigerian American Moslems whose bodies are sent home are buried according to the Islamic tradition.

INTERACTIONS WITH OTHER ETHNIC MINORITIES

Nigerian Americans interact with other ethnic minorities and the community as a whole, though most Nigerian Americans will first seek out people from their own tribes. At one time, as a result of the Biafra War, Nigerian Americans from the Yoruba tribe would not interact with others from the Ibo tribe and vice versa; but this situation has improved in contemporary times. Interaction exists between Nigerian Americans and people from other African countries such as Ghana, Ethiopia, Kenya, and Uganda. Most Africans see themselves as brothers and sisters in the United States since they all left their home countries to come here. There are some Nigerian Americans who prefer not to interact with people of their own heritage. There have been many cases of fraud, crime, and drug smuggling involving Nigerian Americans and some want to avoid any implication in such criminal cases.

RELIGION

As is the case in many African countries, Western religion was imposed on Nigeria. Traditionally, Nigerians believe that there are two types of divinities: the Supreme Being, and the subordinate deities. The Supreme Being can be likened to God and the subordinate deities to the saints and others through whose intercession people can communicate with the Supreme Being. The Ibos, for instance, refer to the Supreme Being in powerful terms, such as *Chukwu*—the Great Providence, and *Chineke*—Creator and Providence. The traditional religion of the Yorubas focuses on different gods, representing aspects of one almighty, all-encompassing God, *Olodumare, Oluwa, Olorun*—owner of heaven and earth, who is too sacred to be directly approached or worshipped.

Through commercial contacts and colonization, Islamic and European religions were introduced in Nigeria. The majority of Nigerian Americans hailing from the northern states in Nigeria are Moslems. Islamic groups in the northern part of Nigeria include the Hausa, Fulani, Kanuris, Kanemis, Bagirimis, and the Wadayans. About 40 percent of the Yoruba population also practice Islam. The majority of Nigerian Americans from the Ibo tribe are Catholics. While many Nigerians worship with the American community in places of worship, members of the Nigerian American community have their own groups in which they can worship together. For example, in Boston, the Igbo community has formed a group that worships in the Catholic tradition, using the native language in both prayers and songs. They inculcate traditional practices such as dancing and drumming into their worship.

A key development in religion in Nigeria was the establishment of *Aladura* or spiritual churches. *Aladura* is a Yoruba word meaning "one who prays." The Aladura movement started among the Yoruba people in Nigeria during the first decades of the twentieth century and spread throughout Africa. Among the many practices of this movement, all participants put on white robes while they worship. They may worship in a church building, along the beach, on top of hills, or by the mouth of rivers praying, confessing their sins, healing, singing and clapping. The *Aladura* movement can be likened to the charismatic movement in the United States. In many cities in the United States, Nigerian Americans have established their own *Aladura* churches where they gather to worship.

EMPLOYMENT AND ECONOMIC TRADITIONS

Early Nigerian Americans came to the United States to study, acquired terminal degrees, and returned home. This ambitious habit was copied by many Nigerian Americans settling in the United States. Through their status as American citizens or permanent residents Nigerian Americans were able to acquire prestigious jobs in academia and other professions. Other Nigerian Americans without the academic qualifications accept jobs in various sectors of society. Many Nigerian Americans establish their own businesses in the United States. For many, trading in Nigerian and other African costumes has become a profitable business. This requires travelling between Nigeria and the United States to arrange importation of items. In many American cities, it is not uncommon to find Nigerian and other African restaurants owned and operated by Nigerian Americans. Nigerian Americans have established their own small businesses, including travel agencies, parking lots, taxi stands, cultural exchange programs, and health and life insurance agencies. Even though they target the general population for their clientele, Nigerian Americans invest time in acquiring Nigerian and other African clientele.

POLITICS AND GOVERNMENT

Nigerian Americans as a group do not have a large political clout in the United States. They do work in small groups through established associations or where they reside to raise political consciousness when appropriate issues arise. When the press in the United States reports sensational stories that create stereotypical impressions about Nigeria, Nigerian Americans react in unison to correct such impressions.

RELATIONS WITH NIGERIA

Nigerian Americans maintain a high sense of pride for their country. They remain attached to Nigeria no matter how long they stay away from it. Many go home to visit occasionally while others make a visit to the motherland an annual obligation. Basketball star Hakeem Olajuwon, who recently became a citizen of the United States, expresses the attachment Nigerians have for their country: "There's no place like home. I will always be from Nigeria" ("Hakeem Becomes U.S. Citizen," *The Houston Chronicle*, April 3, 1993).

When Nigerians first came to the United States, they would gather with other African students to promote nationalism and protest against colonial domination in their homeland. In contemporary times, Nigerian Americans have been vociferous in protesting against injustice and despotic rule in Nigeria. In 1989, when Nigeria's military leader Ibrahim Babaginda summarily dissolved several groups that aspired to be registered as political parties to compete in elections, Nigerian Americans throughout the United States held demonstrations to protest against this act of despotism.

In 1993, when Babaginda refused to accept the June elections and proposed a second elections in August, Nigerian Americans added their voice to those of freedom-loving people around the world to protest against his disrespect for the choice of Nigerian voters, Chief Moshood Abiola. As the political situation in Nigeria remains in turmoil, Nigerian Americans constantly express themselves and gather to ensure that justice will prevail.

Nigerian Americans forge strong ties with their motherland. By working strongly with both private and governmental groups, Nigerian Americans have succeeded in organizing exchanges between business people in the United States and Nigeria. Individual organizations also pool their resources together to assist their motherland. A good example is the Network of Nigerian Engineers and Scientists whose members sometimes offer free services to the government of Nigeria. As a result of these efforts there has been a boost in trade between the United States and America and a boost of tourism in Nigeria. African American tourists visit Nigeria in huge numbers every year to explore their heritage.

By working closely with universities, other institutions of higher learning, and research centers, Nigerian Americans have ensured that prominent authors, artists, and other researchers visit the United States on a regular basis. Wole Soyinka, the Nobel prize winner from Nigeria, has been a regular visitor to many campuses and art centers in the United States. Chinua Achebe, renowned novelist and scholar comes to the United States to lecture on college campuses and at other literary and cultural events. Top known artists and musicians such as King Sunny Ade, Ebenezer Obey, Sonny Okosun, and Fela Anikulapo Kuti have been invited by Nigerian Americans to perform throughout the United States.

INDIVIDUAL AND GROUP CONTRIBUTIONS

Nigerian Americans vividly portray the philosophy of life evident in all African societies: as long as God has given you the strength and power to live, you have to contribute to society as much as you can. Small in percentage as they are to the American population as a whole, Nigerian Americans distinguish themselves. The following is a sample of notable Nigerian Americans working in various arenas.

ACADEMIA

Known as one of the world's top three scientists in the fields of robotics, Bartholomew Nnaji (1957-), came to the United States on an athletic scholarship in 1977 and is currently a professor at the College of Engineering of the University of Massachusetts, Amherst; author of six books and editor in chief of the International Journal of Design and manufacturing, Nnaji has won many awards including the 1988 Young Manufacturing Engineering Award.

JOURNALISM

Through the popular journal *African World*, Bartholomew Nnaji (1957-), professor of industrial engineering and operations research and past interim federal minister for science and technology in Nigeria, has been working with Okey Ndibe, former editor of *African Commentary* to educate Americans about the distortion of the history of Africans and others of African descent.

MUSIC

Titilayo Rachel Adedokun (1973-) was a finalist in the 1993 Miss America pageant and the 1993 Miss Ohio. Adedokun is currently a graduate student at the Cincinnati College Conservatory of Music.

O. J. (Orlando Julius) Ekemode (1942-) born in Ijebu-Ijesha in Nigeria, started playing drums at age eight. His combination of traditional African music with contemporary jazz, religious, reggae, Afro-beat, and soul music in the fashion of James Brown has made him one of the living legends of real African music in the United States.

SCIENCE AND TECHNOLOGY

One of America's top black engineers, Olusola Seriki, currently development director for the Rouse Company in Columbia, Maryland, has distinguished himself; born in Ibadan, Oyo, Nigeria, he is a Howard University graduate who has worked on several large-scale international projects; the countless awards he has received include the prestigious African Business Executive of the Year in 1989; an accomplished author and scholar, Seriki is also active in various professional organizations.

SPORTS

According to George Karl, coach of the Seattle Supersonics, Hakeem Olajuwon (1963-) is the second-best player in the world. Akeem, as he is affectionately known, led the University of Houston to three consecutive trips to the Final Four of the NCAA basketball tournament. In 1985, he led the Houston Rockets to the playoffs with a second-place finish in the Midwest division. Akeem is credited with transforming the Houston Rockets into a defensive force in basketball.

Donald Igwebuike (1961-), kicked five years for the Tampa Bay Buccaneers football team; when he was released in September 1990, he was picked up by the Minnesota Vikings for the 1990 football season; soon after he was arrested and charged with being an accomplice to heroin trafficking; although he was acquitted in a federal court in 1991, no team wanted to sign him; however he is currently a kicker for the Baltimore team. Christian Okoye (1961-), known as the "Nigerian Nightmare" is a superior discus thrower and a great football player; his sports career in the United States started when he came on a track scholarship to the Azusa Pacific University in 1982; he is also a former Kansas City Chiefs running back who became the NFL's leading rusher in 1989.

MEDIA

PRINT

Because Nigeria's official language is English, publications regarding Nigerian Americans come out mainly in the English Language. The following are just a few of the available newspapers and similar types of publications on Nigeria.

Nigeria Trade Journal.

Published quarterly, this journal is an important resource for Nigerian Americans and others interested in establishing businesses in Nigeria.

Contact: Nigerian Consulate General.

Address: 828 Second Avenue, New York, New York, 10017-4301.

Telephone: (212) 752-1670.

Nigerian Financial Review.

Quarterly magazine providing insight into the financial world of Nigeria. Valuable resource for Nigerian Americans and potential American investors in Nigeria.

Contact: Priscilla A. Williams.

Address: Infodata Ltd., U.S.A., 239 Sheridan Avenue, Mount Vernon, New York 10552.

Nigerian Journal.

Quarterly journal published by the Nigerian Consulate in New York. This English language publication provides a vast array of information on Nigeria, and issues of concern to Nigerians at home and those abroad, as well as non-Nigerians interested in Nigeria.

Contact: Nigerian Consulate General.

Address: 828 Second Avenue, New York, New York, 10017-4301.

Telephone: (212) 752-1670.

Nigerian Students Union in the Americas Newsletter.

A monthly publication that provides information on Nigeria and the world at large to Nigerians and Nigerian students studying in the Americas.

Contact: Nigerian Consulate General.

Address: 828 Second Avenue, New York, New York, 10017-4301.

Telephone: (212) 752-1670.

Nigerian Times.

Formerly the *African Enquirer*.

Contact: Chika A. Onyeani, Editor.

Address: 368 Broadway, Suite 307, New York, New York 10013.

Telephone: (212) 791-0777.

RADIO

WABE-FM (90.1).

This is a daily evening music broadcast featuring music from all over the world, including Nigeria.

Contact: Lois Reitzes.

Address: 740 Bismark Road, N.E., Atlanta, Georgia 30324.

Telephone: (404) 827-8900.

WRFG-FM (89.3).

"African Experience" is a two-hour program from 12:00 p.m. to 2:00 p.m. on Saturdays with emphasis on music, opinions, interviews from Africa, including Nigeria.

Contact: Tom Davis.

Address: 1083 Austin Avenue, N.E., Atlanta, Georgia 30307.

Telephone: (404) 523-3471.

ORGANIZATIONS AND ASSOCIATIONS

League of Patriotic Nigerians (LPN).

Founded in 1985, the LPN has a membership of 10,000 Nigerian American professionals, including doctors, lawyers, accountants, and engineers. It promotes professional behavior, and the impor-tance of good citizenship, respect for the law, and community involvement.

Contact: Alex Taire, Vice President.

Nigerian American Alliance (NAA).

Formerly known as the Nigerian American Friendship Fund, the NAA was founded in 1988 and has a membership of 300 business people, government officials, and educators interested in Nigeria and American-Nigerian relations. The NAA promotes improved understanding between the two countries on political, social, and economic issues.

Contact: James E. Obi, Agency Manager.

Address: 2 Penn Plaza, Suite 1700, New York, New York 10121.

Telephone: (212) 560-5500.

Nigerian American Chamber of Commerce (NACC).

The NACC is a trade group trying to develop closer economic ties between Nigeria and the United States.

Address: 575 Lexington Avenue, New York, New York 10021.

Telephone: (212) 715-7200.

Nigerian Students Union in the Americas (NSUA).

Disseminates information about Nigeria and Africa; cooperates with other African student unions in the Americas and with Nigerian student unions in Nigeria and other parts of the world.

Contact: Granville U. Osuji.

Address: 654 Girard Street, N.W., Apartment 512, Washington, D.C. 20001.

Telephone: (202) 462-9124.

Organization of Nigerian Citizens (ONC).

Founded in 1986, the ONC has a membership of 700 in 21 state groups; it is made up of people of Nigerian ancestry, and works to increase the understanding and awareness of Nigeria and its citizens by promoting educational programs. It also serves as a networking link for people interested in Nigeria. The ONC seeks solutions to problems encountered by Nigerian Americans.

Contact: Chuks Eleonu.

Address: P.O. Box 66220, Baltimore, Maryland 21239.

Telephone: (410) 637-5165.

World Union of Nigerians (WUN).

Promotes democratic principles of government, protection of civil liberties, and economic development within Nigeria.

Contact: Sonnie Braih, Executive Chair.
Address: 2147 University Avenue, W., Suite 101, P.O. Box 14265, St. Paul, Minnesota 55114.
Telephone: (612) 776-4997.

MUSEUMS AND RESEARCH CENTERS

The Afro-American Historical and Cultural Museum.

Maintains a vast collection of African sculpture and artifacts relating to Africa and the slave trade. Nigeria is well represented in the collection.

Contact: Nannette A. Clark, Executive Director.
Address: 701 Arch Street, Philadelphia, Pennsylvania 19106-1557.
Telephone: (215) 574-0380.

Black Heritage Museum.

Holds a vast collection of art and artifacts of black heritage, including many tribal artifacts from Nigeria.

Contact: Priscilla G. Stephens Kruize, President.
Address: Miracle Center Mall, 3301 Coral Way, Miami, Florida 33257.
Telephone: (305) 252-3535.

Museum for African Art.

Has an extensive collection of art from all over Africa, including Nigeria.

Contact: Susan M. Vogel, C.E.O and Executive Director.
Address: 593 Broadway, New York, New York, 10012.
Telephone: (212) 966-1313.

Museum of African American Art.

Has preserved a large collection of Arts of African and African descendant peoples, including Nigeria.

Contact: Belinda Fontenote-Jamerson, President.
Address: 4005 Crenshaw Boulevard, Third Floor, Los Angeles, California 90008.
Telephone: (213) 294-7071.

National Museum of African Art.

Part of the Smithsonian Institution, the museum has over 6,000 objects of African art, wood, metal, ceramic, ivory, and fiber. Its collection on Nigerian art is extensive.

Contact: Dylvia H. William, Director.
Address: 950 Independence Avenue, S.W., Washington, D.C., 20560.
Telephone: (202) 357-4600.

SOURCES FOR ADDITIONAL STUDY

Burns, Sir Alan. *History of Nigeria*. London: George Allen and Unwin Ltd., 1929; reprinted, 1976.

Essien, Efiong. *Nigeria Under Structural Adjustment*. Nigeria: Fountain Publications Ltd., 1990.

Hair, Paul Edward Hedley. *The Early Study of Nigerian Languages: Essays and Bibliographies*. London: Cambridge University Press, 1967.

Nigeria: A Country Study, edited by Helen Chapin Metz. Washington D.C.: Federal Research Division, Library of Congress, 1992.

Offoha, Marcellina Ulunm. *Educated Nigerian Settlers in the United States: The Phenomenon of Brain Drain*. Philadelphia, Temple University, 1989.

Shepard, Robert B. *Nigeria, Africa, and the United States: From Kennedy to Reagan*. Bloomington: Indiana University Press, 1991.

Sofola, Johnson Adeyemi. *American-Processed Nigerians: A Study of the Adjustment and Attitudes of the Nigerian Students in the United States of America*. American University, 1967.

U.S. Bureau of the Census. *Detailed Ancestry Groups for States, 1990*. Prepared by the Economic and Statistics Administration, Bureau of the Census. Washington, D.C., August 1993.

NORWEGIAN AMERICANS

by
Odd S. Lovoll

The pioneers on the American frontier were the new Vikings of the West; Leif Ericson became the quintessential icon of a glorified Viking heritage. Norwegians found a second identifying quality by presenting themselves as an ethnic group with wholesome rural values and ideals. And, in fact, Norwegians were the most rural of any major nineteenth-century immigrant group.

OVERVIEW

Occupying the western part of the Scandinavian peninsula in northwestern Europe, and sharing borders with Sweden, Finland, and Russia, Norway is slightly larger than the state of New Mexico, measuring 125,181 square miles (323,878 square kilometers). The country measures 1,095 miles from south to north, and one-third of its land mass lies north of the Arctic Circle, extending farther north than any other European country.

Norway's population is 4,300,000. Save for an indigenous minority of Samis (estimated at no more than 40,000) confined mainly to the northern half of the country, Norway's population is ethnically and culturally homogeneous. Almost 90 percent of the inhabitants belong to the Evangelical Lutheran state church, five percent are members of other denominations and faiths, and only five percent have no religious affiliation. Norway's form of government is a hereditary constitutional monarchy. The capital city is Oslo. The national flag displays a central blue cross with a white border on a red field. Norwegian is the official language, rendered in two different literary forms, the predominant *bokmål* (Dano-Norwegian) and the rural dialect-based *nynorsk* (New Norse).

Norway (Old Norse: *Norvegr* or *Noregr*) designates the sea-lane—the north way—along the country's extensive coastline as viewed from the south. Maritime connections west and south have, as a consequence of Norway's geography, characterized its history. During the Viking Age (800-1030) expansive forces moved the Norse Vikings onto the historical stage of Europe; their westward expansion extended to Iceland, Greenland, and even to the continent of North America. Some time before 890 Harald Finehair consolidated Norway under the Yngling dynasty. The martyrdom of King Olav II of this royal line on July 29, 1030, at the Battle of Stiklestad, made him Norway's patron saint, secured a national monarchy, and established the Christian church as a dominant institution.

Medieval Norway attained its political height under the reign of Haakon IV Haakonson (1217-1263), with territorial dominance to the western islands (the Orkneys, the Shetlands, the Hebrides, the Isle of Man, and the Faroes), Iceland, and Greenland, and three districts in present-day Sweden. It was then that Norway entered fully into close diplomatic and commercial relations with other European states.

Norwegian national decline manifested itself in dynastic unions with the two other Scandinavian nations, Sweden and Denmark. The Bubonic Plague that ravaged Europe in the middle of the fourteenth century hit Norway, a country with greater poverty and fewer natural resources than the other Nordic lands, especially hard. Norway's population was devastated, resulting in a serious loss of income for the great landowners, the church, and the king. The last king of an independent and sovereign Norway died in 1380 and Norway united with Denmark. In 1397 the three Scandinavian states were joined under one ruler in the Kalmar Union; in the case of Norway the union with Denmark lasted until 1814. The Lutheran Reformation in 1537 resulted in Norway's reduction in administrative arrangements to a province within the Danish state. The idea of Norway as a kingdom, however, remained alive throughout the union period and was evidenced in the term "the twin realms."

MODERN PERIOD

The big power politics following the Napoleonic Wars yielded a national rebirth.. Rejecting the terms of the Treaty of Kiel, which transferred Norway to the King of Sweden, a constituent assembly meeting north of Oslo at Eidsvoll on May 17, 1814, signed a constitution establishing a limited and hereditary monarchy, and declared Norway's independence. Mindful of their pledge to the Swedish throne, but also not wishing to quell Norwegian moves toward independence, the European powers endorsed a compromise that established a union under the Swedish king. The union preserved the Eidsvoll constitution and was based on the will of the Norwegian people rather than the Treaty of Kiel.

The Act of Union signed in 1815 declared, in principle, an equal partnership in the double monarchy of Sweden and Norway. In reality, however, Norway held an inferior position. Politically Norway feared Swedish encroachment and sought full equality in the union. Culturally the new nation struggled against Danish hegemony—a result of the 400-year union—and engaged in a quest for national identity and cultural independence. There was a surge of nationalism, which was expressed in an idealized and romantic cultivation of the peasantry as the true carriers of the national spirit. Norway's ultimate goal was a separate and respected national status within the Nordic nations. In 1905 the union with Sweden ended after a dispute over foreign affairs, centering on Norway's demand for an independent consular service. The union was unnatural from the start with few, if any, positive elements linking the two countries.

Prince Carl of Denmark was elected King of Norway, taking the name Haakon VII, which linked him to the old Norwegian royal line. The first half-century of full independence witnessed a rapid transformation from mainly an agricultural society to an industrialized and commercial one. The laboring classes gained political influence and from the mid-1930s the Norwegian Labor Party formed the government. German occupation from 1940 to 1945 suspended the Party's political agenda, but in the postwar era it resumed power and transformed Norway into a prosperous social-democratic welfare state. In foreign affairs, the country abandoned its historically neutral stance and joined the western alliance in the North Atlantic Treaty Organization (NATO). In 1994 Norway completed negotiations for membership in the European Union. A pending national referendum will determine whether or not Norway actually becomes a member.

THE PIONEER IMMIGRATION

Norwegian overseas emigration began earlier than in the other Nordic lands, commencing dramatically on July 4, 1825, with the sailing of the tiny sloop *Restauration* from Stavanger on the southwestern coast of Norway. The initial emigration occurred in a district with historical ties to England where the idea of emigration as an alternative to staying at home originated. As early as 1821 the enigmatic wanderer Cleng Peerson, "the pathfinder of Norwegian emigration," traveled to America as an agent for the pioneer emigrants. Many Lutheran pietists and Quakers chose to emigrate as a result of persecution by the Lutheran clergy because of their defiance of ecclesiastical law. Religious oppression did not enter into the subsequent emigration. In 1824 Peerson returned briefly to Norway to advise the emigrants, but was back in the United States to meet "the Sloopers" (so called because they sailed on a sloop). The *Restauration* landed in New York on October 9, 1825, with a boatload of 53 immigrants—one of them a baby girl born during an adventurous voyage of 14 weeks.

Annual emigration did not commence until 1836, but a contact had been made with the New World. Individuals had gone to America in the intervening years and even visited Norway to report on life there. The Norwegian exodus rose in the 1840s; by 1865, nearly 80,000 Norwegians had entered the United States. From the southwestern coastal areas the "America fever" had moved along the west coast and inland to the central highland region. Even though no part of Norway was entirely untouched by the overseas exodus, the majority of emigrants in this founding phase of the movement came from the inner fjord districts in west Norway and the mountain valleys of east Norway. It was an emigration of rural folk with a strong family composition. Their move was permanent; they sought a new life in America for themselves and their descendants. As a result, the character of the immigrant community that evolved in America reflected traditions, mores, and religious as well as secular values of the people from their districts in the old country and conveyed a strong familial and communal bond.

MASS IMMIGRATION

The end of the Civil War brought about a great increase in Atlantic crossings. The number of Norwegian emigrants leaped from 4,000 in 1865 to 15,726 in 1866, heralding the era of mass migration. The migration occurred until 1873 when, in the course of only eight years, some 110,000 Norwegians left their homeland. The second, and also the greatest, period of emigration lasted 14 years from 1880 to 1893, when on the average 18,290 left annually—ten for every 1,000 Norwegians. During this time Norway's emigration intensity was the second greatest in Europe, surpassed only by Ireland. Norway experienced a final mass exodus in the first decade of the twentieth century, although there was considerable emigration in the 1920s as well. Emigration from its beginning in 1825 until the present has affected some 900,000 people. Of the total emigration, 87 percent, or 780,000 Norwegians, left in the period between 1865 and 1930.

In the nineteenth century, Norwegian emigrants headed almost exclusively for the United States. Only since 1900 have other overseas areas, especially Canada, attracted substantial number of Norwegians. Still, the United States remains the most popular destination. A rapid population growth in the last century and a slow industrial expansion left many young Norwegians unable to find gainful employment at home. Surplus labor was syphoned off through emigration. The United States on the other hand had a great need for people to develop its resources. In periods of expanding economy, American society offered seemingly unlimited possibilities. The response in Norway was a rise in emigration. The migration of families gradually changed in the last quarter of the century to an emigration of individuals. It was dominated by a movement of young male laborers who came from the cities as well as the countryside, though the rural exodus was by far the larger. From the 1880s, youths with education and technical training joined the masses who went to America.

Improved transportation facilitated by steam passenger liners, allowed people to move back and forth across the Atlantic, yielding a two-way migration. The Norwegian Bureau of Statistics has estimated that about 25 percent of the immigrants to North America between 1881 and 1930 have resettled in Norway. Still, as of 1990 there were 3,869,395 residents of Norwegian ancestry in the United States, nearly as many as in the home country.

SETTLEMENT

The majority of the pioneer immigrants, the so-called "Sloopers," assisted by the kindly services of American Quakers, went to Orleans County in western New York state and settled in what became Kendall Township. In the mid-1830s the Kendall settlers gave impetus to the westward movement of Norwegians by founding a settlement in the Fox River area of Illinois. A small urban colony of Norwegians had its genesis in Chicago at about the same time.

Immigrant settlements now stood ready to welcome Norwegian newcomers, who, beginning in 1836, arrived annually. From Illinois, Norwegian pioneers followed the general spread of population northwestward into Wisconsin. Wisconsin remained the center of Norwegian American activity up until the Civil War. In the 1850s Norwegian landseekers began moving into both Iowa and Minnesota, and serious migration to the Dakotas was underway by the 1870s. The majority of Norwegian agrarian settlements developed in the northern region of the so-called Homestead Act Triangle between the Mississippi and the Missouri rivers. The upper Midwest became the home for most immigrants. In 1910 almost 80 percent of the one million or more Norwegian Americans—the immigrants and their children—lived in that part of the United States. In 1990, 51.7 percent of the Norwegian American population lived in the Midwest; Minnesota had the largest number. Minneapolis functioned as a Norwegian American "capital" for secular and religious activities.

"A newcomer from Norway who arrives here will be surprised indeed to find in the heart of the country, more than a thousand miles from his landing place, a town where language and way of life so unmistakably remind him of his native land." Svein Nilsson, a Norwegian American journalist (in *Billed-Magazin*, May 14, 1870).

In the Pacific Northwest, the Puget Sound region, and especially the city of Seattle, became another center of immigrant life. Enclaves of Norwegians emerged as well in greater Brooklyn, New York, in Alaska, and Texas. After Minnesota, Wisconsin had the most Norwegians in 1990, followed by California, Washington, and North Dakota.

In a letter from Chicago dated November 9, 1855, Elling Haaland from Stavanger, Norway, assured his relatives back home that "of all nations Norwegians are those who are most favored by Americans." This sentiment was expressed frequently as the immigrants attempted to seek acceptance and negotiate entrance into the new society. In their segregated farming communities, Norwegians were spared direct prejudice and might indeed have been viewed as a welcome ingredient in a region's development. Still, a sense of inferiority was inherent in their position. The immigrants were occasionally referred to as "guests" in the United States and they were not immune to condescending and disparaging attitudes by old-stock Americans. Economic adaptation required a certain amount of interaction with a larger commercial environment, from working for an American farmer to doing business with the seed dealer, the banker, and the elevator operator. Products had to be grown and sold—all of which pulled Norwegian farmers into social contact with their American neighbors.

In places like Brooklyn, Chicago, Minneapolis, and Seattle, Norwegians interacted with the multicultural environment of the city while constructing a complex ethnic community that met the needs of its members. It might be said that a Scandinavian melting pot existed in the urban setting among Norwegians, Swedes, and Danes, evidenced in residential and occupational patterns, in political mobilization, and in public commemoration. Intermarriage promoted interethnic assimilation. There are no longer any Norwegian enclaves or neighborhoods in America's great cities. Beginning in the 1920s, Norwegians increasingly became suburban, and one might claim, more American.

ACCULTURATION AND ASSIMILATION

Norwegian history in America covers a period of 170 years, beginning with the pioneer immigrants in 1825. Viking ancestors had, however, established colonies in Greenland—outposts of European civilization—as early as 985 A.D. From there they found America, commonly associated with the voyages of the Norse adventurer Leif Ericson, around the year 1000 and formed colonies on Newfoundland. These had no impact on the later European settlement in the New World, but they provided Norwegians, and other Scandinavians, with a claim to a birthright in America and gave them their most expressive identifying ethnic symbols.

The pioneers on the American frontier were the new Vikings of the West; Leif Ericson became the quintessential icon of a glorified Viking heritage. Norwegians found a second identifying quality by presenting themselves as an ethnic group with wholesome rural values and ideals. And, in fact, Norwegians were the most rural of any major nineteenth-century immigrant group. In 1900, for instance, only a little more than a quarter of all Norwegian-born residents in the United States lived in towns with more than 25,000 inhabitants. It was the lowest percentage for any European immigrant population. It has been claimed that the Norwegian farmer in America passed on a special rural bond from one generation to the next. Perhaps the greatest contribution was a dedication to farming as a way of life; in 1900, 54.3 percent of the children of Norwegian immigrants were farmers. No other ethnic group even came close.

In their farming communities Norwegians exhibited a nationalistic solidarity that had no counterpart among other Scandinavian groups. The homeland's quest for a national identity created a patriotic fervor that was transplanted as immigrant clannishness. Even today, as evidenced by the retention of their institutions, Norwegians appear more ethnocentric than their Nordic neighbors in America. For example, a Norwegian-language Lutheran congregation survives in Chicago, whereas the Swedes, with a much larger population, have not maintained a Swedish-language church.

PUBLIC CELEBRATIONS

Norwegians' past in the United States was celebrated at the Norse American Centennial in the Twin Cities of Minneapolis and St. Paul in June 1925. A century had passed since the landing of the *Restauration* in New York harbor. President Calvin Coolidge came to honor the Norwegians for being good Americans and validated their claim of sharing nationality with the original discoverer of America as the Norwegian Americans reflected upon a successful 100 years as an immigrant people. The festivities displayed an attachment to traditional rural values and a cultivation of ancient and heroic Norse roots, but featured heroes from their American experience as well. An impressive pageant centered on the life of Colonel Hans Christian Heg, a hero from the Civil War. The hostilities between the North and the South gave Norwegian Americans a sense of a

These Leikarring Norwegian Dancers are standing in front of a replica of the Valhalia Viking ship in Petersburg, Alaska.

legitimate place in the United States because Norwegian blood had been spilled in its defense.

The symbols and content of a Norwegian ethnic identity emerged among the more successful of their nationality in such urban centers as Chicago and Minneapolis. They were the ones who most eagerly sought acceptable ethnic credentials and gathered their compatriots around the celebration of such holidays as Norwegian Constitution Day on May 17, which became the most important identifying ethnic symbol. The day is still celebrated with a traditional parade featuring flags, banners, music, and speeches in Norwegian centers across America. The event, observed since the early days of settlement, communicates American patriotism as well as Norwegian memories; ethnic identities are firmly rooted in positive views of the group's place in America and images of the homeland's culture are equally prominent in the celebration.

There are numerous folk festivals in Norwegian centers. *Norsk Høstfest* in Minot, North Dakota (for information, contact [701] 852-2368), and Nordic Fest in Decorah, Iowa (for information, contact [800] 382-3378), annually assemble thousands of Norwegian Americans nationwide around a varied program focusing on a Norwegian American heritage.

At such events Norwegian stereotypes are regularly introduced to the amusement of those assembled. Invariably there are stories and jokes poking fun at the ignorance and foolishness of Norwegian types, such as the characters of Ole and Lena, who speak in broken English. New tales are constantly being created. A typical one might go as follows: "Ole and Lena invited a well-to-do Uncle for dinner. Little Ole looked him over and finally approached the old Uncle with a request. 'Uncle Knute ... vill you make a noise like a frog for me?' said Little Ole. 'Vy in the world do you vant me to make a noise like a frog?' exclaimed the Uncle. 'Because,' said Little Ole, 'Papa says ve are going to get a lot of money ven you croak!'" (Red Stangeland, *Ole & Lena Jokes*, Book 4 [Sioux Falls, South Dakota: Norse Press, 1989] p. 14.)

CUSTOMS AND TRADITIONS

In 1879 a Norwegian Unitarian minister and author was amazed after a visit to Wisconsin at "how Norwegians have managed to isolate themselves together in colonies and maintain their Norwegian memories and customs." He had to ask himself if he was really in America. Adjustments were, however, made to American ways in clothing and food, although especially typical Norwegian dishes were retained. These became associated with Christmas celebrations, which in pioneer days were observed for the entire Twelfth-night period, as in Norway. Aaste Wilson of Wisconsin tells how transplanted Norwegians retained such old customs: "They invited one another for Christmas celebration and then they had home-brewed ale, made from malt or molasses or sugar cane.... Nearly everybody slaughtered for Christmas so that they could have meat and sausages. Then they had potatoes and *flatbrød* (flatbread) and *smultringer* (doughnuts) and sauce made from dried apples. And most of them had *rømmegrøt* (cream porridge). We youngsters liked to stay and listen to the old folks and thought it good fun when they told about old things in Norway." (Wilson, Aaste, *"Live blant nybyggjarane." Telesoga*, September 1917.)

A gradual transition to American life weakened immigrant folkways. Some traditions and customs survived and were cultivated, others were reintroduced and given a heightened importance as a part of an ethnic heritage. Toward the end of the century *lutefisk*, dried Norwegian cod soaked in a lye solution, assumed a role as a characteristic Norwegian American dish. It was served at lodge meetings, festive banquets, and church suppers, most regularly during the Christmas season. The dish is served with *lefse*, a thin buttered pancake made from rolled dough. Madison, Minnesota, has erected a statue of a cod in its city park and advertises itself as the "*Lutefisk* Capital of America" because it reportedly consumes more *lutefisk* per capita than any other American city.

Old-country traditions in food, festive dress, folk arts, and entertainment were given a powerful boost with the establishment of *bygdelag*, or old-home societies, around the turn of the century. These groups were rooted in Norwegian locality and loyalties to the old-country home community. The annual reunions of the 50 or so such societies, each bearing the name of a specific Norwegian home district, became grand celebrations of a regional and rural Norwegian cultural heritage.

Women especially revived the use of the festive rural dress, the *bunad*, wearing specific costumes of their old-country districts. A love for jewelry was demonstrated in the use of heavy silver brooches (*sølje*). The peasant costume of Hardanger on Norway's west coast, a favored region for national romantics, inspired the official dress of the Daughters of Norway organization. These colorful outfits are worn at Norwegian American public events.

There was also renewed interest in the traditional Norwegian Harding fiddle, and old rural dances. Even today, groups meet to practice the old figures and demonstrate their mastery of the country dances. The current popularity of the peasant arts of wood carving and *rosemaling* (rose painting) also grew out of the *bygdelag* tradition. Vesterheim, the Norwegian American Museum in Decorah, Iowa, has promoted the folk arts through instruction and exhibitions.

PROVERBS

Norwegians tend to integrate sayings and proverbs into daily conversations. Some common expressions are: All is not gold that glitters; A burnt child avoids the fire; A dear child has many names; All cats are gray in the dark; As we make our bed, so must we also lie; "Cleanliness is a virtue," said the old woman, she turned her slip inside out every Christmas Eve; Crumbs are also bread; Empty barrels make the most noise; If it rains on the pastor it drips on the sexton; Many small brooks make a big river.

CUISINE

Norwegian cuisine is mainly limited to special occasions—family events like weddings and anniversaries, and such holidays as Christmas, when other customs are revived as well. The *kransekake* a cone-shaped cake of almond macaroon rings, is traditionally served at weddings and anniversaries. It is generally decorated with costumed figures and with flags, snappers, flowers, or medallions. The observance of the Christmas season begins on Christmas Eve, when a big meal is served, followed by the reading of the Christmas gospel and the opening of gifts. Hymns and carols are sung later, accompanied in some families by tradition of holding hands and circling the Christmas tree.

A typical old-country Christmas meal consists of *lutefisk*, *rømmegrøt*, pork or mutton spare ribs with pork sausages, as well as *fattigmann*, a deep-fried diamond-shaped cookie; *sandkake*, a cookie made of butter, flour, and almonds, baked in small metal molds; *krumkake*, a wafer baked in a special iron and rolled into a cylindrical shape while still warm; *julekake*, a sweet bread containing raisins, citron, and cardamon, and the essential *lefse*, which appears in many regional variations.

The Norwegian *koldt bord*, or cold table, is basically the same as the better known Swedish *smörgåsbord*, with selected hot dishes. Some of the traditional dishes of the Norwegian "cold table" include herring in many forms; sardines; smoked salmon and other fish; sliced cold ham, lamb, and beef; cheeses like Swiss, *geitost* (goat cheese), and *gammelost* (highly pungent sour milk cheese); *sylte* (pickled pork, pressed into loaf shape and sliced); pickles, cranberries, apple sauce, and spiced apples; and various types of bread, including flatbread. The meal is served with *akevitt* (strong distilled alcoholic drink) and beer.

HEALTH AND MENTAL HEALTH ISSUES

In his investigation of Norwegian immigrants in Minnesota, Ørnulv Ødegaard discovered a much higher incidence of emotional and mental problems than among Norwegians in Norway (Ornulv Òdegaard, *Emigration and Insanity: A Study of Mental Disease among the Norwegian-born Population in Minnesota* [Copenhagen], 1932). The frequency was also much higher than among other ethnic groups in America. At present, no empirical evidence has identified any emotional or cultural causes unique to the Norwegian population.

LANGUAGE

The Norwegian language, along with Danish and Swedish, belongs to the mutually comprehensible northern branch of the Germanic family of languages. During the centuries-long union with Denmark, Norwegians accepted Danish as their written language. Following independence in 1814 efforts to provide a national written standard created conflict between those who worked for a gradual Norwegianization of Danish orthographic forms and those who wished to create a totally new written language. The Norwegian government officially recognizes the existence of the predominant *bokmål* (Dano-Norwegian), which continues the Danish written tradition greatly modified through a series of reforms under the influence of Norwegian speech habits, and *nynorsk* (New Norse), constructed on the basis of modern dialects which most faithfully preserved the forms of Old Norse. Because of the isolated nature of Norwegian rural communities, the local vernacular was distinct with marked dialectal differences from one district to the next.

The cultural baggage of Norwegian immigrants included their specific local dialect and a Danish literary language. The latter played a significant role in the immigrant community, attaining a nearly sacred quality. It was the language of their institutions, secular and religious, and of sacred and profane literature. The immigrants had little appreciation for the linguistic reforms in the homeland; often such changers were viewed as a betrayal to a common cultural heritage. Changes in the official written language in Norway made the older form even more difficult to retain in America. A newspaper such as *Decorah-Posten* in Decorah, Iowa, persisted in using a Dano-Norwegian orthographic tradition from the 1870s well into the 1950s. The situation created confusion among teachers of Norwegian at American high schools, colleges and universities, who felt obligations to the language of the immigrant community. Only just before World War II did they in principle agree to teach the written standard—generally the Dano-Norwegian *bokmål*—which at any one time was recognized as the official one in Norway.

English was another threat to the maintenance of the Norwegian language in America. Rural settlement patterns protected spoken Norwegian so it still can be heard in some Norwegian communities. According to researcher Joshua A. Fishman, about half of second generation Norwegians in the period 1940 to 1960 learned the language; and in 1960 there were as many as 40,000 of the third generation who had learned Norwegian. As of 1990, about 80,000 speakers of Norwegian remained in the United States. In Minnesota, Norwegian, with 16,000 speakers, is the second most common European language after German. Across the country there are still two bilingual newspapers, *Western Viking* in Seattle and *Nordic Times* in Brooklyn. The *bygdelag* promoted the use of rural vernaculars and, indeed, their annual reunions provided an environment where rural speech was honored and encouraged. It was, however, a mixed language with English words and phrases integrated.

GREETINGS AND OTHER POPULAR EXPRESSIONS

Some common Norwegian expressions are: *God dag* ("gooDAAG")—Good Afternoon, How do you do?; *Adjø* ("adyur")—Goodbye; *Hvordan st_r det til?* ("VOORdahn stawr deh til")—How are you?; *Bare bra, takk* ("BAArer braa tahk")—Just fine, thanks; *Takk* ("tahk")—Thank you; *Mange takk* ("MAHNger tahk")—Thank you very much; *Skål* ("skawl")—Cheers; *God jul!* ("goo yewl")—Merry Christmas; *Godt nyttår* ("got newt awr")—Happy New Year; *Gratulerer!* ("grahtewLAYrerr")—Congratulations.

FAMILY AND COMMUNITY DYNAMICS

Early Norwegian immigration exhibited a pronounced family character. In a typical settlement like Spring Grove Township in Minnesota, for instance, there was in 1870 a near gender balance—107 men for each 100 women—as compared to 128 males to 100 females for all Minnesotans. An extended communal and familial network was encouraged by this circumstance. The regional composition of most rural settlements, so that immigrants from a specific Norwegian home community were preponderant, worked to the same end, recreating a familiar and comforting cultural and social environment.

But opportunities in America, where land was cheap and labor expensive, altered immigrant practices. The family farm, lacking the retinue of servants and landless agricultural workers common in Norway, encouraged greater marital fertility to produce needed labor. The immigrant families were large. The sexual division of labor changed as women moved further into domestic

roles. Men took over such farm chores as milking, which had been women's work in Norway.

Norwegian courting patterns were modified in part due to pietistic attitudes rooted in religious awakenings in Norway, but also because they were ridiculed by American neighbors. Greater wealth allowed the immigrants to imitate urban middle-class practices in housing, dress, household amenities (such as pianos), and leisure activities. But the bourgeois lifestyle was colored both by the local Norwegian cultural background and by the dominant position of the immigrant Lutheran church.

The male-dominated youth migration toward the end of the century was also entrenched in kinship and community. Later immigrants traveled increasingly to urban centers to reunite with relatives in America. Carl G. O. Hansen, visiting an aunt in Minneapolis in the 1880s, described the Norwegian environment: "My aunt sent one of her children out to make some purchases. Some things were to be bought at Haugen's, some at Tharaldsen's and some at Olsen & Bakke's. That surely sounded as if it were a Norwegian town." (Carl G. O. Hansen, *My Minneapolis* [Minneapolis, Minnesota: Privately published, 1956], p.52.)

The many single men living as boarders in crowded quarters would foster marriage outside the Norwegian group. Yet, there was a strikingly high percentage of in-marriage only in both the immigrant generation and the American-born second generation. In Chicago in 1910, 77 percent of married first generation Norwegians had wed another Norwegian, and 46 percent of the married second generation had chosen a mate within their ethnic group. When most Norwegian Americans married outside their nationality, their spouse was Scandinavian, or, if German, at least shared a Lutheran culture.

For most Norwegian families the "American Dream" was the security of a middle-class existence. Only a few Norwegians asserted themselves as financiers and captains of industry. Norwegians typically endorsed the American principle of equality and rejected American materialism. This attitude was reinforced by the Lutheran ethic of renouncing worldly pleasure. According to the census of 1990, 4.3 percent of Norwegian American households received public assistance and 5.1 percent lived under the poverty line.

Current specific data on in-marriage and divorce are not available. With regard to the latter, Norwegian Americans do not seem to deviate much from the average for the American population as a whole. Anecdotal evidence also suggests a continued high degree of in-marriage, attributable to community and church relations, and even to loyalty to an ethnic heritage. A persistent sense of family cohesion and values is evident in the common practice of arranging family reunions and the compilation of family histories. Such activities fortify ties to the past.

EDUCATION

Higher education in America is greatly indebted to religion. In the Norwegian immigrant community the Lutheran church recognized the salutary benefits of education in a Christian spirit. It emulated American denominations in establishing Lutheran church academies and colleges.

Norwegians placed themselves in a singular position among Scandinavian groups in America to question the religionless "common" school. The orthodox Lutheran clergy even dreamed of replacing the public schools with Lutheran parochial schools, but lacked the means to do so. The ability to read and write was common among Norwegian immigrants, and it improved greatly after 1860 when Norway enacted new laws to improve public education. The Norwegian Lutheran church in America did manage to operate congregational schools, some continuing into the 1930s. During the summer months these schools offered lessons on Lutheran faith and rudimentary instruction in the Norwegian language.

The academy movement flourished for a while, with approximately 70 such schools being established. They lasted until about World War I and assisted the immigrants in adjusting to American society. Inevitably they also strengthened a national Norwegian identity. Some academies were transformed into four-year liberal arts colleges. The college movement among Norwegians began in 1861 with the founding of Luther College, now located in Decorah, Iowa. The school was a facet of the church's effort to train Lutheran ministers. As such it was a men's school, with nearly half of the graduates entering the ministry. In the 1930s it began to admit women.

Five other Norwegian colleges have since been established. All were founded before 1900 mainly as academies. Three are in Minnesota: St. Olaf College in Northfield, which admitted female students from its inception; Augsburg College in Minneapolis; and Concordia College in Moorhead. Augustana College is located in Sioux Falls, South Dakota, and Pacific Lutheran University is in Tacoma, Washington.

Norwegian women in America obtained higher education at a time when such studies were closed to women in the homeland. Some of these women were trained as physicians at the Women's Medical School which opened in Chicago in 1870. As feminists and as professionals, they became leaders in the Norwegian community.

According to the 1990 census, of those who declared Norwegian as their primary ancestry, 21 percent of the women and 32 percent of the men 25 years or older had earned bachelor's, master's or doctor's degrees. Most attended public institutions rather than one of the "Norwegian" colleges.

RELIGION

The Norwegian Lutheran church was a focal point and conservative force in rural settlements in the upper Midwest. The congregation became an all-encompassing institution for its members, creating a tight social network that touched all aspects of immigrant life. The force of tradition in religious practice made the church a central institution in the urban environment as well. The severe reality of urban life increased the social role of the church.

In the unbridled freedom of America, Norwegian Lutherans exhibited an extreme denominationalism and established a tradition of disharmony. The Church of Norway largely abandoned the immigrants and provided no guidance. As a consequence, no fewer than 14 Lutheran synods were founded by Norwegian immigrants between 1846 and 1900. In 1917 most of the warring Lutheran factions reconciled doctrinal differences and organized the Norwegian Lutheran Church in America. It was one of the church bodies that in 1960 formed the American Lutheran Church, which in 1988 became a constituent part of the newly created Evangelical Lutheran Church in America.

Even though the terms Norwegian and Lutheran might seem synonymous to many, there were in fact substantial numbers of Methodists among Norwegian immigrants. They were concentrated especially in Chicago; a Norwegian Methodist theological seminary was established in Evanston. Some Norwegians converted to the Baptist faith. There were also groups of Quakers, relating back to "the Sloopers," and Mormons who joined the trek to the "New Jerusalem" in Salt Lake City, Utah.

EMPLOYMENT AND ECONOMIC TRADITIONS

Norwegians succeeded in commercial agriculture in pioneer times—following frontier practice—as wheat farmers but soon diversified into other products as dictated by topography, soil, climate, and market. In Wisconsin such considerations drew some Norwegians to tobacco farming. In Iowa they grew corn or raised cattle and hogs; in parts of Minnesota dairy farming was prominent. In the northwestern part of the state Norwegian farmers engaged heavily in spring wheat cultivation. The hard spring wheat region extended into South and North Dakota where Norwegians adapted to the demands of grassland wheat production on the semiarid northern plains.

In the urban economy, Norwegian men, along with other Scandinavians, found a special niche in construction and the building trades. It was a natural transfer of skills from home, as was their work as lumberjacks in the forests of northern Wisconsin and Minnesota. Norwegian men in Minneapolis earned a livelihood in the large flour mills. In the Pacific Northwest logging and employment in sawmills engaged many. Another significant transplanted skill was shipping. On the Great Lakes, Norwegian sailors and boat owners dominated as long as sailing vessels remained an important means of transportation. In 1870 approximately 65 percent of all sailors on Lake Michigan were Norwegian. Shipping was big on the eastern seaboard and the west coast as well. The coastal areas provided rich opportunity for fishing too. Norwegians on the west coast and Alaska began to develop the halibut industry at the turn of the twentieth century. By 1920 about 95 percent of all halibut fishermen and an even higher percentage of the owners of halibut schooners were of Norwegian birth or descent.

Traditional early employment for Norwegian women involved domestic and personal service. Accessibility to higher education gradually opened up new possibilities—especially for the American-born generations—in commerce, education, and in specialized professions. Looking at the occupational picture in 1950, there is a striking social advance both for women and men. Still Norwegians of both the first and second genera-

tion revealed a preference for farming, and men born in Norway were overrepresented in construction work.

The evidence provided in the 1990 census indicates little occupational concentration among Norwegian Americans. Of employed persons 16 years old and over, only 4.5 percent were occupied in farming, forestry, and fishery, and six percent in construction, while 15 percent were employed in manufacturing, and nearly 31 percent in a variety of managerial and specialty occupations. That year 4.4 percent of the civilian labor force was unemployed.

POLITICS AND GOVERNMENT

Norwegians in America have participated in the formation of several aspects of the political culture and are to be found in conservative and liberal camps of both prominent political parties.

Norwegians had a certain passion for the political arena. Familiarity with democratic reform and local self-government in Norway, a dislike of officialdom, and a heightened assertion encouraged them to participate in local government in America. From the community, they made their way to state and even national politics. During the early decades of this century Norwegians in Minnesota and North Dakota were, for instance overrepresented in the state administrations as well as in the legislatures and Congress.

Political affiliation, as expressed in a flourishing Norwegian immigrant press, was strongly influenced by the Free-Soil party. In the late 1850s, this same press abandoned the Democrats for Abraham Lincoln's Republican party, supporting its antislavery stance and its free distribution of frontier land to serious settlers. The Homestead Act of 1862 and the heroic participation of Norwegian Americans in the Civil War assured a strong loyalty to the Republican party and its ideals.

Toward the end of the nineteenth century, however, other issues came to the fore and weakened Republican loyalties. In regions suffering from agricultural depression and exploitation by outside financial interests, independent political thought brought Norwegians into the agricultural protest embodied in the Populist movement. This was especially the case in the wheat-growing regions of North Dakota and western Minnesota.

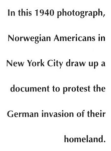

In this 1940 photograph, Norwegian Americans in New York City draw up a document to protest the German invasion of their homeland.

From around the turn of the century the Progressive movement gained a broad Norwegian following and Norwegians exhibited great faith in the benefits of legislative reform. The Nonpartisan League, organized in North Dakota in 1915, was further evidence of agrarian unrest. Norwegian farmers played a prominent role in its activities and advocacy, which included such socialist goals as public control and operation of grain silos, and the sale of wheat. This radical policy was, however, less a consequence of ethnic predispositions toward social reform than of economic self-interest and the problematic local conditions faced by wheat farmers.

Norwegians were also attracted to the Socialist party, joining local socialist clubs, which again became members of the Scandinavian Socialist Union formed in Chicago in 1910. But they did not do so in great numbers. Due to the high concentration of Norwegians in skilled occupations, especially in the building trades, they did, however, join labor unions in large numbers. The efforts of a Norwegian immigrant, Andrew Furuseth, to improve the working conditions for sailors, resulting in the Seamen's Act of 1915, is one example of the significant contributions made by immigrants to the American union movement.

In the 1920s Norwegians joined a national trend toward the Democratic party. The loyalty to the Republican party was significantly frayed as working class and reform-minded Norwegians took part in third-party movements, increasingly for Democrats, who seemed more committed to labor concerns and social justice than the Republicans. Republicanism remained common among middle- and upper-class Norwegian Americans, however.

Norwegian members of both parties were concerned with prohibition. Under the banner of temperance and local prohibition of the sale of intoxicating beverages, Norwegian politicians gained the support of their compatriots and were elected to public office. North Dakota, influenced by the agitation of the Norwegian American press, adopted a prohibition clause in its state constitution in 1889. National prohibition legislation, passed in 1919 as the Volstead Act, was named for Norwegian American Andrew J. Volstead, Republican congressman from Minnesota. Opposition to prohibition and the corruption and crime it yielded, paradoxically, strengthened the move toward the Democratic party, most especially among urban Norwegians.

MILITARY

Most Norwegians have viewed military service as an affirmation of American patriotism. The first fallen hero was a private in the war with Mexico who had Americanized his name to George Pilson. He had immigrated to Chicago and fell in 1847 in the bloody battle of Buena Vista, with

Chicago newspapers claiming that "more patriotic blood does not enrich the field at Buena Vista than that of the Chicago Norwegian volunteer." Norwegian acts of heroism, valor, and sacrifice constituted a watershed experience during the Civil War; Norwegian men had served in great numbers, suffered substantial casualties, and had established themselves in America. Norwegians supported the Spanish-American War and rallied around the American war objectives during World War I. In a patriotic spirit, Norwegian American societies and organizations published lists of "our boys" in the armed forces and memorialized the fallen of their nationality. Occupation of Norway by the Germans during World War II was a calamity that filled Norwegians in America with indignation and sorrow. During the summer of 1942 the U.S. Army established a Norwegian-speaking combat unit, the 99th Infantry Battalion, in case there should be an invasion of Norway. It consisted of immigrants and Norwegians born in America.

RELATIONS WITH NORWAY

Norwegian Americans cultivated bonds with Norway, sending gifts home often and offering aid during natural disasters and other hardships in Norway. Relief in the form of collected funds was forthcoming without delay. Only during conflicts within the Swedish-Norwegian union, however, did Norwegian Americans become involved directly in the political life of Norway. In the 1880s they formed societies to assist Norwegian liberals, collecting money to assist rifle clubs in Norway should the political conflict between liberals and conservatives call for arms. The ongoing tensions between Sweden and Norway and Norway's humiliating retreat in 1895 fueled nationalism and created anguish. Norwegians in America raised money to strengthen Norway's military defenses. The unilateral declaration by Norway on June 7, 1905, to dissolve its union with Sweden yielded a new holiday of patriotic celebration.

INDIVIDUAL AND GROUP CONTRIBUTIONS

As in any large population, certain members of the Norwegian American community have excelled in many disciplines. A sampling of group and individual achievements follows.

ACADEMIA

Thorstein Veblen (1857-1929), a second-generation Norwegian, was a superb social critic. His best known work is *The Theory of the Leisure Class* (1899), a savage attack on the wastefulness of American society. Einar Haugen (1906-) is a prominent linguist and professor emeritus at Harvard University. Marcus Lee Hansen (1892-1938), of Danish and Norwegian descent, was a pioneer immigration historian. Theodore C. Blegen (1891-1969) was also a prominent historian of Norwegians in America. Agnes Mathilde Wergeland (1857-1914) was a professor of history at the state university in Laramie, Wyoming, and the first Norwegian woman to earn a doctoral degree.

ARTS

Olive Fremstad (1868-1951) was an internationally renowned Wagnerian opera singer. Ole Bull (1810-1880) was a well-known concert violinist. F. Melius Christiansen (1871-1955) perfected *a capella* singing as director of the St. Olaf College choir. He has been called the "Music Master of the Middle West." Ole E. Rølvaag (1876-1931), the best-known Norwegian American author, wrote such books as *Giants In the Earth* (1927). Hjalmar Hjorth Boyesen (1848-1895), a realistic novelist, literary critic, and social Darwinist, taught at Cornell and Columbia universities. Kathryn Forbes (1909-1966) authored the best-selling *Mama's Bank Account* (1943), a portrait of a Norwegian family in San Francisco. As *I Remember Mama*, Forbes' work became a hit Broadway play, a motion picture, and a television series. Celeste Holm (1919-), versatile actress of stage and screen, appeared on Broadway and in numerous motion pictures. In 1950 she was an Academy Award nominee for Best Supporting Actress for her role in *All About Eve*.

INDUSTRY AND BUSINESS

Nelson Olson Nelson (1844-1922) founded the N. O. Nelson Manufacturing Company, which became one of the world's largest building and plumbing supply companies. Ole Evinrude (1877-1934), a self-taught mechanical engineer, developed the idea of the outboard motor. He formed the Evinrude Company in 1909. Arthur Andersen (1885-1947) was the founder of the world-famous accounting firm that bears his name. Conrad Hilton (1887-1979), Norwegian on his father's side, established one of the world's largest hotel chains and at the time of his death, owned 260 first-class hotels worldwide.

JOURNALISM

Victor F. Lawson (1850-1925) was editor and publisher of the Chicago *Daily News*, a philanthropist and a community leader. William T. Evjue (1882-1970) gained great influence as the editor of the progressive and reform-minded Madison *Capital Times*. Eric Sevareid (1912-1992), had a distinguished career in journalism and as a radio and television reporter and commentator.

MEDICINE

Ludvig Hektoen (1863-1951) made great progress in cancer research. The Hektoen Institute of Medical Research continues his work. Ingeborg Rasmussen (1854-1938) graduated from the Women's Medical College in Evanston in 1892 and became a prominent physician, feminist, and cultural leader among the Norwegians in Chicago. Helga Ruud (1860-1956) graduated from the Women's Medical College in 1889 and enjoyed a distinguished medical career at the Norwegian American Hospital in Chicago. Ulrikka Feldtman Bruun (1854-1940) was an influential temperance worker among Danes and Norwegians for the Woman's Christian Temperance Union (WCTU).

POLITICS AND GOVERNMENT

Knute Nelson (1843-1923) served as a Republican U.S. senator from Minnesota from 1895 to 1923. Andrew Furuseth (1954-1938) organized American commercial sailors. He was considered their liberator and was referred to as "the Abraham Lincoln of the Sea." Earl Warren (1891-1974) served as Chief Justice of the U.S. Supreme Court from 1953 to 1969. Henry Jackson (1912-1983), Democratic U.S. senator from Washington, served from 1953 to 1983. Hubert Humphrey (1911-1978) served for two terms as U.S. vice president under President Lyndon Johnson and was the Democratic presidential nominee in 1968, losing to Richard Nixon in the national election. Walter Mondale (1928-), served as a U.S. senator from Minnesota (1964-1977); U.S. vice president under President Jimmy Carter (1977-1881); and was the Democratic presidential nominee in 1984. Since 1993, Mondale has been U.S. Ambassador to Japan under the Clinton administration. Warren Christopher (1925-), whose great-grandparents emigrated from Norway in 1853, was named secretary of state in 1993.

SCIENCES

Ernest O. Lawrence (1901-1958), a professor of physics at Yale University, received the Nobel Prize in physics in 1939. Ivar Giaever (1929-), Norwegian-trained engineer and physicist, received the Nobel Prize in physics in 1973. Lars Onsager (1903-1976), received the Nobel Prize in chemistry in 1968. Norman E. Borlaug (1914-), an agricultural scientist, received the 1970 Nobel Peace Prize for his leadership in the "Green Revolution," which helped to dispel the fear of famine in underdeveloped countries. Ole Singstad (1882-1969) was chief engineer for the construction of the Holland Tunnel under the Hudson River.

SPORTS

Norwegian immigrants brought skiing to America in the mid-1800s by introducing cross-country racing and ski jumping, and organizing local clubs, including the National Ski Association. They dominated the sport into the 1930s. Beginning in 1856, John A. "Snowshoe" Thompson (1827-1876) delivered mail on skis across the Sierra Nevada mountains for nearly 20 years during the winter months, ensuring postal connection between Utah Territory and California. Sonja Henie (1912-1969) was an Olympic and World figure skating champion, movie star, and pioneer of ice shows. Torger Tokle (1920-1945), arrived in America in 1939 and was unrivaled by any U.S. ski jumper. Tokle won 42 of 48 competitions and, in so doing, set no fewer than 24 new hill records. He was killed in military action in the mountains of northern Italy while serving in the 86th Mountain Regiment—"The Ski Troops." Knute Rockne (1888-1931), head football coach at the University of Notre Dame from 1918 to 1931, revolutionized American collegiate football; his record consist of 105 wins, 12 losses, and five ties. Mildred "Babe" Didrikson Zaharias (1913-1956), a daughter of Norwegian immigrants, was a champion in basketball, track, and golf. Tommy Moe (1970-) won a gold medal for skiing in the 1994 Olympic Games in 1994.

MEDIA

PRINT

News of Norway.

Address: Royal Norwegian Embassy, 2720 34th Street, N.W., Washington, D.C. 20008.

Telephone: (202) 333-6000.
Fax: (202) 337-0870.

Norway Times/Nordisk Tidende.

Contact: Tom Røren, Editor.
Address: 481 81st Street, Brooklyn, New York 11209.
Telephone: (718) 238-1100.

Western Viking.

Contact: Alf Lunder Knudsen, Editor and Publisher.
Address: 2405 Northwest Market Street, Seattle, Washington 98107.
Telephone: (206) 784-4617.

RADIO

KBLE-AM (1050).

"The Scandinavian Hour" every Saturday morning.

Contact: Ron Olsen.
Address: 1114 Lakeside Avenue, Seattle, Washington. 98112.
Telephone: (206) 324-2000.

WTHE-AM (1520).

"Scandinavian Echoes" every Saturday afternoon.

Contact: Jeanne Widman.
Address: P.O. Box 712, Baldwin, New York 11510.
Telephone: (516) 742-1520.

ORGANIZATIONS AND ASSOCIATIONS

American-Scandinavian Foundation (ASF).

Promotes international understanding by means of educational and cultural exchange with Denmark, Finland, Iceland, Norway, and Sweden. It has an extensive program of fellowships and grants, and publishes the *Scandinavian Review*.

Contact: Lena Bärck Kaplan, President of the Board of Trustees.
Address: 725 Park Avenue, New York, New York 10021.
Telephone: (212) 879-9779.

The Norsemen's Federation (Nordmanns-Forbundet).

An international organization founded in Norway in 1907 to strengthen the ties between men and women of Norwegian heritage in and outside Norway. It functions as a cultural and social orga-

nization and has chapters throughout the United States.

Contact: Johan Fr. Heyerdahl, Secretary General.
Address: Rådhusgt. 23 B, 0158 Oslo, Norway.

Norwegian American Historical Association (NAHA).

Founded in 1925, is the main research center for Norwegian American history. It possesses large documentary archives and extensive library holdings. The Association publishes one to two volumes annually; so far more than 80 volumes of high scholarly merit on the Norwegian American experience have been released under its imprint.

Contact: Lloyd Hustvedt, Executive Secretary.
Address: St. Olaf College, 1520 St. Olaf Avenue, Northfield, Minnesota 55057.
Telephone: (507) 646-3221.

Scandinavian American Genealogical Society (SAGS).

Promotes the study of Danish, Finnish, Icelandic, Norwegian, and Swedish genealogy.

Contact: Barbara Oestreich, President.
Address: P.O. Box 16069, St. Paul, Minnesota 55116-0069.
Telephone: (612) 645-3671.

Sons of Norway.

An international order founded as a fraternal society in Minneapolis in 1895 with lodges throughout the United States as well as in Canada and in Norway. It provides insurance benefits for its members and publishes a monthly magazine, *The Viking*.

Contact: Liv Dahl, Administrative Director.
Address: 1455 West Lake Street, Minneapolis, Minnesota 55408.
Telephone: (612) 827-3611; or, (800) 945-8851.

MUSEUMS AND RESEARCH CENTERS

Little Norway.

Provides guided tours through a Norwegian pioneer homestead settled in 1856, featuring the Norway building patterned after a twelfth century stave church. It was built in Trondheim, Norway, to be exhibited at the Chicago World's Columbian Exposition in 1893.

Contact: Scott Winner, Director.

Address: 3576 Highway JG North, Blue Mounds, Wisconsin 53517.

Telephone: (608) 437-8211.

Nordic Museum.

Opened in 1980 in Seattle, Washington. Its purpose is to collect, preserve, and present the Scandinavian heritage in the Pacific Northwest. It has an extensive collection of objects from Scandinavia and the Pacific Northwest.

Contact: Marianne Forssblad, Director.

Address: 3014 Northwest 67th Street, Seattle, Washington 98117.

Telephone: (206) 789-5707.

Norskedalen Heritage and Nature Center.

Features objects specific to Norwegian immigrants who settled in Vernon and LaCrosse counties, Wisconsin, before 1900, and two separate pioneer homesteads. It arranges an annual Midsummer Festival in late June.

Contact: James Nestingen, Director.

Address: P.O. Box 225, Coon Valley, Wisconsin 54623.

Telephone: (608) 452-3424.

Vesterheim, the Norwegian American Museum.

A major ethnic museum, it maintains high professional standards and supports an outdoor museum as well as a large collection of objects dealing with the Norwegian homeland and life in America. It also features a museum store with Norwegian American crafts and books. It conducts workshops in Norwegian folk crafts.

Contact: Darrell D. Henning, Director.

Address: Decorah, Iowa 52101.

Telephone: (319) 382-9681.

SOURCES FOR ADDITIONAL STUDY

Babcock, Kendrick Charles. *The Scandinavian Element in the United States.* Urbana: University of Illinois Pres, 1914.

Blegen, Theodore C. *Norwegian Migration: The American Transition.* Northfield, Minnesota: NAHA, 1940.

Gjerde, Jon. *From Peasants to Farmers: The Migration from Balestrand, Norway, to the Upper Middle West.* New York: Cambridge University Press, 1985.

Haugen, Einar. *The Norwegian Language in America: A Study in Bilingual Behavior,* two volumes. Bloomington: Indiana University Press, 1969.

Lovoll, Odd S. *A Century of Urban Life: The Norwegians in Chicago before 1930.* Northfield, Minnesota: NAHA, 1988.

————. *The Promise of America: A History of the Norwegian American People.* Minneapolis: University of Minnesota Press, 1984.

Qualey, Carlton C. *Norwegian Settlement in the United States.* Northfield, Minnesota: NAHA, 1938.

U.S. Bureau of the Census. *Ancestry of the Population of the United States, 1990.* Prepared by the Economic and Statistics Administration, Bureau of the Census. Washington, D.C., August 1993.

————. *Detailed Ancestry Groups for States, 1990.* Prepared by the Economic and Statistics Administration, Bureau of the Census, Washington, D.C., October 1992.

In traditional Ojibwa culture, an individual lived in a band and was a member of a clan. Most people from the same clan shared a common ancestor on their father's side of the family. Some clans were matrilinear, and children were affiliated with their mother's clan. People of the same clan claim a common totem, the symbol of a living creature.

OJIBWA

by

Lorene Roy

OVERVIEW

The Ojibwa ("oh-jib-wah") are a woodland Native people who originated in northeastern North America. In the mid-seventeenth century there were approximately 35,000 Ojibwa on the continent. According to the 1990 census, the Ojibwa were the third-largest Native group (with a population of 104,000), after the Cherokee (308,000) and the Navajo (219,000). Federally recognized Ojibwa reservations are found in Minnesota (Fond du Lac, Grand Portage, Leech Lake, Mille Lacs, Nett Lake [Bois Forte Band], Red Lake, and White Earth), Michigan (Bay Mills Indian Community, Grande Traverse, Keweenaw Bay Indian Community, Saginaw, and Sault Sainte Marie), Wisconsin (Bad River, Lac Courte Oreilles, Lac du Flambeau, Mole Lake or Sokaogan Chippewa Community, Red Cliff, and St. Croix), Montana (Rocky Boy's), and North Dakota (Turtle Mountain). Others have petitioned for federal recognition. While Ojibwa reserves are also found in Ontario and Saskatchewan, this account stresses their history in the United States.

HISTORY

The Ojibwa call themselves the Anishinabeg (also spelled Anishinaabeg, or if singular, Anishinabe) for "first" or "original people." In the eighteenth century the French called Ojibwa living near the eastern shore of Lake Superior Salteaux or Salteurs, terms now used only in Canada. The Anishinabe acquired the names Ojibwa and Chippewa from French traders. The English preferred to use Chippewa or Chippeway, names typically employed on the treaties with the British government and later with the U.S. government. In 1951, Inez Hilger noted that more than 70 different names were used for Ojibwa in written accounts (M. Inez Hilger, *Chippewa Child Life and Its Cultural Background* [originally published, 1951; reprinted, St Paul: Minnesota Historical Society Press, 1992], p. 2).

There are several explanations for the derivation of the word "Ojibwa." Some say it is related to the word "puckered" and that it refers either to the distinctive type of moccasin that had high cuffs and a puckered seam or, to adopt a grisly version, to the Anishinabe practice of roasting their enemies until the corpses were puckered. Others say that the French used the word *o-jib-i-weg* or "pictograph" because the Anishinabe employed a written language based on pictures or symbols. And others say that "Ojibwa" is related to "Chippewa," because when pronounced with an accent on the second syllable and a silent final consonant, it sounds the same.

MIGRATION TO THE GREAT LAKES

Early legends indicate that, 500 years ago, the Ojibwa lived near the mouth of the Saint Lawrence River. About 1660 they migrated westward, guided by a vision of a floating seashell referred to as the sacred *miigis*. At the Straits of Mackinac, the channel of water connecting Lake Huron and Lake Michigan, the vision ended, and the Anishinabe divided into three groups. One group, the Potawatomi, moved south and settled in the area between Lake Michigan and Lake Huron. A second group, the Ottawa, moved north of Lake Huron. A third group, the Ojibwa, settled along the eastern shore of Lake Superior. Because of this early association, the Potawatomi, the Ottawa, and the Ojibwa are known collectively as the Three Fires.

FIRST CONTACT

The Ojibwa met non-Native Americans in the 1600s, possibly hearing about Europeans through the Huron people. The first written European accounts about the Ojibwa appeared in Jesuit diaries, published in collected form as the *Jesuit Relations and Allied Documents*. The Jesuits were followed by French explorers and fur traders, who were succeeded by British fur traders, explorers, and soldiers and later by U.S. government officials and citizens.

Fur trading, especially exchange of beaver pelts for goods including firearms, flourished until the 1800s. The Ojibwa traded with representatives of fur companies or indirectly through salaried or independent traders called *coureurs de bois*. In addition to furs, the land around the Great Lakes was rich in copper and iron ore, lumber, and waterpower, all natural resources that were coveted by non-Native Americans. Competition in trading led to intertribal conflict. By the 1700s the Ojibwa, aided with guns, had succeeded in pushing the Fox south into Wisconsin. Ojibwa and Sioux fighting extended over a 100-year period until separate reservations were established.

By the mid-nineteenth century the Ojibwa had enlarged their geographic boundaries and had splintered into four main groups. The Southeastern Ojibwa lived southeast and north of Lake Huron, in present-day Michigan and southern Ontario. The Southwestern Ojibwa lived along the south and north shores of Lake Superior. The Northern Ojibwa lived in northern Ontario. The Plains Ojibwa or Bungi lived in the present-day states and provinces of Montana, North Dakota, Manitoba, and Saskatchewan. The Plains Ojibwa adopted a lifestyle that resembled that of other Plains tribes, living in tepees, riding horses, and relying on buffalo for food and clothing.

RELATIONSHIP BETWEEN OJIBWA AND NON-NATIVE AMERICANS

The history of the contact between non-Native Americans and the Ojibwa dates back more than 350 years. While the Ojibwa did not engage in extended armed conflict with Europeans, the relationship was not always amicable. To the missionaries the Ojibwa were heathens to be converted to Christianity. To the fur traders they were commodities who could be purchased and indentured to company stores through watered-down alcohol and cheaply made goods. To the settlers they were wastrels who did not force the land to release its bounty. To ethnologists the Ojibwa were objects of study. To the government they were impressionable and recalcitrant wards. While there are many people who now value the Ojibwa culture, there are still others who regard the Ojibwa with disinterest or disdain, indicating that long-held stereotypes persist.

KEY ISSUES

Key issues facing the Ojibwa include economic development to reduce the numbers of unemployed, improved medical treatment to combat illnesses such as diabetes and alcoholism, better management of natural resources, protection of treaty rights and attainment of sovereignty, and increased emphasis on higher education to train specialists and renew cultural ties.

ACCULTURATION AND ASSIMILATION

MISCONCEPTIONS AND STEREOTYPES

The Ojibwa face the same misconceptions and stereotypes applied to other Native people. Because they refuse to strip the land of all its bounty, they have been considered lazy and unintelligent. Sports mascots and consumer product labels targeted at the general American public perpetuate Native American stereotypes. Ojibwa have also seen their sacred religious beliefs, such as vision quests, misinterpreted and sold by seekers of New Age thought. Misconceptions about sovereignty are common. Almost all early treaties promised the Ojibwa that they could continue to hunt and fish in ceded land, yet when the Ojibwa attempt to enforce their treaty rights conflicts arise with non-Native outdoors enthusiasts and tourists. From 1989 to 1991 anti-treaty organizations such as Stop Treaty Abuse staged protests against spearfishing that led to racial slurs, verbal threats, stoning, and gunfire aimed at Ojibwa. Two widely publicized antitreaty group slogans were, "Save a Deer, Shoot an Indian," and "Save a Fish, Spear a Squaw." The relationship between the Ojibwa and the federal government is often perceived not as a legal entitlement but as a special privilege; many non-Native Americans have been falsely persuaded that the Ojibwa receive extraordinary benefits.

TRADITIONAL CULTURE

The traditional Ojibwa culture valued generosity, honesty, strength of character, endurance, and wisdom. These qualities were instilled through education, religious practice, and by example within the tribe. The Ojibwa counted time by 24-hour intervals (nights), months (moons), and years (winters). Each month had a name, denoting some natural feature or event. October, for example, was called the "falling leaves moon." Time was sometimes reckoned by making notches on sticks.

Precontact culture was heavily influenced by the natural terrain as the Ojibwa adapted their lifestyle to survive in a heavily forested land traversed by a network of lakes and rivers. The Ojibwa lived a seminomadic life, moving a number of times each year in order to be close to food sources. Except for the Plains Ojibwa, who rode horses, they traveled on land by foot and wore snowshoes during the winter, transporting goods on dog sleds. The portability of Ojibwa lodging—the wigwam—enabled such moves to be made quickly and easily. Wigwams could be built in a day by bending peeled green ironwood saplings into arches; lashing the arches into a circular or oval shape with basswood fiber; and weaving birch bark strips or rush, cedar bark, or cattail mats around the saplings. The dwelling had two openings, a door and a hole on top to emit smoke from the cooking fire located directly below. When they moved to another camp, the Ojibwa left the frame, taking the lightweight birch bark strips and rush mats. During warm months the Ojibwa slept on cedar bough mattresses, each person wrapped in a bearskin or deerskin robe.

Ojibwa lived in hunting camps in late fall and winter. In winter, men trapped and hunted. Families could become isolated during the winter months, and women occupied time by tanning hides and sewing, while families engaged in storytelling. Many tales centered on Nanabush, a half-human, half-spirit trickster, who was often entangled in humorous scrapes and brought innovations, such as medicine, to humankind from the spirits (Nanabush went by many other names: Naanabozho, Nanibush, Nenabozho, Manabozho, Minabozho, Waynaboozhoo, Wenabozho, Wenabozhoo, Wenebojo, Winabojo, or Winneboshoo). Gambling was another popular pastime. In the moccasin game, players on different teams guessed the location of a marked bullet or metal ball hidden under a moccasin. Gambling was a social event often accompanied by drumming and singing.

Before they began to trade with Europeans and Americans, Ojibwa wore clothing made from animal hides, primarily from tanned deerskin. The women wore deerskin dresses, leggings, moccasins, and petticoats made of woven nettle or thistle fibers. The men wore leggings, breechcloths, and moccasins. Girls and women decorated the clothing in geometric designs with bones, feathers, dyed porcupine quills, shells, and stones, using bone or thorn needles and thread made from nettles or animal sinew. Jewelry was made from animal bones, claws, or teeth strung into necklaces. After European contact, the Ojibwa began to wear woven clothing. Europeans introduced the Ojibwa to glass beads inspired by the designs in calico cloth. Both men and women wove and mended fish nets.

Birch bark was a versatile natural product from which the Ojibwa created many items, including canoes, toboggans, and storage containers. The Ojibwa built canoe frames from wood and covered the frame with sewn birch bark strips, sealing the seams with pine or spruce gum. Each canoe weighed from 65 to 125 pounds and was typically 16 feet long, 18 inches deep, and three feet wide across the midpoint. Toboggans also had curved wooden frames covered with birch bark. The Ojibwa decorated birch bark baskets with porcupine quills, sweet grass, birch bark cutouts, or bitten designs that were created by folding thin pieces of birch bark in half and biting them. The dents made dark impressions on the light background. Birch bark torches were fashioned by rolling the bark into tubes and covering the tube with pitch. The Ojibwa also carved wooden objects such as arrows, bowls, boxes, drums, paddles, rattles, spoons, shuttles for weaving fish nets, and war clubs.

TRANSFORMATION OF CULTURE

Traditional life was altered through contact with non-Native Americans. Fur trading resulted in the Ojibwa becoming reliant on traded goods rather than the clothing, utensils, and weapons they had constructed. The establishment of reservations restricted Ojibwa seasonal travel, the formalized educational system removed children from their families, and the government's relocation policies dispersed tribe members. By the late 1980s many Ojibwa lived in one-room log cabins, frame cabins, or tar paper shacks rather than in wigwams. Wigwam construction incorporated new materials: other forms of tree bark were more easily available than long strips of birch bark; blankets covered wigwam doors instead of animal

In this 1938 photograph, a mother and daughter weave baskets in preparation for a celebration commemorating the 1863 Ojibwa treaty with the Sioux.

skins; calico, cardboard, and tar paper replaced the rush matting. The rate of acculturation varied by reservation. By the mid-1940s, only the elderly were bilingual, and most Ojibwa had adopted modern clothing. Birch bark canoes were largely replaced by wooden and later aluminum boats. Few Ojibwa practiced their traditional religion.

Ojibwa culture is currently experiencing a renaissance as natives and nonnatives are studying Ojibwa botany, crafts, myths, and religion. Wild ricing is still part of the culture, although the harvest is now regulated. Making maple sugar is still popular as well, although the sap may be collected in plastic bags rather than in birch bark baskets.

Many Ojibwa are concerned about the degradation of the environment by industry and mismanagement. Logging enterprises have destroyed traditional maple sugar camps, and fish caught in freshwater lakes are contaminated with mercury. It is still common for Ojibwa to hunt, trap, and fish. The *Mide* religion has been revived as well, and traditional importance is still afforded to visions and dreams. Ojibwa gatherings often begin with a prayer and a ritual offering of tobacco as an expression of gratitude and respect to the Heavenly Spirit. Powwows, the modern equivalent of multiband gatherings, are now elaborately staged competitions were costumed dancers perform to the accompaniment of vocalists who sing in Ojibwa while beating on bass drums with padded drumsticks. Clan and band affiliation still exists, and many Ojibwa seek to reclaim lands once tribally owned. If they are nonreservation dwellers, they often maintain ties to reservations, especially if they are enrolled or official members. Tribal newsletters are a means for members to stay abreast of local news, issues, and politics.

CUISINE

Native cuisine was closely influenced by the seasons, as Ojibwa changed camps in seminomadic pattern to locate themselves closer to food sources. For example, because the Ojibwa used maple sugar or maple syrup as a seasoning, during the late spring they lived near maple sugar trees, each family or group of families returning to a traditional location where they had stored utensils and had marked with an ax cut the trees they would tap. A typical sugar camp or sugar bush encompassed an area of some 900 taps or cuttings, with up to three taps made per tree. The Ojibwa collected maple sap in birch bark containers and poured it into vats made of moose hide, wood, or bark, and later into brass kettles, where it was boiled until it became syrup. The syrup was strained, reheated, thickened, and stirred in shallow troughs until it formed granulated sugar. Birch bark cones were packed with sugar, tied together, and hung from the ceiling of the wigwam or storage building. The Ojibwa also poured the sap into wooden molds or directly into snow to form maple sugar candy. Camps were moved in the summer to be close to gardens and wild berry patches. The Ojibwa cultivated gardens of corn, pumpkins, and squash. Dried berries, vegetables, and seeds were stored in underground pits. They drank teas boiled from plants and herbs and sweetened with maple sugar. The Ojibwa fished throughout the year, using hooks, nets, spears, and traps. Fish and meat were dried and smoked so they could be stored.

In late summer the Ojibwa moved again to be near wild rice fields. Wild rice (in Ojibwa, *mahnomin, manomin,* or *manoomin*) is a grain that grows on long grasses in shallow lakes or along streams. As the edible rice seeds began to mature, families marked the area they would harvest by tying the rice stalks together, using knots or dyed rope that would distinguish their claim. The rice harvest was a time of community celebration, starting with the announcement by an annually appointed rice chief or elder that the fields were ready. One team member stood in the canoe pushing a long forked pole to guide the canoe through the grasses. The other team member sat in the canoe, reaching to bend the grass over the canoe and hitting the grass with wooden stocks called beaters in order to shake the wild rice seeds from the grass without permanently injuring the plant. When the canoe was filled, it was poled to shore where the rice was dried, parched to loosen the hull, treaded on to remove the hull, and winnowed to separate the chaff. A medicine man blessed the first rice harvested, and each ricing pair donated rice to a communal fund to feed the poor. Rice was often boiled and sweetened with maple sugar or flavored with venison or duck broth. Up to one-third of the annual harvest was stored, usually in birch bark baskets. The rice season lasted from ten days to three weeks. Ricers often poled through their sections every few days as the rice seeds matured at differing rates. Rice was left to seed the beds for the following year and to be consumed by the birds.

HEALTH AND MENTAL HEALTH ISSUES

During their first contact with non-Native peoples, the Ojibwa were exposed to a number of diseases and suffered through epidemics of smallpox and other illnesses. The transition from traditional living to permanent settlement in villages led to a reduced lifestyle and to a high incidence of communicable diseases including tuberculosis and trachoma. When the Ojibwa ceded land they often did so in exchange for health care, indicating an early concern for health issues. These rights are still in effect, and Ojibwa living on or maintaining social ties with reservations may have access to federally funded programs including Indian Health Service clinics or hospitals. The Ojibwa, along with other Native American groups, share concerns over poor health. There are high incidences of chemical dependency, diabetes, fetal alcohol syndrome, obesity, suicide, and accidental death.

Today the Ojibwa use a blend of traditional and modern treatment methods to improve health. Alcohol consumption and chemical dependency is discouraged. Alcohol and drugs are banned from powwow sites, and some powwows are organized to celebrate sobriety. Mash-Ka-Wisen (Be strong, accept help), the oldest Native-owned and operated chemical treatment center, on the Fond du Lac Reservation, incorporates elements of Ojibwa culture into its services for its clients. The Minneapolis American Indian Center provides an array of social services, including programs on chemical dependency, developmental disabilities, and rehabilitation.

Traditional herbal cures include sumac fruit made into tea with crushed roots to stop bleeding, blackberry roots boiled and drunk to stop diarrhea or prevent miscarriage, wild onions cooked and sweetened with maple sugar to treat children's colds, yarrow roots mashed into creams for treating blemishes, strawberry roots boiled and eaten to treat stomach aches, and plantain leaves chopped and used as a poultice for bruises, rheumatism, and snake bites.

LANGUAGE

Spoken Ojibwa or Ojibwemowin is an Algonquin language with regional dialectical differences. It is related linguistically to the languages not only of the Ottawa and Potawatomi but also of the Fox, Cree, and Menominee. Since it was a spoken rather than a written language, the spelling of Ojibwa words varies. The Ojibwa language is spoken by 40,000 to 50,000 people. While once spoken only by elders, there is currently a resurgence of interest in and promotion of the language. Many Ojibwa demonstrate this interest in native identity by preferring to be called Anishinabe. Instruction is available in some public as well as in tribally directed educational settings. Classes and workshops offered at community colleges and state universities are sometimes broadcast to more distant locations. Language texts as well as instructional material in workbooks, bilingual texts, audiotapes, and multimedia formats have also been developed. Tribal newspapers carry regular Ojibwa-language columns.

GREETINGS AND OTHER POPULAR EXPRESSIONS

Common Ojibwa expressions include: *Boozhoo* ("boo shoo")—Hello, greetings; *Miigwech* ("mee gwitch")—Thank you; *Aaniin ezhi-ayaayan?* ("a neen a shay i an")—How are you?; *Nimino-ayaa* ("nay mi no a yah")—I am fine; *Mino-ayaag!* ("minnow a yog")—All of you be well!

FAMILY AND COMMUNITY DYNAMICS

In traditional Ojibwa culture, an individual lived in a band and was a member of a clan. Most peo-

ple from the same clan shared a common ancestor on their father's side of the family. Some clans were matrilinear, and children were affiliated with their mother's clan. People of the same clan claim a common totem (*dodem, do daim,* or *do dam*), the symbol of a living creature. The seven original clans were the bear, bird, catfish, crane, deer, loon, and marten. Twenty or more clans with additional totems were added later. A totem could denote an attribute such as prowess, leadership, knowledge, healing power, or sustenance. Bands consisted of groups of five to 50 families, up to 400 people, and lived within the same village. Examples are the five large bands of Minnesota: the Superior, Mississippi, Pillager, Red Lake, and Pembina. Bands were formed of people from a number of clans.

SOCIAL ACTIVITIES UNRELATED TO FOOD GATHERING

Traditionally, Ojibwa behavior was controlled by taboos that governed actions during pregnancy, birth, illness, death, and mourning. For example, bereaved relatives were not allowed to participate in food gathering until someone fed them the first wild rice or maple sugar of the season. Within families, Ojibwa humor was expressed through teasing.

Before contact with non-Native Americans, the Ojibwa held annual spring and autumn celebrations at a central location, with singing, dancing, eating, sports competitions, and storytelling. In the early 1700s the celebrations took place in Bowating, near present-day Sault Sainte Marie. In the late 1700s they were held near Lake Superior's Chequamegon Bay and, by the early eighteenth century, at Fort La Pointe on Madeline Island. These celebrations commemorated significant events in an individual's lifetime: the naming of a child, a boy's first hunt, a girl's first menstrual period, marriage, and death. Music played a central part in these events, as singers would perform to the accompaniment of drums, rattles, or, during courtship, flutes.

MARRIAGE

Women were allowed to marry soon after puberty, at age 14 or 15. During a woman's first menstrual period she fasted in a small wigwam from five to ten days. During this time the manitou or spirits were considered a strong spiritual presence in her life. Boys were allowed to marry as soon as they could demonstrate that they could support a family through hunting. During courtship the couple's contact was supervised. If both young people were found acceptable to each other and to their families, the man moved in with the wife's family for a year. There was no formal wedding ceremony. If the marriage proved to be disharmonious or if the wife failed to conceive, then the man returned to his parents. A couple that wished to continue living together after the year would build their own separate dwelling. Marital separation was allowed, and after separation people could remarry. Men who could support more than one family might have more than one wife. Intermarriage was acceptable, and by 1900 most Ojibwa were of mixed heritage, typically French and Ojibwa.

CHILDREARING

Parents appointed an elder to give the baby its sacred, or dream, name. The parents would also give the child one or more nicknames. Ojibwa babies were wrapped in swaddling until they were one year old, then kept in cradle boards—rectangular wooden frames with a backrest or curved headboard to protect the baby's head, and a footrest. Dream catchers—willow hoops encircling woven animal-sinew designs that resembled spider webs—and toys of bone, birch bark, shells, or feathers hung from the headboard. Dried moss, cattail down, and rabbit skins served as diapers. Grandparents typically had living with them at least one grandchild, including at least one granddaughter. Childhood was divided into two periods: the time before the child walked, and the time from walking to puberty.

Until they were around seven years of age, both girls and boys were tended to and taught by their mothers, aunts, and elders. Boys were then taught hunting and fishing skills by the men, while girls continued to learn domestic skills from the women and elders. Moral values were taught by example and through storytelling.

FUNERALS

If a person died inside a wigwam, the body was removed through a hole made in the west-facing side of the dwelling. The body was wrapped in birch bark and buried with items of special significance. During the next four days the individual's spirit or ghost was said to be walking westward to a place where the soul would dwell after death. Food and beverage were left at the grave site for the spirit's consumption during the walk. Grave sites were marked by erecting gabled wood houses over the length of the grave. Placed at the head of the grave was a wooden marker painted with a pictograph illustrating the individual's achievements and clan affiliation; the totem animal was painted upside down, denoting death. Families mourned for periods of up to one year, with some family members expressing grief by blackening their faces, chests, and hands with charcoal and maintaining an unkempt appearance. A Feast of the Dead service, scheduled each fall, was sponsored by families who had lost members over the previous year. Food continued to be left at the grave site at regular intervals over a period of many years.

EDUCATION

Federal policy toward Native education emphasized Native American assimilation into U.S. society. Consequently, instruction in vocational skills was promoted over the teaching of Native traditions. From the 1870s until the 1940s, many Ojibwa children were sent to government day schools, mission schools, or boarding schools (grade schools located as far away as Kansas and Pennsylvania). School attendance for Ojibwa became compulsory in 1893.

A significant step toward Native American education occurred with the passage of the Johnson O'Malley Act in 1934, authorizing states and territories to contract with the Bureau of Indian Affairs (BIA) for services including education. Public schools were encouraged to incorporate information on Native cultures into their curricula.

Today Ojibwa children living off reservations attend public or private schools. Private schools include those operated by Native American organizations, such as the Red School House in St. Paul and the Heart of the Earth Survival School in Minneapolis. Since 1989 public school curricula in Wisconsin are required by law to incorporate lessons on Native American cultures; by 1994 similar legislation was being considered in Minnesota. Ojibwa living on or near reservations may also be taught in tribally run schools or BIA contract schools. Some academic institutions offer degree programs specializing in Ojibwa culture. In addition, four of the 24 tribal colleges in the United States are located on Ojibwa reservations: Bay Mills Community College (Brimley, Michigan), Fond du Lac Community College (Cloquet, Minnesota), Lac Courte Oreilles Ojibwa Community College (Hayward, Wisconsin), and Turtle

Mountain Community College (Belcourt, North Dakota). These institutions offer associate degrees and, in their roles as community centers, serve as focal points of Ojibwa culture.

According to the *Chronicle of Higher Education* (Volume 60, No. 1, August 25, 1993, pp. 13, 15), as of fall 1992, 114,000 (0.8 percent) of 14,359,000 college students in the United States were Native Americans. As with other Native peoples, fewer Ojibwa complete high school and postsecondary education than do other population groups. The composite of Ojibwa students in higher education often differs significantly from that of non-Native American students: they generally are older, drop out or stop out at higher rates, take longer to complete their degrees, and often are married with children. These students face many obstacles including culturally rooted learning differences and homesickness if they relocate. Students requesting financial aid from their tribe may be channeled into certain fields of study such as education, social work, or medicine.

RELIGION

While some aspects of religious observance were communal, traditional Ojibwa religious practice was focused on inward personal experience. There was a belief in spirits, called manitou or manidoo. The creator was referred to as Gitchie Manitou. Manjimanidoo or evil spirits existed; windigos were especially terrifying spirits who dwelled within lakes and practiced cannibalism. Animate and inanimate objects possessed spiritual power, and the Ojibwa considered themselves one element of nature, no greater or less significant than any other living being. The cardinal directions were invested with sacred power and were associated with certain colors: white for the north, red or black for the south, yellow for the east, blue for the west. The Ojibwa recognized three additional directions: heaven, earth, and the position where an individual stands. Tobacco was considered sacred and was smoked in pipes or scattered on lakes to bless a crossing, a harvest, or a herd or to seal agreements between peoples of different tribes.

Dreams carried great significance and were sought through fasting or other purgative ceremonies. Dream catchers were used to capture good dreams. The name "dreamer" was reserved for tribal visionaries who would dream of certain powerful objects—such as stones—that they would then seek on waking. Dreamers might also experience prophetic dreams that they would convey to others to forestall danger. At an early age young boys and girls fasted in order to obtain a vision of how to conduct their future. Some visions provided complete messages and songs; others were incomplete and were revealed in their entirety only with the fullness of time. Visions could come during sleep. Since it was difficult to adhere to the advice imparted by visions, men and women went on annual fasts or retreats to renew the vision and reflect on their lives.

Sweat lodges were used to cure illness or to procure dreams. These were wigwams in which steam was created by pouring water over heated rocks and sealing the entrances. Bark and pine boughs might be added to the steam. Fasting was used to cure sickness and, like sweating, was thought to cleanse the body.

The Ojibwa developed a Grand Medicine Society or *Midewiwin* (*Mitewiwin*) religion. Abbreviated *"Mide,"* *Midewiwin* most likely means "good-hearted" or "resonant," in reference to the belief that the *Mide* priest worked for the betterment of others and employed special sacred drums. The *Mide* culture is a hierarchical priesthood of four to eight degrees, or orders, with each level representing the attainment of certain skills or knowledge. Women as well as men, children as well as adults, could be priests (also referred to as medicine men or women). As many as 20 years of study might be required to progress to the highest degree. After one year of training, an apprentice was initiated as a first-level *Mide* priest and was allowed to perform certain duties. Initiations were held during an annual Grand Medicine Dance in the spring or early fall and lasted from one to five days. Conducted in large wigwams, the ceremonies incorporated the use of a sacred drum and sacred pipe, both of which were guarded by caretakers. Initiates offered gifts such as blankets, cooking utensils, and wild rice. Feasting included wild rice, fresh or dried blueberries, maple sugar, and dog meat. Subsequent training required learning herbology for treating sickness or for acquiring personal power, a skill used much in the way that charms are used. *Mide* priests, therefore, acquired the role of healer. *Mide* members were also reputed to use "bad medicine" to cause sickness or death. *Mide* priests carried personal medicine bundles, cloth squares, or cloth or yarn bags enclosing one or more decorated animal skins called medicine bags. Specific types of skins were associated with each of the *Mide* degrees. At the first level, the *Mide* priest would have a medicine bag made from the skin of an otter, marten, mink, or weasel. Objects found in medicine bags included shells, bear claws decorated with ribbons, glass beads, *kinikinik* (native tobacco), carved figures, dried roots, and herbs. *Mide* songs and instructions were recorded on birch bark scrolls that were placed under the care of an appointed guardian priest.

In the early nineteenth century, many Ojibwa became followers of the Shawnee Prophet and his multitribe Shawano cult whose members advocated a return to traditional living and replacing *Mide* rites with new ceremonies. The Prophet was also known as Lalawethika (Laulewasika) or Tenskwatawa and was the brother of the Shawnee warrior Tecumseh. The Shawano cult lost favor and the *Mide* regained strength after the Prophet's followers failed to defeat the U.S. Army troops in 1811 at the battle of Tippecanoe.

Christianity was adopted slowly, but most modern Ojibwa are Roman Catholics or Protestant Episcopalians. Conflict arose between full-blooded Ojibwa, who tended to follow a more traditional lifestyle focused on *Mide* or Episcopalian values, and the mixed-blood progressive Ojibwa, who typically were Roman Catholic and followed a more acculturated lifestyle. The BIA often settled disagreements between the two factions by siding with the progressives who promoted majority culture values such as agronomy and small business enterprises.

EMPLOYMENT AND ECONOMIC TRADITIONS

Ojibwa culture dictated that excess goods be shared with the less fortunate. With the arrival of the fur trade, the Ojibwa learned to barter for goods that generally could be consumed within a year. They first earned money through the sale of land or timber rights. Since saving money was not a tradition and the amount they received was low, incomes were disposable and might be barely sufficient for a meager living. Often relocated to disadvantaged areas, the Ojibwa faced poverty and bare subsistence through living off the land and/or farming. Reservation life led to reliance on government assistance.

Modern Ojibwa live on reservations and in a variety of nonreservation areas, rural, suburban, and urban. Like other Native peoples, the Ojibwa, particularly those on reservations, have high rates of unemployment. They may support themselves through seasonal work, including forestry, farming, tourism, trapping, and wild ricing. Particularly since the 1970s reservations also support small businesses: bait shops, campgrounds, clothing manufacturing, construction, fish hatcheries, hotels, lumber stores, marinas, restaurants, and service stations.

With the passage of the Indian Gaming Regulatory Act in 1988, reservations were accorded new employment venues related to gaming, including bingo halls, casinos, and spin-off businesses such as gas stations, hotels, and restaurants. While there is some opposition to gaming, profits have contributed to higher employment levels and income. Tribes have invested gaming income in the purchase of ancestral lands, in road and home construction, and in building new social service buildings and/or extending social services. Some reservations have passed employment rights ordinances requiring employers on reservations to give preference to tribal members in hiring, training, and promotion.

Treaty rights allow modern Ojibwa to hunt, fish, and harvest rice on lands once belonging to their ancestors. The Ojibwa right to use the natural resources of reservation lands ceded to the government was reaffirmed by the U.S. Court of Appeals for the Seventh Circuit in the 1983 Voigt Decision. In 1987 federal judge James Doyle found that these rights extended to the use of traditional methods and that the Ojibwa had the right to use their natural resources to the extent that they could support a modest standard of living.

POLITICS AND GOVERNMENT

SIGNIFICANT EVENTS AND DOCUMENTS

Federal policy emphasized the assimilation of the Ojibwa into U.S. society. This policy has taken the following forms: treaty making; establishment of reservations and removal; individual allotments; relocation; and self-determination and cultural affirmation.

TREATY MAKING

Until 1871 the Ojibwa tribes were viewed as sovereign nations. As such, the legal relationship between the Ojibwa and national governments and their citizens was largely defined by treaties. Treaties drew boundaries between Ojibwa lands and lands designated for other tribes and/or non-Native Americans; concentrated tribes on reservations; allowed the government to purchase Ojibwa land; or set regulations concerning commerce. A major treaty was signed by Lakota (Sioux) and Ojibwa representatives at Prairie du Chien (in present-day Wisconsin) in 1825 to stop fighting between the two nations and establish boundaries. In 1827 another treaty set the boundary between Ojibwa and Menominee land. The Ojibwa ceded or sold land rights in Michigan, Minnesota, and Wisconsin to the federal government in a number of treaties, including one signed in 1854 that established permanent Ojibwa reservations in three states: Michigan, Minnesota, and Wisconsin. Bands were dispersed geographically, with members spread out in different reservations. In exchange for land or natural resources, the Ojibwa received annuities or annual payments of goods, livestock, food staples, clearance of debt with fur traders or fur company stores, and the services of blacksmiths, physicians, saw millers, and teachers.

ESTABLISHMENT OF RESERVATIONS AND REMOVAL

Federal and state legislation replaced treaty making in 1871. Later some reservations were created by executive order or by public act. Some reservations closely followed traditional Ojibwa boundaries, while others were established in previously unsettled areas. In the 1860s non-Native Americans put forward a plan to move all Minnesotan Ojibwa to a new reservation in the northwest corner of the state. Members of the four bands living in Minnesota were eventually relocated to the White Earth Reservation, beginning in 1868. The history of White Earth is a particularly disruptive one, with much of the land initially designated for the Ojibwa lost through improper taxation and swindling.

INDIVIDUAL ALLOTMENTS

The General Allotment Act of 1887, also known as the Dawes Act, outlined national adherence to allotment, a policy of encouraging assimilation to white culture, primarily through the adoption of agriculture as a means of subsistence. States also passed their versions of the Dawes Act, such as

Minnesota's Nelson Act of 1889. After Ojibwa families took their allotments, unallotted land on reservations was then sold to the public.

Rather than converting the Ojibwa to self-sufficient living, the allotment system resulted in the loss of Native-held land. There were also environmental and cultural reasons the Ojibwa did not succeed as farmers. In some reservation areas the land was sandy, rocky, swampy, or heavily wooded, and the weather limited the varieties of crops that could mature during the short growing season. Farming was also resisted by some Ojibwa who perceived gardening as women's work and disliked the permanency that farming required.

All Native Americans, including the Ojibwa, became U.S. citizens in 1924. Until this time, Ojibwa could attain citizenship through marriage to a non-Native American, by serving in World War II, or as a reward for living a "civilized life."

In 1934 the passage of the Indian Reorganization Act reversed the allotment system, and tribes held elections to decide whether to reorganize their governments. In 1936 six of the seven Minnesota reservations incorporated as the Minnesota Chippewa Tribe. Red Lake, which elected not to join the Minnesota Chippewa Tribe, is still known for its adherence to traditional culture. The Red Lake Reservation was excluded from the Nelson Act, and, while it did sell some land to the United States, the original tribal areas remained the property of the entire tribe. The six reservations in Wisconsin are governed separately, as are the westernmost Ojibwa in North Dakota and Montana. There are three Ojibwa tribal groups in Michigan. The Sault Sainte Marie band is governed separately as the Bay Mills Indian Community. The Keweenaw Bay Indian Community includes three bands: L'Anse, Lac Vieux Desert, and Ontonagon. The Saginaw Chippewa Tribe comprises the Saginaw, Swan Creek, and Black River bands.

In the 1930s Ojibwa men and women were employed in federal conservation, construction, and manufacturing projects organized under the Civil Works Administration and the Civil Conservation Corps, Indian Division. Ojibwa also received vocational training through Works Progress Administration programs. This brought some economic relief to reservation areas hit hard by the depression.

After World War II federal policy toward Native Americans once again promoted assimilation and integration, a setback for the New Deal

This photograph is of Peter Fontaine, a member of the Ojibwa tribe who worked as an engineer for the Puget Sound Navy Yard. The flags on the locomotive represent war bond purchases.

philosophy encouraging Native culture and autonomy.

RELOCATION

In the 1950s the BIA instituted the Indian Relocation Services campaign. Like the allotment system, relocation focused on individual Ojibwa rather than tribal group and Native culture. Ojibwa were encouraged to move off reservations to assimilate with non-Native culture in urban areas to reduce the need for federal support. Great Lakes Ojibwa moved to urban centers in Minnesota and Wisconsin, most notably Duluth, Milwaukee, and Minneapolis, St. Paul.

SELF-DETERMINATION AND CULTURAL AFFIRMATION

The policy of promoting Native self-sufficiency was termed "self-determination." Under the Johnson administration, the Ojibwa qualified for Office of Economic Opportunity funds to open

social programs, such as Head Start, and Native businesses and housing. Federal legislation in the 1970s, most notably the Indian Education Act of 1972, the Indian Self-Determination Act of 1973, and the Education Assistance Act of 1975, provided funding for culturally based education and afforded tribes more direct control of programs once administered by the BIA.

During the late 1960s some urban Ojibwa in Minneapolis formed a Red Power Organization known as the American Indian Movement (AIM). A modern proponent of the Native warrior ethic, AIM supported tribal civil rights through enforced reform rather than legislation. Activism took a different form in the 1980s and the 1990s, with the Ojibwa seeking to enforce treaty rights and working in the legal arena.

Traditional Ojibwa governance followed a multitiered system of elders, civil chiefs, and when necessary war chiefs. Elders—older and respected tribe members—played vital roles in decision making and educating younger members of the band. Civil chiefs could inherit their position or be nominated. Elders met in councils to identify a potential civil chief who would manage day-to-day operations. The nominee, who could be female or male, could accept the invitation to serve as civil chief, though such acceptance was not mandatory. Chiefs had official assistants, including messengers and orators. Civil chiefs could also summon the council of elders to request assistance. Councils of chiefs and elders from a number of bands met to discuss major decisions that would affect more than one band. War chiefs were self-appointed; a war chief was any man who could convince others to join him in battle. Adult men and women were part of the general council, and while votes were not tallied, each individual could join in the discussion at tribal meetings.

Late twentieth-century reservation areas are striving for home rule—the right to set and follow laws of their own making. Ojibwa reservations in Minnesota are each governed by a Reservation Business Council (RBC, also known as a Reservation Tribal Council). There are three districts on each reservation, each of which elects a representative to the RBC. The entire reservation also elects officials: a chairperson and a secretary-treasurer. Members of the RBC serve four-year terms. The RBC discusses approval of loans, petitions requesting enrollment of official membership in the tribe, and issues relating to economic development and sends reports to the U.S. Secretary of the Interior. Two members from each of the six reservations comprising the Minnesota Chippewa Tribe also serve on the statewide Tribal Executive Committee (TEC), which meets every three months. While the RBC governs the reservation, the TEC governs the tribe, as constituted by its six member reservations.

The Red Lake Reservation has a tribal council consisting of three officers (chairperson, secretary, and treasurer) elected from the entire tribal membership and eight council members, two elected from each of four districts. Red Lake also maintains traditional governance through an advisory council of descendants of civil chiefs.

Modern versions of intertribal councils also exist. The Four-State Intertribal Assembly represents the interests of over 30 tribes in Michigan, Minnesota, Iowa, and Wisconsin. Representatives meet at annual conferences.

BATTLE AND MILITARY SERVICE

The Ojibwa culture traditionally has revered the warrior. The Ojibwa often engaged in battles with and against other Native peoples and joined non-Native Americans in their fighting. During the French and Indian Wars (1754-1763), the Ojibwa sided primarily with the French. Ojibwa also participated in Pontiac's Rebellion (1763-1764), most notably in the capture of the British-held Fort Michilimackinac (in present-day Michigan). Their role during the Revolutionary War (1776-1783) was negligible. During the War of 1812, Ojibwa living west of Lake Superior sided with the Americans, while those living in present-day Michigan sided with the British. During World War I, the Ojibwa responded to the war effort by buying war bonds and donating money to the Red Cross. Ojibwa men also served in active duty. Ojibwa men served during World War II (1941-1945), and both men and women moved to urban areas for employment in war industries. The grand entrance march at many powwows begins with an honor guard of Ojibwa war veterans. Ojibwa may still be awarded eagle feathers in recognition of extraordinary achievement.

INDIVIDUAL AND GROUP CONTRIBUTIONS

The Ojibwa have made a number of significant contributions to American life: they discovered maple sugar and wild rice and invented hammocks, snowshoes, canoeing, and lacrosse. The English language contains a number of Ojibwa words (moccasin, moose) and place-names (Mackinaw, Michigan, Mesabi). Many Ojibwa contributions evolved over centuries, before they could be acknowledged by written record. Notable Ojibwa men and women, primarily those living in the late twentieth century, and their achievements are identified below.

ACADEMIA

White Earth enrollee Will Antell (1935-) has served as an educational consultant on Native education for the State of Minnesota. Edward Benton-Banai (1934-) directs the Heart of the Earth Survival School in Minneapolis and has written a series of coloring books to teach Ojibwa culture to young people. Lester Jack Briggs, Jr., (1948-) is director of the Fond du Lac Community College, Cloquet, Minnesota. Duane Champagne (1951-) serves as director of UCLA's American Indian Studies Center where he is also the editor of the *American Indian Culture and Research Journal*. After completing her Ph.D. at the University of Minnesota, Ojibwa educator Rosemary Ackley Christensen (1939-) has continued to publish, lecture, and consult on topics related to Native education. Gwendolyn A. Hill (1952-), of mixed Ojibwa and Cree heritage, is president of the Sisseton-Wahpeton Community College, Sisseton, South Dakota. Modern scholars have increasingly turned to tribal elders, including Maude Kegg (1904-), for instruction in the Anishinabe culture and language.

GOVERNMENT AND POLITICS

Among those credited with organizing AIM are Dennis Banks (1932-) and Clyde Bellecourt (1939-). Both were instrumental in organizing events such as the 1972 Trail of Broken Treaties caravan to Washington, D.C., resulting in the takeover of the BIA offices. Banks's recent activities include lecturing and acting in the films *The Last of the Mohicans* (1992) and *Thunderheart* (1992). Leonard Peltier (1944-) took part in the 1973 occupation of Wounded Knee, South Dakota. Convicted of killing two FBI agents, he is imprisoned in Marion, Illinois. His controversial conviction is examined in the 1992 film *Incident at Oglala*. A number of foreign countries and organizations regard Peltier as a prisoner of conscience.

LITERATURE

Author and poet Louise Erdrich (1954-) is the best-known modern Ojibwa writer. The characters in Erdrich's fiction follow a rich genealogy of Pillager band Ojibwa and non-Native Americans from the nineteenth century to the modern reservation milieu of gaming and competition dancing. Her novels include: *Love Medicine* (1984), *The Beet Queen* (1986), *Tracks* (1988), and *The Bingo Palace* (1994). Poet, novelist, and journalist, Jim Northrup, Jr., (1943-) writes about modern Anishinabe life on the Fond du Lac Reservation in northeastern Minnesota. A collection of his poems and short stories was published as *Walking the Rez Road* (1993), and his humorous and often biting commentary appears in a column, "Fond du Lac Follies," published in *The Circle* and *News from Indian Country*. Gerald Vizenor (1934-), a member of the Minnesota Chippewa Tribe, is a

professor of Native American Studies at the University of California, Berkeley. A poet and novelist, his writing centers on traditional culture and includes such works as *The Everlasting Sky: New Voices From the People Named Chippewa* (1972); *The People Named the Chippewa: Narrative Histories* (1984); and *Interior Landscapes: Autobiographical Myths and Metaphors* (1990).

MEDIA

PRINT

The Circle.

Published by the Minneapolis American Indian Center, this monthly publication provides international, national, and local news relevant to Indian concerns and tracks issues of importance to the Ojibwa.

Contact: Joe Allen, Editor.

Address: 1530 East Franklin Avenue, Minneapolis, Minnesota 55404.

Telephone: (612) 879-1700.

MASINAIGAN (Talking Paper).

Published by the Great Lakes Indian Fish and Wildlife Commission (GLIFWC). This 40-page quarterly publication reports on GLIFWC activities and on a broader range of issues of importance to the Ojibwa, including antitreaty activity, treaty support, Indian education, Native culture, Native rights, and major federal legislation.

Contact: Susan Erickson, Editor.

Address: P.O. Box 9, Odanah, Wisconsin 54861.

Telephone: (715) 682-4427.

RADIO

WOJB-FM (88.9).

Located on the La Courte Oreilles Reservation, it is a public radio station billed as the Woodland Community Radio, broadcasting news, information, and culture relevant to Native peoples, particularly the Ojibwa.

Address: Lac Courte Oreilles Public Broadcasting Corporation, Route 2, Box 2788, Hayward, Wisconsin 54843.

Telephone: (715) 634-2100.

ORGANIZATIONS AND ASSOCIATIONS

Great Lakes Indian Fish and Wildlife Commission (GLIFWC).
Founded in 1983, the GLWIFC's mission is to assist 13 Ojibwa tribes in Michigan, Minnesota, and Wisconsin to better manage their natural resources in off-reservation areas. The Commission comprises five divisions: Biological Services, Enforcement, Planning and Development, Intergovernmental Affairs, and Public Information. It publishes a free quarterly newsletter, *MASI-NAIGAN (Talking Paper)*.

Contact: James Schlender.
Address: P.O. Box 9, Odanah, Wisconsin 54861.
Telephone: (715) 682-4427.

Minnetrista Council for Great Lakes Native American Studies (MCGLNAS).
Founded in 1990, it is an organization with representatives from more than 20 tribes. MCGLNAS promotes the study and preservation of woodland tribal culture and sponsors annual powwows, conferences, and workshops.

Contact: Nicholas Clark.
Address: P.O. Box 1527, Muncie, Indiana 47308-1527.

MUSEUMS AND RESEARCH CENTERS

D'Arcy McNickle Center for the History of the American Indian.
Located within the Newberry Library, it provides access to scholarly material in the E. E. Ayer Collection; the Center sponsors seminars, exhibits, summer institutes, and fellowships, and publishes occasional papers, bibliographies, and monographs.

Address: 60 West Walton Street, Chicago, Illinois 60610-3394.
Telephone: (312) 943-9090.

Minnesota History Center.
The headquarters of the Minnesota Historical Society, it includes an extensive research and archival collection on the Native peoples of the state. Among its vast and varied exhibits on the Ojibwa is a detailed exhibit on wild ricing.

Address: 345 Kellogg Boulevard West, St. Paul, Minnesota 55102-1906.
Telephone: (612) 296-6126; or, (800) 657-3773.

SOURCES FOR ADDITIONAL STUDY

Broker, Ignatia. *Night Flying Women: An Ojibway Narrative*. St. Paul: Minnesota Historical Society Press, 1983.

Densmore, Frances. *How Indians Use Wild Rice Plants for Food, Medicine and Crafts*. New York: Dover, 1974 (originally published as *Uses of Plants by the Chippewa Indians*, 1928).

Hilger, M. Indez. *Chippewa Child Life and Its Cultural Background*. St. Paul: Minnesota Historical Society Press, 1992 (originally published, 1951).

The Jesuit Relations and Allied Documents: Travels and Explorations of the Jesuit Missionaries in New France, 1610-1791, edited by Rubin G. Thwaites. Cleveland: Burrows Brothers Co., 1896-1901.

Johnston, Basil. *Ojibway Ceremonies*. Lincoln: University of Nebraska Press, 1990.

————. *The Ojibway Heritage*. New York: Columbia University Press, 1976.

Summer in the Spring: Anishinabe Lyric Poems and Stores, edited by Gerald Vizenor. Norman: University of Oklahoma Press, 1993.

Tanner, Helen Hornbeck. *The Ojibway*. New York: Chelsea House, 1992.

Vennum, Thomas, Jr. *Wild Rice and the Ojibway People*. St. Paul: Minnesota Historical Press, 1988.

Warren, William Whipple. *History of the Ojibway People*. St. Paul: Minnesota Historical Society Press, 1984 (originally published, 1885).

Religion figures
prominently in the
life of Pakistani
American families,
and the Holy Quran,
the teachings of the
Holy Prophet, serve
as the guidelines that
Pakistani Muslims
follow throughout
their lives.

PAKISTANI AMERICANS

by
Tinaz Pavri

OVERVIEW

Pakistan received its independence from British India in 1947. It was created on the basis of religious identity, so that Muslims from British India, which had an overwhelming majority of followers of the Hindu religion, would have a nation to call their own. It is bordered by India on the east, Iran and Afghanistan on the west, the great Karakoram mountain range and China on the north, and the Arabian Sea on the south. Modern-day Pakistan is divided into four major geographic divisions known as the North-West Frontier Province (NWFP), Punjab, Sind, and Baluchistan. Each of these regions has its own language and ethnic groups. The capital of Pakistan is the modern city of Rawalpindi, although its cultural and economic centers continue to be Lahore and Karachi.

HISTORY

Pakistan boasts the site of the famed Indus valley civilization (B.C. 2500 to B.C. 1700), including prehistoric remains at Mohenjo-Daro, near the modern Pakistani city of Larkana, and at Harappa, near the city of Lahore. The Indus valley civilization has remained an interest for archaeologists because of the society's high level of sophistication and stability over several centuries.

A considerable Muslim population existed in British India due to conversions of portions of the population by invading Muslim rulers like the Turks, Persians, and Mughuls, who established kingdoms in northern India from the about the eighth century until British dominance began to be strengthened in the eighteenth century. Pakistan's ethnic and cultural diversity has been formed through legacies of invading Persians, Turks, Arabs, Huns, Greeks, and Mongols.

When the struggle for independence from the British colonizers started in India at the beginning of the twentieth century, Hindus, followers of India's majority religion, and Muslims fought side by side for their freedom from British rule. The Indian National Congress, the political party that eventually led India to its independence from the British, had many devoted Muslims members who were willing to give up their lives for the cause of India's freedom.

Mahatma Gandhi's movement of *satyagraha*, or non-violent passive resistance in the face of British oppression, formed the key to India's response to British colonization and gave shape to the drive for independence. Hundreds of thousands of Indians, both Hindu and Muslim, refused to cooperate with their British colonizers on every level of daily life—from the social to the political to the economic. Finally, the British decided that they could no longer rule over India; they formally relinquished its Indian colony in 1947.

However, as the goal of independence appeared more likely to be achieved, a section of the Muslim leadership led by Mohammed Ali Jinnah (1876-1948), who later became independent Pakistan's founder and first governor general, felt that Muslims would never be accorded equal treatment in a largely Hindu India. Because Jinnah feared political, social, and cultural subordination to the Hindu majority, he started a movement to establish a separate state based on Islam for the Indian Muslims. This group felt that in order to be truly free, Indian Muslims needed their own homeland. The independence leaders, both Hindus like Nehru and Mahatma Gandhi, and Muslims like Jinnah and Liaquat Ali Khan, who later became Pakistan's first prime minister, worked together with the British to make the transition from British India into independent India and Pakistan a reality.

When the British finally left India in 1947, two independent states, India and Pakistan, were formed. The separation was a consequence of, and resulted in, feelings of some bitterness between the two nations. Hundreds of thousands of Hindus and Muslims died in the riots that followed independence, as Muslims from India migrated to Pakistan and Hindus who lived in the newly created Pakistan streamed into India. Refugee camps were created on both sides of the border between the two countries to deal with these mass migrations.

These difficult, even tragic, beginnings that marked the two countries at their inception continued to be reflected in the relationship that has developed between them in the post-independence era. India and Pakistan have fought three wars over the years, and have been involved in many other confrontations, particularly over the disputed Kashmir region that lies between the two countries and is today the scene of a protracted, three-way conflict among the Indians, Pakistanis, and Kashmiris, who are seeking independence from both India and Pakistan. However, there are also ties of a shared history and culture that bind the people of the two countries. Many Muslims who chose to remain in India have close family members who moved to Pakistan and some Hindus remained behind in Pakistan, ensuring an intertwined destiny for the two countries.

After the death of Jinnah, Pakistan was ruled by a series of army chiefs under what were called martial law regimes. Pakistan's presidents in the 1950s and 1960s were army generals who assumed the highest political office. In 1971, Pakistan was divided again as a result of ethnic insurgency in its Eastern wing, which was populated mainly by Bengali-speaking Muslims, and the subsequent war with neighboring India. As a result of this division, a new sovereign country—Bangladesh—was created; Pakistan has since recognized Bangladesh and has established diplomatic and trading relations with the new nation.

An overwhelming 98 percent of the Pakistani population are followers of Islam. There are much smaller Hindu, Christian and Zoroastrian minority communities. Pakistan is not a secular state; the state religion is Islam, and religion enters many aspects of Pakistani political and social life. There are also several distinct ethnic and linguistic groups in Pakistan, including Pathans, Punjabis, Sindhis, and Baluchis. The Pathans, also known as the Pushtoons or Pakhtoons, come from the region of the North-West Frontier Province (NWFP). They include tribes on the border of Pakistan and Afghanistan, although the community has become increasingly urbanized in recent years. The Punjabi community is the center of education and industry in Pakistan and includes both rural and urban segments within it. The Baluchis from Baluchistan were originally a semi-nomadic people; today, while many continue to follow ancient traditions, others have moved to the city of Karachi in search of employment. All these communities have their own languages. The Sindhis come from the region of Sind and are a mixture of several different ethnic groups but share a common language, Sindhi. These subcommunities, who are represented in the larger Pakistani American community, have experienced some tension in recent times.

Pakistan has had four constitutions since 1947. Benazir Bhutto, the Harvard-educated daughter of Zulfikar Ali Bhutto, Pakistan's president from 1971 to 1977, was voted into power in 1988, in the country's first largely-free national elections. She led her father's political party, the Pakistan People's Party (PPP) to victory. She then lost the 1990 general election, but is today head of Pakistan's government once again. Under Benazir Bhutto, Pakistan has made significant strides towards the establishment of political democracy, although it still faces internal threats of ethnic strife and religious fundamentalism.

EARLY IMMIGRATION

Since Pakistan only came into existence in 1947, any documentation of the life of Pakistani Americans can technically only commence from that year. However, it should be noted that Muslim immigrants from India and the region that is now Pakistan entered the United States as early as the eighteenth century, working alongside their Hindu or Sikh brethren in agriculture, logging, and mining in the western states of California, Oregon, and Washington.

In 1907, around 2,000 Indians, including Hindus and Muslims, worked alongside other immigrants from China, Japan, Korea, and Italy on the building of the Western Pacific railway in California. Other Indians worked on building bridges and tunnels for California's other railroad projects. As the demand for agricultural labor increased in California, Indians turned to the fields and orchards for employment. Muslim agricultural workers in California sometimes brought an Imam or learned man to the fields with them. The Imam proceeded to pray from the Holy Koran several times a day when the men took their breaks.

Muslims from the Indian subcontinent became successful as land tenants in the early part of the twentieth century, and leased or owned land in many California counties in order to grow rice. Many of these ventures were very successful, and many Indians, Hindu and Muslim, prospered financially as they increased their acreage and even bought small farms and orchards; however, heavy rains in 1920 devastated some rice crops and drove some Indians into bankruptcy.

Like Hindu and Sikh Indian immigrants, some Muslims chose to return to India after they had achieved some amount of financial prosperity. Many others, however, stayed, putting down firm roots in California and the adjoining western states and sometimes marrying Mexican women, since the immigration of Muslim women from the subcontinent was nonexistent.

While all Indian immigrants faced racial prejudice, Muslims from the subcontinent were also subject to added prejudice against their religion, Islam. Among the common misconceptions of the Islamic faith that existed in America during that time were those that viewed Muslims as polygamists and therefore not suitable people to be allowed to enter America; there were also calls for the expulsion of Muslims already in the country. Expulsions of Indians from the communities within which they worked were also attempted by other Euro-American workers. The Asiatic Exclusion League (AEL) was organized in 1907 to encourage the expulsion of Asian workers, including Indian Hindus and Muslims.

The immigration of Indians, Hindu and Muslim, was tightly controlled by the American government during this time, and Indians applying for visas to travel to the United States were often rejected by U.S. diplomats in important Indian cities like Madras and Calcutta. In addition, legislation was introduced in the United States that attempted to legally restrict the entry of Indians and other Asians into America as well as to deny them residency and citizenship rights. Some of these pieces of legislation were defeated, while others were adopted. For instance, a literacy clause was added to a number of bills, requiring that immigrants pass a literacy test to be considered eligible for citizenship. This effectively ensured that most Indians would not be able to meet the requirements. It was only in 1947 that Congress passed a bill allowing naturalization for Indians. Between 1947 and 1965 there were only around 2,500 Pakistani immigrants in the United States according to reports from the Immigration and Naturalization Service.

The largest numbers of Pakistani Americans have migrated to the United States since 1965, when the U.S. government lifted previously existing immigration restrictions and repealed quotas. Numbers of Pakistani immigrants swelled after 1970, with thousands of Pakistanis entering the United States each year since that time. Like their Asian Indian counterparts, they tended to be urban, well educated, and professional. Many of them had come from cities like Karachi and Lahore, and were familiar with Western culture and ways of living. However, the dependents and relatives that they have since sponsored for permanent residence in and citizenship to the United States in the years after 1965 have tended to be characterized by lower levels of education.

Figures from the 1990 U.S. Census indicate that there are about 100,000 Pakistani Americans in the United States. The largest percentage, 32 percent, live in the Northeast, with 27 percent living in the South, 21 percent in the West, and 20 percent in the Midwest. States with the highest concentrations of Pakistani Americans are New York, California, and Illinois. Pakistani Americans tend to settle in large cities, in part a reflection of the large Pakistani cities of Lahore, Karachi, and Rawalpindi that a majority of the post-1965 immigrants came from, and in part a reflection of the availability of jobs. Accordingly, there are significant settlements of Pakistani immigrants in cities such as New York, Chicago, Philadelphia, and Los Angeles.

Although subgroup differences within the larger community are salient, with Pakistani Americans choosing to spend most time with members of their own ethnic and linguistic groups like Sindhis, Punjabis, and Baluchis, the community is also fairly united on a broader level.

ACCULTURATION AND ASSIMILATION

Very little has been written about the Pakistani American community. Many scholars writing about ethnic communities in the United States tend to lump the community together with the larger Asian Indian community, thereby glossing over the distinctiveness of the Pakistani Americans. For instance, in *Arab, Armenian, Syrian, Lebanese, East Indian, Pakistani and Bangladeshi Americans: A Study and Source Book* (San Francisco: E&R Research Associates, 1977), Kananur

Chandras offers little distinction between the Asian Indian, Pakistani American, and Bangladeshi American communities and hence cannot be relied upon for information on Pakistani Americans. Others tend to assume, incorrectly, that Pakistani Americans, because they are overwhelmingly Muslim, can be described as a part of America's Arab Muslim community. In addition, there is no comprehensive listing of Pakistani American organizations across the United States, or a listing of the communities newspapers or other media channels.

CUISINE

There is considerable similarity between the cuisine of northern India and that of Pakistan, the entire region having experienced the same foreign invasions and cultural influences over the centuries. It is hence common to see restaurants featuring Indian and Pakistani cuisine under the same roof in the United States. However, Pakistani cuisine is quite distinctive and has many traditional dishes that are not necessarily shared with Asian Indians.

Although regional variations exist, Pakistani cuisine in general tends to be highly spiced. Spices such as cumin, turmeric, and chili powder are common with Asian Indian cuisine. In addition, Pakistani American cuisine also includes such spices as cloves, cinnamon, and cardamom, a result of Arab influence.

Meat dishes—lamb, goat, and beef—are common. It is also traditional for the meat to be kosher or *halaal*, cut in a way that ensures the slow draining of blood from the animal, for religious reasons. Also in keeping with Islamic tradition, pork is not eaten. Festive rice dishes include *pulao*, a fragrant dish of mildly spiced rice with peas or dried fruits, and *biryani*, which consists of rice and meat marinated in yogurt and spices. *Dals*, or lentils and split peas prepared in spicy sauces, are common. Whole peas like the chickpea prepared in a flavorful sauce called *cholle* ("chollay"), are also popular. Vegetable dishes include *saag* ("sahg") or spinach and *aloo-mattur*—potatoes and peas. Unleavened breads made with white and wheat flour are eaten with many meals; these include the robust *naan*, clay-baked *roti*, and *paratha*.

Traditional Pakistani sweets include *zarda* ("zahrdah"), a sweet, yellow, rice dish, *jalebi* ("jahlaybee"), an orange-colored, fried sweet made of a sugary syrup and flour, *ladoo* ("lahdoo"), a

round ball of sweetened chick-pea flour embellished with pistachios or cashews and *ras malai* ("rahs mahlaee"), a dessert made of heavy cream. Tea flavored with cinnamon and cardamom is also drunk frequently. Another way to round off a meal is to chew *paan*, which is the broad leaf of the betel plant sprinkled with a lime powder and *kaat* and can be mildly euphoric.

Most Pakistani American families eat at least one traditional meal a day, the main meal. It is prepared with fresh ingredients by the woman of the house. Although Western-style short cuts to food preparation like the use of canned or preserved substitutes are increasingly being used, cooking the main meal still remains quite a laborious chore. It is the woman who undertakes the task of cooking for the family, often with the help of daughters. It is still rare for male family members to be engaged in domestic chores like cooking and household cleaning. They would be more likely to work outdoors or be engaged in tasks like household repairs. Pakistani Americans regard the family meal as an important event in their daily lives. It is a time for the family to talk to each other about what events have transpired during the day and a time to be together and maintain contact in the face of busy individual schedules.

TRADITIONAL COSTUMES

Pakistani American men and women wear the traditional *salwar kameez* on festive occasions.

The costume, consisting of a long tunic and tight or loose-fitting leggings or trousers and often including a diaphanous shawl or veil called the *dupatta* ("dooputtah") for women, is commonly made of cotton or silk. Women's costumes tend to be more colorful and intricate, often including exquisite embroidery or *zari*, a technique that involves the weaving of gold or silver thread into the cloth. It is more rare, but not unheard of, for some Pakistani women to wear the sari, the traditional costume of Asian Indian women.

Like their Asian Indian counterparts, Pakistani American women enjoy wearing gold ornaments or jewelry, including bangles, bracelets, rings, and necklaces. Simple ornaments are worn daily, while more opulent ones, with settings of precious stones, are worn at weddings and other celebrations. These precious ornaments are often passed down through the generations as family heirlooms. Often on festive occasions, *mehendi*, or the application of a paste made with henna that dries in delicate, intricate designs on the palms of the hands, is sported by some women and girls in the community.

DANCES AND SONGS

A common dance performed by women in the community on festive occasions like weddings and other celebrations is the *luddi* ("luhd-dee"). Women dance in circles while rhythmically clapping their hands. *Qawaali* ("kawalee"), a genre of music that traces its roots to Sufi Muslim devotional and mystical music and that is meant to encourage religious ecstasy among its listeners, has many adherents within the Pakistani American community, and is also drawing increasing numbers of other Americans into its fold of admirers. It generally encourages intense listener involvement and response. The best-known group performing this music that has toured America in recent times is the Pakistani group Nusrat Fateh Ali Khan and Party. Groups performing the Qawaali generally include several singers and such instruments as harmoniums and *tablas* ("tublah"), a type of drum. The *ghazal*, a mellow, emotional style of ancient Persian lyric verse set to music and sung by both men and women, is also popular among members of the community. Film music, from both popular Pakistani films and Indian films in Hindi, also has many adherents within the community, particularly first-generation and recent immigrants. Pakistani bands that combine Western rock and pop tunes with Urdu lyrics are popular at celebrations.

HOLIDAYS AND CELEBRATIONS

The International New Year is widely celebrated among members of the community. In addition, Pakistani Americans celebrate the creation of Pakistan on August 14 as Independence Day. The birthday of Jinnah, the founder of the Pakistani nation is celebrated on December 25, and Pakistan Day on March 23. Religious celebrations include *Eid-ul-Fitr*, festivities that signify the end of the month of fasting during *Ramadan*, and *Eid-ul-Azha*, a joyous observance of the pilgrimage to Mecca. Pakistani Hindus celebrate *Diwali* ("deevalee"), the festival of lights and *Holi* ("hoelee"), the festival of color that traditionally welcomes the spring.

Celebrations on such days typically include visits to friends and family, the exchange of gifts and sweets, and invitations to feasts. Traditional costumes are worn. Celebratory parades in cities and towns where there are large Pakistani American communities are increasingly being held. *Qawaalis*, *ghazals*, *mushaira* ("mooshaeera") or Urdu poetry readings, and Pakistani and Hindi films might be organized for community celebrations that might be held on festive days at the local community centers. Less common, but no less enjoyed in large cities with great ethnic diversity like New York, is the occasional cricket match that will be organized within the community or across cricket-playing communities like the Asian Indian and West Indian on holidays.

HEALTH AND MENTAL HEALTH ISSUES

Pakistani Americans take health issues seriously and consult health-care providers regularly. Family physicians are often chosen from within the community. Traditional herbal remedies might be employed to battle minor illnesses. Ayurveda and homeopathy are also employed. Ayurveda focuses on spiritual healing as an essential part of physical healing and bases its cures on herbs and other natural ingredients such as raw ginger and garlic. It emphasizes preventive healing. Homeopathy attempts to cure by stimulating the body's own defenses against the illness. The ancient practice of Yoga has some adherents in the community. The practice has a tradition that is several thousand years old, and combines a routine of exercise and meditation.

Members of the community are less likely, however, to seek help for mental health issues, a reflection of the traditionally low levels of consciousness of the subject in Pakistan and the social stigmas and skepticism that continue to be attached to it. Members of the community generally believe that families rather than institutional settings are best suited to take care of the mentally ill.

LANGUAGE

Urdu is the official language of Pakistan, although only about ten percent of all Pakistanis speak it. The majority of the population speaks regional dialects, like Punjabi, Baluchi, and Sindhi, which are taught is the nation's schools along with Urdu. Urdu is a blend of four different languages—Hindi, Arabic, Persian, and Turkish—and is also spoken by Muslims in India. It conforms to a modified version of the Persian script and is therefore written from right to left, whereas Hindi, which utilizes Devanagari script, is written from left to right. English is also used in official interaction in Pakistan.

About 30 percent of Pakistani Americans speak Urdu. A larger percentage, perhaps 50 percent, speak Punjabi. Others might speak Sindhi or Gujrati, reflecting their ethnic heritage and the regions of Pakistan from which they trace their ancestry. As a result of the legacy of British colonization, most Pakistani Americans are also fluent in English. While many first-generation Pakistani Americans continue to speak their native languages at home, offspring generally speak only English but understand their parents' native tongue. Many American words that have no easy translation like subways, cable-TV or microwave oven have inevitably entered everyday Pakistani American communication.

GREETINGS

Pakistani Americans salute each other with the traditional Islamic greeting *Salaam Aleikum* ("sahlaam alaykoom")—Peace be with you. The response to that greeting, conveying the same meaning, is *Aleikum Salaam*. Another common phrase is *Inshallah* ("insha-allah")—God willing.

FAMILY AND COMMUNITY DYNAMICS

Pakistani American families, like their Asian Indian counterparts, tend to be tightly knit and patriarchal. In the case of the early immigrants, often only males had formal educations, and they became the sole breadwinners. The nuclear family is most common, but members of the extended family like grandparents, aunts, and uncles visit frequently and for long periods of time. Siblings and close relatives are encouraged to visit America and are provided with financial and emotional support should they decide to eventually immigrate to the United States. The family, both immediate and extended, is the focus of existence for many Pakistani Americans. Many leisure activities for Pakistani Americans tend to be family and community oriented. Pakistani Americans prefer to reside in areas where there are other Pakistani American families who provide them with a sense of community. Since family ties are so strong, they also try to live close to relatives so that frequent visits are possible.

Most first-generation Pakistani American women continue to fulfill traditional female roles, choosing to take care of the home and family rather than pursuing demanding careers. Second-generation Pakistani American women tend to be more resistant to traditional roles, but the pressures for conformity within the Pakistani community are still quite strong. Some young women report that this results in their "doing it all"—pursuing a demanding career as well as taking on the major responsibility of running the house and caring for the daily needs of the family.

Traditional and religious values are very important to Pakistani Americans, and children are taught their history and culture at an early age. Special classes are held on weekends to teach children these aspects of their identity. Such classes include religious and language education. As is the case with many Muslims, religion tends to provide the guidelines by which the lives of many Pakistani Americans are lived. Dating is discouraged, and marriage between Pakistani Americans within the larger community in general and within the ethnic subcommunities in particular, with parental approval, is actively encouraged. Family and community members are widely consulted in selecting prospective marriage partners for young people. In recent times, there has been some tension between Pakistani American immigrant parents and their American-born children, as children question the need for parental involvement in questions of partner selection and ask for the freedom to date individuals of their choice.

On the whole, education is highly valued among Pakistani Americans. Many first-generation males came to the United States with high levels of education and proceeded to study even further in the United States. The value of education was then transmitted to their children. Both girls and boys are encouraged to study hard, but it is often understood that it will finally be the male's responsibility to be the major financial provider for his family.

As is the case with Asian Indians, Pakistani Americans mingle with their American counterparts or with members of other immigrant ethnic groups in work situations, but often choose to spend their leisure time with members of their own community. Many Pakistani Americans report conflicting feelings about American culture and ways of life. While many aspects of American culture and society are admired, such as personal and political freedom, individualism, the country's achievement in science and technology, and American economic efficiency, other aspects, such as premarital relations, dating, and divorce, are shunned. Again, regional differences prevail, with the more urban immigrants from Karachi tending to be more receptive of American culture and values than the more traditional immigrants who trace their roots to the provinces and rural areas of Pakistan.

Members of the larger Pakistani community hold distinct perceptions of the different subcommunities that the community is composed of. For instance, Pakistanis tracing their roots to Lahore are generally considered to be more traditional and conservative than the more cosmopolitan, Westernized, and sophisticated immigrants from Karachi. The Sindhis and Baluchis are also considered traditional and conservative. Distinctions are also made between immigrants tracing their roots to rural Pakistan and those who have come from large urban centers.

There is some interaction with and overlap between members of the Asian Indian and Pakistani American communities. This is particularly the case with those members of both communities who have the common bond of Islam between them and who might share in prayers at the same mosques and celebrate the same religious festivals.

WEDDINGS AND FUNERALS

A Pakistani wedding is a time for great celebration. Traditional Muslims rites are observed, and friends and relatives are invited to join festivities that might stretch over several days and that include feasting on traditional foods. The legal portion of the ceremony is accomplished with the signing of the *nikaah*, or marital agreement, by the bride and groom. A *mulvi* ("moolvee"), or knowledgeable one, is present at all ceremonies and formally asks the bride and groom whether they accept each other in matrimony. The wedding is held at party centers, not in mosques, and traditional Pakistani music is played before and after the ceremony. While gifts of money and jewelry are traditionally given at weddings in Pakistan, the community in America tends to also give as gifts appliances or other household items that would be of use to the young couple. Jewelry is still frequently passed down from mother to daughter or daughters-in-law at weddings. Pakistani Hindus, on the other hand, follow the traditional Hindu ceremony, with the bride and groom circling the holy fire from three to seven times, and the priest chanting prayers.

Pakistani Americans follow Islamic rites in burying their dead. No separate cemeteries exist for the community in America; rather, available cemeteries are used. In rare cases, the body might be flown to Pakistan for burial. Only males are allowed to participate in the actual burial ceremony. Pakistani Hindus are generally cremated according to Hindu religious tradition. In this ceremony also, males are given greater prominence. A death is a time for the Pakistani community to come together to provide emotional and sometimes financial support for the bereaved family.

RELIGION

Most Pakistani Americans are devout Muslims, who pray five times a day facing the direction of the holy city of Mecca. Religion figures prominently in the life of Pakistani American families, and the Holy Quran, the teachings of the Holy Prophet, serve as the guidelines that Pakistani Muslims follow throughout their lives. Families often visit the mosque once a week, usually on Friday afternoons, where the Imam leads the prayer. If it is not possible to visit the mosque for Friday prayers, Sunday prayers are another popular alternative. Children are encouraged to attend religious education classes held on weekends and during the summer vacation in substantially populated communities. Both men and women must keep their arms and legs covered while in the mosque, and covering the head is also encouraged. The sexes must sit either in separate rooms or in separate groups within the same room for the duration of the prayers.

The majority of Pakistanis belong to the Sunni sect of Islam, although a significant representation may also be found among the Shi'ite sect. Sunnis, or Orthodox Muslims, believe that the community is responsible for maintaining Islamic law. This law, or *shari'a*, is based on four sources, which in descending order of importance are: the Quran; the examples and teachings of the prophet; communal consensus (later the consensus of religious scholars) on Islamic principles and practices; and reasoning by analogy. Shi'ites, who are followers of Muhammad's cousin, Ali, believe that Muslim religious leadership descends through blood lines. They also differ from Sunnis through certain religious procedures.

In smaller towns in America where there may not be mosques within easy access, Pakistani Americans make special trips to attend the nearest one on major religious holidays and occasions. Pakistani Americans worship at mosques alongside other Muslims who might trace their ancestry to all parts of the Islamic world and to India; there are generally no separate Pakistani American mosques.

Pakistani Americans also participate in and contribute to the larger Islamic community, which includes Arab Americans and African

Americans, in America. They are part of the larger community's efforts to educate the country about the ideals of Islam and the teachings of the prophet Mohammed. Pakistani Americans have played important roles in the association the Muslim Students of America (MSA), which caters to the needs of Islamic students across the United States.

Although the overwhelming majority of Pakistani Americans are Muslims, there are also Hindus, Christians, and Zoroastrians within the community. Some Hindus chose to remain in the newly created Pakistan after partition, and they form the core of the Pakistani Hindu community. Hindus are part of a religious tradition that is less structured and less formally organized than other religions like Islam and Christianity. Hinduism is a polytheistic religion, with Hindus generally worshipping many gods, including Brahma, the God of Creation, and Surya, the Sun God. The Hindu community today has access to more than 100 temples all over America, with the oldest one being in San Francisco. It is also common for Hindus in the United States to worship at home, where a small room or portion of a room may be set aside for worship and meditation.

Pakistani Christians, like Asian Indian Christians, worship at churches all over the country and share in the religious life of the dominant Christian culture in America. Zoroastrians or Parsees trace their roots to ninth-century Persia, and form a minuscule religious minority in both India and Pakistan. They have prospered in trade and the professions in both these countries, as also in America, where reports of the earliest Zoroastrians were documented as early as the turn of the century. In recent times, Pakistani Zoroastrians have come to the United States mainly from the Pakistani cities of Lahore and Karachi.

EMPLOYMENT AND ECONOMIC TRADITIONS

The profile of the Pakistani American today is dramatically different from the earliest Muslims immigrants from the Indian subcontinent, who came to the United States as manual and agricultural workers with few skills and little or no education.

Many Pakistani American males who entered the United States after 1965 were highly educated, urban, and sophisticated, and soon found employment in a variety of professions such as law, medicine, and academia. In the post-1965 wave of immigration, many Pakistanis also came to America as students who earned graduate degrees that enabled them to pursue successful careers in a variety of fields. Some members of the community immigrated to the United States with specific educational backgrounds in fields like the law but failed to find positions within that specific field because their qualifications and experience did not transfer readily to the American context. They have either retrained themselves in other professions or fields, or have had to be satisfied with accepting positions that are meant for individuals with lesser educational qualifications than they have. This is the price that some of these immigrants have paid to settle in the United States.

Most of the community today lives a comfortable, middle-class and upper-middle-class existence, although there might be some incidence of poverty among newer uneducated immigrants. These immigrants tend to take low-paying jobs involving manual or unskilled labor and tend to live in big cities where such jobs are readily available. Many Pakistani Americans also own their own businesses, including restaurants, groceries, clothing and appliance stores, newspaper booths, and travel agencies. It is common to include members of the extended and immediate family in the business.

Pakistani Americans tend to follow the residence pattern set by other Americans, in that they move to more affluent suburbs as their prosperity increases. Members of the community believe in the symbolic importance of owning homes; accordingly, Pakistani Americans tend to save and make other monetary sacrifices earlier on in order to purchase their own homes as soon as possible.

Members of the family and the larger community tend to take care of each other, and to assist in times of economic need. Hence, it would be more common to turn to a community member for economic assistance rather than to a government agency. Relatively low levels of the community are therefore on welfare and public assistance.

POLITICS AND GOVERNMENT

In the early part of this century, Muslim immigrants were actively involved, along with their

Hindu Indian brethren, in the struggle for residence and citizenship rights in America. Since the second wave of immigration in 1965, the Pakistani American community has not been politically inclined, but this is now changing, with the community starting to contribute funds to their candidates of choice in both parties, and running for elected office in districts with large Pakistani American populations. In recent times, Pakistani American candidates have run for the state senate in districts of such city boroughs as Brooklyn in New York. Because the community is geographically dispersed, the formation of influential voting blocs has not generally been possible, making it difficult to for the community to make an impact on politics in this particular way. However, there are increasing efforts on the part of community leaders to ensure voter registration and involvement. Like the Asian Indians, Pakistani Americans tend to vote Democratic in larger numbers than Republican.

RELATIONS WITH PAKISTAN

Most Pakistani Americans maintain close links with relatives and friends in Pakistan. First-generation Pakistani Americans travel to their native land at least once every few years, and tens of thousands of airplane tickets are sold to Pakistani Americans every year. They often take back to Pakistan gifts of money, food, and clothing for friends and family, and donate generously to charities. Second-generation Pakistani Americans tend to travel to Pakistan less frequently as ties become attenuated. The relationship of the U.S. and Pakistani governments in the past few decades has been very close, and the Pakistani American community has benefitted from this American interest in the country of their origin.

Pakistani Americans maintain a deep interest in the society and politics of Pakistan. Funds are raised by the community in America for the different political parties and groups in Pakistan. Tensions among ethnic groups like the Sindhis, Punjabis, or Baluchis, in Pakistan tend to be reflected in interaction between these subgroups in America, but to a much lesser extent. Tensions between India and Pakistan also tend to be reflected in the relationships between Asian Indians and Pakistani Americans.

INDIVIDUAL AND GROUP CONTRIBUTIONS

ACADEMIA

Pakistani Americans have achieved success in many fields, particularly in academia, where they hold positions of respect as faculty members in many prestigious universities. Mohammad Asad

Khan (1940-), a geophysicist and educator, is on the faculty of the geophysics and geodesy department at the University of Hawaii. He has also been a visiting scientist at numerous institutions, including NASA's Goddard Space Center. Altaf Wani is an associate professor of Radiology at the Ohio State University. Mazhar Ali Khan Malik is a professor of economics and engineering and founder of the Pakistan League of America (PLA). Samuel Iftikhar (1923-1991) was an Asian scholar and reference librarian at the Library of Congress, Washington, D.C. for more than 25 years. He worked mainly in the Southern Asian section of the library.

ART

Samina Quraeshi (1946-) is the director of design arts at the National Endowment for the Arts (NEA) in Washington, D.C. She holds dual Pakistani and American citizenship and is a graduate of the Yale University School of Art and Architecture. She has been a design consultant who has run her own business.

HEALTH AND MEDICINE

Dr. Salam Shahidi (1933-1992) was a leading medical researcher in the department of Health, New York City. He was also vice-chairman of the Pakistan League of America (PLA) and president of a cultural organization called the National Association of Pakistani Americans. Dr. Muhammad Akhtar is currently the commissioner of Public Health in Washington, D.C., a position he assumed in 1991. He was born in Lahore, Pakistan, and has held important posts in the health departments of the states of Michigan and Missouri during the 1970s and 1980s. Dr. Amanullah Khan (1940-), a physician, served on the faculty of West Pakistan Medical School. He was a fellow in hematology and oncology at the Wadley Institute of Molecular Medicine in Dallas, Texas, between 1966 and 1969, and has been the chair of the department of immunology from 1970. He is the author of several books and has written several articles in scholarly journals in his field. Dr. Shafi Bezar, a Manhattan surgeon, is also publisher of the community newspaper Awan, and president of the Pakistan League of America (PLA). Dr. Mohammed Sayeed Quraishi (1924-) holds a doctorate from the University of Massachusetts. He has served as a member of the United Nations WHO team to Bangladesh and has been an ento-

mologist at the Malaria Institute of Pakistan. He has served at the National Institutes of Health in Bethesda, Maryland and the National Institute of Allergy and Infectious Diseases. He is the author of many books and received the Recognition and Appreciation of Special Achievement Award by the National Institute of Health in 1988.

MEDIA

The news group bit.listserv.pakistan provides news of events in Pakistan.

PRINT

Al-Hilal.

Semi-monthly Pakistani newspaper (Urdu).

Contact: Lateef Owaisi, Editor.

Address: 338 Hollyberry Trail, Willowdale, Ontario, Canada M2H 2P6.

Telephone: (416) 493-4374.

Fax: (416) 493-4374.

Community Digest.

Weekly magazine for Ismaili, Gujarati, Pakistani, South Asian, Iranian, and Afghanian communities in British Columbia.

Address: 1755 Robson Street, Suite 216, Vancouver, British Columbia, Canada V6G 3B7.

Telephone: (604) 875-8313.

Jung.

Published in New Jersey in English and Urdu. Features articles of interest to the community and news from Pakistan.

The Minaret.

A community newspaper that features articles on community engagements, other topics of interest to the community in America and news from Pakistan. It is published in New York City.

New York Crescent.

Includes articles of interest to the community, news about social engagements involving the community in New York and the United States.

Pakeeza International.

Semi-monthly magazine for Pakistani and Muslim Canadians (Urdu).

Contact: Shahtaj Famima, Editor.

Address: 17 Burnhope Drive, Brampton, Ontario, Canada L6X 3R9.

Telephone: (416) 924-7444.

Fax: (416) 455-9839.

Pakistan Calling.

An English language weekly focusing on the Pakistani American community and on events in Pakistan. It is published in New York, by Zafar Qureshi.

TELEVISION

"TV Asia."

A program often shown on international cable channels all over the United States, includes Pakistani soap operas, films, and plays. Cities like New York and Los Angeles with relatively large Pakistani American settlements have weekly Pakistani feature and news programs.

Address: TV Asia, c/o International Channel, 12401 West Olympic Boulevard, Bethesda, Maryland 20814.

Telephone: (310) 826-2429.

ORGANIZATIONS AND ASSOCIATIONS

Many associations tend to be headquartered in big cities with significant Pakistani American populations. Some associations and organizations are restricted to the interests of particular ethnic and regional communities like Punjabis or Sindhis and subsects thereof. The list that follows are pan-Pakistani organizations—those that do not distinguish on the basis of ethnic or regional groups.

Association of Pakistani Physicians (APP).

APP is an organization of Pakistani American physicians and dentists. Focuses on how to better serve the health needs of the Pakistani American community and of all Americans.

Address: 6414 South Cast Avenue, Suite L2, Westmont, Illinois 60559.

Telephone: (708) 968-8585.

Muslim Students of America (MSA).

Founded in 1963 to serve as a voice for Muslim students in American universities and today has chapters in most major cities in the United States and Canada. Pakistanis have played a leading role in the organization from its inception and have held key roles in its administration. Holds conferences annually on subjects relevant to the Muslim academic community.

Pakistan League of America (PLA).

Membership ranges in the thousands. Promotes Pakistani culture in America, holds national conventions and seminars on issues of interest to the community.

Pakistan Society of Atlanta.

Promotes Pakistani culture and heritage within the United States.

Address: 1035 Bridgewater Walk, Snellville, Georgia 30278-2050.

U.S.-Pakistan Economic Council (USPAK).

Promotes trade between the United States and Pakistan. Offers information on economic and social conditions in Pakistan.

Address: 500 Fifth Avenue, Suite 935, New York, New York 10110.

Telephone: (212) 221-7070.

SOURCES FOR ADDITIONAL STUDY

Helwig, Arthur, and Usha M. Helwig. *An Immigrant Success Story: Asian Indians in America.* Philadelphia: University of Pennsylvania Press, 1990.

Jensen, Joan. *Passage From India: Asian Indian Immigrants in North America.* New Haven: Yale University Press, 1988.

Malik, Iftikhar Haider. *Pakistanis in Michigan: A Study of Third Culture and Acculturation.* New York: AMS Press, 1989.

Melendy, H. Brett. *Asians in America: Filipinos, Koreans, and East Indians.* Boston: Twayne Publishers, 1977.

Though Palestinian Americans have generally had a smooth transition to a new culture, many still feel unsettled because of tensions in their homeland and specifically the lack of a Palestinian state.

PALESTINIAN AMERICANS

by
Ken Kurson

OVERVIEW

Historical Palestine stretched from the eastern shore of the Mediterranean Sea to lands east of the Jordan River, according to commentators, and was bordered by Syria on the north and Egypt on the south. Most of this land is now controlled by or part of the State of Israel. The majority of the six million people of Palestinian descent live in Jordan, Syria, and Lebanon (a total of two and a half million), the autonomous territories of the West Bank and Gaza Strip (two million), Israel proper (approximately 750,000), or the United States (approximately 200,000).

The Middle East has long been the crossroads of major trade routes between East and West. The economic and political significance of these lands has made them the object of continual conquest by various armies since Biblical times. This has been particularly true for Palestine; the various peoples who inhabit the region today remain mired in a bitter and deadly conflict that is the direct legacy of the war and terror that proceeded almost without interruption during the first half of the twentieth century.

HISTORY

In addition to the region's significance in terms of trade and political conquest, ancient Palestine was the "Holy Land" and birthplace for two major world religions—Judaism and Christianity—and later became very significant for Islam as well. Thus, Palestine has played a tremendous role in the world's religious and cultural history.

By 1500 B.C. the culture in ancient Palestine had developed to the point where the first known alphabetic writing system was invented. During the late Bronze Age (1500-1200 B.C.) Palestine was controlled by Egypt, and many of the major cities were used by the Egyptians as administrative centers for their rule. This was also a period of great religious activity, when many temples were built and the mythology of the Canaanite gods and goddesses was inscribed in tablets.

The ancient name for Palestine was "Canaan," and the people living there before the arrival of the Israelites were known as "Canaanites." The name "Palestine" resulted from the influx of a number of so-called sea peoples, who traveled east across the Aegean sea to settle in the lands of the eastern Mediterranean in about 1200 B.C. One of these groups, the Philistines, ended up in Palestine after Ramses III refused their entrance into Egypt, and by the eleventh century B.C. they dominated Palestine's Mediterranean coast. Also during this period, the Israelites, who were nomads and farmers from Egypt, moved to the more remote highlands of the central hilly region of Palestine where they settled small villages; the ruins of approximately 250 such villages have been discovered by modern archaeologists. By 1000 B.C. the size and strength of the Israelite tribes was sufficient for them to present a challenge to the Philistines. They wrested control from the Philistines and established a kingdom led by King Saul and his successors David and Solomon, who reigned from approximately 1020 B.C. to 920 B.C. Solomon's reign represented the zenith of this period, when the capital of Jerusalem was established and the Temple constructed. Historians claim that most of the Hebrew scriptures, or Old Testament of the Bible, were composed during this time in ancient Israel.

After Solomon's death the kingdom was divided into two Hebrew states—Israel in the north and Judah (from which the name "Jew" derives) in the south—which were at war for much of the next 400 years. Judah was defeated by the Babylonians in 586 B.C., and this period saw the ascendancy of the Kings Hezekiah and Josiah (who tried to use the teachings of the Deuteronomic writers to rule according to the laws of Moses) and the Hebrew prophets Isaiah, Jeremiah, and Micah. However, the Babylonians were soon conquered by the Persians, and the whole of Palestine came under the Persian Empire.

The conquest of the Persian Empire by Alexander the Great in 332 B.C. ushered in the Hellenistic, or Greek, period in which Hebrew was supplanted by Greek and Aramaic as the dominant language. This influence remained even after Alexander's death (323 B.C.) during a period of Egyptian rule and subsequently under the Seleucid kings from Syria, who took actions to undermine Jewish customs and enforce the worship of Greek gods. The Jews rebelled under the leadership of the Maccabees in 167 B.C. and established a Jewish state, which, by the time of the Roman conquest in 63 B.C., controlled much of Palestine and had converted many to Judaism. Yet a revolt in 132 A.D. led the Romans to evict the Jews from Jerusalem and to establish the city of Aelia Capitolina on its ruins.

In 638 Muslim invaders built a mosque on the site of the ruins of the Jewish Temple in Jerusalem. Some Christians remained in isolated towns on the Mediterranean coast (such as Ramla, Jaffa, and Lydda), and in 1099 Christian Crusaders from western Europe took Jerusalem and imposed a kingdom for nearly a century. For the most part, however, the inhabitants of Palestine became Arabized, converting to Islam and speaking Arabic.

Palestine was conquered by the Ottoman Turks in 1517, whose empire dominated the region for 400 years until its demise in World War I, afterwhich the British controlled the region. There was a period of modernization in Palestine in the 1830s when Ibrahim Pasha established secular schooling and civil rights so that Christians and Jews could exist somewhat on a par with the Muslims. When the rural people rebelled against this secularism, the European powers forced Ibrahim out in 1840, and the Ottoman Empire regained control.

ISRAEL

In 1919 Jews represented ten percent of Palestine's population; by 1944 the number of Jews in Palestine had risen to 32 percent of the total population. Many of the Jewish immigrants came following Hitler's rise to power in 1933 and especially thereafter as refugees of the Holocaust. Their land acquisition during the mandate was aided by financial support from the Jewish National Fund, which allowed them to purchase land from Syrian absentee landholders as well as from Palestinian Arabs. The Arab farmers who had worked the land without owning it were suddenly dispossessed and forced to seek a living in the cities.

This spurred an Arab revolt, which led the British to explore the possibility of a partition of Palestine between a Jewish state and an Arab state. Two commissions attempted fruitlessly to settle on a map that could be agreed upon, and fears that the Arabs would side with the Germans in the incipient war led the colonial government to issue a "white paper" in 1939 limiting Jewish migration to 75,000 over the next five years and guaranteeing an "independent Palestine state" within ten years. The Arabs rejected the delayed independence, and the Jews found the immigration quota unconscionable owing to the plight of the Jews in Europe. Paramilitary groups, the Irgun and the Stern Gang, carried out attacks against British installations and assassinated the British minister of state, Lord Moyne, in order to further Jewish interests.

In 1947 the U.N. General Assembly overwhelmingly passed a resolution calling for the partition of Palestine into separate Jewish and Arab states, with Jerusalem to exist under international administration. Jewish leaders accepted the plan, though they hoped to expand the borders of their state; but the Arabs rejected it on the grounds that the Jewish minority did not deserve a state at their expense, notwithstanding the atrocities committed in Europe.

Jewish leaders declared the establishment of the state of Israel on May 14, 1948, setting the scene for the first of a series of Arab-Israeli wars and military conflicts. While the Palestinian Arabs were still suffering the effects of the British suppression of their revolts a decade earlier, the surrounding Arab countries of Egypt, Syria, Jordan, and Iraq attempted a supporting invasion of Israel on May 15.

When armistices were signed between Israel and the surrounding Arab countries of Egypt, Jordan, Lebanon, and Syria in early 1949, Israel had less than a third of the population of Palestine but controlled three-quarters of its territory. The prospect of further violence spurred a mass exodus of Arabs from their homes. More than half of the 1,300,000 Arabs were living in refugee camps at the end of the war, including about 400,000 from lands designated for the Jewish state by the U.N. partition plan.

MODERN ERA

By 1967 the process of urbanization had begun in Palestine, thus undermining the traditional social institutions that had been grounded in the village and clan. An increase in literacy (owing to six years of compulsory education provided by U.N. schools) and in higher education, and a shift from an agrarian economy to one of industrial, artisan, and white-collar jobs, also led to a change in the character of the Palestinian leadership. Where until 1948 the Palestinians were generally represented by political and religious officials from the upper classes, the new movements were more populist.

Tensions over Israeli diversion of water from the Jordan River to the south of Israel led to the Arab formation of the Palestine Liberation Organization (PLO), which carried out attacks against the diversion project, prompting Israeli military reprisals against Jordan and Syria. Incidents of this kind escalated to the Six Day War in 1967, in which Israel defeated the Arab military forces and conquered the Gaza Strip and the Sinai Peninsula from Egypt; East Jerusalem and the West Bank from Jordan; and the Golan Heights from Syria. The U.N. issued Resolution 242, calling for Israeli withdrawal from these territories in exchange for peace, and this document remained central to the question of peace in Palestine for decades.

In the ensuing decades, the Israelis were generally willing to negotiate on the basis of 242 without any preconditions, though they insisted that Jordan represent the Palestinian people. Many of the more conservative Israelis argued that the lands in question were essential to the security and even existence of Israel as a buffer against the Arab's continued aggression. The Arabs refused to acknowledge Israel's right to exist and objected to the resolution's reference to the Palestinians as refugees rather than as a people with a right to a state of their own. They repeatedly called for Israeli withdrawal from the occupied territories before negotiations could begin.

The 1970s saw continued violence in Palestine, with the PLO committing terrorist acts against Israeli targets, and more radical factions targeting civilians worldwide in an effort to implicate and thus discredit the PLO. After being expelled from Jordan in 1970, the PLO established a base of operations in Lebanon from which to attack northern Israel, as well as a small state within a state, which provided various social welfare services to the Palestinians as well as the

Lebanese before it was destroyed by Israeli invasions in 1982 and 1987.

In December of 1987 Palestinian resistance to the Israeli occupation, which had for some time expressed itself in demonstrations, strikes, and boycotts, coalesced into a popular uprising that has come to be known as the *intifada*, which literally means "shaking off" in Arabic. All sectors of society in the West Bank and Gaza Strip joined the acts of resistance, the most visible being the youths in the streets taking up rocks and gasoline bombs against Israeli forces. Though it was met with a brutal response, the *intifada* seemed to strengthen the Palestinian sense of resilience and self-reliance, as groups were formed in each locality to organize the resistance activities and provide medical services, food, and education to those who were in need. As it continued into the early 1990s this uprising also seemed to increase world awareness of and sympathy for the plight of the Palestinians and their call for self-determination.

The United States pressured Israel to give up its insistence on recognizing only Jordan as the Palestinians' representative, and after much diplomacy Israel finally began negotiations with the PLO as well as with individual Arab countries. In September of 1993 Prime Minister Rabin of Israel and Yasser Arafat, representing the Palestinians, signed a peace agreement that called for a five-year period of limited autonomy for the occu-pied territories and further negotiations on a permanent solution after three years.

The limited autonomy commenced in July of 1994 as Arafat began his administration of Gaza and the West Bank town of Jericho without an effective state apparatus or infrastructure. He also suffered from opposition by radical groups, such as the Hamas and the Islamic Holy War, which took the form of violent provocations that called into question the viability of Palestinian self-rule under present conditions. These serious questions were looming in the fall of 1994 when the Swedish Nobel committee awarded the prestigious peace prize jointly to Arafat, Prime Minister Rabin, and Foreign Minister Shimon Peres in an effort to bolster the fledgling struggle for peaceful coexistence between Jews and Arabs in the Middle East.

PALESTINIAN IMMIGRATION WAVES

Estimates of the number of Palestinian Americans range from 100,000 to 400,000, with a number of researchers settling on 200,000 as a reasonable guess. The difficulty in determining a more precise number results in part from the fact that there has never been an actual state of Palestine that immigrants could call their country of origin. In U.S. immigration and census records up to 1920 all Arabs, Turks, Armenians, and more were classified as coming from "Turkey in Asia," and not until recently did the Immigration and Naturalization Service recognize "Palestinian" as a nationality. Palestinian immigrants may have come from within Israel or the occupied territories; one of the Arab countries that received refugees from the Arab-Israeli wars, especially Egypt, Jordan, Lebanon, and Syria; or a country to which Palestinians immigrated in search of economic opportunity.

Palestine's unique political history makes it difficult to determine exactly when the first Palestinians immigrated to the United States and how many came. Most sources refer to Arab immigrants generally and indicate that while a small number of Palestinians, mainly Christian, came to the United States before 1948, the vast majority have arrived since that year.

Some Middle Eastern Arabs immigrated to the United States after 1908, the year the Ottoman Empire began requiring military service of its subjects in certain areas. The majority of these individuals were Christians, because Muslims feared losing their Islamic culture in a Western, Christian society. Increased tensions during the British Mandate and continuing Jewish migration to Palestine from Europe, however, induced Muslim Palestinian migration. The pioneers were primarily young men, although married men and some families followed when positive reports were received or when individuals returned home and displayed their success. Unlike the Christian Palestinians who preceded them, many of these immigrants sought to make money in the United States in order to return and live a more comfortable life, and often a family pooled its resources to send a member over. Though they had not been peddlers in their homeland, the vast majority of the earliest immigrants (both Christian and Muslim) took up the occupation, with some traveling across the country selling jewelry and other small items. As their numbers grew, a network of services to bring new immigrants over as well as to organize and supply the peddlers added a new level of jobs for the more experienced.

The restrictive Immigration Act of 1924 reflected the isolationism prevalent in America between the World Wars. This, in addition to the Depression in the 1930s and World War II, served to reduce immigration greatly during the second quarter of the century. But the aftermath of World War II and the Arab-Israeli war following the establishment of the state of Israel in 1948 brought greater numbers of Palestinian immigrants, most of whom were refugees.

The greatest wave of Palestinean immigration began after the Six Day War in 1967 and has continued to the present, although it peaked in the 1980s. By 1985 the Palestinean American community was estimated at approximately 90,000; by the end of the decade, the community had nearly doubled. While some Palestinean immigrants came to the United States for political reasons, the vast majority immigrated for economic and educational opportunity. Unlike early immigrants from Palestine, those who came after 1967 were much better educated as a result of the U.N.-sponsored schools and increased attendance at universities in the Middle East and abroad. Thus, many in this third wave of immigrants were professionals who met the requirements of the Immigration and Nationality Act of 1965, which contributed to a "brain drain" of many of the most educated in Palestine specifically and the Middle East in general.

SETTLEMENT PATTERNS

A majority of Palestinian immigrants initially settled on the East Coast, but industrial jobs before and especially after World War II drew the Palestinian immigrants, among many others, to urban industrial centers in the Midwest and later throughout the country. Today, the largest concentrations of Palestinian Americans are in New York and parts of New Jersey, Detroit, Los Angeles, San Francisco, Chicago, Cleveland, Atlanta, Dallas-Fort Worth, and Jacksonville, Florida.

ACCULTURATION AND ASSIMILATION

One of the few studies of the Palestinian experience in the United States was published by Kathleen Christison in the *Journal of Palestine Studies* in 1989. It details how Palestinian Americans for the most part have adapted quickly and successfully to American society while retaining a remarkable level of awareness of and involvement in the culture and politics of the land from which they or their predecessors came. She argues that there is no correlation between the extent of assimilation and the level of Palestinian nationalism: those who identify most strongly with their Palestinian roots are not necessarily the least American of the group.

Alienation seems to be rare among Palestinian Americans, though it does exist for certain segments of the population. Older Palestinians who come to the United States with grown children who support them tend to be the most alienated because they do not need to learn English to survive, they tend to socialize within the group, and they generally have the least amount of contact with the rest of American culture. Women more than men are more prone to feel alienated from American society because, in many cases, they are kept from the mainstream culture so that they may perform the primary role in imparting the Palestinian culture to their children.

Others are simply more tradition-bound and guard against the effects of the more open and liberal Western society. They oppose much that is common in the dominant culture, such as open sexuality, divorce, and drugs and alcohol, for religious and cultural reasons. They worry about raising their children here, especially girls, and some even resort to sending their children back to the Middle East for education during crucial teenage years.

Many Palestinian Americans, however, retain a Palestinian identity while identifying themselves as Americans first and foremost. Christison profiles an owner of a jewelry store in Albuquerque, New Mexico, who came to America from the West Bank when he was seven and is active in local business and politics. He married a woman from his home village and is active in promoting the Palestinian cause through the American political system. He is on the American-Arab Anti-Discrimination Committee's executive committee and was one of eight Palestinian American delegates at the 1988 Democratic convention.

Though Palestinian Americans have generally had a smooth transition to a new culture, many still feel unsettled because of tensions in their homeland and specifically the lack of a Palestinian state. Studies of Palestinian Americans report that few say they have been the subject of overt discrimination based on their ethnicity. However, many say that they are often made to feel foreign, or not fully American. Certain people they encounter want to classify them as "Arab," as if this were incompatible with being an American. Some Palestinian Americans also find that they are accepted personally but that a distinction is drawn between them and their people in the Middle East. Many Americans apparently identify Palestinians with the few extremists who commit terrorist acts to publicize the plight of Palestine or to discredit by association the moderate factions they oppose. The Palestinians in the United States resent this characterization, and they often fault the media coverage of the Arab-Israeli conflict, which, in their view, does not do enough to educate the public about their history and the injustices they continue to suffer. On the other hand, the consensus is that seven years of the *intifada* and Israeli reaction to it has done a lot to dramatize the Palestinians' plight and turn public opinion toward a solution that includes a Palestinian state alongside Israel.

TRADITIONAL CLOTHING

Traditional clothing for men was fairly uniform throughout the Middle East because they did far more traveling than the women. There were various styles that characterized the villagers, townspeople, and Bedouins, but within each group the rich and poor were distinguished primarily by the quality of the fabrics. The male wardrobe generally consisted of pants, a tunic, an overgarment secured with a belt, and sometimes a vest. Both sexes covered their head as a sign of modesty and respect. Men wore a skullcap covered by a simple cloth wrapped around the head, a more elaborate turban, or a *kafiyyeh*, the scarf secured by a cord. In the United States most Palistenian men wear Western dress, although they may sometimes wear the traditional *kafiyyeh* during special occasions.

In Palestine, women traditionally wore an outfit comprising of pants, a dress, an overgarment, a jacket or vest, and a shoulder mantle. They often wore a bonnet-like hat trimmed with coins on their head. In certain areas this was replaced by a *kafiyyeh* held in place by a folded scarf. The dresses were very elaborate, at times having as many as 21 individual pieces sewn together. The colors and embroidered patterns differed from one locality to the next and evolved over time. Fine embroidered dress panels were considered works of art and as such were handed down from mother to daughter. Jewelry was also a very important part of costume in traditional Palestine, and its function went beyond that of adornment and display of wealth. Amulets were worn to ward off the dangers of the Evil Eye, which was believed to take the lives of half of the population. Usually, what the upper classes wore in gold, the lower classes reproduced with baser metals or with less elaboration, such as necklaces whose pendants did not completely encircle the neck. Many women continue to wear traditional clothing in the United States, although their most ornate garments are generally reserved for special occasions.

CUISINE

As in most Arab cultures, beans, chickpeas, lentils, and rice are the staple ingredients in a variety of Palestinian dishes. Water, oil, vegetables, and seasonings are often added to these to produce different kinds of pastes, which are usually scooped up with pita bread—a round, flat, bread with a pocket in it. Sesame seed paste or oil may be used to embellish a meal. Stews are very popular and may be made with a variety of different meats, especially lamb. Fish is also commonly eaten. Various kinds of salads and cooked vegetables complement these dishes, and one of a number of different kinds of yogurt often accompanies a meal. Desserts include such sweet pastries as *baklava*, which is made with honey and chopped nuts, as well as fresh and dried fruits. Coffee and tea are the most common beverages.

LANGUAGE

Though many Palestinians living and/or working in Israel speak Hebrew as a necessary second language, Arabic has been the language of the Palestinians since the seventh century. Arabic is the youngest of the Semitic languages. It developed a sophisticated oral tradition through the poetry of the nomadic Bedouins before it became the language of the Islamic religion and its holy text, the Koran, in the seventh century. As the Arab Empire grew, Arabic replaced the Aramaic, Coptic, Greek, and Latin languages and became the main instrument of Arab culture. The Koran, the *Arabian Nights*, and the *Muqaddama*, a fourteenth-century history of the rise and fall of civilizations, are the great masterpieces of Arabic literature.

Arabic is the native language of virtually all Arabs, from northern Africa to the Arabian Peninsula. The dialects vary widely, though a common form of Arabic called Modern Standard Arabic (MSA), which is a simplified version of the language in the Koran, facilitates communication. MSA is the main form of written Arabic throughout the Arab world, as well as the language used in radio and TV broadcasts and in most schools. Arabic has an alphabet with 28 letters.

GREETINGS

Common Arabic greetings include the following (in transliteration): *issálamu alékum*—peace be upon you; *wi alékuma salám*—and upon you; *nahárik saíd*—good day; *saíd mubárak*—may your day be pleasant; *sabáh ilxér*—good morning; *sabáh innúr*—good morning of light; *misá ilxér*—good evening; *saída*—good-bye; *maássalama*—(go) with safety; *izzáy issíha*—how are you? (how is the health?); *alláh yisallímak*—may God keep you.

FAMILY AND COMMUNITY DYNAMICS

As with many other immigrant groups coming from a more traditional society to a modern Western one, the Palestinian immigrants in the first half of this century experienced a breakdown in the nature of the hierarchical and patriarchal extended family. Whether the father was away from home as an itinerant peddler or just working long hours, his authority decreased, especially in families where the mother was also involved with the family business. The influence of education and economic opportunities and American culture generally led to more nuclear families with fewer children. Women's participation in the economic sphere of the family in time reduced the number of restrictive customs. Except for some families that remained highly traditional, most Muslim women shed their veils when they emigrated, and both Christian and Muslim women generally ceased to cover their heads as they had been required to do in their former culture.

By the time of World War II, women had become increasingly independent. They were more often allowed to remain single and there was much less family control over their choices. The segregation of the sexes was mostly limited to mosques, and marriages occurred later and were usually not arranged. Many saw marriage as the opportunity to be liberated from parental control and to establish their own identity closer to that of the mainstream culture that they had grown up with through school and the media.

Evidence suggests that in the 1990s many families encourage marriage to other Palestinians either through community organizations that foster social contacts with others in the group or even by traveling to hometowns in the Middle East to find potential spouses. Despite these efforts some inter-ethnic and inter-religious marriages take place, and in most cases this does not put insurmountable strain on relations between the generations. However, in the families that remain the most traditional, prohibitions on dating, limits on friendships with non-Palestinians, and even extensive restrictions on the style of dress are all used to limit the influence of American culture. When they exist, though, these conditions are much more likely to be applied, or more severely applied, to girls than to boys.

WEDDINGS

In Palestine, marriage required a gift to the bride's family, usually money but sometimes real estate. Weddings lasted from three days to a week, beginning with celebrations on Tuesday and followed by a procession to the groom's house on Thursday, which was accompanied by singing, drums, and the firing of guns. Islamic law permitted a man to have as many as four wives, but a second wife was usually only taken in cases where the first wife was ill or where male children were not forthcoming. In the United States, many Palestinian marriage traditions have changed somewhat in order to conform to American law. Palestinians are encouraged to marry within their ethnic community and are expected to respect their parents wishes when choosing a spouse. The ceremony itself remains a festive event and celebrations may last several days.

FUNERALS

Upon death, ceremonies are performed within 24 hours. In Palestine, professional mourners were sometimes hired. A meal for the family is prepared after the funeral, and family members and friends bring food and give condolences in the days that follow. Mourning periods last up to a year, and women sometimes cover their dresses with dark cloth.

EDUCATION

Along with the Lebanese, Palestinians have the highest education rate in the Middle East. In the United States approximately 35 percent of Palestinian men and 11 percent of women have at least a college degree. This compares with a rate of just over 20 percent for the American adult population in general. Though they have always been aware of the politics and history of their homeland, Palestinian American students are increasingly taking an interest in studying Arab language and culture more formally in college and graduate school. A number of Palestinian or Arab organizations are also making an effort to monitor and improve the teaching of Arab history and culture in the nation's schools.

RELIGION

Although most Arab Americans are Christian—representing Eastern Orthodox, Roman Catholic, and Protestant churches—the vast majority of Palestinian Americans are Muslim, i.e., followers of Islam. Islam is a religion based on the teachings of Mohammed (c. 570-632), who called on Arabs to surrender to the will of God (Allah) and to commit themselves anew each day. Muslims have five basic religious duties, which are known as the five pillars of Islam.

First, Muslims must repeat their creed, the *shahada:* "There is no God but the one God, and Mohammed is his prophet." The second pillar, *salat,* consists of ritual prayers said five times each day while facing toward Mecca, Mohammed's birthplace. On Fridays Muslims attend a service at a mosque in which an *imam* leads the prayer and usually gives a sermon. *Zakat,* the giving of alms, is the third pillar. The fourth pillar requires the adherent to fast during the month of Ramadan, which means refraining from food, drink and sex during daylight hours. It is also customary to pray and recite the Koran at night during Ramadan. The final pillar entails a pilgrimage, or *hajj,* to the Kaaba, the holy shrine in Mecca, that is to be made at least once in one's lifetime.

The primary Muslim holiday commemorates Mohammed's birthday and involves speeches, meetings, and prayers. The sacred book of the Islamic religion is the Koran. It is believed to be the words of Allah as revealed to Mohammed at different times by the angel Gabriel. The words of previous, lesser prophets, including Moses and Jesus, were also given by Allah, but they were corrupted, and so the Koran was sent to purify the message. This message is known as the *sharia,* which provides guidance for all specific situations in life. Included are proscriptions against drinking wine, eating pork, usury, and gambling.

EMPLOYMENT AND ECONOMIC TRADITIONS

Many of the Palestinian immigrants early in the century became itinerant peddlers in the United States, selling jewelry and trinkets that could be carried easily in a suitcase. They quickly learned enough English to emphasize that their wares were authentic items from the Holy Land. As more Palestinians came over, new opportunities

John (left) and Jacob
Rantisi pose inside their
Kenosha, Wisconsin,
restaurant.

opened up for the more experienced to provide services related to bringing immigrants over and setting them up in business as peddlers.

The large percentage of Palestinian immigrants since the 1967 war who are educated is reflected in the increased numbers of professionals among their ranks. A study of Palestinian Arab immigrants from Israel, the West Bank, and Gaza, published in 1994, used the 1980 census to look at socioeconomic characteristics. Among the 90 percent of Palestinian American men and 40 percent of women who are in the labor force, 40 percent and 31 percent, respectively, have either professional, technical, or managerial positions. There are also large numbers in sales: 26 percent of men, and 23 percent of women. The self-employment rate for men is a significant 36 percent (only 13 percent for women), compared to 11 percent for non-immigrant men. Of the self-employed, 64 percent are in retail trade, with half owning grocery stores. In terms of income, the mean for Palestinian families in 1979 was $25,400, with 24 percent earning over $35,000 and 20 percent earning less than $10,000.

POLITICS AND GOVERNMENT

Christison's study found that while Palestinian

Americans are typically not more politically active than the population at large they are very politically aware of their history and the issues facing their homeland. They are more active in social organizations, such as mosques, churches and local associations, than in political ones, though the former have strong political implications. In the absence of a Palestinian state, the unity and preservation of communities in the diaspora serve to maintain Palestinian identity.

For example, Jacksonville, Florida, has a large contingent of immigrants from the Christian town of Ramallah, in the West Bank just north of Jerusalem. This community was long a close-knit Palestinian social unit, and it was strengthened by the formation in 1958 of the American Federation of Ramallah, Palestine, which now has over 25,000 members nationwide. Until the mid-1960s the community identified primarily with its roots in Ramallah, rather than Palestine generally. George Salem, who grew up in the community, says that in the 1950s and early 1960s, "We knew we were from Ramallah; we didn't really know whether it was Jordan or Palestine or what." But this changed after the PLO was formed and especially since the Israeli occupation of the West Bank. These events, culminating in the *intifada*, have heightened Palestinian American solidarity with those in their homeland and added a sense of urgency to finding a lasting solution to the Arab-Israeli conflict.

INDIVIDUAL AND GROUP CONTRIBUTIONS

In part owing to their small numbers, and perhaps also because of their tendency, as described above, to work more quietly behind the scenes, few Palestinian Americans are widely known. However, based on their educational and professional status there are undoubtedly many Palestinian Americans in positions of prominence in various fields, such as the business leaders and Democratic National Convention delegates mentioned above.

ACADEMIA

Edward Said is professor of English and comparative literature at Columbia University in New York City; author of numerous scholarly and general interest books, including *The Question of Palestine*; he is a member of the Palestine National Council. Born in Jerusalem in 1935, the son of Arab Christians who were Anglican, he was educated in Cairo after the family fled to that city in 1947. Regarding the politics of his homeland he has said, "My endless beef with the Palestinian leadership is that they've never grasped the importance of America as clearly and as early as the Jews. Most Palestinian leaders, like Arafat, grew up in tyrannical countries like Syria or Jordan, where there's no democracy at all. They don't understand the institutions of civil society, and that's the most important thing!"

Mohamed Rabie is another of many Palestinian Americans in academia. He has a Ph.D. in economics and taught at Kuwait University and Georgetown University before moving to the University of Houston. He has authored many books on Middle East Affairs, including *The Other Side of the Arab Defeat*, *The Politics of Foreign Aid*, and *The Making of American Foreign Policy*. Rabie is the president of the Center for Educational Development and a member of various social and professional associations, including the Middle East Economics Association and the Middle East Studies Association.

GOVERNMENT AND POLITICS

George Salem served as Solicitor of Labor in the Reagan administration. He grew up in the Jacksonville, Florida, Ramallah community described above. Even though the community had a strong identity and there were 13 Ramallah families within a three-block radius of his house, his parents discouraged him, unsuccessfully, from running for president of the student council at his high school because they feared his becoming too Americanized. He credits youth clubs and other social organizations with upholding a distinct Ramallan identity long before the turbulent events of the 1960s forged a larger Palestinian one.

MEDIA

PRINT

The American-Arab Message.

A weekly Arabic and English language paper published on Friday with a circulation of 8,700. Founded in 1937.

Address: 17514 Woodward Avenue, Detroit, Michigan 48203.

Telephone: (313) 868-2266.

Islamic Affairs.

A monthly publication since 1969 owned by the National Council on Islamic Affairs. In Arabic and English, with a circulation of 15,000.

Address: P.O. Box 416, New York, New York 10017.

Journal of Palestine Studies.

A publication of the Institute for Palestine Studies and the University of California Press, it was founded in 1971 and appears quarterly with information exclusively devoted to Palestinian affairs and the Arab-Israeli conflict.

Contact: Philip Mattar, Associate Editor.

Address: 3501 M Street, N.W., Washington, D.C. 20007.

Telephone: (800) 874-3614.

Fax: (202) 342-3927.

Middle East Monitor.

Monthly newsletter that focuses on political events in the Middle East and North Africa, paying particular attention to current political changes and economic development.

Contact: Amir N. Ghazaii, Editor.

Address: 402 Godwin, P.O. Box 236, Ridgewood, New Jersey 07450.

Telephone: (201) 670-9623.

News Circle.

A monthly publication since 1972 with a circulation of 5,000. In Arabic and English.

Address: P.O. Box 3684, Glendale, California 91201.

Telephone: (818) 557-1500.

Other Israel.

Founded in 1983 and published four or five times per year, it seeks to promote peace between Israelis and Palestinians.

Contact: Adam Keller, Editor.

Address: Israel Council for Israeli-Palestinian Peace, 4816 Cornell Avenue, Downers Grove, Illinois 60515.

Telephone: (708) 969-7584.

RADIO

WGPR-FM (107.5).

Weekly programming targeting Detroit's large Arab American population.

Address: 3140 East Jefferson, Detroit, Michigan.

Telephone: (313) 259-8862.

WKCR-FM (89.9).

A Sunday night program "In All Languages" periodically features Arabic and addresses concerns of New York's Arabic-speaking community.

Address: Columbia University, New York, New York 10027.

Telephone: (212) 854-5223.

WONX-AM (1590).

Airs occasional programs concerning Arab Americans.

Contact: Judy Selby.

Address: 2100 Lee Street, Evanston, Illinois 60202.

Telephone: (312) 282-9722.

WSOU-FM (89.5).

Approximately one hour per week of programming catering to Arab Americans.

Address: 400 South Orange Avenue, South Orange, New Jersey 07079.

Telephone: (201) 761-9520.

TELEVISION

WGPR (Independent Station 62, Detroit).

"Arab Voice of Detroit" airs Saturday nights from 10:00 p.m. to 12:00 a.m.

Address: 3140 East Jefferson, Detroit, Michigan.

Telephone: (313) 259-8862.

ORGANIZATIONS AND ASSOCIATIONS

American-Arab Anti-Discrimination Committee (ADC).

The committee, founded in 1980, provides legal counseling and general assistance to victims of anti-Arab discrimination, and works to fight stereotypes of Arab Americans by educating the public, particularly through schools.

Contact: Albert Mokhiber, President.

Address: 4201 Connecticut Avenue, N.W., Suite 500, Washington, D.C. 20008.

Telephone: (202) 244-2990.

American Arabic Association (AMARA).

Individuals interested in promoting a better understanding among Americans and Arabs through involvement in charitable and humanitarian causes; supports Palestinian and Lebanese charities that aid orphans, hospitals, and schools.

Contact: Dr. Said Abu Azhra, President.

Address: 29 Mackenzie Lane, Wakefield, Massachusetts 01880.

Telephone: (617) 246-1515.

Arab American Institute (AAI).

This organization was founded in 1985 to promote the interests of the Arab American community through the political system, as well as educate the public about the community's contributions to American society.

Contact: Dr. James Zogby, President.

Address: 918 16th Street, N.W., Suite 601, Washington, D.C. 20006.

Telephone: (202) 429-9210.

Bethlehem Association.

Promotes understanding by the American public of the Arab people, and especially the Palestinian culture.

Contact: Dr. Hanna Canawati, President.

Address: P.O. Box 2029, Downey, California 90242.

Telephone: (310) 943-7167.

Palestine Aid Society of America (PAS).

Founded in 1978, the PAS works to raise American awareness of the Palestinian point of view on issues regarding the Middle East. It also provides financial aid to educational and community empowerment projects in the occupied territories.

Contact: Taleb Salhab, Executive Director.

Address: 2025 Eye Street, N.W., Suite 1020, Washington, D.C. 20006.

Telephone: (202) 728-9425.

Palestine Arab Delegation (PAD).

Presents the views of Palestinian Arabs in the special political committee of the United Nations during the U.N. General Assembly.

Contact: Issa Nakhleh, Chair.

Address: P.O. Box 608, New York, New York 10163.

Telephone: (212) 758-7411.

Palestinian Mission to the United Nations.

In 1974 the U.N. officially recognized the PLO as the representative of the Palestinian people. Since that time it has been given observer status at the U.N.

Address: 115 East 65th Street, New York, New York 10021.

Telephone: (212) 288-8500.

Union of Palestinian Women's Associations in North America (UPWA).

Promotes national and social self-determination and independence for Palestine; strives toward emancipation and empowerment of Palestinian and Arab women.

Contact: Maha Jarad.

Address: P.O. Box 29110, Chicago, Illinois 60629.

Telephone: (312) 436-6060.

MUSEUMS AND RESEARCH CENTERS

Harvard University Institute for Social and Economic Policy in the Middle East.

This institute has coordinated research by Harvard faculty on Middle East affairs since its inception in 1983.

Contact: Leonard J. Hausman, Director.

Address: John F. Kennedy School of Government, 79 JFK Street, Cambridge, Massachusetts 02138.

Telephone: (617) 495-3666.

Institute for Palestine Studies.

The institute was founded in 1963 to study the Arab-Israeli conflict, as well as the Palestinian cultural and economic life in the occupied territories, particularly in Gaza.

Contact: Dr. Philip Mattar, Executive Director.

Address: 3501 M Street, N.W., Washington, D.C. 20007.

Telephone: (202) 342-3990.

Museum of the University of Chicago Oriental Institute.

Founded in 1919 in conjunction with university archaeological work in the ancient Near East, the institute's collection contains art from Palestine.

Address: 1155 East 58th Street, Chicago, Illinois 60637.

Telephone: (312) 753-2475.

University of Pennsylvania Museum.

Founded in 1889, this museum contains materials regarding Syro-Palestinian anthropology and ethnology.

Address: 33rd and Spruce Streets, Philadelphia, Pennsylvania 19104.

Telephone: (215) 243-4000.

SOURCES FOR ADDITIONAL STUDY

Christison, Kathleen. "The American Experience: Palestinians in the U.S.," *Journal of Palestine Studies*, autumn 1989; pp. 18-36.

Clines, Francis X. "A West Bank Village's Sons Return," *New York Times*, February 15, 1988; p. A6.

Cohen, Yinon, and Andrea Tyree. "Palestinian and Jewish Israeli-born Immigrants in the United States," *International Migration Review*, 28, No. 2; pp. 243-254.

Dimbleby, Jonathan. *The Palestinians*. New York: Quartet Books, 1979.

Kifner, John. "New Pride for Palestinian Americans," *New York Times*, December 12, 1988; p. A3.

Sacco, Joe. *Palestine: A Nation Occupied*. Seattle: Fantagraphics Books, 1994.

Said, Edward. *The Question of Palestine*. New York: Times Books, 1979.

Turki, Fawaz. *The Disinherited: Journal of a Palestinian Exile*. New York: Monthly Review Press, 1972.

Wilkerson, Isabel. "Among Arabs in the U.S.: New Dreams," *New York Times*, March 13, 1988; p. A12.

PANAMANIAN AMERICANS

by
Rosetta Sharp Dean

It is often assumed that the Panamanians of Central America and the South Americans share a common culture. Although the majority share a Spanish or Portuguese heritage, they represent very diverse peoples who have been incorporated into nation-states recently.

OVERVIEW

A country slightly smaller than the state of South Carolina, Panama is located in Central America. Its land mass measures 29,762 square miles (77,381 square kilometers), bounded by the Caribbean Sea to the north, Colombia to the east, the Pacific Ocean to the south, and Costa Rica to the west. The climate of the area is tropical with a dry season that extends from January to May and a rainy season from May to December. Rainfall varies from 130 inches on the Atlantic coast to 68 inches on the Pacific side. Temperatures generally range between 73 and 87 degrees Fahrenheit (23-31 degrees Celsius).

Panama has a population of slightly over 2.4 million people; 70 percent are of Mestizo origin (mixed Spanish, and Indian) or mixed Spanish, Indian, Chinese, and West Indian. The rest of the population comprises various ethnic minorities, including West Indian (14 percent), white (ten percent), Indian (six percent). Most of the population is Roman Catholic, however, there are several other denominations as well as Judaic and Islamic faiths represented. The country's official language is Spanish, and its capital city is Panama City. Panama's national flag consists of four rectangles arranged lower left, blue; upper right, red; upper left, white with blue star in the center; lower right, white with red star in the center.

HISTORY

Panama was the native name of a village on the Pacific Coast of the Gulf and Isthmus of Panama. Before its discovery by the Spanish, Panama was inhabited by a large number of Amerindians. The groups lived in organized chiefdoms, depending on the area's fish, birds, and sea turtles, and on starchy root crops for food. Numbering nearly one million when the Spanish arrived in 1501, the largest group was the Cuna. The country's name, which means "land of plenty fish," may also come from the Cuna words *panna mai,* or "far away," a reply to Spaniards who wondered where to find gold. The name Panama is also believed to be a Guarani Indian word meaning "a butterfly," and also signifying a mud fish, perhaps because the flaps of the mudfish resembled the wings of a butterfly.

Panama has been subjected to numerous occupations by foreign powers since the Renaissance period. Since 1513, when the Spanish explorer Vasco Nuñez de Balboa crossed a narrow strip of land and discovered the Pacific Ocean, the Isthmus of Panama has been a major crossroad of the world, linking two great continents and separating two great oceans. His discovery opened up a shorter route to Peru and the gold of the Incas. Fortune seekers from Europe could land at Colón, cross the narrow isthmus, and set sail on the Pacific for Peru. Shortly after his discovery, Balboa was condemned for treason and put to death with the help of a former aide, Juan Pizarro, who then used the route to conquer the Incas. Panama became an important travelway and supply post for the Spanish conquistadores (conquerors).

By 1519 Spanish settlements had been established, and the king's appointed governor, Pedro Arias de Avila, had settled in the village of Panama. Under his rule, Balboa's Indian allies were killed and other Indians were enslaved. Many fled to the jungle or to the swampland and isolated islands on the northeast coast. A priest, Bartolomé de la Casas, was outraged by the Indian enslavement and persuaded Spain's government to send African slaves in their stead. By this time, many Indians had died from disease and mistreatment, while those who escaped had become isolated in the forests and swamps. The separation of Indian groups from Panamanians remains today. African slaves became so important that the British were given a contract to deliver 4,800 slaves a year for 30 years. Slave revolts moved the Spanish king to interrupt the delivery for a time.

From the beginning, the narrowness of the land inspired the idea of a canal. The Spanish, however, were disinclined to build one, wanting to keep rival fortune seekers away from the Pacific Ocean. So for 300 years the only route was a muddy jungle road from the Atlantic Ocean to the Pacific. Outsiders often attacked. British forces captured a fortress on the Atlantic, Portobello, several times, and buccaneers troubled the area in the 1600s. The Scottish attempted to begin a colony and open the land to trade in 1698, but failed due to disease and the resistant Spanish. Spain held on to the land and controlled its markets until 1740, then allowed Panamanians to trade with other countries. Panama, though, seldom had the freedom of self-rule. From 1718 to 1722 the Spanish government in Peru held authority over Panama. Spain's viceroy of Granada (who ruled Panama, Colombia, and Venezuela), assumed control in 1739. When this government was abandoned in 1819, the viceroy moved to Panama and ruled there for two years. Although Spanish occupation of Panama ended in 1821, close relations between the Spanish and Panamanians flourished; mixed marriages and the adoption of Spanish culture and language gradually molded the Spanish and Panamanians into a distinct ethnic entity. The ancestors of the modern Panamanian people managed to preserve their Spanish heritage despite governance by European and Colombian conquests. The Spanish language in Panama has survived as a member of the Romance language group. In 1821 Panama obtained independence from Spain, and joined the new republic of Greater Colombia. The French started a canal in 1879, but after 20 years of struggle with the jungle, disease, financial problems and the sheer enormity of the project, they were forced to abandon it.

The California gold rush in the 1840s renewed interest in travel between the oceans. In 1845, the United States helped build the first transcontinental railroad that crossed Panama. Meanwhile, France, Britain, and the United States explored the possibility of a canal to join the two oceans by way of either Panama or Nicaragua. In 1879 Ferdinand de Lesseps of France, and builder of the Suez Canal, began construction of a canal in Panama under a license from Colombia. However, disease (yellow fever, malaria), rain, and mud made him abandon the project. From 16,000 to 22,000 workers had died.

THE CANAL

In the early 1900s Colombians fought a civil war—the War of a Thousand Days. Colombian rebels operated from bases in Nicaragua, passing through Panama on their way to fight. The United States now had a growing interest in building a canal across Central America. In 1902, it intervened in the war and established a truce. In 1903 and 1904, Panama declared its independence from Colombia, drew up its first constitution, and elected its first president. In 1903, the United States signed the Hay-Ban-Vanilla treaty in which the concession for a public maritime transportation service across the Isthmus was granted; the treaty also granted the United States control over strips of land five miles wide on either side of the canal. The United States did not own the Canal Zone, but the treaty of 1903 allowed it to lease the area "in perpetuity." In return the United States agreed to pay Panama $10 million plus an annual rent of $250,000, which was later increased to $1.93 million.

In 1904, the United States purchased France's rights to the unfinished canal for $40 million and began the Herculean task of carving a canal through the isthmus. Many able and dedicated men were involved in this venture. Among them were Colonel William C. Gorges, an army doctor who achieved a major triumph in wiping out yellow fever and reducing malaria. Colonel George W. Goethals, an army engineer who later became the first governor of the Canal Zone, was put in charge of the operation in 1907. The giant excavation through the mountains of the Continental Divide at Culebra Cut, later renamed Gaillard Cut, was directed by engineer David Gaillard. After seven years of digging and construction, and the expenditure of $380 million, the Panama Canal was officially opened on August 15, 1914, and the U.S. cargo ship *Ancon* made the first transit.

After World War II, Panamanians opposed to U.S. presence in the Canal Zone demanded renegotiation of the 1903 treaty; however, the arrangement of the 1903 treaty between the United States and Panama continued until the 1960s when disputes arose over U.S. control of the canal and zone. The United States agreed to negotiate new treaties relating to the Panama Canal and the Canal Zone. The treaties, which were accepted in 1977 and signed by General Omar Torrijos Herrera, head of the Panamanian

Government, and U.S. President Jimmy Carter, stipulated joint administration of the Canal starting in 1979, and the complete return of the Canal to Panama on December 31, 1999. The treaties, which replaced the treaty of 1903, turned over to Panama the government of the Canal Zone and the territory of the Canal Zone itself, except for areas needed to operate and defend the canal. The United States remains responsible for the operation and military defense of the canal until December 31, 1999, after which it will come under complete Panamanian control.

The presence of the Canal changed lifestyles in the country. A people that had primarily earned their living as subsistence farmers now gained most of their income from the Canal. The canal employs about 3,500 United States citizens and some 10,000 Panamanians. Among the available housing areas assigned to canal employees are Balboa and Ancon on the Pacific side and, on the Atlantic side, Cristobal, Coco Solo, and Margarita. Gatun and Gamboa are communities primarily for people who work at the locks or in dredging and hydroelectric operations.

MODERN ERA

In 1988 General Manuel Noriega used his military prominence to seize control of the Panamanian government, establishing a dictatorship, which brought him great personal wealth. Previously supported by the United States, Noriega became the object of condemnation, based on evidence linking him to drug trafficking, murder, and election fraud. In an attempt to squash Noriega, the United States imposed severe economic sanctions on Panama. Although the Panamanian working class suffered from these actions, Noriega himself was virtually unaffected. In December of 1989, a U.S. invasion of Panama led to the ousting of Noriega, who officially surrendered in January 1990. He was taken to the United States and was convicted on drug charges in 1992.

THE FIRST PANAMANIANS IN AMERICA

Panamanians, among other Central Americans have a recorded presence of almost 175 years on American soil. More than one million immigrants from Central and South America have settled in the United States since 1820, but their role in the development of American society remains uncharted. The U.S. Census Bureau did not tabulate separate statistics for Panama, Central and

South American nations until 1960. The number of Panamanian Americans in the United States increased slowly. In the 1830s, only 44 arrivals were recorded, but by the early twentieth century more than 1,000 came annually. After World War I, immigration tapered off. The 1940 census listed only 7,000 Central Americans; many apparently had died or returned home.

"Getting off Ellis Island, my mother was dressed up. She had been making this suit for a year to land in. And I was dressed up with handmade lace and all. It was jampacked with mostly Europeans. And most of these people were dirty, actually dirty. I was terrified."

Ayleen Watts James in 1923, cited in *Ellis Island: An Illustrated History of the Immigrant Experience*, edited by Ivan Chermayeff et al. (New York: Macmillan, 1991).

SIGNIFICANT IMMIGRATION WAVES

After World War II, the number of immigrants increased rapidly and by 1970 the Central Americans numbered 174,000. Paradoxically, the flow of emigrants from Panama was small for nearly the entire period in which there were no immigration restrictions on applicants from the Western Hemisphere, but increased dramatically after the 1965 Immigration Act, which imposed a ceiling of 120,000 admissions from the hemisphere. By 1970, Panamanians constituted one of the largest of the Central American groups in the United States. Most Panamanians were non-whites. Women outnumbered men among Panamanian immigrants by about one-third. The number of immigrant males per 100 females was very low in the 1960s, falling to 51 for Panama. The percentage of immigrants under 20 years of age was higher for males than for females; most female immigrants were between 20 and 49, many of them service, domestic, or low-paid, white-collar workers who immigrated to earn money to send home. Since 1962 the percentage of employed newcomers who are domestic servants has remained high, ranging from 15 to 28 percent. The entry of homemakers and children after 1968 was eased by the immigration preference system favoring family reunions. As of 1990, there were approximately 86,000 people of Panamanian ancestry living in the United States.

SETTLEMENT

Most Panamanian immigrants live in New England, or on the Gulf Coast, or Pacific Coast, or in Middle Atlantic or Great Lakes areas. New York City contains the largest urban population of Panamanians. A substantial number of Panamanians settled in Florida and California. Over 15,000 Panamanians lived in New York in 1970, with fewer than 600 in San Francisco. Throughout the nineteenth and twentieth centuries, the Panamanians congregated in urban areas, especially in very large metropolitan cities. In 1920, for example, when 49 percent of the U.S. population lived in rural areas, 87 percent of the Panamanians were living in cities. They gravitated to urban centers because their education, occupational skills and lifestyles were suited to urban society. Mestizo, black, and Indian Panamanians are more numerous in New York than in any other U.S. city, numbering over 17,000 in 1970. But the forces that have led these groups to one locale or another (employment opportunities, the nucleus of an ethnic community, transportation links with the homeland) are not well understood.

ACCULTURATION AND ASSIMILATION

Little is known about the early Panamanians in the United States. Indeed, in the past, insufficient knowledge of Panamanian ethnic characteristics generated misconceptions in America. For example, the U.S. Census Bureau did not tabulate separate statistics for individual Central and South American nations until 1960—the characteristics of the individual national groups were buried in aggregated immigration and census statistics.

It is often assumed that the Panamanians of Central America and the South Americans share a common culture. Although the majority share a Spanish or Portuguese heritage, they represent very diverse peoples who have been incorporated into nation-states recently. In the newer version of acculturation and cultural pluralism, an immigrant does not surrender ethnic and cultural identity to become an American. With this approach, America is viewed more realistically, with many diverse ethnic and cultural groups. This view recognizes that one of America's strengths is in its cultural diversity and that this diversity should not be denied but highly valued.

TRADITIONS, CUSTOMS, AND BELIEFS

In the city and country, Panamanians share certain values. One is *personalismo*, a belief in interpersonal trust and in individual honor. With this belief comes a distrust of organizations and a high sensitivity to praise or insult. The most valued unit is the extended family. Another universal is *machismo*, the belief in male dominance and an image of the man as strong and daring. Women are expected to be gentle, forgiving, and dedicated to their children.

Most Panamanians are Roman Catholic, but the church and state are separate and religious freedom is guaranteed by the constitution. The religious feeling of the Panamanians is reflected in their frequent celebrations of religious holidays.

HOLIDAYS CELEBRATED BY PANAMANIAN AMERICANS

Besides Christmas Day, New Year's Day, and Easter, Panamanian Americans celebrate the Independence Day of Panama on November 3. Other holidays such as Good Friday, Mother's Day, Father's Day, Thanksgiving, and Valentine's Day are also celebrated.

FOLK DANCES

Panamanians love festivity, and during their celebrations one can see in their traditional costumes and folk dances some of the more colorful aspects of life in Panama. The national dance is the *tamborito*, in which a man and a woman, surrounded by a circle of other dancers, pretend to flirt with each other while they dance. Other couples take turns dancing in the circle. The dance is performed to the beat of the *Caja* and *Pujador*, drums that were originally used by slaves brought to Panama from Africa and the West Indies during the colonial period. During the dance the woman wears the *pollera*—a full long white dress decorated with embroidery, or the *montuna*—a long skirt with bright floral patterns worn with a white, embroidered, off-the-shoulder blouse. The man's costume, the *montuno*, is a long white cotton shirt, with fringe or embroidered decorations, and knee-length trousers. The *tamborito* is especially popular during Carnival, a four-day period of joyous festivity that precedes Ash Wednesday, the first day of Lent. Lively salsa—a mixture of Latin American popular music, rhythm and blues, jazz, and rock, is a Panamanian specialty.

CUISINE

Panamanians enjoy a variety of international dishes. However, food is similar to that eaten through-

This Panamanian American musician is performing in the 1990 West Indies Festival in Brooklyn, New York.

out Central America. Two popular dishes are *sancocho*—a soup made with meat and vegetables, and *tazajo*—ox meat beaten thin and grilled and covered with a tomato sauce. Other favorites include *ceviche* (raw fish, cured, and mixed in lime juice, with onions, red peppers, and other spices), *empanadas, tortillas*, and *carimanolas* (each made with ground beef that is stuffed in a corn meal or flour dough), tamales (a mixture of chicken or pork, onions, olives, and other hot or mild spices stuffed in a corn meal mixture wrapped in banana leaves, tied with string, then steam cooked). Some nutritious vegetables enjoyed by Panamanians are plantain, yellow yam, yucca, and bread fruit.

Traditionally, every meal is accompanied with rice or a variation of rice and peas or beans. The most popular drinks are *chicha fuerte*, a liquor made with a corn base, beer that comes from the *guanabana* fruit (fruit of the soursop, a tropical American tree), and a beverage called palm wine.

HEALTH AND MENTAL HEALTH ISSUES

There are no documented health problems or medical conditions that are specific to Panamanian Americans. Many families have health insurance coverage underwritten by various ethnic organizations. Like most Americans, Panamanian American business owners and professionals in private practice are insured at their own expense, while employees benefit from their employers' health plans when available.

LANGUAGE

The Panamanian dialect is distinct to its native origin in Panama. For the first generation of immigrants, regardless of the period of arrival in America, Spanish was the primary language. Subsequent generations spoke Spanish less often, eventually switching to English as their principal language.

FAMILY AND COMMUNITY DYNAMICS

During the first three decades of the twentieth century, the Panamanian American family underwent profound changes. The first immigrants were typically single males who had left their families behind temporarily to save enough money to send for them later. They settled first in apartments. Panamanians are among the one million immigrants from Central and South American to have settled in the United States since 1820. In most discussions, Panamanians are not considered apart from other Spanish-surnamed people, although they are not a homogeneous group. The number of African Panamanians, for example, can be inferred only from the count of nonwhites in the 1960 and the 1970 Census. The husband is the usual source of authority in the family.

Panamanians gather at social clubs, and organizations for the maintenance of ethnic ties; there they discuss social, political, economic problems and news from Panama. Since many Panamanian women work outside the home, economic conditions have gradually improved, and immigrants are able to purchase a home, cars, and modern appliances, or rent larger apartments in more prosperous neighborhoods.

The typical Panamanian household features Panamanian art such as the famous Cuna Indians textile *molas*, which generally depicts native wildlife and themes, the Panamanian flag, and other cultural icons displayed in a common area. Panamanians have always held the family in high esteem. Demographics show that Panamanian families usually have two or three children. In 1970, nearly 40 percent had one wage earner, 54 percent had two, and only six percent had no income earner.

WEDDINGS

Most wedding ceremonies involve two requirements: the man and woman must say that they want to become husband and wife; the ceremony must have witnesses, including the official who marries the couple. If the couple has a religious ceremony, it is conducted by a member of the clergy, such as a minister or priest. If a couple is marrying in a civil (nonreligious) ceremony, a judge or other authorized official performs it. Many couples prefer a traditional religious ceremony, though some Panamanians depart from custom. Some even write their own wedding service. The traditional wedding ceremony begins with the bridesmaids and ushers walking slowly down a center aisle to the altar. They stand on each side of the altar throughout the ceremony. The groom enters and waits for the bride at the altar. The bride then walks down the aisle with her father, another male relative, or a family friend. She wears a white dress and veil and carries a bouquet. At the altar, the bride and groom exchange marriage vows and accept each other as husband and wife. The groom puts a wedding ring on the ring finger of the bride's left hand, and the bride may also give the groom a ring. After the ceremony, the bride and groom kiss and then leave down the main aisle.

Many Panamanians follow the traditional wedding ceremonies, but certain religious groups add their own features to it. For example, different Protestant groups have their own versions of the ceremony. Many Roman Catholic weddings take place during a mass, and the bride and groom receive communion. The reception is held either at a private home, hotel, or restaurant. Guests give gifts or money at the reception or bridal shower. The reception is accompanied by music and dancing.

BAPTISMS

When a child is ready for baptism, the parents first select the godparents. The godfather—*padrino*, and godmother—*madrina*, are often the same couple who served as best man and matron of honor at the parents' wedding. The parents bring the child to the church, where the priest confers the grace of God by putting his hand on the child and then anoints the child on the forehead with blessed olive oil. The baptism is completed by sprinkling the child with holy water. It is customary to have a large or small dinner after the baptism.

FUNERALS

A death in the family is followed by a funeral. The practices include public announcement of the death, preparation of the body, religious ceremonies or other services, a procession, a burial or other form of disposal, and mourning. The body typically is washed, embalmed, and then dressed in special garments before being placed into a coffin. Many people hold an all-night watch called a *velorio*. The funeral may include prayers, hymns, and other music, and speeches called *elogio* that recall and praise the dead person. Many funeral services take place at a funeral home with the embalmed body on display. After the funeral, the mourners return with the bereaved family to their house and share food.

EDUCATION

Law requires all Panamanian children aged six through 15 to attend school, but this rule is not rigidly enforced. Particularly in rural areas, enrollment drops greatly in the secondary years as teenagers seek employment to augment their family's income. About half the secondary-age population was enrolled in 1982. The early immigrants cared very much for the children, and instilled in their children the importance of education. Many first-wave immigrants managed to obtain or to hold jobs. Encouraged by their parents, the second generation of Panamanian Americans placed more emphasis on vocational training and college education. While most newcomers are domestic, very few are agricultural or industrial laborers. In the last two decades many Panamanians have embraced professional careers, and others have become white collar workers. Subsequent generations have progressed even further in their educational and professional pursuits. As a result, Panamanian Americans have been able to make many significant contributions to American society.

INTERACTIONS WITH OTHER ETHNIC MINORITIES

Panamanian Americans' social relations with other ethnic groups in the United Stated defy generalization. Their ties with other Hispanic groups in the United States are not well developed; but similarity of religion, lifestyle, and language often draw them together despite country of origin. Although their ethnic group boundaries are permeable and flexible, they may be rigid with respect to class and race. Panamanian workers generally came into contact with other ethnic groups in the workplace; they began to interact with other ethnic groups as they moved into better residential areas and suburbs. All these factors, including the proliferation of mixed marriages, have contributed to the integration of Panamanians into mainstream American society.

RELIGION

Approximately 93 percent of the population nominally belongs to the Roman Catholic church, and six percent are Protestant (Evangelical). Other religious denominations represented in Panama include Seventh-Day Adventists, Baptists, Lutherans, Presbyterians, and Unitarians, as well as the Judaic and Islamic faiths. Women are the ones who attend church with the children. In Panamanian Catholicism, much emphasis is given to the mother of Jesus, Mary, who serves as an example for the women

EMPLOYMENT AND ECONOMIC TRADITIONS

Early Panamanian immigrants and their occupational characteristics have changed little in the latter decades of the twentieth century; 30 to 40 percent are professionals and white-collar workers—highly skilled and educated persons—with very few agricultural or industrial laborers.

It is estimated that Panamanians and other Hispanics represent a consumer market of between $140 billion and $190 billion, and that market will be responsible for much of the consumer market growth in the United States in the future. In addition, revenues of owned businesses were estimated to be $29.6 billion in 1990, up 48 percent from 1987. Many experts expect an upward surge in Panamanian and other Hispanic economic growth and development during the 1990s.

However, as a whole, Panamanian Americans and other Hispanics suffer from high poverty levels compared with non-Hispanics. For example, as determined by assets owned, income,

These Panamanian
American women are
preparing for the Hispanic
Day Parade in New York
City.

employment status, education and other factors, the average net worth of a white household is about eight times that of a Hispanic household ($43,279 as opposed to $5,524).

In the private sector, Panamanian workers are active members in the nation's work force. Panamanians have had some degree of occupational upgrading during the past decade, but they are more likely than the overall work force to be employed in lower-skilled, lower-paid occupations. Most of the increases in the employment of approximately 60 percent of Panamanian women were in mid-level occupations (technical, sales, and administrative support) and the generally lower-paid service occupations. Another 15 percent of Panamanian women were employed in management and professional positions. The occupational levels among Panamanian men have been stable in the managerial, professional, technical, sales, and administrative support positions. Occupational growth for Panamanian men has been concentrated in occupations requiring intermediate skills (operators, laborers, and fabricators), which has accounted for nearly one-third of their employment.

In the federal government, Panamanian presence is evidenced throughout all departments and agencies. No longer are Panamanian Americans limited to the social service sector of government—Department of Education, Health and Human Services, Housing and Development.

They are also in the Commerce, Labor, Interior, the State Departments, and the Pentagon, as well as the White House. During the last two decades, Panamanian Americans and other Hispanics have been ambassadors to numerous Central and South American countries.

POLITICS AND GOVERNMENT

Panamanian Americans are extremely aware that their increasing numbers translate to increased political influence, and they are exerting political power that complements their growing numbers and economic influence. In addition, they are carefully identifying issues that bring a measure of political unity to their diverse population.

Although each Hispanic group has its own identity, they are finding that their commonalities provide them with a more effective political voice. In recent years Hispanic politicians have been rallying around points of commonality as their political involvement increases. Panamanian Americans have also made significant political contributions to United States foreign policy in Latin America. Domestic issues such as civil rights, affirmative action, and bilingual education have often brought them together in a unified front.

Three million Panamanian and other Hispanic voters are concentrated in six states, which, when combined, account for 173 of the 270 electoral votes needed to win a presidential election. This underscores the importance of Hispanics as a voting bloc, particularly in the Southwest. There has been a significant increase in registered Hispanic voters in recent years; and, as more young Hispanics reach voting age, Hispanic strength as a political force will increase even more significantly. Hispanic political influence is directed by such organizations as the Mexican American Legal Defense and Educational Fund (MALDEF) Puerto Rican Legal Defense and Education fund (PRLDEF), National Council of La Raza, League of United Latin American Citizens (LULAC), American G.I. Forum, Cuban National Planning Council, Inc., National Image, Inc., Puerto Rican/Latinos Voting Rights Network, and many others.

MILITARY

The military history of Panamanians and other Hispanics contains a full scope of duty and dedication. No less than 37 Hispanic Americans have received the Medal of Honor, America's highest military decoration. During the Spanish-American War, Hispanic soldiers rode with Theodore Roosevelt's "Rough Riders." Military historians estimate that a quarter to a half million Hispanics served in the armed forces during World War II. Eight Hispanics received the Medal of Honor for actions during the Korean War, and 13 were decorated for actions in the Vietnam conflict. Panamanians played active roles during United States operations in Grenada, Panama, and Saudi Arabia. As of September 1990, Hispanics accounted for 2.1 percent of all active officers. The Army officer ranks had 1.9 percent Hispanic representation, the Navy had 2.4 percent, the Marine Corps 2.4 percent, the Air Force 2.0 percent, and the Coast Guard 1.7 percent.

RELATIONS WITH PANAMA

Panamanian Americans have always been proud of their homeland and have maintained ties beyond normal relations with family or friends left behind. Cultural ties between the two countries are strong, and many Panamanians come to the United States for higher education and advanced training. In cooperation with the United States government, many Panamanian Americans provide needed resources and training, and joint operations with the Drug Enforcement Agency trying to fight illegal narcotics. In addition, Panamanian Americans supported the renewal of democracy and stability in Panama, and a fundamentally strong relationship with the United States, which became severely strained by the Noriega regime during the late 1980s. Presently, some Panamanian Americans are involved in developing business ventures in Panama. There is also a steady flow of scholarly exchanges between Panama and the United States—via grants and scholarships—in which Panamanian Americans take an active role through academic organizations.

INDIVIDUAL AND GROUP CONTRIBUTIONS

Although Panamanian Americans represent only 0.4 percent of America's total population, they have made significant contributions to American popular culture and to the arts and sciences. The following sections list Panamanian Americans and their achievements:

LITERATURE

Panamanian writers did not begin to make a significant contribution to world literature until the early twentieth century. Among the most notable of this group was the poet Ricardo Miró. Panama's best-known contemporary writers are Demetrio Korsi, a poet, and Rogelio Sinan, a poet and novelist. Korsi's works are sometimes critical of United States influence on Panamanian culture. Sinan's works have a cosmopolitan tone that reflects the author's extensive travels.

MUSIC AND FILM

Lucho Azcarraga, an internationally renowned organist and composer, is best known for Panamanian folklore music. Ruben Blades, is an internationally renowned singer, actor, songwriter and producer of Buscando America; noted films are Predator II, and The Landlord.

SPORTS

In boxing, Panama Al Brown was a bantamweight champion in 1929; Roberto Duran became a lightweight champion in 1972 and 1978, a welter-weight champion (WBC) in 1980, and a light-middleweight champion (WBA) from 1983 to 1989; Ismael Laguna was a lightweight champion in 1965 and 1970; Jorge Lujan was a ban-tamweight champion from 1977 to 1980; Ernesto (Nato) Marcel was featherweight champion in 1972 and retired in 1973; Eusebio Pedroza was a featherweight champion from 1978 to 1985; Enrique Pinder was a bantamweight champion (WBC) in 1972; Rigoberto Riasco was a super bantamweight champion in 1976; Hilario Zapata was a flyweight champion in 1985. Famous jock-eys include Braulio Baeza, Lafitte Pincay, Heliodoro Gustines, Jorge Velasques, and Jacinto Vasquez. These jockeys have ridden at race tracks in Panama, Belmont, and Aqueduct. And in base-ball, Rod Carew played for the American League.

MEDIA

PRINT

El Diario/La Prensa.

Published Monday through Friday, since 1913, this publication has focused on general news in Spanish.

Contact: Carlos D. Ramirez.

Address: 143-155 Barick Street, New York, New York 10013.

Telephone: (718) 807-4600.

Mundo Hispanico News.

This publication was founded in 1979 and is pub-lished twice a month in Spanish with some Eng-lish and distributed free, or by subscription.

Contact: Alfredo Duarte.

Address: P.O. Box 13808, Atlanta, Georgia 30324.

Telephone: (404) 881-0441.

The Nuevo Amanecer.

Published by the Tablet Publishing Company, it serves the Hispanic Catholic community of Brooklyn, Queens, and Long Island.

Contact: Alberto Romero, Editor.

Address: 653 Hicks Street, Brooklyn, New York 11231.

Telephone: (718) 858-3838.

Que Pasa Panama!

Bi-monthly newsletter that updates information on Panama and the Panamanian communities in the United States and abroad.

Contact: Fulvia Jordan, Editor.

Address: 290 Lincoln Place, Suite D-2, Grand Central Station, Brooklyn, New York 11238.

Telephone: (718) 638-0862.

RADIO

WAOS-AM (1460).

Operates sunrise to sunset.

Contact: Samuel Zamarron.

Address: P.O. Box 746, Austell, Georgia 30001.

WHCR-FM (90.3).

City College of New York (National Public Radio).

Contact: Frank Allan or Linda Prout.

Address: 138 Convent Avenue, New York, New York 10031.

Telephone: (212) 650-7481.

WKAT-AM (1360).

This is a Latin owned broadcast featuring commu-nity news as well as Hispanic music.

Contact: Julio Romero.

Address: 13499 Biscayne Boulevard, Suite 1, North Miami, Florida 33181.

Telephone: (305) 949-9528.

ORGANIZATIONS AND ASSOCIATIONS

ASPIRA.

Address: 22 East 54th Street, New York, New York 10022.

Association of Hispanic Arts (AHA).

Address: 173 East 116th Street, Second Floor, New York, New York 10029.

Circulo De Arte Latinoamericano (Latin American Art Circle).

Address: Atlanta, Georgia.

Telephone: (404) 733-4200.

Hispanic Association of Colleges and Universities.

Address: 11 Dupont Circle, N.W., Suite 900, Washington, D.C. 20036.

Hispanic Institute.

Address: Colombia University, 612 West 116th Street, New York, New York, 10027.

Telephone: (212) 854-4187.

Hispanic Link News Service, Inc.

Address: 1420 N Street, N.W., Washington, D.C. 20005.

Telephone: (202) 234-0280; or, (202) 234-0737.

Hispanic Organization of Professionals and Executives.

Address: 1625 K Street, N.W., Suite 103, Washington, D.C. 20006.

League of United Latin American Citizens (LULAC).

Address: 342 Wilkens, San Antonio, Texas 78210. **Telephone:** (512) 533-1976.

NALEO Education Fund.

Address: 34 Garnet Street, Los Angeles, California 90023.

Telephone: (213) 262-8503; or, (800) 44-NALEO.

National Alliance of Spanish-Speaking People for Equality.

Address: 1701 16th Street, N.W., Suite 601, Washington, D.C. 20009.

Telephone: (202) 234-8198.

National Association of Latino Elected and Appointed Officials (NALEO).

Address: 708 G Street, S.E., Washington, D.C. 20003.

Telephone: (202) 546-2536.

National Council of La Raza.

Address: 810 First Street, N.E., Suite 300, Washington, D.C. 20002.

Telephone: (202) 289-1380.

National Hispanic Council on Aging.

Address: 2713 Ontario Road, N.W., Washington, D.C. 20009.

Telephone: (202) 265-1288.

National Image, Inc.

Address: P.O. Box 895, Austin, Texas 78701.

Network of Educators' Committees on Central America.

Address: 1188 22nd Street, N.W., Washington, D.C. 20037.

Telephone: (202) 429-0137.

Los PADRES (Padres Asociados para Derechos, Religious, Educatios y Sociales).

Address: 2216 East 108th Street, Los Angeles, California 90040.

Telephone: (212) 569-5951.

Society of Hispanic Professional Engineers.

Address: 5400 East Olympic Boulevard, Suite 225, Los Angeles, California 90022.

Telephone: (213) 725-3970.

La Sociedad Panamena de Atlanta (Panamania Society).

Telephone: (404) 284-3434.

MUSEUMS AND RESEARCH CENTERS

Circulo De Arte Latinoamericano (Latin American Art Circle).

Part of the Twentieth Century Arts Society of the High Museum of Art, it sponsors artist and events at the museum and a Latin American film festival in November.

Telephone: (404) 733-4200.

Panamanian Chamber of Commerce.

Offers membership services between the southeastern United States and Panama for commercial relationships, trade missions to Panama to meet with business and government representatives, information center for trade and business development, cultural and educational exchanges, and networking opportunities for members meeting with distributors from Latin America through the Colon Free Zone.

Address: 260 Peachtree Street, N.W., Suite 1760, Atlanta, Georgia 30303.

La Sociedad Panamena De Atlanta (Panamania Society).

Hosts a Panamanian Independence Day celebration and scholarship drive in November to provide high school scholarships for high school seniors who are Panamanian natives or of Panamanian descent.

Telephone: (404) 284-3434.

SOURCES FOR ADDITIONAL STUDY

The Encyclopedia of World Faiths, edited by P. Bishop and M. Darton. New York: Facts on File, 1989.

Focus on Panama, Volume 10, edited by K. J. Jones. Panama: Focus, 1981.

Harvard Encyclopedia of American Ethnic Groups, edited by S. Thernstrom, A. Orlov, and O. Handlin. Cambridge, Massachusetts: Belknap Press of Harvard, 1980.

Lorimer, L. T., et al. *Lands and Peoples*. Danbury, Connecticut: Grolier, 1993.

Taylor, I. *Names and Their Histories: A Handbook of Historical Geography and Topographical Nomenclature*. Detroit, Michigan: Gale Research, 1969.

U.S. Bureau of the Census. *Panamanian Population in the United States: April 1990*. Washington, D.C., 1990.

Webb, S. C., et al. *A Mosaic: Hispanic People in the United States* (Report). New Orleans, Louisiana: Defense Equal Opportunity Management Institute, Topical Research Intern Program, 1991.

PERUVIAN AMERICANS

by
John Packel

Peruvians are attracted to the political and economic stability of the United States, the work opportunities, and the chance for their children to go to school and have a better future. A majority of these immigrants have family or acquaintances established in the United States who serve as intermediaries in their transition to a new culture.

OVERVIEW

The third-largest country in South America, Peru borders Ecuador and Colombia to the north, Brazil and Bolivia to the east, and Chile to the south. At 496,222 square miles, it is larger than Spain, Portugal, and France combined. In 1993 Peru had a population of over 22 million, and its capital, Lima, was home to fully one-third. This picturesque land is divided into three main geographic regions: the *costa,* along the South Pacific; the *sierra,* or highlands of the Andes mountains; and the *selva,* or jungle, in the east.

The *costa* is a thin, mostly barren strip of desert between the ocean and the mountains. Except for a few valleys where mountain rivers have brought enough water to make farming possible, the Peruvian desert is the driest in the world, with some areas never having seen even an inch of rain in recorded history. This region is prone to earthquakes, such as the one in 1970 that killed 66,000 people. Every few years in late December a warm Pacific current called *El Niño* (the Christ child) brings serious weather conditions that have disastrous effects on Peru's fishing industry and, in turn, its economy.

The upland plateau known as the *sierra* represents about one-fourth of Peru's land and holds a majority of the country's population. Its average elevation is 13,000 feet, making the air rather thin and cold, and ten peaks top 20,000 feet. (The highest is Mt. Huascarán at 22,334 feet.) Called the backbone of the continent, the Andes Mountains stretch from the Caribbean Sea all the way down the Pacific coast. Rivers flowing eastward to the Amazon Basin have cut scenic gorges as deep as 5,000 feet, at the bottom of which the climate becomes tropical. On Peru's southeast border with Bolivia, Lake Titicaca spans 3,200 square miles at an elevation of 12,507 feet, making it the world's highest navigable lake.

Peru's largest geographic area, the *selva* or *montaña* region, begins with the eastern slopes of the Andes and stretches eastward to include part of the Amazon River Basin's tropical rainforest. The lower elevations contain very dense vegetation and there are virtually no roads, with transportation taking place on the rivers.

HISTORY

Most anthropologists believe that the first inhabitants of the Americas crossed over from Asia during an ice age about 30,000 years ago across a land bridge connected to Alaska where the Bering Strait is now. Some of these people migrated down the Pacific coast and arrived in the Andean region about 20,000 years ago. Little is known about this time, but the first settlements were along the coast and relied mainly on fish and wild plants and animals. Agriculture probably began around 4000 B.C., and by 2000 B.C. civilization had advanced to the point where ceremonial centers were being built in coastal areas and the skill of making pottery had developed.

The early peoples of the *montaña* grew river valley plants such as peanuts, cucumbers, manioc, squash, beans, sweet potatoes, and chili peppers. Those in the tropical forests also grew cotton and plants used for medicinal purposes. The coastal peoples farmed the sea for fish, which they at times traded to those in the highlands for the grains and potatoes cultivated there. They probably did not use boats for fishing but rather cotton nets. Anchovy runs allowed for the collection of fresh fish which could by dried and ground into a meal that was preserved for months by covering it with earth. Beached whales provided the opportunity for an immediate feast, as the meat could not be stored.

Up to approximately 900 B.C. the Andean region saw a number of small states existing relatively independently. But advances in agriculture occasioned a growth in population and the first truly urban societies in Peru. These urban environments provided the structure and personnel required for a more specialized society. A measure of communication between neighbor societies helped provide the right conditions for expansion to full-fledged empires, and a number of these rose and fell prior to the Inca empire.

The first known of these empires was the Chavín, which expanded to encompass much of northern Peru and the central coast and lasted perhaps 1500 years. In a narrow Andean valley there are the remains of Chavín de Huántar, a city with extensive architecture. The inhabitants' stone carvings, pottery, textiles, and metalwork feature a god in the form of a fierce puma, or jaguar. The Chavín people's Akaro language was the predecessor of Aymará, which is still spoken by a small minority of Peru's population today. The Chavín were also adept at farming in the mountains and cultivated maize up to elevations of 9,000 feet.

Roughly contemporary with the Chavín was the Paracas civilization in the south. Their elaborate fabrics, woven on looms from cotton and alpaca wool, are known today because they were used in a type of mummification process. The coastal heat created oven-like conditions in the tombs and dried the contents out, thus preserving them.

The Nazca people ruled to the south of the Paracas for over a thousand years beginning about 500 B.C. They also produced wondrous fabrics, but their finest work was colorful pottery featuring birds, fish, fruit, and mythological creatures. The Nazca era is best known, however, for the mysterious lines cut into the earth by scraping away sun-scorched brown rock to reveal the yellow sand underneath. These enormous patterns, some of which are five miles long, form outlines of birds, spiders, monkeys, and other unidentifiable shapes. Scientists speculate that the shapes may have had something to do with astrological studies or an ancient calendar.

The Moche River valley, on Peru's north coast, was home to the Mochicas from about 100 to 750 A.D. They were gifted engineers and developed irrigation systems employing canals and aqueducts. The Mochicas were among the first to build roads in Peru; this facilitated the movement of their armies and made possible a messenger network in which runners carried messages marked on beads. They also pioneered the use of guano—the droppings of coastal birds—as fertilizer, a practice still in use today. They harvested the guano by paddling rafts out to off-shore islands.

The Tiahuanaco culture was based near Lake Titicaca on the high plains of present-day Bolivia at an elevation of about 15,000 feet. Its capital featured a pyramid-shaped fortress called the Acapana and courts that consisted of huge platforms made from stones weighing as much as 100 tons. In about 500 A.D. the Tiahuanacans extended their influence up the coast, bringing a religion that portrayed a weeping god with bands of tears around his eyes. With the fading of this culture came a return to the rural village life of disparate tribes.

This tribal period ended around 1000 A.D. with the ascendence of the Chimu kingdom, which had grown out of the Mochica empire and spanned nearly 600 miles of coast from present-day Lima to Ecuador. The Chimu capital, Chanchan, was a meticulously laid out 14-square-mile city with 40-foot clay walls featuring intricate, repeated patterns of birds, fish, and geometrical shapes. The primary building material was large adobe brick, and huge pyramids towered above the city. The Chimu people's advanced irrigation systems included reservoirs lined with stones.

THE INCAN EMPIRE

The Incas of Peru were one of the most advanced civilizations in pre-Columbian America, rivalled only by the Mayans and the Aztecs of Mesoamerica. We know more about the Incas than their Andean predecessors because of their fateful contact with the Spanish conquistadors in the sixteenth century. Though the Incas never developed a written language, a number of Spaniards chronicled the Incan oral history and legends. One of these was Garcilasa de la Vega, who was born in Cuzco in 1540 to an Inca princess and a Spanish conquistador and governor.

One legend told of the sun-god, Inti, creating a brother and sister, Manco Capac and Mama Ocllo, on an island in Lake Titicaca. He gave them a golden staff and told them to wander until the staff sunk into the ground, at which point they would show humans how to build villages, cultivate the land, and appreciate the sun-god's wisdom. The brother and sister wandered northward through the mountains to a beautiful river valley, where Manco Capac threw the staff and it disappeared into the ground. They named the place Cuzco, "the navel of the world," and the Inca nation was born.

Manco Capac was the first of eight Incan rulers from approximately 1200 to 1400 A.D. who built a small state centered in Cuzco. The expansion to a mighty empire began after 1430, when the powerful Chanca nation to the west of Cuzco attacked the Incas. Prince Yupanqui, who had been exiled to a distant llama ranch by his father, returned and defeated the Chancas. He became the ninth Incan ruler in 1438, renamed himself Pachacuti—"he who transforms the earth"—and set about unifying the Andean tribes into a powerful empire. He expanded the empire to the point where it reached from Lake Titicaca in the southeast to Lake Junin in the northwest.

Pachacuti and his successors would first send ambassadors to a rival tribe to try to persuade them to join the prosperous nation, which had storehouses to guarantee food in times of famine. If neither this nor the sight of the Inca army won the tribe over without a battle, the Incas used their superior weaponry. This included the bola, a series of thongs with stones attached which wrapped around an enemy's legs; rocks propelled by slings swung over the head; stone clubs and double-edged wooden swords; and protective gear such as helmets, shields, and huge spans of heavy cloth, which repelled slingstone attacks.

Pachacuti's son, Topa Inca, expanded the empire northward almost to what is now Quito, Ecuador, and then turned west toward the coast. He persuaded the Chimu people to join in the empire and then continued southward down the coast beyond Lima into the northern territories of present-day Chile, Bolivia, and Argentina. His son, Huayna Capac, became the eleventh Lord Inca in 1493 and pushed the boundaries of Inca control into the highlands of Ecuador. At this point the Inca empire was at its peak, extending 2,500 miles north to south and covering 380,000 square miles. Close to 12 million people, speaking 20 languages and comprising at least 100 distinct tribes, had been unified under the all-important Inca ruler.

When a new tribe was brought into the empire—whether peacefully or through force—Inca soldiers were stationed in the land, and then government officials, called *curacas*, arrived to take a census, divide the land according to the Inca labor structure, and teach the Quechua ("KESH-wah") language. Members of the nobility were brought back to Cuzco to learn the Incan customs, and the tribe's religious idols were taken hostage to dissuade the local people from rebelling. When conflicts arose the Incas were likely to remove the troublesome element of the local population and replace it with loyal Inca *mitimaes*, whose purpose was to set the proper example.

Essential to the Inca empire building was their vast network of roads, which grew to an amazing length of 10,000 miles. The Royal Road was carved out of the mountain walls in the high Andes. Cutting switchbacks to climb mountainsides and at times tunneling through the mountain itself, the road was as narrow as 3 feet in places but stretched from one end of the empire to the other. The coast had a companion highway, wider and straighter, that ran from the southern city of Arequipa to Tumbes in the north. Shorter roads connected these two main ones at periodic intervals spanning the empire. Rest houses called *tampus* dotted the highways and were spaced about a day's journey apart. Storage spaces were often nearby and contained supplies for the 25,000-member Incan army.

The Incas were also adept at engineering bridges over the many rivers and ravines of their mountainous land, as well as causeways over tracts of swampland. A number of the bridges continued to be used during the Spanish colonial era, including the 250-foot suspension bridge over the Apurimac River, which lasted from 1350 to 1890. The suspension bridges consisted of five braided cables, each a foot thick, made from the fibers of the maguey plant. Three of the cables formed the base of the walkway, the other two were the side rails, and all were attached to beams sunk into piles of rock and earth. Though they swayed in the wind, the bridges were crossed safely by people, pack-laden llamas, and later the Spaniards' horses. Other types of bridges included pontoons of reed boats strapped together and baskets suspended from cables which ferried people and supplies across a ravine.

These roads and bridges were used not only by the army and by pedestrians granted permission by the government, but also by those performing a function essential to maintaining the empire—the messengers known as *chasquis*. These runners carried oral messages, small packages, or *quipus* (Incan counting devices made from strings with a series of knots in them) from village to village and from the capital to all parts of the empire. Every mile or two there were two huts, one on either side of the road, which housed runners who would continue the relay on to the next station. This communication system could transmit a message 420 miles from Lima to Cuzco in just three days. This speed was critical for quelling rebellions by conquered peoples.

Also important for Incan military success was their network of fortresses, or *pucaras*. Constructed on hilltops with views of major valleys, the *pucaras* had barracks, houses, reservoirs, and a sun temple. When an enemy tribe approached, the Incas of a nearby city would flee to the fortress for protection. Machu Picchu, the most famous of these *pucaras*, was never found by the Spanish and was only rediscovered by modern explorers in 1911. Machu Picchu had terraces for farming, palaces, and an aqueduct that carried in water from a spring a mile away and channeled it down a series of 16 stone basins. Because the Incas did not use cement to hold their structures together the stones had to be cut with such precision that they would fit together snugly—so close, in fact, that even today a knife blade cannot penetrate the spaces between them.

The Incas relied on a high degree of social stratification and specialization to accomplish their military and organizational feats. Believed to be a direct descendant of the sun, the king was a divine ruler, and he had two classes of nobility serving him. The "Incas by birth," who could claim decent from Manco Capac, made up the Incas' advisory Council of Nobles and were governors and administrators of the empire's provinces. The lower "Incas by privilege" held honorary titles and served as *curacas* responsible for a specific number of people. Military heroes and the leaders of vanquished tribes often had this status conferred upon them by the ruling Inca.

Even before the time of the Incas, the peoples of the Andean highlands had lived and farmed in small groups of related families called *ayllus*. The Incas built on this basic social unit by dividing the people into groups of ten such families. Each group had a leader who, along with nine others like him, reported to one *curaca*. Thus each *curaca* was responsible for 100 families. Ten of these government officials reported in turn to a higher official, and so on in expanding factors of ten up to the regional governors, who sat on the Inca's council.

The *curacas* took a yearly census of the people under their administration and grouped them into 12 labor units according to their age and sex. Boys from age nine to 16 were shepherds, for example, while nine- to 12-year-old girls collected the plants and herbs that were used to make medicines and dyes for clothing. Though the Incas never developed an actual written language, they kept account of this detailed labor system through a device called the *quipu*. The *quipu* had strings of varying thickness and color connected by one main thicker string. Special accountants called *quipucamayocs* made knots in the strings in units of ten and recorded information ranging from population, crop, and herd sizes to birth and death dates.

The Incas also did not have a monetary system, so the people supported the government directly through two kinds of work. First, Incans spent a certain number of days each year in one type of public service, such as working on roads and bridges, mining gold and silver, serving in the army, or running messages. Second, all the agricultural produce was divided between four recipients: the sun temples and priests; the ruler and his government; those who could not work, such as the old, the infirm, and those serving in the army; and finally the *ayllu*. The local *curaca* was responsible for reapportioning an *ayllu*'s land each year, giving more to a family with a new baby and a whole strip (measuring approximately 150 feet by 300 feet) to a newly married couple. These Inca farmers continued the ancient practice of cultivating the mountainsides by building step-like terraces and improved them with irrigation systems consisting of aqueducts, canals, and tunnels. Elevations above 12,000 feet were home to the llama and alpaca herds, which were also divided into four portions.

Judging from their descendants who live in the Andean highlands today, the Incas were short in stature—the men being about five feet tall and the women a few inches shorter—and stocky, with expanded lungs that allowed them to take in more air to compensate for the lack of oxygen at high altitudes. They had dark eyes and straight black hair, high cheekbones, and copper-colored skin. Their clothes were woven from the wool of the llama or alpaca or from coastal cotton. While the nobility wore fancier dress often adorned with gold and silver, peasant clothing was fairly plain and simple except for more colorful outfits reserved for festivals. Men wore loincloths with woolen belts, sleeveless tunics called *uncus*, and cloaks or ponchos of alpaca wool. Women wore tunics that reached their ankles and covered them with shawls or cloaks fastened with a long pin called a *topu*. Both sexes went barefoot or wore sandals made of straw, cloth, or leather.

The Incas worshiped a number of gods, including Viracocha, the creator, Inti, the sun-god, and others representing natural phenomena such as thunder. Their calendar, based on observations of the sun, had 12 months, each with three ten-day weeks, and five days left over for religious festivals honoring the sun and the seasons. Because they believed sickness to be caused by bad spirits or the ill will of other tribes, the Incas used prayers, offerings, and magic to supplement their array of medicines, which included belladonna for eye ailments and small amounts of cocaine from the coca plant as a pain reliever.

In 1525, the Inca Huayna Capac died in an epidemic that may have been smallpox or the measles, diseases introduced by the Spanish for which the native population had no immunity. Because the ruler had failed to designate his successor, two of his sons shared the role for a time—Atahualpa ruling the north from Quito and Huáscar the south from Cuzco. But soon tensions broke out between the two and Atahualpa sent his father's army against Huáscar, who was defeated and later killed. This civil war lasted a number of years and severely weakened the empire at an inopportune time, for reports of strange white-faced, bearded men in "sea houses" were brought to the Inca, who thought it best to ignore them and hope they would go away.

THE SPANISH CONQUEST

In May of 1532, Francisco Pizarro, a Spaniard seeking to conquer land and plunder gold for himself and his king, landed near the coastal city of Tumbes with a force of 180 cavalrymen and foot soldiers. He was aware of the civil war and set out toward the mountain city of Cajamarca, where Atahualpa and 30,000 Incas waited. Apparently, the Inca thought that the foreigners were there to surrender. But when Atahualpa furiously rejected a Spanish priest's offer of a prayerbook and an explanation that Spain now ruled the land, a massacre ensued in which the Spaniards used crossbows, cannons, and muskets to slaughter 2,000 Incas and take their leader prisoner.

Atahualpa tried to ransom himself with the promise of enough gold and silver to fill his cell. For two months works of art made of the precious metals poured in from the surrounding areas and were melted into gold bars, 20 percent going to King Charles I and the remainder to Pizarro and his men. This did not help Atahualpa or the Incas, however, because the invaders feared a rebellion and thought it safer to have the ruler burned at the stake. Atahualpa objected that this would deprive him of proper burial and an afterlife, and so he was given the option of being baptized a Christian and then strangled. The last king of the majestic Incan empire was killed in this manner on August 29, 1533. For a number of years Huáscar's half-brother and his sons battled the Spanish fruitlessly; the last resistor, Topa Amaru, was executed in Cuzco in 1572.

Spain ruled Peru as a viceroyalty for nearly 300 years after the conquest and regarded it more or less as a huge mine that existed to fill the crown's coffers. The Spaniards felt that as a superior culture their customs and particularly the church brought civilized society to the natives. The political and economic system they instituted to carry out their aims, called *encomienda*, granted soldiers and colonists land and mining permits, as well as the slave labor of the natives. Living and working conditions for the native Peruvians on the farms and especially in the mines were horrendous: hard labor, malnutrition (exacerbated by the Spaniards' introduction of European crops and the elimination of many native ones), and especially diseases wiped out an estimated 90 percent of the pre-conquest native population within a century.

During this colonial period Spain passed legislation attempting to protect the native population, but it was virtually ineffectual. Practices specifically outlawed—such as debt peonage, where subjects are trapped in an unending cycle of indebtedness for necessities of life which cannot be overcome through their labor—were in reality widespread. The influx of Spaniards taking advantage of these opportunities, as well as 100,000 African slaves, became part of a highly stratified society with European-born Spaniards at the top, Peruvian-born Spaniards (Creoles) next, and the urban working poor, the black slaves, and the indigenous population at the bottom.

In 1780 a descendant of the last Inca took the name Tupac Amaru and led a rebellion by the indigenous population. The rebellion began to gain wider support by condemning the corruption of colonial officials, but promptly lost it with indiscriminate attacks on Spaniards and Creoles. Ultimately, the campaign for independence resulted from conditions outside Peru and had to be led by outsiders. When Napoleon invaded Spain and imprisoned the king in 1808, the vacuum of authority allowed the Creoles in the colonial capitals set up autonomous regimes. Then between 1820 and 1824, José de San Martín and Simón de Bolívar, two generals who had liberated Argentina, Chile, Venezuela, and Colombia from

Spanish rule, completed the process by adding Peru to the list. Elected president-for-life, Bolívar attempted to modernize the country by cutting taxes, funding schools, and lifting many of the worst abuses against the indigenous population, but conservative Creole opposition forced him to leave after only two years.

INDEPENDENCE AND ECONOMIC INSTABILITY

After two decades of chaos, including wars lost to Bolivia, Colombia, and Chile, General Ramón Castilla brought a measure of stability and prosperity to Peru during his control of the country from 1845 to 1862. He exploited the economic benefits of guano, a bird dung collected from islands off the coast of Peru and sold to Europe for fertilizer, as well as desert deposits of sodium nitrate, which was used to make munitions and fertilizer. The general also organized a public school system, built the country's first railroad, ended the tribute tax paid by indigenous people, and abolished slavery, which led to the importation of Chinese laborers.

Peru's defeat by Chile in the War of the Pacific (1879-1883), fought over lands with rich nitrate deposits, was a humiliating experience that led many to call for an improvement in the lot of indigenous Peruvians so that they might contribute more fully to the society. The late nineteenth and early twentieth centuries showed evidence of efforts to modernize the society and economy. Public administration was improved, the armed forces were professionalized, public education was fostered, and modern labor legislation was enacted. These contributed to the conditions that encouraged foreign investment capital in the burgeoning sugar, cotton, copper, and rubber industries. This, in turn, created an urban industrial proletariat and strengthened the middle class.

In the 1930s the Great Depression had a crippling effect on the Peruvian economy as export markets collapsed and foreign loans dried up. This situation seems to have contributed to the rise of a political movement known as the American Popular Revolutionary Alliance (APRA), which was anti-communist but borrowed from the ideologies of Marxism and Italian fascism and advocated agrarian reform, the nationalization of industry, and opposition to U.S. imperialism. APRA's leader, the formerly exiled student organizer Víctor Raúl Haya de la Torre, never won the presidency, but the party maintained a major presence in the political scene for over 40 years, both through bloody conflicts with the armed forces and through congressional coalitions in the years APRA was not banned.

The Peruvian military had long played a large role in the state, either through generals assuming the presidency or by influencing elections. In 1962, for example, a slight plurality by APRA brought a nullification of the results and the election of Fernando Belaúnde Terry a year later. From 1968 to 1975 General Juan Velasco Alvarado and the Revolutionary Government of the Armed Forces ruled in an attempt to create a new and prosperous Peru that was "neither capitalist nor communist." The general forged ties with socialist countries and made Peru a voice for third world interests. He nationalized most of the country's banks, its railroads and utilities, and many foreign corporations.

Central to this effort to control the economy and increase social justice was Velasco's land reform, which was among the most extensive in Latin America. Ninety percent of Peru's farmland had been owned by a landed aristocracy comprising just two percent of the population, so the administration appropriated 25 million acres of this land and distributed it to worker-owned cooperatives and individual families. This failed to achieve the far-ranging effects hoped, however, in part because of the insufficient amount of arable land relative to the large number of people, and also because of the absence of policies giving the poor a greater share of the benefits.

Civilian rule returned with the reelection of Belaúnde Terry in 1980 after a constituent assembly had drawn up a new constitution. The presidency was transferred peacefully in 1985 to Alan García Perez of the APRA and again in 1990 to Alberto Fujimori, a Peruvian university professor of Japanese decent who won in a run-off against the novelist Mario Vargas Llosa. Peru's poor economic performance, including inflation that soared as high as 2800 percent annually, continued to wreak social havoc. After a period of accepting austerity measures as conditions for aid from the International Monetary Fund, under García, Peru declared a severe reduction in the debt payments it would make to foreign investors and nationalized an American oil company, which resulted in a cut-off of needed credit and U.S. aid.

In addition to these economic woes, Peru suffered from social disruption caused by leftist terrorist groups and the governmental response to them. A guerrilla organization founded by university professor Carlos Abimael Guzmán Reynoso and guided by the principles of the Chinese dictator Mao Zedong, the *Sendero Luminoso* (Shining Path), specialized in assassination and the use of violent intimidation against the peasants, such as cutting off their fingers to prevent them from voting. In a period of less than 20 years, 30,000 people were killed. The Tupac Amarú movement was another group carrying out equally vicious attacks in Peru's urban areas. The coca harvests, which supplied much of the United States' huge cocaine market, also brought violence as U.S. pressure to destroy crops led to terrorist attacks on local officials by those profiting from the drug trade. In the midst of these social woes, the country's pride received a boost in 1981 when the United Nations elected a Peruvian, Javier Pérez de Cuellar, to a five-year term as Secretary General.

In 1992 President Fujimori responded to these economic and social crises by dissolving the congress and judiciary and consolidating power in a Government of Emergency and National Reconstruction, while promising to submit a revised constitution to a referendum and hold elections at some point in the future. Referred to as an *autogolpe*, or self-coup, Fujimori's takeover also involved a suspension of civil liberties. These bold moves were well-received by the public, however, and his popularity increased further when Sendero leader Guzmán was captured and the movement's stronghold on certain rural areas, such as Ayacucho, was broken. As of 1994 Fujimori was attempting to improve Peru's standing with international creditors and lending agencies and to lure foreign investment back to the country, but the task remained a daunting one.

ACCULTURATION AND ASSIMILATION

Peruvians began immigrating to the United States in small numbers early in the twentieth century, but the vast majority have come since World War II and especially in the last 20 years (when the United States has been the destination for more Peruvians than any other country). Official statistics show a Peruvian population of 162,000 in 1990, but other estimates put the number beyond 300,000. Some of the disparity may have to do with illegal immigrants who were not counted in the former number. It is more

clear where the immigrants have settled. The largest concentration, over 80,000, reside in the New York metropolitan area—particularly in Paterson, New Jersey, and in the New York City borough of Queens. Peruvians are also clustered around the cities of Miami, Los Angeles, Houston, Chicago, and Washington, D.C.

Peru's social and economic crises are at the root of internal migration from rural areas to the cities, as well as immigration to the United States. Unemployment rates of over 50 percent have left many without a means to earn the basic necessities of life, and others are chronically underemployed. An unstable political climate and especially political violence by terrorist groups have caused many to flee. Peruvians are attracted to the political and economic stability of the United States, the work opportunities, and the chance for their children to go to school and have a better future. A majority of these immigrants have family or acquaintances established in the United States who serve as intermediaries in their transition to a new culture.

In addition to the family, there are social institutions that aid the Peruvians' assimilation to American culture. The Catholic church is important to newly arrived Peruvians because of its familiarity, the services it often extends in terms of finding work and applying for citizenship, and the opportunity it affords for meeting other Peruvians, including those of a higher social class. Also important is the broader Latino community. Peruvians benefit from sharing a language and many cultural traits with other more established groups. The travel, legal, and labor services that already exist in these communities assist newer immigrants. State social service programs are also available to the most indigent.

Peruvians from the upper class have benefitted economically from their immigration to the United States because on the whole they have been able to transfer their capital and business expertise. They range from owners of factories and large stores to accountants for major banks and corporations to agro-industrial managers.

However, this group has faced major obstacles to its assimilation. Although they are well off financially, these Peruvians do not have the economic or particularly the political power they had in Peru. Yet, because of their background, they tend not to identify with the middle-class Americans whose status they share. Many try to compensate by joining relatively exclusive associations that have social gatherings for holidays and weddings.

Middle-class Peruvian immigrants did not arrive in large numbers until the 1970s, when the exodus was led by doctors and engineers. Assimilation has been relatively easy for this group, and consequently they have been labelled the "children of success." Like those from the upper class, they had been familiar with American cultural practices before their arrival. The difference was that these middle-class Peruvians did not lose any prerogatives or privileges. This group tends to maintain a stronger cultural and religious identity through participation in church and other social activities.

Peru's lower classes were the last to take advantage of the opportunities in America and have immigrated in increasing numbers since the mid-1980s. These immigrants have come from positions ranging from low-level bureaucrats to manual laborers. They have had the most difficulty assimilating on account of their tendency to lack formal education, to have a greater difficulty learning English, and to cling more tightly to their home culture. They generally live in areas of urban poverty and have a lot of pressure to send money back to families in Peru. Many in this group have only recently made the transition from rural to urban life in Peru, where they have learned or improved their Spanish in order to come here.

HEALTH AND MENTAL HEALTH ISSUES

As is the case with the nation's standard of living in general, there is a great disparity between rural and urban health care in Peru. Most health services are located in the cities; residents of Lima have the best access to health care and about 60 percent of the country's hospital beds. Only about one-third of the rural population sees a doctor even once a year. Part of this is owed to the fact that many in Peru's indigenous population are superstitious and reluctant to use Western medicine, preferring instead home remedies and in some cases even ritual magic. Respiratory diseases are common, and many diseases are spread through parasites and infection. The infant mortality rate in Peru is very high—84 per 1,000 live births—and the life expectancy of 61 for men and 65 for women is low.

A major medical catastrophe struck Peru in 1991 when an epidemic of cholera broke out. A result of dismal or nonexistent sanitation systems that left the vast majority of rural residents without clean drinking water, the cholera spread quickly to over 50,000 people and killed hundreds. Health officials estimate that only five percent of those living in rural areas have access to potable water, and in the cities the figure is a still dangerous 80 percent.

LANGUAGE

Spanish has been Peru's official language since the Spanish conquest. Approximately 80 percent of all Peruvians speak Spanish today, including some who also speak one of the indigenous languages, Quechua ("KESH-wah") or Aymará. A language that grew out of the Latin brought to Spain by conquering Romans, Spanish has a vocabulary and structure similar to other Romance languages, such as French and especially Italian. Its alphabet generally overlaps with that of English and contains 28 letters: "k" and "w" occur only in words of foreign origin, and additional letters are "ch" (as in "chest"), "ll" (generally pronounced like the English "y"), "ñ" (like the "ny" in "canyon," which comes from the Spanish *cañón*), and "rr" (a rolled "r" sound). The "b" and "v" are interchangeable in Spanish and are a bit softer than an English "b." The "h" is silent, and the "d" can have a soft "th" sound within a word. Spanish vowels have one primary sound, making spelling and pronunciation on sight much easier than in English: "i" (as in "feet"), "e" (as in "they"), "a" (as in "hot"), "o" (as in "low"), "u" (as in "rude"). Words ending in a vowel, "n" or "s" are accented on the next-to-last syllable, those ending in other consonants have stress on the last syllable, and any exceptions require an accent mark.

Some common greetings and expressions include the following: *hola*—hello; *buenos días*—hello, good day; *buenas tardes*—good afternoon; *buenas noches*—good night; *como está usted*—how are you?; *adiós*—good-bye; *hasta mañana*—good-bye (literally "until tomorrow"); *hasta luego*—good-bye (literally "until later"); *por favor*—please; *grácias*—thank you; *feliz navidad*—Merry Christmas.

When San Martín issued proclamations declaring Peru's independence in 1821, he used both Spanish and Quechua (the Incan language, also known as Runasimi) and made both official languages. Bolívar, however, did not favor Quechua, and thereafter Peruvian governments ignored the language, hoping it would die out. This changed in 1975 when, in an effort to promote cultural pride among the indigenous population as a means to increasing their stake in Peruvian society, the military government declared Quechua an official language along with Spanish. Today Quechua is the most widely spoken of any Native American language, with perhaps seven million speakers in South America. Though there is a social stigma attached to the language because virtually all of its Peruvian speakers are members of the underclass, still the two million Peruvian highlanders who speak only Quechua are proud of their linguistic and cultural heritage and have resisted the forces of Europeanization.

These are a few Quechua expressions: *allillanchu* ("ah-yee-YAN-choo")—how are you?; *allinmi* ("ah-YEEN-me")—I'm fine; *maymantam* ("my-MON-tom")—where are you from?; *imatam sutiyki* ("ee-MAH-tom soo-TEE-kee")—what is your name? The English word "jerky" comes from the Quechua word for dried meat, *charki*, and the Spanish coca plant, which is the source of cocaine, gets its name from the Quechua word *kuka*.

A smaller number of Peru's indigenous highlanders, probably about half a million, speak Aymará, the language of a tribe conquered by the Incas. Also, in the rainforests of eastern Peru the 40 or so tribes speak a number of ancient tribal languages.

FAMILY AND COMMUNITY DYNAMICS

Approximately 45 percent of Peruvians today are descendants of Peru's indigenous population, often referred to as Indian, while about 43 percent are mestizos, people of mixed indigenous and Spanish heritage. Another ten percent are of unmixed European ancestry, almost all Spanish. The blacks who are descendants of the slaves from Africa, and those whose ancestors were imported Chinese and Japanese laborers, together make up less than two percent of the population.

Spanish colonization left a legacy of social stratification that is for the most part unbroken today. Traditionally, the small Spanish upper class ruled the native and mestizo underclass. In the twentieth century a middle class of whites and some mestizos has developed, but most mestizos and almost all of the indigenous population belong to the underclass.

About half of Peru's whites belong to the elite class that runs the country's political and economic affairs. They speak Spanish and dress much like their counterparts in the rest of the Western world. Family ties are particularly important for this group because they help maintain their powerful status in the society. Whites seldom associate with people from other classes, and their children usually marry into other upper-class families. Most of these families live in the prosperous areas of Lima and the other major cities. Most of Peru's upper- and middle-class families have a varied diet consisting of meat, fish, poultry, vegetables, and cereal products. Main dishes are heavily seasoned with onions and hot peppers. Most main dishes are accompanied by rice, potatoes, and bread.

The mestizos also generally speak Spanish and dress according to Western styles. They are the group that has had the closest relations with the ruling elite, such as when they would be hired by the whites to supervise native workers in mines or on plantations. As the middle class has grown the mestizos have found other avenues for advancement, such as going to college and becoming involved in government, business, the military, and various other professions. These opportunities have not been enough, however, to raise a majority out of the underclass.

Peru's indigenous population lives predominately in the rural highlands, the coast, and the *selva*. The people are nearly all poor and lack formal education. They subsist mainly through farming and cling tenaciously to their culture. While the young often wear Western-style clothing, the older Peruvians wear more traditional handwoven garments such as ponchos and sandals. Traditional costumes are increasingly saved for special ceremonial occasions. Rural Peruvians live mainly by agriculture. On the Pacific Coast they grow rice, cotton, sugar cane, and barley for sale. Maize and rice are the food crops along with grapes, olives, and oranges. The coastal dwellers also catch pilchard and white fish. In the highlands the staple crops are maize, potatoes, barley, and wheat. The diet of the poorest Peruvians is a fairly monotonous one and often lacks complete nutritional value—potatoes, beans, corn, squash, wheat or barley soups, and occasionally fish. The highland population frequently chews the leaves of the coca plant to suppress appetite and fatigue.

All social classes and ethnicities in Peru place a great deal of emphasis on family, often extending it to include distant relatives and godparents. Frequently chosen from a superior social class, godparents are sponsors at baptisms and other rites of passage, and this relationship maintains bonds of mutual assistance between the sponsors and the child's family. Peruvian social life often revolves around the extended family, especially among the indigenous Peruvians, who may have few important social ties beyond the family. The extended family commonly serves an economic function, as well, with members working together and pooling their resources. The nuclear family tends to be male dominated, and fathers have great authority over the children even into adulthood.

Though the indigenous families tend to be less patriarchal than white and mestizo families, there, too, the husbands dominate the household. Particularly in the shantytowns around the large urban centers, known as the *pueblos jóvenes* (young towns), harsh economic conditions result in mestizo families that are more fragile than elsewhere. Many marriages among this population consist of consensual unions rather than legal marriages.

EDUCATION

Peru has made great strides this century in educating its people. Education's share of the national budget rose from three percent in 1900 to over 30 percent in the 1960s, and school enrollment increased at double the rate of population growth. The literacy rate of those over 15 years of age is 87 percent, one of the highest in Latin America. Education is free and compulsory between the ages of six and 15. However, the vast majority of the uneducated are those in rural areas where there often are not enough schools and teachers. Great disparities also exist between the sexes in terms of the quality and number of years of education. Most middle- and upper-class students attend private schools in the cities.

Peru has more than 30 national universities, though most of them are relatively new and of lesser quality. They also tend to be very political, engendering student radicals on campus. However, San Marcos University in Lima is the country's most prestigious public university and South America's oldest, having been chartered in 1551. The National Engineering University, the National Agrarian University, and the Superior School for Business Administration are also highly regarded. The elite sectors of society tend to favor private universities, such as Lima's Catholic University, because they are less political. Peru's important research centers include the Institute of the Sea and the International Potato Center.

RELIGION

Peru's constitution guarantees freedom of religion. About 95 percent of Peru's population is at least nominally Roman Catholic, a legacy of the church's deep-rooted involvement in the country's affairs since the Spanish conquest. The state supports the church through an annual grant, and the president is involved in the selection of its hierarchy. There are also small numbers of Protestants, Jews, and Buddhists; they comprise only about one percent of the population.

There is a wide range of religious commitment, and women tend to be far more devout than men. Agnosticism is common in the cities, especially among intellectuals. Despite this, Catholicism is firmly woven into Peruvian culture. The Catholic religion is taught in public schools throughout the country, and fiestas corresponding to Church holidays are among the most important social events of the year, even in larger cities. A list of national holidays reveals religion's prominence: New Year's Day (January 1), Holy Thursday and Good Friday (variable), Labor Day (May 1), Day of the Peasant (June 24), St. Peter and St. Paul's Day (June 29), Independence Day (July 28 and 29), St. Rose of Lima, patroness of Peru (August 30), Battle of Anzamos (October 8), All Saints' Day (November 1), Immaculate Conception (December 8), and Christmas Day (December 25).

While middle-class Peruvians tend to be strict in their religious beliefs and adherence to ritual, farther down the social scale one finds an increasing tendency to blend elements of superstition, folk religion (including the worship of Incan gods), and magic with formal Catholicism. Many of the beliefs and practices of ancient Peru persist in this form. A number of local shrines and icons that have survived earthquakes or other natural disasters are revered as evidence of miracles or divine intervention.

EMPLOYMENT AND ECONOMIC TRADITIONS

Peru's economy is hampered by the inefficiency and obsolescence of many of its structures. In each of the major areas of the economy there are a few productive modern enterprises outnumbered by inefficient traditional counterparts. The modern units of the economy employ about one-third of the work force but are responsible for about two-thirds of the nation's income. The modern sectors also support Peru's politically powerful middle class and its militant labor unions. Another duality in the economy exists between low-income subsistence agriculture in the sierra, and the wealth produced on the large, productive farms of the coast, in off-shore fisheries, and in the city of Lima. Few jobs are available to the more than 200,000 people who enter Peru's work force each year, with the result that fewer than half of the country's workers are fully employed.

Approximately 42 percent of the Peruvian work force is employed in agriculture, fishing, or forestry, though these sectors represent only 14 percent of the national income. Manufacturing, mining, and construction employ 18 percent of workers and generate 38 percent of the gross national product. The service sector (which includes Lima's 200,000 street vendors) employs 40 percent of Peru's workers and contributes 48 percent of the nation's income.

Peru is a net exporter of raw materials and unfinished products and a net importer of manufactured products. It also has to import much of its food because domestic production is inadequate and because transportation is severely limited by the small percentage of roads that are paved. The leading exports are petroleum, copper, silver, zinc, lead, fishmeal, and coffee. Cocaine exports are not part of official figures, but they are estimated to bring in as much foreign currency—almost all U.S. dollars—as petroleum and copper combined. The United States is Peru's largest trading partner, buying one-third of its legal exports and supplying about 40 percent of its imported goods. Japan and Germany are also major trading partners.

POLITICS AND GOVERNMENT

Peru's 1979 constitution was the first in its history to extend the right to vote to all citizens aged 18 and over without any literacy requirement, and voting was made obligatory up to age 60. The people elect the president and two vice-presidents to five-year terms, though the president may not be re-elected to a consecutive term. Since 1985 a presidential candidate must get at least 50 percent of the vote or else a run-off ensues between the top three candidates. The president heads the executive department, which carries out government operations through a cabinet led by a presidentially appointed premier.

The Peruvian legislature is made up of a 60-member Senate and a 180-member Chamber of Deputies, all of whom are elected to five-year terms concurrent with the president's. The congress convenes twice a year, from April 1 to May 31 and from July 27 to December 15, and either house may initiate legislation. The president reviews legislation but has no veto power. The judicial branch consists of judges appointed by the president to terms that end at age 70. The 16 justices of Peru's highest court, the Supreme Court in Lima, are selected by the president from a list submitted by the National Justice Council.

Peru's governments have been highly centralized since Incan times, and this is still true today. There are 24 political departments plus the constitutional province of Callao. Each department is divided into provinces, which are further divided into districts. The departments and provinces are headed by prefects appointed by the president to carry out the policies dictated by the central government. The people elect local councils to govern their districts and municipalities.

At the end of 1994 President Alberto Fujimori still ruled with the virtually dictatorial powers assumed in his 1992 presidential coup, in which he suspended the congress and judiciary, ostensibly to deal more forcefully with Peru's economic and political instability. Elections were scheduled for 1995 to determine the status of the constitution and the future of the country.

INDIVIDUAL AND GROUP CONTRIBUTIONS

Peruvian Americans have contributed to American society in various ways—from the large numbers of doctors and other medical specialists, to those in education and business, to those who provide manual labor or child care. The following is a sample of Peruvian Americans who have achieved recognition in their field.

ARTS

Carlos Llerena Aguirre (1952-) is an artist and educator born in Arequipa, Peru. He received a bachelor of arts degree from the School of Visual Arts in New York City in 1979, a master's from Hunter College in 1982, and a master's of fine arts from the University of Illinois in 1994. He was an instructor at the School of Visual Arts and has been an associate professor at the University of Illinois since 1989. He is a member of the Society of Newspaper Designers and has had exhibitions of his woodcuts and engravings in Urbana, Illinois, Lima, Norway, and London.

Isaac Goldenberg (1945-) is a poet and novelist living in New York City. Born in Peru, he is the co-director of the Instituto de Escritores Latinoamerican in New York as well as the Latin American book fair. Isaac was a New York State Council of the Arts Writer in Residence in 1987-1988. His books include *La Vida Contado* (1992), *Tiempo al Tiempo* (1984), and *La Vida a Plazos de Jacobo Lerner* (1980).

Luís John Kong (1956-) maintains various roles as poet, arts administrator, and TV and radio producer. Born in Pisco, Peru, he attended college in California, receiving a B.A. in English and biol-

ogy from Sonoma State University in 1982. He directed the university's intercultural center and was a producer/programmer for a bilingual public radio program. Most recently Kong has served as poet, teacher, and consultant for the California Poets in the Schools program. He received the Corporation for Public Broadcasting Silver Award for his production "En Camino" in 1989.

BUSINESS

Virginia Patricia Rebata (1953-) is a business executive with the Marriott Corporation. Born in Lima, she graduated from the University of California, Berkeley, with a B.A. in 1975 and received an M.P.A. from California State University, Hayward, in 1980. Virginia served as youth employment services director for the San Mateo (California) County Board of Education before going to work for Marriott as director of Human Resource Field Programs and Services in 1992. She established the first English as a Second Language program for Hispanics at Marriott's headquarters and received the National Alliance for Business President's Award in 1989.

GOVERNMENT AND POLITICS

Maria Azucena Arbulu (1956-) is an official in the Michigan state government. She was born in Pueblo, Colorado, and got her B.A. at Oberlin in 1978 and her M.A. in 1984 at the American Graduate School of International Management. She worked for the Detroit Board of Education and the Motorola Corporation before taking a position as international trade specialist with the state of Michigan. She now serves as the state's trade officer for Canadian operations.

JOURNALISM

Pedro M. Valdivieso (1932-) is the editor of the paper *Actualidad* in Los Angeles. He was born in Piura, Peru, and studied journalism and public relations at San Marcos University and Lima University, respectively. He edited newspapers in Lima before moving to the United States and editing *Noticias del Mundo* (Los Angeles) and *El Diario de Los Angeles*. Valdivieso has reported for Channel 34 TV in Los Angeles and is a member of the Association of Journalists in the Spanish Language and the Federation of Journalists from Peru.

LIBRARY SCIENCE

César Rodríguez (1945-) is a university librarian born in Callao, Peru. He received a B.A. from Queens College in New York City in 1970 and an M.A. from Columbia University in 1983. He was the Yale University Social Science Library's acquisition librarian from 1976 to 1986, after which he became the curator of the library's Latin American collection. Rodríguez is a member of the Latin American Studies Association and a contributor to a number of Latin American bibliographies. He served as a corporal in the U.S. Marine Corps in Vietnam from 1965 to 1969 and received three medals.

MEDICINE AND HEALTH

Graciela Solís Alarcón (1942-) is a physician and educator originally from Chachapoyas, Peru. She earned her M.D. in Peru in 1967 and an M.P.H. from Johns Hopkins University in 1972. She did her residency in Baltimore and in Peru and has been a professor at the University of Alabama at Birmingham since 1980. She is a member of the American College of Rheumatology and the American College of Physicians and has authored a number of articles in her field.

Carlos Castaneda (sometimes Castañeda) is perhaps the best known Peruvian American. While attempting a thesis on medicinal plants for the University of California, Los Angeles, in the late 1960s, he met a Yaqui (Mexican) *brujo*, or medicine man, living in Arizona and became heavily influenced by his way of life. Carlos began a series of best-selling books based on these experiences, beginning with *The Teachings of Don Juan: A Yaqui Way of Knowledge* in 1976. The books relate a hallucinogen-induced search for a non-rational reality and an attempt to become a Yaqui warrior. The author considered them anthropological field studies, and indeed they served as his master's and doctoral theses, though critics within the field of anthropology say they are more properly regarded as fiction. While Castaneda seems to be purposely elusive regarding his biographical details, he is thought to have been born in Cajamarca, Peru, in 1925. He received his B.A., M.A., and Ph.D. from UCLA in 1962, 1964, and 1973, respectively.

SCIENCE

Jaime A. Fernandez-Baca (1954-) is a physicist at the Oak Ridge National Laboratory. He earned his B.S. in Lima in 1977 before coming to the United States for a M.Sc. and Ph.D. at the University of Maryland (1982 and 1986). Fernandez-Baca has done his research at the Instituto de Energia Nuclear in Peru and at the University of Maryland. He was awarded a fellowship by the International Atomic Energy Agency in 1977 and has published numerous technical articles.

MEDIA

PRINT

Chasqui.

A weekly publication in Spanish with 8,000 subscribers, half in New York City and half in New Jersey. It reports on political events in Peru and on Peruvian social and political concerns in the New York area.

Address: 44-17 28th Avenue, Suite 3F, Long Island, New York 11103.

Telephone: (718) 728-8274.

El Diario La Prensa.

Founded in 1913, this Spanish-language daily has a circulation of 67,000 and includes coverage of Peru in its international pages.

Address: 143 Varick Street, New York, New York 10013.

Telephone: (212) 807-4600.

El Heraldo.

This Spanish-language daily with coverage of Peru was founded in 1975 and has a circulation of 20,000.

Address: 70 East Lake Street, Suite 520, Chicago, Illinois 60601.

Telephone: (312) 201-8488.

El Nuevo Herald.

This Spanish-language daily includes Peru in its coverage of South America. It was founded in 1976 and has a circulation of 98,000.

Address: 1 Herald Plaza, Miami, Florida 33132.

Telephone: (305) 376-3535.

RADIO

WADO-AM (1280).

"Perú Cerca de Ti" (Peru Near You), a magazine type program featuring music, news, and tourism information related to Peru, airs on Saturdays from 7:00 p.m. to 8:00 p.m.

Address: 277 Paterson Plank Road, Carlstadt, New Jersey 07072.

Telephone: (201) 438-4171.

TELEVISION

"Perú Ahora" (Peru Now), U.S. Cable of Paterson (New Jersey).
Airs Tuesday nights from 10:00 p.m. to 10:30 p.m. It has features on Peruvian culture and political events as well as items of interest to the local Peruvian community.

Address: 137 Ellison Street, Peterson, New Jersey 07505.
Telephone: (201) 279-6660.

"Perú Aquí" (Peru Here), Queens Cable Channel 66 (New York City).
A weekly program that incorporates interviews with Peruvians and Peruvian Americans, features on Peruvian cities, and presentations of the arts (particularly dance) in the local Peruvian community. It airs Saturday nights from 8:00 p.m. to 9:00 p.m.

Address: 79-07 Roosevelt Avenue, Jamaica Heights, New York 11372.
Telephone: (718) 478-2222.

ORGANIZATIONS AND ASSOCIATIONS

Casa Perú.
This organization is dedicated to the transmission of Peruvian culture. One of its projects is the production of the weekly cable program "Perú Aquí." It also publishes a quarterly newsletter.

Address: 103-15 39th Avenue, Corona, New York 11368.
Telephone: (212) 398-6555.

Centro Cultural Peruano.
Address: 143-45 Sanford Avenue, Flushing, New York 11355.

Club Perú de Nueva York.
This organization promotes Peruvian culture through lectures and other social events. It also raises money for hospitals in Peru.

Contact: Dr. Rodolfo Byrne, Director.

Address: 85-07 Chevy Chase Street, Jamaica Estates, New York 11432.
Telephone: (718) 454-1084.

The Peruvian-American Medical Society.
This professional organization of Peruvian American doctors raises money for equipment needed by Peruvian hospitals.

Address: 313 Heathcote Avenue, Mamaroneck, New York 10543.
Telephone: (914) 381-2001.

MUSEUMS AND RESEARCH CENTERS

American Museum of Natural History.
This New York City landmark museum has a wing dedicated to South American peoples that features Peruvian civilizations, especially the Incas.

Address: Central Park West at 79th Street, New York, New York 10024.
Telephone: (212) 769-5100.

Cornell University.
The university has an exhibit that showcases an ongoing research project in Peru sponsored by its Intercollege Program in Archaeology.

Contact: Professor John S. Henderson, Director.
Address: B59 McGraw Hall, Ithaca, New York 14853.
Telephone: (607) 255-7254.

University of California, Berkeley.
The Center for Latin American Studies, founded in 1956, incorporates social science and the humanities in its scope. It gives particular emphasis to the native populations of South America.

Address: 2334 Bowditch Street, Berkeley, California 94720.
Telephone: (510) 642-2088.

University of California, Los Angeles.
Founded in 1959, the Latin American Center coordinates research on the region's socio-politics, environment, technology, literature, and arts.

Contact: Norris Hundley, Director.
Address: 10343 Bunche Hall, 405 Hilgard Avenue, Los Angeles, California 90024.
Telephone: (310) 825-4571.

University of Florida, Gainesville.

The Institute for Latin American Studies was founded in 1931. It features studies in the humanities and social sciences and has a project on Aymará language and culture.

Contact: Dr. Terry L. McCoy.

Address: 319 Grintner Hall, Gainesville, Florida 32611.

Telephone: (904) 392-0375.

SOURCES FOR ADDITIONAL STUDY

Arden, Harvey. "The Two Souls of Peru," *National Geographic*, March 1982; pp. 284-321.

Blassingame, Wyatt. *The Incas and the Spanish Conquest*. New York: Julian Messner, 1980.

Dostert, Pierre Etienne. *Latin America 1994*. Washington, D.C.: Stryker-Post Publications, 1994.

Martín, Luis. *The Kingdom of the Sun: A Short History of Peru*. New York: Charles Scribner's Sons, 1974.

Stavans, Ilan. "Two Peruvians: How a Novelist and a Terrorist Came to Represent Peru's Divided Soul," *Utne Reader*, July/August 1994; pp. 96-102.

Werlich, David P. *Peru: A Short History*. Carbondale: Southern Illinois University Press, 1978.

Wright, Ronald. *Cut Stones and Crossroads: A Journey in the Two Worlds of Peru*. New York: Viking Press, 1984.

POLISH
by
Syd Jones

AMERICANS

Poles numbered among the earliest colonists in the New World and today, as their numbers exceed ten million, they represent the largest of the Slavic groups in America.

OVERVIEW

Poland, the seventh largest country in Europe, occupies an area of 120,727 square miles—somewhat larger than the state of Nevada. Located in east-central Europe, it is bordered to the east by Russia and the Ukraine, the Czech Republic and Slovakia to the south, Germany to the west, and the Baltic Sea to the north. Drained by the Vistula and Oder Rivers, Poland is a land of varied landscape—from the central lowlands, to the sand dunes and swamps of the Baltic coast, to the mountains of the Carpathians to the south. Its 1990 population of just over 38 million is largely homogeneous ethnically, religiously, and linguistically. Minority groups in the country include Germans, Ukrainians and Belarusans. Ninety-five percent of the population is Roman Catholic, and Polish is the national language. Warsaw, located in the central lowlands, is the nation's capital. Poland's national flag is bicolor: divided in half horizontally, it has a white stripe on the top half and a red one on the bottom. Polish Americans often display a flag similar to this with a crowned eagle at its center.

HISTORY

The very name of Poland harkens back to its origins in the Slavic tribes that inhabited the Vistula valley as early as the second millennium B.C. Migrations of these tribes resulted in three distinct subgroups: the West, East, and South Slavs. It was the West Slavs who became the ancestors of modern Poles, settling in and around the Oder and Vistula valleys. Highly clannish, these tribes were organized in tight kinship groups with commonly held property and a rough-and-ready sort of representative government regarding matters other than military. These West Slavs slowly joined in ever-larger units under the pressure of incursions by Avars and early Germans, ultimately being led by a tribe known as the Polanie. From that point on, these West Slavs, and increasingly the entire region, were referred to as Polania or later, Poland. Under the Polanian duke Mieszko and his Piast dynasty, further consolidation around what is modern Poznan created a true state; and in 966, Mieszko was converted to Christianity. It is this event that is commonly accepted as the founding date of Poland. It is doubly important because Mieszko's conversion to Christianity—Roman Catholicism—would link Poland's fortunes in the future to those of Western Europe. The East Slavs, centered at Kiev, were converted by missionaries from the Greek church, which in turn linked them to the Orthodox east.

Meanwhile, the South Slavs had been coalescing into larger units, forming what is known as Little Poland, as opposed to Great Poland of the Piasts. These South Slavs joined Great Poland under Casimir I and for several generations the new state thrived, checking the tide of German expansionism. But from the twelfth to thirteenth centuries, the new kingdom became fragmented by a duchy system that created political chaos and civil war among rival princes of the Piast lineage. Following devastations caused by Tatar invasions in the early thirteenth century, Poland was defenseless against a further tide of German settlement. One of the last Piasts, Casimir III, succeeded in reunifying the kingdom in 1338, and in 1386 it came under the rule of the Jagiellonian dynasty when the grand duke of Lithuania married the crown princess of the Piasts, Jadwiga. Known as Poland's Golden Age, the next two centuries of Jagiellonian rule enabled Poland-Lithuania to become the dominant power in central Europe, encompassing Hungary and Bohemia in its sphere of influence and producing a rich cultural heritage for the nation, including the achievements of such individuals as Copernicus (Mikołaj Kopernik, 1473-1543). At the same time, Poland enjoyed one of the most representative governments of its day as well as the most tolerant religious climate in Europe.

But with the end of the Jagiellonian dynasty in 1572, the kingdom once again fell apart as the landed gentry increasingly assumed local control, sapping the strength of the central government in Krakow. This state of affairs continued for two centuries until Poland was so weakened that it suffered three partitions: Austria took Galicia in 1772; Prussia acquired the northwestern section in 1793; and Tsarist Russia possessed the northeastern section in 1795). By the end of the three partitions, Poland had been completely wiped off the map of Europe. There would not be an independent Poland again for a century and a half, though a nominal Kingdom of Poland was established within the Russian Empire by the Congress of Vienna in 1815. In both Russia and Germany a strict policy of suppression of the Polish language and autonomous education was enforced.

After World War I, an independent Poland was once again re-established. With Josef Pilsudski (1867-1935) as its president and dictator from 1926 to 1935, Poland maintained an uneasy peace with the Soviet Union and Nazi Germany. But with the onset of World War II, Poland was the first victim, and once again the nation was subsumed into other countries: Germany and the Soviet Union initially, and then solely under German rule. The Nazis used Poland as a killing ground to subdue and eradicate Polish culture by executing its intellectuals and nobles, and to "settle" the Jewish question once and for all by exterminating the Jews of Europe. In camps such as Auschwitz-Birkenau this gruesome strategy was put into effect, and by the end of the war in 1945, Poland had lost a fifth of its population, half of which—over three million—were Jews.

Liberation, however, did not mean freedom, for after the war Poland fell under the Soviet sphere; a communist state was set up and Poland once again had become a fiefdom to a foreign power. In 1956 Poland's workers went on a general strike in protest to Moscow's heavy-handed domination. Though brutally suppressed, the strike did force Poland's new leader Władysław Gomułka to relax some of the totalitarian controls imposed by Warsaw and Moscow, and farms were decollectivized. Through successive leadership of Edward Gierek and General Wojciech Jaruzelski, however, the economic conditions worsened and the Poles struggled increasingly for more autonomy from Moscow. By 1980 three events had coincided that would be decisive for Poland's future: the Soviet Union was going bankrupt; Karol Cardinal Wojtyła became Pope

This 1948 photograph was taken shortly after this Polish woman and her three children arrived in New York City; they settled in Rensselaer, Indiana.

John Paul II; and a new and illegal union, Solidarity, had been formed under Lech Wałesa. These last two especially brought Poland into international focus. By 1989, Solidarity won concessions from the government including participation in free elections. After their overwhelming victory, which brought to power their leader Lech Wałesa as President, Solidarity set up a coalition government with the communists; and with the fall of the Soviet Union, Poland along with all of central Europe, regained new breathing room in its heartland. The difficult task now confronting the country is a transformation from a centrally planned economy to a market economy, one that causes enormous dislocations including unemployment and runaway inflation.

THE FIRST POLES IN AMERICA

Poles numbered among the earliest colonists in the New World and today, as their numbers exceed ten million, they represent the largest of the Slavic groups in America. Though claims have been made for Poles sailing with Viking ships exploring the New World before 1600, there is no hard evidence to support them. By 1609, however, Polish immigrants do appear in the annals of Jamestown, having been recruited by the colony as skilled craftsmen to create products for export. These immigrants were integral in the establishment of both the glassmaking and woodworking industries in the new colonies. An early Polish explorer, Anthony Sadowski, set up a trading post along the Mississippi River which later became the city of Sandusky, Ohio. Two other names of note occur in the early history of what would become the American republic: the noblemen Tadeusz Kościuszko (1746-1817) and Casimir Pułaski (1747-1779) both fought on the rebel side in the Revolutionary War. Pułaski, killed in the battle of Savannah, is still honored by Polish Americans—Polonia as the ethnic community is referred to—by annual marches on October 11, Pułaski Day.

SIGNIFICANT IMMIGRATION WAVES

Since the times of those earliest Polish settlers—romantics, adventurers and men simply seeking a better economic life—there have been four distinct waves of immigration to the United States from Poland. The first and smallest, occasioned by the partitioning of Poland, lasted from roughly 1800 to 1860 and was largely made up of political dissidents and those who fled after the dissolution of their national homeland. The second wave was far more significant and took place between 1860 and World War I. Immigrants during this time were in search of a better economic life and tended to be of the rural class, so-called *za chleben* (for bread) emigrants. A third wave lasted from the end of World War I through the end of the Cold War and again comprised dissidents and political refugees. Since the fall of the Soviet Union and Poland's democratic reforms, there has been yet a fourth wave of a seemingly more temporary immigrant group, the *wakacjusze*, or those who come on tourists visas but find work and stay either illegally or legally. These economic immigrants generally plan to earn money and return to Poland.

The first wave of immigrants, from approximately 1800 to 1860, was largely made up of intellectuals and lesser nobility. Not only the partitioning of Poland, but insurrections in 1830 and 1863 also forced political dissidents from their Polish homeland. Many fled to London, Paris and Geneva, but at the same time New York and Chicago also received its share of such refugees from political oppression. Immigration figures are always a problematic issue, and those for Polish immigrants to the United States are no different. For much of the modern era there was no political entity such as Poland, so immigrants coming to America had an initial difficulty in describing their country of origin. Also, there was with Poles, more so than other ethnic immigrant groups, more back-and-forth travel between host country and home country. Poles have tended to save money and return to their native country in higher numbers than many other ethnic groups. Additionally, minorities within Poland who immigrated to the United States confuse the picture. Nonetheless, what numbers that exist from U.S. Immigration and Naturalization Service records indicate that fewer than 2,000 Poles immigrated to the United States between 1800 and 1860.

The second wave of immigration was inaugurated in 1854 when about 800 Polish Catholics from Silesia founded Panna Maria, a farming colony in Texas. This symbolic opening of America to the Poles also opened the flood gates of immigration. The new arrivals tended to cluster in industrial cities and towns of the Midwest and Middle Atlantic States—New York, Buffalo, Pittsburgh, Cleveland, Detroit, Milwaukee, Minneapolis, Chicago, and St. Louis—where they became steelworkers, meatpackers, miners, and later autoworkers. These cities still retain their large contingents of Polish Americans. A lasting legacy of these Poles in America is the vital role they played in the growth and development of the U.S. labor movement, Joseph Yablonski of the United Mine Workers only one case in point.

Confusion over exact numbers of Polish immigrants again becomes a problem during this period, with large underreporting, especially during the 1890s when immigration was highest. Most agree, however, that between mid-nineteenth century and World War I, some 2.5 million Poles immigrated to the United States. This wave of immigration can be further broken down to two successive movements of Poles from different regions of their partitioned country. The first to come were the German Poles, who tended to be better educated and more skilled craftsmen than the Russian and Austrian Poles. High birthrates, overpopulation, and large-scale farming methods in Prussia, which forced small farmers off the land, all combined to send German Poles into emigration in the second half of the nineteenth century. German policy vis-a-vis restricting the power of the Catholic church also played a part in this exodus. Those arriving in the United States totalled roughly a half million during this period, with numbers dwindling by the end of the century.

However, just as German Polish immigration to the United States was diminishing, that of Russian and Austrian Poles was just getting underway. Again, overpopulation and land hunger drove this emigration, as well as the enthusiastic letters home that new arrivals in the United States sent to their relatives and loved ones. Many young men also fled from military conscription, especially in the years of military build-up just prior to and including the onset of World War I. Moreover, the journey to America itself had become less arduous, with shipping lines such as the North German Line and the Hamburg American Line now booking passage from point to point, combining overland as well as transatlantic passage and thereby simplifying border crossings. Numbers of Galician or Austrian Poles total approximately 800,000, and of Russian Poles—the last large immigration contingent—another 800,000. It has also been estimated that 30 percent of Galician and Russian Poles arriving between 1906 and 1914 returned to their homelands.

The influx of such large numbers of one ethnic group was sure to cause friction with the "established" Americans, and during the last half of the nineteenth century history witnesses intolerance toward many of the immigrants from divergent parts of Europe. That the Poles were strongly Catholic contributed to such friction, and thus Polonia or the Polish Americans formed even tighter links with each other, relying on ethnic cohesiveness not only for moral support, but financial, as well. Polish fraternal, national, and religious organizations such as the Polish National Alliance, the Polish Union, the Polish American Congress, and the Polish Roman Catholic Union have been instrumental in not only maintaining a Polish identity for immigrants, but also in obtaining insurance and home loans to set the new arrivals on their own feet in their new country. Such friction abated as Poles assimilated in their host country, to be supplanted by new waves of immigrants from other countries. Polish Americans have, however, continued to maintain a strong ethnic identity into the late twentieth century.

With the end of World War I and the reestablishment of an independent Polish state, it was believed that there would be a huge exodus of Polish immigrants returning to their homeland. Such an exodus did not materialize, though immigration over the next generation greatly dropped off. U.S. immigration quotas imposed in the 1920s had much to do with this, as did the Great Depression. But political oppression in Europe between the wars, displaced persons brought on by World War II, and the flight of dissidents from the communist regime did account for a further half million immigrants—many of them refugees—from Poland between 1918 and the late 1980s and the fall of communism.

The fourth wave of Polish immigration is now underway. This is comprised mostly of younger people who grew up under communism. Though not significant in numbers because of immigration quotas, this newest wave of post-Cold War immigrants, whether they be the short-term workers, *wakacjusze*, or long-term residents, continue to add new blood to Polish Americans, ensuring that the ethnic community continues to have foreign-born Poles among its contingent. Estimates from the 1970 census placed the number of either foreign born Poles or native born with at least one Polish parent at near three million. Over eight million claimed Polish ancestry in their background in the 1980 census and 9.5 million did so in the 1990 census, 90 percent of whom were concentrated in urban areas. A large part of such identity and cohesiveness was the result of outside conditions. It has been noted that initial friction between Polish immigrants and "established" Americans played some part in this inward looking stance. Additionally, such commonly held beliefs as folk culture and Catholicism provided further incentives for communalism. Newly arrived Poles generally had their closest contacts outside Polish Americans with their former European neighbors: Czechs, Germans, and Lithuanians. Over the years there has been a degree of friction specifically between the Polish American community and Jews and African Americans. However, during the years of partition, Polish Americans kept alive the belief in a free Poland. Such cohesiveness was further heightened in the Polish American community during the Cold War, when Poland was a satellite of the Soviet Union. But since the fall of the Soviet empire and with free elections in Poland, this outer threat to the homeland is no longer a factor in keeping Polish Americans together. The subsequent increase in immigration of the fourth wave of younger Poles escaping difficult transition times at home has added new numbers to immigrants in the United States, but it is yet to be seen what their effect will be on Polish Americans. As yet, these recent immigrants have played no part in the power structure—not being members of the fraternal organizations. What their effect in the future will be is unclear.

ACCULTURATION AND ASSIMILATION

In a society so homogenized by the effects of mass media, such ethnic enclaves as the amorphous reaches of Polish Americans is clearly affected. Despite the recent emphasis on multiculturalism and a resurgent interest in ethnic roots, Polish Americans like other ethnic groups become assimilated more and more rapidly. Using language as a measure, it can be seen how quickly such absorption occurs. In a 1960 survey of children of Polish ethnic leaders, 20 percent reported that they spoke Polish regularly. By 1990, however, the U.S. census reported that only 750,000 Polish Americans spoke Polish in the home.

"We wanted to be Americans so quickly that we were embarrassed if our parents couldn't speak English. My father was reading a Polish paper. And somebody was supposed to come to the house. I remember sticking it under something. We were that ashamed of being foreign."

Louise Nagy in 1913, cited in *Ellis Island: An Illustrated History of the Immigrant Experience,* edited by Ivan Chermayeff et al. (New York: Macmillan, 1991).

As part of the European emigration, Polish immigrants have had an easier time racially than many other non-European groups in assimilating or blending into the American scene. But this is only a surface assimilation. Culturally, the Polish contingent has held tightly to its folk and national roots, making Polonia more than simply a name. It has been at times a country within a country, Poland in the New World. By and large, Poles have competed well and succeeded in their new homeland; they have thrived and built homes and raised families, and in that respect have participated in and added to the American dream. Yet this process of assimilation has been far from smooth as witnessed by one fact: the Polish joke. Such jokes have at their core a negative representation of the Poles as backward and uneducated simpletons. It is perhaps this stereotype that is hardest for Polish Americans to combat, and is a legacy of the second wave of immigrants, the largest contingent between 1860 and 1914 made up of mostly people from Galicia and Russia. Though recent studies have shown Polish Americans to have high income levels as compared to British, German, Italian, and Irish immigrant groups, the same studies demonstrate that they come in last in terms of occupation and education. For many generations, Polish Americans in general did not value higher education, though such a stance has changed radically in the late twentieth century. The professions are now heavily represented with Polish Americans as well as the blue collar world. Yet the Polish joke persists and Polish Americans have been actively fighting it in the past two decades with not only educational programs but also law suits when necessary. The days of Polish Americans anglicizing their names seem to be over; along with other ethnic groups Polish Americans now talk of ethnic pride.

TRADITIONS, CUSTOMS, AND BELIEFS

It had been noted that clans and kinship communities were extremely important in the early formation of Slavic tribes. This early form of communalism has been translated into today's world by the plethora of Polish American fraternal organizations. By the same token, other traditions out of the Polish rural and agrarian past still hold today.

Gospodarz may well be one of the prettiest sounding words in the Polish language—to a Pole. It means a landowner, and it is the land that has always been important in Poland. Ownership of land was one of the things that brought the huge influx of Poles to the United States, but less than ten percent achieved that dream, and these were mainly the German Poles who came first when there was still a frontier to carve out. The remaining Poles were stuck in the urban areas as wage-earners, though many of these managed to save the money to buy a small plot of land in the suburbs. Contrasted to this is the *Górale,* or mountaineer. To the lowlanders of Greater Poland, the stateless peoples of the southern Carpathians represented free human spirit, unbridled by convention and laws. Both of these impulses runs through the Polish peoples and informs their customs.

An agrarian people, many Poles have traditions and beliefs that revolve around the calendar year, the time for sowing and for reaping. And inextricably linked to this rhythm is that of the Catholic church whose saints' days mark the cycle of the year. A strong belief in good versus evil resulted in a corresponding belief in the devil: witches who could make milk cows go dry; the power of the evil eye, which both humans and animals could wield; the belief that if bees build a hive in one's house, the house will catch on fire; and the tradition that while goats are lucky animals, wolves, crows and pigeons all bring bad luck.

PROVERBS

Polish proverbs display the undercurrents of the Polish nature, its belief in simple pragmatism and honesty, and a cynical distrust of human nature: When misfortune knocks at the door, friends are asleep; the mistakes of the doctor are covered by the earth; the rich man has only two holes in his nose, the same as the poor man; listen much and speak little; he whose coach is drawn by hope has poverty for a coachman; if God wills, even a cock will lay an egg; he who lends to a friend makes an enemy; no fish without bones; no woman without

CUISINE

The diet of Polish Americans has also changed over the years. One marked change from Poland is the increased consumption of meat. Polish sausages, especially the *kielbasa*—garlic-flavored pork sausage—have become all but synonymous with Polish cuisine. Other staples include cabbage in the form of sauerkraut or cabbage rolls, dark bread, potatoes, beets, barley, and oatmeal. Of course this traditional diet has been added to by usual American fare, but especially at festivities and celebrations such as Christmas and Easter, Polish Americans still serve their traditional food. Polish Americans have, in addition to the sausage, also contributed staples to American cuisine, including the breakfast roll, *bialys*, the *babka* coffeecake, and potato pancakes.

TRADITIONAL COSTUMES

Traditional clothing is worn less and less by Polish Americans, but such celebrations as Pulaski Day on October 11 of each year witness upwards of 100,000 Polish Americans parading between 26th Street and 52nd Street in New York, many of them wearing traditional dress. For women this means a combination blouse and petticoat covered by a full, brightly colored or embroidered skirt, an apron, and a jacket or bodice, also gaily decorated. Headdress ranges from a simple kerchief to more elaborate affairs made of feathers, flowers, beads, and ribbons decorating stiffened linen. Men also wear headdresses, though usually not as ornate as the women's—felt or straw hats or caps. Trousers are often white with red stripes, tucked into the boots or worn with mountaineering moccasins typical to the Carpathians. Vests or jackets cover white embroidered shirts, and the favorite colors replicate the flag: red and white.

HOLIDAYS CELEBRATED BY POLISH AMERICANS

In addition to Pułaski Day, which President Harry Truman decreed an official remembrance day in 1946, Polish American celebrations consist mainly of the prominent liturgical holidays such as Christmas and Easter. The traditional Christmas Eve dinner, called *wigilia*, begins when the first star of the evening appears. The dinner, which is served upon a white tablecloth under which some straw has been placed, consists of 12 meatless courses—one for each of the apostles. There is also one empty chair kept at the table for a stranger who might chance by. This vigil supper begins with the breaking of a wafer, the *oplatek,* and the exchange of good wishes; it moves on to such traditional fare as apple pancakes, fish, *pierogi* or a type of filled dumpling, potato salad, sauerkraut and nut or poppy seed torte for dessert. To insure good luck in the coming year one must taste all courses, and there must also be an even number of people at the table to ensure good health. The singing of carols follows the supper. In Poland, between Christmas Eve and the Epiphany (January 6, or "Three Kings") "caroling with the manger" takes place in which carolers bearing a manger visit neighbors and are rewarded with money or treats. In Poland, the Christmas season comes to a close with Candelmas day on February 2, when the candles are taken to church to be blessed. It is believed that these blessed candles will protect the home from sickness or bad fortune.

The Tuesday before Ash Wednesday is celebrated by much feasting. Poles traditionally fried *pączki* (fruit-filled doughnuts) in order to use the sugar and fat in the house before the long fast of Lent. In the United States, especially in Polish communities, the day before Ash Wednesday has become popularized as Pączki Day; Poles and non-Poles alike wait in line at Polish bakeries for this pastry. Easter is an especially important holiday for Polish Americans. Originally an agrarian people, the Poles focussed on Easter as the time of rebirth and regeneration not only religiously, but for their fields as well. It marked the beginning of a farmer's year. Consequently, it is still celebrated with feasts which include meats and traditional cakes, butter molded into the shape of a lamb, and elaborately decorated eggs (*pisanki*), and a good deal of drinking and dancing.

HEALTH AND MENTAL ISSUES

There are no documented health problems specific to Polish Americans. Initially skeptical of modern medicine and more likely to try traditional home cures, Polish Americans soon were converted to the more modern practices. The creation of fraternal and insurance societies such as the Polish National Alliance in 1880, the Polish Roman Catholic Union in 1873, and the Polish Women's Alliance in 1898, helped to bring life insurance to a larger segment of Polonia. As with the majority of Americans, Polish Americans acquire health insurance at their own expense, or as part of a benefits package at their place of employment.

LANGUAGE

Polish is a West Slavic language, part of the Lekhite subgroup, and is similar to Czech and Slovak. Modern Polish, written in the Roman alphabet, stems from the sixteenth century. It is still taught in Sunday schools and parochial schools for children. It is also taught in dozens of American universities and colleges. The first written examples of Polish are a list of names in a 1136 Papal Bull. Manuscripts in Polish exist from the fourteenth century. Its vocabulary is in part borrowed from Latin, German, Czech, Ukrainian, Belarusan, and English. Dialects include Great Polish, Pomeranian, Silesian and Mazovian. Spelling is phonetic with every letter pronounced. Consonants in particular have different pronunciation than in English. "Ch," for example is pronounced like "h" in horse; "j" is pronounced like "y" at the beginning of a word; "cz" is pronounced "ch" as in chair; "sz" is pronounced like "sh" as in shoe; "rz" and "z" are pronounced alike as the English "j" in jar; and "w" is pronounced like the English "v" in victory. Various diacriticals are also used in Polish: "ź," "ż," "ń," "ć," "ś," "ą," "ę," and "ł."

GREETINGS AND OTHER POPULAR EXPRESSIONS

Typical Polish greetings and other expressions include: *Dzien dobry* ("gyen dobry")—Good morning; *Dobry wieczor* ("dobry viechoor")—Good evening; *Dowidzenia* ("dovidzenyah")—Good-bye; *Dozobaczenia* ("dozobahchainya")—Till we meet again; *Dziekuje* ("gyen-kuyeh")—Thank you; *Przepraszam* ("psheprasham")—I beg your pardon; *Nie* ("nyeh")—No; *Tak* ("tahk")—Yes.

FAMILY AND COMMUNITY DYNAMICS

Typically, the Polish family structure is strongly nuclear and patriarchal. However, as with other ethnic groups coming to America, Poles too have adapted to the American way of life, which means a stronger role for the woman in the family and in the working world, with a subsequent loosening of

the strong family tie. Initially, single or married men were likely to immigrate alone, living in crowded quarters or rooming houses, saving their money and sending large amounts back to Poland. That immigration trend changed over the years, to be replaced by family units immigrating together. In the 1990s, however, the immigration pattern has come full circle, with many single men and women coming to the United States in search of work.

MARRIAGE AND THE ROLE OF THE WOMAN IN POLISH AMERICA

Until recently, Polish Americans have tended to marry within the community of Poles, but this too has changed over the years. A strong ethnic identity is maintained now not so much through shared traditions or folk culture, but through national pride. As with many European immigrant groups, male children were looked upon as the breadwinners and females as future wives and mothers. This held true through the second wave of immigrants, but with the third wave and with second and third generation families, women in general took a more important role in extra-familial life.

As with many other immigrant groups, the Poles maintain traditions most closely in those ceremonies for which the community holds great value: weddings, christenings and funerals. Weddings are no longer the hugely staged events of Polish heritage, but they are often long and heavy-drinking affairs, involving several of the customary seven steps: inquiry and proposal; betrothal; maiden evening and the symbolic unbraiding of the virgin's hair; baking the wedding cake; marriage ceremony; putting to bed; and removal to the groom's house. Traditional dances such as the *krakowiak*, *oberek*, *mazur*, and the *zbójnicki* will be enjoyed at such occasions, as well as the polka, a popular dance among Polish Americans. (The polka, however, is not a Polish creation.) Also to be enjoyed at such gatherings are the national drink, vodka, and such traditional fare as roast pork, sausages, *barszcs* or beet soup, cabbage rolls and poppy seed cakes.

Christenings generally take place within two weeks of the birth on a Sunday or holiday; and for the devoutly Catholic Poles, it is a vital ceremony. Godparents are chosen who present the baby with gifts, more commonly money now than the traditional linens or caps of rural Poland. The christening feast, once a multi-day affair, has been toned down in modern times, but still involves the panoply of holiday foods. The ceremony itself may include a purification rite for the mother as well as baby, a tradition that goes back to the pre-Christian past.

Funerals also retain some of the old traditions. The word death in Polish (śmierć) is a feminine noun, and is thought of as a tall woman draped in white. Once again, Catholic rites take over for the dead. Often the dead are accompanied in their coffins by strong shoes for the arduous journey ahead or by money as an entrance fee to heaven. The funeral itself is followed by a feast or stypa which may also include music and dancing.

EDUCATION

Education has also taken on more importance. Where a primary education was deemed sufficient for males in the early years of the twentieth century—much of it done in Catholic schools—the value of a university education for children of both sexes now mirrors the trend for American society as a whole. A 1972 study from U.S. Census statistics showed that almost 90 percent of Polish Americans between the ages of 25 and 34 had graduated from high school, as compared to only 45 percent of those over age 35. Additionally, a full quarter of the younger generation, those between the ages 25 and 34, had completed at least a four-year university education. In general, it appears that the higher socio-economic class of the Polish American, the more rapid is the transition from Polish identity to that of the dominant culture. Such rapid change has resulted in generational conflict, as it has throughout American society as a whole in the twentieth century.

RELIGION

Poland is a largely Catholic nation, a religion that survived even under the anti-clerical reign of the communists. It is a deeply ingrained part of the Polish life, and thus immigrants to the United States brought the religion with them, Initially, Polish American parishes were established from simple meetings of the local religious in stores or hotels. These meetings soon became societies, taking on the name of a saint, and later developed into the parish itself, with priests arriving from various areas of Poland. The members of the parish were responsible for everything: financial support of their clergy as well as construction of a church and any other buildings needed by the priest. Polish American Catholics were responsible for the creation of seven religious orders, including the Resurrectionists and the Felicians who in turn created schools and seminaries and brought nuns from Poland to help with orphanages and other social services.

Quickly the new arrivals turned their religious institution into both a parish and an okolica, a local area or neighborhood. There was rapid growth in the number of such ethnic parishes: from 17 in 1870 to 512 only 40 years later. The number peaked in 1935 at 800 and has tapered off since, with 760 in 1960. In the 1970s the level of church attendance was beginning to drop off sharply in the Polish American community, and the use of English in the mass was becoming commonplace. However, the newest contingent of Polish refugees has slowed this trend, raising attendance once again, and helping to restore masses in the Polish language at many churches.

All was not smooth for the Polish American Catholics. A largely Protestant nation in the nineteenth century, America proved somewhat intolerant of Catholics, a fact that only served to separate immigrant Poles from the mainstream even more. Also, within the Church, there was dissension. Footing all the bills for the parish, still Polish American Catholics had little representation in the hierarchy. Such disputes ultimately led to the establishment of the Polish National church in 1904. The founding bishop, Reverend Francis Hodur, built the institution to 34 churches and over 28,000 communicants in a dozen years' time.

EMPLOYMENT AND ECONOMIC TRADITIONS

As has been noted, the Polish immigrants were largely agrarian except for those intellectuals who fled political persecution, By and large they came the United States hoping to find a plot of land, but instead found the frontier closed and were forced instead into urban areas of the Midwest and Middle Atlantic states where they worked in steel mills, coal mines, meatpacking plants, oil refineries and the garment industry. The pay was low for such work: the average annual income for Polish immigrants in 1910 was only $325. The working day was long, as it was all across America at the time, averaging a ten-hour day. But still

In this photograph, taken in 1964, six-year-olds Leonard Sikorasky and Julia Wesoly are watching the Pułaski Day Parade in New York City, which commemorates the death of the Revolutionary War General Casimir Pułaski.

Polish Americans managed to save their money and by 1910 it is estimated that these immigrants had been able to send $40 million back to their relatives and loved ones in Russian and Austrian Poland. The amount was so large in fact, that a federal commission was set up to investigate the damages to the U.S. economy that such an outflow of funds might create.

Families pulled together in Polonia, with education coming second to the need for young boys to contribute to the annual income. The need for such economies began to decline after World War I, however, and by 1920 only ten percent of Polish Americans families derived income from the labor of children, and two-thirds were supported by the head of family. Over the years of the twentieth century—except for the years of the Great Depression—the economic situation of Polish Americans has steadily improved, with education taking on increasing importance, creating a parallel rise in Polish Americans in the white collar labor market. By 1970 only four percent were laborers; 23 percent were craftsmen.

Polish Americans have also been important in the formation of labor unions, not only swelling the membership, but also providing leaders such as David Dubinsky of the CIO and, as has been noted, Joseph Yablonski of the United Mine Workers.

POLITICS AND GOVERNMENT

Though heavily concentrated in nine industrial states, Polish Americans did not, until the 1930s, begin to flex their political muscle. Language barriers played a part in this, but more important was the fact that earlier immigrants were too concerned with family and community issues to pay attention to the national political scene. Even in Chicago, where Polish Americans made up 12 percent of the population, they did not elect one of their own to the U.S. Congress until 1920. The first Polish American congressional representative was elected from Milwaukee in 1918.

Increasingly, however, Polish Americans have begun playing a more active role in domestic politics and have tended to vote in large numbers for the Democrats. Al Smith, a Democrat and Roman Catholic who was opposed to Prohibition, was one of the first beneficiaries of the Polish American block vote. Though he lost the election, Smith received an overwhelming majority of the Polish American vote. The Great Depression mobilized Polish Americans even more politically, organizing the Polish American Democratic Organization and supporting the New Deal policies of Franklin D. Roosevelt. By 1944 this organization could throw large numbers of Polish American votes Roosevelt's way and were correspondingly compensated by federal patronage. Prominent Polish American members of congress have been Representatives Dan Rostenkowski and Roman Pucinski, both Democrats from Illinois, and Senator Barbara Mikulski, a Democrat from Maryland. Maine's Senator Edmund Muskie was also of Polish American heritage.

RELATIONS WITH POLAND

Internationally Polish Americans have been more active politically than domestically. The Polish National Alliance, founded in 1880, was—in addition to being a mutual aid society—a fervent proponent of a free Poland. Such a goal manifested itself in very pragmatic terms: during World War I, Polish Americans not only sent their young to fight, but also the $250 million they subscribed in liberty bonds. Polish Americans also lobbied Washington with the objective of a free Poland in mind. The Polish American Congress (PAC) was created in 1944 to help secure independence for Poland, opposing the Yalta and Potsdam agreements, which established Soviet hegemony in Eastern Europe. During this same time, Polish American socialists formed the Pro-Soviet Polish American Council, but its power waned in the early years of the Cold War. PAC, however, fought on into the 1980s, supporting Solidarity, the union movement in Poland largely responsible for the downfall of the communist government. Gifts of food, clothing and lobbying in Washington were all part of the PAC campaign for an independent Poland and the organization has been very active in the establishment of a free market system in Poland since the fall of the communist government.

INDIVIDUAL AND GROUP CONTRIBUTIONS

Only approximately 2.5 percent of the U.S. population, Polish Americans have nonetheless made significant contributions to the nation's sciences and popular culture.

ACADEMIA

Bronislaw Malinowski (1884-1942), a pioneer of cultural anthropology, emphasized the concept of culture in meeting humankind's basic needs; he taught at Yale late in his life, after writing such important books as *Argonauts of the Western Pacific* and *The Sexual Life of Savages in Northwestern Melanesia*. Linguist Alfred Korzybski (1879-1950), born in Warsaw, came to the United States in 1918; his work in linguistics focussed on the power of the different value and meaning of words in different languages in an effort to reduce misunderstanding; he founded the Institute of General Semantics in 1938 in Chicago, and his research and books—including *Manhood and Humanity* and *Science and Sanity*—have been incorporated in modern psychology and philosophy curricula as well as linguistics.

COMMERCE AND INDUSTRY

Oleg Cassini, Polish Italian, also made a name in fashion. Ruth Handler (1917-), co-founder of Mattel toy company and creator of the Barbie doll, was born to Polish immigrant parents in Colorado. William Filene (1830-1901) was born in Posen and founded Boston's Filene department store. Iowa's largest department store, Younker's, was founded by three Polish immigrant brothers—Samuel, Marcus, and Lipma Younker—in 1850. The food industry in America has also had prominent Polish Americans among its ranks. Mrs. Paul's Fish is the creation of Polish American, Edward J. Piszek (1917-). Leo Gerstenzang (1923-) was a Polish immigrant from Warsaw who invented the Q-Tip cotton swab.

ENTERTAINMENT

Hollywood has had its fair share of Polish-born men and women who have helped to shape that industry, including Harry and Jack Warner of Warner Bros. Entertainers and actors such as Sophie Tucker and Pola Negri also managed to hide their ethnic roots by changing their names. The pianist and performer Liberace (1919-1987), half-Polish and half-Italian, was born Władziu Valentino Liberace.

LITERATURE AND JOURNALISM

Jerzy Kosinski (1933-1991), the Polish-born novelist, came to the United States after World War II; his *Painted Bird* relates the experiences of a small boy in Nazi-occupied Poland and is one of the most stirring and troubling novels to come out of that time. The poet Czesław Miłosz (1911-), naturalized in 1970, won the Nobel Prize for Literature in 1980. Born in Lithuania of Polish parents, Miłosz studied law and served in the diplomatic corps as well as establishing a name for himself as a poet before immigrating in 1960; some of his best known works are *The Captive Mind, The Issa Valley*, and *The Usurpers*. The cartoonist Jules Feiffer (1929-), known for his offbeat and biting wit, was born to Polish immigrant parents in the United States.

MUSIC

Leopold Stokowski (1882-1977), is just one of the musical luminaries to carry on the Ignacy Paderewski tradition; born in London of Polish and Irish parents; Stokowski, a renowned conductor, became a naturalized U.S. citizen in 1915; he was best known as conductor of the Philadelphia Orchestra for many years, and for popularizing classical music in America; his appearance in the 1940 Disney film, *Fantasia*, is an example of such popularizing efforts. The jazz drummer Gene Krupa (1909-1973), the measure for drummers long after, was also of Polish heritage; Krupa was born in Chicago and played with Benny Goodman's orchestra before forming his own band in 1943; he revolutionized the role of the drummer in a jazz band.

POLITICS AND GOVERNMENT

In addition to above-mentioned members of congress, two other recent Polish Americans have made their names in Washington. Leon Jaworski (1905-1982) was the prosecutor in the 1973 Watergate investigation of then President Richard Nixon; and Zbigniew Brzezinski, born in Warsaw in 1928 and naturalized in 1958, was an important advisor to President Carter from 1977 to 1980 on the National Security Council.

SCIENCE

The biochemist Casimir Funk (1884-1967) was, in 1912, the first to discover and use the term vitamin; his so-called vitamin hypothesis postulated that certain diseases such as scurvy and pellagra resulted from lack of crucial substance in the body; Funk also went on to do research in sex hormones and cancer; he lived in the United States from 1939 until his death. Dr. Stanley Dudrick developed the important new method of vein feeding termed IHV—intravenous hyperalimentation.

SPORTS

Many notable Polish Americans have made their names household words in baseball. Included among these are the pitcher Stan Coveleski (1888-1984) whose 17-year career from 1912-1928 earned him a place in the Hall of Fame in 1969; Stan Musial (1920-), right field, another member of the Baseball Hall of Fame, who played for St. Louis from 1941 to 1963; Carl Yastrzemski (1939-), left fielder for the Boston Red Sox, was voted to the Hall of Fame in 1989; and Al Simmons (1902-1956), born Aloysius Harry Szymanski, who played center field for the Philadelphia Athletics from 1924-1944. In football there have been numerous outstanding Polish American players and coaches, Chicago's Mike Ditka (1939-) a stand-out among these, playing as a tight end for the Bears from 1961 to 1972 and later coaching the team to a Super Bowl championship in 1985; a Hall of Fame player, Ditka has most recently worked as a television sports commentator.

VISUAL ARTS

Korczak Ziolkowski (1909-1982), an assistant to Gutzon Borglum in the monumental Mount Rushmore project in South Dakota, continued that monumental style with a 500-foot by 640-foot statue of Chief Crazy Horse still being blasted out of solid rock in the Black Hills by his family.

MEDIA

PRINT

Dziennik Zwiazkowy/Polish Daily News.

Published in Polish, it covers national and international news with a special emphasis on matters effecting the Polish American community.

Contact: Wojciech Bialasiewicz, Editor.

Address: 5711 North Milwaukee Avenue, Chicago, Illinois 60646.

Telephone: (312) 763-3343.

Fax: (312) 763-3450.

Gazeta Polska.

Polish-language newspaper.

Address: 5242 West Diversey Avenue, Chicago, Illinois 60639.

Telephone: (312) 685-1281.

Fax: (312) 283-1675.

Glos.

Polish-language newspaper.

Contact: Andrzej Dobrowolski, Editor.

Address: 140 Greenpoint Avenue, Brooklyn, New York 11222.

Glos Polek/Polish Women's Voice.

Biweekly publication of the Polish Women's Alliance of America.

Contact: Mary Mirecki-Piergies, Editor.

Address: 205 South Northwest Highway, Park Ridge, Illinois 60068.

Fax: (708) 692-2675.

Gwiazda Polarna (Northern Star).

Published weekly in Polish, it provides national and international news for the Polish American community as well as information about Polish activities and organizations domestically.

Contact: Malgorzata Terentiew-Cwiklinski, Editor.

Address: 2619 Post Road, Stevens Point, Wisconsin 54481.

Telephone: (715) 345-0744.

Fax: (715) 345-1913.

Narod Polski.

Publication of the Polish Roman Catholic Union of America.

Contact: Kathryn G. Rosypal, Editor.

Address: 984 Milwaukee Avenue, Chicago, Illinois 60622.

Telephone: (312) 278-3210.

Fax: (312) 278-4595.

New Horizon: Polish American Review.

Contains items of interest to the Polish community.

Contact: B. Wierzbianski, Editor.

Address: 333 West 38th Street, New York, New York 10018-2914.

Telephone: (212) 354-0490.

Nowy Dziennik/Polish Daily News.

Polish-language newspaper.

Contact: Boleslaw Wierzbianski, Editor.

Address: 333 West 38th Street, New York, New York 10018-2914.

Telephone: (212) 594-2266.

Perspectives.

A Polish American educational and cultural bimonthly.

Contact: Krystyna Kusielewicz, Editor.

Address: c/o Marta Korwin Rhodes, 7300 Connecticut Avenue, Bethesda, Maryland 20815-4930.

Telephone: (202) 554-4267.

Polish American Journal.

Official organ of the Polish Union of the United States. Published monthly, it covers national, international, and regional news of interest to Polish Americans.

Contact: Mark Kohan, Editor.

Address: 1275 Harlem Road, Buffalo, New York 14206-1960.

Telephone: (716) 893-5771.

Fax: (716) 893-5783.

Polish American Studies.

A journal of the Polish American Historical Association devoted to Polish American history and culture.

Contact: James S. Pula, Editor.

Address: 984 Milwaukee Avenue, Chicago, Illinois 60622.

Polish American World.

Published weekly, it reports on activities and events in the Polish American community and on life in Poland.

Contact: Thomas Poskropski, Editor.

Address: 3100 Grand Boulevard, Baldwin, New York 11510.

Telephone: (516) 223-6514.

Polish Digest.

Covers history of Poland, news from Poland, and Polish culture.

Contact: Leszek Zielinski, Editor.

Address: c/o Horyzonty, 1924 North Seventh Street, Sheboygan, Wisconsin 53081-2724.

Telephone: (715) 341-6959.

Fax: (715) 346-7516.

Polish Fest News.

Contact: Ray Trzesniewski, Jr., Editor.

Address: Polish Festivals, Inc., 7128 West Rawson Avenue, Franklin, Wisconsin 53132.

Telephone: (414) 529-2140.

Polish Heritage.

A quarterly review of the American Council for Polish Culture.

Contact: Wallace M. West, Editor.

Address: 6507 107th Terrace, Pinellas Park, Florida 34666-2432.

Telephone: (813) 541-7875.

Polish Heritage Society Biuletyn.

Monthly newsletter of the Polish Heritage Society; encourages the preservation and understanding of Polish and Polish American culture and history.

Contact: Pat McBride, Editor.

Address: Box 1844, Grand Rapids, Michigan 49501-1844.

Telephone: (616) 456-5353.

Fax: (616) 456-8929.

Polish Review.

Scholarly journal of the Polish Institute of Arts and Sciences of America devoted to the study of Polish history and culture.

Contact: Joseph W. Wieczerzak, Editor.

Address: 208 East 30th Street, New York, New York 10016.

Telephone: (212) 686-4164.

Fax: (212) 545-1130.

Swiat Polski/Polish World.

Published weekly in Polish.

Contact: Ewa Matuszewski, Editor.

Address: 11903 Joseph Campau Street, Hamtramck, Michigan 48212.

Telephone: (313) 365-1990.

Fax: (313) 365-0850.

Zgoda.

Published by the Polish National Alliance of North America, contains fraternal, cultural, sports, and general news in Polish and English.

Contact: Wojciech A. Wierzewski, Editor.

Address: 6100 North Cicero Avenue, Chicago, Illinois 60646-4385.

Telephone: (312) 286-0500.

Fax: (312) 286-0842.

RADIO

WBRK-AM.

Polish American Programming.

Contact: Tom Wotjkowski.

Address: 100 North Street, Pittsfield, Massachusetts 01201.

Telephone: (413) 442-1553.

WCSS-AM.

"Polka Party."

Contact: Dan Kielbasa.

Address: 6 Genessee Lane, Amsterdam, New York 12010.

Telephone: (518) 843-2500.

WEDC-AM.

"Polish Sunshine Hour."

Contact: Halina Gramza.

Address: 5475 North Milwaukee Avenue, Chicago, Illinois 60630.

Telephone: (312) 631-0700.

TELEVISION

WCIU-TV.

"Polevision," a daily two-hour show airs between 7:00 p.m. and 9:00 p.m. with programs in both Polish and English.

Contact: Robert Lewandowski.

Address: Board of Trade Building, 141 West Jackson Boulevard, Chicago, Illinois 60604.

Telephone: (312) 663-0260.

ORGANIZATIONS AND ASSOCIATIONS

American Council for Polish Culture (ACPC).
National federation of groups devoted to fostering and preserving Polish ethnic heritage in the United States.

Contact: Dr. Kaya Mirecka-Ploss, Executive Director.
Address: 2025 O Street, N.W., Washington, D.C. 20036.
Telephone: (202) 785-2320.

American Institute of Polish Culture (AIPC).
Furthers knowledge of and appreciation for the history, science, art, and culture of Poland.

Contact: Blanka A. Rosenstiel, President.
Address: 1440 79th Street Causeway, Suite 117, Miami, Florida 33141.
Telephone: (305) 864-2349.

Polish American Congress (PAC).
Umbrella organization for local and national Polish organizations in the United States with more than three million combined members. Promotes improved quality of life for Polish Americans and people in Poland.

Contact: Eugene Rosypal, Exeuctive Director.
Address: 5711 North Milwaukee Avenue, Chicago, Illinois 60646-6215.
Telephone: (312) 763-9944.

Polish American Historical Association (PAHA).
Concerned with Polish Americana and the history of Poles in the United States.

Address: 984 North Milwaukee Avenue, Chicago, Illinois 60622.
Telephone: (312) 384-3352.

Polish Falcons of America.
Founded in 1887, the Polish Falcons have a membership of 31,000 in 143 groups or "nests." Established as a fraternal benefit insurance society for people of Polish or Slavic descent, the Falcons also took on a strong nationalist sentiment, demanding a free Poland. The society promotes athletic and educational events and provides a scholarship fund for those majoring in physical education. The Falcons also publish a bi-monthly publication in Polish, *Sokol Polski*.

Contact: Lawrence R. Wujcikowski, President.

Address: 615 Iron City Drive, Pittsburgh, Pennsylvania 15205.
Telephone: (412) 922-2244.

Polish Genealogical Society of America (PGSA).
Promotes Polish genealogical study and establishes communication among researchers.

Contact: Stanley R. Schmidt, President.
Address: 984 North Milwaukee Avenue, Chicago, Illinois 60622.

Polish National Alliance of the United States (PNA).
Founded in 1880, the PNA has a membership of 286,000 made up of nearly 1,000 regional groups. Originally founded as a fraternal life insurance society, PNA continues this original role while also sponsoring education and cultural affairs. It maintains a library of 14,000 volumes.

Contact: Edward Moskal, President.
Address: 6100 North Cicero, Chicago, Illinois 60646.
Telephone: (312) 286-0500.

Polish Roman Catholic Union of America.
Founded in 1873, the Roman Catholic Union has a membership of 90,000 in 529 groups. Founded as a fraternal benefit life insurance society, the union sponsors sports and youth activities, and conducts language school as well as dance and children's programs. It also has a library of 25,000 volumes.

Contact: Josephine Szarowicz, Secretary General.
Address: 984 Milwaukee Avenue, Chicago Illinois 60622.
Telephone: (312) 278-3210.

Polish Surname Network (PSN).
Collects and disseminates genealogical information on surnames of Polish heritage. Provides fee-based research, research analysis, and translation services.

Contact: Mary S. Hartig, Executive Officer.
Address: 158 South Walter Avenue, Newbury Park, California 91320.

Polish Union of the United States.
Founded in 1890, the Polish Union has a membership of 12,000 in 100 groups. This fraternal benefit life insurance society bestows the Copernicus Award to a student excelling in astronomy. Publishes the monthly *Polish American Journal*.

Contact: Wallace S. Piotrowski, President.

Address: 4191 North Buffalo Street, Orchard Park, New York 14127-0684.

Telephone: (716) 667-9782.

Polish Women's Alliance of America.

Founded in 1898, the Polish Women's Alliance has a membership of 65,000 in 775 groups or chapters. It is a fraternal benefit life insurance society administered by women and maintains a library of 7,500 volumes on Polish and American culture and history.

Contact: Helen Wojcik, President.

Address: 205 South Northwest Highway, Park Ridge, Illinois 60068.

Telephone: (708) 384-1200.

MUSEUMS AND RESEARCH CENTERS

Many public libraries, including the Los Angeles Public Library, New York Public Library/Donnell Library Center, Boston Public Library, Denver Public Library, Miami/Dade Public Library, and the Detroit Public Library, have extensive Polish language collections to serve the Polish American communities.

American Institute for Polish Culture.

Founded in 1972 to promote the appreciation for history, culture, science and art of Poland, the American Institute for Polish Culture sponsors exhibits, lectures, and research and maintains a 1,200-volume library and publishes books on history and biography.

Contact: Blank A. Rosenstiel, President.

Address: 1440 79th Street, Causeway, Suite 403, Miami, Florida 33141.

Telephone: (305) 864-2349.

Center for Polish Studies and Culture.

Founded in 1970 at St. Mary's College, the Center for Polish Studies promotes research in the teaching of Polish and arranges educational exchanges. It also maintains a library, art gallery, and a museum of artifacts from Polish Americans.

Contact: Janusz Wrobel.

Address: St. Mary's College, Orchard Lake, Michigan 48034.

Telephone: (810) 682-1885.

Kosciuszko Foundation.

Founded in 1925, the Kosciuszko Foundation is named after the Polish nobleman who fought in the American revolution. The foundation is a clearinghouse for information on Polish and American cultural affairs. Also known as the American Center for Polish Culture, the foundation has a reference library and arranges educational exchanges as well as administers scholarships and stipends.

Contact: Joseph E. Gore, President.

Address: 15 East 65th Street, New York, New York 10021.

Telephone: (212) 734-2130.

Polish Museum of America.

Founded in 1937, the Polish Museum preserves artifacts of the Polish American experience and mounts displays of costumes, religious artifacts and Polish art. It also maintains a 25,000-volume library for researchers and the Polish American Historical Association which is concerned with the history of Poles in America.

Contact: Dr. Christoph Kamyszew, Director and Curator.

Address: 984 North Milwaukee Avenue, Chicago, Illinois 60622.

SOURCES FOR ADDITIONAL STUDY

Bukowczyk, John. *And My Children Did Not Know Me: A History of the Polish-Americans*. Bloomington: Indiana University Press, 1987.

Fox, Paul. *The Poles in America*. New York: Arno Press, 1970.

Lopata, Helena Znaniecka. *Polish Americans: Status Competition in an Ethnic Community*, second edition. New Brunswick, New Jersey: Transactions Publishers, 1974; reprinted, 1994.

Morawska, Ewa. *The Maintenance of Ethnicity: A Case Study of the Polish American Community in Greater Boston*. San Francisco: R&E Associates 1977.

Renkiewicz, Frank. *The Poles in America, 1608-1972: A Chronology and Fact Book*. Dobbs Ferry, New York: Oceana Publications, Inc., 1973.

Wytrwal, Joseph. *America's Polish Heritage: A Social History of the Poles in America.* Detroit, Michigan: Endurance Press, 1961.

Zieleniewicz, Andrzej. *Poland,* translated, revised, and edited by Robert Strybel, Leonard Chrobot, Robert Geryk, Joseph Swastek, and Walter Ziemba. Orchard Lake, Michigan: Center for Polish Studies and Culture, 1971.

Wherever they settled, Portuguese immigrants had to face many disconcerting changes in their new environment. Rather than living in the same town or even the same neighborhood as the rest of their family— grandparents, aunts, uncles, cousins— upon whom they could depend for help when they needed it, they found themselves alone and without the support system that the extended family could provide.

PORTUGUESE AMERICANS

by
Ernest E. Norden

OVERVIEW

Portugal, officially called the Portuguese Republic, is the westernmost country of continental Europe. It is bordered on the east and north by Spain, with which it shares the Iberian Peninsula, and on the west and south by the Atlantic Ocean. It is about the size of Ohio, having an area of 35,553 square miles (92,082 square kilometers), and measuring 360 miles at its longest point and 140 miles at its widest. Portugal also includes the Azores (Açores) and the Madeira Islands in the North Atlantic Ocean and Macao, a tiny territory on the southern coast of China.

Portugal's current population of roughly 9.9 million people is decreasing. Major cities are the capital Lisbon, Porto, and Amadora. However, two-thirds of the people live in rural areas. Nearly 99 percent of the population is of Portuguese origin; the largest ethnic minorities include Cape Verdeans, Brazilians, the Spanish, British, and Americans. Although there is no official religion in Portugal, 94.5 percent of the people are Roman Catholic. Other Christian groups include Protestants, Apostolic Catholics, and Jehovah's Witnesses. There are small minorities of Jews and Muslims. The country's official language is Portuguese, and the national flag has a field of green on the left with a wider field of red on the right; the national emblem is centered on the line dividing the two colors. Portugal's chief products are grapes, potatoes, hogs, beef cattle, corn, sardines, tuna, textiles, paper products, electrical machinery, cork products, ceramics, and shoes.

EARLY HISTORY

The early history of Portugal saw occupation by Iberians from North Africa and then by Celts who migrated from France. Phoenicians and Carthaginians later established themselves in southern Portugal. After the Second Punic War (218-201 B.C.) the Roman domination of Portugal began. The Lusitanians, a warlike Celtic tribe under the leadership of Viriathus, fiercely opposed the Roman armies, but the latter triumphed. Roman contributions to Portugal included roads, buildings, and the Latin language, from which Portuguese developed. Portugal's name derives from Portus Cale, a pre-Roman or Roman settlement near the mouth of the Douro River, where Porto is now located. In the fifth century A.D., as Roman control of the peninsula weakened, the land was overrun by Suevi who were followed by the Visigoths. In 711 the Muslims invaded the peninsula, and Christian forces spent the next 500 years trying to expel them. To fight off the African Almoravids, King Alfonso VI of León and Castile enlisted the aid of Henry of Burgundy, whom he rewarded with the title of Count of Portucale and the hand in marriage of his illegitimate daughter Teresa. Henry's son, Alfonso Henriques, claimed the title Alfonso I, King of Portugal, in 1139. By 1179 his kingdom, occupying the northern third of present-day Portugal, was recognized as autonomous and separate from Castile.

Alfonso I and his son Sancho I reconquered the remaining Portuguese territory from the Muslims. When Sancho II died in 1248 without leaving an heir to the throne, the Count of Boulogne declared himself King Alfonso III. He was responsible for moving the capital from Coimbra to Lisbon, for lessening the power of the church in his land, and for convoking the Cortes at Leiria (1254) at which the commoners were represented for the first time.

Alfonso III's son Diniz, who ruled Portugal from 1279 to 1325, built a navy, founded the University of Coimbra (1290) which was first located in Lisbon, and showed interest in literature, shipbuilding, and agriculture, for which he came to be called the *rei lavradór* (farmer king). His wife, Elizabeth, who worked to maintain peace in Portugal, was known as the Holy Queen (*rainha santa*) and

was later canonized as St. Elizabeth of Portugal. After the death of Ferdinand I in 1383, his wife Leonor Telles married their daughter Beatriz to the King of Castile. There was disagreement as to whether Beatriz should be heiress to the throne, and in 1385 the Cortes chose John, an illegitimate son of Peter I (the Cruel), a former king of Portugal, to rule as John I. John was Master of a religious-military order, the Order of Aviz.

John's son, known as Prince Henry the Navigator, utilized the resources of geographers and navigators to launch a series of explorations beyond the frontiers of Portugal. With the peninsula now reconquered from the Muslims, the Portuguese drive for expansion continued out of a desire to explore unknown lands, to seek a trade route for transporting spices from India, and to spread the Christian religion. Henry financed the expeditions that discovered Madeira and the Azores; these islands were uninhabited but were quickly colonized, and they still belong to Portugal.

Under Manuel I (1495-1521) Vasco da Gama reached India and Pedro Àlvares Cabral discovered Brazil. Manuel, who married Isabella, the eldest daughter of Spain's Ferdinand and Isabella, never realized his dream of uniting Spain and Portugal under his power. As part of his marriage contract with Isabella, he was required to rid Portugal of the Jews who had taken refuge there after being expelled from Spain. A few were allowed to emigrate, but most were forcibly converted to Christianity. Manuel's son, John III (1521-1557) established the Inquisition in Portugal. In 1580, when Portugal again found itself with no heir to the throne upon the death of Cardinal Henry, last of the House of Aviz, Philip II of Spain seized control as Philip I of Portugal (1580-1598). Portugal remained under Spain's control for 60 years until John, Duke of Bragança, defeated the Spanish and founded his own dynasty as John IV in 1640. The Portuguese had increasingly resented Spanish rule because of taxation and because the promises Philip had made to maintain Portugal's autonomy and to name only Portuguese to government posts were soon broken. Spain finally recognized Portuguese independence in 1668.

THE EIGHTEENTH CENTURY

During the eighteenth century, wealth from Brazil began to pour into the country. Gold was discovered in Minas Gerais in 1693, and Brazil became a source of diamonds beginning in 1728. Great wealth was extracted by the Portuguese, and a 20 percent tax on it maintained their monarchs. John V (1706-1750) sought to establish an absolute monarchy. His son Joseph (1750-1777) was weak and allowed his minister Sebastião José de Carvalho e Melo, the Marquis of Pombal, to run the government in a more enlightened fashion. The latter is credited with the competent governmental response to the earthquake that leveled Lisbon in 1755. Pombal also ordered the expulsion of the Jesuits in 1759 and the consequent reform of the educational system. In 1762 Spain invaded Portugal, and peace was not achieved until 1777 through the Treaty of San Ildefonso.

THE NINETEENTH CENTURY

When Napoleon declared war on England Portugal, allied by treaties, was drawn into the struggle. In 1806 Napoleon issued a decree intended to close all continental ports to British ships, and he later invaded Portugal to ensure that his decree was carried out there. As the French army neared Lisbon, the royal family boarded British ships, which carried them to Rio de Janeiro where they remained for 14 years. Meanwhile, the Portuguese and British armies, under the Duke of Wellington, drove the French from the country. Portugal made peace with France in 1814. In 1815 Brazil's status was elevated to that of a kingdom united with Portugal. The royal family did not seem anxious to return to Portugal, and when William Carr Beresford, the British commander in charge in Portugal traveled to Brazil to convince John VI to return, the Portuguese drew up a national constitution and would not allow Beresford back into the country. John VI returned in 1821 and swore to uphold the constitution. His eldest son Peter declared Brazil independent from Portugal in 1822 and became its emperor. John VI recognized Brazil's independence in 1825. John's death in 1826 marked the beginning of a period of political strife that lasted until after mid-century, when party government was established. The main parties were the Historicals and the more moderate Regenerators. The latter part of the century was occupied with disputes over Portugal's claims to territories in Africa.

THE TWENTIETH CENTURY

In the early twentieth century, the republican movement grew in strength. In 1908, King Charles I and his heir, Louis Philip, were assassinated. King Manuel II (1908-1910) was to be the last monarch, for a republican revolution began on October 4, 1910, and Manuel was forced to seek refuge in England until his death in 1932. The revolutionary government gave the vote to adult males and drew up a constitution. It expelled religious orders from the country and disestablished the Roman Catholic church. It founded new universities in Lisbon and Porto. But the republicans were divided into many factions, and there was great political instability. Within 15 years, 45 different regimes held the reins of government. Portugal's bad economic situation became even worse through joining the Allies in World War I (1914-1918). In 1926 the army overthrew the government and set up a dictatorship under General António Oscar de Fragoso Carmona who named António de Oliveira Salazar, an economics professor at the University of Coimbra, as his minister of finance. After his successful handling of the budget, Salazar was named prime minister in 1932. As dictator he managed to keep Portugal out of World War II; he improved the country's roads and its means of transportation; he promoted new industries and other development. However, his government was very conservative; the people enjoyed few rights and were under surveillance by the secret police. The rich enjoyed economic advantages under his regime, but the poor got poorer. Salazar suffered a stroke in mid-1968 and died two years later. Marcelo Caetano then became head of the government and liberalized many governmental policies, but he did not go far enough or fast enough for many Portuguese. Emigration increased, inflation grew, and the country faced a grave economic crisis.

In 1974 a group of military officers, under the leadership of Otelo Saraiva de Carvalho, overthrew Caetano's government; this is often called the "Captains' Revolution" because it was planned by military officers dissatisfied with Portugal's long wars to retain possession of her colonies in Africa. One of the first things accomplished by the new junta called the Armed Forces Movement (Movimento das Forças Armadas) was the granting of independence to Portuguese colonies in Africa. The government also reestablished democratic freedoms. General elections were held in 1976; the government became more stable but had to face the problems of rapid inflation and high unemployment. The constitution was revised in 1982 to limit the powers of the president. Portugal is a member of the United Nations and of the North Atlantic Treaty Organization (NATO). In 1986 Portugal became a member of the European Common Market.

THE PORTUGUESE IN AMERICA

The Portuguese came to America very early. In fact, Portuguese explorers may have reached the Antilles before Columbus. João Rodrigues Cabrillo arrived in San Diego Bay on September 9, 1542, and was the first European to explore the land that is now California. Portuguese Jews emigrated early to America as well as to other countries to escape persecution in their native land. Mathias de Sousa is the first Portuguese immigrant on record; he arrived in Maryland in 1634. Aaron Lopez, another Portuguese Jew, played an important role in introducing the sperm-oil industry to the Newport, Rhode Island, area in the eighteenth century, and Abraham de Lyon introduced the cultivation of grapes into Georgia in 1737. Portuguese from the Azores and the Cape Verde Islands manned New England's whaling ships. They signed on as low-paid laborers in order to avoid military service and to escape the poverty in which they lived at home. Many of them settled in New England, especially around New Bedford, Massachusetts.

IMMIGRATION TRENDS

Portugal has one of the highest rates of emigration in Europe.; and until the middle of the twentieth century, most Portuguese emigrants (about 80 percent of them) went to Brazil. The Portuguese began to arrive in the United States in relatively large numbers around 1870. Shortly after that, there was also increased immigration to the Sandwich Islands (now the state of Hawaii), where the Portuguese went originally to labor on sugar plantations. The majority of the immigrants came to the United States seeking a higher standard of living; they were not drawn by educational opportunity or political or religious freedom. Besides wanting to escape poverty, high taxes, and the lack of economic advancement at home, many males emigrated to avoid eight years of service in Portugal's army. Natural disasters also stimulated many to seek opportunities to live and work elsewhere. The drought in the Cape Verde Islands in 1904 and the volcanic eruptions and earthquakes in the Azores in 1958 sent waves of people abroad. Most of the early Portuguese immigrants to the United States were from the Azores; continental Portuguese did not start arriving in large numbers until the beginning of this century.

Once substantial immigration to the United States started, it increased steadily, peaking between 1910 and 1920. In 1917 the United States government instituted a literacy test requiring that people over the age of 16 had to be able to read and write some language at a basic level in order to settle here. Since the literacy rate in Portugal was extremely low, this test effectively barred many Portuguese from entry; of the Portuguese immigrants admitted shortly before the literacy test was instated, nearly 70 percent were illiterate. In addition, the U.S. Immigration Act of 1924 established a quota system that allowed only a small number of Portuguese immigrants to enter per year. The Great Depression further discouraged immigration to the United States because economic advancement was the Portuguese's main goal. Emigration from the Azores increased in 1958, however, when the Azorean Refugee Act allowed 4,800 to emigrate after the volcanic destruction that took place there. Later, the Immigration and Nationality Act of 1965 abolished the quota system and consequently spurred a sharp increase in Portuguese immigration. At that time the Portuguese began to enter this country at the rate of 11,000 to 12,000 per year. This rate started to decline in the early 1980s and has now stabilized at 3,000 to 4,000 per year. Some of these have returned to Portugal either because they preferred living there or because they were unable to adjust to their new environment. Of those who returned to live in the Azores, at least, the impressions of their life in this country, which they have related to their friends and families, have created a favorable attitude toward the United States. The many Portuguese immigrants who remained here have contributed substantially to American society.

SETTLEMENT PATTERNS

At first the Portuguese tended to settle near their ports of entry. The greatest number made their homes in New England (especially in Massachusetts and Rhode Island), New York, central California, and Hawaii. A small group settled in central Illinois. The Homestead Act encouraged some Portuguese to go west to obtain ownership of land. Those who settled on the East Coast also spread into Connecticut and New Jersey, and most recent immigrants find homes in Connecticut, New York, or New Jersey. The number of Portuguese immigrants now settling in California or Hawaii has been greatly reduced. Because so many Portuguese arrived without skills or education, they tended to remain for a long time in the lower middle class or middle class unless they attained the background necessary for advancement.

ACCULTURATION AND ASSIMILATION

The Portuguese who settled in Hawaii tended to lose their ethnic identity fastest. From the sugar plantations they moved to the large cities where they became involved in trades and service industries. Others went into farming. They tended to intermarry with other ethnic groups and quickly lost their feeling of Portuguese identity.

In California there was a greater effort to maintain ethnicity. The Portuguese immigrants generally settled in rural areas where they farmed or operated dairies. They hired other Portuguese as hands on their farms, and under these semi-isolated conditions, it was easier to preserve their old customs. Fathers were the decision makers of the household. They allowed their daughters to attend school only as long as the law required; after that they kept them at home. Boys enjoyed more freedom than girls, but they also tended to quit school as soon as possible to work on the farm or dairy; and they were expected to marry Portuguese girls. When the rate of arrival of new immigrants slowed and American-born descendants far outnumbered the foreign-born Portuguese, assimilation began. Organizations such as the Cabrillo Civic Clubs, however, were formed to preserve pride in the Portuguese heritage.

The situation on the East Coast was different. There the Portuguese, mainly of rural origin, settled in urban areas. This change in environment forced family life and attitudes to change. When times were bad at the mills, women had to go to work to help support the family. In general, children were expected to leave school at the first opportunity to go to work to contribute to the family's maintenance as well. This tended to keep the Portuguese in the lower middle class, but it freed the women from their traditionally subordinate role and granted them more independence.

Wherever they settled, Portuguese immigrants had to face many disconcerting changes in their new environment. Rather than living in the same town or even the same neighborhood as the rest of their family—grandparents, aunts, uncles, cousins—upon whom they could depend for help when they needed it, they found themselves alone and without the support system that the extended family could provide. Unlike the milieu to which they were accustomed, in the United States education was compulsory for children, women were more emancipated, young people were freer to select the mates of their choice, families were more democratic rather than being dominated by the father, and a generation gap often existed within families because the young had developed better language proficiency and had attended public schools where they were exposed to the attitudes of their American peers.

TRADITIONS, CUSTOMS, AND BELIEFS

The Portuguese have a variety of folk beliefs, many of which coincide with those of other cultures. Some believe that certain people have the power of the evil eye, which endows them with the ability to cast evil spells on others by the use of their eyes. One may ward off the evil eye by making a gesture called "the fig" in which one closes the fist and sticks the thumb between the first and second fingers. For many the devil is real and has the power to work evil. The word "devil" (*diabo*) is avoided for fear of evoking him; he may also be kept away by making the sign of the cross. Fridays and the number 13 are considered bad luck. Some people trust their health to witch doctors called *curandeiros*, who attempt to cure illnesses with herbal medicines or magic. These beliefs disappear or are looked upon as superstitions as immigrants are absorbed into American society.

When people are far from their native countries, they long to preserve some of the customs from their youth that had special significance to them. Early in the twentieth century, Portuguese immigrants revived three celebrations from their homelands—the Festival of the Blessed Sacrament, the Festival of the Holy Ghost, and the Senhor da Pedra Festival.

FESTIVAL OF THE BLESSED SACRAMENT

This celebration from the island of Madeira was initiated in 1915 in New Bedford, Massachusetts. This four-day festival, which takes place the first weekend of August, has grown to be the largest Portuguese American celebration, attracting over 150,000 visitors to New Bedford each year. Throughout the festival there is entertainment, including Portuguese and American music, singing, dancing, and famous entertainers. Decorative arches are erected in the festival area and are covered with bundles of bayberry branches. Colored lights and banners are also used for decoration. Vendors sell American and Madeiran foods including *carne de espeto* (roasted meat on a skewer), *linguiça* (sausage), *cabra* (goat), *bacalhau* (codfish) in spicy Portuguese sauces, *favas* (beans), and Madeiran wine. Local groups perform Portuguese folk music and dances; fireworks and raffles add to the festivities. On Sunday, the final day of the festival, its organizers march with a band to the church for the 11:00 a.m. mass. At 2:00 p.m. there is a colorful parade that includes children in native costumes, bands, floats, and beauty queens. Although this festival includes a mass and a procession, it is basically a secular celebration meant for socializing and having fun.

FESTIVAL OF THE HOLY GHOST

This festival, celebrated in California and in New England, is modeled after an Azorean prototype. Depending on the location, it is celebrated on some weekend between Easter and the end of July. The celebration originated with Queen Elizabeth of Aragon, wife of Portugal's King Diniz, in 1296. As an act of humility, before a mass to which she had invited the poor, she gave the royal scepter to the most indigent and had the royal crown placed on his head. After the mass, the queen and other nobles served a sumptuous meal to the poor. In the modern celebration, the crown is kept in the church throughout the year. Details of the celebration vary from place to place, but sometimes a drawing is held to determine which families will have the honor of keeping the crown at their house for one of seven weeks leading up to the festival. The child of the first winner is crowned as the child-emperor/empress. Amidst a week of feasting and celebration, he keeps the crown in a place of honor in his house, surrounded by candles and flowers, and at the end of the week, he walks in a procession to the house of the second winner, and the second child-emperor/empress is crowned. The crown passes through seven successive households. A few days before the final Sunday of the festival, the priest blesses the food that has been collected for the poor, although today this food is more commonly used for a community banquet. On the final weekend there may be a special mass, procession, and a carnival or fair that includes fireworks, charity auctions, music, ethnic food, and dancing the chamarrita, an Azorean folk square dance.

THE FESTA DE SENHOR DA PEDRA

This festival, begun in New Bedford, Massachusetts, in 1924, is celebrated the last Sunday of August. It is also based on an Azorean festival. Its promoters emphasize the religious aspect of this celebration. After mass the image of Senhor da Pedra and those of nine other church figures are carried in procession on floats through the streets on the shoulders of the faithful. They are accompanied by a band, other church members carrying crucifixes and banners, and children wearing their first-communion outfits or dressed as angels; children also carry six smaller floats topped by the images of saints. The priest marches in the procession carrying the sacrament. As the figure of Senhor da Pedra passes, onlookers attach money to his float. One neighborhood decorates its street with sand paintings and flower petals over which the procession will pass. A carnival with public entertainment, ethnic foods—caçoila (marinated pork), bacalhau, and linguiça, and raffles are also part of the festival.

Other regional celebrations include the Santo Cristo festival in Fall River, Massachusetts, the Festival of Our Lady of Fatima, which commemorates the reported appearance of the Virgin in Fatima, Portugal, in 1917, and the Festival of Our Lady of Good Voyage in Gloucester, Massachusetts, during which the fishing fleet is blessed.

PROVERBS

Proverbs are popular in Portuguese culture, and many have been passed on from one generation to the next:

Não ha rosas sem espinhos—You can't have roses without having thorns too; Amar e saber não póde ser—Love and prudence do not go together; Mais quero asno que me leve, que caballo que me derrube—I'd rather have an ass that carried me than a horse that threw me off; A caridade bem entendida principia por casa—Charity begins at home; A Deus poderás mentir, mas não pódes enganar a Deus—You may lie to God, but you cannot deceive him; Da ma mulher te guarda, e da boa não fies nada—Beware of a bad woman, and don't trust a good one; Aonde o ouro falla, tudo calla—When money speaks, all else is silent; Do mal o menos—Of evils, choose the least.

CUISINE

Portugal's cuisine shows great variety because each of her provinces has its own specialties. Along the coast a shellfish açorda is popular. This is a type of soup made from soaking country bread in a broth used to boil shellfish. Just before serving, hot shellfish and chopped coriander are added, and the dish is topped off by the addition of raw eggs that poach in the hot liquid. The city of Porto is famous for its tripe recipes. Tripe stew, for example, contains tripe, beans, veal, *chouriço* or *linguiça*, *presunto* (mountain-cured ham similar to prosciutto), chicken, onion, carrots, and parsley. The city of Aveiro is know for its *caldeirada*, a fish and shellfish stew seasoned with cumin, parsley, and coriander. Around the city of Coimbra one might find *bife à portuguésa* (steak prepared in a seasoned wine sauce and covered with thin slices of *presunto* ham) and *sopa à portuguésa* (soup made of pork, veal, cabbage, white beans, carrots, and macaroni).

Cod is the most commonly served fish, perhaps as *bolinhos de bacalhau* (codfish cakes), or *bacalhau à Gomes de Sá* (fried with boiled potatoes, onions, eggs and olives). Indeed, since Portugal is surrounded on two sides by the ocean, seafood is fresh and plentiful throughout the country. *Escabeche* consists of fish pickled with carrots and onions and stored in the refrigerator for several days before serving.

The Portuguese, like the Spanish, use olive oil and garlic generously in their cuisine, but they use herbs and spices more widely, especially cumin coriander, and paprika. *Caldo verde* (green soup) is made of fresh kale, potatoes, garlic-seasoned smoked pork sausage (either *linguiça* or *chouriço*), olive oil, and seasonings. It is served with *pão de broa* (rye bread) and red wine. Tender slices of lamprey eel prepared in a spicy curry sauce is also a typical dish.

Cozido à portuguésa is a stew made of beef, chicken, and sausage boiled with chick-peas, potatoes, turnips, carrots, cabbage, turnip greens and rice. Chicken, roasted suckling pig, lamb, and goat are also important in Portuguese cuisine. *Massa sovada*, a delicious Portuguese sweet bread, is even commercially available in parts of the United States.

Typical desserts and confections include *pudim flan* (a baked custard topped with a caramelized sugar sauce), *toucinho do céu* ("bacon of heaven" almond cake), and *ovos moles* (a sweet mixture of egg yolks and sugar syrup), which may be served as dessert or used as icing on a cake. *Figos recheados* (dried figs stuffed with almonds and chocolate) are often served after dinner accompanied by a glass of port wine.

Portuguese wines have a good reputation. Some of the best red wine comes from Colares, the only region that still produces grapes from native European root stock. The best white wines are from Carcavelos and Buçelas. Although they are really either red or white, the so-called green wines (*vinhos verdes*), made from grapes picked before they are fully ripe, are produced in the north. They are crackling wines and have an alcohol content of eight to 11 percent. Portugal is famous for its port wine (named for the city of Oporto); it is a fortified wine whose alcohol content is 20 percent. The best ports are aged for a minimum of ten years, but some are aged for as many as 50. Madeira wine, coming from the Madeira Islands, is similar to port.

TRADITIONAL COSTUMES

The clothing worn in modern-day Portugal is similar to that worn in the United States. However, for certain festivals, traditional costumes are worn. These vary from region to region, but men often wear black, close-fitting trousers with a white shirt and sometimes a bright-colored sash or vest. On their heads they might wear a long green and red stocking cap with a tassel on the end that hangs down to one side. Women wear colorful gathered skirts with aprons and cloth shawls over their shoulders. During the festival of *tabuleiros* in the region around Tomar, the harvest is celebrated by girls clad in ankle-length, long-sleeved white cotton dresses adorned by a wide colored ribbon that goes around the waist and over one shoulder. On their heads they wear a tall crown made of bread and weighing more than 30 pounds. The crown, which is at least as tall as the girl herself, is decorated with paper flowers and sprigs of wheat and is topped by a white dove or a Maltese cross.

PORTUGUESE SONGS AND DANCES

The *fado* is a melancholy type of song from Portugal. It is performed in certain bars of Lisbon late at night and in the early hours of the morning. These songs are believed to have originated among Portuguese sailors who had to spend months or even years at sea, away from their beloved homeland. The *fado*, meaning "fate," praises the beauties of the country for which the singer is homesick or of the love that he left behind. Regional folk dances include the *chula*, the *corridinho* (a polka-like dance from southern Portugal), the *fandango*, the *tirana*, and the *vira*.

HOLIDAYS CELEBRATED BY PORTUGUESE AMERICANS

The Portuguese celebrate the traditional Christian holidays. Their celebration of Christmas (*Dia*

do Natal) includes attending midnight mass on Christmas Eve (*missa do galo*), getting together with the extended family to share a meal and converse, singing carols outside friends' homes, and displaying a manger scene. New Year's Eve is celebrated by picking and eating 12 grapes as the clock is striking midnight in order to assure 12 months of happiness in the new year. On January 6, *Dia de Reis* (Day of the Kings), gifts are exchanged. Families share a ring-shaped cake called a *bolo Rei* which contains toy figures that bring good luck if found in one's portion. During Holy Week there are processions through the streets carrying portrayals of the passion of Jesus. The most famous processions are in the cities of Covilhã and Vila do Conde. On Easter, after attending mass, the family enjoys a special meal. This may include *folar*, a cake made of sweet dough and topped with hard-boiled eggs. On Pentecost (50 days after Easter) Holy Ghost societies in the Azores provide food for the poor in the community. *Véspera de São João* (Saint John's Eve), on June 23, is a celebration in honor of St. John the Baptist. The traditions associated with this festival have to do with fire and water. People build bonfires, dance around them, and leap over their flames. It is said that water possesses a miraculous quality that night, and that contact with it or dew can bring health, good fortune, protection to livestock, marriage, or good luck. On the thirteenth of May and October, people throng to the sanctuary of Our Lady of Fatima in search of miraculous cures or the granting of a prayer. In the United States, all these celebrations have become Americanized or have been abandoned for American equivalents (for example, the *Dia das Almas* has been replaced by Memorial Day), but certain traditions may be retained by some families out of ethnic pride.

HEALTH AND MENTAL HEALTH ISSUES

Portuguese Americans have no specific health problems or medical conditions that afflict them. They take pride in their sturdiness and longevity. They have a reputation for hard work and diligence. The birth rate of Portugal is high compared to the rest of Europe and to the United States, but it has dropped in recent years. Mutual aid societies are an established tradition among Portuguese Americans. Many workers have health insurance through their employer's benefits plan; the self-employed often insure themselves at their own expense.

LANGUAGE

Portuguese is a Romance language derived from Latin. Today it is spoken by people on five continents, including about 300,000 in the United States. Linguists see its development as consisting of two main periods. The language of the twelfth to the sixteenth centuries is called Galician-Portuguese; it was essentially the same as that spoken in northwestern Spain. The language of central Portugal, between Coimbra and Lisbon, came to be considered the standard dialect, and this language, from the sixteenth century on, is called modern Portuguese.

Modern Portuguese is characterized by an abundance of sibilant and palatal consonants and a broad spectrum of vowel sounds (five nasal phonemes and eight to ten oral ones). Portuguese has an uvular "r" similar to the French "r." On occasion, unstressed vowels tend not to be pronounced, for example, *professor* is pronounced "prufsor." Portuguese has a northern and a southern dialect. The northern dialect is more conservative and has retained more traits of Galician-Portuguese; the southern one has evolved further. The Portuguese spoken in the Azores and in Madeira might be considered a third dialect. Brazilian Portuguese differs from continental Portuguese in sound (diphthongs in final positions are not nasalized, and unstressed vowels are not omitted in pronunciation), in vocabulary (words from indigenous languages have been incorporated), and in syntax.

GREETINGS AND OTHER POPULAR EXPRESSIONS

Common Portuguese greetings and other expressions include: *Bom dia* ("bong DEE-uh")—Good morning; *Boa tarde* ("BOH-uh tard")—Good afternoon; *Boa noite* ("BOH-uh noyt")—Good night; *Por favor* ("poor fuh-VOR")—Please; *Obrigado* ("o-bree-GAH-doo")—Thank you; *Adeus* ("a-DEH-oosh")—Goodbye; *Desculpe!* ("dush-KOOLP")—Excuse me!; *Como esta?* ("KOH-moo shta")—How are you?; *Saúde!* ("sa-OOD")—Cheers!; *Feliz Natal* ("Fe-LEEZ na-TA-o")—Merry Christmas; *Próspero Ano Novo* ("PRAHS-pe-roo UN-new NO-voo")—Happy New Year.

FAMILY AND COMMUNITY DYNAMICS

In the earliest years of Portuguese immigration to the United States, most of the new arrivals were young, single males or married men hoping to bring their families over when their financial condition allowed. Most Portuguese immigrants came from rural villages and were illiterate; those who settled in urban areas had great adjustments to make. Their poor educational background and their lack of marketable skills condemned them to unskilled labor. They brought with them an anti-intellectual attitude derived from their belief that the father ruled the household and the children worked under his supervision to contribute to the common good by working on the land that their family was farming. Allowing their children to spend time in school was a luxury that these immigrants could not afford. In their new environment they resisted compulsory education for the young. When they were required to send their children to school, they sent them to public schools rather than to parochial ones. After a generation or two, however, families were more financially able to allow their children to continue their education. As a result, Portuguese American families have produced many physicians, lawyers, and university professors.

Immigrants also had to make adjustments to their diets. Since many of the early arrivals lived in boarding houses, they had to acclimate quickly to American food which generally represented an improvement over the bread, codfish, beans, and wine that were staples in Portugal. On the negative side, it was more difficult and more expensive to obtain fresh fruit, vegetables, and fish in the United States than it had been in Portugal. Children had to adjust to cow's milk after having been used to goat's milk. Immigrants who settled in rural areas, however, were not subject to such sudden changes in diet and could preserve their traditional eating habits more easily.

Because they could no longer depend upon their extended family for support, Portuguese immigrants formed mutual aid societies in the United States. The first was founded around 1847. The early societies were established for men only. Each member would pay a monthly amount into the treasury of the society or periodically would be assessed; in turn he would receive benefits if he lost his job or was unable to work because of illness or disability. These societies sometimes afforded the opportunity to socialize with other Portuguese. Similar organizations for women began to appear about 20 years later.

Women, who traditionally held a subordinate position in the family and in society in Portugal, gained greater equality with men in the United States. Many of them had to leave the home to work in industries in order to help support the family. Their progress is reflected in their participation in organizations founded by Portuguese Americans. At first they did not participate at all; then they established organizations for themselves. Later they served as auxiliaries for men's organizations, and now they enjoy equal membership with men in many of these clubs.

FRAGMENTATION OF PORTUGUESE IMMIGRANT GROUPS

Portuguese immigrants tended to differentiate themselves from other Portuguese-speaking immigrants of different geographical backgrounds. The continental Portuguese, the people from the Cape Verde Islands, those from Madeira, those from the Eastern Azores, and those from the Central Azores felt little affinity for the other groups, and often rivalry existed among them despite their common language. Except for the continentals, they did not think of themselves as Portuguese but as citizens of a particular island. And Azoreans often identified with a particular city rather than with the island as a whole. In the United States, each group tended to settle in clusters to be near others with whom they felt kinship and allegiance. The various groups did not know one another well, and prejudices grew among them. They wanted little to do with one another and even ridiculed each other's dialects. The groups with lighter skin looked down upon those with darker skin. Fraternal organizations founded by one group would not admit members of the other groups. The well-educated Portuguese who belonged to a higher social class felt little in common with those of the lower classes. This internal fragmentation has lessened with time but has inhibited Portuguese immigrants from presenting a united front for their own betterment.

RELIGION

Nearly all Portuguese immigrants to the United States are Roman Catholic. However, whereas the Roman Catholic church was protected by the Portuguese government for many years, church and state are separate in the United States. Immigrants came into conflict with the church because its laws made it difficult and frustrating to try to establish a Portuguese Catholic church in a community. The church, which had to be built with money contributed by the Portuguese immigrants, could be stripped of its Portuguese identity at the discretion of the bishop. Although none was ever built in Hawaii, the mainland United States has several Portuguese Catholic churches in Califor-

nia and about 30 in New England. There are also a few Portuguese Protestant churches in existence. The first was a Portuguese Presbyterian church established in Jacksonville, Illinois, in 1850. It was founded by about 130 newly arrived Madeiran Protestants who left their native land because of religious persecution and settled in this region, after having spent several years in Trinidad. Within a few years, their numbers had grown to 400. There are Portuguese Protestant churches in New England, California, and Hawaii. Many people of Portuguese descent have found a church home in nonethnic Roman Catholic churches and in mainstream American Protestant churches.

EMPLOYMENT AND ECONOMIC TRADITIONS

Portuguese immigrants who settled on the East Coast tended to find work in factories, especially in the textile mills, in whaling and fishing, and in truck farming. Some found jobs as itinerant farm workers, picking cranberries and strawberries. Women worked as seamstresses in garment shops. In California, early Portuguese immigrants participated in gold mining as well as in whaling and fishing. Many there went into various types of farming. The first Portuguese in Hawaii worked on sugar plantations but soon moved to the urban centers to work in more skilled jobs. At first the Portuguese were assigned some of the most undesirable jobs, but as their proficiency in English and their work skills and educational level improved, they rose to higher, more responsible positions. Their success in farming is demonstrated by the fact that, by 1974, 34 percent of all market milk produced in California came from Portuguese American dairies. Many Portuguese American entrepreneurs went into business for themselves and opened restaurants, hotels, and banks. Others took advantage of educational opportunities in the United States and went into the professions. They now occupy a broad spectrum of jobs and careers and are found at all social and economic levels of society.

POLITICS AND GOVERNMENT

Portuguese Americans have assimilated quietly into American society; they have tended not to

This Portuguese American man is fishing off the coast of Newport, Rhode Island.

use politics as a means of promoting their own welfare. They have also tended to avoid political and social protest. They are self-reliant and avail themselves of welfare programs only as a last resort. They have organized themselves, however, through mutual aid societies as well as civic, educational, social, and fraternal organizations. Some of these include the Portuguese Union of the State of California, the Portuguese American Civic League of Massachusetts, the Portuguese Civic League of Rhode Island, the Portuguese Educational Society of New Bedford, Massachusetts, the Luso-American Education Foundation, the Luso-American Federation, the League of Portuguese Fraternal Societies of California, and the Cabrillo Civic Clubs of California. They also have served in elected governmental positions. Their political influence began early in Hawaii; in 1894 three of the 18 elected delegates to the Constitutional Convention were Portuguese. In California the first Portuguese American was elected to the state legislature in 1900. This did not happen in Massachusetts until the early 1940s.

State governments have formally recognized the contributions that some Portuguese have made to the United States. Since 1935 California has celebrated Cabrillo Day on September 28, honoring the discoverer of that state. In 1967 the state of California further proclaimed the second week in March of each year Portuguese Immigrant Week. In 1974 Massachusetts set aside March 15

as Peter Francisco Day. Peter Francisco was a boy of Portuguese origin who, during the Revolutionary War, enlisted in the Continental Army at the age of 16; his courage and patriotism earned the respect of General George Washington. There is a Peter Francisco Park in the Ironbound district of Newark, New Jersey. Portuguese Americans have served with distinction in the United States armed services since the Revolution.

INDIVIDUAL AND GROUP CONTRIBUTIONS

Although most of the Portuguese who arrived on American shores lacked education and skills, and therefore had limited ability to make significant contributions to their new land's popular culture or to its arts and sciences, there have been exceptions. Descendants of Portuguese immigrants, having had greater educational opportunity in America, have gone on to make their mark on American society. In considering their contributions, it must be remembered that Portuguese Americans constitute only a fraction of one percent of the population of the United States, and that they have achieved success in areas besides those listed below, such as business and dairy farming.

ACADEMIA

Dr. Joaquim de Siqueira Coutinho (1885-) was a professor at George Washington University and at the Catholic University of America. From 1910 to 1920 he was in charge of the Brazilian section of the Pan-American Union. Francis Mile Rogers (1914-) was professor of Portuguese at Harvard University where he chaired the Department of Romance Languages and Literatures. He also served as Dean of the School of Arts and Sciences and authored a number of books.

ART AND ARCHITECTURE

William L. Pereira (1909-) is an internationally known architect and city planner. He designed or planned such complexes as Cape Canaveral, CBS Television City, the Los Angeles Museum of Art, the Crocker Citizens Bank in Los Angeles, the Central Library at the University of California (San Diego), and the Union Oil Center. Henrique Medina and Palmira Pimental were painters in the 1930s.

FILM, TELEVISION, AND THEATER

Harold José Pereira de Faria (Hal Peary) (1908-1985) achieved fame in the title role of the series "The Great Gildersleeve," which he played for 16 years on radio and television. He also appeared in motion pictures. John Mendes (1919-1955) performed as a magician under the name of "Prince Mendes." He was also a stage, screen, and television actor. Other Portuguese American motion picture actors include Rod de Medicis and Nestor Pavie. Carmen Miranda (1914-1955), although known as "the Brazilian bombshell," actually was born in Portugal. She was a popular film star of the 1940s known for her humor, her singing, and her extravagant hats piled high with fruit. She popularized Latin American dance music in the United States. Henry da Sylva established a ballet school in Hollywood, acted in films and directed them as well.

GOVERNMENT

Joseph F. Francis and Mary L. Fonseca were senators in the Massachusetts State Legislature. João G. Mattos served in the state legislature of California. Helen L. C. Lawrence became chair of the City Council of San Leandro, California, in 1941. In that position she exercised the power of mayor. Clarence Azevedo was mayor of Sacramento, California. In 1979, Peter "Tony" Coelho of California was elected to the United States House of Representatives; he is probably the first Portuguese American to serve in the national congress. Ernest Ladeira served as President Richard M. Nixon's advisor on social welfare. He was also an assistant to John Volpe, Secretary of Transportation. John M. Arruda was mayor of Fall River, Massachusetts, for six years.

LITERATURE

Some Portuguese immigrants recorded their experiences in their adopted country: Laurinda C. Andrade (1899-) gives a young girl's impressions in her autobiography, The Open Door; Lawrence Oliver (1887-1977) wrote an autobiography titled Never Backward; and Alfred Lewis (1902-1977) wrote an autobiographical novel, Home Is an Island, as well as poetry. Onésimo Almeida, who completed his university training in Portugal and then earned a Ph.D. at Brown University where he later served as professor, wrote Da Vida Quotidiana na LUSAlândia (1975), Ah! Mònim dum Corisco (1978), and (Sapa)teia Americana (1983).

Immigrants who tell of their experiences in poetry include Artur Ávila in his Rimas de Um Imigrante and José Brites in his Poemas sem Poesia and Imigramante (1984). John Roderigo Dos Passos (1896-1970) is the only American novelist of Portuguese descent who has an international reputation. His works include Manhattan Transfer (1925) and the trilogy U.S.A. (1937), for which he is best known. It comprises the novels The 42nd Parallel (1930), 1919 (1932), and The Big Money (1936). He published a second trilogy titled District of Columbia in 1952. Jorge de Sena (1919-1978) came to the United States from Portugal via Brazil. He was a professor at the University of Wisconsin, Madison. At the University of California, Santa Barbara, he was chair of the comparative literature program. He was a well-known literary critic, poet, playwright, novelist and short-story writer. His works include the novels O Físico Prodigioso (translated into English as The Wondrous Physician) and Sinais de fogo as well as the short story collections Génesis and Os grao-capitaes. English readers can obtain his work By the Rivers of Babylon and Other Stories. The novelist and short-story writer José Rodrigues Miguéis (1901-1980) wrote fiction such as Saudades para Dena Genciana and Gente da Terceira Classe.

MUSIC

John Philip Sousa (1854-1932) was director of the U.S. Marine Band from 1880 to 1892. He then founded his own Sousa Band in 1892 which, in its over 40-year existence, became the world's most famous concert band. At the outbreak of World War I, Sousa, at the age of 62, joined the navy to train bands at the Great Lakes Naval Training Center. He is famous as the composer of such marches as "Stars and Stripes Forever," "Semper Fidelis," "The Washington Post March," and "Hands Across the Sea." He also composed several operettas including The Captain, The Charlatan, and The Queen of Hearts, as well as several suites for piano. Ilda Stichini and Maria Silveira were opera divas in the 1930s. Raul da Silva Pereira was a composer and conductor. Elmar de Oliveira (1950-) is a violinist who, in 1978, was the first American to win the gold medal in Moscow's Tchaikovsky competition; he is now on the faculty of the Manhattan School of Music. In the field of popular music, the vocalist Tony Martin (1912-) produced many hit records between 1941 and 1957. He had his own radio show and also appeared in films. His best role was probably in Casbah (1948). He appeared in nightclubs in the 1970s. A general contribution the Portuguese people have made to American music is the ukulele, which originated in Madeira and is now popular in Hawaii.

RELIGION

The charismatic religious leader Marcelino Manoel de Graça (1882-1960), also known as "Sweet Daddy Grace," founded the United House of Prayer for All People in the Harlem area of New York. His congregation, made up mainly of African Americans, included over three million people. Humberto Sousa Medeiros (1915-1983), who had been bishop of Brownsville, Texas, was named to succeed Cardinal Cushing as Archbishop of Boston in 1970. He was the first non-Irish American to fill that position in 124 years. He was elevated to the College of Cardinals in 1973.

SCIENCE AND MEDICINE

José de Sousa Bettencourt (1851-1931) earned degrees in both law and medicine. He practiced medicine and taught at the San Francisco Medical School. João Sérgio Alvares Cabral (d. 1909) practiced medicine in Oakland, California. He gave free consultations to the poor and ones at reduced rate to Portuguese. He also served as editor in chief of A *Pátria*, a Portuguese newspaper published in Oakland. Mathias Figueira (1853-1930) founded the American College of Surgeons. M. M. Enos (1875-) was head of the Portuguese Association of the Portuguese Hospital of Saint Anthony in Oakland, California. He was also director of the Portuguese American Bank and taught at the National Medical School of Chicago. Carlos Fernandes (d. 1977) was director of St. John's Hospital in San Francisco.

SPORTS

Bernie de Viveiros played baseball with the Detroit Tigers and the Oakland Oaks. Manuel Gomes also was a baseball player as was Lew Fonseca (1899-1989) who played for the Cincinnati Reds, the Philadelphia Phillies, the Cleveland Indians, and coached the Chicago White Sox; he was a pioneer in the use of film to analyze players' performance during a game. In boxing, Al Melo participated as a welterweight in the Olympics in 1924. George Araujo, Johnny Gonsalves, and Babe Herman were contenders for the world boxing championships. Justiano Silva was a profes-

sional wrestler. Henrique Santos won the United States fencing championship in 1942. Tony Lema (1934-1966), also known as "Champagne Tony," was the winner of numerous professional golf tournaments. At the time of his death he ranked tenth in all-time earnings in the PGA. Tennis star Vic (E. Victor) Seixas, Jr. (1923-), won the U.S. Open Championship in 1954.

TECHNOLOGY

Abilio de Silva Greaves invented a fire-alarm system as well as devices used in aviation. In the field of textiles, Steve Abrantes invented a wool carding device, and José Pacheco Correia invented one for combing cotton. Sebastião Luiz Dias patented an irrigation control system. John C. Lobato developed a new type of army tank.

MEDIA

People who are interested in Portuguese cultural topics and would like to communicate with those having similar interests may do so through the USENET news group called soc.culture.portuguese. A game or pastime called "MOOsaico" can be played through Telnet by contacting moo.di.uminho. pt 7777. Participants explore a virtual world and talk to other players. The game may be played in Portuguese or English.

PRINT

Jornal Portugues/Portuguese Journal.
Published every Thursday in Portuguese and English; circulation of 2,500.

Contact: Albert Lemos, Editor.
Address: 1912 Church Lane, San Pablo, California 94806.
Telephone: (510) 237-0888.

Journal do Emigrante.
Portuguese newspaper, founded in 1975.

Contact: Isaias Lopes, Editor and Publisher.
Address: 4003 Boulleurent San Laurent, Montreal, Quebec, Canada H2W 1Y4.
Telephone: (514) 843-3863.

Luso-Americano.
Established 1928 and published every Wednesday and Friday with a circulation of 36,000—the largest outside Portugal and Brazil.

Contact: Antonio Matinho, Editor and Publisher.
Address: 88 Ferry, Newark, New Jersey 07105.
Telephone: (201) 589-4600.

O Jornal Portuguese.
Contact: Lou da Silva, Editor.
Address: 410 Second Street, Fall River, Massachusetts 02722.
Telephone: (508) 678-3844.

The Portuguese Post.
Established 1986 and published every Monday; circulation 20,000.

Contact: George Valante, Editor.
Address: 109 Monroe, Newark, New Jersey 07105.
Telephone: (201) 344-5652.

Portuguese Times, Inc.
Published every Thursday; circulation 15,000.

Contact: Manuel Ferreira, Editor.
Address: 1501 Acushnet Avenue, New Bedford, Massachusetts 02740.
Telephone: (508) 997-3118.
Fax: (508) 990-1231.

Portuguese Tribune.
Published bi-monthly. Circulation: 1,800 subscriptions plus sales in more than 250 vending locations.

Contact: Armando Antunes, Editor.
Address: P.O. Box 3477, San Jose, California 95156.
Telephone: (408) 729-6195.

Voz de Portugal/Voice of Portugal.
Semi-monthly magazine published in Portuguese.

Contact: Lourenco Costa Aguiar, Editor and Publisher.
Address: 370 A Street, Hayward, California 94541.
Telephone: (415) 537-9503.

RADIO
KRVE.
"Som da Comunidade."

Address: 227 North Santa Cruz Avenue, Los Gatos, California 95030.
Telephone: (408) 354-6622.

WINE.
Radio Portugal.

Address: 6 Melrose Avenue, Danbury, Connecticut 06810.
Telephone: (203) 743-4709.

WJFD.
Radio Globo.

Address: 270 Union Street, New Bedford, Massachusetts 02740.
Telephone: (617) 997-2929.

WRCP.
Radio Clube Portugues.

Address: 1110 Douglas Avenue, Providence, Rhode Island 02904.
Telephone: (401) 273-7000.

TELEVISION
Full Channel.
Address: 57 Everett Street, Warren, Rhode Island 02885.
Telephone: (401) 247-1250.

A Nossa Gente.
Address: Heritage Cable Vision, 1636 Alum Rock Avenue, San Jose, California 95116.
Telephone: (408) 258-2800.

Portuguese American Hour.
Address: Channel 38, 46921 Warm Springs Boulevard, Fremont, California.
Telephone: (415) 656-3232.

The Portuguese Channel.
Address: Channel 20, 1501 Acushnet Avenue, New Bedford, Massachusetts 02740.
Telephone: (508) 997-3110.
Fax: (508) 996-2151.

Portuguese Television.
Address: Channel 38, P.O. Box 51, Fremont, California 94541.
Telephone: (415) 797-4219

RTP.
This Portuguese television channel can be received from the Hughes Galaxy III satellite. This is a C-band satellite with a horizontal polarization. Its position is 93.5 degrees west, and its transponder number is five.

Address: R.T.P. USA, Adams Street, Newark, New Jersey.
Telephone: (201) 344-8888.

ORGANIZATIONS AND ASSOCIATIONS

American Association of Teachers of Spanish and Portuguese (AATSP).

Founded in 1917. The membership of the AATSP is made up of teachers of Spanish and/or Portuguese from the secondary school through university level as well as other interested persons. There are state and local chapters besides the national organization. Its journal *Hispania* contains articles dealing with Spanish, Portuguese, and Brazilian language, literature, and culture. The organization holds a national conference once a year where there are workshops for teachers and oral presentations of research in the field of Spanish and Portuguese.

Contact: Dr. Lynn A. Sandstedt, Executive Director.

Address: Gunter Hall, Room 106, University of Northern Colorado, Greeley, Colorado 80639.

Telephone: (303) 351-1090.

Fax: (303) 351-1095.

American Portuguese Society.

Founded in 1959. Promotes friendship, understanding, and cultural relations between Portugal and the United States through exhibits, seminars, and cultural exchanges. Publishes the *Journal of the American Portuguese Society* with articles in English about Portuguese culture.

Contact: Michael Teague, Secretary.

Address: 555 Madison Avenue, Seventh Floor, New York, New York 10021.

Telephone: (212) 751-1992.

Cabrillo Civic Clubs.

Social clubs in California for Portuguese-Americans and their spouses. They raise money for various charities (e.g., the American Red Cross, the American Cancer Society) and for university scholarships for descendants of Portuguese and Portuguese Americans.

Contact: Vera Souza, State Secretary.

Address: P.O. Box 374, Stratford, California 93266.

Telephone: (209) 947-3110.

International Conference Group on Portugal.

Founded in 1972. An international network for teaching and research related to Portugal and the Lusophone world, not including Brazil. Their journal, *Portuguese Studies Review*, is published twice a year; it is intended for students, scholars, teachers, and all others who have an interest in Portugal, in Lusophone Africa and Asia, and other Lusophone parts of the world, for the purposes of studying, learning, teaching, writing, general interest, as well as visiting and tourism.

Contact: Professor Douglas L. Wheeler, Coordinator.

Address: Department of History, HSCC 408, University of New Hampshire, Durham, New Hampshire 03824.

Telephone: (603) 862-3018.

Fax: (603) 868-6935.

Portuguese Continental Union USA.

Founded in 1925. A fraternal organization serving the Portuguese community.

Contact: Francisco Mendonca, Supreme Secretary/CEO.

Address: 899 Boylston Street, Boston, Massachusetts 02115.

Telephone: (617) 536-2916.

Portuguese Cultural Foundation, Inc.

Founded in 1979. Promotes Portuguese culture and language in the New England states via events, data base management, and seminars.

Contact: Peter Calvet, Executive Director.

Address: 3 Armstrong Avenue, Providence, Rhode Island 02903.

Telephone: (401) 331-8070.

União Portuguesa do Estado da California (U.P.E.C.).

Founded in August, 1880. The character of this organization is social, charitable, and benevolent; it seeks to protect its members and their families, and to provide aid and relief to its members and to their widows and children by assessments and the payment of dues. This group has extended charity not only to causes in the United States, but also to those in the Azores, Africa, and Italy. It awards scholarships to deserving student members of the society and stipends to members and nonmembers for the study of Portuguese language and culture at the post-graduate and graduate levels.

Contact: Carlos Almeida, Executive Director.

Address: 1120 East 14th Street, San Leandro, California 94577.

Telephone: (510) 483-7676.

MUSEUMS AND RESEARCH CENTERS

The Center for Portuguese Studies.

An affiliated unit at the University of California, Santa Barbara, the center is an autonomous institution within the Department of Spanish and Portuguese. It was created in honor of Jorge de Sena, a distinguished Portuguese professor and writer, to implement Portuguese Studies in California and the United States. The center awards scholarships and stipends to students of Portuguese, sponsors summer course offerings in Portuguese, hosts important international colloquia, and maintains a library. The center is also responsible for a publication series and for the production of *Santa Barbara Portuguese Studies*, a yearly journal devoted to the literature and culture of the Portuguese-speaking world.

Contact: João Camilo dos Santos, Director.

Address: University of California at Santa Barbara, Center for Portuguese Studies, Department of Spanish and Portuguese, 4330 Phelps Hall, Santa Barbara, California 93106-4150.

Telephone: (805) 893-4405; or, (805) 893-3162.

Fax: (805) 893-8341.

The National Museum for Women in the Arts.

Contains drawings, paintings, sculptures, designs, collages, and fashions by some 30 Portuguese women artists. The museum's library includes information on all artists whose works are on exhibition.

Contact: Michele Weber, Librarian; or, Randi Greenberg, Assistant Registrar.

Address: 1250 New York Avenue N.W., Washington, D.C. 20005-3920.

Telephone: (202) 783-5000 and (202) 783-7377.

The Oliveira Lima Library.

Located on the campus of The Catholic University of America in Washington, D.C., this is the oldest and most extensive library of materials specializing in Luso-Brazilian history and culture.

Telephone: (202) 319-5059.

The União Portuguesa do Estado da California Library.

Has 8,000 volumes dealing with Portugal and Portuguese Americans.

Contact: Carlos Almeida.

Address: 1120 East 14th Street, San Leandro, California 94577.

Telephone: (510) 483-7676.

SOURCES FOR ADDITIONAL STUDY

Almeida, Carlos. *Portuguese Immigrants: The Centennial Story of the Portuguese Union of the State of California*. San Leandro, California: Supreme Council of U.P.E.C., 1992.

Cabral, Stephen L. *Tradition and Transformation: Portuguese Feasting in New Bedford*. New York: AMS Press, Inc., 1989.

Cardoso, Manoel da Silveira. *The Portuguese in America: 590 B.C.-1974: A Chronology & Fact Book*. Dobbs Ferry, New York: Oceana Publications, Inc., 1976.

Gilbert, Dorothy Ann. *Recent Portuguese Immigrants to Fall River, Massachusetts: An Analysis of Relative Economic Success*. New York: AMS Press, Inc., 1989.

Pap, Leo. *The Portuguese-Americans*. Boston: Twayne Publishers, 1981.

Ribeiro, José Luís. *Portuguese Immigrants and Education*. Bristol, Rhode Island: Portuguese American Federation, 1982.

Wolforth, Sandra. *The Portuguese in America*. San Francisco: R&E Research Associates, Inc., 1978.

No one knows when Pueblo peoples first arrived in the Southwest, but they are believed to be descended from Archaic desert culture peoples who had been in the region for thousands of years.

PUEBLOS

by
D. L. Birchfield

OVERVIEW

Pueblo peoples have lived in the American Southwest for thousands of years. Their ancient ruins, particularly Anasazi cliff dwellings, are among the most spectacular ancient ruins in North America. By the end of the severe, prolonged droughts in the late fourteenth century they had relocated to the vicinity of their modern communities primarily located within the watershed of the upper Rio Grande River Valley in New Mexico and the watershed of the Little Colorado River in Arizona. The pueblo tribes represent several distantly related language families and dialects, and they have continued to maintain close contact with each other since the arrival of Europeans in the region in the sixteenth century. Today the 19 pueblos of New Mexico cooperate in a loose confederation called the All Indian Pueblo Council. Each pueblo is autonomous and has its own tribal government. The Pueblos have been able to retain a tribal land base, retain a strong sense of community, and maintain their language and culture. The name Pueblo is the Spanish word for village and denotes both the people and their communal homes.

HISTORY

No one knows when Pueblo peoples first arrived in the Southwest, but they are believed to be descended from Archaic desert culture peoples who had been in the region for thousands of years. Archaeologists have developed eight classifications for Pueblo chronology. Basketmaker I spans the period prior to 100 B.C. The Basketmaker II period (100 B.C.-400 A.D.) featured beautifully woven baskets, the cultivation of corn and pumpkins, the first pit houses, and rare, crude gray pottery. The Basketmaker III period (400-700) featured the first cultivation of beans, the domestication of turkeys, the replacing of short spears and the *atlatl* with the bow and arrow, and the increased use of pottery (either gray, or with a black pattern on a white base). The Pueblo I period (700-900) featured the cultivation of cotton; pit houses became ceremonial kivas; houses were built above ground out of stone and set immediately against one another; cradle boards were introduced; and white, red, and orange ceremonial pottery was made with black or red decorations. The Pueblo II period (900-1100) featured multi-storied stone masonry apartments and an elaborate system of roads, in a culture that is also known as the Anasazi. The Pueblo III period (1100-1300) saw the Anasazi culture reach its greatest height in communities such as Chaco Canyon and Mesa Verde; the period featured extensive trade with Mexico and the development of polychrome pottery and pots of diverse shapes. During the Pueblo IV period (1300-1540) glazing was used in pottery for the first time, but only for ornamentation, and paintings appeared on the walls of the kivas; the population centers shifted from the Colorado Plateau to the Little Colorado River and the upper Rio Grande River. The Pueblo V period (1540-present) featured the adjustments Pueblo peoples have had to make due to the arrival of Europeans in the region. By 1700 only Zuni, Acoma, Taos, Picuris, and the Hopi had not moved their locations since the arrival of the Spanish.

The Pueblo people were visited by a number of large Spanish exploratory expeditions in the sixteenth century, beginning with Coronado in 1540. These expeditions brought diseases for which the Pueblos had no resistance and resulted in large population decreases before the Spanish finally colonized New Mexico with the expedition of Juan de Onate in 1598. The Pueblo people suffered severe disruptions of their lives and cultures during the long Spanish colonization of New Mexico. During the Spanish era the number of pueblos in New Mexico was reduced from somewhere between 70 and 100 pueblos to 19. The Spanish tried to force the Pueblos to convert to Christianity and exacted forced labor from them

under the *encomienda* system. Many pueblos were moved or consolidated to benefit Spanish labor demands. In the mid-seventeenth century serious disputes developed between the civil and religious authorities in New Mexico, with the Pueblos caught in the middle. In 1680 the Pueblos revolted and successfully drove the Spanish out of New Mexico for more than a decade, but the Spanish returned in force and reconquered the region by 1694. The historic southward migration of the Comanches onto the Southern Plains, beginning about 1700, displaced the Eastern Apaches from the plains and greatly altered Spanish-Indian relations in New Mexico for the remainder of the Spanish colonial era. Pueblo auxiliaries were often required to fight with Spanish troops against either Apaches, Navajos, Utes, or Comanches, depending upon Spanish Indian policies and alliances at any given time. Pueblos became Mexican citizens in 1820 at the conclusion of the Mexican revolution, the only Indians in the Southwest to be granted Mexican citizenship. As Mexican citizens Pueblos, became citizens of the United States at the conclusion of the Mexican War in 1848, the only Indians in the Southwest to gain U.S. citizenship in that manner. Most Indians in the Southwest did not become U.S. citizens until the Indian Citizenship Act of 1924.

MODERN ERA

Pueblo peoples today are still to be found in their ancestral homeland, primarily along the upper Rio Grande River Valley in the state of New Mexico, along with the Hopi in northeastern Arizona and the small community of Isleta del Sur near El Paso, Texas, just across the border from New Mexico. Census figures have sometimes shown great variation from census to census for some individual pueblos, as have population reports compiled by other federal agencies, such as the Bureau of Indian Affairs Labor Force Report. In both the 1980 and 1990 census, Arizona and New Mexico ranked third and fourth, respectively, for the largest number of Indian residents within each state (Oklahoma and California have the largest Indian populations). Texas ranked eighth. The Pueblo peoples in these states, and their modern tribal governments follow.

NEW MEXICO

The Acoma Pueblo is one of the 12 Southern Pueblos, located west of Albuquerque and the oldest continuously inhabited settlement within the United States, dating from the twelfth century. Called the Sky City, it sits atop a 350-foot mesa. Only about 50 people now inhabit the ancient town year-round. It has no electricity or running water. Most of the Acoma people live in the nearby communities of Acomita, Anzac, and McCarty's.

Cochiti Pueblo, a Southern Pueblo, is located west of Santa Fe. Cochiti pueblo leases land to the town of Cochiti Lake, which offers recreational services. Cochiti drums are well-known craft items made here, as well as pottery, jewelry, and storyteller figures. A portion of the original 1628 church can still be seen in the rebuilt structure.

Isleta Pueblo, a Southern Pueblo, is the largest Tiwa-speaking pueblo, composed of several communities on the Rio Grande River south of Albuquerque.

Jemez Pueblo, another Southern Pueblo, is located north of Albuquerque in an area of wilderness and is the last remaining Towa-speaking pueblo. It absorbed the Towa-speaking survivors of Pecos Pueblo when Pecos was abandoned in the 1830s. The pueblo is known for its baskets made of yucca fronds.

Laguna Pueblo, a Southern Pueblo located west of Albuquerque, is the largest Keresan-speaking pueblo, composed of six villages: Old Laguna, Paguate, Mesita, Paraje, Encinal, and Seama. Each town has its own fair and feast day. A rich uranium mine was located here. Now the Laguna Reclamation Project is attempting to restore the mining site.

Nambe Pueblo, is one of the eight Northern Pueblos, located north of Santa Fe in an area of scenic land formations.

Picuris Pueblo, a Northern Pueblo, located north of Santa Fe, is the smallest of the Tiwa-speaking pueblos. The original pueblo, built in the twelfth century, was abandoned after the Pueblo revolt of 1680 and was reestablished in the early eighteenth century.

Pojoaque Pueblo, the smallest of all the pueblos, is a Northern Pueblo located north of Santa Fe. A late nineteenth century smallpox epidemic almost destroyed this Tewa-speaking people. The present settlement dates from the 1930s, but ruins of the original pueblo are nearby. Also nearby are the ruins of several pueblos deserted after the Pueblo Revolt. Traditional dances were revived in 1973 after having been abandoned for about a century. Revenues from a commercial strip along the highway makes Pojoaque one of the more affluent pueblos.

Sandia Pueblo, a small Southern Pueblo located north of Albuquerque, occupies about 26 acres near the center of the reservation. Its annual feast day is open to the public.

San Felipe Pueblo, a Keresan-speaking pueblo known for its ceremonies is a Southern Pueblo, located north of Albuquerque. Its Green Corn Dance involves hundreds of participants.

San Ildefonso Pueblo, a Northern Pueblo of Tewa-speaking pueblo famous for its pottery is located north of Santa Fe.. San Ildefonso is host to the annual Eight Northern Indian Pueblos Artist and Craftsman Show.

San Juan Pueblo is the largest Tewa-speaking pueblo. A Northern Pueblo located north of Santa Fe, it was the site of the first Spanish capitol of New Mexico.

Santa Ana Pueblo, a Southern Pueblo, is located north of Albuquerque. This Keresan-speaking pueblo is often closed to the public except for several feast days during the year. Many of the residents live on farmland outside the pueblo.

Santa Clara Pueblo, is a Northern Pueblo, located north of Santa Fe. Traditional crafts are available, and tours are available for the ancient 740-room Puye Cliff Dwellings.

Santo Domingo Pueblo, a Southern Pueblo located north of Albuquerque and known for its turquoise and silver jewelry, is the largest of the eastern Keresan-speaking pueblos.

Taos Pueblo, a Northern Pueblo north of Santa Fe is a Tiwa-speaking pueblo, famous for its drums. A National Historic Site, the pueblo is heavily visited by tourists. Taos Pueblo and the nearby town of Taos were famous during the fur trapping era.

Tesuque Pueblo, a Northern Pueblo, located north of Santa Fe, is listed on the National Register of Historic Places. The Pueblo Revolt of 1680 started here.

Zia Pueblo, a Southern Pueblo located north of Albuquerque, is a Keresan-speaking pueblo known for its orange-on-white pottery. The Zia sun symbol was adopted by the state of New Mexico and appears on the state flag. The pueblo overlooks the Jemez River.

Zuni Pueblo is known for its jewelry, sold by the Zuni Craftsmen Cooperative Association at

Juanita Pena, a San Ildefonso Pueblo pottery maker, poses with her child.

the pueblo. There are restaurants and a tribal campground. The Hawikuh ruins are nearby, a Zuni village abandoned after the Pueblo Revolt of 1680. The Zuni Pueblo is a Southern Pueblo located south of Gallup.

ARIZONA

In northeastern Arizona, completely surrounded by the Navajo Nation, are found the villages of the Hopi, occupying approximately one and one-half million acres. The Hopi population exceeds

9,000, found primarily near the center of the nation, with the three ancient villages on top of First Mesa, Second Mesa, and Third Mesa and the three modern communities at the foot of the mesas.

TEXAS

Just across the border from New Mexico, in Texas, is Isleta del Sur Pueblo, This pueblo was founded by Pueblo people who fled New Mexico with the Spanish during the Pueblo Revolt of 1680.

ACCULTURATION AND ASSIMILATION

Pueblo people are at home in both their Native world and in the world of the dominant American culture. They have learned to be U.S. citizens while still remaining Pueblo. Changes, however, have been inevitable. Pueblo culture has long been multilingual. It is now rapidly becoming bilingual. In times past Pueblos might be fluent not only in the language of their pueblo, but also in one or more of the other Pueblo languages or dialects. With the arrival of the Spanish, Pueblos also learned the Spanish language. With the arrival of the Comanches in their vicinity, many Pueblos, especially those on the eastern frontier nearest the plains, learned Comanche, just as some northern Pueblos learned Jicarillan due to close relations with the Jicarilla Apache. Pueblos nearest the Navajos were apt to know Navajo. Spanish is still common among older Pueblo people. But increasingly, Pueblo young people are learning only the language of their pueblo and English. With English being a universal language within the region, and with its hold growing ever stronger by the profound linguistic influences of radio, television, print journalism, and public education, few Pueblos today learn other Native languages besides their own.

TRADITIONS AND CUSTOMS

Ceremonial dances are at the heart of Pueblo culture. Pueblo traditional dance costumes are among the most striking of any Native peoples. Kachinas are masked male dancers who impersonate spirits of nature and who perform ceremonial rituals in the plazas on feast days and other important occasions. Ritual clowns are also a part of some ceremonials. The clowns engage in funny, sexual, and absurd behavior to remind the spectators of the sometimes foolish behavior of all humans. Some ceremonials, such as the Zuni Shalakos, feature kachinas in ten-foot high costumes. Among the Hopi, the kachinas are said to live in the San Francisco peaks near Flagstaff. They come to the Hopi for six months each year, arriving during the February Bean Dance.

LANGUAGE

Zuni is classified as a language isolate of the Penutian Phylum. All other Pueblo languages are classified within the Aztec-Tanoan Phylum: within the Kiowa-Tanoan family are three Tanoan languages, Tiwa, Tewa, and Towa; the Hopi language is an isolate within the Uto-Aztecan family; and Keresan is an unclassified language isolate not yet assigned to any family within the phylum. Zuni is spoken only by the Zuni. Tiwa is spoken by Taos, Picuris, Sandia, and Isleta. Tewa is spoken by San Juan, Santa Clara, San Ildefonso, Nambe, Tesuque, and Pojoaque. Towa is spoken only by the Jemez. Keresan is spoken by Acoma, Cochiti, Laguna, San Felipe, Santa Ana, Santo Domingo, and Zia. Language can be richly expressive and descriptive, as in these Tewa constructions for the lunar cycle: Moon of the cedar dust wind (February); Moon when the leaves break forth (March); Moon when the leaves are dark green (June); Moon when the corn is taken in (September); and Moon when all is gathered in (November).

FAMILY AND COMMUNITY DYNAMICS

Pueblo culture is matrilineal and matrilocal. Children are born into the mother's clan. Wife abuse is uncommon in functioning, matrilocal cultures because the wife is surrounded by the protection of her relatives. Child custody disputes are unknown because the child is a member of the mother's clan and remains with the mother or her relatives should a marriage not endure. In the matrilocal residence pattern, related women, and their husbands and children, live in clusters of apartments within a larger structure, which is a classic description of both Anasazi and Pueblo building requirements. The development of this matrilocal system of residence accounts for the change from pit houses to above-ground masonry apartments. An aspect of life for which Pueblo Indians are perhaps best-known, Pueblo dwellings are interconnected multi-level apartment-like structures made of stone and plaster or adobe bricks. The ceiling of one "apartment" serves as floor and outside courtyard for the one above it. Pueblo structures sometimes reached five stories tall, with inhabitants moving from one floor to the next via ladders that led through holes in the ceilings instead of through outside doorways. This structural design, along with their strategic placement at the tops of mesas, served as safeguards against outside attacks.

Pueblos held community gatherings in pit houses, which were dug into the ground in a central location in the pueblo. A remnant of the pit house survives as the kiva, an underground chamber that is built into the apartments of the southwest. In the kivas, related men, who do not live together in matrilocal communities, meet and hold ceremonies. These groups of related men constitute a clan. The clan affords an important opportunity for maintaining ties between related men in matrilocal cultures, even though the men trace their descent through the female line.

PUEBLOS DANCES AND SONGS

Songs and dances are significant in Pueblo life. Masks, textiles, and body painting are important aspects of Pueblo ritual. The Pueblos use gourd rattles, wooden drums, and rawhide as musical instruments for their ceremonies and dances, which are unique to each tribe and have prescribed roles for the leaders, singers, dancers, and spectators. Many dances, performed usually by men who sing and dance in line formations or in procession, are held in honor of seasonal change and related duties, such as hunting in the winter, or harvest in the autumn. Many dances relate to the bringing of rain. Most of the Pueblos perform a version of the Corn Dance and the Matachina Dance, and many perform dances in honor of buffalo or deer. Pueblo dances are among the best-known Native American customs still practiced, and many of the Pueblos allow the public to come and watch them.

HOLIDAYS CELEBRATED BY PUEBLOS

On January 6 most pueblos celebrate King's Day and the installation of new governors and officials. The first week in February is the Governor's Feast at Acoma. April 19-20 is the Eight Northern Indi-

These Taos Pueblo Indians are performing at the ninth annual Taos Pueblo Buffalo Pasture Powwow, which took place in July 1988.

an Pueblos Spring Arts and Crafts Show at De Vargas Mall in Santa Fe. May 3 is Santa Cruz Day at Cochiti and Taos. June 13 is Grab Day at San Ildefonso, San Juan, Santa Clara, Taos, and Picuris. July 4 is the Nambe Falls Ceremonial at Nambe. July 4 is the Annual Pope Foot Race at San Juan. The last weekend in July is the Puye Cliff Ceremonial at Santa Clara. On August 5-10 all pueblos celebrate the Symbolic Relay Run. August 10 is Grab Day at Laguna and Cochiti. Mid-August is the Intertribal Indian Ceremonial in Gallup. December (date set annually) is the time for the Shalako Ceremonial at Zuni.

RELIGION

To be Pueblo is a way of life, a world view, a part of a community, and perhaps one of the reasons that Pueblo religion is so entrenched is that there is no word for religion in the Pueblo languages. Religious beliefs are deeply interwoven in many aspects of Pueblo culture, including farming, storytelling, dances, art, architecture, and other everyday activities. Especially symbolic for the Hopi is agriculture, which carries a sacred significance and determines a great deal of their work cycles, ceremonies, and feasts. Much Hopi spirituality centers on the belief that when their ancestors emerged from the depths of the earth, they were offered their choice of foods. The Hopi chose an ear of short blue corn, symbolizing a life of hardship, humility, and hardiness, since the short blue corn is the most difficult to harvest successfully but is also the most durable. The planting and harvest of corn is in a real way the Hopi's connection to their earliest ancestors and the creation of the world. Pueblo religious ceremonies and rituals are often tied to the bringing of rain and a successful harvest; and the Pueblo still practice many of them today.

The Hopi story of the creation of the world is based on the concept of emergence, which is a common theme in Pueblo folklore and religion. Hopi believe that their ancestors, themselves a sort of spirit beings, migrated through three underground worlds before arriving on the earth above them—the fourth world. There they made a covenant with the spirit being Masau-u, who allowed them to remain on the land as long as they followed sacred rules that ensure harmony among people, maintain the land, and provide water needed to grow their crops. The Hopi still try to honor this sacred contract today.

Pueblos have also modified Christian teachings to make them compatible with traditional views. The result is a form of Christianity found nowhere else in the world. Pueblo Catholicism nevertheless has much in common with the experiences of Native peoples throughout the middle and southern portions of the hemisphere who are nominally Catholics, but whose practice and beliefs are at great odds with official canon. The church is tolerant of this practice, having found, after exerting great effort, that it cannot uproot traditional Pueblo religious beliefs. The church made its greatest effort, with public hangings and whippings, in the 1660s and 1670s. In the Pueblo Revolt of 1680, 21 of the 33 Catholic priests in New Mexico were killed. The Catholic Christian influence has resulted in the creation and observance of a number of Christian holidays and feast days, which frequently coincide with traditional celebrations and the performance of traditional dances. Some pueblos observe feast days in honor of their patron saints.

EMPLOYMENT AND ECONOMIC TRADITIONS

The Pueblo people are among the most successful dry farmers in the world. They are also skilled at irrigation farming. Today many Pueblos continue the agricultural traditions of their ancestors and continue to cultivate in the same time-honored manner. Many Pueblo people are also employed in the urban areas near their homes, and many of them who now live in these urban areas return to the pueblo frequently, sometimes as often as nearly every weekend. Traditional craftwork in pottery, weaving, jewelry, and drum making are also important sources of income. Tribal enterprise also provides jobs. The Hopi Cultural Center, with its restaurant and motel, offers some employment opportunities. At Acoma the visitor center has a restaurant, crafts shop, and a museum, and a bingo hall is nearby. Cochiti provides services for the town of Cochiti Lake, which leases its land from Cochiti Pueblo and has a commercial center, a marina, and an 18-hole golf course. The majority of Isleta's residents work in Albuquerque, but others operate the bingo hall, grocery stores, and the campgrounds at Isleta Lakes. Some excellent vineyards are found at Jemez. Laguna Industries Inc. manufactures communications shelters for the U.S. Army and is only one of a number of Laguna tribal industries. Some Lagunas found employment in the uranium mining industry and others are now finding employment in the reclamation project that is attempting to restore the mined land. Many of Nambe's residents work in Santa Fe, in Espaniola, or at Los Alamos National Laboratory. Others are employed by the Eight Northern Indian Pueblos Council. Picuris Pueblo Enterprise Cultural Center houses a museum, a restaurant, and a store and operates guided tours. Pojoaque generates revenue by the development of a commercial strip fronting the highway, and the pueblo also operates an official state tourist center. The Sandia Indian Bingo Parlor is one of the largest in New Mexico. Sandia also operates Bien Mur Indian Market Center and Sandia Lakes Recreation Area. At San Ildefonso there is a museum, several trading posts, and a visitor center and the annual Eight Northern Indian Pueblos Artist and Craftsman Show. At San Juan there is the Oke Oweenge Crafts Cooperative. At Santa Ana there is the Ta Ma Myia crafts shop. Santo Domingo is developing commercial property along Interstate 25, where it also operates a museum. Taos operates a horseback riding and guided tour business as well as several trading posts. Tesuque operates a bingo parlor and Camel Rock Campground. Zuni has been a model for tribal enterprise, taking advantage of direct federal grants through the Community Action Programs to gain administrative control of almost all of the Bureau of Indian Affairs contract services on the reservation, which now run more efficiently and

POLITICS AND GOVERNMENT

Under the Indian Reorganization Act of 1934, many Pueblos refused to allow their traditional form of government to be replaced by a foreign system. The tribal council system is modeled somewhat after the U.S. government, but also has much in common with the way corporations are governed. Each tribe within the United States was given the option of reorganizing under the act, and many Pueblos refused to do so. Traditional Pueblo government features leadership from different sources of strength within each community. Clans are an important force in providing leadership, and among some Pueblos specific clans have traditional obligations to provide leaders. This is true of the Bear Clan among the Hopi, the Antelope Clan at Acoma, and the Bow Clan at Zuni. The Tewa pueblos have dual village leaders, where the heads of the winter and summer moieties each exercise responsibility for half the year. In matters of traditional religion, which encompasses much of what white people associate with government, a *cacique* among the Pueblos and a *kikmongwi* among the Hopi have serious responsibilities to the people. Along with their assistants they not only perform ceremonies but also organize hunts and the planting of crops.

Today the Hopi in Arizona and six New Mexico pueblos (Isleta, Laguna, Pojoaque, San Ildefonso, Santa Clara, and Zuni) elect their governors and councils. In New Mexico, the All Indian Pueblo Council had its first recorded meeting in 1598 when Juan de Onate met with 38 Pueblo leaders at Santo Domingo. Pueblo oral history recounts that the various pueblos had been working together long before the arrival of the Spanish and that secret meetings of the council were a major factor in the successful planning of the Pueblo Revolt of 1680. The All Indian Pueblo Council was formed on November 5, 1922 when Pueblo leaders assembled at Santo Domingo to meet with U.S. government officials. Its present constitution was adopted on October 16, 1965. The council is a confederation of New Mexico pueblos that seeks to protect and advance their interests, particularly regarding relations with other governments.

RELATIONS WITH THE UNITED STATES

Because Pueblos were granted full Mexican citizenship while under Mexican rule from 1821 to 1848, they automatically became U.S. citizens when the Southwest was annexed by the United States at the conclusion of the Mexican War in 1848. The Pueblos were the only Indians in the Southwest to become U.S. citizens in that manner. Pueblos had to sue to have their status as Indians recognized by the United States, which was achieved by a decision of the U.S. Supreme Court in 1916. They are now federally recognized Indian tribes. By joining together to form the All Indian Pueblo Council in the 1920s, after a congressional investigation had revealed that 12,000 non-Pueblo claimants were living on Pueblo land, they succeeded in getting the U.S. Congress to pass the Pueblo Lands Act of 1924, which secures some of their traditional land to them. The struggle for water rights has characterized much of their relations with United States in this century. In 1975, after a 30-year struggle, Taos Pueblo succeeded in regaining its sacred Blue Lake and 55,000 acres of surrounding land in the mountains above the pueblo. This marked one of the few times that the United States has returned a major sacred site to Indian control.

INDIVIDUAL AND GROUP CONTRIBUTIONS

ACADEMIA

Ted Jojola (1951-), an educator and administrator of Isleta Pueblo descent, is known for his research on Native American culture. His numerous publications have dealt with subjects ranging from urban planning to teaching, architecture, and ethnography. He is currently a professor at the University of New Mexico. Edward P. Dozier (1916-1971) was a pioneering anthropologist, linguist, and educator who specialized in the study of the Pueblo Indians of the Southwest. He spent much of his career at the University of Arizona and was also prominent as an activist for Indian rights.

Alfonso Ortiz (1939-) is a well-known anthropologist, scholar, and activist whose books on Southwest Indian tribes, including *American Indian Myths and Legends* (1984) and *The Tewa World: Space, Time, Being, and Becoming in a Pueblo Society* (1969), are considered classics in anthropological scholarship. In addition to his academic work, Ortiz was president of the Association of American Indian Affairs (AAIA) in the 1970s. During his term, the organization played a central role in the return of the sacred Blue Lake to the Taos Pueblo people and the passage of the Indian Child Welfare Act, which ensured that Indian orphans are placed in Indian foster homes, among other accomplishments. Ortiz has been a professor in the University of New Mexico's anthropology department since 1974.

ART

Pueblo communities have produced a number of renowned artists, including Maria Montoya Martinez (c. 1887-1980), who has been called perhaps the most famous Indian artist of all time. In her award-winning pottery, she revived and transformed indigenous pottery into high art. Martinez was a San Ildefonso Pueblo who spent much of her career producing pottery with her husband and other family members, including their son Popovi Da, who became a well-known artist in his own right. Martinez and her husband displayed and demonstrated their craft at the 1904 World's Fair in St. Louis, Missouri, as well as in museums and art shows. Martinez was particularly respected for her black-on-black pottery designs, which came to be known as blackware pottery.

Helen Quintana Cordero (1915-) is a Cochiti Pueblo responsible for reviving the nearly lost art of clay dollmaking among her people. Clay dolls, typically embodying women singing to children, had been used by Southwest Indians for centuries for religious purposes and during harvest ceremonies, but this custom had declined with the arrival of white settlers in the region. Cordero specialized in what has come to be known as the "storyteller doll," drawn from her memories of her grandfather, who would gather the Pueblo children around him and tell them traditional Indian tales of the past. She was the first to use the male figure in her pioneering clay doll arrangements, which include the storyteller with up to 30 clay children dolls sitting in various positions around him.

Pablita Velarde (1918-) is a Santa Clara Pueblo artist who is best known for her paintings depicting numerous aspects of daily Pueblo life, including religious ceremonies, tribal government, arts and crafts, costumes, and farming. She painted murals at the Bandelier National Park in New Mexico and at the 1934 World's Fair in an authentic and detailed style that is drawn upon her knowledge and study of her ancestry. Her works are sometimes used as secondary source material for scholars researching the life of ancient Indians. Helen Hardin (1946-1984), a Tewa Pueblo known for her acrylic and casein designs, was a regarded as a premier artist of the Southwest. She used Native American patterns and geometric shapes in her award-winning paintings.

FILM

Hopi producer/director Victor Masayesva, Jr., has created a feature length film, *Imagining Indians*, that succeeds in conveying Native American resentment of the appropriation of its culture for commercial purposes. *Imagining Indians* is a 90-minute film that explores many facets of what happens when Native stories, rituals, and objects become commercial commodities. Masayesva is from Hotevilla, a village of about 500 people on Third Mesa. Hotevilla was constructed, hastily, in 1906 by Hopi women, whose men had been incarcerated by the United States and moved to Alcatraz Island to prevent them from moving to southern Utah. Masayesva had never been to a town larger than Winslow, Arizona, when he went to New York City at age 15. He studied still photography at Princeton University and then began working with video. For some of the editing techniques in *Imagining Indians* he gained access to state of the art equipment, a machine for which only three were available in the United States. Masayesva has screened *Imagining Indians* in Phoenix, Santa Fe, Houston, Boston, New York, and at the University of Oklahoma. A 60-minute version has been edited for television.

LITERATURE

Pueblos have produced some of the most outstanding contemporary Native literary writers. Two of the first three Lifetime Achievement honorees of the Native Writers' Circle of the Americas have been Pueblos: Simon J. Ortiz (Acoma) and Leslie Marmon Silko (Laguna). In the early 1970s Ortiz was editor of *Americans Before Columbus*, the newspaper of the Indian Youth Council. In the 1980s he held official tribal positions as Interpreter and First Lieutenant Governor of Acoma. He has taught at the Institute of American Indian Arts, the University of New Mexico, Navajo Community College, Sinte Gleska College, San Diego State University, the College of Marin, Lewis and Clark College, and Colorado College. He edited one of the most important collections of Native literature, *Earth Power Coming*, published by Navajo Community College Press, and has written many books, among them *From Sand Creek; Going for the Rain; A Good Journey; Fightin': New and Collected Stories; The People Shall Continue;* and *Woven Stone.*

Silko has also taught at a number of universities, including the University of Arizona and the University of New Mexico. Her work has had a profound influence on the Native literary community. Her best known works are *Ceremony, Storyteller,* and *Almanac of the Dead.* Both Ortiz and Silko delivered plenary session speeches at the historic Returning the Gift conference of North American Native writers at the University of Oklahoma in 1992, a conference that drew nearly 400 native literary writers from throughout the upper Western hemisphere.

Paula Gunn Allen (Laguna) is another well-known Pueblo author. She edited the anthology *Spider Woman's Granddaughters.* She has published books of fiction, *The Woman Who Owned the Shadows*; poetry, *Shadow Country,* and *Skin and Bones*; and nonfiction, *The Sacred Hoop,* and *Studies in American Indian Literatures.* Laguna poet Carol Lee Sanchez has published *Excerpt From a Mountain Climber's Handbook, Message Bringer Woman,* and *Conversations From the Nightmare.* Hopi/Miwok writer Wendy Rose is coordinator of American Indian Studies at Fresno City College and has held positions with the Women's Literature Project of Oxford University Press, the Smithsonian Native Writers' Series, the Modern Language Association Commission on Languages and Literature of the Americas, and the Coordinating Council of Literary Magazines. Her books include *Hopi Roadrunner Dancing; Long Division: A Tribal History; Academic Squaw: Reports to the World from the Ivory Tower; Lost Copper; What Happened When the Hopi Hit New York; The Halfbreed Chronicles; Going to War with All My Relations;* and *Bone Dance.*

Laguna educator Lee Francis, director of the American Indian Internship program at American University in Silver Springs, Maryland, is also national director of Wordcraft Circle of Native American Mentor and Apprentice Writers and is editor of its newsletter, *Moccasin Telegraph,* and of its quarterly journal. In 1994 Francis led a team of Native writers who guest edited a special Native American Literatures issue of *Callaloo* for the University of Virginia and Johns Hopkins University Press. Many other Pueblos are literary writers, including Aaron Carr, Joseph L. Concha, Harold Littlebird, Diane Reyna; Veronica Riley, Joe S. Sando, Laura Watchempino, and Aaron Yava. Some of their best early work appears in *The Remembered Earth: An Anthology of Contemporary Native American Literature,* published by the University of New Mexico Press in 1979. Some of the most recent work by a new generation of Pueblo literary figures, including Rachael Arviso, Rosemary Diaz, and Lorenzo Baca can be found in *Neon Powwow: New Native American Voices of the Southwest* (1993).

SCIENCE

Frank C. Dukepoo (1943-), a Hopi-Laguna geneticist, was the first Hopi to earn a doctorate degree. Born in Arizona, he earned a Ph.D. from Arizona State University in 1973 and has held teaching or research positions there and at San Diego State University, Palomar Junior College, and, beginning in 1980, at Northern State University. Dukepoo has also served as director of Indian education at Northern Arizona University, and held administrative positions with the National Science Foundation and the National Cancer Institute. In addition to founding and coordinating the National Native American Honor Society, which assists Native American students, Dukepoo has conducted extensive research on birth defects in Indians.

MEDIA

PRINT

American Indian Law Newsletter.
Address: 1915 Roma Avenue, N.E., Albuquerque, New Mexico, 87106.

Americans Before Columbus.
Address: 318 Elm Street, Albuquerque, New Mexico 87012.

Bear Track.
Address: 1202 West Thomas Road, Phoenix, Arizona 85013.

Cochiti Lake Sun.
Address: P.O. Box 70, Cochiti, New Mexico 87014.

Drumbeat.

Address: Institute of American Indian Arts, Cerrillos Road, Santa Fe, New Mexico 87501.

Four Directions.

Address: 1812 Las Lomas, N.E., Albuquerque, New Mexico 87131.

Eight Northern Pueblos News.

Address: Route 1, Box 71, Santa Fe, New Mexico 87528.

Graduate Indian Center Newsletter.

Address: 4520, Montgomery, N.E., Suite 1B, Albuquerque, New Mexico 87109.

Hopi Action News.

Address: The Winslow Mail, Winslow, Arizona 86047.

Hopi Crier.

Address: Hopi Day School, Oraibi, Arizona 86039.

Hopi Tutu-Veh-Ni.

Address: Box 123, Kykotsmovi, Arizona 86039.

Indian Arizona.

Address: 4560 North 19th Avenue, Suite 200, Phoenix, Arizona 85015-4113.

Indian Education Update.

Address: 2121 South Mill Avenue, Suite 218, Tempe, Arizona 85282.

Indian Extension News.

Address: New Mexico State University, Las Cruces, New Mexico 88001.

Indian Forerunner.

Address: P.O. Box 927, San Juan Pueblo, New Mexico 87566.

Indian Life.

Address: 1664 East Campo Bello Drive, Phoenix, Arizona 85022.

Indian Quest.

Address: 708 South Lindon Lane, Tempe, Arizona 85281.

Indian Resources Development Newsletter.

Address: P.O. Box 30003, Las Cruces, New Mexico 88003-0003.

Indian Trader.

Address: P.O. Box 1421, Gallup, New Mexico 87301.

Indian Voice.

Address: 9169 Coors Road, N.W., Box 10146; Albuquerque, New Mexico 87184.

Institute of American Indian Arts Newsletter.

Address: P.O. Box 20007, Santa Fe, New Mexico 87504.

Isleta Eagle Pride.

Address: P.O. Box 312, Isleta, New Mexico 87022.

Kachina Messenger.

Address: P.O. Box 1210, Gallup, New Mexico 87301.

Keresan.

Address: Box 3151 Laguna, New Mexico 87026.

Native American Smoke Signals.

Address: 13282 Central Avenue, P.O. Box 515, Mayer, Arizona 86333.

Native Images.

Address: P.O. Box 1624, Tempe, Arizona 85280.

Native Peoples Magazine.

Address: 1833 North Third Street, Phoenix, Arizona 85004.

Pueblo Horizon.

Address: 2401 12th Street, N.W., Albuquerque, New Mexico 87102.

Southwest Native News.

Address: P.O. Box 1990, Tuba City, Arizona 86045.

Southern Pueblos Bulletin.

Address: 1000 Indian School Road, N.W., Albuquerque, New Mexico 87103.

Southwind Native News.

Address: P.O. Box 40176, Albuquerque, New Mexico 87196.

Thunderbird.

Address: Albuquerque Indian School, 1000 Indian School Road, N.W., Albuquerque, New Mexico 87103.

Tsa'aszi'.

Address: P.O. Box 12, Pine Hill, New Mexico 87321.

Uts'ittisctaan'i.

Address: Northern Arizona University, Campus Box 5630, Flagstaff, Arizona 86011.

Zuni Tribal Newsletter.

Address: P.O. Box 339, Zuni, New Mexico 87327.

RADIO

KCIE-FM (90.5).

Address: P.O. Box 603, Dulce, New Mexico 87528.

KENN.

Address: P.O. Box 1558, Farmington, New Mexico 87499-1558.

KGAK.

Address: 401 East Coal Road, Gallup, New Mexico 87301-6099.

KGHR-FM (91.5).

Address: P.O. Box 160, Tuba City, Arizona 86045.

KHAC-AM (1110).

Address: Drawer F, Window Rock, Arizona 86515.

KNNB-FM (88.1).

Address: P.O. Box 310, Whitewater, Arizona 85941.

KPGE.

Address: Box 00, Page, Arizona 80640-1969.

KPLZ.

Address: 816 Sixth Street, Parker, Arizona 85344-4599.

KSHI—FM (90.9).

Address: P.O. Box 339, Zuni, New Mexico 87327.

KTDB-FM (89.7).

Address: P.O. Box 89, Pine Hill, New Mexico 87321.

KTNN-AM.

Address: P.O. Box 2569, Window Rock, Arizona 86515.

ORGANIZATIONS AND ASSOCIATIONS

All Indian Pueblo Council (AIPC).

Serves as advocate on behalf of 19 Pueblo Indian tribes on education, health, social, and economic issues; lobbies on those issues before state and national legislatures. Activities are centered in New Mexico.

Contact: James Hena, Chair.

Address: P.O. Box 3256, Albuquerque, New Mexico 87190.

Telephone: (505) 881-1992.

American Indian Law Students Association.

Address: 1117 Stanford, N.E., Albuquerque, New Mexico 87106.

Arizona Commission for Indian Affairs.

Address: 1623 West Adams, Phoenix, Arizona 85007.

Hopi Cultural Center.

Address: P.O. Box 67, Second Mesa, Arizona 86043.

Indian Education Center.

Address: Arizona State University, Tempe, Arizona 85281.

New Mexico Commission on Indian Affairs.

Address: 330 East Palace Avenue, Santa Fe, New Mexico 87501.

New Mexico Indian Advisory Commission.

Address: Box 1667, Albuquerque, New Mexico 87107.

MUSEUMS AND RESEARCH CENTERS

Albuquerque Museum and the Maxwell Museum in Albuquerque, New Mexico; American Research Museum, Ethnology Museum, Fine Arts Museum, Hall of the Modern Indian, and Institute of American Indian Arts, in Santa Fe, New Mexico; Art Center in Roswell, New Mexico; Black Water Draw Museum in Portales, New Mexico; Coronado Monument in Bernalillo, New Mexico; Heard Museum of Anthropology in Phoenix, Arizona; Milicent Rogers Museum in Taos, New Mexico; Northern Arizona Museum in Flagstaff, Arizona; and the State Museum of Arizona in Tempe.

SOURCES FOR ADDITIONAL STUDY

Beck, Warren D., and Ynez D. Hasse. *Historical Atlas of New Mexico*. Norman: University of Oklahoma Press, 1969.

Bruggmann, Maximilien, and Sylvio Acatos. *Pueblos: Prehistoric Indian Cultures of the Southwest,* translated by Barbara Fritzemeier. New York: Facts On File, 1990 (originally published as *Die Pueblos*, U. Bar Verlag, Zurick, Switzerland, 1989).

The Coronado Narrative: Spanish Explorers in the Southern United States, 1528-1543, edited by Frederick W. Hodge and Theodore H. Lewis. New York: Scribners, 1970.

Dominguez, Francisco Atanasio. *The Missions of New Mexico, 1776*, translated and annotated by Eleanor B. Adams and Fray Angelico Chavez. Albuquerque: University of New Mexico Press, 1956.

Eagle/Walking Turtle (Gary McLain). *Indian America: A Traveler's Companion*, third edition. Santa Fe, New Mexico: John Muir Publications, 1993.

Forbes, Jack D. *Apache, Navaho, and Spaniard*. Norman: University of Oklahoma Press, 1969; reprinted with new introduction, 1994.

Marquis, Arnold. *A Guide To America's Indians: Ceremonials, Reservations, and Museums*. Norman: University of Oklahoma Press, 1974.

Minge, Ward Alan. *Acoma: Pueblo in the Sky*, second edition. Albuquerque: University of New Mexico Press, 1991.

New Perspectives on the Pueblos, edited by Alfonso Ortiz. Albuquerque: University of New Mexico Press, 1985.

O'Brien, Sharon. *American Indian Tribal Governments*. Norman: University of Oklahoma Press, 1989.

The Onate Expeditions; Spanish Explorations; Spanish Explorations in the Southwest, 1542-1706, edited by Herbert Eugene Bolton. New York: Scribners, 1908.

Ortiz, Alfonso. *The Pueblo*. New York: Chelsea House, 1994.

Sando, Joe S. *Pueblo Nations: Eight Centuries of Pueblo Indian History*. Santa Fe: Clear Light Publishers, 1992.

Trimble, Stephen. *The People: Indians of the American Southwest*. Santa Fe, New Mexico: Sar Press, 1993.

PUERTO RICAN AMERICANS

by
Derek Green

The history of Puerto Rican American assimilation has been one of great success mixed with serious problems.

OVERVIEW

The island of Puerto Rico (formerly Porto Rico) is the most easterly of the Greater Antilles group of the West Indies island chain. Located more than a thousand miles southeast of Miami, Puerto Rico is bounded on the north by the Atlantic Ocean, on the east by the Virgin Passage (which separates it from the Virgin Islands), on the south by the Caribbean Sea, and on the west by the Mona Passage (which separates it from the Dominican Republic). Puerto Rico is 35 miles wide (from north to south), 95 miles long (from east to west) and has 311 miles of coastline. Its land mass measures 3,423 square miles—about two-thirds the area of the state of Connecticut. Although it is considered to be part of the Torrid Zone, the climate of Puerto Rico is more temperate than tropical. The average January temperature on the island is 73 degrees, while the average July temperature is 79 degrees. The record high and low temperatures recorded in San Juan, Puerto Rico's northeastern capital city, are 94 degrees and 64 degrees, respectively.

According to the 1990 U.S. Census Bureau report, the island of Puerto Rico has a population of 3,522,037. This represents a three-fold increase since 1899—and 810,000 of those new births occurred between the years of 1970 and 1990 alone. Most Puerto Ricans are of Spanish ancestry. Approximately 70 percent of the population is white and about 30 percent is of African or mixed descent. As in many Latin American cultures, Roman Catholicism is the dominant religion, but Protestant faiths of various denominations have some Puerto Rican adherents as well.

Puerto Rico is unique in that it is an autonomous Commonwealth of the United States, and its people think of the island as *un estado libre asociado*, or a "free associate state" of the United States—a closer relationship than the territorial possessions of Guam and the Virgin Islands have to America. Puerto Ricans have their own constitution and elect their own bicameral legislature and governor but are subject to U.S executive authority. The island is represented in the U.S House of Representatives by a resident commissioner, which for many years was a nonvoting position. After the 1992 U.S. presidential election, however, the Puerto Rican delegate was granted the right to vote on the House floor. Because of the Puerto Rico's commonwealth status, Puerto Ricans are born as natural American citizens. Therefore all Puerto Ricans, whether born on the island or the mainland, are Puerto Rican Americans.

Puerto Rico's status as a semiautonomous Commonwealth of the United States has sparked considerable political debate. Historically, the main conflict has been between the nationalists, who support full Puerto Rican independence, and the statists, who advocate U.S. statehood for Puerto Rico. In November of 1992 an island-wide referendum was held on the issue of statehood versus continued Commonwealth status. In a narrow vote of 48 percent to 46 percent, Puerto Ricans opted to remain a Commonwealth.

HISTORY

Fifteenth-century Italian explorer and navigator Christopher Columbus, known in Spanish as Cristobál Colón, "discovered" Puerto Rico for Spain on November 19, 1493. The island was conquered for Spain in 1509 by Spanish nobleman Juan Ponce de León (1460-1521), who became Puerto Rico's first colonial governor. The name Puerto Rico, meaning "rich port," was given to the island by its Spanish *conquistadors* (or conquerors); according to tradition, the name comes from Ponce de León himself, who upon first seeing the port of San Juan is said to have exclaimed, "¡Ay que puerto rico!" ("What a rich port!").

Puerto Rico's indigenous name is *Borinquen* ("bo REEN ken"), a name given by its original inhabitants, members of a native Caribbean and South American people called the Arawaks. A peaceful agricultural people, the Arawaks on the island of Puerto Rico were enslaved and virtually exterminated at the hands of their Spanish colonizers. Although Spanish heritage has been a matter of pride among islander and mainlander Puerto Ricans for hundreds of years—Columbus Day is a traditional Puerto Rican holiday—recent historical revisions have placed the *conquistadors* in a darker light. Like many Latin American cultures, Puerto Ricans, especially younger generations living in the mainland United States, have become increasingly interested in their indigenous as well as their European ancestry. In fact, many Puerto Ricans prefer to use the terms *Boricua* ("bo REE qua") or *Borrinqueño* ("bo reen KEN yo") when referring to each other.

Because of its location, Puerto Rico was a popular target of pirates and privateers during its early colonial period. For protection, the Spanish constructed forts along the shoreline, one of which, El Morro in Old San Juan, still survives. These fortifications also proved effective in repelling the attacks of other European imperial powers, including a 1595 assault from British general Sir Francis Drake. In the mid-1700s, African slaves were brought to Puerto Rico by the Spanish in great numbers. Slaves and native Puerto Ricans mounted rebellions against Spain throughout the early and mid-1800s. The Spanish were successful, however, in resisting these rebellions.

In 1873 Spain abolished slavery on the island of Puerto Rico, freeing black African slaves once and for all. By that time, West African cultural traditions had been deeply intertwined with those of the native Puerto Ricans and the Spanish conquerors. Intermarriage had become a common practice among the three ethnic groups.

MODERN ERA

As a result of the Spanish-American War of 1898, Puerto Rico was ceded by Spain to the United States in the Treaty of Paris on December 19, 1898. In 1900 the U.S. Congress established a civil government on the island. Seventeen years later, in response to the pressure of Puerto Rican activists, President Woodrow Wilson signed the Jones Act, which granted American citizenship to all Puerto Ricans. Following this action, the U.S. government instituted measures to resolve the various economic and social problems of the island, which even then was suffering from over-population. Those measures included the introduction of American currency, health programs, hydroelectric power and irrigation programs, and economic policies designed to attract U.S. industry and provide more employment opportunities for native Puerto Ricans.

In the years following World War II, Puerto Rico became a critical strategic location for the U.S. military. Naval bases were built in San Juan Harbor and on the nearby island of Culebra. In 1948 Puerto Ricans elected Luis Muñoz Marín governor of the island, the first native *puertorriqueño* to hold such a post. Marín favored Commonwealth status for Puerto Rico. The question of whether to continue the Commonwealth relationship with the United States, to push for U.S. statehood, or to rally for total independence has dominated Puerto Rican politics throughout the twentieth century.

Following the 1948 election of Governor Muñoz, there was an uprising of the Nationalist Party, or *independetistas*, whose official party platform included agitation for independence. On November 1, 1950, as part of the uprising, two Puerto Rican nationalists carried out an armed attack on Blair House, which was being used as a temporary residence by U.S. President Harry Truman. Although the president was unharmed in the melee, one of the assailants and one Secret Service presidential guard were killed by gunfire.

After the 1959 Communist revolution in Cuba, Puerto Rican nationalism lost much of its steam; the main political question facing Puerto Ricans in the mid-1990s was whether to seek full statehood or remain a Commonwealth.

EARLY MAINLANDER PUERTO RICANS

Since Puerto Ricans are American citizens, they are considered U.S. migrants as opposed to foreign immigrants. Early Puerto Rican residents on the mainland included Eugenio María de Hostos (b. 1839), a journalist, philosopher, and freedom fighter who arrived in New York in 1874 after being exiled from Spain (where he had studied law) because of his outspoken views on Puerto Rican independence. Among other pro-Puerto Rican activities, María de Hostos founded the League of Patriots to help set up the Puerto Rican civil government in 1900. He was aided by Julio J. Henna, a Puerto Rican physician and expatriate. Nineteenth-century Puerto Rican statesman Luis Muñoz Rivera—the father of Governor Luis Muñoz Marín—lived in Washington D.C., and served as Puerto Rico's ambassador to the States.

SIGNIFICANT MIGRATION WAVES

Although Puerto Ricans began migrating to the United States almost immediately after the island became a U.S. protectorate, the scope of early migration was limited because of the severe poverty of average Puerto Ricans. As conditions on the island improved and the relationship between Puerto Rico and the United States grew closer, the number of Puerto Ricans who moved to the U.S. mainland increased. Still, by 1920, less than 5,000 Puerto Ricans were living in New York City. During World War I, as many as 1,000 Puerto Ricans—all newly naturalized American citizens—served in the U.S. Army. By World War II that number soared to over 100,000 soldiers. The hundred-fold increase reflected the deepening cooperation between Puerto Rico and the mainland States. World War II set the stage for the first major migration wave of Puerto Ricans to the mainland.

That wave, which spanned the decade between 1947 and 1957, was brought on largely by economic factors: Puerto Rico's population had risen to nearly two million people by mid-century, but the standard of living had not followed suit. Unemployment was high on the island while opportunity was dwindling. On the mainland, however, jobs were widely available. According to Ronald Larsen, author of *The Puerto Ricans in America*, many of those jobs were in New York City's garment district. Hard-working Puerto Rican women were especially welcomed in the garment district shops. The city also provided the sort of low-skilled service industry jobs that non-English speakers needed to make a living on the mainland.

New York City became a major focal point for Puerto Rican migration. Between 1951 and 1957 the average annual migration from Puerto Rico to New York was over 48,000. Many settled in East Harlem, located in upper Manhattan between 116th and 145th streets, east of Central Park. Because of its high Latino population, the district soon came to be known as Spanish Harlem. Among New York City *puertorriqueños*, the Latino-populated area was referred to as *el barrio*, or "the neighborhood." Most first-generation migrants to the area were young men who later sent for their wives and children when finances allowed.

By the early 1960s the Puerto Rican migration rate slowed down, and a "revolving door" migratory pattern—a back-and-forth flow of people between the island and the mainland—developed. Since then, there have been occasional bursts of increased migration from the island, especially during the recessions of the late 1970s. In the late 1980s Puerto Rico became increasingly plagued by a number of social problems, including rising violent crime (especially drug-associated crime), increased overcrowding, and worsening unemployment. These conditions kept the flow of migration into the United States steady, even among professional classes, and caused many Puerto Ricans to remain on the mainland permanently. According to U.S. Census Bureau statistics, more than 2.7 million Puerto Ricans were living in the mainland Unites States by 1990, making Puerto Ricans the second-largest Latino group in the nation, behind Mexican Americans, who number nearly 13.5 million.

SETTLEMENT PATTERNS

Most early Puerto Rican migrants settled in New York City and, to a lesser degree, in other urban areas in the northeastern United States. This migration pattern was influenced by the wide availability of industrial and service-industry jobs in the eastern cities. New York remains the chief residence of Puerto Ricans living outside of the island: of the 2.7 million Puerto Ricans living on the mainland, over 900,000 reside in New York City, while another 200,000 live elsewhere in the state of New York.

That pattern has been changing since the 1990s, however. A new group of Puerto Ricans—most of them younger, wealthier, and more highly educated than the urban settlers—have increasingly begun migrating to other states, especially in the South and Midwest. In 1990 the Puerto Rican population of Chicago, for instance, was over 125,000. Cities in Texas, Florida, Pennsylvania, New Jersey, and Massachusetts also have a significant number of Puerto Rican residents.

ACCULTURATION AND ASSIMILATION

The history of Puerto Rican American assimilation has been one of great success mixed with serious problems. Many Puerto Rican mainlanders hold high-paying white collar jobs. Outside of New York City, Puerto Ricans often boast higher college graduation rates and higher per capita incomes than their counterparts in other Latino groups, even when those groups represent a much higher proportion of the local population.

However, U.S. Census Bureau reports indicate that for at least 25 percent of all Puerto Ricans living on the mainland (and 55 percent living on the island) poverty is a serious problem. Despite the presumed advantages of American citizenship, Puerto Ricans are—overall—the most economically disadvantaged Latino group in the United States. Puerto Rican communities in urban areas are plagued by problems such as crime, drug-use, poor educational opportunity, unemployment, and the breakdown of the traditionally strong Puerto Rican family structure. Since a great many Puerto Ricans are of mixed Spanish and African descent, they have had to endure the same sort of racial discrimination often experienced by African Americans. And some Puerto Ricans are further handicapped by the Spanish-to-English language barrier in American cities.

Despite these problems, Puerto Ricans, like other Latino groups, are coming to exert more political power. This is especially true in cities like New York, where the significant Puerto Rican population can represent a major political force when properly organized. In many recent elections Puerto Ricans have found themselves in the position of holding an all-important "swing-vote"— often occupying the sociopolitical ground between African Americans and other minorities on the one hand and white Americans on the other.

TRADITIONS, CUSTOMS, AND BELIEFS

The traditions and beliefs of Puerto Rican islanders are heavily influenced by Puerto Rico's Afro-Spanish history. Many Puerto Rican customs and superstitions blend the Catholic religious traditions of Spaniards and the pagan religious beliefs of the West African slaves who were brought to the island beginning in the sixteenth century. Though most Puerto Ricans are strict Roman Catholics, local customs have given a Caribbean flavor to some standard Catholic ceremonies. Among these are weddings, baptisms and funerals. And like other Caribbean islanders and Latin Americans, Puerto Ricans traditionally believe in *espiritismo*, the notion that the world is populated by spirits who can communicate with the living through dreams.

In addition to the holy days observed by the Catholic church, Puerto Ricans celebrate several other days that hold particular significance for them as a people. For instance, *El Dia de las Candelarias,* or "candlemas," is observed annually on the evening of February 2; people build a massive bonfire around which they drink and dance and chant "¡Viva las candelarias!" or "Long live the flames!" And each December 27 is *El Dia de los Innocentes* or the "Day of the Children." On that day Puerto Rican men dress as women and women dress as men; the community then celebrates as one large group.

Many Puerto Rican customs revolve around the ritual significance of food and drink. As in other Latino cultures, it is considered an insult to turn down a drink offered by a friend or stranger. It is also customary for Puerto Ricans to offer food to any guest, whether invited or not, who might enter the household: failure to do so is said to bring hunger upon one's own children. Puerto Ricans traditionally warn against eating in the presence of a pregnant woman without offering her food, for fear she might miscarry. Many Puerto Ricans also believe that marrying or starting a journey on a Tuesday is bad luck, and that dreams of water or tears are a sign of impending heartache or tragedy. Common centuries-old folk remedies include the avoidance of acidic food during menstruation and the consumption of *asopao* ("ah so POW"), or chicken stew, for minor ailments.

MISCONCEPTIONS AND STEREOTYPES

Although awareness of Puerto Rican culture has increased within mainstream America, many common misconceptions still exist. For instance, many other Americans fail to realize that Puerto Ricans are natural-born American citizens or wrongly view their native island as a primitive tropical land of grass huts and grass skirts. Puerto Rican culture is often confused with other Latino American cultures, especially that of Mexican Americans. And because Puerto Rico is an island, some mainlanders have trouble distinguishing Pacific islanders of Polynesian descent from the Puerto Rican people, who have Euro-African and Caribbean ancestry.

CUISINE

Puerto Rican cuisine is tasty and nutritious and consists mainly of seafood and tropical island veg-

These enthusiastic spectators are watching the 1990 Puerto Rican Day Parade in New York City.

etables, fruits, and meats. Although herbs and spices are used in great abundance, Puerto Rican cuisine is not spicy in the sense of peppery Mexican cuisine. Native dishes are often inexpensive, though they require some skill in preparation. Puerto Rican women are traditionally responsible for the cooking and take great pride in their role.

Many Puerto Rican dishes are seasoned with a savory mixture of spices known as *sofrito* ("so-FREE-toe"). This is made by grinding fresh garlic, seasoned salt, green peppers, and onions in a *pilón* ("pee-LONE"), a wooden bowl similar to a mortar and pestle, and then sautéing the mixture in hot oil. This serves as the spice base for many soups and dishes. Meat is often marinated in a seasoning mixture known as *adobo,* which is made from lemon, garlic, pepper, salt, and other spices. *Achiote* seeds are sautéed as the base for an oily sauce used in many dishes.

Bacalodo ("bah-kah-LAH-doe"), a staple of the Puerto Rican diet, is a flaky, salt-marinated cod fish. It is often eaten boiled with vegetables and rice or on bread with olive oil for breakfast. *Arroz con pollo,* or rice and chicken, another staple dish, is served with *abichuelas guisada* ("ah-bee-CHWE-lahs gee-SAH-dah"), marinated beans, or a native Puerto Rican pea known as *gandules* ("gahn-DOO-lays"). Other popular Puerto Rican foods include *asopao* ("ah-soe-POW"), a rice and chicken stew; *lechón asado* ("le-CHONE ah-SAH-doe"), slow-roasted pig; *pasteles* ("pah-

STAY-lehs"), meat and vegetable patties rolled in dough made from crushed plantains (bananas); *empanadas de jueyes* ("em-pah-NAH-dahs deh WHE-jays"), Puerto Rican crab cakes; *rellenos* ("reh-JEY-nohs"), meat and potato fritters; *griffo* ("GREE-foe"), chicken and potato stew; and *tostones*, battered and deep fried plantains, served with salt and lemon juice. These dishes are often washed down with *cerveza rúbia* ("ser-VEH-sa ROO-bee-ah"), "blond" or light-colored American lager beer, or *ron* ("RONE") the world-famous, dark-colored Puerto Rican rum.

TRADITIONAL COSTUMES

Traditional dress in Puerto Rico is similar to other Caribbean islanders. Men wear baggy *pantalons* (trousers) and a loose cotton shirt known as a *guayaberra*. For certain celebrations, women wear colorful dresses or *trajes* that have African influence. Straw hats or Panama hats (*sombreros de jip-ijipa*) are often worn on Sundays or holidays by men. Spanish-influenced garb is worn by musicians and dancers during performances—often on holidays.

The traditional image of the *jíbaro*, or peasant, has to some extent remained with Puerto Ricans. Often depicted as a wiry, swarthy man wearing a straw hat and holding a guitar in one hand and a *machete* (the long-bladed knife used for cutting sugarcane) in the other, the *jíbaro* to some symbolizes the island's culture and its people. To others, he is an object of derision, akin to the derogatory image of the American hillbilly.

PUERTO RICAN DANCES AND SONGS

Puerto Rican people are famous for throwing big, elaborate parties—with music and dancing—to celebrate special events. Puerto Rican music is polyrhythmic, blending intricate and complex African percussion with melodic Spanish beats. The traditional Puerto Rican group is a trio, made up of a *qauttro* (an eight-stringed native Puerto Rican instrument similar to a mandolin); a *guitarra*, or guitar; and a *basso*, or bass. Larger bands have trumpets and strings as well as extensive percussion sections in which maracas, guiros, and bongos are primary instruments.

Although Puerto Rico has a rich folk music tradition, fast-tempoed *salsa* music is the most widely known indigenous Puerto Rican music. Also the name given to a two-step dance, *salsa*

has gained popularity among non-Latin audiences. The *merengue*, another popular native Puerto Rican dance, is a fast step in which the dancers' hips are in close contact. Both *salsa* and *merengue* are favorites in American barrios. *Bombas* are native Puerto Rican songs sung *a cappella* to African drum rhythms.

HOLIDAYS CELEBRATED BY PUERTO RICANS

Puerto Ricans celebrate most Christian holidays, including *La Navidád* (Christmas) and *Pasquas* (Easter), as well as *El Año Nuevo* (New Year's Day). In addition, Puerto Ricans celebrate *El Dia de Los Tres Reyes*, or "Three King's Day," each January 6. It is on this day that Puerto Rican children expect gifts, which are said to be delivered by *los tres reyes magos* ("the three wise men"). On the days leading up to January 6, Puerto Ricans have continuous celebrations. *Parrandiendo* (stopping by) is a practice similar to American and English caroling, in which neighbors go visiting house to house. Other major celebration days are *El Día de Las Raza* (The Day of the Race—Columbus Day) and *El Fiesta del Apostal Santiago* (St. James Day). Every June, Puerto Ricans in New York and other large cities celebrate Puerto Rican Day. The parades held on this day have come to rival St. Patrick's Day parades and celebrations in popularity.

HEALTH AND MENTAL HEALTH ISSUES

There are no documented health problems or mental health problems specific to Puerto Ricans. However, because of the low economic status of many Puerto Ricans, especially in mainland inner-city settings, the incidence of poverty-related health problems is a very real concern. AIDS, alcohol and drug dependency, and a lack of adequate health care coverage are the biggest health-related concerns facing the Puerto Rican community.

LANGUAGE

There is no such thing as a Puerto Rican language. Rather, Puerto Ricans speak proper Castillian Spanish, which is derived from ancient Latin. While Spanish uses the same Latin alphabet as English, the letters "k" and "w" occur only in foreign words. However, Spanish has three letters not found in English: "ch" ("chay"), "ll" ("EL-yay"), and "ñ" ("AYN-nyay"). Spanish uses word order, rather than noun and pronoun inflection, to encode meaning. In addition, the Spanish language tends to rely on diacritical markings such as the *tilda* (~) and the *accento* (´) much more than English.

The main difference between the Spanish spoken in Spain and the Spanish spoken in Puerto Rico (and other Latin American locales) is pronunciation. Differences in pronunciation are similar to the regional variations between American English in the southern United States and New England. Many Puerto Ricans have a unique tendency among Latin Americans to drop the "s" sound in casual conversation. The word *ustéd* (the proper form of the pronoun "you"), for instance, may be pronounced as "oo TED" rather than "oo STED." Likewise, the participial suffix "*-ado*" is often changed by Puerto Ricans. The word *cemado* (meaning "burned") is thus pronounced "ke MOW" rather than "ke MA do."

Although English is taught to most elementary school children in Puerto Rican public schools, Spanish remains the primary language on the island of Puerto Rico. On the mainland, many first-generation Puerto Rican migrants are less than fluent in English. Subsequent generations are often fluently bilingual, speaking English outside of the home and Spanish in the home. Bilingualism is especially common among young, urbanized, professional Puerto Ricans.

Long exposure of Puerto Ricans to American society, culture, and language has also spawned a unique slang that has come to be known among many Puerto Ricans as "Spanglish." In Spanglish, "New York" becomes *Nuevayork*, and many Puerto Ricans refer to themselves as *Nuevarriqueños*. Puerto Rican teenagers are as likely to attend *un pahry* (a party) as to attend a *fiesta;* children look forward to a visit from *Sahnta Close* on Christmas; and workers often have *un Beeg Mahk y una Coca-Cola* on their lunch breaks.

GREETINGS AND OTHER POPULAR EXPRESSIONS

For the most part, Puerto Rican greetings are standard Spanish greetings: *Hola* ("OH lah")—Hello; *¿Como está?* ("como eh-STAH")—How are you?; *¿Que tal?* ("kay TAHL")—What's up; *Adiós* ("ah DYOSE")—Good-bye; *Por favór* ("pore fah-FORE")—Please; *Grácias* ("GRAH-syahs")—Thank you; *Buena suerte* ("BWE-na SWAYR-tay")—Good luck; *Feliz Año Nuevo* ("feh-LEEZ AHN-yoe NWAY-vo")—Happy New Year.

Some expressions, however, appear to be unique to Puerto Ricans. These include: *Mas enamorado que el cabro cupido* (More in love than a goat shot by Cupid's arrow; or, to be head over heels in love); *Sentado an el baúl* (Seated in a trunk; or, to be henpecked); and *Sacar el ratón* (Let the rat out of the bag; or, to get drunk).

FAMILY AND COMMUNITY DYNAMICS

Puerto Rican family and community dynamics have a strong Spanish influence and still tend to reflect the intensely patriarchal social organization of European Spanish culture. Traditionally, husbands and fathers are heads of households and serve as community leaders. Older male children are expected to be responsible for younger siblings, especially females. *Machismo* (the Spanish conception of manhood) is traditionally a highly regarded virtue among Puerto Rican men. Women, in turn, are held responsible for the day-to-day running of the household.

Both Puerto Rican men and women care very much for their children and have strong roles in childrearing; children are expected to show *respeto* (respect) to parents and other elders, including older siblings. Traditionally, girls are raised to be quiet and diffident, and boys are raised to be more aggressive, though all children are expected to defer to elders and strangers. Young men initiate courtship, though dating rituals have for the most part become Americanized on the mainland. Puerto Ricans place a high value on the education of the young; on the island, Americanized public education is compulsory. And like most Latino groups, Puerto Ricans are traditionally opposed to divorce and birth out of wedlock.

Puerto Rican family structure is extensive; it is based on the Spanish system of *compadrazco* (literally "co-parenting") in which many members—not just parents and siblings—are considered to be part of the immediate family. Thus *los abuelos* (grandparents), and *los tios y las tias* (uncles and aunts) and even *los primos y las primas* (cousins) are considered extremely close relatives in the Puerto Rican family structure. Likewise, *los padrinos* (godparents) have a special role in the Puerto Rican conception of the family: godparents are friends of a child's parents and serve as "second parents" to the child. Close friends often refer to each other as *compadre y comadre* to reinforce the familial bond.

Although the extended family remains standard among many Puerto Rican mainlanders and islanders, the family structure has suffered a serious breakdown in recent decades, especially among urban mainlander Puerto Ricans. This breakdown seems to have been precipitated by economic hardships among Puerto Ricans, as well as by the influence of America's social organization, which de-emphasizes the extended family and accords greater autonomy to children and women.

For Puerto Ricans, the home has special significance, serving as the focal point for family life. Puerto Rican homes, even in the mainland United States, thus reflect Puerto Rican cultural heritage to a great extent. They tend to be ornate and colorful, with rugs and gilt-framed paintings that often reflect a religious theme. In addition, rosaries, busts of *La Virgin* (the Virgin Mary) and other religious icons have a prominent place in the household. For many Puerto Rican mothers and grandmothers, no home is complete without a representation of the suffering of *Jesús Christo* and the Last Supper. As young people increasingly move into mainstream American culture, these traditions and many others seem to be waning, but only slowly over the last few decades.

INTERACTIONS WITH OTHER ETHNIC MINORITIES

Because of the long history of intermarriage among Spanish, Indian, and African ancestry groups, Puerto Ricans are among the most ethnically and racially diverse people in Latin America. As a result, the relations between whites, blacks, and ethnic groups on the island—and to a somewhat lesser extent on the mainland—tend to be cordial.

This is not to say that Puerto Ricans fail to recognize racial variance. On the island of Puerto Rico, skin color ranges from black to fair, and there are many ways of describing a person's color. Light-skinned persons are usually referred to as *blanco* (white) or *rúbio* (blond). Those with darker skin who have Native American features are referred to as *indio*, or "Indian." A person with dark-colored skin, hair, and eyes—like the majority of the islanders—are referred to as *trigeño* (swarthy). Blacks have two designations: African

Puerto Ricans are called people *de colór* or people "of color," while African Americans are referred to as *moreno*. The word *negro*, meaning "black," is quite common among Puerto Ricans, and is used today as a term of endearment for persons of any color.

RELIGION

Most Puerto Ricans are Roman Catholics. Catholicism on the island dates back to the earliest presence of the Spanish *conquistadors*, who brought Catholic missionaries to convert native Arawaks to Christianity and train them in Spanish customs and culture. For over 400 years, Catholicism was the island's dominant religion, with a negligible presence of Protestant Christians. That has changed over the last century. As recently as 1960, over 80 percent of Puerto Ricans identified themselves as Catholics. By the mid-1990s, according to U.S. Census Bureau statistics, that number had decreased to 70 percent. Nearly 30 percent of Puerto Ricans identify themselves as Protestants of various denominations, including Lutheran, Presbyterian, Methodist, Baptist, and Christian Scientist. The Protestant shift is about the same among mainlander Puerto Ricans. Although this trend may be attributable to the overwhelming influence of American culture on the island and among mainland Puerto Ricans, similar changes have been observed throughout the Caribbean and into the rest of Latin America.

Puerto Ricans who practice Catholicism observe traditional church liturgy, rituals, and traditions. These include belief in the Creed of the Apostles and adherence to the doctrine of papal infallibility. Puerto Rican Catholics observe the seven Catholic sacraments: Baptism, Eucharist, Confirmation, Penance, Matrimony, Holy Orders, and Anointing of the Sick. According to the dispensations of Vatican II, Puerto Ricans celebrate mass in vernacular Spanish as opposed to ancient Latin. Catholic churches in Puerto Rico are ornate, rich with candles, paintings, and graphic imagery: like other Latin Americans, Puerto Ricans seem especially moved by the Passion of Christ and place particular emphasis on representations of the Crucifixion.

Among Puerto Rican Catholics, a small minority actively practice some version of *santería* ("sahn-teh-REE-ah"), an African American pagan religion with roots in the Yoruba religion of western Africa. (A *santo* is a saint of the Catholic church who also corresponds to a Yoruban deity.) *Santería* is prominent throughout the Caribbean and in many places in the southern United States and has had a strong influence on Catholic practices on the island.

EMPLOYMENT AND ECONOMIC TRADITIONS

Early Puerto Rican migrants to the mainland, especially those settling in New York City, found jobs in service and industry sectors. Among women, garment industry work was the leading form of employment. Men in urban areas most often worked in the service industry, often at restaurant jobs—bussing tables, bartending, or washing dishes. Men also found work in steel manufacturing, auto assembly, shipping, meat packing, and other related industries. In the early years of mainland migration, a sense of ethnic cohesion, especially in New York City, was created by Puerto Rican men who held jobs of community significance: Puerto Rican barbers, grocers, barmen, and others provided focal points for the Puerto Rican community to gather in the city. Since the 1960s, some Puerto Ricans have been journeying to the mainland as temporary contract laborers—working seasonally to harvest crop vegetables in various states and then returning to Puerto Rico after harvest.

As Puerto Ricans have assimilated into mainstream American culture, many of the younger generations have moved away from New York City and other eastern urban areas, taking high-paying white-collar and professional jobs. Still, less than two percent of Puerto Rican families have a median income above $75,000.

In mainland urban areas, though, unemployment is rising among Puerto Ricans. According to 1990 U.S. Census Bureau statistics, 31 percent of all Puerto Rican men and 59 percent of all Puerto Rican women were not considered part of the American labor force. One reason for these alarming statistics may be the changing face of American employment options. The sort of manufacturing sector jobs that were traditionally held by Puerto Ricans, especially in the garment industry, have become increasingly scarce. Institutionalized racism and the rise in single-parent households in urban areas over the last two decades may also be factors in the employment crisis.

Urban Puerto Rican unemployment—whatever its cause—has emerged as one of the greatest economic challenges facing Puerto Rican community leaders at the dawn of the twenty-first century.

POLITICS AND GOVERNMENT

Throughout the twentieth century, Puerto Rican political activity has followed two distinct paths—one focusing on accepting the association with the United States and working within the American political system, the other pushing for full Puerto Rican independence, often through radical means. In the latter part of the nineteenth century, most Puerto Rican leaders living in New York City fought for Caribbean freedom from Spain in general and Puerto Rican freedom in particular. When Spain ceded control of Puerto Rico to the United States following the Spanish-American War, those freedom fighters turned to working for Puerto Rican independence from the States. Eugenio María de Hostos founded the League of Patriots to help smooth the transition from U.S. control to independence. Although full independence was never achieved, groups like the League paved the way for Puerto Rico's special relationship with the United States. Still, Puerto Ricans were for the most part blocked from wide participation in the American political system.

In 1913 New York Puerto Ricans helped establish *La Prensa*, a Spanish-language daily newspaper, and over the next two decades a number of Puerto Rican and Latino political organizations and groups—some more radical than others—began to form. In 1937 Puerto Ricans elected Oscar García Rivera to a New York City Assembly seat, making him New York's first elected official of Puerto Rican decent. There was some Puerto Rican support in New York City of radical activist Albizu Campos, who staged a riot in the Puerto Rican city of Ponce on the issue of independence that same year; 19 were killed in the riot, and Campos's movement died out.

The 1950s saw wide proliferation of community organizations, called *ausentes*. Over 75 such hometown societies were organized under the umbrella of *El Congresso de Pueblo* (the "Council of Hometowns"). These organizations provided services for Puerto Ricans and served as a springboard for activity in city politics. In 1959 the first New York City Puerto Rican Day parade was

held. Many commentators viewed this as a major cultural and political "coming out" party for the New York Puerto Rican community.

Low participation of Puerto Ricans in electoral politics—in New York and elsewhere in the country—has been a matter of concern for Puerto Rican leaders. This trend is partly attributable to a nationwide decline in American voter turnout. Still, some studies reveal that there is a substantially higher rate of voter participation among Puerto Ricans on the island than on the U.S. mainland. A number of reasons for this have been offered. Some point to the low turnout of other ethnic minorities in U.S. communities. Others suggest that Puerto Ricans have never really been courted by either party in the American system. And still others suggest that the lack of opportunity and education for the migrant population has resulted in widespread political cynicism among Puerto Ricans. The fact remains, however, that the Puerto Rican population can be a major political force when organized.

INDIVIDUAL AND GROUP CONTRIBUTIONS

Although Puerto Ricans have only had a major presence on the mainland since the mid-twentieth century, they have made significant contributions to American society. This is especially true

in the areas of the arts, literature, and sports. The following is a selected list of individual Puerto Ricans and some of their achievements.

ACADEMIA

Frank Bonilla is a political scientist and a pioneer of Hispanic and Puerto Rican Studies in the United States. He is the director of the City University of New York's Centro de Estudios Puertorriqueños and the author of numerous books and monographs. Author and educator Maria Teresa Babín (1910-) served as director of the University of Puerto Rico's Hispanic Studies Program. She also edited one of only two English anthologies of Puerto Rican literature.

ART

Olga Albizu (1924-) came to fame as a painter of Stan Getz's RCA record covers in the 1950s. She later became a leading figure in the New York City arts community. Other well-known contemporary and avant-garde visual artists of Puerto Rican descent include Rafael Ferre (1933-), Rafael Colón (1941-), and Ralph Ortíz (1934-).

BUSINESS

Deborah Aguiar-Veléz (1955-) was trained as a chemical engineer but became one of the most famous female entrepreneurs in the United States. After working for Exxon and the New Jersey Department of Commerce, Aguiar-Veléz founded Sistema Corp. In 1990 she was named the Outstanding Woman of the Year in Economic Development. John Rodriguez (1958-) is the founder of AD-One, a Rochester, New York-based advertising and public relations firm whose clients include Eastman Kodak, Bausch and Lomb, and the Girl Scouts of America.

FILM AND THEATER

San Juan-born actor Raúl Juliá (1940-1994), best known for his work in film, was also a highly regarded figure in the theater. Among his many film credits are *Kiss of the Spider Woman*, based on South American writer Manuel Puig's novel of the same name, *Presumed Innocent*, and the *Addams Family* movies. Singer and dance Rita Moreno (1935-), born Rosita Dolores Alverco in Puerto Rico, began working on Broadway at the age of 13 and hit Hollywood at age 14. She has earned numerous awards for her work in theater, film, and television. Miriam Colón (1945-) is New York City's first lady of Hispanic theater. She has also worked widely in film and television. José Ferrer (1912-), one of cinema's most distinguished leading men, earned a 1950 Academy Award for best actor in the film *Cyrano de Bergerac*.

LITERATURE AND JOURNALISM

Jesús Colón (1901-1974) was the first journalist and short story writer to receive wide attention in English-language literary circles. Born in the small Puerto Rican town of Cayey, Colón stowed away on a boat to New York City at the age of 16. After working as an unskilled laborer, he began writing newspaper articles and short fiction. Colón eventually became a columnist for the *Daily Worker*; some of his works were later collected in *A Puerto Rican in New York and Other Sketches*. Nicholasa Mohr (1935-) is the only Hispanic American woman to write for major U.S. publishing houses, including Dell, Bantam, and Harper. Her books include *Nilda* (1973), *In Nueva York* (1977) and *Gone Home* (1986). Victor Hernández Cruz (1949-) is the most widely acclaimed of the Nuyorican poets, a group of Puerto Rican poets whose work focuses on the Latino world in New York City. His collections include *Mainland* (1973) and *Rhythm, Content, and Flavor* (1989). Tato Laviena (1950-), the best-selling Latino poet in the United States, gave a 1980 reading at the White House for U.S. President Jimmy Carter. Geraldo Rivera (1943-) has won ten Emmy Awards and a Peabody Award for his investigative journalism. Since 1987 this controversial media figure has hosted his own talk show, *Geraldo*.

POLITICS AND LAW

José Cabrenas (1949-) was the first Puerto Rican to be named to a federal court on the U.S. mainland. He graduated from Yale Law School in 1965 and received his LL.M. from England's Cambridge University in 1967. Cabrenas held a position in the Carter administration, and his name has since been raised for a possible U.S. Supreme Court nomination. Antonia Novello (1944-) was the first Hispanic woman to be named U.S. surgeon general. She served in the Bush administration from 1990 until 1993.

SPORTS

Roberto Walker Clemente (1934-1972) was born in Carolina, Puerto Rico, and played center field for the Pittsburgh Pirates from 1955 until his death in 1972. Clemente appeared in two World Series contests, was a four-time National League batting champion, earned MVP honors for the Pirates in 1966, racked up 12 Gold Glove awards for fielding, and was one of only 16 players in the history of the game to have over 3000 hits. After his untimely death in a plane crash en route to aid earthquake victims in Central America, the Baseball Hall of Fame waived the usual five-year waiting period and inducted Clemente immediately. Orlando Cepeda (1937-) was born in Ponce, Puerto Rico, but grew up in New York City, where he played sandlot baseball. He joined the New York Giants in 1958 and was named Rookie of the Year. Nine years later he was voted MVP for the St. Louis Cardinals. Angel Thomas Cordero (1942-), a famous name in the world of horseracing, is the fourth all-time leader in races won— and Number Three in the amount of money won in purses: $109,958,510 as of 1986. Sixto Escobar (1913-) was the first Puerto Rican boxer to win a world championship, knocking out Tony Matino in 1936. Chi Chi Rodriguez (1935-) is one of the best-known American golfers in the world. In a classic rags-to-riches story, he started out as a caddie in his hometown of Rio Piedras and went on to become a millionaire player. The winner of numerous national and world tournaments, Rodriguez is also known for his philanthropy, including his establishment of the Chi Chi Rodriguez Youth Foundation in Florida.

MEDIA

Over 500 U.S. newspapers, periodicals, newsletters, and directories are published in Spanish or have a significant focus on Hispanic Americans. As of 1991 there were five major Spanish-language daily newspapers published in the mainland United States: two in New York, two in Miami, and one in Los Angeles. More than 325 radio and television stations air broadcasts in Spanish, providing music, entertainment, and information to the Hispanic community.

PRINT

El Diario-La Prensa.

Established in 1913, it is a daily Spanish-language newspaper with daily news, opinions, sports, entertainment, and advertising sections. Has wide Puerto Rican readership.

Contact: Carlos D. Ramirez, Publisher.

Address: 143-155 Varick Street, New York, New York 10013.

Telephone: (212) 807-4600.

HISPANIC.

Established in 1988, it covers Hispanic interests and people in a general editorial magazine format on a monthly basis.

Contact: Alfredo Estrada, Publisher.

Address: Hispanic Publishing Corp., 111 Massachusetts Avenue, N.W., Suite 410, Washington, D.C. 20001.

Telephone: (202) 682-3000.

Hispanic Business.

Established in 1979, this is a monthly English-language business magazine that caters to Hispanic professionals.

Contact: Jesus Echevarria, Publisher.

Address: 360 South Hope Avenue, Suite C, Santa Barbara, California 93105-4017.

Telephone: (805) 682-5843.

Hispanic Link Weekly Report.

Established in 1983, this is a weekly bilingual community newspaper covering Hispanic interests.

Contact: Felix Perez, Editor.

Address: 1420 N Street, N.W., Washington, D.C. 20005.

Telephone: (202) 234-0280.

Noticias del Mundo.

Established in 1980, this is a daily general Spanish-language newspaper.

Contact: Bo Hi Pak, Editor.

Address: Philip Sanchez Inc., 401 Fifth Avenue, New York, New York 10016.

Telephone: (212) 684-5656.

Vista.

Established in September 1985, this monthly magazine supplement appears in major daily English-language newspapers.

Contact: Renato Perez, Editor.

Address: 999 Ponce de Leon Boulevard, Suite 600, Coral Gables, Florida 33134.

Telephone: (305) 442-2462.

RADIO

Caballero Radio Network.

Contact: Eduardo Caballero, President.

Address: 261 Madison Avenue, Suite 1800, New York, New York 10016.

Telephone: (212) 697-4120.

CBS Hispanic Radio Network.

Contact: Gerardo Villacres, General Manager.

Address: 51 West 52nd Street, 18th Floor, New York, New York 10019.

Telephone: (212) 975-3005.

Lotus Hispanic Radio Network.

Contact: Richard B. Kraushaar, President.

Address: 50 East 42nd Street, New York, New York 10017.

Telephone: (212) 697-7601.

WHCR-FM (90.3).

Public radio format, operating 18 hours daily with Hispanic news and contemporary programming.

Contact: Frank Allen, Program Director.

Address: City College of New York, 138th and Covenant Avenue, New York, New York 10031.

Telephone: (212) 650-7481.

WKDM-AM (1380).

Independent Hispanic hit radio format with continuous operation.

Contact: Geno Heinemeyer, General Manager.

Address: 570 Seventh Avenue, Suite 1406, New York, New York 10018.

Telephone: (212) 564-1380.

TELEVISION

Galavision.

Hispanic television network.

Contact: Jamie Davila, Division President.

Address: 2121 Avenue of the Stars, Suite 2300, Los Angeles, California 90067.

Telephone: (310) 286-0122.

Telemundo Spanish Television Network.

Contact: Joaquin F. Blaya, President.

Address: 1740 Broadway, 18th Floor, New York, New York 10019-1740.

Telephone: (212) 492-5500.

Univision.

Spanish-language television network, offering news and entertainment programming.

Contact: Joaquin F. Blaya, President.

Address: 605 Third Avenue, 12th Floor, New York, New York 10158-0180.

Telephone: (212) 455-5200.

WCIU-TV, Channel 26.

Commercial television station affiliated with the Univision network.

Contact: Howard Shapiro, Station Manager.

Address: 141 West Jackson Boulevard, Chicago, Illinois 60604.

Telephone: (312) 663-0260.

WNJU-TV, Channel 47.

Commercial television station affiliated with Telemundo.

Contact: Stephen J. Levin, General Manager.

Address: 47 Industrial Avenue, Teterboro, New Jersey 07608.

Telephone: (201) 288-5550.

ORGANIZATIONS AND ASSOCIATIONS

Association for Puerto Rican-Hispanic Culture.
Founded in 1965. Seeks to expose people of various ethnic backgrounds and nationalities to cultural values of Puerto Ricans and Hispanics. Focuses on music, poetry recitals, theatrical events, and art exhibits.

Contact: Peter Bloch.
Address: 83 Park Terrace West, New York, New York 10034.
Telephone: (212) 942-2338.

Council for Puerto Rico-U.S. Affairs.
Founded in 1987, the council was formed to help create a positive awareness of Puerto Rico in the United States and to forge new links between the mainland and the island.

Contact: Roberto Soto.
Address: 14 East 60th Street, Suite 605, New York, New York 10022.
Telephone: (212) 832-0935.

National Association for Puerto Rican Civil Rights (NAPRCR).
Addresses civil rights issues concerning Puerto Ricans in legislative, labor, police, and legal and housing matters, especially in New York City.

Contact: Damaso Emeric, President.
Address: 2134 Third Avenue, New York, New York 10035.
Telephone: (212) 996-9661.

National Conference of Puerto Rican Women (NACOPRW).
Founded in 1972, the conference promotes the participation of Puerto Rican and other Hispanic women in social, political, and economic affairs in the United States and in Puerto Rico. Publishes the quarterly *Ecos Nationales*.

Contact: Ana Fontana.
Address: 5 Thomas Circle, N.W., Washington, D.C. 20005.
Telephone: (202) 387-4716.

National Council of La Raza.
Founded in 1968, this Pan-Hispanic organization provides assistance to local Hispanic groups, serves as an advocate for all Hispanic Americans, and is a national umbrella organization for 80 formal affiliates throughout the United States.

Contact: Raul Yzaguirre.

Address: 810 First Street, N.E., Suite 300, Washington, D.C. 20002.

Telephone: (202) 289-1380.

Fax: (202) 289-8173.

National Puerto Rican Coalition (NPRC).

Founded in 1977, the NPRC advances the social, economic, and political well-being of Puerto Ricans. It evaluates the potential impact of legislative and government proposals and policies affecting the Puerto Rican community and provides technical assistance and training to start-up Puerto Rican organizations. Publishes *National Directory of Puerto Rican Organizations; Bulletin; Annual Report.*

Contact: Louis Nuñez, President.

Address: 1700 K Street, N.W., Suite 500, Washington, D.C. 20006.

Telephone: (202) 223-3915.

Fax: (202) 429-2223.

National Puerto Rican Forum (NPRF).

Concerned with the overall improvement of Puerto Rican and Hispanic communities throughout the United States.

Contact: Hector Velazquez, President.

Address: 31 East 32nd Street, Fourth Floor, New York, New York 10016.

Telephone: (212) 685-2311.

Puerto Rican Family Institute (PRFI).

Established for the preservation of the health, well-being, and integrity of Puerto Rican and Hispanic families in the United States.

Contact: Maria Elena Girone, Executive Director.

Address: 145 West 15th Street, New York, New York 10011.

Telephone: (212) 691-5635.

Museums and Research Centers

Brooklyn College of the City University of New York Center for Latino Studies.

Research institute centered on the study of Puerto Ricans in New York and Puerto Rico. Focuses on history, politics, sociology, and anthropology.

Contact: Maria Sanchez.

Address: 1205 Boylen Hall, Bedford Avenue at Avenue H, Brooklyn, New York 11210.

Telephone: (718) 780-5561.

Hunter College of the City University of New York Centro de Estudios Puertorriqueños.

Founded in 1973, it is the first university-based research center in New York City designed specifically to develop Puerto Rican perspectives on Puerto Rican problems and issues.

Contact: Frank Bonilla.

Address: 695 Park Avenue, New York, New York 10021.

Telephone: (212) 772-5689.

Institute for Puerto Rican Policy.

Founded in 1982, it is a nonprofit, nonpartisan policy-analysis research center focusing on Puerto Rican community issues, the IPRP publishes studies on Puerto Rican political campaign contributors, political participation, public sector employment, and other related subjects.

Contact: Angelo Falcón.

Address: 286 Fifth Avenue, Suite 804, New York, NY 10001.

Telephone: (212) 564-1075.

Institute of Puerto Rican Culture, Archivo General de Puerto Rico.

Maintains extensive archival holdings relating to the history of Puerto Rico.

Contact: Carmen Davila.

Address: 500 Ponce de León, Suite 4184, San Juan, Puerto Rico 00905.

Telephone: (809) 722-2113.

Fax: (809) 724-8393.

Puerto Rican Culture Institute, Luis Muñoz Rivera Library and Museum.

Founded in 1960, it houses collections that emphasize literature and art; institute supports research into the cultural heritage of Puerto Rico.

Address: 10 Muñoz Rivera Street, Barranquitas, Puerto Rico 00618.

Telephone: (809) 857-0230.

SOURCES FOR ADDITIONAL STUDY

Dietz, James L. *Economic History of Puerto Rico: Institutional Change and Capitalist Development.* Princeton, New Jersey: Princeton University Press, 1986.

Falcón, Angelo. *Puerto Rican Political Participation: New York City and Puerto Rico.* Institute for Puerto Rican Policy, 1980.

Fitzpatrick, Joseph P. *Puerto Rican Americans: The Meaning of Migration to the Mainland.* Englewood Cliffs, New Jersey: Prentice Hall, 1987.

Hauberg, Clifford A. *Puerto Rico and the Puerto Ricans.* New York: Twayne, 1975.

Perez y Mena, Andres Isidoro. *Speaking with the Dead: Development of Afro-Latin Religion Among Puerto Ricans in the United States: A Study into Interpenetration of Civilizations in the New World.* New York: AMS Press, 1991.

Puerto Rico: A Political and Cultural History, edited by Arturo Morales Carrion. New York: Norton, 1984

After the Revolution of December 1989, which brought an end to Communism in Romania, thousands of new immigrants of all ages came to the United States, and new arrivals (legal and illegal) continue to enter the country.

ROMANIAN AMERICANS

by
Vladimir F.
Werstman

OVERVIEW

Romania is a country slightly smaller than the state of Oregon, measuring 91,699 square miles (237,500 square kilometers). Located in southeastern Europe, it is bounded by Ukraine and Slovakia to the north, Bulgaria to the south, Serbia to the southwest, Moldavia and the Black Sea to the east, and Hungary to the west.

Romania has a population of slightly over 23 million people. Eighty-eight percent are of Romanian ethnic origin while the rest consist of various ethnic minorities, including Hungarians, Germans, Serbians, Bulgarians, Gypsies, and Armenians. Eighty percent of the population nominally belong to the Romanian Orthodox Church, and approximately ten percent are Catholics of the Byzantine Rite. Other religious denominations represented in Romania include Seventh-Day Adventists, Baptists, Lutherans, Presbyterians, and Unitarians, as well as the Judaic and Islamic faiths. The country's official language is Romanian, and its capital city is Bucharest. Romania's national flag consists of three large stripes (red, yellow, and blue) arranged vertically.

HISTORY

The name Romania, which means "New Rome" in Latin, was given by Roman colonists after

Emperor Trajan (c. 53-117 A.D.) and his legions crossed the Danube River and conquered Dacia (an ancient province located in present-day Transylvania and the Carpathian Mountain region) in 106 A.D. Although Roman occupation of Dacia ended in 271 A.D., the relationship between the Romans and Dacians flourished; mixed marriages and the adoption of Latin culture and language gradually molded the Romans and Dacians into a distinct ethnic entity. The ancestors of the modern Romanian people managed to preserve their Latin heritage despite Gothic, Slavic, Greek, Hungarian, and Turkish conquests, and the Romanian language has survived as a member of the Romance languages group.

Romania has been subjected to numerous occupations by foreign powers since the Middle Ages. In the thirteenth century, the Romanian principalities Moldavia and Wallachia became vassal states of the Ottoman Empire. Bukovina, Transylvania, and Banat were incorporated into the Austro-Hungarian Empire during the 1700s. Czarist Russia occupied Bessarabia in 1812. In 1859 Moldavia and Wallachia became unified through the auspices of the Paris Peace Conference, and Romania became a national state. At the Congress of Berlin in 1878 Romania obtained full independence from the Ottoman Empire but lost Bessarabia to Russia. In 1881, Romania was proclaimed a kingdom and Carol I (1839-1914) was installed as its first monarch.

MODERN ERA

Following the death of Carol I, his nephew, Ferdinand (1865-1927), became king and led the country into World War I against the Central Powers. Romania regained Transylvania, Banat, Bukovina and other territories after the war. In 1940, Carol II (1893-1953) named General Ion Antonescu (1882-1946) premier of Romania, who then forced the monarch to renounce his throne in favor of his son, Michael I (1921-). Under Antonescu's influence, Romania became an ally of Nazi Germany during World War II and fought against the Soviet Union. In the last year of the war, however, Romania switched its alliance to the Soviets and, after the war ended, Antonescu was executed. In national elections held in 1947, members of the Communist party assumed many high-level positions in the new government, and King Michael I was forced to abdicate his throne. Gheorghe Gheorghiu-Dej (1901-1965) of the Romanian Communist party

served as premier (1952-1955) and later as chief of state (1961-1965). Two years after Gheroghiu-Dej's death, Nicholae Ceauşescu (1918-1989), a high-ranking Communist official, assumed the presidency of Romania.

On December 22, 1989, the Communist regime was overthrown and Ceauşescu was executed on Christmas Day. Romania's transitional government (the National Salvation Front) declared Romania a non-Communist state and announced free elections in the spring of 1990. In January 1990, the Romanian Communist party was officially banned and Ion Iliescu (1930-) was elected president on May 20.

THE FIRST ROMANIANS IN AMERICA

Romanians have a recorded presence of almost 250 years on American soil. In the late eighteenth century, a Transylvanian priest named Samuel Damian immigrated to America for scientific reasons. Damian conducted various experiments with electricity and even caught the attention of Benjamin Franklin (they met and had a conversation in Latin). After living in South Carolina for a few years, Damian left for Jamaica and disappeared from historical record. In 1849, a group of Romanians came to California during the Gold Rush but, being unsuccessful, migrated to Mexico. Romanians continued to immigrate to America during this period and some distinguished themselves in the Union Army during the Civil War. George Pomutz (1818-1882) joined the Fifteenth Volunteer Regiment of Iowa and fought at such battlefields as Shiloh, Corinth, and Vicksburg, and was later promoted to the rank of Brigadier General. Nicholas Dunca (1825-1862), a captain serving in the Ninth Volunteer Regiment of New York, died in the battle of Cross Keys, Virginia. Another Romanian-born soldier, Eugen Teodoresco, died in the Spanish-American War in 1898.

SIGNIFICANT IMMIGRATION WAVES

The first major wave of Romanian immigrants to the United States took place between 1895 and 1920, in which 145,000 Romanians entered the country. They came from various regions, including Wallachia and Moldavia. A smaller group called Macedo-Romanians came from Macedonia (a region on the Balkan peninsula) and Albania. The majority of these immigrants—particularly those from Transylvania and Banat—were

Romanian American
Regina Kohn was
permitted to enter the
United States because her
violin playing so
impressed immigration
authorities at Ellis Island
that they deemed her an
artist. This photograph
was taken on
December 28, 1923.

unskilled laborers who left their native regions because of economic depression and forced assimilation, a policy practiced by Hungarian rulers. They were attracted to the economic stability of the United States, which promised better wages and improved working conditions. Many did not plan to establish permanent residency in America, intending instead to save enough money to return to Romania and purchase land. Consequently, tens of thousands of Romanian immigrants who achieved this goal left the United States within a few years, and by 1920 the Romanian American population was approximately 85,000.

Between 1921 and 1939, the number of Romanians entering the United States declined for several reasons. Following World War I, Transylvania, Bukovina, Bessarabia, and other regions under foreign rule officially became part of Romania, thus arresting emigration for a time. In addition, the U.S. Immigration Act of 1924 established a quota system which allowed only 603 persons per year to immigrate from Romania. The Great Depression added to the decline of new Romanian immigrants to the United States; immigration figures reached their lowest level at the beginning of World War II. Romanians who did enter the country during this period, however, included students, professionals, and others who later made notable contributions to American society.

A new surge of immigrants to the United States was generated by the threat of Nazi occu-

pation of Romania during World War II. When the Communists assumed control of the country in 1947 they imposed many political, economic, and social restrictions on the Romanian people. Refugees (who had left the country as a result of persecutions, arrests, or fear of being mistreated) and exiles (who were already abroad and chose not to return to Romania) were admitted into the United States through the auspices of the Displaced Persons Act of 1947 and other legislation passed to help absorb the flood of refugees and other immigrants from postwar Europe. Because of the abrupt and dramatic nature of their departure, the refugees and exiles (estimated at about 30,000) received special moral and financial support from various Romanian organizations—religious and secular—in America. These immigrants infused an important contingent of professionals, including doctors, lawyers, writers, and engineers into the Romanian American community, and were also more active politically. They established new organizations and churches, and fought against Communist rule in their homeland.

After the Revolution of December 1989, which brought an end to Communism in Romania, thousands of new immigrants of all ages came to the United States, and new arrivals (legal and illegal) continue to enter the country. The elimination of Communist travel restrictions; the desire of thousands of people to be reunited with their American relatives and friends; and the precarious economic conditions in the new Romania were powerful incentives to come to America for a new start in life. Among the newcomers were professionals, former political prisoners, and others who were disenchanted with the new leadership in Romania. There were also many Romanian tourists who decided to remain in America. Many of these immigrants spoke English and adjusted relatively well, even if they took lower-paying jobs than those to which their credentials or experience entitled them. However, others found neither employment nor understood the job hunting process, and returned to Romania. Still others left the United States to try their luck in Canada or South America. Those who chose to return to Europe settled in Germany, France, or Italy. According to the 1990 U.S. Census, there were approximately 365,544 people of Romanian ancestry living in the United States.

Because early Romanian immigrants were either peasants or laborers, they settled in the major industrial centers of the East and Midwest and took unskilled jobs in factories. The heaviest concentrations of Romanian Americans can be found in New York, New Jersey, Pennsylvania, Ohio, Illinois, Michigan, and Indiana. A substantial number of Romanians also settled in Florida and California. Living near the factories where they worked, first-generation Romanian Americans established communities which often consisted of extended families or of those who had migrated from the same region in Romania. Second- and third-generation Romanian Americans, having achieved financial security and social status, gradually moved out of the old neighborhoods, settling either in suburban areas or in larger cities, or relocating to another state. Consequently, there are few Romanian American communities left that preserve the social fabric of the first-generation neighborhoods.

ACCULTURATION AND ASSIMILATION

While researching data for her doctoral dissertation on Romanian Americans in 1929, Christine Galitzi Avghi, herself a Romanian, observed that "Romanians in the United States constitute a picturesque, sturdy group of newly made Americans of whom altogether too little is known" (Christine Galitzi Aughi, A Study of Assimilation among the Romanians in the United States [New York: Columbia University Press, 1929]; reprinted in 1969). Indeed, in the past, insufficient knowledge of Romanian ethnic characteristics generated various misconceptions in America. Some authors, such as Wayne Charles Miller, in his A Comprehensive Bibliography for the Study of American Minorities (1976), erroneously considered Romanians Slavs because Romania borders several Slavic countries. Other immigration studies, including Carl Wittke's We Who Built America: The Saga of the Immigrant (1939; revised 1967) and Joseph Hutchmacher's A Nation of Newcomers (1967) completely overlooked Romanians when discussing immigrants from Eastern Europe. In American Fever: The Story of American Immigration (1967), Barbara Kaye Greenleaf stereotyped Romanians as wearing sheepskin coats "during all seasons" even though such coats are worn by farmers and shepherds only in the winter. Romanians who had originally come from Transylvania with ethnic Hungarians (Transylvania was under Hungarian rule before World War I) were also greatly misunderstood. For some Americans, the mere mention of Transylvania and Romania

evoked Hollywood images of vampires and werewolves as depicted in several film adaptations of Bram Stoker's novel Dracula (1897). Such misconceptions did not deter Romanian ethnic pride, however, which reached its peak during World War II. Today, as other groups are reaffirming their cultural past, Romanian Americans are doing the same.

"I never really knew how much my ethnic background meant to me until the Romanian Revolution a few years ago. I was never ashamed of my background, I just never boldly stated it. I guess because I live in America I thought that I was just an American, period."

Veronica Buza, "My Ethnic Experience" in *Romanian American Heritage Center Information Bulletin*, September-October 1993.

TRADITIONS, CUSTOMS, AND BELIEFS

Romanians have a variety of traditions and lore dating back to antiquity. For example, on certain days some farmers would not cut anything with shears so that wolves will not injure their sheep. Tuesdays were considered unlucky days to start a journey or to initiate important business. A plague could be averted by burning a shirt which has been spun, woven, and sewn in less than 24 hours. Girls would not fill their pitchers with water from a well without breathing upon it first and pouring some of it on the ground (a libation to the nymph of the well). Before serving wine, drops were poured on the floor to honor the souls of the dead. A woman who did not want children would be tortured in hell. A black cat crossing in front of a pedestrian brought bad luck. An owl seen on the roof of a house, in a courtyard, or in a tree was a sign of forthcoming bad luck, including death in the family. Such superstitions were gradually forgotten as Romanian immigrants became acculturated into American society.

PROVERBS

A wealth of proverbs from Romanian culture have survived through generations: A good book can take place of a friend, but a friend cannot replace a good book; Whether homes are big or small, a child is a blessing to all; The cheapest article is advice, the most valuable is a good example; Do not leave an old good friend of yours just to please a new one; One thing for sure, each couple can tell, one's home is both paradise and hell; Idleness is the biggest enemy of good luck; Knowledge is like a tower in which you test and build your power; Modesty is the dearest jewel of a man's soul; Enjoy drinking the wine, but do not become drunk by it.

CUISINE

Romanian cuisine is savory, flavorful, and stimulating to the appetite. Herbs and vegetables are used in abundance, and one-dish meals occupy an important place in the repertoire of recipes. These dishes are very nourishing, inexpensive, and easy to prepare. Romanian Americans enjoy cooking, often modifying old country recipes or creating new dishes. *Mamaliga* ("mamalíga"), considered a national dish, is a corn mush eaten with butter, cheese, meats, and even with marmalade or fruit jelly as a dessert. *Ciorba* ("chiórbá") is a popular sour soup, seasoned with sauerkraut or pickled cucumber juice. It contains onions, parsnip, parsley root, rice, and ground beef mixed with pork, and is served after the boiled vegetables are removed. *Gratar* ("gratár") is a steak (usually pork) accompanied by pickled cucumbers and tomatoes and combined with other grilled meats. Garlic is a major ingredient used in preparing the steak. *Mititei* ("meeteetáy"), which is similar to hamburgers, consists of ground beef rolled into cylindrical forms and seasoned with garlic, and is often served with *gratar*.

Sarmale ("sarmálay") is a stuffed cabbage dish prepared with pork shoulder, rice, black pepper, and chopped onion. *Ghiveci* ("gyvéch") is a vegetable stew containing carrots, potatoes, tomatoes, green peppers, onions, celery roots, eggplant, squash, stringbeans, fresh peas, cabbage, and cauliflower. *Cozonac* ("kozonák") and *torte* ("tortáy") are various forms of cakes served as desserts. *Ţuica* ("tsúika") is a brandy made from plums or wheat. *Vin* ("veen") is wine and *bere* ("báyray") is beer. Romanian hosts and hostesses usually serve salads in a variety of shapes and compositions as entre dishes. Christmas dinner often consists of ham, sausages, pastry, fruits, *bere*, *vin*, and a special bread called *colac* ("kolák"). At Easter, lamb, ham, sausages, breads, and painted Easter eggs are prepared, and *vin* and *bere* accompany the feast.

TRADITIONAL COSTUMES

Romanian traditional, or peasant costumes, are made from handwoven linen. Women wear embroidered white blouses and black skirts (or another color, according to region) which cover the knees. The costume is completed with headscarves of various colors (older women usually wear black scarves) arranged according to age and regional traditions. The traditional costume for men consists of tight-fitting white pants, a white embroidered shirt worn over the pants that almost reaches the knees, and a wide leather or cotton belt. Men wear several types of hats according to season; black or grey elongated lambskin hats are customary during the winter and straw hats are usually worn during the summer. On festive occasions, men wear black or grey felt hats adorned with a flower or feather. Moccasins are traditional footwear for both men and women, while boots (with various adornments according to regional traditions) are worn by men. Romanian Americans wear their national costumes only on special occasions, either on national holidays celebrated in churches, at social gatherings, or while performing at local ethnic festivals.

ROMANIAN DANCES AND SONGS

During special occasions, dancers perform the *hora* ("khóra"), a national dance in which men and women hold hands in a circle; the *sîrba* ("syrba"), a quick, spirited dance; and the *invârtite* ("ynvyrtéetay"), a pair dance. These dances are accompanied by popular shoutings (sometimes with humorous connotations) spoken by the leader of the dance who also invites members of the audience to join the dancers. The orchestra consists of fiddles, clarinets, trumpets, flutes, bagpipes and panpipes, drums, and the *cobza* ("kóbza"), an instrument resembling a guitar and mandolin. Popular songs are traditionally performed during social reunions both in America and Romania. The *doina* ("dóiyna"), for example, are multi-verse tunes evoking nostalgic emotions, from a shepherd's loneliness in the mountains to patriotic sentiments. The *romanţa* ("romántsa") is a romantic melody expressing deep feelings of affection.

HOLIDAYS CELEBRATED BY ROMANIAN AMERICANS

In addition to Christmas Day, New Year's Day, and Easter Day, Romanian Americans celebrate the birthday of the Romanian national state on January 24 and Transylvania's reunification with

Romania on December 1. Romanian Americans with pro-monarchist views also celebrate May 10, which marks the ascension of Carol I to the Romanian throne. During these festivities, celebrants sing the Romanian national anthem, "Awake Thee, Romanian," written by Andrei Muresanu (1816-1863), a noted poet and patriot. Monarchists sing the Romanian royal anthem which begins with the words "Long live the king in peace and honor." A semi-official holiday similar to Valentine's Day is celebrated by lovers and friends on March 1, when a white or red silk flower (often hand-made) is presented as an expression of love.

HEALTH AND MENTAL HEALTH ISSUES

There are no documented health problems or medical conditions that are specific to Romanian Americans. Many families have health insurance coverage underwritten by the Union and League of Romanian Societies in America or by other ethnic organizations. Like most Americans, Romanian American business owners and professionals in private practice are insured at their own expense, while employees benefit from their employers' health plans when available.

LANGUAGE

The Romanian language is a Romance language derived from Latin that has survived despite foreign influences (Slavic, Turkish, Greek, and others). In fact, it has many Latin words that are not found in other Romance languages, and is more grammatically complex. Although Romanian uses the Latin alphabet, the letters "k," "q," "w," and "y" appear only in foreign words. In addition, Romanian has specific diacritical marks: "ă," "â," "î," "ţ" "ş" Romanians consider their language sweet and harmonious, bringing "honey to the mouth," and are proud of its Latin origin.

For first-generation Romanian immigrants—regardless of the period they arrived in America—Romanian was the primary language. In a very short time, however, such American words as supermarket, basement, streetcar, laundry, high school, and subway became infused in daily speech; thus, Romanian has evolved into an "Americanized" Romanian. Subsequent generations generally have spoken Romanian less often, eventually switching to English as their principal language. Romanian church services (including

Sunday school) are still conducted in Romanian. In several cities, radio programs are broadcast in Romanian, and there are numerous Romanian-language newspapers and periodicals in circulation.

GREETINGS AND OTHER POPULAR EXPRESSIONS

Common Romanian greetings and other expressions include: Bună seara ("bóona seàra")—Good evening; Bună ziua ("bóona zéeoóa")—Good day; Salut ("salóot")—Greetings, hello; La revedere ("la rayvaydáyray")—Good-bye; Noroc bun ("norók bóon")—Good luck; Mulţumesc ("mooltsóomesk")—Thank you; Felicitări ("feleecheetáry")—Congratulations; La multzi ani ("la múltzi ánee")—Happy New Year; Sărbători fericite "(sarbatóry fayreechéetay")—Happy Holidays (this greeting is used at Christmas time, for there is no expression like Merry Christmas in Romanian); Hristos a inviat ("Khristós a ynveeát")—Christ has Risen (a greeting used at Easter), the reply is Adevărat a inviat ("adevarát a ynveeát")—In truth He has risen; Sănătate ("sanatátay")—To your health, (spoken when raising a toast).

FAMILY AND COMMUNITY DYNAMICS

During the first three decades of the twentieth century, the Romanian American family underwent profound changes. The first immigrants were typically single males or married men who had left their families behind temporarily in order to save enough money to send for them later. They lived in crowded boarding houses and often slept on the floors. On Sundays and holidays, they congregated in saloons or restaurants and at church. Later, Romanian immigrants gathered at the headquarters of mutual aid societies and fraternal organizations where they discussed news from Romania, read or wrote letters, and sang religious or popular songs. Meanwhile, the boarding houses evolved into cooperatives in which a boarder provided his own bed and shared all operating expenses (rent, utilities, food, and laundry services) with the other residents.

As Romanian immigrants became better accustomed to the American way of life, they adopted higher standards of living, prepared more nutritious meals, and engaged in such recreational activities as sports and movie-going. Since most women worked outside the home, economic conditions gradually improved, and the immigrants were able to purchase a home, cars, and modern appliances, or were able to rent larger apartments in more prosperous neighborhoods. The typical Romanian household features Romanian embroidery or rugs, the Romanian flag, and other cultural icons, which are displayed in a common area.

Romanians have always held the family in high esteem and are generally opposed to divorce. Although the first wave of immigrants consisted of large families, subsequent generations chose to have fewer children, a trend that could be attributed to economic factors. Early immigrants cared very much for their children, did not permit child labor, and instilled in their children the importance of education. While approximately 33 percent of the Romanian immigrants who came to America before World War I were illiterate, many of them managed to learn English or improve their education to obtain or to hold jobs. Encouraged by their parents, second-generation Romanian Americans placed more emphasis on vocational training and college education.

While maintaining their place in the industries where their parents worked, second-generation Romanian Americans gradually switched from unskilled to skilled occupations. Others became white collar workers, and many embraced professional careers. Subsequent generations went even further in their educational and professional pursuits. Romanian Americans made such progress that for several decades none of the adult members of this group had less than a high school education. The professional ranks of Romanians (those educated at American universities) were substantially enlarged by the thousands of professionals who immigrated to the United States after World War II, and in the years following the Revolution of 1989. As a result, Romanian Americans were able to make many significant contributions to American society.

WEDDINGS

The bridal shower, a social custom that was never practiced in Romania, has evolved into an often gala affair attended by both sexes. Prior to the wedding ceremony, bans are announced for three consecutive Sundays so that impediments to the marriage—if any—can be brought to the attention of the priest. After that, the couple selects the best man and maid (or matron) of honor, both of whom are called *naşii* ("nashée"), usually a husband and wife or a sister and brother. In most cases, the *naşii* later serve as godparents to the couple's children.

On the day of the wedding, the bridal party meets in the bride's home and leaves for the church, where the groom is waiting along with the best man. In the church there is no instrumental music, and the bridal procession is made in silence. The bride is brought to the altar by her father or another male member of the family, who then relinquishes her to the groom. The ceremony is begun by the priest, assisted by a cantor or church choir that sings the responses. After receiving affirmative answers from the couple about their intention to marry and their mutual commitment, the priest blesses the wedding rings and places them in the hands of the bride and groom. Then, metal or floral crowns are placed on the heads of the couple so that they can rule the family in peace, harmony, and purity of heart. The bride and groom then take three bites of a honey wafer or drink wine from a common cup, which symbolizes their bountiful life together. Finally, the hands of the couple are bound together with a ribbon to share all joys and sorrows together, and the couple walks three times around the tetrapod (a small stand displaying an icon), symbolizing the eternity of their union and obedience to the Holy Trinity. The crowns are removed with a blessing from the priest, who then concludes the ceremony with a few words of advice for the couple. The reception is held either at a private home, hotel, or restaurant. Instead of gifts, guests give money at the reception, which is collected by the *naşii* who publicly announce the amounts received. The reception is accompanied by music and dancing, including popular Romanian songs and folk dances.

BAPTISMS

When a child is ready for baptism, the parents first select the godparents, or *naşii*, who are often the same couple that served as best man and matron of honor at the parents' wedding. The *naşii* bring the child to the church, where the priest confers the grace of God by putting his hand on the child. Then, the priest exorcises the child by breathing on the child's forehead, mouth, and breast. The godmother, or *naşa* ("násha"), renounces the service of Satan in the child's name and promises to believe in Jesus Christ and serve

only Him. In front of the altar, the priest anoints the child with the "oil of joy" (blessed olive oil) on the forehead, breast, shoulders, ears, hands, and feet. The baptism is completed by dipping the child three times in a font or by sprinkling with holy water. Immediately after the baptism follows confirmation, which consists of a new anointment of the child with *mïr* (pronounced "meer," meaning holy chrism), a mixture of 33 spices blessed by the bishop, on the forehead, eyes, nose, mouth, breast, ears, hands, and feet. It is customary to hold a dinner after the baptism, where guests usually bring gifts in the form of money.

FUNERALS

A death in the family is announced by the ringing of church bells three times a day (morning, noon, and evening) until the day of the funeral. Prayers for the dead are recited by the priest and the Gospel is read during the wake, called *saracusta* ("sarakóosta"). At the church, the funeral service consists entirely of singing; with the assistance of the cantor and choir, the priest sings hymns and prayers for the dead. The priest bids farewell to the family in the name of the deceased and asks for forgiveness of sins against family members or friends. At the cemetery prayers are recited and the Gospel is read. Before the coffin is lowered into the grave, the priest sprinkles soil on top of it and recites the following: "The earth is the Lord's, and the fullness thereof." Later, the deceased's family offers a *pomana* ("pomána"), which is either a complete meal or sandwiches and beverages. The purpose of the funeral is to remember the dead, and to seek forgiveness of his or her sins. At least six weeks following the burial, a memorial service called *parastas* ("parastás") is offered. During the *parastas*, the priest recites a few prayers for the deceased, and a large cake-like bread is then cut into small pieces and served with wine in the church's vestibule. After being served, the mourners recite "May his (or her) soul rest in peace" and reminisce about the person who had passed away.

INTERACTIONS WITH OTHER ETHNIC MINORITIES

Romanian Americans began to interact with other ethnic groups as they moved into better residential areas and suburbs. Romanian Orthodox believers established relationships with Orthodox Serbians, Greeks, Russians, and Ukrainians by attending their churches. Similarly, Romanian Catholics were drawn to Hungarian or Polish Catholics, while Romanian Baptists established friendly relations with Serbian, Croatian, and Bulgarian Baptists. Romanian workers came into contact with other ethnic groups in the workplace. All of these factors—including the proliferation of mixed marriages—contributed to the integration of Romanians into mainstream American society.

RELIGION

The first Romanian American churches, St. Mary's Orthodox Church (Cleveland, Ohio) and St. Helen's Catholic Byzantine Rite (East Cleveland, Ohio), were founded in 1904 and 1905, respectively. These churches also served as community centers where immigrants spent a good part of their social life. The vast majority of Romanian American churchgoers are Eastern Orthodox with a membership of about 60,000, organized into 60 parishes under two canonical jurisdictions. Forty-five parishes are subordinated to the Romanian Orthodox Episcopate of America, headed by Bishop Nathaniel Pop. Fifteen parishes—the majority of which are located in Canada—are under the Romanian Orthodox Missionary Episcopate of America, led by Archbishop Victorin Ursache (1912-). The Catholic Church of the Byzantine Rite has 15 parishes, serving approximately 4,000 Romanian members. The church is led by Vasile Puşcaş, the first Byzantine Rite bishop in America. The number of Romanian Protestants is approximately 2,500; most of them are Baptists. The first Romanian Baptist church was founded in Cincinnati, Ohio, in 1910; at present there are nine Romanian Baptist churches and smaller groups of Romanian Seventh-Day Adventists and Pentecostals under various jurisdictions.

The Romanian Orthodox church and the Catholic Church of the Byzantine Rite are essentially sister churches with a common history, liturgy, customs, and traditions. Both follow the teachings of the Apostles but differ in their interpretation of the Pope's infallibility. Members of the Byzantine Rite church believe in the infallibility of the Pope when he speaks *ex cathedra* on faith and morality, while Orthodox followers contend that any person or council in the church is not infallible. Those who embraced the dogma of papal infallibility switched allegiance from the Eastern Orthodox church to the Vatican in 1697 but have preserved all other features and disciplines of the Eastern church. Both churches adhere to the Nicene Creed, and the Liturgy is based on the text of Saint John Chrysostom (c. 347-407 A.D.), modified by Saint Basil the Great (c. 329-379 A.D.). There are seven Sacraments: Eucharist, Baptism, Confirmation, Penance, Matrimony, Holy Orders, and Anointing of the Sick. In the Romanian Orthodox church, the Anointing of the Sick is administered by three priests and may be given to the healthy to prevent illness. Services in both churches are conducted in Romanian accentuated by song and chants. The cathedrals are richly decorated with icons and images of the saints, although carved images are forbidden. The altar is located in the center of the sanctuary, and a screen or partition called an iconostasis separates the sanctuary from the rest of the church. Only priests and deacons can enter the sanctuary; other parishioners are not permitted to cross beyond the iconostasis.

Orthodox and Byzantine Rite priests usually wear black cassocks, but gray and brown are also permitted. During the Liturgy, vestments are colorful and ornate; while a priest's headdress is a cylindrical-shaped black hat, bishops wear a mitre, a crown made of stiff material adorned on top with a cross and various small pictures or icons. At the top of the pastoral scepter are two intertwined serpents surmounted by a cross or an image of a saint. Former liturgical colors (black, red, white) are not observed in modern times. Orthodox priests are permitted to marry before ordination, but only unmarried priests can become bishops. Deacons, subdeacons, and readers assist the priests during services. Clergy and laity (nonclergy) take part in the administration of the church and in the election of the clergy in Orthodox churches, while Byzantine Rite priests are appointed by their bishops.

Romanian Protestant churches conduct their services in the same manner as their American coreligionists, employing Romanian pastors who are subordinated to various local American jurisdictions. Their predecessors were trained by American missionaries in Romania during the nineteenth century.

EMPLOYMENT AND ECONOMIC TRADITIONS

Because early Romanian immigrants settled in the eastern and midwestern regions of the United States, they found work in such industries as iron, rubber, and steel manufacturing; coal mining; meat packing; and automotive assembly. They were assigned the heaviest and dirtiest jobs, as was the custom with all newly arrived immigrants. After accumulating work experience and perfecting their English language skills, some Romanians advanced to more responsible positions. Immigrants who settled in California were employed as gardeners, fruit gatherers and packers, and in freight transportation, while Macedo-Romanians often held jobs as waiters in the hotel and restaurant industries. About nine percent of Romanian immigrants settled in Colorado, North and South Dakota, Idaho, and Wyoming; they became involved in agriculture and ranching either as farm owners or as managers. Romanians were also employed as tailors, bakers, carpenters, and barbers, establishing their own small businesses in Romanian American neighborhoods. Romanian women found employment in light industry, such as cigar and tobacco manufacturing, or as seamstresses. Younger women became clerks or office secretaries, while others worked as manicurists or hairdressers in beauty salons. Many Macedo-Romanian women took jobs in the textile industry. Some Romanians with entrepreneurial skills opened travel agencies, small banks, saloons, boarding houses, and restaurants.

POLITICS AND GOVERNMENT

The formation of the Union and League of Romanian Societies of America (ULRSA) in 1906 marked the beginning of Romanian political activity on a national scale. Founded in Cleveland, ULRSA brought together dozens of mutual aid and cultural societies, clubs, fraternities, and other groups committed to preserving Romanian ethnicity. It provided insurance benefits, assisted thousands of Romanians in completing their education, and taught newly arrived immigrants how to handle their affairs in a democratic way. As ULRSA gained more power and prestige, its leaders were often "courted" by local and national politicians to enlist political support from the Romanian American community.

The leadership of the ULRSA (with a few exceptions) has traditionally held a neutral and unbiased position in American politics. Despite this neutrality, however, many Romanians, especially those who immigrated to America prior to World War II, have pro-Democratic sentiments, while the majority of postwar immigrants and refugees with strong anti-Communist sentiments tilt more toward the Republican party. A small group of Romanian American socialists—primarily workers from Cleveland, Chicago, Detroit, and New York—founded the Federation of the Romanian Socialist Workers of the United States in 1914 and later merged with the pro-Communist International Workers Order (IWO). Many Romanian Americans also joined local labor unions for the practical reason that they could not obtain work otherwise. Later, as employment opportunities improved, they participated in union activities according to their specific interests, benefits needs, and preferences.

MILITARY

During World War I, several hundred Romanian volunteers from Ohio and other states enrolled in the American Expeditionary Force in Europe on the French front. Many of these soldiers received commendations for bravery. Over 5,000 Romanian Americans served in the American Armed Forces during World War II and over 300 died in combat. Lieutenant Alex Vraciu of East Chicago, Indiana, destroyed 19 Japanese planes in 1944; Cornelius and Nicholas Chima, brothers from Akron, Ohio, were the only Romanian American team to fly a combat plane in 1944. Florea Busella of Glassport, Pennsylvania, was the first Romanian American woman to enroll in the Navy's WAVES in 1942, and Lieutenant Eleanor Popa, a registered nurse from Ohio, was one of the first American military women to enter Tokyo, Japan in 1945. Romanian Americans were also represented in significant numbers during the Korean and Vietnam Wars and many were promoted to officer ranks. Nicholas Daramus became the first Romanian American to be promoted to the rank of full commander in the U.S. Navy in 1977.

RELATIONS WITH ROMANIA

Romanian Americans have always been proud of their homeland and have maintained ties beyond normal relations with family or friends left behind. Before and during World War I, Romanian Americans exposed Hungarian persecution of Transylvanians in their newspapers and many organizations called for the unification of Transylvania and Romania. They also gave generous donations of money, food, and clothing for Romania's orphans, widows, and refugees. In 1919 Romanian Americans submitted a Four-Point Motion to the Peace Conference, calling for the reestablishment of Romania's territorial borders (including Transylvania and other regions formerly held by foreign powers), equal rights for ethnic minorities, and the establishment of a democracy based on principles adopted in the United States.

In the 1920s and 1930s many Romanian Americans actively supported the National Peasant Party founded in Transylvania against anti-democratic political forces. Prominent Romanians such as Queen Marie (1875-1938) visited Romanian American communities, and the Romanian government sent a group of students to complete their studies at various American universities. After World War II, Romanian Americans sent food, medicine, and clothing to refugees and other types of aid to help Romania's devastated economy.

During the years of Communist dictatorship, Romanian American groups sent a formal memorandum to President Harry Truman protesting the mass deportations of Romanians by Soviet troops in 1952, and in 1964 called upon President Lyndon B. Johnson to exert pressure on the Communists to release Romanian political prisoners and provide exit visas for individuals desiring to join relatives in the United States. Many Romanian Americans who held pro-monarchist views sought the restoration of Michael I, who was forced by the Communists to abdicate in December 1947. Romanian American Catholics vehemently opposed the suppression of their church in Romania beginning in 1948, in which bishops and priests were arrested and murdered, and church property was confiscated. Many Romanian Catholics were deported.

Romanian Americans continue to aid their native country during difficult times through the auspices of the Union and League of Romanian Societies in America, the International Red Cross, and other philanthropic organizations. Presently, some Romanian Americans are involved in developing business ventures in Romania, given the precarious conditions of the country's economy and unfamiliarity with the capitalist system. There is also a steady flow of scholarly exchanges between Romania and United States—via grants and scholarships—in which Romanian Americans take an active role through the Romanian Studies Association of America, the American Romanian Academy of Arts and Sciences, and other academic organizations.

INDIVIDUAL AND GROUP CONTRIBUTIONS

Although Romanian Americans represent only one-eighth of one percent of America's total population, they have made significant contributions to American popular culture and to the arts and sciences. The following sections list Romanian Americans and their achievements.

ACADEMIA

Mircea Eliade (1907-1986) was a renowned authority on religious studies, mythology, and folklore. His many publications include *The History of Religions: Essays in Methodology* (1959) and *Zalmoxis, the Vanishing God: Comparative Studies in the Religions and Folklore of Dacia and Eastern Europe* (1972). Many of Eliade's works have been translated into several languages. Nicholas Georgescu-Roegen (1906-1994) pioneered mathematical economics and influenced many American economists through his *Analytical Economics: Issues and Problems* (1966). Georgescu-Roegen was considered by his peers "a scholar's scholar and an economist's economist." Mathematician Constantin Corduneanu edits *Libertas Mathematica*. Romance philologist Maria Manoliu-Manea served as president of the American Romanian Academy of Arts and Sciences for many years.

FILM, TELEVISION, AND THEATER

Jean Negulesco (1900-) directed *Singapore Woman* (1941), *Johnny Belinda* (1948), *Titanic* (1953), and *Three Coins in a Fountain* (1954), and was also known as a portrait artist. Television actor Adrian Zmed (c. 1954-) costarred with William Shatner in the police drama "T. J. Hooker" (1982-1986). In theater, Andrei Şerban (1943-) adapted and directed classical plays at LaMama Theater in New York City, while Liviu Ciulei (1923-) is best known for directing classical works.

JOURNALISM

Theodore Andrica (1900-1990) edited and published two successful periodicals, the *New Pioneer* during the 1940s, and the *American Romanian Review* during the 1970s and 1980s. Both publications featured articles on Romanian American life, traditions, customs, and cooking, and documented the achievements of Romanian Americans. Andrica also served as editor of the *Cleveland Press* for 20 years. The Reverend Vasile Haţegan (1915-) of the Romanian Orthodox Church wrote several articles on Romanians residing in New York City, while the Reverend Gheorghe Mureşan of the Romanian Catholic Byzantine Rite Church proved to be a gifted editor for Catholic publications. John Florea (1916-) of *Life* magazine and Ionel Iorgulescu (1918-) of *Redbook* magazine were outstanding photographers during the 1940s and 1950s. For 25 years, broadcaster Liviu Floda of Radio Free Europe hosted programs discussing human rights violations by the Communist regime in Romania. Floda interviewed hundreds of personalities, helped reunite refugee families with American relatives, and wrote dozens of articles on various subjects for Romanian Americans and foreign-language journals.

LITERATURE

Peter Neagoe (1881-1960) was the first major Romanian American author. In such novels as *Easter Sun* (1934) and *There Is My Heart* (1936), he depicted the lives of Transylvanian peasants in realistic detail. Mircea Vasiliu (also an illustrator) wrote *Which Way to the Melting Pot?* (1955) and *The Pleasure Is Mine* (1963), in which he humorously recounts his experiences as an immigrant. Eugene Theodorescu's *Merry Midwife* and Anişoara Stan's (1902-1954) *They Crossed Mountains and Oceans* (1947) also focus on immigrant life in America. Moreover, Stan published *The Romanian Cook Book*, which remains a prototype of Romanian cookery and cuisine. Eli Popa edited and translated *Romania Is a Song: A Sample of Verse in Translation* (1967), a bilingual collection of Romanian classical and folk poetry, and modern verse by Romanian American poets. Andrei Codrescu (1946-), a poet, novelist, and journalist, has added new dimensions to contemporary Romanian American literature through such books as *The Life and Times of an Involuntary Genius* (1975), *In America's Shoes* (1983), and several others which delineate anti-Communist sentiments in Romania and the immigrant experience in America. Codrescu also founded the literary journal *Exquisite Corpse*, and is a contributor to the National Public Radio program "All Things Considered."

MUSIC

George Enesco (1881-1955) was a composer, violinist, and conductor who lived in the United States before and after World War II. Enesco conducted several symphony orchestras, taught at the Manhattan School of Music in New York City, and earned fame for his "Romanian Rhapsodies," which has since been performed by many American and foreign symphony orchestras. Ionel Perlea (1901-1970) served as musical conductor of the New York Metropolitan Opera for over 20 years despite the fact that his right hand was paralyzed; he also taught at the Manhattan School of Music. Stella Roman (1905-1992), an operatic soprano, performed at the Metropolitan Opera in New York during the 1940s and 1950s, specializing in Italian opera spinto roles. Other gifted performers include Christina Caroll (1920-) of the New York Metropolitan Opera; Iosif Cristea and Gloria Vasu, both with the Boston Grand Opera Company; Yolanda Marculescu, soprano and music teacher at the University of Wisconsin at Milwaukee; Lisette Verea, operetta singer and comedienne based in New York City; and Marioara Trifan, an internationally renowned pianist. In addition, the popular tune "And the Angels Sing," which was recorded by the legendary jazz musician Benny Goodman, is in fact a Romanian folk song brought to America by Romanian immigrants.

SCIENCE AND TECHNOLOGY

George Palade (1912-) of the Yale University School of Medicine shared the 1974 Nobel Prize in medicine, for his contributions to research on the structure and function of the internal components of cells. Traian Leucutzia (1893-1970), who began his medical career in Detroit, Michigan, in the 1920s, was one of the first scientists to detect the radiation hazards of X-rays, and served as editor of the *American Journal of Roentgenology, Radium Therapy,* and *Nuclear Medicine* for several years. Valer Barbu (1892-1986) taught psychiatry and psychoanalysis at Cornell University, the New School of Social Research in New York City, and the American Institute of Psychoanalysis before and after World War II. A disciple of Karen Horney, Barbu was critical of Freudian analysis.

Constanin Barbulescu, an aeronautical engineer, devised methods of protecting aircraft flying in severe weather. He published his findings in *Electrical Engineering* and other technical journals during the 1940s. Alexandru Papana (1905-1946) tested gliders and other aircraft for Northrop Aircraft in California. Many of Papana's experiences as a test pilot were documented in *Flying* magazine.

SPORTS

Charlie Stanceu (1916-1969) was the first Romanian American to play baseball in the major leagues. A native of Canton, Ohio, Stanceu pitched for the New York Yankees and the Philadelphia Phillies during the 1940s. Stanceu was followed by Johnny Moldovan, who signed a contract with the Yankees in 1947.

VISUAL ARTS

Constantin Brancuşi (1856-1957) is considered by some art critics to be the father of modern sculpture. He first exhibited his works in America in 1913 at the International Exhibition of Modern Art. Many of Brancusi's pieces ("Miss Pogany," "The Kiss," "Bird in Space," "White Nigress") were acquired by the Museum of Modern Art in New York City, the Philadelphia Museum of Art, and the Art Institute of Chicago. Sculptor George Zolnay (1867-1946) created the Sequoya Statue in the United States Capitol, the Edgar Allan Poe monument at the University of Virginia at Charlottesville, and the War Memorial sculpture of Parthenon in Nashville, Tennessee. Zolnay also served as art commissioner at the 1892 World Columbian Exhibition in Chicago, Illinois. Elie Cristo-Loveanu (c. 1893-1964) distinguished himself as a portrait artist and professor of painting at New York University during the 1940s and 1950s. His portrait of President Dwight Eisenhower is on display at Columbia University. Constantin Aramescu, a Floridian, is noted for paintings on Romanian subjects. Iosif Teodorescu and Eugene Mihaescu (1937-) are illustrators for the *New York Times*, while Mircea Vasiliu (1920-), a former diplomat, is a well known illustrator of children's books. Alexandru Seceni painted icons and saints in several Romanian Orthodox churches in America and also developed a special technique of wood etching for the Romanian Pavilion at the 1939 New York World's Fair.

PRINT

America: Romanian News.
Organ of the Union and League of Romanian Societies in America (ULRSA). It is a monthly publication that focuses on organization activities and achievements of local ULRSA branches and features cultural news and book reviews written in English and Romanian. It is supplemented by an almanac listing important events in the Romanian American community.

Contact: Peter Lucaci, Editor.

Address: 23203 Lorain Road, North Olmstead, Ohio 44070-1625.

Telephone: (216) 779-9913.

Luminatorul (The Illuminator).
Monthly bilingual publication of the Romanian Baptists Association. Prints articles on religious subjects and lists organization activities.

Contact: Marioara Pascu, Editor.

Address: 4112 West Wellington, Chicago, Illinois 60641-5425.

Telephone: (312) 545-8996.

Romanian American Heritage Center Information Bulletin.
Organ of the Valerian Trifa Romanian-American Heritage Center (English language only). Bimonthly publication that contains articles on early Romanian American immigrants and their contributions to American society, and also features book reviews.

Contact: Traian Lascu, Editor.

Address: 2540 Grey Tower Road, Jackson, Michigan 49201.

Telephone: (517) 522-8260.

Solia (The Herald).
Published monthly in a bilingual format by the Romanian Orthodox Episcopate of America. Focuses on parish news and youth and women-auxiliary projects, but also features book reviews and produces an annual supplement listing important events and a religious calendar.

Contact: Manuela Cruga, English Language Editor.

Address: 2522 Grey Tower Road, Jackson, Michigan 49201-9120.

Telephone: (517) 522-8260.

Unirea (The Union).

Monthly bilingual publication of the Association of Romanian Catholics in America. Gathers news from various parishes, features a youth section, and prints book reviews. It also publishes an annual supplement listing important events, a religious calendar, and other information.

Contact: John Halmaghi, Editor.

Address: 4309 Olcott Avenue, East Chicago, Indiana 46312-2649.

Telephone: (219) 398-3760.

RADIO

WCAR-AM (1900).

"Ethnic and Proud," is a weekly one-hour Romanian broadcast featuring religious and community news as well as Romanian music.

Contact: Jimmy Crucian.

Address: 2522 Grey Tower Road, Jackson, Michigan 49204.

Telephone: (517) 522-4800; or, (313) 527-1111.

ORGANIZATIONS AND ASSOCIATIONS

American Romanian Academy of Arts and Sciences (ARA).

Founded in 1975, the ARA has a membership of 250 Romanian scholars who live in the United States. It focuses on research and publishing activities regarding Romanian art, culture, language, history, linguistics, sciences, and economics.

Contact: Maria Manea-Manoliu, President.

Address: Department of French and Italian, University of California, Davis, California 95616.

Telephone: (916) 752-6442.

American Romanian Orthodox Youth (AROY).

Founded in 1950, with approximately 2,000 members, AROY functions as an auxiliary of the Romanian Orthodox Episcopate of America; cultivates religious education and Romanian culture through summer courses, retreats, sports, competitions, scholarships, and other activities.

Contact: Gary Davis, President.

Address: 2522 Grey Tower Road, Jackson, Michigan 49201-9120.

Telephone: (517) 522-4800.

Association of Romanian-American Orthodox Ladies Auxiliaries (ARAOLA).

Founded in 1938, the ARAOLA functions under the aegis of the Romanian Orthodox Episcopate of America. Its 2,600 members are involved in charitable work, cultural programs, and preservation of traditional values. The organization also provides scholarships to female graduate students, and maintains a museum. ARACOLA is also known as Asociatia Reuniunilor Femeilor Ortodoxe Romane-Americane.

Contact: Pauline Trutza, President.

Address: 1466 Waterbury Road, Lakewood, Ohio 44107.

Telephone: (216) 221-2435.

Association of Romanian Catholics of America (ARCA).

Founded in 1948, the ARCA promotes religious education in the tradition of the Romanian Catholic Church of the Byzantine Rite and cultural preservation, and sponsors special programs designed for youths. The Association is also involved in publishing activities.

Contact: Reverend George C. Mureşan, Director.

Address: 1700 Dale Drive, Merrillville, Indiana 46410.

Telephone: (219) 980-0726.

Union and League of Romanian Societies of America (ULRSA).

Founded in 1906, with approximately 5,000 members, ULRSA is the oldest and largest Romanian American organization. It has played an important role in organizing Romanian immigrants and in preserving Romanian culture. Presently, the ULRSA functions as a fraternal benefit insurance organization.

Contact: Virginia Tekushan, Secretary and Treasurer.

Address: 23203 Lorain Road, North Olmsted, Ohio 44070.

Telephone: (216) 779-9913.

MUSEUMS AND RESEARCH CENTERS

Cleveland Cultural and Folk Art Center.

Has preserved a large collection of Romanian national costumes, wood carvings, rugs, icons, furniture, paintings, and over 2,000 Romanian books, as well as English books related to Romania.

Contact: Virginia Martin.

Address: 3256 Warren Road, Cleveland, Ohio 44111.

Telephone: (216) 941-5550.

Iuliu Maniu American Romanian Relief Foundation (IMF).

Has a sizable collection of Romanian peasant costumes, paintings and folk art items. It also manages a library of Romanian books that can be borrowed by mail.

Contact: Ariana A. Popa, President.
Address: P.O. Box 1151 Gracie Square Station, New York, New York 10128.
Telephone: (212) 734-3714.

Romanian American Heritage Center.

Collects and preserves historical records relating to Romanian immigrants and their achievements. The collection consists of religious items, brochures, minutes, flyers, and reports donated by various Romanian American organizations, family and individual photographs, and other materials of interest to researchers.

Contact: Alexandru Nemoianu.
Address: 2540 Grey Tower Road, Jackson, Michigan 49201.
Telephone: (517) 522-8260.

Romanian Cultural Center.

A Romanian government agency similar to the United States Information Agency (USIA), has a sizable collection of Romanian books published in Romania, and a collection of folk art items. The center organizes cultural programs and assists in providing contacts in Romania.

Contact: Liviu Petrescu.
Address: 200 East 38th Street, New York, New York 10016.
Telephone: (212) 941-5550.

Sources for Additional Study

Andrica, Theodore. *Romanian Americans and Their Communities of Cleveland.* Cleveland, Ohio: Cleveland Press, 1977.

Diamond, Arthur. *Romanian Americans.* New York: Chelsea House, 1988.

Galitzi Avghi, Christine. *A Study of Assimilation among the Romanians in the United States.* New York: Columbia University Press, 1929; reprinted, 1969.

Werstman, Vladimir. *The Romanians in America, 1748-1974: A Chronology and Factbook.* Dobbs Ferry, New York: Oceana Publications, 1975.

———. *The Romanians in America and Canada: A Guide to Information Sources.* Detroit: Gale Research Company, 1980.

RUSSIAN AMERICANS

by
Paul Robert
Magocsi

For the most part Russian immigrants and their descendants have succeeded in assimilating into mainstream American life. There are a few groups that have avoided acculturation and maintained the traditional lifestyle they brought from the homeland. Such traditionalists include the Orthodox Christian Old Believers and the non-Orthodox Molokan Christian sect.

OVERVIEW

Since the second half of the nineteenth century, Russia has been the largest country in the world, stretching from the plains of eastern Europe across Siberia as far as the shores of the Pacific Ocean. For centuries, Russia has straddled both Europe and Asia, two continents that are divided by the Ural Mountains.

In a sense, there are two Russian homelands. One is the present-day state of Russia, which coincides with territory inhabited by ethnic Russians. The other includes territories that are beyond Russia proper but were once part of the pre-World War I Russian Empire and later the Soviet Union. Americans who identify their heritage as Russian include first-generation immigrants and their descendants who came from Russia within its present-day borders; people from the Baltic countries, Belarus, and Ukraine who have identified themselves as Russians; East Slavs from the former Austro-Hungarian Empire who have identified themselves as Russians once in the United States; and Jews from the Western regions of the former Russian Empire and the Soviet Union who, aside from their religious background, identify themselves as Russians.

Much of European Russia west of the Urals was part of a medieval state known as *Kievan Rus'*, which existed from the late ninth century to the thirteenth century. During the Kievan period, Orthodox Christianity reached Russia and that religion remained intimately connected with whatever state or culture developed on Russian territory until the twentieth century. It was in a northern part of *Kievan Rus'*, the Duchy of Muscovy, that the birth of a specifically Russian state can be found. The state-building process began in the late thirteenth century, when the Duchy of Muscovy began to consolidate its power and expand its territory. The expansion proved to be phenomenal. By the seventeenth and eighteenth centuries, the growing state included lands along the Baltic Sea, Belarus, Ukraine, Moldova, and large parts of Poland. The country's borders also moved beyond the Ural Mountains into Siberia, a vast land whose annexation together with Central Asia and the Caucasus region were completed in the nineteenth century.

As the country grew, it also changed its name from the Duchy to the Tsardom of Muscovy and in 1721 it became the Russian Empire. Throughout the centuries, Muscovy/Russia functioned as a centralized state ruled by autocratic leaders whose titles changed as their power and influence grew. The grand dukes became the tsars of Muscovy, who in turn became emperors of the Russian Empire. Although the rulers of the empire were formally called emperors (*imperator*), they were still popularly referred to as tsars or tsarinas.

MODERN ERA

During World War I, Russia experienced a revolution, and in March 1917, the tsarist empire collapsed. In November 1917, a second revolution took place, led by the Bolsheviks and headed by a revolutionary named Vladimir Lenin. The Bolshevik Revolution was opposed by a significant portion of the population, and the result was a Civil War that began in 1918 and lasted until early 1921. In the end, the Bolsheviks were victorious, and in late 1922 they created a new state, the Union of Soviet Socialist Republics, or the Soviet Union. The Soviet Union consisted of several national republics, the largest of which was called Russia. Beyond the Russian republic many inhabitants especially in the western regions of the Soviet Union continued to identify themselves as Russians.

The new Soviet state proclaimed the worldwide establishment of Communism as its goal. It intended to achieve that goal by promoting Bolshevik-style revolutions abroad. Since many countries feared such revolutions, they refused to recognize Bolshevik rule. Thus, the Soviet Union was isolated from the rest of the world community for nearly 20 years. That isolation came to an end during World War II, when the Soviet Union, ruled by Lenin's successor Joseph Stalin, joined the Allied Powers in the struggle against Nazi Germany and Japan. Following the Allied victory, the Soviets emerged alongside the United States as one of the two most powerful countries in the world. For nearly the next half-century, the world was divided between two camps: the free or capitalist West led by the United States, and the revolutionary or Communist East led by the Soviet Union.

By the 1980s, the centralized economic and political system of the Soviet Union was unable to function effectively. In 1985, a new Communist leader, Mikhail Gorbachev, tried desperately to reform the system but failed. He did set in motion, however, a new revolution, bringing such enormous changes that by late 1991 the Soviet Union disappeared as a country. In its place, each of the former Soviet republics became an independent country, and among the new countries was Russia.

SIGNIFICANT IMMIGRATION WAVES

The first Russians on U.S. territory were part of Russia's internal migration. During the eighteenth century, Russian traders and missionaries crossing Siberia reached Alaska, which became a colony of the Russian Empire. By 1784 the first permanent Russian settlement was founded on Kodiak, a large island off the Alaskan coast. Soon there were Russian colonies on the Alaskan mainland (Yakutat and Sitka), and by 1812 the Russians pushed as far south as Fort Ross in California, 100 miles north of San Francisco. In 1867 the Russian government sold Alaska to the United States, and most Russians in Alaska (whose numbers never exceeded 500) returned home. Russian influence persisted in Alaska, however, in the form of the Orthodox Church, which succeeded in converting as many as 12,000 of the native Inuit and Aleut people.

Large-scale emigration from Russia to the United States only began in the late nineteenth century. Since that time, four distinct periods of immigration can be identified: 1880s-1914; 1920-1939; 1945-1955; and 1970s-present. The reasons for emigration included economic hardship, political repression, religious discrimination, or a combination of those factors.

The pre-1914 Russian Empire was an economically underdeveloped country comprised primarily of poor peasants and a small but growing percentage of lowly paid or unemployed industrial workers. European Russia also encompassed the so-called Pale of Settlement (present-day Lithuania, Belarus, Moldova, and large parts of Poland, and Ukraine). The Pale was the only place Jews were allowed to reside. The vast majority lived in small towns and villages in their own communities known as the *shtetl*, which were made famous in America through the setting of the Broadway musical *Fiddler on the Roof*.

Between 1881 and 1914, over 3.2 million immigrants arrived from the Russian Empire. Nearly half were Jews; only 65,000 were ethnically Russian, while the remaining immigrants were Belarusans and Ukrainians. Regardless of their ethnoreligious background, their primary motive was to improve their economic status. Many of the 1.6 million Jews who also left did so because they feared *pogroms*—attacks on Jewish property and persons that occurred sporadically in the Russian Empire from the 1880s through the first decade of the twentieth century.

While many Jews from the Russian Empire did not identify themselves as Russians, another group of immigrants adopted a Russian identity in the United States. These were the Carpatho-Rusyns, or Ruthenians, from northeastern Hungary and Galicia in the Austro-Hungarian Empire (today far western Ukraine, eastern Slovakia, and southeastern Poland). Of the estimated 225,000 Carpatho-Rusyns who immigrated to the United States before World War I, perhaps 100,000 eventually joined the Orthodox Church, where they and their descendants still identify themselves as Americans of Russian background.

The second wave of immigration was less diverse in origin. It was directly related to the political upheaval in the former Russian Empire that was brought about by the Bolshevik Revolution and Civil War that followed. Over two million persons fled Russia between 1920 and 1922. Whether they were demobilized soldiers from anti-Bolshevik armies, aristocrats, Orthodox clergy, professionals, businesspersons, artists, intellectuals, or peasants, and whether they were of non-Jewish (the majority) or Jewish background, all these refugees had one thing in common—a deep hatred for the new Bolshevik/Communist regime in their homeland. Because they were opposed to the Communist Reds, these refugees came to be known as the Whites.

The White Russians fled their homeland. They left from the southern Ukraine and the Crimea (the last stronghold of the anti-Bolshevik White Armies) and went first to Istanbul in Turkey before moving on to several countries in the Balkans (especially Yugoslavia and Bulgaria); other countries in east-central Europe; Germany; and France, especially Paris and the French Riviera (Nice and its environs). Others moved directly westward and settled in the newly independent Baltic states, Poland, Czechoslovakia, or farther on to western Europe. A third outlet was in the Russian far east, from where the White émigrés crossed into China, settling in the Manchurian city of Kharbin. As many as 30,000 left the Old World altogether and settled in the United States. This wave of Russian immigration occurred during the early 1920s, although in the late 1930s several thousand more came, fleeing the advance of Nazi Germany and Japan's invasion of Manchuria. During this period, approximately 14,000 immigrants arrived in the United States.

The third wave of Russian immigration to the United States (1945-1955) was a direct outcome of World War II. Large portions of the former Soviet Union had been occupied by Germany, and hundreds of thousands of Russians had been captured or deported to work in Germany. After the war, many were forced to return home. Others lived in displaced-persons camps in Germany and Austria until they were able to immigrate to the United States. During this period, approximately 20,000 of these Russian displaced persons, the so-called DPs, arrived.

Both the tsarist Russian and Soviet governments placed restrictions on emigration. In 1885 the imperial Russian government passed a decree that prohibited all emigration except that of Poles and Jews, which explains the small numbers of non-Jewish Russians in the United States before World War I. By the early 1920s, the Bolshevik/Communist-led Soviet government implemented further controls that effectively banned all emigration. As for the second-wave White Russian refugees who fled between 1920 and 1922, they were stripped of their citizenship in absentia and could never legally return home. This situation was the same for the post-World War II DPs, who were viewed as Nazi collaborators and traitors by the Soviet authorities.

In contrast, the fourth wave of Russian immigration that began in late 1969 was legal. It was formally limited to Jews, who were allowed to leave the Soviet Union for Israel as part of the agreements reached between the United States and the Soviet Union during the era of détente. In return for allowing Jews to leave, the United States and other western powers expanded the economic, cultural, and intellectual ties with their Communist rival. Although Jews leaving the Soviet Union were only granted permission to go to Israel, many had the United States as their true goal; and by 1985 nearly 300,000 had reached the United States.

After 1985 the more liberal policy of the Soviet government under Mikhail Gorbachev allowed anyone to leave the Soviet Union, and thousands more Jewish and non-Jewish Russians immigrated to the United States. Because Russia is an independent country with a democratically elected government, newcomers cannot justify their claim to emigrate on the grounds of political or religious persecution. This has resulted in a slowing of Russian emigration during the last decade of the twentieth century.

SETTLEMENT

Of the 2,953,000 Americans who in 1990 identified themselves wholly (71.6 percent) or partially (28.4 percent) of Russian ancestry, nearly 44 percent reside in the Northeast. This is a reflection of early settlement patterns. The Jews, in particular, went to New York City, Philadelphia, Boston, and other large cities. The non-Jewish Russians from the Russian Empire and the Carpatho-Rusyns settled in these cities as well as Chicago, Cleveland, Pittsburgh, and the coal mining towns of eastern Pennsylvania. Nearly 5,000 members of a Russian Christian religious sect known as the Molokans settled in California during the first decade of the twentieth century. They formed the nucleus of what has become a 20,000-member Russian Molokan community that is concentrated today in San Francisco and Los Angeles.

Most White Russian soldiers, aristocrats, professionals, and intellectuals settled in New York City, Philadelphia, and Chicago. But some moved into farming communities, such as a group of Don and Kuban Cossacks who established what are still vibrant rural centers in southern New Jersey. Those who left from the Russian far east and Chinese Manchuria settled in California, especially San Francisco and Los Angeles. The fourth wave settled almost exclusively in cities where previous Russian immigrants had gone, especially New York City. Certain sections like Brighton Beach in Brooklyn were transformed into vibrant Russian communities by the 1980s.

While the basic settlement pattern established by the first two waves of immigrants may have been maintained, the past three decades have also witnessed migration toward the sun-belt states like Florida, as well as to California where the original Russian communities have been supplemented by newcomers from the northeast.

ACCULTURATION AND ASSIMILATION

For the most part Russian immigrants and their descendants have succeeded in assimilating into mainstream American life. There are a few groups that have avoided acculturation and maintained the traditional lifestyle they brought from the homeland. Such traditionalists include the Orthodox Christian Old Believers and the non-Orthodox Molokan Christian sect. Whether these people live in large cities like San Francisco, Los Angeles, and Erie, Pennsylvania; in rural towns like Woodburn, Oregon; or in the backwoods of Alaska, they have continued to use the Russian language at home and sometimes succeeded in having Russian taught in public schools. The distinct dress and religious-based lifestyle of these groups keep them at a social distance from other Americans and distinguishes them from the rest of the community. A large number of White Russians, especially those of aristocratic background from the immediate post-World War I era, also found it difficult to adapt to an American society that lacked respect for the deference that Russian nobles, princes, princesses, and intellectuals otherwise had come to expect.

The Old Believers, Molokans, and White Russian aristocrats are only a small minority of the Russian American community today. But even among the vast majority who sought to assimilate, the goal was not always easy to accomplish; American society during the past 70 years has had a negative opinion of the Soviet Union and, therefore, of Russian Americans. Russian Americans have frequently been suspected of being potential Communist spies or socialists and anarchists intent on infiltrating and disrupting America's labor movement.

Even before the Soviet Union existed, immigrant workers from Russia, particularly Jews, played a leading role in organizations like the

Taken in 1947, this photograph demonstrates the influence of American fashion on traditional Russian dress. The lace shawls of these women are called *kascinkas*; their high-heeled shoes are American.

American branch of the International Workers' Organization. Leon Trotsky and Nikolai Bukharin, two of Lenin's closest associates, lived in New York City for a time where they edited a Russian-language socialist newspaper. And just before the American branch of the Red Cross was about to assist thousands of White Russians in finding refuge in the United States, authorities in places like New York led raids against the headquarters of the Union of Russian Workers and the Russian-dominated American Communist party. As a result, several thousand aliens were deported, nearly 90 percent of whom were returned to what by then had become Bolshevik-controlled Russia. It is a little known fact that as late as the 1970s some of these returnees and their descendants still maintained an identity as Americans even after living in the Soviet Union nearly half a century.

After World War II the United States was once again struck by a Red Scare, this time even more widely publicized as a result of the congressional investigations led during the 1950s by the demagogic Senator Joseph McCarthy. Again Russians and all things Russian were associated with Communism, so Russian Americans were forced to maintain a low profile, and some felt obligated to renounce their heritage.

Most recently, Russians in the United States have been linked to organized crime. With the break-up of the Soviet Union in the early 1990s, and the radical change in that country's economy,

a number of speculators have tried to take advantage of the situation. Many of these new Russian businessmen have contacts or are themselves residents in Russian American communities like Brighton Beach where they carry out illegal transactions. It is common to find references in today's mainstream American media to the dangers of the Russian mafia and, by implication, of all Russians.

CUISINE

Russian Americans enjoy many traditional dishes. They prepare a variety of rich and tasty soups, which are almost always served with a dollop of sour cream, or *smetana*. Most famous is *borshch*, or borscht, made from beets, cabbage, and meat. In the summer, borscht is served cold. *Shchi*, also made from cabbage, includes as well turnip, carrot, onion, or leek, and beef. Fish soups, such as *solianka*, that include onion, tomato, cucumber, lemon, butter, and sometimes beef, are popular. Many soups also include potatoes or dumplings. The traditional dark Russian bread is made from rye, though wheat is used increasingly. Russian meals are accompanied by vodka.

LANGUAGE

Russian is the largest of the Slavic languages and is spoken today by over 250 million people. For most first-generation immigrants the Russian language was used to communicate with one's family and friends until they attained a knowledge of English. For others the Russian language took on a symbolic function and was maintained to preserve a sense of Russian identity. For these reasons, the Russian language has never died out in the United States and, if anything, the number of native speakers and publications has expanded dramatically during the last two decades.

> "I felt lost, as if there was nothing to hold onto ahead of us. But having my mother and my two brothers with me, we felt we were still a family, though our life would never be the same."
>
> Maria Oogjen in 1923, cited in *Ellis Island: An Illustrated History of the Immigrant Experience,* edited by Ivan Chermayeff et al. (New York: Macmillan, 1991).

The appearance of newspapers, journals, and books in the United States and other countries where Russians lived helped keep traditional Russian culture alive throughout much of the twentieth century. Following the onset of Bolshevik rule in late 1917, the Soviet state eventually banned all forms of cultural and intellectual activity that did not conform to Stalin's version of Communism. Even the Russian language was transformed by the deletion of several letters from the Cyrillic alphabet and the infusion of new words that reflected the changes brought about by the Soviet system. Many of these new words were really abbreviations, such as *gensek* (general secretary), *gosplan* (state plan), *kolkhoz* (collective farm), *Komsomol* (Communist Youth League), *natsmen* (national minority), *vuzy* (colleges and universities), and *zarplata* (salary). At the same time many words were eliminated, such as *gorodovoi* (police officer), *gospodin* (gentleman, Mr.), *gospozha* (lady, Mrs.), and *gubernator* (governor).

Many Russians who emigrated after the Bolshevik Revolution felt they had a moral duty to preserve the old alphabet as the medium for the "true" Russian language. As a result, until the fall of the Soviet Union in late 1991, there existed two Russian literatures: Soviet Russian literature and Russian literature abroad. Schools were also created in an attempt to preserve the Russian language for the descendants of immigrants. Since the late nineteenth century many Orthodox church parishes have had their own Russian-language schools. This tradition is still practiced in some parishes and summer camps conducted by the Russian Scout movement. At a higher level various Orthodox churches operated Russian-language seminaries, and there were even university-level institutions such as the Russian Collegiate Institute in New York City (1918) and the Russian People's University in Chicago (1921). These efforts proved to be short-lived, although today there is no shortage of Russian language, literature, history, and culture courses taught at some high schools and numerous universities throughout the United States.

FAMILY AND COMMUNITY DYNAMICS

The Russian extended family structure of uncles, aunts, cousins, godparents, etc. that prevailed in villages and *shtetls* was difficult, if not impossible, to recreate in the United States. Therefore, families became more inner-directed and isolated than they had been in Russia.

There was also a decrease in the number of children. Among post-World War I White Russian émigrés, there were twice as many men as women. This meant there was a high percentage of unmarried men with no children or marriages with women of other backgrounds. Poverty and unstable economic conditions among émigrés also worked against having children. Even among the pre-World War I Russian Jewish immigration in which the number of males (56 percent) and females (44 percent) was more balanced, the number of children married couples bore was well below the American norm. Statistics from 1969 reveal that Russian American women of the first generation and their descendants had an average of 1.7 to 2.4 children, while women of comparable ages who were of English, German, Irish, or Italian backgrounds had between 2.1 and 3.3 children.

Initially, Russian immigrants strove to have their children choose marriage partners from among their own group. Among Russian Jews, the religious factor was of primary importance. Hence, descendants of pre-World War I Jewish immigrants from Russia largely intermarried with Jews or non-Jews with non-Russian origins. Non-Jewish Russians were more concerned with maintaining a Russian identity within their family, but marriages with non-Russians soon became the norm.

EDUCATION

While their family units may have been smaller than those of other Americans on average, Russian immigrants tended to place greater emphasis on education. This was certainly the case among Jews who brought a strong tradition of learning that had characterized Jewish life for centuries. Non-Jewish White Russians were intent on providing their offspring with the highest possible education (in the Russian language, if possible) so that they could take an appropriate place in Russian society when the Communist regime would collapse and they could return home. Even when it became obvious that returning to a non-Communist Russia was impossible, higher education was still considered useful for adaptation to American society. It is not surprising, then, that by 1971, among Americans of nine different backgrounds (English, Scottish, Welsh, German, Italian, Irish, French, and Polish), Russians between 25 and 34 had on average 16 years of education, while all others had at most only 12.8 years.

WOMEN

In traditional Russian society, women were legally dependent upon their husbands. The Bolshevik Revolution radically changed the status of women under Communist rule. Russian women were offered equal economic and social responsibilities, which resulted in a high percentage of females in the labor force. The majority of physicians and health care workers in general are women. In the family, however, a woman is still expected to perform domestic tasks such as cooking, cleaning, and shopping. Women have played a determining role in maintaining the cultural identity in the family passing on knowledge of Russian language and culture to younger people and by participation in philanthropic work that affects the entire community. Among the oldest of such organizations was the Russian Children's Welfare Society Outside Russia founded in New York City in 1926 to help orphans and poor children. Today the best known is the Tolstoy Foundation, set up in 1939 by Alexandra Tolstoy (1884-1979), daughter of the famous nineteenth-century Russian novelist, Leo Tolstoy. With branches throughout the world, the Tolstoy Foundation still operates a Russian senior citizen's home and cultural center in Nyack, New York, which has helped tens of thousands Russians and other refugees settle in the United States.

RELIGION

Based on religious criteria, Russian Americans are classified in three categories: Orthodox Christians, Jews, and nominal Jews. The large pre-World War I influx of Jews from the Russian Empire consisted mainly of individuals whose lives were governed by Jewish law and tradition in the thousands of *shtetls* throughout European Russia. Whether they were of the conservative Orthodox or Hassidic tradition, attendance at the synagogue; observance of the Sabbath (from sunset on Friday to sunset on Saturday); and deference to the rabbi as community leader, characterized Russian-Jewish life. While the authority of the rabbi over most aspects of daily Jewish life could not be fully maintained in the New World, the pre-World War I Russian-Jewish immigrants maintained their religious traditions within the confines of the home and synagogue. It was their Jewishness and not any association with Russia that made them indistinguishable from the larger Jewish-American society.

The arrival of Russian Jews since the early 1970s stands in stark contrast to their pre-World War I predecessors. For nearly 70 years, the Soviet system frowned on Judaism and other forms of religion. Therefore, by the time of their departure, the vast majority of Soviet Jews had no knowledge of Yiddish or Hebrew and had never been to a synagogue. Living in an officially atheistic Soviet Union, many found it politically and socially expedient to forget or even deny their Jewish heritage. When it became possible for Jews to emigrate legally from the Soviet Union, many quickly reclaimed their ancestral religious identity.

These Russian-speaking nominal Jews found it difficult to relate to English-speaking religious Jews when they arrived in the United States. While a small percentage of the newcomers learned and accepted the Jewish faith while in the United States, most follow no particular religion and have remained simply Russians or Russian Americans who are Jews in name only.

The concept of being a Russian in America is often associated with the Orthodox Christian faith. The Russian Orthodox church traces it roots to the Eastern Christian world. After the Christian church split in 1054 between the western or Latin sphere (centered in Rome) and the eastern or Byzantine-Greek sphere (centered in Constantinople, present-day Istanbul), the Orthodox church in Russia maintained its spiritual allegiance to the Byzantine east. In the second half of the fifteenth century a jurisdictionally independent Russian Orthodox church, with its main seat in Moscow, was founded. At first the church was headed by a patriarch, but after 1721 it was led by a council of bishops known as the Synod.

Eastern Christianity, and thereby Russian Orthodoxy, differed from the western Christian churches in several ways. The Divine Liturgy (not Mass) was conducted in Church Slavonic instead of Latin; priests could marry; and the old Julian calendar was retained. This meant that by the twentieth century fixed feasts like Christmas (January 7) were two weeks behind the commonly used Gregorian calendar.

Russian Orthodox church architecture both in the homeland and in the United States also had distinctive features. Church structures are based on a square floor plan (the so-called Greek cross) covered by a high central dome and surrounded by four or more smaller domes. The domes are usually finished in gold and topped by three-bar crosses. Inside the dominant element is the *iconostasis*, a screen covered by icons that separates the altar from the congregation. Some traditional churches have no pews and there is never an organ because of the Orthodox belief that only the human voice is permitted in the worship of God. Russian Orthodox priests are often clad in colorful vestments laden with gold trim. Some priests also wear long beards, which according to tradition should not be cut. Easter is the most festive of holidays when churches are packed with worshippers at midnight services, include candlelight processions, and are followed by the early morning blessing of Easter baskets filled with food delicacies and hand-painted eggs.

Throughout its history in the United States, the Russian Orthodox church has not only ministered to immigrants from Russia, but has also functioned as a missionary church attracting new adherents. Even before Alaska was purchased by the United States in 1867, the church converted over 12,000 Aleutians and some Eskimos to Orthodoxy. Aside from his spiritual work, the Orthodox Russian Bishop Innokentii Veniaminov (1797-1879) was also the first person to codify a written Aleut language for which he published a dictionary, grammar guide, Bible, and prayer-books.

Nearly 50,000 converts were attracted to Russian Orthodoxy during the 1890s and first decade of the twentieth century. These were Carpatho-Rusyn immigrants of the Greek or Byzantine Catholic faith living in Pennsylvania, New York, New Jersey, Ohio, and other northeastern industrial states. One of their own priests, Father Alexis Toth (1853-1909), convinced many Greek Catholic parishioners to return to the Orthodox faith of their ancestors. For his work, Toth was hailed as the father of Orthodoxy in America, and in 1994 was made an Orthodox saint.

The Russian Orthodox Church also had problems with internal divisions. Some of those divisions had occurred decades or even centuries earlier in the Russian Empire. Consequently among Russian immigrants in the United States there were Old Believers, whose movement dates from the seventeenth century, and the Molokans, whose movement emerged in the nineteenth century. The Old Believers and Molokans have been most fervent in retaining a sense of Russian identity through an active use of the Russian language in their religious services and in their daily lives.

More significant are the splits that occurred in the Russian Orthodox Church after its establishment in the United States. The divisions were the result of developments in the homeland, in particular the reaction of Russians abroad to the Bolshevik/Communist revolution and the existence of the officially atheist Soviet Union.

During the 1920s and 1930s, three factions had developed within Russian Orthodoxy. One faction consisted of the original Russian Orthodox Church that started in Alaska before moving to California and New York. It continued to recognize formally the patriarch, whose office as head of the mother church in Russia was restored in 1917. But as long as Russia was ruled by an uncompromising Soviet government, the American branch of the church governed itself as a distinct jurisdiction known as the *Metropolia*. The second faction consisted of the post-World War I White Russian émigrés, whose numbers included some clergy and laymembers of the church who rejected the idea of a patriarch, and favored a church governed by the Synod. Those who favored rule by the Synod came to be known as the Russian Orthodox Church Abroad, or the Synod. A third group consisted of individual parishes that remained directly under the jurisdiction of the patriarch in Moscow, even though he was living in a godless Soviet Communist state and was subject to governmental pressure.

Each of the three factions of the Russian Orthodox church in the United States had its own bishops, clergy, cathedrals, churches, monasteries, seminaries, publications, and supporting lay organizations. Each of the three also often denounced the others so that much of Russian community life in the United States from the 1920s through the 1960s was characterized by fierce rivalry between competing Russian Orthodox churches.

In 1970 the *Metropolia* reached an agreement with the patriarch in Moscow, was released from its formal subordination to Moscow, and became an independent body known as the Orthodox Church of America. This church is the largest of the three Russian Orthodox churches in the United States. Since 1970 the Orthodox Church of America has conducted all its services in English. The patriarchal parishes have mostly been absorbed by the Orthodox Church of America. The Synod Abroad remains staunchly Russian in terms of religious tradition and language use, and was an enemy of the Soviet Union until that state's demise in 1991.

EMPLOYMENT AND ECONOMIC TRADITIONS

The majority of Russian Jews and other Russians who arrived in the United States between the 1880s and 1914 entered the industrial labor force in the northeastern United States. This was not a particularly difficult adjustment, since 88.7 percent of Jews in European Russia in 1897 had been in manufacturing, commerce, and the equivalent of a white-collar service trade. In contrast, 63.2 percent of non-Jewish Russians worked in agriculture.

Women immigrants of Russian-Jewish background dominated America's garment industry as seamstresses in the small clothing factories and sweatshops of New York City and other urban areas in the northeast. Other Russians, including Belarusans and Carpatho-Rusyns, worked in factories in the large northeastern cities as well as in the coal mines of eastern Pennsylvania, the iron and steel factories in the Pittsburgh area, and the slaughtering and meatpacking plants of Chicago. The Russian presence was so pronounced in certain trades that they established their own unions or branches of unions, such as the Russian branch of the Union of Men's and Women's Garment Workers, the Russian-Polish department of the Union of Cloakmakers, the Society of Russian Bootmakers, and the Society of Russian Mechanics.

The White Russians who came after World War I had a much higher level of education than their predecessors. Although many took on menial jobs at first (there are countless legends of Russian aristocrats employed as waiters, taxi-drivers, or doormen at night clubs), they eventually found employment that took advantage of their skills. This was also the case among the post-World War II DPs, many of whom found their ways into university teaching, federal government employment, publishing, and other jobs that reflected the Cold War interests of the United States in the Soviet Union.

Educational levels and job skills are highest among the most recent Russian-Jewish immigrants. As high as 46.8 percent have had a university education, and 57.6 percent have been employed in the Soviet Union as engineers, economists, skilled workers, or technicians. In the United States, most have been able to find similar jobs and improved their economic status. Among the best known, and highest paid, of the recent immigrants are several hockey players of Russian background from the former Soviet Olympic team who have become a dominant part of teams in the National Hockey League during the 1980s and 1990s.

The descendants of the large pre-World War I immigration have done very well economically. By the 1930s and 1940s, the American-born offspring of the older immigrants remained in the same industries as their parents (clothing, steel, meat-packing, etc.), although some moved into managerial or white-collar positions. The third generation began to enter professions and have become doctors, lawyers, engineers, and businesspeople in larger numbers. By 1970 the median family income for Russian Americans was nearly $14,000, which was three to four thousand dollars higher on average than the median family income among Americans of English, Scottish, Welsh, German, Italian, Irish, and French background.

POLITICS AND GOVERNMENT

Aside from their active participation in the labor movement during the early decades of the twentieth century, Russians have generally not become involved in American political life. In a sense, their labor union activity acted as a deterrent to further political work, since many were accused of being socialists or Communists. In general, Russians have never formed a strong voting bloc that would encourage American politicians to solicit their support. Only in the past decade, in places like the Brighton Beach area of New York City, have local politicians like U.S. Congressman Stephen Solarz successfully courted the Russian vote.

This Russian American

vendor sells handicrafts

from his booth in

Brooklyn, New York.

RELATIONS WITH RUSSIA

While Russians may have avoided American politics, they did not shy away from concern with the homeland. This was particularly the case among the White Russian immigrants. The very fact that they were designated White Russians was a political statement. As refugees and political émigrés, most White Russians felt that their stay abroad was only temporary, and that they must live a Russian life while in temporary exile until the inevitable fall of the Soviet Union would allow them to return to a democratic Russia. This was the basic ideology that held the post-World War I White Russians and the post-World War II DPs together, even though they represented a wide variety of political persuasions. At one extreme some believed in the return of the monarchy. This included a woman living in the New York City area who claimed she was Grand Duchess Anatasia (1901-1918), one of the daughters of the last tsar Nicholas II Romanov who somehow had miraculously survived the mass assassination of the royal family. The legitimacy of this woman's claims were never proved or disproved.

Many rejected the monarchy and awaited the creation of a parliamentary liberal democratic state. The leader of this group was Alexander Kerensky (1881-1970), the last prime minister of Russia before the Bolshevik Revolution. He immigrated to New York City on the eve of World War II to escape the Nazi occupation of Paris where he had been living in exile. There were also regional groups like the Don and Kuban Cossacks who argued for autonomy in a future Russia, several socialist and anarchist groups on the political left, and a Russian Fascist organization based in Connecticut during the late 1930s on the far right. Among the post-World War II DPs there were also those who believed in Lenin's brand of socialism, which they felt had been undermined by his successor, Joseph Stalin.

Each of these political orientations had at least one organization and publication that was closely linked to or was a branch of the same or similar émigré organization based in western Europe. Despite their various social, propagandistic, and fund-raising activities, none of these Russian-American organizations ever achieved the abolition of Soviet rule in their Russian homeland. Realizing their inability to end Communist rule in Russia, some Russian Americans turned their efforts to their community in the United States and its relationship to American society as a whole. These people became concerned with the way they and their culture were perceived and depicted in America's media and public life. In response to those concerns lobbying groups, such as the Congress of Russian Americans and the Russian-American Congress, came into existence in the 1970s.

INDIVIDUAL AND GROUP CONTRIBUTIONS

ACADEMIA

Several researchers from Russia have enriched our knowledge by writing studies about their native land. In fact, much of America's present-day understanding of Russia and the Soviet Union is in large part due to the work of immigrants like historian Michael Rostovtsev (1870-1972); church historians Georges Florovsky (1893-1979), Alexander Schmemann (1921-1983), and John Meyendorff (1926-1993); linguist Roman Jakobson (1896-1982); literary critic Gleb Struve (1898-1985); and historians Michael Florinsky (1894-1981), Michael Karpovich (1888-1959), Alexander Vasiliev (1867-1953), George Vernadsky (1887-1973), Aleksander Riasanovsky (1923-), and Marc Raeff (1926-).

ART

Influential Russian American artists include Gleb Derujinski, a noted sculptor, and Sergey Rossolovsky, a respected painter from Portland, Maine.

LITERATURE

Writers generally have the greatest difficulty adapting to and being accepted in a new environment, since their language is their instrument of creativity, and by its nature a foreign and inaccessible element. Nevertheless, a few Russian authors have flourished on American soil. These include Vladimir Nabokov (1889-1977), who switched from Russian to English in the late 1940s and produced many novels, including the very popular *Lolita* (1958), and the short story writer Nina Berberova. Two other authors, while continuing to write in Russian, have nonetheless enhanced their careers while in the United States. They are Josef Brodsky (1940-) and the historical novelist and social critic Aleksander Solzhenitzyn (1918-), both of whom were awarded the Nobel Prize for literature.

MILITARY

John Basil Turchin (born Ivan Vasilevich Turchinov) served in the Union army during the Civil War and was promoted to the rank of U.S.

Brigadier General—the first Russian American to be elevated to such a high position.

MUSIC, DANCE, AND FILM

Classical music, opera, and ballet in the United States have been enriched for over a century by the presence of Russian composers and performers from Petr Illich Tchaikovsky and Sergei Prokofieff to Fritz Kreisler, Feodor Chaliapin, Sergei Diaghileff, Anna Pavlova, and Rudolf Nureyev, all of whom have graced America's stages for varying periods of time. Others came to stay permanently, including Serge Koussevitsky (1874-1951), conductor of the Boston Symphony Orchestra from 1924 to 1949; composers Sergei Rachmaninoff (1873-1943) and Alexander Gretchaninov (1864-1956); cello virtuoso, conductor, and musical director since 1977 of the National Symphony Orchestra, Mstislav Rostropovich (1927-); choreographer, founder of the School of American Ballet, and from 1948 to his death, director of the New York City Ballet, George Balanchine (1904-1983); and ballet dancers Natalia Makarova (1940-) and Mikhail Baryshnikov (1948). But the most famous of all was Igor Stravinsky (1882-1971), who settled permanently in New York City in 1939, from where he continued to enrich and influence profoundly the course of twentieth-century classical music. Dimitri Tiomkin, noted composer and musical director and author of many musical scores for Hollywood films. Natalie Wood, who was born in San Francisco as Natasha Gurdin (1938-1981) was an actress in numerous American films.

SCIENCE AND TECHNOLOGY

Vladimir Ipatieff (1867-1952) was a prominent research chemist; George Gamow (1904-1968), was a nuclear physicist who popularized the big-bang theory of the origin of the universe; Wassily Leontieff (1906-), is a Nobel Prize-winning economist who formulated the influential input-output system of economic analysis; Alexander Petrunkevitch (1875-1964) wrote numerous works in the field of zoology; Igor Sikorsky (1889-1972) was an aviation industrialist and inventor of the helicopter; Pitirim Sorokin (1889-1968) was a controversial sociologist who argued that western civilization was doomed unless it attained "creative altruism"; and Vladimir Zworykin (1889-1982) was a physicist and electronics engineer who is known as the father of television.

MEDIA

PRINT

Nezavisimaya Gazeta.

Selected version of Russian daily; text in Russian; published semi-monthly in English translation.

Contact: Cynthia Neu, Editor and Publisher.

Address: 7338 Dartford Drive, Suite 9, McLean, Virginia 22102.

Telephone: (703) 827-0414.

Fax: (703) 827-8923.

Novoe Russkoe Slovo/New Russian Word.

This publication is the oldest Russian daily newspaper in the world.

Contact: Andrei Sedych, Editor.

Address: 111 Fifth Avenue, Fifth Floor, New York, New York 10003-1005.

Telephone: (212) 564-8544.

Novyi Zhurnal/New Review.

Scholarly publication covering Russian interests.

Contact: George Kashkarov, Editor.

Address: 611 Broadway, Suite 842, New York, New York 10012-2608.

Telephone: (212) 353-1478.

Panorama.

This is the nation's largest independent American Russian weekly publication.

Contact: Alexander Polovets, Editor.

Address: 501 South Fairfax Avenue, Suite 206, Los Angeles, California 90036.

Telephone: (213) 931-2692.

Russkaia Zhizn'/Russian Life.

Daily newspaper covering Russian interests in Russian.

Address: 2460 Sutter Street, San Francisco, California 94115.

Telephone: (415) 921-5380.

Fax: (415) 921-8726.

Russky Golos/Russian Voice.

Address: 130 East 16th Street, New York, New York 10003.

Telephone: (212) 475-7595.

Zapiski.

Journal of the Association of Russian American Scholars in the United States; covers Russian culture.

Contact: Nadja Jernakoff, Editor.
Address: Box 180035, Richmond Hill, New York 11418-0035.
Telephone: (518) 785-6780.
Fax: (518) 388-6462.

Zerkalo/Russian Reflections.

This is the first Russian-English bilingual weekly in the United States.

Address: 1420 Josephine Street, Denver, Colorado 80206.
Telephone: (303) 377-2306.

RADIO

KMNB.

Address: 7060 Hollywood Boulevard, Suite 919, Los Angeles, California 90028.
Telephone: (213) 463-7224.

WMNB.

Russian American Broadcasting Company.

Address: Fort Lee, New Jersey 07024.
Telephone: (800) 570-2778; or, (800) 772-2080.

TELEVISION

RTN.

Russian Television Network.

Address: Box 3589, Stamford, Connecticut 06903.
Telephone: (800) 222-2786.

WMNB.

Russian American Broadcasting Company.

Address: Fort Lee, New Jersey 07024.
Telephone: (800) 570-2778; or, (800) 772-2080.

ORGANIZATIONS AND ASSOCIATIONS

Association of Russian American Scholars in the United States of America (ARASUSA).

Functions as a Russian scholarly center aimed at cooperating with Russian scholars in their pedagogical work and in their research projects in the United States; also unites persons involved in the study of Russian culture.

Contact: Professor Nadja Jernakoff, President.
Address: P.O. Box 180035, Richmond Hill, New York 11418.
Telephone: (518) 785-6780.

Congress of Russian Americans, Inc.

Political action umbrella group with branches throughout the country; seeks to promote Russian cultural heritage and to protect the legal, economic, and social interests of Russian Americans.

Contact: Katherine P. Lukin, Secretary.
Address: P.O. Box 818, Nyack, New York 10960.
Telephone: (914) 358-7117.

Fund for Relief of Russian Writers and Scientists in Exile (Litfund).

Fund to assist financially writers and scholars of Russian background living abroad.

Address: 519 Eighth Avenue, New York, New York 10018.
Telephone: (212) 564-5564.

Orthodox Church in America.

The largest church with members of Russian background; 12 dioceses throughout North America.

Address: P.O. Box 675, Route 25A, Syosset, New York 11791.
Telephone: (516) 922-0550.

Russian Children's Welfare Society.

Philanthropic group to help needy children of immigrants or refugees, especially from Russia.

Address: 349 West 86th Street, New York, New York 10024.
Telephone: (212) 779-2815.

Russian Independent Mutual Aid Society.

Fraternal organization and insurance company to provide workers and other policy holders with security in old age.

Address: 917 North Wood Street, Chicago, Illinois 60622.
Telephone: (312) 421-2272.

Museums and Research Centers

Immigration History Research Center.

Address: University of Minnesota, 826 Berry Street, Minneapolis, Minnesota 55455.

Telephone: (612) 373-5581.

Museum of Russian Culture.

Includes archival and published materials as well as artifacts pertaining to Russian American life, especially in California.

Address: 2450 Sutter Street, San Francisco, California 94115.

New York Public Library, Slavic and Baltic Division.

Aside from a rich collection of printed materials on the Russian and Soviet homeland, there is much material on Russians in the United States from the 1890s to the present.

Address: Fifth Avenue and 42nd Street, New York, New York 10018.

Telephone: (212) 930-0714.

Orthodox Church in America Archives.

Includes archival and published materials on Russian Orthodox church life in North America from the late nineteenth century to the present.

Address: P.O. Box 675, Route 25A, Syosset, New York 11791.

Telephone: (516) 922-0550.

YIVO Institute for Jewish Research.

Provides the best collection of archival and printed materials on Jews from the former Russian Empire and Soviet Union.

Address: 1048 Fifth Avenue, New York, New York 10028.

Sources for Additional Study

Chevigny, Hector. *Russian America: The Great Alaskan Adventure, 1741-1867*. Portland, Oregon: Binford and Mort, 1979.

Davis, Jerome. *The Russian Immigrant*. New York: Arno Press, 1969.

Eubank, Nancy. *The Russians in America*. Minneapolis, Minnesota: Lerner Publications, 1979.

Magocsi, Paul Robert. *The Russian Americans*. New York and Philadelphia: Chelsea House, 1989.

Ripp, Victor. *Moscow to Main Street: Among the Russian Emigres*. Boston: Little, Brown and Co., 1984.

Studies of the Third Wave: Recent Migration of Soviet Jews to the United States, edited by Dan N. Jacobs and Ellen Frankel Paul. Boulder, Colorado: Westview Press, 1981.

Wertsman, Vladimir. *The Russians in America, 1727-1976*. Dobbs Ferry, New York: Oceana Publications, 1977.

SALVADORAN AMERICANS

by
Jeremy Mumford

Salvadoran immigration to the United States is a fairly recent phenomenon. The movement is small in comparison with some of the great immigration waves of the past, but it has a profound significance for both countries.

OVERVIEW

The smallest of the Central American states, the Republic of El Salvador measures 21,041 square kilometers—about the size of the state of Massachusetts—and has a population of approximately five million. Situated near the northern end of the Central American isthmus, it is bordered by Guatemala to the northwest, Honduras to the northeast, and the Pacific Ocean to the south. A Spanish-speaking country, El Salvador was given its name—which means "the Savior," referring to Jesus Christ—by the Spanish. Its flag consists of horizontal stripes, two blue and one white, with the national coat of arms in the center. This coat of arms contains branches, flags, green mountains, and the words "Republica de El Salvador en la America Central" and "Dios Union Libertad." Also pictured in the center of the flag are a small red liberty cap and the date of El Salvador's independence from Spain: September 15, 1821.

Two volcanic mountain ranges dominate El Salvador's landscape; they run parallel to each other, east to west, along the length of the country. Just to the north of the southern range lies a broad central plain, the most fertile and populous region of El Salvador, which includes the nation's capital city, San Salvador, and a handful of smaller cities. These urban areas have grown significantly in recent years and by the mid-1990s housed more than half the population of El Salvador. But because El Salvador's economy is largely agricultural, a considerable portion of the population remains in the countryside to work the coffee plantations and other farms.

HISTORY

Before fifteenth-century explorer Christopher Columbus discovered the New World, the land now called El Salvador belonged to the Pipil, nomads of the Nahua language group who were related to the Aztecs of central Mexico. From the eleventh century A.D., the Pipil developed their country of Cuzcatlán ("Land of the Jewel") into an organized state and a sophisticated society, with a capital city located near modern San Salvador. But during the 1520s Spanish *conquistadors,* fresh from the conquest of Mexico, invaded the land of the Pipil. Led by a general named Atlacatl, the Pipil resisted the invasion with initial success, but ultimately succumbed to the Spanish forces.

As in Mexico and the rest of Central America, the *conquistadors* created a divided society in the province they named El Salvador. A small ruling class composed of people of Spanish birth or descent grew rich from the labor of the Indian population. Intermarriage gradually softened the racial division; today the majority of Salvadorans are *mestizos,* with both Spanish and Indian ancestors. But there remains in El Salvador an extreme disparity between the powerful and the powerless, between the wealthy landowners—according to legend, the "Fourteen Families"—and the multitudinous poor.

El Salvador became independent from Spain in 1821. The ex-colony initially joined with Guatemala, Honduras, Nicaragua, and Costa Rica to form the United Provinces of Central America. But the regional federation dissolved after 20 years. Then, threatened by Mexican and Guatemalan aggression, the Salvadoran government sought to make the country part of the United States. The request was turned down. El Salvador remained independent but gradually came under the influence of American banks, corporations, and government policies. The nineteenth and twentieth centuries brought considerable political turmoil to El Salvador, with the army and the plantation owners trading places in a series of unstable regimes.

One constant in Salvadoran history has been its economy of single-crop export agriculture. In the sixteenth century El Salvador produced cacao, from which chocolate is made; in the eighteenth century it grew the indigo plant, which yields a blue dye used in clothing. Since the late nineteenth century, El Salvador's great cash crop has been coffee, although in recent decades the country has also grown cotton and sugar. El Salvador organized its economy with factory-like efficiency, consolidating land into huge plantations worked by landless peasants. As markets changed, cycles of boom and bust hit these people hard.

This unstable social order often became explosive. El Salvador has seen repeated rebellions, each one followed by massive, deadly retaliation against the poor. In 1833 an Indian named Anastasio Aquino led an unsuccessful peasant revolt. Nearly a century later, a Marxist landowner named Agustín Farabundo Martí led another. This was followed by the systematic government murder of rural Indians, leaving an estimated 35,000 dead—an event known as *la matanza,* or "the massacre."

MODERN ERA

Between 1979 and 1992, Salvadoran guerrillas waged a civil war against the government, fueled in part by the same inequities that motivated Aquino and Martí. The nation's army fought back with U.S. money, weapons, and training from American military advisers. An estimated 75,000 people died during the conflict, most of them civilians killed by the army or by clandestine death squads linked to the government (Elston Carr, "Pico-Union: 'Trial' Dramatizes Salvadoran Abuses," *Los Angeles Times,* March 21, 1993). The guerrilla war and the "dirty war" that accompanied it were a national catastrophe. But in 1992, after more than a dozen years of fighting, the army signed a peace accord with the guerrillas' Farabundo Martí National Liberation Front (FMLN). Peace has returned to El Salvador, which is now governed by a reasonably democratic constitution.

SALVADORANS IN AMERICA

Salvadoran immigration to the United States is a fairly recent phenomenon. The movement is small in comparison with some of the great immigration waves of the past, but it has a profound significance for both countries. The flight of Salvadorans from their own country was the most dramatic result of El Salvador's civil war, draining that country of between 20 and 30 percent of its population. Half or more of the refugees—between 500,000 and one million—immigrated to the United States, which was home to less than 10,000 Salvadorans before 1960 (Faren Bachelis, *The Central Americans* [New York: Chelsea House, 1990], p. 10; cited hereafter as Bachelis). El Salvador's exiled population is already changing life at home through its influence and its dollars and will undoubtedly play an important role in its future history.

Salvadoran American immigration has changed the face of foreign affairs in the United States. The flood of refugees from a U.S.-supported government forced a national rethinking of foreign policy priorities. This in turn transformed the nature of American support for the Salvadoran government and may have helped to end the war in El Salvador. Salvadoran Americans are at the center of an ongoing national debate about U.S. responsibility toward the world's refugees and the future of immigration in general.

SIGNIFICANT IMMIGRATION WAVES

The exodus of Salvadorans from their homeland was prompted by both economic and political factors. Historically, El Salvador is a very poor and crowded country. Cyclical poverty and overcrowding have led to patterns of intra-Central American immigration in the past. During the 1960s many Salvadorans moved illegally to Honduras, which is less densely populated. Tension over these immigrants led to war between the nations in 1969, forcing the Salvadorans to return home. El Salvador's civil war from 1979 to 1992 created high unemployment and a crisis of survival for the poor. As in the 1960s, many Salvadorans responded by leaving their native land.

The fear of political persecution has led other Salvadorans to seek refuge in another country. During the 1980s death squads—secretly connected with government security forces—murdered many suspected leftists. Operating mostly at night, these groups killed tens of thousands of people during the civil war (Bachelis, pp. 41-42). At the height of the death squad movement, 800 bodies were found each month. As the frenetic pace of assassination continued, the squads resorted to increasingly vague "profiles" by which to identify members of so-called "left-wing" groups— all women wearing blue jeans, for instance (Mark Danner, "The Truth of El Mozote," *New Yorker*, December 6, 1993, p. 10). The bodies of some

In this 1986 photograph, Sarah Martinez poses in the Rescate refugee center in Los Angeles. A Salvadoran refugee, she and her husband were imprisoned and tortured there by the police; her husband was later murdered.

victims were never recovered; these people form the ranks of the "*desaparicinos*" (disappeared).

This climate of pervasive terror prompted many Salvadorans to flee their homeland. Some left after seeing friends or family members murdered or receiving a death threat; others fled violence by the guerrillas or the prospect of forced recruitment into the army. About half of the immigrants ended up in refugee camps in Honduras or in Salvadoran enclaves in Costa Rica, Nicaragua, or Mexico. The other half headed for *el Norte*—the United States.

Because they left quickly and quietly, without property or established connections in the United States, Salvadoran refugees could seldom obtain U.S. visas. They crossed borders illegally, first into Mexico, then into the United States. Refugees trekked through the desert, swam or rowed the Rio Grande, huddled in secret spaces in cars or trucks, or crawled through abandoned sewer tunnels in order to enter the United States. Many sought aid from professional alien smugglers, known as "coyotes," and were sometimes robbed, abandoned in the desert, or kept in virtual slavery until they could buy their freedom.

Once in the United States, Salvadorans remained a secret population. U.S. law provides that aliens (including illegal ones) who can show they have a tenable fear of persecution can receive political asylum and become eligible for a green card. But according to U.S. Immigration and Naturalization Service (INS) figures, political asylum was granted to very few Salvadorans: in the 1980s only 2.1 percent of applications were approved. Those who were turned down faced possible deportation. Therefore, few Salvadorans made their presence known unless they were caught by the INS.

Salvadoran refugees did not at first see themselves as immigrants or Americans. Most hoped to go home as soon as they could do so safely. In the meantime, they clustered together to maintain the language and culture of their homeland. Dense Salvadoran enclaves sprang up in Latino neighborhoods in San Francisco, Chicago, Houston, Washington, D.C., and the New York suburb of Hempstead, Long Island. Wherever a few Salvadorans established themselves, that place became a magnet for friends and relatives; about three quarters of the Salvadoran town of Intipuca, for instance, moved to Washington, D.C. (Segundo Montes and Juan Jose García Vásquez, *Salvadoran Migration to the United States* [Washington, D.C.: Center for Immigration and Refugee Assistance, Georgetown University, 1988]), p. 15; cited hereafter as Montes and Vásquez). But the greatest number of refugees settled in Los Angeles, where Salvadorans soon became the second-largest immigrant community. The Pico-Union and Westlake districts of Los Angeles became a virtual Salvadoran city—by some counts second only to San Salvador.

Salvadoran refugees during the 1980s were only one current in a broad stream of Central American refugees pouring into the United States. Guatemala and Nicaragua, like El Salvador, endured civil wars during this period. Many people from those countries joined the Salvadorans seeking refuge in the United States.

The Central American influx was secret and illegal, and much of mainstream America was at first ignorant of its magnitude. But the INS kept a close eye on the situation. Many Salvadorans who were denied asylum in the States exercised their rights to appeal their cases, sometimes all the way up to the Supreme Court. (Until a final decision is reached, the applicant is entitled to temporary working papers.) INS agents suddenly found a huge new bureaucratic workload dropped in their laps, for which they had little experience or funding. Many agents tried to move immigration cases along by any means necessary: intimidating Salvadorans into signing papers in English which put them on the next plane to El Salvador, or refusing asylum applications after a ten-minute interview

and deporting the applicants before they had a chance to appeal (Ann Crittenden, *Sanctuary: A Story of American Conscience and the Law in Collision* [New York: Weidenfeld & Nicholson, 1988]).

The deportation of Salvadoran refugees led many liberal American activists to take an interest in the Central American influx. Disheartened by the conservative trend in America in the 1980s, these activists found a rallying point in the plight of the refugees. Some saw the Central American refugee crisis as the great moral test of their generation. Likening the deaths in El Salvador and Guatemala to the Holocaust (the systematic slaughter of European Jews by German Nazis during World War II), human rights activists in the United States felt a moral imperative to petition their government for a change in foreign policy.

American activists established a loose network to aid the refugees. Operating in clear violation of federal laws, they took refugees into their houses, aided their travel across the border, hid them from the authorities, helped them find work, and even gave them legal help. Reviving the ancient custom that a fugitive might find sanctuary inside a church and be safe from capture, the activists often housed refugees in church basements and rectories, giving birth to what later became known as "the sanctuary movement."

Throughout the 1980s the U.S. government extended very little sympathy to Salvadoran refugees. Ironically, the government only began to acknowledge the reality of Salvadoran oppression when persecution and war began to taper off in El Salvador. In 1990 a federal lawsuit brought against the INS by the American Baptist Churches (ABC) forced the agency to apply a more lenient standard to Central American asylum applications. The settlement prompted the INS to reopen many Salvadoran applications it had already denied and to approve new ones in greater numbers. By this time, however, many Salvadoran Americans had benefited from an amnesty passed in 1986, which "legalized" illegal immigrants who had entered the States before 1982.

In 1991, after years of debate on the issue, Congress awarded Temporary Protected Status to Salvadorans who had been in the United States since 1990. This status allowed qualifying Salvadorans to live and work in the States for a fixed period of time. Known as the Deferred Enforced Departure (DED), the special status was scheduled to expire at the end of 1994.

Although the war is over in El Salvador, many Salvadoran Americans are still afraid to return to their homeland. ARENA, the political party most closely associated with the death squads, was in power in the mid-1990s, and many of the conditions that brought about the war remained the same. Furthermore, Salvadoran Americans had established roots and a new livelihood in the United States. A 1990 poll found that 70 percent of Salvadorans surveyed did not intend to return to El Salvador, even if they knew they were safe (Robert Lopez, "Salvadorans Turn Eyes Homeward as War Ends," *Los Angeles Times,* December 27, 1992). However, Salvadoran Americans maintain close ties to friends and relatives at home. Within a year after the civil war ended, about 350,000 Salvadoran Americans visited El Salvador (Tracy Wilkinson, "Returning to Reclaim a Dream," *Los Angeles Times,* May 19, 1993).

Due to poor INS records and the low profile of undocumented immigrants, statistics regarding Salvadoran immigration are notoriously unreliable. As of 1995 the total number of Salvadorans in the United States was somewhere between 500,000 and 1 million. Approximately one-third of the immigrant population were green card holders, who could apply for U.S. citizenship after five years. Between one-fifth and one-third had some form of temporary legal status. The remaining third were undocumented and therefore illegal.

ACCULTURATION AND ASSIMILATION

Assimilation is more problematic for Salvadorans in the United States than it has been for other immigrants. Most Salvadorans who have any legal status at all are asylum seekers, motivated to immigrate to the States because of fear of persecution, not a desire to become an American. Asylum laws prohibit many Salvadorans from renewing their ties to their home culture. Most asylum seekers cannot visit El Salvador, even for a loved one's funeral, without losing their legal status in the United States. (The assumption is that anyone who travels to El Salvador—whatever the reason—is not really afraid of persecution there.) Thus, many Salvadoran Americans are torn between embracing the culture of America and maintaining their Salvadoran identities.

Salvadoran Americans form an insular community—with their own social clubs, doctors, even banks—and often have little contact with outsiders. They maintain a tight network, living almost exclusively with other people from their home country, or even their hometown (Pamela Constable, "We Will Stay Together," *Washington Post Magazine,* October 30, 1994; Doreen Cavaja, "Making Ends Meet in a Nether World," *New York Times,* December 13, 1994). Many older immigrants have spent more than ten years in the United States without learning any English.

Although they immigrated largely out of fear rather than a desire for a new life, Salvadorans in the United States, especially the younger generations, are gradually becoming Americanized. While conditions have improved in El Salvador, few refugees have returned home. The United States—once a place of refuge—has become a new home for Salvadoran immigrants. To reflect the changing needs of the Salvadoran American community, the Central American Refugee Center in Los Angeles (CARECEN), one of the largest support organizations for refugees, changed its name to the Central American Resource Center (Elston Carr, "A New Direction," *Los Angeles Times,* May 9, 1993).

TRADITIONS, CUSTOMS, AND BELIEFS

El Salvador has a rich heritage of folk beliefs and customs, which evolved in a landscape of villages, fields, forests, and mountains. Salvadoran Americans seek to preserve their traditional rural culture—a difficult proposition, considering most Salvadorans settle in America's largest cities.

Salvadoran folklore is rooted in supernatural beliefs. Tales of ghosts and spirits have been passed orally from generation to generation. One such spirit is the Siguanaba, a beautiful woman who seduces men she finds alone in the forest at night and drives them mad. Slightly less dangerous are the Cadejos, two huge dogs; the black one brings bad luck, while the white one brings good luck. Another spirit, the Cipitío, is a dwarf with a big hat who eats ashes from fireplaces and strews flower petals in the paths of pretty girls. Such country legends have little meaning in a Los Angeles barrio; they are rapidly dying out among Salvadoran American children, a generation thoroughly immersed in the world of American cartoons and comic book characters.

MISCONCEPTIONS AND STEREOTYPES

Salvadoran Americans have sometimes had tense relations with their neighbors in the cities where they are concentrated. Salvadoran gangs have fought with Mexican gangs in Los Angeles, and in Washington, D.C., a city with a significant Salvadoran population, they have competed with African Americans for jobs and resources. In May of 1991, after a black policewoman shot and killed a Salvadoran man during an arrest, Salvadorans in Washington's Mt. Pleasant neighborhood rioted. This incident, however, is not necessarily representative of relations in all Salvadoran American communities.

Many cultural observers contend that mainstream America has not yet formed a distinct stereotype of Salvadoran Americans. Salvadorans have settled in neighborhoods already populated by Mexican Americans, and outsiders generally have only a vague sense of the various Latino nationalities in those neighborhoods. But Salvadorans certainly share in the widespread discrimination leveled at Latinos. In the New York borough of Brooklyn, for example, a group of white teenagers who beat up a Salvadoran man in a neighborhood park reportedly referred to him as "that Mexican."

PROVERBS

Salvadoran Spanish is rich in proverbs that reflect the country's rural landscape. While a North American might say, "Be quiet, the walls have ears," a Salvadoran would warn, "There are parrots in the field."

CUISINE

Salvadoran food is similar to Mexican food but is sweeter and milder. The foundation of the diet is cornmeal tortillas (thicker than the Mexican variety), rice, salt, and beans. The most popular national snack is the *pupusa*, a cornmeal griddle-cake stuffed with various combinations of cheese, spices, beans, and pork. *Pupusas* are served with *curtido*, a cabbage and carrot salad made with vinegar. A more substantial meal is *salpicón*, minced beef cooked with onions and chilies and served with rice and beans. For dessert, many dishes include fried or stewed bananas. *Chicha*, a sweet drink made from pineapple juice, is a popular beverage. The best Salvadoran food is found in private homes, but many Salvadoran restaurants and food stands have opened in Los Angeles and other cities where Salvadoran Americans live.

Both in El Salvador and in Salvadoran American neighborhoods, people love to buy food from street vendors. Popular street foods include *pupusas* and mango slices—spiced with salt, lime juice, red pepper, and crushed pumpkin and sesame seeds.

TRADITIONAL DRESS

Salvadorans wear the same Western-style clothing worn by most Latin Americans who are not culturally Indian. Salvadorans in the highlands, where nights can be very cold, occasionally wear brightly colored blankets of traditional Mayan design, but they call these Guatemalan blankets, underscoring their foreign origin. Around their necks, many Salvadorans wear small crosses tightly wrapped with colored yarn.

MUSIC

The most popular musical form in El Salvador is the *cumbia*, a style that originated in Colombia. A typical *cumbia* is performed with a male singer (usually a high baritone or tenor) backed by a male chorus, drums (primarily kettledrum and bass drum), electric guitar and bass, and either a brass section or an accordion. The 2/4 beat is slower than most Latin music; the baseline is heavy and up-front. A very danceable musical form, it is popular with non-Latin audiences.

Ranchera music, which originated in Mexico, is also well liked by the country people in El Salvador. In the cities, many people listen to rock and rap music from the United States. Mexican American musical styles such as *salsa*, *merengue*, and *tejano* music have become increasingly popular among Salvadorans in the United States. These and other styles from North America are also gaining more listeners in El Salvador.

HOLIDAYS CELEBRATED BY SALVADORAN AMERICANS

Many Salvadoran Americans celebrate Independence Day for all of Central America on September 15 of each year. The first week in August is the most important national religious festival, honoring Christ, El Salvador's patron and namesake, as the holy savior of the world. Known simply as the National Celebration, this week is marked in both El Salvador and Salvadoran American neighborhoods with processions, carnival rides, fireworks, and soccer matches.

HEALTH AND MENTAL HEALTH ISSUES

The single greatest health problem in El Salvador is malnutrition, which especially affects children. This problem is largely absent among Salvadoran Americans. Still, undocumented Salvadoran Americans are often hesitant to visit American doctors or hospitals, for fear of being reported to the immigration authorities. And many communities—including, through 1994's Proposition 187, the State of California—have sought to deny public health services to undocumented immigrants.

Partly for these reasons, some Salvadoran Americans continue to rely on traditional healers. Such practitioners, known as *curanderos*, use herb teas and poultices, traditional exercises, incantations, and magical touching to heal. Other Salvadoran immigrants are patients of Salvadoran doctors who may have received training at home but have no license to practice in the United States (John McQuiston, "Man Held for Practicing Dentistry without Degree or License," *New York Times*, December 2, 1994).

Some Salvadoran Americans carry deep emotional scars from the torture they suffered or witnessed. Many are tormented by rage, continuing fear, and guilt at escaping the violence that claimed the lives of so many of their loved ones. As a result, some members of the immigrant community suffer from depression, alcoholism, and erratic or violent behavior. Few Salvadoran Americans can afford to receive the psychological help they need to work through their traumatic experiences (Marcelo Suarez-Orozco, *Central American Refugees and U.S. High Schools* [Palo Alto: Stanford University Press, 1989]).

LANGUAGE

Spanish is the first language of almost all Salvadorans. Salvadoran Spanish is very close to the Spanish spoken in Mexico and other Central American countries; it is recognizable only by its accent.

El Salvador stands apart from neighboring countries in that its indigenous languages are virtually dead. One possible explanation for this loss lies in El Salvador's history of widespread violence against the poor. In the aftermath of the 1833 rebellion and during the *matanza* of 1932, government forces singled out Indians to be killed; out of

self-protection, many Salvadoran Indians adopted Spanish language and dress during these times.

Because of their initial determination to return to El Salvador, many immigrants to America at first resisted learning English. However, bilingual education programs, particularly in Los Angeles and Washington, D.C., have been extremely helpful to Salvadoran children (Pamela Constable, "Bilingual Plan Draws Bitter Words in D.C., *Washington Post*, October 26, 1994).

FAMILY AND COMMUNITY DYNAMICS

The traditional family in El Salvador, as in Latin America generally, is large and close-knit. The father exercises final authority in all things, and together the parents maintain firm control over their children, above all their daughters. Among Salvadoran Americans, though, this pattern has begun to change. The immigration process and the vastly different conditions of life in the United States have altered Salvadoran family dynamics in dramatic and at times destructive ways.

Due to the nature of their flight to the United States, many Salvadoran refugees made the journey alone: husbands left their wives, parents their children, teenagers their families. Entire families were separated and often stayed that way. Many refugees married non-Salvadorans, sometimes for immigration benefits, and Salvadoran Americans were barred from returning home for any reason without forfeiting a request for asylum.

Some Salvadoran parents who were separated from their children for a long period of time during the immigration process found—when finally reunited as a family—that they had lost some of their traditional parental authority and control over the youngsters. Likewise, teenagers who settled in the United States alone grew into adulthood under influences very different from those they would have encountered at home. Even when families moved to America together, family dynamics inevitably changed under new cultural influences. Children learned English faster and adapted more readily to their new surroundings than their parents. They often had to translate or explain things to their parents, argue for their parents with English-speaking storekeepers, and in general become more knowledgeable and confident than their parents. This role-reversal proved painful for both generations.

Salvadoran American parents generally fear that their children may stray too far in America's permissive society. Indeed, many young Salvadoran Americans have formed gangs, especially in Los Angeles, where the culture of Latino youth gangs has deep roots. These gangs, including the nationally known Salva Mara Trucha, distribute drugs, extort money from local merchants (especially street vendors), and battle for turf with Mexican gang members (Mike O'Connor, "A New U.S. Import in El Salvador," *New York Times*, July 3, 1994; Anthony Millican, "Street Gang Shakes Down Vendors for Sidewalk 'Rent'," *Los Angeles Times*, December 27, 1992).

RITUALS OF FAMILY LIFE

Salvadoran Catholicism emphasizes all the sacraments that are practiced in other Catholic countries: baptism, confirmation, marriage in the church, communion at mass, and last rites. Other occasions are also celebrated in church, such as graduation from school and a girl's *quinceañera*, or fifteenth birthday. Still, when compared with other Central Americans, a surprising number of Salvadorans do not observe church rituals. Church weddings, for instance, are considered prohibitively expensive for the poor, and common-law marriage is frequently practiced.

One ritual of family life which is common even among the poor is *compadrazgo*, or the naming of godparents. Latin Americans of all nationalities practice this custom. They place special importance in the relationship between a child and his or her *padrino* and *madrina*—and between the parents and their *compadres*, the friends they honored by choosing them for this role.

Some rituals of the old country have been abandoned by members of the immigrant community. For instance, the traditional Salvadoran practice of interring bodies in family crypts has recently given way to a more Americanized approach to burying the dead. In the early 1980s, most Salvadoran Americans who could afford it had their bodies sent to El Salvador for burial after death, a posthumous relocation that could cost thousands of dollars. By the mid-1990s, Salvadoran Americans were beginning to reach the painful conclusion that their families would never return to El Salvador; as a result, more and more immigrants are opting for burials in the United States (Gabriel Escobar, "Latinos Making U.S. Their Home in Life and Death," *Washington Post*, July 12, 1993).

PUBLIC ASSISTANCE

Few Salvadoran American families depend entirely on public assistance; a large portion of the immigrant population is undocumented and therefore does not qualify for government benefits. However, the high rate of poverty in the community forces many to seek whatever help they can find—either through assistance for U.S.-born children or through fraudulently obtained benefits. The extent of reliance on public assistance is hard to estimate due to its underground nature.

EDUCATION

Salvadoran Americans, like many immigrants, place a high value on education as a way to advance in the world. Some Salvadorans cherish education in particular because of their ongoing struggle to achieve it at home: because the National University in San Salvador included a number of Marxist professors and students, the government closed down the campus in 1980. Some professors and students kept classes going in a variety of small buildings and private homes; all Salvadoran university students realized that they could not take access to education for granted.

In the United States access to education has been equally difficult for Salvadorans. Many schools excluded or reported undocumented students, until the U.S. Supreme Court decision in *Plyer v. Doe* (1982) established that all children, even illegal immigrants, have a constitutional right to attend public school. This issue remains controversial: California's Proposition 187, approved by voters in 1994, seeks again to exclude undocumented students from public schools.

At the university level, few institutions allow undocumented immigrants to enroll. California State is one of the few universities to admit students without proof of legal residency. Furthermore, it allows undocumented immigrants in California to pay the low tuition charged to state residents, instead of the much higher out-of-state rates. As the only major university where undocumented immigrants can enroll for less than $2000 per year, it has attracted many Salvadoran American students to its campuses in Southern California. Again, this educational route is threatened by California's Proposition 187.

RELIGION

Most Salvadorans are members of the Roman Catholic church, although various evangelical

Protestant denominations, including Baptists, Seventh-Day Adventists, Assemblies of God, and Mormons, also have Salvadoran adherents. In addition, a small number of Salvadorans are Jewish or Muslim, stemming from late nineteenth-century immigration from the Middle East.

Salvadoran Catholicism bears the strong influence of liberation theology, a Catholic school of thought that evolved in Latin America during the 1960s and 1970s. Liberation theology teaches that Christianity is a religion of the poor. The movement encouraged impoverished Salvadorans to form Christian communities—or "base communities"—to improve their lives. Dedicated both to Bible study and to mutual aid in the secular world, these communities organized credit unions, cooperative stores, labor and peasant unions, and political activist groups.

Liberation theology received an important boost from the approval of the 1968 Latin American Bishops' Conference in Medellín, Colombia. In the late 1970s Salvadoran Archbishop Oscar Romero, though originally selected for his conservative views, became an important patron of the new theology. Young priests carried the message to the Salvadoran countryside with an evangelical fervor, but a shortage of priests in El Salvador necessitated an increase in the involvement of the Catholic laity. Base communities sprang up both in the cities and the country.

Liberation theology's success in organizing the poor had a profound impact on Salvadoran politics. The movement brought new political ideas to the countryside, as the universities did to the cities. Many of the peasants who comprised the rural left during the civil war—guerrillas, farmworker federation members, activists who demonstrated in San Salvador—traced the origins of their political consciousness to participation in a base community.

The Salvadoran army was well aware of the effects of the new theology. Starting in the 1970s, it targeted Catholic organizers for harassment and death. In March of 1980 Archbishop Romero was assassinated while saying mass; the murder was attributed to a right-wing death squad. Nine months later, four U.S. churchwomen who were working in El Salvador were killed, causing outrage in the States. And in November of 1989, six Jesuit priests and two women were killed on the San Salvador campus of the Jesuit-run Central American University.

Salvadoran American Catholics have not reproduced the full-fledged base communities that they left behind in El Salvador. However, many Salvadoran Americans are members of progressive Latino Catholic congregations, influenced by liberation theology and Vatican II, which advocate social justice and self-empowerment among the poor. These same congregations have a history of activity in the sanctuary movement, helping their Salvadoran members gain a foothold in the United States.

In addition to the Catholic church, several evangelical Protestant denominations have Salvadoran churches. These communities were founded throughout the Salvadoran countryside during the twentieth century by missionaries from the United States. In the 1970s and 1980s the evangelical sects increased their missionary efforts, in particular through the influence of American military advisers on soldiers in the Salvadoran army. Both in El Salvador and in the States, Salvadoran evangelicals tend to be more socially and politically conservative than Catholics.

EMPLOYMENT AND ECONOMIC TRADITIONS

Salvadorans have often been referred to as "the Germans of Central America" because of their strong work ethic (Walter LaFeber, *Inevitable Revolutions* [New York: Norton, 1993], p. 10). Salvadorans in the United States are among the hardest-working immigrants, working enough hours at low-paying jobs to send about $800 million home every year.

Although many Salvadoran refugees worked on the land before immigrating to the United States, few of them settled in America's rural areas. In this respect, Salvadorans differ from newly arrived Mexican Americans, many of whom engage in migrant farm labor; Salvadoran immigrants are instead concentrated in unskilled urban jobs that do not require English.

Many Salvadoran American men work in hotel and restaurant kitchens, especially in Los Angeles. Others work as day laborers in the building trades. Many Salvadoran American women work as nannies and maids. Both men and women perform cleaning and janitorial services in hotels, commercial buildings, and homes. Some Salvadorans also work as unlicensed street vendors of food and goods, a line of work which is illegal in Los

In this 1990 photograph, Salvadoran American children protest against conditions in El Salvador along with their parents in New York City.

Angeles and other cities but is nevertheless tolerated and in fact contributes to the life and economy of the city.

Although Salvadoran Americans toil in the lowest-paying sectors of the American economy, they are slowly but inexorably becoming more prosperous. They work long hours, save a great deal, and are gradually moving from the inner cities to the suburbs.

Salvadoran American income is of vital importance to El Salvador. Salvadoran Americans, even those who are poor, have an incentive to send money to family and friends in El Salvador because a U.S. dollar buys much more there than in the States. In all, they send approximately $800 million back home per year—close to $1000 per person. These payments, known as remittances, are the largest source of income for El Salvador—larger than either coffee exports or U.S. government aid. For this reason, El Salvador is sometimes said to have a "remittance economy" (Montes and Vásquez, p. 15). It is in part because of this contribution to the economy at home that Salvadoran politicians lobby Washington for permanent status for Salvadoran Americans.

Salvadoran Americans have also brought large numbers of American consumer goods to El Salvador. By 1994 far more homes in El Salvador had color televisions, stereos, and other modern equipment than they did 15 years earlier. In this way, too, Salvadoran Americans have trans-

formed the texture of life in El Salvador.

In addition to gifts and remittances, Salvadoran Americans have extensive investments in their home country. They may not plan to return permanently, but many are keeping the option open. According to one report, two-thirds of new housing built in San Salvador is bought by Salvadoran Americans (Tom Gibb, "Those Who Didn't Flee Rely on U.S.," *San Francisco Chronicle*, August 30, 1993). Taking as its model the role American Jews played in the growth of Israel, the Los Angeles agency El Rescate hopes to establish a bank that will allow expatriates to invest directly in Salvadoran development (Robert Lopez, "A Piece of the Pie," *Los Angeles Times*, September 19, 1993).

POLITICS AND GOVERNMENT

The Salvadoran American community has not been a significant political force either in the United States or at home. However, the size, concentration, and organization of the community suggest that this may change in the future. Most Salvadoran Americans are not U.S. citizens and therefore do not have the right to vote in elections. Salvadorans do not have nearly as much influence with the political establishment as voting constituencies have. In Los Angeles, for instance, there is a stark contrast between the U.S.-born Chicano neighborhoods of East L.A. and the Pico-Union and Westlake neighborhoods, populated by immigrant Mexicans and Central Americans. The former have many community centers, legal services, and social workers; the latter have very few (Hector Tobar, "No Strength in Numbers for LA's Divided Latinos," *Los Angeles Times*, September 1, 1992). This situation is slowly changing, however: Carlos Vaquerano, the Salvadoran community affairs director of CARE-CEN, was named to the board of Rebuild L.A., organized to help the city recover from the L.A. riots in 1992 (Miles Corwin, "Understanding the Riots," *Los Angeles Times*, November 16, 1992).

One area of U.S. politics in which Salvadoran Americans have played an important role is in legislation regarding their immigration status. In the debate leading to the passage of Temporary Protected Status for Salvadoran refugees and the extensions of that status, Salvadoran organizations lobbied politicians and brought their cases of persecution to the press. At first, refugee organizations were run by Americans, and Salvadorans often appeared in public only with bandannas over their faces. Gradually, Salvadorans and other Central Americans began to take charge of the refugee organizations and assume a higher public profile.

Salvadoran Americans have also contributed significantly to labor union activity. Many refugees fought for the right to organize under repressive conditions in El Salvador, and they brought dedication, even militancy, to American unions. In a 1990 Los Angeles janitors' strike, for instance, Salvadoran union members continued to march and demonstrate even under the threat of police violence. And Salvadoran street vendors in Los Angeles have organized to improve their precarious situation (Tracy Wilkinson, "New Questions Arise for Salvadorans in Los Angeles," *Los Angeles Times*, January 12, 1992).

RELATIONS WITH EL SALVADOR

Most Salvadoran Americans are not active in or outspoken about Salvadoran politics. Those U.S. organizations most actively involved in Salvadoran politics (such as the Committee in Solidarity with the People of El Salvador, CISPES) have attracted little participation by Salvadoran Americans themselves. The immigrants' own organizations have focused not on politics at home, but on relief and jobs in immigrant communities throughout the United States. This relative indifference to home politics may be surprising, given the political passions that have long raged in El Salvador; but the majority of Salvadoran Americans seem interested in putting the hatred of the past behind them.

While the most ideologically committed of the Salvadoran refugees settled in Mexico, Nicaragua, or Costa Rica, those who settled in the United States focused on survival and building a community. Refugees who fled the government and refugees who fled the guerrillas have a lot in common; many will not even discuss their political beliefs, lest it disrupt the fragile solidarity of the refugee community. Furthermore, many Salvadorans on the left became active in politics because of the desperate poverty and class war in El Salvador; when they arrived in the United States, where it seemed for the first time possible to escape poverty through hard work, their political commitment sometimes melted away.

Salvadorans outside El Salvador are not permitted to cast absentee ballots in that country's elections. The majority of the refugee community is thought to favor the left, and the absence of their votes is believed to have helped the right-wing party ARENA win the Salvadoran presidency in 1989 and 1994 (Lisa Leff, "At Peace but Uneasy, Salvadorans Vote Today," *Washington Post,* March 20, 1994).

The relative lack of political influence among Salvadoran Americans is not necessarily permanent. Salvadoran immigrants are densely concentrated in a few cities, and they have a strong infrastructure in refugee organizations. As more Salvadorans become U.S. citizens, the immigrant community will probably play a larger role in local and regional politics. And given their economic contribution, they will almost certainly come to exert more influence in El Salvador.

INDIVIDUAL AND GROUP CONTRIBUTIONS

ARTS

Claribel Alegría (1924-), the most famous living Salvadoran writer, was born in Nicaragua but moved with her family to El Salvador at an early age. She studied at George Washington University in Washington, D.C., and has since visited the United States on a regular basis. With her U.S.-born husband, Darwin Flakoll, she has lived in various parts of the world—particularly Spain and Nicaragua—but she considers herself a Salvadoran. Her autobiographical poetry and fiction (some written in collaboration with her husband) is very popular among both Salvadorans and Salvadoran Americans and provides a rich portrait of bourgeois life in a provincial Salvadoran city.

Many Salvadorans involved in their country's political strife have recorded their feelings in poetry; one such writer, Miguel Huezo Mixco (1954-), was a guerrilla soldier who composed and published verses during campaigns against the army (*Mirrors of War* [New York: Monthly Review Press, 1985], p. 147).

Dagoberto Reyes, a Salvadoran painter and sculptor, immigrated to Los Angeles in the early 1980s. His sculpture "Porque Emigramos" ("Why We Immigrate") was commissioned to stand in Los Angeles's MacArthur Park.

Alvaro Torres, a popular singer of Spanish-language romantic ballads, was born in El Salvador and lived in Guatemala and Mexico before moving to the United States. José Reyes, another popular Salvadoran musician, also lives in the United States.

Christy Turlington (1969-) is an internationally known supermodel. The daughter of a Salvadoran mother, she began modeling at the age of 14. She has appeared on the runways of Paris, Milan, and New York, in the pages of every major fashion magazine, and has contracts with Maybelline, Calvin Klein, and Vidal Sassoon. Turlington is also a noted animal rights activist and has raised money for Salvadoran causes.

EDUCATION

Jorge Catán Zablah (1939-), a Salvadoran who received his Ph.D. from University of California at Santa Barbara, is the chairman of the Spanish Department at the Defense Language Institute in Monterey, California.

GOVERNMENT AND POLITICS

Colonel Nicolás Carranza is an infamous Salvadoran American who commanded El Salvador's Treasury Police in the early 1980s. He has been accused of organizing and overseeing many of the clandestine death squads that operated during those years. In 1988 the *Nation* reported that he was living in Kentucky, supported by active duty pay from the Salvadoran military and an annual stipend from the CIA.

SPORTS

Hugo Perez, a midfielder on the U.S. national soccer team, immigrated from El Salvador to Los Angeles as a child. The second-highest all-time scorer on the U.S. team, he contributed to America's unexpectedly competitive performance in the 1994 World Cup. During World Cup matches played at Pasadena, California, Salvadoran Americans were among the most vociferous fans of the U.S. team. Waldir Guerra (1967-), another great Salvadoran soccer player who learned his craft in L.A.'s highly competitive Salvadoran soccer leagues, immigrated to the United States from his hometown of San Vicente, El Salvador, at age 16. He was a star in college and professional soccer in California and later returned to El Salvador to play professional soccer there. A member of the Santa Ana team, he is considered the second-best player in all of El Salvador.

MEDIA

Most Salvadoran Americans rely on the general Spanish-language media in the United States, which is largely produced by Mexicans, Puerto Ricans, and Cubans. There are very few media outlets geared specifically toward Salvadoran Americans.

RADIO

KPFK-FM (90.7).
Pacifica Radio for Southern California broadcasts a radio show for Salvadorans hosted by Carlos Figueroa, who has also worked with the FMLN's Radio Venceremos in El Salvador.

Address: 3729 Cawenga Boulevard West, North Hollywood, California 91604.
Telephone: (818) 985-2711.

TELEVISION

KMET-TV, Channel 38.
This Los Angeles station airs a 30-minute daily show focusing on Salvadoran American news and culture, hosted by José Trinidad.

Contact: Laura Cohen, Public Relations Director.
Telephone: (213) 469-5638.

ORGANIZATIONS AND ASSOCIATIONS

Central American Refugee Center (CARECEN).
Founded in 1983 as a relief organization for refugees, CARECEN has evolved into a community self-help and advocacy organization for Central Americans. Though largely staffed by non-Central Americans, its director is Salvadoran American. The Los Angeles office has changed its name from the Central American Refugee Center to the Central American Resource Center. CARECEN has independent offices in several U.S. cities.

Contact: Robert Lovato, Executive Director.
Address: 1636 West Eighth Street, Los Angeles, California.
Telephone: (213) 385-1638.

Centro Presente.
A community center for Central Americans in the Boston area.

Address: 54 Essex Street, Cambridge, Massachusetts.
Telephone: (617) 497-9080.

El Rescate.

Established in 1981, El Rescate provides legal, educational, and community economic development services to Central American refugees in the Los Angeles area.

Contact: Oscar Andrade, Director.
Address: 1340 South Bonnie Brae Street, Los Angeles, California.
Telephone: (213) 736-4703.

Interfaith Office on Accompaniment (IOA).

Works to support the refugees and displaced communities of El Salvador. Aims to enhance moral, political, and economic development by sending interfaith delegations and church volunteers to assist the Salvadoran people.

Contact: Lana Dalbert, Chair.
Address: 1050 South Van Ness Avenue, San Francisco, California 94110.
Telephone: (415) 821-7102.

MUSEUMS AND RESEARCH CENTERS

Central America Resource Center (CARC).

This Texas organization releases a bimonthly English-language newsletter with political and cultural news from Central America, selected and translated from a variety of Spanish-language news sources. It also maintains a library and archive in its Austin office. Not to be confused with the social service organization CARECEN.

Address: 2520 Longview, Austin, Texas 78705.
Telephone: (512) 476-9841.

Hemispheric Migration Project, Center for Immigration Policy and Refugee Assistance, Georgetown University.

This project sponsors and publishes research on various population movements within the Americas, including the migration of Central Americans to the United States.

Address: Box 2298, Hoya Station, Washington, D.C. 20057.

Telephone: (202) 687-7032.

SOURCES FOR ADDITIONAL STUDY

Bachelis, Faren. *The Central Americans*. New York: Chelsea House, 1990.

Constable, Pamela. "We Will Stay Together," *Washington Post Magazine*, October 30, 1994.

Crittenden, Ann. *Sanctuary: A Story of American Conscience and the Law in Collision*. New York: Weidenfeld & Nicholson, 1988.

Montes, Segundo, and Juan Jose García Vásquez. *Salvadoran Migration to the United States: An Exploratory Study*. Washington, D.C.: Center for Immigration Policy and Refugee Assistance, Georgetown University, 1988.

Suarez-Orozco, Marcelo. *Central American Refugees and U.S. High Schools*. Palo Alto: Stanford University Press, 1989.

U.S. Senate Committee on the Judiciary. Subcommittee on Immigration and Refugee Affairs. *Central American Migration to the United States*. Washington, D.C.: Government Printing Office, 1990.

SAMOAN AMERICANS

by
Paul Cox

Samoans have an expansive view of familial bonds. A Samoan *a'iga* or family includes all individuals who descend from a common ancestor.

OVERVIEW

The Samoan archipelago consists of 15 inhabited islands in the South Pacific that are located approximately 14 degrees south latitude and between 171 and 173 degrees west longitude. The archipelago is a politically divided one. The eastern group of islands is known as American Samoa, a U.S. territory with a population of 41,000. The total land area of American Samoa is 77 square miles and includes seven major islands: Tutuila (which includes the territorial capital of Pago Pago), Aunu'u, Ta'u, Ofu, Olosega, Swains Island, and Rose Atoll. American Samoa is administered by an elected governor and territorial legislature as well as a non-voting delegate to the U.S. House of Representatives. The native-born residents of American Samoa are considered American nationals. While they do not pay U.S. income taxes or vote in U.S. presidential elections, they may serve in the U.S. armed services.

The western half of the archipelago comprises Western Samoa, an independent country. These islands have a total population of 182,000 and a total land area of 1,104 square miles. Western Samoa includes four inhabited islands: Upolu (which houses Apia, the nation's capital), Manu'a, Apolima, and Savaii, which is the largest but also the most underdeveloped of these islands. A former United Nations protectorate under the administration of New Zealand, Western Samoa is a member of the British Commonwealth.

Samoan weather is usually hot and wet, with a mean temperature of 79.5 degrees fahrenheit and heavy annual rainfall. In the city of Apia, for instance, annual rainfall measures about 80 inches.

The number of Samoans living outside of Samoa easily exceeds the combined population of both American and Western Samoa. Large populations of expatriate Samoans can be found in Auckland, New Zealand; Honolulu, Hawaii; Los Angeles, California; San Francisco, California; and Salt Lake City, Utah. Smaller groups have settled in Wellington, New Zealand; Sydney, Australia; Laie, Hawaii; Oakland, California; and Independence, Missouri. Most older expatriate Samoans are immigrants, although many of their offspring are natural-born citizens of their host countries. Regardless of birthplace, however, peoples of Samoan descent are linked by a distinctive cultural heritage that continues to flourish on those South Pacific islands.

HISTORY

The Samoan islands were colonized between 500 and 800 B.C. by an oceanic people distinguished by their production of Lapita pottery—a unique pottery form named after one of the original sites of pottery shard discovery in Melanesia. Based on archaeological, botanical, and linguistic evidence, it seems almost certain that the ancestors of the Samoans originated in Indo-Malaysia, spent several centuries living along coastal areas of New Guinea, and then colonized Samoa and Tonga, another island in the Pacific Ocean. It is unclear whether Samoa or Tonga was colonized first, but it was within these archipelagos that Polynesian culture developed from its Lapita roots. Over time the descendants of these original immigrants colonized other regions, including Tahiti and other areas of eastern Polynesia, the Marquesas, Hawaii, and New Zealand. The ancestors of the Polynesians brought with them a group of agricultural plants distinguished by a variety of tree crops that produced nuts and fruits (including breadfruit) and a set of starchy tuberous crops, including taro and yams. Once in Samoa, the Lapita potters developed a material culture characterized by a few large stone fortifications, early attempts at irrigation, and a startling talent for producing highly finished boat timbers.

The quality of the ship timbers produced by the Samoans did not escape notice. Indeed, the first European accounts of Samoa speak admiringly of the work of the islands' inhabitants in this respect. The quality of Samoan boats suggested an easy facility with tools of iron, according to the journals of Jacob Roggeveen, the first European to discover Samoa. Roggeveen happened upon the islands in 1722 during his ill-fated voyage from the Netherlands to New Ireland. He recorded that the Samoan seamen were a sturdy, healthy group, although he mistook their tattoos for paint. Although he traded a few nails for coconuts, Roggeveen was unable to entice any of the Samoans to board his ship. Concerned about the lateness of the season and the poor anchoring terrain, Roggeveen decided not to attempt a landing.

The second European explorer to visit Samoa, Louis Antoine de Bougainville, named the archipelago the "Navigator Islands" in honor of the superb sailing vessels manned by the natives. "Their canoes are made with a good deal of skill, and have an outrigger," he wrote. "Though we ran seven or eight knots at this time, yet the [canoes] sailed round us with the same ease as if we had been at anchor."

After sighting Bougainville's ship, the Samoans sent out a party in a canoe to meet him. Bougainville reported they "were naked, excepting their natural parts, and shewed us cocoa-nuts and roots." The "roots" presented to Bougainville were likely those of *Piper methysticum*, used in Samoa to make *kava*, a beverage that is consumed on ceremonial occasions. The present of both coconuts and *kava* to Bougainville constituted a *sua*, or ceremonial offering of respect to a traveling party. *Kava* roots were also ceremonially presented to the next European to visit Samoa, the French explorer La Perouse, on December 6, 1787. The presentation of *Piper methysticum* roots was accompanied, per usual Samoan practice, by soaring rhetoric that added considerably to the ambience of the *kava* ceremony.

Unfortunately, the La Perouse expedition met with tragedy when 11 members of the crew were later killed by Samoans. The French claimed the attack was unprovoked, although they admitted the attack came after they had fired muskets over the heads of a few Samoans to persuade them to release a grapnel rope to a long boat. Later reports indicated that the massacre occurred after the French shot and killed a Samoan attempting to steal an iron bolt. Verification of this report came from the missionary J. B. Stair, who wrote that the massacre occurred after the French had hoisted a Samoan up a mainstay of a long boat by the thumb in retribution for a petty theft (Stair, *Old Samoa*, 1897). Regardless of the root cause of the altercation, La Perouse fostered a myth of barbarity about the Samoans in its wake, bitterly remarking in his memoirs that he would leave the documentation of Samoan history to others.

The massacre of the French sailors from the *Astrolabe* in 1787 gave the Samoans a reputation for savagery that deterred future European exploration of the islands, except for a few brief contacts such as the visit of that H.M.S. *Pandora* in 1791. Only a few whalers and warships called at Samoan ports for the next number of years.

In 1828 Tongan Wesleyan missionaries arrived in Samoa, but they had little success in their proselytizing endeavors. In 1830, however, John Williams sailed the *Messenger of Peace* to Savaii under the guidance of a Samoan convert from Rarotonga. He first traveled to Sapapalii village, home of Malietoa, the highest-ranking chief in Samoa. During an interview on the ship, Williams obtained permission from Malietoa to land Tahitian and Rarotongan missionaries in Samoa. In addition, he secured a commitment from Malietoa to avail himself of the missionaries' teachings.

Williams returned to Samoa in 1832 to find the new Christian faith thriving. Other religious groups were quick to follow. In 1835 Peter Turner formally established the Wesleyan mission on Manono island. Proselytizing activities proceeded at a fast pace, particularly when George Pratt and Charles Wilson of the London Missionary Society translated the Bible into Samoan.

Although the missionaries were explicitly instructed by Williams to confine their activities to the religious sphere, the impact of the European missions on Samoan culture was rapid and profound. Samoans abandoned their former religious beliefs and made dramatic changes to central cultural practices. Warfare as an instrument of political change was discarded, as was polygamy, abortion, "indecent" dances, and certain common articles of clothing (such as the *titi*, a skirt made from *Cordyline terminalis* leaves). The missionaries introduced new agricultural plants and practices, new items of clothing (*siapo* or tapa cloth), and new forms of housing construction. In only a few years, a fundamental restructuring of traditional Samoan society had taken place. *Faifeau* or ministers played a new and pivotal role in this culture, a respected status that continues to this day.

Later, other *papalagi* (foreigners) with less evangelical interests visited Samoa. The U.S. Exploring Expedition visited and mapped Samoa in 1839. Commander Charles Wilkes appointed the son of John Williams as American Vice-Consul. In 1845 George Pritchard joined the diplomatic corps in Apia as British Consul. Both Williams and Pritchard avoided native intrigues and concentrated on assisting in the naval affairs of their respective countries.

The geopolitical importance of Samoa grew over time due to its proximity to southern whaling grounds and the unparalleled harbor of Pago Pago. In 1857 the German firm of Godeffroy greatly expanded copra trade, establishing a regional center in Samoa. This led to the establishment of a German consulate in 1861. This increased interest in Samoa created significant tensions between the three colonial powers on the island. Samoa was finally partitioned between the east (Eastern Samoa) and the west (German Samoa) during the 1880s.

American Samoa was eventually ceded by the chiefs of Tutuila and Manu'a to the United States and administered by the Department of the Navy as a U.S. territory. The region was largely forgotten until the 1960s, when President John F. Kennedy told Governor John Hayden to "get Samoa moving." During the 1960s and 1970s construction on American Samoa increased dramatically. A hospital, television transmission facilities, and schools were built throughout the territory. Steps were taken to institute a popular election to determine the territorial governor, a position previously filled by appointment from Washington, D.C.

Western Samoa's development during the twentieth century was a little more dramatic. Western Samoa changed hands from German ownership to New Zealand administration during the First World War after a bloodless invasion. After the war, Western Samoa was declared a League of Nations Trust Territory under New Zealand Administration. A nascent independence movement, called the "Mau," was ruthlessly crushed by New Zealand colonial administrators. One of the leaders of this movement, a Samoan chief and a man of great wisdom and presence, Tamasese, was shot and killed by New Zealand armed forces during this conflict. Later, though, New Zealand assumed a more benign role in Western Samoa, assisting the country as it prepared for independence in 1962. Today Western Samoa is led by a parliament and prime minister, with His Highness Malietoa Tanumafili II acting as the ceremonial Head of State.

ACCULTURATION AND ASSIMILATION

Immigration of Samoans to New Zealand, Australia, and the United States accelerated during the 1950s. Western Samoa, with its historically close ties to New Zealand, sent a number of scholarship students to pursue college degrees in New Zealand. American Samoa saw many of its citizens enroll in U.S. military services. Samoans who chose to pursue ecclesiastical endeavors were often educated by Anglicans in London. Others entered Catholic seminaries in the South Pacific and studied in Rome, while those who became local leaders in the Church of Jesus Christ of Latter-day Saints (Mormon) traveled to Utah. All these experiences overseas encouraged growing numbers of Samoans to emigrate from Samoa to these distant countries. Since the initial wave of the Samoan emigration overseas numerous second-generation Samoans have been born not on the islands but in their new country. In the 1990 census of the United States, over 55,000 Americans reported themselves to be of Samoan descent. Approximately 26,000 of the respondents resided in California, with another 15,000 in Hawaii, and 2,000 in Utah. But the influence of Samoan Americans has spread far beyond these limited regions.

The contributions made by Samoan Americans have been many and diverse. The courage and valor of Samoan soldiers became legendary during the Korean conflict and the Vietnam war. Prowess on the athletic field led to significant recognition for Samoan Americans in the sports of college and professional football, New Zealand rugby, and even Japanese Sumo wrestling. Samoan American political leaders such as Faleolemavaega Eni Hunkin, who served as staff council for the House Subcommittee on National Parks and Lands and later as the American Samoan delegate to the United States Congress, and Governors Peter Coleman and A. P. Lutali have played an increasingly visible role in formulation of U.S. policy in the Pacific rim.

Many recent immigrants from Samoa, though, have been forced to pursue low-paying jobs as untrained laborers. Others have been forced to rely on governmental entitlement programs for support. A few members of the Samoan community are undocumented aliens who are legally, linguistically, and culturally isolated from their host countries.

As a group, Samoans in America face all the tensions and difficulties encountered by other immigrant groups as they enter new homelands. Many older Samoans, particularly those from Western Samoa, speak English haltingly. Yet in areas of significant Samoan population concentration, even Samoan Americans who are fluent in English have faced considerable prejudice. Just as in the time of the La Perouse expedition, Samoans have in some areas gained unwarranted reputations as perpetrators of violent crime. The involvement of small numbers of Samoan youth in gang activity has led some to dismiss all young Samoan Americans as hoodlums. Such prejudice can have devastating consequences: even impartial observers concede that there have been instances when it has been difficult for a person of Samoan descent to receive a fair criminal trial in Hawaii.

In New Zealand, Hawaii, California, and Utah there is now a reawakening and organization of expatriate Samoan communities in an attempt to reach out to younger people of Samoan ancestry and inform them of the traditional ways and cultures. Samoan culture, while based largely on hospitality, is at times mystifying to Westerners as well as to the offspring of expatriate Samoans who know little of the ways and language of their ancestral home. Scholars are also sometimes confused, and as a result Samoan culture has been the topic of much controversy. In *Coming of Age in Samoa*, Margaret Mead argued that Samoan adolescents are spared the *sturm und drang* of American adolescence. She argued that, unlike their counterparts in Western cultures, young people in Samoa pass relatively easily through adolescence. Her views have been challenged by the anthropologist Derek Freeman, who argued that, contrary to the easy-going Samoan nature portrayed by Mead, Samoan culture is hierarchical, power-conscious, and occasionally violent.

The nature of Samoan society is considerably more complex than either camp may wish to admit. Unlike Mead's assertion that Samoans are a "primitive" people, Samoan culture is elaborate and sophisticated and is exemplified by Samoan rhetorical skills, which are considerable. Samoan villages are equally complex in their structure, with a plethora of different levels of *matai*, or chiefs. Villagers are related in various complex ways from a series of common descent groups.

This Samoan American woman is performing in the Lotus Festival in Los Angeles.

CUISINE AND DIET

Samoan cuisine is fairly bland and varies little. Samoans eat two or three meals a day consisting of boiled taro or rice cooked with coconut milk, fresh fish, breadfruit, and usually some form of tinned or fresh meat. Fruit, although plentiful in the island, is seldom eaten during the mealtime. Raw Samoan cocoa—which for many visitors is an acquired taste, orange leaf tea—lemon grass tea, or coffee is usually served with meals. Samoans do not usually engage in conversation while eating, since the hosts typically do not eat until the guests have finished their meals. Many Samoans have, in recent years, strayed from the traditional diet of starchy roots and fruits to a more westernized diet. The medical community believes that this dietary change has translated into a high incidence of diabetes among Samoan people. Although in traditional villages Samoans tend to be very trim in appearance, in some expatriate communities obesity is common, possibly as a result of a more sedentary lifestyle.

CLOTHING

Clothing in Samoa consists of a *lavalava*, a single piece of cloth that is worn as a wrap-around skirt by both men and women. Brightly colored floral print shirts or blouses, or in more informal settings, T-shirts, complete the typical outfit. In remote villages some women go without tops while washing clothes or performing other household tasks. While Samoans prefer colorful floral designs in both their *lavalava* and tops, darker colors are preferred on formal occasions. In such instances, Samoan men often wear a *lavalava* made from suit cloth material. Such a formal *lavalava,* when combined with leather sandals, white shirt, tie, and suit coat, is considered appropriate dress whether attending a funeral or hosting government dignitaries. In such settings women will wear a *pulu tasi,* a sort of *mu'u-mu'u* designed by the early Christian missionaries. On Sundays, Samoans prefer to wear white clothing to church.

Although Samoan concepts of personal modesty may differ from western concepts, they are very important to Samoans. The area between the calf of the leg and the thigh is considered to be especially inappropriate for public exhibition. Many traditional Samoan villages ban beach wear such as bikinis and swimming suits. Some even ban women from wearing trousers.

While the appearance and garb of Samoan women are subject to a range of cultural restrictions, full-body tattoos are common on Samoan men. The tattooing process is prolonged and painful. It is believed by Samoans to be a means of helping men appreciate the prolonged labor pains involved with childbirth.

HOLIDAYS

Both American Samoa and Western Samoa celebrate their respective national holidays. Christmas, Easter, and other religious holidays are also of great significance to Samoans. In addition, the second Sunday of October is celebrated by most denominations as "White Sunday." On this day, the service revolves around memorized recitations by children. After the service, Samoan children are waited upon by the adults of their family, served a festive meal, and presented with gifts.

HEALTH AND MENTAL HEALTH ISSUES

Samoans have a traditional system of healing that plays a very important role in Samoan culture. Traditional Samoan healers use a variety of massage treatments, counseling techniques, and herbal preparations to treat illness. Recent scientific analysis of Samoan healing practices show them to have some degree of empirical justification: a large number of plants used by Samoans for medical purposes demonstrate pharmacological activity in the laboratory. The National Cancer Institute, for instance, recently licensed the new anti-HIV compound prostratin, which was discovered in a Samoan plant used by traditional healers.

Samoans believe that there are some illnesses that cannot be cured by Western medicine. These include illnesses of the *to'ala*, the reputed center of being located beneath the navel, and cases of spiritual possession. *Musu*, a psychiatric illness of young women characterized by a nearly autistic withdrawal from communication, has been treated successfully in New Zealand by traditional healers. Samoan healers exist and practice, albeit covertly, in most expatriate Samoan communities.

Samoans believe that the major sources of disease are poor diet, poor hygiene, and interpersonal hostility. Since Samoa is a consensus culture with a heavy emphasis on responsibility and family, many believe that an individual who does not support his family, who does not shoulder the responsibilities of village life, and who otherwise does not participate in traditional culture, has a high risk of becoming ill. Linguistic isolation complicates some medical interaction with the older Samoans, but in general Samoans are appreciative of Western medicine and responsive to prescribed courses of medical treatment.

Samoan Americans are particularly susceptible to high rates of diabetes and other illnesses associated with a high-fat diet and decreased patterns of physical activity. As a population, though, Samoans show lower cholesterol levels than would be expected given their diet and patterns of obesity. Coconut oil, which is very rich in saturated fats, plays an important part in the Samoan diet. Many Samoan delicacies such as *palusami* (young taro leaves with coconut cream) are cooked in coconut cream. Such a diet, combined with sedentary lifestyle, is a key contributor to cardiovascular illness.

American Samoa maintains a fine hospital, the L.B.J. Tropical Medical Center in Fagalu, near Pago Pago. The Western Samoa National Hospital at Moto'otua is a fine facility as well, especially for a developing country. When necessary, difficult cases are referred by L.B.J. and Moto'otua to hospitals in Honolulu and Auckland, respectively.

LANGUAGE

The Samoan language is an ancient form of Polynesian dialect. It consists of three basic types of language. Common Samoan is the Samoan language of commerce and normal village interactions, while Respect Samoan includes honorific terms used for others of equal or greater rank. The third language type employed by Samoans, Rhetorical Samoan, is a set of proverbial, genealogical, and poetic allusions.

Samoan vowels are pronounced very simply; the French approach to their vowel pronunciation is similar. Consonants are nearly identical to English consonants with two exceptions: the glottal stop indicated by an apostrophe is an unaspirated consonant produced in the bottom of the throat that can best be approximated as the break in the English expression "oh oh." Thus the Samoan word for "thank you,"—*fa'afetai*—is pronounced "fah-ah-fay-tie." The Samoan "g" sound is also difficult for some foreigners to master. It is pronounced similarly to the "ng" in "sing along;" the Samoan word for gun—*faga*—is thus pronounced as "fah-ngah." The "n" sound is pronounced as "ng" by Samoans as well. Finally, in colloquial Samoan, the "k" sound is pronounced instead of the "t;" hence *fa'afetai* becomes "fa'afekai." Samoans, however, do not like foreigners to use colloquial pronunciation. In Samoan words all syllables are given equal timing with a slight accent placed on the penultimate syllable.

The following are several common Samoan greetings and their English translations: *talofa*—hello; *fa'afetai*—thank you; *tofa*—goodbye; *malo*—congratulations; *lau afioga*—your highness (high chief); *lau tofa*—your highness (orator); *lau susuga*—sir.

RHETORIC

Ceremonial Samoan may be one of the most complex rhetorical forms known on the face of the earth. Eloquent oratory has long been an integral part of the Samoan culture. In the case of a village or district dispute, the victor is often the side represented by the most eloquent orator. Oratorical ability in Samoa is a treasured commodity because it has historically brought its finest practitioners prestige, cultural influence, and material goods.

The importance of rhetoric in Samoa has even been institutionalized in the Samoan system of chiefdoms. In Samoan culture there are two types of chiefs: high chiefs, who function very much as the corporate executive officers of the village; and orators or "talking chiefs" who speak for the village in its dealings with others. Samoan orators are expected to memorize an amazing array of information, including the historical events of Samoa, an exhaustive list of Samoan proverbial expressions, and the genealogies of most of the major families in Samoa. Orators are also expected to be able to speak with power and eloquence in an extemporaneous fashion.

Listening to Samoan oratory at a *kava* ceremony can be an awe-inspiring experience. Sophisticated allusions to ancient events, nuanced proverbial expressions, and powerful political insights are combined with extensive references to the Bible and the genealogies of those present to produce an exquisitely cerebral poetic work. Samoan oratory is delivered in a cadence and clarity of voice that is clear and ringing. Frequently speeches are yelled out as a sign of respect to visitors. Unfortunately, this oral tradition, the highest of all Samoan arts, is the art form most inaccessible to foreigners. Very little Samoan formal rhetoric has ever been translated into English.

FAMILY AND COMMUNITY DYNAMICS

Samoans have an expansive view of familial bonds. A Samoan *a'iga* or family includes all individuals who descend from a common ancestor. Samoan familial ties are complex and highly interwoven, but also very important; all Samoans are expected to support and serve their extended families. Each extended family has one or more chiefs who organize and run the family.

Family pride is a central part of Samoan culture as well. Individuals in Samoan villages fear breaking village rules not only because of any individual consequences but because of the shame it might bring to their family. In cases of serious transgression, the entire family may be penalized by the village council. In extreme cases the transgressor's chief may be stripped of his title and the family disinherited from the land. The fear of shaming one's extended family thus serves as a potent deterrent in the culture. This philosophy extends not only to transgressors but also to victims. An offense committed against anyone, particularly elderly individuals—who are revered in Samoan society—or young women, may be seen as an offense to the victim's entire family. In contrast to western philosophies that laud individualism, Samoan culture emphasizes the importance of family ties and responsibility.

In Samoan culture, serious offenses may be redeemed by an *ifoga* (a lowering). This is a ceremony that reflects deep contrition on the part of the perpetrator. In an *ifoga,* all of a transgressor's extended family and village will gather before dawn in front of the residence of the offended or injured party. There they will sit covered by fine mats as the sun rises. They remain in that position until forgiven and invited into the house. They then present fine mats, pigs, and cash as evidence of their contrition. There is no Western equivalent to an *ifoga,* but performance of an *ifoga* in western Samoa, even for a serious crime, will often result in waiver or dramatic reduction of the criminal penalties that would have otherwise been assessed.

The Samoan concept of family has profound economic consequences. All Samoans are expected to provide financial support for their families. Many expatriate Samoans routinely send a large portion of their earnings back to their relatives in Samoa. Such foreign remittances constitute a significant portion of the income of Western Samoa. Although such remittances are a godsend for the relatively weak economy of Western Samoa, there is concern that the third generation of expatriate Samoans may become so assimilated into western cultures that this practice will not survive.

DATING PRACTICES

While older Samoans enjoy the regard in which they are held, younger members of the culture grapple with the complicated process of courtship. In remote villages dating is frowned upon. The culturally acceptable way for young men and young women to meet each other is for the young man to bring presents and food to the young woman's family and to court his intended in the presence of the woman's family. In traditional villages, even slight deviation from this pattern may place the young man at some risk of physical harm from the young woman's brothers.

Romantic affairs are, of course, difficult to transact. Typically an intermediary called a *soa* (go-between) is used to communicate the amorous intentions of a young man to the *soa* of the young woman. If romantic interest is reciprocated, young men and young women will visit surreptitiously at night under the cover of darkness. Such liaisons, however, are fraught with danger should the young woman's brothers discover them. Brothers in traditional Samoan culture consider it their familial duty to aggressively

screen out unwarranted suitors or inappropriate attempts to court their sister without parental supervision.

Physical contact between the sexes, including kissing and hand holding, is considered to be in poor taste in public. Even married couples avoid physical contact in public. These traditional practices, however, have changed as Samoan culture has become more westernized. In Pago Pago and Apia boys and girls date, attend dances, take in films, and socialize in most of the ways common to Western countries. However, any offense to a young woman, including swearing, is still taken as a deep offense by a young woman's brothers and may result in violence.

MARRIAGE AND CHILDREN

Marriage has become more common since the advent of Christianity, but in Samoa many people live together and even raise children without the benefit of marriage. This custom, called *nofo fa'apouliuli*, sometimes functions as a sort of trial marriage in which a Samoan tests the relationship before settling on a single partner.

Illegitimacy does not have the same negative connotations in Samoan culture that it does in other cultures. Children are warmly welcomed into a family and are frequently raised by grandparents or other relatives as their own offspring. In general, children within the Samoan family have a great deal of mobility. It is not uncommon in Samoa for children to be raised by people other than their biological parents. In many cases children are raised by members of extended family or even friends. All children are, regardless of their genetic relationship to the husband and wife in the family, treated equally and expected to assist with family chores.

Until approximately age seven boys and girls are reared in nearly identical fashion in Samoan culture. But girls from eight to ten years old are expected to play major roles in caring for other infant children. It is not uncommon in Samoan villages to see eight- or nine-year-old girls packing a six-month-old baby on their hip. Once boys and girls approach puberty deep cultural taboos take effect that preclude their continued close association. Past puberty, brothers and sisters are not allowed to be alone in each other's presence.

CEREMONIES

In Samoa infant children and their mothers occupy special status. New mothers are usually presented with *vaisalo*, a rich drink made of grated coconut, coconut milk, manihot, and the grated flesh of the vi apple. On occasion fine mats may also be presented to the mother.

A Samoan wedding typically involves feasting, dancing, and much merriment. Weddings are generally held in accordance with local customs or ecclesiastical protocols, followed by a large reception for the bride and groom.

Conveyance of a chiefly title is another noteworthy cultural event in Samoa. Typically the family of the chief-to-be will prepare kegs of corned beef, fine mats, money, and other items with which to "pay" the village granting the title. Visitors to the ceremony are also hosted in extravagant fashion. Extended and sophisticated rhetoric is exchanged by orators representing the various families in attendance and includes analysis of the genealogical provenance of the title. In some villages the candidate for the chief position is wrapped in a fine mat tied with a bow; he becomes a chief when the bow is untied. Many times paper currency is placed in an ornamental fashion in the chief's headdress. All chief ceremonies, however, regardless of village, culminate in the *kava* ceremony wherein the candidate drinks *kava* for the first time as the new chief. Invitation to attend a chief investiture ceremony or *saufa'i* is a signal honor, one rarely granted to foreigners.

Conveyance of a chiefly title is far more than an honorific. Individuals in the group immediately adopt the chief's title as their own first name. All people in the village, other than the immediate family, refer to the new chief by the new title. Furthermore, in traditional Samoan culture all the dependents of the new chief use the chief's title as their new last name.

Once established, the new chief is expected to attend village councils, act with a sense of decorum and dignity, support village activities via manual labor and cash donations, and behave with the interests of his family and village foremost in his mind. As a member of the village chief council, the new chief will participate in decisions reached in consensus with the other chiefs. Some chieftains in Samoa also have special titles such as *Malietoa, Tamasese, Tupuola,* or *Salamasina.* These titles have national significance. Individuals bearing such titles should be treated as the equivalent of European monarchs.

The conveyance of chief's titles has become a difficult business for expatriate Samoans since in traditional Samoan culture all chief's titles are tied to an identifiable piece of land in Samoa. Expatriate Samoans seeking titles usually must return to Samoa for the ceremonies. In New Zealand some chief investiture ceremonies have been held. However, titles so conferred outside of Samoa are controversial within Samoa. Infrequently, diplomats, aid workers, and other foreign visitors are granted honorific titles that have no validity in terms of Samoan land relationships and are not recognized by the Lands and Title Court. Exceptions to this arrangement are rare but do occur. Although nearly all chiefs are men, several women hold chiefly titles, and in at least one case a village conferred a valid title, registered with and recognized by the Land and Titles Court, on a Samoan-speaking foreigner.

Samoan funerals include important demonstrations of high Samoan culture. In a funeral the extended family of the bereaved prepares money, fine mats, kegs of corned beef, pigs, and case goods to present to visitors at the funeral. Visitors attend with a single palm leaf held aloft in front of them. On arrival at the home of the bereaved, the orator representing the visitors stands outside the hut, addresses the dead person with an honorific string of titles, and then speaks to everyone present. After the speech the visitors are invited to sit and wait as other visitors trickle in. The funeral concludes with an orator who acts as a representative for the bereaved family. The orator speaks before distributing gifts to the visitors.

At funerals and chief investiture ceremonies a great deal of cash and a large number of fine mats—which may take up to six months to complete—exchange hands. In some instances, more than 2,000 fine mats and as much as $20,000 may be redistributed.

MANNERS

The Samoan culture is very hospitable to foreigners. Usual expectations of strict formal behavior and rigorous rhetoric are suspended for visitors. Knowledge of a few simple courtesies, however, will help ensure goodwill in such settings. When entering a Samoan house or cultural event, it is important to quickly glance to see if other people are wearing shoes. It is usually considered disrespectful to walk across a mat in a Samoan house with shoes on. Shoes can be removed and left at the door. When walking in front of anybody one should bend low and say *Tulou* ("too-low").

When entering a room or assembly of Samoans in a cultural setting it is considered good manners to walk around the room and shake each person's hand, smiling and looking them in the eyes. *Talofa* ("tah-low-fah") is the greeting. After greeting everyone present, the visitor should sit where directed. It is considered rude in Samoan culture to stand while addressing someone who is sitting.

It is important to accept whatever hospitality is offered by Samoans. Hence, if everyone is seated on a mat on the floor but the visitor is offered a chair, the visitor should sit on the chair. If seated on the floor a visitor should cross his legs and avoid pointing his feet at anyone. If this position becomes uncomfortable the visitor can place a mat over his extended legs.

The presentation of *kava* is considered to be the highest symbol of respect that can be granted to a visitor. If presented with a cup of *kava*, one may drip a few drops on the ground (symbolic of returning goodness to the earth) and say *Ia manuia* ("ee-ah mahn-wee-ah"), which means "let there be blessings." At that point one can either drink from the cup or return it to the server.

The acceptance of gifts is important in Samoa. No gift offered by a Samoan should be refused. Such refusal might be considered an indication of displeasure with the person presenting the gift. The most common gifts are those of food or mats. Gifts are frequently given as an indication of the status or prestige of both the giver and the receiver. Gifts are given without expectation of reciprocation. During dancing or other fundraising activities, however, cash donations are usually welcomed. It is also considered good manners to publicly offer a significant cash payment to an orator who has given a speech of welcome or greeting.

Samoan culture also features several rules of etiquette concerning food. Never eat in front of a Samoan without offering to share your food. When served by others, it is important to show due respect to the food. While the meal does not have to be eaten in its entirety, the food itself should be handled and treated with respect, since it represents the finest that the hosts can provide.

Display of negative emotions, particularly irritation, anger, or other hostility, is considered to be in very bad taste and a sign of weakness. Samoans treat each other with extraordinary politeness even under difficult circumstances. One who exercises decorum even under stressful circumstances receives high marks in Samoan culture.

EDUCATION

Samoans value education very highly. For a developing country Western Samoa has an astonishingly high rate of literacy—approximately 98 percent. In traditional villages education is first received at a minister's school, where children are taught to read. Later they attend elementary and secondary schools. The emphasis in Samoan education is largely on rote memorization.

Differences in educational philosophy can be found from island to island, however. Western Samoan students, for instance, pursue an education that in many ways resembles the system taught in New Zealand, while children in American Samoa receive an education that resembles, in many respects, the curriculum taught on the American mainland. In Western Samoa the best schools are frequently operated by churches. Some of the Catholic schools are particularly prestigious.

Although there is a community college in American Samoa and two university campuses in Western Samoa, many Samoans pursue higher education either in New Zealand or the United States. Many Samoan Americans major in education, law, or other social sciences.

RELIGION

In Samoa religion plays a huge role that remarkably has been ignored by many anthropologists studying Samoan culture. The Samoan culture is a pious one. Most families in Samoa conduct a nightly *lotu* or vespers service in which the family gathers together, reads from the Bible, and offers prayers. Prayers are offered at every meal. Church attendance in Samoa is almost universal; the major denominations on the islands are Anglican, Methodist, Catholic, and Mormon. Ministers of religion occupy a status in Samoa tantamount to that occupied by high chiefs and are granted extraordinary deference.

Religion in the Samoan setting, however, has a unique Polynesian twist. Most Samoan Americans prefer to organize and participate in Samoan-speaking congregations, with some accommodation made for their non-Samoan speaking offspring. Singing in a Samoan congregation is enthusiastic and beautiful. The Samoan Bible, which was translated directly from Greek, is quoted extensively in most Samoan services. By and large, Samoans are far more familiar with Bible scripture than their Western counterparts.

POLITICS AND GOVERNMENT

Since American Samoans do not vote in national elections and the region has been administered in a fairly bipartisan manner by the Department of Interior, it is difficult to assess Samoan American political leanings. Hawaii, which has been traditionally a strong bastion for the Democratic party, is home to many Samoans, but many Samoan Americans live in the staunchly Republican areas of Orange County, California, and Utah as well. Given their relatively small numbers, however, it is unlikely that any unified voting behavior on their part would have more than local political significance.

A current political issue of interest to Samoans is the minimum wage law. American Samoa received a waiver from obeying the minimum wage law due to the havoc that implementation would likely create for the tuna canneries in American Samoa. Union involvement appears to be fairly minimal among Samoan workers.

Western Samoa has a lively political climate, with much jousting and intrigue between the different political parties. There continues to be, in some circles, discussion of a possible unification of the two Samoan regions into a single independent country. Few American Samoans appear to be in favor of this idea. Their resistance to Samoan unification is driven not only by the tremendous economic disparity between American Samoa and Western Samoa, but also because of different cultural trajectories. Thus, while there are significant cultural and linguistic similarities between Western and American Samoa, unification seems unlikely. Instead, many Western Samoans seek to immigrate to American Samoa. Some have even joined the U.S. armed forces.

INDIVIDUAL AND GROUP CONTRIBUTIONS

The following individuals have made significant contributions to American society. Frank Falaniko, Jr. (1956-) is a landscape construction engineer and president of Green City, Inc.; Eni Faauaa Hunkin Faleomavaega, Jr. (1943-), is a government official; Al Noga (1965-), is a professional football player who has played with the Minnesota Vikings and the Washington Redskins; and Mavis Rivers (c. 1929-1992), was a jazz vocalist who joined her father's band during World War II and sang with the Red Norvo combo, George Shearing, and Andre Previn.

MEDIA

American Samoa maintains a television station that produces local programming under the direction of the territorial government. Three channels are broadcast throughout American Samoa. These carry American network programming in the evening and locally-produced educational programming in the daytime. Western Samoa has recently begun a television production facility as well.

Both American and Western Samoa operate several radio stations. In Western Samoa 2AP is the national radio station and the major means of communication with individuals in remote villages. Every evening messages reporting deaths, births, conferences, or other family news are aired on 2AP as a way of informing people who have no other ready access to information on developments and events on the islands. Samoan-language radio programs are also broadcast by radio stations in Auckland, Honolulu, and Salt Lake City.

PRINT

Samoa Times.

Incorporates *Samoa Bulletin*; presents text in English and Samoan.

Contact: Leulu Felise Va'A., Editor.

Address: Box 1160, Apia, Western Samoa.

ORGANIZATIONS AND ASSOCIATIONS

Polynesian Cultural Center (PCC).

Presents, preserves, and perpetuates the arts, crafts, culture, and lore of Fijian, Hawaiian, Maori, Marquesan, Tahitian, Tongan, Samoan, and other Polynesian peoples.

Contact: Lester W. B. Moore, President.

Address: 55-370 Kamehameha Highway, Laie, Hawaii 96762.

Telephone: (808) 293-3333.

MUSEUMS AND RESEARCH CENTERS

Major libraries on Samoa are the O. F. Nelson Memorial Library in Apia, the Oliveti Library in Pago Pago, the Turnbull Library in Wellington, and the Bernice P. Bishop Library in Honolulu. Major museum collections of Samoan items can be found at the Dominion Museum in Auckland, New Zealand, the Bernice P. Bishop Museum in Honolulu, the Lowie Museum in Berkeley, and the Ethnological Museum in Basel, Switzerland.

SOURCES FOR ADDITIONAL STUDY

Baker, P. T., J. M. Hanna, and T. S. Baker. *The Changing Samoans: Behavior and Health in Transition*. Oxford: Oxford University Press, 1986.

Cox, P. A., and S. A. Banack. *Islands, Plants and Polynesians: An Introduction to Polynesian Ethnobotany*. Portland: Dioscorides Press, 1991.

Davidson, J. M. "Samoa and Tonga," in *The Prehistory of Polynesia*. Cambridge: Harvard University Press, 1979.

Fox, J. W., and K. B. Cumberland. *Western Samoa*. Christchurch, New Zealand: Whitcombe and Tombs, 1962.

Freeman, D. *Margaret Mead and Samoa: The Making and the Unmaking of an Anthropological Myth*. Cambridge: Harvard University Press, 1981.

Kennedy, P. M. *The Samoan Tangle: A Study in Anglo-German-American Relations*. Dublin: Irish University Press, 1974.

Stair, J. B. *Old Samoa*. London: Religious Tract Society, 1897.

Unlike the Scotch-Irish, who emigrated individually, the Scots emigrated in groups, which reflects their early organization in clans.

SCOTTISH AND SCOTCH-IRISH AMERICANS

by
Mary A. Hess

OVERVIEW

Scotland occupies roughly the northern one-third of the British Isles; its area is 30,414 square miles (78,772 square kilometers), or about the size of the state of Maine. A fault line separates the country into the northern Highlands and the southern Lowlands, the agricultural and industrial center of the country. In addition, there are several island groups offshore, notably the Hebrides, Shetland, and Orkney Islands. Two-thirds of the nation's population of 5,100,000 live in the Lowlands, most near the country's two largest cites—Edinburgh, the Scottish capital, and Glasgow. The other major cities of Dundee and Aberdeen reflect Scotland's major industries, particularly fishing and shipbuilding, and its strong ties to maritime commerce. The name Scotland derives from a Gaelic word for "wanderer."

Although the Highlands occupy a greater land mass than the Lowlands, they are more sparsely populated. There are also distinct cultural differences between the two. Highlanders, who were organized in family groups called clans, share a mostly Celtic culture and many are still Roman Catholic; whereas the Lowlanders are mostly Presbyterian, and speak Scots, which is an English-based language.

A land of considerable natural beauty, Scotland is surrounded on three sides by water—the

Atlantic Ocean to the north and west, and the North Sea to the east. Deep and narrow inlets known as *firths* penetrate the coastline of Scotland, while inland are distinctive glacial lakes known as lochs, the most famous of which is Loch Ness, the home of the fabled "Nessie," a prehistoric creature said to live in the deepest part of the lake.

HISTORY

The earliest recorded history concerning the Scots comes from the Romans, who controlled southern Britain in the first century A.D. In 84 A.D., the Romans defeated the tribal armies of Scotland in battle but they were unable to conquer the people. In an attempt to isolate the fierce "barbarians," the Roman emperor Hadrian built a massive stone wall, the remains of which are still visible traversing northern England just south of the Scottish border. By the 600s, four tribal groups had emerged: the Angles of the Southeast, related to the Germanic tribes settling England at the time; the Britons of the southwest, a Celtic people related to the Welsh; the Picts, also Celtic, who dominated the Highlands; and the Scots, a Celtic group that settled the western islands and cost from nearby Ireland. Christianity, brought by missionaries such as St. Ninian and St. Columba, spread slowly among the tribes beginning in about 400.

Following the Viking invasions of the 800s and 900s, the four tribes gradually united under Scottish kings such as Kenneth MacAlpin, who brought the Scots and Picts together in 843 and is often called the first king of Scotland. His descendants succeeded in gaining limited control over rival kings and the feuding clans (groups of families related by blood). One king who briefly unseated the dynasty was Macbeth of Moray, who killed Duncan, a descendant of MacAlpin, in 1040. Eventually, the Scots gave their name to the land and all its people, but the kings often ruled in name only, especially in the remote Highlands where local clan leaders retained their independence.

In 1066 Norman invaders from France gained control of England. Powerful new English rulers such as the thirteenth century's Edward I, who was called "the Hammer of the Scots," gained influence over the Scottish kings and helped shape culture in the Lowlands. Still the Scots resisted English dominance, often allying with England's enemy, France. One brief period of glory came when Robert Bruce, a noble, gained the Scottish crown and wiped out an English army at Bannockburn in 1314. Bruce's daughter married Walter the Steward (steward was a high office of the royal administration). This led to *Stewart*, later spelled *Stuart*, becoming the name of Scotland's royal house.

The English and Scottish royal houses had become closely connected through marriage. On Elizabeth's death in 1603, Mary's son James IV, already king of Scotland, ascended the throne of England. The Catholic Stuart monarchs faced trouble in both England and Scotland as the religious disputes between Catholics and Protestants wreaked the land. His coronation as James I of England settled Scotland's fate, for it was during his reign that the Plantation in Ulster relocated Lowland Scots in an attempt to reconstruct Ireland as a Protestant country. James's son, Charles I, was executed in 1649 by Oliver Cromwell's Protestant regime; after the Stuarts' restoration to the throne, James II was replaced by his Protestant daughter Mary and her husband William of Orange in 1688. While rebellions continued in Scotland, the union of crowns marked the beginning of an increasing bond between Scotland and her more powerful neighbor. The Treaty of Union (1707) formalized the political connection by incorporating Scotland's government into that of England. This created the United Kingdom and laid the foundation for the British Empire—to which the Scots would contribute greatly in coming centuries.

Political turmoil continued in Scotland during the 1700s with rebellions led by James Stuart (son of James II), who was backed by France and Spain—England's Catholic enemies. The most important of these "Jacobite" (from *Jacobus*, Latin for James) campaigns occurred in 1715 and in 1745, when James' son Charles also surprised Britain by invading from Scotland. These failed attempts engendered a vast body of romantic legend, though, particularly around the figure of Charles, called "Bonnie Prince Charlie" or the "Young Pretender" (claimant to the throne). The Jacobites found more support among the fiercely independent Highlanders, who had remained largely Catholic, than among the stern Protestant Lowlanders. The Scots retained their distinctive character, however, even as they contributed to Britain's prosperity and worldwide power.

THE SCOTCH-IRISH

The Scotch-Irish trace their ancestry to Scotland, but through Northern Ireland, which also belongs to the British Empire. Northern Ireland, which is composed of six counties—Antrim, Armagh, Cavan, Down, Monaghan, and Tyrone, occupies an area of 5,452 square miles (14,121 square kilometers), or a territory somewhat larger than the state of Connecticut. Its capital and largest city is Belfast, where approximately one-fifth of the country's population of 1,594,000 resides.

The Scotch-Irish descend from 200,000 Scottish Lowland Presbyterians who were encouraged by the English government to migrate to Ulster in the seventeenth century. Trying to strengthen its control of Ireland, England tried to establish a Protestant population in Ulster. Surrounded by native hostility, though, the group maintained its cultural distinction. The same economic pressures, including steadily increasing rents on their land, frequent crop failures, and the collapse of the linen trade, coupled with the belief in greater opportunity abroad, caused many Scotch-Irish to leave for the American colonies during the eighteenth century. It is estimated that nearly two million descendants of the Scotch-Irish eventually migrated to the American colonies.

"People who had come to this country in the earlier years had told me, you'll be sorry when you get to Ellis Island. But I wasn't really sorry, I was just maybe upset a little bit. What upset me the most was having to go through so many people's hands and take such a long time."

Mary Dunn in 1923, cited in *Ellis Island: An Illustrated History of the Immigrant Experience*, edited by Ivan Chermayeff et al. (New York: Macmillan, 1991).

IMMIGRATION

From 1763 to 1775, 55,000 Scotch-Irish from Ulster and 40,000 Scots arrived in America. Since Scotland was able to pursue its own colonies in the New World, several small colonies were established in the early seventeenth century in East Jersey and South Carolina. These colonies were primarily for Quakers and Presbyterians who were experiencing religious persecution by the then Episcopalian Church of Scotland. Although some Scots were transported to America as prisoners or criminals and were forced into labor as punishment, many voluntarily settled in America as traders or tobacco workers in Virginia. However, the political persecution of the Jacobite sympathizers, combined with economic hard times, forced many Scots to emigrate. Unlike the Scotch-Irish, who emigrated individually, the Scots emigrated in groups, which reflects their early organization in clans. They became a significant presence in the New World, settling in the original colonies with a particularly strong presence in the Southeast.

Many Scotch-Irish joined the mass migrations to the New World brought on by the Potato Famine of the 1840s. Substantial numbers of Scots also immigrated to the United States in the nineteenth century to work in industry. Throughout the twentieth century, immigration would rise when economic conditions in Scotland worsened; this was especially true during the 1920s when an economic depression hit Scotland particularly hard. Because British law then prohibited skilled workers to leave the country, many Scotch-Irish laborers found their way to the United States through Canada.

SETTLEMENT PATTERNS

Because of profound doctrinal differences with New England's Congregationalism, the Scotch-Irish Presbyterians opted for the religious freedom of William Penn's colony; and the earliest settlements there were near Philadelphia in the 1720s. They reached as far west as Pittsburgh before finding greater opportunities in the southern colonies. The Scotch-Irish and Scots alike were strongly represented in the push westward, though, and their participation in military campaigns was significant. Darien, Georgia, was founded by Highland Scots in service to General James Oglethorpe, and their assistance was invaluable in protecting the British colonies of the Southeast from the Spanish in Florida. These Highland Scots strongly protested against the institution of slavery in the colony, setting a precedent for strong anti-slavery sentiment that stood against the Scotch-Irish planters and English colonists who were eager for slavery to help build the colony and amass fortunes.

Today the descendants of the Scotch-Irish number over six million, with about five million identifying themselves as descended from Scottish ancestry. In the 1990 U.S. Census "Scotch-Irish" was the eleventh most populous ethnic group, followed by "Scottish." The states reporting the highest concentration of Scotch-Irish are California, Texas, North Carolina, Florida, and Pennsylvania. Those claiming Scottish descent are also most populous in California, then Florida, Texas, New York, and Michigan. The issue of descent is somewhat confused since not all historians and social scientists count Scotch-Irish as a culturally

distinct group. For the purposes of the 1990 census, "Scotch-Irish" was included as a classification that was a single, rather than a multiple, response to the question of national origin. Also, a significant number of African Americans and Native Americans claim Scotch-Irish ancestry.

ACCULTURATION AND ASSIMILATION

The Scots people were among the first European settlers, and along with the other colonists from the British Isles, helped create what has been recognized as the dominant culture in America: namely, white and Protestant. By working hard and seizing the opportunities of a rapidly growing country, many Scottish immigrants were able to move up rapidly in American society. Unaffected by barriers of race, language, or religion, they earned a reputation for hard work and thrift that was greatly admired in the young republic. Perhaps the most notable among this group is one of America's most successful immigrants—the industrialist Andrew Carnegie. After arriving in America at the age of 13, he worked first in a cotton mill, then as a superintendent for the Pennsylvania Railroad. By shrewd investments, he parlayed his Carnegie Steel Company into a huge fortune. In his famous essay, "The Gospel of Wealth," he described his rationale for philanthropy—

Carnegie donated hundreds of millions of dollars to build public libraries, endow universities, and fund scholarships. His most famous gift is one of New York's most beautiful public buildings, Carnegie Hall, which has hosted the world's most distinguished performers in the lively arts. Carnegie believed that wealth acquired by hard work should be shared with society, but on his terms; for example, Carnegie was bitterly opposed to unionization in his steel plants and was behind the murder of strikers in the Homestead Strike at his plant in Homestead, Pennsylvania, in 1892.

Scots are relatively unscathed by any ethnic stereotyping; however, the phrase, "cold as Presbyterian charity" reflects the long standing belief that Scots are dour and stingy. This seems to be lessening, although brand names such as "Scotch Tape" reinforce the idea that to be Scottish is to be thrifty. There is also the persistence of the "hillbilly" legend, which portrays Appalachian residents as ill-clad, unshod bumpkins fond of brewing "moonshine" (bootleg whiskey). This image became widespread with the "Lil' Abner" comic strip drawn by Al Capp beginning in 1932; the strip reached 60 million readers and became first a Broadway musical and then a film in 1959. In the 1960s, a CBS television series, "The Beverly Hillbillies" and its spinoffs "Petticoat Junction" and "Green Acres" furthered the image of rural people as simpletons. The dignity of most rural Southern life has emerged, however, with the publication of the "Foxfire" books in the 1970s, and the efforts of folklorists to preserve and document a vanishing way of life. Appalshop, a rural arts and education center in Whitesburg, Kentucky, exemplifies the effort to preserve the Scottish and Scotch-Irish heritage of Appalachia on film and also recorded music.

The figure most associated with the best aspects of this tradition is the pioneer Daniel Boone (1734-1820), whose life has been celebrated in song and story, as well as movies and television. Daniel Boone was a trailblazer and patriot who continues to capture the imaginations of Americans. Other famous Scots who immigrated to America were Flora MacDonald, the woman who saved the life of "Bonnie Prince Charlie" by hiding him from his pursuers. Imprisoned by the English until she became too troublesome as a symbol of Jacobite sentiment, she was pardoned and immigrated to North Carolina. John Muir, Scottish-born naturalist (1838-1914), was reared as a strict Calvinist, and reacted to a near loss of his eyesight in an accident by a spiritual quest for the natural world. He began a walk on foot across the continent, and fiercely advocated the preservation of the wilderness; he influenced President Theodore Roosevelt to become a conservationist. The national parks are a tribute to his foresight and love of America's natural beauty.

There is a cliché about "the wandering Scot" which contains an essential truth—that Scottish people have both a wanderlust and a strong affection for Scotland. This attachment can be seen today in the celebration by Americans of their Scottish and Scotch-Irish roots, which often means both a consciousness of ethnicity as well as taking a journey to discover their ancestral heritage. Many genealogical firms in Great Britain and Ireland specialize in helping these Americans trace their ancestry. A family crest, a tartan tie, or an interest in traditional customs is a demonstration of pride in their ethnic identity.

TRADITIONS, CUSTOMS AND BELIEFS

Scottish and Scotch-Irish customs include the *shivaree* (an elaborate courting ritual that involves the serenading of the bride outside her window) and square dancing. The square dance began with reels and other dances enjoyed by the nobility and was transformed to the present popularity of line dancing—steps done to music often featuring the most Scotch-Irish of instruments, the fiddle.

Today's "Texas Two-Step" and "Boot-scooting" evolved from ancient ritual dances.

Scots enjoy large "gatherings of the clan," which celebrate their heritage and offer opportunities to meet others who share membership in the clan. Most states with a large Scottish and Scotch-Irish population (such as New York and Michigan) have "Highland Games," which feature sports such as "tossing the caber," in which men compete to toss a heavy pole the farthest distance. Bagpipe music is a very important part of this celebration, as it is at any celebration of clan identity. North Carolina, which has one of largest concentrations of people of Scottish descent, hosts the biggest gathering at Grandfather Mountain each July. Campbells mingle with MacGregors and Andersons, while enjoying Scotch whisky and traditional cuisine.

CUISINE

Main Scottish staples are oatmeal, barley, and potatoes. Oatmeal is made into a porridge, a thick, hot breakfast cereal traditionally seasoned with salt. Barley is used primarily in the distillation of Scotch whiskey, now a major source of export revenue. Potatoes ("tatties") are most often eaten mashed. There is also the traditional *haggis* (a pudding made from the heart, liver, and other organs of a sheep, chopped with onions and oatmeal and then stuffed into a sheep's stomach and boiled). This unique meal, served with tatties and "a wee dram" (small portion of whiskey), has taken its place with the tartan and the bagpipes as a national symbol. Scots also enjoy rich vegetable soups, seafood in many forms, beef, oatcakes (a tasty biscuit), and shortbread (a rich, cookie-like confection).

TRADITIONAL DRESS

The famous Scottish kilt, a knee-length skirt of a tartan pattern, was created by an Englishman, Thomas Rawlinson, who lived in the 1700s. The older kilts were rectangles of cloth, hanging over the legs, gathered at the waist, and wrapped in folds around the upper body. The blanket-like garment served as a bed-roll for a night spent outdoors. Aside from the kilt, fancy "highland" dress includes a *sporan* (leather purse on a belt), stockings, brogues (shoes), dress jacket, and a number of decorative accessories. The plaid is a length of tartan cloth draped over the shoulder and does not properly refer to the pattern, which is the tartan.

Women's fancy dress is simpler, though elegant, consisting of a white cotton blouse, perhaps with embroidered patterns, and a silk tartan skirt. Her version of the plaid, a tartan also in silk, is hung over the shoulder and pinned in place with a brooch. This finery, like the tartans, is mostly an invention of the modern age but has become traditional and it is taken quite seriously. The tartan shows up elsewhere, commonly worn on ties, caps, and skirts—even on cars and in the costumes of young "punk rockers" in Edinburgh and Glasgow.

MUSIC

There is considerable Scottish influence in the field of country and folk music, directly traceable to the Scots ballad—a traditional form in which a story (usually tragic) is related to the listener in song. The ballad (e.g. "Barbara Allen") originated as an oral tradition, and was brought to the southeastern United States by immigrants who preserved the form while adapting melody and lyrics to suit their purpose. Instruments, especially the fiddle and harp, have been transformed into unique sounding relations such as the hammered dulcimer, pedal steel guitar, and electric mandolins, and are the staples of today's country music, particularly bluegrass, which emphasizes the heritage of country music in its traditional origins in Scotland and Ireland.

HOLIDAYS

Most Scottish holidays are those celebrated throughout Great Britain; however, two holidays are unique to Scotland: Scottish Quarter Day, celebrated 40 days after Christmas, and the commemoration of St. Andrew, patron saint of Scotland, on November 30. A sentimental holiday is the birthday of poet Robert ("Robbie") Burns, born January 25, 1759, who is perhaps best known to Americans for the perennial New Year's anthem, "Auld Lang Syne." The Scotch-Irish also celebrate July 12, the anniversary of William of Orange's victory over the Catholics at the Battle of the Boyne in 1690, with parades.

HEALTH AND MENTAL HEALTH ISSUES

Health concerns are primarily determined by economic factors, and especially by location. Having found, for the most part, economic security due to generations of residence and the economic advantage of an early arrival in America, many Scots and Scotch-Irish are insured through their employers, are self-employed, or have union benefits. The great exception is in Appalachia, where poverty persists despite the initiatives of John F. Kennedy and Lyndon B. Johnson's "War on Poverty" in the 1960s. The dominant industry of the area, coal mining, has left a considerable mark on the health of Scottish and Scotch-Irish Americans. Black lung, a congestive disease of the lungs caused by the inhalation of coal dust, disables and kills miners at a high rate. This and chronic malnutrition, high infant mortality, and low birth weight remain the scourge of mountain people. West Virginia, Kentucky, and Tennessee still have pockets of poverty as a result of high unemployment and isolation. The pattern of early marriage and large families is still typical, as is a significant problem with domestic violence.

LANGUAGE

The Scotch-Irish are unlikely to share speech patterns and the characteristic burr (a distinctive trilled "r") with the Scots. However, linguists who have studied Appalachian accents have found continuity in usage and idiom that can be shown to originate in Scottish phrases. Occasionally remnants of the Scottish idiom survive in words such as "dinna" which means "don't," as in "I dinna ken" (I don't know), but this is increasingly rare as even isolated mountain hollows in the South are penetrated by mass media and its homogenizing influence.

FAMILY AND COMMUNITY DYNAMICS

Traditional family structure, especially in the Highlands, centered around the clan. There are about 90 original clans. Many of the clan names are prefixed by "Mac," meaning "son of." The clans have loosely defined territories, and prolonged wars, often spanning generations, were once common between clans. The most famous feud was that between the Campbells (who supported the English) and the MacDonalds (Jacobites). Even today there are MacDonalds who will not speak to Campbells and vice-versa. Large clans enrolled smaller ones as allies, and the alliances also became traditional. The adjective "clannish," derived from the Gaelic *clann* (descent from a common ancestor) perfectly describes the sentimental attachment

This girl is performing a

Scottish sword dance.

that Scottish Americans feel concerning extended family and heritage. The origin of this term is the tendency of Scots to migrate with their clan and settle in the same location. This tendency was so pronounced that in parts of Kentucky and Ten-nessee, relatives adopted the use of their middle name as a surname since all their kin shared a common last name. One of the most infamous examples in America of the Scottish tendency to clannishness is the Hatfield and McCoy feud of the

880s in the Tug River Valley along the West Virginia and Kentucky border. The murderous vendetta lasted years and involved disputes over a razorback hog, a romance between a Hatfield son and a McCoy daughter, and various other affronts to family dignity. After nationwide publicity, the feud was finally ended in 1897 after the execution of one of the Hatfields and the jailing of several other participants. However, the phrase, "feuding like the Hatfields and McCoys" is still a part of the American vocabulary.

Gatherings were purposeful and practical in frontier America, as in the "quilting bee," which allowed women to enjoy each others' company while creating a patchwork quilt—the essence of thrift. Various small pieces of fabric were sewn together in patterns to create a beautiful and utilitarian bed covering. Today many of these quilts are treasured by the descendants of the women who made them. Quilting is a popular craft that has enjoyed an ever-widening appreciation both as a hobby and folk art; quilts are often displayed in museums, and one of the best collections can be seen in Paducah, Kentucky, home of the American Quilting Society. Another traditional community activity is that of the barn raising and the subsequent dance—a tribute to the pioneer spirit that built America. Neighbors cooperated to erect barns and celebrated their hard work with fiddle music and a square dance late into the night. These gatherings helped shape community in rural areas such as the Midwest and the West.

RELIGION

The traditional dividing line between the Scotch-Irish and the Irish has been religion. While Irish immigrants have been primarily Catholics, the Scotch-Irish are followers of John Knox and John Calvin. The belief in predestination of the soul had a powerful effect on the shaping of the Scots' psyche. The original plantation of Scots in Ulster, which was motivated by economic hard times as much as by politics, was an attempt by England to subdue the native Catholic population. England thereby politicized religion when it initiated the discord between the two groups, a discord that still plays itself out in Northern Ireland. When the Potato Famine of the 1840s caused the Scotch-Irish to migrate to the New World, they brought their faith with them, retaining a tradition that stood them in good stead in the largely Protestant country. Although in Scotland the Church of Scotland was an austere entity, not given to large churches or displays of wealth, it gradually gave way to grand affirmations of material success in America. Today the Presbyterian church still plays a significant role in American religious life. The stirring hymn "Onward Christian Soldiers" (1864) exemplifies the Scottish heritage reflected in today's church: "Onward Christian soldiers / Marching as to war / With the Cross of Jesus / Going on before!" Written first as a children's hymn, it became a favorite in Protestant churches.

EMPLOYMENT AND ECONOMIC TRADITIONS

Scots and Scotch-Irish have been drawn to the land as farmers and herders just as in their home country. Highland Scots, in particular, were attracted to mountain areas that resembled their homeland, and replicated their lives as herders and small scale farmers wherever possible. Others were drawn to work in heavy industry, such as the steel mills and coal mines. The nation's railroads provided employment for many, and in the case of Andrew Carnegie, provided a step up in his career as a capitalist. Many sought higher education and entered the professions at all levels, particularly as physicians and lawyers. For others, isolated in Appalachia or the rural South, hard times during the Great Depression brought scores of Scotch-Irish to the factories of Detroit and Chicago, where they labored in the auto plants and stockyards. Poverty returned for many of these people as plants shut down and downscaled in the 1960s, creating so-called "hillbilly ghettoes" in major Northern industrial cities. Generations of poverty have created an underclass of displaced Southerners which persists as a social problem today. Author Harriette Arnow, born in 1908, wrote movingly of the plight of these economic migrants in her novel *The Dollmaker* (1954). Scottish and Scotch-Irish Americans have, of course, assimilated to a high degree and have benefited much from the opportunities that class mobility and a strong work ethic have brought them.

POLITICS AND GOVERNMENT

Not until the 1970s would Scottish nationalism be a significant force in British politics; nonetheless, in 1979, Scottish voters rejected limited home rule in a referendum. There is a significant presence of Scottish nationalists today despite the historic, economic and cultural ties to Britain.

Scottish and Scotch-Irish Americans have been involved with U.S. government from the founding of the Republic. As landholders and farmers, they were very much the people Thomas Jefferson had in mind as participants in his agrarian democracy. From legislators to presidents, including President Bill Clinton, the passion of Scottish people for government has been felt in America. Presidents who shared this heritage include Andrew Jackson (1767-1845), Ulysses S. Grant (1822-1885), Woodrow Wilson (1856-1924), and Ronald Wilson Reagan (1911-).

MILITARY

Both Scots and the Scotch-Irish were a significant presence in the American Revolution and the Civil War. The divided union was embodied by Generals "Stonewall" Jackson and Jeb Stuart for the Gray and George B. McClellan for the Blue. Many Scots had settled on the frontier and moved westward seeking land and opportunity, and pressed forward to the West, particularly Texas, Oklahoma, and the Gulf Coast. Texas in particular was a land of opportunity for the land-hungry Scots—Sam Houston and his fellows were among the intrepid settlers of that diverse state. They fought the Comanches and settled the Plains, creating a legend of Texan grit and determination not unlike the reputation of their Scottish forebears. The Alamo in San Antonio is a symbol of the tenacity of the Scotch-Irish who were prominent among the defenders of the Texas Republic.

Highland Scots and their descendants (who typically settled in the mountains) were active in the anti-slavery movement, while it was more common for the Lowland Scots and the Scotch-Irish to be proslavery. This created a major rift in the mid-South and the lowland areas, which clung to slavery while the highlands in large part chose the Union during the Civil War. Scots and Scotch-Irish have figured prominently in all the major political parties in American history, and were perhaps most identified as a group with the Populist movement which reached its peak in the 1890s and united farmers for a short time against perceived economic injustice. The South and Midwest were the stronghold of the populists, led by men like Tom Watson and Ignatius Donnelly. Scots and Scots-Irish were also a major force in the union movement, exemplified by the agita-

tion for workers rights in the textile mills of the Southeast and the mines of West Virginia and Kentucky, marked by serious outbreaks of violence and strikes. "Which side are you on?" was a question often heard in these conflicts. Filmmaker Barbara Kopple documented this long and bloody struggle in her prize-winning film, *Harlan County, USA* (1977).

Since the breakup of the so-called Democratic "Solid South", it is difficult to predict how Scottish and Scotch-Americans vote. In addition, because of assimilation, it would be unlikely that there would be a "Scots vote" or "Scotch-Irish" vote.

INDIVIDUAL AND GROUP CONTRIBUTIONS

DANCE

Isadora Duncan (1878-1927) was a major innovator in modern dance, creating a unique expression based on Greek classicism and a belief in liberating the body from the constrictive costumes and especially footwear of classical ballet; her flowing draperies and bare feet made her the sensation of her day; her colorful life story is chronicled in her autobiography, *My Life* (1926).

FILM, TELEVISION, AND THEATER

The influence of Scottish and Scotch-Irish Americans in the performing arts stretches from Oscar winning directors like Leo McCarey (1898-1969) whose films *Going My Way* (1944) and *The Bells of St. Mary's* (1945) are considered classics in Hollywood sentimentality, to the remarkable Huston family whose careers span much of the history of the motion picture in America. Walter Huston (1884-1950), his son John (1906-1987) and John's daughter Angelica (1951-) have all won Academy Awards. Walter Huston was a memorable character actor, perhaps best remembered for one of his son John's best films as a director, *The Treasure of the Sierra Madre* (1948); granddaughter Angelica was directed by her father in three films, notably *Prizzi's Honor* (1985) for which she won as best supporting actress. John Huston's last film, *The Dead*, a 1987 adaptation of James Joyce's story, also starred Angelica and was scripted by her brother Danny. James Stewart (1908-), one of Hollywood's most famous and beloved citizens, is well known for classics such as *Mr. Smith Goes to Washington* (1939), *It's a Wonderful Life* (1947), and *Rear Window* (1954). One of his leading ladies (in *The Philadelphia Story*, 1940) is Katharine Hepburn, (1907 -) a strong-willed and talented actress who portrayed the doomed Mary, Queen of Scots in *Mary of Scotland* (1936). Hepburn, daughter of a prominent Connecticut physician and his wife, a suffragist and birth control activist, has enjoyed a long and honored career on stage and screen; she won three Academy Awards and was nominated for eight. Another remarkable career was that of Fred MacMurray, an actor known for films such as *Double Indemnity* (1944)—a tense *film noir*—and *The Apartment* (1960), was also known as a comic actor. He made a successful transition to Walt Disney films such as *The Absent Minded Professor* (1961) and became a television icon in the 1960s as the widowed father in the popular sitcom "My Three Sons." Two singers, Gordon MacRae (1921-) and John Raitt (1917-), enjoyed Broadway success that transferred to Hollywood musicals; both are known for their portrayal of Curley in *Oklahoma!* (which depicts customs such as the shivaree and the barn dance).

LITERATURE

Writers who have enriched American literature include: Robert Burns (1759-1796), the beloved Scots poet; Sherwood Anderson (1876-1941), author of the pathbreaking novel, *Winesburg, Ohio* (1919); North Carolinian Thomas Wolfe (1900-1938), whose novel, *Look Homeward, Angel* (1929) has been called "the great American novel". Carson McCullers (1917-1967), author of *Member of the Wedding* (1946) and *Reflections in A Golden Eye* (1941), is one of the South's most important novelists. Ellen Glasgow's (1873-1945) best novel, *Vein of Iron* (1935), concerns the fortunes of Ada Fincastle, the daughter of a hardy Scotch-Irish family of Virginia in the early part of the twentieth century. Larry McMurtry, whose novels *The Last Picture Show* and *Lonesome Dove* have enjoyed tremendous success after filmed versions have captured fans for the prolific writer's view of his home state and its rich history.

MUSIC

Michael Nesmith (1943-), son of Bette Nesmith Graham, became famous as a songwriter and performer with the 1960s rock group, the Monkees. Bonnie Raitt (1950-), daughter of John Raitt, is a popular Grammy-winning singer and a noted interpreter of the blues.

SCIENTISTS AND INVENTORS

Cyrus McCormick (1809-1884), an immigrant from Ulster, invented the reaper. Samuel Morse (1791-1872), who revolutionized communications with the telegraph and Morse Code, was also an accomplished portrait painter and a founder of Vassar College in 1861; in 1844, he sent the famous message "What hath God wrought?" from Washington to Baltimore, and between 1857 and 1858 he collaborated with entrepreneur Cyrus Field (1819-1892) in laying the first transatlantic cable. Field later established the Wabash Railroad with financier Jay Gould. A particularly enterprising Scotch-Irish woman, Bette Nesmith Graham (1924-1980), born in Dallas, Texas, died with a net worth over $47.5 million; a poor typist, she devised a product that would cover mistakes and in so doing created "Liquid Paper"—a correction fluid. Claire McCardell (1905-1958) revolutionized fashion design and dance with the invention of the stretch leotard; a pioneer in women's ready-to-wear clothing, she also created the affordable and practical "popover," a wrap-around denim house-dress, and the "Moroccan" tent dress.

VISUAL ARTS

Scottish and Scotch-Irish craftsmen and artists are similarly prominent. Gilbert Stuart (1755-1828), perhaps America's best-known portrait artist, was of Scottish heritage (his paintings of George Washington provide the definitive image of the "father of his country" for many Americans), as was Scots-born portrait artist John Smibert (1688-1751), and sculptor Frederick MacMonnies (1863-1937), whose graceful public sculptures adorn the New York Public Library, among many other locations (his Columbian fountain at the World's Columbian Exposition of 1893 was one of the most celebrated artistic achievements of that fair). Another is Duncan Phyfe, craftsperson (1768-1854), whose name is well-known to generations of Americans who cherish the tables, chairs, and cabinets he created, as well as inspiring imitators of his work—the apex of the Federalist style.

MEDIA

PRINT

Calling All Scots.

Publication of the American Scottish Foundation, Inc.

Contact: Charles H. Haws, Editor.

Address: Box 537, Lenox Hill Station, New York, New York 10021.

Telephone: (212) 988-4468.

Claymore.

Newsletter of Scottish information and services published by the Council of Scottish Clan Associations, Inc.

Address: Box 8947, Richmond, Virginia 23235.

Drochaid/Bridge.

Provides information on Scottish clans, societies, groups, activities and events in Canada and elsewhere.

Address: c/o St. Andrew's Presbyterian Church, 73 Simcoe Street, Toronto, Ontario, Canada M5J 1W9.

Highlander.

A magazine of Scottish heritage.

Contact: Angus J. Ray, Editor.

Address: Box 397, Barrington, Illinois 60011.

Telephone: (708) 382-1035.

Fax: (708) 382-0322.

Rampant Lion.

Published by the Scottish Historic and Research Society of the Delaware Valley; discusses all subjects related to Scotland and the isles.

Contact: Blair C. Stonier, Editor.

Address: 102 St. Pauls Road, Ardmore, Pennsylvania 19003-2811.

Review of Scottish Culture.

Covers all aspects of Scottish ethnology at all social levels over the historical periods.

Contact: Alexander Fenton.

Address: c/o National Museums of Scotland, York Buildings, Queen Street, Edinburgh EH2 1JD, Scotland.

Telephone: 031-255-7534.

Scotia.

An interdisciplinary journal of Scottish studies.

Contact: William S. Rodner.

Address: Old Dominion University, Department of History Arts and Letters Building, Norfolk, Virginia 23529.

Telephone: (804) 683-3933.

Fax: (804) 683-3241.

Scotlands: The Interdisciplinary Journal of Scottish Culture.

Published by Edinburgh University Press; include articles and essays celebrating the richness of Scottish culture found in literature, history music, art, film, and television.

Contact: Christopher MacLachlan, Editor.

Address: 22 George Square, Edinburgh EH8 9LF, Scotland

Telephone: 031-650-4218.

Fax: 031-662-0053.

Scottish Banner.

Contact: Valerie Cairney, Editor.

Address: 755 Center Street, Lewiston, New York 14092.

Telephone: (800) 729-8950.

Fax: (804) 683-3241.

RADIO AND TELEVISION

TNN (The Nashville Network).

The Nashville Network is a 24-hour cable country music channel. Programming is primarily geared toward performance; programming include recorded videos and talk shows, with a strong regional emphasis toward the South and West "The Grand Ole Opry," a radio/television simulcast of the weekly performances of leading country music performers from Nashville's Ryman Auditorium, airs each Saturday evening at 8:00 p.m. on TNN and on a syndicated network of radio stations as well. Begun in 1925, it is the nation's oldest radio program.

WFAE.

"The Thistle and The Shamrock," a weekly Celtic music and cultural appreciation program featuring thematically grouped presentations of Scottish, Irish and Breton music. Carried nationally on National Public Radio.

Contact: Fiona Ritchie.

Address: 1 University Place, Charlotte, North Carolina 28213.

ORGANIZATIONS AND ASSOCIATIONS

American Scottish Foundation.

An organization that promotes Scottish heritage through Scotland House, a cultural center in New York City, and a newsletter, *Calling All Scots.*

Address: 545 Madison Avenue, New York, New York 10022.

Telephone: (212) 605-0338.

Fax: (212) 308-9834.

Association of Scottish Games and Festivals.

Provides information for its members on Highland Games held in the United States; compiles statistics and maintains a computer database.

Address: 47 East Germantown Pike, Plymouth Meeting, Pennsylvania 19462.

Telephone: (215) 825-7268.

Fax: (215) 825-8745.

Council of Scottish Clans and Associations.

Provides information on clan organizations for interested individuals or groups and maintains files of clan newsletters, books, etc. Meets each July at Grandfather Mountain.

Address: Route 1, Box 15A, Lovettsville, Virginia 22080-9703.

Telephone: (703) 822-5292.

Scotch-Irish Foundation.

Members are of Scotch-Irish descent; the foundation compiles records and bibliographic materials on the Scotch-Irish. Affiliated with the Scotch-Irish Society of the United States on America.

Address: 201 Main Street, New Holland, Pennsylvania 17557.

Telephone: (717) 354-4961.

Fax: (717) 355-2227.

Scotch-Irish Society of the United States of America.

An organization of persons of Scotch-Irish heritage; sponsors the work of the Scotch-Irish Foundation.

Contact: Ian Stuart, Esquire.

Address: Box 181, Bryn Mawr, Pennsylvania 19010.

MUSEUMS AND ARCHIVES

There are significant collections on Scotch-Irish and Scottish heritage to be found in university collections; notable ones include the Robert Louis Stevenson Collection at Yale University, the Robert Burns Collection at the University of South Carolina at Columbia, and a new archive of Scottish materials to be housed in Durham, North Carolina, under the sponsorship of North Carolina Central University. There is an important genealogical collection housed at the Ellen Paine Odum Library in Moultrie, Georgia.

SOURCES FOR ADDITIONAL STUDY

An American Odyssey: The Autobiography of Nineteenth Century Scotsman, Robert Brownlee; At the Request of His Children; Napa County, California October 1892, edited by Patricia A. Etter. Fayetteville: University of Arkansas Press, 1986.

Colley, Linda. *Britons: Forging the Nation 1707-1837.* New Haven: Yale University Press, 1992.

A Companion to Scottish Culture, edited by David Daiches. London: Edward Arnold, 1981.

Dobson, David. *Scottish Emigration to Colonial America, 1607-1785.* Athens: University of Georgia Press, 1994.

Finley, John H. *The Coming of the Scot.* New York: Charles Scribner's Sons, 1940.

Finlayson, Iain. *The Scots.* New York: Atheneum, 1987.

Hanna, Charles A. *The Scotch-Irish: The Scot in North Britain, North Ireland, and North America,* two volumes. Baltimore, Maryland: Genealogical Publishing Company, 1968.

Hewitson, Jim. *Tam Blake & Co.: The Story of the Scots in America.* Edinburgh: Canongate Press, 1993.

Jackson, Carlton. *A Social History of the Scotch-Irish*. Lanham, Maryland: Madison Books, 1993.

Johnson, James E. *The Scots and Scotch-Irish in America*. Minneapolis, Minnesota: Lerner Publications, 1966; reprinted, 1991.

Lehmann, William C. *Scottish and Scotch-Irish Contributions to Early American Life and Culture*. Port Washington, New York: Kennikat Press, 1978.

Leyburn, James G. *The Scotch-Irish*. Chapel Hill: The University of North Carolina Press, 1962.

McWhiney, Grady. *Cracker Culture: Celtic Cu toms in the Old South*. Tuscaloosa: University Alabama Press, 1988.

Tichi, Cecelia. *High Lonesome*. Chapel Hill: Ur versity of North Carolina Press, 1994.

Wilson, Charles Reagan and William Ferris. T *Encyclopedia of Southern Culture*. Chapel Hi University of North Carolina Press, 1989.

SERBIAN AMERICANS

by
Bosiljka
Stevanovic

Although Serbian immigrants tended to live in closely knit, homogeneous colonies, they were never so totally isolated as to prevent any penetration of American influence, and that interaction inevitably led to changes in many aspects of their lives.

OVERVIEW

Located in the southeast portion of the former Yugoslavia, Serbia, which occupies 34,116 square miles, is the largest of the former Yugoslavia's six republics. Included in its territory are the autonomous provinces of Kosovo and Vojvodina. Serbia is bordered by Hungary to the north, Romania and Bulgaria to the east, Greece and Albania to the south, Bosnia-Herzegovina to the west, and Croatia to the northwest. Ten million people live in Serbia, 70 percent of whom are Serbian; the remaining 30 percent are of Albanians (especially in Kosovo), Croatians, Hungarians, Slovenenians, and smaller groups of Germans, Gypsies, Romanians, and Turks. Serbians belong to the Eastern Orthodox Church, while the Croatians, Hungarians, and Slovenians are Roman Catholic. The Albanians are primarily Muslim, as are the Turks.

HISTORY

The Serbs settled in the Balkans in the seventh century during the reign of the Byzantine Emperor Heraclius (610-41 A.D.). The Serbs are Slavs, whose prehistoric home had been in the general area of today's Byelorussia and Ukraine. In the sixth century A.D. the Slavs began to leave their land, dispersing themselves to the north, east, west, and south. The Serbs went south, and became known as the South Slavs, or Yugoslavs.

The earliest and the most powerful principalities, or states, were Zeta (located in modern-day Montenegro) and Raska (located in present-day Kosovo). The earliest significant rulers of Zeta were Mutimir (829-917), during whose reign the Serbs accepted Christianity; Cheslav (927-960), an enlightened ruler who created a strong state; and Voislav (1034-1042), who was successful in asserting Zeta's statehood from Byzantium. His son Michael followed (1050-1082), and during his reign the church broke into two: the Western church, or the Roman Catholic church, and the Eastern Orthodox church, headed by a Patriarch and with Constantinople as its papal seat.

In time, Zeta weakened and Raska achieved great political and military power. The ascension to the throne of Raska by the Grand Zupan Stefan Nemanja (1114-1200) marks one of the most important events in Serbian history. Founding the Nemanjic Dynasty, which was to rule for the next 200 years, he ushered in the Golden Age of Serbian medieval history. An able politician and statesman, Stefan Nemanja ruled from 1168 to 1196, consolidating his political power within the state, undertaking Serbia's territorial expansion, and achieving independence from Byzantium. Religiously, however, Serbia became irreversibly tied to the Eastern rites and traditions of Byzantium. In 1196 he called an assembly of nobles and announced his abdication in favor of his son Stefan Prvovencani, or Stefan the First Crowned. Stefan married Anna Dondolo, the granddaughter of the Venetian Doge Enrico Dondolo, thus securing his power. In 1217 Pope Honorius III sent his legate with a royal crown for Stefan, who became Stefan Prvovencani, or the First Crowned. The crowning confirmed the independence of Serbia, and also brought about the recognition of the Serbian state as an European state.

King Stefan then turned his attention to the creation of an independent and national church. His brother Sava undertook numerous diplomatic missions before he was able to attain this goal, and in 1219 he was consecrated as the First Archbishop of the Serbian Autocephalus (autonomous) Church. This event marks another cornerstone in Serbian history and Serbian Orthodoxy, for in 1221 Archbishop Sava was able to crown his brother King Stefan again, this time according to the religious rites and customs of the Eastern Orthodox Church.

Saint Sava is one of the most sacred and the venerated historical figures in the minds and hearts of Serbs. Aside from contributing enormously to education and literacy in general, Saint Sava, together with King Stefan, wrote the first Serbian literary work, a biography of their father.

As the Serbian medieval state matured politically, it also developed a solid and prosperous economy. The state's Golden Age reached its apogee during the reign of Czar Dusan Silni Emperor Dusan the Mighty (1308-1355). An extremely capable ruler, he secured and expanded the Serbian state, while richly endowing the Serbian Orthodox Church, which was the center of learning and artistic creativity, predating even the beginnings of the Italian Renaissance. He elevated the head of the church to the Patriarchy, and consolidated the internal affairs through the Emperor's *Zakonik*, the written Code of Laws, unique in Europe at that time. Emperor Dushan's accomplishments were such that Serbs today continue to draw inspiration and solace from the national pride and glory achieved during his time.

The Battle of Kosovo Polje ("The Field of Blackbirds") on June 28, 1389, fought between the Ottoman Turks led by Sultan Murad I (1319-1389), and the Serbs led by Czar Lazar (1329-1389) changed the course of Serbian history for centuries to come, for the Serbian defeat was followed by 500 years of Turkish rule and domination. Over the centuries Serbia remained totally isolated from the rest of Europe, and could not participate in the enormous political changes or cultural and industrial progress unfolding in other European states.

The land and all other natural resources became the Sultan's domain. The Turks became landowners called *sipahis*, while the Serbs were reduced to the status of *raya*, the populace who worked the land they previously had owned; and their labor was called *kulluk*, a term which to this day denotes the work of slaves. Every four years the countryside was raided; small Serbian male children were forcibly taken from their families and brought to Istanbul, where they were raised and trained to become Janissaries, the Ottoman's elite military unit. Another particularly distasteful practice was to use economic pressures to convert people to Islam.

In 1804 Karadjordje (Black George, or Karadjordjevic) Petrovic (1752-1817), a merchant, led the First Serbian Uprising against the Turks. Severe Turkish reprisals caused many Serbian leaders to escape north to Vojvodina, where he monasteries at Fruska Gora became Serbian cultural strongholds. Among those who escaped was Milos Obrenovic (born Milosh Obrenovich; 1780-1860), a local administrator, who emerged as the leader of the Second Serbian Uprising against the Turks in 1815. In 1829 Serbia was granted autonomy by the Turkish Sultan under a hereditary prince. A lengthy feud between the Karadjordjevic and Obrenovic dynasties ensued.

Serbia's struggle to establish itself as an independent nation in the nineteenth century was marked by many changes of rulers and forms of government, until a monarchy was established in 1882, followed by a constitutional monarchy in 1903. Serbia also emerged as the strongest Balkan state at the conclusion of the First Balkan War against the Ottoman Empire in 1912, when Serbia, Montenegro, Greece, and Bulgaria formed an alliance (the Balkan League) and defeated the Turks.

MODERN ERA

Fearing Serbia and her leading role in the determination to rid the Balkans of all foreign domination, the Austro-Hungarian government systematically pressured Serbia both politically and economically, until the tensions between the two nations led to the events that ignited World War I. When Archduke Franz Ferdinand and his wife, Sophie, chose to review the troops in Sarajevo on St. Vitus Day, June 28, 1914—the most sacred date of the Serbian calendar, commemorating the Battle of Kosovo—a small secret association called "Young Bosnia" had Gavrilo Princip, one its their members, carry out the assassination of the Archduke and his wife. Austria, accusing Serbia of complicity, responded with an immediate ultimatum, compliance with which would have presented a serious threat to the sovereignty of Serbia. Having just fought two Balkan Wars, and not wanting to get involved in another conflict, Serbia offered a compromise. Austria rejected these terms and declared war on Serbia on July 28, 1914, precipitating World War I.

Although heavily outnumbered and drained of resources from the just concluded Balkan Wars, the Serbian army initially fought successfully against Austria-Hungary, but the addition of the German army to the Austrian side tipped the balance against Serbia. Eventually, the ravaged Serbian army had to retreat through Albania toward the southern Adriatic Sea, where the remnants were picked up by French war ships. After being reconstituted and reequipped, this strengthened Serbian army broke through the Salonika Front in late 1916, and over the next year and a half successfully fought its way north, culminating in the recapture of Belgrade in October of 1918. This victory significantly contributed to the final collapse of the Austro-Hungarian monarchy.

The physical destruction of Serbia had been staggering, but the growing significance of the Pan Slavic movement led to the establishment of the Kingdom of the Serbs, Croats, and Slovenes, including Bosnian Muslims and Macedonians, later renamed Yugoslavia ("the land of the South Slavs") by the country's king, Alexander Karadjordjevic (1888-1934).

Despite the 1934 assassination of King Alexander in Marseille, the country prospered as a result of increased trade and growing industrialization. This period was brought to a sudden halt by the bombing of Belgrade on April 6, 1941, which preceded the invading armies of Nazi Germany. The Yugoslav defenses collapsed within two weeks and the country was dismembered. Some parts of Yugoslavia were ceded to Italy, Hungary, and Bulgaria; the remaining areas were divided into two occupation zones: one German, consisting of Serbia proper; the other Italian, consisting of Montenegro and Dalmatia. In less than a week after the beginning of hostilities, an Independent State of Croatia was established as a satellite to the Axis Powers, headed by Ante Pavelic, the leader of the Croat *Ustasi* (Ustashi) Party.

The government and King Peter II fled to London. Some Serbian troops withdrew to the mountains and organized themselves as guerrillas, under the leadership of Colonel Draza Mihailovic, and became known as the Yugoslav Army in the Homeland, or more popularly, *Cetnik* (Chetnik), from the word *ceta*, meaning a small fighting group. Promoted to general and named Minister of War by the government in exile, Mihailovic's aim was to fight alongside the Allies in order to defeat the Axis powers, to liberate his country, and to restore democracy.

After Germany attacked the Soviet Union in June 1941, the Yugoslav Communists, under the leadership of Josip Broz Tito, formed another guerrilla movement, which they called the National Liberation Movement, or Partisans. It soon became clear that the Serbs had to fight not only the Germans, but also the Partisans and the Ustashi, who were joined by two Muslim divisions from Bosnia. The Ustashi instituted a reign of terror which led to a massacre of 500,000 to 700,000

Serbs, as well as 50,000 Jews and 20,000 Gypsies. To counter Mihailovic's guerrilla attacks, the Germans used reprisals against the civilian population, taking 50 hostages for every soldier killed, and 100 for every officer; thus, in one instance alone they executed 7,000 Serbs in a single day (October 21, 1941) in the city of Kragujevac, including school children driven out of their classrooms that morning.

Tito's Partisans, conducting a campaign of anti-Chetnik propaganda, gained the support of the Allies, who withdrew their endorsement of Mihailovic's Chetniks. Operating mainly in Ustashi territory, namely Croatia and the mountain ranges of Bosnia-Herzegovina, the Partisans were joined by many Serbs who were attempting to escape Ustashi terror. However, the communists did not have the support of the Serbian population at large.

Emerging victorious at the end of the war, Tito set out to further secure the power of the Communist Party and his own. Purging the country of its enemies, the new government tried and executed General Draza Mihailovic. After the redrawing of the internal borders, Tito's Yugoslavia became a federation of six republics: Serbia, Croatia, Slovenia, Bosnia-Herzegovina, Montenegro, Makedonija, and two autonomous provinces: Kosovo and Vojvodina, which were carved out of the larger Serbia.

In 1948 Tito successfully achieved a separation from Joseph Stalin, the Soviet leader, and his more radical brand of communism; this prompted the West to view Tito as a communist "with a human face." Though Tito enjoyed a reputation as an able statesman in the eyes of the western nations, he nonetheless left a legacy of political, economic, and ethnic problems, as well as a political system unable to cope with them. Economically, Yugoslavia was never solvent, and politically, unresolved questions along national and genocide lines are, once again, leading to bloodshed and the dismemberment of Yugoslavia, as witnessed by the latest events.

MAJOR IMMIGRATION WAVES

While the earliest Serbian immigrants came to the United States after 1815, the largest wave of immigration took place from 1880 to 1914. There were arrivals between the two world wars followed by refugees and displaced persons after World War II. Lastly, arrivals since 1965 have included the influx resulting from current events in the former Yugoslavia. Generally speaking, it is difficult to determine the exact number of Serbs who came to America in the early waves of immigration because immigration records often did not distinguish between various Slavic and, especially, South Slavic groups. The term Slavonic was most often used in recording immigrants from the various parts of the Eastern Europe. Church records are more helpful in distinguishing the Serbs, for these documents clearly state religious orientation of the parishioners. In addition, census statistics compiled before World War I had further confused the issue by listing immigrants by their country of origin. Thus, the Serbs could be included with the Croats, Slovenians, Austro-Hungarians, Turks, Bulgarians, or Romanians, or simply listed as Yugoslavs after 1929, when the kingdom of the Serbs, Croats, and Slovenes was renamed Yugoslavia. According to the 1990 U.S. Census figures, there are 116,795 Americans of Serbian origin living in the United States. It is impossible to tell, however, how many out of the 257,995 who in 1990 reported Yugoslavian origin actually have Serbian ancestry. It can safely be assumed that the total number of Serbian Americans today might vary from 200,000 to 350,000 and up to 400,000, according to some estimates. By American standards, this is a rather small immigrant group.

The smallest numbers of Serbian immigrants came from Serbia proper. The people there still worked large family lands that formed collectives called *zadruga*, which provided enough economic stability to entice them to stay. In addition, the emergence of Serbia as an independent nation during the nineteenth century offered hope for more political stability.

The historical map of the Balkans in the early 1800s explains the patterns of Serbian immigration. The Serbs who came to America at that time were from the areas which were under the domination of either Austro-Hungarian or the Turkish Empire.

Because the Austrian Empire was constantly subjected to Turkish invasions, it encouraged Serbian families to settle along the frontiers dividing the two powers, giving them land, religious, economic, and political freedom. In exchange, the Serbs agreed to protect the border areas against the Turks and to build fortifications in peacetime. The Austrian Emperor Ferdinand I (1503-1564) officially recognized this agreement in 1538, and granted self-government to the Serbian villages.

In 1691 Emperor Leopold I (1640-1705) signed the "Privilegija," a document which granted the same rights to the Serbs who had fled to the Vojvodina region. Thus, a number of generations of Serbs formed a "buffer population" between the Austro-Hungarian and Turkish Empires. Therefore, the first Serbs to leave their native land for America were from the military frontier areas—Kordun, Krajina, Luka, Slavonija, Vojvodina, Dalmatia, and other coastal areas—precisely the areas where generations earlier had taken refuge from Turkish reprisal. Serbs from Dalmatia were actually the first ones to emigrate because of the close proximity to the sea and relative ease of transportation offered by the steam operated ships.

Poverty and ethnic and religious persecutions were behind the decisions to leave one's village, family, and way of life for America, whose allure as the land of opportunity appealed to able-bodied young men. In 1869 the Austrian Emperor dissolved the age-old agreement with the Granicaris. The Serbs felt betrayed by the Emperor, and in the words of Michael Pupin, who came from Vojvodina, they felt "delivered to the Hungarians," who then subjected them to a severe campaign of Magyarization, insisting on officially the Hungarian language in schools and courts, as well as seeking to convert them to Roman Catholicism.

The greatest numbers of Serbs arrived during the peak period of immigration to America between 1880 and 1914 from Austro-Hungarian Croatia, Slavonia, and Vojvodina, as well as from Montenegro. Although the overwhelming majority of Serbian immigrants were uneducated, unskilled men in their prime working years—mostly peasants from the countryside—they did not come to America particularly to be farmers, and they did not intend to stay. Instead, they wanted to remain in the United States long enough to earn money enabling them to return home and improve the lives of their families, in keeping with a practice called *pecalba* (pechalba). They settled in the mining areas of Pennsylvania, Ohio, West Virginia, northern Minnesota, Montana, Nevada, Arizona, and Colorado, as well as in the big industrial cities of Pittsburgh, Cleveland, and Chicago, working in steel mills and related industries. Others found works with the major meatpacking companies in Chicago, Milwaukee, Kansas City, Omaha, and St. Paul, and in the lumber industries in the Pacific Northwest. The Serbian motto *covek mora da radi*, "a man has to work" served them very well in this country.

ACCULTURATION AND ASSIMILATION

It can be argued that assimilation into American life and society's acceptance of the new immigrants was uneven at best. On the one hand, some Serbians were impressed by the freedom and openness of the Americans as well as by the opportunities available to all. On the other hand, late nineteenth-century Americans, feeling threatened by the large numbers of new immigrants from southern and eastern Europe, increasingly expressed anti-immigrant sentiment. The Immigration Restriction League founded in Boston in 1894 attempted to achieve the curbing of this type of immigrant tide by advocating the literacy test, which required immigrants over 16 years of age to be literate. Since the eastern and southern Europeans were less literate than their counterparts from northern and western Europe, it was clear where the actions of the League were going to lead. The immigration laws from 1921 and 1924 established a national origins system and set annual quotas for each nationality based on the percentage of the total of that nationality already living in America. This was based on the 1890 and 1910 census, which respectively assigned a two percent and a three percent annual quotas, or 671, and later 942, per year for all immigrants from Yugoslavia.

The majority of the earlier Serbian immigrants endured the hardships and found that the degree of freedom and the opportunities available to them in America were worth staying for. However, the Great Depression of the 1930s adversely affected the old Serbian immigrant communities. Discouraged, many returned to their homeland.

The immigrants who arrived after 1945 were refugees from World War II. Among their numbers were former army officers and soldiers who had either been prisoners of war or attached to the Allied Forces; people deported to Nazi Germany as slave-laborers; and supporters of General Mihailovic during the Civil War who fled following the communist takeover. Many Serbs, therefore, found a new home in America under the Displaced Persons Act of 1948 and the Refugee Relief Act of 1953.

The differences between this wave of Serbian immigration and the previous ones are substantial. The new immigrants came mainly from the urban areas in Serbia proper rather than the rural areas outside Serbia; they came for political reasons rather than economic reasons, and tended to see themselves as emigres rather than immigrants. They were on the whole highly educated members of the middle and upper classes, many among them had considerable social status, and they came to join already well-established Serbian communities. Politically minded, many also saw this country as a safehouse in which to develop strategic operations in opposition to the Yugoslav communist state, rather than a new homeland.

Recent immigration resulting from the economic and political failures of the communist system reverts to being motivated by the economy once again, but does not offer the sense of cohesiveness experienced by earlier groups. Until the dissolution of Yugoslavia beginning in 1991, the newest immigrants had come and gone freely between America and Serbia. Some worked for American companies, some for Yugoslav companies in the United States; and many, after staying abroad for a number of years went back to Yugoslavia with hard currency and marketable skills.

In America, the Serbian churches maintain parish Sunday schools where children learn the language, customs and traditions of their ancestors. The Serbian Orthodox Diocese at the St. Sava Monastery in Libertyville, Illinois, runs a summer camp as well as the parish school. The children of immigrants have mostly attended public schools, and in the early days it was often the case that these children were the only source of information about American culture and history for Serbian adults.

ORGANIZATIONS

In the early stages of Serbian immigration, fraternal mutual aid societies and insurance companies preceded the church as the centers of Serbian American community life. These were formed for economic reasons, as the new arrivals needed to find ways to protect themselves against the hazards of dangerous and life-threatening work in mines, foundries, or factories. In the early years the Serbs readily joined other Slavic groups, such as the Slavonic Benevolent Organization founded in San Francisco in 1857, which served all South Slavs.

In time, Serbian immigrants formed their own organizations, starting as local groups, lodges, assemblies, and societies whose goals were the preservation of culture, social welfare, and fraternal sentiment. The first such organization was the Srpsko Crnogorsko Literarno i Dobrotvorno Drustvo (Serbian-Montenegrin Literary and Benevolent

Society) founded in San Francisco in 1880, then Srpsko Jedinstvo (Serbian Unity) in Chicago in 1894. Other societies followed and began to form federations, such as the Srpsko Crnogorski Savez (Serbian-Montenegrin Federation) whose headquarters were in Butte, Montana, and which ceased to exist because most of its members left to fight in the Balkan Wars (1912-1913) and in World War I.

In the eastern section of the United States, eight Serbian lodges, which were part of the Russian Orthodox Society, formed their own organization in McKeesport, Pennsylvania, in 1901. Originally called Srpki Pravoslavni Savez-"Srbobran" (Serbian Orthodox Federation-"Srbobran"), it became known in 1929 as Srpski Narodni Savez (Serbian National Federation, SNF), when other organizations joined it, such as Savez Sjedinjenih Srba-Sloga (Federation of United Serbs-"Concord"). The last organization to join this federation was Srpski Potporni Savez-"Jedinstvo" (Serbian Benevolent Federation-"Unity") from Cleveland, Ohio, in 1963. The events around this merger produced an atmosphere of "politicking" which provided the Serbian American communities with an arena all its own, and although somewhat outside from the mainstream of American political life, it served to reinforce their Serbian identity.

The SNF, whose headquarters were and still are in Pittsburgh, was first an insurance organization, evolving into the single most important Serbian organization. Its founder, Sava Hajdin, said at one point: "We never wished our federation to be only the association of benevolent societies. We wished it to be the matrix of Serbianism in America and the bastion of the idea of St. Sava ." Indeed, the humanitarian side of its work included the cooperation with other organizations to provide aid to Serbia during both World Wars. After the war, the federation sent relief to refugees and prisoners of war, and sponsored thousands of new immigrants.

On the cultural level, since 1906 the SNF has been publishing its weekly bilingual newspaper, "Amerikanski Srbobran"; it provides scholarships and maintains a fund for printing and free distribution of Serbian primers, used by young people to learn the language of their ancestors. It sponsors well-attended events, such as tournaments for soccer, tennis, golf, and bowling, as well as a three-day "Serbian Days" celebration each summer. In the last decade or so it has been actively raising funds for the building of St. Sava Cathedral on Vrachar Hill in Belgrade, and lastly, it is very much involved in providing humanitarian help in the latest conflict.

The oldest and largest Serbian patriotic organization is the Srpska Narodna Odbrana (Serbian National Defense). Organized in 1914 in New York by Michael Pupin, it recruited volunteers for World War I, and also sent large monetary aid to Serbia. Inactive in the 1920s and 1930s, the organization was revived during World War II by the great Serbian poet and diplomat-in-exile, Jovan Ducic (1871-1943). Declaring its support for the Cetniks of General Mihailovic, who instituted a campaign of guerrilla warfare in Yugoslavia, the SND began a radio program in Chicago, and published the periodical *American Serb* from 1944-48.

After the war the SND sent food and relief supplies to thousands of Serbs dispersed in various displaced persons camps, and provided scholarships to Serbian students. In cooperation with the Serbian Orthodox Diocese and Srpska Bratska Pomoc (Serbian Fraternal Aid) the SND brought thousands of displaced persons to America. Much to their chagrin, the sponsors discovered that the new immigrants were politically very much at odds with each other, and soon the ill effects were felt in the organization. Attempts were made to bring back some unity, and in 1947 the SND sponsored an All-Serb Congress in Chicago. The Serbian National Committee was formed, headed by Konstantin Fotic (Constantin Fotitch) the former Yugoslav Ambassador to the United States. Another conference was held in Akron, Ohio, in 1949, during which the Serbian National Council was formed. The highly respected Bishop Nikolaj Velimirovic, himself a refugee, attended, but failed to end the discord. In the 1960s the then president of the organization, Dr. Uros Seffer (Urosh Seferovich), and his followers sided with Bishop Dionisije's autonomous Serbian church, while the supporters of the church in Belgrade organized their own American Serbian National Defense. Srpska Narodna Odbrana survived this turmoil and still publishes *Sloboda (Liberty)*.

Women's organizations among Serbian Americans are various groups of sisterhoods known as Kolo Srpskih Sestara, or Serbian Sisters Circles. They were organized in the beginning of the twentieth century in Pittsburgh, Cincinnati, and Chicago. The federation of Circles of Serbian Sisters was formed in 1945 when representatives of more than thirty sisterhoods met in Libertyville, Illinois. They are active in fundraising activities and support children's camps and charities. Being closely associated with the Serbian church, they, unfortunately, were affected by the schism in the church.

ARTS AND POPULAR CULTURE

Music is a very important role in the Serbian American community. The early Serbian immigrants from the Military Frontier areas brought with them their native mandolin-like string instrument called a tamburica (tamburitza), which varies in five different sizes and ranges. George Kachar, one of the first teachers of tamburitza in America, brought the love for his music from his homeland to a small mining town in Colorado, where he taught during the 1920s. His most remarkable students were four Popovich brothers who later became famous as the Popovich Brothers of South Chicago. Having started by traveling from community to community, they gained prominence by delighting Serbian American audiences for sixty years with their art, while also achieving national recognition by appearances at the White House and by participating in the "Salute to Immigrant Cultures" during the Statue of Liberty celebrations held in 1986.

During the annual Tamburitza Extravaganza Festival, as many as twenty bands from around the country perform for three days, with performers undoubtedly vying for the Tamburitza Hall of Fame in St. Louis, Missouri. The new students and performers are actively recruited and trained by the Duquesne University Tamburitzans, which maintains a folklore institute, grants scholarships for promising students, and makes good use of the enthusiasm generously shared by the junior team called "Tammies." A few active tamburitza manufacturers in the United States continue to assure an adequate supply of this favorite instrument.

The immigrants who came to America after World War II brought in a different style of music performed on accordions. Drums, keyboards, and the amplified modern instruments came into use in the last few decades. These musical groups mostly play the newly composed folk music, which combines traditional instruments, melodies, and styles with modern instruments, lyrics, and production techniques. Generally speaking, be they older or newer immigrants, the Serbs sing of love and death, of parting and hope, of the tragedy that accompanied them throughout their history, and of the heroic deeds that helped them triumph over adversity. One of the most beloved and nostalgic songs is *Tamo deleko*, "Far Away," referring to Serbia's distance from the United States.

Serbian American choirs, performing mainly at social functions, were formed early on, such as the Gorski Vijenac (Mountain Wreath) Choir in Pittsburgh in 1901, and the Branko Radicevic

These women are performing a traditional Serbian dance at the Serbian Festival.

Choir in Chicago in 1906. There were no church choirs in the early part of the twentieth century, until Vladimir Lugonja (1898-1977) founded the Serbian Singing Foundation of the USA and Canada (SSF) in 1931 as an antidote to the Great Depression. Many choirs joined in, connected with the church parishes, and totaled thirty by World War II. Their membership in the federation was contingent on their singing in church. Since 1935, the federation has been sponsoring annual concerts and competitions where both secular and liturgical music are performed. A number of Serbian priests have come from the ranks of the SSF; many are well known directors and conductors such as Adam Popovich, Director of South Chicago's SLOBODA. A respected veteran of the Serbian American choir movement, Popovich and his choir performed at the White House for Dwight D. Eisenhower's presidential inauguration.

The *gusle*, another symbol of Serbianism, is a string instrument similar to a violin. Gusle musicians have used it since the earliest days of the Serbian kingdom in accompanying the chanting of epic poetry. Although this instrument is capable of rendering only a few melancholy notes, the *guslar*, or bard, manages to evoke myriad emotions. During the Ottoman period of Serbian history the guslari traveled from village to village bringing news and keeping alive ancient Serbian heroic epics and ballads, which played a role of utmost importance in the development and

preservation of the Serbian national conscience and character.

The *kolo*, meaning the circle, is the Serbian national dance, and by extention the Serbian American dance. Danced in a circle as well in a single line, the dancers hold each other's hands or belts, and no one, from teenagers to grandparents, can resist the lively tunes and sprightly motions. A good number of folk dancing ensembles throughout America has kept alive the rich repertoire of folk dancing, and it is difficult to imagine any kind of Serbian celebrations without a performance of one such ensemble.

CUISINE

Serbian cuisine over the centuries has adopted the tastes and flavors of Middle Eastern, Turkish Hungarian, and Austrian foods. Roast suckling pig and lamb are still very much appreciated and served on festive occasions. Serbs are also fond of casserole dishes with or without meat; pies (consisting of meat, cheese, or fruit); all kinds of fried foods, and an assortment of cakes, cookies, and condiments that rival the displays in Vienna and Budapest.

A few representative dishes would be *sarma*, stuffed cabbage, made from leaves of sour cabbage, or from wine leaves, and chopped beef or veal, often in combination with chopped pork, onions, smoked meat for added flavor; Serbs especially appreciate *gibanjica*, or *pita gibanjica*, a cheese pie made with feta or cottage cheese (an American substitute for the cheese used in the homeland), or the combination of both, butter, filo pastry leaves, eggs, and milk. *Cevapcici*, the summer time favorite for cook-outs, are small barbecued sausage-like pieces, prepared from a combination of freshly chopped pork, lamb, veal, and beef, and served with raw onions.

Serbs like to drink wine, beer, and especially the plum brandy called *sljivovica*, which is the national drink, made from *sljiva*, or plums, the Serbian national fruit. Another word for sljivovica is *rakija*, which is once-distilled plum brandy; twice-distilled sljivovica is called *prepecenica*. Serbs drink at all kinds of celebrations: weddings, baptisms, and krsna slavas; every raised glass is accompanied with the exclamation: "Ziveli," or "Live long!" It is not surprising that many Serbs found California to be the perfect place for continuing the family tradition of growing grapes to produce wine, or plums for sljivovica.

TRADITIONAL COSTUMES

Serbian traditional clothing consists of richly embroidered, colorful garments, which are worn today only by the dancers in the folkloric dance ensembles, or perhaps at other events inspired by folk motives, such as picnics, harvests, or church festivals. Each region has its own particular motives and ways of wearing these costumes, making it easy to discern one from another. The typical costume for women from Serbia proper consists of a fine linen blouse richly embroidered with floral or folk motifs; a vest called a *jelek*, cut low under the breast, made of velvet, embroidered with silver and gold thread, and worn tightly around the waist; an ample colorful skirt accompanied by an embroidered apron and a white linen petticoat worn longer than the skirt to show off the hand-crocheted lace; knitted and embroidered stockings; and a pair of handmade leather slipper-like footwear called *opanci*. The hair is long and braided; the braids are sometimes worn down the back or twisted in a bun around the head.

The costume for men consists of a head cap called a *sajkaca*, a white linen shirt, a wool jacket, and pants (The jacket is short with sober decorations and the pants are worn tight around the knees.) A richly decorated sash is tied around the waist. The fabrics used were always homegrown, spun, or woven, and the costumes were made at home. The early immigrants stood out in an American crowd by the way their clothes looked, which provided an easy target for ridicule. Today, these costumes have given way to standard dress, and if still in existence, are brought out only at folk festivals.

LANGUAGE

The Serbian language is part of the Slavic language group to which belong Russian, Ukrainian, Polish, Czech, Slovak, Croatian, Bulgarian, and Macedonian. In the seventh century two Greek missionaries, Cyril and Methodius, created the Slavic alphabet, called the Cyrillic, which is still used by the Russians, Serbs, Ukrainians, Bulgarians, and Macedonians. The Old Slavonic, or Staroslovenski, was the original literary language of all the Slavs. It evolved into the Church Slavonic, or Crkvenoslovenski, which in turn engendered the Serb Church Slavonic, the Serb literary language up until the nineteenth century.

In the early nineteenth century Vuk Srefanvoic Karadjic (1787-1864), who become known as the father of the "modern" Serbian language, reconstructed the alphabet to conform it phonetically with the oral language, thus recognizing the spoken language as the literary language; this resulted in reawakening Serbian culture in general. He published the first Serbian dictionary in 1818, and collected and published volumes of epic and lyrical poetry that had survived in the oral tradition in the Serbian countryside. His voluminous correspondence is an important political and literary document.

Immigrants were confronted with the modification of their language as it came into contact with English, resulting in the incorporation of many English words into everyday use, especially those that were needed to communicate in a more complex society and did not exist in their rural vocabulary. Another American influence can be seen in the fact that many immigrants changed their names for simplification. Often the changing of names was done by either the immigration officers at the time of entry into the United States, or by the employers at the factories or mines who were not accustomed to dealing with complicated Slavic names. At other times, the immigrants themselves opted for simpler names, either for business reasons, or to escape being a target for ridicule. Also, some changes were the result of the immigrants' desire to show loyalty to their adopted country; thus, the names were either simply translated—e.g., Ivan into John,

Ivanovic into Johnson—or the diacritical marks over the letters "c" and the "s" were dropped and replaced by English-sounding equivalents such as Sasha for Sasa and Simich for Simic.

GREETINGS

Here are a few basic greetings and saying in Serbian: *dobro jutro* ("dobro yutro")—good morning; *dobar dan* (pronounced as written)—good day; *dobro vece* ("dobro vetche")—good evening; *zdravo* (pronounced as written)—greetings; *hvala* ("khvala")—thank you; *dobro dosli* ("dobro doshli")—welcome.

FAMILY AND COMMUNITY DYNAMICS

Although though Serbian immigrants tended to live in closely knit, homogeneous colonies, they were never so totally isolated as to prevent any penetration of American influence, and that interaction inevitably led to changes in many aspects of their lives. Their children and grandchildren only rarely adhere to the old ways, and as a result the immigrant heritage becomes a strange mixture of old-country and American cultural elements.

In their homeland the immigrants had been primarily farmers; all the family members lived together in *zadrugas*, large family cooperatives, where everyone worked on the family land, maintaining strong family ties, as well as observing a strict hierarchical order from the head of the *zadruga*, called *srareshina*, down to the youngest child. In America, each family member's occupation could be different, leading to less interdependence among the family members, without, however, destroying the closeness of family ties. To a great extent Serbian and Serbian American households still include grandparents, or other elderly relatives needing care and help. It is also a common practice to have grandparents care for young children while the parents are working, as well as take charge of housekeeping in general. Elderly parents (or close relatives) live out their lives at home surrounded by their children and grandchildren. The structure of a typical Serbian American family also retains close relationships with the extended family—aunts, uncles, and cousins—going back a few generations, thus plac-

ing emphasis on strong emotional ties as well as offering a good family support system.

RELIGION

The Serbs accepted Christianity in the ninth century due to the work of the two Greek brothers, missionaries from Salonika, Cyril and Methodius, also called "Apostles of the Slavs." Since that time, and especially since the 1219 establishment of the Serbian Orthodox Autonomous church by King Stefan Prvovencani, the Serbs have strongly identified their religion with their ethnic heritage. *Srpstvo*, or being Serbian, expresses this concept of the Serbian identity as encompassing the nation, its historic heritage, church, language, and other cultural traditions. Serbian communal life in the United States mainly evolved and, to a large degree, still revolves around the church parish.

Orthodoxy, which means "correct worship", partly differs from other Christian practices in that priests are allowed to marry and in its use of the Julian calendar, which is 13 days behind the Gregorian calendar. Thus, for example, the Serbs celebrate Christmas on January 7th instead of December 25th.

Serbian churches, both in America and in the homeland, feature the Altar, a carved Iconostasis, and richly painted icons. A pedestal called *Nalonj*, placed at a respectable distance from the altar, is used to exhibit the icon of the Saint the particular church is named after, and upon entering the church everyone stops there to make the sign of the cross and kiss the icon.

The first Serbian churches in America were established in Jackson, California, in 1893, followed by McKeesport, Pennsylvania (1901), and Steelton, Pennsylvania (1903). At that time all Serbian churches were under the jurisdiction of the Russian Orthodox church, although served by Serbian priests. The first American-born Serbian Orthodox priest, the Reverend Sebastian Dabovich (1863-1940), the son of a Serbian pioneer in California, was appointed head of the Serbian mission in the United States by the Patriarch in Moscow in 1905.

In 1919 a separate Serbian Orthodox Diocese in North America and Canada was created under the leadership of the Reverend Mardary Uskokovich (d. 1935), who later became the first bishop of the new Diocese, establishing his seat in Libertyville, Illinois, in 1927. From 1940 to 1963 the Diocese was headed by Bishop Dionisije Milivojevic. During World War II the Diocese was instrumental in arranging for the immigration of refugees, as well as placing refugee priests. The Diocese published the first English language Serbian newspaper, the *Serbian Orthodox Herald*. In 1949 the Clergy Association of the Serbian Orthodox Diocese of the United States and Canada formed their united headquarters in Pittsburgh, Pennsylvania. *Orthodoxy* was their official publication.

In 1963 the Serbian Diocese of North America suffered a painful schism and split into two groups: one wanted an independent Serbian Orthodox church in America; the other insisted on keeping the alliance with the Patriarchy in Belgrade. The immigrant community became bitterly divided. The old settlers felt that the primary role of the church was to uphold Orthodoxy and to maintain the spiritual life in the communities, while the newer immigrants saw the need to defend themselves against the Communist threat.

The church remains divided, although it officially reconciled during the Holy Liturgy jointly celebrated on February 15, 1992 by the Patriarch Pavle of Belgrade and the Metropolitan Irinej, the head of the Free Church in America, whose seat is in New Gracancia (Third Lake, Illinois). The two contending factions have worked on a new church constitution, a document expected to be administratively complete in 1995 and intended to seal the reunification.

The two most important religious holidays of the year for Serbian Americans are *Bozic* (Christmas), and *Uskrs* (Easter). Both are celebrated for three days. Bozich starts with *Tucindan* (two days before Christmas) when a young pig is prepared to be barbecued for Christmas dinner, or *Bozicna vecera*. On the day before Christmas—called *Badnji Dan*—the *badnjak*, or Yule Log, is placed outside the house, and the *pecenica*, or roasted pig, is prepared. In the evening straw is placed under the table to represent the manger, the Yule log is cut and brought in for burning, and the family gathers for a Lenten Christmas Eve dinner. *Bozicni Post*, the Christmas Lenten, is observed for six weeks prior to Christmas, during which a diet without milk, dairy products, meat, or eggs is maintained. This strict observance is practiced by fewer people today, as most are willing to fast only for a week prior to Christmas.

On Christmas Day, *cesnica*, a round bread, is baked from wheat flour. A coin placed inside the bread brings good luck throughout the year to the person who finds it. The family goes to church early on Christmas Day, and upon return home the most festive meal of the year is served. The father lights a candle and incense, and says a prayer. The family turns the *Chesnica* from left to right and sings the Christmas hymn *Rozdestvo Tvoje*, which glorifies the birth of Christ. The cesnica is broken and each member of the family receives a piece, leaving one portion for an unexpected guest. Each person kisses the person next to him three times with the greeting *Hristos se rodi*, "Christ is born," and receives in reply *Vaistinu se rodi*, "Indeed He is born."

In America, the burning of the *badnjak* is done at church after Christmas Eve mass, and an elaborate Lenten Christmas Eve dinner is served in the parish hall for those who wish to participate.

Traditionally, three Sundays before Christmas are dedicated to the family: *Detinjci*, the Children's Day; *Materice*, the Mother's Day; and *Ocevi*, Father's Day. On each of these days the celebrants are tied to an object and their release is obtained with a gift.

Uskrs (Easter), is considered the holiest of holidays, and is celebrated from Good Friday to Easter Sunday. A seven-week Lenten period is observed, also without fish, meat, eggs, milk, or dairy products, which is practiced today in altered fashion as well. *Vrbica*, or Palm Sunday, is observed on the last Sunday before Easter when the willow branches are blessed and distributed to all present. This service is rendered especially beautiful and significant by the presence of children, dressed in fine new clothes worn for the first time, with little bells hanging from their necks on Serbian tricolor ribbons—red, blue, and white—waiting for the whole congregation to start an outside procession encircling the church three times.

Easter celebrations cannot be conceived without roasted lamb and colored eggs. The eggs symbolize spring and the renewal of the life cycle as well as *Vaskrsenje*, the Easter Resurrection. Each color as well as each design has a specific meaning in this age old folk art form of egg decorating.

The Easter Mass is the most splendid one. The doors of the iconostasis, which remain closed until the symbolic moment of *Hristovo Voskresenje*, or "Christ's Resurrection," open wide; the church bells ring, and the priest dressed in his gold vestments steps forward. The congregation sings a hymn of rejoicing, and a procession led by the banner of Resurrection encircles the church three times while the worshippers carry lit candles. The greetings *Hristos voskrese*, "Christ has risen," and *Vaistinu voskrese*, "He has risen indeed," are exchanged three times.

The most important Serbian tradition is the yearly observance of *Krsna Slava*, the Patron Saint's Day. This uniquely Serbian religious holiday, reminiscent of the prehistoric harvest festivals, is celebrated once a year in commemoration of the family's conversion to Christianity, when each family chose its patron saint, which derived from the custom of worshipping protective spirits. Passing from father to son, this joyous holiday is observed with friends and family enjoying sumptuous foods, often with music and dancing as well. The central elements which enhance the solemnity of *Krsna Slava* are: *slavska sveca*, a long candle which must burn all day; the votive light lit in front of the icon representing the picture of the family patron saint; and incense burning. Two foods are specially prepared: *koljivo*, or sometimes called *zito*, made with boiled wheat, sugar, and ground nuts; and *krsni kolac*, which is a ritual round bread baked solely for this occasion. It is decorated with dough replicas of birds, wheat, grapes, barrels of wine, or whatever else an inspired mother of the family can think of, aside from the obligatory religious seal representing the cross and the symbolic four S's: *Samo Sloga Srbina Spasava*, "Only Unity Will Save the Serbs." The priest visits the homes and conducts a ceremony in which the *kolac* is raised three times symbolizing the Holy Trinity. He and the head of the family cut a cross on the bottom of the kolac into which a little wine is poured to symbolize the blood of Christ.

Every year on June 28 the Serbs commemorate *Vidovdan*, or Saint Vitus Day. One of the most sacred holidays, it commemorates a defeat on June 28, 1389, when the Serbs led by Czar Lazar lost their kingdom to the Turks. The heroism and death of Czar Lazar and his Martyrs who died that day for *krst casni i zlatnu slobodu*, or the "venerable cross and golden freedom," is commemorated in epic songs and celebrated each year by churches and communities across America. The Serbs might be the only people who celebrate a disastrous defeat as a national holiday, but what they are really celebrating is the ability to withstand adversity. For the last 600 years the Serbs have maintained the tradition of respecting their ancestors for living out the old proverb *bolje grob nego rob*, or "better a grave than a slave."

Kumstvo, or godparenthood, is another tradition deeply embedded in the Serbian culture. The parents of an unborn child choose a *kum* or a *kuma* (a man or a woman to be a godparent), who names the baby at the baptismal ceremony. The godparents also have the responsibility of ensuring the moral and material well being of the child if need be, and are considered very close family.

Some customs are remnants of pagan days and were inspired by the closeness with nature; in June, when daisies are abloom in the fields, young girls of marrying age make wreaths that they hang outside their houses. A young man confesses his love by taking the wreath away, leaving the young woman to hope that it should only be the right one. The *dodola*, or the rain dance, is another example; a young girl dressed in flowers, plants, and grasses, goes from house to house and sings a prayerful chant, which is supposed to bring rain. Helpful housewives drench her with buckets of water and small gifts.

Beliefs derived from superstitions are many, such as: a black cat crossing the road in front of a person will bring bad luck; a horse in a dream will bring good luck; black birds are a bad omen; an itching left palm presages money.

EMPLOYMENT AND ECONOMIC TRADITIONS

Although historically Serbs have placed high value on education, early immigrants were largely illiterate or had very little education, due to their circumstances living under Turkish occupation. In America, they worked, as already stated, in predominantly heavy industrial areas. In time, they began to attend evening English-language classes offered by the adult-education programs in public schools, which proved to be enormously valuable to them, and especially to their children.

The younger generations took an increased interest in education, and slowly began to break away from the factory jobs and move to white-collar occupations. In recent decades the Serbs have gone on to higher education. Although Serbian American professionals can be found in nearly every American industry, a great many tend to opt for engineering, medicine, law, or other professions. Lately, however, more and more young people are attracted by financial service industries, such as banking, insurance, and stock brokerage. Boys and girls are educated alike, and everyone is free to set career goals to his or her own liking. The number of women in professions traditionally held by men, especially medicine and engineering, is very high among Serbs.

POLITICS AND GOVERNMENT

Although their participation in American political life has evolved slowly, Serbs have demonstrated a great deal of fervor for politics. Generally speaking, most Serbian Americans are more likely to be concerned with the government's policies and attitude toward Yugoslavia than in local politics.

World War I was the turning point in political activities and unity with other Slavic groups, and, again, such activities had more to do with the politics in the homeland rather than in America. President Woodrow Wilson encouraged Serbian, Croatian, and Slovenian leaders in America to meet and call for the union of the South Slavs then within the Austro-Hungarian Empire, and for the unification with Serbia in an independent Serbian kingdom. The creation of the Yugoslav National Council resulted, its purpose being to inform and influence the American people, as well as to recruit for war and raise money. Thousands of South Slavs joined either the Serbian army or the American army, and thousands of Serbian emigrants returned from the United States to fight for Serbia.

Of the many immigrants who arrived in the United States after 1945, many were very politically engaged, and considered America as a base for pursuing political goals related to Yugoslavia. A number of political organizations were formed to reflect the differing views carried over from the mother country concerning the new regime and the affiliations with particular groups during World War II. After 1945, most of the large numbers of newcomers who joined the Serbian American community in America were Cetniks. Forming political organizations they continued their fight against Tito's communist dictatorship as best they could. Another faction, albeit much smaller in numbers, was an ultra right-wing group called Ljoticevci, a party that was founded by Dimitrije Ljotic (d. 1945). These two groups polarized the attention of the Serbian American immigrants and heightened political awareness among Serbian American communities.

Many older immigrants felt overwhelmed and bewildered by the number of factions and their nuances. Some were alienated, and others fell victim to the communist infiltration and propaganda. However, the vast majority of both the older immigrants and those who arrived after 1945 remain loyal to the American ideals of freedom and liberty.

Many men and women of Serbian descent who have joined the mainstream of American politics today as mayors, governors, and senators have testified to the fact that a degree of "American" political maturity has been reached by this ethnic group in spite of its still intense identification with their motherland, as exemplified by Rose Ann Vuich, the first woman senator from California in 1976.

Given the Serbian penchant for politics, the political issues of the former Yugoslavia have always been and are still being passionately debated among Serbian Americans. Political issues in the Balkans have always been a matter of life and death for the Serbs, who after a flourishing independence in the late Middle Ages, survived centuries of subjugation and, since the early 1800s, have gradually succeeded in the fight for freedom and the unification of their homeland.

The current conflict in the former Yugoslavia, which brought about a new period of intense political activity among Serbian Americans, was prompted by the premature recognition of the independence of Slovenia, Croatia, and Bosnia-Herzegovina, first by most of the member-states of the European community, and then by the United States on April 7, 1992. The Serbs in Croatia's Krajina Region, who had been turned into a minority by the declaration of independence on the part of Croatia, voted to secede from Croatia in 1991. In Bosnia-Herzegovina, they expressed their wishes not to live in minority status among the Muslims by boycotting the referendum for Bosnian independence held in late February 1992. They had reasons to fear for their lives again, because having sided with the Axis Powers during World War II, the fascist Croat Ustashi and their Muslim allies had conducted the systematic extermination of the Serbs. The Nazi-puppet Independent State of Croatia instituted death camps, among which Jasenovac is the most well known.

In Croatia, the resurgence of the old Nazi-Croat symbols at the onset of the conflict, including the use of the Fascist Ustashi flag, the renaming of streets and squares, blatant antisemitism, and the renaming of the national currency to "kuna," which was the currency's name during the Nazi period, are reminders of a painful and not too distant past.

These facts, coupled with the unilateral 1992 declaration of independence of Bosnia against the

wishes of the Serbian minority, which represented approximately one-third of the population, effectively turning them for a second time into second class citizens after 500 years of Turkish/Muslim domination, and reviving the memories of persecutions during World War II, have politically galvanized the Serbian American community in the last several years.

Once again, the Serbian American community is at great odds with the Yugoslav President Slobodan Miloshevic, and to a large degree, and for the first time, with the U.S. government, which they perceive to be one-sided. The Serbs in America are now deeply disappointed, for not only have they shared American principles of freedom and justice for many centuries, but they, unlike the Croats and Bosnian Muslims, have fought with Americans and their allies through two World Wars in the twentieth century.

PARTICIPATION IN THE ARMED FORCES

The degree of participation of Serbian Americans in the armed forces, as well as in the intelligence community, is high. During World War I thousands of American Serbs went to Serbia, an ally, to fight, while others established a number of humanitarian organizations to send help abroad. The response was overwhelming during World War II as well. A large number distinguished themselves in battle and some were awarded the Congressional Medal of Honor.

Many Serbian Americans had distinguished careers in the military, such as Colonel Nicholas Stepanovich, U.S. Army, who had a brilliant career as a lawyer and military leader and was appointed by President Dwight D. Eisenhower to the U.S. ambassadorial staff to the United Nations; Colonel Tyrus Cobb, U.S. Army, who served in Vietnam both in war and in peace missions. The recipient of the Defense Superior Service Medal, the "highest peace time award," Colonel Cobb was appointed to the National Security Council and was selected by President Ronald Reagan to accompany him on summits to Geneva, Moscow, and Iceland. Many other Serbian Americans served in the Office of Strategic Services (later known as the Central Intelligence Agency [CIA]), including Nick Lalich, George Vujnovic, and Joe Veselinovich. The Vietnam War and the Persian Gulf War have also claimed Serbian American decorated heroes as well, such as Lance Sijan, for whom a building is named at the U.S. Air Force Academy in Colorado Springs, Colorado.

LABOR UNIONS

The labor movement and the labor unions in America found some of their staunchest supporters among the Serbs. Having worked very hard to earn their living and having given strength and youth to their new homeland, they felt, as many other Americans did, that strong unions presented opportunities to rectify many poor work situations. They were active with the United Mine Workers of America, the American Federation of Labor, the Congress of Industrial Organizations, and the Textile Workers Union of America, among others. The contributions of the Serbs to the labor movement are numerous, as exemplified by Eli Zivkovich, who organized behind the story of the unionization of textile workers in North Carolina as depicted in the film *Norma Rae*.

Related to the labor movement and union organizing is the work done by Serbian Americans in the field of labor laws as exemplified by the tireless efforts of Robert Lagather, an attorney. The son of a mine worker and a miner himself as a young man, Lagather had a deep commitment to improving the working conditions in the mines, and the role he played in the Federal Mine and Safety and Health Act of 1977 testifies to his determination and dedication.

INDIVIDUAL AND GROUP CONTRIBUTIONS

The contributions of Serbian Americans were best summarized by Jerome Kisslinger: "[From] the Louisiana oyster fishermen of the 1830s and the California innkeeper of the 1850s to the Pittsburgh steel worker of 1910, the political refugee of the 1950s and the engineer today, Serbians have proved themselves to be more than a colorful fringe on our (American) social fabric—they are woven into its very fiber."

ACADEMIA

Political science professor Alex N. Dragnich (1912-) served in the Office of Strategic Services during World War II and as the Cultural Attache and Public Affairs Officer in the American Embassy in Yugoslavia. Dragnich wrote extensively on Serbian subjects; his latest publication is entitled *Serbs and Croats: The Struggle in Yugoslavia* (1992).

FILM, TELEVISION, AND THEATER

Actor Karl Malden (born Mladen Sekulovich in 1913) received an Academy Award for his performance in *A Streetcar Named Desire* in 1951 and was nominated for a second Oscar in 1954 for his work in *On the Waterfront*. Malden is best known for his starring role in the television series "The Streets of San Francisco," and for his series of television commercials for American Express.

Actor John Malkovich (1954-) founded the Steppenwolf Theatre Company in Chicago. An accomplished film actor as well, Malkovich appeared in such films as *Dangerous Liaisons*, *In the Line of Fire*, and *Places in the Heart*, for which he received an Academy Award nomination.

Steve Tesich (born Stoyan Tesich in 1942) is a well-known screenwriter, playwright, and novelist who received an Academy Award for Best Screenplay in 1979 for *Breaking Away*. His other screenplays include *Eleni*, *The World According to Garp*, and *Passing Game*.

LITERATURE

Novelist and publishing executive William (Iliya) Jovanovich (1920-) has written many works, including *Now, Barabbas* (1964), *Madmen Must* (1978), and *A Slow Suicide* (1991). Jovanovich is also the president and chief executive officer of Harcourt Brace Jovanovich.

Poet and translator Charles Simic (1938-) was awarded the 1990 Pulitzer Prize for Poetry for his collection, *The World Doesn't End*.

POLITICS

Born in 1795 as Djordje Sagic in a Serbian settlement in western Hungary, George Fisher came to America in 1815, having agreed to become a bond servant upon his arrival. He jumped ship at the mouth of Delaware River in order to escape his pledge, and was named Fisher by the bystanders who watched him swim ashore. He then wandered from Pennsylvania to Mississippi to Mexico; and eventually to Texas, where he joined in the battle for independence from Mexico, helped to organize the first Supreme Court of the Republic; and held a number of positions in the Texas state government. Fisher also published a liberal Spanish-language newspaper. In 1851 he went to Panama, and from there to San Francisco. While in California he served as secretary of the land commission, justice of the peace, county judge. He finished his wandering and wondrous life as the council for Greece in 1873.

Awarded the GOP Woman of the Year Award in 1972, Helen Delich Bently (1923-) is currently a congresswoman from Maryland. Rose

Ann Vuich served in the California State Senate from 1976 to 1992 and received the Democrat of the Year Award in 1975. Joyce George (1936-), attorney and politician, was appointed U.S. Attorney from the Northern District of Ohio by President George Bush in 1989.

SCIENCE

Nikola Tesla (1856-1943), "the electrical wizard," astonished the world with his demonstration of the wonders of alternating current at the World Columbian Exposition in Chicago in 1893; in the first half of the twentieth century, this became the standard method of generating electrical power. Tesla also designed the first hydro-electric power plant in Niagara Falls, New York. Having introduced the fundamentals of robotry, fluorescent light, the laser beam, wireless communication and transmission of electrical energy, the turbine and vertical take-off aircraft, computers, and missile science, Tesla was possibly the greatest inventor the world has ever known. His work spawned technology such as satellites, beam weapons, and nuclear fusion.

Michael Idvorsky Pupin's (1858-1935) scientific contributions in the field of radiology include rapid X-ray photography (1896), which cut the usual hour-long exposure time to seconds; the discovery of the secondary X-ray radiation; and the development of the first X-ray picture used in surgery. His other interests covered the field of telecommunications. The "Pupin coil," which uses alternate current, made long distance telephone lines and cables possible. He also invented the means to eliminate static from radio receivers as well the tuning devises for radios. Pupin successfully experimented with sonar U-boat detectors and underwater radars, as well as the passage of electricity through gases. In addition to his scientific contributions, he was a prominent Serbian patriot. He tirelessly campaigned on behalf of Serbia during World War I. In his Pulitzer Prize-winning autobiography *From Immigrant to Inventor* (1925) Pupin stated: "[I] brought to America something ... which I valued very highly, and that was: a knowledge of and a profound respect and admiration for the best traditions of my race ... no other lesson had ever made a deeper impression upon me." The Pupin Institute at Columbia University was founded in his memory.

Milan Panic (1929-) founded ICN Pharmaceuticals, Inc. in Pasadena, California. At one time his company employed 6,000 people, with sales of over $150 million. In 1992 Panic served as the Prime Minister of Yugoslavia.

SPORTS

Professional basketball player Pete Maravich (1948-1987) was perhaps best known as "Pistol Pete" Maravich.

VISUAL ARTS

John David Brcin (1899-1982) was a sculptor who immigrated to America in 1914. Drawing his inspiration from American subjects, Brcin sculpted busts of President Abraham Lincoln, Mark Twain, and many others. He also created large reliefs depicting scenes from American history.

MEDIA

PRINT

Amerikanski Srbobran (The American Serb Defender).

Published by the Serb National Federation since 1906, this is the oldest and largest circulating Serbian bilingual weekly newspaper in the United States, covering cultural, political, and sporting events of interest to Serbian Americans.

Contact: Robert Rade Stone, Coordinating Editor.

Address: 1 Fifth Avenue, seventh floor, Pittsburgh, Pennsylvania 15222.

Telephone: (412) 642-7371.

Fax: (412) 642-1372.

Glasnik Srpskog Istoriskog Kulturnog Drustva "Njegos" (Herald of the Serbian Historical-Cultural Society "Njegos").

Founded in 1959, this historical and literary review is published biannually.

Contact: Drasko Braunovic, Editor.

Address: 774 Emroy Avenue, Elmhurst, Illinois 60126.

Telephone: (708) 833-3721.

Serb World U.S.A.

A continuation of *Serb World* (1979-83), this bimonthly, illustrated magazine was established in 1984. It features articles about Serbian American immigrants' cultural heritage and history, as well as other topics relating to Serbian Americans.

Serbian Studies.

Founded in 1980, this scholarly journal is published biannually by the North American Society for Serbian Studies. It offers broad coverage of history, political science, art, and the humanities.

Contact: Dr. Nikola Moravcevich, Editor.

Address: P.O. Box 4348, University Hall, Room 1202, Chicago, Illinois 60680.

Telephone: (312) 996-7068.

Sloboda (Liberty).

Founded in 1952 by the Serb National Defense Council of America, this publication is an illustrated biweekly featuring articles on Serbian history and culture.

Address: 5782 N. Elston Avenue, Chicago, Illinois 60646.

Telephone: (312) 775-7772.

Srpska Borba (The Serbian Struggle).

Monthly journal published by the Serbian Literary Association (Srpsko Literarno Udruzenje) since 1953. It features articles on political, social, historical, and cultural topics.

Contact: Budimir D. Streckovic, Editor.

Address: 448 Bari Avenue, Chicago, Illinois 60657.

Telephone: (312) 549-1099.

Unity Herald (Glas Sabora Ujedinjenja).

Established in 1992 by the Serbian Unity Congress, this quarterly bilingual journal features reports on the latest events in the former Yugoslavia, as well as the SUC activities.

Contact: Ljiljana Obradovich-Knezevich, Editor.

Address: P.O. Box 2146, Napa, California 94558.

Fax: (707) 224-6593.

RADIO

"American Serbian Radio Hour," WSLR-AM 1350, Akron, Ohio.

Weekly broadcast since 1955, featuring Serbian recorded music and news related to the Serbian American community.

Contact: Mike Malen, Director.

Address: 964 Charlada Way, Akron, Ohio 44313.

Telephone: (216) 864-9991.

"'Drina' Broadcasting—Voice of American Serbs," WNWK-FM 105.9, Ridgewood, New York.

Established in 1992, this program airs on Sundays. It presents world news, particularly news from the former Yugoslavia, and other topics pertinent to Serbian Americans.

Contact: Dusan Radovic, Director.

Address: 72-04 Forest Avenue, Ridgewood, New York 11385.

"Serbian Radio Hour" ("Srpske Melodije I Novosti"), WCPN-FM 90.3, Cleveland, Ohio.

Weekly three-hour program featuring Serbian music and news, especially from Belgrade, Pale, and Knin.

Contact: Djordje Djelic, Director.

Address: 6364 Pearl Road, Cleveland, Ohio 44130.

Telephone: (216) 842-6161.

Fax: (216) 842-6163.

"Serbian Radio Hour," WLTH-AM, Gary, Indiana.

Weekly broadcast since 1954. Presents social, religious, and cultural news of interest to the Serbian community.

Contact: Helen Pavicevich, Director.

Address: 11228 South Avenue L, Chicago, Illinois 60617.

Telephone: (312) 221-4143.

"Serbian Radio Program," KTYM-AM 1460 and KORG-AM 1190.

Program is broadcasted twice a day on Saturdays, featuring world news, special reportage from Beograd, Pale, and Knin and music of Serbian origin.

Contact: Veroljub Radivojevic, Director.

Address: 23128 Gainford Street, Woodland Hills, California 91364.

Telephone: (818) 222-5073.

Fax: (818) 591-9678.

ORGANIZATIONS AND ASSOCIATIONS

Belgrade Club, Inc.

Founded in 1982. A non-profit membership organization engaged in such cultural programs as lectures on art and art history, and film screenings. Publishes a quarterly bulletin covering the arts.

Contact: Donya-Dobrila Schimansky, President.

Address: P.O. Box 6235, Yorkville Station, New York, New York 10128.

Serb National Defense Council of America (Sprska Narodna Odbrana).

Established in 1941 with chapters throughout the United States and abroad. Activities focus on political and cultural Serbian interests.

Contact: Slavko Panovic, President.

Address: 5782 N. Elston, Chicago, Illinois 60646.

Telephone: (312) 775-7772.

Serb National Federation (SNF).

Founded in 1906, the SNF has lodges throughout the United States and Canada. Its activities transcend business interests to include sponsoring and promoting many programs from sports to scholarship within the Serbian American community.

Contact: Robert Rade Stone, President.

Address: 1 Fifth Avenue, Seventh floor, Pittsburgh, Pennsylvania 15222.

Telephone: (412) 642-7372.

Fax: (412) 642-1372.

Serbian American Affairs Office (SAAO).

Established in 1992, SAAO serves as a clearinghouse for information and research on current events occurring in the former Yugoslavia, and arranges guest appearances on radio and television stations across the United States.

Contact: Danielle Sremac, Director.

Address: P.O. Box 32238, Washington, D.C., 20007.

Telephone: (202) 965-2141.

Fax: (202) 965-2187.

Serbian Cultural Club "St. Sava" (Srpski Kulturni Klub "Sv. Sava").

Founded in 1951, this organization has chapters throughout the United States and abroad. Activities promote Serbian culture and political awareness among the host nations and the hosts' culture among the Serbs.

Contact: Budimir D. Sreckovic, President.

Address: 448 Barry Avenue, Chicago, Illinois 60657.

Telephone: (312) 549-1099.

MUSEUMS AND RESEARCH CENTERS

North American Society for Serbian Studies.

Founded in 1980 within the framework of the American Association for the Advancement of Slavic Studies (AAASS) to research and promote Serbian literature, history, and culture. Attracts Serbian scholars from the United States, Canada, and Mexico, who meet at annual conferences of the AAASS. (Note: The address of this organization varies according to the location of the president, elected for a one year term during the conference. At this writing, the president is Ljubica Popovic, professor of Medieval Art at Vanderbilt University).

Tesla Memorial Society.

Established in 1979, this scientific, educational, and cultural society is dedicated to commemorating and popularizing the life and work of Nikola Tesla.

Contact: Nicholas Kosanovic, Executive Director.

Address: 453 Martin Road, Lackawanna, New York 14218.

SOURCES FOR ADDITIONAL STUDY

Beloff, Nora. *Tito's Flawed Legacy: Yugoslavia and the West since 1939*. Boulder: Westview Press, 1985.

Kaplan, Robert D. *Balkan Ghosts: A Journey through History*. New York: St. Martin's Press, 1993.

Lees, Michael. *The Rape of Serbia: The British Role in Tito's Grab for Power, 1943-1944*. San Diego: Harcourt Brace Jovanovich, 1990.

Martin, David. *The Web of Disinformation: Churchill's Yugoslav Blunder*. San Diego: Harcourt Brace Jovanovich, 1990.

Paris, Edmond. *Genocide in Satellite Croatia, 1941-1945: A Record of Racial and Religious Persecutions and Massacres*. Chicago: The American Institute for Balkan Affairs, 1961.

Pavlovich, Paul. *The Serbians: The Story of a People*. Toronto: Serbian Heritage Books, 1988.

Pupin, Michael. *From Immigrant to Inventor*. New York: Charles Scribner's Sons, 1924.

West, Rebecca. *Black Lamb and Grey Falcon: A Journey throughout Yugoslavia*. New York: The Viking Press, 1941; revised 1982 (Penguin Books).

Acculturation, assimilation, and intermarriage have made inroads into Sioux traditional family and community relationships. The more isolated and rural portions of the population tend to be more traditional.

SIOUX

by
D. L. Birchfield

OVERVIEW

The Siouan-language peoples comprise one of the largest language groups north of Mexico, second only to the Algonquian family of languages. Many Siouan-language peoples are no longer identified as Sioux, but have evolved their own separate tribal identities centuries ago, long before contact with non-Indians. The name Sioux originates from a French version of the Chippewa *Nadouessioux* (snakes). The immense geographical spread of Siouan-language peoples, from the Rocky Mountains to the Atlantic Ocean, from the Great Lakes to the Gulf of Mexico, attests to their importance in the history of the North American continent—most of that history having occurred before the arrival of non-Indians. Those known today as Sioux (the Dakota, the Lakota, and the Nakota), living primarily in the upper Great Plains region, are among the best-known Indians within American popular culture due to their participation in what Americans perceive to have been dramatic events within their own history, such as the Battle of the Little Big Horn in the late nineteenth century. American students have been told for more than a century that there were no survivors, despite the fact that approximately 2,500 Indian participants survived the battle. The lands of the Sioux have also been a focal point for some of the most dramatic events in the American Indian Movement of recent times, especially

the 71-day occupation of Wounded Knee, South Dakota, in 1973, which brought national media attention to the Pine Ridge Reservation. Sioux writers, poets, and political leaders are today among the most influential leaders in the North American Native American community of nations, and the Sioux religion can be found to have an influence far beyond the Sioux people.

HISTORY

The Sioux had the misfortune of becoming intimately acquainted with the westward thrust of American expansion at a time when American attitudes toward Indians had grown cynical. In the East and Southeast, from early colonial times, there was much disagreement regarding the nature of the relations with the Indian nations. There was also a constant need to have allies among the Indian nations during the period of European colonial rivalry on the North American continent, a need that the newly formed United States felt with great urgency during the first generation of its existence. After the War of 1812, things changed rapidly in the East and Southeast. Indians as allies became much less necessary. It was the discovery of gold in 1828, however, at the far southern end of the Cherokee Nation near the border with Georgia that set off a Southern gold rush and brought an urgency to long-debated questions of what the nature of relations with the Indian nations should be.

Greed for gold would play a pivotal role in the undermining of Sioux national independence. At mid-century streams of men from the East first passed through Sioux lands on their way to the gold fields of California. They brought with them smallpox, measles, and other contagious diseases for which the Sioux had no immunity, and which ravaged their population by an estimated one-half. Later, in the 1870s, the discovery of gold in the heart of *Paha Sapa* (the Black Hills), the sacred land of the Sioux, brought hordes of miners and the U.S. Army, led by Lieutenant Colonel George Armstrong Custer, into the center of their sacred "heart of everything that is" in a blatant violation of the Treaty of Fort Laramie of 1868.

The Sioux had no way of knowing about the process that had worked itself out in the East and Southeast, whereby, in direct contravention of a U.S. Supreme Court decision (*Worchester vs. Georgia*), Indians would no longer be dealt with as sovereign nations. No longer needed as allies, and looked upon as merely being in the way, Indians entered a perilous time of being regarded as dependent domestic minorities. Many Eastern and Southern Indian nations were uprooted and forced to remove themselves beyond the Mississippi River. By the time American expansion reached Texas, attitudes had hardened to a point at which Texans systematically expelled or exterminated nearly all of the Indians within their borders; however, Sam Houston, during his terms as president of the republic of Texas and as governor of the state of Texas, unsuccessfully attempted to accommodate the needs of Indians into Texas governmental policy.

To the Sioux in the second half of the nineteenth century, the U.S. government was duplicitous, greedy, corrupt, and without conscience. The Sioux watched the great buffalo herds be deliberately exterminated by U.S. Army policy; and within a generation they found themselves paupers in their native land, with no alternative but to accept reservation life. They found it impossible to maintain honorable, peaceful relations with the United States. At first, attempts were made to acculturate the Sioux, to assimilate them out of existence as a separate people; then in the mid-twentieth century, the government attempted to legislate them out of existence through an official policy of "termination" of Indian nations. Only within recent decades have there been attempts on the part of the U.S. government to redress past wrongs. In the 1960s, under the occasional prod of court decisions and a national consciousness focused on civil rights legislation for minorities, attempts were made to recognize and respect significant remaining vestiges of Indian sovereignty. Finally, by legislation in 1979 Indians were allowed to openly practice their religions without threat of criminal prosecution. The gains have not come without bloodshed and strife, however, especially in the lands of the Sioux and especially during the mid-1970s—a time of virtual civil war on the Pine Ridge Reservation. Alarmed by the bold actions and the extent of the demands by some groups of Indians, particularly the American Indian Movement (AIM), the U.S. government tried to slow the pace of change by exploiting differences between the more acculturated Indians and the more traditional Indians. Since that time, much healing has occurred; but the question of what the nature of the relations between the Native peoples of this continent and the people of the United States will be remains open.

MODERN ERA

Federally recognized contemporary Sioux tribal governments are located in Minnesota, Nebraska, North Dakota, South Dakota, and Montana. According to the 1990 census, South Dakota ranked eleventh among all states for the number of Indians represented in its population (50,575, which was 7.3 percent of the South Dakota population, up from 6.5 percent in 1980). Minnesota ranked twelfth with a reported total of 49,909 Indians, or 1.1 percent of its population (up from 0.9 percent in 1980). Montana ranked thirteenth with a reported total of 47,679 Indians, or 6.0 percent of its population (up from 4.7 percent in 1980). North Dakota ranked eighteenth with a reported total of 25,917 Indians, or 4.1 percent of its population (up from 3.1 percent in 1980). Nebraska ranked thirty-fifth with a reported total of 12,410 Indians, or 0.8 percent of its population (up from 0.6 percent in 1980).

Many Native Americans from these areas have migrated to urban industrial centers throughout the continent. Contemporary estimates are that at least 50 percent of the Indian population in the United States now resides in urban areas, frequently within the region of the tribal homeland but often at great distances from it. Other populations of Sioux are to be found in the prairie provinces of Canada.

ACCULTURATION AND ASSIMILATION

Beginning in the late nineteenth century the U.S. government attempted to force the Sioux to assimilate into American culture. The prime weapon of cultural genocide as practiced by the United States was a school system contracted to missionaries who had little regard for traditional Sioux culture, language, or beliefs. Sioux children, isolated from their families, were punished if they were caught speaking their Native tongue. Their hair was cropped, and school and dormitory life was conducted on a military model. Many children attended the school located at Flandreau, South Dakota. Some Sioux children were removed to schools in the East, to Hampton Institute in Virginia, or to the Indian school at Carlisle, Pennsylvania, while others attended the Santa Fe Indian School and the Haskell Institute in Lawrence, Kansas. Throughout this ordeal, the Sioux were able to retain their language and religion, while learning English and adjusting to the demands of American culture. Some Sioux began attaining distinction early in this process, such as physician Charles Eastman. Today, the Sioux people are at home in both worlds. Sioux intellectuals and academicians, such as noted author Vine Deloria Jr., and poet and scholar Elizabeth Cook-Lynn, who also edits *Wicazo Sa Review*, a scholarly journal for Native American Studies professionals, are leaders within their respective fields within the North American Native American community.

TRADITIONAL CRAFTS

The Sioux are skilled artisans at beadwork, quillwork, carving, pipe making, drum making, flute making, and leatherwork of all kinds—from competition powwow regalia to saddles and tack. These are crafts that have been handed down from generation to generation. Intertribal powwow competitions, festivals, and tribal fairs bring forth impressive displays of Sioux traditional crafts. A large tribal arts and crafts fair is held annually at New Town, North Dakota, September 17-19.

SIOUX DANCES AND SONGS

Summer is the most popular season for powwows. Intertribal powwows featuring dance competitions are the ones at which visitors are most welcome. A number of powwows tend to occur annually on the same date. Powwows are held at a number of communities in South Dakota on May 7, including the communities of Wounded Knee, Kyle, Oglala, Allen, and Porcupine. A Memorial Day weekend powwow is held by the Devil's Lake Sioux at Fort Totten, North Dakota. Powwows are held in mid-June at Fort Yates, North Dakota, and at Grass Mountain, South Dakota. Powwows are held July 2-4 at La Creek, South Dakota; July 2-5 at Cannon Ball, North Dakota; July 3-5 at Spring Creek, South Dakota, at Greenwood, South Dakota, and at Fort Thompson, North Dakota; July 14-16 at Mission South Dakota; July 15-16 at Flandreau, South Dakota; July 17-19 at New Town, North Dakota; July 21-23 at Cherry Creek, South Dakota; July 28-30 at Little Eagle, South Dakota; and the last weekend of July at Belcourt, North Dakota. August and September are also popular months, with powwows held at Lake Andes, South Dakota, each weekend during the first half of August; at Fort Yates, North Dakota, August 4-6; at Rosebud, South Dakota, August 11-13; at Bull Head, North Dakota, August 13-15; at Bull Creek and Soldier Creek, South Dakota, September 2-4; and at Sisseton, South Dakota, and Fort Totten, North Dakota, over the Labor Day holiday.

HOLIDAYS CELEBRATED BY THE SIOUX

The Spotted Tail Memorial Celebration is held in late June at Rosebud, South Dakota. July 1-4 is the date of the Sioux Ceremonial at Sisseton, South Dakota. The Sioux Coronation is held in early October at Fort Totten, North Dakota. Tribal fairs are held July 23-25 at Fort Totten, North Dakota; August 7-9 at Lower Brule, South Dakota; August 21-23 at Rosebud, South Dakota; August 27-29 at Eagle Butte, South Dakota; and Labor Day weekend at Devils Lake and Fort Totten, North Dakota.

HEALTH AND MENTAL HEALTH ISSUES

All of the health problems associated with poverty in the United States can be found among the contemporary Sioux people. Alcoholism has proven to be especially debilitating. Many traditional Indian movements, including AIM, have worked toward regaining pride in Native culture, including efforts to combat alcohol abuse and the toll that it takes among contemporary Native peoples.

LANGUAGE

The Iroquoian language family, the Caddoan language family, the Yuchi language family, and the Siouan language family all belong to the Macro-Siouan language phylum, indicating a probable divergence in the distant past from a common ancestor language. Geographically, the Iroquoian family of languages (Seneca, Cayuga, Onondaga, Mohawk, Oneida, and Wyandot—also known as Huron), are found in the Northeast, primarily in New York state and the adjacent areas of Canada, and in the Southeast (Tuscarora, originally in North Carolina, later in New York; and Cherokee, in the Southern Appalachians, and later in Oklahoma). The Caddoan language family includes the Caddo, Wichita, Pawnee, and Arikara languages, which are found on the central Plains. Yuchi is a language isolate of the Southern Appalachians.

Members of the Siouan language family proper are to be found practically everywhere east of the Rocky Mountains except on the southern Plains and in the Northeast. On the northern Plains are found the Crow, Hidatsa, and Dakota (also known as Sioux) languages. On the central Plains are found the Omaha, Osage, Ponca, Kansa, and Quapaw languages; in Wisconsin one finds the Winnebago language; on the Gulf Coast are the Tutelo, Ofo, and Biloxi languages; and in the Southeast one finds Catawba. The immense geographical spread of the languages within this family is testimony to the importance of Siouan-speaking peoples in the history of the continent. They have been a people on the move for a very long time.

Oral traditions among some of the Siouan-speaking peoples document the approximate point of divergence for the development of a separate tribal identity and, eventually, the evolution of a separate language unintelligible to their former kinspeople. Siouan-speaking peoples of all contemporary tribal identities, however, share creation stories accounting for their origin as a people. They come from the stars, which can be contrasted, for example, with the Macro-Algonkian phylum, Muskogean-speaking Choctaws who emerged from a hole in the earth near the sacred mother mound, *Nanih Waiya*. It can be contrasted also with the Aztec-Tanoan phylum, Uto-Aztecan-speaking Hopi, who believe they have ascended upward through successive layers of worlds to the one they presently occupy.

Siouan-speaking peoples also exhibit a reverence for the number seven, whereas Choctaws hold that the sacred number is four. There are fundamental cultural differences between Native American peoples whom Europeans and Americans have considered more similar than different. For example, the Macro-Siouan phylum, Iroquoian-speaking Cherokees and the Macro-Algonkian phylum, Muskogean-speaking Choctaws have both been categorized by non-Indians as members of the so-called "Five Civilized Tribes" due to similarities in their material culture; whereas knowledgeable Choctaws consider the Cherokees to have about three too many sacred numbers.

Today the Sioux language consists of three principal, mutually intelligible dialects: Dakota (Santee), Lakota (Teton), and Nakota (Yankton). The Sioux language is not restricted to the United States but also extends far into the prairie provinces of Canada. The Sioux were also masters of sign language, an ancient vehicle of communication among peoples who are native to the North American continent. The Sioux language can be heard in a video documentary (*Wiping The Tears of Seven Generations*, directed by Gary Rhine and Fidel Moreno, Kafaru Productions, 1992), which records interviews with a number of Sioux members of the Wounded Knee Survivors' Association, as they relate what their grandparents told them about the 1890 massacre at Wounded Knee.

FAMILY AND COMMUNITY DYNAMICS

The basic unit of traditional Sioux family and community life is the *tiyospaye*, a small group of related families. In the era of the buffalo, the *tiyospaye* was a highly mobile unit capable of daily movement if necessary. A *tiyospaye* might include 30 or more households. From these related households a headman achieved the position of leadership by demonstrating characteristics valued by the group, such as generosity, wisdom, fortitude, and spiritual power gained through dreams and visions. Acculturation, assimilation, and intermarriage have made inroads into Sioux traditional family and community relationships. The more isolated and rural portions of the population tend to be more traditional.

In traditional Lakota community life, fraternal societies, called *akicitas*, are significant within the life of the group. During the era of the buffalo when Lakota society was highly mobile, fraternal societies helped young men develop leadership skills by assigning them roles in maintaining orderly camp movements. Membership was by invitation only and restricted to the most promising young men. Another kind of fraternity, the *nacas*, was composed of older men with proven abilities. The most important of the *nacas* societies, the *Naca Omincia*, functioned as something of a tribal council. Operating by consensus, it had the power to declare war and to negotiate peace. A few members of the *Naca Ominicia* were appointed *wicasa itancans*, who were responsible for implementing decisions of the *Naca Ominicia*. Many vestiges of traditional Lakota community organizational structure have been replaced, at least on the surface, by structures forced upon the Lakota by the U.S. government. One important leader in the society was the *wicasa wakan*, a healer respected for wisdom as well as curative powers. This healer was consulted on important tribal decisions by the *wicasa itancans*, and is still consulted on important matters by the Lakota people today.

RELIGION

The Sun Dance, also known as the Offerings Lodge ceremonial, is one of the seven sacred ceremonials of the Sioux and is a ceremonial for which they have come to be widely known. The most famous Sun Dance occurs in early August at Pine Ridge. The Sun Dance takes place in early July at Rosebud, and at other times among other Sioux communities. The ceremonials, however, are not performed for the benefit of tourists. Attendance by tourists is discouraged.

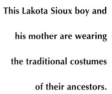

This Lakota Sioux boy and his mother are wearing the traditional costumes of their ancestors.

No American Indian religion has been more closely studied or more widely known than the Sioux religion, partly due to the appeal of John Niehardt's book, *Black Elk Speaks,* in which he recorded his interviews with the Sioux spiritual leader earlier this century. Another reason for its prominence is because the American Indian Movement adopted many of the practices of the Sioux religion for its own and carried those practices to many areas of the continent where they had not been widely known. The so-called New Age movement within American culture has also become captivated by the religious practices of the northern Plains Indians, primarily the Cheyenne and the Sioux (practices that are largely foreign to Indians in many other areas of the continent, but which are perceived by many Americans as representative of Indians in general). Yet, until by act of Congress, the American Indians Religious Freedom Act of 1978, the practice of Indian religions was a crime in the United States.

The practice of many Native American religions throughout the continent was forced underground in the late nineteenth century as news spread about the massacre of 153 unarmed Minneconjou Sioux men, women, and children by the U.S. Army at Wounded Knee on the Pine Ridge Reservation on December 29, 1890. The Minneconjous, camped at Wounded Knee Creek, had been holding a Ghost Dance, attempting to fulfill the prophecies of the Paiute visionary Wovoka.

While fleeing their own agency after the murder of Sitting Bull, they tried to reach what they perceived to be the safety of the protection of Chief Red Cloud at Pine Ridge, who was on friendly terms with the U.S. government.

Perhaps because the massacre at Wounded Knee was one of Sioux people on Sioux land, the Sioux have been strong contemporary leaders in asserting the religious rights of Native peoples. These efforts have also been vigorously pursued on behalf of incarcerated Native Americans, where penal authorities in practically every state historically have been contemptuous of the religious rights of Native American inmates.

While the ceremonials of the Sioux, the Sun Dance, the Sweat Lodge, and other aspects of their religion may be foreign to many other Native Americans (for example, the sweat lodge, a religious ceremonial among the Sioux, is merely a fraternal and communal event among the Choctaws and many other Native peoples), one aspect of the Sioux religion is nearly universal among North America's Indians—the sanctity of land and the reverence for particular sacred lands. For the Sioux and for the Cheyenne, the sacred land is *Paha Sapa,* known in American culture as the Black Hills, and their major contemporary struggle is to regain it. They have won a decision from the U.S. Indian Claims Commission that *Paha Sapa* was taken from them illegally by the United States, and that they are entitled to $122 million in compensation. The Sioux have rejected the award of money, which, being held in trust for them, has now accumulated interest to a total of more than $400 million. They are not interested in money; they want *Paha Sapa*; and there is precedent for their demand. In 1970 Congress passed, and President Richard Nixon signed, legislation returning Blue Lake—the sacred lake of Taos Pueblo—and 48,000 surrounding acres to Taos Pueblo. This was the first return of land to Indians for religious purposes by the United States.

EMPLOYMENT AND ECONOMIC TRADITIONS

In the late nineteenth and early twentieth centuries the U.S. government tried to force the Sioux to become farmers. Cattle ranching, however, has become more important to them and many Sioux derive some economic benefit from the cattle industry. Sioux have distinguished themselves on the professional rodeo and all-Indian rodeo circuits.

Sioux reservations are isolated from urban industrial centers, have attracted very little industry, and experience some of the highest levels of unemployment and the highest levels of poverty of any communities within the United States. For example, on the Cheyenne River Reservation in the mid-1980s, unemployment averaged roughly 80 percent and 65 percent of all families were living on less than $3,000 per year. Many Sioux have found it necessary to leave their communities to find employment. Like many Indian reservations, various agencies of the U.S. government and programs funded by the government account for the largest percentage of jobs. Extractive industries also provide some employment, but the economic benefits go largely to non-Indians, and many traditional Sioux refuse to participate in economic activities that scar and pollute their land. The discovery of uranium on Sioux lands, which has raised questions regarding if and how it should be extracted, has been a divisive issue within Sioux communities.

POLITICS AND GOVERNMENT

The structure and operation of the contemporary government of the Lakota tribal division of the Sioux serves as an example of that of other Sioux governments. The contemporary national government of the Lakota nation is the National Sioux Council, which is composed of delegates from the Lakota reservations at Cheyenne River, Standing Rock, Lower Brule, Crow Creek, Pine Ridge, Rosebud, Santee, and Fort Peck. The council meets annually to discuss matters affecting the entire Lakota nation. It is based on the traditional model of Lakota government, where the headman of each band represented the band's tribe, and the headman of each Lakota tribe represented the Greater Sioux Council. Essentially a federal structure, it also functions by the imposition of vote counting rather than consensus—a quintessential American Indian method of decision making.

Each contemporary Lakota reservation is governed by an elected tribal council. The organization of the Cheyenne River Reservation tribal council, for example, is a supreme governing body for the Cheyenne River Sioux. It is empowered to enter into negotiations with foreign governments, such as the government of the United States, to pass laws and establish courts, appoint tribal officials, and administer the tribal budget. Certain kinds of actions by the tribal council, however, are subject to the authority of the secretary of the interior of the U.S. government, a reminder that the Sioux are not alone in their land. The council consists of 18 members, 15 of which are elected from six voting districts (the districts being apportioned according to population), and three who are elected at large—the chairperson, the secretary, and the treasurer. The council elects a vice-chairperson from among its members. Each tribal council member reports to the district tribal council for the district from which the council member was elected. These district councils are locally elected.

To vote or hold office at Cheyenne River one must be an enrolled tribal member and meet residency requirements. For enrollment, one must be one-quarter blood or more Cheyenne River Sioux and one's parents must also have been residents of the reservation. However, a two-thirds vote of the tribal council may enroll a person of Cheyenne River Indian blood who does not meet either the blood quantum or the parental residency requirements. To vote, one must meet a 30-day residency requirement; to hold office, the residency requirement is one year.

THE "INCIDENT AT OGLALA"

No other event typifies the problems encountered by traditional Indians in seeking the redress of long-standing grievances with the United States more than the 71-day siege of Wounded Knee in 1973, known as the "Incident at Oglala." When the siege ended in May of 1973, and when no network correspondents remained to tell the world what was happening on the Pine Ridge Reservation, traditional Indians and supporters of the American Indian Movement (AIM) endured a reign of terror that lasted for more than two years. Frightened by the takeover of the Bureau of Indian Affairs building in Washington, D.C., and by the occupation of Wounded Knee, the mixed-blood leadership of the Oglala Lakota tribal government moved to crush political activism on the reservation while the AIM leadership was in court. Federal authorities allowed and funded heavily armed vigilantes, called goon squads (Guardians Of the Oglala Nation), who patrolled the roads and created a police state. Freedom of assembly, freedom of association, and freedom of speech ceased to exist. Violence reigned. Drive-by shootings, cars run off the road, firebombings and murders became the norm.

During one 12-month period there were more murders on the Pine Ridge Reservation than in all the other parts of South Dakota combined. The reservation had the highest per capita murder rate in the United States. By June of 1975 there had been more than 60 unsolved murders of traditional Indians and AIM supporters. The FBI, charged with solving crimes on Indian reservations, took little interest in the killings. But when two FBI agents were killed near the community of Oglala on the Pine Ridge Reservation on June 26, 1975, 350 FBI agents were on the scene within three days.

Two FBI agents, new to the area and unknown to its residents, were dressed in plain clothes and driving unmarked cars; they reported that they were following a red pickup truck, which they believed contained a man who was wanted for stealing a pair of boots. The vehicle actually contained a load of explosives destined for an encampment of about a dozen members of the AIM, not far from the community of Oglala. When the two FBI agents followed the red pickup off the road and into a field, to a point within earshot of the encampment, a firefight erupted between the two FBI agents and the occupants of the vehicle, who have never been identified. Armed only with their handguns, the agents attempted to get their rifles out of the trunks of their cars, and in so doing exposed themselves to the gunfire. Hearing the shooting, and thinking

themselves under attack, men and women from the encampment came running, carrying rifles. They took up positions on a ridge overlooking the vehicles; when fired at, they returned the fire. Within a few minutes a third FBI agent arrived but not before the first two FBI agents lay dead near their vehicles. The red pickup fled the scene, but it had been seen and reported, and the report preserved in the records of FBI radio transmissions. The AIM members on the ridge from the encampment, went down to the vehicles and discovered the bodies of the two FBI agents. Bewildered and frightened, they fled the area on foot, under heavy fire, as law enforcement authorities began arriving *en masse*, but not before an Indian man lay dead—shot through the head at long range. The two FBI agents, already wounded, had been shot through the head at point blank range.

The full fury of the FBI descended on Pine Ridge Reservation. The director of the FBI appeared on television and announced a nationwide search for the red pickup. In the months that followed, the FBI was unable to find the red pickup or its occupants. Three men who had been at the AIM encampment that day, Darrelle Butler, Bob Robideau, and Leonard Peltier, were arrested and charged with killing the two FBI agents. No one was ever charged with killing the Indian. Peltier, in Canada, fought extradition. Butler and Robideau, however, were tried and acquitted by a jury that believed they had acted in self-defense and that they had not been the ones who executed the wounded agents. The fury of the government then fell on the third defendant, Leonard Peltier. The United States presented coerced, perjured documents to the Canadian authorities to secure Peltier's extradition from Canada. At the trial, the red pickup truck now became a red and white van, like the one to which Leonard Peltier could be linked. FBI agents who had filed reports the day of the shooting, reporting the red pickup, now testified differently, saying their reports had been in error. The government now claimed that the two dead FBI agents who had reported that they were following a red pickup did not know the difference between a red pickup and a red and white van.

With the first trial as a blueprint for everything it had done wrong in the courtroom, the government found a sympathetic judge in another jurisdiction who ruled favorably for the prosecution, and against the defense, disallowing testimony about the climate of violence and fear on the reservation, and effectively thwarting the defense of self-defense. Also, by withholding the results of crucial FBI ballistics tests, which showed that Leonard Peltier's weapon had not fired the fatal shots), the government got a conviction against Peltier. He was sentenced to two life terms in the federal penitentiary. A recent documentary (*Incident At Oglala: The Leonard Peltier Story*), through interviews with numerous participants, examines in detail the events of the day the two FBI agents were killed, and the government case against Peltier, revealing that in a fair trial Peltier would have been acquitted, as Butler and Robideau were, and that the nature of his involvement was the same as theirs.

INDIVIDUAL AND GROUP CONTRIBUTIONS

ACADEMIA

Sioux author, professor, and attorney Vine Deloria, Jr. (1933-), has been one of the most articulate speakers for the recognition of Indian political and religious rights. Born at Standing Rock on the Pine Ridge Reservation, he holds degrees in divinity from the Lutheran School of Theology and in law from the University of Colorado. His writings include *Custer Died For Your Sins* (1969), *We Talk, You Listen: New Tribes, New Turf* (1970).

LITERATURE

Sioux poet, author, and professor Elizabeth Cook-Lynn (1930-), born on the Crow Creek Reservation, is a granddaughter of Gabriel Renville, a linguist who helped develop Dakota dictionaries; a Dakota speaker herself, Cook-Lynn has gained prominence as a professor, editor, poet, and scholar; she is emeritus professor of American and Indian studies at Eastern Washington State University, and in 1985 she became a founding editor of *Wicazo Sa Review*, a bi-annual scholarly journal for Native American studies professionals; her book of poetry, *Then Badger Said This*, and her short fiction in journals have established her as a leader among American Indian creative voices. Virginia Driving Hawk Sneve, a Rosebud Sioux, is the author of eight children's books and other works of historical nonfiction for adults; in 1992 she won the Native American Prose Award from the University of Nebraska Press for her book *Closing The Circle*. Oglala Sioux Robert L. Perea (1944-), born in Wheatland, Wyoming, is also half Chi-

cano; a graduate of the University of New Mexico, he has published short stories in anthologies such as *Mestizo: An Anthology of Chicano Literature* and *The Remembered Earth*; in 1992 Perea won the inaugural Louis Littlecoon Oliver Memorial Prose Award from his fellow creative writers and poets in the Native Writers' Circle of the Americas for his short story, "Stacey's Story." Philip H. Red-Eagle, Jr., a Wahpeton-Sisseton Sioux, is a founding editor of *The Raven Chronicles*, a multi-cultural journal of literature and the arts in Seattle; in 1993, Red-Eagle won the Louis Littlecoon Oliver Memorial Prose Award for his manuscript novel, *Red Earth*, which is drawn from his experiences in the Viet Nam War. Fellow Seattle resident and Sioux poet, Tiffany Midge, who is also enrolled at Standing Rock, captured the 1994 Diane Decorah Memorial Poetry Award from the Native Writers' Circle of the Americas for her book-length poetry manuscript, *Diary of a Mixed-Up Half-Breed*. Susan Power, who is also enrolled at Standing Rock, gained national attention with the 1994 publication of her first novel, *The Grass Dancer*.

VISUAL ARTS

Yankton Sioux graphic artist Oscar Howe (1915-1984) has become one of the best known Native American artists in the United States. Known as *Mazuha Koshina* (trader boy), Howe was born at Joe Creek on the Crow Creek Reservation in South Dakota. He earned degrees from Dakota Wesleyan University and the University of Oklahoma, and was a professor of fine arts and artist in residence at the University of South Dakota for 15 years. His work is characterized by poignant images of Indian culture in transition and is depicted in a modern style.

MEDIA

PRINT

Blue Cloud Quarterly.
Address: Blue Cloud Abbey, Marvin, South Dakota 57251.

Camp Crier.
Address: Fort Belknap Agency, Harlem, Montana 59526.

Indian Youth of America Newsletter.
Covers educational, recreational, cultural, and social issues pertinent to Indian youth and those working with Indian youths and families.

Contact: Paige Gordon, Editor.

Address: 609 Badgerow Building, Box 2786, Sioux City, Iowa 51106.

Telephone: (712) 252-3230.

Fax: (712) 252-3712.

Lakota Times.

Address: 1920 Lombardy Drive, Rapid City, South Dakota 57701.

Native Times.

Address: P.O. Box 3300, Rapid City, South Dakota 57709.

News.

Address: United Sioux Tribes, Star Route 3, Pierre, South Dakota 57501.

Oglala Nation News.

Address: Pine Ridge, South Dakota 57770.

Paha Sapa Wahosi.

Address: South Dakota State College, Spearfish, South Dakota 57783.

Rosebud Sioux Herald.

Address: Rosebud, South Dakota 57570.

Sioux Journal.

Address: Eagle Butte, South Dakota 57625.

Sisseton Agency News.

Address: Sisseton BIA Agency, Sisseton, South Dakota 57262.

Spirit Talk Magazine.

Address: Postal Drawer V, Browning, Montana 59417.

Standing Rock Star.

Address: Box 202, Bullhead, South Dakota 57621.

Rosebud Sioux Herald.

Address: P.O. Box 65, Rosebud, South Dakota 57570.

Three Tribes Herald.

Address: Parshall, North Dakota 58770.

Wawatay News.

Published by Wawatay Native Communications Society; reports on events, issues, and news affecting Native people across Ontario.

Contact: Diane Millar, Editor.

Address: 16 Fifth Avenue, P.O. Box 1180, Sioux Lookout, Ontario, Canada P8T 1B7.

Telephone: (807) 737-2951.

Fax: (807) 737-3224.

Wicazo Sa Review.

Address: Route 8, Box 510, Rapid City, South Dakota 57702.

Wotanin-Wowapi.

Newspaper of the Fort Peck Assiniboine and Sioux tribes.

Contact: Bonnie Red Elk, Editor.

Address: Box 1027, Poplar, Montana 59255.

Telephone: (406) 768-5155.

Fax: (406) 768-5478.

RADIO

KCCR.

Address: Box 766, Pierre, South Dakota 57501.

KEYA.

Address: P.O. Box 190, Belcourt, North Dakota 58316.

KILI.

Address: P.O. Box 150, Porcupine, South Dakota 57772.

KINI.

Address: P.O. Box 146, St. Francis, South Dakota 57572.

KOJM.

Address: Box 391, Harve, Montana 59501.

KOLY.

Address: 322 Sixth Street West, Mobridge, South Dakota 57601.

KRBN.

Address: Box 908, Red Lodge, Montana 59068.

ORGANIZATIONS AND ASSOCIATIONS

American Indian Center.

Address: 475 Cedar Street, St. Paul, Minnesota 55102.

Cheyenne River Sioux.

Sioux tribal divisions represented on this reservation include the Sihasapa, Minneconjou, Sans Arcs, and the Oohenonpa.

Address: P.O. Box 590, Eagle Butte, South Dakota 57625.
Telephone: (605) 964-4155.
Fax: (605) 964-4151.

Crow Creek Sioux.

The Sioux on this reservation include descendants of a number of Sioux tribal divisions, including the Minneconjou, Oohenonpa, Lower Brule, and Lower Yanktonai.

Address: P.O. Box 658, Fort Thompson, South Dakota 57339.
Telephone: (605) 245-2221.
Fax (605) 245-2216.

Devils Lake Sioux.

The Sioux on this reservation include Assiniboine, Pabaksa, Santee, Sisseton, Yanktonai, and Wahpeton Sioux.

Address: Sioux Community Center, Fort Totten, North Dakota 58335.
Telephone: (701) 766-4221.
Fax: (701) 766-4854.

Flandreau Santee Sioux.

Represented are descendants of the Santee Sioux who separated from the Mdewakanton and Wahpekute Sioux in 1870 and settled at Flandreau in 1876.

Address: Flandreau Field Office, Box 283, Flandreau, South Dakota 57028.
Telephone: (605) 997-3871.
Fax: (605) 997-3878).

Fort Belknap Sioux.

Represented are the Assiniboine-Sioux and Gros Ventre.

Address: P.O. Box 249, Harlem, Montana 59526.
Telephone: (406) 353-2205.
Fax: (406) 353-2797.

Fort Peck Assiniboine-Sioux.

Represented are the Assiniboine-Sioux, closely related to the Yanktonai.

Address: P.O. Box 1027, Poplar, Montana 59255.
Telephone: (406) 768-5155.
Fax: (406) 768-5478).

Indian Center.

Address: 5633 Regent Avenue North, Minneapolis, Minnesota 55440.

Indian Center.

Address: Box 288, Yankton, South Dakota 57078.

Indian Community Center.

Address: 2957 Farnum, Omaha, Nebraska 68131.

Indian Student Association.

Address: University of Minnesota, Minneapolis, Minnesota 55455.

Lower Brule Sioux.

Represented are the Lower Brule and Yanktonai Sioux.

Address: Lower Brule, South Dakota 57548.
Telephone: (605) 473-5561.
Fax: (605) 473-5606.

Lower Sioux.

Represented are the Mdewakanton and Wahpekute divisions of the Santee Sioux.

Address: Route 1, Box 308, Morton, Minnesota 56270.
Telephone: (507) 697-6185.
Fax: (507) 697-6110.

Montana Department of Indian Affairs.

Address: Mitchell Building, Helena, Montana 59601.

North Dakota Indian Affairs Commission.

Address: 2021 Third Street North, Bismark, North Dakota 58501.

Oglala Sioux.

Represented are predominantly Oglala Sioux, also Brule Sioux and Northern Cheyenne.

Address: Pine Ridge, South Dakota 57770.
Telephone: (605) 867-5821.
Fax: (605) 867-5659.

Prairie Island Sioux.

Represented are the Mdewakanton division of the Santee Sioux.

Address: 5750 Sturgeon Lake Road, Welch, Minnesota 55089.
Telephone: (612) 385-2536.

Fax: (612) 388-1576).

Rosebud Sioux.
Represented are the Oglala, Oohenonpa, Minneconjou, Upper Brule, Waglukhe, and Wahzhazhe Sioux.

Address: Rosebud, South Dakota 57570.
Telephone: (605) 747-2381.
Fax: (605) 747-2243.

Santee Sioux.
Represented are the Santee Sioux, including Mdewakanton, Wahpekute, Sisseton, and Wahpeton.

Address: Route 2, Niobrara, Nebraska 68760.
Telephone: (402) 857-3302.
Fax: (402) 857-3307.

Sioux Tribes of South Dakota Development Corporation.
Promotes employment opportunities for Native Americans; offers job training services.

Address: 919 Main Street, Suite 114, Rapid City, South Dakota 57701-2686.
Telephone: (605) 343-1100.

Sisseton-Wahpeton Sioux.
Represented are the Sisseton Sioux.

Address: Route 2, Agency Village, Sisseton, South Dakota 57262.
Telephone: (605) 698-3911.
Fax: (605) 698-3708).

Skakopee Sioux.
Represented are the Mdewakanton division of the Santee Sioux.

Address: 2330 Sioux Trail, Prior Lake, Minnesota 55372.
Telephone: (612) 445-8900.
Fax: (612) 445-8906).

South Dakota Commission on Indian Affairs.
Address: Pierre, South Dakota 57501.

Standing Rock Sioux.
Represented are predominantly the Teton Sioux, including Hunkpapa and Sihasapa, but also including Lower and Upper Yanktonai.

Address: Fort Yates, North Dakota 58538.
Telephone: (701) 854-7231.

Fax: (701) 854-7299.

Upper Sioux Community.
Represented are predominantly the Sisseton and Wahpeton divisions of the Santee Sioux, but Devil's Lake, Flandreau, and Yanktonai Sioux are also included.

Address: P.O. Box 147, Granite Falls, Minnesota 56241.
Telephone: (612) 564-2360.
Fax: (612) 564-3264.

Urban Sisseton-Wahpeton Sioux.
Address: 1128 Fifth Street, N.E., Minneapolis, Minnesota 55418.

Yankton Sioux.
Represented are the Yanktonai Sioux tribal division.

Address: P.O. Box 248, Marty, South Dakota 57361.
Telephone: (605) 384-3641.
Fax: (605) 384-5687.

MUSEUMS AND RESEARCH CENTERS

Museums that focus on the Sioux include: the Minnesota Historical Society Museum in St. Paul, Minnesota; the Plains Indian Museum in Browning, Montana; the Affiliated Tribes Museum in New Town, North Dakota; the Indian Arts Museum in Martin, South Dakota; the Land of the Sioux Museum in Mobridge, South Dakota; the Mari Sandoz Museum on the Pine Ridge Reservation, South Dakota; the Sioux Indian Museum in Rapid City, South Dakota; and the University of South Dakota Museum in Vermillion.

SOURCES FOR ADDITIONAL STUDY

Incident At Oglala: The Leonard Peltier Story (video documentary), directed by Michael Apted, narrated by Robert Redford. Carolco International N.V. and Spanish Fork Motion Picture Company, 1991.

Marquis, Arnold. *A Guide to America's Indians: Ceremonials, Reservations, and Museums*. Norman: University of Oklahoma Press, 1974.

McClain, Gary (Eagle Walking Turtle). *Indian America: A Traveler's Companion*, third edition. Santa Fe, New Mexico: John Muir Publications, 1993.

Native America: Portrait of the Peoples, edited by Duane Champagne, foreword by Dennis Banks. Detroit: Gale Research, 1994.

Neihardt, Hilda. *Black Elk and Flaming Rainbow: Personal Memories of the Lakota Holy Man and John Neihardt*. Lincoln: University of Nebraska Press, 1995.

Neihardt, John. *Black Elk Speaks: Being the Life Story of a Holy Man of the Oglala Sioux*. Lincoln: University of Nebraska Press, 1961.

O'Brien, Sharon. *American Indian Tribal Governments* (Civilization of the American Indian Series). Norman: University of Oklahoma Press, 1989.

Paha Sapa: The Struggle for the Black Hills (video documentary), directed by Mel Lawrence. HBO Studio Productions, 1993.

Wiping the Tears of Seven Generations (video documentary), directed by Gary Rhine and Fidel Moreno. Kifaru Productions, 1992.

SLOVAK

by
**June Granatir
Alexander**

AMERICANS

**Slovak immigrants
exemplified the
pattern evident
among most ethnic
groups in the United
States: they adjusted
to American society
and preserved some
traditions and values
while altering
others.**

OVERVIEW

Slovakia is at the crossroads between eastern and western Europe. It is bordered by Poland to the north, Hungary to the south, the Czech Republic to the west, and the Ukraine to the east. Although a small country, with a land mass of 18,919 square miles, Slovakia's topography varies widely. Its territory includes rugged mountains, dense forests, and low fertile plains. The vast Carpathian mountain range that stretches along Slovakia's northern border also juts into central Slovakia. In this central region the Tatras, which cap the Carpathian system, reach altitudes as high as 8,711 feet. The capital, Bratislava, is located in southwestern Slovakia on the Danube River.

Slovakia's population is 5,297,000. Although the country is ethnically diverse, Slovaks are the overwhelming majority accounting for 4.5 million (85.6 percent) of the inhabitants. The populace also includes approximately 600,000 (10.8 percent) Hungarians and 79,500 (1.5 percent) Gypsies. The remaining population consists primarily of Czechs, Jews, and Carpatho-Rusyns. The official language is Slovak.

Slightly more than 60 percent of Slovakia's inhabitants are Roman Catholic while 8.4 percent are Protestant. Although most ethnic Hungarians belong to the Reformed church, Lutherans constitute the country's largest Protestant denomination.

Other faiths include Judaism, Greek Catholic, and Orthodox. The religion of an estimated 27.2 percent of the population is either unidentifiable (17.5 percent) or atheist (9.7 percent).

HISTORY

Throughout most of its history modern-day Slovakia was not an independent country. Its inhabitants were subject peoples of multi-national empires. When the Austro-Hungarian Empire collapsed in 1918, Slovaks joined with Czechs to create an independent Czechoslovakia. Except for a short period of independence during World War II (1939-1945), Slovakia remained part of that multi-national state until 1993.

The history of Slovakia reaches back to the fifth and sixth centuries when Slavic tribes migrated into the region south of the Carpathian Mountains. These ancestors of modern-day Slovaks established villages and developed an agricultural economy in the Middle Danube Basin. In the mid-ninth century Slavs from Bohemia, Moravia, and the Danube region united to form the Great Moravian Empire, which comprised most of latter-day Czechoslovakia, southern Poland, and western Hungary. The empire was the first unification of Czech (Bohemian and Moravian) and Slovak peoples. In the 860s Christianity was introduced into the empire. In 907 Magyars, a semi-nomadic people from the northeast, invaded the empire and established the Kingdom of Hungary, which incorporated modern-day Slovakia. The collapse of the Great Moravian Empire split the Czechs and Slovaks, and they stayed separate for the next one thousand years. Until 1918 the Slovak lands remained part of Hungary, but the region was known as Upper Hungary, not Slovakia.

During the fifteenth century, the Protestant Reformation spread into Upper Hungary, and most Slovaks converted to the Lutheran faith. In 1526, after the Ottoman Turks conquered the southern section of its kingdom, Hungary became part of the Hapsburg Empire. During the Counter-Reformation which accompanied Hapsburg rule, most Slovaks returned to Roman Catholicism, although a significant minority remained Protestant.

MODERN ERA

In the nineteenth century Slovaks and Hungary's other ethnic minorities were subjected to Magyarization, an official policy of forced assimilation. The government made Magyar (Hungarian) the official language and outlawed all other languages. It closed schools and adopted other measures to abolish ethnic cultures in Hungary. By the early twentieth century, the Magyarization policy had enjoyed significant success in Upper Hungary. In general, Slovaks living in the region did not view themselves as a separate people.

World War I opened the way for dismembering the Austro-Hungarian Empire and letting its subject nationalities create independent countries. As a result the Czech and Slovak lands were united, and Czechoslovakia was created on October 28, 1918. Many Slovak supporters of an independent Czechoslovakia had envisioned the new state as a federation of two independent people. Instead, the country's constitution established a centralized government with a single capital city, Prague. Instituting a centralized government, instead of a system that granted Slovaks autonomy, led to tensions between Czechs and Slovaks in the 1920s and 1930s. As result of the Munich Agreement (1938) and Hitler's invasion of Czechoslovakia in March 1939, Slovakia's political leaders declared Slovakia independent. Independent Slovakia was in reality a puppet government of Germany.

In 1945 Slovakia and the Czech lands were reunified. In postwar elections the Communist party enjoyed significant victories, and in 1948 party leaders engineered a coup and took over the government. For the next 40 years Slovakia remained part of Czechoslovakia and under communist control. In 1969 the government granted Slovakia autonomy within the country and designated Bratislava as the capital city. In the fall of 1989 Slovaks joined Czechs in the Velvet Revolution that toppled the communist-controlled government in December. In April 1990 Czechoslovakia was renamed the Czech and Slovak Federative Republic. The first free elections since 1945 occurred in June 1990. As reforms and measures to privatize the economy were introduced, relations between Czechs and Slovaks became strained. After the June 1992 elections, Czech and Slovak government officials decided that the two regions should separate. Because it was achieved without bloodshed or serious animosities, the breakup of the former Czechoslovakia is often called the Velvet Divorce. On January 1, 1993, Slovakia became independent. Slovakia's first prime minister was Vladimir Meciar.

IMMIGRATION

A few Slovaks immigrated to the United States before the American Civil War but their numbers were small. Large-scale Slovak immigration to the United States began in the late 1870s, steadily increased during the following two decades, and peaked in 1905 when 52,368 Slovaks entered. Slovak immigration declined precipitously during World War I and started up again after hostilities ended in 1918. The movement came almost to a complete halt in the 1920s when American immigration laws virtually stopped East European immigration into the United States. According to immigration records 480,201 Slovaks entered the country between 1899 and 1918. The 1920 census found that there were 274,948 foreign-born Slovaks in the United States. Slovak immigrants and their children totaled 619,866.

Statistics on Slovak immigration, however, are imprecise and it is difficult to determine the number that actually immigrated to the United States. Before 1899 U.S. immigration officials listed immigrants by country of birth. Thus, until 1899 Slovaks were recorded as Hungarians. Even after immigrants were enumerated by nationality, the Magyarization policies had been so effective that many Slovaks did not identify themselves as such. Also, perhaps one-third of the Slovaks who came to the United States were not immigrants but instead migrants. Often called "birds of passage," they worked temporarily in America and then returned to Europe. They wanted to earn money to buy property in their homeland. It was common for Slovaks to make several trips between the United States and Upper Hungary. At least 19 percent of the Slovaks who entered an American port from 1899 to 1910 had been in the United States one or more times before. Not until 1908 did immigration officials subtract the number of immigrants leaving from the total numbers entering the United States. Still, it is clear that temporary migrants formed an especially large contingent of the early stages of the Slovak immigration and remained a common feature of the movement. Between 1908 and 1910, for example, 80,797 Slovaks entered the United States while 41,726 left. Its temporary nature also affected the composition of the Slovak immigration. Most Slovak immigrants were unskilled laborers, and men typically outnumbered women by more than two to one. Between 1899 and 1910, 266,262 Slovak males and 111,265 Slovak females entered the United States.

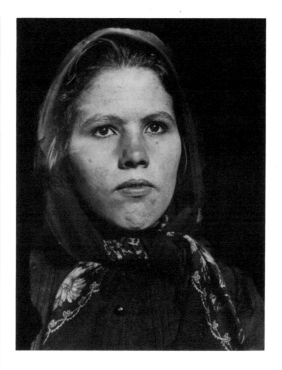

This Slovak woman's photograph was taken shortly after her arrival to Ellis Island.

Over time, many birds of passage decided to stay in America and sent for their families. The reasons for staying varied. Some were unable to save enough money to buy land and in some regions of their homeland no land was available. Others decided that America promised a better future while others married and decided to stay. Whatever their motives, between 1880 and the mid-1920s probably between 450,000 and 500,000 Slovaks moved permanently to the United States.

Slovak immigrants were committed to saving money and fulfilling obligations to families left behind. As a result they routinely sent money to Europe. In 1899 alone more than $4 million was channeled to the Slovak region of Hungary. The determination to save money, compounded by the fact that so many Slovaks were males who had come alone, influenced living standards. In general, Slovaks tried to live cheaply. Laborers often roomed in boardinghouses where they could get a bed and daily meals for as little as ten dollars per month. These boardinghouses were typically run by Slovak immigrants, a husband and wife who either owned or rented a large house. For these Slovak families, taking in boarders became an important source of additional income.

Slovak immigration began during a period when anti-foreign sentiment was on the rise in the United States. The response by Americans to Slovaks reflected the common anti-foreign attitude.

Furthermore, the desire by Slovaks to live cheaply, the large number of males, and their concentration in unskilled industrial jobs reinforced beliefs that immigrants were creating social and economic problems for the United States. Although criticized for drinking and living in crowded conditions Slovaks were not usually singled out as presenting special problems. Since Slovaks did not have a separate identifiable homeland and most Americans did not know that there was a Slovak people, they often referred to Slovak immigrants simply as Slavs, Slavic, Slavish, or by the pejorative terms Hunky or Bohunk. Based on their geographic origin, Slovaks fell into the general category of undesirable immigrants. Judging persons from both eastern and southern Europe as biologically and intellectually inferior and a threat to American society, some native-born Americans demanded that these "undesirables" be barred from the country. The immigration laws of the 1920s that curtailed southern and east European immigration severely reduced the number of Slovaks who could enter the United States. Between 1929 and 1965 American quotas permitted only 2,874 persons from Czechoslovakia to immigrate annually to the United States. In the decades after immigration restriction went into effect, Slovaks were lost in popular perceptions and culture, as they were lumped into generalizations about the massive turn-of-the-century immigration.

Slovak Americans rank as the second largest Slavic group in the United States. The 1990 census revealed that 1,882,897 Americans claimed Slovak descent: 1,210,652 listed Slovak as their "first ancestry," and another 672,245 designated it as "second." Nearly three-fourths (74.7 percent) of Americans acknowledging some Slovak descent resided in the Northeast and Midwest. Less than .03 percent of the 1990 Slovak American population was foreign born, and 74 percent of these immigrants had come before World War II.

SETTLEMENT

Slovaks gravitated to areas where industries were expanding and needed unskilled labor. More than half the Slovak immigrants went to Pennsylvania and primarily to the milltowns and coal mining districts in the state's western region. Other popular destinations included Ohio, New Jersey, New York, and Illinois. Slovaks "chain migrated," that is they went to places where previous Slovak immigrants already lived. Between 1908 and 1910 an astounding 98.4 percent of Slovaks entering the country were joining relatives or friends.

ACCULTURATION AND ASSIMILATION

Slovak immigrants exemplified the pattern evident among most ethnic groups in the United States: they adjusted to American society and preserved some traditions and values while altering others. Values and beliefs that Slovaks brought with them were rooted in their rural past and reflected the concerns of agricultural communities. Slovaks placed great value on owning property and a home. They valued the family and the honoring of family obligations.

TRADITIONS, CUSTOMS, AND BELIEFS

Slovaks were a deeply religious people. Some religious holy days were customarily observed with village processions while others were less dramatic. On some saints' feast days Slovak villagers came together as a community to pray for a favor associated by legend with a saint. For example, on the feast of Saint Mark (April 25) they prayed for rain and good weather during the upcoming growing season. Although Slovaks were fervently religious, their beliefs and customs were a blend of folklore and superstitions linked to the Christian calendar. A vast array of superstitions permeated their culture. For example, Slovaks performed rituals to rid or protect their villages from demons and witches.

Slovaks also carried out numerous rituals, especially during the Christmas season, which they believed foretold their future. On November 30 at the beginning of the season they poured lead into boiling water and relied on the shape of the cooled droplets to make predictions about the forthcoming year. Young women had several rituals that they believed might reveal who their husbands would be. On Christmas Eve Slovaks cracked nuts and used the condition of the meat as an indicator of what the upcoming year might hold for them. They also took measures that they hoped would control the future. On Christmas Eve, the head of the household gave food from the dinner table to the family's animals in the hope of ensuring the livestock's health.

TRADITIONAL COSTUMES

The typical folk costume for women consisted of a puffed-sleeve blouse, a vest, a short but full skirt, an apron, a bonnet or headscarf, and calf-high boots. Male costumes included a hat, a shirt overlaid with a vest, trousers, and boots. Men's trousers, typically form-fitting but occasionally flared, were usually white with colorful embroidery. Both male and female folk costumes made of homespun cloth and sheepskin were multi-colored and featured intricate embroidery. Specific styles, colors, and items included in the attire varied from village to village and from region to region. In fact, peasant costumes could be so distinctive that they simultaneously indicated a person's village and religion. A headdress also revealed a woman's marital status. In the United States, Slovak folk costumes have become nostalgic or quaint artifacts worn only for interethnic or Slovak events.

CUISINE

Soup is a staple of the Slovak daily diet. Cabbage, potatoes, and dumplings, all prepared in a variety of ways, are regular fare on Slovak tables. Meat, especially in Slovakia's poorer eastern region, was not a common ingredient in soups or main dishes; though some traditional dishes served throughout Slovakia are meat-based. *Klobasa* (a sausage with garlic) and *holubky* (cabbage leaves stuffed with pork, rice, and onions) are the most popular. Duck and chicken are reserved for special occasions, but for particularly festive celebrations goose is preferred. Although desserts are not part of the daily diet, Slovak culinary specialities include several filled *kolacy* (sweet yeast baked goods). The most popular *kolac* contains prune, ground nut, or crushed poppyseed fillings. Depending on the filling, *pirohy* (small dumplings) are served as main dishes or as desserts.

Slovaks attach great importance to serving traditional foods on Christmas and Easter, the only major holidays observed by Slovaks in both the homeland and the United States. Although in regional variations, several dishes served at Christmas and Easter are considered authentic Slovak cuisine. On Christmas Eve the main dishes consist of *bobalky* (bite-size rolls in either sauerkraut and butter or in a poppyseed sauce) and a special mushroom soup. Traditional Easter specialties include Slovak *paska* (a sweet, yeast bread with raisins) and homemade *hrudka* also known as *syrek* (a bland, custard-style imitation cheese).

HOLIDAYS CELEBRATED BY SLOVAK AMERICANS

In their Slovak homeland, the celebration of Christmas and Easter was an event for both family

and village. While Slovak American Christmas celebrations have taken on American features with a greater emphasis on gifts and a midday turkey dinner, many Americans of Slovak descent adhere to the custom of the family coming together for traditional Slovak foods on Christmas Eve. Visiting family during both the Christmas and Easter seasons has also remained an obligatory custom among Slovak Americans.

HEALTH AND MENTAL HEALTH ISSUES

Neither Slovak immigrants nor their descendants have unique health problems. The 1990 census data indicate that average rates of disability among both young and elderly Slovaks are the same as for most other ethnic groups in the United States. The same is true for the number of Slovaks institutionalized. Immigrants and subsequent generations did suffer from afflictions characteristic of other working-class Americans, especially at the turn of the century. In addition to a high rate of tuberculosis, workers were killed or permanently maimed in industrial accidents. Some Slovaks who toiled in mines have been stricken with the respiratory problems that afflict that segment of workers.

Slovaks had local folk remedies. It has not been documented how extensively immigrants practiced these folk cures or how long they persisted in the United States. Although no systematic study of Slovak health attitudes has been done, there is no evidence that folk cures had any real impact on Slovak health practices in the United States.

LANGUAGE

Slovak belongs to the Slavic language group. Although similar to other Slavic languages, especially Czech, Slovak is linguistically distinct with its own grammar and vocabulary. Slovak has three dialects (western, central, and eastern) that roughly correspond with geographical areas in Slovakia. Each dialect also has numerous local and regional variations. Slovak, like other Slavic languages, has diacritical marks that govern the pronunciation of both consonants and vowels. The accent is on the first syllable.

The roots of the Slovak language predate the introduction of Christianity in the ninth century, but it did not become a written language until centuries later. The first serious attempt to codify a Slovak literary language occurred in the late eighteenth century. This early version was later rejected for one codified in the mid-1840s based on the central Slovak dialect.

Slovak was the primary language spoken among immigrants and between them and their children. The language has not persisted among successive generations in the United States. Several factors contributed to this decline. First, children gave way to the pressure in American society to abandon foreign languages. Second, immigrants were often barely literate. Although they taught their children, especially the older sons and daughters, to speak Slovak they could not teach them to read and write the language. Slovaks established parochial schools where language instructions were provided, but these classes often either proved inadequate or students did not remain in school long enough to become literate in Slovak. However, Slovak is taught in various Sunday schools for children and in universities, including Kent State University. Several American libraries have Slovak-language collections.

The Slovak language was modified slightly in the United States as English, or modern, technical terms were introduced into the vocabulary. The absence of diacritical marks in English meant that either the spelling or the pronunciation of many Slovak names was changed. For example, a person with the name Karcis (pronounced "kar-chis") had the option to change the pronunciation to the English ("kar-kis") or keep the pronunciation and change the spelling to Karchish.

GREETINGS AND OTHER POPULAR EXPRESSIONS

Common Slovak greetings include: *Dobre rano* ("dobre rahno")—Good morning; *Dobry den* ("dobre den")—Good day; *Dobry vecer* ("dobre vecher")—Good evening; *Dobru noc* ("dobroo nots")—Good night; *Prosim* ("prosem")—please, if you please, excuse me; *Dakujem* ("djakooyem")—Thank you; *Dobru chut'* ("dobroo kootye")—Eat well!, bon appetit!; *Na zdravie* ("nazdravye")—To [your] health!, cheers! (a toast); *Vesele Vianoce* ("veseleh veanotse")—Merry Christmas.

FAMILY AND COMMUNITY DYNAMICS

Immigration is a disruptive process, especially for families. Although chain migration meant that

Slovaks typically went to where relatives and friends had already settled, families were temporarily torn apart. Men immigrated alone, lived in boardinghouses, and later summoned their families or fiancees to join them. The process also worked in reverse as children emigrated first and then sent for elderly parents left behind in Europe. Although Slovaks typically maintained a close-knit family system, by mid-twentieth century Slovak Americans were moving from cities to suburbs. During the latter decades the third and fourth generations were also moving from dying milltowns to metropolitan regions.

Marriage patterns influenced family and community dynamics. For the immigrant generation, the norm was marriage between Slovaks. The second generation followed the same trend into the 1920s and 1930s, but by the post-World War II era interethnic marriages proved more common. Dating patterns differed from generation to generation and even within the same generation. Immigrants recalled that, for them, dating in the United States was limited to events sponsored by Slovak fraternals, churches, or social groups. Attending religious services and sharing in a family dinner also were common among couples. By the mid-1920s the Slovak youth had adopted the dating practices common among their American peers. They enjoyed dances, movies, amusement parks, and other entertainment characteristic of the changing contemporary popular culture.

Both traditional culture and religious values combined to make divorce uncommon among Slovak immigrants. Reliable data on divorce rates for specific ethnic groups are unavailable but, given general trends in the United States, the empirical evidence suggests that dissolutions involving Slovaks surely rose in the latter part of the twentieth century.

WEDDINGS

Weddings were lengthy affairs that, depending on the village's size, could involve nearly all the inhabitants. Preparatory rituals for the marriage, the ceremony, and subsequent celebrations could last a week. During the festivities, usually three days after the actual marriage ceremony, the bonneting of the bride took place. A bonnet was placed on her head, and she was accepted as a married woman.

Christening the newborn traditionally occurred within a few days of birth but godparents were selected long before the child was born. Slovaks chose godparents carefully because these persons were expected to assume responsibility for the child's welfare should misfortune befall the parents. Following both Protestant and Catholic ceremonies, the celebrators retired to the home of the parents or godparents to partake in a celebratory feast. In some areas, after a son's birth or christening a bottle of *slivovica* (plumb brandy), was buried only to be retrieved and consumed on his wedding day.

FUNERALS

Proper burial of the dead was a ritual that spanned several days. The deceased's body usually lay in his or her home for two days, and on the third a procession of villagers accompanied the coffin to the cemetery for burial. Deaths also triggered a host of superstitions. Immediately following a person's demise, Slovaks covered all the mirrors and closed all the windows in the deceased's home. They believed that these measures would prevent the dead from returning.

EDUCATION

Slovak culture traditionally did not place a high emphasis on education. The Hungarian government's Magyarization policy, together with the agricultural nature of Slovak society, worked against developing a culture that valued formal education. Between 24 percent and 30 percent of the turn-of-the-century Slovak immigrants over the age of 14 could neither read nor write. Those who had attended school had gone for only a few years. With this background many immigrant parents, especially during the pre-World War I era, did not hesitate to put their children to work at early ages. In the 1920s more Slovak children regularly attended school and more completed 12 years of education. Nevertheless, Slovak parents generally advocated practical learning over an education in the sciences or liberal arts. Rather than stressing social mobility, both first- and second-generation parents typically encouraged children to get a secure job even if that meant working in a factory. The value system of both first- and second-generation Slovaks placed women in the traditional role of wife, mother, and home-maker; therefore, education was considered even less valuable for daughters than for sons.

The tendency to downplay formal education did have an impact. Based on the 1990 census nearly 21 percent of native-born Slovak Americans over the age of 24 had not received a high school diploma. This percentage undoubtedly includes a significant number of elderly persons who were forced to leave school in the earlier half of the century. Americans of Slovak descent have attended college but not in large numbers. In 1990 only 14.3 percent (123,341) of Slovak Americans older than 24 had a bachelor's degree from a four-year college, and 6.3 percent (54,008) had an associate's degree. Census figures also showed that only 7.5 percent (64,998) of this age group held a professional, master's, or doctoral degree. However, the data also reveal that more than one-half (52.6 percent) of Slovak Americans who received a bachelor's degree continued their education and obtained an advanced degree. Fewer Slovak American women than men have received college degrees. Women represented only 42.4 percent (52,237) of the Slovak Americans with a bachelor's degree, while men accounted for 57.6 percent (71,104). The discrepancy between men and women who received advanced degrees is more pronounced. Only 37.5 percent (5,196) of the Slovak Americans with professional degrees in 1990 were women while the percentage of men accounted for 62.5 percent (8,668). Women with doctorates represented 19.6 percent (1,072) of the total while men claimed 80.4 percent (4,391).

The stress on traditional roles for Slovak women has influenced their educational achievements and community activities. During World War II, Slovak women led local drives to sell war bonds and helped raise money for the International Red Cross and other relief projects. Otherwise, Slovak American women have typically limited their activities to their churches, fraternals, schools, and community events.

RELIGION

Slovak immigrants include Catholics, Lutherans, and Calvinists, but the majority of Slovaks are Roman Catholic. The first Slovak Roman Catholic churches were founded in 1885 in Hazleton, Pennsylvania, and Streator, Illinois. During the next four decades Slovak Catholics established nearly 250 churches in the United States. The universality of the Latin mass and Catholic theology meant that Slovaks continued to practice their religion as they had done in their homeland. The requirement that individual congregations pay all church expenses was the most significant difference between Slovak Catholic churches in Europe and the United States. Because parishes had to be self-supporting, lay organizations sponsored numerous fund-raising social events, and ethnic churches became centers of community activities.

A small number of Slovak Byzantine rite Catholics also migrated to the United States. They organized a few churches but more often they cooperated with other Byzantine rite Catholics, especially Carpatho-Rusyns, to found ethnically mixed parishes. Byzantine rite Catholics professed the same creed as followers of the Roman rite, and both were under papal authority. However, services in the Byzantine rite were conducted in Old Church Slavonic, which used the Cyrillic alphabet. The fact that Byzantine rite clergymen could marry while Roman Catholic rite priests could not became a significant difference in the United States. Having a married clergy created problems for Byzantine rite Catholics because some American bishops refused to accept wedded priests in their dioceses. This refusal caused some Byzantine rite Catholic Slovaks to join an Orthodox church.

Lutherans comprised the second largest body of Slovak immigrants. They organized their first congregation in 1883 in Freeland, Pennsylvania, and during the next half century Slovak Lutherans established more than 70 congregations and missions. In 1902 Slovak Lutherans formed their own synod, an executive and judicial body made up of clergy and laypersons. Conflicts developed when the Slovak Synod became affiliated with the Evangelical Lutheran Synodical Conference of America in 1908. Some Slovak Lutheran clergy and laypersons refused to adopt liturgical changes subsequently demanded by the conference and, as a result, serious divisions developed. Continued disagreements over liturgical and theological principles led to the formation of the Slovak Zion Synod in 1919, which affiliated with the United Lutheran Church in America in 1962. Most Slovak Lutherans belong to congregations associated either with the Lutheran Church of America or the Synodical Conference.

Only a small number of Slovak Calvinists immigrated to the United States. A few of these Protestants affiliated with Reformed churches but most became Presbyterians. They founded 15 Slovak Presbyterian churches. A tiny number of Slovak immigrants converted to other Protestant religions, primarily to the Congregational church. In 1916, there were three Slovak Congregational churches and another that included both Czechs and Slovaks. These four churches had only 308 adult members.

Slovak churches survived for decades as ethnic institutions while experiencing some change. By the 1930s Slovak Protestant churches were introducing English into their services. Catholics continued to use Latin until the 1960s when the Catholic church began to use the vernacular. As the immigrant generation died and their descendants moved out of ethnic neighborhoods, some Slovak churches declined or were taken over by new immigrant groups. Nevertheless, in cities and small towns especially in Pennsylvania, Ohio, New York, and New Jersey, vibrant Slovak Lutheran and Catholic churches still exist.

EMPLOYMENT AND ECONOMIC TRADITIONS

Eighty percent of Slovak immigrants had been common or farm laborers in their homeland. Having few skills Slovaks found jobs as manual laborers in heavy industries, especially in steel and allied industries that produced durable goods. A large number of Slovaks also toiled in coal mines. In 1910 surveys revealed that 82 percent of Slovak males labored as miners or in iron and steel mills. Some Slovak women were employed as domestics, but in cities they often worked in food processing plants. Fewer employment opportunities existed for women in small milltowns. Those who were unable to find domestic service jobs typically remained unemployed and helped at home until they married. Widows and married women often ran boardinghouses where they cooked and did the laundry for residents.

The majority of second-generation Slovak males followed their fathers' paths and became industrial laborers, although some did enter the professions or acquired skills. Subsequent generations have deviated from this course. The 1990 census found that only 5.7 percent of Slovak Americans were self-employed while the vast majority remained wage and salary workers; however, in the type of jobs they differed from their parents or grandparents. In 1990 only 26 percent of Slovaks had jobs in manufacturing, mining, and construction. Most Slovaks were employed in white-collar jobs.

The evidence does not yet indicate what impact corporate downsizing has had on Slovak Americans holding white-collar positions but the process has clearly affected laborers. The closing of plants in the industrial Northeast and Midwest has adversely affected second- and third-generation Slovaks, especially persons beyond middle age. Still, the unemployment rate of 4.4 percent among Slovak Americans is below the national average. The median income for Slovak families in 1989 was just over $40,000, and only 3.7 percent had incomes below the poverty level.

POLITICS AND GOVERNMENT

Slovak involvement in politics has changed over the decades. At the turn of the century few immigrant workers regularly participated in political activities. Such involvement was typically limited to leaders of Slovak fraternal societies. Founded to provide insurance, disability benefits, and unemployment compensation, and to stimulate ethnic consciousness among Slovaks, fraternals also encouraged or required members to become American citizens. Fraternal leaders believed that having a membership composed mainly of American citizens would enhance the fraternals' political clout. These organizations worked hard to influence legislation that affected immigrants. They also became involved in American domestic issues, especially those that concerned working-class Americans. During the 1930s, fraternals actively lobbied for social security, unemployment benefits, minimum wage-maximum hours legislation, and the legalization of unions. Slovak immigrants and their children helped organize and joined unions, especially in the steel and mining industries where so many of them worked. In his powerful novel, *Out of This Furnace* (1941), Thomas Bell, a second-generation Slovak, vividly describes the work experiences and union activities of Slovaks in western Pennsylvania where he grew up during the Great Depression.

An accurate picture of the political activities of Slovak immigrants and successive generations is difficult to discern. In 1920 when citizenship data was recorded by "country of birth" only 45.8 percent of persons from Czechoslovakia had become American citizens and could vote. During the 1930s the New Deal programs drew working-class Slovaks to the Democratic Party. Through the 1950s Slovaks seemed to remain loyal to the Democratic Party in state and local elections but the pattern in national elections is less clear. In 1960 John F. Kennedy's Catholicism and Cold War liberalism attracted Slovak American Catholics. The specific voting patterns and political activities of Slovak Americans during the following three decades have not been studied, but empirical evidence suggests that the same religious, class, regional, and related differences that divide the country's population and influence political behavior in general also fragment Americans of Slovak descent. In geographic areas where Slovaks have concentrated, they have been elected to local and state offices. But only one Slovak American has been elected to the United States Congress—Joseph M. Gaydos (1926-), who represented Pennsylvania's twentieth district from 1968 through 1992. Joseph Yasko of Bethlehem, Pennsylvania, was a state representative in the 1930s, and a state senator in the 1950s.

"Identification with an ethnic group is a source of values, instincts, ideas, and perceptions that throw original light on the meaning of America."

Michael Novak, an American philosopher and theologian of Slovak descent, from his *The Rise of the Unmeltable Ethnics,* 1972.

RELATIONS WITH SLOVAKIA

Slovak organizations also became involved in the politics of their homeland. Specifically to counter the Hungarian government's intensified Magyarization efforts, in 1907 Slovak journalists and national fraternal leaders organized the Slovak League of America. During World War I, the league and Slovak fraternal societies worked to secure American and international support for the creation of an independent Czecho-Slovakia. Their activities included lobbying American politicians and trying to influence public opinion. The league and its supporters pressured Thomas Masaryk, the future first president of Czechoslovakia, into signing the Pittsburgh Agreement on May 30, 1918. The document ostensibly provided for Slovak autonomy within the newly created state. According to the agreement's provisions Slovakia was to have its own independent administration, parliament, and court system. The Pittsburgh Agreement subsequently became one of the most controversial documents in Czechoslovakia's history. Its provisions were not incorporated into Czechoslovakia's constitution, and a centralized government was established instead. During the 1920s and 1930s several Slovak American organizations tried unsuccessfully to persuade Czechoslovakia's government to implement the Pittsburgh Agreement. During the Cold War, Slovak organizations actively supported American policies and those of other countries that opposed the totalitarian government in Czechoslovakia.

MILITARY

The precise number of Slovaks who served in World War I cannot be determined. Military records for the period after 1920 categorize Slovaks and Czechs together as Czechoslovaks. According to the 1990 census, 6,566 persons, including 635 women, of Slovak ancestry were serving in the United States military.

INDIVIDUAL AND GROUP CONTRIBUTIONS

The Americanization of names as well as intermarriage among ethnic groups precludes identifying many persons of Slovak ancestry who have made a significant contribution to American society or to the arts, sciences, education, industry, and government.

AEROSPACE

Astronaut Eugene Cernan (1935-) participated in Gemini space flights and Apollo-Saturn moon missions; his father came to the United States from Kysuce in Slovakia.

ARTS AND ENTERTAINMENT

Andy Warhol, (1928-1987), pop artist, famous for his paintings of soup cans and other modern art, was the son of immigrants who came to the United States from Slovakia in 1913. Actor Jack Palance (1920-) received the 1991 Academy Award for best supporting actor for his role in *City Slickers*.

LITERATURE

Thomas Bell (1903-1961), originally Belejcak, was a second-generation Slovak author of six novels; his best and most famous novel, *Out of This Furnace*, vividly portrays the life of Slovak immigrants, their children, and grandchildren from the turn of the century into the Great Depression of the 1930s. Michael Novak (1933-), author of *Naked I Leave*, is also a theologian and conservative commentator who received the 1994 Templeton Prize for Progress in Religion; Sonya Jason (1927-) is the author of *Concomitant Soldier*. Paul Wilkes (1938-) is also a noted writer.

MILITARY

In World War I, Michael Kocak (1882-c.1918), who was born in Gbely in western Slovakia, received both an Army and a Navy Congressional Medal of Honor; he singlehandedly and under fire eliminated a German machine-gun nest and then organized 25 French colonial troops and led them in a successful attack on another machine-gun position. Michael Strank (d. 1945), a Slovak who came to the United States in 1922, was one of the six men immortalized by the famous photograph of the raising of the American flag atop Mount Suribachi, Iwo Jima, on February 23, 1945; the U.S. Marine Corps Memorial monument located adjacent to Arlington National Cemetery is based on that photograph.

SPORTS

George Blanda (1927-) is a football legend. Chicago Black Hawks star Stan Mikita (1940-) was born in Slovakia.

MEDIA

PRINT

Fraternally Yours, Zenska Jednota.

A monthly publication of the First Catholic Slovak Ladies Association.

Contact: Dolores J. Soska, Editor.

Address: Box 184, Vandergrift, Pennsylvania 15690.

Telephone: (412) 567-5224.

Jednota.

A monthly publication of the First Catholic Slovak Union.

Contact: Joseph C. Krajsa, Editor.

Address: Jednota Press, Rosedale and Jednota Lane, Middletown, Pennsylvania 17057.

Telephone: (717) 944-0461.

Narodne noviny.

A monthly publication of the National Slovak Society.

Contact: Lori Crowley, Associate Editor.

Address: 2325 East Carson Street, Pittsburgh, Pennsylvania 15203.

Telephone: (412) 488-1890.

Slovak Catholic Falcon.

A weekly publication of the Slovak Catholic Sokol.

Contact: Daniel S. Tanzone, Editor.

Address: 205 Madison Street, Passaic, New Jersey 07055.

Telephone: (201) 777-4010.

Zornicka.

A monthly publication of the Ladies Pennsylvania Slovak Catholic Union.

Contact: Cecilia Gaughan, Editor.

Address: 69 Public Square, Suite 922, Wilkes-Barre, Pennsylvania 18701.

Telephone: (717) 823-3513.

RADIO

WCPN-FM (90.3).

"Slovak Radio Hour" is a weekly one-hour cultural program that also includes local Slovak community items.

Contact: Vlado E. Mlynek.

Address: 8211 Essen Avenue, Parma, Ohio 44129.

Telephone: (216) 884-3705.

WEDO-AM (810).

"McKeesport Slovak Radio Hour" is a weekly one-hour program that features folk music, news from Slovakia, and local Slovak community items.

Address: Midtown Plaza Mall, 516 Sinclair Street, McKeesport, Pennsylvania 15132.

Telephone: (412) 664-4431.

WERE-AM (1300).

"Slovak Radio Program" is a weekly one-hour cultural program that also includes local Slovak community items.

Contact: Johanna Oros.

Address: 1041 Huron Road, Cleveland, Ohio 44124.

Telephone: (216) 696-1300.

WMBS-AM (590).

"Slovak Hour" is a weekly one-hour program featuring music and news.

Contact: Rudolph Faix.

Address: 82 West Lafayette Street, Uniontown, Pennsylvania 15401.

Telephone: (412) 438-3900.

WPIT-AM (730).

"Western Pennsylvania Slovak Radio Hour" is a weekly one-hour program that features folk music and local Slovak community items.

Address: 200 Gateway Towers, Suite 1615, Pittsburgh, Pennsylvania 15222.

Telephone: (412) 281-1900.

ORGANIZATIONS AND ASSOCIATIONS

First Catholic Slovak Ladies Association (FCSLA).

Founded in August 1892, the FCSLA is a religious fraternal organization that provides insurance benefits to more than 105,000 members. It also promotes the preservation of Catholicism and ethnic culture among Slovak American Catholics.

Contact: Anna S. Granchay, President.

Address: 24950 Chagrin Boulevard, Beechwood, Ohio 44122.

Telephone: (216) 464-8015.

First Catholic Slovak Union of the U.S.A. and Canada (FCSU).

Founded in September 1890, the FCSU is a religious fraternal organization that provides insurance benefits to more than 88,300 members. It promotes the preservation of Catholicism and ethnic culture among Slovak American Catholics. The FCSU also operates an orphanage and a publishing house, the Jednota Press, in Middletown, Pennsylvania.

Contact: Joseph R. Kristofik, President.

Address: 6611 Rockside Road, Independence, Ohio 44131.

Telephone: (216) 642-9406.

National Slovak Society (NSS).

Founded in 1890, the NSS is a secular fraternal organization that provides insurance benefits to more than 13,700 members. It also promotes the preservation of ethnic culture among Slovak Americans.

Contact: David G. Blazek, President.

Address: 2325 East Carson Street, Pittsburgh, Pennsylvania 15203.

Telephone: (412) 488-1890.

Slovak Catholic Sokol (SCS).

Founded in 1905, the SCS is a religious organization that provides insurance benefits to nearly 41,400 members. It promotes athletic and gymnastic programs as well as the preservation of Catholicism and ethnic culture among Slovak Americans.

Contact: George J. Kostelnik, President.

Address: 205 Madison Street, Passaic, New Jersey 07055.

Telephone: (201) 777-2605.

Slovak League of America.

Founded in 1907, the Slovak League is a secular organization that promotes the preservation of Slovak culture in the United States. It also provides funds for projects to assist cultural and religious institutions in Slovakia.

Contact: John A. Holy, Secretary-Treasurer.

Address: 205 Madison Street, Passaic, New Jersey 07055.

Telephone: (201) 777-2605.

MUSEUM AND RESEARCH CENTERS

Balch Institute for Ethnic Studies.

Institute has Slovak books and periodicals. Its manuscript collections include some fraternal and organizational records as well as papers of a few Slovak Americans.

Contact: Joseph Anderson, Librarian.

Address: 18 South Seventh Street, Philadelphia, Pennsylvania 19106.

Telephone: (215) 925-8090.

Immigration History Research Center.

Located at the University of Minnesota, it is the largest repository in the world of materials on immigrants from eastern and southern Europe. Among its holdings are Slovak newspapers, fraternal and non-fraternal publications, and books. Its manuscript collections include the records of several Slovak organizations, fraternal societies, churches, and prominent persons.

Contact: Joel Wurl, Curator.

Address: 826 Berry Street, St. Paul, Minnesota 55114.

Telephone: (612) 627-4208.

Jankola Library and Archives Center.

This is the largest Slovak Library in the United States with more than 30,000 volumes. It also contains manuscript collections and Slovak artifacts.

Contact: Sister Martina Tybor.

Address: Danville Academy, Danville, Pennsylvania 17821.

Telephone: (717) 275-5606.

Jednota Museum and Archives Center.

This museum houses books, Slovak memorabilia, costumes, and artifacts. It also contains First Catholic Slovak Union publications and materials as well as records from some local FCSU lodges.

Contact: Edward Tuleja.

Address: Rosedale and Jednota Lane, Middletown, Pennsylvania 17057.

Telephone: (717) 944-2403.

Slovak Institute.

This institute has extensive holdings of books, newspapers, periodicals, and other documents related to Slovak immigration and life in the United States.

Contact: Reverend Father Andrew Pier.

Address: 2900 Martin Luther King Jr. Drive, Cleveland, Ohio 44104.

Telephone: (216) 721-5300.

Slovak World Congress (SWC).

Seeks to make known the history and aspirations of Slovak people and strives to preserve cultural heritage and provide those of Slovankian descent with a sense of their historical background.

Contact: Vida Capay, Secretary General.

Address: 1243 Islington Avenue, Suite 805, Toronto, Ontario, Canada M8X 1Y9.

Telephone: (416) 503-1918.

SOURCES FOR ADDITIONAL STUDY

Capek, Thomas Jr., "The Slovaks in America," in his *The Cech (Bohemian) Community of New York.* New York: Czechoslovak Section of America's Making, 1921; reprinted, San Francisco: R & E Research Associates, 1969; pp. 77-93.

Krause, Paul. *The Battle for Homestead, 1880-1992: Politics, Culture, and Steel.* Pittsburgh: University of Pittsburgh Press, 1992.

Miller, Kenneth. *The Czecho-Slovaks in America.* New York: George H. Doran Company, 1922.

Slovaks in America: Historical and Cultural Studies: A Bicentennial Study, compiled by Joseph Krajsa, et al. Middletown, Pennsylvania: Jednota Press, 1978.

Stasko, Jozef. *Slovaks in the United States of America: Brief Sketches of Their History, National Heritage, and Activites.* Cambridge, Ontario: Good Books Press, 1974.

Stolarik, M. Mark. *Growing Up on the South Side: Three Generations of Slovaks in Bethlehem, Pennsylvania, 1880-1976.* Lewisburg, Pennsylvania: Bucknell University Press, 1985.

————. *The Slovak Americans.* New York: Chelsea House, 1988.

SLOVENIAN AMERICANS

by
Edward Gobetz

The belief that the American and Slovenian cultures at their best are not only compatible but complement and enrich each other seems to appeal to large numbers of Slovenian Americans who have visited the country of their ancestors.

OVERVIEW

Slovenia measures 7,896 square miles (20,256 square kilometers), which is slightly less than Massachusetts or half the size of Switzerland. About two-thirds of Slovenia is located in the Alps, the remaining third gradually melts into the Pannonian Plains. Correspondingly, the climate of tiny Slovenia is Mediterranean along the Adriatic Sea, alpine in the mountains, and continental (Central European) in the plains. Bordering on Italy to the west, Austria to the north, Hungary to the east, and Croatia to the south, Slovenia has a population of just a little over two million. Approximately 88 percent of the population is Slovenian, a decrease due to the influx of migrants and refugees from the southern republics of former Yugoslavia. In addition, there have also been very small national minorities: about 10,000 Hungarians and over 2,200 Italians. Much larger Slovenian national minorities continue to live in Italy and Austria, plus a smaller population in Hungary.

Slovenians, the westernmost Slavic people, have always been geographically and culturally a part of Central Europe rather than of the Balkans. Because of Slovenia's smallness and centuries of subjugation by other countries, it has been relatively unknown to the world. Many people confuse it with other countries, especially with Slovakia. In recent years the Slovenian government and tourist agencies have tried to pinpoint its location and improve its image by publicizing the country as "Slovenia, on the sunny side of the Alps."

HISTORY

While most historians believe that Slovenia was settled between 568 and 650 A.D., this has been challenged by a group of writers who argue that Slovenians are descendants of an ancient West Slavic people called Veneti, Vendi or Wends—a people that predate the Romans. All scholars agree that Slovenians settled in present-day Slovenia by 650 A.D. They enjoyed a brief independence at the dawn of their known history when they developed a form of representative democracy, which was well known to several leading figures, including Thomas Jefferson; this ancient Slovenian democracy was, according to Harvard historian Crane Brinton in the *Catholic Historical Review*, a variable that "went into the making of modern Western institutions."

After allying themselves with the Bavarians against the warlike Avars and jointly defeating them in 743, the northern Karantanian Slovenians lost their independence to their Bavarian allies who refused to leave, and a year or two later to the Franks who subdued the Bavarians. After the mysterious disappearance of Prince Kocelj, the Slovenians of Pannonia came under the rule of a Frankish overlord in 874. For over a millennium the Slovenian people were under the political administration of their more powerful neighbors: the Bavarians, the Franks, the Holy Roman Empire, and the Austrian Empire.

The Christianization of the Slovenians had been conducted by missionaries from Aquileia (now in northern Italy) and Salzburg (then an ethnically mixed territory). The most famous missionaries were the Irish bishop St. Modestus in the mid-eighth century who labored in Karantania, and the brothers St. Cyril and St. Methodius from Salonica who spread the Christian faith in Slovenian Pannonia in the late 860s and 870s and established a seminary to educate Slovenian boys for the priesthood.

In addition to constant Germanization pressures, which began with the Christianization process, the Slovenians suffered almost two centuries of sporadic Turkish raids, especially from 1408 to 1578. An estimated 100,000 Slovenians perished and an equal number of young boys and girls were taken to Turkey where boys were trained as Turkish soldiers (*janizaries*) and the girls were put into harems. In 1593, however, the united Slovenian and Croatian forces decisively defeated the Turks in the battle of Sisak, Croatia. Due to the leadership of Count Andrej Turjaski (Andreas of Turjak, Slovenia), the threat of subsequent Turkish raids on Slovenian lands was considerably diminished. Slovenians were also involved in numerous uprisings against the exploitative foreign nobility, the most famous of which was the joint Slovenian-Croatian revolt of 1573 in which over a third of the revolutionaries perished in battle, while many of the survivors were tortured and executed. Although German-speaking Austrians and Germans wanted to Germanize the Slovenians in order to establish a secure land-bridge to the Adriatic and the Mediterranean Seas, the bulk of Slovenians resisted bribes and threats, occasionally gaining genuine friends and supporters, thus preserving their ethnic and cultural identity.

Slovenians learned to read and write as early as the 860s. The Slovenians established the Jesuit College in Ljubljana in 1595, *Academia operosorum*—the first Slovenian Academy of Arts and Sciences—in 1673, and *Academia philhamionicorum* in 1701. They created a beautiful literature, culminating in the poetry of Dr. France Preseren (1800-1849), and in the prose of Ivan Cankar (1876-1918), and share with the Scandinavians the reputation of being the best-read people of Europe. They have also made numerous contributions to the world, including Jurij Slatkonia, who became the first regular bishop of Vienna in 1513 and founded the internationally acclaimed Vienna Boys choir. Many prominent scholars and scientists were Slovenian, including: Joseph Stefan (1835-1893), a physicist and author of Stefan's fourth-power law, who was also one of the many Slovenian rectors of the University of Vienna; Frederic Pregl (1869-1930), father of microanalysis and Nobel prize winner in chemistry in 1923; Leo Caprivi (Kopriva; 1831-1899), the chancellor of Germany in 1890s; Kurt von Schuschnigg (Susnik; 1897-1977), the last chancellor of Austria prior to Hitler's Anschluss; Misha Lajovic (1921-), the first immigrant and the first non-Anglo-Saxon federal senator of Australia; and Dr. Aloysius M. Ambrožič (1930-), the first immigrant and Slavic archbishop of Toronto, the largest Catholic diocese of Canada.

THE MODERN ERA

A part of Austria until 1918 and then Yugoslavia, with a period of German and Italian occupation and the brutal communist revolution between 1941 and 1945, Slovenia organized the first free post-war elections in the spring of 1990. Slovenia declared independence on June 25, 1991, and after inflicting surprising defeats on the communist-led Yugoslav Army under the leadership of defense minister Janez Jansa, achieved peace on July 7, 1991. On December 23, 1991, the Slovenian Constitution was adopted. On January 15, 1992, while Christian Democrat Lojze Peterle was prime minister, the European Commmunity led by Christian Democratic governments, recognized independent Slovenia. On May 22, 1992, Slovenia became a permanent member of the United Nations. Although still struggling to fully liberate itself from communism, Slovenia has been described by western analysts and journalists as having the best prospects for genuine democracy and prosperity among all formerly communist countries.

"The first night in America I spent, with hundreds of other recently arrived immigrants, in an immense hall with tiers of narrow iron-and-canvas bunks, four deep.... The bunk immediately beneath mine was occupied by a Turk.... I thought how curious it was that I should be spending a night in such proximity to a Turk, for Turks were traditional enemies of Balkan peoples, including my own nation.... Now here I was, trying to sleep directly above a Turk, with only a sheet of canvas between us."

Louis Adamic, 1913, cited in *Ellis Island: An illustrated History of the Immigrant Experience,* edited by Ivan Chermayeff et al. (New York: Macmillan, 1991).

THE FIRST SLOVENIANS IN AMERICA

The first proven settler of mixed Slovenian-Croatian ancestry was Ivan Ratkaj, a Jesuit priest who reached the New World in 1680. He was followed by Mark Anton Kappus, S. J., who came to America in 1687 and distinguished himself as missionary, educator, writer, and explorer. In the 1730s Slovenians and Croatians established small agricultural settlements in Georgia. A number of Slovenian soldiers fought in George Washington's revolutionary forces. Between 1831 and 1868, the Slovenian-born scholar, missionary, and bishop, Frederic Baraga, labored on a vast 80,000 square mile piece of virgin territory, including parts of Michigan, Wisconsin, Minnesota, and Canada, where he and his followers built some of the first churches and schools. Father Andreas Skopec (Skopez) reached Fryburg, Pennsylvania, in 1846 and was joined by several of his Slovenian compatriots. Other Slovenian settlements followed in the mining town of Calumet, Michigan, in 1856, the farming community of Brockway, Minnesota, in 1865, and several rural areas in Michigan, Illinois, and Iowa. Settlements were also established in Omaha, Nebraska, in 1868, Joliet, Illinois, in 1873; New York City in 1878, and Cleveland, Ohio, in 1881. Following the missionaries and other trailblazers, the largest numbers of Slovenian immigrants reached America between 1880 and World War I, particularly from 1905 to 1913, although the exact numbers are impossible to pinpoint because Slovenians were then shown either as Austrians or jointly with Croatians, or under a number of other broader labels.

The 1910 census reported 183,431 persons of Slovenian mother tongue, 123,631 "foreign-born" and 59,800 born in America. These numbers are clearly an underestimate of the actual Slovenian population since descendants of earlier settlers often no longer knew Slovenian. Many Slovenians coming from Austria tried to escape the anti-Slavic prejudice by identifying themselves as Austrians, and many who should have been reported as Slovenian appeared under such general headings as Slav, Slavic, Slavish, or Slavonian. The actual number of Americans of Slovenian descent was probably somewhere between 200,000 and 300,000. The underestimate was even more pronounced in the 1990 census, which listed only 124,427 Americans of "Slovene" ancestry. Since the ancestry was the identifying criterion, including persons with single and multiple ethnic ancestry, regardless of whether or not they knew the Slovenian language, the actual numbers of Slovenian Americans probably has been growing approximately to the same extent as the total population of the United States.

SETTLEMENT

From the very beginning, Slovenian immigrants have been widely scattered in many states. However, despite the underestimates, the U.S. census probably identifies correctly the states with the highest concentration of Slovenian Americans. Ohio, where about 40 percent live, is the unrivaled leader, with greater Cleveland as the home of the largest Slovenian community. It is followed by Pennsylvania, with about 12 percent, and Illinois with less than ten percent. Minnesota and Wisconsin each have a little over five percent Slovenian population, followed in descending order by California, Colorado, Michigan, Florida, New York, Texas, Indiana, Washington, Kansas, and Maryland. There is, however, no single American state in which Slovenians have not been represented in the 1990 census.

ACCULTURATION AND ASSIMILATION

Until 1918 the bulk of Slovenian immigrants were Slovenian by ethnicity and Austrian by citizenship or statehood. They usually knew German, which facilitated their adjustment in the American work place where, at that time, many foremen were from German-speaking countries. Yet, the American population began to differentiate between genuine German Austrians, other German-nationality members, and various non-German ethnic groups, including the Slovenians who were looked down upon as inferior and given such pejorative labels as "Polacks," "Hunkies," and "Bohunks." Residents of cities with larger settlements of immigrants became aware of further subdivisions and reserved "Hunkies" for Hungarians, "Bohunks" for Czechs and Slovaks, and "Grainers" or "Grenish" (a corruption of the term "Krainers," i.e., from the Slovenian province of Krain, Kranjska, or Carniola) for Slovenians. Numerous accounts and studies suggest that for over half a century after 1880 there was strong anti-Slavic and anti-Slovenian prejudice in America. Although Slovenians were not included among the 40 "races" or ethnic groups whose hierarchical position in America has been studied since 1926 by means of the Bogardus Social Distance Scale, statistical scores and narrative reports in leading textbooks suggest that there was an intense and widespread prejudice against all Slavic groups.

Initially most Slovenians coped with the problems of being low-status or despised strangers in a foreign land by establishing their own ethnic communities, including churches, schools, and business establishments. They also organized self-help groups such as fraternal societies, social and political clubs, and national homes as their new community centers. A high degree of self-sufficiency among Slovenians helped them adjust relatively well within their own ethnic community and facilitated adjustment in the American work place and in society at large. Many applied the leadership skills they had learned in their ethnic neighborhoods to wider American society, rising from club or lodge officers to become members of city councils, mayors, and other American political, business, and civic leaders. With few exceptions this piecemeal adjustment to America seemed to proceed remarkably well. Similarly, the Slovenians avoided being on welfare; in times of crises they helped each other.

Slovenian Americans have acquired English with impressive speed and facility. They have been anxious to own homes, often with vegetable and flower gardens. Approximately 48 percent of Slovenian refugees bought their homes after being in America on the average of ten years. Yet, in the spirit of a pluralistic, multicultural America, many are anxious also to preserve the best elements of their ethnic culture. Since the 1970s there has been an unprecedented surge of interest in Slovenian music (especially the accordion as the national instrument), language, genealogy, history, culture, customs, folklore, and other aspects of Slovenian heritage. The belief that the American and Slovenian cultures at their best are not only compatible but complement and enrich each other seems to appeal to large numbers of Slovenian Americans who have visited the country of their ancestors.

CUISINE

Slovenian immigrant women and many of their descendants traditionally have been excellent cooks and bakers; many of their culinary specialties are sold in ethnic communities today at fund raising projects. Some of the most popular goodies include *potica,* which is as Slovenian as apple pie is American. Among the usual varieties are walnut, raisin, and tarragon *poticas.* Apple, cherry, apricot, cheese, and other varieties of *strudel* are also tempting delicacies, as are *krofi,* the Slovenian variety of doughnuts, and *flancati,* a flaky, deep-fried pastry. Dumplings (*cmoki* and *struklji*), meat-filled or liver-filled for soups, are also popular, as well as those filled with apricots, plums, finely ground meat, or cheese, which can be served as the main meal, or as dessert. In addition to all kinds of chicken and other meats, the Carniolan sausage (*kranjske klobase*) and for Easter, "filled stomach" (*želodec*) are also favorites. Slovenian wines have won many international prizes and some Slovenian Americans continue to make their own wine, even if they no longer grow their own grapes. Slovenians in the "old" country traditionally have been known for their hospitality.

TRADITIONS, CUSTOMS, AND BELIEFS

In several Slovenian communities some group-specific customs survive. One of these is *miklavževanje*, celebrations of *sv. Miklavž* or the old St. Nick's feast when the good saint, dressed up as a bishop and accompanied by angels and *parkelji* (little devils), visits Slovenian communities, exhorts children to be good, and distributes gifts, usually from a throne put in the center of the stage. Vintage festivals (*trgatve*) at recreation farms or parks and in national halls attract merrymakers, with dancing or socializing under clusters of tempting grapes; those who reach for them and are caught by the "police," are taken to the "court" and sent to a "jail" where all can see their sad "fate." Then, a loved one pays the ransom or fine, which is used for a worthy cause, while the "thief" (or *tat*) is set free. There is also *martino-vanje*, a public celebration of St. Martin's feast when the good saint changes lowly grape juice into tasty wine. This is another good excuse for socializing, a banquet with wine-tasting, and a dance of waltzes and polkas. Concerts and festivals, plays and sports events, bazaars and exhibits, benefit brunches, lunches, and suppers all keep Slovenians in ethnic communities busy and happy.

HEALTH AND MENTAL HEALTH ISSUES

Slovenian culture has emphasized the value of good health. One of the most frequently quoted sayings states, "*Zdravje je največje bogastvo*"—"Health is the greatest wealth." Following the Czech lead, the most influential Slovenian youth organizations that often included "youngsters" 50 or 70 years old, were the Eagles (*Orli*) and the Falcons (*Sokoli*), which adopted an ancient Roman guideline as their own slogan, "*Mens sana in corpore sano*"—"A heathy mind in a healthy body," paying attention to development of both good character and physical fitness. Active participation in athletics, gymnastics, walks, hikes, mountain climbing, and a variety of sports, including skiing, contribute to good health. Alcohol consumption and smoking, on the other hand, are among the unhealthy practices in which large numbers of Slovenians indulged.

In America, overcrowded boarding houses and life in depressing urban areas with air, water, and noise pollution contributed a new variety of health hazards. In places such as steel mills and coal mines, occupational risks lurked for workers. Many often experienced unavoidable accidents, increased air pollution, extremes of heat and cold, and pollution with coal dust resulting in black lung disease that has shortened the life of countless miners. In some mining towns, from Pennsylvania to Wyoming, there is an alarming absence of older men; and their widows survive with nothing but their modest homes and low retirement pensions to compensate them for their families' share in building a more prosperous America.

As working and living conditions have generally improved, and some good health habits learned in childhood have persisted, the health and mental health of Slovenian Americans now compares with that of other Americans. It is unclear whether or not home remedies, such as a small pharmacy of medicinal herbs that many Slovenian immigrant households maintained, have been among the contributing factors to better health. A conclusion of "slightly better" than "national health" was reached by Dr. Sylvia J. O'Kicki, who examined a group of Slovenian Americans with comparable cohorts selected from the National Health Interview Survey of 1985. She states in *Ethnicity and Health* that "when the group of Slovene Americans without any regard to the level of ethnicity is compared to the national American sample they differ favorably in health status and the practice of health behaviors.... Those who are actively involved in the heritage and traditions of the ethnic group report a more favorable health status and practice of more favorable health behaviors."

In general, there was a remarkable resilience among earlier immigrants who were confronted by adverse conditions and problems that few could imagine today. Post-World War II refugees also went through years of deprivations, hardships of camp life, and a series of new problems in a strange new country, which often left them physically and emotionally exhausted and penniless. Some of them even survived death camps such as Dachau; two of them, Milan Zajec and Frank Dejak, miraculously escaped from a communist mass grave.

LANGUAGE

Slovenian is the language of the oldest preserved written documents of any Slavic people, the so-called *Brižinski spomeniki* (the Freising Monuments), dating from 1000 A.D. Prlmož Trubar published the first printed books in Slovenian starting in 1551, less than a century after the invention of the Guttenberg press. Through the millennium of incorporation into German-speaking lands the Slovenian language was the pivotal vehicle of Slovenian culture, consciousness, identity, and national survival. Because the Slovenians were few in number they were anxious to preserve their mother tongue while simultaneously learning other languages.

Slovenian is a difficult language to learn because of its many inflections. Its grammar makes understanding other languages easier, and Slovenians have long been noted for their exceptional linguistic skills. Many Slovenian missionaries in America preached in five or more languages. A study of post-World War II refugees shows that over 37 percent of those with only grade school education could "get along" in five languages; among the most highly educated ones, all could do so. Several colleges and universities teach the Slovenian language: University of Illinois, Indiana University, University of Kansas, Kent State University, Ohio State University, and the University of Pittsburgh. There are also several libraries with Slovenian-language collections, which contributes to preservation of the language.

The Slovenian writing system is phonetically precise in that a letter, with very few exceptions, has the same sound. Most letters are the same as in English (except that Slovenian lacks the letters "w"and "y"), and many letters have the same sound as in English. For the rest, the following pronunciation guide may be of help: "a" is pronounced as in art; "e" as in get (never as in eve); "i" as in ill (never as in like); "o" as in awe; "u" as in ruler (never as in use); "c" as in tsar (never as in cat); "č" as the "ch" in church; "g" as in go (never as in age); "j" as the "y" in yes (never as in just); "lj" as "lli" in million; "nj" as the "gn" in monsignor; "š" as in she; "z" as in zipper; and "ž" as the "ge" in garage.

GREETINGS AND OTHER POPULAR EXPRESSIONS

Dobro jutro—good morning; *dober dan*—good day; *dober večer*—good evening; *dobrodošli*—welcome; *jaz sem (Janez Zupan)*—I am (John Zupan); *to je gospod (gospa, gospodična) Stropnik*—this is Mr. (Mrs., Miss) Stropnik; *kako ste*—how are you; *hvala, dobro*—thank you, well; *na svidenje*—so long; *zbogom*—goodbye; *lahko noč*—good night; *prosim*—please; *hvala*—thank you; *na zdravje*—to your health; *dober tek*—enjoy your meal; *vse najboljše*—the best of everything; *oprosite*—excuse me; *čestitke*—congratulations; *kje je*—where is; *kje je restavracija (hotel)*—where is a restaurant

(hotel); *kje je ta naslov*—where is this address; *me veseli*—I am pleased; *žal mi je*—I am sorry; *sem ameriski Slovenec (ameriška Slovenka)*—I am an American Slovenian; *vse je zelo lepo*—everything is very nice; *Slovenija je krasna*—Slovenia is beautiful; *se pridite*—come again; *srečno pot*—have a happy trip!

FAMILY AND COMMUNITY DYNAMICS

Until World War I, men usually emigrated first; after they had saved enough money, they arranged for their wives or sweethearts to follow. Early entrepreneurs, such as owners of boarding houses, restaurants, and saloons, also lured many young women to come and work for them in America; however, the men were anxious to marry them as soon as they could get to know them. As in Slovenia, divorce among Slovenian Americans has been extremely rare, although it has recently increased especially in ethnically and religiously mixed families. In general, immigrant parents are anxious for their children to marry someone from their own ethnic and religious group, although ethnic homogamy has been decreasing among members of American-born generations.

Until recently, Slovenians have also frowned upon putting their parents or elderly relatives into homes for the aged. Since employment of women has increased and families have become more mobile, an increasing proportion of the elderly are now being placed into homes for the aged. Extended families were common among early immigrants, while nuclear families prevail today. Increasingly, children move away from their parental homes once they are permanently employed, believing that this is expected in America. However, many parents still prefer to have their children live at home until marriage and save money for their own home. The oldest child is often expected to be responsible and a role model for younger children; the youngest child is widely believed to be given most affection by all, although actual differences by order of birth are now probably comparable to those of American families. Women have played a pivotal role not only as homemakers but also in Slovenian ethnic churches, language schools, charity projects, and increasingly in political campaigns. There is a Slovenian proverb: "*Žena tri vogle podpira*"—"The woman supports three corners [of a four-corner home]."

WEDDINGS

Young people have adopted such American wedding customs as showers. However, they often still prefer huge ethnic weddings with hundreds of guests in attendance, delicious meals, and Slovenian varieties of pastries.

FUNERALS

At wakes and funerals, organizations to which the deceased belonged are represented; occasionally there are honor guards in uniforms or national costumes. After the funeral all guests are invited to a meal to show the bereaved family's appreciation for their attendance and to ease the transition for the family and community deprived of one of its members.

RELIGION

Coming from a country with strong Catholic traditions where hills and valleys are dotted with many beautiful, century-old churches, most Slovenian immigrants cling to their religious roots. They have built their own churches and other religious institutions all over America. Following the example of the missionaries, priests and seminarians came from Slovenia, and American-born descendants of immigrants gradually joined the clergy. Since 1924 the Slovenian Franciscan Commissariat of the Holy Cross in Lemont, Illinois, has played a pivotal role among Slovenian Catholics in America. It established the Mary Help of Christians Shrine (with a replica painting from Brezje, Slovenia)—the most popular Slovenian pilgrimage in North America. It comprises a monastery and seminary, a high school, a retreat house, the Alvernia Manor for the Aged, annual *Koledars,* and a Slovenian Cultural and Pastoral Center of Lemont scheduled for completion in 1994. It also publishes the religious monthly *Ave Maria.* In 1971 a Slovenian Chapel of Our Lady of Brezje was dedicated inside the National Shrine of the Immaculate Conception in Washington, D.C., becoming another significant Slovenian religious landmark in America.

Many Slovenian parishes have been struggling for survival in recent years, mostly because of the changing nature of neighborhoods, the flight of Slovenian population to the suburbs, increased Americanization and secularization of the younger generation, and the lack of Slovenian priests. In very rare instances, ethnic churches that have closed have been replaced by new ones in new neighborhoods, as happened in Milwaukee-West Allis, Wisconsin, or in Bridgeport-Fairfield in Connecticut.

There is also a small number of Slovenian Protestants who refer to themselves as Windish. Although numerically small, this community has long used a Slovenian dialect in interaction, its services, and its press, and has displayed considerable ethnic and religious vitality, as exemplified by St. John's Windish Lutheran Church in Bethlehem, Pennsylvania, and a few other Slovenian Protestant institutions.

Many Slovenians worship in other American Catholic parishes, while an extremely small number have joined other religions. Geographic and social mobility and intermarriage have caused the absorption into other Catholic churches. The children of young couples are frequently enrolled in local Catholic schools, which means that their parents also join the usually non-Slovenian parish. Many of these people still return to Slovenian parishes on special occasions—Christmas and Easter, annual festivals, celebrations of holidays, Corpus Christi processions, Palm Sunday festivities with Slovenian *butare* (ornamented bundles of branches). St. Mary's Parish in Cleveland even presents the Passion liturgy in Slovenian, all conducted by school children in biblical attire (ranging from Roman soldiers to Mary and Christ).

EMPLOYMENT AND ECONOMIC TRADITIONS

With the exception of missionaries, priests, and some 6,000 to 10,000 ideological dissenters, especially post-World War II refugees from Marshall Tito's communism, the bulk of Slovenians in America were economic immigrants. As in most groups, they tended to come from the poorest areas and most economically disadvantaged families. With the exception of persons who wanted to avoid being drafted, a few adventurers, socialist or other political dissenters, post-1947 refugees, and farm laborers have also immigrated in significant numbers.

The earliest immigrants often took advantage of the open lands and homesteading, and established such Slovenian pioneer farming communities as St. Stephen's and St. Anthony's in Minnesota, or later Traunik in Michigan. Many immigrants initially intended to return to Slovenia after they had earned enough money to establish themselves in their native country. When the land became more difficult to obtain, however, the major wave of Slovenian immigrants settled in industrial cities and mining towns where their unskilled labor was sold for meager wages.

It is impossible to discover an exact breakdown of employment since Slovenians were shown as Austrians or Yugoslavs, or combined with Croatians or South Slavs on most documents. While Slovenians were better educated than other South Slav groups, the statistical distribution was probably more favorable for them than shown. The available data on the South Slavs in general are nevertheless suggestive. Thus, in 1921, 42 percent of the South Slavs were workers in steel, iron, and zinc mines, smelters, and refineries; 12 percent worked in the coal mines; 6.5 percent in the lumber industry; six percent in stockyards, and five percent in fruit growing; chemical works, railroads, and electrical manufacturing employed four percent each; professions accounted for 3.5 percent, and farming for only three percent.

Considerable numbers of Slovenian immigrants, however, soon became skilled workers. In the early decades of the twentieth century many Slovenian Americans worked in the automobile industry in Detroit, Toledo, Cleveland, and Pittsburgh. They were also well represented in the manufacture of hats in New York. They were highly appreciated and much sought-after because of their skill and experience, having learned the trade in their home country. Included in this group were both men and women. Thus, hat making, especially straw-hat making, was a group-specific skill that many Slovenians found useful in their American employment. Other skills survived as useful hobbies: home-building and carpentry skills; butchering, sausage making, and meat-processing skills; wine making; and apiculture, which helped many Slovenian immigrants provide honey for family and friends. Women were highly skilled cooks, bakers, and gardeners, and canned large quantities of fruit and vegetables. Habits of hard work, honesty, frugality, and mutual help, particularly in times of hardship, helped Slovenian immigrants survive and succeed in a strange land.

Today, Slovenian Americans can be found in all occupations. Many are now professionals; others own businesses, agencies, and factories; still others are workers, foremen, or executives with large American companies. As research on Slovenian contributions to America shows, a large number of Slovenian Americans have achieved positions of leadership and prominence in American society.

POLITICS AND GOVERNMENT

Like other ethnic groups, Slovenian Americans were targeted by American politicians as soon as they had become citizens and were able to vote. As a rule, Slovenian Americans were attracted to the Democratic Party, viewed as the party of the working class people. Republicans have recently won a substantial number of adherents. Rising from minor political positions, such as ward leaders and members of council, Slovenian American politicians now increasingly reflect the American political spectrum, including a presidential candidate.

Slovenian American congressional representatives include John A. Blatnik (1911-) from northeastern Minnesota, who served from 1947 to 1975; he was succeeded by James L. Oberstar (1934-); Ray P. Kogovsek (1941-), was elected from Colorado in 1978; Philip Ruppe (1927-) represented Michigan between 1967 and 1979. The last was a Republican while the others were Democratic. While very few Slovenians are attracted to Independent candidates, there was a substantial number of Slovenian American Democrats for Republican Ronald Reagan.

In numerous towns, such as Ely, Eveleth, Chisholm, and Gilbert in Minnesota, Slovenian Americans have long been strongly represented on city councils, and as mayors of such larger communities as Euclid and Wickliffe, Ohio. Slovenian candidates were also elected mayor in such cities as Portland, Oregon, and Indianapolis, Indiana, where the proportion of Slovenian voters was insignificant. In Cleveland, the city with the largest number of Slovenians in America, Slovenians have long served as ward leaders, council members, and heads of various branches of municipal government. They also served in Cleveland as judges, a chief of police, a council president, and a mayor. Frank J. Lausche first won national attention as a fearless judge who, with the help of Gus Korach, a Slovenian worker, broke up the widespread organized crime and corruption in a true-life drama that resulted in local and national publicity.

MILITARY

A relatively small number of Slovenian Americans have been well represented in the military. Slovenian immigrant Louis Dobnikar, serving on the destroyer *Keamey*, was the first Clevelander and one of the first 11 Americans to be killed during World War II. John Hribar, a volunteer marine from Krayn, Pennsylvania (named after Kranj, Slovenia), was one of several Slovenian heroes of Iwo Jima. At least seven Slovenian Americans became generals, including three-star general Anthony Burshnick of the U.S. Air Force and four-star general of the U.S. Army Ferdinand Chesarek. The Archives of the Slovenian Research Center of America also contain materials on six Slovenian American admirals (with the seventh still being researched), including Ronald Zlatoper who received his fourth star in 1994.

RELATIONS WITH SLOVENIA

Slovenian Americans have not established permanent lobbying organizations in Washington, D.C., but they frequently have used existing societies and institutions, *ad hoc* committees, or temporary councils or unions to advocate or support various causes on behalf of their home country. These include: the Slovenian League, Slovenian National Union, and Slovenian Republican Alliance during World War I; various relief committees, the Union of Slovenian Parishes, and Slovenian American National Council during World War II; the Slovenian American Council, which substantially supported the first free elections that toppled the communist dictatorship in Slovenia in 1990. A special *ad hoc* committee, Americans for Free Slovenia, together with scores of other organizations and institutions, especially the *American Home* newspaper, the Slovenian Research Center of America, and thousands of individuals, helped secure the American recognition of independent Slovenia in 1992. For several decades after World War II, the Slovenian Language section of Voice of America Information Agency, played an important role by bringing objective information to its listeners in Slovenia.

INDIVIDUAL AND GROUP CONTRIBUTIONS

Slovenia, despite its small size, has made many important contributions to the world.

ACADEMIA

Emil Mrak, chancellor of University of California at Davis, and Frederick Stare, founder of Harvard University's Department of Nutrition, were America's foremost authorities on nutrition. John Nielsen (Sesek) was a leading metallurgist; Joseph Koffolt was a leader in chemical engineering; Anton Peterlin was a leader in macromolecular chemistry; Stephen Malaker was prominent in nuclear physics and cryogenics; Robert A. Pucel contributed to microwave science and technology; Anton Mavretic and Mark Dragovan distingushed themselves in astronomy; and Daniel Siewiorek was a leader in computer architecture.

AERONAUTICS

Max Stupar, an early designer and manufacturer of airplanes, was considered the father of mass airplane production. Dr. August Raspet, a noted inventor and designer of modern airplanes, was president of American Aerophysics Institute. Adrian Kisovec invented the Convertiplane-Rotafrx models. Dr. Ronald Sega became the first Slovenian astronaut.

ARCHITECTURE

Araldo Cossutta, who designed L'Enfant Plaza in Washington and numerous landmark buildings throughout America and in Europe, won, with I. M. Pei, the 1968 Architectural Firm Award. Alexander Papesh became America's foremost designer of stadiums, including the Robert F. Kennedy Stadium in Washington, D.C. Simon Kregar won national awards for design of industrial buildings.

ART

Slovenian American artists include Gregory Prusheck, Michael Lah, Stephen Rebeck, France Gorse, Donald Orehek, Lillian Brulc, Lucille Dragovan, Frank Wolcansek, John Hapel, Paul Kos, Bogdan Grom, three generations of Prazens, Joseph Opalek, Nancy Bukovnik, and Gary Bukovnik, Emilia Bucik-Razman, Miro Zupancic, Joseph Vodlan, Erica Bajuk, Vlasta Radisek, August Pust, and Damian Kreze, to mention but a few.

FILM, TELEVISION, AND DANCE

Among movie and television personalities, Laura LaPlante and Audrey Totterare are part Slovenian. Also Slovenian are actors George Dolenz and Frank Gorshin; ballerinas Veronica Mlakar of the New York City Ballet Theater and Isabella Kralj of Chamber Dance Theater in Milwaukee. Anton Schubel was director of the International Ballet Company in New York; Milko Sparemblek, a Slovenian immigrant, served as ballet director of Metropolitan Opera at Lincoln Center; Charles Kuralt, widely known as a CBS correspondent and a capable writer, has also recently discovered his Slovenian roots.

LITERATURE

Karl Mauser (1918-1977) was an author whose work was translated into German, French, and Spanish. Frank Mlakar (1913-1967), author of the acclaimed novel, *He, the Father*. Louis Adamic (1899-1951), whose widely translated books have been included as Book-of-the-Month Club and *Obras Famosas* selections, became a pioneer of multiculturalism in America with the publication of his *From Many Lands, My America* and *A Nation of Nations*.

MISSIONARIES

There is also a proud, if seldom known, record of contributions made to America by Slovenian missionaries. Mark Anton Kappus, a Slovenian-born Jesuit missionary, scholar, and superior of Jesuit missions in the enormous territory of Sonora and Pimeria Alta in northern Mexico and southern Arizona, came to America in 1687 and returned to Europe in 1701 to report that California was not an island, as it then had been generally believed; the most prominent Slovenian missionary was Frederic Baraga, who from 1831 to 1868, labored among Native Americans of the Upper Great Lakes region on an enormous territory of over 80,000 square miles and wrote several books, including Indian dictionaries and grammars still in use today. In numerous areas of Michigan, Wisconsin, Minnesota, and elsewhere Slovenian missionaries built the first churches and schools; they pioneered in the establishment of dioceses of Marquette, Duluth, and St. Cloud; they secured financial support from several European courts and religious organizations, while importing to America shipments of seedlings, vestments, and religious art.

MUSIC

Notable musicians include: Grammy Award-winning Polka King of America, Frankie Yankovic; the "Polka Ambassador" Tony Petkovsek; Polka Priest Frank Perkovich; America's Tamburitzan King Professor Mat Gouze; Metropolitan Opera singer Anton Schubel, who was also the talent scout for Carnegie Hall where he gave concerts with finalists of his nationwide auditions, among them his 13-year-old discovery Van Cliburn; Ivan Zorman, Dr. Sergij Delak, and Dr. Vendelin Spendov, who enriched Slovenian American music with their compositions; and John Ivanusch, known as the Father of Slovenian Opera in America; Paul Sifler is an internationally known organist and composer of such works as *Despair and Agony of Dachau*; Professor Raymond Premru's *Concerto for Orchestra* was selected in 1976 for the famous Cleveland Orchestra's Bicentennial Program conducted by Lorin Maazel.

POLITICS

Senator Tom Harkin, whose mother was a Slovenian immigrant, was one of the 1992 presidential candidates; he pioneered legislation on behalf of the disabled. George Voinovich served as mayor of Cleveland and governor of Ohio. Ludwig Andolsek was a U.S. Civil Service commissioner. John Blatnik, U.S. congressional representative from Minnesota from 1946 to 1974, chaired the Congressional Public Works committee and authored legislation that opened the St. Lawrence Seaway, established the current interstate highway system, and initiated standards for clean air and water.

SCIENCE AND TECHNOLOGY

Frederic Pregl pioneered the field of organic chemistry; Hermann Potočnik Noordung, a pioneer in space science, authored the first scientific book on manned space travel and had a considerable impact on the development of American space program. John Bucik's car of the future was one of America's leading attractions at the New York World Fair in 1964-1965. Dr. France Rode co-invented HP-35 pocket calculators, which Richard Nixon's party took to China as an example of modern U.S. technology.

SPORTS

Notable sports figures include: football players Tony and Mike Adamie, Randy Gradishar, Mark

Debevc, Don Vicic, and Ken Novak; baseball players Frank Doljack, Joe Kuhel, Al Vidmar, Walter Judnich, and Al Milnar; bowlers Charles Lausche, Marge Slogar, Mary "Whitey" Primosh Doljack, "Stevie" Rozman Balough, Sophie Rozman Kenny, Andrew Stanonik, Vince Bovitz, and Jim Stefanich; the Marolt brothers in skiing; Olympic swimmer Ann Govednik; Vicki Foltz (Sega); long-distance running champion; and Hubby Habjan, National Golf Professional of the Year (1965); Eric Heiden, winner of five gold medals at the Winter Olympics of 1980; Peter Vidmar, U.S. team captain and winner of two gold medals and a silver medal in the 1984 Olympics, was the highest scoring gymnast in U.S. history (with a 9.89 average).

MEDIA

PRINT

Amerika Domovina (The American Home).
This was published under a variety of names, starting as *Narodna Beseda (The Word of the People)* in 1899. Privately owned and long a Slovenian-language daily, it is now a bilingual weekly newspaper, with about 3,000 subscribers. It publishes news about Slovenian communities and individuals, various ethnic affairs, and Slovenian reprints. It is the only one of the many non-fraternal Slovenian newspapers that has survived to this day.

Contact: Jim Debevec, Publisher and English Section Editor; or, Dr. Rudolph Susel, Slovenian Language Section Editor.

Address: 6117 St. Clair Avenue, Cleveland, Ohio 44103.

Telephone: (216) 431-0628.

Amerikanski Slovenec (American Slovenian).
This is the oldest Slovenian paper, published without interruption since 1891. Since 1946, when it merged with the *Glasilo KSKJ (Herald of KSKJ)*, it has been an official organ of KSKJ, the American Slovenian Catholic Union. While most of the materials published pertain to activities of the KSKJ, it also caries a variety of news and comments pertaining of ethnic and general human interest. It is currently a bilingual (English and Slovenian) biweekly, with 10,700 subscribers.

Contact: John T. Nemec, Managing Editor.

Address: 708 East 159 Street, Cleveland, Ohio 44110.

Telephone: (216) 541-7243.

Our Voice—Glas ADZ.
This is a biweekly bilingual official organ of American Mutual Life Association (AMLA). While *Clevelandska Amerika* (now *Ameriska Domovina*) was chosen as the official organ of what was then *Slovenska Dobrodelna Zveza* (Slovenian Benefit Society), the seventh convention approved the establishment of its own official organ and the first issue was published early in 1932. In addition to news items about AMLA's lodge activities, *Our Voice* publishes many reprints from Slovenian magazines, both in Slovenian and English languages, and numerous photographs of banquets, parties, and other social and cultural affairs.

Contact: Dr. Rudolph Susel, Editor.

Address: 19424 South Waterloo Road, Cleveland, Ohio 44119.

Telephone: (216) 531-1900.

Prosveta (Enlightenment).
Long a Slovenian daily, it is now an English weekly organ of the Slovene National Benefit Society (SNPJ), devoted predominantly to news items about the fraternal organization and its local lodges and their activities. It also publishes selected items of Slovenian and general human interest, including news on various cultural programs and reprints from Slovenia. By 1994, the Slovenian language entries have been reduced to a single weekly page or less. *Prosveta* has 20,000 subscribers.

Contact: Jay Sedmak, Editor.

Address: 247 West Allegheny Road, Imperial, Pennsylvania 15126.

Telephone: (412) 695-1100.

Slovenian National Directory.
Published by United Slovenian Society; concerned with all aspects of Slovenian culture.

Contact: Cecilia Dolgan, Editor.

Address: 971 East 185th Street, Cleveland, Ohio 44119.

Telephone: (216) 481-8669.

Slovenska Drzava.
Monthly magazine published by Slovenian National Federation of Canada.

Contact: Vladimir Mauko, Editor.

Address: 412 Bloor Street West, Toronto, Ontario, Canada M5S 1X6.

Telephone: (416) 229-9906.

Fax: (416) 924-2502.

Zarja—The Dawn.

This is the official organ of Slovenian Women's Union (SŽZ) and was established as its monthly magazine in 1928. This bilingual magazine, with 6,500 subscribers, remains the only surviving Slovenian American monthly magazine. It is rich with news items about activities of its sponsoring organization, as well as with articles on Slovenian American families, with an emphasis on the role of mothers, and on Slovenian heritage.

Contact: Corinne Leskovar, Editor.

Address: 431 North Chicago Street, Joliet, Illinois 60432.

Telephone: (815) 727-1926.

Fax: (312) 268-7744.

RADIO

WCEV.

American Slovenian Radio Program is an 85 percent Slovenian-language program that has served the Greater Chicago area since 1950. The program presents an impressive variety of Slovenian music, community announcements and electronically submitted news from Slovenia. It is currently broadcast every Friday, from 7:00 to 8:00 p.m., with a 15-minute section presented by the Franciscan Fathers of Lemont, Illinois.

Contact: Corinne Leskovar.

Address: 5100 North Marine Drive, Chicago, Illinois 60640.

Telephone: (312) 275-1115.

WCSB-FM (89.3).

"Songs and Melodies from Beautiful Slovenia" presents a rich variety of Slovenian songs and music, community news and news from Slovenia, excerpts from Slovenian literature, the Sunday spiritual thoughts, special occasion programs, interviews, and political commentaries, all in Slovenian language. It is currently broadcast on Sundays, 9:00 to 10:00 a.m., and on Wednesdays, 6:00 to 7:00 p.m.

Contact: Dr. Milan Pavlovčič, Producer.

Address: WCSB, Cleveland State University, Rhodes Tower, Room 956, Cleveland, Ohio 44115.

Telephone: (216) 687-3523.

WELW-AM (1330).

Tony Petkovsek's radio program broadcasts Slovenian and other polka music daily, 3:30 to 5:00 p.m., in addition to providing current community news and news from Slovenia, interviews, and radiothons in support of charitable and civic causes. Together with the Cleveland Slovenian Radio Club it has also organized annual Tony's Thanksgiving Polka Parties, which have been among the best attended Greater Cleveland community affairs.

Contact: Tony Petkovsek, Producer.

Address: 971 East 185 Street, Cleveland, Ohio 44119.

Telephone: (216) 481-8669.

WKTX-AM (830).

"Slovenia Radio" presents Slovenian and other ethnic music, together with Slovenian and English broadcasts of community news, commentaries, and transmission of news from Slovenia. It is aired on Saturdays, 9:00 to 10:00 a.m.

Contact: Paul M. Lavrisha, Producer.

Address: 6507 St. Clair Ave., Cleveland, Ohio 44103.

Telephone: (216) 391-7225.

WYMS-FM (89.9).

"Slovenian Radio Cultural Hour" presents customs, literature, songs, and music of Slovenia, together with programs dedicated to special cultural topics and news items about the Slovenian community and Slovenia. It has been conducted since 1963 by Vladislav and Isabella Kralj. The program is currently broadcast each Saturday from 11:00 a.m. until 12:00 p.m.

Contact: Vladislav Kralj, Producer.

Address: 690 Meadow Lane, Elm Grove, Wisconsin 53122.

Telephone: (414) 785-2775.

ORGANIZATIONS AND ASSOCIATIONS

American Mutual Life Association (SDZ).

Organized in 1910, it functions through 40 lodges, with a total of 12,769 members in Ohio. In addition to non-profit insurance programs and promotion of Slovenian traditions and customs, the association lists the following activities: Christmas parties for children, bowling and golf tournaments, family day picnics, clambakes, anniversary banquets honoring 50-year members, scholarship award banquets, and Christmas open house for lodge officers and board members.

Contact: Joseph F. Petric, Jr., Secretary.

Address: 19424 South Waterloo Road, Cleveland, Ohio 44119.

Telephone: (216) 531-1900.

American Slovenian Catholic Union (KSKJ).

Established in 1894 as a self-help organization which would also strive to preserve and promote Catholic and Slovenian heritage, while helping its members to be active American citizens, has 28,685 members and is the largest Slovenian Catholic organization in USA. Like SNPJ, it functions through local lodges scattered throughout America, but is coordinated by a national board of directors and an executive committee. It provides to its members payments of death and sickness benefits, scholarships, low-interest loans; it promotes friendship and true Catholic charity and conducts numerous religious, educational, cultural, recreational, and social activities.

Contact: Robert M. Verbiscer, Chief Executive Officer; or Anthony Mravle, Secretary/Treasurer.
Address: 2439 Glenwood Avenue, Joliet, Illinois 60435.
Telephone: (815) 741-2001.

Progressive Slovene Women of America (PSWA).

Founded in 1934, it has 575 members, and its purpose is: to arouse interest in knowledge; to improve social and economic conditions of women, family, and humanity in general; to promote familiarity and understanding of New and Old World cultures; and to encourage members to be good citizens and useful members of society. A philanthropic and service organization, it raises money for humanitarian/cultural causes.

Contact: Florence Unetich, National President.
Address: 19808 Arrowhead Avenue, Cleveland, Ohio 44110.
Telephone: (216) 481-0830.

Slovene National Benefit Society (SNPJ).

Founded in 1904, it is currently, with about 40,000 members, the largest Slovenian American organization. Once a stronghold of labor movement, with some prominent socialists among its leaders, it is now administered mostly by American-born, English-speaking leaders of Slovenian descent. As a non-profit fraternal benefit society, it offers low-cost insurance, tax-deferred savings plans, scholarships, pageants and debutante balls, singing and music circles, Slovenefests and other heritage programs, and a wide variety of various other benefits and activities, athletic, cultural and social projects, and recreational facilities.

Contact: Joseph C. Evanish, National President.
Address: 247 West Allegheny Road, Imperial, Pennsylvania 15126.
Telephone: (412) 695-1100.

Slovenian Research Center of America (SRCA).

Conducts worldwide research on Slovenian heritage, culture, and history; promotes the study of Slovenian language, culture, and ethnic contributions to the United States.

Contact: Dr. Edward Gobetz, Executive Director.
Address: 29227 Eddy Road, Willoughby Hills, Ohio 44092.
Telephone: (216) 944-7237.

Slovenian Women's Union (SŽZ).

Organized in 1926, this organization of 6,100 members has united American Slovenian women of Catholic orientation. Fraternal activities are organized on local (lodge), regional and national basis and include scholarship and educational programs, heritage projects, visits of sick members and paying tribute to deceased members, numerous charity and athletic projects, tributes to honorees such as mothers of the year; uniformed, baton-twirling drill teams, cooking classes and contests.

Contact: Olga Ancel, National Secretary.
Address: 431 North Chicago Street, Joliet, Illinois 60432.
Telephone: (815) 727-1926.

MUSEUMS AND RESEARCH CENTERS

Museum of the Slovenian Women's Union of America.

The museum has a collection of Slovenian memorabilia, books, pictures, slides, records, Slovenian national costumes, and handicrafts. It also functions as a gift shop where various Slovenian items, including books and souvenirs, can be purchased.

Contact: Mollie Gregorich.
Address: 431 North Chicago Street, Joliet, Illinois 60432.
Telephone: (815) 723-4514.

Slovenian Heritage Center.

The center has a museum with three specified categories. One is dedicated to Slovenia alone, with maps, coats of arms, books, pictures, and artifacts. The second covers the Slovenian American history and houses a library of Slovenian and Slovenian American authors. The third area deals with the SNPJ history and also serves as a lecture and conference room.

Contact: Lou Serjak.

Address: 674 North Market, East Palestine, Ohio 44413.

Telephone: (412) 336-5180.

Slovenian Research Center of America, Inc.

This organization is dedicated to research, education, exhibits, publications, and information service on Slovenian heritage. An American and international network of Slovenian volunteer associates assist in research on Slovenian contributions to America and the world, establishing the richest contemporary collection of its kind. Other areas of research include activities and integration of Slovenian immigrants and their descendants, and their organizations.

Contact: Dr. Edward Gobetz, Director.

Address: 29227 Eddy Road, Willoughby Hills, Ohio 44092.

Telephone: (216) 944-7237.

Studia Slovenica.

This organization has been dedicated to research and publishing activities on Slovenia and Slovenian Americans. Its director, Dr. John Arnez, until recently professor of economics at St. Joseph's College in New York, has devoted his knowledge and energies to preparation and/or publication of several valuable books since the late 1950s. In 1991 he appealed to Slovenian American community for materials about Slovenian Americans and those from Slovenian refugee camps to establish a research library at his new location in Slovenia.

Contact: Dr. Janez Arnez, Director.

Address: p.p. 28, 61210 Ljubljana—Sentvid, Slovenia, Europe.

SOURCES FOR ADDITIONAL STUDY

Adamic, Louis. *The Native's Return*. New York: Harper, 1934.

Anthology of Slovenian American Literature, edited by G. Edward Gobetz and Adele Donchenko. Willoughby Hills, Ohio: Slovenian Research Center of America, 1977.

Arnez, John. *Slovenia in European Affairs*. New York: League of CSA, 1958.

————. *Slovenian Community in Bridgeport, Connecticut*. New York: Studia Slovenica, 1971.

Gobetz, G. Edward. *Adjustment and Assimilation of Slovenian Refugees*. New York: Arno Press, 1980.

Govorchin, Gerald Gilbert. *Americans from Yugoslavia*. Gainesville: University of Florida Press, 1961.

Kuhar, Aloysius L. *The Conversion of the Slovenes and the German-Slav Ethnic Boundary in the Eastern Alps*. New York: Studia Slovenica, 1967.

Odorizzi, Irene M. Planinsek. *Footsteps Through Time*. Washington, D.C.: Washington Landmark Tours, 1978.

Prisland, Marie. *From Slovenia to America: Recollections and Collections*. Milwaukee: Bruce Publishing, 1968.

Slovenian Heritage, Volume I, edited by Edward Gobetz. Willoughby Hills, Ohio: Slovenian Research Center of America, 1980.

Strong believers in
the value of their
culture, Spanish
Americans make
every effort to keep
the language alive in
the home.

SPANISH AMERICANS

by
Clark Colahan

OVERVIEW

Similar in climatic zones, area, and population to California, Spain occupies the greater part of the Iberian peninsula in southwestern Europe. Spain's Latin name, Hispania (Land of Rabbits), was given by Carthaginian settlers at the dawn of recorded history. Colonized by a series of important civilizations, it became heir to the cultures not only of Carthage but also of Greece and Rome. It was the home country of legionaries, several emperors, and philosophers, including Seneca, the founder of Stoicism. Later, with the fall of the empire, it was settled by Germanic Visigoths, then Arabs and Moors. As the center of the first world empire of the modern era, Spain imposed its culture and language on peoples in many parts of the globe. By the beginning of the twenty-first century it is estimated that there will be more people in the world who speak Spanish (330 million) than English.

Although politically unified since the reign of the Catholic monarchs Ferdinand and Isabel in the late fifteenth century, Spain continues to be divided by regional loyalties. Individual Spaniards, whether living in Spain or abroad, usually think of the *patria* (the fatherland) not as the entire nation, but rather as the area of the country where they were raised. This tendency has not diminished in recent years; in fact, the government has moved toward a less centralized form of rule by dividing the country into *autonomías* (autonomous areas) linked to Madrid (Spain's capital city) in a loose federalism that accommodates and even encourages more local control than the country has known for centuries.

Among the major regions in Spain are Castile, which includes the capital city of Madrid; Cataluña, which includes the city of Barcelona; Andalucía, which includes Seville; Extremadura; Galicia; and the Basque Country.

While centralist regimes of the past favored a standard national language, the Spanish government today encourages the schooling in and general use of regional dialects and languages. Galicians, for example, who occupy the northwest corner of the peninsula, speak Gallego. It is a language that reflects in vocabulary and structure the region's proximity to Portugal, to the south, and Castile, to the east. Residents of Cataluña speak Catalan, a Romance language that shares many features with other Romance languages such as Spanish and French but that is distinct from them. In Castile, the country's central region, the residents speak Castellano, which is also the language of most Latin American countries and, outside of Spain, is commonly thought of as the standard Spanish language.

Basques, who call themselves Euskaldunak, meaning "speakers of Euskera," occupy a small area of Spain known as the Basque Country; the Basque word for this region is Euzkadi. Located in the north central part of the country, and no more than 100 miles long in any direction, Euzkadi is considered by its inhabitants as part of the same ethnic nation found across the border in southwestern France. In contrast to Gallego, the Basque ancestral language, Euskera, appears unrelated to any other dialect in Spain or elsewhere, with the possible exception of some vocabulary items found in the area of the Black Sea. Basque culture is considered the oldest in Europe, predating even the prehistoric arrival of the Indo-European peoples.

Today, with the exception of enclaves on the north coast of Morocco, the Spanish empire is gone; it has been replaced by a constitutional monarchy modeled on the British system. While emigration is currently at low levels, from 1882 to 1947 some five million Spaniards emigrated (eventually about 3.8 million of those returned to Spain). Half went to Argentina, which, as a large, sparsely populated country, took active measures to attract Europeans; historically, Argentina is second only to the United States in the number of all immigrants received. A number of Spanish immigrants settled in Cuba, a colony of Spain until the Spanish-American War in 1898, and many Spaniards moved to what is now the United States.

EMIGRATION FROM SPAIN

In the first century of Spain's presence in the New World, many of the explorers and soldiers came from Andalucía (in the South) and Extremadura (in the West), two of the poorest regions of the country. The early and lasting influence of these immigrants explains why the standard dialect spoken today in the Western Hemisphere retains the pronunciation used in the South, instead of the characteristics of the older variant still spoken by those living north of Madrid. In the nineteenth and twentieth centuries the region that has produced the most emigrants has been Galicia, together with similar parts of Old Castile that border it on the south. During most of this time Galicia has been an isolated, un-industrialized corner of the peninsula. Its inheritance laws either divided farms among all the siblings in a family, resulting in unworkably small *minifundios*, or denied land entirely to all but the first born. In either case the competition for land was intense, compelling many Galicians to seek their fortunes elsewhere.

Adjoining Galicia to the east on Spain's north coast is Asturias, which also sent large numbers of immigrants overseas. Until the nineteenth century its economic situation was similar to that in Galicia, but it later became a national leader in industrial development based on coal mining, metal working, and ship building. The above-average level of occupational skills possessed by the Asturian immigrants contributed significantly to the characterization of Spanish immigrants as highly skilled workers.

The southern provinces of Spain, which include Almería, Málaga, Granada, and the Canary Islands, have been another major source of Spanish immigration to the United States. A number of factors combined to compel citizens to leave these regions: the hot, dry climate; the absence of industry; and a *latifundio* system of large ranches that placed agriculture under the control of a landed caste.

Basques have also immigrated to the United States in large numbers. Traditionally both hardy mountain farmers as well as seafaring people, they may well have reached the coasts of the New World before Columbus. Basques stood out in the exploration of the Americas, both as soldiers and members of the crews that did the sailing for Spaniards. Prominent in the civil service and colonial administration, they were accustomed to overseas travel and residence. In addition to the restrictive inheritance laws in the Basque Country, another reason for emigration was the devastation from the Napoleonic Wars in the first half of the nineteenth century—campaigns that were followed by defeats in the two Carlist civil wars.

Accustomed to the hardships of mountainous farming and stock raising, Basques found they could make a good living as herders, and later as ranchers, in both Argentina and California. The Spanish pattern of transhumance (the driving of flocks over long distances between summer and winter pastures), provided Basques with seasonal experience related to the lonely, far-flung operations of the New World. It was Spanish shepherds in search of summer pasture that extended the New Mexico colony to the north into what is now Colorado.

MAJOR IMMIGRATION WAVES

In colonial times there were a number of Spanish populations in the New World with governments answerable to Madrid. The first settlement was in Florida, followed by New Mexico, California, Arizona, Texas, and Louisiana. In 1598, when the first New Mexican town was established, there were about 1,000 Spaniards north of Mexico; today, their descendants are estimated at 900,000. Since the founding of the United States, an additional 250,000 immigrants have arrived either directly from Spain or following a relatively short sojourn in a Latin American country.

The earliest Spanish settlements north of Mexico (known then as New Spain) were the result of the same forces that later led the English to come to that area. Exploration had been fueled in part by imperial hopes for the discovery of wealthy civilizations. In addition, like those aboard the Mayflower, most Spaniards came to the New World seeking land to farm, or occasionally, as historians have recently established, freedom from religious persecution. A substantial number of the first settlers to New Mexico, for instance, were descendants of Spanish Jews who had been compelled to leave Spain.

Immigration to the United States from Spain was minimal but steady during the first half of the nineteenth century, with an increase during the 1850s and 1860s resulting from the social disruption of the Carlist civil wars. Much larger numbers of Spanish immigrants entered the country in the first quarter of the twentieth century—27,000 in the first decade and 68,000 in the second—due to the same circumstances of rural poverty and urban congestion that led other Europeans to emigrate in that period. In 1921, however, the U.S. government enacted a quota system that favored northern Europeans, limiting the number of entering Spaniards to 912 per year, an amount soon reduced further to 131.

The Spanish presence in the United States continued to diminish, declining sharply between 1930 and 1940 from a total of 110,000 to 85,000. Many immigrants moved either back to Spain or to another Hispanic country. Historically, Spaniards have often lived abroad, usually in order to make enough money to return home to an enhanced standard of living and higher social status. In Spanish cities located in regions that experienced heavy emigration at the beginning of the twentieth century, such as the port city of Gijón in Asturias, there are wealthy neighborhoods usually referred to as concentrations of *indianos,* people who became rich in the New World and then returned to their home region.

Beginning with the Fascist revolt against the Spanish Republic in 1936 and the devastating civil war that ensued, General Francisco Franco established a reactionary dictatorship that ruled Spain for 40 years. At the time of the Fascist takeover, a small but prominent group of liberal intellectuals fled into exile in the United States. After the civil war the country endured 20 years of extreme poverty. As a result, when relations between Spain and most other countries were at last normalized in the mid-1960s, 44,000 Spaniards immigrated to the United States in that decade alone. In the 1970s, with prosperity emerging in Spain, the numbers declined to about 3,000 per year. Europe enjoyed an economic boom in the 1980s, and the total number of Spanish immigrants for the ten years dropped to only 15,000. The 1990 U.S. census recorded 76,000 foreign-born Spaniards in the country, representing only four-tenths of a percent of the total populace. In contrast, the largest Hispanic group—Mexicans born outside the United States—numbered over two million, approximately 21 percent.

Five areas of the United States have had significant concentrations of Spaniards: New York City, Florida, California, the Mountain West, and the industrial areas of the Midwest. For nineteenth-century immigrants, New York City was the most common destination in the United States. Until 1890 most Spaniards in this country lived either in the city itself, with a heavy concentration in Brooklyn, or in communities in New Jersey and Connecticut. By the 1930s, however, these neighborhoods had largely disintegrated, with the second generation moving to the suburbs and assimilating into the mainstream of American life.

At the end of the nineteenth century, Florida attracted the second largest group of Spaniards in the country through its ties to the Cuban cigar industry. Most of the owners of factories were originally from Asturias, and in the second half of the century they immigrated in substantial numbers, first to Cuba, then later to Key West, and eventually Tampa, taking thousands of workers with them. Several thousands of their descendants still live in the vicinity.

In nineteenth-century California the Basques were an influential segment of American society. At one time they held all the government posts in California and Mexico, including the position of governor. Missionaries, soldiers, and merchants from the Basque Country were also prominent until 1848, when the United States took control of the area that is now California, imposing the English language and American government. In general, urban Basques, with their strong educational backgrounds and professions inseparable from Spanish language and social institutions, went to Spanish-speaking countries where their skills could be used. In Argentina, for example, they form a large and respected component of all branches of professional activity. In contrast, English-speaking areas like the United States and Australia attracted rural, relatively uneducated Basques whose success depended on commitment to physically demanding work.

The presence of rural Basques in California began with the gold rush. Many Basques, emigrating primarily from the province of Navarra and the adjoining French provinces of Labourd, Soule, and Basse Navarre, first sought their fortunes in South America, and later moved on to California in search of mineral wealth. But, as with many groups of '49ers—people seeking gold—the Basques realized that it was not necessarily the mines that would provide riches. The mining camps were filled with people in need of food and supplies, and the demand for animal products was high. Within a few years, Basques were doing well in sheep ranching, first as contract herders and then as owners. Throughout the rest of the nineteenth century and in the early years of the twentieth century, they spread east and north in the Mountain West into California's central San Joaquin Valley, as well as Nevada, Montana, Wyoming, Colorado, New Mexico, and Arizona.

In the 1880s a second wave of Basques emigrated primarily from the Spanish provinces of Vizcaya and Guipuzcoa, located west of France on the shore of the Bay of Biscay. They settled in northern Nevada, southern Idaho, and northeastern Oregon. In Boise they became an important segment of the business community, and the city is now sometimes called the Basque capital of America.

California is also home to descendants of southern Spanish pineapple and sugar cane workers who had moved to Hawaii at the beginning of the twentieth century. The great majority of those immigrants moved on to the San Francisco area in search of greater opportunity. In Southern California's heavy industry, there have been substantial numbers of skilled workers from northern Spain.

The steel and metalworking centers of the Midwest also attracted northern Spaniards. In the censuses of 1920, 1930, and 1940, due to sizable contingents of Asturian coal miners, West Virginia was among the top seven states in number of Spanish immigrants. Rubber production and other kinds of heavy industry accounted for large groups of Spaniards in Ohio, Illinois, Michigan, and Pennsylvania. With the decline of this sector of the American economy in the second half of the twentieth century such centers of industry have largely lost their drawing power, accelerating the dispersal and assimilation of these Spanish communities.

ACCULTURATION AND ASSIMILATION

The decrease in the flow of Spaniards to the United States in recent decades, combined with their ability and willingness to form part of both the Hispanic sector and the society at large, has largely obscured any specifically Spanish presence in the States. As the European segment of the American Hispanic population, and therefore in some ways the least different from the country's predominantly European cultural and racial origins, they are often perceived as less alien than Latin Americans, and are more readily accepted into American society.

SPANISH CHARACTERISTICS

Because of the widely divergent traits of the several Spanish regions, any descriptions of Spanish character can only be approximate. During the last 100 years Spanish writers have engaged in national soulsearching and debate, spurred in part by the country's disastrous loss to the United States in the Spanish-American War of 1898. Early analysts, like philosopher Ortega y Gassett and literary historian Américo Castro, questioned what it was that separated Spain from its European neighbors. Since 1975 the stress has been on reintegrating Spain into the family of nations, which it led at the beginning of the modern era. One trait the discussion has demonstrated is that Spaniards often hold strong opinions at variance with those of other Spaniards. Still, some points of agreement emerge.

Castilians have an austere mystical tradition that goes hand in hand with the region's image of itself as a heroic and Christian civilizer of a world empire. In contrast, Andalucians, in the South, are often censured by those living to the north for their decidedly more outward religiosity, highly visible in Holy Week processions.

A number of factors combined to make the warrior class Spain's dominant sector in centuries past. Like the Castilian hero of the *Poem of the Cid*, members of that class made a practice of limiting their work to warfare and politics, leaving the more intellectual professions to the powerful Jewish minority, and the beginnings of modern industry and agriculture to the vanquished Muslims. When these two minorities were expelled from the country—the Jews in 1492 and the Muslims in 1610—the activities associated with them were considered somewhat tainted. The resulting social pattern was that of advancement through family connections and government service rather than commercial or intellectual distinction.

In the eighteenth century, there were efforts at Europeanization as the Bourbons, the French royal family, came to the Spanish throne with ideas of Enlightenment reform. Growing acceptance of scientific and democratic ideals closed much of the gap between Spain and the rest of Europe in the nineteenth century, though segments of both the aristocracy and the common people continued to resist such notions. These ideals were the focus of civil friction and wars for two-and-a-half centuries, finally emerging victorious only with the democracy established upon the death of Franco in 1975.

Features of a knightly ruling class still indirectly influence Hispanic societies, including those in the United States. These features include a firm grounding in family and other personal relations, a thorough *personalismo* that leads to loyalty in business and politics and to friendships in personal life. *Personalismo*, especially among males, is felt to be deeper and more common than among Anglos and is felt to provide greater security for one's self and family than the provisions of government.

The Spanish work ethic is compatible with the values of both pre- and post-industrial Europe. While often working long, intensive hours, Spaniards have generally not felt work itself to be a pursuit that will guarantee either success or happiness. Instead, leisure has a primary value: it is used to maintain essential social contacts and is identified with upward social movement. Another element of the Spanish character is an aristocratic concern with a public image in harmony with group standards, even if at variance with the private reality. As in other cultures that motivate people through the fear of shame rather than the sting of guilt, the achievement of these goals is substantially validated through the opinions held by others. This notion is exemplified by the Spanish phrase *¿Qué dirán?* (What will they say?).

Stereotypes of Spanish immigrants derive in part from the *leyenda negra*, the "black legend," created and spread by the English in the sixteenth and seventeenth centuries when the two countries were rivals for European domination. Revulsion is expressed at the alleged cruelty of bull fighting, a sport that is believed by supporters to exalt individual worth through the demonstration of almost chivalric courage. Other stereotypical images, including exaggerated ideas of wild emotional intensity, create the misperception of Spain as the land of the tambourine and castanets, fiery flamenco dancing, and the reckless sensualism of Bizet's opera heroine, Carmen. Most of these elements are only connected, and in a much attenuated degree, with the southern region, Andalucía. As in matters of religion, northern Spaniards often view the character of life in their own regions as profoundly different.

BASQUE CHARACTERISTICS AND ASSIMILATION

Scholars have described the Basque character as an insistence on individual achievement combined with an expectation of community involvement. They view the world as a challenge, and life as somber. Fundamental values for men and women alike are *indarra* (strength) and *sendotasuna* (referring to physical and emotional endurance). At Basque festivals the importance of these two qualities is evident in events such as the repeated lifting of a steel cylinder weighing 225 pounds, chopping wood, walking for some distance while carrying two 110-pound weights, and the dragging of large stones. Similarly, Basque folk dancing, involving spectacular kicks and jumps, is highly athletic. Handball and its variant, *jai alai,* are Basque games requiring strength and stamina as well as agility, and male bravado in this regard is typical. That Basque American social life centers on sporting events reflects the degree to which they measure self-worth through effort and achievement.

During the first century of Basque presence in the United States, the institution most responsible for the immigrants' assimilation was the Basque Hotel. It provided a non-threatening atmosphere for orientation to American society, a haven for relaxing and living during vacations and the slow winter months, and it also served as an employment bureau. The Basque maids and waitresses arriving from Spain soon found husbands among the herders, then lived in the hotel during pregnancies. In the second half of the twentieth century the hotels have also been frequented by non-Basque tourists who are attracted by the exotic yet homey atmosphere and hearty family-style meals.

CUISINE

Spanish food varies from region to region, though the use of olive oil instead of butter is widespread. Seafood is also a common element of Spanish meals; few parts of the peninsula are without daily deliveries of fresh fish and shellfish from the coast, and these items are the featured ingredients in the rice-based casserole of the Mediterranean coast called *paella*. Much of the agriculture in the South is involved with olive production, and a typical dish of the southern zone is *gazpacho*, a thick, cold tomato and vegetable soup originally concocted to be served during the heat of the day to harvest workers. One southern town, Jérez de la Frontera, contributed to the English language the word "sherry." In the opposite corner of the country, the Galicians and Asturians drink hard cider and eat a stew called *favada*, made from two kinds of sausage, garlic, saffron, and white beans.

The four- and five-course meals served in the Basque hotels in the American West reproduced those served on holidays in the Old Country, including garbanzo beans, stew, chicken, and meat. Only the traditional seafood dishes of the maritime Basque provinces could not be prepared in the Mountain West. A popular Basque drink, brought to the New World around the turn of the twentieth century but now forgotten in Spain, is picón punch, a mixture of picón liqueur, grenadine, brandy, and soda.

TRADITIONAL HOLIDAYS AND FESTIVE CLOTHING

Most Spanish holidays are also found in American culture through the shared influence of the Catholic church. One exception is the sixth of January, *Día de los Reyes Magos,* "Day of the Three Wise Men." Known in English as Epiphany (formerly Twelfth Night), this holiday has remained vital in Spain as the occasion on which Christmas gifts are given. In the United States, Spanish children usually are the beneficiaries of a biculturalism that supplies them with gifts on January 6 as well as Christmas Eve.

The most commonly pictured Spanish clothing—as in representations of the annual spring fair in Seville that served as the prototype for the California Rose Parade—is the traditional Andalucian ruffled dress for women and the short, tightly fitted jacket for men. This jacket is cut for display both while on horseback and in the atmosphere of stylized energy and romance that characterizes flamenco dancing. Throughout much of Spain, however, holiday attire is based on everyday work clothes, but richly embroidered and appointed. The western region surrounding Salamanca has an economy based on cattle raising, and the extravagantly large hat and embroidered jacket worn by that province's *charros* were passed on to the Mexican cowboys.

Traditional festive Basque clothing is worn by dancers during the annual festivals. This clothing includes, for women, skirts with horizontal stripes, white leggings, blouses with corsets, and

In this 1933 photograph, Isabel Arevalo, a descendent of one of California's oldest Spanish American families, displays the four combs brought to America by her ancestors in the seventeenth century.

scarves worn over the hair. Men's trousers, shirts, and shoes are often all white, set off by dark sashes and berets.

FLAMENCO

Though known throughout the world as a "Spanish" style of music and dance, flamenco is mainly associated with the southern region of Andalucía, where Arabic and Gypsy influences are strong. Flamenco music is characterized by rapid, rhythmic hand clapping and a specialized form of guitar playing. The dancing that accompanies this music is typically done in duet fashion and includes feet stomping and castanet playing. Dancers generally wear the traditional Andalucian costumes described above: ornate, ruffled dresses for women and short, tightly fitting jackets for men. Although flamenco has not become widely popular in America, it can be found—especially in restaurants in major urban areas that have significant Spanish American populations.

LANGUAGE

As Spanish becomes more and more the second language in the United States, the American-born generations of families that emigrated from Spain have been increasingly likely to retain it in both its spoken and written forms. Current communication with Hispanic countries is highly developed, including such media as newspapers, magazines, films, and even Spanish-language television networks. Consequently immigrants arriving in recent years have found themselves less obliged to learn English than did their counterparts of 30 years ago. These newcomers integrate easily into the new Latin American communities that in several parts of the country function mainly in Spanish.

Strong believers in the value of their culture, Spanish Americans make every effort to keep the language alive in the home. Many, however, are opposed to bilingual education in the schools, a position grounded in their awareness of the need to assimilate linguistically in order to compete in an English-speaking society.

Many Basque immigrants, living in remote areas and having minimal contact with other American groups, learned little or no English. Their sons and daughters often entered school knowing only Basque, and consequently did not do well at first. Some members of the first generation were trilingual, speaking Basque, English, and Spanish or French, though their Basque typically eroded as they grew older. Second- and third-generation Basque Americans usually know little Basque or Spanish; the former is more likely to be partially retained. In the last 30 years the Basque Studies Program at the University of Nevada in Reno and the Basque Center in Boise have taught the language as part of the national renaissance of ethnic pride that is particularly visible among Basques.

A common greeting among Spaniards is *¿Qué hay?* ("kay I")—What's new?", and *Hasta luego* ("ahsta lwego")—See you later. Spaniards can easily be distinguished from other Spanish speakers by their ubiquitous use of *vale* ("bahlay"), employed identically to the American "okay." Two commonly heard proverbs are, *En boca cerrada no entra mosca* ("en boca therrada no entra mosca")—Don't put your foot in your mouth (literally, "If you keep your mouth shut you keep out the flies"), and *Uvas y queso saben un beso* ("oobas ee keso saben un beso")—Grapes and cheese together taste as good as a kiss. A customary toast before drinking is *Salud, dinero y amor, y tiempo para disfrutarlos* ("saluth, deenayro, ee ahmor, ee tyempo pahra deesfrutahrlos")—Health, wealth, and love, and time to enjoy them.

Basques greet each other with *Egun on* ("agoon ohn")—Good day, or *Arratsalde on* ("ahrrahtsalday ohn")—Good evening. "Hello" and "Good-bye" are both *agur* ("ahgoorr"). *Eskarrik asko* ("eskahrreek ahsko") expresses thanks. Their strong work ethic is reflected in the proverb, *Alperkeria, askoren ondamendia* ("ahlperkereea, ahskohren ohndahmendeea")—Laziness has ruined many people. The culture's stress on keeping one's word has produced the maxim, *Agindua zorra, esan oi da* ("ahgindooah zorra, esahn oy da")—A promise is a debt, as the saying goes. A useful expression in Basque restaurants is *Gorria bi* ("gorreea bee")—Red wine for two.

FAMILY AND COMMUNITY DYNAMICS

FAMILY STRUCTURE

The structure of the Spanish family has come to resemble the American and European pattern. Grandparents often live in their own house or a retirement home; women frequently work outside the home. The obligation of children to personally care for elderly parents, however, is somewhat stronger among Spaniards—even those raised in the United States—than among the general American population; a parent often lives part of the year with one child and part with another. The traditional practice of one daughter not marrying in order to live with and care for the parents during their last years has not been maintained in this country. The traditional pattern of Hispanic mothers being completely devoted to their children—especially the boys—while fathers spent much of their time socializing outside the home has diminished. Despite various changes within the family structure that broadened women's roles, most community leaders are men.

In the Basque Country, extended families living together were traditionally the rule. The residents of the large farm houses typically included grandparents, a husband and wife (one of whom was the heir of the grandparents), the couple's unmarried children and unmarried brothers or sisters, and servants. Basque women enjoy equal respect with men, their duties being considered equally important and in some cases interchangeable; this feature of the culture is so old and pronounced that it was the subject of comments made by the ancient Greek geographer Strabo.

At one time, young Spanish women were allowed to date only when accompanied by a chaperon, but this custom has been entirely discarded. Family pressure for a "respectable" courtship—a vestige of the strongly emphasized Spanish sense of honor—has been largely eroded in both Spain and the United States. Long engagements, however, have persisted, helping to solidify family alliances while children are still relatively young, and giving the couple and their relatives a chance to get to know each other well before the marriage is formally established.

As far as the Basque culture, marriage to non-Basques was traditionally prohibited, and immigrants to the United States generally either postponed marriage until they returned to live in their home region, or brought a woman to the

United States from the Basque Country to marry. Basque Americans born in the United States, on the other hand, have intermarried freely with other ethnic groups, especially with other Catholics. Their spouses have been welcomed into the group in keeping with the general principle followed in the Old World that the spouse's relatives are also one's own. Despite widespread intermarriage, Basque Americans faithfully maintain their customs due in part to a strong sense of obligation to their parents.

Because careers outside the home are now the norm for Spanish women, differences in the schooling men and women pursue are minimal. A large segment of the community stresses higher education, and, in line with the sharper class distinctions that differentiate Spain from the United States, professional pursuits are highly respected. A significant number of Spanish physicians, engineers, and college professors have become successful in the United States.

COMMUNITY LIFE

Spanish communities in the United States, in keeping with their strong regional identification in Spain, have established centers for Galicians, Asturians, Andalucians, and other such groups. Writing in 1992, Moisés Llordén Miñambres—the specialist in emigration patterns from Spain—regarded this as a given, a natural condition, and referred in passing to the "ethnic" grouping of

recent Spanish emigrants reflecting the individual characteristics of the "countries" from which they come. But these were certainly not the only type of community organizations to spring up in the United States; a variety of clubs and associations were formed. The listing by Llordén Miñambres shows 23 in New York City, eight in New Jersey, five in Pennsylvania, four in California, and lesser numbers in Indiana, Ohio, Illinois, Massachusetts, Michigan, New York State, Rhode Island, Vermont, and Florida.

Llordén Miñambres divides these organizations into several categories. Beneficent societies, such as the Unión Benéfica Española of New York, have aimed to provide charitable help for the needy, bury the poor, and provide information and recommendations to Spanish immigrants. Mutual aid societies, such as the Española de Socorros Mutuos "La Nacional," founded in New York in 1868, began as examples of trade union associations, and were important in providing families with medical care and help in times of economic crisis. The members of educational and recreational societies usually were drawn from among the more successful members of the local Spanish community; activities included literary readings and musical performances, banquets, and dances. There have also been athletic associations, such as the Sporting Club of New York; Spanish chambers of commerce; and purely cultural associations that set up lectures, museums, and plays, such as the Club Cervantes in

Philadelphia. And finally, there have been associations based on religious and political beliefs, such as those that supported the Spanish Republic during and after the Fascist uprising.

Community life in the Basque Country was exceptionally tight-knit, regulated since the tenth century by regional codes known as *fueros* that spelled out the obligations not of subject to ruler but of each resident to the others. The use of communal lands for woodcutting and grazing, found also in other regions of Spain and in colonial New Mexico, is part of this cooperative pattern and was very likely an encouragement to small Basque herders to risk making a living on American public lands.

American-born Basques have formed social clubs, which now sponsor an annual summer or spring festival as their principal activity. Since social as well as traditional folk dancing is popular, a Christmas or New Year's dance is also customary. As the festivals, initiated in 1959, have become more popular, and Basque folkdancing has become better known through groups like Boise's Oinkari Dancers, the impression has been conveyed to the public that the culture grants special importance to sport, dance, and convivial eating. Yet this is only half the picture, as American Basques also have a seemingly contradictory capacity for aloofness and pragmatism.

RELIGION

Many Spanish Americans are less active in Catholic church activities than was common in past generations in Spain; they rarely change their religious affiliation, though, and still participate frequently in family-centered ecclesiastical rituals. In both Spain and the United States events such as first communions and baptisms are felt to be important social obligations that strengthen clan identity.

Basques are devout Catholics but differ from many other Spaniards in a stress on asceticism; the Jesuit Order was founded and first developed in the Basque Country. Another difference is that all members of a congregation, men as well as women, are expected to participate actively in religious services and projects. In the Basque farm areas, schooling was considered important only for boys who were to enter the priesthood. Divorce is uncommon and is regarded negatively.

The most important religious ceremony for Basques is the funeral, which involves several days of rituals and communal meals. American Basques reflect this custom in the obligation they feel to attend the funerals of business associates, friends, and distant relatives. It is not uncommon for them to drive great distances to attend a funeral; such a ceremony might well include representatives from four or five states. In the vast American West this custom also enables the renewal of personal contacts. Funeral insurance is a central feature of the Basque mutual aid societies in both New York and Boise.

In the Basque Country, as throughout Spain, the church has usually opposed emigration, objecting to both the immediate loss of parishioners and the weakening of religious commitment experienced by emigrants. In some cases, members of the clergy denounced the practice of leaving the Basque Country to find work herding sheep because they were concerned about the hardships suffered in the New World.

EMPLOYMENT AND ECONOMIC TRADITIONS

Since Spanish American entrance into the middle class has been widespread, the employment patterns described above have largely disappeared. This social mobility has followed logically from the fact that throughout the history of Spanish immigration to the United States, the percentage of skilled workers remained uniformly high. In the first quarter of the twentieth century, for example, 85 percent of Spanish immigrants were literate, and 36 percent were either professionals or skilled craftsmen. A combination of aptitude, motivation, and high expectations led to successful entry into a variety of fields.

The situation of Basques in the United States has been more complex, with dramatic changes to the employment profile in recent decades. Since the late 1960s, very few Basques have emigrated with the plan of being a sheepherder. With economic conditions improving after Franco's death, past notions of achieving success by making one's fortune in America are no longer prevalent.

At the same time second- and third-generation American Basques have often preferred to leave sheepherding due to the hardship and the isolation. Another factor compelling sheepherders to switch careers in recent decades has been a decline in the value of sheep products due to widespread use of synthetic fabrics and stiff international competition. Those who stay in stock raising sometimes switch to cattle in the interests of a lighter work load and seemingly higher social status. Still, many of the largest open-range sheep operations are owned by Basque Americans.

In California in the mid-twentieth century many Basque Americans found work either as gardeners, in the San Francisco area, or as expert milkers, in the areas around Chino and La Puente. In Miami a certain number of professional *jai alai* players, recruited directly from the Basque Country for American teams, have settled and joined the community of Spaniards there; *jai alai* players and their families also live in Connecticut and Rhode Island. As the port of entry, New York developed a fairly compact Basque neighborhood of as many as 8,000 in the peak years of immigration around 1920, with occupations ranging from laborer to factory owner.

Basque immigrants to the United States, due to their rural background, have rarely been intellectuals, and the number who have entered the professional community is much lower than those who have succeeded in business. Basques did not establish their own schools as other ethnic groups did. Their children usually did well in American classrooms, but they typically remained involved in the family business rather than go to college. In recent years, however, language barriers and other obstacles have been surmounted, and Basque families have come to accept the American belief in education as a primary path to success. The group's overall employment experience has been one of pronounced upward social mobility in occupations clustered around skilled labor and ownership of small businesses.

POLITICS AND GOVERNMENT

With the outbreak of the Spanish civil war in 1936 a number of intellectual political refugees found asylum in the United States. Supporters of the overthrown Spanish Republic, which had received aid from the Soviet Union while under attack from fascist forces, were sometimes incorrectly identified with communism, but their arrival in the United States well before the "red scare" of the early 1950s spared them the worst excesses of McCarthyism.

Reacting against the political climate in Franco's Spain, Spanish Americans have tended to vote Democratic. Until the end of the dictatorship in Spain in 1975 political exiles in the United States actively campaigned against the abuses of the Franco regime. They gained the sympathy of many Americans, some of whom, during the war, formed the Abraham Lincoln Brigade and fought in Spain against the Fascists.

The political orientation of American Basques, due to the often violent separatist movement in the Basque Country, is once again more complicated. Unlike many Basques living in urban settings in Latin America, Basques in the United States have generally been unsympathetic to the cause of Basque nationalists in Spain. This lack of sympathy can be attributed in part to the conservatism of Basque Americans, as well as the harm done to their reputation in this country by recurring accounts of Basque terrorist killings in Spain. The one North American exception took place in New York City, where from 1926 to 1938 pro-nationalist Basques formed their own club in Brooklyn called Aberria.

In the late 1960s an effort was made to unionize Basques employed as sheepherders. The effort was headed by a Basque priest, Santos Recalde, working for the Bishop of Boise as chaplain to the shepherds. He was emphatically opposed by the herders and their associations, who argued that the industry was too threatened by other factors to survive collective bargaining. Although the organizers publicized what they considered shamefully primitive living conditions and low wages, response was not forthcoming from most of the herders. As contract laborers in a foreign country they were either less dissatisfied than Recalde thought or unprepared to face a legal confrontation with their employers. In the past three decades, however, Basque Americans have begun to enter local and state politics much more than they had previously. They are usually affiliated with the Republican party and seek to capitalize on their reputation for honesty and diligence.

INDIVIDUAL AND GROUP CONTRIBUTIONS

ARTS AND HUMANITIES

Among the political refugees from the Spanish civil war was Pablo Casals (1876-1973), an internationally celebrated cellist. In addition to his lyrically beautiful playing, he was known for his adaptations of Spanish folk music, especially from his own region of Cataluña. He was also active in efforts to help other victims of the civil war.

Similar in terms of political position was the novelist Ramón Sender (1902-1982); after fleeing the Franco regime to Mexico and then Guatemala, he finally settled in the United States. Professor of Spanish literature at the University of New Mexico, University of Southern California, and University of California, he published in this country under the pen name of José Losángeles. He is well known for his depiction of the impact of political events on human lives, as in the short novel *Requiem por un campesino español* (*Requiem for a Spanish Peasant*). He managed to keep a sense of humor throughout the aftermath of the Spanish civil war, and humor is paramount in his Nancy novels, in which the protagonist is a typical American undergraduate student.

The poet Angel González (1925-), an Asturian from a republican family who experienced the civil war as a child, has been the clearest and most honored lyrical voice to describe the emotional fatigue and near despair of life under the Franco dictatorship. Living in the United States but traveling frequently throughout the Hispanic world from the 1960s until 1992, he taught during most of that period at the University of New Mexico and has now retired in Spain.

His colleague at the same university is the novelist Alfred Rodriguez (1932-), winner of literary prizes in both Spain and the United States, including the Spanish government's *Golden Letters* award for outstanding Spanish-language narrative written in the United States. Born in Brooklyn to immigrants from Andalucía, he sojourned in Spain during the bleakest years that followed the civil war. His work continues the classic Spanish tradition of the picaresque tale, a penetrating and grimly humorous exploration of the strategies for survival in decayed or traumatized societies.

Until very recently Basques have had little tradition of written literature, with the exception of Catholic documents and devotional materials. Folk tales and legends were told by the improvising oral poet, the *bertsolari*. In the United States verses composed in this spontaneous manner about the trials and hopes of herders have on occasion been preserved. The best known of such poets is Paulo Yanzi, whose poems in Basque include an exchange of letters in verse. His works explore topics that examine the herder's life with poignant detail and philosophical reflection.

The one well-known Basque American literary figure is Robert Laxalt. Born to a sheepherder and raised on the range in Nevada and California, he recreates the Basque experience in North America in poetic, impressionistic prose. *Sweet Promised Land* describes his father's life, while *In a Thousand Graves* takes the reader with him on a journey of self-discovery back to the Basque Country.

POLITICS

A highly successful Basque American in politics is Pete Cenarrusa (1917-); he was the secretary of state for Idaho from 1967 to 1994. He has been a rancher and woolgrower in Idaho since 1946, having earned a degree in agriculture from the University of Idaho. A major in the U.S. Marine Corps from 1942 to 1946, he was an advisor to the Bureau of Land Management and has been elected to several halls of fame: Agriculture, Republican Administrators, Idaho Athletic, and Basque.

SCIENCE AND INDUSTRY

Neurologist Luis García-Buñuel (1931-) was born in Madrid and immigrated to the United States in 1956. He has headed neurology services in several American hospitals, and since 1984 has been chief of staff at the Veterans Administration Medical Center in Phoenix. Thomas García-Borras (1926-), a leading figure in the American heating oil business, was born in Barcelona and arrived in the United States in 1955. In 1983 he published *Manual for Improving Boiler and Furnace Performance*, and he is the president of U.S. Products Corporation in Las Vegas.

MEDIA

PRINT

El Diario/La Prensa.

A major newspaper founded in 1913.

Contact: Carlos D. Ramírez, Publisher.

Address: 143-155 Varick Street, New York, New York 10013.

Telephone: (212) 807-4600.

La Gaceta.

A community newspaper.

Contact: Roland Manteiga, Editor and Publisher.
Address: P.O. Box 5536, Tampa, Florida 33675.
Telephone: (813) 248-3921.

Geomundo.

A magazine on travel, geography, and natural science.

Contact: Elvira Mendoza, Editor.
Address: De Armas Publishing Group, Vanidades Continental Building, 6355 Northwest 36th Street, Virginia Gardens, Florida 33166.
Telephone: (305) 871-6400.

RADIO
WADO-AM.

Contact: Herbert M. Levin, General Manager.
Address: 666 Third Avenue, New York, New York 10017.
Telephone: (212) 687-9236.

WAMA-AM.

Contact: Edraín Archilla-Roig, General Manager.
Address: 5203 North Armenia Avenue, Tampa, Florida 33603.
Telephone: (813) 875-0086.

WKDM-AM.

Contact: Jimmy Jiménez, General Manager.
Address: 570 Seventh Avenue, Suite 1406, New York, New York 10036.
Telephone: (212) 594-1380.

WLCH-FM (91.3).

Contact: Enid Vazquez, General Manager.
Address: Spanish American Civic Association, 30 North Ann Street, Second Floor, Lancaster, Pennsylvania 17602.
Telephone: (717) 295-7760.
Fax: (717) 295-7759.

TELEVISION
Telemundo.

Contact: Henry R. Silverman, President.
Address: 1740 Broadway, 18th Floor, New York, New York 10019.
Telephone: (212) 492-5500.

Univisión.

Contact: Deborah Durham, Washington Bureau Chief.
Address: 444 North Capitol Street, N.W., Suite 601-G, Washington, D.C. 20001; or, 9405 Northwest 41st Street, Miami, Florida 33178.
Telephone: (202) 783-7155; or, (305) 471-3900.

WLTV-Channel 23 (local station).

Contact: José Cancela, General Manager.
Address: 2600 Southwest Third Avenue, Miami, Florida 33129.
Telephone: (305) 856-2323.

ORGANIZATIONS AND ASSOCIATIONS

Hispanic Institute.

Offers lectures and concerts, maintains archives on Spanish and Portuguese literature and linguistics, and publishes a journal of literary criticism entitled *Revista Hispánica Moderna Nueva Epoca.*

Contact: Susana Redondo de Feldman, Director.
Address: 612 West 116th Street, Columbia University, New York, New York 10027.
Telephone: (212) 854-4187.

Música Hispana.

Presents concerts of Spanish, Latin American, and classical chamber music, disseminates information about Hispanic music, and offers referral services to musicians and composers.

Contact: Pablo Zinger, Director.
Address: 600 West 111 Street, 3E-1, New York, New York.
Telephone: (212) 864-1527.

Repertorio Español.

Presents and tours Spanish classic plays, contemporary Latin American plays, *zarzuela* (Spanish light opera), and dance.

Contact: Gilberto Zaldívar, Producer.
Address: 138 East 27th Street, New York, New York 10016.
Telephone: (212) 889-2850.

Twentieth Century Spanish Association of America (TCSAA).

Individuals interested in the study of twentieth-century Spanish literature.

Contact: Luis T. Gonzalez-del-Valle, Executive Secretary.

Address: University of Colorado at Boulder, Department of Spanish and Portuguese, McKenna Language Building, Campus Box 278, Boulder, Colorado 80309-0278.

Telephone: (303) 492-7308.

Unión Española de California.

Organizes cultural events from the traditions of Spain.

Contact: Julián Miguel, President.

Address: 2850 Alemany Boulevard, San Francisco, California 94112.

Telephone: (415) 587-5117.

MUSEUMS AND RESEARCH CENTERS

Basque Studies Program, University of Nevada.

Teaches courses in Basque language and civilization and publishes a newsletter for the general Basque American community.

Contact: William A. Douglas, Director.

Address: Basque Studies Program/322, University of Nevada-Reno, University Library, Reno, Nevada 89557-0012.

Telephone: (702) 784-4854.

Hispanic Society of America.

Free museum exhibits paintings, sculpture, ceramics, textiles, costumes, and decorative arts representative of the Hispanic culture.

Contact: Theodore S. Beardsley, Jr., Director.

Address: 613 West 155th Street, New York, New York 10032.

Telephone: (212) 926-2234.

Southwest Museum.

Collections include artifacts from the Spanish colonial and Mexican eras.

Contact: Thomas H. Wilson, Director.

Address: 234 Museum Drive, Los Angeles, California 90065.

Telephone: (213) 221-2164.

SOURCES FOR ADDITIONAL STUDY

Douglas, William A., and Jon Bilbao. Amerikanuak: *Basques in the New World*. Reno: University of Nevada Press, 1975.

Gómez, R. A. "Spanish Immigration to the United States," *The Americas,* Volume 19, 1962; pp. 59-77.

McCall, Grant. *Basque Americans*. Saratoga, California: R & R Research Associates, 1973.

Michener, James A. *Iberia: Spanish Travels and Reflections*. Greenwich, Connecticut: Fawcett, 1968.

Pereda, Prudencio de. *Windmills in Brooklyn*. [New York], 1960.

"Spaniards," in *Harvard Encyclopedia of American Ethnic Groups*. Cambridge, Massachusetts: Harvard University Press, 1980; pp. 948-950.

SWEDISH AMERICANS

by
Mark A.
Granquist

Swedish immigrants made a fairly quick and smooth transition to life in their new country and most became quickly Americanized. As a northern European people, the Swedes shared with Americans a common religious and social heritage, and a common linguistic base.

OVERVIEW

The Kingdom of Sweden is a constitutional monarchy that is located on the eastern half of the Scandinavian peninsula in Northern Europe. It measures 173,648 square miles (449,750 square kilometers), sharing the Scandinavian peninsula with Norway to the west and north. Across the Baltic Sea, Sweden borders Finland, Estonia, Latvia, and Lithuania to the East, Poland, Germany, and Denmark to the south.

As of 1992, Sweden had a population of 8,602,000. The vast majority are ethnic Swedes, with minorities of Laplanders (Sami), Finns, Estonians, Latvians, Norwegians, and Danes, and, in the late twentieth century, immigrants from southeastern Europe and the Middle East. Virtually all Swedes officially belong to the Lutheran State Church of Sweden; there are smaller groups of Pentecostalists, Methodists, Covenant, Baptists, and Roman Catholics. The country's official language is Swedish, and the capital is Stockholm. The Swedish flag is a yellow cross on a medium blue field.

HISTORY

The Swedes are descended from the Gothic tribes that moved into Sweden following the melting glaciers, probably during the Neolithic period.

The various Gothic settlements were centered in eastern Sweden and the island of Gotland in the Baltic. During the Viking period (800-1050 A.D.) the Swedes pushed eastward into Russia, and were trading as far south as the Black Sea. In Russia, the Swedes (labeled by the Slavs as the "Rus") ruled many areas, especially in the trading town of Novgorod. By about 1000, most of central and eastern Sweden was united in the kingdom of the Svear, although this was disputed by their powerful neighbors, the Danes and the Norwegians. Christianity was introduced to the Swedes by St. Ansgar in 829, although it was slow to take hold and was not fully established until the late twelfth century, under the rule of King Eric IX. Medieval Sweden was slowly incorporated into the European world, and began to form the political and social structures characteristic to its society even up to this day. King Magnus VII was able to unite Norway and Sweden under his rule in 1319, but the arrangement was unstable and did not last. In 1397 Norway and Sweden were united with Denmark, under the rule of the Danish Queen Margaret in the Union of Kalmar. Sweden felt slighted in the Danish-dominated Union, however, and after a Danish massacre of Swedish nobles in 1520, the Swedes rose against the Danes and, led by King Gustav Vasa, freed themselves from Danish rule in 1523. King Gustavus Adolphus fought for the Protestants during the 30 Years War (1618-1648), and gained possessions for Sweden in northern Germany; King Charles X gained further territory in Poland and the Baltic States. Sweden's age of glory ended with the rise of Russia, which defeated the Swedes in the Northern War (1700-1721). Sweden lost Finland to Russia in 1809, but received Norway in compensation in 1814 (a union that lasted until 1905). During the nineteenth century, Sweden underwent economic, social, and political transformation that only partially offset a large-scale immigration to North America. In the twentieth century, Sweden has maintained its political and military neutrality, and has become one of the most highly developed industrialized countries in the world, with stable politics and an extensive social welfare system.

SIGNIFICANT IMMIGRATION WAVES

In 1638, during Sweden's era as a European power, a Swedish merchant company founded the colony of New Sweden in Delaware. This became an official Swedish colony under the leadership of Governor Johan Printz, but struggled because of indifference from the Swedish government; the

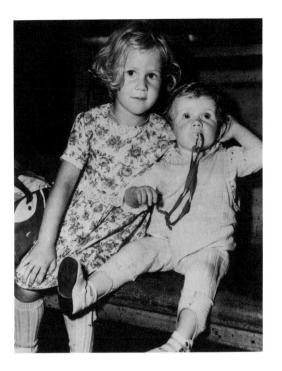

Four-year-old Astrid and one-year-old Ingrid Sjdbeck immigrated to the United States from Sweden with their parents in 1949. The family settled in Pontiac, Michigan.

colony never prospered, reaching a total of only about 500 inhabitants. In 1655 the Dutch took the colony by force; the Dutch were in turn defeated by the English 11 years later. A Swedish-speaking enclave existed in the Delaware River valley until the nineteenth century, however. Swedes played a role in early U.S. history. They were a force in the Revolutionary War. John Hanson of Maryland was the first president of the United States Congress from 1781-1782. Trade and adventure brought a number of Swedes to America in the early national period, but this immigration was rather limited.

Serious emigration from Sweden to America began after 1840, and this flow became a torrent after 1860. From 1851 to 1930, more than 1.2 million Swedes immigrated to America, a number that represented perhaps 25 percent of the total population of Sweden during this period. The country had one of the highest rates of emigration of all of the European nations. The rates of immigration to America fluctuated from year to year, however, reflecting economic conditions in both Sweden and America. The first great wave arrived between 1868 and 1873, as famine in Sweden and opportunity for land in America drove 100,000 Swedes, mainly farm families, from their homeland. They relocated primarily in the upper Midwest. The largest wave of immigrants, approximately 475,000, arrived between 1880 and 1893, again due to economic conditions. This time not only farm families emigrated, but also loggers, miners, and factory workers from the cities. The American Depression of 1893 slowed Swedish immigration until the first decade of the twentieth century, when 220,000 Swedes came to America. World War I halted emigration, and improved economic conditions in Sweden kept it to a trickle after 1920.

The immigration of Swedes to America during the nineteenth century was a movement of youth—young Swedes leaving their homeland for improved economic opportunity in America. The first waves of immigration were more rural and family oriented, but as the immigration progressed this pattern changed; young single men (and later women) left Sweden to find employment in American cities. Economic advancement was the primary reason they emigrated. There were those who resented the political, social, and religious confinement of nineteenth-century Sweden, of course, but research has shown that the overwhelming motivation driving the emigrants westward over the Atlantic was economic.

SETTLEMENT PATTERNS

The patterns of Swedish immigrant settlement changed during the course of the nineteenth century, varying with economic conditions and opportunities. The initial wave of immigration in the 1840s and 1850s was directed toward rural areas of Illinois and Iowa, especially the Mississippi River valley and Chicago. In the 1860s and 1870s immigration shifted toward Minnesota and the upper Midwest, and the Swedish population of Minneapolis grew substantially. In the 1880s rural migration spread to Kansas, Nebraska, and the Dakotas. With the changing complexion of immigration later in the century (more single youth heading toward urban areas) came the growth of immigration to the East and West Coasts. Significant Swedish-American centers were established in Connecticut, Massachusetts, and Maine in the East, and Washington and California in the West, along with a Swedish colony in Texas. By the turn of the century, Swedish Americans were about 60 percent urban; Chicago was the second largest Swedish city in the world, followed by Minneapolis, New York City, Seattle/Tacoma, Omaha, and San Francisco. Smaller cities with a concentration of Swedes included Worchester, Massachusetts, Jamestown, New York, and Rockford, Illinois. By 1930 Swedish America (first- and second-generation

Swedish Americans) had peaked at 1.5 million people; secondary internal migrations had dispersed the Swedes around the country. The 1990 census reported that almost 4.7 million Americans claimed some Swedish ancestry (making it the thirteenth largest ethnic group), with almost 40 percent in the Midwest, 30 percent in the West, and 15 percent each in the South and Northeast. California leads all states with 590,000 Swedish Americans, followed by Minnesota (535,000), Illinois (374,000), Washington (258,000), and Michigan (194,000).

RELATIONS WITH SETTLED AMERICANS

Swedish immigrants were generally well accepted by mainstream America and tended to blend in easily with their neighbors, especially in the Midwest. Coming from a Protestant, northern European country, the Swedes were seen as desirable immigrants. Overall, they were a literate, skilled, and hard-working group, and found employment on farms and in mines and factories. Young Swedish women were especially sought as domestic servants in American homes. In many areas, especially in the upper Midwest, Swedes settled in close proximity to other Scandinavian and German immigrants. Despite some ethnic frictions, these European immigrants had a dominant influence on the culture and society of the region.

ACCULTURATION AND ASSIMILATION

In general, Swedish immigrants made a fairly quick and smooth transition to life in their new country and most became quickly Americanized. As a northern European people, the Swedes shared with Americans a common religious and social heritage, and a common linguistic base. Swedish immigrants settled over a wide range of areas. Because they were drawn mostly to cities, rather than tight-knit rural settlements, they were immersed immediately in American culture. In addition, there was a growing interest in, and influence from, America in nineteenth-century Sweden. During the years prior to 1914, the Swedish American community was continually replenished by newcomers; however, World War I brought with it anti-foreign attitudes, which resulted in a drastic drop in emigration and forced the Swedish American community to Americanize rapidly.

The concept of Swedish America furthered the acculturation process. In an essay in *The Immigration of Ideas*, Conrad Bergendoff described the community as "a state of thinking and feeling that bridged the Atlantic." In this enclave, which existed from the Civil War until the Great Depression, first- and second-generation immigrants created their own society, helping one another make the transition to a new culture. After World War I this community was rapidly integrated into the larger American society. The most telling indicator of this was the transition from the use of Swedish to English. By 1935 the majority of Swedish Americans primarily spoke the language of their new home.

With assimilation and acculturation, though, came a renewed interest in Swedish history and culture as children and grandchildren of immigrants sought to preserve some of the traditions of their homeland. Many institutions dedicated to this preservation were established: historical and fraternal societies, museums, and foundations. It was this dynamic that historian Marcus Hansen observed in his own generation, and which prompted his famous axiom, "What the son wishes to forget, the grandson wishes to remember." (Marcus Lee Hansen, *The Problem of the Third Generation Immigrant,* Rock Island, Illinois: Augustana Historical Society, 1938; p. 9).

INTERACTION WITH OTHER ETHNIC GROUPS

The Swedish immigrants interacted most readily with other Nordic-American groups, namely Danes, Norwegians, and Finns. There was a close affinity with the Finns, many of whom were Swedish-speaking settlers from western Finland (Sweden had ruled Finland from the Middle Ages until 1809). There was a special, good-natured rivalry between the Swedes and the Norwegians in America, which still results in quite a few "Swede" and "Norwegian" jokes. Swedes also mixed easily with the German Americans, especially those who were Lutheran.

CUISINE

Swedish American cooking is quite ordinary; traditional dishes represent the cooking of the Swedish countryside, which is heavily weighted toward meat, fish, potatoes, and other starches. In the area of baked goods, however, Swedish American cooks produce delicious breads, cookies, and other delights. The holiday seasons, especially Christmas, are times for special ethnic dishes such as *lutefisk* (baked cod), meatballs, and ham, which are arranged on a buffet-style Smorgasbord table, surrounded by mountains of baked goods, and washed down with gallons of strong, thick Swedish coffee.

TRADITIONAL DRESS

The immigrants did not have a particularly distinctive way of dressing, and generally adopted the clothing styles of their new homeland. Some brought with them the colorful, festive clothing representative of their region of Sweden, but such ethnic costumes were not worn often. The distinctive regional festive dress of nineteenth-century Sweden has, however, been revived by some Americans of Swedish descent, seeking to get in touch with their roots. This dress is sometimes worn for ethnic celebrations or dance competitions.

HOLIDAYS CELEBRATED BY SWEDISH AMERICANS

Along with the traditional holidays celebrated by Americans, many Swedish Americans celebrate two additional holidays. Along with other Scandinavians, Swedes celebrate the summer solstice, or Midsummer's Day, on June 21. This is a time for feasting and outdoor activities. In many areas of Swedish America this day is celebrated as "Svenskarnas dag" (Swedes' Day), a special festival of Swedish American culture and solidarity, with picnics, parades, and ethnic activities. December 13 is Saint Lucia Day. Remembering an early Christian saint who brought light in the darkness of the world, a young woman is selected to be the "Lucia bride." Dressed in a white gown with a wreath of candles on her head, she leads a procession through town and serves special breads and sweet rolls. The Luciafest is an important holiday leading into the celebration of Christmas.

HEALTH AND MENTAL HEALTH ISSUES

America in the nineteenth century was often a dangerous place for immigrants; many worked hazardous jobs, and health care was frequently lacking. As the Swedish American community began to form, various immigrant groups, especially the churches, established medical and other types of organizations to care for the arriving Swedes. Hospitals, clinics, nursing homes, sanitariums, and orphanages were all a part of the network of care for the immigrants. Especially in the urban centers of the Midwest, Swedish American medical institutions remain in operation to this day.

Some Swedish immigrants and their Swedish American descendants sought medical careers, receiving their training mainly in the United States. After completing their education, some returned to Sweden to practice there. The only significant Swedish influence on American medicine was in the field of physical therapy, where techniques from Sweden were introduced into American medical centers.

There are few diseases or conditions that seem to be specific to the Swedish American community; problems that are prominent in Sweden, such as heart disease, depression, and alcoholism, are also seen within the Swedish American community, as well as in the rest of the United States.

LANGUAGE

Swedish is a North Germanic language, related to Norwegian, Danish, and German. There are no significant linguistic minorities in Sweden. Into the modern period there were some dialects present in various regions of the country, but by the twentieth century these variations had largely disappeared. Swedish uses the standard Roman alphabet, along with the additional vowels "ä," "ö", and "å." The language is pronounced with a particular "sing-song" lilt, and in areas of heavy Scandinavian settlement in the United States (especially the upper Midwest) this lilt is apparent among English-speaking descendants of the Scandinavian immigrants.

For the immigrants in America, Swedish remained the standard language, especially at home and at church, but the settlers soon learned enough English to manage their affairs. Some picked up a fractured combination of English and Swedish, which was derisively called "Swinglish." As the cultural world of Swedish America developed, English words and expressions crept into the community and a distinctive form of American Swedish developed that maintained older linguistic traditions of the Sweden of the 1860s and 1870s. The immigrant community was divided over the question of language, with some urging the retention of Swedish, and others seeking a rapid transition to English. For many older immigrants, especially of the first generation, English remained a very foreign language with which they were not comfortable. Swedish remained the language of the churches and social organizations, but the transition to English was rapid especially among the children of the immigrants. By 1920 English was beginning to replace Swedish in the immigrant community. Bilingual approaches were a temporary measure in many immigrant organizations, in order to meet the needs of both younger and older members of the immigrant community.

GREETINGS AND OTHER POPULAR EXPRESSIONS

Common Swedish greeting and other expressions include: God morgon ("goo mor-on")—Good morning; God dag ("goo dahg")—Good day, or good afternoon; God afton ("goo ahf-ton")—Good evening; God natt ("goo naht")—Good night; På återseende ("poh oh-ter-seh-en-deh")—I'll be seeing you; Adjö ("ah-yoe")—Good-bye; Hur står det till? ("hewr stohr deh teel")—How are you?; Tak ("tahk")—Thanks!; Förlåt ("foer-loht")—Excuse me; Var så god ("vahr soh goo")—You're welcome; Lycka till! ("leuk-kah teel")—Good luck; Vi ses i morgon ("vee sehs ee mor-on")—See you tomorrow.

FAMILY AND COMMUNITY DYNAMICS

When the first wave of immigrants came from Sweden to America in the 1840s and 1850s, the settlers traveled in large groups composed of entire families and led by a pastor or other community leader. These groups established the beginnings of the ethnic communities that are still today identifiably Swedish American. Family and social structures became the bedrock of the larger community, and often these communal settlements maintained the characteristics and customs of the areas in Sweden from which the immigrants had come.

Swedish America was thus founded on a tight communal and familial structure, and these characteristics were present both in rural and urban settlements. But this pattern was soon altered by a number of factors, including the increased immigration of single young people, the geographical dispersion of the Swedish immigrants, and secondary migrations within the United States. Although Swedish Americans rarely inter-married (and then usually only with other Scandinavian American groups), Swedes assimilated rapidly into American society, and by the second or third generation were indistinguishable from the general Anglo-American population. Their family patterns and social organization also became indistinct from that of the wider populations.

EDUCATION

Because of widespread literacy in nineteenth-century Sweden, Swedish immigrants were almost universally literate (at least in Swedish), and education was of primary importance to them. They eagerly embraced the American public school system, enrolling their children and organizing their own public schools wherever they were lacking. Swedish immigrants saw education as the primary means for their children to advance in America. Besides participating in the formation of public institutions of higher education (the University of Minnesota is one good example), Swedish Americans also formed their own private colleges; many remain today, including Augustana College (Rock Island, Illinois), Gustavus Adolphus College (St. Peter, Minnesota), Bethany College (Lindsborg, Kansas), Uppsala College (East Orange, New Jersey), North Park College (Chicago, Illinois), and Bethel College (St. Paul, Minnesota). Other colleges and secondary schools operated for a time in the immigrant community, but many of these did not survive. Swedish American churches founded most of these schools, along with theological seminaries to train their own pastors. Literary and publishing activities were strong in the immigrant communities; presses brought forth streams of newspapers, journals, and books representing a broad spectrum of Swedish American opinions.

RELIGION

The Church of Sweden, the official state church of the country, is a part of the Lutheran family of Protestant Christianity and is by far the largest religious institution in Sweden. Having converted to Christianity rather late in the medieval period, Sweden early on joined the Protestant Reformation of the sixteenth century. Under the direction of King Gustav Vasa the Catholic church organization in Sweden was transformed to Lutheranism, which became the official religion of the state. In fact, until the mid-nineteenth century it was illegal for Swedes to be anything *but* Lutheran, or to engage in private religious devotions or study outside of church sponsorship. The priests of the Church of Sweden were civil servants. Besides their religious duties these priests kept the citizenship and tax records, and functioned as the local representatives of governmental power. This state church system was prone to abuse and stagnation, and many Swedes, both clergy and laity, sought to reform and renew the church.

"Most dear to me are the shoes my mother wore when she first set foot on the soil of America. You must see these shoes to appreciate the courage my parents had and the sacrifices they made giving up family and security to try for a better life, but not knowing what lay ahead. We came to this country as many others did, POOR! My mother's shoes tell a whole story." Birgitta Hedman Fichter, 1924, cited in *Ellis Island: An Illustrated History of the Immigrant Experience,* edited by Ivan Chermayeff et al. (New York: Macmillan, 1991).

In the eighteenth and nineteenth centuries a movement called Pietism made its way from Germany into Scandinavia, seeking to reform the church and the lives of individual believers. Stressing personal conversion and morality, the Pietists were critical of the state church and pressed for reform of both the church and the government. They also sought a change in governmental policy to allow for more freedom of religious expression in Sweden, including religious practice outside the Church of Sweden. Over the course of the century many of the changes proposed by the Pietists were enacted by the church and the government.

It is from this religious background that Swedish immigrants came to America. They were officially Lutheran, but many were unhappy with state church Christianity in Sweden and sought different forms of religious expression. A few early immigrants came to America to escape religious persecution. For the vast majority, however, the motivation for emigration was economic, although they welcomed the chance to worship in their own way. Some found other forms of Protestantism were more to their liking, and they formed Swedish Baptist and Swedish Methodist groups, which in turn exported these movements back to Sweden.

In the 1840s and 1850s various Swedish Americans began religious activities among their fellow immigrants. Notable names include: Gustav Unonius (Episcopalian); Olof and Jonas Hedstrom (Methodist); Gustaf Palmquist and F. O. Nilsson (Baptist); and L. P. Esbjörn, T. N. Hasselquist, Erland Carlsson, and Eric Norelius (Lutherans). In 1851 the Swedish American Lutherans organized as part of an American Lutheran denomination, but they later broke away to form the independent Augustana Synod, the largest religious group in Swedish America. The Baptists and Methodists also formed their own denominational groups, related to their American counterparts. The growth of these groups was fueled by the waves of immigrants after 1865, and the denominations struggled to keep up with the demand for pastors and congregations.

The Augustana Synod practiced a Lutheranism influenced by Pietism. Other immigrants thought that Augustana was still too Lutheran, and sought a freer type of Christian organization that relied more heavily on Pietist traditions. Both within and outside Augustana congregations these immigrants formed Mission Societies that were the core of future congregations. During the 1870s and 1880s, despite the wishes of Augustana leaders, this movement broke away from Augustana and Lutheranism, forming independent congregations. The movement eventually yielded two other Swedish American denominations, the Swedish Mission Covenant Church (1885) and the Swedish Evangelical Free Church (1884). These two groups, along with the Lutherans, Methodists, and Baptists were the largest religious groups in the Swedish American community.

The immigrant religious denominations were easily the largest and most influential organizations within Swedish America. These groups soon began to form congregations, schools, hospitals, nursing homes, orphanages, and seminaries to serve the needs of their community. Much of the cultural and social life of the immigrant communities was channeled through the churches. Still, these religious groups only formally enrolled about 20 percent of all immigrants with 70 percent in Augustana and the remaining 30 percent in the other denominations. The churches reached out beyond their membership to serve many others in the immigrant community, but some Swedes chose to join American churches or to join no church at all. It was a tremendous change for these immigrants, leaving the state church for a system where they had to intentionally join and financially support a specific congregation.

These immigrant churches weathered acculturation and assimilation better than other immigrant institutions. Most churches made the transition to English during the 1920s and 1930s and continued to grow in the twentieth century. Augustana joined with other American Lutherans in 1962, the Methodists merged into American Methodism in 1942, and the Evangelical Free Church began to encompass other Scandinavian free church movements in 1950. The Baptist General Conference and the Evangelical Covenant Church remain independent organizations. Many of the congregations and colleges of these immigrant religious groups retain a strong interest in their ethnic heritage.

EMPLOYMENT AND ECONOMIC TRADITIONS

A common stereotype of nineteenth-century Swedish immigrants was that they were either farmers and agricultural laborers in the rural areas, or domestic servants in urban areas. There was a grain of truth in this stereotype since such occupations were often filled by newly arrived immigrants. For the most part, Swedish immigrants were literate, skilled, and ambitious, quickly moving up the employment ladder into skilled positions or even white-collar jobs. Many Swedes exhibit a streak of stubborn independence and, accordingly, most sought economic activities that would allow them to work with their own talents and skills. For some this meant work within the Swedish American community, serving the needs of the immigrants. For others this meant independent work in the larger American community as skilled workers or independent businesspeople in low-capital, high-labor fields such as wood and metal work, printing, and building contracting.

At the turn of the twentieth century, Swedish American men were employed in agriculture (33 percent), industry (35 percent), business and communication (14 percent), and as servants and laborers (16 percent). Among women, common occupations included servants and waitresses (56 percent), and seamstresses or laundresses (13 percent), with smaller groups of laborers and factory workers. As the Swedes adapted to American society, their employment patterns began to emulate that of the society as a whole, and they moved into educated positions in teaching, business, and industry.

Coming from a country that in the nineteenth century was largely rural, many Swedish immigrants were attracted to America by the prospect of free or cheap agricultural land, mainly in the upper Midwest or Great Plains states. By 1920 there were over 60,000 Swedish American farmers in the United State on more than 11 million cultivated acres, and five out of six of these farmers owned their land. Swedish American farmers were industrious and intelligent and soon picked up American agricultural methods for use on their farms. For the most part, the older agricultural techniques from Sweden were not applicable to American farms, and Swedish Americans made few unique contributions to American agriculture. Later immigrants often headed to the forests and mines of the upper Midwest and increasingly to the Pacific Northwest. Here they worked as lumberjacks and miners, two professions that were common in Sweden.

In the urban areas, Swedish Americans were best known for their skilled work in construction trades, and in the wood- and metal-working industries. Swedish contractors dominated the construction business in the Midwest; at one point it was estimated that 80 percent of the construction in Minneapolis and 35 percent in Chicago was carried out by Swedes. The Swedish contractors also employed many of their fellow immigrants as carpenters, plumbers, masons, and painters, providing vital employment for new arrivals. Over half the Swedish American industrial workers in 1900 were occupied in wood and metal working. In addition, Swedes were represented in the printing and graphics, as well as the design industries.

Swedes were also employed in the engineering and architecture fields, with many designing industrial and military machinery. Two Swedish Americans, Captain John Ericsson and Admiral John Dahlgren, revolutionized American naval power during the Civil War with their invention of the ironclad warship and the modern naval cannon, respectively. Other technical achievements and inventions of Swedish Americans include an improved zipper (Peter Aronsson and Gideon Sundback), the Bendix drive (Vincent Bendix), an improved disc clutch (George William Borg), and xerographic dry-copying (Chester Carlson). Swedish Americans have also made notable contributions in publishing, art, acting, writing, education, ministry, and politics.

POLITICS AND GOVERNMENT

Sweden has a long history of representative government, with the nobles, the clergy, and the peasants all represented in the Swedish Parliament. This tradition was never overcome, even by the most autocratic of Swedish kings. At the beginning of the nineteenth century the voting franchise in Sweden was rather limited, although this changed drastically toward the end of the century.

One of the reasons Swedes came to America was to experience greater political freedom and to help shape their local communities. Swedish Americans from the old Delaware colony were active in the politics of colonial America, and were elected to the legislatures of Delaware and Pennsylvania. The Swedes were also generally on the American side of the Revolutionary War and remained politically active when it ended. John Morton (1724-1777) of Pennsylvania was a delegate to the Continental Congress, and voted for and signed the Declaration of Independence in 1776. John Hanson (1715-1783) of Maryland was one the leading political figures of that state, and was elected to the Continental Congress three times. In 1781 Hanson was elected by Congress as the first president of the United States in Congress Assembled, literally the chief executive of Congress, before the office of the presidency was established.

Through the early national period Swedish Americans usually favored the Democrats over the Whigs, but later they broke with the Democrats over the issue of slavery. Swedish Americans became enthusiastic supporters of the newly rising Republican Party and of Abraham Lincoln. The Swedes' relationship with the Republican Party became so firm and widespread as to be axiomatic; it was said that the average Swedish American believed in three things: the Swedish culture, the Lutheran church, and the Republican Party. In the late nineteenth century Swedes became a powerful force in local Republican politics in the upper Midwest, especially in Minnesota and Illinois. In 1886 John Lind (1854-1930) of Minnesota became the first Swedish American elected to

Congress. Lind uncharacteristically switched to the Democratic party, and was then elected the first Swedish American governor of Minnesota in 1898.

Not all Swedish Americans subscribed to the Republican philosophy, of course. Many immigrants, especially those who arrived in the later waves, were strongly influenced by socialism in Sweden, and brought this philosophy with them to America. Swedish American socialists founded their own organizations and newspapers, and became active within the American socialist community. Most of this socialistic activity was local in nature, but some Swedes became involved on a national level. Joe Hill (Joel Hägglund) was a celebrated leader in the Industrial Workers of the World, but was accused of murder and executed in Utah in 1915.

Although socialism was a minority movement among the Swedish Americans, it did reflect many of their concerns. Swedes tended to be progressives within their parties. They believed strongly in the right of the individual, were deeply suspicious of big business and foreign entanglements, and pushed progressive social legislation and reforms. One of the early leaders in this movement was Charles Lindbergh, Sr. (1859-1924), father of the aviator, who was elected as a Republican to Congress from Minnesota in 1906. In Congress he espoused midwestern Populist ideals, opposed big business interests, and spoke forcefully against American involvement in World War I. After the war, many Scandinavians in Minnesota left the Republican Party for the new Farmer Labor Party, which adopted many of the Populist ideals common among the Swedes. Magnus Johnson was elected as a Farmer Labor senator from Minnesota in 1923, and Floyd Olson served that party as governor of Minnesota from 1931 to 1936. Many Swedes left the Republican Party in 1932 to vote for Franklin D. Roosevelt in the presidential election, and some remained in the Democratic Party. A split occurred within the Swedish American community after Roosevelt's presidency, and that division exists to this day. Urban Swedish Americans are evenly divided between the Democratic and Republican Parties, while rural Swedish Americans remain overwhelmingly Republican.

As with many ethnic immigrant groups, Swedish Americans have been under-represented in national politics, with about 13 senators and 50 representatives, mainly from the Midwest. On the state level there have been at least 28 governors (10 in Minnesota), and many state and local officials. Modern Swedish American politicians have included Governors Orville Freeman (Minnesota), James Thompson (Illinois), and Kay Orr (Nebraska), Senator Warren Magnusson (Washington), and Representative John B. Anderson (Illinois). Swedish Americans have achieved notable success on the Supreme Court, including the appointment of two chief justices, Earl Warren and William Rehnquist.

UNION ACTIVITY

As small independent farmers and business owners, Swedish Americans have not been overwhelmingly involved in American union activities. Many in skilled professions in the wood and metal industries were involved in the formation of craft unions. In addition, given the Swedish domination of the building trades in the Midwest, there were many who became involved with the construction trade unions, most notably Lawrence Lindelof, president of the International Brotherhood of Painters and Allied Trades from 1929 to 1952. Some Swedish American women were involved in the garment and textile unions; Mary Anderson joined a trade union as a shoe stitcher in Chicago, was hired by the International Boot and Show Workers Union, and eventually was appointed director of the U.S. Department of Labor's Women's Bureau.

MILITARY

Swedish Americans have fought for America in all of its wars, from the Revolution to the present day. During the Revolutionary War, Swedes from Maryland and Delaware fought for the most part on the revolutionary side, some in the Army, but many more in the new American Navy. About 90 Army and Navy officers from Sweden came over temporarily to fight on the American side, either directly with American troops, or more typically, with French forces (Sweden was allied with France at the time). One of these officers, Baron von Stedingk, who would become a field marshal in the Swedish Army and Ambassador to Russia.

At the start of the Civil War the Swedish American population numbered about 20,000, and their enthusiasm for Lincoln and the northern cause is seen in the fact that at least 3,000 Swedes served in the Union army, mainly in Illinois and Minnesota regiments. A number of others served in the Union navy, and it was here that Swedish Americans were best known. Admiral John Dahlgren was in command of a fleet blockading southern ports, and introduced a number of modern advances in the area of naval weaponry. Captain John Ericsson, a naval engineer, developed the North's first practical ironclad ships, which fought with great effectiveness and revolutionized naval architecture. The Swedish-American population in the South at the time was concentrated mainly in Texas, and their numbers were small, although some did enlist to fight for the Confederacy.

Leading up to World War I, Swedish American sympathies were typically with Germany, although the strongest sentiments were toward neutrality and isolationism, as espoused by Charles Lindbergh, Sr. When the United States did enter the war on the Allied side in 1917, however, many Swedish Americans rushed to show their patriotism by enlisting in the Army and by buying war bonds. In the 1920s and 1930s, Swedes generally returned to their isolationist and neutralist ways, and Charles Lindberg, Jr. took up this cause where his father left off. However, another famous Swedish American, writer Carl Sandburg, forcefully urged American intervention in Europe against the Nazis, writing many articles and works opposing the German regime. In both World Wars many Swedish Americans served with great distinction, including Major Richard Bong, who received the Medal of Honor in 1944 for destroying 36 Japanese planes in combat. Given their general engineering and technical expertise, many Swedish Americans rose to positions of importance in command, such as John Dahlquist, deputy chief of staff to General Eisenhower, and Arleigh Burke and Theodore Lonnquest, who eventually rose to the rank of admiral in the Navy. Many other Swedish Americans rose to prominence in the defense industry, especially Philip Johnson who headed Boeing Aircraft Company during World War II.

RELATIONS WITH SWEDEN

Swedish Americans have historically been very interested in the development of Sweden, and a lively correspondence is still maintained between Swedes on both sides of the Atlantic. Modern Sweden is a dramatically different country than the one the immigrants left; while Swedish Americans often have a hazy impression of a backward, rural country, reality is quite different. The Sweden of the twentieth century has often been characterized as taking the "middle way," a neutral, socialist country between the capitalist West and the communist East, ruled for most of 50 years by the Social Democratic Party. Some Swedish Americans have applauded the changes that have occurred in modern Sweden, while others have deplored them. During the Vietnam era of the 1960s and 1970s relations between Sweden and the United States were somewhat strained, but the rapport between the two nations has improved significantly since then.

INDIVIDUAL AND GROUP CONTRIBUTIONS

Even though Swedish Americans represent only a small fraction of the total American population, many have made notable contributions to American life and culture.

BUSINESS

Many Swedish Americans have made names for themselves in American business. Eric Wickman (1887-1954) founded Greyhound Corporation and built it into a national enterprise. Charles R. Walgreen (1873-1939) started the national chain of drugstores, and Curtis Carlson parlayed business and service sectors into the Carlson Companies, which operates hotels (Marriot), restaurants, and travel agencies. John W. Nordstrom of Seattle founded the department store chain that bears his name. Some Swedish Americans rose through the ranks to become leaders in American industry, including Eric Mattson (Midland National Bank), Robert O. Anderson (Atlantic Richfield), Rudolph Peterson (Bank of America), Philip G. Johnson (Boeing), and Rand V. Araskog (ITT).

EXPLORATION

One of the best known of all Swedish Americans is the aviator Charles Lindbergh, Jr. (1902-1974); his father and namesake was a congressman and politician, but the younger Lindbergh is known for the first solo flight across the Atlantic in 1927; a national hero, Lindberg served as a civilian employee of the War Department. Another famous explorer was Edwin (Buzz) Aldrin (1930-), the Apollo 11 astronaut who in 1969 was the second person to step on the moon.

FILM, TELEVISION, AND THEATER

The most famous Swedish immigrant in this field was Greta Garbo (1905-1990) who was born in Sweden and came to the United States in 1925; enigmatic, Garbo made 24 films in the United States, after which she abruptly retired and sought seclusion from public view. Other Swedish American actresses have included Viveca Lindfors, Ann-Margaret (Olson), Gloria Swanson, and Candace Bergen—the daughter of Edgar Bergen (1903-1978), well known for his ventriloquism on television. Other Swedish American actors have included Werner Oland and Richard Widmark.

LITERATURE

Although Swedish Americans produced a vast quantity of written literature, some of it was written in Swedish and is unknown outside the immigrant community. With the coming of the second and third generations, however, Swedish Americans have produced a number of writers in English who have earned national reputations. The most famous of these authors was Carl Sandberg (1878-1967), who produced nationally known poetry and novels, but whose most famous work is his four-volume biography of Abraham Lincoln, a work which won Sandberg a Pulitzer prize. Another contemporary Swedish American writer in Nelson Algren (1909-1981), who has written extensively about the hard realities of urban and working class life.

MUSIC

The most famous Swedish American composer is Howard Hanson (1896-1981) who grew up in the immigrant community of Wahoo, Nebraska; for many years Hanson was director of the Eastman School of Music in Rochester, New York, and he is one of the best known twentieth-century American composers of serious classical music. A number of immigrants from Sweden have become important singers of classical music and opera. Best known of all of was Jenny Lind (1820-1887), referred to as the "Swedish Nightingale," she was already famous in Europe when P. T. Barnum brought her to America in 1850 for the first of over 90 concerts in three years; Lind took America by storm; eventually she returned to Europe, but gave generously in support of charities within the Swedish American community. Following Lind to America were such singers as Christiana Nilsson, lyric tenor Jussi Björling, and soprano Birgit Nilsson.

SCIENCE

Many Swedish Americans have become distinguished in the field of science, especially in chemistry and physics. Carl David Anderson (1905-) won a Nobel prize in Physics for his discovery of positronic particles. Another Nobel prize winner is Glenn Seaborg (1912-), who in 1951 won in chemistry for his work with transuranium elements.

VISUAL ARTS

The most widely known Swedish American painter is Birger Sandzén (1871-1945), who lived and worked in the rolling prairies of central Kansas around Lindsborg; his works are found in many museums in Europe and America. A more recent artist, known for his "Pop" art, is Claes Oldenburg (1929-). Other notable artists have included Henry Mattson, John F. Carlson, and Bror Julius Nordfeldt. In sculpture, the best known Swedish American is Carl Milles (1875-1955), who has achieved international fame for his work, especially for his outdoor sculpture; Milles studied with August Rodin in Paris, and went on to be artist-in-residence at Cranbrook Academy of Art in Michigan.

MEDIA

PRINT

Nordenstjernan Svea.
Established in 1872, this weekly is one of the few remaining Swedish American newspapers, printed in English and Swedish.

Contact: Alvalene Karlsson, Editor.
Address: 123 West 44th Street, New York, New York 10036.

Svenska Amerikanaren Tribunen.
Established in 1876, this newspaper is published in Swedish and English.

Contact: Jane Hendricks, Editor.
Address: 10921 Paramount Boulevard, Downey, California 90241.

Sweden and America.
Published by the Swedish Council of America, this quarterly contains general news and articles about Swedish Americans and about develop-

ments in Sweden, and is the most widely circulated periodical about Swedish Americans.

Contact: Christopher Olsson, Editor.
Address: 2600 Park Avenue, Minneapolis, Minnesota 55407.
Telephone: (612) 871-0593.

Swedish-American Genealogist.

This quarterly is published by the Swenson Swedish Immigration Research Center and contains articles on genealogical research, local and family history.

Contact: Dr. Nils William Olsson, Editor.
Address: Swenson Swedish Immigration Research Center, Augustana College, Rock Island, Illinois 61201.
Telephone: (309) 794-7204.

Swedish-American Historical Quarterly.

Published by the Swedish-American Historical Society, this periodical contains articles on the history and culture of Swedish Americans.

Contact: Dr. Raymond Jarvi, Editor.
Address: 5125 North Spaulding Avenue, Chicago, Illinois 60625.
Telephone: (312) 583-2700.

ORGANIZATIONS AND ASSOCIATIONS

American Swedish Historical Foundation.

Founded in 1926, this group maintains a museum, library, and archives on Swedish American culture and history, and sponsors exchanges programs and cultural events. It also publishes an annual *Yearbook*, and other occasional publications.

Contact: Esther C. Meixner, Executive Secretary.
Address: 1900 Pattison Avenue, Philadelphia, Pennsylvania 19145.
Telephone: (215) 389-1776.

American Swedish Institute.

Founded in 1929, the American Swedish Institute seeks to preserve the Swedish cultural heritage in America. The institute, housed in the mansion of a former Swedish American journalist, offers classes, activities, exhibits, concerts and workshops, along with a library and archives.

Contact: Bruce N. Karlstadt, Director.
Address: 2600 Park Avenue, Minneapolis, Minnesota 55407.
Telephone: (612) 871-4907.

Swedish-American Historical Society.

Founded in 1950, the society is dedicated to the preservation and documentation of the heritage of Swedish Americans. Publishes a quarterly journal, *Swedish-American Historical Quarterly* and *Pioneer Newsletter* as well as books in this area.

Contact: Dr. Raymond Jarvi.
Address: 5125 North Spaulding Avenue, Chicago, Illinois 60625.
Telephone: (312) 583-2700.

Swedish Council of America.

Formed in 1973, the Swedish Council of America is a cooperative agency that coordinates the efforts of over 100 different Swedish American historical, cultural, and fraternal organizations. The Swedish Council publishes a monthly magazine called *Sweden and America*, which is a useful forum for current Swedish American activities.

Address: 2600 Park Avenue, Minneapolis, Minnesota 55407.
Telephone: (612) 871-0593.

United Swedish Societies/Svenska Central Forbundet.

Federation of 50 Swedish American organizations.

Contact: Harry Hedin, President.
Address: 20 Bristol Avenue, Staten Island, New York 10301.
Telephone: (718) 442-1096.

Vasa Order of America.

Founded in 1896, it is the largest Swedish American fraternal organization in America with over 31,000 members in 326 lodges nationwide.

Contact: Gladys Birtwistle.
Address: 65 Bryant Road, Cranston, Rhode Island 02910.
Telephone: (401) 461-0016.

MUSEUMS AND RESEARCH CENTERS

American Swedish Historical Museum.

This museum collects and displays artifacts and documents of Swedish Americans to preserve the Swedish American culture. The building is modeled after a seventeenth-century Swedish manor house.

Contact: Ann Barton Brown, Director.

Address: 1900 Pattison Avenue, Philadelphia, Pennsylvania 19145.

Telephone: (215) 389-1776.

American Swedish Institute Museum.

This museum provides exhibits and activities for and about Swedish Americans, including displays of the Institute's collections, as well as traveling exhibits.

Contact: Bruce Karlstadt, Director.

Address: 2600 Park Avenue, Minneapolis, Minnesota 55407.

Telephone: (612) 871-4907.

Bishop Hill.

Located in Western Illinois, this is a fully preserved folk museum, dedicated to preserving the life of the pioneer Swedish immigrants in America. Founded in 1846, Bishop Hill was the home of a religious communal settlement organized by Erik Jansson; though the communal settlement collapsed after Jansson's death, a community remained. In the twentieth century the Bishop Hill Heritage Association began restoring the settlement to its original condition.

Contact: Morris Nelson.

Address: P.O. Box 1853, Bishop Hill, Illinois 61419.

Telephone: (309) 927-3513.

Swedish American Museum Center of Chicago.

Located in Andersonville, an area of historical immigrant settlement, this museum collects and displays artifacts and documents of Swedish immigration, maintains an archives, and sponsors special exhibits and activities.

Contact: Kerstin Lane, Executive Director.

Address: 5211 North Clark Street, Chicago, Illinois 60640.

Telephone: (312) 728-8111.

Swenson Immigrant Research Center.

Situated on the campus of Augustana College, this center has a large collection of historical documents, records, and artifacts on Swedish Americans in the country. The Swenson center is especially good for genealogical and historical study.

Contact: Dag Blanck, Director.

Address: Augustana College, Box 175, Rock Island, Illinois 61201.

Telephone: (309) 794-7204.

SOURCES FOR FURTHER STUDY

American-Swedish Handbook, eleventh edition, edited by Christopher Olsson and Ruth McLaughlin. Minneapolis: Swedish Council of America, 1992.

Benson, Adolph, and Naboth Hedin. *Americans From Sweden*. Philadelphia: J. B. Lippincott Company, 1950.

Bergendoff, Conrad. "The Role of Augustana in Transplanting of a Culture Across the Atlantic," in *The Immigration of Ideas: Studies in the North Atlantic Community*, edited by J. Iverne Dowie and J. Thomas Tredway. Rock Island, Illinois: Augustana Historical Society, 1968.

Carlsson, Sten. *Swedes in North America 1638-1988: Technical, Cultural, and Political Achievements*. Stockholm: Streiffert and Co., 1988.

From Sweden to America: A History of the Migration, edited by Harald Rundblom and Hans Norman. Minneapolis: University of Minnesota Press, 1976.

Hasselmo, Nils. *Swedish America: An Introduction*. Minneapolis: Brings Press, 1976.

Kastrup, Allan. *The Swedish Heritage in America*. St. Paul, Minnesota: Swedish Council of America, 1975.

Letters from the Promised Land: Swedes in America, 1840-1914, edited by H. Arnold Barton. Minneapolis: University of Minnesota Press, 1975.

Ljungmark, Lars. *Swedish Exodus*, translated by Kermit Westerberg. Carbondale: Southern Illinois University Press, 1979.

Moberg, Vilhelm. *The Emigrants* (first novel in trilogy). New York: Simon and Schuster, 1951.

———. *Unto a Good Land* (second novel in trilogy). New York: Simon and Schuster, 1954.

———. *Last Letter Home* (third novel in trilogy). New York: Simon and Schuster, 1960.

Scott, Franklin. *Sweden: The Nation's History*, revised edition. Carbondale: Southern Illinois University Press, 1988.

Skårdahl, Dorothy Burton. *The Divided Heart: The Scandinavian Immigrant Experience Through Literary Sources*. Lincoln: University of Nebraska Press, 1974.

Since the Swiss came from western Europe's oldest democracy and have forged a national unity out of ethnically diverse constituencies, they find American culture compatible with their own.

SWISS

by
Leo Schelbert

AMERICANS

OVERVIEW

Switzerland lies in the central part of the Alps, a 500-mile-long European mountain range, which stretches westward from France's Riviera into what was northern Yugoslavia. Four main passes (Grimsel, Furka, St. Gotthard, and Oberalp) allow passage from Northern Europe across the Alps to Italy, making Switzerland a country of transit. The country covers 15,941 square miles and borders Germany to the north, France to the west, Italy to the south, and Austria and the Principality of Liechtenstein to the east. The Swiss nation is a confederation of 26 member states called cantons, and the nation's capital is Bern, a city that began about 1160 and was officially founded in 1191. The national flag consists of a square red field with a white equilateral cross at its center.

In 1992 Switzerland counted 6.9 million inhabitants, including one million foreign nationals. The country is ethnically diverse, indicated by its four language groups. Religiously the Swiss people are nearly evenly divided between Catholics and Swiss Reformed, but there are also small groups of other Christian denominations and other faiths.

HISTORY

The Swiss Confederation emerged in the late thirteenth century from an alliance of three regions:

the modern-day cantons Uri, Schwyz, and Unter-walden. The so-called *Bundesbrief* of 1291 documents their alliance. In it the three regions pledge mutual support to keep internal order and to resist aggression. The Confederation grew by wars of conquest and by alliances arranged with important towns located at the access routes of the passes to Italy, such as Luzern, Zürich, and Bern. By 1513, 13 cantons had united the rural population with the urban elite of artisans and entrepreneurs. Both groups were intent on gaining and preserving independence from the nobility, a unique development in European history. The Confederation's defeat at the battle of Marignano in upper Italy in 1515 ended the nation's expansion. This loss led to the gradual emergence of armed neutrality, a basic feature of Switzerland's political tradition. However, the Reformation split the people into Catholic and Swiss Reformed hostile camps and nearly destroyed the Confederation.

MODERN ERA

During the seventeenth and eighteenth centuries increasingly smaller oligarchies came to power in the Swiss cantons but were overthrown in 1798 in the wake of the French Revolution. In 1848, after five decades of foreign intervention and internal uncertainty, a new constitution was adopted. The previous system of autonomous states became one federal state, though the people remain the actual sovereign. The Swiss are called upon to vote on numerous issues several times a year. This process occurs either by constitutional requirement or more often by initiative and referendum which, given a sufficient number of signatories, force the government to submit issues to the popular vote. The executive branch, called *Bundesrat*, consists of seven members chosen by Parliament and acts as a unit. The presidency is an honorary position and rotates annually. The legislative power rests with citizens of voting age and with a Parliament, divided into a Council of States (*Ständerat*) and a National Council (*Nationalrat*). In addition, the cantons and over 3,000 communes (*Gemeinden*) have preserved their autonomy and decide numerous issues by popular vote. The Swiss are involved in political decision-making throughout the year on the local, cantonal, and federal level.

Neutrality in foreign affairs and universal military service of men are considered central to the Swiss political tradition, which may have kept the country out of two devastating world wars. Switzerland's economy, however, is fully dependent on the export of quality products and on spe-cial expertise in finance as well as the production of machinery, pharmaceuticals, watches, and precision instruments.

SWISS IN BRITISH NORTH AMERICA

The first known Swiss in what is now the territory of the United States was Theobald von Erlach (1541-1565). In 1564 he was a leading member of a French attempt to create a permanent foothold in North America. He perished when some 900 French soldiers were shipwrecked by a hurricane in September 1565, and killed by the Spanish. Some "Switzers" also lived at Jamestown during the regime of Captain Smith. In 1657 the French Swiss Jean Gignilliat received a large land grant from the proprietors of South Carolina. In 1710 some 100 Swiss joined Christoph von Graffenried (1661-1743) who founded New Bern in present-day North Carolina.

Between 1710 and 1750, some 25,000 Swiss are estimated to have settled in British North America, especially in Pennsylvania, Virginia, and South Carolina. Many were members of the Reformed church and were actively recruited by entrepreneurs such as Jean Pierre Purry (1675-1736), the founder of Purrysburg, South Carolina. About 4,000 Swiss Mennonites settled in Pennsylvania, many of whom had first gone to the Palatinate from which the next generation emigrated in search of fertile, affordable land and greater toleration of their creed.

In the late 1750s an influential group of French Swiss officers in the British service assumed leadership roles in the fight against indigenous peoples resisting white incursions into the trans-Appalachian West, the French, and the insurgent colonials. In the middle decades of the eighteenth century a group of Swiss Jesuits labored in the Southwest of the present United States to promote the northward expansion of New Spain.

SWISS IMMIGRATION 1820 TO 1930

Between 1798 and 1850, about 100,000 Swiss went abroad (the proportions between temporary and permanent migrations cannot be determined) and some 50,000 foreigners located in Switzerland. Between 1850 and 1914 those leaving the Confederation numbered about 410,000, those entering it from abroad about 409,000. Those leaving were attracted by the newly conquered lands taken from indigenous peoples in Australia, New Zealand, and in the Western Hemisphere by expanding neo-

European nations such as Argentina, Brazil, or the United States. The emigrants seem to have been rooted in the lure of faraway lands or in the desire to escape parental control, intolerable marriages, or oppressive village traditions.

"My mother had to try and keep track of us. She finally took us and tied us all together so that we would stay together. And that's the way we came off the boat." Gertrude Schneider Smith, in 1921, cited in *Ellis Island: An Illustrated History of the Immigrant Experience,* edited by Ivan Chermayeff et al. (New York: Macmillan, 1991).

Between 1820 and 1930, some 290,000 people went from Switzerland to the United States. About 12,500 arrived between 1820 and 1850; some 76,500 between 1851 and 1880; and some 82,000 in the 1880s. Between 1891 and 1920, about 89,000 arrived and nearly 30,000 in the 1920s. No reliable figures exist for Swiss return migration, but it was numerically substantial. For instance, nearly 7,000 of the more than 8,200 Swiss of military service age who had gone to the United States returned to Switzerland between 1926 and 1930.

In the first half of the nineteenth century large numbers of Swiss settled in the rural Midwest, especially in Ohio, Indiana, Illinois, and Wisconsin, and after 1848 in California. Some 40 percent of Swiss went to urban areas such as New York, Philadelphia, Cincinnati, Chicago, St. Louis, San Francisco, and Los Angeles. In 1920, for instance, New York counted 9,233 Swiss, Chicago 3,452, San Francisco 2,105, and Philadelphia 1,889. As to states, in 1930 California numbered 20,063 Swiss, New York 16,571, New Jersey 8,765, and Wisconsin, Ohio, and Illinois some 7,000 each.

The socio-economic status of newcomers from Switzerland spanned the spectrum from well-to-do to the poor. A sample analysis from 1915 of 5,000 Swiss men in the United States yielded the following distribution: a third belonged to the lower income and status groups; approximately 44 percent were solidly middle class; and about 22 percent were well situated.

NINETEENTH CENTURY SWISS SETTLEMENTS

In 1804 a special grant of Congress enabled a group of French Swiss winegrowers to settle on the Ohio and establish the town of Vevay, Indiana. This viticulture, which they had hoped to introduce as a permanent feature into the Midwestern economy, became insignificant by mid-century and was replaced by the cultivation of maize and other staples. In 1817 and 1825 Swiss Mennonites founded the agricultural settlements of Sonnenberg and Chippewa in Ohio, and in 1838 Berne, Indiana, the latter still conscious of its Swiss origin. By the efforts of the Köpfli and Suppiger families the town of Highland emerged in southern Illinois in 1831 and eventually attracted some 1,500 Swiss settlers. In the same decade John August Sutter (1803-1880) established New Helvetia in California, then still under Mexican sovereignty. When gold was discovered on his property in 1848, thousands of goldseekers overran his extensive domain, and the city of Sacramento was platted, and became California's capital in 1854.

In 1825 several Swiss, who had joined Lord Selkirk's Red River colony in Canada in 1821, settled at Gratiot's Grove northeast of Galena, Illinois. In 1845 New Glarus was founded in southern Wisconsin's Green County, today the best known settlement of Swiss origin. Numerous Swiss also settled in the towns of Monroe, Washington, and Mount Pleasant. In 1848 Bernese Swiss established Alma on the Mississippi, which counted some 900 Swiss in 1870. A French-Swiss group connected with the Protestant Plymouth Brethren established a community in Knoxville, Tennessee, in the same year.

In the spring of 1856 a group of Swiss and Germans established a Swiss Colonization Society in Cincinnati, Ohio, to create a culturally homogeneous settlement. After an extensive search Tell City was laid out in 1858 on the Ohio River in Perry County, Indiana. In the post-Civil War era Helvetia was founded in West Virginia in 1867 as a result of active recruitment by that state. In the 1880s Peter Staub (1827-1904) initiated the settlement of Grütli in Grundy County, Tennessee. During the same decade 1,000 Swiss who had converted to Mormonism went to Utah and settled mainly at Midway near Salt Lake City and at St. George on Utah's southwestern border. Between 1870 and 1914 several thousand Italian Swiss went to California where they established vineyards and dairy farms.

IMMIGRATION SINCE 1930

The Great Depression and World War II diminished Swiss immigration. Between 1931 and 1960

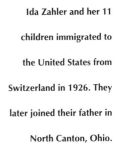

Ida Zahler and her 11 children immigrated to the United States from Switzerland in 1926. They later joined their father in North Canton, Ohio.

some 23,700 Swiss arrived, and 29,100 between 1961 and 1990. Many of these Swiss did not stay permanently. They are mainly professionals and business people employed in American branches of Swiss firms. The 1980 census counted 235,355 people of single, and 746,188 of multiple, Swiss ancestry. In 1990 there was a total of 607,833 persons of Swiss ancestry of whom 35,900 (5.9 percent) were Swiss-born, and of these 57.6 percent were naturalized.

ACCULTURATION AND ASSIMILATION

Although Swiss in the United States are often mistaken for German, French, or Italian, their involvement in American life has been quite extensive. Since the Swiss came from western Europe's oldest democracy and have forged a national unity out of ethnically diverse constituencies, they find American culture compatible with their own. For instance, when John J. Zubly, a delegate to the Second Continental Congress, published the widely distributed pamphlet *The Law of Liberty* in 1775, he appended "A Short and Concise Account of the Struggles of Swisserland for Liberty" to it. He paralleled the Swiss with American colonials, the Austrian emperor with the British king, and viewed their struggle as the same quest for liberty.

TRADITIONS, CUSTOMS, BELIEFS

Although Switzerland is a highly industrialized country with a powerful financial and industrial elite involved in global markets, Swiss culture remains identified with an idealized rural tradition. In New Glarus, a major tourist attraction in southern Wisconsin, a William Tell and Heidi festival is held each year. The chalet, a house style of rural origin, remains identified with the Swiss, although it is common only in certain Swiss regions.

Yodeling and the Alphorn, again native only to some rural Swiss regions, continue to serve as emblems of Swiss culture as do the various *Trachten*—colorful and often beautifully crafted garb for women and men. *Trachten* originate in distinct regions, but tend to become fused into a blended version, sometimes mixed with Tyrolian or Bavarian motifs. The so-called Swiss barn is also widely found in Pennsylvania and some midwestern states. It is built into an incline with a large entrance to the hayloft on an upper level and the entrances to the stables on the opposite lower level. The dominance of rural motifs in Swiss American culture points to a central feature of Swiss self-interpretation: Switzerland's origins are shaped by the traditions of rural communities. Their emblems symbolize Swiss culture however far removed they might be from modern day Swiss and Swiss American reality.

CUISINE

Predictably, Swiss cuisine varies according to ethnic influences. Another historic division is equally telling, however: that between country and city. Thus, two dishes eaten today by all Swiss are the simple cheese fondue, eaten for centuries by Swiss in rural regions, and veal with a sauce of white wine and cream, formerly enjoyed by city dwellers. Cheese, however, is popular in almost any form. As for other regional cuisine, German areas favor pork, often accompanied by *rosti*, a dish of diced potatoes mixed with herbs, bacon, or cheese, and fried to a golden brown.

HEALTH AND MENTAL HEALTH ISSUES

Swiss Americans follow general trends in Western medicine and health care. People in rural areas have remained connected with healing traditions based on telepathic methods and herbs and herbal ointments. In mental health the influence of Carl Gustav Jung (1875-1961) has been significant. Jung viewed mental problems as soluble in part by a skillful evocation of symbols shared by all in a postulated collective subconscious that transcends cultural boundaries. Numerous Jung Institutes of the United States promote Jungian ideas, which also have influenced American literary scholarship.

LANGUAGE

Some 73 percent of Swiss speak High German and in everyday life forms of various Low German dialects, *Schwyzerdütsch* (Swiss-German); 20 percent speak French and several regional dialects (five percent Italian, and one percent Romansh, which is divided into three groups called *Rhaeto-Romontsch, Oberhalbsteinisch,* and *Ladin*). Most Swiss learn as their first language a regional and older form of German, French, or Italian, which remains the principal form of communication. Since the establishment of formal schooling, however, Swiss children learn a new, yet related, language such as High German, standard French or standard Italian. The children of the Romansh region learn German or French. To enter a different linguistic world was, therefore, for most Swiss immigrants not a new experience, and they mastered multiculturalism with relative ease.

GREETINGS AND OTHER POPULAR EXPRESSIONS

Depending on their local origin Swiss greet each other in many forms. Widespread among German

Swiss is *Grüezi* ("groitsee") or *Grüezi wohl*, derived from [Ich] *grüsse dich*—I greet you; also the French-derived *Salü* ("saly") and *Tschau* from the Italian *Ciao*, used both when first meeting and at its conclusion. In Raetoromontsch people say *Bien Dí* ("biandee")—Good day; on parting the French Swiss will use the form *a revere* for the standard French *au revoir* and the German Swiss *uf wiederluäge* ("oof weederlooaga")—See you. In German-speaking rural Switzerland the standard form for goodbye is still widespread, *Bhüet di Gott*—May God protect you.

FAMILY AND COMMUNITY DYNAMICS

Swiss family life is well-regulated and conservative. Few women hold careers outside the family, and young people tend to be cooperative and well-behaved. The Swiss American family is indistinguishable from other American families, which have changed from a patriarchal to an egalitarian and child-centered outlook. The Swiss American family is predominantly middle class. According to the 1990 census the median income of Swiss American families was over $42,000 and only 3.8 percent had an income below the poverty line. Over 40.3 percent of the 153,812 owner-occupied Swiss American housing units were mortgage-free and 46.5 percent had two wage earners in the family.

Swiss Americans recreate organizations they have known at home for mutual support as well as for enjoyment and social contact. They celebrate August 1 as the Swiss national holiday and commemorate important battles of the fifteenth century Swiss struggle for independence with parades, speeches and conviviality. At such events there is yodeling, singing, flag throwing—an artful throwing and catching of a Swiss flag on a short handle high into the air, and sometimes a reading of the *Bundesbrief* of 1291. The festivities also include traditional dishes such as *röschti* (hash browns), and *bratwurst*, in addition to dancing and the playing of folk music on the accordion, clarinet and fiddle.

RELIGION

Swiss immigrants belong to various religions. The first Swiss to arrive in North America in large numbers were the Swiss Mennonites, a group that derived from the Anabaptist communities of the Radical Reformation of the 1520s. They rejected infant baptism, thus declaring the whole of ecclesiastical Christendom as heathen. They also repudiated the state as symbolized by the sword and the oath. The Swiss Mennonite settlements that emerged in Pennsylvania and Virginia in the first half of the eighteenth century were expert in farming, and formed congregations of some 25 to 30 families. Each religious community was semiautonomous and guided by a bishop and by preachers and deacons who were not specially schooled. The only full members were adults who had proven their faith by a virtuous life, the demands of the community, and accepted baptism as a symbol of submission to God's will. Rules set by the religious leaders ordered the manner of dress, forms of courtship, the schooling of children, and dealings with the outside world. If a member failed to conform, the person would be banned and avoided even by the next of kin. In the late nineteenth century many Mennonite congregations, influenced by the Dutch Mennonites, American Protestantism, and American secular culture, gave up the older traditions. They moved into towns and took up occupations increasingly removed from farming. Only some conservative Swiss Mennonites and Amish still hold on to the sixteenth-century forms of their creed.

Numerous Swiss immigrants belong to the Swiss Reformed church, as formulated by Huldrych Zwingli (1484-1531). He adapted Christian doctrine to the needs of a rising urban bourgeoisie. Municipal power increased, monastic institutions were secularized, and the rule of the urban elites strengthened. Many members of the Swiss Reformed church settled in colonial Pennsylvania, Virginia, and the Carolinas. Their views and ecclesiastical organization were similar to those of Presbyterians, with whom they easily merged.

Some 50,000 Swiss Catholics arrived in the United States after the 1820s, including about 20,000 Italian Swiss who settled in California between 1887 and 1938. Depending on their language, Swiss Catholics joined either German, French, Italian, or ethnically undefined American parishes. They found, however, a very different parish organization in the United States that curtailed the Swiss practice of lay jurisdiction over secular affairs.

Several Swiss religious orders were actively engaged in establishing the Catholic church in the United States. In 1842 Franz von Sales Brun-

Theologian Hans Küng signs one of his books during the 1993 Parliament of World Religions in Chicago.

ner (1795-1859) introduced the Order of the Precious Blood into Ohio. In 1852 monks from the ancient Benedictine monastery of Einsiedeln founded St. Meinrad, Indiana, the nucleus of the Swiss Benedictine Congregation of the United States formed in 1881. In 1956 the congregation united some 12 foundations with 645 monks. Benedictine sisters were also deeply involved in promoting Catholic education and charity. Anselma Felber (1843-1883) established a community at Conception, Missouri, which later moved to Clyde. Gertrude Leupi (1825-1904) founded a convent in Maryville, later transferred to Yankton, South Dakota.

EMPLOYMENT AND ECONOMIC TRADITIONS

In the eighteenth century Swiss immigrants were mainly farmers and artisans. Like other German-speaking newcomers, their methods of farming differed from those of the English. Mennonite and Amish farmers fenced their properties, built stables for their cattle, sometimes even before their houses, and tilled well-manured fields. By the mid-eighteenth century they also had developed the Conestoga wagon, a large, heavily built structure that was suited for the arduous trek across the Alleghenies.

The occupational profile of Swiss immigrants reflected the general trends of Western economies. A statistical analysis for the years 1887 to 1938 counted 42 percent in the industrial work force; 25 percent in agriculture; 6.5 percent in commerce; 4.5 percent in the hotel and restaurant business; and 4.3 percent in the professions. A large percentage of Swiss immigrants also worked as domestics.

Viticulture was introduced into the Midwest by French Swiss farmers and was also extensively practiced by Italian Swiss from Canton Tessin who went to California in large numbers after the 1870s. Bernese Swiss used their expertise in dairy farming, especially in Wisconsin. Nicolas Gerber (1836-1908), for instance, opened a Limburger cheese factory in New Glarus in 1868, as did Jacob Karlen (1840-1920) in nearby Monroe in 1878. Gottlieb Beller (1850-1902) developed a system of storage that allowed cheese production to remain responsive to fluctuating market demand. Leon de Montreux Chevalley (1854-1926) founded butter, cheese, and condensed milk factories in Portland, Oregon. Jacques Huber (1851-1918) introduced silk manufacturing to New Jersey; by 1900 he had established a firm with plants in Union City, Hackensack, and other cities of the mid-Atlantic states. Albert Wittnauer (1856-1908) used his Swiss training in watchmaking to establish a successful business in New York City.

By 1900 world-renowned firms such as Nestlé had established plants in the United States. The Swiss pharmaceutical companies Ciba-Geigy, Hoffmann-La Roche, and Sandoz emerged in the twentieth century as important forces in the United States economy and diversified their productive activities. Aargauische Portlandcement-Fabrik Holderbank Wildegg, a Swiss cement company, incorporated in 1912 with original seat in Glarus, Switzerland, and introduced superior, cost-efficient cement production into North America and dominates today's cement market.

POLITICS AND GOVERNMENT

In the eighteenth century Geneva was an autonomous city-state, but allied with the Swiss Confederation. The writings of two of its citizens influenced the founders of the United States engaged in creating a new governmental structure. Jean Jacques Rousseau (1712-1778) expounded the idea that government rested on a social contract. Jean Jacques Burlamaqui (1694-1748) stressed in his *Principles of Natural and Political Law* that a government should guarantee its citizens secure happiness.

The relations between the United States and Switzerland have been generally friendly, but not without tensions. At times outsiders view Swiss neutrality and direct democracy as inefficient; yet Switzerland's neutral stand allows it to represent American interests in nations with which the United States has broken off diplomatic ties.

INDIVIDUAL AND GROUP CONTRIBUTIONS

The Swiss have had easy access to all aspects of life in the United States, although most did not come to public attention. The selection given below features a few according to field of endeavor.

ARCHITECTURE

William Lescaze (1896-1969), born and educated in Geneva, Switzerland, moved to the United States in 1921 and rose to prominence as a builder of skyscrapers; he also authored several treatises on modern architecture. In bridge-building Othmar Ammann (1879-1965), born in Feuerthalen, Canton Schaffhausen, achieved world renown; after studies in Zurich he went to New York City in 1904 and in 1925 was appointed chief engineer of the Port Authority of New York; he built the George Washington and other suspension bridges noted for innovative engineering and bold and esthetic design.

ARTS

Mari Sandoz (1896-1966), the daughter of Swiss immigrants, published several works of enduring value, among them the biography of her father, titled *Old Jules*, and a biography of Crazy Horse, the noted leader of the Sioux; her works reveal not only an unusual understanding of the world of the white settlers, but also of the mental universe of indigenous peoples such as the Sioux and Cheyenne. Jeremias Theus (1719-1774) worked in Charleston, South Carolina, as a successful portrait painter. Peter Rindisbacher (1806-1834) produced valuable paintings documenting his family's move to Canada's Red River colony in 1821 and to Wisconsin in 1826; his works featuring Native Americans are also highly valued for their accuracy. The same holds for the numerous works of Karl Bodmer (1809-1893) who served for 13 months as pictorial chronicler for the Prince zu Neuwied's journey to the Upper Missouri in 1832. Fritz Glarner (1899-1972), like Bodmer a native of Zurich, began working in New York in 1936 where, influenced by Mondrian, he created works in the style of constructivism.

BUSINESS AND INDUSTRY

At age 19 Lorenzo Delmonico (1813-1881) from Marengo, Canton Tessin, went to New York and opened the Delmonico Hotel in 1843 which popularized continental European cuisine in American cooking.

MEDICINE

Adolf Meyer (1866-1950), born in Niederwenigen, Canton Zurich, was influential in American psychiatry; after studies at European universities he worked in various American psychiatric institutions and insisted on the study of symptoms, on bedside note-taking, the counseling of the families of patients, and their further care after discharge; in 1898 he published a classical work on neurology and after 1910 chaired the department of psychiatry at Johns Hopkins Medical School and also directed the Henry Phipps Clinic. Henry E. Sigerist (1891-1957) taught at Johns Hopkins University from 1932 to 1942, directing its Institute of History and Medicine; he had previously been a professor at the University of Leipzig, Germany, and emerged as a leading historian and as an advocate of socialized medicine.

MILITARY

In the American Revolution John André (1751-1780), born in Geneva, Switzerland, and an officer in the British army, was captured as a spy in 1780 and hanged by the revolutionaries; the British honored his bravery by a tomb in Westminster Abbey. At the end of the Civil War another Swiss named Henry Wirz (1823-1865) was also hanged for his alleged crimes as commander of the Confederacy's Andersonville Prison where some 12,000 Union soldiers perished; his responsibility for the terrible conditions at Andersonville remains controversial.

MUSIC

Rudolf Ganz (1877-1972), who immigrated to the United States in 1900, became an influential pianist, the conductor of the St. Louis Symphony Orchestra from 1921 to 1927, and president of the Chicago Musical College of Roosevelt University from 1933 to 1954. The composer Ernest Bloch (1880-1957) of Geneva, Switzerland, taught and wrote music at various American institutions of the Midwest and the West Coast; among his works the orchestral poems titled *Helvetia, America,* and *Israel* intimate his threefold cultural orientation. In film William Wyler (1902-1981), born in Mulhouse, France, of Swiss parents, became one of Hollywood's most respected directors; his *Ben Hur* won an Oscar for him as well as for 11 of his actors. The singer, actor, and television producer Yul Brynner, actually Julius Brynner (1915-1985), was of Swiss and Mongolian descent; he starred in various movies, among them *The King and I.*

POLITICS

In the 1770s John Joachim Zubly (1724-1781) of St. Gallen, Switzerland, emerged as a leading critic of the British; he was an ordained Swiss Reformed minister, a member of the Georgia Provincial Congress, and delegate to the Second Continental Congress; yet he rejected independence and viewed the union between the colonies and Great Britain as sacred and perpetual; on his return to Georgia he was tried and ended his life in obscurity. Albert Gallatin (1761-1849) became successful in the early years of the American republic; he arrived from Geneva in 1780 and eventually moved to western Pennsylvania where he entered politics; he was elected to the state legislature in 1792 but was disbarred by the Federalists; he served instead in the House and emerged as a leader of Jefferson's party; from 1801 to 1813 he served as secretary of the treasury, then as diplomat in France, England, and Russia; after his retirement from politics he became a scholar of Native American languages, co-founded New York University, and was a leading opponent of the War against Mexico in 1847. Another leading Jeffersonian was William Wirt (1772-1834), the son of Swiss immigrants; he was a noted orator and jurist and served as attorney general of the United States from 1817 to 1829. Emanuel Lorenz Philipp (1861-1925) rose to prominence in Wisconsin politics, which he entered in 1903; he served as governor from 1915 to 1921 and promoted cooperation between farmers, workers, and business.

RELIGION

Michael Schlatter (1716-1790) from St. Gallen, Switzerland, went to Pennsylvania in 1746 and there organized numerous parishes of the Swiss Reformed church. Johann Martin Henni (1805-1881) became in 1875 the first Catholic archbishop of Milwaukee; he was born in Misanenga, Canton Graubünden, went to the United States in 1828, became vicar general of the diocese of Cincinnati and editor of the *Wahrheitsfreund*, the first Catholic German-language newspaper. Philip Schaff (1819-1893) of Chur, Canton Graubünden, was a major historian of church history at Union Theological Seminary in New York for 25 years; he was a strong advocate of Christian ecumenism, author of numerous scholarly works, and stressed the historical approach to questions of theology.

SCIENCE

Ferdinand Hassler (1770-1843) was born in Aarau, Switzerland, and studied in Jena, Göttingen, and Paris, then accepted an appointment as professor of mathematics and natural philosophy at West Point; his 1807 plan for a coastal survey of the United States was began in 1817 and the precision of Hassler's work makes it still valid today. Louis Rodolphe Agassiz (1807-1873) became internationally known as a scientist and explorer; born in Motier, Canton Fribourg, he studied the natural sciences at various European universities and published a major work on fish and proposed the theory of a previous ice age he went to Boston in 1846, undertook scientific expeditions to South America, and was appointed to the chair of zoology and geology at Harvard University; there he began work on his influential ten-volume *Contributions to the Natural History of the United States*; his son Alexander Agassiz (1835-1910) also became a noted natural scientist in his own right. A pioneer in the ethnology and archeology of the American Southwest was Adolphe Bandelier (1840-1914); he was born in Bern, Switzerland, went with his family to Highland, Illinois, in 1848, and returned to Switzerland in 1857 to study geology at the University of Bern; on his return he did extended research in Mexico and the American Southwest, later also in Bolivia, and authored numerous studies on Native American cultures of those regions.

TECHNOLOGY

Machinist John Heinrich Kruesi (1843-1899), born in Heiden, Canton Appenzell, joined Thomas A. Edison in Newark, New Jersey, in the early 1870s and transformed Edison's ideas into workable instruments; in 1887 he became general manager and chief engineer of the Edison Machine Works in Schenectady. The Swiss Louis Joseph Chevrolet (1878-1941) came to the United States in 1900, became a successful racing car champion, winning the 500-mile Indianapolis race in 1919; in 1911 he co-founded the Chevrolet Motor Car Company in Detroit, but soon left the enterprise; in 1929 he built a workable airplane engine, and later designed a helicopter.

MEDIA

PRINT

Swiss American.

Published by North American Swiss Alliance; explores shared ethnic and bi-cultural interests of the Swiss American community.

Address: 2590 Lakeside Avenue, N.W., Canton, Ohio 44708.

Telephone: (216) 456-1983.

Swiss American Historical Society Review.

Published three times a year with a circulation of 400, this journal offers scholarly and popular articles of Swiss American interest relating to history, literature, genealogy, and personal experience.

Contact: Leo Schelbert, Editor.

Address: 2523 Asbury Avenue, Evanston, Illinois 60201.

Telephone: (708) 328-3514.

Swiss American Review.

Founded in 1860 under the name *Nordamerikanische Schweizerzeitung*, this weekly publication provides material in English, German, French, Italian, and Romansh. It has an estimated circulation of 3,000 and features news from Switzerland as well as the Swiss American communities and organizations of the United States.

Address: 608 Fifth Avenue, Room 609, New York, New York 10020.

Telephone: (212) 247-0459.

Swiss Journal (Schweizer Journal).
Founded in 1918, it is published bimonthly and has a circulation of 10,000. It presents articles in German, English, Italian, and French.

Contact: Louis M. Muschi, Chief Editor.
Address: 548 Columbus Avenue, P.O. Box 330082, San Francisco, California 94133.
Telephone: (415) 362-8072.

Swiss Review.
Founded in 1973, this quarterly magazine has a circulation of over 300,000. It publishes regional news from Swiss communities for the Swiss abroad, and has editions in German, French, Italian, English, and Spanish.

Contact: Gertrude Jeffries, U.S. Swiss American Editor.
Address: 1430 Cape Cod Way, Concord, California 94521.
Telephone: (510) 370-3571; or (510) 689-2740.

RADIO

Swiss Radio International
Broadcasts via Intercontinental Short Wave transmissions daily (UTC—Universal Time): At 3:30 in German, 4:00 in English, 4:30 in French, and 5:00 in Italian; frequencies 6135, 9860, 9885.

ORGANIZATIONS AND ASSOCIATIONS

American-Swiss Association (ASA).
American and Swiss corporations and individuals interested in maintaining cultural exchange; provides forum for meetings and discussions.

Contact: Anne Yoakam, Executive Director.
Address: 450 Lexington Avenue, Suite 1600, New York, New York 10017-3904.
Telephone: (212) 878-3809.

Swiss American Historical Society (SAHS).
Founded in 1927 it is today the only national organization. Formerly located in Chicago, it moved to Madison, Wisconson, in 1940; it became dormant in the 1950s, but was reactivated in 1963 under the leadership of Heinz K. Meier (1929-1989). It publishes the *SAHS Review* three times a year, holds annual and occasional regional meetings, and supports the SAHS Publication Series with Lang Publishers, New York.

Contact: Erdmann Schmocker, President.

Address: 6440 North Bosworth Avenue, Chicago, Illinois 60626.
Telephone: (312) 262-8336.

MUSEUMS AND RESEARCH CENTERS

Archives of the Archabbey St. Meinrad.
This collection houses 13 volumes of transcripts of materials located at the Benedictine Abbey of Einsiedeln, Switzerland, relating to St. Meinrad's founding in 1854. Despite the fire of 1887 that destroyed valuable sources, letters of the founding generation and extensive correspondence with other monasteries and ecclesiastical institutions are preserved and provide insight into the Benedictine dimension of transplanted Swiss Catholicism.

Address: St. Meinrad College and School of Theology, St. Meinrad, Indiana 47577.
Telephone: (812) 357-6566.

Balch Institute for Ethnic Studies.
Dedicated to preserving and documenting the multicultural heritage of the United States, this organization also houses a collection on the Swiss, including papers of the Swiss American Historical Society.

Contact: Ira Glazer, Director.
Address: 18 S Street, Philadelphia, Pennsylvania 19106.
Telephone: (215) 925-8090.

Lovejoy Library.
Located at Southern Illinois University in Ewardsville, this library houses the Highland, Koepfli, and Suppiger Collections. The materials highlight the founding and evolution of the Highland settlement, which began in 1831, as well as the Swiss in Illinois. They are complemented by materials at the Madison County Historical Museum, also at Edwardsville, and by the Illinois Historical Survey Library at the University of Illinois at Urbana.

Mennonite Historical Library.
Located at Bluffton College, this library has an extensive collection of works on Swiss Mennonite history, and of Swiss Mennonite and Amish family histories and genealogies.

Contact: Harvey Hiebert, Librarian.
Address: 280 West College Avenue, Bluffton, Ohio 45817.
Telephone: (419) 358-3272.

New Glarus Historical Village.

This attraction presents artifacts from its early history in several, thematically arranged buildings. An exhibition hall features the town's history and special exhibits of Swiss American interest.

Contact: Bill Hoesly, President.

Address: P.O. Box 745, New Glarus, Wisconsin 53574-0745.

Telephone: (608) 527-2317.

SOURCES FOR ADDITIONAL STUDY

American Letters: Eighteenth and Nineteenth Century Accounts of Swiss Immigrants, edited by Leo Schelbert. Camden, Maine: Picton Press, 1995.

A Frontier Family in Minnesota: Letters of Theodore and Sophie Bost, 1851-1920, edited and translated by H. Ralph Bowen. Minneapolis: University of Minnesota Press, 1981.

Gratz, Delbert L. *Bernese Anabaptists and Their American Descendants*. Scottdale, Pennsylvania: Herald Press, 1953.

Josephy, Alvin M., Jr. *The Artist Was a Young Man: The Life Story of Peter Rindisbacher.* Fort Worth: Amon Carter Museum, 1970.

Kleber, Albert. *History of St. Meinrad Archabbey 1854-1954.* St. Meinrad, Indiana: St. Meinrad Archabbey, 1954.

Schelbert, Leo. "On Becoming an Emigrant: A Structural View of Eighteenth and Nineteenth Century Swiss Data," *Perspectives in American History*, Volume 7. Cambridge, Massachusetts: Harvard University Press, 1973; pp. 440-495.

The Swiss in the United States, edited by Paul von Grueningen. Madison, Wisconsin: Swiss American Historical Society, 1940.

The United States and Switzerland: Aspects of an Enmeshment; Yearbook of German American Studies 1990, Volume 25, edited by Leo Schelbert. Lawrence: University of Kansas for the Society for German American Studies, 1991.

SYRIAN-LEBANESE AMERICANS

by
Paula Hajar

Traditionally, Syrian-Lebanese families and extended families operate as a unit, relying on each other implicitly in social, financial, and business affairs.

OVERVIEW

Syrian-Lebanese account for close to two-thirds of the estimated 2.5 million people in the United States who are of Arabic descent. Christian Syrian-Lebanese were the first Arabic-speaking people to come to the Americas in large numbers. Their earliest immigration to the United States began in the late 1870s, peaked in 1914 at 9,023, dropped to a few hundred a year during World War I, and rose again during the early 1920s, fluctuating between 1,600 and 5,000. Later, with the Immigration Quota Act (1929-1965), it dropped to a few hundred a year. When the second wave of Arab immigrants began in the late 1960s, the descendants of the early Syrian-Lebanese immigrants were in their third generation and had almost completely assimilated into mainstream America. However, in the 1970s and 1980s, the Arabic-speaking population of the United States began to grow again, and Syrian-Lebanese assumed a higher ethnic profile. Some began to adopt the larger collective cultural identity of Arab American, which is evident today in associations that are as often Arab American as Syrian or Lebanese American.

Syria and Lebanon are located at the extreme eastern end of the Mediterranean Sea. Syria forms Lebanon's northern and eastern borders. Directly south of Lebanon is Israel; the

Mediterranean Sea is to the west. Lebanon's land mass is 4,015 square miles. Syria has a land mass of 71,498 square miles and is bounded by Turkey to the north, Iraq to the east, Jordan to the south, and Lebanon to the southwest. Syria also has a short Mediterranean coastline (about 100 miles) to the north of Lebanon, and borders Israel for about 40 miles on its southern flank.

Syria's population is estimated at between 12 and 14 million. About 80 percent of Syrians are Sunni Moslems; about 10 percent of Syrians are Christians. Minority Moslem populations include Alawites, Druzes, and Shi'a. Only a small portion of the old Syrian Jewish community (about 4,000) remains. Significantly smaller than that of Syria, Lebanon's population is estimated at between 3 and 3.5 million. In Lebanon there is no religious majority; both Moslems and Christians have many sectarian subdivisions, 17 in all. Among them, the Shi'a are the most numerous with about 35 percent, the Sunni are about 23 percent, the Druzes, about six percent. Christians, who account for under two-fifths of the total, include the Maronites (the most numerous and the most powerful) at 22 percent, the Eastern Orthodox at ten percent; Melkites (Greek Catholics) and Armenians, each at six percent, and Protestants at 2.5 percent. Through Lebanon's unwritten National Pact of 1943, political power is apportioned among the religious sects (originally in a ratio of six to five, Christian to Moslem, divided equally since 1992). Various government offices are still reserved for specific sects: the prime minister is always a Sunni Moslem; the president is always a Maronite, the speaker of the house is always a Shiite. Throughout its history there have been movements in Lebanon to "deconfessionalize"—to create a one-person, one-vote system, instead of apportioning representation and political offices by religious affiliation; these efforts continue today.

HISTORY

From 1516 until 1916, when the Ottoman Empire was dismembered by the victors of World War I, the areas that are now Syria and Lebanon were part of the Ottoman province of Greater Syria. At the time of the first immigration wave to the West, Syria and Lebanon were not yet sovereign nations; because of this and also because the Ottomans administered their subject peoples according to their religious affiliation rather than as nationals, early immigrants from Greater Syria

identified with their religious sect, rather than as Turks or Syrians. A sense of national identity did not begin to form among Syrians until the 1920s, when Syria and Lebanon became separate French protectorates. It further developed in the 1940s when the protectorates gained independence. During these developments many former Syrians began to identify themselves as Lebanese.

Since ancient times, Syria has had a succession of rulers, including the Mesopotamians, Hittites, Egyptians, Assyrians, Babylonians, Persians, and Greeks. In 63 B.C., Syria became a Roman province. After the Christian era began, there were periods of unrest as the Church divided into many sects. This unrest lasted until the Islamic conquest of Syria in A.D. 635. During the Abbasid Dynasty, a series of local dynasties ruled Syria and Syria was comprised of independent states. The Crusades to recapture the Holy Land began in 1095 and during the next 200 years, European Christians established beachheads in Antioch, Tripoli, and Jerusalem. In 1174 Saladin recaptured Damascus and expelled most of the Crusaders. In 1260, 1270, and 1300, Mongol invasions wreaked havoc on Syria. In 1516 the Ottomans, who were to rule for the next 400 years, conquered Syria. During this time, Syria's culture, industry, and educational life declined.

While witness to the rise and fall of empires in the area, coastal Lebanon experienced aspects of history that were distinctly its own. In the second and early first millennium B.C., the Canaanites, who became known as Phoenicians, were the first inhabitants of Lebanon. Concentrated in the ports of Tyre, Sidon, and Biblos on the Lebanese coast, and famous as sailors and traders, they founded colonies in North Africa, Europe, and the Mediterranean. Persians, Greeks, and Romans, in succession, challenged Phoenician power. When the Islamic Empire rose in the East, the population took on the Arabic culture, but also maintained its multi-religious character as the mountains of Lebanon became a haven for various religious sects. After the Ottoman Empire gained general control of the area in 1516, Lebanon continued to maintain a feudal system of rule by local chieftains. After 1860, the year many Christians were massacred by Druze in Lebanon and Damascus; the French, who had had an economic and strategic interest in Mount Lebanon since the Crusades, assumed a protector role. During the next 50 years the people of the area became increasingly interested in Western culture, independence from the Ottomans, and a revival of the Arabic language.

MODERN ERA

With the fall of the Ottoman Empire during World War I, England and France divided the area into English and French protectorates. England assumed control of what became Palestine and Jordan, and France took over what became Syria and Lebanon. At this time, France divided Mount Lebanon from Syria and, adding the coastal area, created an entity called "The State of Greater Lebanon." In 1926 the Republics of Lebanon and Syria were created, but it was not until 1941 that each gained full independence, and 1946 when the last French troops departed.

Modern Syrian history has been checkered by a series of mostly bloodless coups. In 1958 Syria and Egypt united to form the United Arab Republic; four years later this union was dissolved by an army coup, and more coups were to follow. In 1970 Hafez al-Assad took power. Among the most enduring of Arab political heads of state, he has generally ruled by extensive repression of his own people.

After independence from the French in 1943, Lebanon became known as the "Switzerland of the Middle East." Its delicate political and demographic equilibrium was tested in 1975, however, and the country erupted into civil war. The political inequities were exacerbated by severe economic divisions, the resistance of those in power to address the needs of the poor, and the weakness of the public sector. At present Lebanon is at peace, though in political and foreign policy matters it is under Syrian quasi-control, a situation that most Lebanese resent. Meanwhile, Lebanon is striving to reconstruct itself physically, economically, and politically. Its new prime minister is billionaire Rafiq Hariri, whose personal fortune has long been dedicated to rebuilding Lebanon's infrastructure.

SYRIANS AND LEBANESE COME TO AMERICA

In 1849 Flavianous Kfoury, a Lebanese Catholic priest, came to America for two years to raise funds for his church. Five years later, Antonious Bishallany, a young Lebanese who had met American Protestants when he guided them through the "Holy Land," came to America to become a missionary. His friendships with many prominent New Yorkers were cut short by his untimely death from tuberculosis two years later.

Many factors spurred large-scale Syrian-Lebanese immigration to America in the late nineteenth century. First, many emigrants found inspiration in the tales of American missionaries (doctors and teachers) about American norms of freedom and equality. Also, the world fairs that took place in Philadelphia (1876), Chicago (1893), and St. Louis (1904) exposed participating Syrians to Americans and American ways. Many who came to perform in the Arab exhibits stayed. For the majority, however, the determinants were economic ambition and family competition. For many families, having a son or daughter in America became a visible mark of status, for the money that the children sent back often went toward refurbishing village homes inside and out. Young men were the first to immigrate, followed by young women and later wives and whole families. (Not infrequently, the wives came first and laid the groundwork for the rest of their families to come.) Some villages lost the best of their youth very quickly. In fact, between the late 1870s and World War I, Lebanon lost over a quarter of its population to emigration. (During World War I, it lost about another fifth to famine.) Immigrants abroad played a major role in the country's post-war reconstruction and subsequent independence.

During the years of American quota restrictions, many Syrians and Lebanese immigrated to Central and South America. Many went to Brazil, Australia, and the countries of West Africa. Today these countries have flourishing Syrian-Lebanese communities.

When in the 1970s and 1980s the Lebanese civil war spawned a new wave of emigrants, many went to Europe—to Athens and Paris in particular. Those who came to the United States reinvigorated Syrian-Lebanese ethnic life. Meanwhile, a smaller number of emigrants from Syria have continued to seek graduate degrees and work in their fields. The new immigrants have reinvigorated Syrian-Lebanese institutions. Better educated and coming from independent nations, recent emigrants have been much more conscious of their Arab identity than their early counterparts. In addition, at least half are Moslems who are deeply invested in maintaining their Islamic traditions and thus are more cautious about assimilating into American culture.

SETTLEMENT PATTERNS

Syrians and Lebanese have settled all over the United States. But from the beginning, New York City has been the largest and most influential community, the "mother colony." New England and upstate New York communities as well as those in the Midwest and the West were often discovered by peddlers who stayed on and opened general stores. Syrians and Lebanese developed important communities in Utica, New York; Boston, Lawrence, Lowell, and Springfield, Massachusetts; Fall River, Rhode Island; and Danbury, Connecticut. They also settled in New Orleans, in Jacksonville, Florida, in Detroit and Dearborn, Michigan, and in Toledo, Ohio. Today the largest concentrations are still in the Northeast and Midwest. Detroit is the largest community in the country, but there are new communities in Los Angeles and Houston.

RELATIONS WITH MAINSTREAM SOCIETY

The first Syrian Lebanese who came to America were considered exotic—their baggy pants (*shirwal*) and fezzes made them stand out even among other immigrants. Later, when enclave living and the ubiquitous Syrian peddler made Syrians a visible presence, attitudes toward them darkened; xenophobia toward non-Northern Europeans increased. During a Senate debate on immigration quotas in 1929, Senator David Reed of Pennsylvania referred to Syrian-Lebanese as the "trash of the Mediterranean." Not surprisingly, Syrians became bent on rapid assimilation into mainstream American society. Many Anglicized their names and joined western churches; most focused their energies on becoming financial successes. By the third generation, they had become virtually invisible as an ethnic group, at least to outsiders. Even the ethnicity of famous Syrian-Lebanese Americans was not generally known by their American publics.

The situation of the group as a whole began to change when large scale immigration resumed in the late 1960s. Much better educated than the first wave, the new immigrants were also more occupationally and religiously diverse. In general, they were both more conscious of their Arab identity and more open in their criticism of the United States' Middle Eastern policies.

KEY ISSUES FACING SYRIAN-LEBANESE AMERICANS

Today Syrian and Lebanese Americans face the same problems as all Arab Americans. One issue is negative stereotyping. For various economic and political reasons, there has been a dramatic upsurge in negative stereotyping of Arabs. Until quite recently, when Arab Americans united to combat such derision, it went unchallenged in all types of venues (e.g., theater, films, books, cartoons, and political discourse). Another issue is an anti-Arab climate in domestic politics. Because the United States has strong ties with Israel, Arab Americans have felt stifled on issues that involve the Arab-Israeli conflict. In fact, some political candidates of the 1980s actually rejected financial support from Arab Americans so as not to be labeled as sympathetic to Arabs. Such a climate obviously creates problems for Arab American participation in the political process.

ACCULTURATION AND ASSIMILATION

Syrians and Lebanese came to America eager to embrace American culture. One factor that hastened assimilation was peddling; on the road the immigrants dealt with Americans in rural areas, thus absorbing the English language and American culture more quickly than if they had stayed within their urban enclaves and worked in factories with other immigrants. Another factor hastening assimilation was service in the American armed forces during the two World Wars. Here young male immigrants befriended Americans, were exposed to American ways of thinking, and absorbed the American values of individualism and independence. Not until a generation later, however, did Syrian-Lebanese women have the opportunity for similar exposure. Though they had come to the United States to work, Syrian women's activities were invariably framed by the needs and resources of their families. By the end of World War II, however, it was not uncommon for Syrian women to work outside the home or outside the family business.

TRADITIONAL BELIEFS, ATTITUDES AND CUSTOMS

Like other Arabs, Syrian-Lebanese are a religious people. They believe that faith in God can move mountains, and that whatever happens is God's will. In Syrian-Lebanese culture, age is greatly respected, and respect for parents is most important. Unlike in many parts of American society, breaking from parents is not considered an essential rite of passage. Family is at the core of Syrian-Lebanese social identity. Even in other family-oriented communities, the strong family ties of Syrian-Lebanese stand out. Loyalty to family has

Syrian American brothers Albert (left) and Louis (middle) Ajamy stand in front of their Detroit, Michigan, grocery store on its opening day in 1916.

traditionally superseded all other allegiances. Each person (particularly the woman) is expected to protect the family's honor. In Syrian-Lebanese culture, roles are often defined by gender, and this social definition anchors both men and women in their respective roles. Women are seen not as repressed, but protected; and men, the undisputed heads of families, take the concerns of others into consideration. The emphasis in Syrian-Lebanese families, in fact, is on the needs and welfare of the group rather than on the needs and interests of the individual. Syrian-Lebanese also emphasize hospitality. No matter the circumstances, it is considered rude not to offer a guest food and drink. Syrian-Lebanese are known for their elaborate and warm hospitality.

Americanization, with its emphasis on youth, personal achievement, individualism, and independence, has eroded some of these traditional practices while leaving others virtually untouched. Syrian-Lebanese continue to find support in their religious institutions, and their core belief in the power of God does not seem to have altered over time. The American emphasis on youth has lessened the Arab respect for age, though it is still a much stronger value in this community than in the American population at large. Though family is highly valued among Syrian-Lebanese, the power of family honor and fear of family shame has dwindled, partly because (with the exception of new immigrants) Syrian-Lebanese are no longer living in such close social circles. Family roles are less gender-defined than they once were in Syrian-Lebanese households, but the deference of females for males and the protection by males of females is still valued among the newest immigrants. Though extended family living has declined markedly, parents can still depend on the loyalty of their children. Hospitality has changed in the United States: doors are locked, schedules are tight, everyone is overloaded with his or her own concerns. New immigrants who come expecting the kind of help from settled relatives that they themselves would have offered back in the village are often sorely disappointed; they soon discover that they are expected, like everyone else in America, to make it on their own.

COMMONLY HELD MISCONCEPTIONS

Because they were coming from an area ruled by the Ottoman Turks, when Syrians first arrived on American shores Americans thought they were Turks. Although the majority of early immigrants were Christian, many Americans assumed that they were Moslems. In addition, Eastern-rite Catholics often found that American Catholics knew little about their religion, and even suspected them of heresy.

More troublesome is the current association of Lebanese with terrorism. This is a relatively recent development with historical and geographic roots. Beginning in the late 1960s (and continuing through the present), animosity between Israel and Lebanon has led to violent acts committed by both parties. Because of its frequent support of Israel, the United States has been a target of Lebanese terrorism. In 1983, a Lebanese group blew up the American marine barracks in Beirut. In the late 1980s, various Lebanese militia groups hijacked airplanes and kidnapped westerners. The groups often committed such acts to draw attention to specific injustices they wanted rectified; but toward the end of the civil war, many terrorist actions had no particular political content at all. In any case, since 1990 the activities of the militias, most of which have been disarmed, have quieted down.

CUISINE

As Syrian-Lebanese have become more numerous and more visible, Syrian-Lebanese food has come out of private homes and church halls into gourmet food shops and health food restaurants. As certain items have become common in mainstream cuisines, their Syrian-Lebanese origins have almost been forgotten. Known for generations as "Syrian bread" by the Syrian-Lebanese, pita has achieved an almost universal popularity. *Hommos* and *baba ghanouj* (chickpea and eggplant dips), and *tabouli* (parsley and bulgur, or cracked wheat, salad), have become mainstays of health food menus.

Fresh fruits and vegetables figure heavily in the Syrian-Lebanese diet, as do cheese, yogurt and yogurt cheese (*labnee*), pickles, hot peppers, olives, and pistachio nuts. Seasoning is always subtle; allspice is used in the stews, mint in the salads, pine nuts in the rice, and rose water in the desserts.

Lamb and chicken are the favored meats; pork is forbidden to Moslems. Many dishes feature lamb stews with vegetables in a tomato sauce. *Kibbee* is ground lamb meat mixed with bulgur wheat and eaten either baked or raw. Yellow and green squash, called *koosa*, are hollowed out and stuffed with rice and ground lamb meat, later cooked in a tomato sauce. The insides of the squash are often fried in olive oil as a separate dish. The ground lamb and rice stuffing mixture (*mahshee*) is sometimes wrapped in grape leaves (*wara' 'anab*) and served with yogurt, or in cabbage leaves (*malfoof*) and served with lemon juice. *Sfeeha* are small open square pies of ground lamb meat and pine nuts, sometimes made with a thin tomato sauce; spinach pies are closed and triangular. One of the most popular sweets is *baqlawa*—filo dough laced with sugar syrup and wrapped around finely chopped walnuts. The national alcoholic beverage of Lebanon is *'arak*, an anisette drink.

TRADITIONAL CLOTHING

Among Christians and some Moslems, traditional Syrian-Lebanese clothing is worn only by performers at ethnic dance festivals. The men's outfit includes the *shirwal* (baggy black pants that fit at the shin), high black boots, white blousy shirts, dark vests, and sometimes the fez. The women's costumes consist of long dresses with embroidered bodices and side panels, and tall hats with long white veils.

On the whole, Western dress is the norm in Syria and Lebanon and among the Syrian-Lebanese in the United States. However, the public dress of religiously observant Moslem women, particularly the Lebanese Shi'a, is the *hijab*, a long-sleeved long coat or dress, and a scarf (often white) that completely covers the hair. Often the scarf alone is considered the *hijab*. Wearing the *hijab* enables Moslem women to abide by the Islamic teaching that a woman should cover herself, particularly her hair, before non-family men so as not to sexually arouse them. Young girls and married women can decide whether or not to wear the *hijab*.

HOLIDAYS

Religion is important to Lebanese and Syrians. Different sects celebrate different religious holidays. Christians celebrate certain saints' days as well as Easter and Christmas. Easter is the Sunday after the first full moon following the vernal equinox. The Orthodox Easter must also come after Passover, and thus Western Easter often falls on a different Sunday from Orthodox Easter. Moslems celebrate three major holidays: *Ramadan* (the 30-day period of daytime fasting); *'Eid al Fitr,* a five-day holiday that marks the end of *Ramadan;* and *'Eid al-Adha,* the "Feast of the Sacrifice," which commemorates the agreement of Abraham with God to sacrifice his son Ishmael. The National Independence Days—November 22 for the Lebanese and April 17 for Syrians, receive little or no notice among Syrians and Lebanese in America.

HEALTH AND MENTAL HEALTH ISSUES

Except for higher-than-average incidences of anemia and lactose intolerance, Syrians and Lebanese have no incidence of medical disease specific to them as a group. As a rule, they support the conventional medical establishment; since many are medical doctors, they are an important part of it. On the other hand, as a group, they probably consult psychiatrists at a much lower rate than others in their educational echelon, which reflects not any higher immunity to stress but rather the enduring cultural belief that problems should be kept within the family. Many American cultural values are considered dysfunctional by Syrian-Lebanese and vice versa. For example, Syrian-Lebanese consider a focus on attaining individual happiness inappropriate (in any case, happiness can only be attained when *everyone* is happy); the issue of finding oneself is also considered strange since the group—family, religion, and place—endow each person with his or her identity and role in life. On the other hand, Americans often find Middle Eastern norms of family closeness smothering; they also find the clear role divisions between the parents and the social engineering of children's lives by their parents limiting. In any case, when serious psychological problems do arise it becomes difficult to find Arabic-speaking clinicians to treat Arabic-speaking patients.

LANGUAGE

Both Syrians and Lebanese speak Arabic. While different regions and cities of the Arab world have their own distinct accents and vocabularies, Arabic speakers are bound linguistically throughout the Arab world by the modern, standard, written Arabic found in newspapers and radio broadcasts throughout the Arab world.

Arabic is a poetic language and poets are prized in Arab culture. In its first 50 years in America, the American Syrian-Lebanese community enjoyed a golden age of letters, with the literature of such New York experimental poets as Khalil Gibran, Ameen Rihany, and Elia Abu-Madey casting their influence on literary circles of the Middle East. However, in their efforts to acculturate, the immigrant generation did little to teach their American-born children to read Arabic. The immigration quota restrictions exacerbated the language decline, for without a continuous influx of new readership, once-flourishing Arab American newspaper and journal publishing fell precipitously. By the second generation even spoken Arabic was disappearing. Churches streamlined their Arabic liturgies, changing much of them to English. The new Syrian-Lebanese immigrants, however, have reinvigorated Arabic language usage in the community. Many Arabic churches now have bilingual announcements, bulletins and sermons, and the business signs in Arab commercial neighborhoods are often painted prominently in Arabic. New Moslem immigrants in particular have contributed to the increase in Arabic usage and have developed Arabic-language classes for children.

Greetings in Arabic are elaborate and there is usually a response and counter-response to every one. *Ahlein*—Welcome; or the longer *Ahlan wa Sahlan*—You are with your people and in a level place (a greeting appropriate at the door or when being introduced to someone for the first time); the more casual *Marhaba*—Hello, responded to with *Marhabteen*—Two hellos; to which the response is *Maraahib*—A bunch of hellos. Similarly, the response to the morning greeting, *Sabaah al-kheir*—The morning is good, is *Sabaah an-noor*—The morning is light. The evening greeting and response are *Masa al-kheir* and *Masa n-noor.* Leavetakings are extremely elaborate: the person leaving says, *Bkhatrak;* to a woman, *Khatrik;* and to a group, *Khatirkum,* which translates as By your leave. The response is *Ma'a salaame*—With safety, or Go in peace; to which the counter response is *Allay salmak,* or *Allay salmik* to a female, and *Allay salimkum* to a group—May God keep you safe. The holiday greeting is *'Eid Mubarak*—Holiday blessings; and *Kull sane w'inte saalim*—Every year and you are safe. *Sahteen* is the Arabic toast—May your good health be twofold. Arabic is filled with references to God. For example, the most com-

Professional Lebanese American boxer Tarick Salamaci and his father, Maruf, pause during practice in Redford, Michigan. Tattooed on Tarick's arm is the phrase "Allah Akbar," meaning "God is great."

mon response to *Keif haalak?*—How are you? is *Nushkar Allah*—(We) Thank God. Often heard after a statement of intention are the words *In sha Allah*—If God wills it. Such phrases imply the belief in human impotence to control the affairs of the world.

FAMILY AND COMMUNITY DYNAMICS

Traditionally, Syrian-Lebanese families and extended families operate as a unit, relying on each other implicitly in social, financial, and business affairs. The father is the decision-maker, and the mother his close advisor; her domain is the daily life of the children and all that happens within the home; his, the things outside. The firstborn son plays a special role in the family, for he brings his bride to live with his parents, raises his family in his parents' household, and cares for them in their old age.

Over the generations, though, as families have assimilated to the American nuclear pattern, the dividing line between gender roles has blurred. Fathers spend more time with their small children, and mothers frequently represent the families in public, for example, at school meetings. Independent households are now the norm, and daughters no longer become part of their marital families. Consequently sisters share responsibility with their brothers for aging parents. The price for this: older women will no longer rule an expanding household or enjoy an increase in power and influence as they age.

MARRIAGE AND CHILDREARING

Because marriage was traditionally an opportunity for a family to strengthen its prestige and economic situation, marriages in the Old World were often arranged. This custom is still practiced among some conservative, new immigrants. To arrange a marriage, parents and other relatives seek out mates for their children. They set up a chaperoned meeting during which the prospective couple can get acquainted. Courtship is conducted under the watchful eye of family members and always carries with it a sense of responsibility and purpose. Casual dating is frowned upon by the more conservative Syrian-Lebanese because it can jeopardize the reputations of the parties and families involved.

Among assimilated Syrian-Lebanese, however, dating is the usual form of courtship. The men and women themselves make the decision to marry. However, just as it is rare for traditional parents to force their children into unwanted arranged marriages, among today's modern couples, young people rarely go against the wishes of their parents.

The majority of Syrian and Lebanese immigrants of the early wave married within their ethnic (and religious) groups; many men returned to their homeland for brides, particularly in the years when single men outnumbered single women in the immigrant community. The majority of the first American-born generation also married within the community. However, by the next generation, ethnic intermarriage was more the norm than the exception. Still, religious intermarriage continues to be frowned upon among new immigrants.

Divorce is less common in arranged marriages than in marriages based on love. The basis of the arranged marriage is a contract of shared responsibility and self-sacrifice; these couples do not expect that individual needs will be satisfied through the marriage. The purpose of such marriages is to build a family. In fact, divorce for reasons of personal unhappiness continues to be frowned upon. Because divorce has traditionally been seen as a shame on the family and a threat to its social fortune, families often get involved in solving marital problems. Though to some extent American-born Syrian-Lebanese have acculturated to the American pattern of divorce, recent Syrian-Lebanese immigrants are dismayed by it and say that in America, "they divorce to marry and marry to divorce." Syrian-Lebanese boast that, by contrast, they "spend 20 years solving problems." They look down upon the multiple divorces and remarriages of America's mainstream.

Syrian-Lebanese families often indulge babies and younger children. As do other traditional cultures, however, Syrian-Lebanese parents use physical punishment. Boys are both coddled and expected to be strong and independent; girls are restrained, taught to work within existing social schemes, and trained to be dependable as well as interdependent. As they mature, girls assume many household responsibilities and become their mothers' right hand. They often take charge of the younger siblings or, in the case of a mother's absence, the entire household. These responsibilities seem onerous to members of the youth-focused culture of modern America, particularly when compared to the freedom given to American teenagers.

EDUCATION

By the time they began immigrating to the United States, the Syrian-Lebanese had attended British, French, Russian, and American schools (including the Syrian Protestant College, later renamed the American University of Beirut) in their homeland for half a century or longer. These foreign schools had also stimulated the establishment of local government schools, and many of them schools encouraged the education of girls.

When they arrived in the United States, Syrian-Lebanese adapted to the American school system and culture. Their attitudes paralleled the evolution of the attitudes of other Americans toward school. By the third generation, the education of girls was considered equal in importance to that of boys. The generation born after World War II attended college at the same rate as the rest of the nation's youth, studying business, medicine, law, pharmacy, computer science, and engineering. Because the vast majority of American-born third generation Syrian-Lebanese descendants are middle class, and because many recent immigrants are educated and/or seeking graduate education, they enjoy a higher educational level than Americans on average.

By nature a conservative, patriarchal society, Catholic Syrian-Lebanese have often favored Catholic schools. Moslem immigrants (like their counterparts back home) occasionally send their children to Catholic schools, where there is more discipline and emphasis on respect for authority. Many Moslem immigrants have set up Islamic schools, some as supplements to their children's education, and a few as full-day parochial schools that teach Arabic language, history, and culture in addition to basic subjects.

THE ROLE OF WOMEN

Women have always been the heart of the Syrian-Lebanese family, and in many cases the real head. Although for the sake of appearances all decisions are cleared with the husbands (and in fact seem to be coming from the men), women's opinions often form the basis of decisions. Husbands depend on their wives to maintain the household and raise the children. Though many Syrian-Lebanese women work outside the home, many say they do so to help the family economically rather than to find personal satisfaction. Many play central roles in the family business, and often take over if their husbands die or become incapacitated. They are good community and church workers as well; many communities have Syrian Ladies Aid Societies—benevolent societies started by the first immigrant generation before World War I and still active today. As Syrian-Lebanese men have become more active in American public life, Syrian-Lebanese women have also begun to participate. Donna Shalala, a Lebanese-American woman, was formerly chancellor of the University of Wisconsin and before that president of Hunter College in New York City, prior to becoming President Clinton's Secretary of Health, Education and Welfare.

PHILANTHROPIC TRADITIONS

Just as each family must take care of its own, each religious community traditionally takes care of its members. Syrian-Lebanese Moslems are enjoined to give 2.5 percent of their income (a tithe called *zakkat*) to the needy within the community. Philanthropic efforts in the Syrian-Lebanese community also cut across religious sects. One is Save Lebanon, an organization formed in 1982 to bring Lebanese children injured in Israel's 1982 invasion of Lebanon to the United States for medical treatment. More prominent is the Saint Jude Children's Research Hospital in Memphis, Tennessee. Established in 1962, it is funded by an organization called Aiding Leukemia-Stricken American Children (ALSAC, established in 1957), American Lebanese Syrian Associated Charities, and individual donations. Founded by entertainer Danny Thomas (1914-1991), who was for a generation the most visible (or only visible) Lebanese American in the United States, ALSAC and St. Jude's have assumed the leading position in the field of research and treatment of childhood leukemia.

RELIGION

Though Syrians and Lebanese in America today are both Christian and Moslem, Christians remain the majority. There are also many Jews from the earliest migration, particularly from Aleppo, Syria, as well as a smaller number of Druze from both immigration waves.

For centuries, religious affiliation in Syria was tantamount to membership in a small nation, or at least a political party. The Ottomans' millet system (which divided people into political entities according to religion) gave religion social and political meaning. The millet system served to create a sense of boundaries among differing sects that went beyond doctrinal disputes. Because brides often converted to the faith of their husbands, the sense of competition among religions heightened. Interfaith marriage was traditionally resented and resisted because it resulted in the automatic loss not only of the bride but of the children she would bear.

In the Arab world today, all the religions—Islam, Christian, Druze, and Jewish—share a cultural context permeated by the same (some say Islamic) values. Thus, they all value hospitality, charity, respect for authority and orthodoxy, piety, and age. The various religions and sects often lose focus of these commonalities as they concentrate instead on their differences.

The vast majority of Syrian-Lebanese Christians in America belong to one of three Eastern rite Christian churches: the Maronite, the Eastern Orthodox, and the Melkite/Greek Catholic. Orthodox and Melkite liturgies are in Arabic and Greek; Maronite liturgy is in Arabic and Aramaic. In the United States, all three are sung partly in English.

The differences among these churches are jurisdictional rather than dogmatic; in particular, they differ on the question of the infallibility of the Pope in matters of faith. All have histories of persecutions (by each other as often as by Moslems) that serve to preserve group identity. Since its beginnings in the fourth century, the Maronite Church has been steadfast in its allegiance to Rome and the West, as well as resistant to the Arabic identity embraced by the other two.

Eastern rite churches have existed in the United States since the early twentieth century. Today there are 178 churches and missions among the Orthodox, 76 among the Maronites, and 45 among the Melkites. Though Melkite and Orthodox faiths do not share Eucharistic privileges, Orthodox and Melkite priests in the United States are discussing sharing sacraments and even reuniting.

All three churches administer confirmation at Baptism. All three use bread soaked in wine for the Eucharist. The marriage ceremony in each rite contains similar components: the blessing of the rings, the crowning of the bride and groom as queen and king, and the sharing of bread and wine—the couple's first meal together. Only the Orthodox and the Melkites have the bride and groom walk around the altar as the couple's first marital journey.

Orthodox priests can marry, but those who do cannot climb the clerical hierarchy. While Melkite and Maronite Catholic priests in the Middle East are encouraged by their own Eastern canon law to marry, they are forbidden to by Western canon. Unlike the Latin Catholic church, Eastern rite churches have icons rather than statuary. As for saints, Maronites especially honor St. Maron and St. Charbel; Melkites, St. Basil; Orthodox, St. Nicholas and St. George; and all three, St. Barbara.

Most Syrian and Lebanese American Moslems arrived after 1965. Moslems did not participate in the earlier migration because they feared that maintaining their religious practices in a Christian country would be difficult. Indeed, accommodation has been more difficult for them than for Christians. In general, Moslems pray five times a day and attend Friday prayers. When no mosque is available, they rent rooms in commercial and business districts where they can go for mid-day prayers (these small prayer places are called *masjids*); however, the mosque or *masjid* is not necessary for prayer. Moslems are supposed to fast during the daylight hours for the month of *Ramadan*. Many, including young schoolchildren, do keep the fast.

EMPLOYMENT AND ECONOMIC TRADITIONS

Upon arrival, many Syrians and Lebanese engaged in peddling. The peddlers carved out routes from New England through the West, travelling their circuits on foot. They were human precursors to department stores. Many developed regular clientele, and many eventually opened their own general stores. Some of those who stayed in the city developed small dry goods busi-

nesses into import/export empires. Already by 1908 the *Syrian Business Directory* cited roughly 3,000 Syrian-owned businesses across the country. The business directory reflected activity in the professions and the service occupations as well as in small industry and import/export. By 1910 there were a handful of Syrian American millionaires. Today there are several clothing empires—Farah and Haggar pants, for example—that are still thriving from the early days.

In some regions Syrian immigrants were factory workers. This was particularly true in Detroit and Dearborn, Michigan, where many Lebanese went to work in the auto industry.

Today the Syrian-Lebanese occupational profile is very broad, though still disproportionately retail-related. Syrian-Lebanese also tend to be self-employed and in managerial and professional capacities at a higher rate than Americans as a whole. Popular fields include medicine, law, banking, engineering, and computer science.

While turn-of-the-century America presented a golden economic opportunity for early Syrian-Lebanese immigrants, America in the 1980s and 1990s has provided a rougher road for recent immigrants. All sectors have been affected. While those with less education are able to support themselves doing whatever work is available (such as construction or service jobs, or restaurant or grocery store work), those with more education are finding themselves vulnerable. Some have even returned to Lebanon because of the American recession.

Starting in the 1980s, particularly in areas hard-hit by the failure of the auto industry, Syrian-Lebanese have been engaging in what once would have been unthinkable even during the Depression years—taking public assistance. Though only a small proportion of the community is on welfare, it is significant because it signals a change in attitudes toward family self-reliance and pride.

POLITICS AND GOVERNMENT

Syrian-Lebanese were a quiet group when they first arrived in America. They admired American democracy and economic freedoms and resisted joining labor unions or engaging in political activity. One issue that did rouse them to protest, though, came in the first generation, when Syrian-born immigrants were being rejected for citizenship in certain states. The Dow case (1914) in Georgia established that Syrians were Caucasian and therefore eligible for naturalization.

Until very recently, most Syrian-Lebanese political involvement has revolved around American policies in the Middle East, particularly those relating to Israel. Through the Eastern Federation of Syrian-Lebanese Organizations, which was established in 1932, Syrian-Lebanese quietly protested to President Harry Truman the 1948 partitioning of Palestine. But it was not until the aftermath of the 1967 war between Israel and its Arab neighbors that Lebanese and Syrians began to coalesce with other Arabs (mostly the new, educated immigrants) to form organizations to promote their common interests.

The members of the Association of Arab American University Graduates (AAUG, established in 1967) focused on educating the American public on the Arab-Israeli conflict. Five years later the National Association of Arab Americans formed to lobby the American Congress and White House administrations on Middle Eastern issues. In 1980 former Senator James Abourezk established the American Arab Anti-Discrimination Committee to combat defamation of Arab Americans in the media. As tensions in the Middle East grew, the task became more complex and Syrians and Lebanese, like all Arab Americans, became the victims of surveillance and civil rights infringements. When the United States bombed Libya in 1986, for example, it was revealed that the Immigration and Naturalization Services (INS) had a list of thousands of Arab (including Lebanese and Syrian) and Iranian students, permanent residents and even U.S. citizens, for possible detention in internment camps in the United States.

Since 1985 it has been illegal for Americans to visit Lebanon. Among the Arab American organizations lobbying to have the ban lifted is the American Task Force for Lebanon, a group of prominent Lebanese Americans who meet regularly with congressional and administration officials to advise on American support for the reconstruction of Lebanon and for the normalization of United States relations with the country.

Many Syrian-Lebanese have traditionally voted Republican, both because of their small business interests, and because of the Democratic party's support of Israel. However, a number of third-generation Syrian-Lebanese Americans, like other American activist counterparts, were influenced by the populism of the 1960s and 1970s,

becoming Democrats and trying to change the Democratic Party's resistance to open discussion on Middle East issues.

Much of this new Syrian-Lebanese political participation has been facilitated by the Arab American Institute (AAI), founded in 1985. AAI's mission is to nurture Arab-American participation in the American political process. AAI encourages Arab Americans to run for political office, to actively support favored candidates, and to become delegates to national conventions. Between 1985 and 1988, 20 Arab American political clubs were chartered around the United States. By the 1988 election AAI had mobilized over 300 Arab Americans to run as delegates to the national Democratic convention, and 60 won slots as Jesse Jackson delegates. At the Democratic Convention in Atlanta Syrian-Lebanese succeeded in introducing planks on such issues as support for Palestinian statehood and sovereignty of Lebanon. For the first time Arab Americans had leverage: after African Americans, they constituted the largest ethnic constituency of Jackson supporters. For the first time they had access to the political process as an ethnic group. Though there were disappointments—in the end the delegates had to settle for a debate on the Middle East planks but no recorded vote, it was clear that they had become players. The heavy Arab American participation in this convention gained the community the first Arab American co-chair of the Democratic National Committee, Ruth Ann Skaff.

INDIVIDUAL AND GROUP CONTRIBUTIONS

ENTERTAINMENT

Casey Kasem, (1933-) is America's most famous disc jockey and originator of radio show *American Top 40,* the host of *American Top 10,* and the principal voice-over for NBC-TV.

FASHION

Norma Kamali (1945-) and Joseph Abboud (1950-) are prominent New York fashion designers. J. M. Haggar (1892-1987) started the largest manufacturer of slacks in the world; and Mansour Farah (1895-1937) established Farah Brothers, a large competitive slack manufacturer.

FILM AND TELEVISION

Jamie Farr (1934-) played Corporal Klinger for 11 years on the popular TV series "M*A*S*H;" the late actor-singer-comedian Danny Thomas (1914-1991) starred in the 1950s' series, "Make Room For Daddy"—the television situation comedy that brought the Lebanese American father into American living rooms; his daughter Marlo Thomas (1943-) is an Emmy-winning actress; his son Tony Thomas (1948-) is a television and film producer and has won many Emmys for "Golden Girls" and other TV series; Tony Shalhoub plays in TV's "Wings;" the late Vic Tayback (1930-1990) played Mel in TV's "Alice;" Moustapha Akkad directed *Lion of the Desert* and *The Message*; Kristy McNichol (1962-) is one of the co-stars of "Empty Nest;" Kathy Najimy (1957-) was a co-star of *Sister Act* with Whoopie Goldberg; F. Murray Abraham (1939-) is the first Syrian American to win an Oscar, for his role in *Amadeus*; the late rock musician Frank Zappa (1940-1993) was a legend in the rock world; Callie Khoury (1957-) was the first woman to receive an Oscar for Best Original Screenplay, for *Thelma and Louise*.

GOVERNMENT SERVICE AND DIPLOMACY

Career diplomat Philip Habib (1920-1992) helped negotiate the end to the war in Vietnam and the end to the Israeli War in Lebanon. Senator James Abourezk (1931-) from South Dakota was the first Lebanese American to serve in the U.S. Senate, 1974-1980, and founded the American Arab Anti-Discrimination Committee. Nick Rahal (1949-) has been a U.S. congressman from West Virginia since 1976. Donna Shalala (1941-) was the president of New York City's Hunter College, later chancellor of the University of Wisconsin, and then Secretary of Health, Education, and Welfare in the Clinton administration. Democratic senator from Maine George Mitchell (1933-) is the senate majority Leader.

LITERATURE AND JOURNALISM

William Blatty (1928-) is the author of the book and screenplay *The Exorcist*. Vance Bourjaily (1922-) is the author of *Confessions of a Spent Youth*, and *The Man Who Knew Kennedy*. Khalil Gibran (1883-1931), poet and artist, is the author of *The Prophet*, perhaps the best-selling volume, after the Bible, of all time; Gibran's exhortation "Ask not what your country can do for you; ask what you can do for your country" in his "Letter to Syrian Youth" was quoted in John F. Kennedy's inaugural address and remains the most-quoted sentence of any inaugural address in American history. American-born Syrian-Lebanese poets include D. H. Milhelm (1926-), Sam Hazo (1928-), Joseph Awad (1929-) Sam Hamod (1936-), Lawrence Joseph (1948-), Gregory Orfalea (1949-), and Elmaz Abinader (1954-). Journalist Helen Thomas (1920-) has been the UPI White House correspondent for half a century and opens and closes every White House press conference.

MUSIC AND DANCE

Paul Anka (1941-), wrote and recorded popular hit songs beginning in the 1950s, including "Diana", "She's a Lady" and "My Way." Rosalind Elias (1931-) is a soprano with the New York City Metropolitan Opera; Elie Chaib (1950-) is a 20-year veteran dancer with the Paul Taylor Company.

PIONEERS

Ralph Nader (1934-) is the country's most prominent consumer advocate and literally invented consumer advocacy; he is the author of *Unsafe at Any Speed*, and founder and head of Public Citizen, an organization that has spawned a number of other citizen action groups such as Congress Watch, the Tax Reform Research Group. Najeeb Halaby (1915-) is the former head of the Federal Aviation Agency and was CEO of Pan-American Airlines. Candy Lightner (1946-) is the founder of MADD (Mothers Against Drunk Driving). Christa McAuliffe (1948-1986) was the teacher aboard the ill-fated space shuttle *Challenger*. Paul Orfalea (1946-) founded Kinko's, the world's largest international chain of copying and business service stores.

SCIENCE AND MEDICINE

Houston heart surgeon Michael DeBakey (1908-) invented the heart pump and pioneered the bypass operation in this country. Harvard University professor Elias J. Corey, (1928-) won the Nobel Prize for Chemistry in 1990. The St. Jude Research Hospital in Memphis, Tennessee, started by Danny Thomas (1914-1991) is the leader in the field of research and treatment of childhood leukemia.

SPORTS

Race-car driver Bobby Rahall won the Indianapolis 500 in 1986; the late Joe Robbie (1916-1990) was owner of the Miami Dolphins.

MEDIA

PRINT

Jusoor (Bridges).
An Arabic/English quarterly periodical that publishes poetry and essays on politics and the arts.

Address: P.O. Box 34163, Bethesda, Maryland 20817.
Telephone: (301) 869-5853.

Lebanon Report.
A monthly magazine that describes in great detail what is happening politically in Lebanon.

Contact: Michael Bacos Young, Editor.
Address: Lebanese Center for Policy Studies, Box 1377, Highland Park, New Jersey 08904.
Telephone: (908) 220-0885.

News Circle.
Published in English, it is a socially oriented magazine that reports on the activities of West Coast Arabs.

Contact: Joseph Haiek, Publisher.
Address: P.O. Box 3684, Glendale, California 91201-0684.

RADIO

Arab Network of America.
Every city with any concentration of Arabic-speaking people, including Lebanese and Syrians, has at least one or two hours of radio programming a week. It is a national Arabic-language radio network whose programs are broadcast in Washington, D.C., Detroit, Chicago, Pittsburgh, Los Angeles, and San Francisco.

Contact: Bruce Finland, CEO.
Address: 150 South Gordon Street, Alexandria, Virginia 22304.
Telephone: (703) 823-8364.

TELEVISION

Arab Network of America (ANA).
Contact: Bruce Finland, CEO.
Address: 150 South Gordon Street, Alexandria, Virginia 22304.
Telephone: (703) 823-8364.

TAC—Arabic Channel.
Contact: Jamil Tawfiq, Director.
Address: P.O. Box 936, New York, New York, 10005.
Telephone: (212) 425-8822.

ORGANIZATIONS AND ASSOCIATIONS

American Arab Anti-Discrimination Committee (ADC).
The largest grassroots Arab American organization; combats stereotyping and defamation in the media and in other venues of public life, including politics.

Address: 4201 Connecticut Avenue, Washington, D.C. 20008.
Telephone: (202) 244-2990.

American Task Force for Lebanon (ATFL).
Lobbies Congress and various administrations on issues related to Lebanon and its reconstruction.

Contact: George Cody, Executive Director.
Address: 2213 M Street, N.W., Third Floor, Washington, D.C. 20037.
Telephone: (202) 223-1399.

Arab American Institute (AAI).
Fosters participation of Arab Americans in the political process at all levels.

Contact: James Zogby, Executive Director.
Address: 918 16th Street, N.W., Suite 601, Washington, D.C. 20006.
Telephone: (202) 429-9210.

Association of Arab American University Graduates (AAUG).
Publishes monographs and books on Arab interests; holds symposia and conferences on current Middle East issues.

Contact: Ziad Asali, President.
Address: P.O. Box 408, Normal, Illinois 61761-0408.
Telephone: (309) 452-6588.

National Association of Arab Americans.
Lobbies capital hill and current administrations vis-a-vis Arab interests.

Contact: Khalil Jahshan, Executive Director.
Address: 1212 New York Avenue, N.W., Suite 300, Washington, D.C. 20005.
Telephone: (202) 842-1840.

MUSEUMS AND RESEARCH CENTERS

Communities and churches have begun to archive some of the memorabilia of the Arab American experience. The two centers of national importance are:

Faris and Yamna Naff Family Arab American Collection Archives Center, National Museum of History, Smithsonian Institution, Washington, D.C.

Contains artifacts, books, personal documents, photographs, oral histories, and doctoral dissertations pertaining to the Arab American immigrant experience, beginning with the earliest wave of immigrants.

Contact: Alixa Naff.

Telephone: (202) 357-3270.

Near Eastern American Collection, Immigration History Research Center, University of Minnesota.

Contains the Philip Hitti archives.

Contact: Rudoph Vecoli.

Address: 826 Berry Street, St. Paul, Minnesota 55114.

Telephone: (612) 627-4208.

SOURCES FOR ADDITIONAL STUDY

The Arab American Almanac, third edition, edited by Joseph R. Haiek. Glendale, California: News Circle Publishing Company, 1984.

Arab Americans: Continuity and Change, edited by Baha Abu-Laban and Michael Suleiman. Normal, Illinois: Association of Arab American University Graduates, Inc. 1989.

Hoogland, Eric. *Crossing the Water*. Washington, D.C.: Smithsonian Institution Press, 1987.

Kayal, Philip, and Joseph Kayal. *The Syrian Lebanese in America: A Study in Religion and Assimilation*. Boston: Twayne, 1975.

The Lebanese in the World: A Century of Immigration, edited by Nadim Shehadi and Albert Hourani. London: Centre for Lebanese Studies in association with I. B. Taurus, 1992.

Naff, Alixa. *Becoming American: The Early Arab Immigrant Experience*. Carbondale and Edwardsville: Southern Illinois University Press, 1985.

Orfalea, Gregory. *Before the Flames*. Austin: University of Texas Press, 1988.

Taking Root, Bearing Fruit, Volume 1, edited by James Zogby; Volume 2, edited by Eric Hooglund. Washington, D.C.: ADC Research Institute, 1984; 1985.

Wakin, Edward. *The Syrians and the Lebanese in America*. Chicago: Claretian Publishers, 1974.

Zogby, John. *Arab America Today: A Demographic Profile of Arab Americans*. Washington, D.C.: Arab American Institute, 1990.

The Thai family is highly structured, and each member has his or her specific place based on age, gender, and rank within the family. They can expect help and security as long as they remain within the confines of this order.

THAI AMERICANS

by
Megan Ratner

OVERVIEW

The Kingdom of Thailand was known as Siam until 1939. The Thai name for this nation is Prathet Thai or Muang Thai (Land of the Free). Located in Southeast Asia, it is somewhat smaller than Texas. The country covers an area of 198,456 square miles (514,000 square kilometers) and shares a northern border with Burma and Laos; an eastern boundary with Laos, Kampuchea, and the Gulf of Thailand; and a southern border with Malaysia. Burma and the Andaman Sea lie on its western edge.

Thailand has a population of just over 58 million people. Nearly 90 percent of the Thai people are Mongoloid, with lighter complexions than their Burmese, Kampuchean, and Malay neighbors. The largest minority group, about ten percent of the population, is Chinese, followed by the Malay and various tribal groups, including the Hmong, Iu Mien, Lisu, Luwa, Shan, and Karen. There are also 60,000 to 70,000 Vietnamese who live in Thailand. Nearly all people in the country follow the teachings of Buddhism. The 1932 constitution required that the king be a Buddhist, but it also called for freedom of worship, designating the monarch as "Defender of the Faith." The present king, Bhumibol Adulyadei, thus protects and improves the welfare of the small groups of Muslims (five percent), Christians (less than one percent), and Hindus (less than one percent) who also worship in Thailand. The Western name of the capital city is Bangkok; in Thai, it is *Krung Thep* (City of Angels) or *Pra Nakhorn* (Heavenly Capital). It is the seat of the Royal House, Government, and Parliament. Thai is the official language of the country, with English the most widely spoken second language; Chinese and Malay are also spoken. Thailand's flag consists of a broad blue horizontal band at the center, with narrower bands of stripes above and below it; the inner ones are white, the outer ones red.

HISTORY

The Thai have an ancient and complex history. Early Thai people migrated south from China in the early centuries A.D. Despite the fact that their former kingdom was located in Yunnan, China, the Thai, or T'ai, are a distinct linguistic and cultural group whose southward migration led to the establishment of several nation states now known as Thailand, Laos, and Shan State in Myanma (Burma). By the sixth century A.D. an important network of agricultural communities had spread as far south as Pattani, close to Thailand's modern border with Malaysia, and to the northeastern area of present-day Thailand. The Thai nation became officially known as "Syam" in 1851 under the reign of King Mongkrut. Eventually, this name became synonymous with the Thai kingdom and the name by which it was known for many years. In the thirteenth and fourteenth centuries, several Thai principalities united and sought to break from their Khmer (early Cambodian) rulers. Sukothai, which the Thai consider the first independent Siamese state, declared its independence in 1238 (1219, according to some records). The new kingdom expanded into Khmer territory and onto the Malay peninsula. Sri Indradit, the Thai leader in the independence movement, became king of the Sukothai Dynasty. He was succeeded by his son, Ram Khamhaeng, who is regarded in Thai history as a hero. He organized a writing system (the basis for modern Thai) and codified the Thai form of Theravada Buddhism. This period is often viewed by modern-day Thais as a golden age of Siamese religion, politics, and culture. It was also one of great expansion: under Ram Khamheng, the monarchy extended to Nakhon Si Thammarat in the south, to Vientiane and Luang Prabang in Laos, and to Pegu in southern Burma.

Ayutthaya, the capital city, was established after Ram Khamheng's death in 1317. The Thai kings of Ayutthaya became quite powerful in the fourteenth and fifteenth centuries, adopting Khmer court customs and language and gaining more absolute authority. During this period, Europeans—the Dutch, Portuguese, French, English, and Spanish—began to pay visits to Siam, establishing diplomatic links and Christian missions within the kingdom. Early accounts note that the city and port of Ayutthaya astonished its European guests, who noted that London was nothing more than a village in comparison. On the whole, the Thai kingdom distrusted foreigners, but maintained a cordial relationship with the then-expanding colonial powers. During the reign of King Narai, two Thai diplomatic groups were sent on a friendship mission to King Louis XIV of France.

In 1765 Ayutthaya suffered a devastating invasion from the Burmese, with whom the Thais had endured hostile relations for at least 200 years. After several years of savage battle, the capital fell and the Burmese set about destroying anything the Thais held sacred, including temples, religious sculpture, and manuscripts. But the Burmese could not maintain a solid base of control, and they were ousted by Phraya Taksin, a first-generation Chinese Thai general who declared himself king in 1769 and ruled from a new capital, Thonburi, across the river from Bangkok.

Chao Phraya Chakri, another general, was crowned in 1782 under the title Rama I. He moved the capital across the river to Bangkok. In 1809, Rama II, Chakri's son, assumed the throne and reigned until 1824. Rama III, also known as Phraya Nang Klao, ruled from 1824 through 1851; like his predecessor, he worked hard to restore the Thai culture that had been almost completely destroyed in the Burmese invasion. Not until the reign of Rama IV, or King Mongkut, which began in 1851, did the Thai strengthen relations with Europeans. Rama IV worked with the British to establish trade treaties and modernize the government, while managing to avoid British and French colonization. During the reign of his son, Rama V (King Chulalongkorn), who ruled from 1868 to 1910, Siam lost some territory to French Laos and British Burma. The short rule of Rama VI (1910-1925) saw the introduction of compulsory education and other educational reforms.

MODERN ERA

In the late 1920s and early 1930s, a group of Thai intellectuals and military personnel (many of whom had been educated in Europe) embraced democratic ideology and were able to effect a successful—and bloodless—*coup d'etat* against the absolute monarchy in Siam. This occurred during the reign of Rama VII, between 1925 and 1935. In its stead, the Thai developed a constitutional monarchy based on the British model, with a combined military-civilian group in charge of governing the country. The country's name was officially changed to Thailand in 1939 during prime minister Phibul Songkhram's government. (He had been a key military figure in the 1932 coup.)

Japan occupied Thailand during World War II and Phibul declared war on the United States and Great Britain. The Thai ambassador in Washington, however, refused to make the declaration. Seri Thai (Free Thai) underground groups worked with the allied powers both outside and within Thailand. The end of World War II terminated Phibul's regime. After a short stint of democratic civilian control, Phibul regained control in 1948, only to have much of his power taken away by General Sarit Thanarat, another military dictator. By 1958, Sarit had abolished the constitution, dissolved the parliament, and outlawed all political parties. He maintained power until his death in 1963.

Army officers ruled the country from 1964 to 1973, during which time the United States was given permission to establish army bases on Thai soil to support the troops fighting in Vietnam. The generals who ran the country during the 1970s closely aligned Thailand with the United States during the war. Civilian participation in government was allowed intermittently. In 1983 the constitution was amended to allow for a more democratically elected National Assembly, and the monarch exerted a moderating influence on the military and on civilian politicians.

The success of a promilitary coalition in the March 1992 elections touched off a series of disturbances in which 50 citizens died. The military violently suppressed a "pro-democracy" movement on the streets of Bangkok in May 1992. Following the intervention of the king, another round of elections was held in September of that year, when the current prime minister, Chuan Leekphai, the leader of the Democrat Party, was elected.

THAIS IN AMERICA

Thai immigration to America was nearly nonexistent before 1960, when U.S. armed forces began arriving in Thailand during the Vietnam war. After interacting with Americans, Thais became more aware of the possibility for immigration to the United States. By the 1970s, some 5,000 Thais had emigrated to this country, at a ratio of three women to every man. The largest concentration of Thai immigrants can be found in Los Angeles and New York City. These new immigrants consisted of professionals, especially medical doctors and nurses, business entrepreneurs, and wives of men in the U.S. Air Force who had either been stationed in Thailand or had spent their vacations there while on active duty in Southeast Asia.

In 1980 the U.S. Census recorded concentrations of Thai near military installations, especially Air Force bases, in certain U.S. counties, ranging from Aroostook County (Loring Air Force Base) in Maine to Bossier Parish (Barksdale Air Force Base) in Louisiana and New Mexico's Curry County (Cannon Air Force Base). A few counties with a larger military presence such as Sarpy County in Nebraska, where the Strategic Air Command has been headquartered, and Solano County, California, where Travis Air Force Base is located, became home to larger groups. Fairly large concentrations of Thai were also found in Davis County, Indiana, the location of Hill Air Force Base, Eglin Air Force Base in Okaloosa County, Florida, and Wayne County, North Carolina, where Seymour Johnson Air Force Base is located.

The Thai Dam, an ethnic group from the mountain valleys of northern Vietnam and Laos were also counted as immigrants of Thai ancestry by the U.S. Census Bureau, though they are actually refugees from other countries. They are centered in Des Moines, Iowa. Like other Southeast Asian refugees of this area, they have coped with problems of housing, crime, social isolation, and depression. Most of them are employed, but in low-paying menial jobs that offer little in the way of advancement.

During the 1980s, Thais immigrated to the United States at an average rate of 6,500 per year. Student or temporary visitor visas were a frequent venue to the United States. The main attraction of the United States is the wide array of opportunities and higher wages. However, unlike people from other countries in Indochina, none whose original homes were in Thailand has been forced to come to the United States as refugees.

In general, Thai communities are tightly knit and mimic the social networks of their native land. As of 1990, there were approximately

91,275 people of Thai ancestry living in the United States. The greatest number of Thais are in California, some 32,064. Most of these people are clustered in the Los Angeles area, some 19,016. There are also high numbers of people whose temporary visas have expired who are believed to be in this area. The homes and businesses of Thai immigrants are dispersed throughout the city, but there is a high concentration in Hollywood, between Hollywood and Olympic boulevards and near Western Avenue. Thais own banks, gas stations, beauty parlors, travel agencies, grocery stores, and restaurants. Further exposure to the English language and American culture has caused the population to disperse somewhat. New York, with a Thai population of 6,230 (most in New York City) and Texas with 5,816 (primarily Houston and Dallas) have the second and third largest Thai populations, respectively.

ACCULTURATION AND ASSIMILATION

Thai Americans have adapted well to American society. Although they maintain their culture and ethnic traditions, they accept the norms as practiced in this society. This flexibility and adaptability has had a profound effect on first-generation American-born Thais, who tend to be quite assimilated or Americanized. According to members of the community, the young people's acceptance of American ways has made these new changes more acceptable to their parents, facilitating relations between "established" Americans and newcomers. With the high concentration of Thais in California and recent efforts to define who is and is not "native," members of the Thai community have expressed fears that there may be problems in the future.

Although many traditional beliefs are retained by Thai Americans, Thais often try to adjust their beliefs in order to live in the United States comfortably. Thais are often perceived as too adaptable and lacking in innovation. A common expression, *mai pen rai*, meaning "never mind" or "it doesn't matter," has been seen by some Americans as an indication of Thais' unwillingness to expand or develop ideas. Also, Thais are often mistaken for Chinese or Indochinese, which has led to misunderstandings, and offended Thais since Thai culture is bound up with Buddhism and has its own traditions, different from Chinese culture. In addition, Thais are often assumed to be refugees rather than immigrants by choice. Thai Americans are anxious that their presence be seen as a benefit, not a burden, to American society.

TRADITIONS, CUSTOMS, AND BELIEFS

Thais do not shake hands when they meet. Instead, they keep their elbows at their sides and press their palms together at about chest height in a prayer-like gesture called *wai*. The head is bent in this greeting; the lower the head, the more respect one shows. Children are supposed to *wai* adults and they receive an acknowledgement in the form of *wai* or a smile in return. In Thai culture the feet are considered the lowest part of the body, both spiritually and physically. When visiting any religious edifice, feet must be pointed away from any Buddha images, which are always kept in high places and shown great respect. Thais consider pointing at something with one's feet to be the epitome of bad manners. The head is regarded as the highest part of the body; therefore Thais do not touch each other's hair, nor do they pat each other on the head. A favorite Thai proverb is: Do good and receive good; do evil and receive evil.

CUISINE

Perhaps the greatest contribution from the small Thai American community has been their cuisine. Thai restaurants remain a popular choice in large cities, and the Thai style of cooking has even begun to appear in frozen dinners. Thai cooking is light, pungent, and flavorful, and some dishes can be quite spicy. The mainstay of Thai cooking, as in the rest of Southeast Asia, is rice. In fact, the Thai words for "rice" and "food" are synonymous. Meals often include one spicy dish, such as a curry, with other meat and vegetable side dishes. Thai food is eaten with a spoon.

Presentation of food for the Thai is a work of art, especially if the meal marks a special occasion. Thais are renowned for their ability to carve fruit; melons, mandarins, and pomelos, to name just a few, are carved in the shapes of intricate flowers, classic designs, or birds. Staples of Thai cuisine include coriander roots, peppercorns, and garlic (which are often ground together), lemon grass, *nam pla* (fish sauce), and *kapi* (shrimp paste). The meal generally includes soup, one or two *kaengs* (dishes that include thin, clear, soup-like gravy; though Thais describe these sauces as

"curry," it is not what most Westerners know as curry), and as many *krueng kieng* (side dishes) as possible. Among these, there might be a *phad* (stir-fried) dish, something with *phrik* (hot chili peppers) in it, or a *thawd* (deep-fried) dish. Thai cooks use very few recipes, preferring to taste and adjust seasonings as they cook.

TRADITIONAL THAI COSTUMES

Traditional clothing for Thai women consists of a *prasin*, or a wrap-around skirt (sarong), which is worn with a fitted, long-sleeved jacket. Among the most beautiful costumes are those worn by dancers of classical Thai ballet. Women wear a tight-fitting under jacket and a *panung*, or skirt, which is made of silk, silver, or gold brocade. The *panung* is pleated in front, and a belt holds it in place. A pailletted and jeweled velvet cape fastens to the front of the belt and drapes down behind to nearly the hem of the *panung*. A wide jewelled collar, armlets, necklace, and bracelets make up the rest of the costume, which is capped with a *chadah*, the temple-style headdress. Dancers are sewn into their costumes before a performance. The jewels and metal thread can make the costume weigh nearly 40 pounds. Men's costumes feature tight-fitting silver thread brocade jackets with epaulets and an ornately embroidered collar. Embroidered panels hang from his belt, and his calf-length pants are made of silk. His jewelled headdress has a tassel on the right, while the woman's is on the left. Dancers wear no shoes. For everyday life, Thais wear sandals or Western-style footwear. Shoes are always removed when entering a house. For the last 100 years, Western clothing has become the standard form of clothing in Thailand's urban areas. Thai Americans wear ordinary American clothes for everyday occasions.

HOLIDAYS CELEBRATED BY THAI AMERICANS

Thais are well known for enjoying festivities and holidays, even if they are not part of their culture; Bangkok residents were known to take part in the Christmas and even Bastille Day celebrations of the resident foreign communities. Thai holidays include New Year's Day (January 1); Chinese New Year (February 15); Magha Puja, which occurs on the full moon of the third lunar month (February) and commemorates the day when 1,250 disciples heard the Buddha's first sermon; Chakri Day (April 6), which marks the enthronement of King Rama I; Songkran (mid-April), the Thai New Year, an occasion when caged birds and fish are set free and water is thrown by everyone on everyone else; Coronation Day (May 5); Visakha Puja (May, on the full moon of the sixth lunar month) is the holiest of Buddhist days, celebrating Lord Buddha's birth, enlightenment, and death; Queen's Birthday, August 12; King's Birthday, December 5.

LANGUAGE

A member of the Sino-Tibetan family of languages, Thai is one of the oldest languages in East or Southeast Asia. Some anthropologists have hypothesized that it may even predate Chinese. The two languages share certain similarities since they are monosyllabic tonal languages; that is, since there are only 420 phonetically different words in Thai, a single syllable can have multiple meanings. Meanings are determined by five different tones (in Thai): a high or low tone; a level tone; and a falling or rising tone. For example, depending on the inflection, the syllable *mai* can mean "widow," "silk," "burn," "wood," "new," "not?" or "not." In addition to the tonal similarities with Chinese, Thai has also borrowed from Pali and Sanskrit, notably the phonetic alphabet conceived by King Ram Khamhaeng in 1283 and still in use today. The signs of the alphabet take their pattern from Sanskrit; there are also supplemental signs for tones, which are like vowels and can stand beside or above the consonant to which they belong. This alphabet is similar to the alphabets of the neighboring countries of Burma, Laos, and Kampuchea. Compulsory education in Thailand is up to the sixth grade and the literacy rate is over 90 percent. There are 39 universities and colleges and 36 Teachers Training Colleges in Thailand to meet the needs of thousands of secondary school students who want higher educational attainment.

GREETINGS AND POPULAR EXPRESSIONS

Common Thai greetings are: *Sa wat dee*—Good morning, afternoon, or evening, as well as good-bye (by the host); *Lah kon*—Good-bye (by the guest); *Krab*— sir; *Ka*—madam; *Kob kun*—Thank you; *Prode*—Please; *Kor hai choke dee*—Good luck; *Farang*—foreigner; *Chern krab* (if the speaker is male), or *Chern kra* (if the speaker is female)—Please, you are welcome, it's all right, go ahead, you first (depending on the circumstances).

FAMILY AND COMMUNITY DYNAMICS

Traditional Thai families are closely knit, often incorporating servants and employees. Togetherness is a hallmark of the family structure: people never sleep alone, even in houses with ample room, unless they ask to do so. Virtually no one is left to live alone in an apartment or house. As a consequence, Thais make few complaints about academic dormitories or the dormitories provided by factories.

The Thai family is highly structured, and each member has his or her specific place based on age, gender, and rank within the family. They can expect help and security as long as they remain within the confines of this order. Relationships are strictly defined and named with terms so precise that they reveal the relation (parental, sibling, uncle, aunt, cousin), the relative age (younger, older), and side of the family (maternal or paternal). These terms are used more often in conversation than the person's given name. The biggest change that settlement in the United States has brought has been the diminishing of extended families. These are prevalent in Thailand, but the lifestyle and mobility of American society has made the extended Thai family hard to maintain.

SPIRIT HOUSES

In Thailand, many houses and buildings have an accompanying spirit house, or a place for the property guardian spirit (*Phra phum*) to reside. Some Thais believe that families living in a home without a spirit house cause spirits to live with the family, which invites trouble. Spirit houses, which are usually about the same size as a birdhouse, are mounted on a pedestal and resemble Thai temples. In Thailand, large buildings such as hotels may have a spirit house as large as an average family dwelling. The spirit house is given the best location on the property and is shaded by the main house. Its position is planned at the time of the building's construction; then it is ceremonially erected. Corresponding improvements, including additions, are also made to the spirit house whenever modifications are made to the main house.

WEDDINGS

Arrival in the United States has brought an increase in self-determined marriages. Unlike other Asian countries, Thailand has been far more permissive toward marriages of personal choice, though parents generally have some say in the matter. Marriages tend to take place between families of equal social and economic status. There are no ethnic or religious restrictions, and intermarriage in Thailand is quite common, especially between Thai and Chinese, and Thai and Westerners.

Wedding ceremonies can be ornate affairs, or there may be no ceremony at all. If a couple lives together for a while and has a child together, they are recognized as "de facto married." Most Thais do have a ceremony, however, and wealthier members of the community consider this essential. Prior to the wedding, the two families agree on the expenses of the ceremony and the "bride price." The couple begins their wedding day with a religious ritual in the early morning and by receiving blessings from monks. During the ceremony, the couple kneels side by side. An astrologer or a monk chooses a favorable time for the couple's heads to be linked with joined loops of *sai mongkon* (white thread) by a senior elder. He pours sacred water over their hands, which they allow to drip into bowls of flowers. Guests bless the couple by pouring sacred water in the same way. The second part of the ceremony is essentially a secular practice. Thais do not make any vows to one another. Rather, the two linked but independent circles of the white thread serve to symbolically emphasize that the man and woman have each retained their individual identities while, at the same time, joining their destinies.

One tradition, practiced primarily in the countryside, is to have "sympathetic magic" performed by an older, successfully married couple. This duo lies in the marriage bed before the newlyweds, where they say many auspicious things about the bed and its superiority as a place for conception. They then get off the bed and strew it with symbols of fertility, such as a tomcat, bags of rice, sesame seeds and coins, a stone pestle, or a bowl of rainwater. The newlyweds are supposed to keep these objects (except the tomcat) in their bed for three days.

DIVORCE

Even in cases in which the marriage has been sealed by a ceremony, divorce is a simple matter: if both parties consent, they sign a mutual statement to this effect at the district office. If only one party wants the divorce, he or she must show proof of the other's desertion or lack of support for one year. The divorce rate among Thais, both officially and unofficially, is relatively low compared to the American divorce rate, and the remarriage rate is high.

BIRTH

Pregnant women are not given any gifts before a baby is born so as to keep them from being scared by evil spirits. These evil spirits are thought to be the spirits of women who died childless and unmarried. For a minimum of three days to a month after birth, the baby is still considered a spirit child. It is customary to refer to a newborn as frog, dog, toad, or other animal terms that are seen as helpful in escaping the attention of evil spirits. Parents often ask a monk or an elder to select an appropriate name for their child, usually of two or more syllables, which is used for legal and official purposes. Nearly all Thais have a one-syllable nickname, which usually translates as frog, rat, pig, fatty, or many versions of tiny. Like the formal name, a nickname is intended to keep the evil spirits away.

FUNERALS

Many Thais consider *ngarn sop* (the cremation ceremony) the most important of all the rites. It is a family occasion and the presence of Buddhist monks is necessary. One *baht* coin is placed in the mouth of the corpse (to enable the dead person to buy his or her way into purgatory), and the hands are arranged into a *wai* and tied with white thread. A banknote, two flowers, and two candles are placed between the hands. White thread is used to tie the ankles as well, and the mouth and eyes are sealed with wax. The corpse is placed in a coffin with the feet facing west, the direction of the setting sun and of death.

Dressed in mourning black or white, the relatives gather around the body to hear the sutras of the monks who sit in a row on raised padded seats or on a platform. On the day that the body is cremated, which for persons of high rank can be as long as a year after the funeral ceremony, the coffin is carried to the site feet first. In order to appease the spirits who are drawn to the funeral activities, rice is scattered on the ground. All the mourners are given candles and incense bouquets. As tokens of respect for the deceased, these are thrown on the funeral pyre, which consists of piles of wood under an ornate paste pagoda. The most exalted guest then officiates at the cremation by being the first to light this structure. The actual cremation that follows is attended by the next of kin only and is usually held a few yards from the ritual funeral pyre. The occasion is sometimes followed by a meal for guests who may have traveled from far away to attend the ceremony. On that evening and the two following, monks come to the house to chant blessings for the departed soul and for the protection of the living. According to Thai tradition, the departed family member is advancing along the cycle of death and rebirth toward the state of perfect peace; thus, sadness has no place at this rite.

EDUCATION

Education has traditionally been of paramount importance to Thais. Educational accomplishment is considered a status-enhancing achievement. Until the late nineteenth century, the responsibility for educating the young lay entirely with the monks in the temple. Since the beginning of this century, however, overseas study and degrees have been actively sought and highly prized. Originally, this sort of education was open only to royalty, but, according to Immigration and Naturalization

Services information, some 835 Thai students came to study in the United States in 1991.

RELIGION

Nearly 95 percent of all Thais identify themselves as Theravada Buddhists. Theravada Buddhism originated in India and stresses three principal aspects of existence: *dukkha* (suffering, dissatisfaction, "dis-ease"), *annicaa* (impermanence, transiency of all things), and *anatta* (non-substantiality of reality; no permanence of the soul). These principles, which were articulated by Siddhartha Gautama in the sixth century B.C., contrasted with the Hindu belief in an eternal, blissful Self. Buddhism, therefore, was originally a heresy against India's Brahman religion.

Gautama was given the title Buddha, or "enlightened one." He advocated the "eight-fold path" (*atthangika-magga*) which requires high ethical standards and conquering desire. The concept of reincarnation is central. By feeding monks, making regular donations to temples, and worshipping regularly at the *wat* (temple), Thais try to improve their situation—acquire enough merit (*bun*)—to lessen the number of rebirths, or subsequent reincarnations, a person must undergo before reaching Nirvana. In addition, the accumulation of merit helps determine the quality of the individual's station in future lives. *Tham bun*, or merit making, is an important social and religious activity for Thais. Because Buddhist teachings emphasize philanthropic donations as part of achieving merit, Thais tend to be supportive of a wide range of charities. The emphasis, however, is on charities that assist the indigent in Thailand.

Ordination into the Buddhist order of monks often serves to mark the entry into the adult world. Ordination is for men only, though women can become nuns by shaving their heads, wearing white robes, and obtaining permission to reside in the nun's quarters on grounds within the temple. They do not officiate at any rituals. Most Thai men *Buat Phra* (enter the monkhood) at some point in their lives, often just prior to their marriage. Many only stay for a short period, sometimes as little as a few days, but in general they remain for at least one *phansa*, the three-month Buddhist Lent that coincides with the rainy season. Among the prerequisites for ordination is four years' education. Most ordinations occur in July, just before Lent.

The *thankwan nak* ceremony serves to strengthen the *kwan*, or the soul, the life essence, of the person to be ordained. During this time, he is called a *nak*, which means dragon, referring to a Buddhist myth about a dragon who became a monk. In the ceremony, the *nak*'s head and eyebrows are shaved to symbolize his rejection of vanity. For three to four hours, a professional master of ceremonies sings of the mother's pain in giving birth to the child and emphasizes the many filial obligations of the young man. The ceremony concludes with all relatives and friends gathered in a circle holding a white thread and then passing three lighted candles in a clockwise direction. Guests generally give gifts of money.

The following morning, the *nak*, dressed in white (to symbolize purity), is carried on the shoulders of his friends under tall umbrellas in a colorful procession. He bows before his father, who hands him the saffron robes he will wear as a monk. He leads his son to the abbot and the four or more other monks who are seated on a raised platform before the main Buddha image. The *nak* asks permission for ordination after prostrating himself three times to the abbot. The abbot reads a scripture and drapes a yellow sash on the *nak*'s body to symbolize acceptance for ordination. He is then taken out of view and dressed in the saffron robes by the two monks who will oversee his instruction. He then requests the ten basic vows of a novice monk and repeats each as it is recited to him.

The father presents alms bowls and other gifts to the abbot. Facing the Buddha, the candidate then answers questions to show that he has met the conditions for entry into the monkhood. The ceremony concludes with all the monks chanting and the new monk pouring water from a silver container into a bowl to symbolize the transference of all merit he has acquired from being a monk to his parents. They in turn perform the same ritual to transfer some of their new merit to other relatives. The ritual's emphasis is on his identity as a Buddhist and his newfound adult maturity. At the same time, the rite reinforces the link between generations and the importance of family and community.

Thai Americans have accommodated themselves to the environment here by adapting their religious practices when necessary. One of the most far-reaching of these changes was the switch from lunar calendar days to the conventional Saturday or Sunday services that are offered in the United States.

This photograph, taken during the Thai New Year in Los Angeles, shows the traditional ceremony of pouring water on monks' palms.

EMPLOYMENT AND ECONOMIC TRADITIONS

Thai men tend to aspire to military or civil service jobs. Rural women have been traditionally engaged in running businesses, while educated women are involved in all types of professions. In the United States, most Thais own small businesses or work as skilled laborers. Many women have opted for nursing careers. There are no Thai-only labor unions, nor do Thais particularly dominate one profession.

POLITICS AND GOVERNMENT

Thai Americans tend not to be active in community politics in this country, but are more concerned with issues in Thailand. This reflects the general insulation of the community, where there are specific delineations between northern and southern Thais and where intercommunity outreach with other groups has been almost nonexistent. Thai Americans are quite active in Thai politics and they keep an active watch on economic, political and social movements there.

INDIVIDUAL AND GROUP CONTRIBUTIONS

Many Thai Americans work in the health-care industry. Boondharm Wongananda (1935-) is a noted surgeon in Silver Spring, Maryland, and the executive director of the Thais for Thai Association. Also worthy of mention is Phongpan Tana (1946-), the director of nurses in a Long Beach, California hospital. Several other Thai Americans have become educators, company executives, and engineers. Some Thai Americans are also beginning to enter the field of American politics; Asuntha Maria Ming-Yee Chiang (1970-) is a legislative correspondent in Washington, D.C. Yet because their community is so small, Thai Americans' statistics are generally tabulated with those of other Asian Americans; presumably this will change as the community grows.

MEDIA

PRINT

Thailand: A World of Growing Investment Opportunites.

Published by Euromoney Publications; lists Thai government offices worldwide; principal content is information on Thailand's legal system, corporate structure, economy, direct investment efforts, and history of its foreign relations.

Address: Nestor House, Playhouse Yard, London EC4V 5EX, England.

Telephone: 71 2363288.

TELEVISION

THAI-TV USA.

Offers programming in Thai in the Los Angeles area.

Contact: Paul Khongwittaya.

Address: 1123 North Vine Street, Los Angeles, California 90038.

Telephone: (213) 962-6696.

Fax: (213) 464-2312.

ORGANIZATIONS AND ASSOCIATIONS

American Siam Society.

Cultural organization that encourages investigation of art, science, and literature in relation to Thailand and its neighboring countries.

Address: 633 24th Street, Santa Monica, California 90402-3135.

Telephone: (213) 393-1176.

Thai Society of Southern California.

Contact: K. Jongsatityoo, Public Relations Officer.

Address: 2002 South Atlantic Boulevard, Monterey Park, California 91754.

Telephone: (213) 720-1596.

Fax: (213) 726-2666.

MUSEUMS AND RESEARCH CENTERS

Asia Resource Center.

Founded in 1974. The center includes among its holdings 15 drawers of clippings on East and Southeast Asia, from 1976 through the present, as well as photograph files, films video cassettes, and slide programs.

Contact: Roger Rumpf, Executive Director.

Address: Box 15275, Washington, D.C. 20003.

Telephone: (202) 547-1114.

Fax: (202)543-7891.

Cornell University Southeast Asia Program.

The center concentrates its activities on the social and political conditions in Southeast Asian countries, including the history and culture of Thailand. It studies cultural stability and change, especially the consequences of Western influences and offers Thai lessons and distributes Thai cultural readers.

Contact: Randolph Barker, Director.

Address: 180 Uris Hall, Ithaca, New York 14853.

Telephone: (607) 255-2378.

Fax: (607) 254-5000.

University of California, Berkeley South/Southeast Asia Library.

This library contains a special Thai collection in addition to its substantial holdings on the social sciences and humanities of Southeast Asia. The entire collection comprises some 400,000 monographs, dissertations, microfilm, pamphlets, manuscripts, videotapes, sound recordings, and maps.

Contact: Rebecca Darby Williams.

Address: 438 Library, Berkeley, California 94720.

Telephone: (510) 642-3095.

Fax: (510) 643-7891.

Yale University Southeast Asia Collection.

This collection of materials centers on the social sciences and humanities of Southeast Asia. Holdings include some 200,000 volumes.

Contact: Charles R. Bryant, Curator.

Address: Sterling Memorial Library, Yale University, New Haven, Connecticut 06520.

Telephone: (203) 432-1859.

Fax: (203) 432-7231.

SOURCES FOR ADDITIONAL STUDY

Audric, John. *Siam: The Land and the People*. New York: A. S. Barnes, 1969.

Cooper, Robert, and Nanthapa Cooper. *Culture Shock*. Portland, Oregon: Graphic Arts Center Publishing Company, 1990.

Detailed Ancestry Groups for States, 1990. Washington, D.C.: Economic Statistics Administration, Bureau of the Census, 1992.

Harvard Encyclopedia of American Ethnic Groups, edited by Stephan Thernstrom. Boston: Harvard University Press, 1980.

Statistical Yearbook of the Immigration and Naturalization Service. Washington, D.C.: Immigration and Naturalization Service, 1993.

Thailand and Burma. London: The Economist Intelligence Unit, 1994.

TLINGIT

by

Diane E. Benson

('Lxeis')

Tlingit people
believe that all life is
of equal value;
plants, trees, birds,
fish, animals, and
human beings are all
equally respected.

OVERVIEW

Alaska is a huge land mass that contains many different environments ranging from the frigid streams and tundra above the Arctic circle to the windy islands of the Aleutians to the mild rainy weather of southeast Alaska. Alaska consists of over 533,000 square miles, with a coastline as long that of the rest of the continental United States. The southern end of the Alaska coastline, a region known as Southeast Alaska, is home to the primary Tlingit (pronounced "klingit") communities. This area covers the narrow coastal strip of the continental shore along British Columbia; it is similar in size and shape to the state of Florida, but with few communities connected by road. Tlingit communities are located from just south of Ketchikan and are scattered northward across islands and mainland as far as the Icy Bay area. Tlingit people also occupy some inland area on the Canadian side of the border in British Columbia and the Yukon Territory. The mainland Tlingit of Alaska occupy a range of mountains from 50 to 100 miles inland. The northern portion of Tlingit country is glacial with the majesty of the Fairweather and Saint Elias mountains overlooking the northern shores of the Gulf of Alaska. Fjords, mountains that dive into the sea, islands, and ancient trees make up most of this wet country that is part of one of the largest temperate rain forests in the world.

The total population of Alaska is just under 600,000. Approximately 86,000 Alaska Natives, the indigenous peoples of Alaska, live there. The Tlingit population at time of contact by Europeans is estimated to have been 15,000. Some reports include the Haida in population estimates, since Tlingit and Haida are almost always grouped together for statistical purposes. Today, Tlingit and Haida Central Council tribal enrollment figures show a total of 20,713 Tlingit and Haida, of which 16,771 are Tlingit. Most of the Tlingit population live in urban communities of southeastern Alaska, though a significant number have made their homes all across the continent. Euro-Americans dominate the Southeast population, with the Tlingit people being the largest minority group in the region.

EARLY HISTORY

The name Tlingit essentially means human beings. The word was originally used simply to distinguish a human being from an animal, since Tlingits believed that there was little difference between humans and animals. Over time the word came to be a national name. It is speculated that human occupation of southeast Alaska occurred 11,000 years ago by Tlingit people. Haida people, with whom the Tlingit have frequent interaction, have only been in the area about 200 years, and the Tsimpsian migrated only recently from the Canadian interior mainland.

Tlingit legends speak of migrations into the area from several possible directions, either from the north as a possible result of the Bering Sea land bridge, or from the southwest, after a maritime journey from the Polynesian islands across the Pacific. Oral traditions hold that the Tlingit came from the head of the rivers. As one story goes, Nass-aa-ge-yeil' (Raven from the head of the Nass River) brought light and stars and moon to the world. The Tlingit are unique and unrelated to other tribes around them. They have no linguistic relationship to any other language except for a vague similarity to the Athabaskan language. They also share some cultural similarity with the Athabaskan, with whom the Tlingit have interacted and traded for centuries. There may also be a connection between the Haida and the Tlingit, but this issue is debated. Essentially, the origin of the Tlingit is unknown.

Tlingit people are grouped and divided into units called *kwan*. Some anthropological accounts estimate that 15 to 20 *kwan* existed at the time of European contact. A *kwan* was a group of people who lived in a mutual area, shared residence, intermarried, and lived in peace. Communities containing a Tlingit population may be called the *Sitka-kwan*, the *Taku-kwan*, or the *Heenya-kwan*, depending on their social ties and/or location. Most of the urban communities of Southeast Alaska occupy the sites of many of the traditional *kwan* communities. Before the arrival of explorers and settlers, groups of Tlingit people would travel by canoe through treacherous waters for hundreds of miles to engage in war, attend ceremonies, trade, or marry.

Through trade with other tribes as far south as the Olympic Peninsula and even northern California, the Tlingit people had established sophisticated skills. In the mid-1700s, the Spaniards and the British, attracted by the fur trade, penetrated the Northwest via the Juan de Fuca Islands (in the Nootka Sound area). The Russians, also in search of furs, invaded the Aleutian Islands and moved throughout the southwestern coast of Alaska toward Tlingit country. The Tlingit traders may have heard stories of these strangers coming but took little heed.

FIRST CONTACT WITH EUROPEANS

Europeans arrived in Tlingit country for the first time in 1741, when Russian explorer Aleksey Chirikov sent a boatload of men to land for water near the modern site of Sitka. When the group did not return for several days, he sent another boat of men to shore; they also did not return. Thereafter, contact with Tlingit people was limited until well into the 1800s.

Russian invaders subdued the Aleut people, and moving southward, began their occupation of Tlingit country. Having monopolized trade routes in any direction from or to Southeast Alaska, the Tlingit people engaged in somewhat friendly but profitable trading with the newcomers until the Russians became more aggressive in their attempts to colonize and control trade routes. In 1802 Chief Katlian of the Kiksadi Tlingit of the Sitka area successfully led his warriors against the Russians, who had set up a fort in Sitka with the limited permission of the Tlingit. Eventually the Russians recaptured Sitka and maintained a base they called New Archangel, but they had little contact with the Sitka clans. For years the Tlingit resisted occupation and the use of their trade routes by outsiders. In 1854 a Chilkat Tlingit war party travelled hundreds of miles into the interior and destroyed a Hudson Bay Company post in the Yukon Valley.

Eventually, diseases and other hardships took their toll on the Tlingit people, making them more vulnerable. In a period between 1836 and 1840, it is estimated that one-half of the Tlingit people at or near Sitka were wiped out by smallpox, influenza, and tuberculosis. At about this time, Americans came into Tlingit country for gold, and in the process sought to occupy and control the land and its people. The Tlingit loss to disease only made American occupation more swift, and Americans became firmly established in the land with the 1867 Treaty of Purchase of Alaska. The Tlingit continually fought American development of canneries, mines, and logging, which conflicted with the Tlingit lifestyle. Disputes between the Americans and the decreasing Tlingit people proved futile for the Tlingit, since Americans displayed impressive military strength, technology, and an unwavering desire for settlement and expansion. The destruction of the Tlingit villages of Kake in the 1860s and of Angoon in 1882 by the American military (due to a disagreement involving the death of two Native people) further established American power and occupancy.

THE LAND CLAIMS PERIOD

The Treaty of Cession (1867) referred to indigenous people of Alaska as "uncivilized tribes." Such designation in legislation and other agreements caused Alaska Natives to be subject to the same regulations and policies as American Indians in the United States. Statements by the Office of the Solicitor in the U.S. Department of Interior in 1932 further supported the federal government's treatment of Alaska Natives as American Indians. As a result, Tlingit people were subject to such policies as the 1884 First Organic Act, which affected their claims to land and settlements, and the 1885 Major Crimes Act, which was intended to strip tribes of their right to deal with criminal matters according to traditional customs. By the turn of the century, the Tlingit people were threatened politically, territorially, culturally, and socially.

In response, the Tlingit people organized the Alaska Native Brotherhood (ANB). The ANB was founded in Sitka in 1912 by nine Tlingit and one Tsimpsian. The ANB's goals were to gain equality for the Native people of Southeast Alaska and to obtain for them the same citizenship and education rights as non-Natives. In 1915, due to the efforts of the ANB (and the newly orga-

These Tlingit girls from Cooper River, Alaska, were photographed in 1903.

nized Alaska Native Sisterhood), the territorial legislature adopted a position similar to the Dawes Act to allow Natives to become citizens, provided that the Natives became "civilized" by rejecting certain tribal customs and relationships. As a result, few Native people became citizens at this time; most did not become American citizens until the U.S. Congress adopted the Citizenship Act of 1924.

Tlingit people also actively pursued the right to vote. Unlike many Alaska Native people at the time who wanted to continue living as they had for many generations, Tlingit leaders sought increased political power. In 1924, William Paul, a Tlingit, won election to the Territorial House of Representatives, marking the beginning of a trend toward Native political power.

In 1929 the ANB began discussing land issues, and as a result Congress passed a law in 1935 allowing Tlingits and Haidas to sue the United States for the loss of their lands. By this time large sections of Tlingit country had become the Tongass National Forest. Glacier Bay had become a National Monument, and further south in Tlingit country, Annette Island was set aside as a reservation for Tsimpsian Indians from Canada. In 1959—the same year that Alaska was admitted as a state—the Court of Claims decided in favor of the Tlingit and Haida for payment of land that was taken from them. The Tlingit-Haida land claims involved 16 million acres without a defined monetary value; an actual settlement took years to conclude. In 1971, the Alaska Native Claims Settlement Act (ANCSA) was passed, which called for the settlement of all claims against the United States and the state of Alaska that are based on aboriginal right, title, use, or occupancy of land or water areas in Alaska.

Tlingit individuals did not receive title to lands as a result of ANCSA. Instead, lands claimed by southeast Natives under this act were placed under the control of the ANCSA-established regional corporation, Sealaska, and the ANCSA-established village corporations. Some village corporations had the option to provide individuals with land in some cases, but most villages designated the land for future development.

The Native Allotment Act of 1906 did result in some Tlingit lands being placed in the hands of individual Tlingits. This law provided for conveyance of 160 acres to adult Natives as long as no tract of ground contained mineral deposits. Only a few allotments were issued in southeast Alaska. The Native Townsite Act of 1926 also provided only for the conveyance of "restricted" title lands, meaning such property could not be sold or leased without the approval of the Secretary of the Interior. Despite these gains, lands reobtained this way by the villages or by individuals failed to sufficiently meet the needs of a hunting and fishing people.

The issues of Native citizenship, their right to vote, fishing, and fishing trap disputes, and the activities of ANCSA contributed to the rising tensions between the Tlingit and the newcomers. In the 1930s, 1940s, and 1950s, it was not uncommon to see signs that read "No Indians Allowed" on the doors of business establishments. The Alaska Native Brotherhood did much to fight these prejudices and elevate the social status of the Tlingit and Haida people as American citizens. Today, although Tlingit people are much more accepted, their fight for survival continues. Their ability to subsist off the land and sea is constantly endangered by logging, pulp mills, overharvesting of the waters by commercial fisheries, government regulations, and the area's increasing population.

ACCULTURATION AND ASSIMILATION

Throughout the nineteenth century, many Tlingit communities were affected by the influx of vari-

ous industries. Fish canneries were established in Sitka and Klawock, gold mining began at Windham Bay, and a Presbyterian mission station was constructed at the place now known as Haines. New settlements like Juneau (1880) and Ketchikan (1888) dramatically changed Tlingit lands and economic systems. A mixed cash-subsistence economy developed, changing traditional trade and material acquisition systems. Missionary schools determined to acculturate the Tlingit and other Alaska Natives instructed the Tlingit in English and American ways and denied the indigenous students access to their traditional language, foods, dances, songs, and healing methods. Although change was overwhelming and Americanization pervasive, Tlingit clan structures remained intact, and traditions survived in the original communities. At the turn of the century it was not uncommon for southeast factories to employ clan leaders to prevent disputes and keep order between their employees and the Native communities.

The destruction and death brought on by disease caused many to abandon their faith in the shaman and traditional healing by the turn of the century. Smallpox and other epidemics of the early nineteenth century recurred well into the twentieth century. A number of communities, including Dry Bay and Lituya Bay, were devastated in 1918 and thereafter by bouts of influenza. Important and culturally fundamental traditional gatherings, or potlatches, became almost nonexistent in Tlingit country during the tuberculosis epidemics of the 1900s. These epidemics caused hundreds of Tlingit and other southeast people to be institutionalized; many of those who fell victim to these diseases were subsequently buried in mass graves. Tlingit people turned to the churches for relief, and in the process many were given new names to replace their Tlingit names, an important basis of identity and status in Tlingit society. Demoralization and hopelessness ensued and worsened with the government-sponsored internment of Aleut people in Tlingit country during World War II. Some Tlingit families adopted Aleut children who had been orphaned as a result of widespread disease and intolerable living conditions.

When they were established, the Alaska Native Brotherhood and Sisterhood accepted acculturation as a goal for their members, believing that the abandonment of cultural traditions was in the peoples' best interest. Their organizational structure, however, reflected a traditional form of government to manage tribal and clan operations. Social and clan interactions and relationships continue to exist to this day despite all outside influences and despite the marked adaptations of Tlingit people to American society. The relatively recent revival of dances, songs, potlatches, language, and stories has strengthened continuing clan interactions and identities.

TRADITIONS, CUSTOMS AND BELIEFS

Tlingit people believe that all life is of equal value; plants, trees, birds, fish, animals, and human beings are all equally respected. Clans and Clan Houses have identifying crests; a clan is equally proud whether its crest is a killer whale or a snail. There are no recognized superior species. When any "crested" living being dies, homage is expected, and appropriate respects are paid. Today, some communities of the southeast are still very sensitive to this tradition.

Tlingit people do not tolerate misuse or misappropriation of their crests, names, songs, designs, stories, or other properties. Each crest has stories and songs associated with it that belong to the crest and thereby to its clan. Ownership recognition of these things among the Tlingit is profound. Almost a century ago, two clans began a dispute over who owned a particular crest. This conflict is discussed in detail in Frederica de Laguna's 1972 work, *Under Mt. St. Elias: The History and Culture of the Yakatat Tlingit*. The issue developed into a social, political, and legal battle that ensued for decades, and in many ways remains unresolved. Using a killer whale song, story, or crest design without acknowledging the owning clan or without its permission, for example, can be considered stealing. Crest ownership sometimes conflicts with American notions of public domain. This conflict, along with a growing interest by the general public in Tlingit art and culture, has raised concerns among the clans about how to protect their birthrights from distortion and acquisition.

Tlingits demand that respect be shown toward other individuals and clans. When a person feels insulted by another, payment must be made by the person or clan who was responsible for the insult, or a process performed to remove the damage publicly. If this does not happen, bad feelings persist, negatively affecting relationships between clans. In the old ways, if a Tlingit person was seriously harmed or murdered by another Tlingit person, the "eye for an eye" philosophy would determine punishment: someone from the opposing clan would have to die. Today, that philosophy is adapted to remain within legal boundaries. Criminal cases are tried strictly by American law, but the family of the perpetrator is subject to social ostracism. Payment by the perpetrator's clan to the harmed clan for the wrongdoing is also conceivable.

Many newcomers to Tlingit country, including some missionaries, erroneously reported that the Tlingit people worshipped totems, idolized animals or birds as gods, and held heathen rituals. As a result some religious leaders instructed their Native congregations to burn or destroy various elements of their art and culture, and a good deal of Tlingit heirlooms were destroyed in this way. These misconceptions undermined the complexity and power of Tlingit culture and society.

POTLATCHES

Potlatches are an integral part of Tlingit history and modern-day life. A potlatch is a giant feast that marks a time for showing respect, paying debts, and displaying wealth. Tlingit people give grandly at potlatches to raise their stature. The respect and honor held toward one's ancestry, name, house crest, and family, and the extent of one's wealth might determine how elaborate a potlatch would be; these ceremonies are not, however, forms of worship to any gods. Potlatches are given for various reasons and may be planned for years in advance. The most common potlatches given today are funeral potlatches, the 40-Day Party, memorial potlatches, adoption potlatches, naming potlatches, totem-pole-raising potlatches, and house- or lodge-building potlatches.

A person's death requires a three-stage potlatch process to properly attend to the deceased person's transfer to the spirit world or future life. The first potlatch includes the mourning and burial of the deceased, lasting from one to four days. George Emmons reports in his book *The Tlingit Indians* that this process traditionally took four to eight days. During this time, the body is prepared for cremation or burial (which is more common today). Attendees sing songs of grief; sometimes the family fasts. Feasts are prepared for guests of the opposite clan (see below for explanation of opposite clans); afterward the person is buried. During the second stage, a party is held for the deceased person's clan. The third stage, or memorial potlatch, which can take place at any time, usually occurs about a year later. The memorial potlatch is a ritual process of letting go emotionally of the deceased. It marks the final release of the deceased to their future life as well as the final mourning, speeches, and deceased person's clan's payments to the opposite clan. The conclusion of the potlatch is a celebration of life and happy stories and song.

Sometimes less elaborate potlatches are held to give names to youngsters, or to those who have earned a new or second name. Naming potlatches may be held in conjunction with a memorial potlatch, as can adoption potlatches. Adoption ceremonies are held for one or more individuals who have proven themselves to a clan by their long term commitment to a Tlingit family or community and who have become members of the clan. The new members receive gifts and names, and are obligated from that day forward to uphold the ways of that clan. For whatever reason potlatches are held, ceremony is ever present. Participants wear traditional dress, make painstaking preparations, give formal speeches in Tlingit and English, and observe proper Tlingit etiquette.

CUISINE AND DIET

The traditional diet of the Tlingit people relies heavily on the sea. Fish, seal, seaweed, clams, cockles, gum boots (chitons—a shell fish), herring, eggs and salmon eggs, berries, and venison make up the primary foods of most Tlingit people. Fish, such as halibut, cod, herring, and primarily salmon, (king, reds, silver, and sockeye) are prepared in many forms—most commonly smoked, dried, baked, roasted, or boiled. Dog, silver, humpy, and sockeye salmon are the fish best utilized for smoking and drying. The drying process takes about a week and involves several stages of cleaning, deboning, and cutting strips and hanging the fish usually near an open fire until firm. These strips serve as a food source throughout the year, as they are easily stored and carried.

The land of southeastern Alaska is abundant with ocean and wildlife, and because of this the Tlingit people could easily find and prepare foods in the warmer seasons, saving colder months for art, crafts, and elaborate gatherings. Today, although food sources have been impacted by population and industry, the traditional foods are still gathered and prepared in traditional ways as well as in new and creative ways influenced by the various ethnic groups who have immigrated into the area, especially Filipino (rice has become a staple of almost any Tlingit meal). Pilot bread, brought in by various seafaring merchants, is also common as it stores well, and softens, for the individual, the consumption of oil delicacies such as the eulochon and seal oils. Fry-bread is also an element of many meals and special occasions. Other influences on diet and food preparation besides standard American include Norwegian, Russian, and Chinese foods.

Other foods of the Tlingit include such pungent dishes as *xákwl´ee*, soap berries (whipped berries often mixed with fish or seal oil), seal liver, dried seaweed, fermented fish eggs, abalone, grouse, crab, deer jerky, sea greens, *-suktéitl´*— goose tongue (a plant food), rosehips, rhubarb, roots, *yaana.eit* (wild celery), and *s´ikshaldéen* (Hudson Bay tea).

TRADITIONAL GARMENTS AND REGALIA

Traditionally Tlingit men and women wore loincloths and skirts made of cedar bark. Because of the rainy weather in southeastern Alaska, raincoats were worn, which were also made from natural elements such as spruce root or cedar bark. Today, Tlingit people no longer wear loincloths and cedar bark skirts, dressing very much as other contemporary Americans. Although modern, Tlingit people display their clan or family emblem on clothing or through jewelry, as has been the custom for centuries.

The most distinctive form of ceremonial dress prior to Americanization and still the most admired is the Chilkat robe. Although called the Chilkat robe after the Chilkat tribe of Tlingit who specialized in weaving, its origin is Tsimpsian. The robe is made from mountain goat wool and cedar bark strips and generally exhibits an emblem of the clan. This garment takes a weaver one to five years to make. The technique not only involves a horizontal weaving similar to that found in other cultures, but also a symmetrical and circular (curvilinear) design as well. This complex art form came dangerously close to extinction in the twentieth century, but through the perseverance of individuals in and outside the tribe there are now several weavers, elder and younger, in Tlingit and other northwest nations today. This is also true of the recently revived art of the Raven's Tail robe, another complexly woven garment of black and white worn over the shoulders in the same cape fashion as the Chilkat robe. Raven's Tail weaving of geometric and herring bone patterns is a skill that had not been practiced in nearly two centuries, but with the

This photograph shows Tlingit Indians in traditional dress.

resurgence of cultural interest is now being practiced throughout the northwest coast. Chilkat and Raven's Tail weaving is also used to make leggings, medicine bags, dance purses, dance aprons, tunics, and shirts.

In 1982 the Sealaska Heritage Foundation in Juneau began what is called *Celebration*. It occurs every even year as a gathering to celebrate culture. At Celebration today, many Chilkat robes can be seen. Chilkat robes are never worn as daily dress, but are worn with pride at potlatches, celebrations, and sometimes for burial, if the person was of a particular social stature. Chilkat robes are a sign of wealth, and traditionally if one owned such an item, he was generally a clan leader of great prestige. Giving away a Chilkat robe meant greater glory since only the wealthiest could afford to be so generous.

Modern regalia today consists primarily of the button blanket, or dancing robe, which although time consuming and expensive to make, is much more available to the people than the Chilkat or Raven's Tail robe. Russian influence played a great part in the evolution of the button blanket, since trade provided the Tlingit people with felt of usually red, black, or blue from which the button blanket is made. These robes are often intricately decorated with one's clan emblems through appliqué variations and mother of pearl (shell) button outlines or solid beading of the design. These robes are worn to display one's lineage and family crest at gatherings, in much the same way as the Chilkat robe.

Robes of any type are almost always worn with an appropriate headdress. Headdresses can be as varied and simple as a headband or as intricate and rich as a carved cedar potlatch hat, displaying one's crest, decorated with color, inlaid with abalone shell, and finished with ermine. Russian influence inspired the sailor style hat that many women wear for dancing. These are made of the same felt as the button blanket and completed with beaded tassels. Ornamentation traditionally included some hair dressing, ear and nose piercing, labrets, bracelets, face painting, and tattooing. Most of these facets of adornment are practiced today, excluding the labret.

The formal dress of the Tlingit people is not only a show of power, wealth, or even lineage, but is an integral part of the social practices of the Tlingit. Tlingit people practice the respect of honoring the opposite clan and honoring one's ancestors in the making and handling of a garment. Importance is placed also on the maker of the garment, and the relationship of his or her clan to the clan of the wearer. Dress in Tlingit culture is an acknowledgment of all who came before.

HEALTH AND MENTAL HEALTH ISSUES

Existing traditional health-care centers consist primarily of physical healing through diet and local medicines, although this practice is rather limited. A few people today still use teas brewed from the devil's club, Hudson bay tea leaves, roots, leaves, and flowers of various plants that cleanse the body, boost the immune system, and even heal wounds and illnesses. Overall, the Tlingit people primarily use modern medical treatment through the existing federally established health-care systems.

Contemporary health-care methods are only marginally effective. Some of the Tlingit believe that people have a relationships with spirits, can communicate with animals and birds, and can learn from all life forms. Those who vocalize these experiences or abilities, however, feel vulnerable about being labelled as mentally ill. Still considered a radical idea by most modernized Tlingit and mental health specialists, this aspect of Tlingit culture is only now beginning to be discussed.

Health problems among the Tlingit are not much different than they are with other Alaska Native peoples. Extensive and continuous Indian Health Service data demonstrate their susceptibility to such illnesses as influenza, arthritis, hepatitis, cancer, and diabetes. Alcoholism is a more common disease that has taken its toll on the people, and although suicide is not as high amongst the Tlingit as it seems to be in more northern Native communities, it too has caused havoc and despair for some Tlingit communities. Providing social and emotional support for individuals as well as for the family structure has become a concern for health-care professionals and concerned tribal citizens. Since the Alaska Natives Commission's 1994 report was released

stressing the link between health and culture, more and more communities are discussing the psychology of various forms of cultural and social oppression and how to recover spiritually, mentally, and physically.

LANGUAGE

The Tlingit language is a tone language that has 24 sounds not found in English. Tlingit is phonemic in that the difference in meaning between words often depends entirely on tone. Much of the Tlingit language is guttural and some of the sounds are similar to that of German. Almost all Alaska Native languages have guttural or "back-in-the-mouth" sounds. Tlingit is unique in that it is not only guttural but has glottalized stops and a series of linguistically related sounds called glottalized fricatives. The sounds of Tlingit are difficult and varied and include not only the more familiar rolling and drawn out vowel sounds and deeper guttural sounds, but also pinched and air driven sounds with consonants which are "voiceless" (except for the "n" sound, as in "naa"). Many of the consonants have no English equivalents.

In the nineteenth century, the first attempts were made to communicate in Tlingit through writing. The Russian Orthodox Church through Bishop Innocent (Veniaminov) created the first alphabet for the Tlingit language and developed a Tlingit literacy program. The Orthodox Church supported bilingual education in its schools, but the Americans discouraged it, and ultimately sought to suppress the use of the language completely. It was not until the 1960s that a Native language literacy movement was resumed through the efforts of such linguists as Constantine Naish and Gillian Story. These linguists created the Tlingit alphabet that is more commonly used today.

Unlike the English alphabet of 26 letters, the Tlingit language has at least 32 consonants and eight vowels. The alphabet was created with not only the familiar lettering of English but also with periods, underlines on letters, and apostrophes to distinguish particular sounds. For example; the word yéil means Raven, and yéil' (with the apostrophe) means elderberry.

Tlingit grammar does not indicate concern with time, whereas English conveys some sense of time with almost any verb usage. Tlingit verbs may provide the information about an action's frequency or indicate the stopping or starting of an action. The grammatical and phonological features of the language make it a difficult one to learn if it has not been taught since birth, but it is not impossible. Unfortunately, due to past efforts to suppress the language there are not many young speakers, although the need to keep the language alive is crucial. The need to maintain indigenous languages is urgently stated in the 1994 *Final Report of the Alaska Natives Commission:* "At the core of many problems in the Alaska Native community are unhealed psychological and spiritual wounds and unresolved grief brought on by a century-long history of deaths by epidemics and cultural and political deprivation at others' hands; some of the more tragic consequences include the erosion of Native languages in which are couched the full cultural understanding, and the erosion of cultural values."

COMMON EXPRESSIONS

Tlingit people do not use such greetings as hello, good-bye, good afternoon, or good evening. Some common expressions are: *Yoo xat duwasaakw*—my name is; *Gunalchéesh*—Thank you; *Yak'éi ixwsiteení*—It's good to see you; *Wáa sá iyatee*—How are you (feeling?; *Wa.é ku.aa?*—Where are you going?; and *Haa kaa gaa kuwatee*—It's good weather for us.

FAMILY AND COMMUNITY DYNAMICS

Tlingit society is divided into two primary ("opposite") clans or moieties, subclans or clans, and houses. The moieties are Raven and Eagle, and all Tlingits are either Raven or Eagle by birthright. The structure is matrilineal, meaning each person is born with the moiety of their mother, which is typically the opposite of the father: If the mother is Eagle, then the father is Raven or vice versa. Traditionally moiety intramarriage was not allowed even if the two Ravens or two Eagles were not at all blood related. Today, although frowned upon, moiety intramarriage occasionally occurs without the social ostracizing of the past.

Clans exist under the Raven moiety and the Eagle moiety. Clans are a subdivision of the moieties; each has its own crest. A person can be Eagle and of the Killer Whale or Brown Bear Clan, or of several other existing clans; Ravens may be of the Frog Clan, Sea Tern Clan, Coho Clan, and so forth. Houses, or extended families, are subdivisions of the clans. Prior to contact houses would literally be houses or lodges in which members of that clan or family coexisted. Today houses are one of the ways in which Tlingit people identify themselves and their relationship to others. Some examples of houses include the Snail House, Brown Bear Den House, Owl House, Crescent Moon House, Coho House, and Thunderbird House.

Tlingits are born with specific and permanent clan identities. Today these identities and relationships are intact and still acknowledged by the tribe. Biological relationships are one part of the family and clan structure; the other is the reincarnate relationships. Tlingit social structures and relationships are also effected by the belief that all Tlingits are reincarnates of an ancestor. This aspect of Tlingit lineage is understood by the elders but is not as likely to be understood and acknowledged by the younger Tlingit, although clan conferences are being held to educate people about this complex social system.

In Tlingit society today, even though many Tlingits marry other Tlingits, there exists a great deal of interracial marriage, which has changed some of the dynamics of family and clan relationships. Many Tlingit people marry Euro-Americans, and a few marry into other races or other tribes. Some of the interracial families choose to move away from the Tlingit communities and from Tlingit life. Others live in the communities but do not participate in traditional Tlingit activities. A few of the non-Tlingit people intermarried with Tlingit become adopted by the opposite clan of their Tlingit spouse and thereby further their children's participation in Tlingit society.

Traditionally boys and girls were raised with a great deal of family and community support. The uncles and aunts of the children played a major role in the children's development into adulthood. Uncles and aunts often taught the children how to physically survive and participate in society, and anyone from the clan could conceivably reprimand or guide the child. Today the role of the aunts and uncles has diminished, but in the smaller and dominantly Tlingit communities some children are still raised this way. Most Tlingit children are raised in typical American one-family environments, and are instructed in American schools as are other American children. Tlingit people place a strong importance on education and many people go on to receive higher education degrees. Traditional education is usually found in dance groups, traditional survival camps, art camps, and Native education projects through the standard education systems.

RELIGION

Traditionally, spiritual acknowledgment was present in every aspect of the culture, and healing involved the belief that an ailing physical condition was a manifestation of a spiritual problem, invasion, or disturbance. In these cases, a specialist, or shaman-*ixt'*, would be called in to combat spirit(s) *yéiks*, or the negative forces of a witch or "medicine man." Today, anyone addressing such spiritual forces does so quietly, and most people are silent on the subject. The Indian Religious Freedom Act was passed in 1978, but to date has had little effect other than to provide some legal support for Tlingit potlatch and traditional burial practices.

Institutionalized religion, or places of worship, were not always a part of the traditional Tlingit way of life, although they are now. The Russian Orthodox and Presbyterian faiths have had the longest and most profound impact on Tlingit society and are well established in the Tlingit communities. Other religions have become popular in southeast Alaska, and a few Tlingit people are members of the Jehovah Witnesses, the Bahai's, and the fundamentalist Baptist churches.

EMPLOYMENT AND ECONOMIC TRADITIONS

The Tlingit economy at time of contact was a subsistence economy supported by intense trade. The cash economy and the American systems of ownership have altered the lifestyle of Tlingit people dramatically; however, many Tlingits have adapted successfully. Job seekers find occupations primarily in logging and forestry, fishing and the marine industry, tourism, and other business enterprises. Because of the emphasis on education, a significant number of Tlingit people work in professional positions as lawyers, health-care specialists, and educators. The Sealaska Corporation and village corporations created under ANCSA also provide some employment in blue collar work, office work, and corporate management. Not all positions within the corporations are held by Tlingit and Haida, as a large number of jobs are filled by non-Natives. The corporations provide dividends—the only ANCSA compensation families receive for land they have lost, but these are generally rather modest. Some of the village corporations have produced some hefty lump sum dividends out of timber sales and one-time sale of NOL's (net operating losses) sold to other corporations for tax purposes, but these windfalls are infrequent.

Since the ANCSA bill passed in 1971, differences in wealth distribution among the Tlingit have arisen that did not previously exist. Some of the Tlingit people are economically disadvantaged and have less opportunities today to rely on subsistence for survival. Welfare reliance has become an all-too-common reality for many families, while those in political and corporate positions seem to become more financially independent. As a result shareholder dissension has increased annually and become rather public.

POLITICS AND GOVERNMENT

Tlingit and Haida people have been and continue to be very active in both community and clan politics and tribal governments as well as in state and city issues. Many Tlingits since the 1920s have won seats in the Territorial legislature, setting in motion Tlingit involvement in all aspects of politics and government. Tlingit activist and ANS leader Elizabeth Peratrovich made the plea for justice and equality regardless of race to the territorial legislature on February 8, 1945 that prompted the signing of an anti-discrimination bill. Her efforts as a civil rights leader became officially recognized by the State of Alaska in 1988 with the "Annual Elizabeth Peratrovich Day." She is the only person in Alaska to be so honored for political and social efforts.

The ANCSA-created corporations wield a great deal of political power, and Tlingit and Haida corporate officials are often courted by legislators and businessmen. The corporations are a strong lobby group in Alaska's capital since they not only control lands and assets but represent over 16,000 Tlingit and Haida shareholders. Tlingit people cast their individual ballots based on their own choices and results show they tend to support the Democratic party. Tlingit people running for office also tend to run on a Democratic ticket.

The Indian Child Welfare Act of 1978 provided the first real means for traditional Tlingit law to be practiced and recognized by American government. Since 1978 several tribal courts have been created and tribal judges placed. A very active tribal court exists in Sitka with Tlingit judges presiding over civil matters brought before the court. Tribal courts in Tlingit country are not yet active in determining criminal cases as might be found in other tribal courts of the continental United States, but tribal councils are considering such jurisdiction. Tribal councils and tribal courts are much more a part of the communities than they were 20 years ago, and many issues today are addressed and resolved by Tlingit communities at this level.

Although no statistics are immediately available, many Tlingit men have fought in the World Wars, Korea, and Vietnam. Tlingit participation in the U.S. armed forces is common and generally supported by the families and their communities.

INDIVIDUAL AND GROUP CONTRIBUTIONS

In the twentieth century the Tlingit people have made many contributions. The following mentions some notable Tlingit Americans and their achievements:

ACADEMIA

Elaine Abraham (1929-), bilingual educator, was the first Tlingit to enter the nursing profession. In her early years, she cared for people on the Navajo reservation during a diphtheria epidemic, and in Alaska, patients of tuberculosis and diphtheria during a time when many indigenous tribes feared modern medicine. Thereafter she served in major hospital supervisory positions and initiated such health programs as the original Southeast Health Aid Program and the Alaska Board of Health (now called the Alaska Native Health Board). An outstanding educator, she began as assistant dean of students at Sheldon Jackson College and was appointed vice-president in 1972. In Fairbanks she cofounded the Alaska Native Language Center and went on to become Vice-President of Rural Education and Extension Centers (1975).

Abraham also established the Native Student Services office for Native students while teaching the Tlingit language at the Anchorage Community College. Her work in student services and indigenous understanding continues as Director of Alaska Native Studies for the University of Alaska in Anchorage.

GOVERNMENT

Elizabeth Peratrovich (1911-1958), civil rights activist, is recognized by Alaskans for her contributions to the equal rights struggle in the state of Alaska. February 17 is celebrated as Elizabeth Peratrovich Day. She is also listed in the Alaska Women's Hall of Fame (1989) and honored annually by the Alaska Native Sisterhood (which she served as Grand Camp President) and by the Alaska Native Brotherhood. Roy Peratrovich (1910-1989), Elizabeth's husband, is also honored by the Alaska Native Brotherhood and other Alaskans for his dedication to bettering the education system and for actively promoting school and social integration. His efforts frequently involved satirical letters to the newspapers that stimulated controversy and debate.

William L. Paul (1885-1977) began as a law school graduate and practicing attorney and became the first Alaska Native and first Tlingit in Alaska's territorial House of Representatives. He contributed to equal rights, racial understanding, and settlement of land issues. Frank J. Peratrovich (1895-1984) received a University of Alaska honorary doctorate for public service, serving as the Mayor of Klawock and as a territorial legislator in the Alaska House and Senate. He was the first Alaska Native not only to serve in the Senate but also to become Senate President (1948).

Andrew P. Hope (1896-1968) was an active politician and contributed to the advancement of Tlingit people and social change. He was instrumental in the development of the Alaska Native Brotherhood (ANB) and was one of Alaska's few Native legislators. Frank See (b. 1915) from Hoonah was also a notable legislator, mayor, and businessman, as was Frank Johnson (1894-1982), a teacher, legislator, and lobbyist. Frank Price was also elected to the territorial legislature.

LITERATURE AND ORATORS

Nora Marks Dauenhauer (1927-), poet, scholar, and linguist, has dedicated her work to the survival of the Tlingit language; she has stressed the importance of story in culture. Besides such published works in poetry as *The Droning Shaman*, she has edited a number of works with her husband, Richard Dauenhauer, including the bilingual editions of Tlingit oral literature, *Haa Shuka, Our Ancestors: Tlingit Oral Narratives* (1987), and *Haa Tuwunaagu Yis, for Healing Our Spirit: Tlingit Oratory* (1990). Together they have developed Tlingit language instruction materials, *Beginning Tlingit* (1976), the *Tlingit Spelling Book (1984)*, and instructional audio tapes. She has written numerous papers on the subjects of Tlingit language oratory and culture, and she has co-authored many other articles. Another active writer is Andy Hope III, essayist, poet, and editor of *Raven's Bones Journal*.

Orators and storytellers in Tlingit history and within the society today are numerous, but some of the noteworthy include Amy Marvin/Ḵooteen (1912-); Chookan sháa, who also serves as songleader and as a lead drummer for the Mt. Fairweather Dancers; Robert Zuboff/Shaadaax' (1893-1974) traditional storyteller and humorist; Johnny Jackson/Ḡooch Éesh (1893-1985), storyteller, singer, and orator; and Jessie Dalton/Naa Tlaa (1903-), an influential bilingual orator. Another well-respected orator was Austin Hammond/Daanawáaḵ (1910-1993), a traditions bearer and activist. Hammond dedicated a song to the Tlingit people just before he died for use in traditional gatherings and ceremony as the Tlingit national anthem.

PERFORMANCE AND DANCE

A widespread interest in Tlingit dancing, singing, and stories has generated the revival and development of a large number of traditional performance groups. The renowned Geisan Dancers of Haines have scheduled national and international engagements as have Kake's, Ḵeex̱' Ḵwaan Dancers, and Sealaska Heritage Foundation's NaaKahidi Theatre. Other major dance groups include the Noow Tlein Dancers of Sitka, led by Vida Davis, the acclaimed children's group, Ḡájaa Héen Dancers of Sitka, and the Mt. Fairweather Dancers (led many for years by the late T'aḵdeintaan matriarch, Katherine Mills). Other notable performance groups include the Tlingit and Haida Dancers of Anchorage, the Angoon Eagles, the Angoon Ravens, the Marks Trail Dancers, the Mt. Juneau Tlingit Dancers, the Mt. St. Elias Dancers, the Seetka Kwaan Dancers, the Killerwhale Clan, the Klukwan Chilkat Dancers, and the Klawock Heinya Dancers.

Gary Waid (1948-), has bridged the Western stage and traditional performance for nearly two decades, performing nationally and internationally in such productions as *Coyote Builds North America*, (Perseverance Theatre, as a solo actor), and *Fires on the Water* (NaaKahidi Theatre, as a leading storyteller); he has also performed in educational films such as *Shadow Walkers* (Alaska State Department of Education and Sealaska Heritage Foundation). Besides performing regularly in Alaska and on tour, Waid performed in New York with *Summer Faced Woman* (1986) and *Lilac and Flag* (1994), a Perseverance Theatre Production coproduced with the Talking Band. He also performs Shakespeare and standard western repertoire. David Kadashan/Kaatyé (1893-1976) was an avid musician in both Tlingit and contemporary Western music during the big band era, and became a traditional orator and song leader of standing. Archie James Cavanaugh is a jazz musician and recording artist, best known for his album *Black and White Raven* (1980), with some selections recorded with the late great Native American jazz saxophonist, Jim Pepper.

VISUAL ARTS

Nathan Jackson is a master carver who has exhibited his works—totem poles, masks, bentwood boxes and house fronts—in New York, London, Chicago, Salt Lake City, and Seattle. His eagle frontlet is the first aspect of Native culture to greet airline passengers deplaning in Ketchikan. Two of his 40-foot totem poles decorate the entrance to the Centennial Building in Juneau, and other areas display his restoration and reproduction work. Reggie B. Peterson (1948-) is a woodcarver, silversmith, and instructor of Northwest Coast art in Sitka, sharing his work with cultural centers and museums.

Jennie Thlunaut/Shax´saani Kéek' (1890-1986), Kaagwaantaan, award-winning master Chilkat weaver, taught the ancient weaving style to others, and thereby kept the art alive. Jennie has woven over 50 robes and tunics, and received many honors and awards. In 1983 Alaska's Governor Sheffield named a day in her honor, but she chose to share the honor by naming her day Yanwaa Sháa Day to recognize her clanswomen. Emma Marks/Seigeigéi (1913-), Lukaax̱ádi, is also acclaimed for her award-winning beadwork. Esther Littlefield of Sitka has her beaded ceremonial robes, aprons, and dance shirts on display in lodges and museums, and a younger artist, Ernestine Hanlon of Hoonah creates, sells, and displays her intricate cedar and spruce basket weavings throughout southeast Alaska.

Sue Folletti/Shax´saani Kéek' (named after Jenni Thlunaut) (1953-), Kaagwaantaan, silver carver, creates clan and story bracelets of silver and gold, traditionally designed earrings, and pendants that are sold and displayed in numerous art shows and were featured at the Smithsonian Institute during the Crossroads of the Continents traveling exhibit. Other exceptional Tlingit art craftsmen include Ed Kasko; master carver and silversmith from Klukwan, Louis Minard; master silversmith from Sitka; and developing artists like Norm Jackson, a silversmith and mask maker from Kake, and Odin Lonning (1953-), carver, silversmith, and drum maker.

MEDIA

PRINT

Naa Kaani.

The Sealaska Heritage Foundation Newsletter; provides updates on Sealaska Heritage Foundations cultural and literary projects. (English language only.)

Address: 1 Sealaska Plaza, Suite 201, Juneau, Alaska 99801.

Raven's Bones Journal.

A literary newsletter; contains reports and essays on tribal and publication issues along with listings of Native American writers and publications. (English language only.)

Contact: Andy Hope III, Editor.
Address: 523 Fourth Street, Juneau, Alaska 99801.

Sealaska Shareholder Newsletter.

A bimonthly publication of the Sealaska Corporation. The primary focus is on corporate and shareholder issues, but also reports on Tlingit, Haida, and Tsimpsian achievements and celebrations. Each issue provides a calendar of cultural, corporate, and social events. (English language only.)

Contact: Vikki Mata, Director of Corporate Communications.
Address: 1 Sealaska Plaza, Suite 400, Juneau, Alaska 99801-1276.
Telephone: (907) 586-1827.

RADIO AND TELEVISION

KTOO-FM.

A local radio and television broadcast station; does a 15-minute Native report five mornings a week. "Raincountry," a weekly program on television deals with Native affairs in Alaska focusing on issues in Tlingit country and the southeast as a whole. On Mondays the station airs the "Alaska Native News," a half-hour program, and Ray Peck Jr., Tlingit, hosts a radio jazz show. No Tlingit person is otherwise on staff for these programs.

Contact: Scott Foster.
Address: 224 Fourth Street, Juneau, Alaska 99801.
Telephone: (907) 586-1670.

ORGANIZATIONS AND ASSOCIATIONS

Alaska Native Brotherhood (ANB)/Alaska Native Sisterhood (ANS).

ANB (founded in 1912) and ANS (founded in 1915) promote community, education, and justice through a governing grand camp and operating subordinate camps (local ANB and ANS groups). Native education and equal rights are some of the many issues addressed by the membership, as are Tlingit and Haida well being and social standing.

Contact: Ron Williams, President.
Address: 320 West Willoughby Avenue, Juneau, Alaska 99801.
Telephone: (907) 586-2049.

Central Council of the Tlingit and Haida Indian Tribes of Alaska (CCTHITA).

Founded in 1965. Provides trust services through Bureau of Indian Affairs (BIA) to Tlingit and Haida people and Tlingit and Haida villages in land allotment cases, operates health and tribal employment programs, and issues educational grants and scholarships.

Contact: Edward Thomas, President.
Address: 320 West Willoughby Avenue, Suite 300, Juneau, Alaska 99801-9983.
Telephone: (907) 586-1432.

Organized Village of Kake.

Founded in 1947 under the Indian Reorganization Act. Contracts with the Bureau of Indian Affairs (BIA) to provide services to the tribe such as counseling referral, general assistance, assistance in Indian Child Welfare Act (ICWA) issues, education and cultural development, scholarships, and housing improvement. Through a Johnson O'Malley BIA contract they provide supplemental education and culture/language classes. The organization also handles its own tribal land trust responsibilities.

Contact: Gary Williams, Executive Director; or, Henrich Kadake, President.

Address: P.O. Box 316, Kake, Alaska 99830.

Telephone: (907) 785-6471.

Sitka Tribe of Alaska (STA).

Chartered in 1938 under the Indian Reorganization Act as the Sitka Community Association, STA is a federally recognized tribe and operates contracts under the Bureau of Indian Affairs (BIA). STA has an extensive social services program, providing counseling, crisis intervention, employment services, housing improvement, youth and education programs, economic development, and historic preservation. STA also supports a tribal court.

Contact: Ted Wright, General Manager; or, Larry Widmark, Tribal Chair.

Address: 456 Katlian Street, Sitka, Alaska 99835.

Telephone: (907) 747-3207.

Yakutat Native Association (YNA).

Founded in 1983. Provides family services to the tribe through Bureau of Indian Affairs (BIA) contracts. YNA's Johnson O'Malley program provides dance instruction, runs a culture camp in the summer, and is in the processes of developing a language program.

Contact: Nellie Valle.

Address: P.O. Box 418, Yakutat, Alaska 99689.

Telephone: (907) 784-3238.

MUSEUMS AND RESEARCH CENTERS

Alaska State Museum.

Houses a varied collection of southeast Alaska Indian art, with elaborate displays of traditional Tlingit regalia, carvings, artifacts, and totem designs.

Address: 395 Whittier Street, Juneau, Alaska.

Telephone: (907) 465-2901.

Sheldon Jackson Museum.

Houses Tlingit regalia, a canoe, a large spruce root basket collection, and other traditional items and artifacts including house posts, hooks, woodworking tools, bentwood boxes, and armor. The museum also contains a large variety of Aleut and Eskimo art. The museum's gift shop sells baskets and other Tlingit art.

Address: 104 College Drive, Sitka, Alaska 99835.

Telephone: (907) 747-8981.

Sheldon Museum and Cultural Center.

Shares the history of Haines, the gold rush era, and Tlingit art in the displays. The center provides books and flyers on different aspects of Tlingit art and history, as well as live demonstrations in traditional crafts.

Address: P.O. Box 623, Haines, Alaska 99827.

Telephone: (907) 766-2366.

Southeast Alaska Indian Cultural Center.

Displays a model panorama of the Tlingit battles against the Russians in 1802 and 1804, elaborate carved house posts, and artifacts. The center shows historic films and has a large totem park outside the structure. Classes are conducted in Tlingit carving, silversmithing, and beadwork, and artists remain in-house to complete their own projects.

Address: 106 Metlakatla, Sitka, Alaska 99835.

Telephone: (907) 747-8061.

Totem Heritage Center.

Promotes Tlingit and Haida carving and traditional art forms and designs by firsthand instruction. The center maintains brochures and other information on artists in the area as well as instructional literature.

Address: City of Ketchikan, Museum Department, 629 Dock Street, Ketchikan, Alaska 99901.

Telephone: (907) 225-5600.

SOURCES FOR ADDITIONAL STUDY

Case, David S. *Alaska Natives and American Laws.* University of Alaska Press, 1984.

Cole, Douglas. *Captured Heritage: The Scramble for Northwest Coast Artifacts.* Seattle: University of Washington Press, 1985.

Dauenhauer, Nora Marks, and Richard Dauenhauer. *Haa Ḵusteeyí, Our Culture: Tlingit Life Stories.* Seattle: University of Washington Press; and Juneau, Alaska: Sealaska Heritage Foundation, 1994.

Dauenhauer, Nora Marks, and Richard Dauenhauer. *Haa Tuwunáagu Yís, for Healing Our Spirit: Tlingit Oratory.* Seattle: University of Washington Press; and Juneau, Alaska: Sealaska Heritage Foundation, 1990.

Emmons, George Thornton. *The Tlingit Indians.* Seattle: University of Washington Press, 1991.

Garfield, Viola E., and Linn A. Forrest. *The Wolf and The Raven: Totem Poles of Southeastern Alaska.* Seattle: University of Washington Press, 1993.

Jonaitis, Aldona. *Art of the Northern Tlingit.* Seattle, Washington: University of Washington Press, 1986.

Langdon, Steve J. *The Native People of Alaska.* Anchorage, Alaska: Greatland Graphics, 1987.

Samuel, Cheryl. *The Chilkat Dancing Blanket.* Seattle: Pacific Search Press, 1982.

Steward, Hilary. *Looking at Totem Poles.* Seattle: University of Washington Press, 1993.

Despite Trinidad and Tobago's culturally diverse people, the family, regardless of ethnic background, fulfills certain basic roles. In the United States, it is the family's responsibility to maintain traditions and enforce strong family values in the community.

TRINIDADIAN AND TOBAGONIAN AMERICANS

by
N. Samuel
Murrell

OVERVIEW

Located on the northeastern coast of Venezuela, the Republic of Trinidad and Tobago comprises the two most southerly islands in the West Indies. Tobago, which lies 20 miles northeast of Trinidad, measures only 117 square miles. Trinidad, which has a land mass of 1,865 square miles, is about the size of Delaware. The Republic's capital, Port of Spain, is an important commercial center, producing beer, rum, plastics, lumber, and textiles. Chief exports of Trinidad and Tobago include oil, sugar, citrus fruit, asphalt, and coffee.

Trinidad and Tobago have approximately 1.27 million residents, most of whom live on Trinidad. While the population of Tobago is predominantly black, Trinidad supports several ethnic groups, including Asian Indians (40.3 percent), blacks (39.6 percent), Europeans, Chinese, and Lebanese (one percent). The remaining 18 percent includes individuals of mixed heritage. Roman Catholics (29.4 percent), Hindus (23.8 percent), Protestant Christians (12 percent), Anglicans (10.9 percent), and Muslims (5.8 percent) are the dominant religious groups of the islands.

The Republic's national flag has a black diagonal band edged with white on a red background. Trinidad and Tobago's national anthem "Side By Side We Stand" echoes the country's commitment to racial and ethnic diversity: "Forged from the love of liberty, / In the fires of hope and prayer, / With boundless faith in our destiny, / We solemnly declare. / Side by side we stand. / Islands of the blue Caribbean sea, / This is our native land. / We pledge our lives to thee, / Here every creed and race / Finds an equal place, / And may God bless our nation."

HISTORY

The history of Trinidad and Tobago is one of invasion, conquest, and colonization. On July 31, 1498, Christopher Columbus discovered the islands, which were inhabited by about 40,000 native peoples (Arawaks and Caribs) whom he called Indians. Columbus named the larger island Trinidad, in honor of the Holy Trinity, and called Tobago (the legendary island of *Robinson Crusoe*) Concepcion. The islands' native population began disappearing, largely from exposure to European diseases and poor treatment, shortly after the founding of the first city, San Josef de Quna (Saint Joseph), in 1592. By 1783 the native population was reduced to less than 1,490 people and by 1800 they were virtually extinct.

Trinidad remained an underdeveloped outpost for almost 200 years until the King of Spain issued the Cedular of Population in 1783 and began enticing planters to migrate to Trinidad with their slaves. In 1791 thousands of French colonists, fleeing the French Revolution in Saint Domingue, settled in Trinidad, bringing enslaved Africans with them. While Trinidad was largely ignored during the early years of colonization, Tobago fell to a number of European explorers. The island passed through the hands of Great Britain, France, Holland, and other invading European countries at least 22 times during its history, until it was finally ceded to Britain in 1814. In January 1889 Trinidad and Tobago united as one nation under British rule. Africans were brought to Tobago as slaves in the early 1600s but were not imported into Trinidad in great numbers until the early 1700s. After the British government abolished slavery in 1834, Asian Indian and Chinese laborers were brought to Trinidad as indentured servants. Between 1842 and 1917, over 170,000 Asian Indians, Chinese, and Portuguese (from Madeira) were enticed into working on the islands' vast plantations. Lured by the fertile soil and unexplored natural resources, many former American slaves migrated to the island as well. Consequently, by 1900 more than 70,000 blacks had settled in Trinidad and Tobago.

MODERN ERA

Trinidad and Tobago was governed by British royalists and dominated by Scottish, French, and Spanish colonists until its independence in 1962. Prior to independence, non-whites had little or no voice in government affairs. After World War I, however, they began protesting through strikes and demonstrations organized by such civil rights leaders as Arthur Cipriani, Uriah Buzz Butler, and others involved with the powerful Oil Field Workers Trade Union and the Manual and Metal Workers Union.

In 1947 the British Government plotted the formation of a West Indian federation, which came to fruition in 1958. They chose Port of Spain as the capital. The federation was designed to foster political and cultural solidarity and to break down economic barriers among the islands. The federation collapsed in 1961, however, when Jamaica seceded from the union, becoming an independent nation. Trinidad and Tobago attained independence on August 31, 1962, and became a republic within The Commonwealth in 1976. In 1965 Trinidad and Tobago joined the Organization of American States (OAS) and the Caribbean Free Trade Area (Carifta) which was renamed the Caribbean Community (Caricom) in 1974. Trinidad and Tobago enjoyed substantial prosperity from the 1960s to the early 1980s due to the success of the oil industry, but prices plummeted in the late 1980s, sending the country into a serious recession.

THE FIRST TRINIDADIANS AND TOBAGONIANS IN THE UNITED STATES

Trinidadian and Tobagonian immigration to the United States, which dates back to the seventeenth century, was spasmodic and is best studied in relation to the major waves of Caribbean immigration. The first documented account of black immigration to the United States from the Caribbean dates back to 1619, when a small group of voluntary indentured workers arrived in Jamestown, Virginia, on a Dutch frigate. The immigrants worked as free people until 1629 when a Portuguese vessel arrived with the first shipload of blacks captured off the west coast of Africa. In the 1640s Virginia and other states began instituting laws that took away the freedom of blacks and redefined them as chattel, or personal property. Trinidad, like many other islands in the British West Indies, served as a clearinghouse for slaves en route to North America. The region also acted as a "seasoning camp" where newly arrived blacks were "broken-in" psychologically and physically to a life of slavery, as well as a place where they acquired biological resistance to deadly European diseases.

SIGNIFICANT IMMIGRATION WAVES

Since the turn of the twentieth century, there have been three distinct waves of Caribbean immigrants into the United States. The first wave was modest and lasted from about 1900 to the 1920s. Between 1899 and 1924, the number of documented, English-speaking Caribbean immigrants entering the United States increased annually from 412 in 1899 to 12,245 in 1924, although the actual number of Caribbean residents in the United States was probably twice as high. Immigration fell substantially after 1924 when the U.S. government established national quotas on African and Caribbean countries. By 1930 there were only 177,981 documented foreign blacks in the United States—less than two percent of the aggregate black population. Approximately 72,200 of the foreign blacks were first-generation emigrants from the English-speaking Caribbean.

Most Trinidadians and Tobagonians who entered the United States during that period were industrial workers, civil servants, laborers, and former soldiers disillusioned by the high unemployment rate in Trinidad and Tobago after World War I. The number of new arrivals dropped significantly during the Great Depression (1932-1937) when more blacks returned to the Caribbean than came to the United States. Only a small number of professionals and graduate students migrated to America prior to World War II, some with the intention of staying for a short time on a student or worker's visa, and others planning to remain permanently.

The second and weakest immigration wave from the Caribbean to the United States was rather sporadic and occurred between the late 1930s and the passage of new immigration policies in the 1960s. As late as the 1950s, the number of Trinidadians and Tobagonians arriving in the United States was low in comparison to other foreign countries. This was partially due to the passage of the 1952 McCarran-Walter Act, which reaffirmed the quota bill and further restricted Caribbean immigration to America. The differential treatment of African and Caribbean peoples by immigration authorities, in contrast to Europeans, also discouraged the migration of Trinidadians and Tobagonians. After the Republic achieved independence in 1962, only 100 Trinidadian and Tobagonian immigrants were permitted to enter the United States annually.

Still, a small group, mainly from Trinidad's middle class, migrated between the waning of the Depression and the changing of U.S. immigration laws. This group consisted mainly of white-collar workers, students, and people joining their families already living in the United States. With the opening of a U.S. Naval Base on Trinidad in 1940, Trinidadian and Tobagonian military personnel were stationed in the U.S. Virgin Islands and Florida, and some served under U.S. and British command in Europe. After World War II, some of these soldiers migrated to America in search of jobs and improved economic opportunity. Because of laws restricting immigration, only 2,598 documented Trinidadian and Tobagonian immigrants entered the United States between 1960 and 1965.

The third and largest wave of Caribbean immigration began in 1965 and continues into the present. It was greatly influenced by the American civil rights movement, which exposed the racism inherent in U.S. immigration policy. The 1965 Hart-Cellar Immigration Reform Act, which established uniform limits of no more than 20,000 persons per country annually for the eastern hemisphere, enabled Trinidadian and Tobagonian immigrants to seek legal immigration and naturalization status in larger numbers. A clause in the Act of 1965, which gave preference to immigrants whose relatives were already U.S. citizens and therefore capable of sponsoring immigrants, also encouraged many Trinidadian and Tobagonian residents to migrate to the United States.

From 1966 to 1970, 23,367 Trinidadian and Tobagonian immigrants, primarily from the educated elite and rural poor classes, legally migrated to the United States. From 1971 to 1975, the figure climbed to 33,278. It dropped to 28,498 from 1976 to 1980, and only half that amount between 1981 and 1984, when the Reagan administration began placing greater restrictions on U.S. immigration policy. Less than 2,300 Trinidadian and Tobagonian immigrants arrived in 1984 and that number scarcely increased during President Reagan's second term of office. A few European-Trinidadians migrated during the latter half of the twentieth century, primarily because they were loosing their grip on political power in the Republic with the rise of nationalism and independence. The majority of those immigrants came to the United States because Britain had restricted immigration from the Commonwealth islands to the British Isles. A larger number migrated in the late 1980s when oil prices fell,

This family portrait of Charles Petioni (seated), along with his brother and sister, was taken before he left Trinidad and Tobago for the United States in 1918.

sending the Republic into a deep recession. Trinidadians and Tobagonians are now the second largest group of English-speaking immigrants in the United States.

SETTLEMENT

A total of 76,270 Trinidadians and Tobagonians, who reported at least one specific ancestry, are documented in the 1990 U.S Census. Of this number, 71,720, or 94 percent, of the aggregate are first generation Trinidadian Tobagonian Americans, and the remaining 4,550 are of the second generation. There were 58,473 such persons in the northeast, 1,760 in the midwest, 18,215 in the south, and 3,822 in the west. Regionally, there were 3,746 Trinidadian and Tobagonian immigrants in New England, 48,727 in the middle Atlantic, 1,523 in east north central United States, 237 in the west north central, 15,096 in the south Atlantic, 549 in east south central, 2,570 in the west south central, 446 in the mountain region, and 3,376 in the Pacific region. The largest percentage of Trinidadians and Tobagonians live in the northeast and the smallest percentage in the midwest. They ranked sixth in the 1965-1980 census report of newcomers into New York City, and rank eighth in the city's 15 largest ethnic groups. By 1982, over half of the Trinidadians and Tobagonians in America resided in New York City.

According to the 1990 Census, the six states that have the largest Trinidadian and Tobagonian populations are: New York (42,973), Florida (7,500), Maryland (4,493), New Jersey (4,245), California (3,100), and Massachusetts (2,590). Family connections, employment opportunities, racial tolerance, access to higher education, and weather conditions are some of the reasons given for the heavy concentration of Trinidadian and Tobagonian immigrants on the eastern seaboard.

ACCULTURATION AND ASSIMILATION

Trinidadian and Tobagonian immigrants generally select one of two options: they either make a quick livelihood in the United States before returning home, or they join American society permanently, usually immersing themselves in black culture and working for the betterment of African American and Caribbean American communities. Many of the early Trinidadians and Tobagonians aged 35 and older did return to their native land. Later immigrants often chose the second option and increasingly became part of the distinctly Caribbean community in New York City and Florida.

Trinidadian and Tobagonian immigrants have had to adjust in a number of ways while assimilating into American society. First, those who are permanent residents must adjust nationally, which often means giving up their Trinidad and Tobago citizenship and strong ties to Caribbean nationalism for American citizenship and values. Secondly, they must adjust to the cultural traditions, social roles, and stereotypes of the racial and ethnic groups with which they identify. Trinidadian and Tobagonian immigrants of the first and second waves arrived in the United States at the height of Jim Crow segregation and, consequently, suffered tremendous racial prejudice. Even though they came from a society where racial categories and stereotypes were not unknown, they resented having to fight virtually every social, political, and economic issue in American society. Third, they must adjust to severe variations in weather patterns, particularly in the north, which, for older generations, is especially difficult. Some immigrants have also had to adjust to life in some of America's roughest neighborhoods. Although friends, relatives, and other sponsors advise them of dangerous neighborhoods, many become casualties of urban crime. Traditionally "safe" Caribbean neighborhoods in New York City, for example, have become battle zones for gangs and drug dealers. Moreover, Trinidadian and Tobagonian immigrants living in non-Caribbean communities often feel isolated; they carry the dual burden of speaking with a foreign accent and being visibly identifiable as a minority in a European-based society. Finally, these immigrants come from a country where they represented the majority and many of them were highly respected leaders. In the United States, however, they must adjust to their new status of "resident aliens."

TRADITIONS, CUSTOMS, AND BELIEFS

Trinidad and Tobago is a multi-faceted country with a perfusion of customs and traditions that meet to form the "Trinibago" culture. Two of the most dominant cultures in Trinidad and Tobago are mixed-black (often called Creole) and Asian Indian. The first is a mixture of African, English, Spanish, and French cultures. Spanish influence is evident in the islands' music, festivals (especially the Parang festival), and dance. Even though France never occupied Trinidad, French planters on the island left their unmistakable mark in terms of language, religion, and class consciousness. The Republic's Asian Indian culture is celebrated through *Divali* (Festival of Lights), *Hosay* (Muslim New Year festival), East Indian music, and various philosophical beliefs and practices foreign to western cultures. For example, everyone is expected to take off their shoes at the door before stepping inside an Indian Muslim house, and new homes are often blessed in a special ceremony. There are rites for conception, birth, puberty, marriage, death, and the planting and harvesting of crops.

CUISINE

Trinidadians and Tobagonians have retained many of their cooking traditions in the United States, although eating habits have changed somewhat to better suit America's fast pace. Breakfast often varies from a full meal to a very light one and may include fresh coconut water and coconut jelly. Because Trinidad and Tobago is a highly Westernized nation, oatmeal, cornflakes, cocoa, coffee, and rolls are also common breakfast foods. Lunches and dinners generally consist of meat, rice, green vegetables, and fruits. One popular Trinidadian and Tobagonian dish is *pelau*, or rice mixed with pork or chicken and various local vegetables. *Calaloo* (a green, leafy vegetable that is served cooked) is sometimes combined with taro, dasheen, or tania leaves, okra, pumpkin, and crab to make a dish called calaloo and crab. Other popular dishes are dumpling and pig-tail or cow-heel soup, *souse* (well-cooked pickled pigs feet), and chicken stew. Most dishes contain meat, or fish although many of the favorites in Trinidad and Tobago (manicou, tatoo, venison, armadillo, lappe, quenk, duck, shark, flying fish, shrimp, kingfish, chip-chip, and cascadou) are not readily available in the United States. Such vegetables as pumpkin, cabbage, onion, and *melongenes* (eggplant) are also well liked. Coconut ice cream and fruits are popular Trinidadian and Tobagonian desserts. Many meals, especially during special occasions, are served with *mauby* (a drink made from the bark of a tree), Guinness stout, and Carib and Stag beers.

Asian Indian dishes of Trinidad and Tobago include *roti* (usually made of beef, chicken, or goat with potatoes and spices wrapped in flat bread), *dalpori* (balled spiced dough usually accompanied by a sauce), channa, and curry goat. Two special dishes of Tobago are curry crab and dumplings and *accra*, which is seasoned salt fish pounded and shaped into small cakes and fried. Some foods are eaten seasonally, in keeping with harvest time and religious traditions. Trinidadians and Tobagonians in the United States often substitute their native dishes with American foods, and prepare traditional foods only when dining with family or during special occasions.

TRADITIONAL COSTUMES

In their homeland, Trinidadians and Tobagonians wear a variety of clothing suited for the tropics. In the United States, however, only people of Asian Indian descent have retained their unique cultural dress. Blacks from the Republic have no special costumes, except for carnival dress, which cuts across racial and ethnic lines. Carnival costumes are elaborate and costly, ranging in form, shape, size, design, and taste; some festival clothing is simply massive and requires the support of cars and trucks, while other pieces may consist of loin cloths and beads. Carnival costuming in Trinidad and Tobago and in New York City (where a Carnival takes place every year) is an extremely expensive cultural and commercial affair, providing department, fabric, hardware, and other stores with hundreds of millions of dollars in revenue every year. Designers Peter Minshall, Peter Samuel, and Edmond Hart are especially well known in the United States for their costume talents.

TRINIDADIAN AND TOBAGONIAN MUSIC AND DANCE

In New York City and Miami it is not uncommon to hear *paring* (music sung in Castilian) and *chawta* (Asian Indian drumming and vocals) in predominantly Caribbean neighborhoods. But the most popular Trinidadian and Tobagonian music in the United States is calypso and *soca* (a derivation of calypso). These sounds are known for their fast beat, heavy percussion, and social expression.

Calypso originated in Trinidad among African slaves in the 1800s. Although it has its roots in African oral traditions, it was sung in French dialect until 1883 when calypsonians began singing in English. Calypsonians play an important role in Caribbean society, functioning as poets, philosophers, and social commentators within social, political, and religious circles. The Mighty Sparrow's "Jean and Dinah," which won the Carnival crown in 1956, represents the linkage between calypso, society, culture, and politics. Sparrow's 1962 calypso, "Model Nation," captures the feelings of Trinidadians and Tobagonians toward their newly achieved status of independence: "The whole population of our little nation / Is not a lot; / But, oh what a mixture of races and culture / That's what we got; / Still no major indifference / Of race, color, religion, or finance; / It's amazing to you, I'm sure, / We didn't get our independence before."

These Trinidadian and Tobagonian musicians are playing steel drums for the Carnival celebration in Brooklyn, New York.

During the 1980s, calypso also became a forum for discussing women's rights. Although they may be less popular than The Mighty Sparrow, such female calypsonians as Singing Francine, Lady Jane, Twiggy, and Denise Plummer have established their voices in Trinidadian and Tobagonian society. Their message is two-fold: women should not tolerate abuse and men should treat women as equals, especially in domestic partnerships.

Trinidad and Tobago is known for its lively rhythmic dances set to the tunes of calypso and steelband music. Immigrants from the Republic perform a variety of dances, including ballet, folk dancing, limbo, wining, hula hoop, *gayelle* (stick dancing), and *mocojumby* (a costumed dancer on stilts). Jump up, a celebrative, emotionally charged, and physically exhausting dance, has a free-for-all style, and is usually performed during Carnival.

HOLIDAYS

Special holidays celebrated by Trinidadians and Tobagonians include: Emancipation Day (August 1), Independence Day (August 31), Republic Day (September 24), and Boxing Day (December 26). Other popular festivals in Trinidad and Tobago are *Phagwa* (honoring the Hindu god Lord Krishna), *Divali* (a Hindu celebration with millions of lights honoring Mother Laskami), and *Hosay* (the

Muslim New Year festival). However, Carnival is perhaps the best known of Trinidadian and Tobagonian holidays; it takes place from Friday through Tuesday before Ash Wednesday of the Lenten season.

Carnival was introduced to Trinidad by the French as an urban festival celebrated by the upper class until emancipation. It then became a festival for all classes, allowing people to break from their normal routine and, through calypso, indirectly attack and ridicule the government. Preparation for this festival begins immediately after Christmas and Panorama (the Grand Steel Drum tournament), or one week before Carnival. On the first night of Carnival there is a "pan around the neck" competition. The "junior carnival" takes place on Saturday and the "panorama finals" on Saturday night. On Sunday night, able calypsonians vie for the title of "calypso monarch" at the *Dimanche Gras,* and the "King and Queen of Carnival" are named. (In 1994 Americans were able to view the *Dimanche Gras* via satellite.) Monday and Tuesday see lots of "carnivalling," or dancing and masquerading with fantastic costumes. On the final day of Carnival, celebrants drink and dance to the point of exhaustion.

In the United States Carnival is a method by which Trinidadian and Tobagonian immigrants maintain their Afro-Caribbean heritage. It was first celebrated in New York in the 1920s as a privately sponsored indoor family affair during the pre-Lenten season, but later evolved into New York City's Labor Day Carnival (called West Indian Day Carnival). The celebration, modeled after Trinidad and Tobago's Carnival, is one of the largest scheduled street events in New York, rivaling Saint Patrick's Day and Macy's Thanksgiving Day Parades. The celebration, held since 1969, was first organized by Jesse Wattle on the streets of Harlem and was moved to the Eastern Parkway in Brooklyn a few years later by Rufus Gorin. The festival features four nights of concerts, a steel band contest, and children's pageants on the grounds of the Brooklyn Museum. The Labor Day Carnival climaxes with a lengthy procession on the Eastern Parkway. Its overall purpose is to promote unity among Caribbeans and Americans.

PROVERBS

Many of the proverbs in Trinidad and Tobago are European in origin but some sayings from Afro-Caribbean and Asian Indian cultures have been preserved as well. British-inspired proverbs include: In for a penny, in for a pound; A penny wise and a pound foolish; and, Make hay while the sun shines. Popular Afro-Caribbean sayings include: Do not cut you nose to patch you bottom; If you see you neighbor house catch fire wet yours; No money no love; A man who cannot rule his house is *tootoolbay*; What you head consent you bottom pay for; and Don't dance with two left feet. Two common Asian Indian proverbs are: Corn "nuh" grow where rain "nuh" fall; and Don't trust you neighbor unless you neighbor trusts you.

HEALTH AND MENTAL HEALTH ISSUES

There are no documented medical problems unique to Trinidadians and Tobagonians in the United States or in Trinidad and Tobago. A few cases of leprosy were found in Trinidad and Tobago but these were isolated and did not pose a national threat to either the Republic or the United States. During the 1970s, alcohol and drug abuse was relatively low but it has increased steadily in the last decade. In 1987 alcoholism was named the most serious drug abuse problem in the nation with marijuana and cocaine following close behind.

The average life expectancy in Trinidad and Tobago is 73 years for women, and 68 years for men. Major causes of death among adults include heart disease, cerebrovascular disease, malignant neoplasms, and diabetes mellitus. The infant mortality rate is relatively low; 17 of every 1,000 babies die in their first year. In the United States, life expectancy among Trinidadians and Tobagonians has decreased somewhat due to socio-economic, health, and crime conditions. Most Trinidadians and Tobagonians use either free or low-cost medical care provided by the government of Trinidad and Tobago, and, compared to other developing countries, they enjoy relatively good health. Some families living in the United States have health insurance coverage through their jobs. The unemployed must depend upon the good will of others and the U.S. government.

LANGUAGE

As a former British colony, the official language of Trinidad and Tobago is English, although Hindi is also spoken widely in Indian communities, both in the Republic and in the United States. French, Spanish, and English patios are also common, as well as Hindustani, a dialect of Phojpuri Hindi. Trinidadians and Tobagonians speak English with a wide variety of accents and innovations due to the impact of Spanish, French, Indian, and African languages. The styles of English therefore range from standard British English, usually spoken in formal conversations, to the more common Trinidad English, a mixture of Spanish, French, British, and African. It must be noted, however, that no sharp break exists between Trinidad English and standard English.

GREETINGS AND OTHER POPULAR EXPRESSIONS

Trinidadian and Tobagonian greetings include: "Wah happenen day?" (casual); "How is the daughter doing?" (casual); "Take care daughter" (good-bye to a young woman friend); "Good morning" (with a heavy accent on morning); "good evening;" "good night;" "Merry Christmas;" "Happy holiday;" "Happy Birthday;" "Happy Easter" (Some Christians say "Christ is Risen"); "Happy New Year;" "Good luck;" and "God's Speed." Some devout Hindus and Muslims greet with the name *Krishna* or *Allah*, respectively.

FAMILY AND COMMUNITY DYNAMICS

Despite Trinidad and Tobago's culturally diverse people, the family, regardless of ethnic background, fulfills certain basic roles. In the United States, it is the family's responsibility to maintain traditions and enforce strong family values in the community. Traditionally, Trinidadian and Tobagonian men were the sole providers of income for their families while women were held accountable for raising children and managing the home. Since the mid-1970s, however, family planning and sexual abuse legislation have enabled Trinidadian and Tobagonian women to enjoy the same educational, professional, and proprietorial rights as men. Many of these women have entered traditionally male-dominated fields such as medicine, law, and journalism. In the United States, where two-income families are often the rule rather than the exception, Trinidadian and Tobagonian women often work as office clerks, nurses, and domestics. They also participate in community government, money management, and child care.

Trinidadian and Tobagonian immigrants with legal status are often active in civic and political affairs and take a keen interest in their children's education by joining the Parent Teacher Association, attending school board meetings, and participating in neighborhood watch programs. There is a high literacy rate among Trinidadian and Tobagonian immigrants in the United States, resulting from the high premium they place on education. In fact, they are often critical of the American education system, which contrasts sharply with the strong British educational system of their homeland. Some Trinidadian and Tobagonian immigrants try to shield their children from racism and miseducation by sending them to private schools either taught or founded by Caribbean people. St. Mark's Academy, founded in Crown Heights, New York, in 1977 by a Guyanese man, has educated hundreds of Caribbean students, many of whom are now leaders in their communities.

WEDDINGS

In ancient Indian traditions, Hindu authorities prescribed eight different forms of marriages, or *ashrams*, but only two of these were ever practiced among Trinidadian and Tobagonian Asian Indians. The more traditional of these, which is no longer practiced, was called *aqua* (matchmaker) and dictated that parents choose their children's partners. Such marriages took place at a young age, usually puberty because it was believed that postponing the wedding of a daughter for too long would bring bad luck. The ritual itself (*panigrahana* and *homa*) involved performing a *saptapadi* (a seven-steps ritual) around a fire. While the selection process occurred when the children were very young, the couple usually did not know their mates' identity until they became teenagers. In most traditional Hindu weddings, the groom is not allowed to see his bride until late in the ceremony, after she exchanges her yellow sari for a red one.

In modern times, Hindu marriages involve bargaining between the two sets of parents and a change of status for the bride and groom. Often there is a short preliminary ceremony, or *chheka*, during which the family priest and the father of the bride travel to the house of the prospective groom to deliver a dowry. By accepting the token sum, the groom is obligated to marry the young woman. The main ceremony takes place at the bride's home, and friends and relatives assist in setting up the *mantro* (nuptial tent). The wedding is followed by a large reception, with music, jokes,

singing, chanting, beating drums, and the throwing of oil, rice, and flowers in the air. Often there is another ceremony and feast at the groom's home. Muslim marriages allow the groom up to four wives but Hindu weddings join only two people and their families. Because of their legal entanglements and non-Christian nature, Muslim marriages were not recognized in Trinidad and Tobago before 1930, and Hindu weddings were not considered legal before 1946. In the United States, Trinidadian and Tobagonian Muslims and Hindus marry according to U.S. laws but retain some of their ceremonial traditions.

Most Afro-Caribbean weddings follow Christian traditions. There is an engagement period which lasts from a few months to many years. Traditionally, the bride's parents were responsible for supplying the bride's dress and the cost of the reception, and the groom and his parents provided the ring and the new home. In the United States this practice varies. In some cases, the parties are already living together and the wedding ceremony only legalizes the relationship in the eyes of the law and the community. In Trinidad and Tobago, young working women occasionally rent a flat and invite a man to live with them. Lovers who are strict Christians, however, generally do not live together before marriage. In the wedding ceremony, the bride wears white, symbolizing chastity, and large numbers of people are invited to observe the event. In Trinidad and Tobago, most wedding receptions are community events, marked by large quantities of food and rum.

BAPTISMS

Trinidadians and Tobagonians generally practice two forms of baptism: infant baptisms and adult baptisms. Among the more traditional Christian denominations (Catholics, Anglicans, Lutherans, Presbyterians, and Methodists), infants are baptized by sprinkling water on their heads. When they reach the age of accountability, a confirmation ceremony is performed. In other Protestant Christian and Afro-centric Christian traditions, the infants are blessed at a dedication ceremony and baptized after their faith in Christ is confessed voluntarily. The subjects are dipped into a river, the sea, or a baptismal fount near the sanctuary by a minister or an elder of the Church. Shangoes and Spiritual Baptists often dip blindfolded individuals three times into the river or sea. Some of these baptismal practices operate underground in the United States.

FUNERALS

Because of the multifaceted nature of its religious culture, Trinidad and Tobago have many different funeral practices. Since Hindus believe that death cannot harm the immortal soul, a dying person is administered a tulsi leaf and water. Asian Indians in Trinidad and Tobago began cremating their dead after 1930 and the practice was carried over to the United States. The funeral is an elaborate ceremony and males may shave their heads, leaving only a lock of hair in the center, on the tenth day of mourning for an immediate family member.

Afro-centric religions (Obeah, Shango, and Shouter Baptist) and Christians bury their dead after performing special rites or conducting a formal funeral church service. A Catholic priest recites the last rites to a dying member of the Church and may offer mass for a soul that may have departed to purgatory before making peace with God. On the night before the funeral, there is a wake for the dead, during which friends and family come to offer condolences, sing dirges, and drink rum. Afro-centric religions have a Nine Night service to ensure that the shadow of the deceased does not return on the ninth evening after death to visit family members. This practice is occasionally performed after Christian, Muslim, and Hindu deaths as well.

INTERACTION WITH OTHER ETHNIC GROUPS

Given their peculiar circumstances, Trinidadians and Tobagonians have adjusted remarkably well to American society by establishing strong social, religious, economic, and political ties with both black and white communities and institutions, a dualism which often puzzles many African Americans. Both Trinidadian and Tobagonian immigrants and native-born blacks often misunderstand one another as a result of stereotypes and misconceptions. This often leads to interracial conflict. Nonetheless, in Crown Heights, Flatbush, and other New York City neighborhoods, Trinidadians have some of the largest churches and most successful businesses in the black community, and are a vital part of the city's economy.

RELIGION

Because of British, Spanish, and French influences, most Trinidadian and Tobagonian citizens are associated, in some way, with Christianity. People of Asian Indian descent on the islands practice Hindu and Islam. Still, a small number of people (nine percent) follow the African-centered religions of Shango, Rada, Spiritual Baptist, Obeah, and Rastafari. Shango and Spiritual Baptist, also known as "Shouters," are the two most common Afro-centric religious traditions, although Rastafari is growing in popularity. Trinidadian Shango, which is part of the legacy of African traditional culture and religion, incorporates a mixture of Catholic rituals and elements of African spiritual beliefs. Spiritual Baptists place great emphasis on participatory worship, while the Shango religion focuses on animal sacrifices, drums, and supernatural manifestations. "Obeah people," sometimes called "shadow catchers," believe they have supernatural powers and can control the spirits of the living and the dead. Followers of this religion believe that they can harness a shadow by forcing it to do specific protective tasks. Because of the negative stigma that other religious groups and the general Trinidadian and Tobagonian public have attached to these folk religions, it is difficult to tell how many immigrants are Spiritual Baptist, Shango, or Obeah followers in the United States. In order to be inconspicuous, many followers of such religions meet in private.

EMPLOYMENT AND ECONOMIC TRADITIONS

Economically, Trinidadian and Tobagonian experiences in the United States have been mixed. Individuals who are not living in America legally, as well as those who are waiting for legal status, tend to be exploited by employers and landlords. Conversely, legal immigrants from Trinidad and Tobago, who are often well educated, work in a variety of occupations.

POLITICS AND GOVERNMENT

Caribbean people have been active in American politics since the early 1800s. After slavery was abolished in the British West Indies in 1834, a number of Trinidadians, Jamaicans, and Barbadians supported the African repatriation movement and worked for the abolition of slavery in collaboration with their black counterparts in the United States. This political activity led to what became known as the Pan-African Movement, supported by W.E.B. DuBois, Marcus Garvey, and others.

The Trinidad-born attorney, H. Sylvester Williams, who had ties to the United States, was one of the leaders of the first Pan-African Congress which met in London in 1900.

During the 1920s, Caribbean immigrants were drawn to Socialist and Black Nationalist groups in the United States; the majority of the members in Marcus Garvey's Universal Negro Improvement Association were from the West Indies. Caribbean American political activity reached a new level in the mid-1930s when Trinidadian and Tobagonian immigrants began playing an important role in the Democratic party in New York. Mervyn Dymally, a Trinidadian immigrant, founded the Caribbean Action Lobby to mobilize ethnic ties into a political interest group focusing on international and local relations. The first black to serve as Lt. Governor in California and the first foreign-born person elected to the U.S. Congress, he was a leading proponent for aid to the English-speaking Caribbean. Other notable politicians were Maurice Gumbs, the founder of The Harriet Tubman Democratic Club, and Ernest Skinner, who ran for City Council in Flatbush, New York, in 1985. While Skinner lost the election, he paved the way for other West Indian Americans.

George Padmore, the great pan-Africanist who was highly decorated in Ghana, founded the International African Service Bureau. In the 1930s and 1940s Padmore, C.L.R. James, and Eric Williams joined W. E. B. DuBois and others in criticizing foreign interference in Africa and discrimination against blacks in the United States. In the 1960s Trinidadian Stokely Carmichael (1941- ; also known as Kwame Toure), a black nationalist and civil rights organizer, served as a major force behind the Student Nonviolent Coordinating Committee (SNCC). His two books, *Black Power Politics of Liberation in America* and *Stokely Speaks: Black Power Back to Pan-Africanism*, are highly regarded in political circles. In the late 1960s, the Black Power Movement in the United States attracted the Caribbean's urban poor and many organizations were formed throughout Trinidad and Tobago using its slogan. Among these were the Black Panthers, the African Unity Brothers, the African Cultural Association, and the National Freedom Organization.

MILITARY

Trinidad's rich deposit of oil and its strategic location have attracted many foreign powers over the years, most notably the United States. In 1940 President Franklin Delano Roosevelt leased three strategic military bases in British-Caribbean territories (one of which was Trinidad and Tobago) from Winston Churchill's British government. The Americans then built a sizable air strip in Port of Spain and a superb naval installation at Trinidad's well-placed deep-water harbor at Chaguaramas Bay. These actions resulted in increased employment and major development projects (through the U.S. Navy and Public Works Department), including the building of roads and bridges for wartime operations, and the recruitment of many Trinidadians and Tobagonians by the U.S. Navy during World War II. Furthermore, American interest in the Republic eased the immigration process to the United States. Many Trinidadian and Tobagonian immigrants who have become naturalized U.S. citizens continue to serve in the U.S. military, though in smaller numbers than during World War II. Because few of these individuals identify themselves as Trinidadian and Tobagonian immigrants, it is difficult to accurately access their number in the U.S. armed forces.

RELATIONS WITH TRINIDAD AND TOBAGO

The government of Trinidad and Tobago does not allow for Trinidadians and Tobagonians to hold dual citizenship abroad. Therefore, naturalized U.S. citizens do not vote in the Republic's elections. Nonetheless, whether they are U.S. citizens or temporary residents, most Trinidadian and Tobagonian immigrants maintain constant communication with their home country. They read the *Trinidad Guardian*, the *Punch*, the *Bomb*, the *Express*, and other national papers and watch news programs broadcast over satellite dishes. Temporary residents also vote in Trinidad and Tobago's general elections and remit funds regularly to family and relatives in the Republic.

Historically, the U.S. government has maintained good diplomatic relations with Trinidad and Tobago, which in recent years has received federal loans to recover from its economic recession. In spite of strained diplomatic relations between the U.S. government and the late Prime Minister, Eric Williams, over the closing of the U.S. naval base in Chaguaramas in the 1970s, the oil boom in Trinidad (between the 1960s and the early 1980s) kept Trindadians and Tobagonians among America's favorite peoples of the Caribbean Basin.

INDIVIDUAL AND GROUP CONTRIBUTIONS

Trinidadians and Tobagonians have enriched American culture in many ways. The following individuals are most notable.

ACADEMIA

Trinidadian and Tobagonian Americans were among the first blacks to enter American academy. Eric Williams, the late Prime Minister of Trinidad and Tobago and Vice Chancellor of the University of the West Indies, taught at Howard University and gave lectures at several other distinguished American colleges and universities. His books *Capitalism and Slavery* and *Columbus to Castro* have been reprinted dozens of times since they were first published in the 1940s and continue to attract interest in the United States. The works of C.L.R. James (one of Trinidad and Tobago's first political philosophers) and Stokley Carmichael, have likewise inspired political thinking on American campuses.

FILM, TELEVISION, THEATER, AND VISUAL ARTS

Errol John is an internationally acclaimed actor and playwright who produced the well-known *Moon On A Rainbow Shawl*. Geoffrey Holder (1930-), an outstanding American producer, director, and choreographer was born in Port of Spain and has lived in the United States for over 50 years. In 1975 he won a Tony Award for directing and designing costumes for *The Wiz*. Other Trinidadian artists who are well known in the United States include: Boscoe Holder, Noel Vaucrosson, Pat Chu Foon, painter M. P. Aladdin, and sculptor Francisco Caballo.

JOURNALISM

Trinidadians have been involved in American journalism since the early 1800s. The literary genius and political scientist C. L. R. James edited the *International African Opinion* and wrote many books on Caribbean and American history and politics. One of James' most renown works is *Black Jacobins*, which documents the black struggle in the Haitian Revolution. John Stewart, a popular Trinidadian writer who did his undergraduate and graduate study in the United States, was also a lecturer for California State University.

LITERATURE

Several of Trinidad and Tobago's most brilliant minds have left their indelible marks on North American and Caribbean literature. V. S. Naipaul (Vidiadhar Surajprasad), Trinidad's premier novelist, is well known in the United States as a prolific writer of nonfiction and fiction whose works often address violent race relations. Born in Trinidad in 1932, he has studied, traveled, lectured, and written in the United States. Among his nonfiction writings are the following: *Finding the Center*, *Among the Believers*, *The Return of Eva Peron with the Killings in Trinidad*, *India: A Wounded Civilization*, *The Overcrowded Barracoon*, *The Loss of El Dorado*, *An Area of Darkness*, *Middle Passage*, and *A Turn in The South*. This last book gives an elegant, but disturbing first-hand encounter of the darker side of American race relations and racial injustice in Atlanta, Charleston, Selma, Birmingham, Tallahassee, Nashville, Tuskegee, and other southern cities. Naipaul's fiction is equally impressive and includes: *The Enigma of Arrival*, *A Bend in the River*, *Guerrillas*, *In a Free State*, *A Flag on the Island*, *The Mimic Men*, *Mr. Stone and the Knights Companion*, *A House for Mr. Biswas*, *Miguel Street*, *The Suffrage of Elvira and The Mystic Masseur*, and more recent works. Lynn Joseph, a Trinidadian-born author who migrated to the United States during her college years, writes children books for Trinidadians and Tobagonians in the United States and the Caribbean.

MUSIC

Trinidadian-Tobagonian American Denise Plummer became the World's Calypso Queen in 1992-1993. Billy Ocean (1950-), a well-known Trinidadian recording artist from London, won fame in the United States with the hit single "Caribbean Queen." Many less well-known Trinidadians and Tobagonians have studied and taught classical music and dance in American colleges and universities. Carol LaChapelle, for example, is a highly regarded educator who teaches choreography at the School for the Performing Arts in New York City.

SPORTS

Trinidad and Tobago's primary sports are cricket and soccer but basketball, netball, table tennis, track and field, golf, horse racing, and water sports are also popular. Among the Republic's most famous athletes is Kareem Abdul-Jabbar (1947-), born Ferdinand Lewis Alcindor, Jr., a first-generation Trinidadian American who became one of the greatest centers in basketball history and was named Most Valuable Player by the National Basketball Association six times. Lesley Stewart and Claude Noel were well-known boxers who lived in the United States and had many title fights in Las Vegas, Atlantic City, and elsewhere. Sir Larry Constantine, who lived for a short time in the United States, was one of the world's greatest cricket players. Hasley Crawford, a sprinter who lived and trained in the United States, was a 1978 Olympic gold medalist for Trinidad and Tobago.

MEDIA

There are many periodicals, papers, radio stations, and television networks in the United States that cater to the Caribbean population.

PRINT

Cimmarron.

A quarterly journal established in 1985 by the City University of New York's Association of Caribbean Studies to discuss and publish issues of importance to Caribbean Americans.

Enquiry.

A quarterly publication established in 1970 by Trinidad & Tobago Association; contains items of interest to the West Indian community.

Contact: C. J. Mungo, Editor.

Address: 380 Green Lanes, London, N4, England.

Everybody's.

A New York magazine, founded in 1977 by a Grenadian who lived in Trinidad and New York, it reflects the demographic interest and views of the American Caribbean community.

New York Carib News.

Founded in 1981, it is a weekly newspaper tabloid that covers Caribbean politics in New York.

RADIO

KISS-FM, WBLS, and 95.2.

These New York stations play calypso at designated hours.

WLIB.

A New York Caribbean radio station that plays music from Trinidad and Tobago and other countries.

TELEVISION

CSN, the Caribbean Station Network.

This station is a major news center in New York.

ORGANIZATIONS AND ASSOCIATIONS

Caribbean Community (CARICOM).

Governments of Antigua and Barbuda, Bahamas, Barbados, Belize, Dominica, Grenada, Guyana, Jamaica, Montserrat, Saint Christopher-Nevis, Saint Lucia, Saint Vincent and the Grenadines, and Trinidad and Tobago. Objects are to promote cooperation and understanding among member states; integrate the economies of member states through the Caribbean Common Market; coordinate the foreign policies of member states; harmonize the policies of member states concerning commerce, health, education, and social affairs. Maintains reference library of 50,000 books, periodicals, and archival material. Publishes *CARICOM Perspective* three times a year.

Contact: Edwin W. Carrington, Secretary General.

Address: Bank of Guyana Building, P.O. Box 10827, Georgetown, Guyana.

Telephone: (2) 69281.

There are a number of important Trinidadian and Tobagonian organizations in the United States: Trinidad Alliance; Caribbean Action Lobby (founded by Mervyn Dymally); West Indian American Day Carnival Association (founded by Rufus Gorin in New York); West Indian Cricket Club (with branches in Ohio, New York, Washington, D.C., Florida, and other states); Brooklyn Council for the Arts, and Trinidad and Tobago-New York Steel Band Club. There is also the Caribbean American Chamber of Commerce and the Caribbean American Media Studies Inc., which is dedicated to the study and dissemination of information about recent West Indian immigrants.

MUSEUMS AND RESEARCH CENTERS

Carib Culture Center.

Contact: Laura B. Moreno, Assistant Director.

Address: 408 West 58th Street, New York, New York 10019.

Telephone: (212) 307-7420.

SOURCES FOR ADDITIONAL STUDY

Foner, Nancy. *New Immigrants in New York*. New York: Columbia University Press, 1987.

Gordon, Monica, and Suzanne Michael. *Emerging Perspectives on the Black Diaspora*. Maryland: University Press of Americans Inc., 1990.

Kasinitz, Philip. *Caribbean New York*. New York: Cornell University Press, 1992.

Kessner, Thomas, and Betty Boyd Caroli. *Today's Immigrant*. London, England: Oxford University Press, 1982.

Langley, Lester. *The United States and the Caribbean in the Twentieth Century*. Georgia: The University of Georgia Press, 1985.

Sander, Reinhardt W. *The Trinidad Awakening: West Indian Literature of the 1930s*. Connecticut: Greenwood Press, 1988.

Sowell, Thomas. *American Ethnic Groups*. Massachusetts: The Urban Institute, 1978.

Williams, A.R. "The Wild Mix of Trinidad and Tobago," *National Geographic*, 185, No. 3, March 1984; pp. 66-88.

Worthman, O. C. *Contemporary American Immigration*. Boston: Twayne Publishers, 1982.

In Turkey family life centers around the male head of the household as he is the one who traditionally provides for his family. Children are expected to obey their parents, even after reaching adulthood, and must also show respect for all persons older than themselves, including older siblings.

TURKISH AMERICANS

by
Donald Altschiller

OVERVIEW

Slightly smaller than Texas and Louisiana combined, Turkey straddles both Europe and Asia, bordering Greece, Bulgaria, Armenia, Georgia, Azerbaijan, Iran, Iraq, and Syria. Its location on two continents has been a crucial factor in its variegated history and culture. The country's area of almost 300,000 square miles includes almost 10,000 square miles of European Turkey, known as Thrace, and approximately 290,000 square miles of Asian Turkey, known as Anatolia or Asia Minor. Lying between the Black Sea and the Mediterranean, modern Turkey spans bustling cosmopolitan centers, pastoral farming communities, barren wastelands, placid Aegean islands and steep mountain ranges.

Turkey's population is estimated at 59 million people, with an annual growth rate of 2.5 percent. Istanbul, Ankara, and Adana are the largest cities. The population has been a racial melting pot since prehistoric days. Settled or ruled by Hittites, Gauls, Greeks, Macedonians, and Mongols, Turks became the decisive influence, introducing a Mediterranean-Mongoloid admixture into the country's ethnic composition. It is difficult to describe the appearance of an average Turk. The individual may be blond and blue-eyed or round-headed with dark eyes or hair. Some Turks have long-headed Mediterranean looks while others possess Mongoloid features with high cheekbones.

Almost 98 percent of the population is Muslim. Turkey, however, is a secular state and Jews and Christians can fully practice their religious faiths. Kurds, who are also mainly Muslims, are the largest ethnic minority in Turkey. Other minorities include Greeks, Armenians, and Jews.

HISTORY

The Turks, who did not arrive in the Anatolian Peninsula until the eleventh century, are relative newcomers to a land that had seen many successive civilizations before their arrival. Beginning around 2000 B.C., pre-Hittites, Hittites, Phrygians, Lydians, Persians, Greeks, and Romans had lived or ruled in the region. After the collapse of Roman power in the west about 450 A.D. Anatolia became the heartland of the Byzantine Empire (a Greek continuation of Roman rule in the eastern Mediterranean).

Originally nomadic peoples from the steppes of Central Asia, Turkish tribes began moving west toward Europe around the first century A.D. In the middle of the 400s, the first group, known as the Huns, reached western Europe. Others established kingdoms in Turkestan and Persia before the 900s, by which time they had converted to Islam. In the late 900s a new Turkish dynasty, the Seljuqs, came to power in Turkestan and then Persia, from where they began to make incursions into Anatolia in the early 1000s. In 1071 the Seljuqs crushed the Byzantine army at Manzikert in eastern Anatolia, capturing the emperor himself. This important battle marked the effective end of Byzantine power in Anatolia, and the beginning of Turkish dominance.

The main branch of the Seljuqs continued to rule in Persia and Mesopotamia (Iran and Iraq), while another branch known as the Seljuqs of Rum (Rome), quickly penetrated the entire Anatolian Peninsula. Of the original population, some fled to Constantinople or the west, a few remained Christian under the generally tolerant rule of the Muslim Turkish tribes, but over the centuries most converted to Islam. Gradually, too, these former Christians, mostly Greek or Armenian speakers, began to speak Turkish, melding with the dominant Turks, whom they had originally outnumbered.

During the 1100s the Seljuqs contended with the Byzantines and with Christian Crusaders from Europe for control in Anatolia, especially along the Aegean coast, from which the Byzantines and the Crusaders had driven the Turkish tribes for over 200 years. The strongly centralized Seljuq state reached the peak of its power in the early 1200s; shortly thereafter local internal revolts, combined with the Mongol invasions from the east, began to erode its authority. By the early 1300s it had collapsed completely.

Of the ten local emirates, or kingdoms, that arose in Turkish Anatolia after the Seljuq's disintegration, one quickly came to preeminence: that of Osman, who ruled in northwestern Anatolia and founded the Osmanli or Ottoman dynasty. Osman's son, Orhan, expanded his father's dominions in Anatolia and in the 1350s undertook the first Ottoman conquests in Europe, wrestling several towns in eastern Thrace from the Byzantines and crushing the Bulgars and Serbs in battle. His successors Murad and Bayezid continued the string of Asian and European conquests.

By the early 1400s the territory of the once mighty Byzantine Empire had been reduced to a small island of land around Constantinople surrounded by Ottoman territory. As Ottoman power had increased, so had the pomp of those who wielded it. Murad, for example, had taken the title *sultan* (meaning "authority" or "power"), rather than the less majestic *bey* or *emir*, which were military ranks. Ottoman capitals also became increasingly grand. Muhammad II undertook a massive building program in Constantinople, constructing houses, baths, bazaars, inns, fountains, gardens, a huge mosque, and an imperial palace. He also encouraged the original inhabitants who had fled to return—Jews, Greeks, and Armenians, many of whom were craftsmen, scholars, or artists—and made trade agreements with Venetian and Florentine merchants. Renamed Istanbul, the city became a hub of culture and commerce.

The Ottoman Empire reached its peak under Muhammad's great-grandson, Suleiman, who took power in 1520. During his rule, the vast Ottoman Empire controlled huge areas of northern Africa, southern Europe, and western Asia. Shortly after Suleiman's death in 1566, however, Ottoman might began to wane. A series of military defeats, internal conflict, and the Empire's inability to successfully counter European political, scientific, and social developments resulted in the loss of most of its territory outside Anatolia. After World War I, when Turkey was defeated by the Allies, its position was further weakened.

Heripsima Hovnanian is welcomed to the United States by 31 members of her family in this 1961 photograph. A bill signed by President Kennedy enabled her to enter the country.

MODERN ERA

Mustafa Kemal (1881-1938), a Turkish World War I hero later known as "Ataturk" or "father of the Turks," organized the Turkish army, drove the Greeks from Turkey, and founded the Republic of Turkey in 1923. After assuming the office of president, Ataturk began a series of revolutionary reforms which transformed Turkey into a modern nation. In a symbolic break with the Ottoman past, he moved the capital from Istanbul to Ankara, the heartland of his nationalist movement. Ataturk replaced religious law with civil, criminal, and commercial laws based on those of Switzerland. Ataturk also encouraged Turks to dress like Europeans. He outlawed the wearing of the *fez* and even promoted ballroom dancing at state functions.

Language reform also transformed the political culture of the country in revolutionary ways. Ataturk changed the Islamic call to prayer from Arabic to Turkish and replaced the Arabic alphabet, in which Turkish had been written, with a modified Latin alphabet. Historians believe that language reform was generally a positive development. Literacy is now more commonplace. Modern Turkish is apparently more adaptable to scientific and technical language than Ottoman Turkish and the language gap between economic classes has also been reduced.

From a one-party system under Ataturk's Republican Peoples' Party, Turkey's government evolved into a parliamentary democracy which, despite interference from the military in the early 1970s, has largely managed to maintain its independence from the powerful army.

SIGNIFICANT IMMIGRATION WAVES

The history of Turkish American immigration to the United States is not well documented and is generally unknown. Although many immigrants came to America to flee religious or political persecution, the primary motivation of many Turks was economic or educational opportunity.

Precise statistics on Turkish American immigration are difficult to obtain. According to U.S. government statistics, the number of immigrants from the Ottoman Empire was minuscule from 1820 through 1860, averaging less than 20 per year. The majority of these individuals (86 percent) returned to Turkey following the establishment of the Republic by Ataturk. Although about 360,000 immigrants from Ottoman Turkey came between 1820 and 1950, only an estimated 45,000 to 65,000 immigrants were Muslim Turks. The majority of arrivals were from the numerous ethnic minorities in the Ottoman Empire, primarily Greeks, Armenians, Jews, and Syrians.

Some historians believe that a large percentage of early Turkish Americans were illiterate but their literacy rate was much higher than that of the Ottoman Empire. According to historian Talat Sait Halman, most of the well-educated immigrants in this group eventually returned to Turkey but the less-educated remained in the United States. These remaining Turks, some studies indicate, retained their Turkish customs throughout the 1940s and 1950s without assimilating into the lifestyle of their newly adopted country.

Unlike the earlier wave of immigrants, the post-World War II generation was highly educated and included almost 4,000 engineers and physicians. These numbers would have undoubtedly been higher but strict U.S. immigration regulations—which were enforced from the mid-1920s until 1965—placed an annual quota of 100 on Turkish immigrants. Again, many of these professionals returned to Turkey after living in the United States for a brief period.

Since the 1970s, the number of Turkish immigrants has risen to more than 2,000 per year. Members of this most recent immigrant group vary widely. Many opened small businesses in the United States and created Turkish American organizations, thus developing Turkish enclaves, particularly in New York City. Still others came for educational purposes. Estimates of the total population of Turkish Americans vary widely, ranging from 100,000 to 400,000.

SETTLEMENT PATTERNS

From the beginning of Turkish immigration to the United States, many immigrants have settled in or around large urban centers. The greatest number have settled in New York City, Boston, Chicago, Detroit, Los Angeles, San Francisco, and Rochester. Other concentrations of Turkish Americans may be found along the East Coast in Connecticut, New Jersey, Maryland, and Virginia, and some have ventured into Minnesota, Indiana, Texas, and Alabama. Many of these communities are served by various local community associations. Membership totals are hard to obtain but range from 50 members to almost 500 members.

ACCULTURATION AND ASSIMILATION

The early Turkish immigrants were almost entirely male. In the culture of Anatolian Turkey, men did not feel comfortable bringing their wives and families until they were able to plant secure economic roots in the United States. Many Americans, however, believed that the Turks were prohibited from bringing their wives because of other reasons. According to Frank Ahmed, author of *Turks in America: The Ottoman Turk's Immigrant Experience,* the *Salem Evening News* falsely claimed that the Turks did not bring their wives because of Islamic religious strictures. The newspaper wrote extensively about the sizable Turkish community on the North Shore of Boston, including the towns of Peabody, Salem, and Lynn.

These immigrants often settled into rooming houses. Frequently, a Turk would rent the house and sublease rooms to his fellow countrymen. Although the accommodations were spare, the newly arriving immigrants somewhat replicated their village life. They ate Turkish food (pilaf, lamb, vegetable dishes) and slept on mattresses without a bedstead.

Although they were hardworking and industrious, many Turks did not escape the prejudice frequently directed at newcomers. Occasionally, they were called "Ali Hassans" or "Abdul Hamids" and some newspapers would ridicule the "terrible Turk" or Islam. Among the Turks, however, there was much tolerance for Turkish minorities, especially Turkish Jews, who were fully accepted and respected by their recently arriving compatriots.

Turks obtained work in factories in New York, Detroit, and Chicago and also in the New England leather industry. Sizable numbers worked in Massachusetts, in the leather factories of Lynn and Salem and the wire factories of Worcester. Forced to work long hours at low pay in unsanitary and unsafe conditions, some Turkish workers were involved in strikes against management, who generally viewed the Turks as "good workers."

Because of the precarious situation in Turkey and concern for their families, most Turks—one estimate was 35,000—stayed for a decade or less and then returned to their Anatolian villages before the Great Depression. A small number of Turks stayed in the United States, learned English, and married American women. According to one estimate, only a few hundred remained in this country.

As a result, the diminished Turkish American community became more close-knit. Social life revolved around coffee houses and benevolent societies. In Peabody, Massachusetts, coffee houses on Walnut Street became a congregating place for the Turks living in the area. It was here that community members would exchange news about their villages while sipping Turkish coffee and noshing on sweet pastry.

CUISINE

Turkish food is widely regarded as one of the world's major cuisines. It is noted for its careful preparation and rich ingredients. A typical Turkish meal begins with soup or *meze* (hors d'oeuvres), followed in succession by the main course (usually red meat, chicken, or fish), vegetables cooked in olive oil, dessert, and fresh fruit. Turkish coffee completes the feast and is served in small cups.

Favorite soups include wedding soup, which combines chicken and beef broth, eggs, lemon, and vegetables; lentil soup, which flavors the basic bean with beef broth, flour, butter, and paprika; and *tarhana* soup, which is made with a dried preparation of flour, yogurt, tomato, and red pepper flakes. Although most meals begin with soup, tripe soup—featuring a sauce of vinegar and garlic—is served after a complete dinner and is usually accompanied by alcoholic drinks.

Borek, which is a pastry roll filled with cheese or ground meat, and *dolma*, made from stuffed grape leaves, green pepper or eggplant are most often served prior to the meal. The *meze* tray features salads and purees, but may also include eggplant, caviar, lamb or veal, fried vegetables with yogurt sauce, and a wide variety of seafood.

The main course sometimes consists of seafood, which may be grilled, fried, or stewed. *Kofte* (meatballs) are another specialty, served grilled, fried, or stewed with vegetables. Fresh vegetables are widely used, served either hot or cold. Vegetables cooked with olive oil are essential to Turkish cuisine. Eggplant, peppers, green beans, and peas are the primary vegetables cooked with olive oil, which is also used as a main ingredient in salads. Rice pilaf, which sometimes contains currants and pine nuts, is served as a side dish. Buttermilk, made of yogurt and water, is preferred with meat dishes. *Rakl*, a drink similar to anisette, is often consumed as an alternative to wine.

The final touch to a meal is a tray of fresh fruits, including peaches, apples, pears, raisins, figs, oranges, and melons. Dessert treats include: *baklava*, a flaky pastry dipped in syrup; *bulbul yuvasi*, thin pastry leaves with walnut filling and lemon peel syrup; *sekerpare*, sweet cookies; and *lokma*, Turkish fritters. Puddings are also popular, including *muhallebi*, milk pudding, and *sutlac*, rice pudding.

At the beginning or end of a meal, it is customary to hear "Afiyet Olsun," which means, "May what you eat bring you well-being." To praise the chef, one says "*Elinize saglik*," or "Bless your hands."

TRADITIONAL COSTUMES

Along with his many other reforms, Ataturk succeeded in making Western-style dress, at least among men, widespread in Turkey. Consequently, Turkish Americans dress no differently than most other Americans. Ataturk also outlawed the traditional *fez*, a brimless, cone-shaped, red hat and made brimmed felt hats mandatory, because with them on men could not touch their foreheads to the ground in prayer. Traditional dress for women requires that they be covered from head to foot. Most Turkish garments are made from wool. The *kepenek*, a heavy hooded mantle shaped from a single piece of felt, sheltered herders from the rain and cold, as well as served as a blanket and tent.

HOLIDAYS CELEBRATED BY TURKISH AMERICANS

Turkey observes both civil and religious holidays. While dates for civil holidays are determined by the same calendar used in the United States, religious holidays are set by the Muslim lunar calendar, resulting in observance on different days each year. Offices of the Turkish government are closed on all these days, and frequently a day or two before or after as well. In the United States many Turkish Americans celebrate New Year's Day on January 1 and National Sovereignty and Children's

The armor featured in this photograph, taken during a Turkish parade in New York City, dates back to the fourteenth century.

Day on April 23. This holiday commemorates the founding of the Grand National Assembly in 1923. At the same time, Ataturk proclaimed it a day to honor children, making it a unique international holiday. Ataturk's birthday is honored on May 19 (officially known as Ataturk Memorial and Youth and Sports Day) and his death is commemorated on November 10. In Turkey, this day is marked by a national moment of silence throughout the nation at precisely 9:05 a.m., the time of Ataturk's death.

Victory Day (August 30) celebrates the victory over the Greeks in 1922 and Turkish Independence Day (October 29) recognizes the proclamation of the Republic by Ataturk in 1923. A unique American tradition, begun on April 24, 1984, is Turkish American Day, during which Turkish Americans march down New York's Fifth Avenue.

RELATIONS WITH OTHER ETHNIC GROUPS

There are many conflicts between Turkish Americans and Armenian Americans, stemming from the tragic genocide of an estimated 1.5 million Armenians by Turks perpetrated more than 70 years ago. Between 1973 and the mid-1980s, Armenian terrorist organizations assassinated several Turkish diplomats in Los Angeles and Boston. These violent actions declined by the late 1980s.

LANGUAGE

Like Mongolian, Korean, and Japanese, Turkish is part of the Ural-Altaic linguistic group. More than 100 million people living in Turkey and Central Asia speak Turkic languages. During the Ottoman era, Turkish was written in Arabic script, from right to left. Ottoman Turkish borrowed heavily from other languages, and its varying forms of Arabic script made it difficult to use.

Ataturk eliminated Arabic script, substituting the Latin alphabet with some letter modifications to distinguish certain Turkish sounds. Many Arabic and Persian loan words were removed, while words from European languages were phoneticized. The alphabet consists of 29 letters—21 consonants and eight vowels. Six of these letters do not occur in English. Turkish has no genders and there is no distinction between he, she, and it. The Turks are very expressive and often use "body language" to communicate.

There are several Turkish American organizations and community centers in the United States that teach the Turkish language to the children of Turkish Americans. Despite this effort, relatively few second- and third-generation Turkish Americans speak Turkish, a trend that will greatly affect the future of this community.

GREETINGS AND OTHER POPULAR EXPRESSIONS

Common expressions among Turks and Turkish Americans include: *Merhaba*—Hello; *Gun aylin*—Good Morning; *Iyi aksamlar*—Good Evening; *Nasilsiniz*—How are you?; *Iyiyim*—I'm fine; *Tessekkur ederim*—Thank you; *Saatler olsun!*—May it last for hours! (said to one after a bath, shave, or haircut); *Gecmis olsun!*—May it be in the past! (said in case of illness).

FAMILY AND COMMUNITY DYNAMICS

In Turkey family life centers around the male head of the household as he is the one who traditionally provides for his family. Children are expected to obey their parents, even after reaching adulthood, and must also show respect for all persons older than themselves, including older siblings. Parental authority in Turkey is so great that parents often arrange for the marriages of their children. The extended family is of extreme importance in Turkey as family members often work in the same business. Men dominate in community affairs. Women are expected to manage the household. In the United States, while the roles of men and women have changed somewhat, the Turkish American family remains close-knit.

There are many political factions in Turkey, which are often reflected in the Turkish American community. All Turkish Americans, however, are united in their concern for Turkey and take great pride in their ethnic heritage. Many Turks living in the United States refuse to abandon their Turkish citizenship. Those who do apply for American visas are generally ostracized by the community.

RELIGION

Most Turkish Americans practice Islam, or "submission to god." In 610A.D., according to Muslim belief, the angel Gabriel ordered Muhammad to recite the Word of God as it was delivered to him. This was the same basic message that had earlier been revealed to the Jews and later to the Christians, but the Word had been misinterpreted over the years and had to be restated. Over a period of 22 years, Muhammad received revelations from the angel, revelations incorporated in the Muslim holy book, the *Koran*. This is a detailed guide to behavior toward God, fellow humans, and the self. Islam therefore provides the basis of personal identity and social life to its followers.

There are five basic requirements of the faith known as the Pillars of Islam: Confession that there is "no god but God" and that Muhammad is the messenger of God; Daily prayer (five times); Giving of alms; Fasting in daylight hours for the Muhammadan month of *Ramadan;* and, Pilgrimage to Mecca at least once in a lifetime.

Prayers are said five times daily wherever one finds oneself, but on Friday the community gathers at the mosque for noon prayer. The religion also bans the eating of pork, drinking alcohol, gambling, and usury (lending money with excessive interest). There are also specific laws concerning marriage, divorce, and inheritance. In some representations, art representing human figures is discouraged. The prophet Muhammad is never portrayed unless veiled, even in motion pictures.

Islam is further divided into two major sects: *Sunni* and *Shi'ite.* Most Turkish Americans, as well as the majority of Muslims in general, are *Sunni* Muslims. They believe that the community as a whole is the guardian and guarantor of Islamic law. This law, shari'a, is based on four sources, which in descending order of importance are: the *Koran,* the examples and teachings of the prophet, communal consensus on Islamic principles and practices, and reasoning by analogy. In later years the consensus was reduced to a consensus of religious scholars. This four-pronged determinant of the law provides great unity, but also provides for a variety of interpretations. Perhaps the most graphic example of this is the treatment of the law relating to modesty among women. In some places this law is accommodated by the wearing of a veil in public; in others, simply by avoiding male company when possible; and in others, is left to the discretion of local leaders.

In the United States, many Turkish Americans worship in Arab or Pakistani mosques. Very few have converted to Christianity or Judaism. One notable exception is Halouk Fikret (1895-1965), who was born to a prominent Muslim family in Turkey, immigrated to the United States, and, in the 1920s, became a Presbyterian minister.

EMPLOYMENT AND ECONOMIC TRADITIONS

Early Turkish immigrants to the United States were predominantly from Turkey's rural community. They settled in large, industrial cities and found employment as unskilled laborers. The majority came to earn money so that they could improve their economic situation and that of their families in Turkey. After the 1950s, a well-skilled and highly educated class immigrated to the United States, the majority being medical doctors, engineers, and scientists. Today, Turkish Americans are visible in virtually every field. The majority are professionals and enjoy a middle-class lifestyle.

POLITICS AND GOVERNMENT

Before the 1970s, there was very little Turkish American involvement in American politics. The Turkish invasion of Cyprus in 1974, however, mobilized many individuals because of U.S. government support for the Greeks. Nonetheless, the small Turkish American community was not able to counter the influence of the much larger and more powerful Greek American organizations. Turkish Americans proudly point to Turkey's membership in NATO and its military and political support of the U.S. government during the 1991 Persian Gulf War.

INDIVIDUAL AND GROUP CONTRIBUTIONS

Turkish Americans have made numerous contributions to American society, particularly in the fields of education, medicine, and science. Others, including Tunç Yalman, artistic director of the Milwaukee Repertory Theater, and Osmar Karakas, who was awarded the 1991 National Press Award for the best news photograph, have contributed significantly to the arts. The following individuals are especially notable.

MUSIC INDUSTRY

Arif Mardin (1932-) is one of the major popular music producers and arrangers in America. His clients include Aretha Franklin, the Bee Gees, Carly Simon, Roberta Flack, and Bette Midler. Born into a prominent Istanbul family, he received a scholarship and B.A. in music at Boston's Berklee School of Music in 1958. After briefly meeting Ahmet Ertegun at the Newport

Jazz Festival, he joined Atlantic Records and is currently its Vice President.

Chief Executive Officer of Atlantic Records, Ahmet Ertegun (1924-) is an influential force in the music business. The son of Turkey's ambassador to the United States, he attended St. John's College in Annapolis, Maryland. The young Ahmet always loved jazz, especially the music of black musicians. He and his brother Nesuhi promoted jazz concerts in Washington, D.C., at locales ranging from the Jewish Community Center, the National Press Club, and even the Turkish embassy. Duke Ellington and Lester Young attended some of these informal jazz sessions. He soon invested $10,000 with a record collector friend and started Atlantic Records. Now, four decades later, it is a conglomerate worth $600 million. Ertegun has been dubbed the "Greatest Rock 'n' Roll Mogul in the World."

SCIENCE AND MATHEMATICS

Feza Gursey (1921-1993) was the J. Willard Gibbs Professor Emeritus of Physics at Yale University. He contributed major studies on the group structure of elementary particles and the symmetries of interactions. Professor Gursoy helped bridge the gap between physicists and mathematicians at Yale. He was the winner of the prestigious Oppenheimer Prize and Wigner Medal.

MEDIA

PRINT

ATS Bulletin.

Quarterly newsletter of the American Turkish Society.

Address: 850 Third Avenue, New York, New York 10022.

Telephone: (212) 319-2452.

Turkish Daily News—Almanac.

Published annually; contains information about the economy and government of Turkey.

Contact: Ilnur Cevik, Editor.

Address: Ilhan Cevik Tunus Cad. 50 A No. 7, 06680 Ankara Kavaklidere, Turkey.

Telephone: 4 4282956.

Fax: 4 4278890.

Turkish Newsletter.

Monthly publication of the Turkish American Association.

Contact: Inci Fenik, Editor.

Address: 1600 Broadway, Suite 318, New York, New York 10019.

Telephone: (212) 956-1560.

The Turkish Times.

Biweekly newspaper of the Assembly of Turkish American Associations. Covers Turkish American issues with news articles, editorials, and business information.

Contact: Dr. Ugur Akimci, Editor.

Address: 1602 Connecticut Avenue, Suite 303, Washington, D.C. 20009.

Telephone: (202) 483-9090.

ORGANIZATIONS AND ASSOCIATIONS

American Turkish Friendship Council (ATFC).

Devoted to increasing understanding of commercial, defense, and cultural issues involving the United States and Turkey; provides information on the history and economical and social advancement of Turkey.

Contact: G. Lincoln McCurdy, Executive Director.

Address: 1010 Vermont Avenue, N.W., Suite 1020, Washington, D.C. 20005.

Telephone: (202) 783-0483.

American Turkish Society (ATS).

Founded in 1949, the ATS has a membership of 400 American and Turkish diplomats, banks, corporations, businessmen, and educators. It promotes economic and commercial relations as well as cultural understanding between the people of the United States and Turkey.

Contact: Ahnet Birsel, Executive Director.

Address: 850 Third Avenue, New York, New York 10022.

Telephone: (212) 319-2452.

Assembly of Turkish American Associations (ATAA).

Founded in 1979, the ATAA has approximately 10,500 members and coordinates activities of regional associations for the purpose of presenting an objective view of Turkey and Turkish Americans and enhancing understanding between these two groups.

Contact: Dr. Bulent Basol, President.

Address: 1601 Connecticut Avenue, N.W., Suite 303, Washington, D.C. 20009.

Telephone: (202) 483-9090.

Federation of Turkish-American Associations (FTAA).

Founded in 1956 and composed of about 30 local organizations of Turkish Americans, it works to advance educational interests and to maintain and preserve knowledge of Turkey's cultural heritage.

Contact: Egemen Bagis, Executive Director.

Address: 821 United Nations Plaza, Second Floor, New York, New York 10017.

Telephone: (212) 682-7688.

Turkish American Associations (TAA).

Founded in 1965, the TAA has approximately 15,000 members and promotes cultural relations between the United States and Turkey.

Contact: Inci Fenik, Secretary.

Address: 1600 Broadway, Suite 318, New York, New York 10019.

Telephone: (212) 956-1560.

Turkish Women's League of America (TWLA).

Founded in 1958, the TWLA comprises Americans of Turkish origin united to promote equality and justice for women. The organization encourages cultural and recreational activities to foster relations between the people of Turkey, the United States, and other countries, including the new Turkish republics of the former Soviet Union.

Contact: Ayten Sandikcioglu, President.

Address: 821 United Nations Plaza, Second floor, New York, New York 10017.

Telephone: (212) 682-8525.

SOURCES FOR ADDITIONAL STUDY

Ahmed, Frank. *Turks in America: The Ottoman Turk's Immigrant Experience*. Greenwich, Connecticut: Columbia International, 1986.

Halman, Talat Sait. "Turks," *Harvard Encyclopedia of American Ethnic Groups*. Cambridge, Massachusetts: Harvard University Press, 1980.

Spencer, William. *The Land and People of Turkey*. New York: J.P. Lippincott, 1990.

UKRAINIAN AMERICANS

by
**Marianne P.
Fedunkiw**

OVERVIEW

Ukraine is officially named Ukrayina, which
means "borderland." After Russia, it is the second-largest country in Europe in area. It is comparable, both in population (about 52 million)
and size (233,089 square miles) to France. It is
bordered by the Black Sea, the Sea of Azov,
Moldova, and Romania to the south; Hungary,
Slovakia, and Poland to the west; Belarus to the
north; and Russia to the north and northeast.

Of its population, 73 percent are of Ukrainian ethnic origin. The country's official language,
since the dissolution of the Soviet Union in 1991,
is Ukrainian. The capital city is Kiev, and the
national flag has two broad horizontal bands of
blue and yellow, the blue on top representing the
sky and the yellow representing fields of wheat.

Although most of western Ukraine is agricultural—it is a country that has served as the
"breadbasket of Europe"—there are large petroleum and natural gas fields as well. Major industrial
products include refined sugar, iron, steel, trac-
tors, cement, glass, paper, and fertilizer.

HISTORY

The earliest evidence of human settlement in
Ukraine dates back 150,000 years. Early inhabi-

tants of the territory included the Balkans, the Cimmerians (the first nomadic horsemen to appear in Ukraine in about 1500 to 1000 B.C.), the Scythians (early seventh century B.C.), and colonies set up by the Greek Empire (by the fourth century B.C.).

The direct ancestors of Ukraine's population today were the Slavs. The Slavs made their way into the Balkans in the early seventh century A.D. By the middle of the ninth century, however, what was to become known as Kievan Rus was still relatively underdeveloped. Much of the ensuing progress is attributed to the Varangians (or Vikings or Normans) who visited Rus in the mid-ninth century.

Following the reign of Oleh, Prince Ihor, and then his wife Olha ruled. Olha took over leadership when her husband, Ihor, was killed and their son Sviatoslav was still too young to rule. Her influence was especially apparent years later when her grandson Volodymyr became prince. Olha had converted from paganism to Christianity in 955 and, with Volodymyr, is credited with bringing Christianity to a pagan land in 988.

The reign of Jaroslav the Wise (1036-1054) is often seen as the pinnacle in the history of Kievan Russia. Among his contributions were more than 400 churches in Kiev alone, and the establishment of *Ruska pravda* (Rus' Justice), the basic legal code of the country. Jaroslav's reign was followed by a period of relative decline, beginning with feuds among his sons and grandsons. Jaroslav divided his kingdom among his sons with the idea that the eldest hold a position of seniority in maintaining unity, but Kiev declined as the political and economic center of Ukraine as each principality lived almost autonomously. Eventually Kiev fell to the Mongols in 1240, under Ogodei Khan and Batu, the latter being the grandson of Genghis.

From the latter half of the thirteenth century until the sixteenth century, Ukraine fell under the rule of first Lithuania (Grand Prince Algirdas moved in to occupy Kiev in 1362) and then Poland, led by Casimir the Great (1310-1370). Ukrainians, or Ruthenians (from Rus', as they called themselves during this period), preferred to be ruled by the Lithuanians, who treated them as equals. In 1385, to consolidate power against a growing Muscovy, an alliance between Lithuania and Poland was struck. Thus, the fourteenth and fifteenth centuries were years of struggle to keep Ukrainian lands from Poland, Hungary, and Lithuania, as well as free of the *boyars* or noble-men who tried to take control. At the heart of many of these battles was religion—since Poland was overwhelmingly Catholic and even Lithuania converted to Catholicism in 1385, the Orthodox Ukrainians were effectively shut out.

The late sixteenth and early seventeenth centuries were periods of recolonization in Ukraine, particularly in the provinces of Kiev and Bratslav. In 1569 the regions of Kiev, Volhynia, and Bratslav (Podillia) were annexed to the Kingdom of Poland. Another part of this development included a new society which grew out of the plains of the Dnieper River—the Cossacks. These men were free, as opposed to the serfs of the sixteenth century, and organized to fend off marauding Tatars. They ruled for decades, freeing Ukraine from Polish rule and helping to defend the country from Turkish, Tatar, and other invaders. One of the most notable of the Cossack leaders (hetmans) was Bohdan Khmelnytsky, who ruled from 1648 to 1657. During this time he led an uprising and mass peasant revolt against the ruling Poles. This led to a new ruling state with the hetman as leader and a tumultuous relationship with Russia in order to fight Poland. There was also a treaty signed with Muscovy in 1654 to help protect against invaders. After Khmelnytsky died in 1657, Ukraine's position weakened and it was eventually betrayed by its ally, Russia, who entered into an agreement with Poland which divided Ukraine between Russia and Poland.

Ukraine often tried to loosen the grip of Russia and Poland. In 1708-1709 Hetman Ivan Mazepa led the Cossacks to fight alongside Sweden's King Charles XII in the Swedish king's war with Russia's Peter I. But the Swedes and Cossacks lost, and Peter destroyed the hetman's capital and the hetmanate itself. By the late seventeenth century, in any case, not much was left of the hetmanate—only about one-third of that which Khmelnytsky controlled in his heyday as leader.

MODERN ERA

In the late eighteenth century, Russia annexed much of eastern Ukraine, taking the provinces of Kiev, Volhynia, and Podillia away from Poland, and taking the Crimea from the Turks. This transfer meant not only that the Orthodox religion could be practiced (it had been persecuted under Polish rule), but that by 1831 Russian became the official language, replacing Polish. This remained basically unchanged until 1918.

Austria gained possession of much of western Ukraine, including the province of Ruthenia and what had been Galicia, also in the late eighteenth century, and it remained Austrian land until the end of World War I. The bid for a free Ukraine was a never-ending one. A major figure was the nationalistic poet and painter Taras Shevchenko (1814-1861). This influential figure, born a serf, established the Ukrainian language as a language of literature, and his work tells the story of the glories and sufferings of the nation—all of this during a time when Ukrainian was banned from schools, books, and the performing arts.

World War I saw the Ukraine caught between the Austrians and Russia, each as potential allies against the other. By 1915-1916, little of Ukraine was left in Russian control. When the Bolsheviks overthrew the Czar and later the provisional government in 1917, Ukraine was poised for freedom. On January 22, 1918, Ukraine declared itself to be independent of Russia and used the help of German and Austrian troops to clear Russians from Ukraine. But the tenuous alliance with Germany and Austria quickly broke down, and freedom was short-lived. By April 1918 a new government, acceptable to the Germans, was set up. Galicia, which had freed itself of Austrian rule, found itself independent in 1918—but that was brief too, and it soon fell to Poland. Four years of war followed, and the new Union of Soviet Socialist Republics (USSR) reconquered Ukraine in 1922 and made it one of the original republics. Aside from being lost and rewon during the Second World War, Ukraine remained part of the USSR until the USSR was dissolved in 1991.

THE FIRST WAVE OF UKRAINIAN IMMIGRATION TO AMERICA

Although individual Ukrainians had come to the United States earlier, the first mass wave immigrated in the late nineteenth century, coinciding with the period of American industrialization. This group, numbering more than 350,000, began to arrive in 1877 as strikebreakers to work the Pennsylvania mines. Most of them came from western Ukraine, particularly the Lemko and Transcarpathian regions. In search of prosperity, they read advertisements which promised earnings ten to 20 times greater than they could hope for in the Ukraine. So they left their families, traveled to the ports of Bremen, Hamburg, Rotterdam, and Antwerp, and were packed into steerage on ships for the long journey to America.

When they reached the immigration check at Ellis Island, they waited in fear since a good number each trip were sent back. Those who made it through concentrated in the factories, steel mills, and foundries in Cleveland, Akron, Rochester, Buffalo, Syracuse, Chicago, and Detroit, as well as in Pennsylvania cities. Before World War I, 98 percent of Ukrainians settled in the northeastern states, with 70 percent in Pennsylvania. Men who had left wives and children in Ukraine first worked and then, when they could support them, brought their families over. They settled in urban villages near other Slavs, Poles, Jews, and Slovaks, seeking a sense of community to replace the one they had left. Their lives centered on the neighborhood church, saloon, general store, and boarding houses.

Unlike the Ukrainian Canadians, few of the early Ukrainian Americans farmed. By the time the first wave crossed the ocean, most of the free land had been distributed already and these new immigrants had no money to buy land. There were, however, isolated groups such as the Stundists (Baptist Evangelicals) who did farm, first in Virginia then in North Dakota. There were also small groups who chose to follow Orthodox priest Ahapii Honcharenko (1832-1916)—often considered the first nationality-conscious Ukrainian—to Alaska in the 1860s and Dr. Nicholas Sudzilovsky-Russel to Hawaii in 1895. Sudzilovsky-Russel was elected to the Hawaiian Senate in 1901 and, in this position, greatly aided more than 375 Ukrainians who were lured to Hawaii by dishonest agents and forced to work as slaves on plantations until they paid the costs of their four-month sea voyages. Eventually they were released from their contracts, and most returned to North America.

THE SECOND WAVE: BETWEEN THE WORLD WARS

This wave of immigrants, covering the period between the two world wars, was considerably smaller than the first, numbering only about 15,000. It was also different in that these were immigrants who were aware of and vocal about their nationalism and politicized to the point of infighting. Until that time, Ukrainian Americans tended to be polarized along religious lines; now there were socialists and conservatives on either end of the political spectrum. Furthermore, assimilation had gained momentum by the time of the second wave, and adjustments to clothing and language came more quickly than to the first immigrants.

THE THIRD WAVE: DISPLACEMENT AFTER WORLD WAR II

The final major wave was one of refugees following the Second World War. These often well-educated Ukrainians (including 2,000 university students, 1,200 teachers and scholars, 400 engineers, 350 lawyers, and 300 physicians) had fled their homes during the war and had little interest in returning while the Soviet government was in place. They saw both the United States and Canada as temporary homes, although most would never return to live in the Ukraine.

Most of these immigrants had spent time in the postwar refugee camps in Austria and Germany. Eight of these DP (displaced person) camps housed two-thirds of the Ukrainian refugees, with the rest in private accommodation. Between 1947 and 1951, these DPs were resettled, with the greatest number (80,000) going to the United States (30,000 went to Canada, 20,000 to Australia, and the same number to Great Britain, 13,000 to Brazil and Argentina, and 10,000 each to Belgium and France).

The DPs concentrated in large cities, particularly New York City, Philadelphia, Chicago, Detroit, Rochester, Syracuse, Buffalo, and Cleveland. They gravitated to neighborhoods where Ukrainian Americans already lived, where churches and a community infrastructure had been set up by previous immigrants. This newest group enjoyed the benefits of often being better educated, and of social assistance systems, schools, and immigrant aid societies already in place. Although educated, professionals may have had to work in menial jobs until they grasped the language and had enough money to set up as doctors, lawyers, and engineers. Some found the adjustment difficult and never returned to their professions and instead took jobs administering Ukrainian institutions and organizations, many of which were brought from Ukraine by the immigrants.

SETTLEMENT PATTERNS

Before World War II, 98 percent of Ukrainian Americans settled in the northeastern United States with almost three-quarters in Pennsylvania. Between the wars, the numbers in Pennsylvania dropped, while the Ukrainian American population of New York and New Jersey grew (especially that of New York City) and sizable communities sprang up in Ohio and Illinois.

The 1990 Census of Population states that 740,803 individuals reported their ancestry as Ukrainian, or 0.3 percent of the total. Of those who said they were Ukrainian Americans, just over two-thirds listed it as "first ancestry." It is interesting to note that the census also gave, as ethnicity choices, Carpath Rusyn, Central European, Russian and Slavic; when many of the first Ukrainians arrived in America, they were identified with labels other than Ukrainian, including some of these choices.

The majority of Ukrainian Americans, the census notes, settled in the Northeast. The state with the greatest number is Pennsylvania (129,753 reported in 1990), followed by New York (121,113), and New Jersey (73,935). Although regionally, the fewest number of Ukrainians are to be found in the American West, California is the fourth-ranked state with 56,211 reported in 1990.

RELATIONSHIP WITH "ESTABLISHED" AMERICANS

Because the first wave of Ukrainians came as strikebreakers, there was tension between them and the established English, Irish, and Welsh miners in the area. Ukrainians were also the first large group of non-English-speaking immigrants, and so they stood out as "different"—they spoke a foreign language, ate different food, and, at least upon arrival, wore different clothes. They also tended to group together, further isolating themselves from the Americans. This, however, changed quickly with the generation of children who grew up in America. It was not unusual for these children, who played in the streets with other non-Ukrainian children, to pick up the language and customs quickly and assimilate thoroughly.

Discrimination, though, was part of life at the start. Ukrainians were called "Hunkies" (having come from the Hungarian part of the Austrian empire) or "Bohunks" (a derivative of Bohemians) by those who reviled these immigrants, who were often illiterate, dirty with miner's dust, and willing to do work no one else would to get a foothold toward a better life. In fact, in his *Ukrainians in North America: An Illustrated History*, Orest Subtelny notes that this so-called "scum of Europe" were thought to be contaminating once civilized towns in Pennsylvania by forcing out those who had given stability to the area: the English, Irish,

Welsh, and Scottish. In fact, in 1897 a discriminatory measure passed the state of Pennsylvania, which required that nonnaturalized American miners and workers pay an additional tax.

KEY ISSUES FACING UKRAINIAN AMERICANS IN THE FUTURE

The most striking issue is the state of the free Ukraine since it gained its independence in 1991, with the breakup of the USSR. The country must deal with new governments and democracy as well as with the transition to economic and social independence. Much of the infrastructure of business and government has been redesigned entirely, and Ukrainian Americans are eagerly monitoring the progress of change.

Another concern is the continuing effects of the Chernobyl nuclear disaster in eastern Ukraine in the 1980s. Considerable aid, both financial and material, has been coordinated to aid victims, particularly the orphans, of the disaster.

There has always been great interest in events "in the old country." Ukrainian American organizations based in the United States have, for decades, been formed to make political pleas on behalf of those in the occupied homeland and to send material and financial aid. This included marches on the White House protesting the Polish Occupation of Eastern Galicia in 1922 and a 1933 march by Detroit Ukrainian Americans to protest the Soviet man-made famine that year.

ACCULTURATION AND ASSIMILATION

Because the United States has modeled itself as a "melting pot" for newly arrived immigrants, Ukrainian Americans have become assimilated more thoroughly and more quickly than their neighbors to the north, the Ukrainian Canadians. This is in part because the first immigrants moved to heavily populated urban centers where they tended to get "lost" more readily among other immigrants and American citizens. As the decades have passed, too, the number of new immigrants has dropped. Couple this with the thoroughness of assimilation—in 1980, less than 17 percent of people of Ukrainian descent said Ukrainian was their primary language—and the future of the Ukrainian American community can seem uncertain.

This does not, however, mean that all is bleak. Through church, cultural, and political-business organizations, Ukrainian Americans and their children and grandchildren have places to go to celebrate their heritage. This is aided by the fact that traditionally Ukrainian Americans have not moved far from their original settlement sites in the northeastern states of Pennsylvania, New York, and New Jersey. Some of the strongest organizations, too, are those which were established early in the history of immigration. The most forward-thinking have changed with the times and deemphasized nationalist concerns in favor of drawing members with cultural, business, and social activities. Credit unions, youth organizations, and professional and business clubs are strong in the communities they serve.

MISCONCEPTIONS ABOUT UKRAINIAN AMERICANS

One of the most common misconceptions about Ukrainian Americans is that they were Russians, Poles, Hungarians, or Austrians. This was the case because depending on when they arrived, Ukraine was occupied by Russia or the USSR, Poland, or the Austro-Hungarian Empire.

TRADITIONS, BELIEFS, AND CUSTOMS

Before Ukraine adopted Christianity in 988, the inhabitants believed in pagan gods who ruled over the sun, stars, and moon. Folk beliefs are still connected to the sun, stars, and moon, as well as to dreams, the seasons, and agriculture. In fact, many of the pagan customs blended, over time, with Christian beliefs. These centered on the family (e.g., birth, marriage, and funeral customs), the community, and seasonal agricultural rites.

Songs and folk tales play a significant role in these ancient customs. There are specific songs for harvest festivals, New Year's celebrations, and Christmas and Easter, all celebrating both pagan beliefs and Christian traditions. Songs and music have always been important to the Ukrainian Americans; the earliest settlers, who had little money, often spent their rare free hours gathered together playing and singing. This has continued, not only in established choirs and ensembles, but as part of Ukrainian youth groups, camps, and Saturday language classes. The language classes are also a place where children of immigrants have been taught about their country's history, geography, and culture.

Examples of ancient customs still practiced today include the spring rites and songs (*vesnianky*) and the traditions associated with the harvest or Kupalo festival in which young maidens make wreaths of wildflowers, and set them afloat in a nearby stream; their fortune is determined by the young man who retrieves the wreath while facing the spirits of the night. Often these are still practiced by Ukrainian American youth at summer camps or through youth organizations and cultural festivals.

PROVERBS

Proverbs are a rich part of the Ukrainian culture and are handed down from generation to generation: A smart man seeks all from himself, a fool looks for everything in others; Fear God—and you will not fear any person; He who thinks rarely always has time to talk; Snow falls upon a pursuit that is put off; A wise man does not always say what he knows, but a fool does not always know what he says; Life is the road to death; It is difficult to learn to thank God if we cannot thank people; The rich man is not he who has great riches but he who squanders little money; A good heart does not know pridefulness; Brotherhood is greater than riches; A black dog or a white dog is still a dog.

CUISINE

Ukrainian cooking is a robust mix of meat, vegetable, and grain dishes. It is similar to, and has been influenced by, the cuisine of Poland, Russia, Turkey, Hungary, Romania, and Moldova. Although the selection and availability of food is more varied for Ukrainian Americans than it is for Ukrainians, many of the traditional foods survive in the United States.

Breads figure prominently in both immigrant and Ukrainian households—Ukraine is, after all, known as the "breadbasket of Europe"—and particular breads such as *paska* for Easter are featured during the holidays and at weddings, often decorated with braids or birds of dough. Bread is featured as a ceremonial ingredient in all special occasions, whether to bring divine blessing to the start of a farm task, to welcome guests to a celebration, or to symbolically part with the dead at the *tryzna*, or wake.

The dishes most readily associated with Ukrainians are likely *borscht* (a soup of red beets), *holubtsi* (cabbage rolls), *pyrohy* or *varenyky* (dough dumplings filled with potatoes and cheeses, sauerkraut, or various fruits such as cherries), and *kielbassa* (smoked sausage). The potato is the most readily used vegetable in traditional Ukrainian cooking, although garlic, onions, cabbage, cucumbers, tomatoes, and beets are also staples. Mushrooms are also a common ingredient, used to spice up a meal and often included in stuffings.

The best showcase for traditional Ukrainian cuisine is the Christmas Eve meatless meal prepared for January 6 (under the Julian calendar for traditionalists). This meal features 12 courses, symbolic of the 12 apostles present at the Last Supper. The meal begins with *kutya* (cooked wheat, ground poppy seed, and honey) and then moves on to pickled herring or pickled mushrooms, *borscht*, one or more preparations of fish, *holubtsi* with buckwheat or rice, *varenyky* with sauerkraut or potatoes, beans with prunes, sauerkraut with peas, baked beets, mushroom sauce, and ends with a dessert of pastries—*makivnyk* (poppy seed cake), *khrusty* (fried bands of dough cookies sprinkled with icing sugar), *pampushky* (doughnuts), *medivnyk* (honey cake) or *compote* (stewed dried fruit).

There is a religious context to Ukrainian festive dinners. At Christmas, a place is set at the table to welcome the spirits of dead relatives. And at Easter, the food that makes up the ceremonial meal is taken to church in a basket decorated with the finest embroidered linens to be blessed.

TRADITIONAL COSTUMES

Although today Ukrainians dress in clothes basically indistinguishable from the rest of modern Europe, there are traditional costumes of Ukraine, which vary from region to region. In Kuvijovyc and Struk's *Encyclopedia of Ukraine*, Ukrainian folk dress is divided into five different regional forms: the Middle Dnieper region, Polisia, Podillia, central Galicia and Volhynia, and Subcarpathia and the Carpathian Mountain region.

The first region around the Dnieper River is characterized by women wearing a *plakhta* (a wraparound skirt), a *kersetka* (a blouse with wide sleeves and a bodice), and an *ochipok* (a headdress), while the men wore cut shirts. These clothes date back to the time of the ruling hetmanate.

In Polisia the clothes date back even further, to the princely era. It is here that the well-known

Ukrainian embroidered blouse ablaze with red and a colorful woven skirt is worn by the women. Men dress in a shirt worn outside their trousers and a grey woolen cap (*maherka*) or a tall felt hat (*iolomok*).

The third region, Podillia, is recognized by the women's multicolored, embroidered blouses and the men's mantle. In central Galicia and Volhynia, linen is a popular fabric, and women wear corsets and head wraps which resemble turbans. The men don caftans, felt overcoats, or jackets. Finally, one of the most recognizable and colorful costumes comes from the Carpathian Mountain region, or Lemkivschyna. Women's skirts are decorated with folds and pleats, while men wear tunics and *leibyks*—the Lemko felt vests.

The greatest showcase for native folk dress for Ukrainian Americans is at dance festivals. The swirling ribbons of color and flashes of billowing satin pants tucked into red boots mix with the linen shirts, laced leather slippers, and felt hats as dancers representing different regions of Ukraine share the stage.

UKRAINIAN SONGS AND DANCES

There is a rich history of Ukrainian music. Some of the oldest traditions survive to this day through Christmas carols, originally sung in pagan times to celebrate the first long day of the season, and the Easter songs, or *hayivky*, also known as songs of spring. There were also songs to herald the arrival of summer and the harvest.

During the era of Cossack rule, other forms of music arose. The lyrico-epic "dumas" told of the struggles of the Cossacks. Music flourished in the seventeenth and eighteenth centuries—there were even organized singing guilds. Notable composers include Semen Artemovsky, author of the opera *Zaporozhian Beyond the Danube* (written in 1863), and Mykola Lysenko (1842-1912), who collected thousands of folk songs in addition to composing original songs and operas. In the United States, the first Ukrainian American choir was organized in 1887 in Shenandoah, Pennsylvania.

Traditional instruments include the *bandura* or *kobza*, whose strings are plucked to make music, the free-reed wind instrument (*sopilka*), the stringed percussion dulcimer, or *tsymbaly*, played by hitting the strings with small hammers, and the violin.

Ukrainian folk dance differs in style and costume, depending on the region being represented and the occasion being celebrated. While dancers from central Ukraine wear bright pants, embroidered shirts, and swirling skirts and aprons, Hutsul dancers from the Carpathian mountain region wear linen trousers tucked into leather slippers and felt hats, and brandish long wooden axes over which the men leap or on which they balance the women. Dance themes deal with relations between men and women as well as particular occupations such as the dances of reapers, cobblers, coopers, and smiths.

Among the most popular dances, though, are the *hopak* and *kozachok*. The *hopak* was first danced by the Cossack of the Zaporhizian Sich in the sixteenth century and spread to the rest of Ukraine. Today it is predominantly associated with the Kiev region and incorporates both male and female dances. It is a fast-tempoed, improvised dance with complex acrobatic movements with the men leaping over one another and high into the air, while the women spin and step around them.

The *kozachok* also originated during the Cossack period in the sixteenth century. It is a folk dance with male and female roles, and often begins with a slow, melodic introduction before breaking into a quick tempo. During the seventeenth and eighteenth centuries it was performed, not only in Ukraine, but also in the royal courts of Russia, France, Hungary, and Poland. Both the *hopak* and *kozachok* are standards of Ukrainian folk dance today.

The 1920s and 1930s were decades of growth in Ukrainian dance, theater and music in the United States. A number of theaters and music halls, beginning with the first in New York City in 1924, were opened. Ukrainian American singers and dancers performed in a concert commemorating the bicentennial of George Washington's birth in 1932, and the New York Association of Friends of Ukrainian Music was created in 1934. Another highlight of the period was a performance by more than 300 Ukrainian American dancers from Vasile Avramenko's dance school at the Metropolitan Opera House in New York City in 1931.

HOLIDAYS CELEBRATED BY UKRAINIAN AMERICANS

Ukrainian Americans all celebrate the same holidays but at different times, depending on which calendar they use. The major holidays are religious. According to the "old" or Julian calendar, Christmas is celebrated January 7, with the ritual dinner the night before. Easter cycles and falls on a different weekend each year. For those who adhere to a more modern model, Christmas and Easter would still be celebrated in a Ukrainian church, in the respective rite, but on December 25 and whatever weekend "English Easter" falls on.

One occasion Ukrainians do not traditionally celebrate is birthdays. More important are the "name days," days during the year which are named for certain saints. For example, friends would gather to help celebrate the name day of any Stephens or Stepany on January 9 by the Julian calendar, St. Stephen's Day.

The other major holiday is on January 22, commemorating the establishment of a free Ukraine on that date in 1917.

HEALTH AND MENTAL HEALTH ISSUES

There are no known afflictions specific to ethnic Ukrainians, although the most recent immigrants from the Chernobyl area are wary of the radiation exposure they received during the reactor meltdown of the late 1980s.

To some degree, folk medicine retains its place in the community in both attitude and practice. The mentally challenged were often considered to be "God's people." Physical diseases were often driven out by squeezing or sucking or were "frightened away" by shouting or beating. Diseases could also be "charmed away" by using magic incantations and prayers or treated with medicinal plants or, more "traditionally," using baths, bleeding (using leeches or cupping), or massages. These methods tended to fall out of favor as Ukrainians were assimilated into the American mode of health care.

Ukrainians have readily joined the American medical establishment. In addition to the health-care professionals who emigrated to the United States, Ukrainian Americans are well represented in the medical fields, including dentistry and chiropractic. In fact, regional associations of physicians were quick to spring up in the major northeastern centers of Ukrainian American concentration.

LANGUAGE

Ukrainian belongs to the Slavic group of Indo-European languages. It is the second most widely spoken language of the 12 surviving members of this group. Historically, there used to exist a literary language called Old Church Slavonic which

This Ukrainian American woman is demonstrating the art of painting Russian Easter eggs.

was common to all of Ukraine, in addition to the dialects of the regions. Unlike other languages such as German or English, the three main dialect groups—northern, southeastern and southwestern—are not particularly different from each other. The alphabet is made up of 33 Cyrillic characters, the last of which is a character which does not stand alone but follows various consonants to soften the sound. Each letter has a particular sound so reading is relatively simple, words being pronounced phonetically.

Ukrainian was the primary language of almost all first-generation Ukrainian Americans. Because of the political situation which they left at home, many also spoke Polish, Russian, or German. In 1980 less than 17 percent listed their primary language as Ukrainian. The Ukrainian language is taught in several universities and colleges, including Stanford University, University of Chicago, University of Illinois at Urbana-Champaign, Harvard University, University of Michigan, and Kent State University. Ukrainian language collections can be found in many public libraries including those in Denver, New York, Brooklyn, Detroit, Minneapolis, and Cleveland.

GREETINGS AND OTHER POPULAR EXPRESSIONS

Common Ukrainian greetings based upon the time of day include: *Dobredeyn*—Good day;

Dobrey ranok—Good morning; and *Dobra nych*—Good night. Other often used expressions include: *Diakoyu*—Thank you; *proshu* (used both for "please" and "you're welcome"), and *dopobachynya* (literally, "until we see each other again", although more commonly translated as "goodbye"). For festive occasions the phrase *mnohaya lita* is used, which means "many happy years"; a corresponding song entitled "*Mnohaya lita*" is the standard birthday song as well as being used for toasts for any happy occasion such as an anniversary or wedding.

There are standard, specific greetings and replies for Christmas and Easter. During the Christmas season, a visitor would enter a home saying, *Christos rodevsia*—Christ is born, and the host's reply would be *Slavim yoho*—Let us praise him. At Easter the greeting changes to *Christos voskrys*—Christ has risen, and the reply changes to *Voistenu voskrys*—He is risen indeed.

FAMILY AND COMMUNITY DYNAMICS

Particularly during the early waves of immigration, men came to America, settled, and then brought over their wives and children. Those who were single, after getting a job and a place to live, often sought to start a family and tended to seek a woman who was of the same ethnic background, if only for ease of communication. With each passing generation there has been a greater tolerance and incidence of marriage outside the Ukrainian culture. Similarly, divorce was and is still relatively rare; it made little economic sense in the beginning and was forbidden in the Catholic faith to which the majority of immigrants subscribed.

Because of geography and time, finding a wife or husband was not always easy. Dating, for early immigrants, was a quick practice centered on Ukrainian community social events—these new Americans worked long hours and had relatively little free time. The couple might attend a dance in a church hall or a concert. Even today, *zabavas* (dances) are prime meetings places for young people.

Around the turn of the century, Passaic, New Jersey, had a high concentration of single Ukrainian women. Most women were employed as domestics, often far from the foundry towns in large coastal cities. Some men left a wife behind in Ukraine and married again in America. A newspaper story published in 1896 told of such a case one step more unusual—the immigrant from Galicia left a wife there and married once in New Jersey and again in Michigan. After being arrested and then returning to his wife in Ukraine, he discovered his two children had grown to number four.

Like many other European immigrants, as the first generation of Ukrainian Americans aged, they often lived with one of their children to serve as babysitters for grandchildren, thereby freeing the parents to work. This also helped to continue the culture and language, and many children went to school speaking only Ukrainian.

Although the duties may have differed, both boys and girls were expected to help with household chores, especially in households where part of the income came from taking in boarders. Considerable responsibility fell on the older siblings to take care of those younger, and much was expected of them so that they could become successful and productive American citizens.

WEDDINGS

Weddings are a major celebration beginning with the negotiations for the bride's hand in marriage. The groom's family appoints a *starosty* (negotiator), who serves as an intermediary between the families of the prospective bride and groom. Originally, this figure did much of the work, even to haggling over the dowry of the bride. Today, if couples wish to include a *starosty*, it is more a symbolic role for a close relative or family friend and often translates into serving as master or mistress of ceremonies.

Before the wedding, a shower or *divych vechir* (maidens' evening) is hosted by the close friends and relatives of the bride. These are often large gatherings of women held in community banquet halls, although today they may be smaller, more intimate affairs hosted in homes. The groom and bride attend and sit beneath a wreath, after a full meal, opening the gifts which guests have brought.

One wedding day custom that is often retained is a blessing, at the home of the bride's parents, that precedes the church wedding ceremony. The bride, groom, and members of the immediate family join a priest to bless the impending union. Then everyone moves on to the church where a ceremony, which may include a full mass, takes place. During the ceremony there are certain customs; which are still kept up, such as placing crowns or wreaths of myrrh on the heads of the pair or binding the bride's and groom's hands with a long embroidered linen called a *rushnychok* and then having the priest lead them about the altar three times. The bride may also say a prayer at the altar and give a gift of flowers to the Virgin Mary, in hopes that she will bless the bride as both wife and mother.

Ukrainian wedding celebrations are large—it is not unusual to have more than 300 guests filling a church hall or banquet room—alive with song and dance, and lots of food. At the beginning of the reception, the bride and groom are greeted with bread and salt by their godparents. The bread represents the wish that they should never know hunger and the salt that they should never know bitterness. After the greeting, the newlyweds and their attendants sit at the head table and dinner begins.

A wedding dinner today reflects the tastes of the couple and their families and can include favorite Ukrainian and American dishes—*perogies* and roast beef. Although many couples have some sort of wedding cake, they may also have a traditional *kolach*; this is a bread with decorative flour, stalks of wheat and braids of dough adorning the top. The name is derived from the word *kolo* which means a circle, a symbol of eternity.

After dinner the dancing starts. Dancing is an integral part of any Ukrainian wedding, and there are a number of traditions built around the dancing segment. At one point in the evening, the bride's veil is removed and replaced with a kerchief, symbolizing her change from maiden to married woman. As the guests watch, encircling the bride and groom, the veil is then placed by the bridesmaids on the heads of single women in the circle who dance with their boyfriends, their fiancés, or groomsmen. Some couples also choose to incorporate throwing the bouquet and garter into the festivities.

BAPTISMS

Within the first year of a baby's birth, the child is christened. Close family friends or relatives are chosen as godparents and participate in the religious ceremony. This is a festive occasion which is often followed by a banquet hosted by the new parents. The link between godparent and child is maintained throughout the child's life and often the godparents are simply referred to as *chresna* (godmother) and *chresny* (godfather) for years after.

FUNERALS

Ukrainians are ritualistic and religious in their funeral rites as well. The actual religious ceremony and burial are preceded by one or two *panachydy*. These brief evening ceremonies are held in the funeral home, and friends and family of the deceased join for a memorial service. The ceremony is conducted by a priest and ends with the singing of the funeral song, "Vichnaya Pam'yat" (Ever Remembered).

The funeral itself is a religious occasion and can include a funeral mass in a church. Family and friends then accompany the casket to the gravesite (few people are cremated) and then repair to a church or community hall or family member's home for a *tryzna* (funeral remembrance luncheon).

One of the most significant features of a Ukrainian funeral is that the memorial service is repeated 40 days after the person dies, and then again annually. There is also a festival, originally associated with the pagan cult of the dead, called Zeleni *sviata* or Rosalia, which is dedicated to visiting and celebrating the dead. It is held 50 days after Easter, and today people meet at the cemetery to have a special mass said in honor of the dead.

EDUCATION

Education for the initial immigrants was a luxury few could afford. With each new wave, Ukrainians came to the United States with more and more education. Many of the artists and professionals who arrived between the wars had been educated in Europe and, as soon as they learned English, were able to pursue their work in the United States. There was also a growing number who studied at American schools and whose children were encouraged to do the same, both boys and girls. Wherever possible, children were educated in parochial schools because religion played a large role in their lives. Those who went on to post-secondary education tended to concentrate in the professions: medicine, law, engineering, graduate studies, and the arts.

Ukrainian American students decided to establish a network based on their common ethnic background soon after the third major wave of immigration. For example, the Federation of Ukrainian Students Organization of America, based in New York City, held its first congress April 10-12, 1953. This included 22 regional and university associations of students across America.

These young dancers from the United Ukrainian organization are performing the Zaporozhian Knight's Battle at the 1946 National Folk Festival in Cleveland, Ohio.

In addition to supporting religion, Ukrainian Americans also support political causes, the arts, sports, and education. The Shevchenko Scientific Society, which was founded in the United States in 1947 and included Albert Einstein among its members in the 1950s, supports science and research activities; the Ukrainian Congress Committee of America, Inc., founded in 1940, coordinates legal and material support for Ukrainians in Europe while raising the profile of Ukraine in America; and the Ukrainian National Association of America, originally established in 1894 as a fraternal benefit society to provide insurance to Ukrainian immigrants, supports the social education and welfare of Ukrainian immigrants while providing aid to the "old country."

THE ROLE OF WOMEN

As well as raising their families, women played a large role by adding to the family income, working as domestics, taking in boarders, working in kitchens or factories, or contributing to the family business. This was hard work; for example, working as a domestic meant seven-day work weeks, almost 13 hours each day, with just Sunday evenings free.

Women were also responsible for maintaining the language and culture, specifically through festive occasions such as Christmas and Easter. The wife and mother would spend hours baking and cooking the multicourse celebratory dinners, participating in the religious life of her family and community, and serving on various women's nationalistic committees.

Many women joined the organizations whose purpose was to promote Ukrainian interests in the diaspora. In addition to joining those groups which accepted men, women also formed their own associations such as the Ukrainian National Women's League of America, Inc. (a national nonpartisan, nonsectarian organization founded in 1925), whose purpose is to unite women of Ukrainian birth and descent living in the United States to promote their common philanthropic, educational, civic, and artistic interests in addition to assisting Ukrainians in Europe, the Ukrainian Women's Alliance, and the United Ukrainian Women's Organizations of America. The first congress of Ukrainian Women in America was held in New York in 1932. Women's organizations managed to combine Ukrainian and American interests (celebrating the birthdays of female poet Lesia Ukrainka along with those of George Washington and Abraham Lincoln in February) and tended to be less insular than men's organizations.

INTERACTIONS WITH OTHER ETHNIC MINORITIES

Even in their early settlement patterns, new Ukrainian immigrants tended to settle near other immigrants, particularly others from Eastern and Central Europe such as Polish, Russian, and Jewish immigrants. Because of the similarities in language (and the fact that many Ukrainians emigrated while their country was under the occupation of Russia, Poland, or Austro-Hungary), Ukrainians, Poles, and Russians could communicate easily even before they learned English. It also gave them the sense of community which they had left behind when they crossed the ocean to America.

RELIGION

Most Ukrainian Americans belong to one of two faiths, Catholic (Eastern, or Byzantine, Rite) and Eastern Orthodox. The Catholics are greater in number, almost twice as numerous as the Orthodox group. The first Ukrainian Catholic church in the United States, St. Michael the Archangel, was built in Shenandoah, Pennsylvania, in 1885 under the direction of the Reverend Ivan Volansky, an immigrant priest who had arrived the year before.

In the late nineteenth century there was a struggle within the Church and in 1899 the Reverend Volansky was called back to Lviv by his superiors, who had buckled under pressure from Vatican authorities who said that Volansky was an Eastern Rite Catholic and that the Latin Rite American Catholic bishops opposed the organization of separate Ukrainian Catholic parishes. This led some Ukrainians to switch to the Russian Orthodox faith. Finally, in 1913 the Vatican acceded to the demands of Ukrainian Catholics in the United States and established an exarchate which made all Ukrainian Catholic parishes, which numbered more than 200 at the time, a separate administrative unit which reported only to the Pope.

The Ukrainian Orthodox church in America was set up in 1928 by ex-Catholic Ukrainians. In addition, thousands of Catholic Ukrainians converted to the Russian Orthodox church after the consecrated priest of a Minneapolis parish, Alexis Toth, who was a widower, was not accepted by the Roman Catholic archbishop (because he had been married). Toth broke away to join the Orthodoxy; his 365 parishioners followed him, and tens of thousands of immigrants from Galicia, Lemkivschyna, and Transcarpathia filled out the ranks.

Ultimately, there were many battles among the dominant religious groups, which included Byzantine Rite Catholic Ruthenians/Ruthyns as they called themselves, Ukrainian Catholics, and Orthodox "Russians." Today the Ukrainian Catholic church (Byzantine Rite) and Orthodoxy remain strong in the United States.

There are also Ukrainian Protestants, including the Stundinst sect, a Baptist denomination which settled in the United States in 1890. This group settled first in Virginia and then went west to North Dakota, where they established a settlement called Kiev, named after the city in which they had lived in Ukraine.

In 1905 Ukrainian Protestants founded the Ukrainian Evangelical Alliance of North America. In 1922, the Union of Ukrainian Evangelical Baptist Churches was established to consolidate the Ukrainian Protestant parishes.

EMPLOYMENT AND ECONOMIC TRADITIONS

Most of the early immigrants of the late nineteenth century worked in the steel mills and foundries of the northeastern states. Within the ethnic urban communities where they lived, other entrepreneurial Ukrainian Americans opened grocery or general stores, butcher shops, and taverns. Women contributed to the family income by taking in boarders and doing their laundry and cooking. Overall, it was characteristic of this first generation of settlers to remain in the job, or at least the industry, with which they began.

Although their pay was not substantial, Ukrainian Americans as a group rarely took advantage of government assistance (where available) or unemployment benefits. They were also among the most law-abiding immigrants—in his *Ukrainians in North America: An Illustrated History*, Orest Subtelny notes that between 1904 and 1908, only 0.02 percent were accused of breaking any law.

By the time of the second immigration wave between the world wars, there was a shift in employment trends. Second-generation Ukrainian Americans had greater opportunity for higher education, and the second influx of immigrants tended to be better educated themselves. From that point forward, the university graduation rate grew, with medicine, law, engineering, and teaching being the principal professions. This is reflected in the growth of Ukrainian American professional and business clubs across the United States. For example, membership in the Society of Ukrainian Engineers in America grew from 82 members at the end of 1949 to 363 just five years later.

POLITICS AND GOVERNMENT

Ukrainian Americans were involved in local, state, and national politics from the earliest years of mass immigration. Dr. Nicholas Sudzilovsky-Russel was elected to and became presiding officer of the Hawaiian senate on February 10, 1901.

In 1925, George Chylak began a five-year term as mayor of Oliphant, Pennsylvania. Mary Beck (Mariia Bek), born in 1908 in Ford City, Pennsylvania, was the first woman elected to the Detroit Common Council. She served as the council's president from 1952 to 1962 and was the acting mayor of Detroit from 1958 to 1962.

In state politics, the lawyer O. Malena took a seat in the Pennsylvania legislature in 1932, the lawyer S. Jarema won a seat in the New York legislature in 1935, and Judge John S. Gonas (b. 1907) took a seat in the Indiana legislature in 1936. Gonas was also a senator from 1940-1948 and a Democratic candidate for vice president in 1960.

Ukrainian Americans also garnered the attention of government rather quickly. On March 16, 1917, President Woodrow Wilson proclaimed April 21 a day "upon which the people of the United States may make such contributions as they feel disposed to aid the stricken Ruthenians (Ukrainians) in the belligerent countries," following discussion in Congress on the Ukrainian cause. And it was President Dwight D. Eisenhower who unveiled a stature of poet and nationalist Taras Shevchenko in Washington, D.C., to commemorate the 150th anniversary of the poet's birth.

Ukrainians, although some belonged to Communist organizations such as the Haidamaky (established in 1907 in New York), tend to be conservative in their politics and, therefore, tend to support the Republican party. But in 1910, the Ukrainian National Association of America (UNA) actually encouraged people to vote for the socialists since neither Republicans nor Democrats were addressing the concerns of the workers. Leftist factions included the Ukrainian Workers Association which broke away from the UNA in 1918 and the Ukrainian Federation of Socialist Parties in America. The other choice for Ukrainian Americans in the 1920s was the conservative-monarchist Sich movement.

Ukrainian Americans are also involved in supporting political change in Ukraine itself. Demonstrations were frequent in the 1920s and 1930s and included the participation of thousands of men, women, and children: the White House was picketed in 1922 on the issues of Polish occupation of Eastern Galicia; about 20,000 Ukrainian Americans marched in Philadelphia in 1930 to protest this same Polish occupation of Western Ukraine; and a 1933 march in Detroit was held to protest the Soviet-induced famine in Ukraine.

MILITARY

Early records reveal that Ukrainian Americans served in George Washington's army during the American Revolution. Mykola Bizun, Ivan Lator, Petro Polyn, and Stephen Zubley are just some of the Ukrainian names that are listed in Washington's register. There was also a group that fought in the Union Army during the American Civil War. Officers Joseph Krynicky, Ivan Mara, and Andrey Ripka served, and the Union dead included Ukrainian Americans Julius Koblansky, Petro Semen, and I. H. Yarosh. All of this, however, was relatively limited involvement since the major waves of immigration were to follow.

Most significant for the Ukrainian Americans during the years of World War I was the concurrent bid for a free Ukraine. World War I was heralded as an opportunity to defeat Austria or Russia, both of which ruled parts of Ukraine at the time. The Federation of Ukrainians in America was formed in 1915 to inform the American public about Ukrainian goals. In 1917—the same year that President Woodrow Wilson declared April 21 as "Ukrainian Day"—dreams were realized and the Ukrainian Peoples Republic was established. But Wilson supported the Russian empire, and not long after, the free Ukraine fell. In addition, many Ukrainians, particularly in Canada, were deemed to be Austrian citizens and, hence, on the wrong side; thousands were incarcerated as enemy aliens.

During World War II thousands of Ukrainian Americans served in the armed forces. Nicholas Minue of Carteret, New Jersey, was posthumously awarded the Congressional Medal of Honor for his single-handed destruction of a German machine gun position. Nestor Chylak, Jr., who went on to be an American League baseball umpire, received the Purple Heart and Silver Star and was almost blinded during the Battle of the Bulge. And Lt. Colonel Theodore Kalakula was awarded the Silver Star and two oak leaf clusters for saving medical supplies during a Japanese air raid and for his attack against the Japanese after the company commander had been wounded. Kalakula was also the first Ukrainian American graduate of West Point.

INDIVIDUAL AND GROUP CONTRIBUTIONS

Ukrainian Americans, in all areas of endeavor, have made lasting contributions to American life. Some of these individuals and their accomplishments follow.

ACADEMIA

George Kistiakovsky (1900-1982), a research chemist, immigrated in 1925 to the United States, where he became a research fellow at Princeton University, after which he joined the faculty of Harvard University in 1930. He was the author of more than 200 articles on chemical kinetic gas-phase reactions, molecular spectroscopy, and thermochemistry of organic compounds. He received many awards including the U.S. President's Medal of Merit in 1946, the Exceptional Service Award of the U.S. Air Force in 1957, and the National Medal of Sciences from the president in 1965. He also served as a consultant to the Manhattan Project, the initiative to develop the atomic bomb in the early 1940s and was appointed head of the explosives division of the Los Alamos Laboratory. In 1959 he was named Special Assistant for Science and Technology by President Dwight D. Eisenhower. Kistiakovsky's daughter, Vera (born in 1928 in Princeton, New Jersey) is an accomplished academic in her own right. She completed her Ph.D. in nuclear chemistry at the University of California, Berkeley, in 1952 and became a professor of physics at the Massachusetts Institute of Technology in 1963.

Other Ukrainian American academics include George Vernadsky, (1897-1972) a historian at Yale University from 1946-1956 and author of a five-volume history of Russian and a biography of Hetman Bohdan Khmelnytsky; Stephen Timoshenko (1878-1972), a specialist in theoretical and applied mechanics, vibration, and elasticity who taught at the University of Michigan and Stanford University from 1927 to 1960; Lew Dobriansky, (b. 1918), economist and author of *Decisions for a Better America*, published in 1960; and Myron Kuropas (b. 1932), professor of educational foundations at Northern Illinois University and special assistant for ethnic affairs to President Gerald Ford in 1976-1977. Kuropas has written several books on Ukrainians in North America including *To Preserve a Heritage: The Story of the Ukrainian Immigration in the United States*, published in 1984.

FILM, TELEVISION, AND THEATRE

Ukrainian Americans who found their way to Hollywood include director Edward Dmytryk (1908-) and Academy Award winner Jack Palance. Dmytryk directed a number of Hollywood films including *Murder My Sweet, Crossfire*, and *The Caine Mutiny*.

Jack Palance, born Walter Palahniuk on February 12, 1920, in Lattimer, Pennsylvania, made his first film, *Panic in the Streets*, in 1950. He began his career as a professional boxer in the 1940s after he returned from a tour of duty in the U.S. Army Air Corps. He made his stage debut on Broadway in *Silver Tassel* in 1949, and also appeared in stage productions of *Julius Caesar, The Tempest* and *A Streetcar Named Desire*. Among his more than 50 films are *Shane, Batman*, and *City Slickers*, for which he won an Academy Award as Best Supporting Actor in 1991. He had his own television series, "Bronk," in 1975, and appeared on various programs over more than four decades.

One of the most versatile individuals in Ukrainian dance and film was Wasyl Avramenko. Born in 1895 in Stebliv, Ukraine, he founded the First School of Ukrainian National Dances in Kalisz, Poland, in 1921. After he immigrated to the United States he directed performances at the Metropolitan Opera House, the 1893 World's Fair in Chicago, the White House in 1935, and took dance tours to Brazil, Argentina, Australia, and Israel throughout the 1950s, 1960s, and 1970s. He established his own dance studio in New York in 1952. Avramenko also did work in film; in 1936, he organized a Ukrainian film company and produced two movies using the texts of two Ukrainian classic plays, *Zaporozhetz Za Dunaem* (*The Cossack from Beyond the Danube*) and *Natalka Poltavka* (Natalka from Poltava).

William Tytla (1904-1968) made his mark in Hollywood animation. He was born in Yonkers, New York, and worked at Walt Disney Studios as an animator, creating Dumbo and the Seven Dwarfs before moving to Paramount, Famous Studios, and Twentieth Century-Fox, where he was director of a cartoon series including Popeye, Little Audrey, and Little Lulu.

Among others in this area of the arts were: Nick Adams, born Adamschock (1931-1968); Anna Sten, born Stenski-Sujakevich (1908-1993), star of *The Brothers Karamazov* and *Nana*; and 1940s Hollywood leading man, John Hodiak (1914-1955) who was married to actress Anne Baxter and starred in Alfred Hitchcock's *Lifeboat* with Tallulah Bankhead and *The Harvey Girls* opposite Judy Garland.

JOURNALISM

There are many Ukrainian Americans who have contributed to a rich heritage of Ukrainian-language journalism in the United States. Reverend Ivan Volansky (1857-1926) published *Ameryka*, the first Ukrainian newspaper in the United States in 1886.

Because of the rapid growth of the Ukrainian press in the United States, there are hundreds of women and men who could be listed here. A partial list includes: Cecelia Gardetska (b. 1898), who worked on journals in Ukraine and America including *Nashe Zhitia* (*Our Life*) in Philadelphia and served as the head of the Department of Journalists for the Federation of Ukrainian Women's Organizations in the United States; Bohdan Krawciw (b. 1904), who in addition to editing more than 15 journals and newspapers was general editor of Volume 2 of *Ukraine: A Concise Encyclopedia*, published in 1971; and Volodymyr Nestorovych (b. 1893), also an editor of a number of Ukrainian-language newspapers in the United States, although he was an engineer and economist by occupation.

LITERATURE

Tania Kroitor Bishop, born Shevchuk, published *An Overture to Future Days* in 1954. This volume of poetry was written in both English and Ukrainian. Bishop also translated other works from Ukrainian into English.

A circle of young poets who called themselves the New York Group of Poets, among them Bohdan Boychuk (1927-), Patricia Kylyna (P. Warren), Yurii (George) Tarnavsky (1934-), and B. Pevny (1931-), published its first volume of modern poetry in 1959. Boychuk became a U.S. citizen in 1955 and worked as an engineer in addition to publishing plays and poetry.

MUSIC

Professor Alexander Koshetz (1875-1944) directed the first concert of Ukrainian church music to an American audience at Carnegie Hall, New York City, in 1936. Hryhorii Kytastyi (1907-1984), musical director, composer and bandurist, is the author of more than 30 melodies of Ukrainian songs for solo and choir with bandura (a traditional stringed instrument) or piano accompaniment. He directed the Bandurists Ensemble in numerous concerts throughout Europe, the United States, and Canada.

Other notables in music include: Nicholas Malko, director of the Chicago Symphony Orchestra from 1945 to 1957; Mykhailo Haivoronsky (1892-1949), composer and founder of the United Ukrainian Chorus in the United States in 1930; Paul Pecheniha-Ouglitzky (Uhlytsky) (1892-1948), double-bass player, composer, and conductor, who lived and worked in New York and was orchestrator for NBC radio; and Virko Baley (1938-), pianist, composer, champion of Ukrainian modern music and chamber music, and conductor of the Las Vegas Symphony Orchestra.

SCIENCE AND TECHNOLOGY

Aeronautical engineer Igor Sikorsky, born in Kiev in 1889 (d. 1972), immigrated to the United States and formed the Sikorsky Aero Engineering Company in 1923. This company built the S-29, the first twin-engine plane made in the United States. Sikorsky is also credited with designing the first helicopter (the VS-300, first flown in 1939) and the S-40 (the first large American four-engine clipper, built in 1931).

Michael Yarymovich (1933-) served as chief scientist of the U.S. Air Force and assistant director to the Apollo Flight Systems in the 1960s. In 1975, he was appointed Assistant Administrator for Laboratory and Field Coordination of the Energy Research and Development Adminstration.

SPORTS

Many Ukrainian Americans became successful in the National Hockey League (NHL). Terry Sawchuk (1929-1970) was elected to the Hockey Hall of Fame in 1971 with 103 career shutouts as a goalie having played 21 seasons with Detroit and Toronto. Bill Moisenko (d. 1994), a right wing for the Chicago Black Hawks, was selected for the all-star team in 1947 and scored a record three goals in 21 seconds in one 1952 game. New York Ranger teammates Walter Tkaczuk and Dave Balon were two-thirds of the NHL's highest scoring line during the 1969-1970 season. And in 1971, Johnny Bucyk, Vic Stasiuk, and Bronko Horvath formed the famous "Uke" line in the all-star game. More recently, Ukrainian American hockey players have included Mike Bossy, Dale Hawerchuk, and Mike Krushelyski.

In baseball, there was umpire Nestor Chylak, Jr. (1922-1982). Chylak was born in Peckville, Pennsylvania and studied engineering at Rutgers University before going to war from 1942 to 1946. He was nearly blinded at the Battle of the Bulge and was awarded the Silver Star and Purple Heart. His major league officiating career spanned three decades, from 1954 to 1978, when he retired as an umpire in the American League.

Football was another sport in which Ukrainian Americans excelled. Bronko (Bronislav) Nagurski (1908-1990) was a famous tackle for the Chicago Bears in the 1930s and 1940s. He helped lift the Bears from ninth to third place in the league and was an all-league player for three consecutive years. Nagurski was elected to the National Football Hall of Fame in 1951. He also made a career as a professional wrestler and won the world heavyweight title in 1937 and 1939. Charles Bednarick, center for the Philadelphia Eagles from 1949 until 1962, was elected to the National Football Hall of Fame in 1967.

Ukrainian American boxers included Steve Halaiko, a member of the 1932 U.S. Olympic team and Golden Gloves champion; and John Jadick, junior heavyweight champion in the 1930s. Wrestler Mike Mazurki (1909-1990) (born Michael Mazurski) went on to a career in films in the 1940s. In the 1960s there were golfers Mike Souchak and Steve Melnik, and soccer star Zenon Snylyk, a member of the 1964 U.S. Olympic soccer team and World Cup team.

VISUAL ARTS

Two of the best-known Ukrainian American artists celebrated their birthdays one day apart. Edward Kozak was born January 26, 1902, in Hirne, Ukraine. Having studied at the Art Acade-

my in Lviv he immigrated to the United States, becoming a citizen in 1956. In addition to participating in exhibitions across the United States, Canada, and Europe, he has illustrated a number of books and from 1951-1954 was a performer on WWJ-TV in Detroit. He established his own painting studios in Detroit and Warren, Michigan, in 1950 and for his efforts in educational films was twice awarded first prize by the American Teachers' Association. Fellow artist Jacques Hnizdovsky, born January 27, 1915, in Pylypcze, Ukraine, studied at the Academy of Fine Arts in Warsaw and Zagreb before settling in New York City in 1949. His career has included a number of one-man shows in North America and Europe. He is best known for his woodcuts, and his work is featured in collections in the Boston Museum of Fine Arts, the Philadelphia Museum of Art, the White House, and the Museum of Modern Arts, Spain.

Another influential figure in the arts community was sculptor Alexander Archipenko (1887-1964), who settled in the United States in 1923. He opened his own art school in New York City in 1939 and served as sculptor in residence at a number of American universities. At the time of his death, he had just completed his 199th one-man exhibition.

Ukrainian American artists established their own association in 1952. More than 100 painters, graphic artists, and sculptors were part of the original group, which included Kozak, Hnizdovsky, Michael Moroz, Michael Chereshnovsky (1911-), and Nicholas Mukhyn.

Yaroslava Surmach-Mills is another well-known artist. Born in New York City in 1925, she graduated from the Cooper Union Art School and has worked as an art instructor, as art editor for *Humpty Dumpty Magazine*, and as an illustrator for numerous children's books. Her work, "Carol Singers," was chosen as a UNICEF Christmas card design in 1965.

MEDIA

PRINT

America.

Published by the Providence Association, an insurance company, it is a weekly tabloid with separate issues in Ukrainian and English, with a circulation of about 6,000. First printed in 1912, this Catholic paper covers politics, sports, and news about Ukraine and the United States.

Contact: Osip Roshka, Editor.

Address: 817 North Franklin Street, Philadelphia, Pennsylvania 19123.

Telephone: (215) 627-0233.

Narodnia Volya.

Published by the Ukrainian Fraternal Association (UFA). First printed in 1911, this weekly publication has a circulation of about 3,000. There are two editors, one for the Ukrainian pages and another for *The Ukrainian Herald*—the English-language section. The paper includes a literary section, news from Ukraine and the United States as it concerns Ukrainian Americans, and updates on the life of the Association. The UFA also publishes an English-language quarterly called *Forum* on the arts and history of Ukraine.

Contact: Nicholas Duplak, Ukrainian Editor; or Serge Kowalchuk, Jr., English Editor.

Address: 440 Wyoming Avenue, Scranton, Pennsylvania 18503.

Telephone: (717) 342-8897.

New Star Ukrainian Catholic Newspaper.

The organ of the St. Nicholas Diocese in Chicago, this bulletin of church news has a circulation of 3,500 and is published in both Ukrainian and English every three weeks.

Contact: Ivana Gorchynsky, Editor.

Address: 2208 West Chicago Avenue, Chicago, Illinois 60622.

Telephone: (312) 772-1919.

Svoboda.

A daily Ukrainian-language newspaper with a circulation of 14,000, it includes local and Ukrainian news stories and advertisements. A weekly English-language newspaper, *Ukrainian Weekly*, is published out of the same location.

Contact: Zenon Snylyk, Editor of *Svoboda*; or Roma Hadzewych, Editor of *Ukrainian Weekly*.

Address: 30 Montgomery Street, Jersey City, New Jersey 07302.

Telephone: (201) 434-0237.

Ukrainian News.

Originally published in Germany in 1944, this Detroit-based paper has an international circulation. It is published weekly by the Bahriany Foun-

dation (a foundation of writers named for Ukrainian writer and political leader Ivan Bahriany). The content includes news as well as literary articles.

Contact: Serhiy Kozak, Editor.

Address: 19411 West Warren Avenue, Detroit, Michigan 48228.

Telephone: (313) 336-8291.

RADIO

WCEV and WVVX.

"Ukrainian Variety Hour," hosted by Maria Chychula from 9:00 to 10:00 a.m. daily on FM 103.1, and on Monday, Wednesday, and Thursday evenings, 7:00 to 8:00 pm on AM 1450. She has been hosting these cultural radio programs since the late 1960s.

Contact: Maria Chychula.

Address: 2224 West Chicago Avenue, Chicago, Illinois 60622.

Telephone: (312) 278-1836.

WHLD (1270).

"Sharvan's Ukrainian Radio Program," hosted by Wasyl Sharvan for more than 45 years, is a weekly program that airs from 1:30 to 4:30 p.m. on Saturdays and includes includes commentary, news, and music.

Contact: Wasyl Sharvan.

Address: 701 Fillmore Avenue, Buffalo, New York 14212.

Telephone: (716) 895-0700.

WNZK.

"Song of Ukraine," "Slovo," and "Ukrainian Catholic Hour" comprise three hours of Ukrainian programming weekly for the more than 100,000 Ukrainian Americans in the metro Detroit area. "Song of Ukraine" is a commentary program, airing Tuesdays at 9:00 p.m.; "Slovo," airing Fridays at 8:00 p.m., is a program hosted by and for new immigrants; and "Ukrainian Catholic Hour," airing on Saturdays at noon, combines information, sermons, and music for Catholics of the Byzantine Rite.

Contact: Jerry Tertzakian.

Address: 1837 Torquay, Royal Oak, Michigan 48073.

Telephone: (810) 557-3500.

ORGANIZATIONS AND ASSOCIATIONS

Ukrainian Academy of Arts and Sciences in the United States.

Founded in 1950, it was established to organize and sponsor scholars pursuing Ukrainian studies. The facilities include a museum and library which has material on the history of Ukrainian immigration to the United States and books on Ukrainian history and literature. It also publishes a scholarly journal, *Annals of the Ukrainian Academy of Arts and Sciences*.

Contact: Dr. Marko Antonovych, President.

Address: 206 West 100th Street, New York, New York 10025.

Telephone: (212) 222-1866.

Ukrainian American Youth Association.

Operates summer camps and offers various cultural and recreational activities.

Contact: Stefa Hryckowian, President.

Address: 136 Second Avenue, New York, New York 10003.

Telephone: (212) 477-3084.

Ukrainian Catholic Church.

First parish in the United States, established in 1885 in Shenandoah, Pennsylvania.

Contact: Archbishop Metropolitan Stephen Sulyk.

Address: Archdiocese of Philadelphia, 827 North Franklin Street, Philadelphia, Pennsylvania 19123.

Telephone: (215) 627-0143.

Ukrainian National Women's League of America.

A non-partisan, non-sectarian organization that sponsors educational scholarships and cultural events.

Contact: Anna Krawczuk, President.

Address: 108 Second Avenue, New York, New York 10003.

Telephone: (212) 533-4646.

Ukrainian Orthodox Church in America.

Founded in 1928 by Ukrainians who emigrated from Russia, Bukovina, Galicia, and Poland.

Contact: Father F. Istochyn, Secretary to the Archbishop.

Address: Ukrainian Orthodox Church of St. Vladimir, 6729 North Fifth Street, Philadelphia, Pennsylvania 19126.

Telephone: (212) 927-2287.

MUSEUMS AND RESEARCH CENTERS

Harvard Ukrainian Research Institute.

Established January 22, 1968, with financial and moral support from large numbers of Ukrainian Americans, Ukrainian Studies at Harvard began in 1957.

Contact: George Grabowicz, Director.

Address: Harvard University, 1583 Massachusetts Avenue, Cambridge, Massachusetts 02138.

Telephone: (617) 495-4053.

Shevchenko Scientific Society.

Founded in 1947 in New York City to support research and to assist immigrant Ukrainian scholars in adjusting to life in the United States, it was named for the famous nineteenth-century Ukrainian poet, Taras Shevchenko. The society organizes scientific sessions, lectures, and conferences as well as maintaining archives and a library.

Contact: Leonid Rudnytzky, President.

Address: 63 Fourth Avenue, New York, New York 10003.

Telephone: (212) 254-5130.

Ukrainian Institute of America.

Founded in 1948, the Institute maintains a permanent exhibition of Ukrainian folk arts, sponsors lectures, concerts and conferences, and houses a Ukrainian historical gallery. It was established with funds from Volodymyr Dzus, a wealthy Ukrainian industrialist.

Contact: Volodymyr Barenecki, President.

Address: 2 East 79th Street, New York, New York 10021.

Telephone: (212) 772-8489.

Ukrainian Museum-Archives Inc.

Established in 1952, the archives emphasize the period of the Ukrainian Revolution and Ukrainian immigration to the United States after World War II. The archives include about 20,000 volumes in addition to archival materials.

Contact: Stepan Malanczuk, Director.

Address: 1202 Kenilworth Avenue, Cleveland, Ohio 44113.

Telephone: (216) 781-4329.

Ukrainian National Museum.
Established in 1958 through the merger of the Ukrainian Archive-Museum in Chicago and the Ukrainian National Museum and Library of Ontario, Canada.

Address: 2453 West Chicago Avenue, Chicago, Illinois.

Telephone: (312) 276-6565.

SOURCES FOR ADDITIONAL STUDY

Encyclopedia of Ukraine, five volumes, edited by Volodymyr Kubijovyc and Danylo Husar Struk. Toronto: University of Toronto Press, 1984-1993.

Kuropas, Myron B. *The Ukrainian Americans: Roots and Aspirations 1884-1954*. Toronto: University of Toronto Press, 1991.

Subtelny, Orest. *Ukrainians in North America: An Illustrated History*. Toronto: University of Toronto Press, 1991.

Ukraine and Ukrainians Throughout the World: A Demographic and Sociological Guide to the Homeland and Its Diaspora, edited by Ann Lencyk Pawliczko. Toronto: University of Toronto Press for the Shevchenko Scientific Society, Inc., 1994.

Ukrainians in North America, edited by Dmytro M. Shtohryn. Champaign, Illinois: Association for the Advancement of Ukrainian Studies, 1975.

Werstman, Vladimir. *The Ukrainians in America 1608-1975*. New York: Oceana Publications, 1976.

VIETNAMESE AMERICANS

by
Carl L. Bankston III

The extended family
is the heart of
Vietnamese culture,
and preservation of
family life in their
new home is one of
the most important
concerns of
Vietnamese
Americans.

OVERVIEW

The Socialist Republic of Vietnam is a long, narrow, "S"-shaped country of 127,243 square miles (329,556 square kilometers). It extends about 1,000 miles from southern China southward to the Gulf of Thailand. It is bordered on the west by Laos and Cambodia and on the east by the south China Sea. At the center of the "S," Vietnam is less than 30 miles wide. The northern and southern parts of the country are somewhat wider, with the north reaching a maximum width of 350 miles.

This southeast Asian nation has a population of about 69 million people. The ethnic Vietnamese, who make up nearly 90 percent of the population, are thought to be descendants of peoples who migrated into the Mekong Delta of northern Vietnam from southern China. There are also about three million members of mountain tribes, found mainly in the Central Highlands and in the Annamese Cordillera mountain chain in the north; about two million ethnic Chinese, most of whom live in large cities; about 500,000 Khmer, or ethnic Cambodians; and about 50,000 Cham, descendants of a Malayo-Polynesian people who dominated the area that is now southern Vietnam before the arrival of the Vietnamese.

Religions include Buddhism, Confucianism, Taoism, Roman Catholicism, Cao Dai (a mixture of aspects of Roman Catholicism and various Asian religions), Hoa Hao (a Vietnamese offshoot of Buddhism), Islam, Protestantism, and animism. Most Vietnamese practice the mutually compatible religions of Buddhism, Confucianism, and Taoism. About three million are Catholics, concentrated in the southern part of the country. About one million practice the Cao Dai religion and about one million belong to the Hoa Hao sect. The number of Protestants is small, and they are mostly found among the tribesmen of the mountains, where American and European missionaries were active until recently. Almost all of the Cham are Muslims.

The country's official language is Vietnamese and the capital city is Hanoi. The official flag is red with a large yellow star in the center, but many Vietnamese Americans object to this flag, viewing it as an emblem of the communist government. They identify instead with the flag of former South Vietnam, which is yellow with three horizontal red stripes in the center.

EARLY HISTORY

Although the Vietnamese are newcomers to North America, they are heirs to a culture far older than the United States, and even older than any of the national societies of Europe. The first known historical records of the Viets in the Red River Delta of what is now northern Vietnam were written by the Chinese in the second century B.C. Vietnamese archaeologists have traced their civilization back even further, to the *Phung-Nguyen* culture that existed before 2000 B.C.

While the village constituted the basis of rural Vietnamese folk culture, many of the nation's formal institutions were introduced from the great neighbor to the north, China. Even the name of the smaller country is derived from Chinese, "*Viet*" being a variant pronunciation of the Chinese word "*Yueh*", which was an ancient southern Chinese state, and "*Nam*" being the same as the Chinese word "*nan*", or "south." Vietnam's close but troubled relations with its huge northern neighbor have shaped many of its political and social structures and have, in recent years, played a crucial role in the creation of a refugee crisis.

As the Chinese empire of the Han dynasty extended its control over the area to the south, the Viets accepted Chinese administrative designations for their territory and the local rulers were redefined as prefectural and district officers.

Despite some early rebellions against Chinese rule (one in particular was instigated by the Trung sisters, who remain Vietnamese national heroes for their struggles against the Chinese in the first century A.D.), Vietnam was a part of the Chinese empire until the successful war for independence in the tenth century. Despite the adoption of Chinese forms of government, Chinese written characters, and Chinese-style Buddhism, the Vietnamese have continued to be wary of their powerful neighbor.

Until the fifteenth century, the Vietnamese occupied only the northern part of what we now know as their country. The southern part constituted the empire of the Cham, Champa, and part of the Khmer, or Cambodian, empire. By 1471, however, under the rulers of the Le dynasty (modeled after the Chinese "emperors"), Vietnam succeeded in conquering almost the whole of Champa. This success not only brought the newly enlarged country into conflict with the Khmers, but it also gave the country its present elongated shape, wide at the top and bottom and exceedingly narrow in the middle where the mountains that run down its center approach the sea coast. This geographical feature, often described as two heads and a little body, divided the country into two regions.

MODERN VIETNAM

While Vietnam's early history was dominated by its struggles with neighboring China, modern Vietnam has been greatly influenced by the European nation of France. Vietnam's early contacts with Europe were primarily forged through Catholic missionaries, particularly Jesuits, who arrived in 1615, after they had been prohibited from entering Japan. France, as the most powerful of Catholic nations in the seventeenth century, was especially active in supporting these religious endeavors, through the Societe des Missions Etrangeres. Alexandre des Rhodes, a French Jesuit, was instrumental in establishing a formidable French Catholic presence in Vietnam, and distributed Christian literature printed in a romanized system of writing, later adopted throughout Vietnam and called *quoc ngu* (corresponding to the Chinese words *kuo-yu*, or "national language").

Through the work of missionaries, the French gained influence in Vietnam long before the arrival of a single French soldier or administrator. When a peasant rebellion, known as the

Tay-son rebellion, reunified the country in 1788 under the rule of a rebel leader who had himself proclaimed emperor, the surviving heir of the southern Nguyen family, Nguyen Anh, sought the assistance of France. Through the missionaries, this claimant to the throne received French ships and volunteer troops that helped him reestablish himself at Saigon in 1789. The French also constructed forts for him and trained his troops, which enabled Nguyen Anh to take control of the entire country by 1802.

Nguyen Anh's son, the Emperor Minh-mang, facilitated a revival of the Confucian religion to reestablish order in the country and to support his own position as an emperor. The spread of Catholicism presented a danger to the Confucian order in the eyes of Minh-mang and his advisors and Minh-mang consequently initiated a policy of persecution against Catholics in 1825. The missionaries, however, continued to fight against the imperial prohibition of mission-work.

By the nineteenth century, the French were struggling to catch up to other European countries in the competition for colonies. The French Emperor Napoleon III took up the cause of the Catholics in Vietnam and used their persecution as a pretext for invading the country and seizing Saigon and the three surrounding provinces in 1859. Minh-mang's grandson, Tu-duc, had to choose between opposing a rebellion in the north and effectively fighting the French; in 1862 he ceded the three provinces to France and agreed to the establishment of a French protectorate over Vietnamese foreign relations. In the 1880s, following a war between France and China, which still claimed sovereignty over Vietnam, the French extended their control over the rest of Vietnam. They held the southern part, known as Cochin China, as a colony, and central and northern Vietnam as protectorates, under the nominal rule of French-controlled emperors of the Nguyen dynasty.

As in other parts of Southeast Asia, the system of colonial domination created in the late nineteenth century was maintained until the rise of an Asian imperial power, Japan. A variety of Vietnamese nationalist movements had developed in response to French rule. The anti-imperialist stance expressed in Lenin's analysis of colonialism attracted some, including the young man who joined the French Socialist Party in 1920 and later became known by the adopted name of Ho Chi Minh. Following the surrender of France to Japan's ally, Germany, Ho Chi Minh's forces were left as the only effective resistance to Japan in Vietnam.

When Japan surrendered in August 1945, the Communist-dominated nationalist forces known as the Viet Minh suddenly found themselves in power. The last of the French-controlled Vietnamese emperors, Bao-dai, abdicated and Ho Chi Minh declared the independence of Vietnam, now known as the Democratic Republic of Vietnam, on September 2, 1945. Japanese forces remained in Vietnam, however, and the Allies moved in to disarm them and send them home. China, still under the Nationalist government of Chiang Kai Chek, was given the task of disarming the Japanese in northern Vietnam, while Britain was assigned the south. Vietnam's French citizens were concentrated in Saigon and the British military was accompanied by French troops. While the Chinese allowed the Viet Minh to retain control of Hanoi and the north, the British helped the French seize control of the south and reestablish French colonial power. After the British left in January 1946 and the Chinese left in the spring of that same year, the country was divided into north and south once again.

At first the French and the new Vietnamese government accepted one another, albeit uneasily, as neither was prepared for open conflict. In March 1946, Ho Chi Minh signed an agreement with the French in which he accepted the deployment of French troops in the north, while France agreed to recognize the Democratic Republic of Vietnam, on the condition that this state would remain part of the Indochinese Federation (including the parts of Vietnam under direct French rule, Cambodia, and Laos) and part of the French Union. Ho Chi Minh and the French also agreed to hold a popular referendum on reuniting the country.

France was not interested in seeing a truly independent power in Vietnam, and the Viet Minh had no desire to see their country continue under colonial rule. In late 1946 and early 1947, tensions between the two sides erupted into combat and the first Vietnam War began. In February 1947, following the Battle of Hanoi, France reoccupied Hanoi and the Viet Minh once again assumed the position of guerrillas, fighting in the mountains.

It was a long time before either side was able to gain a decisive victory. In the early 1950s, however, the growing army of the Democratic Republic of Vietnam, under the command of General Vo Nguyen Giap, began a series of offenses against the French, achieving a famous victory at the city of Dien Bien Phu in May 1954. The French defeat at Dien Bien Phu pushed an international conference on Vietnam in Geneva to recognize a temporary division of the country into North and South Vietnam. In the North, the communist-led Democratic Republic of Vietnam ruled from Hanoi. In the South, the Republic of Vietnam, under the French-supported Emperor Bao-dai, ruled from Saigon, with Ngo Dinh Diem as premier. Some South Vietnamese who sympathized with Ho Chi Minh's government moved north. About one million northerners, between 600,000 and 800,000 of whom were Catholics, fled south on U.S. and French aircraft and naval vessels.

Ngo Dinh Diem proved to be an energetic leader, who put down armed religious sects and criminal groups. In 1955, Diem organized and won elections that forced Bao-dai to abdicate and Diem named himself president of the Republic. Supported by the United States, Diem refused to take part in the elections for national re-unification that had been promised by the Geneva Conference, which led to terrorism and other forms of resistance to his regime in many parts of South Vietnam.

VIETNAM AND THE UNITED STATES

Before 1975, there were almost no Vietnamese people in the United States, but the destinies of Vietnam and the United States became increasingly intertwined during the 1950s and 1960s. Since the war, the Vietnamese have become one of the largest Asian American groups. The American government began to show an interest in Vietnam during World War II, when it gave supplies and other forms of assistance to Ho Chi Minh's anti-Japanese forces. After the war, however, containment of international communism became America's primary foreign policy objective, and the Americans became increasingly dedicated to preserving the anti-communist South Vietnamese government of Ngo Dinh Diem in order to keep the North Vietnamese from taking over the whole country.

Diem, a Catholic, relied heavily on South Vietnamese Catholics and on the large numbers of Catholic refugees from the north. This created resentment in the Buddhist majority, which created opportunities for the North Vietnamese-supported insurgents, who organized themselves as the National Liberation Front and became known

as the Viet Cong. Many volunteer agencies based in the United States, including CARE, Catholic Relief Services, and Church World Services, became active in South Vietnam in the 1950s in response to the social disruption of war. It was through these organizations that many of the South Vietnamese were first acquainted with Americans and American culture.

In 1961 President Kennedy sent military advisors to South Vietnam to assist the beleaguered Diem government. Diem became increasingly unpopular in his own country, however; and in 1963 he was overthrown by a military coup, apparently with the knowledge and consent of the American government. The new leaders of South Vietnam proved less able to maintain control than Diem and by 1965, with the South Vietnamese government on the verge of collapse, President Johnson sent in ground troops.

American military and political leaders believed they were winning the war through the end of 1967. At the beginning of 1968, the Viet Cong and North Vietnamese troops launched the *Tet* offensive, which convinced American leaders that victory, if possible at all, would not be quick or easy. It also increased the American public's opposition to the war. In 1973 the Paris peace talks ended with the United States agreeing on a timetable for withdrawing its troops and turning the war over to the South Vietnamese army. The South Vietnamese government was no better prepared to defend itself than it had been in 1965, and in April 1975 the South Vietnamese capital of Saigon fell to an invasion of North Vietnamese troops.

MAJOR VIETNAMESE IMMIGRATION WAVES

On April 18, 1975, less than two weeks before the fall of Saigon, President Ford authorized the entry of 130,000 refugees from the three countries of Indochina into the United States, 125,000 of whom were Vietnamese. This first large group of Vietnamese in America has become known as "the first wave." Those in the first wave who arrived in the mid- to late-1970s, typically had close ties with the American military and therefore tended to be the elite of South Vietnam. According to data collected by the United States Department of State in 1975, over 30 percent of the heads of households in the first wave were trained in the medical professions or in technical or managerial occupations, 16.9 percent were in transportation occupations, and 11.7 percent were in clerical and sales occupations. Only 4.9 percent were fishermen or farmers—occupations of the majority of people in Vietnam. Over 70 percent of the first wave refugees from this overwhelmingly rural nation came from urban areas.

During the months of April and May 1975, six camps opened in the United States to receive refugees and prepare them for resettlement. After refugees were interviewed, given medical examinations, and assigned to living quarters, they were sent to one of nine voluntary agencies, or VOLAGs. These VOLAGs, the largest of which was the United States Catholic Conference, assumed the task of finding sponsors, individuals, or groups who would assume financial and personal responsibility for refugee families for up to two years.

Despite the fact that many first wave arrivals were from privileged backgrounds, few were well-prepared to take up a new life in America. The majority did not speak English and all found themselves in the midst of a strange culture. The American refugee agencies attempted to scatter them around the country, so that this new Asian population would not be too visible in any one place, and so that no one city or state would be burdened with caring for a large number of new arrivals. Nevertheless, although at least one percent of the southeast Asian population in 1976 resided in each of 29 states, California had already become home to the largest number of refugees, with 21.6 percent of all the Southeast Asians in the United States.

The beginning of the first wave in 1975 was followed by smaller numbers, with only 3,200 Vietnamese arriving in 1976 and 1,900 arriving in 1977. These numbers increased dramatically in 1978 as a result of an enlarged resettlement program developed in response to the lobbying of concerned American citizens and organizations; 11,100 Vietnamese entered the country that year. Political and economic conditions in Vietnam at this time were driving large numbers of Vietnamese from their country, often in small unseaworthy boats. News of their hostile reception in neighboring countries and their sufferings at the hands of pirates created pressure in the United States to expand further the refugee program. Then in January 1979 Vietnam invaded neighboring Cambodia and the following month war broke out between Vietnam and China. As a result the number of Vietnamese admitted to the United States in 1979 rose to 44,500. Many of this sec-

ond wave were Chinese citizens of Vietnam. As the war continued, the number of fleeing Indochinese rose steadily. Many were Cambodians or Laotians but Vietnam, with its larger population, was the homeland of the majority of refugees. In 1980, 167,000 southeast Asians, 95,200 of whom were Vietnamese, arrived in the United States. They were followed in 1981 by 132,000 southeast Asians, 86,100 of whom were Vietnamese.

Unlike the first refugees, the second wave came overwhelmingly from rural backgrounds and usually had limited education. Indeed, they appear to have been the least educated and the least skilled of any legal immigrants to the United States in recent history. Their hardships were increased by their time of arrival: 1980 was a year of high inflation rates, and 1981 to 1983 saw the most severe economic recession of the previous 50 years.

While first wave refugees came directly to the United States, those in the second wave tended to come through refugee camps in southeast Asia. Agencies under contract to the United States Department of State organized classes to teach English and familiarize refugees with American culture. VOLAGs were still charged with finding sponsors prior to resettlement, but these sponsors were usually found before the refugees departed for the United States.

By the early 1980s, secondary migration (moving a second time after migrating to the United States) had somewhat concentrated the Vietnamese American population. While California had always been home to the greatest number of southeast Asians, by 1984 over 40 percent of these refugees were located in California, mostly in the large urban centers. Texas, the state with the next largest number of southeast Asians, held 7.2 percent. This trend toward concentration continued throughout the 1980s, so that the 1990 census showed 50 percent of Vietnamese Americans living in California, and a little over 11 percent living in Texas. Other states with large numbers of Vietnamese were Virginia, Washington, Florida, New York, Louisiana, Massachusetts, and Pennsylvania.

The number of Vietnamese and other Indochinese coming to the United States never again reached the high points of 1980 and 1981. The influx did continue, however, with roughly 24,000 Vietnamese reaching America every year through 1986. Many of those leaving Vietnam for the United States in the 1980s emigrated legally

through the Orderly Departure Program (ODP). This was a program formed by the governments of the United States and Vietnam, despite the fact that there were no formal diplomatic relations between the two countries, which allowed those interviewed and approved by U.S. officials in Vietnam to leave the country. Two of the groups in which the United States was particularly interested were the former South Vietnamese soldiers, who were in prisons and re-education camps, and the Amerasians, the roughly 8,000 children of American fathers and Vietnamese mothers who had been left behind at the end of the war. Although an estimated 50,000 Vietnamese were resettled in the United States through the Orderly Departure Program between late 1979 and 1987, refugees also continued to pour out of Vietnam by boat and on land, across war-torn Cambodia to Thailand.

Although the number of Vietnamese to enter the United States diminished in the late 1980s and early 1990s, the group continued to grow as a part of American society. While the 1980 U.S. census placed the number of Vietnamese in this country at 245,025, the 1990 census listed 614,545 Vietnamese. This increase of over 150 percent made the Vietnamese America's fifth largest Asian group. Because they have large families (the average number of persons in Vietnamese families in 1990 was 4.36 compared with 3.06 for white Americans and 3.48 for African

Americans), by the year 2000 the Vietnamese are expected to be the third largest group among Asians and Pacific Islanders, outnumbered only by Chinese and Filipinos.

ACCULTURATION AND ASSIMILATION

When the first group of Vietnamese arrived in the United States, there was concern about how well this large group of people, from a vastly different culture with limited English and traumatic experiences of war, would fit into American society. The Vietnamese remain newcomers; nearly half are immigrants who arrived after 1980 and only 18.6 percent of Vietnamese living in the United States were born here. Despite these obstacles, their adaptation has been rapid. By 1990 almost three-fourths of Vietnamese in the United States could speak English well or very well. Only 20.5 percent did not speak English well, and only 4.7 percent could not speak English at all. There were differences between those who arrived before 1980 and those who arrived after 1980, but both groups showed high levels of English-language ability. Among the pre-1980 immigrants, 86.9 percent reported that they could speak English well or very well and only 2.0 percent reported that they could not speak English at all. Among the post-1980 immigrants, 62.8 percent said that they could speak English well or very well, and 7.3 percent said that they could not speak English at all.

Despite the general success in adapting to the new country, many Vietnamese Americans continue to face hardships. Nearly a quarter lived below the poverty level in 1990. Moreover, many Vietnamese have had to face prejudice and discrimination from other sectors of the American population.

Maintaining Vietnamese traditions is a major concern in most Vietnamese American communities and adult Vietnamese Americans often worry that their children may be losing distinctive cultural characteristics. Since Vietnamese Americans are such new arrivals, it is difficult to judge to what extent these concerns are justified. Some Vietnamese Americans have made a conscious effort to assimilate completely into American society (for instance, by changing the last name "Nguyen" to "Newman" or "Winn"), but most retain their sense of ethnicity. Those who live in areas largely populated by Vietnamese typically remain more culturally distinctive than those who reside in suburban areas, surrounded by Americans of other ethnic backgrounds.

American views of the Vietnamese have been dominated by American involvement in the Vietnam War. Books and movies about Vietnam and the Vietnamese, such as the films *Apocalypse Now* and *The Deer Hunter,* tend to be ethnocentric, addressing the American experience in Vietnam, rather than Vietnamese life. Vietnamese Americans are often stereotyped in the popular press as chronic overachievers or desperate refugees. These stereotypes may lose some of their force as the Vietnamese presence in America continues.

CUISINE

Rice is the basis of most Vietnamese meals. In fact, the word *com* (pronounced "gum"), which means "cooked rice," is also used to mean "food" in general. In Vietnamese, to ask "have you eaten yet?" one literally asks "have you eaten rice yet?" Rice is eaten with a variety of side dishes, which are usually quite spicy. Popular dishes include *ca kho* (braised fish, pronounced "ga khaw"), *ca chien* (fried fish, pronounced "ga cheeyen"), *thit ga kho sa* (chicken braised with lemon grass, pronounced "tit ga khaw sa"), *thit bo xao* (stir-fried beef, pronounced "tit baw sow"), and *suon xao chua ngot* (sweet and sour spare ribs, pronounced "sow chewa ngawt"). Egg rolls, known as *cha gio* ("cha yaw"), are served with many Vietnamese meals and at almost all Vietnamese festive occasions. A rice noodle soup, *pho* ("fuh"), is one of the most popular breakfast and lunch foods. Vietnamese restaurants have become common in the United States, and their delicious foods are one of the most widely appreciated contributions of Vietnamese Americans to American life.

TRADITIONAL DRESS

Vietnamese men, even in Vietnam, long ago adopted western dress. Women, however, still wear the traditional *ao dai* (pronounced "ow yai") on most special occasions. The *ao dai* consists of a long mandarin-collared shirt that extends to the calves, slit at both sides to the waist. This is worn over loose black or white pants. *Ao dais* may come in many colors, and their flowing simplicity makes them among the most graceful forms of dress.

The conical Vietnamese hat known as the *non la* (literally, "leaf hat") may be seen often in areas where large numbers of Vietnamese Americans reside. Designed for protection from the hot sun of southeast Asia, the *non la* is light and provides comfortable shade when working outdoors.

HOLIDAYS

The most important Vietnamese holiday is *Tet,* which marks both the beginning of the lunar New Year and the beginning of spring. *Tet* usually falls in late January or early February. In traditional families, a ceremony may be held on the afternoon before *Tet,* during which deceased ancestors are invited to come back and spend the festival days with the living. As in the western New Year, fireworks may be heard at midnight, heralding the coming year. Several young men dressed up as a dragon, the symbol of power and nobility, perform the dragon dance on the streets or other open spaces. The dragon dance also has become an important part of the cultural exhibitions in schools and other places. On the morning of *Tet,* families awaken early and dress in their best clothes. People offer each other New Year wishes and give the children lucky red envelopes containing money. *Tet* is considered a time for visiting and entertaining guests, and non-Vietnamese are heartily welcomed to most of the celebrations and ceremonies.

Many Vietnamese Americans, especially Buddhists, also celebrate the traditional holiday of *Trung Nguyen,* or "Wandering Souls Day," which falls in the middle of the seventh lunar month. On this holiday, tables are filled with food offered to the wandering souls of ancestors. In some cases, money and clothes made of special paper may be burned at this time.

Trung Thu, or the "Mid-Autumn Festival", held on the fifteenth day of the eighth lunar month is one of the loveliest of Vietnamese holidays. Bakers in Vietnamese communities begin to prepare weeks before the festival by making moon cakes of sticky rice. People fashion lanterns of cellophane paper in many different shapes, and place candles inside. On the night of the festival, children form a procession and travel through the streets with their bright lanterns, dancing to the beat of drums and cymbals.

PROVERBS

Like the proverbs of many other peoples, traditional Vietnamese proverbs form a treasury of popular wisdom, offering insights into the society and into its beliefs about how relations among people are or ought to be. The following are a few of the countless proverbs that have been quoted by generations of Vietnamese people: Birds have nests, people have ancestors; If a branch is broken from a tree, the branch dies; Big fish eat little ones; From our own thoughts we can guess the thoughts of others; Even the fierce tiger will not devour its kittens; The city has its laws, the village has its customs; The law of the Emperor must give way before the customs of the village; The higher one climbs, the more painful the fall; Life is ten times more valuable than wealth; Chew when you eat, think when you speak.

HEALTH AND MENTAL HEALTH ISSUES

Many older Vietnamese suffer from the strains of war and exile. Younger Vietnamese, who sometimes find themselves straddling two cultures, express confusion over discrepancies between the expectations of their parents and those of the larger society. Nevertheless, Vietnamese Americans as a whole do not exhibit mental health problems that prevent them from functioning in American society.

Vietnamese Americans generally have a high opinion of the American medical establishment. The profession of medical doctor is the most highly rated by Vietnamese Americans in terms of prestige, and it is a source of great pride to Vietnamese American parents to have a child who is a doctor or a nurse.

Tuberculosis was a serious problem among Vietnamese refugees to the United States, but they were kept in refugee camps overseas until it was determined that the disease was cured. As a result, the incidence of tuberculosis among Vietnamese Americans now appears to be very low.

LANGUAGE

Vietnamese is generally a monosyllabic language. Two or more one-syllable words may be joined together, however, usually connected by a hyphen, to form a compound word. Vietnamese is a tonal language; the meanings of words are determined by the pitch or tone at which the words are spoken, as well as by the arrangement of vowels and consonants. Several of these tones are also found in English, but English does not use the tones in the same way as Vietnamese. In Vietnamese, the sound "*ma*" pronounced with a falling tone and the sound "*ma*" pronounced with a low rising tone are actually two different words. The first means "but" and the second means "tomb." There are six of these tones in Vietnamese. In modern written Vietnamese, which uses the romanized system of writing introduced by European missionaries, the tones are indicated by diacritical marks, or marks written above and below the vowel in each syllable. A word without any mark is spoken with a mid-level tone. When the word has an acute accent over the vowel, it is pronounced with a voice that starts high and then rises sharply. When the word has a grave accent over the vowel, it is pronounced with a voice that starts at a low level and then falls even lower. A tilde over the vowel indicates a high broken tone, in which the voice starts slightly above the middle of the normal speaking voice range, drops and then rises abruptly. A diacritical mark that looks like a question mark without the dot at the bottom is written over a vowel to indicate the low rising tone that sounds like the questioning tone in English. A dot written under a vowel means that the word should be pronounced with a voice that starts low, drops a little bit lower, and is then cut off abruptly. Most non-Vietnamese who study the language agree that the tones are the most difficult part of learning to speak it properly.

One of the most interesting features of Vietnamese is its use of status-related pronouns, a feature that it shares with many other Asian languages. While English has only one singular first-person, one singular second-person, and two singular third-person pronouns, Vietnamese has words that perform the function of pronouns. The word that is used for a pronoun depends on the relationship between the speaker and the person addressed. When a student addresses a teacher, for example, the word used for "you" is the respectful "*thay*," which means "teacher." Many of the words used as pronouns express family relations, even when the Vietnamese are speaking with non-family members. Close friends are addressed as "*anh*" ("older brother") or "*chi*" ("older sister"). To address someone more politely, especially someone older than oneself, one uses the words "*ong*" (literally, "grandfather") or "*ba*" (literally, "grandmother"). In this way, the fundamental Vietnamese values of respect for age, education, and social prestige and the central place of the extended family in Vietnamese life are embodied in the language itself.

The dialect of northern Vietnam, known as *tieng bac*, is slightly different from that of southern Vietnam, known as *tieng nam*. One of the most notable differences is that the Vietnamese letter "*d*" is pronounced like the consonant "y" in the southern dialect and somewhat like the "z" in the northern dialect. Although the southern dialect is more common among Vietnamese Americans, many Vietnamese Americans who are from families that moved south in 1954 speak the northern dialect.

Although most of Vietnamese Americans speak English well and use it outside the home, the vast majority retain the Vietnamese language. In 1990, about 80 percent of those who identified themselves as Vietnamese in the U.S. census said they spoke Vietnamese at home, while another 4.7 percent said they spoke Chinese, and only 14.1 percent reported speaking English at home. Even among those who came to the United States before 1980, over 70 percent reported speaking Vietnamese at home. Vietnamese Americans generally regard their language as an important part of their cultural identity, and make efforts to pass it on to their young people.

GREETINGS AND OTHER POPULAR EXPRESSIONS

Some common Vietnamese greetings and expressions are: *Chao ong* ("jow ohm")—Hello (to an older man or to one to whom one wishes to show respect); *Chao anh*—Hello (to a male friend); *Chao ba* ("jow ba")—Hello (to an older woman); *Chao co* ("jow go")—Hello (to a younger woman); *Di Dao* ("dee dow")—Where are you going? (commonly used as a greeting); *Ong* (or *anh, ba, co*, depending on the gender and relationship of the person addressed) *manh gioi khong* ("ohm mahn yoi kohm")—Are you well? (used in the sense of the English "How are you?"); *Cam on* ("gahm ung")—Thank you; *Khong co gi* ("kohm gaw yi")—You're welcome; *Chuc mung nam moi* ("chook meung nam meuey")—Happy New Year. Since Vietnamese uses tones and also contains some sounds not found in English, the suggested pronunciations are only approximate.

LITERATURE

Until the twentieth century, Vietnamese literature was written in Chinese characters adapted to the Vietnamese language, known as *chu nom*. The Vietnamese people have a wealth of folktales that were usually passed on by storytelling, but many were also collected in anthologies in *chu nom* writing. The folktales include stories about animals, fairy tales, fables with moral lessons, Buddhist legends, and stories about historical figures. There are several good collections of Vietnamese folktales in English that can be enjoyed by children and adults alike. Among these are *Under the Starfruit Tree: Folktales from Vietnam* (Honolulu: University of Hawaii Press, 1989), collected by Alice M. Terada; *The Beggar in the Blanket and Other Vietnamese Tales* (New York: Dial Press, 1970), retold by Gail Graham; and *The Wishing Pearl and Other Tales of Vietnam* (New York: Harvey House, 1969), translated by Lam Chan Quan and edited by Jon and Kay Nielsen.

The earliest works of formal literature composed in *chu nom* are poems that date from the Tran dynasty in the thirteenth century A.D. The most important early Vietnamese author, however, was Nguyen Trai, a poet heavily influenced by Chinese models who lived in the early 1400s. Ironically, Nguyen Trai was a minister in the court of the Vietnamese ruler Le Loi (also known as the Emperor Le Thai To), who waged a successful war of liberation against China. This emperor was himself a poet and his writings are included in one of the first anthologies of Vietnamese poetry, which is still read today.

The seventeenth and eighteenth centuries were something of a golden age for narrative and lyric verse in *chu nom* characters. The six- and eight-syllable verse known as *luc-bat* became the most important and widely used literary form at this time. At the beginning of the nineteenth century, the poet Nguyen Du used the six-eight syllable *luc-bat* to compose the long narrative *Kim Van Kieu*, or the *Tale of Khieu* (translated into English by Huynh Sanh Thong and published in the United States by Yale University Press, 1983), which is considered the national literary masterpiece of Vietnam.

The early- to mid-twentieth century saw a flowering of Vietnamese literature, due largely to the spread of the *quoc ngu*, or romanized system of writing. The older Chinese-based writing system was difficult to learn and to use, and the new writing made mass literacy possible, creating new readers and writers. In the twentieth century also, western forms of literature, such as the novel, journalism, and literary criticism, took root. One of the most popular contemporary novelists in Vietnam is Duong Thu Huong, whose novel *Paradise of the Blind* (translated into English by Nina McPherson and Phan Huy Duong, William Morrow and

Co, 1993) became the first novel from Vietnam to appear in English in the United States.

Vietnamese Americans, struggling to adjust to life in a new country and a new language, are only beginning to establish a literature of their own. Most Vietnamese communities have their own newspapers, which frequently offer poems and stories in Vietnamese. The memoir has become an important literary form for Vietnamese American authors attempting to reach a wider English-speaking audience. Two important memoirs by Vietnamese American authors are *The Vietnamese Gulag* (Simon and Schuster, 1986), by Doan Van Toai, and *When Heaven and Earth Changed Places* (Doubleday, 1989), by Le Ly Hayslip. The latter work has also been made into a film by Oliver Stone, and Hayslip has published a second memoir entitled *Child of War, Woman of Peace* (Doubleday, 1993). Jade Ngoc Quang Huynh's *South Wind Changing: A Memoir* (Graywolf Press, 1994), which tells of the author's youth and university education in Saigon, imprisonment in a reeducation camp, flight to America, and his efforts to become a writer, met with great critical acclaim. Robert Olen Butler, an American author with wide experience with the Vietnamese, won the Pulitzer Prize in 1993 for *A Good Scent from a Strange Mountain* (Penguin Books, 1992), a volume of short stories about Vietnamese Americans living in Louisiana and Texas.

FAMILY AND COMMUNITY DYNAMICS

The extended family is the heart of Vietnamese culture, and preservation of family life in their new home is one of the most important concerns of Vietnamese Americans. While American families are generally nuclear, consisting of parents and their children, the Vietnamese tend to think of the family as including maternal and paternal grandparents, uncles, aunts, and cousins. Traditionally minded Vietnamese Americans think of all social relations on the model of family relations. Many Vietnamese Americans have taken on family patterns similar to the nuclear families of other Americans, but many of them still attempt to retain close ties with their extended families, so that even when adult children marry and leave the household, parents often encourage them to live nearby.

Older and newly arrived Vietnamese Americans often display indirectness and extreme politeness in dealing with others. They will tend to avoid looking other people in the eyes out of respect, and they frequently try not to express open disagreement with others. U.S.-born Vietnamese youth often have the mannerisms and cultural traits of other American adolescents, which sometimes leads to intergenerational conflict, and to complaints by older people that the younger people are "disrespectful."

Vietnamese American family ties are strong and their families generally remain intact, despite the strains of exile and adaptation to a new country. In the 1990 U.S. census, 84 percent of Vietnamese people over 15 years of age who had been married were still married. Only 5.3 percent were divorced and only 4.5 percent were separated.

Although Vietnamese Americans often express a distaste for public assistance, most Vietnamese families who arrive in the United States as refugees receive public assistance for about six months from the time of arrival. In 1990, about a fourth of Vietnamese American families were receiving some form of public assistance.

COURTSHIP AND MARRIAGE

Dating is almost unknown in Vietnam, where couples are almost always accompanied by chaperons, and many Vietnamese American parents feel very uncomfortable with the idea of their daughters going out alone with young men. Still, American-style dating has become fairly common among young Vietnamese Americans. Most Vietnamese Americans marry within their ethnic group, but Vietnamese American women are much more likely to marry non-Vietnamese than are Vietnamese American men.

EDUCATION

Education is highly valued in Vietnamese culture, and the knowledge attained by children is viewed as a reflection on the entire family. In a study of achievement among southeast Asian refugees, Nathan Caplan, John K. Whitmore, and Marcella H. Choy found that with both grades and scores on standardized tests, Vietnamese American children ranked higher than other American children, although they did show deficiencies in language and reading. Even Catholic Vietnamese Americans usually attend public schools. Both males and females pursue higher education. A degree in engineering is by far the most popular degree, although this occupation tends to be pursued by males more than by females.

The high value placed on learning leads a large proportion of young Vietnamese Americans to pursue higher education. Almost half of Vietnamese Americans between the ages of 18 and 24 in 1990 were in college, compared with 39.5 percent of white Americans and 28.1 percent of black Americans in the same age group. High school dropout rates among young Vietnamese Americans were also lower than those of other Americans. Only 6.5 percent of Vietnamese Americans from ages 16 to 19 were neither enrolled in high school nor high school graduates, compared to 9.8 percent of white American youth and 13.7 percent of black American youth.

MALE-FEMALE RELATIONS

Vietnamese culture is patriarchal, but relations between male and female Vietnamese in the United States have become much more egalitarian. Vietnamese families strongly encourage higher education for both young men and young women. Still, almost all community leaders are men and young Vietnamese American women often voice frustration at the expectation that they should be primarily wives and mothers, even if they work outside the home.

It is common for Vietnamese American women to work outside the home (55.8 percent contribute to the labor force), but they are often employed in low-paying, marginal, part-time jobs. Although over 90 percent of the female civilian labor force for this group was currently employed in the 1990 census, only 66.6 percent were employed full-time.

RELIGION

Although Buddhism is the religion of the overwhelming majority of people in Vietnam, probably about 30 percent of Vietnamese Americans are Catholics. The rituals and practices of Vietnamese Catholics are the same as those of Catholics everywhere, but some observers, such as Jesse Nash, author of *Vietnamese Catholicism* (New Orleans, Art Review Press, 1992) have claimed that the Vietnamese Catholic outlook is heavily influenced by Confucianism.

Vietnamese Buddhists are almost always Mahayana Buddhists, the general school of Buddhism found in China, Japan, Korea, and Tibet. Vietnamese Buddhism is heavily influenced by the tradition known in Vietnamese as *Tien*, which is more commonly known in the West by its Japanese name *Zen*. This discipline emphasizes the achievement of enlightenment through meditation. Thich Nhat Hanh, a Vietnamese Zen master who was nominated for the Nobel Peace Prize by Martin Luther King, Jr., is widely known in the United States, even outside the Vietnamese American community, for his stories, poems, and sermons.

EMPLOYMENT AND ECONOMIC TRADITIONS

Vietnamese Americans may be found in almost all occupations, but they seem to show a preference for technical jobs, such as electrical engineering and machinery assembling. In the southern states along the Gulf Coast, Vietnamese fishermen and shrimpers play an important role in the fishing industry. High rates of employment have helped to earn Vietnamese Americans a reputation for being hard-working and energetic. In 1990, male Vietnamese Americans over the age of 26 had an unemployment rate of only 5.3 percent and even second-wave refugees, with an unemployment rate of only 6.3 percent, showed less joblessness than most others in the country.

About ten percent of Vietnamese Americans were self-employed in 1990. According to a United States census report on minority-owned businesses, in 1987, Vietnamese in America owned 25,671 firms, with 13,357 employees. This means that the number of Vietnamese-owned businesses had increased by about 415 percent since 1982. Of these businesses, 46 percent (11,855 firms) were in California and a little over one-fifth of these businesses (5,443) were in Texas. This remarkable growth in business ownership among Vietnamese Americans appears to have continued into the 1990s, suggesting that they are adapting well to the U.S. economy.

POLITICS AND GOVERNMENT

Vietnamese Americans are not yet heavily involved in American politics. Most Vietnamese American communities have a branch of the Vietnamese American Voters' Association, a decen-

tralized set of grass-roots groups that functions primarily to prepare Vietnamese people to apply for U.S. citizenship and to advise Vietnamese Americans on voting in local elections.

The relationship between Vietnam and the United States is the major political issue for most Vietnamese Americans, and it is a highly divisive one. Some Vietnamese Americans favor closer relations to Vietnam, feeling that this will lead to greater prosperity for their parent country and contribute to its liberalization. Others strongly oppose any relations between the United States and Vietnam, in the belief that any relations between the two countries help to support the current socialist Vietnamese government.

Young Vietnamese Americans have only begun to serve in the American military. Nevertheless, military service is popular among new college graduates. Vietnamese American cadets at the major American military academies, although few in number, have received widespread attention in the media.

INDIVIDUAL AND GROUP CONTRIBUTIONS

Because the arrival of Vietnamese Americans is so recent, they have only begun to make their mark on American culture.

ACADEMIA

Huynh Sanh Thong is a scholar and translator of Vietnamese literature. Thong was the first editor of *The Vietnam Forum* and *Lac Viet,* two series of collections of literary works on Vietnamese history, folklore, economics, and politics. Both of these collections are part of The Southeast Asian Refugee Project of the Yale Council on Southeast Asia Studies.

ARTS AND ENTERTAINMENT

Dustin Nguyen, born Nguyen Xuan Tri in Saigon, fled with his family to the United States in 1975 when he was 12 years old. Nguyen graduated from high school in Missouri and attended Orange Coast College in California, where he became interested in acting. He moved to Hollywood to pursue this interest and became famous for the character he played on the T.V. series "21 Jump Street" from 1986 to 1990.

JOURNALISM

Andrew Lam is an associate editor with the Pacific News Service. The son of a South Vietnamese army officer, he fled Vietnam with his family in 1975, the day before Saigon fell. He has published essays and news stories in a wide variety of publications. His memoir "My Vietnam, My America" (published in the December 10, 1990 issue of *The*

Nation), gives a young Vietnamese American's reflections on his dual heritage.

MILITARY

Jean Nguyen and Hung Vu, in 1985, became the first Vietnamese immigrants to graduate from the United States Military Academy at West Point. Both had arrived in the United States just ten years earlier, unable to speak English.

MEDIA

PRINT

Most Vietnamese American communities have small Vietnamese-language newspapers with limited circulation. However, there are only a few national publications that are accessible to the public at large.

Across the Sea.

A magazine published twice a year by Vietnamese American Student Publications.

Contact: Jeffrey Hung Nguygen and Quyen Le, Editors.
Address: 700 Eshleman Hall, University of California-Berkeley, Berkeley, California 94720.

Gia Dinh Moi (New Family).

Monthly Catholic magazine in Vietnamese.

Address: 841 Lenzen Avenue, Third Floor, San Jose, California 95126-2736.

Horizons: Of Vietnamese Thought and Culture.

A magazine for Vietnamese American young adults.

Contact: Huy Thanh Cao, Editor.
Address: 415 South Park Victoria, Suite 350, Milpitas, California 95035.

Journal of Vietnamese Music: Nhac Viet.

Formerly *Nhac Viet Newsletter*. Published by International Association for Research in Vietnamese Music; a research journal focusing on the music of Vietnam and Asia.

Address: P.O. Box 16, Kent, Ohio 44240.
Telephone: (216) 677-9703.

Khang Chien.

A monthly Vietnamese-language magazine covering events and developments in Vietnam.

Contact: Vu Quang Vinh, Distributing Manager.
Address: P.O. Box 7826, San Jose, California 95150.
Telephone: (408) 363-1078.
Fax: (408) 363-1178.

Nguoi Vet.

Daily newspaper in Vietnamese.

Contact: Do Ngoc Yen, Publisher.
Address: 14891 Moren Street, Westminster, California 92683.
Telephone: (714) 892-9414.
Fax: (714) 894-1381.

Thoi Luan.

A weekly Vietnamese community newspaper.

Contact: Do Dien Duc, Publisher.
Address: 1685 Beverly Boulevard, Los Angeles, California 90026.
Telephone: (213) 483-8817.

Tin Viet.

Weekly Vietnamese community newspaper.

Contact: Nguyen Thuong Hieb, Editor.
Address: 9872 Chapman Avenue, Suite 12, Garden Grove, California 92641.
Telephone: (714) 530-6521.

Van Hoc.

A major Vietnamese American literary magazine entirely in Vietnamese.

Address: P.O. Box 3192, Tustin, California 92680.

Vietnam Daily Newspaper.

Daily community newspaper serving the greater San Francisco area.

Contact: Giang Nguyen, Publisher.
Address: 575 Tully Road, San Jose, California 95111.
Telephone: (408) 292-3422.
Fax: (408) 292-4088.

The Viet Nam Forum.

A journal published by the Southeast Asian Refugee Project of the Yale Council on Southeast Asian Studies. This project was founded as an archive for written material by refugees from Southeast Asia. The Council also publishes *Lac*

Viet, a series of anthologies of works on Vietnamese history, folklore, economics, and politics.

Contact: Dan Duffy, Editor.
Address: Yale Council on Southeast Asian Studies, Box 13A Yale Station, New Haven, Connecticut 06520.

The Viet Nam Generation.

A press established for the purpose of publishing scholarship and literature about the war in Vietnam; it also publishes material on contemporary Vietnamese Americans.

Address: 18 Center Road, Woodbridge, Connecticut 06525.

Viet Nam Hai Ngoai.

Monthly Vietnamese magazine.

Contact: Dinh Thach Bich, Editor and Publisher.
Address: P.O. Box 33627, San Diego, California 92103-0580.

ORGANIZATIONS
AND ASSOCIATIONS

Vietnamese Americans have formed a wide variety of organizations during the short time they have been a part of American society. Most of these exist to help newly arrived Vietnamese adjust to American society, but they also provide information about Vietnamese American culture, business, and other aspects of Vietnamese life in this country.

Center for Southeast Asian Refugee Resettlement.

Provides services to newly arrived Indochinese refugees.

Contact: Vu-Duc Vuong, Executive Director.
Address: 875 O'Farrell Street, San Francisco, California 94109.
Telephone: (415) 885-2743.

Federation of American Cultural and Language Communities (FACLC).

A coalition of ethnic organizations representing Americans of Armenian, French, German, Hispanic, Hungarian, Italian, Japapese, Sicilian, Ukrainian, and Vietnamese descent; works to address areas of common interest to ethnic communities; seeks to further the rights of ethnic Americans, especially their cultural and linguistic rights. Publishes quarterly newsletter.

Contact: Alfred M. Rotondaro, Executive Director.
Address: 666 11th Street, N.W., Suite 800 NIAF, Washington, D.C. 20001.
Telephone: (202) 638-0220.

Vietnamese American Civic Organization.

Promotes the participation of Vietnamese Americans in voting and other civic activities.

Contact: Hiep Chu, Executive Director.
Address: 1486 Dorchester Avenue, Dorchester, Massachusetts 02122.
Telephone: (617) 288-7344.

Vietnamese American Cultural and Social Council.

Devoted to the social welfare of Vietnamese Americans, as well as to the maintenance of Vietnamese culture in America.

Contact: Paul Phu Tran, Executive Director.
Address: 1211 Garbo Way, Suite 304, San Jose, California 95117.
Telephone: (408) 971-8285.

Vietnamese American Cultural Organization.

Concerned with furthering Vietnamese culture and traditions in the United States.

Contact: Father Joseph Hien.
Address: 213 West 30th Street, New York, New York 10001.
Telephone: (212) 343-0762.

Vietnamese Chamber of Commerce in America.

Serves minority groups; provides help with small businesses.

Contact: Tuong Ngyen, Executive Director.
Address: 9938 Bolsa Avenue, Suite 216, Westminister, California 92683.
Telephone: (714) 839-2257.

Vietnamese Fishermen Association of America.

Represents the interests of the large number of Vietnamese Americans who fish off the Pacific and Gulf Coasts.

Contact: John Nguyen, Executive Director.
Address: 570 Tenth Street, Suite 306, Oakland, California 94607.
Telephone: (510) 834-7971.

Vietnamese Heritage Society (VHS).

Works to preserve Vietnamese culture and heritage and to increase understanding between ethnic groups.

Contact: Trang T. Le, President.

Address: 9750 West Wheaton Circle, New Orleans, Louisiana 70127.

Telephone: (504) 254-1857.

SOURCES FOR ADDITIONAL STUDY

Caplan, Nathan, John K. Whitmore, and Marcella H. Choy. *The Boat People and Achievement in America: A Study of Family Life and Cultural Values.* Ann Arbor: University of Michigan Press, 1989.

Refugees as Immigrants: Cambodians, Laotians, and Vietnamese in America, edited by David Haines. Totowa, New Jersey: Rowman & Littlefield, 1989.

Southeast Asian-American Communities, edited by Kali Tal. Woodbridge, Connecticut: Viet Nam Generation, 1992.

Tenhula, John. *Voices from Southeast Asia: The Refugee Experience in the United States.* New York and London: Holmes & Meier, 1991.

Toai, Doan Van, and David Chanoff. *The Vietnamese Gulag.* New York: Simon & Schuster, 1986.

Tollefson, James W. *Alien Winds: The Reeducation of America's Indochinese Refugees.* New York: Praeger, c. 1990.

Welsh American culture still blooms in singing festivals, which stem from the traditional Welsh *eisteddfod*, which calls for Welsh writing and oratory.

WELSH AMERICANS

by
Evan Heimlich

OVERVIEW

Wales, the western, mountainous peninsula of the island of Great Britain, occupies an area just slightly larger than the state of New Jersey. Wales is shaped roughly like a rectangle with a section taken out of the west side—Cardigan Bay, facing Ireland across the Irish Channel. North of Cardigan Bay the island of Anglesey and the Lleyn peninsula jut westward; to the south, also stretching west, lies the larger Pembroke peninsula. Bounded by water on three sides, Wales itself constitutes a peninsula with its eastern border formed by England. Much of the terrain is mountainous. In the northwest, the rugged Snowdonia range is named for Mount Snowdon, at 3,560 feet the highest in Britain south of Scotland. Lesser mountains and hills run south through central Wales into Pembroke and the famous coalfields of South Wales.

Principal cities and towns lie mostly along the coast. Through these busy seaports come the ore and slate from Welsh mines and quarries. Notable seaports spread from Cardiff, Wales' capital and largest city, which lies on the Bristol Channel in the south, to Caernarfon ("car-nar-vin") and Bangor opposite Anglesey in the north. The Welsh climate is temperate and wet.

The country was named after its inhabitants. The Welsh trace their ancestry to two distinct groups of people—the Iberians who arrived from southwestern Europe in Neolithic times and the Celtic tribes who arrived on the island in the late Bronze Age. Fierce fighters, they resisted the Anglo-Saxon invaders, who could not understand their language and called them *wealas* (strangers). They called themselves *Cmry* (fellow country-men); and, although populations and cultures overlap between Wales and England, Wales and its culture remain distinct. Wales occupies about 8,000 square miles and is the size of a small New England state. Since virtually all farms are no more than 50 miles from the shore, Wales has main-tained its own connections with the outside world.

HISTORY

With the collapse of Roman power in the 400s, Germanic tribes from Northern Europe began set-tling in southeastern Britain. Most numerous were the Angles and the Saxons, related peoples who became the English. The Celts resisted this long influx of alien settlers but were gradually pushed west. By about 800, they occupied only Britain's remotest reaches where their descen-dants live today: the Highland Scots, the Cornish of the southwest coast, and the Welsh. The Irish are also Celtic.

Over the coming centuries, the Welsh, iso-lated from other Celts, developed their own dis-tinctive culture. However, their identity would always be shaped by the presence of their power-ful English neighbors. Wales became a western refuge from the invasion and conquest by hostile tribes from Europe, as well as for puritanical dis-senters against English culture. Not only did this refuge lie farther west than most conquerors could effectively extend, its geography made it inacces-sible. Later, Wales became a site from which Eng-land extracted resources and prefigured the posi-tion that colonial America assumed.

The Roman empire took Wales along with Britain in the first century A.D.: "Wales, however, was always a frontier area of the Empire, and remained scarcely changed throughout the Roman period of occupation," except by the introduction of Christianity (George Edward Hartman, *Ameri-cans from Wales* [New York: Farrar, Straus and Giroux, 1978], pp. 27-28; cited hereafter as Hart-man). In the fifth century A.D., early Welsh Chris-tianity blossomed with the monasteries of St. David. Historically, in literature and legend, Ger-manic invaders took what is now England, isolat-ing the Celts in the mountainous area of Wales.

In the late eighth century, Anglo-Saxon invaders—who were not yet Christians—built

Offa's Dike (named after Offa, the Anglo-Saxon king of Mercia), a physical, earthen barrier to keep Welsh people from raiding eastward. This boundary still marks the separation between Wales and England.

In 1066, William the Conqueror defeated the English and, with his French-born Norman nobles and knights, took power in England and determined to subdue the unruly Welsh. Over the next century, the Normans built a series of wood-en forts throughout Wales from which Norman lords held control over surrounding lands. In the late 1100s, they replaced the wooden strongholds with massive, turreted stone castles. From about 1140-1240, Welsh princes such as Rhys ap Gruffy-dd and Llewellyn the Great rose up against the Normans, capturing some castles and briefly regaining power in the land. After Llewellyn's death in 1240, Welsh unity weakened. The Eng-lish King Edward I conquered Wales in the late 1200s, building another series of massive castles to reinforce his rule. The Welsh successfully resisted the invaders for over hundreds of years, until in 1282, they were brought under the politi-cal jurisdiction of England under Edward I. Under Edward and his successors, Welsh revolts contin-ued against the English. Most important was the rebellion of Owain Glyndwr in the 1400s. Despite his failure, Glyndwr strikes a heroic chord in Welsh memory as the last great leader to envision and fight for an independent Wales.

During the 1400s, the Welsh increasingly became involved in English affairs, taking part in the War of the Roses. In 1485, a young Welsh nobleman named Henry Tudor won the Battle of Bosworth Field against King Richard III, thus securing his claim to the English throne. The Welsh rejoiced at having a Welshman as king of England. King Henry VII, as he was called, restored many of the rights that the Welsh had lost under English occupation. Under his son, Henry VIII, Wales and England became unified under one political system. Elizabeth I, daughter of Henry VIII, was the last Tudor monarch. When she died in 1603, English language, law, and cus-toms had become entrenched in Welsh life. Since that time, the history of the Welsh people has been closely tied to that of their English neigh-bors. Wales has become a highly industrialized, mining region of Great Britain. About four of five Welsh people have adopted English as their lan-guage. Yet the Welsh remain a people apart, proud, independent-minded, and always con-scious of their own national character.

WAVES OF MIGRATIONS

As explorers, migrants, settlers, and missionaries, the Welsh people—themselves descended from Europe's seekers of western refuge—led early waves of westering Europeans to America. Myths of their ancestors' independence prompted them, as did Anglican labeling of their Christianity as Dissent. Generally, Welsh people came to the United States within waves of British migrants. Many valued religious freedom, especially Welsh emigrants whose Christianity did not conform to the Church of England. Furthermore, explorations, rich lands, and higher-paying industrial jobs lured them from Wales to America. Some important early British settlers in North America—including Pilgrims and founders of the United States—were Welsh or Anglo-Welsh, and not English at all.

Popular belief in pre-Columbian contact between Wales and the New World supported Welsh migration to America. According to this popular belief, centuries before Columbus, Welsh migrants had crossed the Atlantic, reached North America, and mixed with Indians. Thus some Welsh missionaries sought to reunite with and Christianize their long-lost cousins.

In Wales, many published reports circulated from those who claimed to have found Welsh Indians in North America. Though no one ever proved the legends, they nevertheless helped propel Welsh immigration. They also motivated important exploration. For example, in 1792 (seven years before the Louis and Clarke Expedition), John Evans, a Welsh Methodist, searched for Welsh Indians in the northern reaches of the Missouri River (David Williams, *Cymru Ac America: Wales and America* [Cardiff: University of Wales Press, 1976], pp. 7, 19); cited hereafter as Williams). Contemporary artifacts commemorate the legend. According to a plaque to Madoc ap Owain Gwynedd on the wall of the Fine Arts Center of the South in Mobile, Alabama, visitors can see where Prince Madoc, the Welsh explorer of America, is believed to have arrived with three ships. Also, the plaque of the Daughters of the American Revolution, which is located on the public strand of Mobile Bay, reads: "In memory of Prince Madoc, a Welsh explorer, who landed on the shores of Mobile Bay in 1170 and left behind, with the Indians, the Welsh language." (David Greenslade, *Welsh Fever: Welsh Activities in the United States and Canada Today* [Cowbridge, Wales: D. Brown and Sons, 1986], p. 17; cited hereafter as Greenslade). Although the various claims of the existence of Welsh-speaking Indians

have not been proved, the finding (after Columbus) of Americans descended from Welsh and Indian ancestors offers some corroboration. However, even discounting the legendary Madoc, the Welsh came to the American continent early, relative to other Europeans.

After Britain's Religious Toleration Act of 1689, Welsh emigration subsided until agricultural economics motivated a late eighteenth-century wave. Welsh farmers had reaped poor harvests for years when they heard of America's expansion into the fertile Ohio valley; meanwhile in Wales, acts of British parliament enclosed commons and open moorlands. Concerned by the streams of emigrants leaving Wales, the British government passed measures to prevent skilled workmen from emigrating.

As industrialists built America's factories, skilled industrial workers migrated in large numbers from Wales to America beginning in the 1830s. Near the end of that century, skilled industrial workers mostly took over from their farming countrymen as newly arrived Welsh Americans. These workers, many of whom developed their industries, came here mostly from southern Wales, Britain's main source of coal and iron.

Knowledgeable Welsh industrialists came here to fill positions in ironworks not only as workers, but also as industrial pioneers and leaders. After David Thomas perfected techniques of burning anthracite coal to smelt iron ore, an American coal company in 1839 brought him from Wales to the great anthracite coalfields in Pennsylvania, where he developed America's anthracite iron industry. The new industry drew the Welsh by the thousands. By the beginning of the twentieth century, Scranton recorded nearly 5,000 natives of Wales, and more than 2,000 in Wilkes-Barre, who came to mine coal for David Thomas' process (Williams, p. 81). From the time of the Civil War to the end of World War I, Scranton claimed the largest concentration of Welsh people in the world outside Wales and England (William D. Jones, Wales in America: Scranton and the Welsh 1860-1920 [Scranton: University of Scranton Press, 1993], p. xvi; cited hereafter as Jones).

Another segment of Welsh American migration followed the tinplate-production industry. Glamorganshire, in southern Wales, dominated the world market as the main producer of tinplate until America, a principal market for Welsh tinplate, captured for itself the role of tinplate producer. To protect its own young tinplate industry, America's 1890 McKinley Tariff raised prices of imported tinplate, throwing the Welsh industry into a depression and effectively drawing hundreds of workers from Wales to its new tinplate works (Williams, p. 85). The Welsh American tinplate producers centered in Philadelphia and Ohio, monopolized their industrial science, and then dominated the field for several generations. Many Welsh immigrants developed into important figures of the industry business, becoming executives and capitalists in their own right (Hartman, p. 86). In addition to their major roles in the development of American coal, iron, and steel industries, Welsh Americans in the mid-nineteenth century also built the American slate industry. Immigrants from North Wales prospected for and dug America's early slate quarries along the borders between Pennsylvania and Maryland, and between New York and Vermont.

Robert D. Thomas, a Congregational minister, authored what became for the Welsh of the post-Civil War period a convenient and detailed guidebook in their own language concerning the available land opportunities in America. After its publication in 1872, *Hanes Cymry America* ("History of the Welsh in America") became popular in Wales and probably figured in encouraging further emigration.

Immigration of Welsh farmers in the closing decades of the nineteenth century swelled America's Welsh communities into the tens of thousands, until about 1890, when the immigration of Welsh farmers to America ebbed. Australia and other destinations began to draw their share of emigrant farmers from Wales who were forced from their farms because they opposed the Anglican Church in Wales. Their emigration helped to improve the harvests by balancing the Welsh population level (Hartman, pp. 75-76).

REGIONS OF SETTLEMENT IN AMERICA

At first, Welsh Americans settled in or near British colonies, among fellow Welsh Americans who shared their religious denomination, such as Baptist, Methodist, or Quaker. Many tried to found a new homeland for their people. Following the missionaries and farmers were the skilled industrial workers and artisans. Baptists led the way. John Miles, founder of the first Baptist church in Wales in 1649, suffered religious persecution as a Baptist, both before and after he led Welsh Baptists to Massachusetts in 1662. Though at first the colony refused to tolerate them, eventually Massachusetts granted them land, where they established the town of Swansea and the First Baptist Church, which stands today as the oldest Welsh church in America.

Two decades after Baptists first arrived, Welsh members of the Society of Friends, or Quakers, founded the second and much larger Welsh group settlement in America. Quakers suffered the worst religious persecutions in Wales, because they professed to value their "inner light" over Church and Bible. Many people of all classes joined the Quakers in England, among them William Penn, who supposedly had a Welsh grandfather. In 1681, Penn obtained a vast tract of territory south of New York. "He [said] that he originally intended to call it New Wales, as it was 'a pretty hilly country,' but the authorities in London did not like the name, and it was called Pennsylvania" (Williams, pp. 24-25). Penn led the Quakers there, including many from Wales, and Pennsylvania became the heart of Welsh settlement.

"There was a man that came around every morning and every afternoon, with a stainless steel cart, sort of like a Good Humor cart. And the man was dressed in white and he had warm milk for the kids. And they would blow a whistle or ring a bell, and all the kids would line up, and he had small little paper cups and every kid got a little warm milk."

Donald Roberts, in 1925, cited in *Ellis Island: An Illustrated History of the Immigrant,* edited by Ivan Chermayeff et al. (New York: Macmillan, 1991).

Preacher Morgan John Rhys founded a new homeland for Welsh Americans in western Pennsylvania where they could live together and preserve their language and customs. Although Beulah, the center of the settlement that he established, has not survived, Ebensburg, its second township, has lasted. Meanwhile, Philadelphia, with its large Welsh population, soon flourished and became one of the most important cities in America.

American regions from New York to Wisconsin and Minnesota to Oregon offered Welsh immigrants work in their traditional occupations and drew concentrations of descendants of Welsh shepherds and dairy farmers. After the Civil War, in Wisconsin, Iowa, Minnesota, Missouri, and Kansas, men entered trades and Welsh American young women found service work in private homes. Some Welsh American fruit growers became pioneers of orchard industries in the Pacific Northwest. Copper workers came to Baltimore, silver miners to Colorado, and prospectors for gold, after 1849, rushed to California. Slate quarrymen came to New England and the Delaware Valley. Because so many Welsh immigrants were coal miners, they came in the greatest concentrations to the coal regions of Pottsville, Wilkes-Barre, and Scranton. Steelworkers came to Pittsburgh, Cleveland and Chicago. (Islyn Thomas, *Our Welsh Heritage* [New York: St. David's Society of New York, 1972], p. 27). Scranton led Welsh American communities in maintaining a Welsh American identity. On the 1990 census, two million Americans reported their ancestry as Welsh.

MIGRATION PATTERNS

Welsh Americans, like other British Americans, spread throughout the United States. Americans reporting Welsh ancestry on the 1990 census, in fact, divide evenly between the Northeast, Midwest, South, and West—more evenly than any other European-American group. Early Welsh American Baptists, who first settled in Massachusetts, branched out to other places. They moved to Pennsylvania because it was especially tolerant of their religion. Others bought land in what is now the state of Delaware, which they called the Welsh Tract.

Some Welsh setters sought not only toleration, but further isolation, to ensure that their children did not lose their national characteristics. To escape Anglo-Americanization, Ezickiel Hughes, of Paddy's Run, Ohio, a sponsor of Welsh immigrants, "decided to place his colony in the open waste lands of Patagonia," at the remote, under-colonized southern tip of South America, where it still exists (Williams, p. 73). Other intramigration followed economic opportunities, such as the move of the industrial town of Lackawanna from Pennsylvania to western New York. Largely accepted by dominant Anglo-Americans, Welsh Americans frequently dominated their industries; non-Welsh coal miners often complained that Welsh American supervisors favored their brethren. Irish American workers suffered categorically at the hands of some Welsh American mining bosses (Jones, p. 37).

ACCULTURATION AND ASSIMILATION

In America, as in Wales, members of this ethnic group forged their identity through their church-es, language, and education. Traditional Welsh American ethnic identity, which depended also on the domination of particular fields of employment, has since flourished in singing festivals.

Especially since nineteenth-century modernization linked the Welsh to England and Welsh Americans to America, the two minority groups have acculturated to the respective cultural dominance of England and America. When England industrialized Wales, extracting its abundant coal and iron ore, it divided the inhabitants into a rural group in which Welsh was spoken and an urban group in which English was the primary language. Late in the nineteenth century, battles over Welsh culture moved into the field of education as England prohibited Welsh public schools from teaching in Welsh. The Welsh maintained their culture, though, through their traditional Sunday schools and through nationalism. Although the Welsh fought and won from the British the legal right to use their own language in courts and schools, the use of the Welsh language declined.

Welsh traditional beliefs, attitudes, and customs stem largely from the strength and nonconformity of Welsh churches. In seventeenth- and eighteenth-century Wales, religious nonconformity preserved Welsh identity when it "arrested the inroads of Anglicanization and the complete absorption of Wales into England" (Hartman, p. 26). Although this resurgent nationalism was crucial for Welsh identity, it was less important to Welsh American identity. At Sunday Schools, Welsh churches campaigned to perpetuate the Welsh language by teaching men, women, girls, and boys to read their Bible in Welsh. Because of the Sunday School movement, many Welsh Americans became literate in their own language. Welsh culture has struggled not only against the English church, but also against the English language. The Welsh flag itself displays a red dragon who legendarily champions the ancient Welsh language. The dragon, called Y *Ddraig Goch*, which is said to keep the faith that "three things, yea four, will endure forever, the earth, the sea, the sky and the speech of the *Cymry*," leads the Welsh people "in an unending war for the perpetuation of [their] language" (Thomas, p. 49).

Welsh American communities waxed and waned with their churches. At first, as new territories opened in North America, Welsh missionary work expanded to fill the opportunities to convert new souls. In eighteenth-century Pennsylvania, Quaker, Baptist, and Presbyterian churches anchored communities in which Sunday

Schools helped shaped Welsh American identities; nevertheless, these early Welsh Americans eventually became Americanized in their habits and English in their speech. During the nineteenth century, however, an increasingly Welsh-minded clergy led Welsh American congregations. Their work, coupled with frequent exchanges of visitors from Wales and between Welsh American communities, drew together a Welsh American identity which better resisted acculturation.

Toward the turn of the twentieth century, in Scranton and elsewhere, Welsh Americans acculturated. More immigrants joined occupations outside their traditional industries. The contexts of their ethnic identities also changed as Eastern European and Italian immigrants entered the coal mines: to the newcomers, Welsh immigrants and Welsh Americans seemed more similar than ever to Anglo-, Yankee, or established "mainstream" Americans. Churches, organizations, and festivals sustain Welsh American culture. America's Welshness manifests itself in placenames such as Bangor, Bryn Mawr, and Haverford. Welsh American places include not only Scranton, but small towns such as Emporia, Kansas, and Cambria, Wisconsin, population 600, "a stronghold of Welshness" near Madison, which bears Welsh street signs (Greenslade, pp. 68, 87).

WELSH AMERICAN SINGING

Welsh American culture still blooms in singing festivals, which stem from the traditional Welsh *eisteddfod*, which calls for Welsh writing and oratory. The *eisteddfod* arose in 1568, when Queen Elizabeth commissioned a qualifying competition to license some of "the multitude of persons calling themselves minstrels, rhymers and bards" (Thomas, p. 24). At the end of the eighteenth century, Romanticism revived Welsh cultural promotion and the *eisteddfod*. Today, the United States usually sends the largest delegation of "Welshmen in Exile" to the annual *eisteddfod* in Wales. The "exiles" marsh in ranks by country to the singing of the Welsh nostalgic hymn, "*Unwaith Eto Yng Nghymru Annwyl*" ("Once Again in Dear Wales"). The revived *eisteddfod*, popular in Wales since 1819, features reconstructed Druidic rites, in "an atmosphere of mysticism always associated with the Celtic spirit" (Hartman, p. 143).

Since the 1830s, Welsh Americans also compete in their own *eisteddfod*. Especially in Pennsylvania, Ohio, Iowa, and Utah, strong traditions of

eisteddfod have inspired expert choirs in their performances of Bach, Handel, Mendelssohn, and other classical composers of sacred music. Utica sponsors the oldest continuously *eisteddfod* in the United States. However, because few Welsh Americans speak or write in Welsh, Welsh Americans focused on singing and mostly replaced the *eisteddfod* with the *Gymanfa Ganu* or Welsh singing festival. The *Gymanfa Ganu* started in Wales in 1859 and spread through America by the 1920s. Unlike in Wales, where each church denomination sponsors its own *Gymanfa Ganu*, Welsh American ones include all denominations. The National Gymanfa Ganu Association of the United States and Canada, founded by Welsh Americans, represents the only successful attempt at forming an all-over national association of Welsh Americans. It originated at Niagara Falls with a gathering of 2,400 Welsh Americans and meets at key American centers each year on Labor Day.

CUISINE

Welsh cuisine uses the basic ingredients of dairy products, eggs, seafood, lamb or beef, and simple vegetables such as potatoes, carrots, and leeks. A national symbol, leeks are waved at rugby football matches by Welsh fans. The leek is Wales' most popular vegetable, being featured in soups and stews. One favorite dish, Anglesey Eggs, includes leeks, cheese, and potatoes. Welsh Rabbit (often called Rarebit by the English) combines eggs, cheese, milk, Worcestershire sauce, and beer. The rich melted mixture is poured over toast.

CLOTHING

The Welsh dress much as Europeans and North Americans do, though perhaps a bit more formally than the latter. Among young people, however, jeans, a t-shirt, and running shoes are as common in Wales as everywhere else. Traditional costumes, commonly worn at events such as an *eisteddfod*, feature colorful stripes and checks, with a wide-brimmed hat for women that looks like a witch's hat with the top half of the cone removed.

LANGUAGE

Cymraeg, the Welsh language, has long been a separate branch of Indo-European languages. It descends from Celtic and relates closely to Breton, the language of Brittany, to Highland Scots Gaelic, and to Irish Gaelic. The language looks difficult to an outsider; it also sounds strange with lilting, musical tones in which one word seems to slur into the next. And in a sense, it may—the first letter of a word may change depending on the word before it. This is called *treiglo*, and it achieves a smoothness treasured by the Welsh ear. Welsh also contains elusive sounds such as "ll" (in the name Llewellyn or Lloyd, for example), which is pronounced almost like a combination of "f," "th," and "ch," though not quite. Welsh words nearly always accent their second-to-last syllable.

The Welsh language's age and its supposed migratory path across Eurasia prompts some linguists to make extraordinary claims about etymologies of certain words. For example, the ancient name for the Caucasian chain of mountains forming an immense barrier between Europe on the north and Asia to the south, may come from the same words as the Welsh "Caun," which means "to shut up, to fence in, to encompass", and "Cas," which translates as "separated" or "insulated" (Jenkins, p. 55).

The Welsh alphabet uses the letters "a, b, c, ch, d, dd, e, f, ff, g, ng, h, I, l, ll, m, n, o, p, ph, rh, r, s, t, th, u, w," and "y" to make such words such as: *Cymru* (Wales); *Cymry* (Welsh people); *Ninnau* (We Welsh), the title of a Welsh American periodical; *noson lawen* (an informal evening of song, recitation, and other entertainment); *te*

bach (light refreshments, usually tea and Welsh cakes); *cymdeithas* (society); *cwrs Cymraeg* (Welsh language course); and *bore da, syr* (good morning, sir). Welsh spelling lacks silent letters; in different words, too, the same letter nearly always has the same sound. The Welsh language, which lacks the letter "k," always sounds "c" as the English "k": thus "Celt" is pronounced "Kelt."

Celt, which first referred to "a wild or covert," and the people who lived there, became a loose term to refer to a grouping of disparate peoples living in certain areas of Great Britain. Romans called *Cymry* who lived on open plains Gauls, which the *Cymry* pronounced as Gaels, and the Saxons, in turn, as *Waels* or Wales, home of the *Waelsh* or Welsh (Jenkins, pp. 38, 40, 97).

Welsh surnames have their own story. When English law in 1536 required Welshmen to take surnames, many simply added an "s" to their father's first name. Common first names such as William or Evan (the Welsh equivalent of John) begot the common surnames of Williams and Evans.

The Welsh pride their language on its musicality and expressiveness, and cherish traditional oratorical skills of poets and priests. In literature, the canonization of poet Dylan Thomas is a matter of Welsh American pride. Thomas wrote and recited in Wales and America English-language poems that drew from Welsh culture and preaching styles. The art of oral storytelling which flourished in medieval Wales left as its written legacy the *Mabinogion* (translated into English by Jeffrey Gantz). Preachers of sermons mastered versions of a chanting style "marked by a great variety of intonations" called *hwyl* and each preacher characteristically followed "his own peculiar melody" through a major key to climax in a minor key (Hartman, p. 105). With their *hwyl*, Welsh preachers led congregations in fervent evangelical revivals.

RELIGION

In pre-Christian Wales, the Druids (a special class of leaders) dominated a religion in which Celts worshipped a number of deities according to rites associated with nature (Hartman, p. 27). However, Welsh and Welsh American identities have centered on religious traditions of strictness, evangelicalism, and reform. From the breach between Welsh and Anglican churches stemmed modern Welsh nationalism itself. Also, Mormonism and scattered versions of pre-Christian paganism figure in Welsh American religion.

The patron saint of the Welsh, St. David (born circa 520) "organized a system of monastic regulations for his abbey ... which became the awe of Christian Britain because of its severity of discipline" (Hartman, p. 28). St. David's Day commemorates his death. On the first day of March, Episcopalian churches such as St. David's Episcopalian Church in San Diego (the cornerstone of which comes from St. David's Cathedral in Wales) hold memorial services (Greenslade, p. 33). For all denominations of Welsh Americans, the day represents an occasion for the annual rallying of Welsh consciousness.

As Welsh churches pitted their religious fundamentalism against the English establishment, their progressivism foreshadowed contributions of Welsh Americans to American puritanism and progress. Around the year 1700, when English rule still dominated Welsh religion, the reform movement came from within the church and received its great stimulus from the pietistic evangelism introduced by John Wesley and George Whitfield. Soon these men, and Welshmen of similar beliefs, were emphasizing the necessity of abundant preaching within the church and the need for experiencing a rebirth in religious conviction as a necessary part in the salvation of the individual.

After this evangelical Methodism spread through Wales, Welsh Methodists split from Wesley and from English Methodists and followed Whitfield into Calvinism, calling themselves Calvinist Methodists. Welsh Methodists, furthermore, withdrew from the Anglican Church and precipitated a consolidation of Welsh culture. "Within a few decades, the Calvinist-Methodists, the Congregationalists, and the Baptists had won over the great majority of the masses of Wales from the established [Anglican] church," and at Sunday Schools taught Welsh people to read the Bible (Hartman, p. 33).

Welsh Christian nonconformists shared fundamentalism and puritanism, yet did not lack for internal controversy. Unifyingly, their shared religion demanded "rigid observance of the marriage vows, discouragement of divorce, austere observance of conduct of life generally" and the strict reservation of Sundays for religious activities; on the other hand, divisive religious differences arose "over the issues of church organization, Calvinism, and infant baptism" (Hartman, pp. 103-104).

Congregations and denominations guarded their independence.

In America, as in Wales, Welsh churches pioneered Sunday Schools; children and adults attended separate classes in which teachers used Socratic methods of questioning. Welsh American churchgoers sang hymns and testified, respectively, on Tuesday and Thursday nights, and regularly held *gymanvas*, preaching festivals.

The first groups of Welsh converts to Mormonism came to America in the 1840s and 1850s. Mormon founder Joseph Smith converted Captain Dan Jones to the religion, then sent him on a mission to Wales. Captain Jones in turn converted thousands, most of whom resettled in Utah and contributed much to Mormon culture. As a prime example, Welsh Americans founded the Mormon Tabernacle Choir.

Since the 1960s, versions of Celtic nature-worship have gained popularity in America and Britain. Two members of the Parent Kindred of the Old Religion in Wales brought Hereditary Welsh Paganism to the United States in the early 1960s. Today, Welsh Pagans can be found in Georgia, Wisconsin, Minnesota, Michigan, California, and West Virginia. Welsh pagans form circles with names like The Cauldron, Forever Forests, and Y *Tylwyth Teg*. Members take symbolic Welsh names like Lord Myrddin Pendevig, Lady Gleannon or Gwyddion, Tiron, and Siani. Welsh pagans in America also use the Welsh language in their rituals. Although the Druids, who led the pre-Christian Welsh religion, have not survived, some of their practices have.

EMPLOYMENT AND ECONOMIC TRADITIONS

Welsh Americans traditionally worked in farming or, during the Industrial Age, in the heavy industries of coal, iron, and steel. Because these industries had developed earlier in Wales, immigrants tended to know their work better than workers from elsewhere. Thus Welsh immigrants took leading roles in America's developing industries. Welsh American industrial bosses especially preferred to hire Welsh American workers, and more specifically, ones from their own religious denomination. As a result, Welsh Americans dominated coal mining, and many coal mines filled mostly with a particular denomination of Welsh Americans. Bosses themselves held membership in the

Freemasons. Across the coal region, though only men worked as miners and bosses, boys, girls, and women worked around the mines.

POLITICS AND GOVERNMENT

George Washington once noted, "Good Welshman Make Good Americans" (Thomas, p. 27). In the founding of the United States of America, cultural history positioned Welsh immigrants as American revolutionaries. The Welsh, who already tended to resent English control, were strongly inclined toward revolution in France, Britain, and America. The United States can trace the derivation of its trial-by-jury system through England to Wales. Though it is unclear exactly where Welsh culture contributed to the founding moments of America, Welsh Americans claim the Welshness of Jeffersonian principles, especially that certain rights are inalienable, that rights not assigned to governments are reserved for the people, and that church and state must remain separate. In February of 1776, one month after the publication of Thomas Paine's *Common Sense*, a Welshman, Dr. Richard Price, published in London *The Nature of Civil Liberty*, appealing "to the natural rights of all men, those rights which no government should have the power to take away"; five months later, Welsh American Thomas Jefferson published similar ideas in the Declaration of Independence (Williams, p. 45).

For decades, nearly 75 percent of Welsh immigrants became citizens, higher than any other group (Williams, p. 87). In accord with their religion, Welsh Americans have helped to lobby for temperance, Prohibition, and Sabbath-enforcing Blue Laws. Welsh American abolitionists included workers on the underground railroad, such as Rebecca Lewis Fussell (1820-1893), and authors such as Harriet Beecher Stowe, who wrote *Uncle Tom's Cabin*. Author Helen Hamilton Gardiner (1853-1925) joined several other Welsh American leaders in the fight for women's suffrage.

Welsh Americans also have been labor leaders. In 1871, Welsh American coal miners led their union in a historic strike in which they protested a 30 percent wage decrease, ultimately to no avail. They won only disapproval and prejudice from more established classes of Americans (Jones, p. 53).

INDIVIDUAL AND GROUP CONTRIBUTIONS

ARTS AND ENTERTAINMENT

Illustrator Alice Barber Stephens (1858-1932), and architect Frank Lloyd Wright; pioneer film-producer D. W. Griffith (1869-1959); Bob Hope (1903-); talk show host Dick Cavett (1936-); stage and screen actor Richard Burton (1925-1984); actor Ray Milland (1907-1986); actress Bette Davis (1908-1989).

COMMUNITY SERVICE

Luther Hammond Lewis founded the Big Brother Movement.

EDUCATION

Elihu Yale launched Yale University; Morgan Edwards and Dr. William Richards established Brown University; Carey Thomas (1857-1935) founded and served as president of Bryn Mawr College. Catharine E. Beecher (1800-1858), sister of Harriet Beecher Stowe, founded seminaries for women. Helen Parkhurst (1887-1973), originator of the Dalton Plan of individualized student contracts, established the Dalton School in New York.

EXPLORERS

In the 1780s Jacques Clamorgan, a Welsh West Indian, whose real name was Charles Morgan, led an important scientific exploration of the West before Lewis and Clark; Clamorgan ventured up the Missouri for the fur-trading Spanish who wanted to ally with the Mandans, who seemed to be the remaining Welsh Indians. Meriwether Lewis himself was Welsh American, as was frontiersman Daniel Boone, and John Lloyd Stevens, who discovered Mayan ruins and authored travel narratives.

GOVERNMENT

Roger Williams (born in Wales in 1599) was the first European to establish a democracy on this continent, based upon the principles of civil and religious liberty, at Providence plantations, Rhode Island. Thomas Jefferson (1743-1826), was the greatest Welsh American colonial patriot, whose ancestors came from the foot of Mount Snowden in Wales to the colony of Virginia. Another Welsh American, Gouverneur Morris (1752-1816), later wrote the final draft of the Constitution of the United States. Supreme Court Chief Justice John Marshall (1755-1835) fathered American constitutional law. Welsh American presidents of the United States include not only James Monroe and Calvin Coolidge, but moreover, Abraham Lincoln. Robert E. Lee, General of the Confederate Army, and Jefferson Davis, president of the Confederacy, also were Welsh Americans. So were Supreme Court Chief Justice Charles Evans Hughes, Secretaries of State Daniel Webster and William H. Seward, and first Lady Hillary Clinton. At least 30 state governors also were Welsh American.

LITERATURE

Emlyn Williams, actor and playwright, author of *The Corn Is Green*; Jack London (1876-1916), author of *The Call of the Wild* and *White Fang*; Kate Wiggin (1856-1923), author of *Rebecca of Sunnybrooke Farm*; and Harriet Beecher Stowe (1811-1896), author of *Uncle Tom's Cabin*. Medical scientist Alice Catherine Evans (1881-1975), first woman president of the society of American Bacteriologists; pioneer nutritionists Mary Swartz Rose (1874-1941) and Ruth Wheeler (1877-1948); as well as women's health reformer Mary Nichols. Mary Whiton Calkins (1863-1930), was the first female president of the American Psychological Association, and became the first president of the American Philosophical Association.

MILITARY

Spirited Welsh Americans led the American Revolutionary War. Robert Morris (1734-1806) financed the American effort, in which Major General Charles Lee, born in Wales in 1731, served as second in command to Washington. General "Mad Anthony" Wayne (born in 1745), a Pennsylvania-born Welsh American, fought the Battle of Monmouth. General Isaac Shelby (born in 1750), a Maryland-born Welsh American, fought with his father, Evan Shelby, and other Welsh generals and soldiers in 1774 at the Battle of Point Pleasant, New Jersey.

MUSIC

Opera star Margaret Price; popular vocalists Shirley Bassey and Tom Jones, known as the "Welsh Elvis."

RELIGION

Welsh preacher Morgan John Rys, who came to America in 1794, preached that slavery contradicted the principles of the Christian religion and the rights of man; he also stirred controversy by preaching a sermon in which he said that no land should be taken from the Red Indians without payment.

MEDIA

PRINT

The Bard.

Published in Phoenix, Arizona, by the Annwn Temple of Gwynfyd, a circle of hereditary Welsh pagans.

Enfys.

Newsletter in English and Welsh; keeps people of Welsh descent in touch with Wales.

Contact: Gerwyn Morgan, Editor.

Address: Wales International, Muriau Gwyn, Beulah, Newcastle Emlyn, Dyfed SA38 9QE, Wales.

Telephone: 0239-811655.

Ninnau.

Monthly magazine containing news and information for Americans and Canadians of Welsh ancestry.

Contact: Arturo Lewis Roberts, Editor and Publisher.

Address: 11 Post Terrace, Basking Ridge, New Jersey 07920.

Telephone: (908) 766-6736.

Fax: (908) 221-0744.

Welsh Studies.

Address Edwin Mellen Press, 415 Ridge Street, Box 450, Lewiston, New York 1409992.

Telephone: (716) 754-2788.

Fax: (716) 754-4056.

Y Drych (The Mirror).

Monthly newspaper on Welsh social and political news; also covers Welsh events in the United States and Canada; includes regular cultural, genealogical, and Welsh-language features.

Contact: Mary Morris Mergenthal, Editor.
Address: P.O. Box 8089, St. Paul, Minnesota 55108.
Telephone: (612) 642-1653.
Fax: (612) 642-1943.

Yr Enfys (The Rainbow).

Published since 1949 by Undeb Y Cymry Ar Wasgar (Wales International), it is the only international periodical for Welsh exiles.

ORGANIZATIONS AND ASSOCIATIONS

National Welsh American Foundation (NWAF).

Has bestowed charitable awards since 1980, and lobbies for a Presidential proclamation of the first of March as the official Welsh American Day.

Contact: Wilfred Greenway.
Address: 216-03 43rd Avenue, Bayside, New York 11361.
Telephone: (212) 224-9333.

Welsh American Genealogical Society (WAGS).

Publishes a newsletter.

Welsh American Historical Society.

Contact: Mildred Jenkins, Secretary.
Address: c/o Welsh American Heritage Museum, 412 East Main Street, Oak Hill, Ohio 45656.

Welsh Associated Youth of Canada and the United States (WAY).

Launched in 1970 to involve young Welsh Americans in their heritage; a decade later, the Welsh National Gymanfa Ganu Association board of trustees granted WAY a permanent seat.

Contact: Claire Tallman.
Address: P.O. Box 3246, Ventura, California 93006.

Welsh Harp Society of America.

Founded by the St. David's Society of Kansas City in 1984.

Contact: Judith Brougham.
Address: 4202 Clark, Kansas City, Missouri 64111.
Telephone: (816) 561-6066.

Welsh Heritage Week.

Contact: Anne Habermehl.
Address: 3925 North Main, Marion, New York 14505.
Telephone: (315) 926-5318.

Welsh National Gymanfa Ganu Association (WNGGA).

Contact: David E. Thomas.
Address: 5908 Hansen Road, Edina, Minnesota 55436.
Telephone: (612) 920-1454.

Welsh Society.

Seeks to keep alive Welsh culture and heritage; assists immigrants to the United States from Wales; maintains charitable programs.

Contact: Daniel E. Williams, Secretary.
Address: 450 Broadway, Camden, New Jersey 08103.
Telephone: (609) 964-0891.

MUSEUMS AND RESEARCH CENTERS

Cymdeithas Madog—The Welsh Studies Institute.

Contact: Donna Lloyd-Kolkin.
Address: 1352 American Way, Menlo Park, California 94025.
Telephone: (415) 565-3320.

SOURCES FOR ADDITIONAL STUDY

The Cymry of '76. Baltimore: Genealogical Publishing Co., Inc., 1855.

Dodd, A. H. The Character of Early Welsh Emigration to the United States. Cardiff: University of Wales Press, 1957.

Greenslade, David. Welsh Fever: Welsh Activities in the United States and Canada Today. Cowbridge, Wales: D. Brown and Sons, 1986.

Hartmann, George Edward. *Americans from Wales*. New York: Farrar, Straus and Giroux, 1978.

Holt, Constance Wall. *Welsh Women: An Annotated Bibliography of Women in Wales and Women of Welsh Descent in America*. Metuchen, New Jersey: Scarecrow, 1993.

Jones, William D. *Wales in America: Scranton and the Welsh 1860-1920*. Scranton: University of Scranton Press, 1993.

Morris, Jan. *The Matter of Wales*. Oxford: Oxford University Press, 1984.

Thomas, Islyn. *Our Welsh Heritage*. New York: St. David's Society of New York, 1972.

Thomas, R. D. Hanes. *Cymry America: A History of the Welsh in America,* translated by Phillips G. Davies. Lanham, Maryland: University Press of America, 1983 (originally published in 1872).

Williams, David. *Cymru Ac America: Wales and America*. Cardiff: University of Wales Press, 1975 (first published in 1946).

———. *A Short History of Modern Wales*. London: John Murray, Ltd., 1961.

The Yupiaq people believe that everything of the earth possesses a spirit. Having a spirit means that all things possess consciousness or awareness; and having awareness means that they are mindful of who they give themselves to and how they are treated.

YUPIAT

by
Oscar Kawagley

OVERVIEW

An estimated 86,000 Native people inhabit 87 percent of the Alaskan land mass, or 493,461 square miles. Approximately one-fourth of the Alaskan Native or Yupiat (pronounced "yu-pee-at") live in the southwest area of the state. This floodplain of the Yukon and the Kuskokwim Rivers composes the Arctic and Subarctic region. Villages are located along the Bering Sea and Bristol Bay coasts as well as the delta of the two rivers. There are approximately 21,415 Yupiat living in 62 villages, although the majority are concentrated in the villages of Bethel and Dillingham. Approximately 40 to 50 percent of the populace are non-Native in these two villages.

The Native people of Alaska migrated from Asia. Anthropologists theorize that they originated in Mongolia because their physical features resemble those of Mongoloids. According to Yupiaq creation mythology, the Yupiat were created by the Raven in the area in which they are presently located.

Approximately 32 percent of Alaska Native people have migrated to Anchorage (the biggest city in Alaska) and the Matanuska-Susitna area. Most of these people are looking for opportunities for a better life and living. Many live in poverty because they do not possess marketable skills. Many Alaskan Native people are now campaigning for an educational system that respects their own languages, ways of knowing, skills, and problem-solving methods and tools. They feel this will lead to a Native state of well-being with a positive identity and cultural pride leading to self-reliance, self-determination, and spiritual strength.

ACCULTURATION AND ASSIMILATION

The Yupiaq people did not readily accept education in the coastal, Yukon and Kuskokwim delta villages. The resistance was lead by shamans, village leaders, and elders. It was not the superior knowledge, weapons, or methods of non-Natives that defeated the leaders, but the diseases that members of the dominant society brought with them. The Yupiaq people had no resistance to these new illnesses. The shamans, who treated ailments using spiritual methods, stood by helplessly while many of their people succumbed to these foreign diseases. Whole villages were wiped out, orphaning many children and young adults. It was during this time that the missionaries were able to establish their churches and orphanages, building schools to teach a different language and way of life. The cognitive and cultural imperialism of the dominant society forced the Yupiat to conform to this system. Under the teachings of the missionary-teachers, the youngsters were faced with corporal punishment for using their mother tongue and practicing their strange ways. Being told their language and ways were inferior mentally scarred many students. To this day, the Yupiaq people suffer many psycho-social problems.

The goal of traditional Yupiaq education was to teach the youth to live in harmony in the human world, as well as the natural and spiritual worlds. It was their belief that everything in the universe (plants, animals, rivers, winds, and so forth) had a spirit, which mandated respect. Everything possessing a spirit meant that everything had a consciousness or awareness, and therefore must be accorded human respect. The Yupiat did not practice pantheism; they merely treated everything with respect and honor. Such a way of life led the Yupiat to possess only that which was absolutely necessary and taught them to enjoy to the utmost the little they had. The Yupiaq people have been bombarded by Western society's institutions for a little over 100 years. These strange outside values and ways have wreaked havoc with their world view. Most Yupi-

at are aware of who they are and where they came from, but the continuing barrage of foreign values and ideas causes confusion. The clash of Western and Yupiaq values and traditions has caused many Yupiaq people to suffer from a depression that is spiritual in nature. There is a need for them to regain harmony with Nature. This is what fosters their identity.

TRADITIONS AND CUSTOMS

In the past, Yupiaq clothing was made from the pelts of such animals as Alaskan ground squirrels, muskrat, mink, land otter, wolf, beaver, red fox, caribou, and moose, in addition to fish and waterfowl skins. Yupiaq women made parkas, pants, boots, and gloves from these skins. For special occasions, the women wore squirrel-skin parkas with many designs and tassels on them. A well-made parka shows that the owner has fine skills; if a woman with a beautiful parka is of marrying age, parents of young men assess her as a possible wife for the son.

The Yupiaq people observe the Western holidays, although they practice Yupiaq singing and dancing. In this way they have begun to Yupiakize many of the Western holidays. Of the several original ceremonies, it is only the Messenger Feast that is still observed. The celebration, which takes place in the spring, experienced a resurgence around 1990. None of the other traditional ceremonies are practiced anymore. The reason may be that few elders remain who remember the songs and dances. All traditional ceremonies required singing songs in a prescribed order, and making changes was taboo. Often these require very elaborate paraphernalia such as masks, drums, clay lamps, food, and designated leaders with special costumes. Much time was spent in preparation for the performances. The rehearsals for traditional ceremonies were not to be observed by the villagers.

The Yupiaq people have returned to practicing their songs and dances, which are a form of prayer. Since Yupiaq culture is based on oral traditions, songs have been passed down from generation to generation for centuries. Five dominant ceremonies and several minor ceremonies are observed throughout the year. The dominant ceremonies are: *Nakaciuq* (Bladder Festival), *Elriq* (Festival of the Dead), *Kevgiq* (invitation ceremony), *Petugtaq* (request certain items), and *Keleq* (invitation). These were ceremonies of thanksgiving to the *Ellam Yua* (Spirit of the Universe) and Mother Earth for the many gifts. Ceremonies focus on three things: centering or balancing within oneself and with the world; reciprocation to the plants and animals that must be killed in order to live; and expression of joy and humor. All Yupiaq rituals and ceremonies incorporate meditation on the integration of the human, natural, and spiritual worlds.

CUISINE

The Yupiaq region is rich with waterfowl, fish, and sea and land mammals. Salmon are a staple source of food and are caught in setnets, or drifting downriver. The nets are let out of a boat perpendicular to the river shoreline and allowed to drift downriver for approximately one-half mile. When the net is pulled in, fishers remove their catch. The fish are taken to the fish camp, where they are unloaded into holding boxes. The fish are beheaded and split by the women. The split fish are hung to dry. When the surface of the flesh begins to harden, they are moved to the smoke house where they are smoked and preserved for winter use. Some of the fish are salted, frozen, or buried underground for later use. Today about half the food is supplied by subsistence activities; the other half is purchased from the commercial stores.

The tundra provides berries for making jams, jellies, and a Yupiaq delicacy commonly called Eskimo ice cream—a concoction of vegetable shortening, berries, and sugar. Today there are many variations of this dessert. Yupiaq women have incorporated many new ingredients, such as raisins, strawberries, dried peaches, apples, and mashed potatoes to create innovative and tasty mixtures.

HEALTH AND MENTAL HEALTH ISSUES

Traditionally the Yupiaq people were a healthy people in spite of occasional famines and diseases. Presently, the two biggest problems with the growing population are water and sewage. Water from the rivers and lakes is no longer potable as a result of pollution. Wells must be drilled and sewage lagoons built, but there are inherent problems as well. The land on which this must take place is marshy and presents difficulties for control. Federal and state agencies are constantly asked to grant more funding for these activities. However, the matter becomes more problematic each year. The solutions require expensive undertakings.

Suicide among young Yupiaq men is high. This is generally attributed to problems Native youth have with identity and finding a meaningful place in society. The Bethel and Dillingham region has a wide range of chronic health problems, including otitis media, cancer, cardiovascular disease, diabetes, tooth and gum disease, obesity, and sexually transmitted diseases. The Yupiaq people are only now beginning to have a role in stemming these maladies.

LANGUAGE

The language of the Dillingham and Bethel regions is Yupiaq. There are four dialects: Yupiaq of the delta region; Cupiaq of the coastal; Suqpiaq of the Alaska Peninsula; and Siberian Yupiaq of St. Lawrence Island. These dialects are becoming grammatically impoverished. There has been much debate among the Yupiat over whether their language should be taught at home or in the schools. As a result, English is becoming the dominant language. Some villages still prefer to speak primarily Yupiaq and regard English as the second language. Even these villages, however, are losing pieces of language. The younger generation communicates mainly in English. For the first time in the history of the Yupiaq people a generation gap is steadily widening. The Yupiaq people realize their world view is imbedded in the language; that its webbing is ineluctably intertwined in the nuances, inflections, and subtleties of the words. Therefore many Yupiaq people wish the language be revived, retaught, and maintained by parents, village members, and the schools.

FAMILY AND COMMUNITY DYNAMICS

According to Yupiaq tradition, the father is the head of the family but the mother's role as preparer of food is equally important. She tends to the plants and animals, giving proper care and observing taboos. In Yupiaq culture, plant and animal foods have consciousness and are aware of how the woman takes care of them. If pleased with the care, they give of themselves to the hunter again after reincarnation. Some of these beliefs are still observed by traditional families.

Many traditions are being lost, however, due to the pressure to make money and to satisfy advertisement-induced "needs." As with the dominant society, divorce and one-parent families are on the rise among Yupiaq people. The number of single teenage mothers has increased. The nuclear family, which was once very important to Yupiaq people, today is crumbling. Few Yupiaq youth really know who the members of their extended family are. This knowledge was important for survival in the past.

Traditionally there was no dating among the Yupiaq people. Marriages were arranged by parents. Today many Yupiaq people date and fall in love. Only very traditional families arrange marriages. With new modes of transportation, such as, three- and four-wheelers, snow machines, airplanes, and boats with powerful outboard motors, Yupiaq people can visit loved ones in distant villages.

In times past, men and women had very distinct roles in the village. The men were providers, the women were caregivers. Children were treasured by the parents, as they were insurance that the elders would be taken care of in later years. Father, grandfather, and males of the extended family and community educated the boys. Mothers, grandmothers, and women of the extended family and community taught the girls. It was said that the community raised the children.

EDUCATION

Today education of the young is haphazard. Many young people do not want to learn and do not see the value of traditional ways. The schools provide inferior schooling for Native youth. They graduate without mastering either the Yupiaq language or English. They are usually very weak in mathematics and the sciences. Many do not pursue higher education, which accounts for the growing number of high school graduates in the villages who are unable to acclimate to the subsistence way of life and the outside world. The majority of the few who enter the universities end up as drop-outs. Only about 2.3 percent have made it through institutions of higher learning. Nevertheless, they are taxing the village need for housing, subsistence products, recreational facilities, health services, general assistance, and so forth.

All village schools are publicly funded by the state of Alaska. Ancillary funds are received from the federal government, required by such laws as the Indian Education, Johnson-O'Malley, Title VII Bilingual, and the Migratory Education acts. Today, there is a growing number of Yupiaq students dropping out of elementary and high schools because they do not see any value in the knowledge and skills taught there. The cognitive and cultural imperialism of the dominant society is alive and well. Those few that do make it through the universities do not return to their villages for their new knowledge and skills cannot fit into the community nor does a position exist. It might be said that there is a brain drain from the delta. Many students who enroll in the University of Alaska system will register in education programs. When successfully completed they have the opportunity to return to their home villages to teach. Most graduate students will continue in education, working for a master's degree in administration (for a principal's certificate) or in cross-cultural education. A few will enroll in anthropology. There are very few Native students who enroll in mathematics and the sciences.

The Yupiaq elders, community members, parents, teachers' aides, teachers, and university professors have been pioneers in exploring mathematics and the sciences in Yupiaq thought. This effort attempts to use the Yupiaq skills and ways of thinking as the basis for mathematics and sciences curricula. Yupiaq people have begun to realize they have knowledge which is not understood by the dominant society. Schooling has been based on the outside world with a concomitant feeling that what the Yupiat know is of little importance. Today the Yupiat are challenging this train of thought and have taken a keen interest in changing it. They are promoting education that focuses on their language, knowledge, and skills from elementary through high school. Making their community their laboratory will edify and strengthen the identity of the Yupiaq youth. This will be their most important contribution to education, arts, mathematics, sciences, industry, and government.

RELIGION

The Yupiaq people believe in a *Ellam Yua* ("thlam yu-a"), a Spirit of the Universe. The most important god, however, is the Raven, the creator of earth and human beings. The Raven-god is given powers of the spirits, yet has the weaknesses of human beings. It has provided many wonderful things for the Yupiat such as the sun, moon, and stars for light, and life for all the earth's inhabitants. But the Raven possesses human frailties such as greed, making mistakes, hurting others and itself. It is the indomitable trickster and often has other animals and humans play tricks. The Raven is a survivor. It, as a pronoun designating the Raven, is fitting because it changes in form to a human, a plant, and is often a messenger in its existing form.

The Yupiaq people believe that everything of the earth possesses a spirit. Having a spirit means that all things possess consciousness or awareness; having awareness means that they are mindful of who they give themselves to and how they are treated. A hunter who cares for and heeds taboos, and whose wife does the same, will be a successful provider. The animals will give of themselves to the hunter knowing that they will be well taken care of. Since the Yupiaq people believe that everything in nature has a spirit, some anthropologists say that they are pantheistic. This is not the case. Because animals and other things possess spirits means they are honored and respected, but not necessarily worshipped. The purpose of this spirituality is to live in harmony with everything of the human, natural, and spiritual worlds. To live in harmony is to be balanced in living and doing things that feel right in the heart.

Medicine people were specialists among the Yupiaq people. Some specialized in bone healing, others used herbs for curing diseases, still others called upon spirits of animals, such as the bear and eagle, or spiritual beings for aid. Yupiaq people believed that animal spirits and spirit helpers lived on the moon. Powerful medicine people would experience out-of-body travel to the moon, the sea, the spiritual world, other villages, animal kingdoms, and other far-off places. They were citizens of two worlds—the earth and places where the spirits dwelled. They travelled readily and learned much from their experiences, which they conveyed to their village.

The Yupiaq people believed human beings were inherently good, which is quite different from most modern day religions. If a person did something wrong, the community would seek out some activity to help the wrongdoer correct his or her behavior, to become rehabilitated, and again become a positive member of the community. This differs from the punishment that is dispensed by the modern-day justice system.

Since the Yupiaq people had to kill living things in order to survive, they developed rituals and ceremonies to regain a sense of peace with the world and its creatures. This was their method of reciprocation to Mother Earth. The Yupiaq people could never become vegetarians because they needed the animal protein and fat to live in a harsh environment.

Land is important to the Yupiaq people, for human beings and spirits occupy the same space. The land is described in action words, therefore it is a process, on-going and dynamic. By careful and patient observation the Yupiaq people learned how they are to interact with other people, nature, and the spirits. Nature became their metaphysic. Today, the Yupiaq people are not living as close to nature and, as a result, suffer from a spiritual depression.

EMPLOYMENT AND ECONOMIC TRADITIONS

Well over 50 percent of villagers qualify for government assistance. Yupiaq unemployment is as high as 80 percent in some villages. Jobs are scarce and the Alaska Native Commission claims that the few subsidized public service positions are generally occupied by transient or permanently settled non-Natives. The regional and village corporations, created by the Alaska Native Claims Settlement Act, are barely surviving, unable to develop business ventures from natural resources that are accessible to transportation and do not require a large initial capital investment. The main industries in the Bethel and Dillingham regions are seasonal fisheries and government-funded jobs. These regions are not rich in natural resources. Some small pockets of gold, platinum, and cinnabar exist. Profiting from such resources, however, conflicts with the Native concept of living in harmony with nature. Mining activities require that the surface of the environment be altered and make it unproductive for animal habitats, berries, and edible plants. Thus corporate leaders in the Yupiaq community are reluctant to invest in ventures that will alter the environment.

Since the women's role requires them to stay in the village, some have assumed leadership roles as village corporations' presidents. The men's role requires them to leave the village for subsistence hunting and trapping. Traditionally a man and woman have always been a team. It makes sense that women assume some of the modern roles, which a growing number are doing. Many women have become bilingual teachers and counseling aides in the schools. Others are community health aides and practitioners. These women generally receive a rudimentary introduction to health practices, including diagnosis, medication, and emergency care from the Kuskokwim Community College in Bethel. As they advance, they receive more training. If they encounter a situation about which they know little, they call a physician in the Public Health Service Hospital in Bethel. Critical situations require the patient be transported to the hospital with one of the many local air services. The female aides with their nurturing ways and knowledge of traditional healing practices are well suited to this service. If modern treatment and pharmaceuticals do not work, the Yupiaq practitioners often try Yupiaq treatments. Often, the two treatments will work in concert to heal the patient. The health practitioners are the bridge between the patient and the medical doctor.

POLITICS AND GOVERNMENT

The Yupiaq people were governed by egalitarianism whereby each member of the village had the same rights and responsibilities. They had a traditional council composed of elders who held meetings to address problems and issues affecting the village. They chose a chief, a servant-leader who often was the best hunter-provider in the village. The chief and council would address a problem, striving for consensus to arrive at a solution. Sometimes there would be an issue that no one agreed upon. It would be tabled for the next meeting. If, at the succeeding meeting, there still was no agreement, the matter would be dropped. The chief was kept in power as long as he or she used common sense and did not become arrogant or try to make decisions on his or her own. The chief was strictly a servant of the people and was expected to uphold their will.

Several forms of governmental entities usually operate within the modern village, which is confusing to the local people as well as agents of other institutions. Villagers and agents wonder with which entity they are supposed to work. Each village has a traditional or Indian Reorganization Act (IRA) council, a municipal office funded by the state of Alaska, a health center funded by the federal government, and a village corporation. Each has a prescribed function within the village. The IRA or tribal council was established under the auspices of the federal government, the health center is under the Yukon-Kuskokwim Health Corporation funded by the

Dr. Daryl Graves (left) and Yupiat John Kameroff display a salmon they caught in the Kuskokwim River in southwestern Alaska.

federal Indian Health Service, and the village corporation established under the Alaska Native Claims Settlement Act (ANCSA) has responsibilities for business ventures and village lands.

The Indian Self-Determination and Education Act has had the biggest impact on the Yupiaq villages. This law allows the Yupiaq villages to contract services operated by the federal government, including schools, social services, general assistance, child welfare, health services, and game management. Many of these services have been taken over by regional corporations or by organized clusters of villages. Funding for these activities is always a problem. The sources are consistently looking for ways to cut programs.

The Yupiaq region belongs to the Alaskan Federation of Natives, Inc. (AFN), which is a statewide organization representing all Native regions. This organization functions year-round with one annual meeting of representatives from every region. They try to address all issues affecting the Alaskan Native people. They present many resolutions to various government agencies and institutions whose activities affect the Native people. The Yupiaq people are always well represented. Being from a region where there are many elderly people who do not speak English, they have purchased communications technology that translates English to Yupiaq for the duration of the meeting. They are the only native group to use translators. This shows the importance given to the AFN annual meeting by the Yupiaq people.

The people of the Bethel and Dillingham regions vote heavily democratic. The majority of the Alaskan Native people belong to the Democratic Party.

MILITARY

Since World War II, many Yupiaq men have joined the armed forces. Today, many young men are members of the Army National Guard. Most villages have a guard unit. The headquarters of the 297th Infantry Battalion is in Bethel. It provides opportunities for income as well as training. Many Yupiaq young men have become officers.

MEDIA

RADIO AND TELEVISION
KYUK and KYUK-TV.

Has many tapes of Yupiaq songs, myths, legends and stories, and videotapes of the Yupiaq people.

Address: Bethel, Alaska.

MUSEUMS AND RESEARCH CENTERS

Alaska State Museum.
Address: 395 Whittier Street, Juneau, Alaska 99801-1718.
Telephone: (970) 465-2901.
Fax: (907) 465-2976.

Anchorage Museum of History and Art.
Address: 121 West Seventh Avenue, Anchorage, Alaska 99501.
Telephone: (907) 343-4326.

Institute of Alaska Native Arts, Inc.
Address: Box 70769, Fairbanks, Alaska 99707.
Telephone: (907) 456-7406.
Fax: (907) 451-7268.

Sheldon Jackson Museum.
Address: 801 Lincoln Drive, Stika, Alaska 99835.
Telephone: (907) 747-5222.
Fax: (907) 747-5212.

UAF Museum.
Address: 907 Yukon Drive, P.O. Box 756960, Fairbanks, Alaska 99775-6960.
Telephone: (907) 474-7505.
Fax: (907) 474-5469.

Yugtarvik Museum.
Address: Bethel, Alaska 99559.
Telephone: (907) 543-3521.
Fax: (907) 543-3596.

SOURCES FOR ADDITIONAL STUDY

Alexie, O., and H. Morris. *The Elders' Conference 1984*. Bethel, Alaska: Orutsararmiut Native Council, 1985.

Barnhardt, R. "Administrative Influences in Alaskan Native Education," in *Cross-Cultural Issues in Alaskan Education*, edited by R. Barnhardt. Fairbanks: Center for Northern Educational Research, 1977; pp. 57-63.

Bielawski, E. *Cross-Cultural Epistemology: Cultural Readaptation through the Pursuit of Knowledge* (paper presented at the Seventh Inuit Studies Conference). Fairbanks: University of Alaska Fairbanks, 1990.

Collier, J. J. A *Film Study of Classrooms in Western Alaska*. Fairbanks: Center for Cross-Cultural Studies, University of Alaska Fairbanks, 1979.

Darnell, F. "Education among the Native Peoples of Alaska," *Polar Record*, 19, No. 122, 1979; pp. 431-446.

Fienup-Riordan, A. *Eskimo Essays Yup'ik Lives and How We See Them*. New Brunswick and London: Rutgers University Press, 1990.

———. A. *The Real People and the Children of Thunder: The Yup'ik Eskimo Encounter with Moravian Missionaries John and Edith Kilbuck*. Norman and London: University of Oklahoma Press, 1991.

Henkelman, J. W., and K. H. Vitt. *Harmonious to Dwell*. Bethel: Tundra Press, 1985.

Kawagley, O. "Yup'ik Ways of Knowing," *Canadian Journal of Native Education*, 17, No. 2, 1990; pp. 5-17.

Napoleon, H. *Yuuyaraq: the Way of the Human Being*. Fairbanks: Center for Cross-Cultural Studies, University of Alaska Fairbanks, 1990.

Oswalt, W. *Mission of Change in Alaska: Eskimos and Moravians on the Kuskokwim*. San Marino, California: Huntington Library, 1963.

Oswalt, W. H. *Bashful No Longer*. Norman: University of Oklahoma Press, 1990.

Schwalbe, A. B. *Dayspring on the Kuskokwim*. Bethlehem, Pennsylvania: Moravian Church, 1951.

BOOKS

Alba, Richard. *Ethnic Identity: The Transformation of White America*. New Haven, Connecticut: Yale University Press, 1990.

    Discusses relations between white and ethnic minority groups in contemporary American society.

Albyn, Carol Lisa, and Lois Sinako Webb. *The Multicultural Cookbook for Students*. Phoenix, Arizona: The Oryx Press, 1993.

    Covers the cuisines of 122 countries, providing at least two traditional recipes per country. Glossary of terms.

Ashabranner, Brent. *Still a Nation of Immigrants*. New York: Cobble Hill Books/Dutton, 1993.

    Illuminates recent trends in American immigration. Photographs.

Backus, Karen, and Julia Furtaw, eds. *Asian American Information Directory*. Detroit: Gale Research, 1992.

    Comprehensive resource covering Asian American organizations, museums, agencies, institutions, programs, services, and publications.

Beard, Timothy Field. *How to Find Your Family Roots*. New York: McGraw-Hill, 1977.

    Guide for tracing ethnic backgrounds in America and abroad (180 countries).

Bernardo, Stephanie. *The Ethnic Almanac*. New York: Doubleday, 1981.

    Reference source covering 40 ethnic groups that includes statistical data, short essays, biographies, customs, and bibliographies.

Boland, Emily. *An American Christmas: A Celebration of Our Heredity from around the World*. New York: Philosophical Library, 1989.

    Explores the ethnic folklore, customs, and social life of several ethnic groups.

Brown, Francis J., and Joseph Roucek. *One America: The History, Contributions, and Present Problems of Our Racial and National Minorities*. New York: Prentice Hall, 1952.

Reference book covering almost 100 ethnic groups that includes information on immigration, settlement, and major contributions, as well as statistical data and bibliographies.

Bruhn, Wolfgang, and Max Tilke. *A Pictorial History of Costume*. London: A. Zwemmer, 1955.

    Contains excellent color illustrations of ethnic costumes from Europe, Asia, and Africa.

Buenker, John, and Lorman Ratner. *Multiculturalism in the United States: A Comparative Guide to Acculturation and Ethnicity*. New York: Greenwood Press, 1992.

    Discusses minority groups in America, focusing on pluralism and ethnic relations.

Buttlar, Lois, and Lubomyr R. Wynar. *Building Ethnic Collections: An Annotated Guide for School Media Centers and Public Libraries*. Littleton, Colorado: Libraries Unlimited, 1977.

    Recommends books covering over 50 ethnic groups.

Cardasco, Francesco. *American Ethnic Groups, the European Heritage: A Bibliography of Doctoral Dissertations at American Universities*. Metuchen, New Jersey: Scarecrow Press, 1981.

    Lists over 1,400 dissertations that cover 30 ethnic groups.

Casey, Betty. *International Folk Dancing, USA*. Garden City, New York: Doubleday, 1981.

    Describes folk dancing in several European, Asian, and Latin American countries. Illustrated.

Champagne, Duane, ed. *The Native North American Almanac: A Reference Work on Native North Americans in the United States and Canada*. Detroit: Gale Research, 1994.

    Comprehensive guide covering North American tribes, their history, language, arts, education, literature, media, and prominent Native Americans.

Champion, Selwyn G. *Racial Proverbs: A Selection of the World's Proverbs Arranged Linguistically*. New York: Macmillan, 1965.

    Offers hundreds of proverbs from 27 countries.

Chiswick, Barry. *Immigration, Language, and Ethnicity: Canada and the United States*. Washington, D.C.: AEI Press, 1994.

    Explores immigration patterns, ethnic and linguistic minorities, and language policy in both countries.

Coppa, Frank J., and Thomas J. Curran, eds. *The Immigrant Experience in America*. Boston: Twayne, 1976.

    Provides historical coverage of European, Hispanic, and Asian immigration to the United States.

Daniels, Roger. *Coming to America: A History of Immigration and Ethnicity in American Life*. New York: HarperCollins, 1990.

    Historical overview of immigration and settlement patterns in the United States. Photographs.

Davis, Hillary. *Celebrate: Traditional Ethnic Entertaining in America*. New York: Crescent Books, 1992.

> Explores the folklore, festivals, cookery, and heritage of various ethnic groups.

Dinnerstein, Leonard. *Ethnic Americans: A History of Immigration*, third edition. New York: Harper & Row, 1988.

> Historical overview of immigration and ethnic relations.

Dinnerstein, Leonard et al. *Natives and Strangers: Blacks, Indians, and Immigrants in America*, second edition. New York: Oxford University Press, 1990.

> Historical account of various ethnic groups in the United States and their relationships with one another. Illustrated.

Di Pietro, Robert. *Ethnic Perspectives in American Literature: Selected Essays on the European Contribution*. New York: Modern Languages Association, 1983.

> Illuminates European ethnic groups. Bibliography.

Dunbar, Nelia, and Brian Rajewski, eds. *Countries of the World and Their Leaders Yearbook*. 2 vols. Detroit: Gale Research, 1995.

> Comprehensive study of more than 200 countries that includes information on religion, education, media, and politics and government.

Eiseman, Alberta. *From Many Lands*. New York: Atheneum, 1970.

> Documents the immigrant experiences from the past 200 years through journals, newspapers, and literature.

Estell, Kenneth, ed. *The African American Almanac*. Detroit: Gale Research, 1994.

> Comprehensive reference source covering history, organizations, politics, religion, music, sports, science, the arts, and notable persons.

Ferraro, Thomas J. *Ethnic Passages: Literary Immigrants in Twentieth Century America*. Chicago: Chicago University Press, 1993.

> Discusses the impact of emigration and immigration on twentieth-century American fiction.

Friedman, Lester D. *Unspeakable Images: Ethnicity and the American Cinema*. Urbana: University of Illinois Press, 1991.

> Traces ethnic influences in American motion pictures.

Georges, Robert A. *American and Canadian Immigrant Folklore: An Annotated Bibliography*. Hartford, Connecticut: Garland Press, 1982.

> Includes coverage of 50 ethnic groups, primarily Europeans, but also Asian and African peoples.

Gold, Milton J., and Carl Grant. *In Praise of Diversity: A Resource Book for Multicultural Education*. Washington, D.C.: Association of Teacher Educators, 1977.

> Contains essays praising various cultures and ethnic groups for their contributions to American society.

Greene, Victor R. *American Immigrant Leaders, 1800-1910: Marginality and Identity*. Baltimore, Maryland: Johns Hopkins University, 1987.

> Recognizes Irish, German, Norwegian, Swedish, Jewish, Polish, and Italian leaders in various fields. Bibliography.

Handlin, Oscar. *The Uprooted: The Epic Story of the Great Migrations that Made the American People*. Boston: Little Brown, 1990.

> Reference source that compares immigrant groups, emphasizing how they altered American culture.

Hayden, Carla. *Venture into Cultures: A Resource Book of Multicultural Materials and Programs*. Chicago: American Library Association, 1992.

> Discusses the culture, holidays, games, arts, crafts, dances, foods, and juvenile literature of African Americans, Asians, Arabs, Hispanic Americans, Jews, Africans, Persians, and Native Americans.

Hecker, Melvin. *Ethnic America, 1970-1977: Updating the Ethnic Chronology Series*. Dobbs Ferry, New York: Oceana Publications, 1979.

> Provides chronology information on 31 ethnic groups.

Hoerder, Dick. *The Immigrant Labor Press in North America, 1840s-1970s: An Annotated Bibliography*. New York: Greenwood Press, 1987.

> Includes essays, statistical data, and bibliographies on 30 ethnic groups, most of which are European.

Hutchinson, Edward Prince. *Immigrants and Their Children, 1850-1950*. New York: Wiley, 1956.

> Comprehensive study illuminating the generation gaps within numerous ethnic groups over the past 100 years, focusing on economic, social, professional, and linguistic issues.

James, J.P., and E. James. *We the People of America: An Atlas of America's Ethnic Diversity*. New York: Macmillan, 1988.

> Identifies American ethnic groups on national, regional, and city scales, providing good annotations, maps, and statistical data based on the 1980 U.S. Census.

Johnson, Harry A. *Ethnic American Minorities: A Guide to Media and Materials*. New York: R & R Bowker, 1976.

> Includes audio-visual aids, catalogs, and bibliographies.

Johnson, Michael. *The Native Tribes of North America: A Concise Encyclopedia*. New York: Macmillan, 1992.

> Guide to 400 tribes in North America, centering on identity, religion, culture, kinship, and location. Excellent Illustrations.

Kanellos, Nicolas, ed. *The Hispanic American Almanac: A Reference Work on Hispanics in the United States*. Detroit: Gale Research, 1993.

> Comprehensive reference source that examines history, religion, the arts, media, music, science, sports, education, and notable Hispanics. Illustrated.

Katz, William Loren. *The Great Migrations, 1880s-1912*. Austin, Texas: Raintree, Steck-Vaughn, 1993.

> Recounts major immigration waves from Europe, the Middle East, and Asia.

Kivisto, Peter. *The Ethnic Enigma: The Salience of Ethnicity for European Origin Groups*. Philadelphia: The Balch Institute Press, 1989.

> Addresses ethnic relations between European American groups.

Kraus, Barbara. *The Barbara Kraus International Cook Book: Fabulous Meals from the Cuisines of More than 100 Countries*. New York: Perigree Books, 1991.

> Contains typical dishes indexed by the names of meals and by country. Bibliography.

Lee, Joan F. *Asian American Experiences in the United States: Oral Histories of First to Fourth Generation Americans from China, the Philippines, Japan, India, Pacific Islands, Vietnam and Cambodia*. New York: McFarland, 1991.

Supplemental source to other sources on Asian Americans. Illustrated.

Lieberson, Stanley. *From Many Strands: Ethnic and Racial Groups in Contemporary America*. New York: Russell Sage Foundation, 1988.

Analysis of American ethnic and racial groups based on 1980 U.S. Census data.

Liebman, Lance. *Ethnic Relations in America*. Englewood Cliffs, New Jersey: Prentice-Hall, 1982.

Provides essays on ethnic history, immigration, and language, as well as political and legal issues.

McCabe, Cynthia Jaffe. *The American Experience: Contemporary Immigrant Artists*. New York: Independent Curators; Philadelphia: The Balch Institute for Ethnic Studies, 1985.

Examines the artistic contributions of various ethnic groups in America.

Mangiafico, Luciano. *Contemporary American Immigrants: Patterns of Filipino, Korean, and Chinese Settlement in the United States*. New York: Praeger, 1988.

Reviews settlement patterns and social adjustment.

Manoogian, Sylvia, and Natalia Bezugloff. *Directory of Language Collections in North American Public Libraries*. Chicago: American Library Association, 1986.

Locates language collections in over 200 libraries, arranging them by foreign language and by geographic location.

Mead, Frank S. *Handbook of Denominations in the United States*, nineteenth edition. Nashville, Tennessee: Abingdon Press, 1990.

Reference source that includes the religious bodies of several American ethnic groups.

Melton, J. Gordon, ed. *Encyclopedia of American Religions*, fourth edition. Detroit: Gale Research, 1993.

Offers comprehensive coverage of over 1700 religious groups.

———. *Directory of Religious Organizations in the United States*, third edition. Detroit: Gale Research, 1993.

Provides information on over 2,500 religious organizations.

Meltzer, Milton. *The Hispanic Americans*. New York: Crowell, 1982.

Reference source for young people, focusing on the social and economic conditions of various Hispanic American groups.

Miller, Sally. *The Ethnic Press in the United States: A Historical Analysis and Handbook*. New York: Greenwood Press, 1987.

Furnishes essays and bibliographies on over 25 ethnic groups.

Miller, Wayne Charles. *A Comprehensive Bibliography for the Study of American Minorities*. 2 vols. New York: New York University Press, 1976.

Covers several dozen ethnic groups (not only minorities) in short essays and bibliographies.

———. *A Handbook of American Minorities*. New York: New York University Press, 1976.

A condensed version of *A Comprehensive Bibliography for the Study of American Minorities* (1976) by the same author that is useful for quick reference.

Minority Organizations: A National Directory, fourth edition. Garret Park, Maryland: Garret Press, 1992.

Provides information on 9,700 organizations representing African American, Native American, Hispanic American, and Asian American groups.

Morrison, Joan, and Charlote Fox Zabusky. *American Mosaic: The Immigrant Experience in the Words of Those Who Lived It*. Pittsburgh, Pennsylvania: University of Pittsburgh Press, 1980.

Collection of experiences by American immigrants from Europe, Asia, the Middle East, South America, and South Africa.

Newman, Jaqueline. *Melting Pot: An Annotated Bibliography and Guide to Food and Nutrition Information for Ethnic Groups in America*. New York: Garland Publications, 1993.

Contains information on the food habits, cookery, and nutrition of several dozen American ethnic groups.

Palmer, Ransford R. *In Search of a Better Life: Perspectives on Migration from the Caribbean*. New York: Praeger, 1990.

Comparative study centering on the migration of Caribbean peoples to the United States, Canada, and Great Britain.

Parillo, Vincent. *Strangers to These Shores: Race and Ethnic Relations in the United States*, fourth edition. New York: Macmillan, 1990.

Examines America's pluralism in a multiracial society, covering more than 100 ethnic groups.

Pozzetta, George. *Folklore, Culture, and the Immigrant*. New York: Garland, 1991.

Discusses immigration, ethnicity, and acculturation in the United States.

Racinet, Albert. *The Historical Encyclopedia of Costumes*. New York: Facts on File, 1988.

Includes traditional costumes from Africa, Asia, Europe, Oceania, and North America. Illustrated.

Santoli, Al. *New Americans: An Oral History, Immigrants and Refugees in the U.S. Today*. New York: Viking Press, 1988.

Personal accounts of American immigrants from several ethnic groups.

Schon, Isabel. *A Hispanic Heritage: A Guide to Juvenile Books about Hispanic People and Culture*. Metuchen, New Jersey: Scarecrow Press, 1980.

Includes information on several Hispanic American groups.

Schorr, Alan. *Hispanic Resource Directory, 1992-1994: A Comprehensive Guide to Over 6,000 National, State, and Local Organizations Concerned with Hispanic Americans*. Juno, Alaska: Denali Group, 1992.

Includes information on several Hispanic American groups.

Schwartz, Carol, and Rebecca Turner, eds. *Encyclopedia of Associations*. 3 vols. Detroit: Gale Research, 1994.

Reference source covering over 100 ethnic organizations.

Shenton, James P. *Ethnic Groups in American Life*. New York: Arno Press, 1978.

Contains reproduced articles from *The New York Times* dealing with American ethnic groups and their concerns.

Shorris, Earl. *Latinos: A Biography of the People*. New York: W.W. Norton, 1992.

Provides Hispanic American history and biographies of notable Latinos.

Sowell, Thomas. *Ethnic America: A History*. New York: Basic Books, 1981.

Includes ethnic groups from Africa, Asia, Europe, and Latin America.

Standard Periodical Directory. New York: Oxbridge Press, 1995.

Annual directory containing English and bilingual titles that covers over 60 American ethnic groups.

Statistical Abstract of the United States. Washington, D.C.: U.S. Bureau of the Census, 1995.

Reference source published annually that presents immigration statistics by country of origin along with comparative data dating back to the nineteenth century.

Stave, Bruce, and John Sutherland. *From the Old Country: An Oral History of European Migration to America*. New York: Twain Publishers, 1994.

Furnishes oral histories from the 1930s through the 1970s, including discussions on crossing the ocean, work, family, love and marriage, community life, and other topics.

Takaki, Ronald. *Strangers from a Different Shore: A History of Asian Americans*. Boston: Little Brown, 1989.

Investigates Chinese, Japanese, Korean, Indian, Filipino, and Vietnamese groups. Illustrated.

Thernstrom, Stephan et al. *Harvard Encyclopedia of American Ethnic Groups*. Cambridge, Massachusetts: Belknap Press/Harvard University Press, 1980.

Scholarly source covering over 100 ethnic groups that includes discussions of immigration, settlement, organizations, religions, and major contributions. Bibliographies.

Tilke, Max. *National Costumes from East Europe, Africa and Asia*. New York: Hastings House, 1978.

Treats various ethnic groups. Color illustrations.

Tilton, Jeff Todd. *Worlds of Music: An Introduction to the Music of the World's Peoples*. New York: Schirmer Books, 1992.

Addresses Native American, African American, European, Asian, Latin American, and American (folk) music.

Upton, Dell. *America's Architectural Roots: Ethinic Groups that Built America*. Washington, D.C.: Preservation Press, 1986.

Provides examples of American ethnic architecture. Illustrated.

U.S. Census of the Population and Housing. Washington, D.C.: U.S. Bureau of the Census, 1991-1992.

Contains the latest numerical data on American ethnic groups, their geographical location, language preservation, and other relevant topics.

Veliana-Suarez, Ana. *Hispanic Media, USA: A Narrative Guide to Print and Electronic News Media in the United States*. Washington, D.C.: Media Institute, 1987.

Supplies Hispanic American newspapers, directories, and mass media information.

Waldman, Carl. *Encyclopedia of Native American Tribes*. New York: Facts on File, 1988.

Describes 150 North American tribes, their locations, migration patterns, life styles, languages, and other relevant topics. Color illustrations.

Warren, Lee. *The Dance of Africa: An Introduction*. Englewood Cliffs, New Jersey: Prentice Hall, 1972.

Covers several African dances. Photographs and dance instructions.

Wasserman, Fred. *Ellis Island: An Illustrated History of the Immigrant Experience*. New York: Macmillan, 1991.

Records the experiences of individuals who entered America through Ellis Island through photographs.

Wasserman, Paul, and Alice Kennington, eds. *Ethnic Information Sources of the United States*, second edition. 2 vols. Detroit: Gale Research, 1995.

Comprehensive source covering over 120 American ethnic groups that includes organizations, periodicals, research centers, radio, and other subjects. Bibliography.

Wasserman, Paul et al. *Festival Sourcebook*. Detroit: Gale Research, 1977.

Includes discussions of ethnic celebrations.

Waters, Mary C. *Ethnic Options: Choosing Identities in America*. Berkeley: University of California Press, 1990.

Reviews the ethnic composition of America, focusing on mixed marriages and the freedom to choose ethnic backgrounds.

Weiser, Marjorie K. *Ethnic America*. New York: Wilson, 1978.

Supplies articles on different ethnic groups in the United States, especially Native Americans and African Americans, and their acculturation.

Wertsman, Vladimir F. *What's Cooking in Multicultural America: 400 Ethnic Cuisines at Your Finger Tips*. Metuchen, New Jersey: Scarecrow Press, 1995.

Presents cuisines from every continent, including 120 Native American tribes. Annotated bibliographies.

———. *Career Opportunities for Bilinguals and Multilinguals: A Directory of Resources in Education, Employment, and Business*, second edition. Metuchen, New Jersey: Scarecrow Press, 1994.

Employment guide that identifies educational institutions specializing in languages and targets prospective employers in the United States and abroad who are interested in hiring individuals with language skills.

Westin, Jeane Eddy. *Finding Your Roots: How Every American Can Trace His Ancestors at Home and Abroad*. Los Angeles: J.P. Tarcher, 1977.

Guide for tracing one's background in the United States and beyond.

Weyr, Thomas. *Hispanic USA: Breaking the Melting Pot*. New York: Harper and Row, 1988.

Discusses Hispanic American culture, ethnic identity, and assimilation.

Wilde, Larry. *Larry Wilde's Complete Book of Ethnic Humor.* New York: Bell Publishing Co./Crown Publishers, 1984.

Reveals the ethnic wisdom, expressed through humor, of various ethnic groups.

Williams, Robin Murphy. *Mutual Accomodation: Ethnic Conflict and Cooperation.* Minneapolis: University of Minnesota Press, 1977.

Explores intercultural communication.

Wittke, Carol Frederick. *We Who Built America: The Saga of the Immigrant.* Rev. ed. Cleveland, Ohio: Case Western University, 1967.

Provides concise coverage of several American ethnic groups.

Wynar, Lubomyr. *Encyclopedic Directory of Ethnic Newspapers and Periodicals in the United States.* Littleton, Colorado: Libraries Unlimited, 1976.

Pioneer work covering over 50 ethnic groups.

———. *Guide to Ethnic Museums, Libraries and Archives in the United States.* Kent, Ohio: Kent State University, 1978.

Includes information on over 60 ethnic groups.

———. *Ethnic Film Strip Guide for Libraries and Media Centers.* Littleton, Colorado: Libraries Unlimited, 1980.

Covers several dozen groups.

———. *Encyclopedic Directory of Ethnic Organizations in the United States.* Littleton, Colorado: Libraries Unlimited, 1985.

Contains information on over 70 ethnic groups.

Yinger, J. Milton. *Ethnicity: Source of Strength; Source of Conflict.* New York: State University of New York Press, 1994.

Evaluates the pros and cons of ethnicity, ethnic relations, and assimilation.

PERIODICALS

Emie Bulletin (1976-). New York: Ethnic Materials Information Exchange Round Table/ALA, Queens College Graduate School of Library and Information Studies. Quarterly.

Multiethnic coverage featuring short articles, bibliographies, and book reviews.

Ethnic Forum (1980-). Kent, Ohio: Center of Study of Ethnic Publications, Kent State University. Semi-Annual.

Contains essays on American ethnic groups, book reviews, and bibliographies.

Ethnic Groups (1976-). New York: Gordon & Breach Science Publishers. Quarterly.

Treats ethnic identity, social, and cultural policies.

Ethnic Newswatch (1992-). Stamford, Connecticut: Softline Information. Quarterly.

CD ROM containing articles form over 90 ethnic and minority newspapers and magazines.

Ethnic Resource Guide (1975-). Bloomington: Ethnic Heritage Studies Program, Indiana University. Annual.

Provides articles on African American and European groups.

Explorations in Ethnic Studies (1978-). Tempe: National Association of Ethnic Studies, Arizona State University. Monthly.

Focuses on cultural activity and inter-ethnic group relations.

Melus (1973-). Huntington, West Virginia: Society of Multicultural Literature in the USA, Marshall University. Quarterly.

Studies ethnicity in American literature and media.

Multicultural Review (1990-). Westport, Connecticut: Greenwood Publishers. Quarterly.

Contains articles, book reviews, and bibliographies, providing excellent coverage of numerous American ethnic groups.

Anka, Paul   95, 247, 1321
Anna Marinkovich   381
Anne of Green Gables   247
Annesley, Robert   279
Anschluss   152, 1257
Antall, József   694
Antarctic Ocean   99, 138
Antell, Will   1027
Anthony F. Lucas Medal   381
Anti-Defamation League of B'nai B'rith   834
Antioch College   589
Antipodes   138
Antipoems, New and Selected   613
Antonescu, Ion   1145
Antwerp   185, 189, 194, 1376
Anxiety Disorders Institute   612
Anzac Day   145
Apache Indians   71-83, 279, 375, 956-958,
    963, 967, 1117, 1120, 1128
Apache Tribal Cultural Center   80
Apache Tribal Fair   76, 78
apartheid   18, 307
Apartment, The   160, 1207
Apollo 8   407
Apollo 10   407
Apostle Thomas   263
Apostolic church   116-117, 121, 529
Appaduravi, Arjun   132
Appalachian State University   483
Apple Computer Company   527
Aquino, Benigno S. Jr.   503
Aquino, Corazon   503
Arab American & Chaldean Communities Social
    Council   269
Arab American Historical Society   96
Arab American Institute   94, 97, 1052, 1320,
    1322-1323
Arab American University Graduates, Inc.   94,
    97-98, 1320, 1322-1323
Arab Americans   84-98, 264, 266, 268-269,
    465, 468, 470, 1037, 1049, 1052, 1309, 1312,
    1315, 1320, 1322-1323
Arab Israeli War   86, 94, 97, 464, 1046
Arab Women's Council   97
Arabian Peninsula   84, 1048
Arabian Sea   123, 1030
Arabic   24, 84, 88-90, 95, 262, 264-267, 466,
    468, 470, 713, 720, 725, 728, 822, 900, 1035,
    1043, 1045, 1048, 1051-1052, 1276, 1309-
    1310, 1315, 1317-1318, 1322, 1366, 1370
Aracata, Colombia   336
Arafat, Yasir   87
Aragón, Sergio Ramiro   612
Arai, Clarence Takeya   810
Aramaic   93, 262-266, 1043, 1048, 1318

Araucanians   100
Arbulu, Maria Azucena   1079
Arcadia, California   382
Archipenko, Alexander   1389
architecture   57, 61, 113, 152, 157-158, 186,
    310, 362, 477, 491, 495, 527, 533, 575, 587,
    597, 683, 799, 809, 850, 901, 905, 948, 970,
    1040, 1068, 1110, 1121, 1123, 1166, 1264,
    1291, 1293, 1304
Ardoin, Amédé   13
Are You Being Served   484
Arendt, Hannah   832
Arevalo, Juan Jose   597
Argentina   44, 99-108, 196, 282, 294, 458,
    483, 597, 983, 1069, 1072, 1271-1273, 1300,
    1377, 1387
Argentine Association of Los Angeles   108
Argentine-American Chamber of Commerce
    101, 108
Argentine-North American Association for the
    Advancement of Science, Technology and
    Culture   101, 108
Argentinean Americans   99-108
Argentinean Independence Day   108
Argentinean Information Service Center   108
Arias, Arturo   613
Arias Foundation   340
Arias Sánchez, Oscar   340
Aristide, Jean-Bertrand   644, 652
Ariyoshi, George Ryoichi   810
Arizona   71-76, 78, 80-83, 161, 235, 242, 246,
    249, 254, 496, 519, 600, 603, 659, 767, 778,
    808, 843, 907-908, 924, 928, 934-938, 952,
    955, 958-960, 962-968, 987, 1080, 1116-
    1117, 1119, 1123-1128, 1215, 1265, 1272-
    1273, 1417
Arizona Commission for Indian Affairs   82,
    967, 1127
Arizona State University   82, 235, 937, 965,
    967, 1125, 1127
Arkansas   274, 278, 310, 312, 317, 323, 348,
    581, 630, 892, 1209
Arkansas River   323
Arlen, Michael   119
Arlington Heights, Illinois   222
Armen, Kay   119
Armenia   45, 109-112, 114-117, 119-121, 628,
    1282, 1364
Armenian American Radio Hour   120
Armenian Americans   109-122, 1370
Armenian Assembly of America   120
Armenian church   116, 118
Armenian Evangelical Social Service Center
    112
Armenian Evangelical Union   117

Boston Tea Party   543
Boston University   51, 495, 513-514, 591
Bosworth Field   1409
Botany Bay   138-139, 145
Botero, Fernando   336
Boucher, Georges-Alphonse   559
Boucher, Jean-Claude   557
Boudinot, Frank   279
Boulpaep, Emile   192, 194
Bounty Island   138
Bourgeois, Ulric   561
Bourjaily, Vance   1321
Bousma, William   444
Boutros-Ghali, Boutros   469
Bowdoin College   543
Boxing Day   167, 788, 1356
Boychuk, Bohdan   1388
Boyer, Charles   542
Boyesen, Hjalmar Hjorth   1012
Brademas, John   589-590
Brady, Anthony Nicholas   744
Brady, Mathew   744
Brahman   129-130, 1331
Brahms, Johannes   150
Braithwaite, E. R.   626
Brancuşi, Constantin   1156
Brandeis, Louis D.   407, 831
Brandeis University   152, 157
Brantford, Ontario   248
Brasil   196, 205
Brasseaux, Carl A.   370, 545
Bratt, James H   445
Brault, Gérard J.   550, 556, 558, 564
Brazil   99, 163-164, 196-207, 326, 435, 617,
    817, 831, 1067, 1101-1103, 1111-1112,
    1114, 1300, 1311, 1377, 1387
Brazil Alive!   199
Brazil Watch   205
Brazilian American Chamber of Commerce
    206
Brazilian American Cultural Center   206
Brazilian American Cultural Institute   206-207
Brazilian Americans   198-207
Brazilian Independence Day   200, 204
Brcin, John David   1226
Brees, Antoon   193
Brennan, Walter   278
Brennan, William G.   745
Brenner, Victor D.   891
Brentano, August   158
Brescia, William Jr.   325
Bridenbaugh, Carl   485
Bridgetown, Barbados   171
Briggs, Lester Jack Jr.   1027
Brill, A. A.   159

British Americans   479-480, 484, 1412
British Broadcasting Corporation   480, 484
British Crown   139, 141, 733, 988
British Empire   240, 471, 480, 484, 1199-1200
British Guiana   617, 619
British India   124, 1030-1031
British Information Services   484
British Museum   316
British Nationality Act   620
British North America Act   241
British Parliament   164-165, 170, 988, 1410
British Royal Collection   80
Brittany   1, 9, 1414
Broch, Hermann   159
Brockton, Massachusetts   559
Broder, David   831
Bronson, Charles   890
Bronx, New York   47, 49, 52, 135, 497, 686,
    690, 746
Bronze Age   579, 589, 1043, 1409
Brookings Institution   132, 576
Brookline, Massachusetts   205, 261
Brooklyn Art Academy   542
Brooklyn Bridge   651
Brooklyn College   248, 1142
Brooklyn Dodgers   560, 891
Brooklyn, New York   53, 90, 171-172, 461,
    529, 626, 653-654, 781, 833, 874, 878, 893,
    983, 1004, 1014, 1059, 1064, 1095, 1142,
    1168, 1283, 1356
Brooks, Mel   831
Brooks, Van Wyck   443
Brotherhood of Sleeping Car Porters   37
Broumas, Olga   590
Brown, Francis   54, 498, 880, 894
Brown, Jim   38
Brown, Marianne Wargelin   532
Brown University   119, 205, 680, 728, 1111,
    1416
Brown v. Board of Education of Topeka   26
Bruce, Louis R. Jr.   762
Bruckner, Anton   154
Brumidi, Constantino   779
Brunswick   1, 3, 111, 122, 182, 238-239, 241,
    243, 245-246, 369, 439, 444, 446, 546-547,
    562, 594, 698, 706, 708-709, 1098, 1426
Brussels, Belgium   189, 193, 195, 560
Bruun, Ulrikka Feldtman   1013
Bryan, Violet Harrington   361, 369
Bryant, Anita   278
Bryant, Lane   890
Brynner, Julius   1305
Bryson, Bill   485
Bucharest, Romania   1144
Buchwald, Art   831

Chen, Steven 309

Cher 119, 278

Chereshnovsky, Michael 1389

Cherokee Indian Nation Campout 275

Cherokee Indians 271-281, 314-315, 317, 320, 349, 358, 751, 891, 1016, 1231, 1233-1234

Cherokee Museum 280

Cherokee National Historical Society 280

Cherokee National Museum 280

Cherokee, North Carolina 280

Cherry Hill, New Jersey 593

Chervenkov, Vulko 211

Cheslav 1212

Chevalley, Montreux 1304

Cheviot Hills 471

Chevrolet, Louis Joseph 1306

Chiang, Asuntha Maria Ming-Yee 1332

Chiang Kai-shek 298, 302, 308

Chicago Bears 407, 891, 1389

Chicago Black Hawks 382, 408, 1252, 1389

Chicago Cubs 52, 591

Chicago, Illinois 39, 135, 161, 178, 213, 222-223, 262, 337-338, 382, 408, 545, 575, 592-594, 614, 681, 747, 780-781, 811, 813, 833, 891-894, 937-938, 1029, 1053, 1080, 1095-1098, 1141, 1156, 1171, 1227-1228, 1267, 1289, 1295-1296, 1307, 1390, 1392

Chicago Opera Ballet 406

Chicago Public Library 47, 886

Chicago Sun Times 147

Chicago Symphony Orchestra 407, 528, 1388

Chicago Tribune 338, 559

chicanas 919-920, 922, 934, 937

chicanos 601, 608, 655, 910-912, 916, 919-922, 925, 931-933, 935, 937-939, 1182, 1238

Chickamaugans 272

Chickasaha, Oklahoma 323

Chickasaw Indians 273, 320

Chico, Modesto 672

Chien-Hsiung Wu 310

Chierici, Rose-Marie Cassagnol 655

Childers, Ernest 357

Children's Day 303, 1221

Chile 100, 282-295, 458, 604, 923, 1067, 1069, 1072

Chilean Americans 282-295

China 103, 123, 125, 141, 225-227, 233, 296-305, 307-312, 375, 459-460, 500, 619, 661, 670-671, 798-799, 804-805, 837-841, 849, 857-858, 864, 923, 1030, 1032, 1100, 1161, 1265, 1325, 1393-1395, 1397, 1401, 1403

Chinamen 309

Chinatowns 299-307, 310-312, 814

Chinese American Citizens Alliance 311

Chinese American Citizens Outlook 311

Chinese American Forum 311

Chinese Americans 165, 296-312, 499

Chinese Consolidated Benevolent Association 311

Chinese Culture Foundation of San Francisco 311

Chinese for Affirmative Action 308, 312, 337, 383

Chinese Historical Society of America 312

Chinese New Year 302-303, 1328

Chino, Eusebio 766, 778

Chios 580-581

Chiquinquira 334

Chiricahua 73, 77, 79, 83, 279, 958

Chisholm, Minnesota 531

Chisholm, Shirley 171

Choctaw Civil War 316

Choctaw Indian Fair 321-322

Choctaw Indians 271, 273, 313-325, 349, 963, 968, 1234-1235

Chomsky, Noam 830

Chopin, Kate O'Flaherty 367

Chopin, Oscar 367

Chopra, Kuldeep Prakash 132

Chou Enlai 298

Choy, Herbert Y. C. 853

Chretien, Alfred J. 556

Christensen, Carl Christian Anton 421

Christensen, Rosemary Ackley 1028

Christian III 411

Christian IV 412

Christian Methodist Episcopal churches 29

Christian Reformed church 441, 444

Christiansen, F. Melius 1012

Christie, Agatha 480

Christmas 8, 22, 59, 61, 93, 103-105, 114-115, 118, 128, 145, 154-155, 167-168, 179, 187-189, 200, 216, 227, 257, 289, 330, 334, 342, 377-378, 400-401, 412, 414-417, 438, 454, 465, 468, 490, 522-523, 552-553, 570, 583-584, 587, 589, 606, 622, 647, 651, 687, 699, 713, 768, 771, 788, 809, 832, 846, 873-874, 878, 899, 925-927, 991, 1006-1008, 1059, 1075, 1077, 1089, 1106-1108, 1134-1135, 1145, 1148-1149, 1166, 1190, 1203, 1220-1221, 1246-1248, 1262, 1267, 1275, 1279, 1287, 1314, 1328, 1356-1357, 1378-1382, 1384, 1389

Christoffel Plantin prize 192

Christopher, Warren 1013

Christowe, Stoyan 214, 222-223

Chrysler, Walter 443

Chrysostom, Saint John 1152

Chubak, Sadeq-i 728

D

Halpern, Ben   830
Halpern, Otto   159
Hamer, Fannie Lou   37
Hamlisch, Marvin   832
Hammerstein, Oscar   832
Hamod, Sam   1321
Hampton, Lionel   36
Han Dynasty   297, 1394
Han-fei   297
Handler, Ruth   1093
Handlin, Oscar   830
Handy, W. C.   36
Hansberry, Lorraine   36
Hansen, Alvin Harvey   419
Hansen, Marcus Lee   419, 1012, 1287
Hansen, Niels Ebbesen   421
Hanson, Howard   1294
Hanson, John   1285, 1291
Harald Bluetooth   411
Hardin, Helen   1124
Harjo, Joy   349, 357, 359
Harris, Wilson   625-626
Harrison, Richard B.   35
Harvey, Laurence   890
Hassler, Ferdinand   1306
Hatathli, Ned   963
Haugen, Einar   1012, 1015
Hauschka, Spaeth   159
Hawaii   143, 192, 312, 375, 500-508, 510-515,
    574, 657-669, 799-800, 804, 808-813, 839-
    844, 847-849, 852-853, 856, 946, 1040,
    1103-1104, 1109-1110, 1112, 1187, 1189,
    1196, 1273, 1376, 1401
Hawaiian Cable Vision Co.   668
Hawaiian Sugar Planters Association   504,
    511, 841
Hawaiians   375, 504, 508, 511, 657-669, 800,
    808-809, 841-852, 1196, 1376, 1386
Hayakawa, S. I.   810
Hayakawa, Sessue   810
Hayashi, Harvey Saburo   811
Hazo, Sam   95, 1321
Hébert, Félix   557
Heifetz, Jascha   832
Hekman, John   443
Hektoen, Ludvig   1013
Heller, Joseph   831
Hellman, Lillian   832
Henie, Sonja   1013
Henius, Max   421
Hennepin, Father   192
Henni, Johann Martin   1306
Hentoff, Nat   831
Hepburn, Katharine   1207
Heraclius   1211

Herbert, Victor   744
Hersh, Seymour   831
Hersholt, Jean   419
Hertz, John David   158
Hess, Victor Franz   574
Hesselink, Ira John   444
Hevesy, Georg Karl   705
Hidalgo, Cecilia   292
Hijuelos, Oscar   393
Hill, Gwendolyn A.   1028
Hill, Joan   279, 358
Hill, Joe   1292
Hill, Richard   762
Hillman, Sydney   890
Hilton, Conrad   1012
Hindemith, Paul   574
Hinduism   124-132, 170, 225, 327, 618, 622,
    637, 711, 715, 793, 857, 1030-1039, 1331,
    1356, 1358-1359
Hindus   123-132, 623, 627, 634, 715, 1030-
    1039, 1325, 1350, 1357-1359
Hinojosa, Rolando   935
Hispania   101, 1114, 1270
Hispanic Americans   102, 232, 286, 387-391,
    637, 685, 804, 911, 916, 919, 929, 944, 1063,
    1139-1141, 1278
Hispaniola   163, 384, 425-426, 642-643, 784
Hmong Americans   670, 681
Hmong National Development   679-680
Ho, Don   667
Hoa Hao   1394
Hobson, Geary   279
Hodiak, John   1388
Hoekstra, Peter   443
Hoffman, Dustin   831
Hofstadter, Robert   832
Hogan, Ben   745
Holder, Geoffrey   1361
Holland, John Philip   744
Hollo, Anselm   528
Hollywood   88, 111, 159-161, 222, 260, 302,
    318, 330, 469, 480, 561, 705, 810, 830, 877,
    892, 902, 990, 1094, 1111, 1139, 1147,
    1170-1171, 1184, 1206-1207, 1305, 1327,
    1387-1388, 1404, 1413
Holm, Celeste   1012
Holocaust   157, 631, 693, 820, 822, 826, 829,
    835, 888, 1043, 1176
Homestead Act   413, 437, 1004, 1010, 1103
Homolka, Oscar   160
Honduran Americans   682-691
Honduras   596, 599, 969-970, 974, 979, 982,
    1173-1175
Hope, Andrew P.   1345
Horn, Gyula   695

John V   1102
John and Mary   589
Johnny Belinda   1154
Johnson, Earvin "Magic"   38
Johnson, Frank   1345
Johnson, James Weldon   37
Johnson, Lyndon B.   933, 1154, 1203
Johnson, Melvin   528
Johnson, Philip G.   1293
Johnson, Sargent   38
Johnson, William   745
Joint Baltic American National Committee
    489, 886
Jojola, Ted   1123
Joliet, Louis   549
Jonás, Charles   405-406
Jones, Alan   147
Jones, Tom   1413, 1417
Jong, Erica   831
Jordan, Michael   38
Jornal Portugues   1112
Joseph, Franz   150, 693
Josiah   1043
Journal do Emigrante   1112
Judaism   170, 297, 441, 467, 815-836, 1043,
    1165, 1244, 1371
Juht, Ludvig   495
Juliá, Raúl   1139
Julien, Percy Lavon   37
Junaluska, Arthur   279
Juneteenth   22
Jung, Carl Gustav   1302
Just, Ernest Everett   37

K

Kádár, János   694
Kalb, Marvin   831
Kamali, Norma   1320
Kamen, George   222
Kanagawa, Tooru J.   811
Kang, Younghill   853
Kanjobal Americans   603, 607, 613
Kann, Robert A.   157
Kansas   246, 399, 402, 527, 560, 569, 573, 576,
    617, 640, 952, 964, 984, 998, 1022, 1215,
    1232, 1259, 1261, 1286, 1289, 1294, 1308,
    1411, 1413, 1418
Kantonen, Taisto   528
Karabian, Walter   119
Karadjic, Vuk Srefanvoic   1219
Karadjordjevic, Alexander   1213
Karklins, Ingrid   878
Karlen, Jacob   1304
Karpovich, Michael   1169

Karras, Alex   591
Kasem, Casey   95, 1320
Katolikus Magyarok Vasárnapja   706
Kaufmanis, Kãrlis   878
Kaukonen, Jorma   528
Kaye, Danny   831
Kazan, Elia   589
Kazanjian, Varaztad   119
Kazin, Alfred   832
Keaton, Buster   744
Kegg, Maude   1028
Kelly, Emmett   744
Kelly, Gene   745
Kelly, Grace   745
Kelly, James E.   744
Kemal, Mustafa   1366
Kemény, John George   705
Kennedy Center Honors   247
Kennedy, David M.   951
Kennedy, John F.   29, 33, 310, 574, 933, 951,
    1053, 1188, 1203, 1251, 1321, 1366, 1396
Kenny, Maurice   762
Kentucky   13, 98, 185, 272, 712, 941, 1184,
    1202-1203, 1205-1206
Keppler, Joseph   158
Kerensky, Alexander   1169
Kerkorian, Kirk   119
Kerouac, Jack   559
Khan, Amanullah   1040
Khmer   224-237, 858, 862, 1325, 1393-1394
Khomeini, Ayatollah Ruhollah   721, 729
Khorana, Har Gobind   134
Khosana   236, 866
Khoury, Callie   1321
Kiesler, Frederick John   158
Kihss, Peter   878
Kilkson, Rein   496
Kilpatrick, Jack F.   279
Kilpatrick, William Heard   744
Kim, Elaine H.   852
Kim Hyung-Soon   853
Kim Young Ik   853
Kimball, Spencer W.   944, 950
King, Carole   832
King, Martin Luther Jr.   22, 32, 36, 38, 40-41,
    59, 811, 1254, 1403
King, Thomas   279
Kistiakovsky, George   1387
Kitano, Harry H. L.   809
Knaves Wager   52
Knoll, Erwin   158
Knudsen, William S.   421
Kocak, Michael   1252
Kogovesk, Ray P.   1263
Kohl, Herbert   831

571, 574, 580-581, 583, 586-587, 589-590,
600, 603, 612, 620-621, 624-625, 630, 639,
644-645, 651-652, 684, 686-689, 695-696,
698, 702, 712, 721-722, 724, 732, 734-738,
742, 744, 752-755, 757, 759, 761-762, 766-
769, 772, 786-790, 792-795, 809, 817-819,
825, 827-832, 843, 845, 847, 849-853, 861,
870, 874-876, 882-884, 886, 890, 897, 902,
908, 941, 943, 950, 976, 978, 983, 990, 992,
1003-1005, 1011, 1033, 1035, 1039, 1046,
1058-1059, 1062, 1074, 1078-1079, 1085-
1086, 1088-1089, 1092, 1103, 1124, 1131-
1135, 1137-1139, 1145, 1147, 1153-1155,
1162-1169, 1175-1185, 1200-1202, 1207,
1217, 1224, 1233, 1246, 1250, 1258-1259,
1263, 1265, 1269, 1273, 1278-1280, 1286,
1289, 1300, 1304-1305, 1311-1312, 1315,
1318, 1320-1321, 1326-1327, 1346, 1354-
1356, 1358-1361, 1367, 1369-1370, 1377-
1378, 1380-1381, 1383-1384, 1386-1388,
1397, 1401, 1409, 1411-1412
New York Nichibei   812
New York Public Library   41, 47, 119, 490,
709, 728, 782, 886, 1098, 1172, 1207
New York State   170-171, 471, 550-551, 558,
581, 590, 613, 750, 752-753, 761-762, 1004,
1079, 1233, 1278
New Zealand   137-148, 484, 657, 663, 1187-
1189, 1191, 1194-1195, 1197, 1299
New Zealander Americans   137-148
Newcombe, John   147
Newton-John, Olivia   145, 147
Ng, Faye Myenne   309
Nicaragua   339-340, 599, 611, 682, 684, 969-
986, 1056-1057, 1174-1176, 1183
Nicaragua Center for Community Action   984
Nicaraguan Americans   969-986
Nicaraguan Interfaith Committee for Action
979, 984
Nicaraguan Perspectives   984
Nicholson, Jack   355, 745
Nicole, Christopher   626
Niebaum, Gustave   527
Nielsen, Leslie   419
Nigerian American Alliance   999, 1342, 1346-
1347
Nigerian American Chamber of Commerce
999
Nigerian Americans   987-1000
Nigerian Students Union in the Americas   999
Nigerian Times   999
Niño   18, 342, 1067
Nippon Club   813
Nisei   802-803, 805, 809-811, 814
Nixon, Richard M.   742, 1111

Nnaji, Bartholomew   997
No Adam in Eden   559
Noah, Mordecai M.   831
Nobel Peace Prize   33, 235, 241, 340, 832, 839,
1013, 1403
Noël, Philip W.   557
Noga, Al   1196
Noli, Fan Stylian   51
Norden News   530
Norman, Greg   147
Norsemen's Federation, The   1014
North American Committee   250
North American Post   812
North Americans   2, 385, 1414
North Atlantic Treaty Organization   184, 241,
411, 419, 574, 579, 951, 1002, 1064, 1102,
1371
North Carolina   46, 237, 271-272, 280, 306,
373, 475, 483, 600, 752, 1200, 1202, 1208-
1210, 1225, 1233, 1299, 1326
North Dakota   101, 185, 213, 414, 417, 570,
808, 1004-1005, 1010-1011, 1016-1017,
1023, 1025, 1232-1233, 1239-1241, 1376,
1385
North Korea   837-840, 842
North Vietnam   226, 671, 858
North-West Frontier Province   1030-1031
Northern Ireland   473-474, 731, 733, 738, 743-
744, 1199-1200, 1205
Northern Ireland Aid Committee   743
Northern War   487, 869, 1285
Northwest Nikkei   812
Northrup, Jim Jr.   1028
Norway   125, 410-411, 516, 518, 666, 1001-
1015, 1079, 1284-1285
Norwegian American Historical Association
1014-1015
Norwegian Americans   1001-1015
Norwegian Constitution Day   1005
Novak, Kim   406
Novak, Michael   1251-1252
Novello, Antonia   1139
Novy, Frederick George   407
Now, Barabbas   1225
Nureyev, Rudolf   1170
Nurske, Ragnar   495
Nye, Naomi Shihab   95
Nysted, Nebraska   414, 417

O

O'Brien, Pat   744
O'Connor, Carroll   745
O'Connor, Mary Flannery   744
O'Connor, Sandra Day   745

United Swedish Societies   1295
Union and League of Romanian Societies of
      America   1153, 1156-1157
Union Jack   472, 484, 659
Union Saint-Jean-Baptiste   561
Unitas, Johnny   891
United Baltic Appeal   497, 877
United Cambodian Council   237
United Farm Workers Organizing Committee
      509-510
United Force   619, 1302
United Hellenic American Congress   589, 594
United South and Eastern Tribes   324
United States Information Agency   1158
Universal Negro Improvement Association
      794, 1360
Urban, Joseph   157
Urich, Robert   260
Uris, Leon   89, 832
Ursache, Archbishop Victorin   1152
Uskokovich, Mardary   1220
Utah   309, 412-413, 417, 421, 445, 485, 594,
      843, 857, 941-953, 955, 958-959, 963, 1010,
      1013, 1124, 1187, 1189, 1196, 1292, 1300,
      1413, 1415
Utrecht, Treaty of   2, 548

V

Valdez, Luis   910, 934
Valdivieso, Pedro M.   1079
Valtman, Edmund   495
Van Andel, Jay   443
Van Biesbroeck, Georges   193
Van Buren, Martin   443
Van de Poele, Karel J.   193
Van den Broek, Theodore J.   437
Van Kley, Dale   444
Van Raalte, Albertus   437, 441
Vandenberg, Arthur   443
Vander Heide, Jan   443
Vanderbilt, Cornelius   442
Vanity of Duluoz   559
Vartan, Sylvie   119
Vasiliev, Alexander   1169
Vasiliu, Mircea   1155-1156
Vaska, Lauri   496
Vasquez-Ajmac, Luis Alfredo   612
Vassileva, Ralitsa   221
Vasu, Gloria   1155
Vatt Khmer   236
Veblen, Thorstein   1012
Vein of Iron   1207
Velarde, Pablita   1124
Velichki, Bishop Andrei   220

Venezuela   196, 326-328, 449-450, 460, 617-
      618, 1056, 1072, 1350
Veniaminov, Innokentii   1166
Venti di settembre   768
Vermont   35, 184, 222, 251, 258, 261, 548,
      550-551, 556, 558, 561, 615, 706, 854-856,
      954, 1278, 1372, 1411
Vernadsky, George   1169, 1387
Véspera de São João   1107
Vézina, Elie   557
Victory Day   490, 899, 1370
Vida a Plazos de Jacobo Lerner   1079
Vida Contado   1079
Vienna, Austria   149-150, 152, 154-155, 158-
      161, 213, 221-222, 381, 569, 574, 619, 693,
      817, 1084, 1218, 1257
Viet Cong   671, 858, 1395-1396
Vietnam   34, 138, 191, 224-228, 231, 233, 237,
      293, 298-299, 306, 310, 357, 494, 652, 670-
      672, 743, 770, 857-858, 864, 902, 1063,
      1080, 1153, 1189, 1224, 1293, 1321, 1326,
      1345, 1393-1399, 1401-1406
Vietnam War   225-227, 293, 743, 1189, 1224,
      1326, 1395, 1399
Vietnamese Americans   237, 866, 1393-1407
Vietnamese Heritage Society   1407
Vig, Peter Sørensen "P.S."   419
Viking Age   1002
Virgin Passage   1129
Virginia   18-19, 26, 34, 96, 108, 111, 132, 176-
      177, 185, 194, 222, 228, 235, 250, 260, 272,
      278, 289, 294-295, 339, 361, 363, 369, 375,
      381, 397, 460, 474-475, 479, 537, 576, 631,
      655, 682, 696, 717, 733, 746, 785, 790, 814,
      843, 949, 951, 1079, 1125, 1145, 1156-1157,
      1170, 1200, 1203, 1205-1209, 1215, 1232,
      1238, 1273, 1282, 1299-1300, 1303, 1321-
      1322, 1351, 1367, 1376, 1385, 1397, 1415,
      1417
Visakha Puja   1328
Visions of Gerard   559
Vitas Valaitis   890
Vizenor, Gerald   1028-1029
Vlissingen   131, 328, 435, 451, 812-813, 843,
      1081
Voislav   1212
Volansky, Ivan   1385, 1388
Vööbus, Arthur   495
Voodoo   166, 390, 643, 646-647, 649-651, 653
Voralberg, John Michael Kohler   158
Vorkapic, Slavko   381
Voz de Portugal   1113
Voz Summary   984
Vraciu, Lieutenant Alex   1153
Vuich, Rose Ann   1223

W

Waid, Gary   1346

Waihee, John   667

Wales   138, 140, 357, 471-474, 638, 736, 964, 1408-1419

Walgreen, Charles R.   1293

Walking the Rez Road   1028

Walking Turtle   83, 324, 1128, 1242

Wallace, Mike   831

Walter, Bruno   159, 574

Walter-Pastori Refugee Relief Acts   437

Walters, Barbara   831

Walz, Maggie   528

War of 1812   34, 240-241, 367, 475, 477, 483, 543, 1027, 1231

Warehousemen's Union   510-511, 513, 667

Wargelin, John   523

Warhol, Andy   259-260, 408, 1252

Warner, Albert   831

Warner, Harry   831

Warner, Jack   831, 1094

Warner, Sam   831

Warren, Earl   1013, 1292

Washington   19, 26, 30-31, 33-34, 37, 45, 51, 112, 125, 133, 140-141, 157, 185, 192, 198, 211, 213, 235, 241, 247, 258, 287, 292, 316-317, 319, 329, 355, 380, 406, 412, 414, 427, 430, 432, 437, 443, 467, 488, 502, 504-506, 509-510, 512, 518-519, 521, 526-527, 542-543, 570, 600, 612, 645, 686, 712, 742, 752, 777, 787, 794-795, 800, 806, 808, 810, 818, 831, 840, 843, 847, 851, 859, 902, 907-908, 961-962, 973, 983, 1004, 1009, 1032, 1074, 1093-1094, 1110-1111, 1131, 1176-1180, 1182-1183, 1188, 1196, 1207, 1237, 1258-1259, 1262, 1264, 1286, 1292, 1300, 1304, 1326, 1380, 1384, 1386, 1397, 1416

Washington, Booker T.   26, 31

Washington, D.C.   19, 45, 198, 235, 287, 292, 317, 329, 406, 467, 506, 526-527, 542-543, 600, 612, 645, 781, 787, 818, 851, 902, 907, 961-962, 973, 983, 1074, 1131, 1140-1142, 1176, 1178-1179, 1183, 1188, 1237, 1262, 1264, 1386

Washington Heights   427, 430, 432-433, 818

Waters, Muddy   36

Wauneka, Annie Dodge   963

Way Home, The   247, 625

Wayne, Anthony   1417

Wayne, John   460, 744

Weaver, Dennis   279

Weill, Kurt   574

Weinstein, Joe   158

Weitling, Wilhelm   573

Wellek, René   407

Wells, Emmaline Blanche   950

Wellstone, Paul   831

Welsh   99, 471-475, 479, 743, 1165, 1167, 1199, 1377-1378, 1408-1419

Welsh American Genealogical Society   1418

Welsh Americans   1408-1419

Welsh National Gymanfa Ganu Association   1418

Wenceslas the Holy   397

Weninger, Francis Xavier   151

Werfel, Franz   114, 152, 159

Wergeland, Agnes Mathilde   1012

Werner, Heinz   159

West Africa   22, 28-29, 168, 388, 390, 431, 618, 646, 651, 686, 987, 991, 1130, 1132, 1311

West Cemetery of Eleusis, The   589

West Denmark, Wisconsin   417-418

West Indian Americans   794, 1360

West Indian Sugar Company   785

West Indies   2, 17-18, 162, 165, 170, 360, 412, 419, 619, 626, 642, 655, 733, 794-795, 896, 1059, 1129, 1350-1351, 1359-1361

West, Nathaniel   832

West Side Story   589, 832

West Virginia   185, 194, 250, 272, 339, 479, 696, 790, 1203, 1205-1206, 1215, 1273, 1300, 1321, 1415

Westinghouse, George   575

Weydemeyer, Joseph   573

Wheeler, Ruth   1417

Which Way to the Melting Pot?   1155

Whipple, Maurine   951

White Anglo-Saxon Protestant   483

White Russians   175, 1161-1163, 1165, 1167-1169

White, Theodore H.   831

Whiteman, Roberta Hill   762

Whitman, Walt   293, 443, 559

Whittier, John Greenleaf   542

Wickman, Eric   1293

Widstoe, John A.   951

Wieghorst, Olaf   421

Wiesel, Elie   832

Wiggin, Kate   1417

Wigner, Eugene   705

Wilder, Billy   160

Wilder, Gene   831

Wilkes, Paul   1252

William Penn Association   506, 706, 708

William the Silent   435

Williams, Roger   474, 1416

Wilson, Woodrow   259, 372, 419, 442, 502, 526, 993, 1130, 1206, 1223, 1386

Windmill Herald, The   444